Gillette®

LEAGUE
Publications Ltd

RUGBY LEAGUE
2010-2011
Back to the future

League Publications Ltd

First published in Great Britain in 2010 by
League Publications Ltd
Wellington House
Briggate
Brighouse
West Yorkshire HD6 1DN

A CIP catalogue record for this book is available from the British Library
ISBN 978-1-901347-22-7

Designed and Typeset by League Publications Limited
Printed by H Charlesworth & Co Ltd, Wakefield

Contributing Editor	Tim Butcher	
Statistics, production and design	Daniel Spencer	

Contributors

Gareth Walker	**Pictures** Rugby League
Malcolm Andrews	Photos
Tom Coates	SWPix
Lorraine Marsden	Peter Morley
Raymond Fletcher	Varley Picture Agency
John Drake	Action Photographics,
David Kuzio	Australia
James Coldman	CameraSport
Ricky Wilby	Getty Images
Mike Sterriker	Gordon Clayton
Phil Caplan	Ian Lovell
Ian Bridge	Allan McKenzie
Neil Barraclough	Mike McKenzie
Martyn Sadler	Magi Haroun
Simon Fitzjohn	Paul English
Ross Heppenstall	Paul Keevil
Phil Hodgson	Steve Jones
David Parkinson	Richard Land
Sian Couch	Bill Watkinson
Ian Golden	
Steve Mascord	
Mike Rylance	
Richard de la Riviere	
Ben Collins	
Keith McGhie	
Joanna Lester	
Conor Kelly	

CONTENTS

ACKNOWLEDGEMENTS

Gillette Rugby League 2010-2011 is the 15th in League Publications Ltd's annual series of Rugby League Yearbooks, the eighth year of its production with the backing of world-leading brand Gillette.

In compiling this historical record of the Rugby League year, we rely on the hard work and dedication of all the contributors to *Rugby Leaguer & Rugby League Express* and *Rugby League World* magazine. Without their efforts this yearbook would not be possible.

We are able to include some wonderful action photography provided by, in particular, SWPix, Varley Picture Agency, RLphotos.com, Action Photographics in Sydney and Peter Morley of RL Images.

Thanks are due to the Rugby Football League for their help during the year, and in particular Gavin Wild and Tom Hoyle for their assistance in helping track down the dates of birth of players.

Acknowledgement also to the Rothmans Yearbook 1999, compiled by Ray Fletcher, the British Rugby Records Book from London Publications, and to the club officials who helped us verify records.

The magnificent statistical review was put together meticulously, as always, by Daniel Spencer, who also designed the book.

Special mentions for Gareth Walker and Malcolm Andrews who wrote the Championship and NRL/State of Origin sections and to Tom Coates for his assistance in compiling the Other Internationals section. Thanks also to Opta Sportdata, who compiled the Opta Index Analysis in our jam-packed statistical section.

TIM BUTCHER
Contributing Editor
Gillette Rugby League 2010-2011

INTRODUCTION

2010 was the year Wigan made it back to the top of the Rugby League tree; that Warrington established themselves as one of the game's elite; Featherstone Rovers enjoyed a renaissance, despite losing a dramatic Championship Grand Final to Halifax; Batley won their first trophy for 86 years; and England again came third in an end-of-season international tournament.

A change of coach at Wigan, with Melbourne assistant coach Michael Maguire succeeding Brian Noble, did the trick. After three years of reaching the final eliminator from a variety of finishing positions, the Warriors finally made it to Old Trafford and had old foes St Helens beaten by half-time with an opening that epitomised their year as a whole, as they combined crushing defence with lightning handling to race into a 16-nil lead after only 20 minutes.

Having finished four points clear at the top of the table at the end of the regular season, there was no doubting Wigan as the champion side of 2010. Their winger Pat Richards and halfback turned fullback Sam Tomkins shared the Albert Goldthorpe Medal, Tomkins having been the Rookie of the Year the season before, while Richards, in his fifth season at the club, smashed the Wigan points-in-a-season record of Andy Farrell.

The Warriors ended Leeds' three-year reign as champions. The Rhinos' early-season form had them out of the play-off places at one point, and, when they did start to come with a late charge, they saw their Grand Final chances slip away with an injury to Jamie Peacock in round 25. That blow also scuppered Leeds' chances in the Challenge Cup final at Wembley, where Warrington retained the trophy with a consummate performance. Chris Hicks became the first player to score a hat-trick at the new Wembley, although he was beaten to the Lance Todd Trophy as man of the match by the brilliance on the day of Lee Briers. The Rhinos had the consolation of knocking Wigan out of the Cup in a quarter-final at Headingley, in the most dramatic of finishes.

The Wolves enjoyed a much more consistent campaign in 2010, edged into third by the most slender of points differences, and they beat Wigan at the DW Stadium, having come within inches of victory against them at home in round 3. They did make the play-offs this year, although they couldn't progress, losing at St Helens and at home to Huddersfield.

A new era dawns at Leeds, as coach Brian McClennan, despite signing a new one-year contract in mid-season, decided it was time to take his family back down under, bringing the succession plan a year forward. Brian McDermott, after four solid years developing the Harlequins' first-grade squad, was supposed to be McClennan's assistant for a year, but was elevated to head coach for the 2011 season.

St Helens lost a Grand Final for the fourth time in a row, and they lost their coach Mick Potter who was appointed the new Bradford mentor for 2011. Keiron Cunningham finally played his last game, at Old Trafford, after 17 years at the very top of the game. Potter had done a remarkable job, with injury robbing him of both his halfbacks, Leon Pryce and Kyle Eastmond, in the vital run-in.

Huddersfield Giants came within one game of the Grand Final, and they had a

Wigan and St Helens take to the Old Trafford pitch for the 2010 Super League Grand Final

traumatic season, with a rape charge that proved to be groundless hanging over some of their players for the first half of the season. Their captain Brett Hodgson revealed he would be signing for Warrington at the end of Super League XV, and coach Nathan Brown announced he was going home two years into his three-year contract, but then changed his mind. The Giants' play-off run from fifth spot and the selection of six of their players in England's Four Nations squad meant their season finished on a major high.

The team they edged in the Elimination Play-off, Crusaders, had a year that in many ways was symmetrical. 2010 started with uncertainty about the future of Wales' Super League presence, when it was bought by Wrexham FC, and it ended with similar concern, with the club in financial administration, though new head coach Iestyn Harris was appointed and player re-signings were announced. Harris was promoted from assistant to Brian Noble, who stepped out of the role after a progressive season with a group of players he recruited at short notice. One of those, Jarrod Sammut, who arrived mid-season, became one of the true characters of the game with his trademark ponytail and flamboyant try celebrations. Almost a thousand Welsh supporters made the trip to Huddersfield for the Elimination Play-off, and roared their heads off as only two late tries prevented them making further progress.

The two Hull clubs were nip and tuck all year, with the Black and Whites winning both regular-season contests between the two, but the Robins getting their revenge with a 21-4 win at the KC Stadium when they met in a Super League play-off for the first time. Rovers fell at Wigan in the next round.

Hull coach Richard Agar made Sean Long his captain at the start of the year, but the Airlie Birds misfired during his three periods of injury and Richard Horne was also missing for long spells. Rovers coach Justin Morgan was under intense pressure, after a couple of thrashings by St Helens in May, but he turned it around for the end-of-season run-in.

Introduction

Castleford Tigers finished just outside the top eight, edged out by Crusaders on the last weekend, but had key injuries to Dean Widders and Richard Owen in mitigation, as well as fitness concerns over Brent Sherwin, who left for the Catalans Dragons half way through the season.

Sherwin couldn't prevent the Dragons finishing in last place, with coach Kevin Walters making his departure at the end of the season. The Dragons did make the Challenge Cup semi-finals though, before meekly exiting at the hands of Warrington. Discipline problems dogged them all through the year, with Dimitri Pelo and Setaimata Sa both escaping a custodial sentence after a fight in Leeds city centre in the early hours after their round 1 defeat at Wakefield, the same players being suspended by the club for another matter, and Chris Walker also suspended by the club. Add in a pre-season training injury to Thomas Bosc, a broken leg to Clint Greenshields and a broken neck vertebra for Walker, and you have the ingredients for a wooden spoon.

Harlequins finished just above the Dragons after another season of struggle, hit by pre-season injuries to Rob Purdham and Luke Dorn, and, bar a couple of shocks along the way - the astounding win at Wigan the biggest of them - there were very few highlights. Apart, that is, from the emergence of players from London and the South, and it was no coincidence that two players from that area, Tony Clubb and Darrell Griffin, made their full international debuts for England in the Four Nations.

Of the other teams not to make the play-offs, Bradford were going well until it became apparent that marquee signing Matt Orford needed season-ending surgery after injuring his shoulder at Murrayfield on Magic Weekend. Orford went home to Australia for treatment, and decided he didn't want to come back to fulfil the last two years of his contract. The Bulls lost 13 of their last 14 games, and new England coach Steve McNamara left Odsal after eight of those defeats.

Salford were never real play-off material, but they produced a few feisty performances along the way, probably the best a 42-34 home win over St Helens. Wakefield were riding high in the early stages, but they suffered a series of blows, with the drugs ban imposed on hooker Terry Newton, who only played two games for his new club, the departure of homesick prop Shane Tronc and the mid-season transfer of their star man, Danny Brough, to Huddersfield.

The Terry Newton story had one tragic final chapter, the former Great Britain hooker taking his own life in September. A year that also saw a crazed gunman randomly shoot and kill former Whitehaven and Workington player Garry Purdham, and 12 other people in Cumbria, put the fortunes of Rugby League clubs into true perspective.

The Gillette Yearbook contains the full story of the domestic year, full details of the international season and the Australian NRL season, and match facts for every Super League and Challenge Cup game involving professional teams, Championship and Championship One and Northern Rail Cup game. Every player who has played Super League is also listed, along with those players who made their debuts this year. We have also selected five individuals who we judge to have made the biggest impact on Rugby League in 2010.

League Publications publishes the weekly newspaper *Rugby Leaguer & Rugby League Express*, as well as the monthly glossy magazine *Rugby League World* and the website *'totalrugbyleague.com'*.

Many thanks once again to Gillette for their support for both this yearbook, and for the sport of Rugby League.

TIM BUTCHER
Contributing Editor
Gillette Rugby League 2010-2011

1
THE 2010 SEASON

DECEMBER 2009
A new crusade

Super League XV served up a dramatic twist even before the new year had begun. In the week following Australia's win over England in the 2009 Gillette Four Nations final, the Rugby Football League released the details of the following year's Super League fixtures. Champions Leeds Rhinos were to travel to Wrexham to begin the defence of their Super League title against the Crusaders in a round-four game brought forward to accommodate the World Club Challenge. It was to be the earliest start to a Super League season since the competition began in 1996, and the first time a Super League match would be played in January. The season was to start a week earlier than in 2009 because of England's involvement in the 2010 Four Nations to be played in the southern hemisphere in October and November.

The south Wales-based Crusaders planned to play home matches both at Rodney Parade in Newport and in north Wales at Wrexham. But rumours suggested the club's major shareholder Leighton Samuel was ready to pull out of the club. It emerged that, behind the scenes, the RFL was involved in negotiations to find a buyer. On Friday 11th December, it was confirmed the club had been sold to Wrexham AFC, with a new Championship 1 club to be based in Neath. Derek Twigg, the Member of Parliament for Halton, whose constituency covered Widnes, slammed the RFL for allowing the Crusaders to move to Wrexham, claiming that the decision to award them a Super League licence in 2009 had proved to be a mistake.

The draw for the fourth Magic Weekend saw the 14 Super League clubs split into two pools. The top eight sides from Super League XIV were in one pool and were drawn against each other to provide four fixtures, whilst the bottom six were in a second pool.

Tony Smith's departure from the England coaching job the morning after England's resounding 46-16 defeat to Australia in the Gillette Four Nations Final led to a flurry of names being linked with the job. Former Great Britain and St Helens coach Ellery Hanley, out of the game since leading Doncaster to promotion from National League 2 in 2008, was championed by Martin Offiah. Offiah thought that ex-Oldham coach Mike Ford, the bookies favourite for the job, was unlikely to give up his 'cushy number (defence coach) with England rugby union' to take up what many saw as a poisoned chalice. Wakefield coach John Kear, who had coached England in the 2000 World Cup was second favourite.

Super League clubs were already into their pre-season preparations. Bradford Bulls signed Australian halfback Matt Orford from NRL club Manly on a three-year contract and had to inform Chris Walker of the Gold Coast Titans they wouldn't be going through with a deal the player thought was signed, sealed and delivered in August. Orford's capture enabled the Bulls to allow their long-standing captain Paul Deacon to move to home-town Wigan.

Salford City Reds signed Daniel Holdsworth from Canterbury Bulldogs, while Leeds' new signing Brett Delaney went straight into a rehabilitation group as pre-season training started, though Rhinos coach Brian McClennan dismissed fears about the centre not starting the season. The 2009 NRL season had ended with 24-year-old Delaney on the sidelines at Gold Coast Titans following a hamstring injury.

Hull KR coach Justin Morgan admitted he was interested in signing Brisbane Broncos prop forward Joel Clinton, a Kangaroo tourist in 2004. Wakefield prop forward James Stosic's contract at Wakefield Trinity Wildcats was cancelled after the player failed in his attempt to obtain a Macedonian passport. The New Zealander had applied for a European passport to avoid exceeding the club's overseas quota. A week later the Wildcats signed experienced prop forward Paul King from Hull FC.

The Wildcats were one of the few clubs to play over a snowy Christmas period. Half of the ten pre-season fixtures scheduled for the weekend were called off due to the severe weather conditions that had affected most of the country. Workington Town were hammered at home 60-6 by neighbours Whitehaven, while Dewsbury Rams, unbeaten in Championship 1 in 2009, lost 20-12 in the snow at home to Heavy Woollen rivals Batley Bulldogs.

Castleford Tigers went down 26-12 against Bradford Bulls at the Jungle, while Leeds Rhinos were the only team to register a home win, defeating Wakefield 32-12 in front of 8,797 spectators. The Wildcats picked up several injury worries in their Boxing Day clash. Damien Blanch was ruled out of the start of the season proper with a broken hand, while Terry Newton picked up a minor calf tear and Kyle Bibb damaged a knee in the first tackle.

Huddersfield's signing from Wakefield, Brad Drew, was set to miss the start of Super League XV after undergoing a knee operation he'd delayed the year before. The Giants were also resigned to being without Danny Kirmond (knee) and Simon Finnigan (shoulder and neck) for the start of the new campaign after off-season operations.

Another Giants signing, New Zealand World Cup winner David Fa'alogo jetted into England to take up his three-year contract. The second-row forward's career at South Sydney ended controversially when he punched his coach Jason Taylor during end-of-season celebrations. Giants star David Faiumu pleaded guilty that month in Rockhampton District Court in Central Queensland to a charge of causing grievous bodily harm. Faiumu received an 18-month suspended prison sentence. Catalans Dragons' hopes of re-signing 2009 captain Greg Bird faded. Bird was expected to agree a one-year contract with the Gold Coast Titans after winning his appeal against an assault conviction.

Warrington's new signing Richie Myler was rated the fourth best teenager in the world game in Rugby League World magazine's annual list and was joined in the top ten by Hull winger Tom Briscoe and Castleford fullback Richard Owen. Canberra fullback Josh Dugan was rated number one. A former world-ranked teenager, Kyle Eastmond, dispelled rumours about a move to rugby union by signing a two-year contract extension with St Helens.

The disruption caused by the end-of-year cold spell not only affected the holiday games of professional clubs. On the last weekend before Christmas, the amateur Rugby League programme suffered its first total wipe-out in recent memory.

* The inquest on Leon Walker, who collapsed and died during a Wakefield reserve team game against Celtic Crusaders at Maesteg in 2009, found that the 20-year-old had a rare, undiagnosed heart defect.

JANUARY
Snow business...

The snow and ice had Britain, and much of Europe, in its grip going into the new year of 2010. Of four scheduled professional pre-season games on the New Year holiday weekend, only one - the clash between Batley and Huddersfield on the Saturday - went ahead. The Bulldogs enjoyed a 40-12 victory against a Giants team made up of Academy players. The amateur Rugby League programme almost suffered another wipeout over the weekend. The only game played was the Hull ARL's GMB Union Tom Beautiman Cup Final between Reckitts and Holderness Vikings. The Carnegie Challenge Cup preliminary round was also victim to the weather. All the Elite 1 and 2 matches in France were postponed.

The weather didn't improve for much of the month. Eorl Crabtree's Testimonial Match between the Giants and Halifax was postponed on the second Sunday of January and was re-scheduled for the start of the 2011 season.

Meanwhile, England captain Jamie Peacock called for Super League to be reduced to ten clubs. Peacock told Rugby League World he believed fewer sides would result in a shorter season and higher standards, to the benefit of the England team. Leeds Rhinos captain Kevin Sinfield was voted the Super League Player of 2009 by the readers of League Express, beating Man of Steel Brett Hodgson into second place.

Steve Prescott received an MBE in the Queen's New Year's honours list for services to Rugby League and to charity. The former St Helens, Hull, Wakefield and Ireland fullback had raised hundreds of thousands of pounds for charity through the Steve Prescott Foundation after being diagnosed with a rare form of cancer in September 2006.

The Crusaders, with coach Brian Noble desperately trying to assemble a competitive squad, were linked with former Australian international Willie Mason. The Crusaders finalised deals for Tony Martin and scrum-half Michael Witt. Martin, who won an NRL Grand Final with Melbourne Storm in 1999, made his Super League debut with London Broncos in 1996, returning for a second spell from 2001 to 2003. He had spent the last two seasons with Wakefield Trinity Wildcats, and had signed a contract with Castleford Tigers for 2010, before the Tigers realised he would occupy a spot on the overseas quota and pulled out of the deal. Witt, who had been a sensation in his first year at Parramatta in 2003, had been released by NZ Warriors midway through 2009 and had a short spell in rugby union in New Zealand.

Hull FC and Great Britain winger Gareth Raynor was signed by Noble after being released by the Airlie Birds from the final year of his contract, alongside two other players released by Hull, Jamie Thackray and Tommy Lee. Raynor, due to make a court appearance in April to answer fraud charges in connection with an alleged internet scam, signed a short-term contract until his court case had been settled. The Crusaders also announced the signing of Vince Mellars, a centre with previous NRL experience, from the Auckland Vulcans club.

Castleford played a pre-season warm-up game at the end of a training camp in the south of France, beating the Dragons 14-12. It was a memorable trip for Tigers coach Terry Matterson, who lost a finger in a bizarre accident. The Tigers were 24 hours into their five-day stay in Perpignan when, at the end of a training session, Matterson climbed a fence to retrieve a stray ball. His wedding ring got caught, causing the finger to be ripped out.

New Wigan head coach Michael Maguire announced that captain Sean O'Loughlin would be one of a five-man leadership team that would rotate the job game by game. Richard Agar appointed Sean Long as the new captain of Hull FC; Thomas Bosc was named captain of the Dragons and Andy Lynch was to skipper Bradford Bulls.

The weather relented for the pre-season Hull derby, which served as a testimonial for long-serving Hull FC halfback Richard Horne and attracted a big crowd of 16,204, with both sets of supporters giving Horne a standing ovation as he led the two teams onto the pitch. Despite no points being at stake, it was a compelling Hull derby, with Hull, in a 28-16 win, giving debuts to new skipper Long, Australian signings Craig Fitzgibbon and Mark O'Meley, and Jordan Turner, who arrived from Salford in the close-season.

Warrington signing Richie Myler scored four tries in a friendly at Leigh Centurions after returning from a training camp in Tenerife. Warrington beat Leigh 60-16, with Ryan Atkins also marking his debut with a try. Warrington paid tribute to one of the club's other heroes, former captain Mike Gregory, when it unveiled 'Mike Gregory Way' at The Halliwell Jones Stadium.

Paul Deacon and Karl Pryce missed Wigan's 40-38 victory at Wakefield, while Bulls coach Steve McNamara decided not to give his 2010 marquee signing Matt Orford a run in Matt Diskin's testimonial match at Headingley. Leeds won a tight game 12-10.

Harlequins skipper Rob Purdham was left cursing his luck after tearing shoulder ligaments in a pre-season training camp at an Army base. The loose forward had missed the second half of the 2009 campaign after suffering a blood clot in his wrist. Purdham faced another 12 weeks on the sidelines, with Chad Randall standing-in as skipper.

The RFL made two small changes to the interpretations of the rules for the 2010 season. The first change meant a referee would call 'held' in a tackle when a ball carrier's leg was lifted by the defending team, as opposed to both legs. The second was intended to outlaw the practice of dragging tackled players into touch, or back towards their own in-goal area. From now, as soon as the referee saw a tackler dragging the ball carrier in a tackle that involved more than one tackler, he would call 'held'. The RFL appointed James Child to its senior refereeing squad, taking the number of full-time employed officials to seven.

Huddersfield Giants faced an uncertain start to the season. A 22-year-old woman alleged that six players from the club had raped her in an incident at a hotel at which the players were staying in Newcastle while on a training week at a venue in the city. The police arrested the players and all six were granted bail. Their identity was not revealed.

Round 4

Leeds centre Keith Senior set up the opening game of the season on the last Friday night in January in Wrexham by claiming the Crusaders shouldn't have been in Super League. Senior told the Sunday Mirror. 'They have shot themselves in the foot by moving to Wrexham and so close to Widnes.'

Hundreds of fans were unable to get into the sold-out stadium for the opening clash at Wrexham's Racecourse Ground, 10,344 spectators turning out despite the freezing conditions, which made a return at the end of the month, heavy snow falling during the day in Wrexham.

The Rhinos confirmed their pre-season favouritism to retain the title for a fourth consecutive year with an eventual 34-6 victory. But the Crusaders - whose only pre-season game against Harlequins had been cancelled because of snow - were solid and showed great spirit until they succumbed to Leeds' late onslaught. New halfback Michael Witt took the eye early on, but, like the Crusaders, he faded as fatigue set in. PNG international Jason Chan was the standout in an industrious home pack.

January

Leeds were without the rested Jamie Peacock and Brent Webb but eventually had enough patience, guile and speed to overcome the Welsh side, with new centre Brett Delaney producing a robust performance. The other new signing, Greg Eastwood, came on for 50 minutes and showed glimpses of his ability.

To the delight of the home crowd, it was 6-6 at the break. After an early Witt penalty goal, a Delaney kick nutmegged Nick Youngquest and stopped just short of the dead-ball line for Scott Donald to dive on the ball. Kevin Sinfield kicked the touchline conversion. The Welsh side drew level when a half break by Chan gave Witt the position to put up a bomb to the left. Left centre Vince Mellars took the ball out of the air and turned to feed Gareth Raynor, who shot into the corner. Witt was short with the kick.

Crusaders looked to have weathered a second-half Leeds storm and by the 65th minute they were mounting an attack in the Leeds '20'. Youngquest put up an angled kick that stand-in fullback Kallum Watkins collected five metres from his own posts. Watkins took the tackle and audaciously back-flicked the ball to Danny Buderus. Quick-thinking saw him feed the ball right to Donald, who did the same to Delaney, who set off downfield. Spotting Crusaders' prop and skipper Ryan O'Hara as the only cover tackler, he fed Danny McGuire on his right shoulder and the 60-metre chase was a procession. Sinfield converted from out wide.

The try that killed off the Crusaders was more fortunate, when McGuire collected Sinfield's chip and his pass out of the tackle hit Youngquest and ricocheted for Ali Lauitiiti to shoot under the posts. Sinfield converted. Tries to Sinfield, Delaney and Lauitiiti gave the score a lopsided look that the Crusaders didn't deserve. Several thousand remained at the end gave their new heroes a standing ovation.

More than 350,000 TV viewers tuned in for the game, one of the biggest audiences ever attracted to a club game other than for the Grand Final.

Round 3

The returning Ben Jeffries scored a try as he led from the front in Wakefield Trinity Wildcats' 18-10 win at Harlequins on the Saturday - the round three game brought forward so the London club could give Melbourne a warm-up before the World Club Challenge. The sides went at it hammer and tongs from the first whistle to the final hooter, with a flare-up at a scrum close to the end, Richard Moore and Louie McCarthy-Scarsbrook receiving their marching orders. They both got a one-match ban.

Wakefield debutant Darryl Millard opened the scoring when he leapt above Chris Melling to haul in Danny Brough's bomb and touch down. The hosts were quickly back in the contest, Luke Gale and Chad Randall combining at speed to create some space which debutant fullback Ben Jones-Bishop - on loan for the season from Leeds - stepped into to scorch home.

The Wildcats scored the try of the game. A kick from Gale was gathered in front of his own posts by fullback Aaron Murphy and after evading a clutch of tacklers he set off downfield before offloading for Jeffries to stride home from distance. Jones-Bishop hauled Quins back into it once more, stretching out to score despite being held up short of the line.

With just two points in it, the contest could have gone either way, but Murphy sealed matters when he rounded off more Wakefield pressure midway through the half.

CARNEGIE CHALLENGE CUP - ROUND 1

Saturday 23rd January 2010
Bradford Dudley Hill 18 Castleford Panthers 20; Castleford Lock Lane 34 Thornhill Trojans 10; Crosfields 12 Rochdale Mayfield 22; East Hull 36 Stanley Rangers 12; East Leeds 0 Ovenden 8; Eccles & Salford 14 Leigh East 42; Featherstone Lions 14 British Army 24; Heworth 0 Hunslet Warriors 56; Ince Rose Bridge 26 Oulton Raiders 30; Milford Marlins 28 Eastmoor Dragons 12; Saddleworth Rangers 8 Siddal 22; Wath Brow Hornets 14 Kells 6; York Acorn 32 Thatto Heath Crusaders 36

Sunday 24th January 2010
Blackwood Bulldogs 42 Edge Hill University 16; British Police 46 Dewsbury Celtic 16; Gloucestershire Warriors 32 Edinburgh Eagles 36; Leeds Met University 28 Loughborough University 4; Northumbria University 4 Royal Navy 54

Sunday 31st January 2010
Royal Air Force 24 Warrington Wizards 28

Saturday 6th February 2010
Drighlington 26 West Hull 10; Hull Dockers 26 Pilkington Recs 12; Myton Warriors 20 Halton Simms Cross 15; Normanton Knights 6 Wigan St Patricks 4; Shaw Cross Sharks 8 Leigh Miners Rangers 44; Stanningley 0 Wigan St Judes 22

Sunday 7th February 2010
West London Sharks 16 Nottingham Outlaws 38

16

FEBRUARY
Changing of the guard?

Round 1

Sean Long made the perfect return to St Helens on the first Saturday night of February, scoring a try and playing the leading role as Hull FC completely dominated his old club in a 32-12 victory. Snow and ice wasn't a problem, but the fog in St Helens was so intense that many of the 12,142 spectators at the ground and the live Saturday-night TV audience were unable to see major parts of a game which came close to being called off 30 minutes before kick-off.

A trio of former Sydney Roosters made their Super League debuts; Saints centre Sia Soliola facing ex-teammates in Craig Fitzgibbon and Mark O'Meley. It wasn't an auspicious start for Kiwi Test star Soliola, who was withdrawn at half-time with an ankle problem. Winger Ade Gardner had already left the field with a rib injury after only 12 minutes and James Graham was to follow with a bruised sternum. Gary Wheeler filled in on the left flank for Francis Meli, back in New Zealand on compassionate leave.

With a try and two assists, Long aced his eagerly anticipated clash with his former under-study Kyle Eastmond. Long's try at the start of the second half was the coup de grace; Danny Tickle - with a superb pass out of the tackle - Jordan Tansey and Richard Horne combining to split the Saints defence in a superb 80-metre break that ended with Long diving over by the posts. Tickle's conversion made it 20-nil and sent the Old Faithful into raptures. Eleven minutes later Tom Briscoe romped out of a half-completed tackle metres from his own line to sprint the length of the field and Fitzgibbon converted for 26-0.

After Tansey was sin-binned for a professional foul, Saints finally cracked Hull's defence, Matt Gidley forcing his way over in the right corner. Chris Flannery added another, 11 minutes from the end, with Eastmond again adding the goal. But fittingly Hull wrapped up an impressive victory with the final try, Kirk Yeaman pouncing on Long's kick and Fitzgibbon's dribble, and Fitzgibbon again converting.

Big-spending Warrington got off to a flyer with a 58-0 home win over Harlequins, winger Chris Riley, in for the injured Chris Hicks, scoring five tries in 24 minutes. Harlequins were already looking shot before kick-off with Danny Ward and Ben Jones-Bishop having joined their already crippling injury list. Quins were 12-0 down after 20 minutes and prop Matt James's fumble on the Wolves' tryline followed by stand-in skipper Chad Randall's immediate sin-binning for slowing down a 20-metre restart ended any hope.

Defending champions Leeds were stunned by visitors Castleford at Headingley on the Friday night, the Tigers recording a 24-10 win. Leeds prop Jamie Peacock had been installed as 8-1 favourite to win the Engage Super League Man of Steel crown in 2010 and made his

17

seasonal debut, but the Tigers played a brilliant tactical game on a rutted, sand-filled Headingley pitch. Rangi Chase marshalled the Tigers majestically, his and Brent Sherwin's boot securing a 6-1 goal-line drop-out count and two tries, while his short inside ball caught out the home sliding defence, accounting for the other two touchdowns.

Leeds' defeat meant that Wakefield were the early Super League leaders, after following up their win at Harlequins with a hard-fought 28-20 home victory against the Catalans Dragons on the Sunday. Catalans were missing Thomas Bosc and Jamal Fakir due to training injuries in midweek and their plans were dealt a further blow by the late withdrawal of star fullback Clint Greenshields through illness.

At 10-10 the Dragons had new forward Dallas Johnson sin-binned just before the break and regained the lead through a Sebastian Martins try while still down to 12 men. But two tries in three minutes put the hosts back in front, with Dale Morton touching down in the 51st minute before Glenn Morrison crossed for his first Wakefield try. A second try for 19-year-old winger Morton sealed victory with 12 minutes left, making Chris Walker's late debut try a consolation. Paul Johnson came off the bench for his Wakefield debut but was cleaned out almost immediately by a Rémi Casty tackle. Johnson didn't return until the middle of April. Casty was referred by the RFL Match Review Panel and was suspended for one game.

The following morning the Catalans Dragons confirmed five of their players had been arrested by West Yorkshire Police following a street fight in Leeds city centre.

Huddersfield Giants also got off to a positive start - despite losing prop Keith Mason to a pectoral injury in the first minute - with a 24-12 opening-round home victory over Bradford Bulls, new Kiwi back-rower David Fa'alogo scoring a try after coming off the bench on 25 minutes for his first competitive outing since close-season knee and ankle surgery. Within 16 minutes of the kick-off, Brett Hodgson had set up the first two tries for Leroy Cudjoe and was already looking a good bet to retain his Man of Steel title. The first came from Hodgson's long pass and the second from a slide-rule kick that plopped comfortably into the winger's hands. Hodgson went close to scoring a try himself when he hacked on a loose ball and won the chase, only to be fooled by an awkward last bounce in the in-goal area, three minutes after Shaun Lunt's dummy-half try had made it 16-0.

Bradford's new Australian duo of Brett Kearney and Matt Orford showed one or two promising signs in the Galpharm fog. Orford had the most success with a key part in Bradford's first two tries; his smart pass enabling Chris Nero to put in Stuart Reardon and a few minutes later his kick being well taken by Paul Sykes, who sent Rikki Sheriffe over to pull back to 16-8 at half-time. Fa'alogo's converted try early in the second half extended Huddersfield's lead to 22-8 and Bradford never looked like catching up, despite coming back strongly in the last quarter.

Hull Kingston Rovers coach Justin Morgan was happy to start on a winning note with a 30-12 victory over Salford City Reds at Craven Park on the Sunday. The absence of Ben Galea with a knee injury meant that Morgan played Paul Cooke at loose forward, switching centre Jake Webster to stand-off. Behind an impressive pack, with Rhys Lovegrove outstanding, Michael Dobson led Rovers superbly and chipped in with a try and five goals from five attempts.

New Wigan coach Michael Maguire celebrated his 36th birthday on the Friday by picking up two points in his first competitive game in charge, as his side demolished the Crusaders 38-6, on Brian Noble's first return to the DW Stadium. Thomas Leuluai marked his announcement as one of Wigan's team of leaders with a man-of-the-match display, starting at scrum-half before moving to hooker to accommodate the introduction from the bench of debutant Paul Deacon, who entered the field of play in the first half to a rousing reception from an appreciative crowd of 13,680. Cameron Phelps just pipped two-try hero Amos Roberts to the gamestar award with two clever kicks for tries in the first half and a well-taken try for himself.

Round 2

England captain Jamie Peacock criticised the decision of the Super League clubs to keep 14 sides in the competition. A cut to 12 or even ten teams had been proposed at the February meting of Super League clubs.

On the field, Paul Wellens scored four tries on the Sunday as St Helens clinically despatched Bradford Bulls at Odsal by 38-6. It was the first time Saints had scored more than 15 points since a 44-24 win against Harlequins at the Stoop on 25th July 2009. They were missing Ade Gardner, out with a rib cartilage injury sustained in the defeat by Hull, and Iosia Soliola, who injured his ankle in the same game. Keiron Cunningham was another absentee due to his mother's death. Francis Meli was back from compassionate leave.

Kyle Eastmond kicked impeccably on his way to an 18-point haul and Leon Pryce was back on form. Wellens' second try was a blinder, reminiscent of Saints at their best. Jon Wilkin's break initially set James Roby clear, and Jonny Lomax, Meli, Scott Moore and Tony Puletua all handled the ball before Wellens touched down. It looked certain that Saints would nil Bradford at Odsal for the first time since Leeds went away with a 30-0 victory in May 2006 until Matt Orford scrambled over for a consolation in the last seconds.

Wakefield coach John Kear paid tribute to scrum-half and matchwinner Danny Brough, who played a key role with 16 points in the Wildcats' 28-18 home win over Leeds on the Sunday. Brough was a constant thorn in the side of the Rhinos and snared a 75-metre interception try at the start of the second half to give his side a 14-point lead, which proved too much for the Rhinos to overhaul.

Brian McClennan hit out at the second-half sin-binning of his captain Kevin Sinfield, for dissent, by new full-time referee James Child and the penalty count ended 17-7 against Leeds. Darryl Millard's 55th minute try when he plucked Brough's crossfield kick out of the air four minutes after Sinfield's yellow card was the gamebreaker.

The Wildcats had now won their last eight regular-round Super League matches, a run stretching back to July 2009, and sat top of the current table with three consecutive wins in 2010.

A magnificent defensive first-half performance allowed Wigan to eventually canter to a comfortable 32-6 home victory against Hull KR. Wigan led 10-0 after only seven minutes through Amos Roberts and Martin Gleeson tries but had to withstand a bombardment from the Robins for the rest of the half that yielded only a Ben Fisher try five minutes before the break. Both fullbacks, Cameron Phelps and Shaun Briscoe didn't return for the second half, with ankle and knee injuries respectively. Sean O'Loughlin's try nine minutes after the break halted Hull KR's momentum, and from that moment the Warriors never looked back, Pat Richards, Joel Tomkins and the form player of this stage of the season, Roberts, adding further tries.

Warrington also made it two from two with a 28-16 Saturday-night win at Castleford, Lee Briers the matchwinner. After tries to James Evans and Joe Westerman, two excellent kicks from Briers turned a ten-point deficit into a share of the spoils at half-time, and he then produced a trademark interception try before setting up Richie Myler's late clincher.

Bad news for the Tigers was a knee injury to Dean Widders that needed surgery. The Wolves had two players up before the RFL Disciplinary Committee the following Tuesday. Adrian Morley was found not guilty of a high tackle on Sherwin after he had passed the ball and Garreth Carvell was found guilty of leading with the forearm to the head of Paul Jackson, having a one-match ban reduced to a fine on appeal.

Catalans Dragons were having a tough start to the season. The week after five of their players were arrested in Leeds city centre after an early Monday morning fracas they sunk to a 16-4 defeat at Harlequins. The Dragons were still missing Thomas Bosc, giving

February

William Barthau a Super League debut, although Clint Greenshields made his seasonal bow. Rémi Casty was out suspended and they suffered the dismissal of David Ferriol for punching Jason Golden in the 65th minute. Ferriol escaped suspension. Quins had Ben Jones-Bishop, Danny Ward and Louie McCarthy-Scarsbrook back after the Wolves defeat, though Luke Gale broke his jaw. Will Sharp's hat-trick proved decisive.

Hull gave an indication they were genuine contenders with a tough 14-6 home win over Huddersfield Giants at the KC Stadium on the Friday night. None epitomised Hull's work ethic more than 32-year-old Craig Fitzgibbon, while fellow back-rower Danny Tickle scored a try and kicked three goals. Hull's new-found confidence was evident after only seven minutes when they spurned a penalty near the posts and were rewarded with Tickle's try from Shaun Berrigan's pass. Tickle added the goal and another to a second try in the 26th minute on the back of the game's best piece of rugby, Epalahame Lauaki putting Richard Whiting away in classic centre style before he handed on for winger Craig Hall to go in at the corner.

Lauaki undid his fine work early in the second half when he was penalised for dissent and Scott Grix scored a try from the position gained. Leroy Cudjoe added the goal. The complexion of the game had changed and Hull were ready to take the penalty points when offered, Tickle banging over their only second-half score from 30 metres. The late withdrawal of Brett Hodgson with a back injury was a blow to the Giants.

Brian Noble led the Crusaders to their first win of the season on the Friday night as they demolished Salford 36-16 with a clinical display at the Willows. Centre Vince Mellars was one of the heroes, scoring a hat-trick of tries thanks, largely, to the boot of Michael Witt. Elliot Kear, the young Welsh fullback, also impressed in his first outing of the new season.

Round 3

On the weekend of round three, Wakefield's new hooker Terry Newton confessed to having taken a human growth hormone that was detected by a doping test during pre-season training on 24th November. Newton said he would not contest the charge against him brought by the UK Anti-Doping Agency. The 31-year-old former Great Britain international was suspended by the Rugby Football League after becoming the first athlete in world sport to be caught for taking the banned substance.

The Wildcats had a rest weekend, having played their round-three game to accommodate Harlequins' game against Melbourne Storm, which the Australian Premiers won 34-10. That allowed Wigan to jump above Wakefield to the top of the table after one of the best contests for many years, as they beat Warrington at the Halliwell Jones Stadium in the Saturday-night TV game, by 22-20.

The Wolves looked likely to be the side maintaining their unbeaten record, leading 16-4 with just under half an hour to go before the departure of Lee Briers, whose left ankle was twisted in a tackle before he was carried from the field. Wigan went on to win, although they were grateful that Warrington's David Solomona lost the ball in the act of scoring what would have been the winning try in the final minutes.

After Warrington made the better start, Amos Roberts broke through Ben Harrison's tackle on the halfway line after taking Andy Coley's pass, used Sam Tomkins as a foil, stepped past Matt King and arced away to the corner for a glorious score. It came against the run of play and nine minutes later Warrington made their territorial advantage count as Michael Monaghan probed from dummy-half close to Wigan's line and found Richie Myler, whose eye for the gap was sharp. Briers tagged on the goal to edge his side ahead by a couple of points.

The Wolves extended that lead in the 28th minute when they moved the ball from left to right with a speed and crispness that saw them score in the corner courtesy of the prolific Chris Riley. Solomona then crashed over and Briers' second conversion opened up a well-deserved 12-point buffer as the Wolves left the field at half-time to a standing ovation.

After Briers' exit, Wigan began their fightback with another try from Roberts. Before the Wolves touched the ball again, the Warriors had closed the gap further as Roberts' jinking run foxed Warrington's defence before he offloaded to the supporting Darrell Goulding who touched down. Richards' touchline goal was a pearler and the gap was down to just two. The visitors were soon back on level terms as Richards potted an easy penalty goal after Adrian Morley's high tackle. Then Wigan produced one of the plays of the night when Sam Tomkins, who had had a quiet game, chipped over the defence, regathered and freed Thomas Leuluai who sent Tomkins' brother Joel to the line. Richards' goal opened up a six-point gap.

Chris Bridge couldn't convert a 73rd minute Louis Anderson try, leaving the Wolves two points adrift, and, when Sam Tomkins kicked out on the full with just two minutes remaining it gave them a final chance to win the game, Solomona losing possession in a mass tackle when going over the line a minute later.

St Helens, still missing Keiron Cunningham, overturned an early 8-0 deficit in Perpignan, aided by the first-half dismissal of the France captain Olivier Elima for a high tackle on Jonny Lomax, to win 42-12. Dragons officials and fans were infuriated by the dismissal of Elima in the 23rd minute of the clash. The Dragons were leading 8-4 when their captain shoulder-charged Lomax, appearing to make contact with the player's head. Elima was immediately red-carded by referee Steve Ganson and got a one-game suspension the following Tuesday. Lomax managed to score a try on the next play before being led groggily from the field.

The Catalan faithful in the stands at one point turned their back on the game as they vented their anger at Ganson in a one-way second half that saw Saints run in four converted tries in the 19 minutes after half-time.

On the Sunday, Crusaders kicked on from their first win at Salford with a thrilling 18-16 victory over previously unbeaten Hull FC at the Racecourse Ground. Michael Witt was at the heart of every Crusaders attack and Nick Youngquest's second try ten minutes from time sealed the win after Kirk Yeaman's four-pointer on 61 minutes had given Hull - without Sean Long, out with a hamstring injury - a 16-12 lead. The game had been in doubt as the snow and ice returned on then Sunday, but 6,794 turned out for Wrexham's second Super League game. Eight of the ten Northern Rail Cup games scheduled for that day fell victim to the weather.

The under-fire Bradford Bulls bounced back from a disappointing brace of early defeats to beat Castleford 41-22 at the Grattan Stadium on the Friday. Matt Orford sprayed out the passes that brought two tries and produced the perfect cross field kick for another. In addition he banged over seven goals, including a 30-metre field goal. Brett Kearney ripped through for two tries, made a slashing run that almost brought another and added his own creative touch to put in Paul Sykes for the last touchdown.

Castleford coach Terry Matterson, without Brent Sherwin, expressed concern about a fast-freezing Odsal playing surface after the Tigers' young star Richard Owen suffered a broken leg and was ruled out for the season.

Brett Hodgson illustrated his importance to Huddersfield Giants with a triumphant return from a back injury in a 30-0 win at Hull KR. Hodgson provided the final pass for three Huddersfield tries and kicked a 40/20 to set up another. His namesake David provided the Giants' cutting edge out wide to finish with a well-taken hat-trick of tries.

Leeds coach Brian McClennan insisted things would be 'all right on the night' when the Rhinos faced Melbourne Storm in the following Sunday's World Club Challenge clash at Elland Road. Inconsistent Leeds again struggled on the Friday, when they edged past Salford 22-10 at Headingley. Only a last-minute try by Ian Kirke added an air of comfort to the final scoreline. Scott Donald was set to miss the Melbourne clash, however, after dislocating a shoulder.

Round 4

Wigan went clear at the top of the table with a 58-0 hammering of Catalans Dragons at the DW Stadium on the Friday night. Pat Richards scored 38 points, with five tries and nine goals, just four short of former Leeds star Iestyn Harris's Super League record of 42 points scored against Huddersfield in 1999. Richards would have got two more points if he hadn't hit the post with his last conversion attempt and he started and finished the rout, claiming his second Super League hat-trick inside just 20 minutes before completing the scoring with his fifth try late on, his haul the biggest-ever Super League points tally by a Wigan player.

The Warriors posted a 36-0 lead by half-time and continued to run riot against Catalans' right-hand defence, with George Carmont adding a second-half brace. Catalans had now conceded 144 points in losing their opening four games, leaving them rooted to the foot of the Super League table.

Wigan were the only undefeated club in Super League after Wakefield lost 22-16 on the same night at St Helens. Saints rallied from 12-0 down to wreck the resolute Wildcats' 100 per cent record in a real arm wrestle. James Graham's non-stop effort was outstanding, though it was Keiron Cunningham's emotional return to the line-up that sparked the Saints' comeback. Cunningham had missed Saints' last two games following the death of his mother and a minute's silence was observed before the game in her memory. It was the 500th appearance of Cunningham's career.

It was fitting that Cunningham grabbed the go-ahead score with a trademark try from dummy-half as the Wildcats, who refused to concede defeat and ended the game camped in Saints' '20'.

Saints found themselves 12-0 adrift thanks to two breakaway tries to Dale Morton and Darryl Millard. Wakefield almost added a third on 23 minutes, when Glenn Morrison just failed to ground a deft dab in-goal by Obst.

Saints finally opened their scoring account on 28 minutes when Leon Pryce's bustling diagonal run through right centre ended with a lobbed pass to send Jonny Lomax in at the corner. Kyle Eastmond goaled from the touchline. After the break, Eastmond - hanging back behind the line to follow Graham's charge - erupted into space and on a 30-metre diagonal dash to the right corner. Eastmond's kick from the touchline drifted wide right. Cunningham's trademark try and Eastmond's goal made it 16-12. Francis Meli's converted try in the left corner edged the home side further ahead. The Wildcats weren't finished though. Murphy palmed Ben Jeffries' cross-field kick to Millard who scored in the left corner to make it 22-16, with Obst just missing the kick from the touchline. It set up a tense end to the game.

Despite captain Sean Long's absence, the Airlie Birds returned to winning ways on the Friday with a convincing 28-4 home win over Harlequins. Former England winger Mark Calderwood made his first appearance of the season after recovering from a hamstring injury, though fullback Jordan Tansey missed the game after being disciplined by the club for being late for training the day after Hull's loss to the Crusaders. His replacement, Richard Whiting, never put a foot wrong in an impressive display. Craig Hall and Danny Tickle tries in five minutes at the start of the second half put the game beyond the under-strength Quins.

Bradford condemned Salford to their fourth consecutive Super League defeat in a tight encounter at the Willows, by 7-0. A game littered with errors due to the cold and wet weather conditions provided plenty of tension, as Matt Orford helped the Bulls dominate possession in the first half, his high and low kicks causing Salford problems all night. Bradford deservedly took the lead on 23 minutes when the Brett Kearney made a half-break and offloaded to Paul Sykes who, after juggling with the ball, fed Steve Menzies to go in under the posts. Orford failed to add the simple conversion as the Bulls led 4-0, but kicked a 65th minute penalty before the game was sealed with two minutes remaining when Sykes slotted over a field goal.

The only try of a pulsating second half from Chris Hicks settled a bruising battle at the Galpharm Stadium on the Sunday between Huddersfield and Warrington in the Wolves' favour, 14-10. Warrington were minus Lee Briers and Chris Bridge (both ankle injuries) but 2009 top try-scorer Hicks was making his first appearance of the season and showed his prowess near the line when breaking a long-standing deadlock with the winning score 15 minutes from time. Matt King, back in the centre after several starts on the wing, was in great form, scoring two first-half tries that the Giants matched with scores from Kevin Brown and Paul Whatuira.

Castleford coach Terry Matterson admitted to feeling frustrated after his team suffered a narrow 24-20 defeat to Hull KR at the Jungle on the Saturday evening - the Tigers' second home defeat of the season. The game turned on a decision by video referee Steve Ganson to award a late try to the Robins when prop forward Liam Watts juggled the ball as he went over the line, with most observers convinced he hadn't touched down properly. The Tigers had 20-year-old Wigan winger Shaun Ainscough on debut, and he scored a hat-trick in the first match of his month-long loan deal at the club, after a three-match loan spell at Widnes in which he scored four times. He had scored 24 tries in just 16 games and his hat-trick against Hull KR was the third of his career.

In Championship 1, new club South Wales Scorpions made an outstanding debut at Neath, beating Workington Town 22-20 in their first ever game.

SUPER LEAGUE TABLE - *Sunday 28th February*

	P	W	D	L	F	A	D	PTS
Wigan Warriors	4	4	0	0	150	32	118	8
Warrington Wolves	4	3	0	1	120	48	72	6
Hull FC	4	3	0	1	90	40	50	6
St Helens	4	3	0	1	114	66	48	6
Wakefield T Wildcats	4	3	0	1	90	70	20	6
Huddersfield Giants	4	2	0	2	70	40	30	4
Leeds Rhinos	4	2	0	2	84	68	16	4
Bradford Bulls	4	2	0	2	66	84	-18	4
Hull Kingston Rovers	4	2	0	2	60	94	-34	4
Crusaders	4	2	0	2	66	104	-38	4
Castleford Tigers	4	1	0	3	82	103	-21	2
Harlequins	4	1	0	3	30	108	-78	2
Salford City Reds	4	0	0	4	38	95	-57	0
Catalans Dragons	4	0	0	4	36	144	-108	0

World Club Challenge

On a cold and rainy night at Elland Road, Leeds, Melbourne Storm adapted their tactics ruthlessly to suit the slower play-the-ball of the English game and gain revenge over Leeds Rhinos for the World Club Challenge defeat of 2007. Kangaroo Cameron Smith, who started the game in the unfamiliar role of scrum-half before moving to hooker, was the man of the match in an 18-10 Storm win. Smith slotted five goals from as many attempts, and constantly kept his side moving forward in what was at times a titanic forward battle.

It was a close encounter, but the loss of skipper Kevin Sinfield after half an hour with a deadleg scuppered Leeds' chances. The Rhinos also missed dislocated-shoulder victim Scott Donald, with his

replacement, centre Kallum Watkins, millimetres away from grounding the ball on two occasions as he went in at the right corner on the 13th and 74th minutes. The Rhinos players were often visibly frustrated by what they saw as constant holding down from the Storm, with Keith Senior penalised for dissent in the second half after voicing his opinions too loudly.

Two penalties each had the scores locked at 4-4 at half-time. Leeds attacked first after the restart, with Luke MacDougall on hand to defuse a Rob Burrow wide kick behind

Billy Slater's challenge forces Kallum Watkins to lose possession over the tryline

his own line. But it was Melbourne who were on the front foot when Danny McGuire grabbed the game's first try moments later. On the last tackle of an attacking set, Smith's hopeful grubber bounced off the leg of Delaney and into the arms of McGuire, who sprinted 80 metres to the try-line. Richard Silverwood referred the decision to video referee Phil Bentham and after several viewings, taking over two minutes, he ruled that McGuire was onside and the score stood. Burrow converted superbly to briefly open up a six-point gap.

The Storm response was almost immediate. The Australians took a quick tap when Kylie Leuluai was pinged for taking out Billy Slater off the ball and Brett Finch, Adam Blair and Dane Nielsen combined to send MacDougall over for a debut try. This time it was Smith producing the extras to tie the scores up again, and the Storm skipper was soon putting his side ahead for the first time with a penalty that was a real 'coach killer'. Senior was penalised for dissent while in possession and Smith made no mistake from 35 metres out.

Leeds struggled to mount any real pressure on the Storm line throughout the second half, but they did fashion one final chance with six minutes remaining. Running the ball on the last tackle, Jamie Jones-Buchanan's wide pass gave Watkins another sniff of the line, but Slater was again on hand to do just enough and force the Leeds youngster to lose the ball again over the line. With just over two minutes on the clock, after a mistake at the play-the-ball from Ali Lauitiiti, Anthony Quinn squeezed over in the left corner to seal matters.

GILLETTE FUSION WORLD CLUB CHALLENGE

Sunday 28th February 2010

LEEDS RHINOS 10 MELBOURNE STORM 18

RHINOS: 1 Brent Webb; 23 Kallum Watkins; 3 Brett Delaney; 4 Keith Senior; 5 Ryan Hall; 6 Danny McGuire; 7 Rob Burrow; 8 Kylie Leuluai; 14 Matt Diskin; 10 Jamie Peacock; 11 Jamie Jones-Buchanan; 17 Ian Kirke; 13 Kevin Sinfield (C). Subs (all used): 9 Danny Buderus; 12 Ali Lauitiiti; 15 Greg Eastwood; 16 Ryan Bailey.
Try: McGuire (47); **Goals:** Sinfield 1/1, Burrow 2/2.
STORM: 1 Billy Slater; 2 Luke MacDougall; 3 Dane Nielsen; 4 Greg Inglis; 5 Anthony Quinn; 6 Brett Finch; 7 Cameron Smith (C); 8 Aiden Tolman; 9 Ryan Hinchcliffe; 10 Jeff Lima; 11 Adam Blair; 12 Ryan Hoffman; 13 Todd Lowrie. Subs (all used): 14 Rory Kostjasyn; 15 Kevin Procter; 16 Hep Cahill; 17 Jesse Bromwich.
Tries: MacDougall (50), Quinn (78); **Goals:** Smith 5/5.
Rugby Leaguer & League Express Men of the Match:
Rhinos: Greg Eastwood; *Storm:* Cameron Smith.
Penalty count: 10-11; **Half-time:** 4-4;
Referee: Richard Silverwood;
Attendance: 27,697 *(at Elland Road, Leeds).*

MARCH
No doubting Thomas

Round 5

Paul Deacon made his first return to Bradford since his winter switch to home-town club Wigan, but afterwards it was all about the man who had replaced him as scrum-half at Odsal as Matt Orford led an amazing second-half revival, scoring two tries as the Bulls came back from 20-0 down to beat the undefeated Warriors 22-20.

The table-topping Warriors, on the crest of a wave after winning their first four games of the season, bossed the opening half and could easily have been further ahead at the break. At 20-0 there seemed no way back for the Bulls but, in the ultimate game of two halves, Steve McNamara's men clawed their way back into contention then stole victory as Orford slotted the winning conversion with less than a minute remaining.

It was an unthinkable outcome after a dominant Wigan performance in the first half with Darrell Goulding, Harrison Hansen and Pat Richards, twice, getting tries to put Wigan almost out of sight at 20-0.

Orford completely stole the show with his second-half performance. First he combined with Craig Kopczak and Wayne Godwin to send Brett Kearney racing in beside the posts. Two minutes later an opportunist Orford, at first receiver, spotted a gap and dived over from close range and, with the former Manly Sea Eagle slotting both conversions, it was game on again.

Wigan still seemed on course to maintain their 100 per cent record until another moment of Orford magic set up the grandstand finish. He bamboozled the Warriors defence with a determined diagonal charge and, despite badly missing the conversion, left his team within a score of victory. Again Wigan seemed to have steadied the ship. But Amos Roberts lost possession in a fierce tackle from Paul Sykes and Glenn Hall and seconds later Heath L'Estrange sent Glenn Hall thundering under the posts to leave Orford with the simplest of match-winning kicks.

Warrington picked up a fourth win in five outings to claim joint-top spot in the table, a killer 18-point blitz either side of the break enough to see off a brave Crusaders challenge at the Halliwell Jones Stadium by 46-12. The direction of Michael Monaghan was key and the incisive running of Matt King saw him denied a hat-trick of tries only by some desperate Crusaders defence.

Richard Horne scored two tries and earned three Albert Goldthorpe points for his performance for Hull FC in their 42-22 victory against Castleford Tigers at the KC Stadium on the Friday. The 27-year-old former Great Britain star returned to his best form as Hull also registered their fourth win in five games, with Horne occupying the missing Sean Long's scrum-half berth, alongside former Salford youngster Jordan Turner at stand-off. Horne's 47th-minute touchdown sparked a scoring burst that brought four converted tries in 11 minutes to take Hull from 12-12 to a 36-12 lead.

Despite the absence of reigning Man of Steel Brett Hodgson on the Saturday, the Giants were magnificent in clinically disposing of Wakefield 52-0 at Belle Vue. The visitors scored five times in each half and nilled a team for the second time in a fortnight, having achieved a 30-0 victory at Hull KR the previous month. Kevin Brown, Larne Patrick and Scott Grix – on his first return to Belle Vue – were all outstanding, but it was Kiwi centre Paul Whatuira who stole the show. Leroy Cudjoe filled Hodgson's boots in fine style, scoring a try and kicking six goals as well as being safe in defence. Whatuira's eighth-minute try put Huddersfield 12-0 clear and signalled a long night for the Wildcats. Former Great Britain forward Lee Gilmour registered his first Huddersfield try when he made the most of Whatuira's break early in the second half.

Catalans picked up a first win of the season, by 24-12 at the Willows on the Friday night at the expense of an off-colour Salford side. Shaun McRae again opted to overlook his on-loan halfback Matty Smith, preferring to pair Daniel Holdsworth and Stefan Ratchford for successive matches, while the Dragons, still missing Thomas Bosc, suffered the pre-match hammer blow of losing his halfback partner Adam Mogg. The excellent Setaimata Sa moved to stand-off, while Kane Bentley started at hooker with Casey McGuire at scrum-half. Gregory Mounis's second conversion opened up an eight-point lead going into the final quarter - too much for an impotent Reds to claw back.

Leeds hammered Harlequins 62-4 at Headingley on the Friday night, with Danny Buderus scoring two tries. After a report in Sydney's Daily Telegraph claiming his old club, Newcastle Knights, were eager to re-sign him with immediate effect, Buderus ruled out a return before his Leeds Rhinos contract expired at the end of the season. The highlight of a one-sided game was when Danny McGuire scored a brilliant individual try, kicking the ball twice over the defence and collecting it each time. Wakefield Wildcats prop Kyle Bibb made his debut after joining embattled Harlequins on a month's loan. The Rhinos suffered a blow after specialists confirmed that New Zealand international Greg Eastwood had suffered a wrist injury that could rule him out for ten weeks.

A try by Ben Fisher two minutes from time finally settled an enthralling clash at Craven Park between Hull KR and St Helens in the home side's favour by 28-24. The lead changed hands five times and the result was in balance until the dying seconds. Former Wigan winger Liam Colbon notched a hat-trick for the Robins. Rovers introduced Ben Galea for his first Super League start of the year and retained Chaz I'Anson at stand-off. The Robins' matchwinner at the Jungle the week before, Liam Watts, was also in the side but there was still no place for out-of-favour Paul Cooke. But Craven Park fans finally got a look at their latest signing, former Brisbane prop Joel Clinton, who made his long-awaited home debut.

Saints arrived at Craven Park on the back of three straight wins but were without the services of a handful of their squad including Ade Gardner, Matt Gidley, Sia Soliola, Chris Flannery and Jon Wilkin. That week a town-centre statue of Keiron Cunningham was unveiled by St Helens Borough Council.

* Halifax amateurs Siddal made Challenge Cup history on the Sunday by beating the professionals of Doncaster 26-0 at the Keepmoat Stadium - the biggest ever margin of victory for an amateur team against a professional side.

Round 6

Hull coach Richard Agar warned that Super League might need to copy the NRL and employ two referees in order to avoid driving fans away from the game after the Warriors beat Hull 48-24 at the DW Stadium. Agar maintained Wigan's wrestling techniques spoiled the top-of-the-table clash.

Sean O'Loughlin masterminded a comprehensive Wigan victory as the Super League leaders bounced back from the previous week's defeat at Bradford. The Warriors ran in eight tries, including two each for Darrell Goulding and Sam Tomkins, to inflict Hull's second loss of the season. Three Hull tries in the last 13 minutes added a different complexion to the final score but there was no denying Wigan's all-round superiority.

Winger Pat Richards finished with a personal haul of 20 points after adding eight goals to his 15th-minute try.

St Helens saw off a brave challenge from the much-improved Crusaders at Knowsley Road on the Friday night, holding on for a 37-30 win. The Welsh side showed grit and skill in overcoming a 24-6 half-time deficit to put the frighteners on a St Helens outfit that looked to be cruising. In the end it took a Kyle Eastmond field goal to settle home nerves and seal the win. After the game James Graham laughed off speculation that he was on the verge of agreeing to join NRL side Sydney Roosters.

Castleford Tigers overturned a ten-point deficit in Perpignan to record their second win of the season by 20-16 on a chilly, subdued evening, the Gilbert Brutus pitch surrounded with cleared snow. Over 100 Dragons supporters had been out in force after over 40 centimetres of snow had fallen on the Catalan region over the course of Monday and Tuesday.

Chances were few and far between, but Rangi Chase stood apart from the rest, so much so, that the majority of the locals stayed behind and applauded him off the field after the Tigers came back from a 10-nil deficit. Clint Greenshields broke his fibula three minutes from time in the Dragons' fifth loss of the season.

Only Harlequins lay below the French side after their 26-22 defeat by Salford at the Stoop on the Sunday as the Reds earned their first points of the season, and themselves moved off the foot of the league. Quins led 18-4 after Lamont Bryan's 48th minute try but four minutes later Steve Tyrer scored the first of a hat-trick with a Jodie Broughton touchdown sandwiched in between, before Ben Jones-Bishop's last minute effort for Quins. Salford scrum-half Jeremy Smith was suspended for two games after pleading guilty to striking Harlequins' Danny Orr with his forearm.

Adrian Morley was a tower of strength while Ryan Atkins and Matt King terrorised the Bradford defence out wide, as Warrington scored 27-unanswered second-half points to complete a 33-8 home victory and keep pace with Wigan at the top. The Bulls were full value for an 8-6 interval advantage, but once their former junior, Atkins, crossed 11 minutes after the restart they rarely looked like scoring. Atkins had an outstanding game despite being woken at 6.30am on the day of a game for a random drugs test.

Having been dismantled 52-0 at Hearwell Stadium by Huddersfield the week before, Wakefield's confidence looked shot when they found themselves trailing 18-6 at the interval of the Friday-night TV game at Craven Park. Hull KR dominated the opening half with tries from Liam Colbon, Jake Webster and Scott Murrell and were expected to go on and win the game comfortably after Danny Brough's sin-binning on the half-time hooter. But a devastating ten-minute spell from a 12-man Wildcats side inspired by Sam Obst helped them back into the game and ensured Brough's professional did no damage. Two further converted scores and a field goal saw the Wildcats, who scored 25-unanswered points during the second half, pull away to a 31-18 win. Form prop Shane Tronc scored two tries.

Huddersfield turned over Leeds 26-20 in a thrilling game at the Galpharm Stadium on the Sunday, ending a run of 12 successive defeats to the Rhinos. The Giants were 20-12 down after 44 minutes, but retained their belief and came up with the winning try 17 minutes from the end when Martin Aspinwall went in from close range off Scott Grix's pass. Leroy Cudjoe kicked the goal and added a 74th minute penalty to cap the victory. Giants' Andy Raleigh was sin-binned for punching Ali Lauitiiti but escaped suspension.

The RFL that week had fined Leeds Rhinos' Keith Senior £1,000 – half of it suspended for the remainder of the season - for criticising referee Richard Silverwood in the aftermath of the previous month's Gillette World Club Challenge. By co-incidence Silverwood was the referee at the Galpharm Stadium. Huddersfield scrum-half Luke Robinson celebrated a new two-year contract extension even though his scrum-half place was threatened by the club's imminent signing of Wakefield's Danny Brough.

Wigan and Warrington lay in first and second positions in the Super League table after six rounds, with ten points each. But despite being four points ahead of Leeds and two ahead of St Helens, the two clubs that had contested the last three Grand Finals, the bookmakers refused to translate the leaders' early season form into favouritism to win the Super League trophy. The Rhinos remained the favourites, according to William Hill, although they had drifted from 11/10 before the start of the season to 6/4. St Helens were second favourites, but had also drifted to 4/1 from their early season price of 11/4. Warrington and Wigan were joint third favourites, with both clubs priced at 9/2, having moved from 9/1 and 10/1 respectively at the start of the season. Huddersfield Giants were fifth in the betting at 8/1.

Round 7

On a cold, wet Friday night in Wrexham, Crusaders unveiled high-profile capture Gareth Thomas in a 14-6 win against the Catalans, though the former Welsh rugby union captain and British Lion was helped from the field after just half an hour of his debut. Thomas suffered from blurred vision after a heavy knock in the first minute with his first touch as he ran the ball at David Ferriol. The hit left him wobbly and caused him to knock on the play the ball. He was then forced to withdraw after another tough tackle, this time from Jamal Fakir. The win meant Crusaders had equalled 2009's tally of three wins, in just their seventh game - the same number that champions Leeds had managed. Peter Lupton's 69th-minute try opened up an eight-point gap for the home side to decide a dour battle.

The Dragons' season appeared to be lurching from crisis to crisis. Adam Mogg, who made the Super League Dream Team in 2007, had left the club to re-join Canberra Raiders. Without injured star backs Clint Greenshields, Thomas Bosc, Jean-Philippe Baile and Mogg, they didn't have the creativity in them to score more than one try - and that came from a kick. And they lost top tryscorer Chris Walker to a calf strain minutes before the kick-off. His replacement at fullback was debutant David Guasch, whose normal position was in the halves.

St Helens coach Mick Potter insisted more was to come from Kyle Eastmond after the 20-year-old put in a match-winning performance in the win over Warrington at the GPW Recruitment Stadium on the Friday night. The England international grabbed a try and six goals as Saints ran out 28-18 winners in front of a sell-out crowd in horrible wet and cold conditions. Ade Gardner's second try, in the 67th minute, took the wind out of Warrington's sail after a blistering seven-minute spell brought them to within two points of Saints.

The defeat, only Warrington's second of the season, meant the Wolves had not beaten Saints on their home turf since January 1994 and still only had one Super League win under their belt against them since the move to summer in 1996.

While Saints were finding their touch, their great rivals Leeds were still struggling, losing 17-10 at home to Hull Kingston Rovers on the Friday night. Jamie Peacock joined the Rhinos' injury list, damaging ligaments in his foot. Rovers hung on for their first success at Headingley in a quarter of a century after leading 16-6 at half-time. Michael Dobson's guile and control and Ben Galea's work rate saw Justin Morgan's men through and Dobson's 77th minute field goal sealed the win.

Leeds fielded three debutants - Chris Clarkson, Michael Coady and Kyle Amor - and were thought ready to negotiate to take their former player Lee Smith back on loan at Headingley. Smith joined rugby union club London Wasps after the end of the 2009 Gillette Four Nations tournament, but had only played one first-team game for them.

Danny Tickle kicked three out of three goals for Hull against Bradford Bulls on a busy Friday night, helping the Airlie Birds to an 18-6 home victory. Hull suffered a major pre-match blow when in-form Richard Horne was a late withdrawal with a rib injury but Jordan Turner stepped in at stand-off with a match-winning display. Turner's try-saving tackle prevented Bradford extending their early 2-0 lead in the 24th minute - Stuart Reardon looked to be a certain scorer as raced to the corner until Turner flew across and smashed him into touch just short of the flag. Then, with only a few seconds of the first half remaining, Hull quickly formed a scrum near the Bulls' line and Turner was equally alert. Picking up the ball from the base of the scrum he put in a superb little kick under pressure that Jordan Tansey dived on between the posts.

Bradford did not deserve to be behind and they suffered their own pre-match blow when play-maker Matt Orford was laid low with a virus. His regular halfback partner Brett Kearney was also a few degrees under, but he switched to scrum-half and belied his state of health with a tireless effort. It was not until Lee Radford's 70th-minute converted try extended their lead to 18-2 that Hull could be certain of victory.

In midweek Bradford learned close-season signing Danny Sculthorpe would remain on the long-term sick list after picking up an infection following pre-season back surgery.

Paul Cooke made his Wakefield debut on the Sunday after joining the club from Hull KR on a short-term deal to the end of the season. Cooke made his entrance from the bench with the Wildcats already 28-0 ahead against Salford, eventually winning 36-6. The omission of Danny Brough from Wakefield's starting line-up added to speculation around his departure to Huddersfield, who travelled to London to beat Harlequins 32-18. Brett Hodgson was involved in most of the good things the Giants did in teeming West London rain, though it was Leroy Cudjoe who stole the headlines with a hat-trick of tries. Harlequins winger Jon Wells announced his retirement that weekend after failing to shake off the effects of neck surgery carried out during the off-season.

The Warriors emerged 36-22 winners at the Jungle on the Sunday afternoon to remain top of Super League. A flurry of three tries shortly after the break in the space of seven minutes, including the second of the electric Amos Roberts' hat-trick, helped the Super League leaders to register an ultimately comfortable victory over the battling Tigers

* France coach Bobbie Goulding received a reprimand for his alleged drunken behaviour at the Rugby League International Federation Player of the Year Dinner during the Four Nations tournament in 2009.

Round 8

A clinical second-half performance from Wigan in a bruising encounter at the DW Stadium kept them clear at the top of the Super League ladder with a 24-4 win and condemned Leeds to their third consecutive defeat and their fifth of the first eight rounds.

It was a creditable effort from the Rhinos. Leeds skipper Kevin Sinfield had still not recovered from the leg injury sustained in the World Club Challenge, while Ryan Bailey replaced Jamie Peacock (foot ligaments). Luke Ambler made his Rhinos debut from the substitutes bench.

With Wigan leading 6-0 at the break, an unconverted Ryan Hall try for Leeds six minutes after the restart could have set up a real shock. But a great run from Amos Roberts was followed by Pat Richards ghosting through some tired defence, before Sean O'Loughlin's cut-out pass was collected by winger Darrell Goulding, who dived over in the corner to extend Wigan's lead. Richards coolly added the goal for a 12-4 advantage. Then the on-form Joel Tomkins scored from close range and Goulding's second decided the contest. O'Loughlin was the top performer and that week was named the Rugby League World Player of the Month.

Warrington remained second after beating Wakefield at home 32-16, the 16-point margin flattering the Wildcats. Chris Riley scored his eighth, ninth and tenth tries of the season, Ryan Atkins picked up a brace against his old club, and Chris Bridge was outstanding. To Wakefield's credit, they kept coming back at Warrington, but without the departed Danny Brough and with Ben Jeffries still on the sick list, they lacked direction. Danny Kirmond did show some good debut touches after arriving on loan as part of the Brough transfer deal with Huddersfield. Kirmond's appearance was his first since picking up a knee injury the previous August that kept him out of the Giants' Challenge Cup final appearance.

March

The Giants unveiled Brough in the Sunday clash against St Helens at the Galpharm Stadium. But his debut off the bench ended in disappointment, as the Giants slipped to a 24-6 defeat against red-hot St Helens. Saints were beginning to look a real threat. James Graham worked tirelessly, Keiron Cunningham was superb and Kyle Eastmond added the finishing touches with a 78th-minute try that saw him duck under David Faiumu and Eorl Crabtree.

Salford club captain Rob Parker broke his hand in the Reds' shock 27-20 win over Hull FC at the Willows in the Saturday TV game. The Reds had a 100 per cent completion rate in the second 40 minutes after allowing a bright opening to slip away, and that saw Australian halfback Daniel Holdsworth control the contest, while former loan Hull winger Jodie Broughton scored two crucial and well-taken second-half tries. Fullback Karl Fitzpatrick also showed a poacher's instinct to help himself to his own double – the second after a touch of magic from Steve Tyrer – while the Reds' forwards, led by an impressive start from Adam Sidlow, got the better of their more illustrious opponents. Tyrer's moment of absolute brilliance came in the 57th minute as the Reds regained the lead after Broughton had levelled with his first try four minutes after the break. Holdsworth's kick to the right looked to be far too strong, but Tyrer reached skywards, flicked the ball back in play as he headed over the dead-ball line, and Fitzpatrick followed through to score.

Hull KR winger Liam Colbon was released from hospital in Perpignan on the Sunday after being cleared to return to England with his teammates. Colbon was admitted to hospital and detained overnight with a broken jaw sustained in the closing minutes of Rovers' 16-10 defeat by the Catalans Dragons at Stade Gilbert Brutus the previous night. Medical staff at the stadium took more than seven minutes to take him from the field, after he was involved in a collision with Dragons' fullback Chris Walker in the build-up to the Robins' last try. Man of the match Walker received a two-match ban for reckless contact with the head and neck. Catalans' vital win came as Thomas Bosc returned from pre-season injury to give the Dragons some much-needed direction from the halves. Cyrille Gossard's try 16 minutes from time made it 16-0 as Hull KR failed to finish off plenty of chances.

Another club with an injury crisis, Castleford, signed a second Wigan player in forward Chris Tuson on a month's loan and he was concussed on debut in the Tigers' 22-16 home win over Crusaders. It was the Tigers' first home win since beating the same club the previous September. Castleford owed much to Rangi Chase. The stand-off produced the pass for their first try and a kick that led to the fourth and final touchdown. In between he was also involved in the moves that brought their other two tries. Jordan Thompson's 72nd-minute try grew in importance as Crusaders' strong finish closed the gap to six points.

Bulls coach Steve McNamara's decision to switch Brett Kearney to fullback for the first time since his arrival in England tipped the balance as Bradford won their first game in the last three, by 19-12, to leave Harlequins still rooted to the bottom of the table. Never-say-die Quins were always in with a shout of something until Matt Orford's late field goal.

SUPER LEAGUE TABLE - *Sunday 28th March*

	P	W	D	L	F	A	D	PTS
Wigan Warriors	8	7	0	1	278	104	174	14
Warrington Wolves	8	6	0	2	249	112	137	12
St Helens	8	6	0	2	227	148	79	12
Huddersfield Giants	8	5	0	3	186	102	84	10
Hull FC	8	5	0	3	194	143	51	10
Wakefield T Wildcats	8	5	0	3	173	178	-5	10
Hull Kingston Rovers	8	4	0	4	133	175	-42	8
Bradford Bulls	8	4	0	4	121	167	-46	8
Leeds Rhinos	8	3	0	5	180	139	41	6
Castleford Tigers	8	3	0	5	168	213	-45	6
Crusaders	8	3	0	5	138	215	-77	6
Salford City Reds	8	2	0	6	109	197	-88	4
Catalans Dragons	8	2	0	6	98	200	-102	4
Harlequins	8	1	0	7	86	247	-161	2

* Former Wigan coach Denis Betts was one of four Englishmen interviewed for the vacant England coaching position, along with Richard Agar, Steve McNamara and Brian McDermott.

APRIL
New Order

Round 9

Super League leaders Wigan assumed outright favouritism to win the SLXV Grand Final in October, with official bookmakers William Hill quoting odds of 9/4, in from 10/1 before the season started, after their 18-10 win at St Helens on Good Friday.

Pre-season favourites Leeds drifted in the betting from 11/10 to 11/4, after registering only three wins from nine rounds. They did however manage to salvage a 20-20 draw from their Thursday-night derby at Headingley with the previously unfancied Bradford Bulls. Lee Smith, who had left at the end of 2009 to play rugby union but returned to his old club, was the Rhinos' hero with two tries, including the score in the right corner that finally levelled three minutes from time. The Bulls should have taken both points after dominating three-quarters of a dramatic, helter-skelter clash and building what appeared to be a match-winning 20-6 lead with centre Chris Nero's second try on 52 minutes. According to the Bulls, there were question marks about whether Smith should have actually played at Headingley. The Rhinos named a 19-man squad that didn't include Smith's name on the Tuesday, but they were then given special permission by the RFL.

After Smith's leveller that Sinfield could not convert, Andy Lynch for the Bulls and Rob Burrow and Jamie Jones-Buchanan all missed with field-goal attempts.

St Helens coach Mick Potter felt that referee Ben Thaler should have been brave enough to send Wigan fullback Amos Roberts to the sin bin for a second time during Saints' Good Friday 18-10 defeat to Wigan, who recorded their first victory at Knowsley Road since September 2003. It was the last Good Friday Super League clash between the two at the famous old ground, Saints expecting to be in a new stadium for the 2011 season.

Roberts, filling in at fullback for the injured Cameron Phelps, received a yellow card after 45 minutes for preventing Leon Pryce taking a quick tap penalty. While he was off the field Saints cut a 16-0 deficit down to just six points, thanks to tries from Ade Gardner and Tony Puletua. After Roberts returned he was again penalised on 66 minutes, this time for obstructing Saints forward Jon Wilkin after Wilkin had chipped past the Australian. Only a penalty ensued.

It was a pulsating 80 minutes in the driving rain. After an early Pat Richards penalty, Wigan applied most of the pressure and it eventually told when video referee Phil Bentham gave Darrell Goulding the nod after Francis Meli and James Roby spilled a high kick which allowed the winger to pounce for his eighth try of the season, Richards adding the extras as Wigan led 8-0. Another two quick penalties for Wigan kept the pressure on before hooker Mike Mcllorum ignored the pleas to go for goal and tapped the ball to Iafeta Palea'aesina, who bulldozed his way over from close range to extend Wigan's lead. Richards again added the two for 14-0.

St Helens needed to score first in the second half to give them a chance of forcing a comeback, but it was the Warriors who extended their advantage as Richards slotted over his fourth goal after Leon Pryce interfered at the play-the-ball. Three successive penalties on Wigan's line eventually saw Roberts sent to the sin bin and Saints thought they had crossed for their first score but Bentham ruled that James Roby was held up by a great tackle from Richards. But from the next play-the-ball the home side made their extra man count as Eastmond's neat kick to the corner was collected on the full by Gardner and touched down. Eastmond added the extras for 16-6.

Saints again made their extra man count on 56 minutes as Puletua forced his way over from close range from Keiron Cunningham's short ball. Just as Roberts prepared to come back into the game. Eastmond failed to add the conversion and Wigan led 16-10. Wigan wasted a glorious opportunity to put the game to bed following a break from Sam Tomkins, but he put in an ill-judged kick when a pass inside to Thomas Leuluai was the better option. Two minutes later a penalty from Pryce for an attack on Sam Tomkins' head while the scrum-half was on the floor allowed Richards to slot over his fifth goal for an 18-10 winning lead.

In the Hull derby, Hull FC edged Rovers 18-14 at Craven Park, as heroic defence won the day. A succession of errors and penalties put Hull FC under enormous pressure, but they made up for that with defiant backs-to-the-wall defence. Rovers were eight points ahead after as many minutes and their fans were in good voice when they led 14-6 midway through the first half. But it was Hull's Old Faithful that was ringing out towards the end. Jordan Tansey's try on the hour was a beauty. Halfbacks Sean Long and Richard Horne fanned the ball out to the left, with the latter finding Tansey gliding up from the rear to go on a 20-metre curving run to the corner, where a little swerve took him away from the covering Shaun Briscoe.

Wakefield beat Castleford at Belle Vue 19-6 to move within four points of leaders Wigan. The old rivals had gone in at the break on level terms at 6-6, with both sides struggling to control the ball in testing, greasy conditions. But Paul Cooke took a grip in the second period to help steer the Wildcats to a comfortable victory after the previous week's indifferent display at Warrington. Cooke had a hand in the first try of the second period when, five minutes after the restart, he fired a long ball to centre Darryl Millard, who sent winger Dale Morton over in the corner with a peach of a pass. Cooke, who had previously converted Sam Obst's first-half try from the touchline, stepped up again to land a difficult conversion. Castleford found themselves back on their own line five minutes later, following Obst's 40/20, and when Ben Jeffries sent a telling chip over the visitors' line, Tevita Leo-Latu rose above a tiring defence for a crucial score. Cooke again added the extras and after his 65th minute penalty Trinity effectively had the game in the bag. Cooke's 71st-minute field goal confirmed that.

Warrington weren't at their best but still managed to rack up seven tries in despatching Salford 32-2 on Good Friday. If they'd had a goalkicker they would have surpassed 40 points. Chris Bridge only managed two from seven. Chris Riley got two of the tries to take him clear at the top of the Super League try-scoring charts with 12.

Danny Brough treated fans to a masterclass in his first start for Huddersfield as the Giants returned to winning ways with a resounding 48-6 Good Friday home triumph over Catalans Dragons. The 28-year-old scrum-half was at his best, turning in a man-of-the-match performance that saw him score two and create two of his side's nine tries against the injury and suspension-hit French outfit. Brett Hodgson scored a try and kicked six goals to claim a personal haul of 16 points.

The Thursday-night fixture between Crusaders and Harlequins was postponed because of a waterlogged pitch at the Gnoll in Neath.

Round 10

Salford City Reds caused the shock of the Easter Monday programme with a 30-18 defeat of Huddersfield at the Willows. Daniel Holdsworth kicked seven goals from seven attempts for the home side, who got the ball rolling in the fifth minute with a try to Adam Sidlow. Wingman Ashley Gibson added Salford's second on 34 minutes, with Holdsworth also kicking two penalties during the first period. Holdsworth then crossed for a try of his own a minute after the restart to put daylight between the sides. The Giants registered their first points through Brett Hodgson's try, with Larne Patrick, Leroy Cudjoe and Paul Whatuira also crossing. But Steve Tyrer's try on 62 minutes, coupled with Danny Brough's failure to convert three of the Giants' four-pointers, ensured a comfortable Reds victory.

Danny McGuire's magnificent 76th-minute try was enough to secure a 34-24 victory in Perpignan for a Rhinos side that looked unstoppable in the first half. The Dragons, who were backing up from a heavy defeat at Huddersfield three days earlier, came back strongly in the second half after four tries in eleven first-half minutes had given the Rhinos a commanding lead. Ali Lauitiiti, Jamie Jones-Buchanan, Keith Senior and Danny McGuire all touched down to silence the home fans after Jerome Guisset and had given the French team an early advantage. Brett Delaney's try five minutes before the break looked decisive, but it was cancelled out by Dallas Johnson's effort, controversially awarded by video referee Stuart Cummings, which set the platform for an unlikely Dragons comeback.

Kylie Leuluai was sin-binned early in the second half after a late challenge on Dimitri Pelo as he kicked on the last tackle, and the Catalans took advantage with a Julien Touxagas try, with Bosc's goal reducing the deficit to eight points. Sinfield kicked a penalty, but then made a blunder on the last tackle, trying to shepherd Bosc's grubber dead, but failing to see Kane Bentley sneaking in on his blind side to touch down. Bosc's goal put the Catalans in sight of an unlikely victory, but then Sinfield made amends with a brilliant pass on the break to the supporting McGuire, who evaded Steven Bell to cross for the matchwinner.

Warrington scored 19-unanswered points in the second half at the KC Stadium to break Hull FC's resistance and tarnish their unbeaten 2010 home record with a 29-10 win. It took the Wolves just three minutes to take the lead when Chris Hicks crossed. The Airlie Birds battled back though and Willie Manu's try just before the half-hour mark, after Craig Hall's 16th-minute opener, had given them the lead. But their advantage lasted just four minutes. Hicks grabbed his second before half-time to tie the game, with Richard Whiting and the returning Lee Briers kicking one from two for their respective sides.

The second half was tightly contested before Warrington pulled away in the final ten minutes. Richard Myler's 49th-minute effort gave the Wolves the lead, before Michael Monaghan's try and Briers' field goal settled the contest. There was still time for Hicks to complete his hat-trick.

Wigan remained two points clear after a 54-14 home win over Wakefield, though an injury to Super League's form winger Amos Roberts put a dampener on a great Wigan performance. Roberts was stretchered off after rupturing his posterior cruciate knee ligament while scoring his second try. The former Sydney Roosters star beat four defenders on his way to the line before colliding awkwardly with one of the post protectors.

Roberts' two first-half tries were complemented by Pat Richards' brace and tries to Darrell Goulding and Joel Tomkins, as the Warriors coasted into a 32-0 interval lead. They began the second half in similar fashion, with Goulding adding his second three minutes in. Wakefield never really threatened to cause an upset, but were able to stifle the rampant Warriors with three tries in the third quarter, one from Damien Blanch and two from Matt Blaymire. Goulding and Richards completed their hat-tricks, with six conversions taking Richards' personal points tally on the day to 24.

Two quick-fire Saints tries after the break ensured a return to winning ways for St Helens as they hammered Castleford at the Jungle 52-18. The first half was a close-run affair, with Saints taking an early lead through tries from Kyle Eastmond and Francis Meli. At the end of the first quarter the Tigers struck back, thanks to tries by Craig Huby and

Ryan Clayton which, with Joe Westerman converting the first, saw them back on level terms. Maurie Fa'asavalu's try before the interval again put Saints in front, before James Roby and Meli, with his second, put daylight between the sides. Westerman responded for the Tigers but, by this stage, Saints were home and dry. Eastmond's second on the hour was quickly followed by tries to Tony Puletua and Leon Pryce, before Roby wrapped things up for Saints with his second. Michael Shenton's consolation try in the final minute did little to lift the spirits of the Castleford faithful, who had endured a miserable Easter weekend after their defeat at neighbours Wakefield three days earlier.

Bradford Bulls made it three points from a tough Easter weekend by battling to a 20-16 home win over former coach Brian Noble's Crusaders. The Bulls were far from their best following their gruelling draw at Leeds, but they battled hard for the full 80 minutes against a side playing its first match in ten days. Michael Platt's try eight minutes from time finally settled the game in the Bulls' favour. Former State of Origin fullback Clinton Schifcofske made his League comeback for Crusaders after a three-year spell in rugby union.

Hull KR bounced back from Good Friday's agonising derby defeat with a ruthless performance at the Stoop, condemning Harlequins to their sixth consecutive league defeat - by 52-12. With Quins' scheduled match against Crusaders on the Thursday postponed, and captain Rob Purdham playing his first game of the season. many expected the Robins to struggle. The rest did little to rejuvenate the struggling Londoners, however, as the men from east Hull raced into a 16-0 lead inside 15 minutes through tries from Ben Galea, Matt Cook and Michael Dobson. Kris Welham then grabbed his first try just after the half-hour mark, with scrum-half Dobson kicking three from four to give Hull KR a commanding lead at the interval.

Despite managing to get off the mark with tries to Danny Orr and Luke Williamson, things didn't improve for the struggling Londoners in the second half. Welham crossed for his second five minutes in, before completing his hat-trick and then adding a fourth in the final ten minutes. Further tries from Rhys Lovegrove and Galea piled on the misery for Quins.

Round 11

Wigan's dominance of SLXV continued as they moved four points clear at the top of the table, after Warrington suffered their third defeat of the season - a 36-16 reverse at Hull Kingston Rovers.

The Warriors were made to work hard in the blazing sun to record their tenth victory of the season, by 18-4, over a battling Salford at the Willows. The game was no classic but strong defence from both sides and some clinical finishing from winger Pat Richards proved to be the difference in front of over six and half thousand fans. Salford coach Shaun McRae was back in the dug-out for the City Reds after missing the win over Huddersfield Giants through illness and his side trailed only 6-4 at half-time. But Richards scored the only two tries of the second half and his second with 20 minutes remaining left Salford with too much to do.

In front of another big, vocal home crowd, Hull Kingston Rovers produced a magnificent Sunday-afternoon performance to inflict a 20-point defeat on the in-form Wolves. Chris Riley's 54th minute try levelled at 16-all, but Rovers finished with a late flurry and were deserved winners of a wonderfully entertaining clash. Coach Justin Morgan paid tribute to England winger Peter Fox after an outstanding display which saw him pick up three Albert Goldthorpe points, scoring two tries in an energetic performance.

Castleford duo Joe Westerman and Rangi Chase missed the 24-0 defeat at Huddersfield on the Friday night. The pair were stood down by Cas coach Terry Matterson for an undisclosed breach of the club's disciplinary code. The Tigers already had seven first-team players out injured before Matterson chose to leave two of his most potent attacking threats in the stands. The makeshift pairing of Ryan McGoldrick and Kirk Netherton at halfback did their best, and there were plenty of other willing workers, including 17-year-old substitute Oliver Holmes making his debut. All four Giants tries came from wingers, including a David Hodgson hat-trick, plus four great conversions by Brett Hodgson in what was a hard forward slog.

Crusaders notched their fourth win of the season and moved up to tenth in the table with a 20-10 win over Wakefield at Belle Vue. Two second-half tries swung the contest in the Welsh side's favour. Gareth Thomas scored his first try since switching from rugby union. Brian Noble was forced into a late re-shuffle after halfback Luke Dyer's wife went into labour on the Saturday night, but he was able to debut former Wests Tigers' utility back Rhys Hanbury from the bench following his belated acquisition of a visa.

Michael Witt's varied kicking kept maximum pressure on Trinity, continually turning them round and forcing them to attack from deep. Nick Youngquest's spectacular long-range 54th-minute try to make it 16-10 after the sides remained level at the break buoyed the Crusaders.

St Helens found the going tough at the Stoop as a double-header with rugby union saw a crowd of over five thousand watch Harlequins put in a feisty effort before going down 32-24. Quins had winger Kevin Penny on debut at the start of a loan spell from Warrington. He scored a try but the gamestar was Kyle Eastmond, with a try and six from six goals. James Roby's second try with eight minutes to play finally opened up a winning margin for the Saints.

The Bulls looked impressive in their 36-14 win over the Dragons in boiling-hot Perpignan. Gamestar Steve Menzies' touchdown 19 minutes from time killed off any hope of a Dragons comeback, as Rikki Sheriffe finished with a hat-trick of tries. Catalans received a blow with the news that their new signing from Australia, Chris Walker, would miss at least 12 weeks after fracturing his neck in his comeback match from a two-game suspension.

The Bulls moved up to fifth as Hull FC lost at Leeds 46-30. The Rhinos built a 16-point lead in an impressive opening half hour and posted five tries in 20 minutes to win the contest and they looked very good, with skipper Kevin Sinfield in near complete control. But, having seemingly rediscovered the ruthlessness of champions, they allowed the initiative to be wrested from them. Keith Senior's first try in the 57th minute, a product of his searing long-range break, to make it 28-14, snuffed out Hull's hope, after they had clawed back a 16-point deficit to near parity.

Young Hull winger Tom Briscoe bagged four tries, thanks predominantly to some sterling centre play from Kirk Yeaman, but the Airlie Birds lost Shaun Berrigan with a broken collar-bone. First choice halfbacks Sean Long and Richard Horne, Craig Fitzgibbon and Danny Tickle were already on the injury list.

Challenge Cup Round 4

Steve McNamara led the Bulls to a 50-0 Challenge Cup victory over Dewsbury Rams on the Sunday of the Challenge Cup weekend and the following Wednesday was announced as the new England coach, on a part-time basis alongside his Bradford job until the end of the season.

McNamara was urged to build the national team around Wigan's Sam Tomkins by Sheffield Eagles boss Mark Aston, after his side was beaten by Wigan at Bramall Lane on the Saturday. The Warriors star turned on the skills, scoring a hat-trick of tries as Wigan struggled at times to beat the Championship team 50-34.

Huddersfield coach Nathan Brown advised McNamara to draft Kevin Brown into his plans for the Four Nations. The Huddersfield stand-off was outstanding during his side's televised 40-12 Carnegie Challenge Cup triumph over Hull Kingston Rovers on the

Sunday, having a hand in four of the Giants' seven tries.

Castleford coach Terry Matterson insisted his position would not change after his side was dumped out of the Carnegie Challenge Cup by Championship club Barrow at the Jungle on the Sunday. The Raiders clinched a thrilling Cup-tie 34-28 with Ned Catic's last-minute try against his former club – the first time a Super League side had been beaten by lower division opposition since 2006, when Warrington lost to Hull KR.

Luke Dorn made his first start of the campaign after shoulder surgery in the Saturday 23-16 win over Wakefield Wildcats at the Stoop. Luke Gale's last-minute field goal finally secured a Quins victory. Wakefield were without home-sick Shane Tronc, on his way back to Australia where he joined Brisbane Broncos.

Amateurs Siddal made their exit to Batley by 34-2 at the Shay. Batley winger Lee Greenwood was left out of the Bulldogs team to concentrate on his role of coaching the National Conference League champions.

Former Wigan and Salford scrum-half Martin Crompton watched his Championship One side come from 18-6 down at the break to upset higher-division Whitehaven and claim the biggest win in Blackpool Panthers' short history by 24-18.

Blackpool were rewarded with a fifth-round tie at Leeds, who were made the firm 9/4 favourites to win the Cup in the wake of their 48-24 victory over Hull FC at the KC Stadium on the Saturday, with Hull suffering a record home defeat. Although Ryan Hall produced excellent finishing to score four tries, the Leeds victory was forged on a tremendous first-half performance by Carl Ablett. After a promising start, Hull - missing Sean Long and Shaun Berrigan and losing Lee Radford, Danny Tickle and Kirk Yeaman during the game - were always doing the chasing and were out-classed in almost every department.

There was still one fourth round tie to be completed, as the game between Widnes and French club Lezignan was postponed after the French club's flight to England was cancelled due to a volcanic ash cloud emanating from Iceland that had brought airports across Europe to a standstill. Lezignan's attempts to sub-charter a flight to bring them to England were thwarted by the continued closure of British airspace. Widnes won the tie 44-24 when it was finally played on the following Thursday after Lezignan travelled by coach.

Salford had been forced to make the long journey to Perpignan for their tie against Catalans Dragons by coach, before they eventually went down 30-8 to their French hosts. Leigh Centurions endured a similar nightmare coach journey for their 32-20 Challenge Cup win in Limoux on the Saturday. The Centurions arrived in Limoux just 12 hours before kick-off, but recovered from a 12-10 half-time deficit to book their place in the last 16 of the competition.

Toulouse Olympique completed a 50-hour, 1,836 mile round trip to fulfil their fixture with St Helens on the Saturday night. They set off at 6pm on Friday night from Toulouse, heading to Bilbao in northern Spain before catching an overnight ferry to Portsmouth. They then drove straight to St Helens, arriving at 6.45pm – just 75 minutes before a kick-off time that had already been pushed back two hours. St Helens emerged 56-16 winners, but Olympique put in a brave performance and even led when Vincent Duport went over after just two minutes.

Warrington started their defence of the Carnegie Challenge Cup with a 48-24 home victory, running in nine tries, against a determined Featherstone Rovers.

Round 12

Harlequins travelled to leaders Wigan on the Friday night of the last round of April with only one win to their name all season and produced the biggest shock of the year with a 38-26 win. Amazingly, Quins were losing 24-6 at the break but won the second half by 30 points to leave a crowd of 18,605 absolutely stunned. The Londoners spoilt the Warriors' much-publicised St George's Day celebration by inflicting a second defeat of the season on the league leaders.

Danny Orr was magnificent on his return to Wigan, kicking seven goals out of seven and inspiring Quins throughout, having been switched permanently it seemed from scrum-half to hooker, with Chad Randall at halfback. Two tries from Luke Dorn in the first twelve minutes of the second half signalled the start of the comeback and Randall's late try finally put the game to bed. The only downside for Harlequins was that loanee from Leeds, Ben Jones-Bishop, was expected to be out for six weeks with a fractured skull.

One bright spot for the Warriors was the performance of young back-rower Liam Farrell, cousin of Wigan great Andy, who started his first game for the club and scored two tries, was held up over the line in attempting to score a third, and put in a big defensive shift. Shaun Ainscough played his first Wigan game of the season after being recalled from his loan spell at Castleford, but was subsequently sent to Widnes for a second spell of the season on a dual-registration.

The big game of the weekend was on the Saturday at Knowsley Road. Injury-hit Saints fielded twelve players who had previously played for their Academy side, and beat the reigning champions Leeds 41-20. Keiron Cunningham and James Roby combined to terrorise Leeds and move St Helens to within two points of leaders Wigan. Cunningham's typically shrewd distribution laid on three Saints tries, while Roby crossed twice himself.

With a third hooker, Scott Moore – playing at half with Leon Pryce a late withdrawal due to a broken foot – also playing his full part, the home side shrugged off the absence of a host of key men. Alongside Pryce, Mick Potter was also missing Jon Wilkin, Matt Gidley, Sia Soliola and Francis Meli, but after a stuttering start they overwhelmed a Rhinos side that had now lost half of its opening 12 matches.

Leeds were missing their own first-choice players in Brent Webb and Carl Ablett, but still started the game superbly with Lee Smith crossing after just 56 seconds. But the momentum of the game shifted significantly after Ryan Hall had a 12th minute try disallowed by the video referee for a shepherd, with the home side – aided by six straight penalties – dominating possession and field possession. The Rhinos briefly mounted a second-half comeback but the first-half defensive stint had sapped them.

Young winger Jamie Foster came in for praise after kicking eight goals on his Super League debut and his 66th-minute penalty goal re-established Saints' control when Leeds got to within eleven points. The Rhinos did have the final say when Rob Burrow swooped on a loose ball right on his own line and raced 100 metres, with James Graham chasing in vain.

Brett Hodgson told League Express he was to leave Huddersfield Giants - who would only offer him a one-year extension on his contract - at the end of the season and sign a two-year deal with Warrington. But the Giants rejected a report in the Sydney press suggesting coach Nathan Brown, in the second year of a three-year contract, would be returning home to coach in the NRL in 2011.

Hodgson was out with a deadleg on the Sunday at the Racecourse Ground as Kevin Brown inspired Huddersfield Giants to a seven-try, 38-10 victory over the Crusaders. Brad Drew played his first game since re-signing from Wakefield in 2009. Scott Grix's try five minutes after the break gave the Welsh side too much to do in the second half as winger David Hodgson finished with a hat-trick.

That week, Crusaders winger Gareth Raynor was warned by a judge that he could face jail, after admitting his involvement in a £36,000 ink cartridge counterfeiting scam.

Castleford coach Terry Matterson paid tribute to 18-year-old fullback Jordan Thompson, a try scorer in the Tigers' 30-12 win over Salford as they bounced back from the Challenge Cup defeat to Championship side Barrow. The Tigers, while never behind, were unable to shake Salford off until deep into the closing quarter, and ultimately Castleford were grateful to Joe Westerman, whose seven goals from as many attempts were a significant factor in a first win in five outings. Salford coach Shaun McRae refused to blame the effects of the previous weekend's arduous return journey to the south of

April

France by coach for his side's defeat. The Reds were on the road from Friday to Tuesday.

Hull FC battled to their first win in four games, edging their televised home clash with Wakefield 12-8 in an unimaginative spectacle at the KC Stadium. Twenty penalties and 20 scrums made for a stoppage every two minutes and despite enterprising starts from both sides, a stop-start encounter never really hit the heights. It was a vital two points for the Black and Whites, whose defence had shipped 120 points in their previous three-game losing streak. Despite falling behind to a Darryl Millard score, two converted first-half tries for Richard Whiting proved just enough as the injury-hit East Yorkshire side ended their winless run with a huge defensive effort.

The Wildcats had an early lead but were 12-4 down for almost the whole of the second half. They needed to score twice and managed a fine try from Damien Blanch late on. With a minute remaining, the Wildcats opted not to take the conversion but, as they attacked after the restart, hopes of a comeback were ended by the final hooter.

The Sunday after Steve McNamara was unveiled officially as the new England coach, Bradford out-classed Hull KR at Odsal in a 40-4 victory. Bradford's most comprehensive Super League win of the season came on the back of an almost watertight defensive display that so nearly yielded a second successive shut out (following their 50-0 cup win at Dewsbury). And having frustrated Hull KR for over an hour, the Bulls attack cut loose with four tries in the final quarter that left a hitherto subdued crowd cheering their favourites off the pitch. Two early second-half penalties distanced Rovers before Rikki Sheriffe's brace of tries just after the hour put the result beyond doubt.

Warrington - whose coach Tony Smith had that week extended his contract to the end of 2013 - moved to within two points of Wigan as they cruised home 40-6 in an ill-tempered home clash with Catalans Dragons. The Wolves bounced back from defeat at Hull KR a fortnight before with an impressive first-half performance, after which they led 28-0. Gamestar Richie Mathers - thought likely to be ousted by the arrival of Brett Hodgson at the end of the season - grabbed two of Warrington's five first-half tries while Chris Riley and Jean-Philippe Baile were sin-binned in the 29th minute.

The pick of the Wolves' seven tries came within seconds of the half-time hooter as Riley scored a 50-metre effort just seconds after coming back on. Subs Mike Cooper - back from a loan spell at Castleford - and Mickey Higham claimed their first tries of the season after the break while David Ferriol scored the only try for the dismal Dragons, who slipped to the bottom of the table after their fourth Super League game without a win.

SUPER LEAGUE TABLE - *Sunday 25th April*

	P	W	D	L	F	A	D	PTS
Wigan Warriors	12	10	0	2	394	170	224	20
Warrington Wolves	12	9	0	3	366	166	200	18
St Helens	12	9	0	3	362	228	134	18
Huddersfield Giants	12	8	0	4	314	148	166	16
Bradford Bulls	12	7	1	4	237	221	16	15
Hull FC	12	7	0	5	264	240	24	14
Hull Kingston Rovers	12	6	0	6	239	261	-22	12
Wakefield T Wildcats	12	6	0	6	224	270	-46	12
Leeds Rhinos	12	5	1	6	300	254	46	11
Castleford Tigers	12	4	0	8	222	320	-98	8
Crusaders	11	4	0	7	184	283	-99	8
Salford City Reds	12	3	0	9	157	295	-138	6
Harlequins	11	2	0	9	160	357	-197	4
Catalans Dragons	12	2	0	10	148	358	-210	4

* The big story of April unfolded in Australia where Melbourne Storm were stripped of two NRL titles, three minor premierships, fined $500,000 and ordered to repay $1.1 million in prize money for breaching the salary cap by $1.7m over the previous five years. They would also not be able to accrue league points during the 2010 campaign, ensuring they would finish the season with the wooden spoon.

MAY
It's a kind of Magic

Round 13

RFL Chief Executive Nigel Wood hailed the 2010 Magic Weekend as 'another great example of the Rugby League family coming together to enjoy the big occasion.' After two years at the Millennium Stadium, Cardiff, the Magic Weekend had moved to Edinburgh in 2009 and in SLXV around 52,000 people attended the seven fixtures.

The exact attendance for the weekend was 52,043 – 26,642 on the Saturday, when there were four matches played, and 25,401 for the three games on Sunday. The figure was slightly down on 2009. Wood said he was not overly disappointed, although the future of the event was to be decided.

The first game on the Saturday provided a shock for Bradford - in search of a fourth successive victory - as a first-half Michael Witt masterclass produced a 19-0 Crusaders win. Witt emerged with 15 points from two tries, three goals and a field goal, while fellow Australian Jarrod Sammut, barely 48 hours after landing in the UK, added the other four points through a dazzling touchdown at the end of an eye-catching 45-minute debut. Sammut, who had suffered a lengthy delay en route in Bangkok, started on the bench, and came onto the field after 36 minutes. He was a livewire for the rest of the game before his sensational try secured the Crusaders' fifth win of the season. He juggled a Weller Hauraki pass into his grasp, kicked over the head of Jason Crookes, re-gathered and sparked joyous celebrations as he rolled across the whitewash.

Hull coach Richard Agar accused some of his players of not trying after the 25-8 defeat to Harlequins, while bemoaning the club's worsening injury crisis, with Epalahame Lauaki limping off with a torn calf muscle. The entertaining victory, which was built around a commanding first half in which they established a 15-0 lead, was Quins' second in eight days following their stunning win at Wigan. Playmakers Chad Randall, Luke Dorn and Luke Gale were all in fine form while centre David Howell made a big contribution to a dominant first-half display.

Richie Myler put one over his old club Salford by scoring two tries and having a hand in countless others as Warrington hammered the Reds 68-16. Even without Matt King, Mickey Higham, Paul Wood, Garreth Carvell and Richie Mathers the Wolves were far too good for Shaun McRae's side in every department. Most of the Warrington backline were on fire, and Lee Briers' distribution and kicking was magnificent.

The best game of the Saturday was saved for last, as three unanswered tries in the second half, including a crucial late effort from hooker Danny Buderus, gave Leeds a 34-30 win over Wakefield - only their sixth Super League win of the season.

After going twelve points behind in as many minutes to a Ben Jeffries-inspired Wildcats, who shrugged off the loss of Danny Kirmond in the warm-up with a back spasm, two touchdowns in five minutes seemed to have the defending champions back on track, only for them to fall 28-10 behind going into the break. Their revival began with Ryan Hall's second touchdown, two seconds before the interval, fashioned by Danny McGuire, Brent Webb and Keith Senior with a perfect flat pass, coupled with a touchline conversion from Kevin Sinfield, who had won back possession with a cunning short kick-off. Five minutes into the second period, young back-rower Chris Clarkson – who was a standout throughout – confirmed the comeback with his first try for the club, rolling out of four tacklers to plant the ball down. Hall completed his hat-trick and Buderus's expertly-crafted try with barely three minutes remaining gave the Rhinos the lead for the first and ultimately decisive time. Leeds were the only club to have won all their four Magic fixtures, while Wakefield's fourth straight defeat left them clinging with their fingernails to a top-eight spot.

Sunday opened with Castleford winning a Magic fixture for the first time as they beat Catalans 34-18. Tigers halfbacks Rangi Chase and, especially, Brent Sherwin constantly pinned the French back in their own half with the boot, and forced a total of five goal-line drop-outs. With Joe Westerman outshining his counterpart Gregory Mounis in the conversion stakes in what was a close contest until the final stages, kicking proved a key element. Sherwin also finished with a rare try double, as did Ryan McGoldrick, whose knack of being in the right place at the right time proved invaluable.

Catalans improved on their defeat at Warrington, according to coach Kevin Walters, who only arrived back in the UK on the Saturday after returning to Australia for a family funeral. Mounis never stopped working in the back row and Jean-Philippe Baile made some eye-catching plays from the unfamiliar position of hooker, but it was not enough to haul them off the bottom of the table.

Huddersfield-Wigan was billed as the game of the weekend and the Warriors remained top of the table with a 28-10 win built on a fine first-half defensive stint, before they ruthlessly cut loose in the second. Wigan's 38-26 defeat to Quins had come on the heels of an unconvincing Cup win over Championship side Sheffield and Michael Maguire brought back Andy Coley, Thomas Leuluai and Darrell Goulding, while handing a maiden Super League appearance to Academy product Stefan Marsh. Karl Pryce came in on the wing, in Cameron Phelps' absence, for his first start since the previous July and scored a four-pointer in a blitz of three tries in the opening 14 minutes of the second half.

After the game, Huddersfield coach Nathan Brown suggested that a 'vigilante movement' could enter Rugby League if referees didn't offer more protection to the smaller players in the game. His comments came after Wigan skipper Sean O'Loughlin conceded no more than a penalty after flattening Giants hooker Luke Robinson with a late tackle during the first half.

St Helens coach Mick Potter was delighted to see his team rack up the biggest win of the Magic Weekend as they hammered Hull KR 54-0, surpassing the margin of Warrington's 68-16 win over Salford. Leon Pryce was at the centre of an 11-try rout, with Kyle Eastmond and James Roby also outstanding in a Saints masterclass. Potter had emerged as joint favourite with Harlequins' Brian McDermott to become the new coach of Bradford Bulls in 2011. Speculation was mounting that Saints would not renew Potter's contract at the end of the season.

Rovers never recovered from the shock of conceding two tries in the first six minutes and had leaked 134 points in their last four matches to increase the worries for coach Justin Morgan, who denied rumours in the Australian press that scrum-half Michael Dobson was return home to Canberra Raiders.

Challenge Cup Round 5

Round five of the Challenge Cup took place on the weekend after the general election had resulted in a hung parliament and with negotiations under way between the Liberal Democrats and the two main parties, Conservative and Labour, to form a coalition.

The political uncertainty had no effect on Cup-holders Warrington Wolves in their TV rematch on the Saturday with the team they had beaten at Wembley on 2009, Huddersfield, at the Galpharm Stadium. It was meant to be too close to call but the

Wolves crossed for 12 tries - centre Chris Bridge for five of them - in a 60-4 blow out.

The brilliant Wolves were 24 points up by half-time and the off-colour Giants continued to cough up possession. Brett Hodgson returned early from injury with his thigh heavily strapped and the usually consummate fullback was one of several players who dropped the ball in front of his own posts. Hodgson insisted that thoughts of his impending move to Warrington were the furthest thing from his mind.

Giants coach Nathan Brown was thought to be returning to Australia at the end of the season, with form stand-off Kevin Brown also rumoured to be heading back to home-town Wigan.

Wigan overcame the challenge of Widnes on the Saturday night by 64-10 in a 12-try demolition at Stobart Stadium Halton. Sam Tomkins wreaked havoc in the Widnes defence, helping himself to a hat-trick of tries in the final quarter of the match. The draw, made live on TV on Sunday afternoon, drew Wigan away to Leeds in the quarter-finals, the Rhinos having beaten Championship One Blackpool Panthers by 70-22 on the Friday night.

Giantkillers Barrow, who had accounted for Super League Castleford in the previous round, were pushed all the way by Hunslet Hawks before earning a quarter-final tie at St Helens with a 42-24 home win. The Raiders were in total control on 35 minutes, leading 30-4, but a great second half by the Hawks had them on the back foot and it took a 75th minute Zeb Luisi try to see them through.

St Helens eventually eased to a 30-10 win at the Stoop against a Harlequins side on a run of three straight wins. The home side took a 10-6 lead right on the hooter, Luke Gale finishing off a neat move that saw the Londoners go from inside their own half to touch down. But with injuries to both Danny Ward and Ben Jones stripping the Quins bench to the bare bones, Saints upped the ante after the interval. Twice within the opening five minutes of the second half huge bombs caused chaos in the London defence, with both Ade Gardner and Francis Meli cashing in with tries. When Meli rounded off a move with a further score on 50 minutes, a canter looked on the cards. But back came Quins, with David Howell held up as he tried to ground and Ryan Esders wasting a four-man overlap as the hosts went close. Kyle Eastmond booted Saints to safety with two penalties, and Leon Pryce finished things off when he strolled through a tiring Quins defence to touch down minutes from time.

Bradford progressed with a 58-16 home win over Leigh Centurions, denying former Bulls great Robbie Paul a dream return to Odsal. Four first-half tries gave the Bulls a 24-6 lead to kill off any thoughts of a famous upset for the man who made his name with a 1996 Challenge Cup final hat-trick. In this tie, centre Chris Nero was the hat-trick hero.

A dramatic last-second field goal from Thomas Bosc settled a fantastic end-to-end encounter against Crusaders in Wrexham, by 35-34, to guide the Catalans Dragons into the quarter-finals. The game looked dead and buried after 60 minutes when the Dragons led 34-14, but the spirit of the Crusaders came through to level matters with 11 minutes to go before Bosc landed his killer blow to set up a last-eight clash away at Halifax or Batley Bulldogs.

That tie was sensationally called off hours before kick-off, with Halifax facing the prospect of expulsion from the Challenge Cup after it emerged that the Championship club were guilty of fielding an ineligible player during their fourth-round victory over Swinton. Michael Ostick had turned out for previous club Rochdale in the third round, before playing for Halifax against Swinton. RFL operational guidelines stated that no player was allowed to play for more than one club in the same competition.

Chaos reigned as news of the breach trickled into the public domain, and Bulldogs coach Karl Harrison was left fuming at the 'farcical' timing of the RFL's intervention. The breach only came to light when it was pointed out on a fans' Internet messageboard, with no one at the RFL having identified the problem until the weekend. On the Monday, Halifax were indeed expelled and Batley ordered to play the fourth-round tie at Swinton, which they duly won 58-6, Swinton becoming the first club to be knocked out of the Cup twice in one season.

Round 14

England captain Jamie Peacock was a major injury worry for both club and country - with a mid-season international against France scheduled for June 12th - after limping out of the early stages of Leeds' 26-16 win over Warrington on the Friday evening with a knee injury suffered while making a tackle on international teammate Adrian Morley.

Leeds were back to Championship form against a major challenger for their crown. At the season's half-way point, coach Brian McClennan had asked his men to draw a line in the sand following an underwhelming start to their 2010 Super League campaign and he got the desired response. With the Rhinos' replacement rotation limited - and Chris Clarkson also unable to return after half-time - substitutes Ryan Bailey and Carl Ablett played major roles.

By the hour mark Leeds had taken complete control as the Wolves undermined their best efforts with indiscipline at crucial moments. Having already lost Richie Myler for the foreseeable future with knee ligament damage, making him also unavailable for England, Warrington also had to contend with the withdrawal of in-form decision maker Michael Monaghan with a calf strain picked up in training. Chris Hicks' sin-binning around the hour, when he held on too long to halt a Lee Smith/Ryan Hall breakout, coupled with Kevin Sinfield's resulting successful penalty to make it 20-6, gave Leeds the breathing space they ultimately needed.

The TV game on that Friday night was at Wakefield where Bradford were forced to fight back from 10-0 down for a bruising 29-10 victory, Brett Kearney suffering a foot injury in the first half and never re-appearing after half-time. Chris Nero also left the field after adding two tries, at vital times, to the hat-trick he notched against Leigh in the Challenge Cup a week earlier. Nero's first touchdown - 30 seconds before the break - set the Bulls on their way. His second, six minutes after the interval, gave the Odsal side the lead for the first time.

The Wildcats' form stand-off Ben Jeffries missed the game after injuring a quad in the Magic Weekend game against Leeds. The Wildcats had lost five Super League matches in a row since their Good Friday win over Castleford.

John Kear's side dropped out of the top eight after Hull KR beat the Crusaders 54-10 at Craven Park on the Sunday. Michael Dobson raced over for a first-half hat-trick of tries and ended the game with a personal haul of 30 points as Hull KR racked-up their biggest ever Super League score against the out-enthused Crusaders.

Salford City Reds stunned St Helens with a 42-34 victory in the Saturday TV game. Saints halfback Matty Smith, who was on a season-long loan at Salford, scored twice in the first half and once after the break, as the Reds beat St Helens for the second successive season at the Willows. It was a remarkable turnaround for Salford in the wake of their Murrayfield Magic thrashing by Warrington

The 22-year-old Smith's current deal with St Helens was due to expire at the end of the season. In a dramatic, thrilling contest, Smith's contribution, and that of his halfback partner Daniel Holdsworth, proved crucial in a game in which the Reds led from the second minute to last, without ever pulling clear. The game was in the balance right until the closing stages, when a Smith grubber resulted in Ryan Boyle's match-clinching try.

Catalans' Jamal Fakir revealed he was set to switch codes at the end of the season as the Dragons fell to a 28-14 home defeat to Hull FC on an unusually cold day in Perpignan. Hull's win was built on a wind-assisted first half and some gritty defence in the second that took them back above Leeds and into sixth spot. Jordan Tansey's try fifteen minutes from the ended all Catalan hopes of coming back after they trailed 22-4 at half-time. Hull youngster Liam Cunningham made his debut, coming off the bench, and did not look out of place amongst the other star-name forwards.

It was a brutal game as Dallas Johnson, Dane Carlaw, Dimitri Pelo and Tony Gigot all suffered broken noses and Jean-Philippe Baile was set to miss the rest of the season after fracturing an arm. David Ferriol was sin-binned in the 15th minute after landing a series of punches on Danny Washbrook and Kirk Yeaman went with him. Ferriol was later banned for a game, although Ewan Dowes, who had run into the incident and thrown punches escaped with a fine.

Harlequins' bubble looked set to burst at the Stoop as they stared an eight-point deficit in the face with barely ten minutes to play against Castleford. But a stunning four-try blitz in those closing minutes turned the game on its head and produced a 40-24 home win. Cas, with Dean Widders back for his first outing since round two, held an 18-16 interval advantage and things got better for the visitors after the break, as Steve Snitch touched down at the sticks after a break from Joe Westerman, whose conversion produced an eight-point lead. But instead of pressing on, the visitors elected to adopt a safety-first approach, and Quins began to throw the ball around with abandon. When Chad Randall cashed in on a Luke Williamson break it was game on. Minutes after that Williamson himself got on the scoresheet as Quins retook the lead. The Tigers were stunned, and Quins pressed home their late advantage with further late tries from Danny Orr and David Howell.

Wigan's 38-30 win at Huddersfield extended the Warriors' lead at the top of the table to four points after Warrington's and St Helens' defeats. Martin Gleeson was missing from the Warriors line-up, the former Great Britain centre dropped to the under-20s for disciplinary reasons and replaced by Stefan Marsh.

David Hodgson's fourth hat-trick of the year wasn't enough to stop Wigan's relentless pursuit of the minor premiership in a 12-try thriller. The Warriors twice found themselves reduced to 12 men, after Joel Tomkins and Andy Coley were shown yellow cards either side of half-time, but Michael Maguire's men found the resilience to repel their opponents to grab the points. In the end, only Pat Richards' kicking separated the sides. Both clubs engineered six tries apiece but whereas Brett Hodgson could only land three conversions, Richards booted five conversions and two further penalties for good measure. Wigan back-row forward Lee Mossop dislocated a shoulder in the win.

Giants coach Nathan Brown had confirmed he would return to Australia at the end of the season. In the week leading up to the game, Northumbria Police confirmed they would be taking no action against the six unnamed Huddersfield players at the centre of rape allegations made following the club's pre-season training trip to Newcastle.

Round 15

Wigan stayed four points clear of the chasing pack as winger Karl Pryce crossed for four tries in Wigan's 46-26 win over the Crusaders at The Racecourse on the Saturday, making it eight tries in his four appearances for the Warriors in SLXV.

The majority of Pryce's tries in Wrexham were simple scores on the end of overlaps as the Warriors targetted inexperienced wingman Gareth Thomas. The Warriors, who ran in eight tries, were 28-4 up at the break after a dominant start before a spirited home comeback. Pat Richards was once again Wigan's star man. The stand-in fullback chimed in with a try and seven goals and was also faultless under the high ball.

Crusaders' halfback Jarrod Sammut fractured a cheekbone and was expected to be out for at least six weeks. The Crusaders had been hit in the week before the game when Gareth Raynor was jailed for 15 months after pleading guilty to 14 counts of fraud and counterfeiting, the day after his comeback game at Hull KR after a neck injury. The 32-year-old former Great Britain international had his contract with the Crusaders cancelled, but club maintained the door remained open for a return after his release. Raynor had made seven appearances for the Crusaders, scoring four tries.

The rest of the top four - Warrington, St Helens and Hull FC - all recorded victories. Adrian Morley produced another titanic performance up front and Chris Bridge sparkled out wide as Warrington put Huddersfield to the sword for the second time in three weeks, with a 36-20 win at the Halliwell Jones. It was a world away from the 60-4 thrashing the Wolves had handed out in the Challenge Cup, but Tony Smith's side rarely looked in danger of losing. Matt King's 56th minute try gave the improving Giants too much of a mountain to climb at 30-10. Bridge – playing at scrum-half in the injury absence of Richie Myler – couldn't replicate his five tries from the Galpharm Stadium, but scored once and created two others in an excellent display.

Defeat for Huddersfield marked four in a row amidst the news that Brett Hodgson and Nathan Brown were to leave the club at the end of the season.

St Helens recorded a 68-12 Friday-night home victory over inconsistent Hull KR, running in 13 tries on, bringing their total points scored against the Robins in May to 122. Saints bounced back in style from their shock Salford defeat by hammering Justin Morgan's men for the second time in three weeks in a one-sided romp. Rovers' preparations had been thrown into disarray when their coach broke down on the M62, but a combination of cars and a replacement coach ensured they arrived in time for kick-off. Justin Morgan joked: 'Maybe we should have turned around.'

In a brilliant team effort Ade Gardner crossed for four well-taken tries, with James Roby the pick after slotting into numerous playing positions. Paul Wellens missed the game with a head injury after catching a loose knee as he fielded a kick in the defeat at Salford the week before.

Hull FC had the toughest game of the top four, eventually winning 34-26 in a Sunday game at Castleford. The Airlie Birds trailed 16-10 at the interval, but after the break they took control of the game, scoring 24 consecutive points as they followed up the previous weekend's 28-14 win against Catalans in Perpignan. Sean Long had a hand in several of his side's scores and chipped in with a great solo effort which saw him race 80 metres to score in front of the travelling fans.

Cas did rally late in the day with Rangi Chase scoring a length-of-the-field effort and Michael Wainwright claiming his second of the afternoon a minute from time, but it was too little too late. Kyle Wood made his Tigers debut after arriving on loan from Huddersfield, after being dual-registered with Championship side Batley. Wood was drafted straight into the Tigers side following the departure of Brent Sherwin to Catalans Dragons.

Sherwin made his debut as a Catalans player on the Saturday, after the Dragons' failed attempt to land Melbourne halfback Brett Finch, although he couldn't prevent the Dragons from going down to a 22-14 home defeat to Salford City Reds. Daniel Holdsworth outshone his opposite number, creating the opening try and was deadly with the boot for Salford's second win on the bounce. Gregory Mounis was dismissed five minutes from time for a spear tackle on Luke Swain. He received a one-match suspension.

Wakefield ended a losing run of five games with a thunderous 54-12 win over Harlequins at Belle Vue, with scrum-half Sam Obst in explosive mood off a solid platform set by props Paul King, Richard Moore and Michael Korkidas. The Wildcats closed their account four minutes from time when Paul Cooke sauntered through a tiring defence, adding his seventh goal from ten efforts in an 18-point contribution.

A hot and balmy weekend ended on the Sunday evening with the big west Yorkshire derby at Odsal. Danny McGuire scored a brilliantly taken hat-trick as the resurgent Rhinos climbed back up to fifth in the table with a hard-fought 26-12 victory.

SUPER LEAGUE TABLE - *Sunday 23rd May*

	P	W	D	L	F	A	D	PTS
Wigan Warriors	15	13	0	2	506	236	270	26
Warrington Wolves	15	11	0	4	486	228	258	22
St Helens	15	11	0	4	518	282	236	22
Hull FC	15	9	0	6	334	305	29	18
Leeds Rhinos	15	8	1	6	386	312	74	17
Bradford Bulls	15	8	1	6	278	276	2	17
Huddersfield Giants	15	8	0	7	374	250	124	16
Wakefield T Wildcats	15	7	0	8	318	345	-27	14
Hull Kingston Rovers	15	7	0	8	305	393	-88	14
Castleford Tigers	15	5	0	10	306	412	-106	10
Crusaders	14	5	0	9	239	383	-144	10
Salford City Reds	15	5	0	10	237	411	-174	10
Harlequins	14	4	0	10	237	443	-206	8
Catalans Dragons	15	2	0	13	194	442	-248	4

Challenge Cup Quarter Finals

St Helens were joint favourites to win the Challenge Cup, alongside Leeds Rhinos, after their 32-12 home victory over Barrow, with both clubs priced at 13/8 by bookmaker William Hill.

England skipper Jamie Peacock made a miraculous return to inspire Leeds into the semi-finals with a dramatic 12-10 win over Wigan at rain-soaked Headingley. The prop had damaged knee ligaments and hobbled off against Warrington a fortnight before, being put in brace and told that he could be out for up to two months. But it was Peacock - with Wigan leading 10-8 - whose almost superhuman effort set up position for Lee Smith to score the only try of the game on 78 minutes. First Peacock battered Stuart Fielden, and then produced exceptional harassment of Sam Tomkins on the next, last tackle as the young stand-off attempted a kick, to force a turnover on the Wigan '35'.

In a rain-soaked match that had seen endless ball spilt, the other key element in the win was Amos Roberts needlessly sticking out a hand to propel the ball forward when diverting McGuire's long pass in the vicinity of Ryan Hall to concede a telling late scrum. Smith's sole four-pointer, one of barely a handful of clear-cut chances created by either side, took some scoring as he burst onto an inside pass from Kevin Sinfield from the base of the scrum, evaded Martin Gleeson, trampled through Pat Richards and took desperate Sean O'Loughlin over the line with him.

Warrington threatened to put on a repeat of their astonishing destruction of Huddersfield in the previous round as they led 12-0 against the Bulls at Odsal in the Sunday TV game. But the Bulls - with Matt Orford back from a shoulder injury - never gave up, Chris Hicks' 61st minute try just about seeing the Wolves home to a 26-22 win.

James Graham paid tribute to Barrow after the Co-operative Championship Champions gave St Helens a real test in a Saturday Challenge Cup quarter-final. The Raiders were only 16-12 behind with half an hour remaining before Saints ran in three late tries to secure their passage to a tenth consecutive Cup semi-final, 32-12 the final score. Kyle Eastmond limped off with an ankle injury that ruled him out of England's game with France.

Two cracking tries in the space of ten minutes either side of the interval raised hopes that Batley Bulldogs might spring a surprise over Catalans. But once their Super League visitors got into their stride they smashed any upset hopes with eight unanswered tries to complete a 74-12 victory at Mount Pleasant.

The semi-final draw was made live on BBC radio the following Wednesday by Colin Clarke and Arthur Bunting, the coaches of Wigan and Hull FC in the 1985 Challenge Cup Final, the match that had been selected as the commemorative final for 2010. Leeds and St Helens were drawn together, with holders Warrington paired with 2006 finalists Catalans Dragons.

* RFL Chief Executive Nigel Wood expressed his delight at the new Coalition Government's confirmation that it would support the Rugby League World Cup in 2013 as new Prime Minister David Cameron launched an agreement outlining the Government's policies for the new Parliament.

Also in May, Wales became the twelfth full member of the Rugby League International Federation, following a meeting of the Federation board in Melbourne last Thursday. They were also granted automatic qualification into the 2013 World Cup.

JUNE
A game in mourning

Round 16

The first round of June was the most sombre in living memory as the game, and Cumbria in particular, mourned the murder of former Whitehaven and Workington back-rower Garry Purdham. The 31-year-old, who had retired from the professional game and had returned to play with his amateur club, Egremont, was one of 12 people shot dead in West Cumbria by a crazed gunman who then took his own life. Purdham, elder brother of Harlequins captain Rob, was cutting hedges on a lane when the killer drove by. A minute's silence was held at all matches and Rob Purdham was granted indefinite compassionate leave by Harlequins.

With a real air of mourning hanging over the Stoop in the build-up to their TV game with Crusaders, Quins put in one of their better shows in tribute to their missing skipper. Luke Dorn scored four tries in a 50-22 win and it was 50-10 with eight minutes remaining when 17-year-old Olsi Krasniqi, a Londoner of Albanian descent, scored a try on debut. Late tries by Peter Lupton and Rhys Hanbury made it look slightly more respectable for the Welsh side.

On the Friday night, Danny Tickle's last-gasp field goal gave Hull FC their first league double over St Helens in over 20 years as they announced themselves serious title contenders with a 27-26 win at the KC Stadium. Not since the 1988-89 season had Hull beaten Saints home and away in the same season, but having won 32-12 at Knowsley Road on the opening round of SLXV they came from behind to claim a historic victory.

Francis Meli's first-half hat-trick of tries and a Keiron Cunningham score ensured Tom Briscoe's opener was quickly forgotten. Meli's fourth after the break signalled more of the same but the hosts dug deep with Jordan Turner, Danny Houghton, Willie Manu and Danny Tickle pulling them level. With tensions mounting Tickle struck the match-winner.

In the Friday-night TV game at Headingley, Leeds won a late 28-22 victory over Wakefield for the second time within a month, following their 34-30 Magic Weekend win over their local rivals. On a rainy night, the Wildcats led 12-0 after as many minutes and then held the Rhinos at 18-all until eight minutes from time when a Kevin Sinfield penalty gave Leeds a two-point advantage and a Danny Buderus try - crafted by Sinfield - gave the home side a lead just big enough to hold. It was tough luck again for the industrious Wildcats who had Glenn Morrison back. The back-rower had been out of action for almost two months since breaking his thumb against the Crusaders on 11th April and he made 52 tackles as well as scoring the opening try.

Sean O'Loughlin led from the front as Wigan Warriors maintained their grip on the leadership of Super League with a 38-22 home win against dogged Castleford. O'Loughlin scored two second-half tries and was heavily involved throughout a Warriors performance that appeared to be suffering from a Challenge Cup hangover. That heart-breaking last-minute defeat at Leeds certainly seemed to be having an impact when the Tigers pulled the scores level early in the second half. But with right winger Darrell Goulding collecting a hat-trick that had a significant helping hand from his centre Martin

Gleeson, and Thomas Leuluai buzzing around to good effect from scrum-half, the Warriors pulled away from their opponents in the third quarter of the game.

Warrington Wolves kept the pressure on the league leaders by claiming a hard-fought 27-10 victory at Salford. The home side pressed Warrington hard throughout after a pre-match downpour contributed to a night for difficult handling. The Wolves led 16-6 at half-time but Jodie Broughton's try meant they needed a Lee Briers field goal to nudge them two scores clear with 17 minutes left. Late tries by Mickey Higham and David Solomona sealed a third straight win for Warrington after their victory at Bradford the previous week to reach the Challenge Cup semi-finals.

A 90-metre interception try by Michael Dobson three minutes from time finally settled a dour game with the struggling Catalans at Craven Park by 24-6, as Hull KR moved back into the top-eight with their eighth win of the season. The Robins' only win from their previous five games had been a convincing 54-10 home victory against the Crusaders. They welcomed back Jake Webster, but Liam Colbon who was expected to return after suffering a broken jaw - coincidentally against the Dragons in March - and missing the last eight games was again on the sidelines after picking up a knee ligament injury in training. Rovers' impressive start saw them 12-0 ahead after 20 minutes, a lead that Catalans never looked likely to pull back in the deteriorating conditions.

The big blowout of the weekend came at Odsal on the Sunday as the Giants ran away to a 52-6 win. Nathan Brown's side had lost their last four games and slipped down to seventh in the Super League but skipper Brett Hodgson was imperious as Huddersfield recaptured their best form. Winger Jermaine McGillvary marked his Super League debut with two well-taken tries as Huddersfield raced into a 28-0 lead by half-time.

* The shocking events in Cumbria were felt as far away as South Africa, where nine West Cumbrians were on tour with the BARLA Young Lions side. The Lions, coached by Garry Schofield, completed the tour with five wins from their five-match tour.

Round 17

The RFL's decision to stage the England-France Gillette Fusion international at Leigh almost at the same time as the England soccer team was playing its first game in their World Cup in South Africa led to a crowd of just under 8,000 at the Leigh Sports Village to witness Steve McNamara's first game in charge.

The new coach was left to field questions over the value of the international against France after his side completed an eleven-try 60-6 rout. Sam Tomkins claimed a record-equalling four tries; Melbourne reserve fullback Gareth Widdop impressed with a debut score, while Gareth Ellis and Michael Shenton claimed doubles, with Tom Briscoe and Chris Bridge getting a try each.

International commitments had an effect on Super League in that players were ruled out of club games played on the Friday, but were able to back up if their club fixture was on Sunday. There was even one game on the Saturday at the same time as the international. Leeds Rhinos - without Kevin Sinfield, who started at hooker for England - beat Harlequins at the Stoop 42-22. Former England international Lee Smith, still finding his feet after returning from union side Wasps in April, crossed for three tries and booted 14 points to claim a contest-deciding 26 points. With Danny McGuire having dropped out of the England squad through injury and Rob Burrow still sidelined, the Rhinos halfback pairing was hooker Paul McShane and back-rower Carl Ablett.

On the Friday night, threadbare St Helens kept the pressure on Wigan and Warrington with a 30-22 win over the Giants at Knowsley Road. Depleted by injury and international selections, Mick Potter was without seven first-choice regulars against a team that had found its feet in the previous week's crushing win at Bradford.

When the Giants roared back from a 16-4 deficit to twice level the scores at 16-16 and

22-22, momentum seemed to have switched their way. But Saints' youngsters showed maturity beyond their years when it really mattered. Jamie Foster kept his nerve to boot over a penalty goal from wide on the right when Matt Gidley had been obstructed chasing his own kick. Then Andrew Dixon ran a perfect line to collect Leon Pryce's inside pass for the match-clinching try just eight minutes from time. The Giants were missing England stand-off Kevin Brown, who had committed his long-term future to Huddersfield by signing a contract to keep him at the Galpharm Stadium until 2015

The Wolves ran away from Hull KR in the Friday-night TV game at the Halliwell Jones Stadium to end with a 35-16 win, but it was an almighty battle. Lee Briers scored a try in each half and added five goals and a field goal for a 19-point haul as Warrington avenged their 36-16 defeat at Craven Park in April. Although Warrington enjoyed most of the possession and territory, they only led 6-4 at half-time. But a couple of contentious calls, including the 53rd minute sin-binning of Rovers' Clint Newton, turned the game. The hosts ran in three tries in Newton's absence, with Louis Anderson, Briers and Ryan Atkins crossing to give them an unassailable lead. The two sides then exchanged tries in a frantic finale, with Michael Monaghan replying after Mike Ratu's effort while Matt King followed Ben Fisher's with Warrington's sixth and final try as the Wolves claimed their fourth straight win.

Also on the Friday, Hull made a case for a top-two finish with a 34-12 win over Salford at the KC Stadium. The win, a fourth in a row and a seventh out of eight on home soil kept them in touch with leading duo Wigan and Warrington with ten games remaining. Unlike in each of their previous three campaigns, Hull had players returning from injury rather than dropping out of the side. Epalahame Lauaki made his return, while star hooker Shaun Berrigan was also back after a two-month absence with a shoulder injury. Gamestar Jordan Tansey's try shortly after the half-time interval gave Hull a two-score cushion and all-but ended Salford's challenge.

On the Sunday, Wigan coach Michael Maguire heaped praise on his England international trio of Sean O'Loughlin, and Joel and Sam Tomkins after Wigan re-asserted their four-point cushion at the top of the table by comfortably taming the Wildcats 48-6 in the West Yorkshire rain. O'Loughlin lasted just eight minutes before limping off with a quad strain but the Tomkins brothers gave sterling performances as the Warriors ran in nine tries, including a hat-trick for in-form winger Karl Pryce and two for the league's leading points scorer Pat Richards. The visitors scored three tries in the opening 17 minutes.

Wakefield coach John Kear was being linked with the position of head coach at Catalan Dragons, which was to become vacant when Kevin Walters returned to Australia at the end of the season. Speculation began when Kear was spotted with Catalans director Christophe Jouffret at their match at Hull KR the previous week.

Crusaders boosted their hopes of a play-off place as they produced an amazing performance to put their coach's former employers, Bradford Bulls to the sword at Wrexham by 44-20. The Crusaders entered the clash on the back of three heavy Super League defeats and had not tasted victory since Murrayfield Magic, when they outclassed the Bulls 19-0. Tony Martin was back after a nine-week absence with a hamstring problem and Rhys Hanbury, filling in at halfback with Michael Witt and Jarrod Sammut still out injured, was in brilliant form. The only downside for the Welsh was the sight of Gareth Thomas, who scored the opening try of the game, limping off on 36 minutes with a groin problem.

In a game postponed until the following Tuesday because of the international match, Castleford ended a three-match losing run as they edged Catalans 24-20 at the Jungle. For the Tigers, Michael Wainwright grabbed two vital touchdowns and pulled off three try-saving tackles. Catalans had now lost their last nine games but were much improved with Casey McGuire back at hooker.

* *England Academy beat the France under-18 side 40-16 at the Stade Max Rousie, Villeneuve-sur-Lot the previous Wednesday. The England side ran in eight tries with Wigan Warriors centre Ian Thornley grabbing two and Bradford Bulls halfback Cain Southernwood scoring ten points with a try and three conversions.*

Round 18

The best was saved for last on the weekend of round 18 as over 20,000 fans basked in the Sunday evening sunshine at the DW Stadium to see St Helens edge Wigan 26-24. Wigan were without Sean O'Loughlin, missing after sustaining a quad injury during the previous Sunday's win over Wakefield, and he was replaced at loose forward by Liam Farrell. The only other change for the Warriors was Chris Tuson, who was making only his fourth career appearance for the club, starting from the bench to cover for Farrell. England stars James Graham and James Roby were back for Saints from international duty, while Kyle Eastmond had not recovered from the ankle injury that saw him miss the clash with France. Youngster Paul Johnson kept his spot in the 17 after impressing against the Giants.

After Pat Richards had kicked an early penalty goal, Saints racked up three tries to go into a 16-2 lead. First Leon Pryce ghosted through straight from a scrum he had won with a 40/20; Francis Meli then performed acrobatics to touch down his own grubber in the corner without going into touch and James Roby got the nod of the video referee despite replays being inconclusive when he shot over from dummy-half.

Wigan scored a superb try just before the break when Sam Tomkins fired out a long pass to Karl Pryce, and scored their second when Thomas Leuluai stepped Scott Moore after just a minute of the second half, reducing the gap to four points. After ten minutes a posse of Wigan players pushed James Roby back over the Saints' tryline, and the momentum was clearly with Wigan. But then Mark Riddell gave a forward pass to Phil Bailey from dummy-half, when Wigan were in a dominant position, and the game swung again. Shortly afterwards Sam Tomkins gave away a penalty in a tackle on Leon Pryce, and suddenly Paul Wellens, making his 400th career appearance, was touching down after a great offload by Bryn Hargreaves. Shortly afterwards Wellens pulled off an unbelievable tackle on George Carmont near the corner post. Wellens was magnificent throughout the game, later on pulling off another wonderful tackle on Martin Gleeson.

There was still time for Michael McIlorum and Gleeson to touch down with five minutes remaining. The game had one final act when Pat Richards' drop-out bounced into touch to win a scrum for his team. But when Jamie Foster caught Sam Tomkins' kick under extreme pressure, the game was finally up. Saints, in third place, now trailed Wigan by just four points and that week announced the signing of Australian international prop Josh Perry for 2011.

Clint Greenshields made his long awaited return from injury on the Saturday in the Dragons' 30-23 victory against Wakefield. Greenshields had been out of action since breaking his ankle during March's home defeat to Castleford, and he had been sorely missed by the Dragons, who won just one game in his absence. Thomas Bosc and Dimitri Pelo also made their return. New Wakefield loan signing Julien Rinaldi made a try-scoring second debut for the Wildcats as Bosc's penalty five minutes from time gave the Dragons a seven-point lead and ensured the win.

Bradford were hit with the news that Matt Orford, who damaged his shoulder in May's Murrayfield Magic defeat to the Crusaders, was out for the season. The halfback had played only once since, in the Challenge Cup quarter-final defeat to Warrington, and needed surgery. That weekend the Bulls crashed to a fifth straight defeat – by 40-28 to Warrington at Odsal. Steve McNamara's squad were missing three of their most senior players in Orford, Andy Lynch and Jamie Langley and five more injuries meant McNamara was forced to field one of the youngest benches in Super League history.

Brett Hodgson spearheaded a remarkable Huddersfield comeback at the Galpharm Stadium as the Giants overturned an 18-0 deficit to end Hull's four-match winning run by 32-18. The Black and Whites dominated the majority of the first half and were good value for their 18-point lead when Hodgson sent his namesake David over just before half-time to drag the Giants back into the contest. Hull did not receive a single penalty during the second half and conceded the last nine of the match. Jamahl Lolesi's 68th minute try ensured the balance of play had shifted completely in Huddersfield's favour.

Castleford held off a second-half fightback by Salford at the Willows to claim their second win in six days – by 28-22 - and maintain hope of snatching a play-off spot. Dean Widders helped Cas to a 22-6 half-time lead by claiming a first-half hat-trick. But the Reds hit back with two tries within six minutes of the restart through Stuart Littler and Jodie Broughton before Ian Sibbit's converted try made it 22-22 with 19 minutes left. But Brett Ferres claimed Cas's fifth and final try in the 74th minute to take the Tigers to within three points of the top eight.

2009 Albert Goldthorpe Medal winner Michael Dobson was in top form as he scored two tries and kicked seven goals in Hull KR's fourth successive home win, a 42-6 home success over Harlequins, who had skipper Rob Purdham back. On top of Dobson's contribution, Clint Newton crossed twice in an eye-catching display and there were also tries for Shaun Briscoe, Joel Clinton and Scott Wheeldon as Rovers romped to victory, with Quins' solitary try coming from Danny Ward.

There was a huge shock at Headingley where Crusaders came away with a 32-26 win, though Leeds almost salvaged a point. With Crusaders six points ahead and two minutes left, the Rhinos threw the kitchen sink at them; Rhys Hanbury, Frank Winterstein and Clinton Schifcofske getting across to take Ian Kirke into touch near the corner flag.

Round 19

The last weekend of June saw all the RFL fixture times changed to avoid a clash with England soccer team's World Cup game with Germany, scheduled for Sunday at 3pm. It caused chaos for supporters as clubs hastily brought forward or pushed back kick-off times to enable fans to attend matches and catch the action from South Africa on TV. Confusion reigned, as clubs negotiated alternative schedules with their opponents, with some clubs making announcements as late as Friday afternoon.

Crusaders' match against Wakefield on the Sunday was moved to 6pm, but then had to be put back even further, to 8pm, after the Wildcats were held up by police closing part of the M62 after an incident had disrupted traffic.

Castleford's clash with Bradford was brought forward to 11.30am, while the televised match between Warrington and Leeds, which kicked off at 5.45pm, remained unaffected. The kick-off time of every match in the Championship and Championship 1 was changed.

Friday and Saturday games were unaffected and Wigan re-established their four point lead at the top of the table with a 36-12 win at Harlequins. Pat Richards picked up two Albert Goldthorpe Medal points for his contribution to Wigan's 36-12 win over Harlequins in the capital on Sunday, which saw him leap-frog Michael Witt and teammate Sean O' Loughlin at the top of the table. Richards crossed for two tries and kicked six goals. Sam Tomkins - at fullback following the dropping of Karl Pryce - had another blinder. Ben Jones-Bishop, on loan for the season at Harlequins from Leeds, made a try-scoring return to action after being told he needed to wear a headguard for the rest of the season, after fracturing his skull at Wigan earlier in the campaign.

Sean Long trudged off the field in considerable pain just after the hour mark of Hull FC's 10-8 home win over Catalans, making full use of gas and air, helped by two of the club's medical staff and nursing a dislocated elbow.

Jordan Turner and Richard Whiting put Hull in front before the break, with Casey McGuire mustering a response for the Catalans. However, the sides went in on level terms when Thomas Bosc kicked a penalty on the half-time hooter. Hull eventually clinched the win as Danny Tickle stepped up to make amends for two missed conversions with a penalty in a closely fought second period.

In the TV game at the Galpharm Stadium, Huddersfield and Hull KR shared the points after a dramatic 16-16 draw, as Brett Hodgson kicked a magnificent equalising penalty from near touch after the final hooter had sounded. With about two minutes left, Rovers were apparently heading for a 16-14 victory, with Huddersfield back in their own quarter. Then Kevin Brown plonked a kick right into the hands of Jamahl Lolesi out on the wing. Lolesi strode out of a tackle, loped down the touchline and lobbed over his own kick. It was a frantic chase between Brown and Rovers' Ben Galea. Brown got to the ball first just short of the line, but could not control it as Galea impeded him from behind. Video referee Richard Silverwood ruled 'no try and scrum defence', implying that Brown had knocked the ball on.

The home fans thought it should have at least been a penalty to Huddersfield, and a higher power seemed to agree as, remarkably, the Giants won a rare scrum against the head and a few seconds later the video referee was awarding the match-saving penalty. It came after Danny Brough lofted a kick towards the corner, and David Hodgson leapt high to take it and touch down as he hit the corner flag. Rovers winger Peter Fox was ruled to have tackled him in mid-air. Brett Hodgson had nerves of steel, and from a metre in from the left touchline made it four out of four on the night.

St Helens were at their clinical best as they swept away Salford at Knowsley Road 58-34, to follow up the previous week's win over league leaders Wigan. Again Saints were on course for victory after a first-half blitz, which saw four tries in ten minutes, and again the key men were Leon Pryce and Paul Wellens. Chris Flannery's converted try early in the second half killed off any hope Salford still had.

On the Sunday, England centre Michael Shenton, back in the Castleford line-up after missing the previous week's game at Salford through a knee injury, celebrated his return to action with a hat-trick as the Tigers extended their winning sequence to three matches with a 28-22 home win over Bradford. Shenton's hat-trick score, plus Joe Westerman's first goal, opened up a ten-point buffer with two minutes to go.

Bradford learned they would be without prop Nick Scruton for up to ten weeks due to a knee injury. Scruton suffered a grade-three medial ligament strain in the Bulls' Engage Super League loss to Warrington 11 days before.

Warrington themselves suffered a 37-30 home defeat to Leeds. Adrian Morley was magnificent for the home side but in a nip and tuck game, Kevin Sinfield's wonderful field goal from over 40 metres with five minutes left gave the Wolves too much to do. Wolves centre Chris Bridge aggravated a shoulder injury and was ruled out for three months after undergoing surgery.

John Kear confirmed he would remain in charge of Wakefield Trinity Wildcats for the foreseeable future after it was announced Catalans Dragons would not be pursuing the signature of the 55-year-old. The former Sheffield Eagles and Hull FC boss had been in contact with the French club about the vacant coaching position, but a compensation package could not be agreed between the two clubs. The Wildcats celebrated the news by shrugging off their five-hour coach journey to Wrexham and hammering Crusaders 41-0, ending a three-match losing run. Darryl Millard scored a try on his return from the leg injury he sustained at Hull FC in round 12.

SUPER LEAGUE TABLE - *Sunday 27th June*

	P	W	D	L	F	A	D	PTS
Wigan Warriors	19	16	0	3	652	302	350	32
Warrington Wolves	19	14	0	5	618	319	299	28
St Helens	19	14	0	5	658	389	269	28
Hull FC	19	12	0	7	423	383	40	24
Leeds Rhinos	19	11	1	7	519	418	101	23
Huddersfield Giants	19	10	1	8	496	320	176	21
Hull Kingston Rovers	19	9	1	9	403	456	-53	19
Bradford Bulls	19	8	1	10	354	440	-86	17
Wakefield T Wildcats	19	8	0	11	410	451	-41	16
Castleford Tigers	19	8	0	11	408	514	-106	16
Crusaders	18	7	0	11	337	520	-183	14
Salford City Reds	19	5	0	14	315	558	-243	10
Harlequins	18	5	0	13	327	585	-258	10
Catalans Dragons	19	3	0	16	258	523	-265	6

51

JULY
3D Vision

Round 20

Castleford Tigers promised to appeal against the £40,000 fine handed to them by the RFL after an incident at the Tigers' home match against the Crusaders in March, during which winger Gareth Thomas was subjected to homophobic abuse by a tiny section of home supporters. A tribunal criticised the club 'for failing to take steps to stop the homophobic chanting, for failing to identify the perpetrators, for failing to challenge the chanting and for their failure to undertake a meaningful inquiry afterwards.' Half of the fine was suspended until the end of 2011. But a further £20,000 was payable, as the suspended fine relating to a bottle throwing incident during the Tigers' home game against Catalans Dragons in 2009 was now payable.

The club did appeal and in September the fine was halved and the 2009 fine further suspended after Castleford were able to demonstrate they had taken steps which led to the identification and banning of some of the supporters responsible.

The Tigers responded in spectacular style the Sunday after the initial punishment when a Rangi Chase masterclass stunned Huddersfield - who led 10-0 after eight minutes - with a 44-18 win at the Jungle. The win propelled the Tigers back into the top eight after poor early-season form that had culminated in their Challenge Cup exit at home to Barrow, and left Tigers fans calling for the sacking of coach Terry Matterson.

Despite having one player – substitute Adam Milner – on debut, and another youngster, in Jonathan Walker, with only one first team outing behind him, plus yet another rookie in Jordan Thompson on the bench, Castleford were ultimately comfortable winners over the Giants.

Hull FC held off a second-half fightback from a valiant Bradford side to register a 28-22 win at Odsal. The Bulls came from 22-6 down at the break to level the scores with 20 minutes remaining and had the momentum to go on and win. But a moment of magic from Jordan Tansey enabled Craig Hall to cap a move which started on Hull's ten-metre line and won the match. The former Leeds and Sydney Roosters fullback collected a towering Paul Sykes kick, looked up, seared through the Bulls back line and travelled 70 metres unopposed. Rikki Sheriffe provided a chase but was fended off and evaded, but when Mike Worrincy grabbed Tansey, he slipped the ball out of the back door for Hall to finish off.

It was the Bulls' seventh successive defeat in all competitions at the end of a week in which the Grattan Stadium hosted the Coalition Government's first regional Cabinet meeting.

On the Sunday night Wigan Warriors were always in control in a 34-16 win at Catalans. They led 14-0 at half-time and, but for a five-minute spell, were not threatened during a first half they largely dominated. They then cut loose in a second half, running in four more tries as the Dragons struggled to cope. Wigan's major blip came when referee James Child sent off Andy Coley for a high tackle on Jamal Fakir in the final quarter. By then, the result was already established. Only the final score was in any kind of doubt, with Catalans managing to scrape three late tries to reclaim some pride as they made the most of the extra man. Harrison Hansen was back after missing the last 16 games with a shoulder injury, and Pat Richards, whose involvement was in doubt due to the imminent arrival of a new baby, also played. Sam Tomkins, now a regular at fullback, had a hand in most of Wigan's tries. Coley got a two-match ban.

Former Toulouse player Trent Robinson, assistant coach under Brian Smith at the Sydney Roosters, signed a three-year contract to coach the Catalans Dragon from 2011.

Hull KR recorded a crucial 46-14 away victory over play-off rivals Wakefield as the experienced Ben Galea steered a ship hit by injuries before and during the match. Galea was forced to switch to stand-off when Scott Murrell was helped out of the action with a calf injury, with Clint Newton already starting at centre following the late withdrawal of Mike Ratu.

By the end of the game Justin Morgan's reshuffle had extended to playing Michael Vella at centre, but despite the adversity, they were far too good for a tame Wildcats side, with Galea laying on four of their seven tries. The crucial period came in the first five minutes of the second half. Darryl Millard's disallowed try was quickly followed by Peter Fox's first effort at the other end – a real 12-point swing with the game still in the balance.

On the Friday night Salford kept alive their slim play-off hopes with a 17-14 home win over struggling Harlequins, who lost Chad Randall for the season with a dislocated shoulder. Salford led 14-4 at half-time as Daniel Holdsworth controlled things. Quins improved after the break and the Reds' task was to hold on to a lead that was narrowed by two Ben Jones-Bishop tries. Matty Smith's 73rd-minute field goal ultimately proved the difference – without it, Quins would have snatched a point from a late penalty. Instead they were forced to run it and couldn't get over Salford's line.

The Wolves bounced back from their loss at home to Leeds with a 30-10 win at Crusaders on the Sunday. Warrington coach Tony Smith rested skipper Adrian Morley in a bid to keep his squad fresh as the Wolves moved two points clear of St Helens in second with a six-try victory. Mickey Higham's try on 49 minutes after the Wolves had withstood wave after wave of attacks from the Crusaders, proved the gamebreaker.

Jarrod Sammut, sidelined for six weeks after fracturing his cheekbone against Wigan returned but hooker Lincoln Withers pulled up with injury in the warm-up. Gareth Thomas was ruled out for the rest of the season after breaking down on his comeback game. Thomas, who was returning after a two-match absence because of a groin problem, lasted just 19 minutes before having to be helped from the field after going down in agony clutching his groin.

The game of the round was the Saturday-evening TV game at Headingley as Leeds beat St Helens 28-24. Across the sides an entire team was missing before the kick-off – the Rhinos without seven players and Saints six – but the likes of Jonny Lomax, Chris Clarkson and excellent Matty Ashurst produced a great game.

Saints lost both their playmakers during the game. With Andrew Dixon already sidelined early, Kyle Eastmond suffered a recurrence of his ankle injury before Leeds took first-half control and – just as he was commanding the midfield coming up to the mid-way point of the second half – Leon Pryce suffered a back spasm. Saints were leading 24-16 as Leeds were given a penalty on their own '20' for offside. On the back of drives by Ian Kirke, Carl Ablett and Clarkson, Danny McGuire set Ryan Bailey free and he turned the ball back inside for the stand-off to claim his 17th touchdown of the season.

From the re-start, Jake Emmitt went high on Jamie Peacock, Jamie Jones-Buchanan was prominent and, along with Kevin Sinfield, Lee Smith and Ablett, set the position for the decisive score. Danny Buderus and McGuire sent Bailey on the charge, he was pushed back by Paul Wellens and Matt Gidley but managed a flicked offload that video referee Thierry Alibert deemed bounced away from McGuire's hand. Buderus collected and released Ryan Hall, who finished superbly in the corner.

In the week, Saints prop James Graham admitted his interest in a potential switch to the NRL - but insisted his immediate future lay at St Helens. His current St Helens contract ran until the end of 2011, and Graham moved to quash any rumours about a move a year early.

Round 21

Champions Leeds missed the chance to move into the top four after a 25-6 defeat at Hull KR on the Friday night of round 21. The Rovers supporters joyously celebrated a fifth successive home win and their first double over Leeds for quarter of a century, opening up the race for a top four-spot for a host of aspiring clubs.

With Brett Finch being linked with the club, scrum-half Michael Dobson was at his best. His varied kicking options and choice of pass – expertly backed up by Ben Galea and Scott Murrell – continually tormented the visitors - a final goal-line drop out count of 6-1 testimony to that. Skipper Michael Vella stood out at prop and loan signing from Wigan, Josh Charnley, made an impressive Super League debut in the centre for the Robins. The gamebreaker came just before the break when Peter Fox stole in to sweep up a wayward Kevin Sinfield pass near half way to establish a defining three-score lead.

Rovers' next game was the crunch derby with Hull FC the following Thursday. The Airlie Birds missed their chance to go three points clear of Leeds in fourth with a lacklustre display at Wakefield. The Wildcats, smarting from the previous Sunday's home humiliation by Hull KR, scored 29-unanswered points after slipping behind to an early Jordan Turner try and were ultimately good value for their much-needed 29-6 success.

Hull FC were still missing the key trio of Sean Long, Craig Fitzgibbon and Mark O'Meley, though Richard Horne made his long-awaited comeback off of the bench, having missed Hull's last seven games with a knee injury, although he didn't look match fit. The coup de grace came when Darryl Millard swooped onto a loose Horne pass and ran 70 metres up-field, stepping Richard Whiting and fending Jordan Tansey to score a spectacular breakaway try.

Nathan Brown confirmed he would remain as coach of Huddersfield Giants for the 2011 season, despite announcing in May that he was to return to Australia at the end of 2010 for personal reasons, two years into a three-year contract. Brown confirmed his personal circumstances – which included his house in Australia burning down – had changed. Brown explained his decision in the press conference after the Giants' 30-12 home win over the Crusaders on the Sunday – a victory that moved them back above Hull Kingston Rovers and into sixth place in Super League.

With hooker Shaun Lunt in the unfamiliar position of wide-running second row, and Luke Robinson causing problems from scrum-half, the Giants established enough of a lead to hold off a brief second-half comeback from the Crusaders. Winger Jermaine McGillvary also crossed for two well-taken tries, leaving Brown a relatively satisfied man after the heavy defeat at Castleford the previous week. It was Lunt's huge hit on Rhys Hanbury that led directly to Kevin Brown's crucial 73rd minute try after Crusaders got back to 20-12.

The Wolves ran in nine tries on the Sunday afternoon to end Castleford's four-match winning run with a 54-30 triumph at the Halliwell Jones Stadium, after leading 30-4 at half-time. Adrian Morley was back after being rested against the Crusaders, while Lee Briers missed out after picking up a couple of knocks in the same game. Wolves hooker Jon Clarke was named as one of the substitutes, to make his first appearance in the first-team for over ten months following a broken ankle.

It took Warrington just two minutes to score the opening try and it was a contender for try of the season. Simon Grix and Richie Myler combined before David Solomona sent an outrageous ball round the back of a defender to release centre Ryan Atkins, who then allowed Chris Riley to stroll in for his 22nd try of the season. The match was virtually over as a contest in the final minute of the first half when Michael Monaghan ghosted through some poor Castleford defending and offloaded to the impressive Richie Myler who raced to the line. Ben Westwood's fifth conversion made it 30-4 and the result was not in doubt, despite a mini-comeback by the Tigers.

Catalans won 30-20 at injury-hit St Helens on the Friday night to move within four points of second-last Salford. Clint Greenshields was the two-try hero as Thomas Bosc and Brent Sherwin dovetailed beautifully and Casey McGuire was prominent throughout. Sherwin's 54th-minute try was Catalans' fifth of the game and put them out of reach at 30-16. McGuire had confirmed he would end his four-year association with the Dragons at the end of the season and return to Australia.

Sam Tomkins scored two tries, created a series of others and tormented Salford all night as Wigan took another step towards clinching the League Leaders' Shield with a 60-10 win at the DW Stadium. Ryan Boyle's 21st-minute dismissal, following a high tackle on Stuart Fielden, left 12-man Salford to battle for an hour in vain. They were already 18-0 down when referee Ben Thaler showed the red card to the visiting prop. Boyle received a one-match ban.

Matty Smith signed a two-year contract with the Reds. St Helens' Smith moved on loan to The Willows at the start of the season, after having spent the previous season on loan at Celtic Crusaders. Phillip Leuluai had signed a deal with French side Lezignan for 2011.

Brian McDermott ruled himself out of the running to become the new Bradford head coach before Harlequins' 35-18 home victory against the Bulls on the Friday night. He was also openly critical of the RFL's disciplinary code the following week when the Bulls' Paul Sykes received only a two-game suspension after upending and dumping Harlequins' Oliver Wilkes.

It was a historic game for the Quins. Fullback Luke Dorn was the only overseas player in the Quins' team, the lowest overseas representation in a London squad since the club entered Super League in 1996. The 17-man squad included seven players who had come through the ranks of Rugby League in the south-east.

Round 22

Super League drew a new record aggregate crowd of 89,356 for the weekend's seven-game round-22 programme. The total was 4,981 higher than the previous record of 84,375, set in Round 8 of 2009.

On Thursday night 20,079 people filled the KC Stadium to see Hull FC defeat their neighbours Hull Kingston Rovers, 20-16, in a memorable 210th Hull derby, a tense thriller, featuring a 26-man brawl, six tries, spurned chances aplenty, late drama, and a fierce forward battle.

Hull winger Tom Briscoe's last-minute try-saving tackle ultimately won the game for the Black and Whites and went down in Hull sporting folklore. The nip-and-tuck affair could have gone the way of the Robins, right up until the moment Peter Fox was dumped into touch with 41 seconds remaining by 20-year-old Briscoe. It was a seasonal double for Hull, who had lost seven of their previous ten meetings against Rovers before battling to an 18-14 victory during a brutal Good Friday contest at Craven Park at the beginning of April. The win strengthened the Airlie Birds' hold on a place in the top four and stalled the momentum of Rovers, who came into the game on the back of a four-match unbeaten run.

Hull KR's stand-in captain Clint Newton reacted angrily after Hull FC coach Richard Agar labelled him and his Robins teammates 'cocky'. Newton and Peter Fox took to the field with dyed blond hair - believed to be a forfeit for missing a recent club event. 'It's none of his business and it has nothing to do with being cocky,' Newton told the Hull Daily Mail, after contacting the newspaper himself to respond. 'If his team-talks before a game as big as the derby are about the colour of a player's hair in the opposition, then he has big problems.'

The aftermath of the 68th-minute brawl was that Ben Cockayne received a two-game ban for striking and instigating the fracas, while Robins teammate Jason Netherton received a caution for running in and punching. Hull's Danny Tickle was suspended for one match while forwards Liam Watts and Sam Moa were also found guilty of fighting but avoided suspensions. Hull fullback Jordan Tansey was issued with a caution for his part in the melee.

On the Friday night the biggest crowd of 2010, 22,701, turned out for the 'Big One 2' at the DW Stadium to see the Wolves edge Wigan, 23-16. Warrington withstood a tough opening 20 minutes almost all in their own half as they spilled possession repeatedly in the wake of a pre-match deluge. But Wigan only scored six points through a Pat Richards penalty and Mark Riddell try in that period. It took 24 minutes for Warrington to launch their first real attack, and they crossed for their first try with Lee Briers and Matt King combining to send Chris Hicks over in the corner. Ben Westwood, who kicked nine from nine the previous week, failed to add the goal.

Warrington took the lead on the half-hour when Briers fired in a kick along the greasy turf, and Richie Myler got to the ball just before Roberts to slide in under the posts, taking a knock in the face from Joel Tomkins for his troubles, Westwood made no mistake with the conversion as the Wolves led 10-6. It could have been a lot worse for the Warriors had Myler been awarded any of his two other efforts in the final ten minutes.

The big hits continued in the second half, with Martin Gleeson dropping the ball in a tackle by Adrian Morley to put the Wolves on the front foot, and they took advantage straight away when Ryan Atkins forced his way over after collecting a clever kick through from the knee of Chris Riley. Westwood coolly made it 16-6 from the touchline.

Wigan pulled one back on 50 minutes, when substitute Chris Tuson used his strength to evade the clutches of Atkins and Mathers to cross following an amazing pass from Sam Tomkins. Richards made no mistake and Wigan trailed 16-12. The Wigan crowd was on its feet again moments later when Goulding put in a monster hit on Richie Mathers, causing him to spill the ball while the Wolves had an overlap. Wigan then got back on level terms with a try out of nothing. Warrington looked certain to score on the right-hand side, but Mathers dropped the ball. Richards picked up and raced 90 metres to score despite a brave effort from Riley, though the Australian missed with the conversion.

Warrington edged themselves back in front with ten minutes remaining, when Ben Westwood burst on to a short pass from Riley to score in front of his own supporters, and the second-rower added the goal for a 22-16 lead. Warrington's first win at the DW Stadium since 2007 was sealed with five minutes remaining, when Briers slotted home a field goal to extend the advantage to seven points.

The following Monday, Wigan unveiled a trio of signings from Melbourne Storm - coach Michael Maguire's old club - forwards Ryan Hoffman and Jeff Lima, and stand-off Brett Finch.

The pulsating clash was the first ever game of Super League to be broadcast live in 3D.

On the same night, Leeds Rhinos' 21-20 home victory over the Giants kept them within a point of the top four. It had been just over 50 years since Huddersfield last won a league game at Headingley, and they looked to have broken their hoodoo when Larne Patrick smashed his way over near the posts with six minutes remaining. But the Rhinos manufactured a route to victory, starting with a converted Danny McGuire try, and culminating in Kevin Sinfield's, literally, last-second field goal. The Giants had that week announced the signing of Australian international Luke O'Donnell on a four-year deal.

On the Sunday Castleford stole a march on local rivals Wakefield with a comprehensive 40-16 home win that lifted them above the Wildcats and into eighth place on the Super League ladder. Inspired by a stirring second-half performance from stand-off Dean Widders, who scored two tries and created another after the break, the Tigers were comfortable winners in the end, despite a see-saw opening hour. Wakefield had been in the contest right up until Widders crossed twice either side of the hour mark, turning a two-point Tigers lead into a commanding 14-point advantage.

Victory for Castleford also meant lifting the Adam Watene Trophy awarded in memory of the Kiwi front-rower who played for both clubs before his untimely death in 2008.

Before the game, it appeared both Castleford's and Wakefield's plans for new stadia ahead of the next round of franchise applications in 2011 had been scuppered by the news that Wakefield Council - with funding by the new central government expected to be slashed - was no longer prepared to provide funding for both projects. Talks were taking place between the two clubs and the local authority to resolve the issue, with a ground share believed to be firmly on the agenda.

St Helens avoided a third consecutive loss with an uninspiring 32-18 home win against enterprising Harlequins, but it took a 67th minute breakaway score from Chris Dean following a Quins error in midfield to finally turn the game their way. Leon Pryce returned and his class was evident every time had the ball as he created Saints' key chances.

Catalans Dragons president Bernard Guasch gave his players a 15-minute tongue-lashing immediately after the 26-22 home defeat by Crusaders and the Dragons players looked visibly shocked as they left the Gilbert Brutus Stadium. Peter Lupton's try four minutes from time saw the Crusaders home.

Lee St Hilaire lost his first game as acting head coach, the Bulls going down 30-26 at home to Salford on the Sunday. The former Huddersfield hooker was handed the reins after England coach Steve McNamara left Odsal by mutual consent following eight successive defeats that had seen Bradford slip from fourth in the league to tenth.

St Hilaire fielded an inexperienced side against the Reds, after the loss of Paul Sykes to a two-match suspension as the Reds recorded a first victory at Odsal for 23 years. Their clinical finishing, often from long range, with Karl Fitzpatrick outstanding, carved out a 30-10 advantage going into the last quarter of an hour.

Bradford overcame their attacking deficiencies to storm back with three tries in five minutes, too late to avoid a Super-League era, record-extending ninth successive defeat.

* Batley Bulldogs celebrated their first major trophy for 86 years, after a thrilling 25-24 victory against Widnes Vikings in the Northern Rail Cup Final at Blackpool's Bloomfield Road on the Sunday. The Bulldogs secured victory with a late try from Alex Brown, their dual-registered winger from Huddersfield Giants. The last time Batley had lifted a major trophy was in 1924, when they won the Championship after beating Wigan 13-7 in the play-off final at The Cliff, Broughton. A crowd of 8,138 witnessed a thrilling Northern Rail Cup Final. Despite now having the opportunity to apply for Super League, the Bulldogs were not expected to put their name forward.

Round 23

Crusaders' 30-24 win over Castleford Tigers on the Sunday put them well and truly in the play-off mix. It was a thrilling see-saw match at the Gnoll Stadium, Neath that was decided by a cart-wheel Jarrod Sammut try three minutes from time, after the Tigers had led 24-16 with seven minutes to go.

The Tigers confirmed that England centre Michael Shenton was to leave the club at the end of the season, though Danny Orr would end a four-year spell in the capital and return to the Jungle for the 2011 campaign, taking up a player-coaching role with the Tigers.

Former Australia hooker Royce Simmons accepted a two-year deal with St Helens to replace Bradford-bound Mick Potter. On the Sunday, top displays from Leon Pryce and

July

James Roby helped St Helens keep alive their hopes of second place with a 50-6 away win at Wakefield, whose top-eight hopes were sinking fast. Potter hailed the performance of Pryce, who was omitted from Steve McNamara's 37-man England squad in midweek. Trailing 16-6 at half-time - that after Kieran Hyde had scored a try on his debut - Wakefield needed to score first after the break to have any chance. But Jon Wilkin's 47th-minute effort opened the floodgates.

At half-time, the Wildcats announced they were to press on with their development of a new facility at Newmarket, and that sharing a ground with Castleford in Glasshoughton was 'not an option'. The Wildcats had previously stated that any sporting club within the district boundaries would be welcome to play at their new facility.

On the Friday night the much-anticipated clash between fourth-placed Hull and leaders Wigan turned into a rout as Pat Richards led the way with a hat-trick of tries and seven goals in a 46-0 win at the KC Stadium. For Hull, still basking in a derby triumph over Hull KR last time out, it was always going to be tough, with six first-team players missing. Danny Tickle was suspended, while Richard Whiting, Mark Calderwood, Mark O'Meley, Sean Long and Craig Fitzgibbon all missed out through injury.

Stand-in Wigan coach Shaun Wane was pleased to get a win for the absent Michael Maguire, who was back in Australia with his ailing father. Sam Tomkins' try just before the interval put the game beyond Hull, who had briefly managed to stem the flow after they went 12-0 down in the first 14 minutes.

A day later Wigan were four points clear again at the top when their nemesis the week before, the Wolves, were edged 29-28 in the south of France. The Dragons were welcoming the 100,000th English supporter to Perpignan, and with it had planned a big weekend of celebrations. Warrington planned to spoil the party. But from the off the Dragons looked to rip up the form book, and they played with the freedom and style that had seen them go within eighty minutes of the Grand Final in 2009. Brent Sherwin's field goal 17 minutes from time gave the Dragons a seven-point cushion, and, when Lee Briers went over four minutes from time, that proved vital.

That week, prop Jamal Fakir completed a U-turn and abandoned plans to quit Rugby League, instead opting to extend his stay with the Dragons for another three years.

Leeds Rhinos jumped into the top four with a 31-22 win at Salford on the Sunday. The City Reds were head and shoulders above the Rhinos in the opening 40 minutes and with a little bit more composure they could have been out of sight. But the Rhinos came out a different side after the break and three tries in ten second-half minutes, from Ryan Hall, Kevin Sinfield and Scott Donald, set the platform for a come-from-behind victory.

The Giants also need a second-half revival to see off Harlequins at the Galpharm Stadium, eventually cruising to a 40-4 victory to leapfrog back over Hull KR into fifth spot in the table. It continued a stranglehold of eight Giants' victories in their last nine encounters with the London side. The final eight-try-to-one margin was a fair reflection but when Quins' Luke Dorn snatched an interception score seconds before the interval, to make it just 8-4, it cast a few doubts. Kevin Brown got the Giants going and finished either scoring or having a significant hand in four of their tries, amid a towering defensive display.

The Saturday TV game saw Hull KR inflict a tenth successive defeat on Bradford at Craven Park, Peter Fox scoring a hat-trick in a 49-24 win. Rovers were not brilliant but they were never going to lose from the moment they went 16-0 clear midway through the first half.

SUPER LEAGUE TABLE - *Sunday 25th July*

	P	W	D	L	F	A	D	PTS
Wigan Warriors	23	19	0	4	808	351	457	38
Warrington Wolves	23	17	0	6	753	404	349	34
St Helens	23	16	0	7	784	471	313	32
Leeds Rhinos	23	14	1	8	605	509	96	29
Hull FC	23	14	0	9	477	496	-19	28
Huddersfield Giants	23	12	1	10	604	401	203	25
Hull Kingston Rovers	23	12	1	10	539	520	19	25
Castleford Tigers	23	10	0	13	546	632	-86	20
Wakefield T Wildcats	23	9	0	14	475	593	-118	18
Crusaders	22	9	0	13	415	626	-211	18
Bradford Bulls	23	8	1	14	444	582	-138	17
Salford City Reds	23	7	0	16	394	689	-295	14
Harlequins	22	6	0	16	398	692	-294	12
Catalans Dragons	23	5	0	18	355	631	-276	10

AUGUST
Top Warriors

Round 24

Wigan Warriors moved six points clear at the top of the table after a 26-12 win at Leeds on the last Friday of July, with Warrington slipping up at home to their long-time nemesis St Helens the following evening.

At Headingley on a wet Friday evening, the Warriors were 12-0 up a minute before half-time through Thomas Leuluai and George Carmont tries - Leeds' Carl Ablett and Ryan Bailey both already on report (Ablett the following Tuesday copped a three-match ban for a late high challenge on fullback Sam Tomkins). A try from rookie loose forward Chris Clarkson after great work from Brent Webb had Leeds back in the game at half-time at 12-6. A Keith Senior try two minutes after the break brought the scores level.

Ten minutes after a Pat Richards penalty, the try that gave Wigan breathing space just after the hour mark was a beauty. Following a scrum on half-way, Sean O'Loughlin and Paul Deacon, with a superb short pass, sent Harrison Hansen, who had returned after numerous stitches in a gashed head, on a glorious 30-metre canter outside Webb for Wigan's third try, with Richards' fourth goal making the gap eight points.

Jamie Peacock tried to galvanise the home troops with a step and 50-metre charge up the middle, but he lost possession. Martin Gleeson's try, after O'Loughlin's long ball was well gathered by a limping Darrell Goulding, settled matters, despite Richards missing the touchline conversion. There could have still been a grandstand finish if Ryan Hall had not had a touchdown disallowed when juggling Kevin Sinfield's grubber, the ball hitting Sam Tomkins as he tried to reel it in.

To ensure there were no late dramas, Stuart Fielden won a penalty and Richards landed his fifth goal, while Sam Tomkins was wide with a late field-goal attempt, to make it two wins from two for Shaun Wane before Michael Maguire returned from compassionate leave.

St Helens drew level on points with the second-placed Wolves after clinging on to win 26-24 in a pulsating derby at the Halliwell Jones Stadium that saw the lead change hands five times, with the result remaining in doubt until the final seconds, when Ade Gardner cradled Chris Riley's cross-field kick safely in hand. Warrington still hadn't beaten Saints since 2001.

The closing ten minutes of the game found Saints clinging to a six-point advantage and the Wolves laying siege to their line. And when Wolves standout Ben Westwood pounced on Lee Briers' kick through, hanging on in the face of a mighty tackle from Paul Wellens to score, they seemed set to end the curse.

There were great performances on both sides, but Westwood's effort outshone them all. So it was a cruel twist that he was unable to convert his own try to tie the game, instead giving Saints' scrambling defence the chance to hold on for victory.

On the same night, Hull FC recorded a first win at the Stoop, and overtook Leeds to move into fourth spot in Super League. They welcomed back influential pack men Craig Fitzgibbon and Mark O'Meley. The 42-18 victory was O'Meley's first run-out since tearing his calf during the win over St Helens at the beginning of June, while Fitzgibbon was forced to sit out of the two previous games with an Achilles tendon problem. Danny Tickle was also back in the squad after serving a one-week suspension for his role in the brawl during the Hull derby. Sam Moa's try on 30 minutes ended the game as a contest as Tickle's fifth conversion made it 30-0 at the break.

Huddersfield were loitering with intent in sixth spot, their play-off place secured with a 58-6 home hammering of Wakefield. Brad Drew, Danny Brough and gamestar Kevin Brown enjoyed field days as Huddersfield Giants showed little mercy against the injury-hit Wildcats.

Brown was the star of a first half that ended with the Giants leading 36-0, before Drew and Brough took centre stage against their former club after the break. With the likes of Scott Grix, Leroy Cudjoe, Shaun Lunt and David Faiumu providing willing runs for the three pivots, Huddersfield cut their opponents to pieces. Darrell Griffin also had a tremendous game up front to continue the trend of ex-Wildcats impressing against their old club.

Michael Dobson kicked a 46-metre penalty after the final hooter to book Hull KR's place in the Super League play-offs for a second straight year with a 28-26 home win over Castleford.

With a pulsating match level at 26-26 just seconds before the hooter, Rovers were awarded a dubious penalty. And Dobson held his nerve to make it six kicks from six and clinch a thrilling victory for Rovers, who had come from 20-12 down to win 24-20 at Cas in February.

The Robins led 12-8 after an entertaining first quarter and then 18-12 at the break, with on-loan Wigan centre Josh Charnley scoring two first-half tries. Rangi Chase then came to the fore, scoring one fine try and making another for Stuart Jones for Cas to lead 24-20 heading into the last 20 minutes. But Charnley completed his first-ever first-class hat-trick to edge Rovers back in front before Joe Westerman's late penalty levelled things up and set the stage for Dobson.

The heartbreaking defeat left the Tigers in a four-way battle for the last play-off spot with Crusaders, Wakefield and Bradford.

Salford's 60-16 defeat by the Crusaders in Wrexham on the Sunday extinguished any faint hopes the Reds harboured of a late surge for the eight. The game was over by half-time and if it had been a boxing fight it would have been stopped as Brian Noble's men ran riot led by Rhys Hanbury, Jarrod Sammut and Weller Hauraki. The victory moved the Crusaders level on points with eighth-placed Castleford, with Clinton Schifcofske's two tries and eight goals the standout of a great team performance.

Bradford Bulls went down to their eleventh straight defeat, at home to the Catalans by 24-22 on the Sunday. A second successive win lifted the Dragons off the foot of the table ahead of the following Sunday's Challenge Cup semi-final against Warrington. Bradford fought back from a 16-6 deficit to lead 22-16 but simply couldn't put their opponents away. A 72nd-minute Thomas Bosc penalty finally separated the sides, four minutes after Olivier Elima's levelling try.

Laurent Frayssinous was in charge in the absence of head coach Kevin Walters, who had to return home to Australia following the death of his father. Frayssinous was able to name wingman Chris Walker for the first time in three months, following his career-threatening neck injury, but opted to rest Clint Greenshields for another week and was also without the equally influential Casey McGuire, Jerome Guisset and Dallas Johnson.

The Bulls again dismissed rumours that Matt Orford, their Australian halfback who joined them from Manly Sea Eagles at the start of the season, would not return to Odsal to fulfil the remaining two years of his contract. Reports suggested that Orford, who was in Australia recuperating from surgery on his injured shoulder, suffered from homesickness while in England. Bulls chairman Peter Hood insisted Orford would see out the remainder of his contract at Odsal.

* *Off the field, Crusaders winger Gareth Thomas was named joint-top, with television personality Mary Portas, on a list of influential British homosexuals. The pair replaced last year's number one, the former Secretary of State Lord Mandelson.*

Carnegie Challenge Cup Semi-finals

In a non-stop clash that yielded some truly memorable moments, Leeds Rhinos held off St Helens in the Saturday semi-final at the Galpharm Stadium to return to Wembley for the first time since 1999 after a 32-28 win. An outstanding combination between Jamie Peacock and Danny McGuire sealed a classic game.

Mick Potter's Saints were already dealing with the blow of not having ankle-injury victim Kyle Eastmond fit, when it was confirmed on the Friday that stand-off Leon Pryce would also miss the game with a neck complaint, resulting in a makeshift halfback partnership of Scott Moore and Jon Wilkin. But despite that, St Helens led by two points with seven minutes of the clash remaining. That was when Peacock – fresh off the bench – took on the Saints defence and offloaded inside for McGuire, who raced to the line to seal his man of the match award.

Paul Wellens rolled back the years with a terrific performance which was mirrored by fellow veteran Keith Senior in the Leeds ranks. Leeds coach Brian McClennan also hailed the performances of Lee Smith and Ryan Bailey among others, after deciding to omit Scott Donald and use Smith on the right wing.

While McGuire was fully deserving of his man of the match prize, the role of the two experienced hookers, Danny Buderus and Keiron Cunningham, inspired the best spells in their teams during their time on the field.

Leeds' Danny McGuire looks for support under pressure from St Helens' Jon Wilkin

On the Sunday, there was little drama as Cup-holders Warrington Wolves won a one-way tie against Catalans Dragons at Widnes by 54-12. From the opening minutes, it was apparent that Warrington were going to win after Ben Harrison's opening try. From that point things got quickly worse for the French team, as the Wolves opened them up with ease. Lee Briers was at his best in his 350th career appearance, and Michael Monaghan was in great form.

The Catalans could point to an unfair selection of a 'neutral' venue, or the loss of tackling machine Dallas Johnson, whose wife was due to give birth, but were totally outclassed.

In the build-up to the game, Dragons prop David Ferriol had been quoted by the News of the World, claiming that Wolves prop Adrian Morley was no longer feared by opponents. It turned out his quotes had been made up by the RFL with the Dragons' media manager's approval.

The French club, losing finalists in 2007, had beaten Tony Smith's side 29-28 in Perpignan just a fortnight before, but there was no chance of another upset as the Wolves ran in nine tries to seal their return to Wembley.

Louis Anderson's hat-trick led the way with Harrison, Matt King, Chris Riley, Lee Briers, Richie Myler and Jon Clarke the other scorers, while Clint Greenshields twice crossed for the Dragons.

Round 9

Crusaders' head coach Brian Noble was ecstatic as his side moved into the top eight on the Friday night in a game postponed earlier in the season because of waterlogging.

The Crusaders beat Harlequins 16-12 in the weekend's only Super League match, and with just three rounds to go a play-off spot was now within their grasp. It was the Welsh side's fourth win in a row, a record for them in Super League, and the third game in four they had to produce a great escape to secure the two points. Danny Orr kicked a penalty on 71 minutes to give the Londoners what seemed like an unassailable lead. But the Crusaders snatched victory at the death. Jason Chan got a try back after a thrilling run from former London player Tony Martin created the opportunity. Schifcofske's kick put the Crusaders to within two points.

And, straight away, Crusaders recovered the ball from a short Quins kick-off, which led to Rhys Hanbury charging over for their third try which was again goaled. The halfback attempted a field goal in the final minute but it swung wide of the posts. There was a nervous last 90 seconds for home fans as Quins threw all they could to try to regain the lead, but it was to no avail as the Welsh held on.

The game in Neath kicked off at 6pm on the Friday after several last-minute rearrangements of time and date. Noble explained that moving the kick-off gave his side a full week to prepare for a tough away trip to Hull FC. It also produced the lowest attendance in 15 years of Super League.

Round 25

Leeds followed up their Challenge Cup semi-final success with an overwhelming 38-6 Friday-night victory over Castleford at the Jungle. But they suffered a double injury blow. Luke Burgess broke his jaw in two places during the closing stages. The 23-year-old prop forward was involved in a collision with opposite number Jonathan Walker after returning the restart from Ryan Hall's second try. Even more worrying for Leeds was the sight of Jamie Peacock being helped off the field with what proved to be a season-ending knee injury.

The first half in particular belonged to the mercurial Danny McGuire who scored a picture solo try. Rob Burrow's try eight minutes later wasn't a bad one either as he ducked under Stuart Jones and Liam Higgins' tackle, causing them to near-embrace, and scampered home.

On the same night, Crusaders coach Brian Noble was set to face an investigation by the RFL after he confronted referee James Child after his team went down 18-16 in a crucial clash against Hull FC at the KC Stadium.

The Crusaders appeared to be holding on for a draw, which would almost have guaranteed them a place in the Super League play-offs, until Child awarded a penalty to Hull in the dying seconds of the game for a late hit by Luke Dyer on Hull winger Reece Lyne.

A visibly angry Noble attempt to enter the field to confront Child, but he was held back by the fourth official. He continued, however, to complain from the sidelines as Danny Tickle converted from the touchline to win the game, while the Hull players celebrated their victory.

Five minutes before the end of the game Child had dismissed Hull fullback Jordan Tansey, subsequently banned for two matches, for an illegal tackle on Clinton Schifcofske that left the Crusaders star in a heap. No action was taken by the RFL against Noble.

St Helens went someway towards banishing memories of their Challenge Cup semi-final defeat to Leeds with an 11-try, 60-12 home demolition of hapless Bradford. It was a bittersweet evening for Saints coach Mick Potter whose current employers, led by Jamie Foster's personal haul of 24 points, emphatically dispatched his future ones; the Bulls slumping to their 12th Super League defeat in a row. It wasn't Bradford's worst defeat in Super League – Saints had already beaten them 66-4 back in 2005 – but it came very close.

On the Sunday, Lee Briers pulled the strings as Warrington's assault on second place and preparations for Wembley were boosted by a 36-18 defeat of Wakefield at Belle Vue. Stand-off Briers scored one try – a trademark interception effort - and had a hand in the six others as they had too much for a Wakefield side whose play-off hopes were all but over. Matt King, playing on the left wing, helped himself to a well-taken hat-trick.

It was just enough to edge the Wolves back above St Helens into second, in a race that would now go to the final day of the season. And it also confirmed that the Wolves would record their best ever Super League finish. Before kick-off, the Wakefield players formed a guard of honour for skipper Jason Demetriou in his last game for the club at Belle Vue.

Salford City Reds were swept aside by a 13-minute five-try torrent in the second half by Hull KR, who returned east from the Willows with a 44-18 win. Michael Dobson's 43rd minute 40/20 started the Robins' red-hot spell and he finished with a try, six goals and had a hand or foot in five other tries.

Wigan coach Michael Maguire insisted his team would still win the League Leaders' Shield despite a Sunday night shock 18-16 defeat by Huddersfield at the DW Stadium.

Maguire was forced to make two changes to his team that defeated Leeds Rhinos two weeks before, with Martin Gleeson dropping out following a hernia operation, and Stefan Marsh starting. Darrell Goulding was a late withdrawal, with Karl Pryce coming in to replace him on the wing. The Giants welcomed back fullback Brett Hodgson after a three-game absence with a shoulder injury, while Keith Mason and David Fa'alogo returned to the pack, with Eorl Crabtree and Shaun Lunt dropping to the bench.

Things got a bit tasty after quarter of an hour when Sam Tomkins broke clear to send Pat Richards racing away. Kevin Brown took Tomkins out and was despatched to the sin bin. A minute later an all-in brawl got the crowd on its feet as Stuart Fielden took exception to a stamp on his ankle from Keith Mason and remonstrated, ending with the pair exchanging punches. Both men were sent to sin bin for ten minutes. Mason was suspended for three matches at the following Tuesday's disciplinary hearing. Fielden and Darrell Griffin both received a match each for their parts.

Sam Tomkins' 64th minute wonder-try looked to have sealed top spot for the Warriors. But Leroy Cudjoe's second try, nine minutes from time, was enough to give the

Giants a dramatic win.

Wigan remained top of the table, clear by four points with two matches remaining and hoped to claim the League Leaders Shield at Hull KR the following week.

* That week the RFL announced the opening fixtures of Super League XVI would be staged at the Millennium Stadium in Cardiff. Matches were to take place under the closed roof over the weekend commencing February 12, 2011.

Round 26

Wigan confirmed the Minor Premiership at Hull Kingston Rovers on the Sunday before the Challenge Cup final, with a 38-18 victory at Craven Park. But they were forced to overcome a huge scare after Rovers threatened an upset by scoring three quick-fire tries at the start of the second half. After conceding three tries in seven minutes to go from 14-0 up to 18-14 down, Michael Maguire's men appeared ready to choke for a second successive week. But with Pat Richards ending with 22 points from two tries and seven goals and the Tomkins brothers, Sean O'Loughlin, Mark Riddell and Paul Deacon all oozing authority, the Warriors ended well on top. Sam Tomkins' 62nd-minute try put Wigan back in front and Rovers had no answer to a devastating final ten minutes.

The jockeying for position below Wigan was set to continue right to the last round. St Helens went back into second on points difference with a 36-10 win over the Crusaders in Wrexham on the Saturday night. Saints needed to win by 20 points or more to go above Warrington and up until a contentious decision from the video referee it looked like being a frustrating night for them.

The killer blow came on 65 minutes when James Roby was awarded a try when television replays showed he was short of the line before losing the ball and, with Saints only leading by eight points at the time, it was a crucial decision that seemed to knock the stuffing out of the home side.

Warrington had already got the better of Hull FC at the Halliwell Jones Stadium by 36-18 on the Friday. Having been dominated during the opening exchanges, the Wolves eventually found their rhythm and began to control things, with Ben Westwood a standout and Michael Monaghan, Ryan Atkins and Adrian Morley also impressive. Winger Chris Riley's two tries kept the Wolves in it at 12-all at half-time after Hull had been the better side.

Tony Smith's decision to leave out Lee Briers and Garreth Carvell appeared to have backfired as the hosts struggled to contain Hull during a torrid opening quarter. Smith's side needed 12 minutes before they even touched the ball in Hull's half after the Airlie Birds' pack got the upper hand. Shaun Berrigan was architect-in-chief for the visitors, and by the time Warrington did venture forward, they were already 6-0 down as England winger Tom Briscoe sidestepped Riley and got the ball down despite pressure from Ryan Atkins.

However, Riley quickly made amends when he raced on to Louis Anderson's cut-out pass for Warrington's first try. Substitute forward Epalahame Lauaki powered on to Craig Fitzgibbon's pass to restore Hull's advantage. But Riley was on hand to finish a sweeping move involving Vinnie Anderson, Richie Myler and Atkins just before the break.

Hull continued to fight after the interval and were in with a chance until referee Ian Smith sin-binned Danny Tickle for holding down Michael Monaghan after he had supported a superb Myler break from his own flat pass. The visitors' reduced numbers could not hold out against a Wolves side determined to keep the ball alive. Jon Clarke dived over after Monaghan and Westwood had combined, then Westwood wriggled over after two offloads had stretched Hull to breaking point. Lee Radford kept the visitors in contention with a late score from Sam Moa's pass, but the Wolves were in no mood for a late collapse. Adrian Morley stepped past one defender and carried another over with him, before Myler burst on to Jon Clarke's well-timed pass.

Hull's defeat meant Leeds went back into fourth after a routine 52-6 home win over a dispirited-looking Catalans Dragons, Danny McGuire and Ryan Hall both registering hat-tricks.

Dragons duo Setaimata Sa and Dimitri Pelo had that week been handed suspended jail sentences after being found guilty of an affray. The charges related to a brawl in Leeds city centre after their round-one defeat at Wakefield.

Huddersfield remained within a point of Hull in sixth after outclassing Salford by 52-4 at the Galpharm, Kevin Brown once again at the centre of the Giants attack.

Castleford jumped back into eighth with a 40-28 win at the Jungle over Harlequins. St Helens-bound Michael Shenton and the retiring Mitchell Sargent scored farewell Jungle tries as Castleford Tigers ensured the race for the last play-off spot would go down to the final day of the season. The Tigers had the game effectively won by the hour mark when youngster Adam Milner's try made it 34-12.

That week Brian McDermott had confirmed that 2010 would be his last as Harlequins coach, having agreed to take up a post with Leeds Rhinos as assistant to Brian McClennan. After admitting the decision to return north for family reasons was made with a heavy heart, the former Bradford Bulls prop forward expressed his concern for the future of the London club.

The Wildcats' outside chance of a play-off spot were ended with a 38-28 defeat at Odsal, in what was the Bulls' first win after 12 straight defeats. Their last success had been a 29-10 win at Wakefield on May 10th when they stood fourth in the table. Wakefield strode into a 12-0 lead but the Bulls bounced back to score five tries without reply for caretaker coach Lee St Hilaire's first, and only, win in charge.

Round 27

The Super League XV regular-season reached its climax in the first week of September after a week's interlude for the Challenge Cup final.

Wigan collected the League Leaders Shield after their 34-12 home win over Bradford. Two tries and three goals were enough for Pat Richards to equal Andy Farrell's Super League regular-season points-scoring record of 388 points. The prolific goal-kicking wingman uncharacteristically missed four of his seven conversion attempts.

Nearly all of the 17,058 crowd came to party and were not to be disappointed as four first-half tries quickly put the result beyond doubt. Richards' try a minute after the break was the killer.

The Crusaders went into the play-offs for the first time in their history after grinding out a hard-fought 30-24 win over seventh-placed Hull KR at the Racecourse Ground on the Saturday evening to finish in eighth spot. They eventually sealed the win when Jarrod Sammut collected his own chip and chase to feed Tony Martin, who sent Luke Dyer in for the match-winning try

The Crusaders then had to wait anxiously for the final minutes of St Helens' clash with Castleford to unfold before they knew they had overtaken the Tigers to finish eighth. After their win, the whole squad and coaching staff remained on the field staring at the scoreboard awaiting the conclusion of the game at Knowsley Road.

St Helens needed to beat Castleford at the last league game at the old stadium by nine points to secure a second-place finish. Midway through the second half they led 30-10 and it looked a formality. But, incredibly, Castleford - who needed a win to assure themselves a play-off spot for the second year running - levelled the scores with three minutes left – only for Matt Gidley to snatch back the lead, before Keiron Cunningham bundled himself over under the posts with nine seconds to spare. Jamie Foster's conversion made it 40-30. Saints were second and Crusaders' win on the same night meant the Tigers were out.

August

Second spot ensured a home tie with third-placed Warrington the following Friday, with Kyle Eastmond a major injury concern with a recurrence of the ankle injury. Saints were boosted, though, by the shock return of Sia Soliola. The New Zealand international came off the bench early in the second half.

The Wolves' 36-22 victory over Harlequins at the Stoop on the Friday evening proved not to be enough to earn a home tie. Chris Bridge marked his return to Super League following shoulder surgery with two tries and six goals for Warrington. It was the goal-kicking centre's second outing, after his comeback in the Carnegie Floodlit 9s, won on the Wednesday before Wembley by a young Wigan side.

Tony Smith selected from a largely understrength squad for the Wolves' final game of the regular Super League season, and 17-year-old Rhys Evans came on as substitute for Richie Mathers at fullback in the 54th minute. Adrian Morley, Matt King, Ben Westwood, Lee Briers and Louis Anderson were all rested.

It was an emotional night at the Stoop as Brian McDermott ended his four-year reign as coach. Louie McCarthy-Scarsbrook's seven-year association with the London club was also over after he signed a four-year deal with St Helens. Before the game, Quins chairman David Hughes announced to the crowd that the financial future of the club was secure after negotiations with the RFL.

After their 18-14 Saturday victory over Hull FC at the KC Stadium, champions Leeds Rhinos sealed fourth place. In a clash packed with incident throughout, the game centred around the tenth-minute dismissal of Hull captain Lee Radford, who was shown the red card after punching Ryan Bailey. But despite being a man short for virtually the entire game, Hull – with their loose forward Craig Fitzgibbon getting through a mountain of work and Sean Long back after recovering from a dislocated elbow sustained against Catalans Dragons in June – led for much of the contest, and were 12-0 ahead at half-time.

The expected Rhinos charge came after the break, but Richard Agar's side were still 14-12 ahead with ten minutes remaining. That was when Danny McGuire stepped through a tiring home defence for the second time in the space of six minutes, sealing an opening play-off game for Leeds at table-toppers Wigan.

Radford had been dismissed by referee Ian Smith when he punched Bailey after being caught with a stray elbow as the tackled Leeds prop tried to regain his feet. Bailey was forced to have four stitches in his head, and was immediately sent to the blood-bin. A subsequent one-match ban ruled Radford out of the play-off derby with local rivals Hull KR, who had won the race to sign former Australian Test star Willie Mason for 2011.

Hull averted the threat of punishment from the RFL by signalling their intention to ban for life one supporter who ran on to the pitch and attempted to tackle the Leeds wing Scott Donald during the game.

The Airlie Birds were edged into sixth spot by Huddersfield's 26-12 win in Perpignan on the Saturday night. Luke Robinson's try 16 minutes from time sealed the win for the Giants after a ten-minute spell where Catalans had rallied from a 22-0 deficit.

Jason Demetriou finished a seven-season stint with Wakefield at the Willows in disappointment in the only game on the Sunday, as the Wildcats went down 16-12 to Salford at the Willows. Another player hanging up his boots, Malcolm Alker, wasn't able to take his place because of injury and was set to join the Reds' coaching staff in 2011.

FINAL SUPER LEAGUE TABLE - *Sunday 5th September*

	P	W	D	L	F	A	D	PTS
Wigan Warriors	27	22	0	5	922	411	511	44
St Helens	27	20	0	7	946	547	399	40
Warrington Wolves	27	20	0	7	885	488	397	40
Leeds Rhinos	27	17	1	9	725	561	164	35
Huddersfield Giants	27	16	1	10	758	439	319	33
Hull FC	27	16	0	11	569	584	-15	32
Hull Kingston Rovers	27	14	1	12	653	632	21	29
Crusaders	27	12	0	15	547	732	-185	24
Castleford Tigers	27	11	0	16	648	766	-118	22
Bradford Bulls	27	9	1	17	528	728	-200	19
Wakefield T Wildcats	27	9	0	18	539	741	-202	18
Salford City Reds	27	8	0	19	448	857	-409	16
Harlequins	27	7	0	20	494	838	-344	14
Catalans Dragons	27	6	0	21	409	747	-338	12

CHALLENGE CUP FINAL
Big bad Wolves

Warrington Wolves brushed aside Leeds Rhinos in front of 85,217 spectators as they retained the Challenge Cup trophy with a 30-6 victory – the first time in the club's history they had won back-to-back Challenge Cups.

It was an excellent Warrington performance that saw every player on song, with Lance Todd trophy-winner Lee Briers controlling the game behind the powerhouse front row of Adrian Morley, Garreth Carvell, Paul Wood and David Solomona, and the goal-line defence of an inspired Richie Mathers denying Leeds on at least three occasions.

Briers received 34 of the 40 votes cast for the Lance Todd Trophy, despite Chris Hicks becoming only the third man in history to score a hat-trick in the showpiece event.

CARNEGIE CHALLENGE CUP FINAL

Saturday 28th August 2010

LEEDS RHINOS 6 WARRINGTON WOLVES 30

RHINOS: 1 Brent Webb; 28 Lee Smith; 3 Brett Delaney; 4 Keith Senior; 5 Ryan Hall; 6 Danny McGuire; 7 Rob Burrow; 8 Kylie Leuluai; 9 Danny Buderus; 16 Ryan Bailey; 27 Chris Clarkson; 11 Jamie Jones-Buchanan; 13 Kevin Sinfield (C). Subs (all used): 14 Matt Diskin; 15 Greg Eastwood; 17 Ian Kirke; 18 Carl Ablett.
Try: Smith (66); **Goals:** Sinfield 1/1.
WOLVES: 1 Richard Mathers; 5 Chris Hicks; 3 Matt King; 23 Ryan Atkins; 2 Chris Riley; 6 Lee Briers; 9 Michael Monaghan; 8 Adrian Morley (C); 15 Jon Clarke; 10 Garreth Carvell; 11 Louis Anderson; 12 Ben Westwood; 13 Ben Harrison. Subs (all used): 16 Paul Wood; 26 David Solomona; 14 Mick Higham; 27 Vinnie Anderson.
Tries: Atkins (4, 35), Hicks (18, 62, 72), L Anderson (76); **Goals:** Westwood 3/6.
Rugby Leaguer & League Express Men of the Match:
Rhinos: Lee Smith; *Wolves:* Lee Briers.
Penalty count: 5-6; **Half-time:** 0-14;
Referee: Richard Silverwood;
Attendance: 85,217 *(at Wembley Stadium).*

After a display from his team full of guts, commitment and skill, Wolves coach Tony Smith couldn't be faulted for his team selection, although his omission of 20-year-old England scrum-half Richie Myler attracted some pre-match attention. Myler was forced to watch from the sidelines as Smith opted to play Jon Clarke and Mickey Higham, with Michael Monaghan lining up alongside Briers in the halves.

Leeds coach Brian McClennan opted for rookie forward Chris Clarkson ahead of Ali Lauitiiti, although his biggest loss was in the front row, with broken-jaw victim Luke Burgess, and more significantly Jamie Peacock, out for the season with a knee injury, unavailable for the biggest day of the year.

The atmosphere inside Wembley was electric with both sets of fans in good voice as Briers got the game underway. From his kick-off the game took a strange turn when Danny Buderus gifted possession to the Wolves ten metres out as he misjudged the flight of the ball and knocked on. But, in an incredible opening, from the resultant scrum a blind-side play saw Ryan Atkins scrambled into touch by a posse of Rhinos, and before the end of the first set, it was Leeds laying siege to the Warrington line.

A smart Rhinos move sent the ball wide to Smith who raced down the right wing and chipped ahead into open space. Chris Riley fumbled, Kevin Sinfield picked the ball up cleanly and offloaded brilliantly to Brent Webb who was hauled down. Leeds kept up the pressure and in another repeat set after a Warrington knock down, Ryan Bailey charged over the Warrington line on the third tackle for what looked a certain score. But video referee Ian Smith correctly turned down the try as the Leeds prop was held up by a superb effort from Mathers and Louis Anderson.

The Rhinos continued to press as Keith Senior, Buderus and Rob Burrow all went within inches of opening the scores, but the Warrington online defence managed to scramble to cut them down. The pressure relented when a wide kick to the right corner from Danny McGuire evaded the Rhinos' attackers and bounced into touch.

Leeds looked well on top, but that was as good as it got for the Rhinos as Warrington turned in some enterprising play. Coming out of defence, Morley and Carvell offloaded to Ben Westwood, who in turn found Matt King out wide. The big centre was tackled by Burrow and, minutes later, King found open space again but was just brought to ground metres from the line by Burrow and Ryan Hall. From the play-the-ball, Hicks found Briers and he delivered a pin-point high kick to the left that Brett Delaney mis-judged but Ryan Atkins read perfectly to catch cleanly and touch down. Westwood missed the conversion and three minutes later the lead was doubled before Leeds could get the ball in hand.

An imperious 40/20 on the third tackle after the restart by Briers handed the Wolves a perfect field position. Slick passing took the ball from the right side of the field to the far left and then back again. Briers was again involved as his wide cut-out pass to King allowed the centre to bring Hicks inside. The winger had plenty to do as he jinked and stepped his way to the Leeds line and reached out to touch down, despite the efforts of Senior and Bailey. Westwood hit the post with his conversion attempt and the lead was still only eight points.

That double effort by Warrington shook Leeds and it took them time to recover, but every time the Rhinos looked to make a break, the Wolves kept coming up with big-plays to cut them down - exemplified by Westwood, who managed to bring Ryan Hall to ground and into touch after a superb behind-the-back pass by Jamie Jones-Buchanan. Minutes later, Hall was away down the left wing again but was called back for a forward pass.

Just as the Rhinos looked to be working their way back into the game with five minutes remaining of the half, Warrington hit them with a sucker punch. Sinfield's high kick was allowed to bounce by Mathers and ricocheted forwards off his thigh. Chris Riley collected the ball in what TV replays proved to be an offside position and raced up field in thrilling style. Only a cover tackle by Webb prevented the speedster from going the full length of the field. But from the play-the-ball, Atkins attacked the back-tracking Leeds defence and embarrassed Hall and Ian Kirke before racing through to touch the ball down under the posts. Westwood did convert this time, gifting the Wolves a 14-point lead heading into half-time.

There was still time for sub David Solomona to put on a party piece for the huge crowd as he dummied his trademark one-handed backflick, sidestepped a couple of defenders, threw another one off and as he was tackled still managed to get the ball away.

After the break, Leeds continued to pound the line and after the game was held up of for lengthy treatment on a McGuire injury, although he played on, Brett Delaney was held just short by another monster effort from the Mathers-led Warrington defence.

Six minutes later, Westwood spilled a pass bringing the ball away from his own line, and gifted field position to Leeds. This time, as Burrow fed his centre Delaney, the big Australian looked like he would break Leeds' duck. But he was held up by some more awesome goal-line defence as Mathers and Atkins combined to repel the latest Leeds attack.

Briers' high kick into the sun lifted the siege. Lee Smith couldn't get near it and Riley cleaned up again. Three minutes later, Briers' bomb to the right corner was defused by Hall who had jumped from the field of play.

Leeds got back upfield but Riley dropped on Sinfield's kick in the corner before the Wolves launched a great attack from deep. Michael Monaghan, who had another superb game, and Briers got Hicks clear down the right, although he was tracked and brought down as he came infield. With the Rhinos scrambling back, Briers chipped to the right wing for the chasing King, the ball bouncing on the touchline to end a marvellous attack.

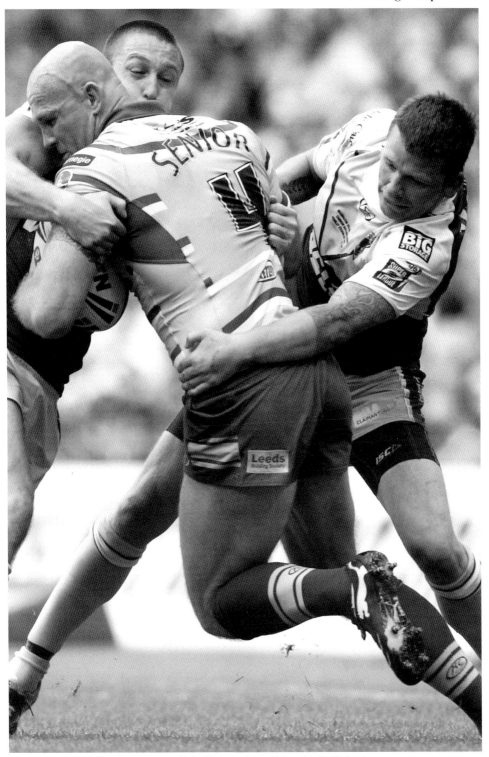

No way past Chris Hicks and Lee Briers for Keith Senior

Ben Harrison and Wolves coach Tony Smith show off the Challenge Cup

Just after the hour, the Warrington spirit of adventure paid dividends as Briers decided to put up another high kick to the right corner and this time Hick rose above Hall in spectacular fashion to catch and get the ball down as he fell to earth. Westwood nailed the conversion attempt from out wide and gave the Wolves a 20-point lead with 19 minutes remaining.

Leeds needed to hit back, and quickly, if they were to give themselves a chance of a comeback but Sinfield's re-start didn't go ten metres. But the Rhinos, now lacking the injured Jones-Buchanan, did get some reward for their blood and sweat, as a wide McGuire pass found Smith, who out-paced the Warrington defence to score in the right corner, in Atkins tackle, with the video referee again consulted. Sinfield added the touchline goal with ease to reduce the arrears.

Just three minutes later, hopes of a Rhinos revival looked to have ended when Mathers ghosted in to score, but his effort was ruled out by the video ref – for an obstruction after decoy Westwood had taken Kirke out earlier in the play.

With Leeds trying everything to score, a wayward Greg Eastwood offload was pounced on by Atkins. After more hard work by Riley, Warrington extended their lead and ended any hopes of a comeback as Hicks completed his hat-trick with seven minutes remaining. Briers was involved, again, darting towards the line before offloading to Louis Anderson who dunked a pass to Mathers. Mathers flicked the ball on to Westwood. He had to turn and collect on the bounce before sending wide to Hicks who managed to step his way to the line to earn his place in Challenge Cup Final folklore.

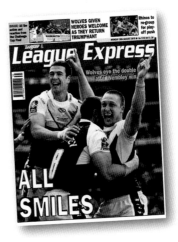

Westwood missed the conversion attempt but did convert after Louis Anderson sprinted over through the left channel, following a superb pass in the tackle from Mathers, to put the cherry on top of the cake and send the Warrington fans into raptures.

SUPER LEAGUE PLAY-OFFS
Nap hand for Saints

Week One

Qualifying Play-offs

ST HELENS 28 WARRINGTON WOLVES 12

St Helens ensured there would be one more game at Knowsley Road before the bulldozers moved in by guaranteeing a home tie in the penultimate play-off round. They had to come back from an opening Wolves blitz that saw the Challenge Cup-holders ease to an 8-0 lead after only six minutes with two slick tries down the right for Matt King.

It looked like plain sailing for Warrington, especially as Saints lacked halfbacks Leon Pryce (neck) and Kyle Eastmond (ankle) with Matty Smith, having signed a contract for 2011 at Salford - the club to which he had been loaned for SLXV - recalled by coach Mick Potter. Smith produced a man-of-the-match performance in his first game for St Helens since March 2008, having spent 2009 on loan with the Crusaders.

Smith orchestrated the Saints fightback as his grubber led to Saints' opening try for Paul Wellens before Keiron Cunningham rolled back the years with a dummy and burst for the corner to give Saints a lead they never looked like relinquishing. As the rain got heavier the Saints pack began to pummel Warrington down the middle and Smith's superb kicking kept the visitors at arm's length. Another academy product, Jamie Foster, also impressed on the wing and kicked six goals, including four penalties that pushed Saints out of reach.

Before the break, James Graham marked his 25th birthday by crashing between Michael Monaghan and Mike Cooper to touch down from James Roby's pass, and a Foster conversion and penalty made it 18-8 at half-time. Shortly after the restart following interference by Ben Westwood, Foster stretched Saints' lead to two converted tries. Foster kicked his third penalty from 35 metres after Mike Cooper went high on Jake Emmitt.

Warrington came into the game on the back of five straight wins, which included their convincing win over Leeds to clinch back-to-back Challenge Cups. But their woeful record against Saints was set to continue when Smith's bomb was spilled by Chris Riley, although the winger appeared to be tackled in the air by Foster. Wellens swept up the loose ball before offloading for Chris Flannery to slide over.

Warrington rallied, with Chris Bridge touching down after charging down Jon Wilkin's kick on the last before Foster added another penalty after Adrian Morley's high tackle on Tony Puletua.

WIGAN WARRIORS 26 LEEDS RHINOS 27

In a game played on Sunday night because of soccer commitments at the DW Stadium, defending champions Leeds, who had only guaranteed fourth spot with a win at Hull in the last game of the regular season, shocked the League Leaders in dramatic fashion. There was controversy right up until the final hooter as Danny McGuire pulled George Carmont back off the ball when he tried to support Pat Richards' last-second break down the left, injuring himself in the process. But the penalty was awarded for obstruction on Richards, taken out by Scott Donald as he kicked ahead. Wigan were given one last shot at goal with five seconds remaining, but Richards' attempt from the touchline 42 metres out was short and off target.

Wigan started like a house on fire, with Sam Tomkins bossing the show, the fullback scoring a brace of tries inside five minutes, but Leeds hit back from 14-0 to lead 20-14 after McGuire's superb try three minutes into the second half. Liam Farrell and Donald then swapped tries before Richards scored a try in the left corner, which he couldn't convert. Tempers flared with nine minutes to go when Ali Lauitiiti was penalised for a high tackle on Joel Tomkins, seconds after Thomas Leuluai pulled off an amazing tackle on Donald in full flight. Richards opted to go for goal from 40 metres, but again was unsuccessful as time was running out for the Warriors.

A brawl almost started when Kevin Sinfield took Stuart Fielden high. Wigan were awarded another penalty and again Richards went for goal and this time he was successful - the scores were tied at 26-26.

But an error from Leuluai from the restart gave the ball back to Leeds via a scrum and they capitalised, with Sinfield slotting over a field goal to once again edge the Rhinos in front, before that dramatic finish meant second-placed St Helens would take up the number-one seeding.

The Warriors would have to do it all again the following Friday against Hull Kingston Rovers.

Elimination Play-offs

HULL FC 4 HULL KINGSTON ROVERS 21

Hull Kingston Rovers recorded a first ever Super League play-off win as their well-organised defence laid the foundations for a memorable win at the KC Stadium, in the first play-off game between the city rivals. With stand-off Scott Murrell outstanding, the Robins swamped the Hull FC attack time after time. Murrell had plenty of support around him, with hooker Ben Fisher scoring one try, having a hand in another and working prolifically in general play. With heavy rain characterising the second half, the match developed into a war of attrition in which the home side did not have the firepower for victory.

Hull FC's cause wasn't helped by a fifth-minute knee injury to fullback Craig Hall, who was selected ahead of the omitted Jordan Tansey, meaning Richard Horne was forced to drop to the back and Danny Washbrook entered the fray to partner Sean Long at halfback.

Rovers took the lead in the tenth minute. Murrell's wide kick was pinpoint and Peter Fox had time and space to collect the ball and finish in the corner. Michael Dobson's towering conversion gave his side an early six-point advantage. Just before the half hour Fisher started and finished the move for the second try, splitting the home defence on halfway before handing on to Shaun Briscoe. He returned the favour and the hooker plunged for the line and a 12-0 lead.

With the rain now teeming down, an Hull KR error allowed the home side back into the game. Substitute Matt Cook lost the ball in Lee Radford's tackle, and quick thinking from Jordan Turner released Tom Briscoe, who displayed outstanding finishing skills to beat Clint Newton and namesake Shaun to touch down in the corner. Tickle could not covert from the touchline, but the game was now very much alive at 12-4.

That became 14-4 on 67 minutes when Dobson slotted a penalty awarded for Willie Manu's high tackle on a side-stepping Ben Cockayne before the Robins applied the crucial final try. It came with little over five minutes left on the clock, as Dobson's hopeful kicked rebounded to Mick Vella, who offloaded smartly to Fisher. The hooker immediately put in a kick that again bounced off a Hull defender, and it was Kris Welham who was the quickest to react, hacking on and diving to touch down in front of the visiting support.

HUDDERSFIELD GIANTS 18 CRUSADERS 12

Two tries in the final eight minutes gave nervous Huddersfield their first taste of play-off success while ending brave Crusaders' near fairy-tale first season. Huddersfield lost their play-off debut in 2007, then were beaten twice after finishing in the top four in 2009, and they had to come back from eight points down after conceding two scores in as many minutes just before half-time against the Welsh club. It was a match that could have gone either way in the closing exchanges.

Amid a rain-soaked arm-wrestle, the first half remained pointless for 37 minutes and penalty-less for over half and hour. Huddersfield, chasing a sixth successive win and defending an unbeaten record against Crusaders, were the more inventive but their own worst enemies with some ambitious offloads giving possession away. As the sun repeatedly traded places with rain showers, and Brian Noble's charges continued to stifle their hosts, neither side was able to break the deadlock until a stray Danny Brough pass was intercepted by Rhys Hanbury who raced in from halfway. Clinton Schifcofske converted, then added a penalty almost immediately after, when the Giants were caught offside after David Hodgson lost possession, to send the visitors in with an 8-0 half-time lead.

Luke Robinson responded in thrilling style to put the Giants back in contention soon after the restart but a couple of penalties from the boot of fullback Schifcofske looked likely to give the large contingent of singing Welsh fans the chance of a celebratory encore. But a late indiscretion earned Jordan James a sin-binning - the prop needlessly knocking the ball out of Leroy Cudjoe's hands after he defused a bomb and moved to the 20-metre restart - and the Giants quickly capitalised. Within three minutes Darrell Griffin burst towards the posts and offloaded out of the back of one hand for Larne Patrick to score and Brett Hodgson's conversion edged Huddersfield in front for the first time.

But the Giants were immediately pulled up for obstruction fielding the short kick-off and Schifcofske continued his 100 per cent record with the boot from 35 metres out.

A field goal or even extra time seemed likely but, as Crusaders pressed forward, Weller Hauraki's attempted pass failed to find Vince Mellars and an alert Brough kicked the loose ball over the halfway line before sending Leroy Cudjoe on a free run to the line and the Giants into week two of the play-offs.

Week Two

Preliminary semi-finals

WARRINGTON WOLVES 22 HUDDERSFIELD GIANTS 34

A classic play-off match at Halliwell Jones saw the Giants establish what looked an unassailable 23-point advantage before the Wolves roared back in the second half to almost steal a game that was decided in spectacular fashion.

With Luke Robinson, Kevin Brown and especially Danny Brough - whose quick feet and clever kicking game were features - flourishing on the back of a solid forward platform and Brett Hodgson – set to join the Wolves for the next two years – providing several vital contributions from the back, not least his six goals, Huddersfield completely dominated the first 40 minutes and looked to be home and dry in difficult, wet conditions.

But the Wolves mounted a comeback that was still going strong when Leroy Cudjoe picked off a Richie Mathers pass two minutes from time. Had Cudjoe not reached high and taken the ball, the home side would have had a walk-in at the corner, providing Ben Westwood with a chance to send the game into golden-point extra-time. Instead, it was Cudjoe grabbing the glory, coach Nathan Brown caught by TV cameras shouting his winger home in the driving rain. The Giants' first-half effort had proved just enough, as a Warrington side inspired by the introduction of substitutes Chris Bridge and two-try Mickey Higham fell agonisingly short.

Warrington found themselves six points down with just two minutes on the clock as Luke Robinson and Kevin Brown combined to put Stephen Wild through a big gap and over the line. Brett Hodgson added the extras. The pick of Huddersfield's 23 first-half points was their second try. There appeared to be nothing on when Brough looked to kick down field from dummy-half and seemed to run himself into a corner. But the halfback signed from Wakefield in mid-season suddenly spotted a gap, accelerated through it, and released Danny Kirmond - recalled from his loan spell at Wakefield - who ran over the top of Chris Riley to score.

Brough booted a 40-metre field goal just before the half-time hooter but the second half, two Brett Hodgson penalty goals aside, belonged to the Wolves. Two tries apiece from Higham and Chris Hicks gave them the momentum that looked likely to take them into extra time with seven minutes remaining and five points between the teams. That soon became six when Brough's second field goal just scraped over the cross bar, before Warrington retained the kick-off to spark the events that led to Cudjoe's clincher.

WIGAN WARRIORS 42 HULL KINGSTON ROVERS 18

Wigan took their second chance with both hands as they put Hull KR to the sword with a clinical second-half display to set up a trip to Headingley the following Saturday. Albert Goldthorpe Medal winners Sam Tomkins and Pat Richards both put in a big shift in attack and defence, while hooker Mark Riddell worked tirelessly in his farewell game at the DW Stadium. The scoreline flattered Wigan in some respects as they were made to work hard in defence, but they stood strong before hitting the Robins on the break.

Warriors coach Michael Maguire was forced into one major change, with Paul Deacon missing out after picking up a groin injury against Leeds. He was replaced at stand-off by Sean O'Loughlin. Darrell Goulding's second try just before the interval that gave Wigan a 24-14 lead knocked the wind out of Hull KR's sails and set the platform for a clinical second-half performance.

Rovers had led 12-6 on ten minutes after Peter Fox and Ben Cockayne tries - the second a beauty as two clever kicks through the right centre from Scott Murrell and Ben Fisher ended with Cockayne racing over - Pat Richards having opened the scoring with a try. But tries to Goulding and Liam Farrell had Wigan back in front before Sam Tomkins threw a number of dummies as he streaked acrossfield before sending Goulding in for his second try.

After the break a high tackle from Josh Hodgson on Martin Gleeson saw the Warriors march deep into Hull KR's half and O'Loughlin went close before Thomas Leuluai burrowed his way over from acting halfback. Richards added his fifth conversion to stretch Wigan's lead to 30-14. Then Gleeson broke down the right before throwing a fine dummy to waltz in behind the posts for Wigan's sixth try. Richards again made no mistake as Wigan led 36-14 and they put the game to bed after Fox grabbed his second as Joel Tomkins stepped and forced his way over following a neat offload from Riddell. Richards kept up his 100 per cent record with the boot as the Warriors went past the 40-point mark.

Week Three

Qualifying semi-finals

LEEDS RHINOS 6 WIGAN WARRIORS 26

Wigan went one step further than the previous three campaigns, clearing the penultimate hurdle to appear at Old Trafford for the first time since 2003 by reversing the result of the controversial meeting between the sides a fortnight before. Three tries either side of half-time saw off the Champions but, had as been their hallmark all season, it was stifling, scrambling defence from the Warriors that ensured their league leaders ranking was deservedly rewarded.

Wigan's unflinching commitment to keep their line intact after conceding the opening try was of the highest order, with George Carmont, Pat Richards, Sam Tomkins, Paul Deacon and Mark Riddell all pulling off notable try-savers, while Paul Prescott and Michael McIlorum were huge influences off the bench.

Pat Richards opened the scoring with his first of five goals but the lead lasted barely two minutes. Danny Buderus and Ian Kirke forced Martin Gleeson into what the video referee deemed a knock on rather than two-man steal, the back-from-injury Jamie Jones-Buchanan quickly shifting the ball to Kevin Sinfield who went on the outside of Harrison Hansen and converted his own effort for the only points the home side scored.

Five minutes from the break, Wigan were back in the lead. From a scrum on the Leeds 'ten', Thomas Leuluai and Sam Tomkins set Joel Tomkins on a romp, his flick pass rolling along the deck away from Scott Donald for Darrell Goulding to gather and run a diagonal line to reach the whitewash. Richards converted to edge the visitors ahead and missed a long-range field goal but, five minutes into the second half, Wigan had a three-score margin. Paul Deacon - Wigan's only signing for 2010 - hoisted a bomb which Donald misjudged. The ball bounced away from Keith Senior, Joel Tomkins juggling before reeling it in and touching down near the posts. Sam Tomkins' superb 30-metre kick return and a marker penalty set up the next score, McIlorum losing the ball in contact but Carmont reacting decisively, hacking on and diving past Matt Diskin to claim a merited score.

Ali Lauitiiti's ball steal set up the final Leeds throw. Rob Burrow's flat pass sending Kylie Leuluai into a gap but Danny Buderus, backing up and taking the scoring pass, had come from an offside position at the play-the-ball.

Instead of being eight points in arrears with four minutes to go, Leeds found themselves 20 points down in the final minute, the Warriors gaining reward for electing to run a late penalty for a high shot. Prescott, O'Loughlin, Carmont, Hansen and Joel Tomkins slipped the ball wide for Gleeson to go over in the corner, Richards - in contrast to his last-second penalty miss at the DW - landing the touchline conversion.

ST HELENS 42 HUDDERSFIELD GIANTS 22

As the final curtain came down at Knowsley Road, Keiron Cunningham provided another fairytale finish to help his side to a fifth consecutive Grand Final. After scoring the final league try on the famous old ground against Castleford in round 27, the Saints number nine repeated the feat against a Huddersfield side that had led 22-18 early in the second half. At that point Cunningham climbed off the bench, having left it with his side 12-0 up courtesy of his two assists and four St Helens tries in the closing 25 minutes booked another Old Trafford trip.

The home side made the perfect start, scoring two converted tries within the first 12 minutes, both to Bradford-bound prop Bryn Hargreaves, who had until then failed to cross the whitewash all season. Cunningham created both tries, the first with a neat grubber kick on the final tackle, the second with a dummy-half pass that allowed Hargreaves to twist out of Shaun Lunt's tackle and over the line.

It had been all St Helens up until that point, but after the introduction of Giants substitutes Eorl Crabtree and David Faiumu the visitors managed to pull level. Brett Hodgson was the architect of both tries, first providing a sharp dummy-half pass for Lunt to stroll over with ease from five metres out, before sending Lawrence over in the opposite corner. Hodgson converted both tries from different touchlines to make it 12-12.

Saints had barely got out of their own half during that period, and went almost half an hour without a penalty. When they were awarded one for Stephen Wild's high tackle on Jamie Foster, they took full advantage. A superb quick inside ball from Paul Clough freed Wellens, who arced around opposite number Hodgson and stretched out to score in Lee Gilmour's cover tackle. But back came the Giants before the break. With Kyle Eastmond struggling out wide, Danny Brough kicked for Lawrence, who showed superb skill to grubber around Francis Meli and touch down himself to close the gap to 18-16 at half-time.

Eastmond surprisingly reappeared for the second half, but lasted only four minutes before limping off. Moments later Brett Hodgson's dummy-half grubber kick was touched down by former Saints hero Gilmour. Hodgson's conversion made it 22-18, and with Eastmond out of the game, Huddersfield had a scent of Old Trafford.

But the re-emergence of Cunningham from the bench changed everything again. James Roby laid on the next St Helens try, as the trend of kicking from the play-the-ball continued for Wellens to show tremendous desire for his second. Then Cunningham produced his third assist, bringing Tony Puletua onto a crash ball. Foster maintained his perfect record with the boot for 30-22. Saints then took a decisive grip on the game as they worked an overlap out wide for Francis Meli to dive over in the left corner. Again, Foster made no mistake, and at 36-22, a fifth Grand Final was all but assured. Cunningham put the rubber stamp on matters as, with six minutes remaining, he forced his way over from dummy-half in trademark style.

Paul Wellens stretches out to score against Huddersfield, as St Helens bid farewell to Knowsley Road

SUPER LEAGUE GRAND FINAL
Irresistible Warriors

The relentless Warriors inexorably staked their claim to the Champion's tag with their first Super League Grand Final victory since 1998, a wonderful opening quarter consigning Saints to heartbreak for the fourth consecutive time.

Thomas Leuluai flew his father, former Hull centre James, and mother over from New Zealand and did them proud, awarded the Harry Sunderland Trophy as man of the match after providing the perfect link between a dominant pack and a supremely efficient back line. Leuluai was at his best when he figured twice in Martin Gleeson's brilliant second try, releasing Sam Tomkins from deep inside his own half and then being there to take the return pass before handing on for Paul Deacon to provide the final pass to Gleeson. Five minutes later Leuluai was there again, when he moved wide to whip the ball out for Gleeson to send in Darrell Goulding.

Leuluai's best solo effort came just after half-time, when he went so close to scoring a superb try. Taking the ball 20 metres out, he weaved and teased his way across field before suddenly straightening up and shooting between two defenders. Despite being brought down just short of the line he appeared to have scored, until the video referee spotted the ball had been ripped from his grasp, and his only reward was a penalty.

The Warriors, fitter and more durable than any of their challengers throughout Super League XV, executed their 2010 game plan to perfection in the final 80 minutes of the season. Wigan's tough defence had got them to the pinnacle but they also showed their exciting side at Old Trafford. Their second try, completing a quick-fire brace for former Saints favourite Gleeson, was as good as any seen in 13 years of Grand Finals.

Much of the build-up centred on Saints' modern-day totem, departing hooker and captain Keiron Cunningham in his final match of a glittering, glorious career. That he did not get the chance to be at his most effective was, in part, down to a selection masterstroke from coach Michael Maguire. He sprang something of a surprise by electing to start with young rake Michael McIlorum ahead of Mark Riddell and his speed out of dummy-half and constant involvement in that crucial opening 20 minutes, when the

ENGAGE SUPER LEAGUE GRAND FINAL

Saturday 2nd October 2010

ST HELENS 10 WIGAN WARRIORS 22

SAINTS: 1 Paul Wellens; 30 Jamie Foster; 3 Matt Gidley; 5 Francis Meli; 24 Jonny Lomax; 12 Jon Wilkin; 34 Matty Smith; 10 James Graham; 9 Keiron Cunningham (C); 15 Bryn Hargreaves; 4 Iosia Soliola; 13 Chris Flannery; 11 Tony Puletua. Subs (all used): 17 Paul Clough; 14 James Roby; 22 Andrew Dixon; 25 Jacob Emmitt.
Tries: Dixon (28), Meli (74); **Goals:** Foster 1/2.
WARRIORS: 6 Sam Tomkins; 24 Darrell Goulding; 3 Martin Gleeson; 4 George Carmont; 5 Pat Richards; 19 Paul Deacon; 7 Thomas Leuluai; 8 Stuart Fielden; 15 Michael McIlorum; 10 Andy Coley; 11 Harrison Hansen; 12 Joel Tomkins; 13 Sean O'Loughlin (C). Subs (all used): 9 Mark Riddell; 17 Iafeta Palea'aesina; 25 Liam Farrell; 14 Paul Prescott.
Tries: Gleeson (4, 16), Goulding (20), S Tomkins (53); **Goals:** Richards 2/3, Riddell 1/3, S Tomkins 0/1.
Rugby Leaguer & League Express Men of the Match: *Saints:* Tony Puletua; *Warriors:* Thomas Leuluai.
Penalty count: 6-11; **Half time:** 6-16;
Referee: Richard Silverwood;
Attendance: 71,526 *(at Old Trafford, Manchester).*

Super League Grand Final

Warriors dominated possession, was vital in drawing Cunningham's and Saints' sting. What also caught up with St Helens, after a season of crippling injuries in key positions, was their understandable lack of midfield creativity and variation. Despite a week devoid of likely selection dilemmas, with Kyle Eastmond, Leon Pryce and Scott Moore ruled out early, Saints chose to again omit Ade Gardner and bring back Jonny Lomax.

Unusually because of the earlier date to accommodate England's Four Nations campaign down under, the sides came out in fading light. There was no torrential Manchester rain to greet them and the start was preceded by a minute's silence for Wigan's-own Terry Newton, who had tragically taken his own life a week before.

It was appropriate that Gleeson, one of Newton's best friends, should capitalise on Wigan's early momentum. Sia Soliola's rolling ball along the ground on his own '30' was snaffled by Pat Richards and Wigan exhibited another of their Super League XV characteristics, the ability to punish mistakes. Sam Tomkins gave depth to swept passes from Paul Deacon and Leuluai and, with the overlap made, Gleeson backed himself and powered over in the fourth minute, Richards missing the conversion attempt from out wide.

Just as Saints felt a reprieve, with Tony Puletua their reliever-in-chief, they conceded a penalty and were put under immense pressure in their own quarter. Deacon and George Carmont tested the left, Jamie Foster's saving hand conceding a scrum on the ten-metre line; a cross-field kick from Sean O'Loughlin palmed back by Richards forcing a similar outcome, after Puletua had hauled down Gleeson on the Saints line. Matty Smith similarly denied Carmont, the Tomkins combined in a raid and, on the last, Richards and Carmont looked to fashion an opening from McIlorum's kick, only for Richards' pass to find touch.

It seemed as though Saints had weathered that storm but, on the next raid from deep, Wigan produced the sparkling moment of the match, ripping inside and down the right for Deacon's long pass to send Gleeson in for his double. Controlling the tempo of the game and dominating the ball, the Warriors – through Deacon and Leuluai and on the back of charges by Coley and O'Loughlin's mediation - garnered a third try. Deacon's long pass this time freed Richards and then his bomb was spilled in front of the St Helens posts, O'Loughlin re-gathering and Leuluai and Gleeson sending arguably the season's most improved player, Darrell Goulding, over in the corner.

Richards landed the touchline conversion before Puletua's return and the introduction of James Roby brought Saints back into the contest. Roby, who elicited a penalty with a bludgeoning run, James Graham and Smith sought to prise an opening in a move that seemed as though it would flounder without a genuine halfback, but a lateral Wilkin found the perfect pass for Andrew Dixon to canter to the posts.

With completion rates high, the first respite a slowly packed scrum on the half hour, Sam Tomkins dealt assuredly with Smith's kicks as Wigan lost Richards with an Achilles tear late in the first half.

Leuluai's magic nearly opened the second period as the Warriors had the first one, his wonderful weaving, near-crawling run after an audacious show of the ball ended by Roby and Lomax as they conceded a penalty in a try-saving ball steal; Riddell missing the shot at goal.

Roby's lovely short ball saw Wellens through a gap but Sam Tomkins' harassment of his pass led to an interception. George Carmont, covering on the wing for Richards, knocked on a Wilkin bomb on his own '20' and from the scrum Puletua went close before Wilkin knocked on and Saints' hopes appeared dashed.

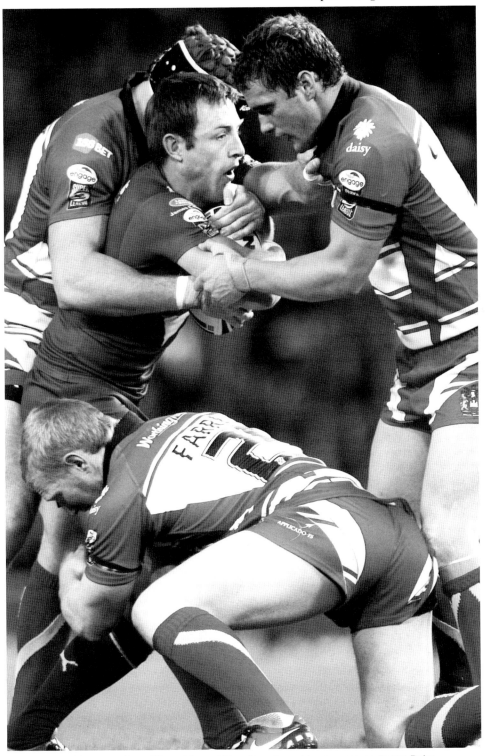

Paul Prescott, Sean O'Loughlin and Liam Farrell combine to wrap up James Roby

Super League Grand Final

Three minutes later, that spurned opportunity came home to roost, Sam Tomkins showing great presence to bulldoze his way through Francis Meli and Lomax and reach out a long arm for the touchdown. He then took a high shot from Meli, a kickable penalty which Wigan ran, although on the next occasion they were offered two they took the points on offer, Riddell's idiosyncratic routine joyously mimicked by the Wigan fans as he put his name in the record book on his last appearance for the club.

With penalties mounting against them and frustration evident, Saints were saved from conceding more points, Liam Farrell obstructing a defender in the build-up to his own touchdown from a peach of an offload from O'Loughlin. Sam Tomkins missed a penalty from 25 metres following a Wilkin ball steal and, after exchanged drop outs conceded and fashioned by Foster, Smith sent in Meli for a fine winger's score in the left corner. In the closing stages Deacon missed a field-goal attempt and Sam Tomkins was just denied a 40/20, Wigan ending the season with the kind of stranglehold they had exerted throughout it.

Harry Sunderland Trophy winner Thomas Leuluai and coach Michael Maguire celebrate Wigan's Super League Grand Final win

---

SUPER LEAGUE XV AWARDS

MAN OF STEEL
Pat Richards (Wigan Warriors)

(chosen by players poll)

YOUNG PLAYER OF THE YEAR
Sam Tomkins (Wigan Warriors)

COACH OF THE YEAR
Michael Maguire (Wigan Warriors)

CLUB OF THE YEAR
Wigan Warriors

TOP TRY SCORER Pat Richards (Wigan Warriors)
for scoring 29 regular season tries

TOP METRE-MAKER James Graham (St Helens)
for making 4,036 regular season metres

TOP TACKLER Dallas Johnson (Catalans Dragons)
for making 1,106 regular season tackles

MIKE GREGORY SPIRIT OF RUGBY LEAGUE AWARD
Ray French

SUPER LEAGUE DREAM TEAM
(previous appearances in italics)
1 Paul Wellens (St Helens) *2005, 2006, 2007*
2 Pat Richards (Wigan Warriors)
3 Matt King (Warrington Wolves)
4 Keith Senior (Leeds Rhinos)
2002, 2003, 2004, 2009
5 Ryan Hall (Leeds Rhinos) *2009*
6 Sam Tomkins (Wigan Warriors) *2009*
7 Michael Dobson (Hull Kingston Rovers) *2009*
8 James Graham (St Helens) *2008*
9 James Roby (St Helens) *2007*
10 Adrian Morley (Warrington Wolves)
1998, 1999, 2009
11 Ben Westwood (Warrington Wolves) *2008*
12 Joel Tomkins (Wigan Warriors)
13 Sean O'Loughlin (Wigan Warriors)

ALBERT GOLDTHORPE MEDAL
(joint winners)
Pat Richards (Wigan Warriors)
& Sam Tomkins (Wigan Warriors)

ROOKIE OF THE YEAR
Liam Watts
(Hull Kingston Rovers)

LIFETIME ACHIEVEMENT AWARD
Malcolm Alker

2
CHAMPIONSHIPS 2010

CHAMPIONSHIP SEASON
Rovers learn Fax of life

HALIFAX emerged as Championship champions with the very last kick of the season, after what must have been one of the most tumultuous campaigns in Rugby League history.

Ben Black's dramatic golden-point field goal against Featherstone completed a stunning 18-point Grand Final comeback by Matt Calland's side and helped put to bed a series of controversies at the Shay in 2010.

The club started by losing a significant sponsor early in the year when a local company went bust, and they were then ejected from the Challenge Cup for fielding the ineligible Michael Ostick.

Coach Calland was temporarily suspended over that matter and director of football Martin Hall later resigned, while around the same time, chief executive Graham Clay and former chairman Howard Posner also left the club.

Fax failed to make the knock-out stages of the Northern Rail Cup when they were dumped out at home by Championship One side Hunslet, and then in September they became caught up in a very public row with rivals Sheffield, who threatened legal action when Sam Barlow was named to start in the Final Eliminator, despite a written agreement between the two that he couldn't play against his former club.

In addition, Halifax were also taken to a tribunal by Stanley Gene, and several key players suffered long-term injuries.

But all of that was forgotten when Aussie halfback Black slotted the winning one-pointer in the Grand Final, landing Fax the £100,000 prize money that helped ease the financial burden of previous crises.

Bradford-bound Shad Royston marked his last year at the club by again finishing as top try scorer and making the sponsors' All Stars team. Rob Worrincy, Bob Beswick, Sean Penkywicz, Dave Larder, Lee Paterson, Dylan Nash, Luke Branighan and David Wrench were all key performers, while Calland deserved immense credit for the way he held his team together and guided them to ultimate success.

FEATHERSTONE ROVERS had looked set to complete a near perfect season under Daryl Powell until Black's field goal broke their hearts in Warrington. Powell's side led 22-4 in the Grand Final before Halifax's stirring late comeback, leaving Rovers to reflect on what might have been.

They lost just two league matches all season, and both by just two points – at home to Toulouse and Sheffield.

Other than that they were incredibly consistent, with halfback Liam Finn backing up his Championship One Player of the Year award in 2009 with the equivalent prize at the higher level in his first season at Featherstone.

Powell was named Coach of the Year and winger Zak Hardaker completed a Rovers treble by sharing the Young Player prize with Batley's Gareth Moore, before earning a big-money move to Leeds after a stunning debut campaign in which he scored 22 tries in 14 appearances. Remarkably, Featherstone also had three other nominees for the main awards in Stuart Dickens, Kyle Briggs and Sam Smeaton.

Hardaker and Smeaton were products of the club's rapidly-expanding youth set-up, while Tom Saxton, Ian Hardman and Tony Tonks also deserved recognition for their efforts.

And while Rovers may have fallen just short of ultimate success, the season was still a fitting tribute to their young player Gareth Swift, who was killed in a car accident in April.

LEIGH CENTURIONS made a blistering start to the Championship season under returning coach Ian Millward, but their 2010 season will ultimately be remembered for two key defeats.

The Centurions missed out on a place in the Northern Rail Cup final when they were beaten at home by eventual winners Batley, losing a chance to tick the much-coveted Super League licence box. And their second opportunity also fell by the wayside when they crashed out of the play-offs to Sheffield, again at home, in September.

But still, there was much to be positive about for a club that had been relegated the previous year, only to be re-instated in the Championship following the financial decline of Gateshead. Millward introduced a host of promising young players into his side, including dual registration quartet Jacob Emmitt, Matty Blythe, Lee Mitchell and Tyrone McCarthy.

Of Leigh's own youngsters, Macgraff Leuluai had a big debut campaign and Martyn Ridyard became a key player over the course of the year. Long-serving James Taylor and Chris Hill were cornerstones of the pack, while perennial top scorer Mick Nanyn racked up another 20 tries and 286 points.

The campaign did finish in disappointing style after the Centurions were undefeated in their first nine Championship matches – but the club remained positive that they could kick on again in 2011.

BARROW RAIDERS failed to match the dizzy heights of 2009, despite plenty of pre-season promise.

The arrival of the experienced Steve McCormack and the retention of much of their Grand Final-winning squad had pointed to another year of success at Craven Park. But McCormack had to deal with a crippling injury list right from the off, and his side rarely looked capable of repeating their feat of making two finals the previous year. Widnes Vikings dumped them out of the Northern Rail Cup, and though Barrow got their revenge in the play-offs, they couldn't overcome the challenge of Sheffield Eagles the following week.

Australian Ned Catic had an outstanding campaign, however, and was deservedly named in the All Stars team alongside stand-off Jamie Rooney. Other key performers were Zebastien Luisi, Nathan Mossop and the evergreen Gary Broadbent, while Andy Ballard, Liam Campbell and Liam Harrison were regularly among the tries during the course of a season that again included a change of coach.

McCormack left his role to take up a new full-time career as a teacher, and the campaign ended with his predecessor Dave Clark in temporary charge. But Clark couldn't quite revive the spirit of 2009, and the Raiders were looking to rebuild the next year.

Fifth place and no silverware may have equated to disappointment for **WIDNES VIKINGS**, but there was still much to admire about the club in 2010. By their own admission they fell short of expectations on the field, but the Vikings' outstanding youth set-up was beginning to bear very real fruit as they pressed ahead for a Super League licence.

Youngsters Danny Craven, Danny Hulme and Tom Kelly all made notable impressions on the first team after making their debuts. And the Vikings insisted that there were plenty more waiting in the wings – opinion backed up by the fact that their under-18s and under-16s were dominant against Super League opposition in 2010.

At first-team level, there was much to contend with for coach Paul Cullen, most notably personal circumstances that meant he was on compassionate leave at different stages of the campaign.

Widnes also had possibly the worst injury list in the competition, forcing them to use no less than 40 players during the course of the campaign. Of those, Jim Gannon, Paddy Flynn and Lee Doran were among the most consistent, though there can be little doubt about their most influential performer.

Championship Season

Halfback Anthony Thackeray was named Rugby League World magazine's Player of the Year after crossing 24 times, and he would again be a linchpin as a new-look Vikings side searched for more success in 2011.

SHEFFIELD EAGLES fell one game short of the Grand Final after a stirring play-off campaign. Mark Aston's side knocked out Leigh and Barrow on their own grounds in consecutive weekends, before eventually being falling to eventual winners Halifax.

Those games showed the potential that Sheffield had promised for much of the year before they finally started to deliver, after a stuttering start to their campaign threatened their place in the top six. Aston's side went five games without a win at one point, before finishing strongly, providing a fitting farewell to the influential and long-serving Australian stand-off Brendon Lindsay. He was yet again a key figure for the Eagles, along with top try scorer and ever-present Craig Cook.

Misi Taulapapa emerged as one of the most dangerous players in the competition after switching to fullback following Johnny Woodcock's injury, while PNG star Menzie Yere again terrorised Championship defences. Irish winger Tim Bergin was a real find out wide, and props Alex Rowe, Jack Howieson, Mitchell Stringer and Ryan Hepworth all had their moments.

BATLEY BULLDOGS' 2010 season will be forever characterised by one afternoon in Blackpool in mid-July. Karl Harrison's side ended the club's lengthy wait for silverware when they beat Widnes Vikings 25-24 to lift the Northern Rail Cup.

Winger Alex Brown's two late tries helped completed a stunning comeback for the big outsiders and provide a genuine Rugby League fairytale for one of the game's most popular clubs.

Harrison rightly made much of the fact that his side was made up almost completely of players living in the local area, and he had a host of stand-out performers among his ranks. Johnny Campbell made the Rugby League World Team of the Year after scoring 30 tries in all competitions, and was joined by impressive prop Sean Hesketh, while Gareth Moore was the joint Young Player of the Year.

His halfback partner Paul Handforth was outstanding for much of the campaign, while back-rower Jason Walton proved a real find after joining from Harrison's former club Salford. The consistent Ashley Lindsay, Danny Maun and Kris Lythe will also have relished the club's long-awaited success after spending much of their careers at Mount Pleasant.

And while the Blackpool victory undoubtedly impacted on their league campaign – they won just one of five matches after the final – the Bulldogs' trophy-winning exploits will live long in the memory of people in the Heavy Woollen town.

TOULOUSE OLYMPIQUE improved on their debut campaign in the Championship and would have made the play-offs but for a disappointing end to the season.

The French side lost their last six league matches to drop out of top-six contention and end what had been a promising year. But they again showed they could compete with the competition's leading lights, being one of only two sides to beat league leaders Featherstone Rovers.

That televised 26-24 win in May was a definite highlight, along with high-scoring and narrow victories at Widnes and Batley. If anything, their home form let them down a little and that should be an area of improvement for respected coach Gilles Dumas next year.

Australian fullback Rory Bromley again stood out for Dumas' side, finishing with 15 tries in all competitions. Fellow imports Nathan Wynn, Brendan Worth and Mike Mitchell were also key figures again, though perhaps the most positive part of the whole campaign was the emergence of several talented youngsters amid an injury crisis that claimed key stand-off Constant Villegas among others.

Portuguese-born winger Carlos Mendes Varela was another potential star of the future, and the French were keen to make the top six at the third attempt in 2011.

DEWSBURY RAMS recovered from a nightmare start at the higher level to become one of the competition's form teams in surviving relegation. The Rams lost their first 12 Championship matches, though the fact that they picked up seven bonus points during that spell pointed to the fact that they were not far away.

Coach Warren Jowitt kept faith in his charges, who produced a stirring end to the campaign, winning six of their last eight games. At the hub of most of the things for Dewsbury was scrum-half Dominic Brambani, whose season mirrored that of the team as he recovered from a slow start to become one of the most influential players in the competition.

Experienced winger Bryn Powell finished as top try scorer with 13 and youngster Scott Turner impressed out wide, but it was in the pack where the Rams' success was built. The likes of Andrew Bostock, Anthony England, Mike Emmett, Luke Blake and James Lockwood played key roles, while Rob Spicer had a big impact on his return from long-term injury late in the season.

It earned Jowitt a nomination for Coach of the Year, and raised hopes that the club could mount a genuine play-off push next time around.

Many people involved with **WHITEHAVEN** would happily forget the 2010 campaign, as the club was relegated, hit serious financial difficulties and was forced to re-form late in the year.

After winning their opening Championship game at home to Toulouse, matters steadily got worse for the West Cumbrian side, as they lost 16 of their next 17 league matches. Late wins over Keighley and Batley came too late in the day to save coach Ged Stokes, who was eventually replaced by local legend David Seeds when the club was forced to relaunch.

That came after a spell of uncertainty and financial administration, but at least now Haven can start to look forward again – although they will start their 2011 season on minus nine points.

Seeds undoubtedly has a big job on his hands, but he will be aided by a youth development system that saw the likes of Jay Rossi, Loz Hamzat and Reece Fox make an impact in the first team in 2010.

Stalwarts Graeme Mattinson and Marc Jackson left for neighbours Workington after doing their utmost to turn the club's fortunes around on the field, but other key figures such as Scott McAvoy and Craig Calvert will remain. Veteran Kiwi Leroy Joe was typically unstinting in his efforts to save the club from relegation, with Howard Hill, Spencer Miller and Andy Thornley others to stand out. But the club was embarking on a new era – with record try scorer Seeds set to be their figurehead for coming campaigns.

KEIGHLEY COUGARS were always going to be up against it in 2010, having started the season on minus nine points after entering administration. And despite a fine effort that hinted at their own version of the Great Escape, Barry Eaton's were ultimately relegated back to Championship One at the end of the year.

A televised May win at much-fancied Sheffield Eagles gave the Cougars a real shout of doing what looked like the impossible, but a home defeat to relegation rivals Dewsbury two weeks later put a significant dent in their hopes.

They would win just one more match, against Toulouse, though Eaton's team was competitive throughout the year.

Halfbacks Danny Jones and Jon Presley were key men for most of the season, and their departures to Halifax and York respectively will leave Keighley with big holes to fill in Championship One.

But the vast majority of the rest of the team remained, maintaining continuity that Eaton has strived for and ensuring props Brendan Rawlins, Scott Law, Andy Shickell and Ryan Benjafield would again team up together. Back-rower Oliver Pursglove was one of the Championship's most improved players, while top try scorer Gavin Duffy, hookers Jamaine Wray and James Feather, plus emerging utility James Haythornthwaite all deserve mention for their contributions to the Cougar cause.

CHAMPIONSHIP ONE SEASON
Soaring Hawks

HUNSLET HAWKS lifted the Championship One title and earned automatic promotion to the higher level after a season of tremendous consistency under player-coach Paul March. The Hawks lost just two matches all season – their opening game at home to rivals Oldham and a shock loss at Rochdale Hornets – and finished three points clear of the Roughyeds.

In his first full campaign in charge of the Hawks, March proved an outstanding guiding influence, and was named the Championship One Player of the Year, edging out his twin brother David, who also had a superb campaign.

. The pair were both named in the Rugby League World Team of the Year alongside experienced back-rower Tommy Haughey and powerful prop James Houston. Among those who were unfortunate to miss out were and talented stand-off Danny Grimshaw and prolific threequarter duo Waine Pryce and Wayne McHugh, who terrorised opposition defences all season.

Paul March himself was a shock omission from the list of nominees for Coach of the Year, although his achievement in winning the league probably helped ease any disappointment. March had recruited heavily from his former club York City Knights during the off-season, effectively maintaining the nucleus of a side that had been together for almost three years. He anticipated minimal changes to his squad for the 2011 campaign in the Championship – and a Northern Rail Cup victory at Halifax in 2010 encouraged the Hawks in making an impact at the higher level.

OLDHAM were forced to don the bridesmaid's dress yet again as a fourth consecutive Grand Final loss ended a campaign of much achievement in ultimate disappointment. Tony Benson's side lost just three times in the league and then reached the Warrington showpiece at the first attempt by beating the Knights at their new Whitebank Stadium home. But they crashed to a 25-4 defeat in the final, after losing the equivalent matches to Featherstone, Doncaster and Keighley in previous years.

Still, there was much to admire about Oldham's 2010 under the popular Benson, not least the emergence of a host of talented young players such as Joe Chandler, Chris Clarke, Danny Whitmore and Ben Heaton.

Centre Mick Fogerty and front-rowers Dave Ellison and Jason Boults were among others to impress, while scrum-half Gregg McNally made a significant late-season impact on loan from Huddersfield Giants.

Fullback Paul O'Connor was one of the stars of the entire competition, earning a nomination for Player of the Year and a place in the Rugby League World team alongside Fogerty and the ever-reliable and influential Neil Roden at stand-off.

But undoubtedly the biggest news of the club's season was their move to their own ground at Whitebank, giving hope that they could lay firm roots in the town after years of switching around various venues.

Australian coach Dave Woods proved again that he has the Midas touch, as he steered **YORK CITY KNIGHTS** to Grand Final glory.

Woods initially arrived at the club as director of rugby, during an often controversial campaign at the club that saw coach Ratcliffe suspended from his job earlier in the year following a racism investigation by the Rugby Football League. A run of disappointing displays then cost Ratcliffe his job, and he was replaced by Woods, who had already steered Castleford to promotion in 2005, repeating the feat with Gateshead in 2008.

And he repeated the trick after a matter of months in charge of the Knights, as Chris Thorman's influential display helped them to Grand Final glory over Oldham at the Halliwell Jones Stadium. Woods had a massive contribution from his captain and second-rower Jordan Ross, who grew in stature as the campaign unfolded and had a big game in the final.

So too did hooker Jack Lee and fullback James Haynes, the latter of whom joined the club midway through the season and allowed Danny Ratcliffe to move to halfback, where he also made an impression.

Free-scoring centre Lee Waterman was named in the sponsors' All Stars team after finishing up as the club's top try scorer, while young winger Tom Lineham was nominated for the competition's Young Player of the Year award.

BLACKPOOL PANTHERS would have finished third but for a mid-season points deduction that characterised a turbulent campaign.

The Panthers were docked ten points by the Rugby Football League for "salary cap irregularities", though coach Martin Crompton then managed to galvanise his players to come within one game of a Grand Final place. Crompton's achievements earned him a third consecutive nomination for Coach of the Year, but by November he had resigned from his post as the club entered administration, and eventually had their membership of the Rugby Football League withdrawn.

Blackpool had plenty of stand-out performances in 2010, with prolific winger Damian Munro, centre Casey Mayberry and prop Andy Hobson making the Rugby League World Team of the Year. It was part of a roller-coaster campaign for veteran prop Hobson, who also earned a number of suspensions and finished the year in Crown Court on an assault charge on York prop Nathan Freer during a Championship One match.

Hooker John Clough was a model of consistency for the club, while halfbacks Tom Hemingway and Carl Forber, plus centre or fullback Martin Ainscough and loose forward Kurt Haggerty, all stood out at different times. The club racked up a record 132-0 win over Gateshead in May.

But reports of points-scoring bonuses for that game were one of the reasons for the RFL's investigation of their finances; something which could yet define the club's history.

ROCHDALE HORNETS made significant progress under their new coach John Stankevitch, finishing in fifth place despite having one of the lowest budgets in the competition. Hornets – now run by a fans' co-operative – made a public stance of only paying the 17 players that took the field each Sunday, and Stankevitch built a team that tested the best sides in the competition.

They were one of only two teams to beat champions Hunslet and produced some outstanding displays at Spotland, including a play-off demolition of South Wales Scorpions. But their away form let them down badly, with only two wins all season, at Gateshead and Swinton, robbing them a chance of finishing in the crucial third position.

Hornets had two members of the sponsors' All Stars team in hard-working duo Craig Ashall and Phil Wood, who rarely allowed their high standard of performance to dip. The same can be said of local fullback Wayne English, in his first season at the club, and he was a constant menace to opposition sides throughout the year. Back-rowers Danny Samuel and Danny Smith, scrum-half Stephen Roper and stand-off Paul Crook all made important contributions as well. Stankevitch managed to retain the majority of his side for 2011.

Championship One Season

SOUTH WALES SCORPIONS were arguably the success story of the season after finishing in a play-off place in their first year of existence. Formed following the switch of Celtic Crusaders to Wrexham, the Scorpions aimed to field a side of primarily young talented Welshmen – and succeeded with style.

Coach Anthony Seibold brought together his hastily assembled squad and they were rarely not competitive, while chalking up a host of impressive results thought the campaign. The best was a head-turning 42-24 win at Oldham in August that effectively ended the Roughyeds' automatic promotion hopes.

Their achievements deservedly earned popular Australian Seibold the Coach of the Year award, though soon afterwards he announced that he would return Down Under for family reasons, leaving a new man to pick up the Scorpions baton. He would inherit a talented, motivated squad that would again be boosted by a close and productive link-up with the Crusaders.

Their dual registration forward Gil Dudson made the sponsors' All Stars team, while Christian Roets and Andrew Gay cannot have been too far away after impressive campaigns.

Aled James, Neil Dallimore, Jamie Murphy, Lloyd White and Loz Wildbore were other influential members of the side. In local hooker and top try-scorer Steve Parry the club unearthed one of the finds of the entire competition, and he just missed out on the Young Player of the Year award after a stunning debut campaign.

WORKINGTON TOWN completed the play-off line up after a dramatic final day on which they almost saw a season's hard work go to waste. Eighth-placed Swinton Lions had to overhaul a 134-point difference as Town faced Doncaster, and the unthinkable was possible until Mike Whitehead's late try spared the Cumbrians' blushes.

It also provided just reward for a season of overall progression, and one that earned joint bosses Martin Oglanby and Gary Charlton a nomination for the Coach of the Year award. Town also took home one of the major prizes, as Rugby League World Team of the Year member Jarrad Stack was deservedly named Young Player of the Year after an outstanding campaign from the Australian. Stack's decision to remain at the club for 2011 was seen as a major coup for Town.

Workington had come close to stunning fancied Blackpool in the play-offs before eventually allowing a 14-0 lead to slip at the Woodlands.

Alongside Stack, winger Neil Frazer, halfbacks Scott Kaighan and Darren Holt, plus prop Kris Coward all had big years.

And with the club having managed to snare a handful of players from rivals Whitehaven during the close season – headed by highly-rated hooker Graeme Mattinson - there was much to be positive about again at Derwent Park.

SWINTON LIONS saw another season that promised much deliver little, as their high-profile squad failed to make the play-offs.

A host of figures with top-flight experienced joined player-coach Paul Smith for the start of the campaign, but after a run of poor results, Smith parted company with the club midway through the season. A number of other players also left for differing reasons around that time, and Swinton had something of a shake-up of personnel, with a host of amateurs from the Huddersfield area joining the club.

Back-rower Darren Hawkyard was among those to impress under a new coaching regime of Paul Kidd and his assistant Ian Watson, who never allowed his efforts on the field to waver. The Lions also had big efforts from the likes of Phil Joseph, Richie Hawkyard and Rob Foxen through the year.

It was all change again at the end of the season, with the experienced Steve McCormack taking over as coach and bringing in the vastly experienced Mark Smith for his 2011 squad. With the club moving to the Willows ahead of a proposed permanent return to the borough at Agecroft from 2012, Swinton were hoping for brighter times ahead.

DONCASTER started the season with new owners and a fresh outlook, but coach Tony Miller was always going to be up against it with a late start and a dramatically reduced budget.

They didn't win a game in the group stages of the Northern Rail Cup, but the real low came with a record 26-0 home defeat to amateurs Siddal in the third round of the Challenge Cup.

It would be the end of March before Miller's side recorded their first victory of the year, but that 40-24 win over York inspired renewed confidence for the rest of the campaign.

They were rarely genuine play-off contenders, but produced several eye-catching performances, not least beating Rochdale at home and pushing a host of the division's high flyers close.

They also finished on a genuine high, beating Workington 46-12 at the Keepmoat Stadium in a display that bode well for the 2011 prospects.

Miller made several mid-season signings that had a big impact at the club, not least loose forward Rob Lunt who was one of the best players in Championship One in the closing weeks of the campaign.

Hookers Paul Hughes, Jack Ely and Kyle Kesik also made their mark, along with talented outside backs Aaron Henry, Tommy Griffiths and Mick Butterfield.

With most of the squad retained for next year along with a sprinkling of new additions, the Dons were in a much stronger position to succeed the next season.

LONDON SKOLARS won just two matches all season, but it was still something of a shock when they decided not to renew the contract of coach James Massara before the end of the campaign.

Skolars had been improving steadily under the rookie coach, and stunned high-flying Rochdale in the capital before recording a comprehensive win over Gateshead Thunder in the closing weeks of the campaign. But it wasn't enough to save Massara's job, and next year the club would be coached by London product Joe Mbu.

It completes a full circle for Mbu, who started his playing career as a junior at the Skolars, who are as keen as ever to push capital talent through. The former Harlequins back-rower will undoubtedly have a tough job on his hands in his first professional coaching job, but he also has plenty of talent at his disposal.

Neil Thorman joined his brother Paul in London for the second half of the season, and the pair are set to combine to good effect again in 2011. Stephen Ball, Sam Gee and Austen Aggrey also made big contributions during the course of the year, and Skolars were hoping to start winning on a more regular basis again in 2011.

It was always going to be an incredibly tough season for **GATESHEAD THUNDER** in 2010. Chris Hood's young, inexperienced squad started the campaign on minus nine points after the club entered administration during the previous close season.

The club set off with a new, more realistic outlook based around talented local players, but their lack of experience shone through at times and they suffered several heavy defeats. A major low point was the 132-0 thrashing at Blackpool Panthers, but the club continued to battle on until the end of the campaign.

There were high spots as well, including an early win over London Skolars and four bonus points over the course of the year.

Ryan Clarke, Matt Barron, Jason Payne and Joe Brown all deserved immense credit for their efforts under Hood, who switched to become director of rugby at the club at the end of the season. Former Castleford Tigers Academy boss Richard Pell came in as coach, and a sprinkling of new signings was expected to help the club improve results-wise.

NORTHERN RAIL CUP FINAL
Who let the Dogs out?

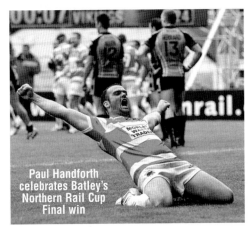

Paul Handforth celebrates Batley's Northern Rail Cup Final win

NORTHERN RAIL CUP FINAL

Sunday 18th July 2010

BATLEY BULLDOGS 25 WIDNES VIKINGS 24

BULLDOGS: 5 John Campbell; 24 Alex Brown; 12 Mark Toohey; 4 Danny Maun; 2 Lee Greenwood; 6 Paul Handforth; 7 Gareth Moore; 8 Byron Smith; 9 Kris Lythe; 10 Sean Hesketh; 26 Jason Walton; 31 John Gallagher; 13 Ashley Lindsay. Subs (all used): 33 Mick Govin; 11 Tommy Gallagher; 20 David Tootill; 21 James Martin.
Tries: Walton (3), Hesketh (8), Brown (68, 78); **Goals:** Moore 4/5; **Field goal:** Moore (33).
VIKINGS: 5 Paddy Flynn; 26 Shaun Ainscough; 19 Matt Gardner; 15 Shane Grady; 2 Dean Gaskell; 6 Anthony Thackeray; 14 Thomas Coyle; 16 Gareth Haggerty; 32 Kirk Netherton; 10 Jim Gannon; 11 Lee Doran; 12 Dave Allen; 13 Chris Gerrard. Subs (all used): 8 Steve Pickersgill; 9 Mark Smith; 17 Ben Kavanagh; 28 Ben Davies.
Tries: Davies (14), Thackeray (17), Flynn (50), C Gerrard (65); **Goals:** Grady 4/4.
Rugby Leaguer & League Express Men of the Match: *Bulldogs:* Paul Handforth; *Vikings:* Ben Davies.
Penalty count: 7-7; **Half-time:** 15-12; **Referee:** Robert Hicks; **Attendance:** 8,138 *(at Bloomfield Road, Blackpool).*

Winger Alex Brown was the hero as Batley Bulldogs lifted their first piece of major silverware for 86 years.

Brown scored two late tries as Karl Harrison's side snatched the Northern Rail Cup from Widnes's grasp with a 25-24 success.

The Vikings looked to have retained the trophy after recovering from 12-0 and 15-12 down to lead 24-15 with just 12 minutes remaining at Blackpool's Bloomfield Road.

But a compelling encounter took a dramatic twist as Brown scored out wide and then clinched the contest by brilliantly catching a high ball to touch down.

Forward Jason Walton and Sean Hesketh had scored the tries to give Batley their early lead, before Widnes roared back. Ben Davies and Anthony Thackeray scored in quick succession to level the scores, before Gareth Moore kicked a field goal and penalty to make it 15-12.

The Vikings then had another purple patch as Paddy Flynn touched down and Chris Gerrard jinked his way over under the posts quarter of an hour from the end. But then Brown stepped forward to write his name in Bulldogs' folklore with his stunning late double.

CHAMPIONSHIP PLAY-OFFS
The Golden Shot

Leigh Centurions saw their Super League application hopes fade to dust as Sheffield Eagles ended their play-off hopes at the first hurdle.

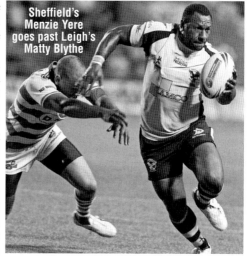

Sheffield's Menzie Yere goes past Leigh's Matty Blythe

The Centurions – desperate to reach the final and tick the box to apply for a 2012 licence – led 18-12 at half-time, with Mick Nanyn scoring a try as part of his eventual 12-point haul. But Sheffield shrugged off a serious injury to fullback Misi Taulapapa to edge home 26-24, with impressive threequarters Menzie Yere and Tim Bergin both grabbing try doubles.

In the other elimination semi-final of the opening weekend, Barrow Raiders put Widnes Vikings to the sword 38-0 at Craven Park. Widnes had been marginal favourites with the bookmakers going into the game against a Raiders side that had Grand Final-winning coach Dave Clark back in temporary charge. But Barrow dominated virtually from the off, and lively halfback Liam Campbell scored a brace of tries in the one-sided win.

That set up a home clash with Sheffield, but the Eagles managed to soar away from home once again, as Craig Cook's late try sealed an outstanding 21-14 win. The teams had been locked at 8-8 at the break after a tense first half, and Martin Ostler's try then gave Barrow a six-point lead. But Sheffield finished strongly and, after Cook scampered over, Simon Brown clinched the win with a late field goal.

Featherstone Rovers had already booked their Grand Final place at that point having dismantled Halifax 46-16 just 48 hours earlier. Kyle Briggs finished with a hat-trick of tries in a dominant Rovers display that gave little indication of what was to unfold between the teams two weeks later.

Fax got their second bite of the play-off cherry with a match against Sheffield that attracted plenty of controversy when the home side decided to field Sam Barlow, despite an agreement between the clubs that he would not face the Eagles in 2010. Loose forward Barlow was inevitably among the try scorers as Fax raced into a commanding 24-6 interval lead.

Matt Calland's side proved far too strong after the break as well, as seven different try scorers helped book their place at the Halliwell Jones Stadium and end the Eagles' brave run.

CHAMPIONSHIP GRAND FINAL

Halifax halfback Ben Black provided a remarkable end to the most dramatic of afternoons to help his side lift the Co-operative Championship title after golden-point extra time.

Australian Black, who had been central to a second-half comeback that saw Fax recover from a 22-4 deficit, kept his nerve to slot the winning field goal just 90 seconds into add-on time. His side had looked completely out of the contest when they trailed by 18 points after Zak Hardaker's second try 52 minutes in. But Black scored one try and laid on another in the space of three incredible minutes around the hour mark, before Stephen Bannister's effort levelled matters in the closing stages.

With Sean Penkywicz also to the fore after emerging for a second spell off the bench, Matt Calland's side then earned the position to have first crack at a field goal in extra-time – and Black made no mistake

It provided a dramatic finale to an unforgettable afternoon that had seen the game rocked by news of Terry Newton's death, and the final then held up for 45 minutes following a fire in the West Stand of the Halliwell Jones Stadium.

Featherstone initially looked to have dealt better with the significant delay caused by Halifax fans having to move to the opposite stand, scoring twice soon after half-time. But ultimately, Fax found the greater staying power to record their first win over Rovers in four attempts over the course of the year.

There were other heroes in the Fax side with forwards Makali Aizue and Sam Barlow making their presence felt throughout, David Wrench never wavering in his efforts, and Shad Royston and Rob Worrincy providing danger out wide.

For Rovers, it was a cruel way to end a season of much achievement under Daryl Powell. He had two of the game's outstanding performers in wingers Zak Hardaker and especially Tom Saxton, while Stuart Dickens, Liam Finn and Kyle Briggs all made big contributions. But ultimately, it was not enough.

Fax had opened the scoring with a stunning length-of-the-field Worrincy try, before Rovers scored twice in quick succession, with Briggs crossing first. Powell's side then scored on the very next set as Saxton bounced away from four Halifax defenders to burst clear from deep, and handed on to fellow winger Hardaker, who sprinted clear for a brilliant breakaway try.

Briggs converted both, before the 45-minute hold-up for the fire. The remaining seven and a half minutes of the half were scoreless, but soon after the restart Rovers scored again through Matty Dale, and when Hardaker crossed again soon after the game looked over at 22-4.

But Halifax then roared back, as a Frank Watene offload sparked good hands that resulted in Black breaking clear and releasing Royston. He was hauled

THE CO-OPERATIVE CHAMPIONSHIP GRAND FINAL

Sunday 26th September 2010

FEATHERSTONE ROVERS 22 HALIFAX 23
(after golden point extra time)

ROVERS: 1 Ian Hardman; 26 Zak Hardaker; 3 Sam Smeaton; 4 Liam Welham; 2 Tom Saxton; 6 Kyle Briggs; 9 Liam Finn; 17 Tony Tonks; 31 Ben Kaye; 10 Stuart Dickens; 18 Tim Spears; 13 Jamie Field; 11 Matty Dale. Subs (all used): 19 Ross Divorty; 16 Dane Manning; 12 Jon Grayshon; 7 Andy Kain.
Tries: Briggs (28), Hardaker (30, 52), Dale (45); **Goals:** Briggs 3/4.
HALIFAX: 4 Shad Royston; 2 Lee Paterson; 6 Luke Branighan; 18 Dylan Nash; 23 Rob Worrincy; 26 Graham Holroyd; 7 Ben Black; 10 Neil Cherryholme; 13 Bob Beswick; 8 Makali Aizue; 11 David Larder; 22 David Wrench; 27 Sam Barlow. Subs (all used): 9 Sean Penkywicz; 17 Frank Watene; 19 Dominic Maloney; 24 Steve Bannister.
Tries: Worrincy (20), Black (58), Branighan (60), Bannister (75);
Goals: Paterson 3/4; **Field goal:** Black (82).
On report: Barlow (35) - alleged high tackle on Divorty.
Rugby Leaguer & League Express Men of the Match:
Rovers: Tom Saxton; *Halifax:* Ben Black.
Penalty count: 6-3; **Half-time:** 12-4; **Full-time:** 22-22;
Referee: Robert Hicks;
Attendance: 9,443 *(at Halliwell Jones Stadium, Warrington).*

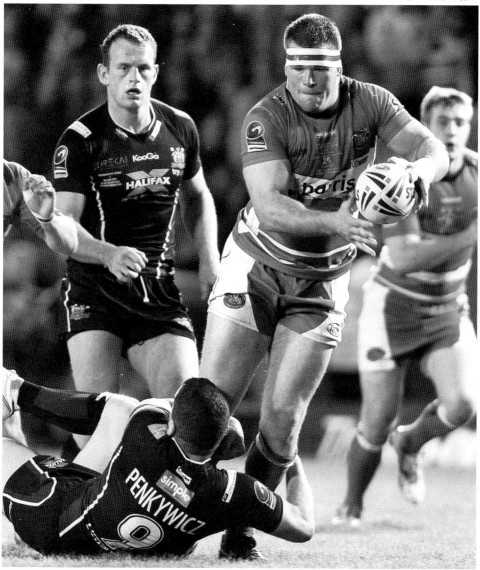

Featherstone's Stuart Dickens tries to escape from Halifax's Sean Penkywicz

down a metre short but Black showed great speed of thought at the play-the-ball to plunge under the posts and close the gap to 12 points. Moments later Hardman failed to deal with a spiralling Holroyd kick, Black was the quickest to react again and Branighan supported to race under the posts.

And with five minutes remaining, Fax were level, as Steve Bannister ran a terrific line to score. Lee Paterson's conversion made it 22-22, and with Holroyd twice unsuccessfully attempting field goals and Smeaton once, the game headed to golden-point extra time.

Extra time lasted just 90 seconds. Featherstone chose to kick off – something Calland confirmed Fax would have done as well if they won the toss – and their first set of six ended with Finn charging down Black's first one-point attempt.

Referee Robert Hicks wiped the tackle count clear and moments later Black sent the Fax fans into raptures with his winning kick.

CHAMPIONSHIP ONE PLAY-OFFS
Phoenix Knights

South Wales Scorpions' season of remarkable progression ended in cruel style at Rochdale, with Hornets running out 60-26 winners. Halfbacks Paul Crook and Steve Roper had fine matches in Hornets' best display of the season, while man of the match Craig Ashall was among three double try scorers.

But Scorpions coach Anthony Seibold was quick to point out the considerable positives of 2010 after the game, with his young Welsh side battling right until the end.

Elsewhere, Blackpool Panthers recovered from a 14-0 half-time deficit to edge past plucky Workington 36-26. Young Player of the Year Jarrad Stack was among the tries as Town dominated the first half with the help of a strong wind. But Martin Crompton's side hit back after the break, with Martin Ainscough crossing for two of their six tries.

That set up a home game with Rochdale, and Ainscough was again among their scorers in a 34-26 win. Hornets were chasing the game for much of the contest, and a further two tries to another ex-Rochdale centre Casey Mayberry ended their season.

Blackpool's Casey Mayberry wrapped up against Rochdale

On the same day, Oldham reached the Grand Final with a thrilling 41-32 win over York City Knights. The Knights had led 18-16 at half-time but a fine display from on-loan halfback Gregg McNally, who finished with eight goals and a field goal, helped steer the Roughyeds into their fourth consecutive final.

York had to regroup quickly and face Blackpool, but they did that in style at the Huntington Stadium, running out 38-18 winners. Much of the damage was done in the first half as Dave Woods' side established a formidable 20-6 advantage. And with Danny Ratcliffe crossing for two tries and Lee Waterman finishing with 18 points, the Knights booked a repeat showdown with Oldham at the Halliwell Jones Stadium.

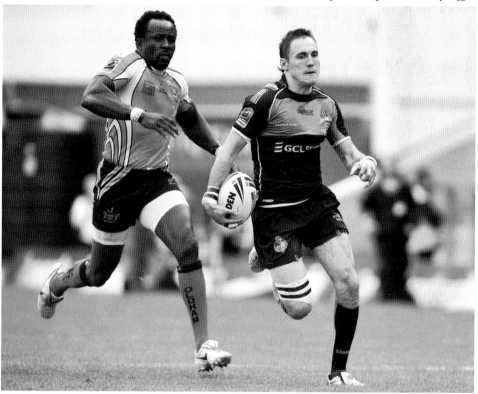

York's Danny Ratcliffe races away from Oldham's Lucas Onyango

CHAMPIONSHIP ONE GRAND FINAL

Chris Thorman guided York City Knights to Grand Final glory and promotion as his side overwhelmed hapless Oldham. The Roughyeds fell at the final hurdle for a fourth season in a row, as York's Australian coach Dave Woods secured a third personal promotion following success with Castleford and Gateshead.

Player-assistant coach Thorman scored one try, kicked two goals and a field goal as the Knights proved too strong for a side that finished 13 points above them in the league. They dominated the final in Warrington almost from start to finish to claim an emphatic victory.

THE CO-OPERATIVE CHAMPIONSHIP ONE GRAND FINAL

Sunday 26th September 2010

OLDHAM 4 YORK CITY KNIGHTS 25

OLDHAM: 1 Paul O'Connor; 2 Lucas Onyango; 24 Marcus St Hilaire; 4 Mick Fogerty; 5 John Gillam; 6 Neil Roden; 28 Gregg McNally; 8 Jason Boults; 9 Martin Roden; 16 Wayne Kerr; 18 Chris Clarke; 13 Joe Chandler; 21 Valu Bentley. Subs (all used): 10 Dave Ellison; 19 Ben Heaton; 17 Danny Whitmore; 7 Matt Ashe.
Try: Fogerty (20); **Goals:** McNally 0/1.
CITY KNIGHTS: 31 James Haynes; 2 Wayne Reittie; 3 Mike Mitchell; 4 Lee Waterman; 28 Danny Wilson; 6 Chris Thorman; 1 Danny Ratcliffe; 17 Nathan Freer; 33 Jack Lee; 10 Alex Benson; 11 Jordan Ross; 29 Ryan Esders; 15 Luke Hardbottle. Subs (all used): 32 Paul Stamp; 36 Callum Dinsdale; 26 Steve Lewis; 30 Jack Stearman.
Tries: Reittie (7), Haynes (26), Thorman (64), Lewis (74);
Goals: Waterman 2/3, Thorman 2/2; **Field goal:** Thorman (69).
Rugby Leaguer & League Express Men of the Match:
Oldham: Neil Roden; *City Knights:* Chris Thorman.
Penalty count: 2-7; **Half-time:** 4-10; **Referee:** Gareth Hewer.
(at Halliwell Jones Stadium, Warrington).

After Wayne Reittie's opener, Mick Fogerty scored Oldham's solitary points with a 19th-minute try that briefly brought them level at 4-4. But impressive fullback James Haynes ran in try number two for a 10-4 half-time lead, and with Thorman and Steve Lewis running in further scores, the Knights proved far too strong.

"They've worked extremely hard over the last few weeks, and we knew we had to dig deep today," said Woods, whose side had lost at Oldham two weeks earlier. "We asked the lads for a big commitment and they gave it to us."

THE CO-OPERATIVE CHAMPIONSHIP AWARDS

CHAMPIONSHIP PLAYER OF THE YEAR
Liam Finn
(Featherstone Rovers)

CHAMPIONSHIP ONE PLAYER OF THE YEAR
Paul March
(Hunslet Hawks)

CHAMPIONSHIP

PLAYER OF THE YEAR
Liam Finn (Featherstone Rovers)
Other nominees: Kyle Briggs (Featherstone Rovers)
Stuart Dickens (Featherstone Rovers)

YOUNG PLAYER OF THE YEAR *(Joint winners)*
Zak Hardaker (Featherstone Rovers)
& Gareth Moore (Batley Bulldogs)
Other nominee: Sam Smeaton (Featherstone Rovers)

COACH OF THE YEAR
Daryl Powell (Featherstone Rovers)
Other nominees: Karl Harrison (Batley Bulldogs)
Warren Jowitt (Dewsbury Rams)

RUGBY LEAGUE WORLD TEAM OF THE YEAR
1 John Campbell (Batley Bulldogs)
2 Tom Saxton (Featherstone Rovers)
3 Lee Paterson (Halifax)
4 Jessie Joe Parker (Featherstone Rovers)
5 Tim Bergin (Sheffield Eagles)
6 Anthony Thackeray (Widnes Vikings)
7 Dominic Brambani (Dewsbury Rams)
8 Sean Hesketh (Batley Bulldogs)
9 Bob Beswick (Halifax)
10 Ricky Bibey (Leigh Centurions)
11 Ned Catic (Barrow Raiders)
12 James Taylor (Leigh Centurions)
13 Matty Dale (Featherstone Rovers)

CLUB OF THE YEAR
Widnes Vikings

BEST COMMUNITY PROGRAMME
Leigh Centurions

REFEREE OF THE YEAR
Robert Hicks

CHAMPIONSHIP ONE

PLAYER OF THE YEAR
Paul March (Hunslet Hawks)
Other nominees: David March (Hunslet Hawks)
Paul O'Connor (Oldham)

YOUNG PLAYER OF THE YEAR
Jarrad Stack (Workington Town)
Other nominees: Tom Lineham (York City Knights)
Steve Parry (South Wales Scorpions)

COACH OF THE YEAR
Anthony Seibold (South Wales Scorpions)
Other nominees: Gary Charlton (Workington Town)
Martin Crompton (Blackpool Panthers)

RUGBY LEAGUE WORLD TEAM OF THE YEAR
1 Paul O'Connor (Oldham)
2 Neil Frazer (Workington Town)
3 Casey Mayberry (Blackpool Panthers)
4 Mick Fogerty (Oldham)
5 Damian Munro (Blackpool Panthers)
6 Neil Roden (Oldham)
7 Paul March (Hunslet Hawks)
8 James Houston (Hunslet Hawks)
9 Phil Wood (Rochdale Hornets)
10 Andy Hobson (Blackpool Panthers)
11 Jarrad Stack (Workington Town)
12 Tom Haughey (Hunslet Hawks)
13 David March (Hunslet Hawks)

RUGBY LEAGUE CONFERENCE NATIONAL

PLAYER OF THE YEAR
Jono Smith (Warrington Wizards)

YOUNG PLAYER OF THE YEAR
Adam Ryder (Huddersfield Underbank Rangers)

COACH OF THE YEAR
Dean Buckler (Kippax Knights)

2010 SUPER LEAGUE SEASON

ROUND BY ROUND

ROUND 4

RIGHT: Controversy at The Jungle as Liam Watts beats Ryan McGoldrick to score a late winning try for Hull KR

ABOVE: Leeds' Ryan Hall and Scott Donald arrive at the Racecourse Ground in Wrexham for Super League's opening game

BELOW: Gareth Raynor beats Kallum Watkins to score in the snow during Crusaders' battling defeat to champions Leeds

ROUND 2

RIGHT: Sean Gleeson shows his delight at scoring during Wakefield's win over Leeds

ROUND 1

LEFT: A triumphant Sean Long returns to Knowsley Road in Hull colours, and celebrates his side's win over St Helens with Danny Tickle and Craig Hall

BELOW: Castleford's James Evans touches down during the Tigers' win at Headingley

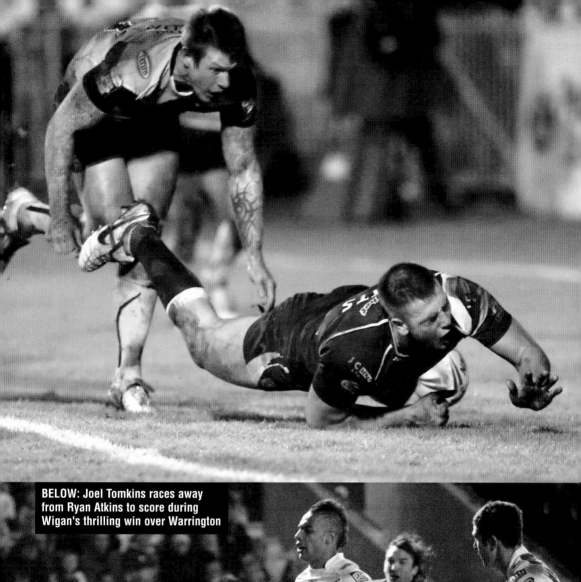

BELOW: Joel Tomkins races away from Ryan Atkins to score during Wigan's thrilling win over Warrington

ROUND 3

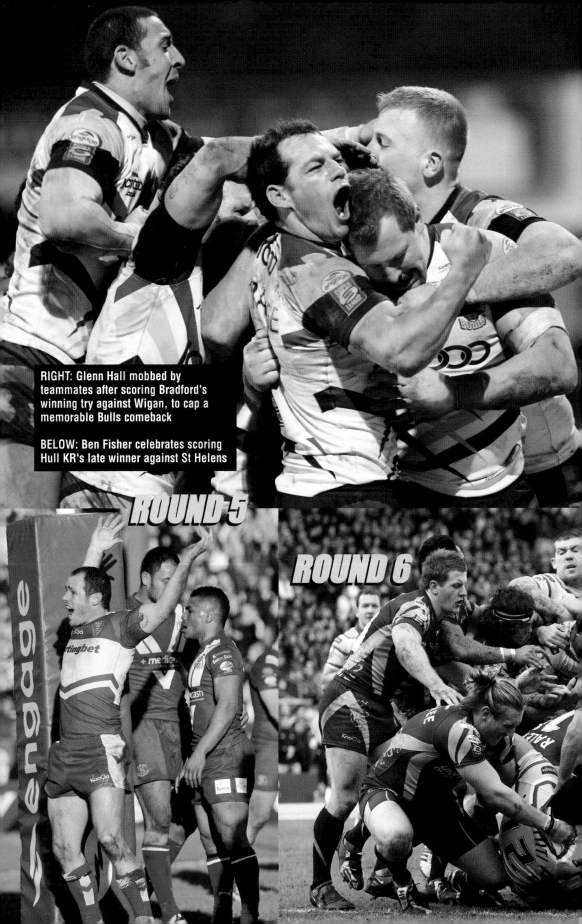

RIGHT: Glenn Hall mobbed by teammates after scoring Bradford's winning try against Wigan, to cap a memorable Bulls comeback

BELOW: Ben Fisher celebrates scoring Hull KR's late winner against St Helens

ROUND 5

ROUND 6

ROUND 7

ABOVE: Catalans' Dimitri Pelo evades Crusaders' Gareth Thomas, making his debut after making the switch from rugby union

ABOVE: Iosia Soliola takes on Richie Myler and Matt King as St Helens edge Warrington

LEFT: Things get heated during Huddersfield's home victory over Leeds

RIGHT: Salford's Daniel Holdsworth, congratulated by Karl Fitzpatrick and Matty Smith, jumps for joy after his field goal ensures victory against Hull

ROUND 8

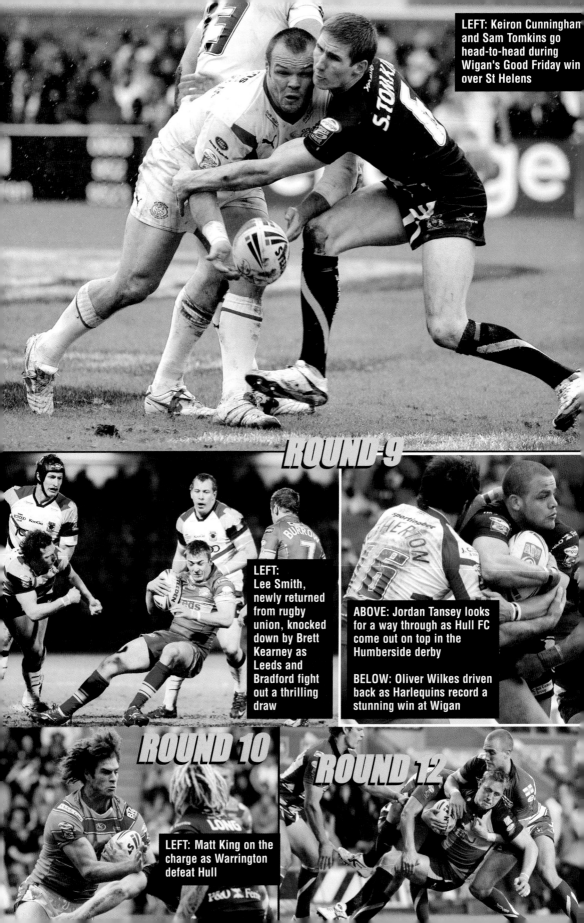

LEFT: Keiron Cunningham and Sam Tomkins go head-to-head during Wigan's Good Friday win over St Helens

ROUND 9

LEFT: Lee Smith, newly returned from rugby union, knocked down by Brett Kearney as Leeds and Bradford fight out a thrilling draw

ABOVE: Jordan Tansey looks for a way through as Hull FC come out on top in the Humberside derby

BELOW: Oliver Wilkes driven back as Harlequins record a stunning win at Wigan

ROUND 10

ROUND 12

LEFT: Matt King on the charge as Warrington defeat Hull

ROUND 11

ABOVE: Michael Witt races away from Darryl Millard on the way to a try during Crusaders' victory at Wakefield

ROUND 13 - MURRAYFIELD MAGIC

RIGHT: Danny Buderus swamped by jubilant teammates after scoring Leeds' decisive late try against Wakefield at Murrayfield

ROUND 16

LEFT: Kyle Eastmond wrapped up by Salford's Matty Smith - on loan from St Helens - who inspires the City Reds to victory over his parent club

BELOW: Greg Eastwood holds off the challenge of Michael Worrincy as Leeds edge Bradford at Odsal

RIGHT: Sean Long grounds former teammate Paul Wellens as Hull pull off an astonishing comeback to defeat St Helens

ROUND 14

RIGHT: Tony Puletua chased by Keith Mason during St Helens' victory over Huddersfield

BELOW: Vince Mellars shows his delight at scoring during Crusaders' win over Bradford

ROUND 15

ABOVE: Lee Smith loses the ball over the tryline under heavy Crusaders pressure as Leeds suffer a shock home defeat

ROUND 18

ROUND 17

LEFT: Leon Pryce beats Liam Farrell to score during St Helens' thrilling derby success over Wigan

RIGHT: Michael Dobson tackled by Luke Ambler and Ian Kirke as Hull KR power past Leeds

FAR RIGHT: Dallas Johnson halted by Nick Fozzard as Catalans upset St Helens

BELOW: Danny McGuire dives past Chris Hicks during Leeds' victory against Warrington in a high-scoring clash

ROUND 19

ABOVE: Michael Platt and Ryan McGoldrick contest a high ball during Castleford's win over Bradford

ROUND 20

LEFT: Craig Hall leaves Bradford's Paul Sykes trailing to score Hull's clinching try at Odsal

RIGHT: Chris Flannery twists over the tryline to score during St Helens' narrow loss at Leeds

ROUND 21

ROUND 22

LEFT: Ben Westwood surrounded by the Wigan defence as Warrington win the first Rugby League game to be broadcast in 3D

BELOW: Tom Briscoe pulls off a late wonder tackle on Hull KR's Peter Fox to win the derby for Hull FC

ROUND 23

ABOVE: Ryan Atkins grounded by Dane Carlaw as Catalans edge Warrington

ABOVE: Stuart Fielden collared by Willie Manu as Wigan take apart Hull

RIGHT: Michael Dobson jumps for joy following his last-gasp winning penalty against Castleford

BELOW: Harrison Hansen leaves Scott Donald and Brent Webb trailing as he scores during Wigan's win at Leeds

ROUND 24

ROUND 25

RIGHT: Huddersfield's David Fa'alogo takes on Mark Riddell and Andy Coley as the Giants triumph at Wigan

BELOW: Keiron Cunningham crashes over for a late try against Castleford that secures second place for St Helens

ROUND 26

ROUND 27

ABOVE: Elliott Whitehead beats Danny Kirmond to score as Bradford end their losing run against Wakefield

LEFT: Danny McGuire goes past Hull's Danny Houghton and Sean Long as Leeds win the battle for fourth place

RIGHT: Brent Webb tackled by Wigan's Martin Gleeson and Darrell Goulding as Leeds come out on top in a controversial thriller

ABOVE: Matty Smith feels the force of Adrian Morley as St Helens deny Warrington

QUALIFYING PLAY-OFFS

LEFT: Ben Fisher celebrates scoring as Hul end the season of their bitter rivals Hull FC

BELOW: Michael Lawrence looks for suppo under pressure from Vince Mellars as Huddersfield battle past Crusaders

ELIMINATION PLAY-OFFS

PRELIMINARY SEMI-FINALS

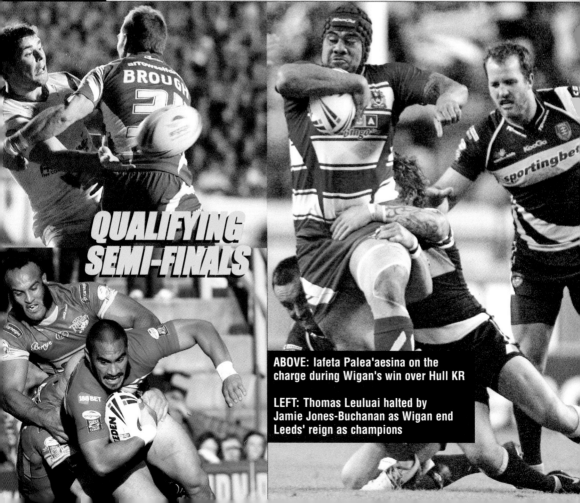

QUALIFYING SEMI-FINALS

ABOVE: Iafeta Palea'aesina on the charge during Wigan's win over Hull KR

LEFT: Thomas Leuluai halted by Jamie Jones-Buchanan as Wigan end Leeds' reign as champions

GRAND FINAL

Sam Tomkins stretches out to score as Martin Gleeson celebrates

ST HELENS 10
WIGAN WARRIORS 22

RIGHT: Man of Steel Pat Richards collects his winners medal, despite picking up an injury

LEFT: Paul Wellens ducks under the challenge of Sean O'Loughlin

champions 2010

Fireworks and champagne as Wigan clinch their first Super League title since 1998

3
PERSONALITIES OF 2010

Pat Richards

Pat Richards collected just about every individual accolade the game had to offer in 2010 and became one of a select group of players to win NRL Premiership and Super League Championship rings.

The Ireland international - who made his first-grade debut for Parramatta in 2000 - scored a try in Wests Tigers' NRL Grand Final win over North Queensland Cowboys in 2005 having pledged his future for the next two years to a Wigan club desperate to get back to the top table. His first season, 2006, at the JJB Stadium was traumatic as the coach who had signed him, Ian Millward, was dismissed and replaced by Brian Noble, the Warriors failing to make the play-offs and at one time looking candidates for relegation. A modest points return that season of 74 (Danny Tickle and Michael Dobson shared most of the goal kicks) gave little indication of the part Richards would play in Wigan's rehabilitation.

Given the goal-kicking duties from then on, Richards became a pointscoring machine, coming second in the Super League points list in 2007 and 2009 and finishing as top pointscorer in 2008. In his first five seasons in Super League he had amassed 1,533 points in all competitions.

The year 2010 was the year of Pat Richards as he smashed Wigan's club points-in-a-season record of 427 set by Andy Farrell in 2001. Richards' 462 points was made up of 32 tries (equal most with Warrington's Chris Hicks) and 167 goals, 53 more than any other Super League player in all competitions.

No surprise then he attracted the individual awards like a magnet, being joint-winner of the Albert Goldthorpe Medal with clubmate Sam Tomkins - a mark of his consistency - and named as the Rugby League Writers' Player of the Year. Then Richards polled more votes among his peers than the two other players on the short-list, Wolves captain Adrian Morley and Sam Tomkins, to become only the fifth Australian to be crowned Man of Steel since the award was instigated in 1977.

Tall and athletic, Richards is an accomplished fielder of the high ball, either in attack or defence and a powerful runner. A natural winger, he has been able to fill in at fullback on many occasions with equal effect and his ability to land a goal-line drop-out 60 metres down field was a huge asset for Wigan in their first Championship year since 1998.

It wasn't quite a perfect ending for Richards in 2010 as he collected his Grand Final ring at Old Trafford with the aid of crutches after suffering an Achilles injury 37 minutes into the game.

Richards is contracted with Wigan for another year and won't surpass Jim Sullivan's career record of 4,883 points set between 1921 and 1946. But he will go down in history as one of the great point scorers in Rugby League.

Keiron Cunningham

Keiron Cunningham brought an end to a remarkable Rugby League career in 2010, though there was no fairytale ending as his St Helens side fell at the the last hurdle for the fourth consecutive season.

Wigan's 22-10 triumph over St Helens at Old Trafford denied Cunningham the perfect finish, but he left an indelible mark on the club he had represented for 17 years and on the game of Rugby League.

A seventeen-year-old Cunningham made his debut 24 August 1994, in the days before Super League, in a defeat at Warrington. During his marvellous career, St Helens have been the most successful club in Super League, enjoying three periods of domination - the double-winning side of 1996; the one that spanned the turn of the century; and the one that won the Super League title in 2006 and the Challenge Cup in 2006, 2007 and 2008. Cunningham was the common thread between those eras, making 496 appearances for Saints, and scoring 175 tries - an impressive strike-rate for a hooker/dummy-half. A double winner in 1996 and 2006, Cunningham played in all St Helens' biggest days and won five Championships and seven Challenge Cups in total.

He had already achieved everything in the domestic game when the Welsh RU tried to sign him in 2001, desperate for a high-profile player to help lift their game out of the doldrums. With huge money on offer, Cunningham decided to stick with Rugby League.

Cunningham's 15 Great Britain caps could have been many more had it not been for injury and his decisions not to be considered for some end-of-season series. He made his last Great Britain appearance in the mid-season Test against New Zealand in 2006, fittingly at Knowsley Road.

In Super League XV, at the age of 33, he remained one of the most dangerous players in Super League, with his strength and speed from dummy-half, and consistent ability to bounce out of tackles. He was as strong as a prop and as wily as a halfback, the archetypal Super League player.

The year 2010 was also St Helens' last at Knowsley Road, and in the last game at Saints' home since 1890 - a 42-22 Qualifying semi-final win over Huddersfield Giants on the last weekend of September - there was only one man who could score the last try. With six minutes remaining, Cunningham forced his way over from dummy-half in trademark style, three weeks after scoring the final regular-season try on the famous old ground against Castleford in round 27.

When a poll was taken amongst St Helens supporters to discover which of their heroes they wanted to be cast as a statue in the town, Cunningham beat the likes of legends Tom van Vollenhoven and Alex Murphy. It was a measure of the esteem with which Keiron Cunningham will be remembered, in St Helens and beyond.

Gareth Thomas

No player's profile was as high as that of former rugby union player Gareth Thomas in 2010, and he only became a Rugby League player in March of that year. As the most-capped Wales player in rugby union history, the player known as Alfie gave a Crusaders team assembled at the last minute by coach Brian Noble a face instantly recognisable by the Welsh public.

In December 2009 Thomas had announced publicly he was gay and with it came widespread recognition outside sport. He was voted top of the 'Pink List' in 2010, ranking the 101 most influential gay people in the UK and he received Stonewall's 'Hero of the Year' award in October 2010.

He made his Crusaders debut in round seven in a televised home game against Catalans Dragons on 19 March, a dour 14-6 win, and it was hardly a dream debut for Thomas. Taking the ball up in the first set, he was met with a solid hit from David Ferriol. Shaken, Thomas fumbled the ball as he tried to play it, and clearly struggled with the requirements of his new game from then on. On the half-hour mark, Jamal Fakir hit Thomas with another hard tackle and the new bloke was led groggily from the pitch, not returning that night.

Thomas only played eleven Super League games, with a modest return of two tries, scoring his first League try in Crusaders' 20-10 away victory against Wakefield Trinity in round 11.

His most headline-grabbing contribution came in his second game, at Castleford when he was subject to homophobic taunting by a small section of the crowd. Later in the year, in June, Thomas hailed the Rugby Football League for sending out "an amazing message" by fining the Castleford club $40,000.

In round 17, he limped off just before half-time of the 44-20 win at Bradford with a groin injury and in his comeback on 4 July he suffered a recurrence in a 30-10 home defeat by Warrington and was sidelined for the rest of the domestic season.

Despite the injury setbacks, he took up the option of another one-year contract in August

If his early efforts in club Rugby League met with mixed results, Thomas's season finished with a bang. He recovered in time to become a dual-code international when he represented Wales in a friendly against Italy at the Racecourse Ground on 6 October, scoring their only try, although Italy went on to win 13-6.

He scored again the following Sunday in Wales' 60-22 European Cup win against Scotland in Glasgow. And when Lee Briers was sidelined with an injury after the 31-30 win against Ireland, Thomas was appointed captain by coach Iestyn Harris for the last game of the tournament - a winner-takes-all showdown with France in Albi.

Thomas scored a try, helping Wales to a 12-11 win to secure both the Alitalia European Cup and a spot in the 2011 Rugby League Four Nations. It was a significant step in the rehabilitation of Welsh Rugby League.

Luke Robinson

If there was one positive note of England's Four Nations campaign, it was the international emergence of Huddersfield Giants halfback Luke Robinson. Having postponed his wedding, to be held in Cyprus, and missed his stag trip to Las Vegas to have the chance to represent his country for the first time, the 26-year-old deserved his success.

Robinson started on the bench in England's opening game with New Zealand in Wellington after he had played a key role in the warm-up with the Maori the week before. In that game, Robinson's first touch after he had substituted James Roby produced England's second try, when he collected Eorl Crabtree's offload from the tackle on his own 30-metre line. The Giants halfback skipped and danced, then shot away from the Maori defence, timing his pass to the supporting Sam Tomkins to perfection.

In the dying seconds of the first half, Robinson looked to have helped bury the Maori's hopes after Tom Briscoe had rolled back the ball as he was being tackled 20 metres out. In a flash the Huddersfield halfback had scooped it up, shot through and found Sean O'Loughlin on his left to go in under the posts. But a tired England went from 18-0 up, and seemingly in total control, to 18-all, and could easily have faced a morale-sapping defeat had it not been for Robinson and Sam Burgess blocking stand-off Arana Taumata's last-minute field-goal attempt.

Robinson did enough in the New Zealand game, including a 70-metre breakaway interception - to earn a starting spot against Australia and it was his try from dummy-half three minutes after the break that got England back into the game that at 26-8 had looked like running away from them.

In the 36-10 win over Papua New Guinea, Robinson was over for two tries before dislocating and breaking an elbow just after half time. It wasn't an ideal finish but Robinson had done enough to establish his international credentials.

On his return home, he was already booked in for surgery on his right shoulder but that had to be postponed for an operation on his other elbow. In between, he was finally getting married to his patient and understanding fiancée, in Halifax, not Cyprus.

What a year it had been. Robinson could quite easily have taken his bat home early in the season when it became apparent Huddersfield coach Nathan Brown was keen to bring Danny Brough in at scrum-half. Despite that, Robinson signed a contract extension with the Giants to the end of 2012, who he joined in 2007 from Salford, after starting his first-grade career at Wigan in 2002.

Two weeks later the Giants signed Brough and Robinson made a highly successful switch to hooker that saw the Giants go to within one game of the Grand Final, before they bowed out at St Helens in the Qualifying Semi-final.

Benji Marshall

Benji Marshall dominated the international scene in 2010, leading New Zealand to success in the Four Nations tournament and was a landslide winner of the *Rugby League World* Golden Boot.

The 25 year-old showed flashes of true brilliance in the pool games of the Four Nations. In New Zealand's 24-10 win over England, he set up his team for victory in the first half, creating a brilliant try for Lance Hohaia. And in the second half he ended England's comeback, engineering and scoring the killer try in the right corner.

The Kiwis came under some criticism after their 34-20 defeat in Auckland by Australia, but two pieces of Benji wizardry in the last ten minutes were memorable. He set up a try for winger Nightingale with one of his characteristic backhand flicks that tied Lote Tuqiri in knots and, with eight minutes left on the clock, almost scored himself. Then he set up a late try for Shaun Kenny-Dowall with another backflick and made two more breaks that could well have resulted in tries.

GOLDEN BOOT - ROLL OF HONOUR
1985 Wally Lewis (Australia)
1986 Brett Kenny (Australia)
1987 Garry Jack (Australia)
1988 Hugh McGahan (New Zealand) & Peter Sterling (Australia)
1989 Ellery Hanley (Great Britain)
1990 Mal Meninga (Australia)
1991-1998 *No award given*
1999 Andrew Johns (Australia)
2000 Brad Fittler (Australia)
2001 Andrew Johns (Australia)
2002 Stacey Jones (New Zealand)
2003 Darren Lockyer (Australia)
2004 Andrew Farrell (Great Britain)
2005 Anthony Minichiello (Australia)
2006 Darren Lockyer (Australia)
2007 Cameron Smith (Australia)
2008 Billy Slater (Australia)
2009 Greg Inglis (Australia)
2010 Benji Marshall (New Zealand)

But he saved his piece de resistance for last. With the Kiwis trailing 12-6 going into the last ten minutes of the final in Brisbane, Marshall won the game with two pieces of magic, although he revealed after the game that he was roused in the closing minutes by the normally mild-mannered Kiwis coach Stephen Kearney sending him messages liberally laced with expletives.

First he put in a spinning kick along the ground, finding his unmarked teammate Jason Nightingale, who sped across the tryline to narrow the lead. His conversion attempt bounced away off the right-hand upright, but Marshall still had some tricks up his sleeve. With time running out, he started a move from 40 metres out, sending Shaun Kenny-Dowall away. The big centre sent Nightingale down the right touchline and he put a pass back to Marshall who, when collared on the tryline, flung the ball blindly over his left shoulder. Scrum-half Nathan Fien was trailing in support, and touched down for the winning try. There were just 93 seconds left on the clock. And it was the first time New Zealand had been in front all night.

4
INTERNATIONAL YEAR

FOUR NATIONS
Kiwis back at number one

New Zealand, coached by Stephen Kearney, won the 2010 Four Nations, tournament held down under, with a dramatic last-minute try to scrum-half Nathan Fien securing a 16-12 victory in the final in Brisbane. The result secured a second tournament-final success against Australia after their World Cup win at the same venue in 2008.

England took a new coach into the Four Nations and Steve McNamara's team fulfilled pre-tournament predictions of a third-place finish. England were eliminated two games in, after defeats to New Zealand and Australia; their third game - a 36-10 win over Papua New Guinea - a dead rubber.

McNamara's first match in charge was a comfortable enough 60-6 win over France at Leigh in June, the highlight four tries by Sam Tomkins and an impressive international debut from Halifax-born Melbourne Storm reserve fullback Gareth Widdop.

When appointed in April, McNamara was supposed to see out the season with his club Bradford, conducting his England job on a part-time basis - with Sydney Roosters coach Brian Smith acting as performance advisor - but he left Odsal by mutual consent in July after a run of eight straight defeats.

McNamara's international squad selection wasn't helped by a serious knee injury sustained in round 25 by captain Jamie Peacock. Peacock's teammate at Leeds, Kevin Sinfield, who had played hooker in the France game, was also unavailable with an Achilles problem that needed surgery. Another Rhinos player, stand-off Danny McGuire was out with a knee injury suffered in the play-off game at Wigan. Warrington's Chris Bridge, a star of the mid-season Test, declared himself unavailable due to the imminent arrival of his first child.

2010 FOUR NATIONS SQUADS

AUSTRALIA: Greg Bird (Gold Coast Titans), Darius Boyd (St George Illawarra Dragons), Todd Carney (Sydney Roosters), Petero Civoniceva (Penrith Panthers), Cooper Cronk (Melbourne Storm), Robbie Farah (Wests Tigers), Paul Gallen (Cronulla Sharks), Kurt Gidley (Newcastle Knights), Jarryd Hayne (Parramatta Eels), Chris Lawrence (Wests Tigers), Tom Learoyd-Lahrs (Canberra Raiders), Luke Lewis (Penrith Panthers), Darren Lockyer (Brisbane Broncos) (C), Brett Morris (St George Illawarra Dragons), Nate Myles (Sydney Roosters), Matt Scott (North Queensland Cowboys), David Shillington (Canberra Raiders), Billy Slater (Melbourne Storm), Cameron Smith (Melbourne Storm), Brent Tate (New Zealand Warriors), Sam Thaiday (Brisbane Broncos), Willie Tonga (North Queensland Cowboys), Anthony Watmough (Manly Sea Eagles), Dean Young (St George Illawarra Dragons).

Jarryd Hayne withdrew with a hamstring injury and was replaced by Lote Tuqiri (Wests Tigers).

ENGLAND: Ryan Atkins (Warrington Wolves), Tom Briscoe (Hull FC), Kevin Brown (Huddersfield Giants), Sam Burgess (South Sydney Rabbitohs), Tony Clubb (Harlequins), Eorl Crabtree (Huddersfield Giants), Leroy Cudjoe (Huddersfield Giants), Gareth Ellis (Wests Tigers), Stuart Fielden (Wigan Warriors), Darrell Goulding (Wigan Warriors), James Graham (St Helens), Darrell Griffin (Huddersfield Giants), Ryan Hall (Leeds Rhinos), Ben Harrison (Warrington Wolves), Shaun Lunt (Huddersfield Giants), Adrian Morley (Warrington Wolves) (C), Sean O'Loughlin (Wigan Warriors), Luke Robinson (Huddersfield Giants), James Roby (St Helens), Michael Shenton (Castleford Tigers), Joel Tomkins (Wigan Warriors), Sam Tomkins (Wigan Warriors), Ben Westwood (Warrington Wolves), Gareth Widdop (Melbourne Storm).

Adrian Morley ruptured a bicep in the warm-up game against New Zealand Maori and was replaced by Garreth Carvell (Warrington Wolves). The captaincy was taken by James Graham.

NEW ZEALAND: Adam Blair (Melbourne Storm), Lewis Brown (New Zealand Warriors), Greg Eastwood (Leeds Rhinos), Nathan Fien (St George Illawarra Dragons), Bronson Harrison (Canberra Raiders), Lance Hohaia (New Zealand Warriors), Shaun Kenny-Dowall (Sydney Roosters), Thomas Leuluai (Wigan Warriors), Issac Luke (South Sydney Rabbitohs), Simon Mannering (New Zealand Warriors), Benji Marshall (Wests Tigers) (C), Ben Matulino (New Zealand Warriors), Fuifui Moimoi (Parramatta Eels), Jason Nightingale (St George Illawarra Dragons), Frank-Paul Nuuausala (Sydney Roosters), Sam Perrett (Sydney Roosters), Frank Pritchard (Penrith Panthers), Junior Sa'u (Newcastle Knights), Jeremy Smith (St George Illawarra Dragons), Manu Vatuvei (New Zealand Warriors), Jared Waerea-Hargreaves (Sydney Roosters), Antonio Winterstein (Brisbane Broncos).

Fuifui Moimoi withdrew after suffering a broken arm and was replaced by Sam McKendry (Penrith Panthers).

PAPUA NEW GUINEA: Paul Aiton (Cronulla Sharks) (C), Dion Aiye (Rabaul Gurias), Makali Aizue (Halifax), Tony Dai (Goroka Lahanis), Sigfred Gande (Rabaul Gurias), Rodney Griffin (Northern Pride), Benjamin John (Parkes Spacemen), Richard Kambo (Newtown Jets), Nickson Kolo (Port Moresby Rangers), Johnson Kuike (Port Moresby Rangers), David Loko (Enga Mioks), Larsen Marabe (Rabaul Gurias), Michael Mark (Hunslet Hawks), Desmond Mok (Ipswich Jets), George Moni (Rabaul Gurias), Glen Nami (Goroka Lahanis), Jessie Joe Parker (Port Moresby Vipers), Joseph Pombo (Canterbury Bulls), Rodney Pora (Rabaul Gurias), Elijah Riyong (Port Moresby Vipers), Andrew Sam (Mendi Muruks), Pidi Tongap (Rabaul Gurias), Ryan Tongia (Gold Coast Titans), Charlie Wabo (Hunslet Hawks), Menzie Yere (Sheffield Eagles).

St Helens' Kyle Eastmond was also out with ankle ligament damage, leaving McNamara's halfback options severely restricted, and he opted for Huddersfield's Luke Robinson over clubmate Danny Brough and Leeds' Rob Burrow in the scrum-half role.

The leadership of the side fell to Adrian Morley but when he ruptured a biceps in the warm-up game against the Maori in the week before the tournament proper, the captaincy was handed to St Helens prop James Graham. Garreth Carvell, a surprise omission from the original 24-man squad, was flown out to replace Morley. Huddersfield had the biggest representation with six players. Three of them, Robinson, Leroy Cudjoe and Shaun Lunt were uncapped before the tournament, as were Wigan winger Darrell Goulding and Warrington forward Ben Harrison.

Australia had six players in their 24-man squad - Tom Learoyd-Lahrs (Canberra), Matthew Scott (North Queensland), Dean Young (St George Illawarra), Todd Carney (Roosters), Nate Myles (Roosters) and Chris Lawrence (Wests Tigers) - set to make their international debuts. Darren Lockyer was to captain the side, while Cooper Cronk won the halfback position ahead of Scott Prince and Mitchell Pearce, with Johnathan Thurston out injured.

Other high-profile injuries ruled Greg Inglis, winger Josh Morris (both shoulder), Michael Jennings and Jamie Lyon (both ankle) out of contention. Jarryd Hayne was initially named but then dropped out with a hamstring tear. He was replaced by Wests Tigers' Lote Tuqiri who would become the first player in history to switch from one international code to the other and back again.

New Zealand included two debutants in their 23-man squad - New Zealand Warriors back-rower Lewis Brown and Brisbane Broncos winger Antonio Winterstein, though neither of the pair got a run. Sydney Roosters centre Shaun Kenny-Dowall - named New Zealand Player of the Year - was recalled after making his only previous appearance against France in 2007.

Of the remaining 17 players chosen, 16 were involved in the 2009 Gillette Four Nations in England, including Wigan scrum-half Thomas Leuluai and Leeds back-rower Greg Eastwood. Wests Tigers' Benji Marshall captained the side.

Warriors centre Jerome Ropati and Manly halfback Kieran Foran were ruled out with shoulder injuries, while centre Steve Matai was suspended for a high tackle in an NRL game and prop Sam Rapira made himself unavailable for family reasons. Fuifui Moimoi was named in the original squad but withdrew with a broken arm. He was replaced by Penrith prop Sam McKendry.

Papua New Guinea had won the right to be the fourth team alongside England, Australia and New Zealand by winning the Pacific Cup in 2009. Their chances of competing were hit only weeks before the Four Nations kick-off by a political fall-out. Former chairman Albert Veratau and his successor Gary Juffa had been involved in year-long dispute which came to a head in September 2010. Kumuls coach Adrian Lam and his coaching team quit in the lead up to the Four Nations, primarily due to Juffa's demand that the Kumuls squad be largely comprised of domestic players.

The in-fighting in the PNGRL also raised doubts about the viability of the country's NRL bid. Three board members of the bid organisation - including Queensland coach Mal Meninga - resigned.

Lam was replaced as coach by another Kumuls legend, Stanley Gene, who was left with less than a month to prepare his team. Several players based in Australia were unavailable, including star Gold Coast winger David Mead (Moore has had been in the World Cup in 2008) and the Australian Rugby League prevented St George Illawarra's Neville Costigan from playing for his country of birth because he had played Origin.

Only seven of the side that had won the Pacific Cup remained in the squad, and only captain Paul Aiton from Cronulla Sharks was from an NRL club, although there was a sprinkling of English Championship experience. The bulk of the players were selected from the local PNG competition. The result was three heavy defeats, despite some flashes of attacking brilliance and brutal defence throughout.

Four Nations

A sub-standard opening quarter in Wellington's Westpac Stadium scuppered England's chances of getting their Four Nations campaign off to a winning start after the bodyblow of the opening try from centre Junior Sa'u - in New Zealand's very first set of the game. Fullback Lance Hohaia doubled the Kiwi lead to 12 points before the half-time break. And four minutes after the turnaround, Shaun Kenny-Dowall embarrassed the English defence to step over for New Zealand's third try.

At 18-0 down, a rout was on the cards. But England's revival was spirited, and, had they got the rub of the green, they could easily have pinched the points. James Roby broke England's duck when his grubber from dummy-half hit a post-protector, and he scrambled through to ground the ball. Gareth Widdop converted, and two tackles later England were in again. Coming out of their own '20', captain James Graham and Roby both offloaded in tackles for Sam Tomkins and brother Joel to ship the ball right to Michael Shenton. Despite an ankle injury that after the game ruled him out of the rest of the tour, Shenton stepped inside before showing wonderful pace to break away, finding Kevin Brown on his inside. Brown shipped on for Widdop to score the try., though Widdop fluffed the conversion attempt.

Brown looked to have got England back to within two points when he got a hand to Sam Tomkins' banana kick into the in-goal but the video referees ruled he had shoved the challenging Greg Eastwood in order to touch down.

At the end of the next set, Kiwi captain Benji Marshall was engineering and then scoring the killer try in the right corner. It was a significant blow by the brilliant Marshall, who tormented England, managing to get the ball down one-handed a millisecond before Tom Briscoe forced him into the corner post. Marshall then made it a three-score margin with a majestic touchline conversion.

Kiwi winger Manu Vatuvei left the field after only two minutes clutching a broken arm and was ruled out of the rest of the tournament.

Australia began their defence of the Four Nations title with an easy – if scrappy – victory over the Kumuls at Parramatta Stadium, Sydney. Heavy rain that drenched the small crowd of just 11,308 didn't help. The Kumuls went into the game with bookmakers offering them a 52 points start – and those who took the odds must have been delighted when New Zealand referee Shane Rehm handed the Aussies a 12-2 penalty advantage.

The floodgates opened after five minutes when a cross-pitch kick by Darren Lockyer bounced off the left upright and Billy Slater was on hand to touch down. The enthusiastic Kumuls came up with some big hits, including one from Menzie Yere that winded Lockyer. However their handling was poor and a dropped ball gave the Australians their second try, Brent Tate running across the line off a crisp Slater pass.

It was the start of a procession. Cooper Cronk scored when he chased a Cameron Smith kick from inside his own 40-metre line; another mistake gifted a try to Willie Tonga. When winger Brett Morris went over for his ninth try in six Test appearances the Australians were well ahead of the clock with a 24-nil lead. However, some solid defence by the Kumuls halted the points flood until half-time.

FOUR NATIONS - GAME 1

Saturday 23rd October 2010

NEW ZEALAND 24 ENGLAND 10

NEW ZEALAND: 1 Lance Hohaia (New Zealand Warriors); 2 Jason Nightingale (St George Illawarra Dragons); 3 Shaun Kenny-Dowall (Sydney Roosters); 4 Junior Sa'u (Newcastle Knights); 5 Manu Vatuvei (New Zealand Warriors); 6 Benji Marshall (Wests Tigers) (C); 7 Nathan Fien (St George Illawarra Dragons); 8 Greg Eastwood (Leeds Rhinos); 9 Thomas Leuluai (Wigan Warriors); 10 Adam Blair (Melbourne Storm); 11 Simon Mannering (New Zealand Warriors); 12 Bronson Harrison (Canberra Raiders); 13 Jeremy Smith (St George Illawarra Dragons). Subs (all used): 14 Ben Matulino (New Zealand Warriors); 15 Issac Luke (South Sydney Rabbitohs); 16 Frank Pritchard (Penrith Panthers); 17 Frank-Paul Nuuausala (Sydney Roosters).
Tries: Sa'u (4), Hohaia (34), Kenny-Dowall (44), Marshall (66);
Goals: Marshall 4/5.
ENGLAND: 1 Gareth Widdop (Melbourne Storm); 2 Darrell Goulding (Wigan Warriors); 3 Michael Shenton (Castleford Tigers); 4 Ryan Atkins (Warrington Wolves); 5 Tom Briscoe (Hull FC); 6 Kevin Brown (Huddersfield Giants); 7 Sam Tomkins (Wigan Warriors); 8 Stuart Fielden (Wigan Warriors); 9 James Roby (St Helens); 10 James Graham (St Helens) (C); 11 Gareth Ellis (Wests Tigers); 12 Sam Burgess (South Sydney Rabbitohs); 13 Sean O'Loughlin (Wigan Warriors). Subs (all used): 14 Luke Robinson (Huddersfield Giants); 15 Darrell Griffin (Huddersfield Giants); 16 Ben Westwood (Warrington Wolves); 17 Joel Tomkins (Wigan Warriors).
Tries: Roby (56), Widdop (58); **Goals:** Widdop 1/2.
Rugby Leaguer & League Express Men of the Match:
New Zealand: Benji Marshall; *England:* Michael Shenton.
Penalty count: 7-5; **Half-time:** 12-0; **Referee:** Tony Archer (Australia); **Attendance:** 20,681 *(at Westpac Stadium, Wellington).*

In the 51st minute a penalty got the Kumuls inside Australia's 20-metre line for the first time. But a forward pass was ruled and when PNG second-rower Rodney Griffin lost the ball, Australia pounced.

Despite three would-be defenders trying to hold him up Smith, the Aussie hooker, spun around in the tackle and slammed the ball down behind the whitewash. It broke a 30-minute scoring drought. Within five minutes Lockyer was over for his 34th try in ARL Test colours – he had also grabbed two in the 1997 Super League Tests. It was a record that beat the 33 ARL mark he shared with Ken Irvine. Tonga went over for his second try with five minutes left on the clock.

FOUR NATIONS - GAME 2

Sunday 24th October 2010

AUSTRALIA 42 PAPUA NEW GUINEA 0

AUSTRALIA: 1 Billy Slater (Melbourne Storm); 2 Brett Morris (St George Illawarra Dragons); 3 Brent Tate (New Zealand Warriors); 4 Willie Tonga (North Queensland Cowboys); 5 Lote Tuqiri (Wests Tigers); 6 Darren Lockyer (Brisbane Broncos) (C); 7 Cooper Cronk (Melbourne Storm); 8 Nate Myles (Sydney Roosters); 9 Cameron Smith (Melbourne Storm); 10 Petero Civoniceva (Penrith Panthers); 11 Luke Lewis (Penrith Panthers); 12 Sam Thaiday (Brisbane Broncos); 13 Paul Gallen (Cronulla Sharks). Subs (all used): 14 David Shillington (Canberra Raiders); 15 Tom Learoyd-Lahrs (Canberra Raiders); 16 Anthony Watmough (Manly Sea Eagles); 17 Kurt Gidley (Newcastle Knights). **Tries:** Slater (5), Tate (14), Cronk (16), Tonga (21, 75), Morris (24), Smith (54), Lockyer (59); **Goals:** Smith 5/8.
PAPUA NEW GUINEA: 1 Ryan Tongia (Gold Coast Titans); 2 Michael Mark (Hunslet Hawks); 3 Jessie Joe Parker (Port Moresby Vipers); 4 Menzie Yere (Sheffield Eagles); 5 Elijah Riyong (Port Moresby Vipers); 6 Glen Nami (Goroka Lahanis); 7 Dion Aiye (Rabaul Gurias); 8 Makali Aizue (Halifax); 9 Benjamin John (Parkes Spacemen); 10 George Moni (Rabaul Gurias); 11 Rodney Griffin (Northern Pride); 12 David Loko (Enga Mioks); 13 Paul Aiton (Cronulla Sharks) (C). Subs (all used): 14 Charlie Wabo (Hunslet Hawks); 15 Nickson Kolo (Port Moresby Rangers); 16 Johnson Kuike (Port Moresby Rangers); 17 Larsen Marabe (Rabaul Gurias).
Rugby Leaguer & League Express Men of the Match:
Australia: Billy Slater; *Papua New Guinea:* Menzie Yere.
Penalty count: 12-2; **Half-time:** 26-0; **Referee:** Shane Rehm (New Zealand); **Attendance:** 11,308 *(at Parramatta Stadium).*

The Kiwis ran up a cricket score with a 76-12 flogging of the hapless Kumuls at Rotorua on the second Saturday of the tournament. They fell just 12 points short of their best-ever score in a Test match – the 84-12 thrashing of the Cook Islands at the 2000 World Cup.

New Zealand ran in 14 tries, despite Adam Blair, Ben Matulino and Frank Pritchard being rested. Sam Perrett, in for the injured folk hero Manu Vatuvei, scored the first of a hat-trick of tries to set the ball rolling, Simon Mannering, Jeremy Smith twice and Junior Sa'u stretching the lead to 28-nil after 24 minutes. Late in the half, Lance Hohaia dummied his way across and when Greg Eastwood powered across the stripe and substitute hooker Issac Luke darted under some very ordinary tackles to score, the Kiwis went to the break with a 46-nil lead.

The procession continued in the second half with two tries to Sa'u within the space of two minutes stretching the lead to 56 points. Sa'u could have scored a fourth try but unselfishly sent Perrett across the whitewash moments later.

Two quick tries midway through the second half cheered up the Kumuls – the first to Sheffield centre Menzie Yere when he stepped inside the NZ cover to go over untouched. The other, to stand-off Glen Nami, two minutes later demonstrated that the Kumuls could excite. Hunslet Hawks utility Charlie Wabo caught the Kiwis napping from dummy-half when he chipped over and collected on half-way. In support at speed was Gold Coast junior Ryan Tongia, who sidestepped Hohaia

FOUR NATIONS - GAME 3

Saturday 30th October 2010

NEW ZEALAND 76 PAPUA NEW GUINEA 12

NEW ZEALAND: 1 Lance Hohaia (New Zealand Warriors); 2 Jason Nightingale (St George Illawarra Dragons); 3 Shaun Kenny-Dowall (Sydney Roosters); 4 Junior Sa'u (Newcastle Knights); 5 Sam Perrett (Sydney Roosters); 6 Benji Marshall (Wests Tigers) (C); 7 Nathan Fien (St George Illawarra Dragons); 8 Sam McKendry (Penrith Panthers); 9 Thomas Leuluai (Wigan Warriors); 10 Frank-Paul Nuuausala (Sydney Roosters); 11 Sika Manu (Melbourne Storm); 12 Simon Mannering (New Zealand Warriors); 13 Jeremy Smith (St George Illawarra Dragons). Subs (all used): 14 Issac Luke (South Sydney Rabbitohs); 15 Jared Waerea-Hargreaves (Sydney Roosters); 16 Bronson Harrison (Canberra Raiders); 17 Greg Eastwood (Leeds Rhinos).
Tries: Perrett (2, 48, 62), Mannering (7), Smith (11, 16), Sa'u (24, 42, 44), Hohaia (32), Eastwood (36), Luke (40), Nightingale (71), Manu (74); **Goals:** Marshall 8/10, Luke 2/4.
PAPUA NEW GUINEA: 1 Ryan Tongia (Gold Coast Titans); 2 Michael Mark (Hunslet Hawks); 3 Jessie Joe Parker (Port Moresby Vipers); 4 Menzie Yere (Sheffield Eagles); 5 Elijah Riyong (Port Moresby Vipers); 6 Glen Nami (Goroka Lahanis); 7 Dion Aiye (Rabaul Gurias); 8 Makali Aizue (Halifax); 9 Charlie Wabo (Hunslet Hawks); 10 James Nightingale (North Sydney Bears); 11 Rodney Griffin (Northern Pride); 12 Johnson Kuike (Port Moresby Rangers); 13 Paul Aiton (Cronulla Sharks) (C). Subs (all used): 14 Benjamin John (Parkes Spacemen); 15 Rodney Pora (Rabaul Gurias); 16 Pidi Tongap (Rabaul Gurias); 17 Nickson Kolo (Port Moresby Rangers).
Tries: Yere (52), Nami (54); **Goals:** Tongia 2/2.
On report: Yere (27) – alleged dangerous tackle.
Rugby Leaguer & League Express Men of the Match:
New Zealand: Nathan Fien; *Papua New Guinea:* Menzie Yere.
Half-time: 46-0; **Referee:** Ben Cummins (Australia); **Attendance:** 11,500 *(at Rotorua International Stadium).*

and, as Nightingale came across to cover, sent Nami away to the posts. It was scant consolation for a PNG side off the pace for most of the game.

Four Nations

England coach Steve McNamara made 11 changes for the must-win Four Nations clash with Australia at AAMI Park in Melbourne. Only six players occupied the positions they took in the 24-10 defeat by New Zealand, as McNamara dropped the Melbourne fullback Gareth Widdop, who was denied the chance to play for his country on his home ground, and stand-off Kevin Brown and gave debuts to Huddersfield duo Leroy Cudjoe and Shaun Lunt and the Warrington forward Ben Harrison.

Sam Tomkins moved from scrum-half to fullback, Sean O'Loughlin from loose forward to stand-off and Luke Robinson got his first full cap at scrum-half. In contrast, Australia coach Tim Sheens went for stability, keeping the same team that had faced Papua New Guinea a week earlier.

Luke Lewis gave the Australians an ominous early lead but Sam Burgess got England's first try four minutes later off a crisp pass from James Roby. A penalty goal by Ben Westwood after a high tackle by Paul Gallen put England in front.

Lewis was in again when Darren Lockyer put in a cross-pitch kick behind the posts. The hand of Cooper Cronk appeared to knock the ball on, but video-referee Steve Clark gave Lewis the benefit of the doubt. The blow rocked England as they conceded three tries before the break, to Billy Slater, Brent Tate and Willie Tonga to send the Australians to the break with a solid 26-8 lead.

Robinson darted ten metres from dummy-half to score after less than three minutes of the second half but Lote Tuqiri replied with a try from a Cronk lob after a blatant forward pass from Lewis.

Lunt was denied a try when Clark sent the decision back to Archer for a ref's call, and he ruled that the Huddersfield player had been tackled short of the line. Burgess got his hand to a Robinson kick across the whitewash on the next play but was ruled offside. And then Sean O'Loughlin was held up over the line in a four-man tackle.

England ended their Four Nations on a winning but unconvincing note at Eden Park as Harlequins centre Tony Clubb scored four tries on his full Test debut. McNamara also gave Adrian Morley's replacement, Garreth Carvell, his first call-up of the tournament.

The Kumuls gave England the physical battle they were expecting, Kevin Brown, Sam Burgess and Luke Robinson all suffering game-ending injuries as McNamara was left with 14 fit men standing.

Robinson's nifty footwork left the PNG defence standing still as he shot in for the first try. England were almost immediately in again with a superb try. James Graham rampaged from the kick-off and spread the ball left to Tom Briscoe. The Hull winger was away and when stand-in fullback Jessie Joe Parker moved in for the tackle, Briscoe fed on to Clubb, who powered down the wing to score, Ben Westwood adding the extras.

On the half-hour mark Clubb scythed through the PNG defence for a dubious grounding and minutes later Robinson grabbed his second score, sprinting diagonally into the right corner from 20 metres out for an unconverted try. Sean O'Loughlin's quick pass allowed Clubb to score his hat-trick in the final minute of the first half.

After quarter of an hour of the second half Ben Harrison crossed under the posts, after

FOUR NATIONS - GAME 4

Sunday 31st October 2010

AUSTRALIA 34 ENGLAND 14

AUSTRALIA: 1 Billy Slater (Melbourne Storm); 2 Brett Morris (St George Illawarra Dragons); 3 Brent Tate (New Zealand Warriors); 4 Willie Tonga (North Queensland Cowboys); 5 Lote Tuqiri (Wests Tigers); 6 Darren Lockyer (Brisbane Broncos) (C); 7 Cooper Cronk (Melbourne Storm); 8 Nate Myles (Sydney Roosters); 9 Cameron Smith (Melbourne Storm); 10 Petero Civoniceva (Penrith Panthers); 11 Luke Lewis (Penrith Panthers); 12 Sam Thaiday (Brisbane Broncos) 13 Paul Gallen (Cronulla Sharks). Subs (all used): 14 David Shillington (Canberra Raiders); 15 Tom Learoyd-Lahrs (Canberra Raiders); 16 Anthony Watmough (Manly Sea Eagles); 17 Kurt Gidley (Newcastle Knights).
Tries: Lewis (4, 17), Slater (22), Tate (27), Tonga (30), Tuqiri (46);
Goals: Smith 5/7.
ENGLAND: 1 Sam Tomkins (Wigan Warriors); 2 Darrell Goulding (Wigan Warriors); 3 Leroy Cudjoe (Huddersfield Giants); 4 Ryan Atkins (Warrington Wolves); 5 Tom Briscoe (Hull FC); 6 Sean O'Loughlin (Wigan Warriors); 7 Luke Robinson (Huddersfield Giants); 8 Sam Burgess (South Sydney Rabbitohs); 9 James Roby (St Helens); 10 James Graham (St Helens) (C); 11 Gareth Ellis (Wests Tigers); 12 Joel Tomkins (Wigan Warriors); 13 Ben Westwood (Warrington Wolves). Subs (all used): 14 Stuart Fielden (Wigan Warriors); 15 Eorl Crabtree (Huddersfield Giants); 16 Ben Harrison (Warrington Wolves); 17 Shaun Lunt (Huddersfield Giants).
Tries: Burgess (8), Robinson (43); **Goals:** Westwood 2/2, Cudjoe 1/1.
Rugby Leaguer & League Express Men of the Match:
Australia: Luke Lewis; *England:* Sam Burgess.
Penalty count: 7-7; **Half-time:** 26-8; **Referee:** Tony Archer (Australia); **Attendance:** 18,894 *(at AAMI Park, Melbourne).*

a one-handed pass from the floor by Sam Tomkins. Westwood added the extras to bring up a 30-0 margin, but with England comfortably ahead and lacking substitutes, PNG found their way back into the game. Makali Aizue powered in under the posts before Glen Nami chipped through and re-gathered his own kick, Paul Aiton spreading the ball wide at speed to Menzie Yere, who crashed over the line.

England had one more try in them, as Clubb brushed aside two defenders from first receiver. Westwood's conversion rounded off the scoring.

Captain Darren Lockyer and fullback Billy Slater were rested but Australia never looked likely to lose the second game of the international double-header at Auckland's Eden Park. They led 34-10 midway through the second half before easing off and allowing a couple of late Kiwi tries, created by the wizardry of New Zealand captain Benji Marshall.

Sections of the Eden Park crowd booed during the Australian national anthem. Others threw rubbish at the visitors but it didn't take long for the Australians to show their dominance. Six-and-a-half minutes into the action, scrum-half Cooper Cronk fended Marshall and was across the stripe for the first try. After a penalty for a high tackle by Jeremy Smith, New Zealand surprisingly took a simple two points for a goal instead of searching for a try and moments later Paul Gallen and Brent Tate set up winger Brett Morris for his tenth try in eight Tests.

Minutes later Tate scored his own try. But the Kiwis fought back after some clever work from Marshall. Frank Pritchard scored a wonderful try by powering over stand-off Todd Carney, who was making his Test debut, days after being named International Player of the Year at the RLIF dinner!

After a punch-up between the smallest player on the pitch, New Zealand substitute hooker Issac Luke, and arguably the largest, Aussie prop David Shillington, English referee Richard Silverwood awarded the home side a penalty. Once again the Kiwis accepted the two points to go to the break trailing by eight.

Early in the second half Morris danced along the sideline before flinging a pass inside for Dragons teammate Darius Boyd to touch down. Then sub Robbie Farah put in a kick behind the tryline and his clubmate Chris Lawrence pounced to score on his international debut. Four minutes later Morris was in for his second try. But Marshall was not finished, setting up a tries for Jason Nightingale and Shaun Kenny-Dowall.

FOUR NATIONS - GAME 5

Saturday 6th November 2010

ENGLAND 36 PAPUA NEW GUINEA 10

ENGLAND: 1 Sam Tomkins (Wigan Warriors); 2 Ryan Hall (Leeds Rhinos); 3 Leroy Cudjoe (Huddersfield Giants); 4 Tony Clubb (Harlequins); 5 Tom Briscoe (Hull FC); 6 Kevin Brown (Huddersfield Giants); 7 Luke Robinson (Huddersfield Giants); 8 James Graham (St Helens) (C); 9 James Roby (St Helens); 10 Sam Burgess (South Sydney Rabbitohs); 11 Gareth Ellis (Wests Tigers); 12 Ben Westwood (Warrington Wolves); 13 Sean O'Loughlin (Wigan Warriors). Subs (all used): 14 Darrell Griffin (Huddersfield Giants); 15 Garreth Carvell (Warrington Wolves); 16 Ben Harrison (Warrington Wolves); 17 Gareth Widdop (Melbourne Storm).
Tries: Robinson (15, 36), Clubb (18, 30, 40, 76), Harrison (55);
Goals: Westwood 3/4, Widdop 1/3.
PAPUA NEW GUINEA: 1 Jessie Joe Parker (Port Moresby Vipers); 2 Michael Mark (Hunslet Hawks); 3 Elijah Riyong (Port Moresby Vipers); 4 Menzie Yere (Sheffield Eagles); 5 Richard Kambo (Newtown Jets); 6 Glen Nami (Goroka Lahanis); 7 Dion Aiye (Rabaul Gurias); 8 Makali Aizue (Halifax); 9 Charlie Wabo (Hunslet Hawks); 10 Nickson Kolo (Port Moresby Rangers); 11 Rodney Griffin (Northern Pride); 12 David Loko (Enga Mioks); 13 Paul Aiton (Cronulla Sharks) (C). Subs (all used): 14 Benjamin John (Parkes Spacemen); 15 George Moni (Rabaul Gurias); 16 Joseph Pombo (Canterbury Bulls); 17 Johnson Kuike (Port Moresby Rangers).
Tries: Aizue (57), Yere (65); **Goals:** Aiye 1/2.
Rugby Leaguer & League Express Men of the Match:
England: Tony Clubb; *Papua New Guinea:* Glen Nami.
Penalty count: 8-2; **Half-time:** 24-0; **Referee:** Shane Rehm (New Zealand); **Attendance:** 44,324 *(at Eden Park, Auckland).*

FOUR NATIONS - GAME 6

Saturday 6th November 2010

NEW ZEALAND 20 AUSTRALIA 34

NEW ZEALAND: 1 Lance Hohaia (New Zealand Warriors); 2 Jason Nightingale (St George Illawarra Dragons); 3 Shaun Kenny-Dowall (Sydney Roosters); 4 Junior Sa'u (Newcastle Knights); 5 Sam Perrett (Sydney Roosters); 6 Benji Marshall (Wests Tigers) (C); 7 Nathan Fien (St George Illawarra Dragons); 8 Frank-Paul Nuuausala (Sydney Roosters); 9 Thomas Leuluai (Wigan Warriors); 10 Adam Blair (Melbourne Storm); 11 Sika Manu (Melbourne Storm); 12 Simon Mannering (New Zealand Warriors); 13 Jeremy Smith (St George Illawarra Dragons). Subs (all used): 14 Issac Luke (South Sydney Rabbitohs); 15 Greg Eastwood (Leeds Rhinos); 16 Frank Pritchard (Penrith Panthers); 17 Ben Matulino (New Zealand Warriors).
Tries: Pritchard (29), Nightingale (64), Kenny-Dowall (77);
Goals: Marshall 4/5.
AUSTRALIA: 1 Darius Boyd (St George Illawarra Dragons); 2 Brett Morris (St George Illawarra Dragons); 3 Brent Tate (New Zealand Warriors); 4 Chris Lawrence (Wests Tigers); 5 Lote Tuqiri (Wests Tigers); 6 Todd Carney (Sydney Roosters); 7 Cooper Cronk (Melbourne Storm); 8 Matt Scott (North Queensland Cowboys); 9 Cameron Smith (Melbourne Storm) (C); 10 David Shillington (Canberra Raiders); 11 Greg Bird (Gold Coast Titans); 12 Sam Thaiday (Brisbane Broncos); 13 Paul Gallen (Cronulla Sharks). Subs (all used): 14 Dean Young (St George Illawarra Dragons); 15 Petero Civoniceva (Penrith Panthers); 16 Tom Learoyd-Lahrs (Canberra Raiders); 17 Robbie Farah (Wests Tigers).
Tries: Cronk (6), Morris (20, 58), Tate (23), Boyd (36), Lawrence (54);
Goals: Smith 3/4, Carney 2/2.
Rugby Leaguer & League Express Men of the Match:
New Zealand: Benji Marshall; *Australia:* Paul Gallen.
Penalty count: 7-7; **Half-time:** 10-18; **Referee:** Richard Silverwood (England); **Attendance:** 44,324 *(at Eden Park, Auckland).*

FOUR NATIONS - FINAL TABLE								
	P	W	D	L	F	A	D	Pts
Australia	3	3	0	0	110	34	76	6
New Zealand	3	2	0	1	120	56	64	4
England	3	1	0	2	60	68	-8	2
Papua New Guinea	3	0	0	3	22	154	-132	0

Four Nations

Two pieces of magic from captain Benji Marshall won the 2010 Four Nations for the Kiwis. With ten minutes of the final remaining, and the Australians ahead 12-6, the New Zealand captain put in a spinning kick along the ground, finding his unmarked teammate Jason Nightingale, who sped across the tryline to narrow the lead.

And although his conversion attempt bounced away off the right-hand upright, Marshall still had some tricks up his sleeve. With time running out, Marshall started a move from 40 metres out, sending Shaun Kenny-Dowall away down the right. The big centre sent Nightingale down the right touchline. He put a pass back to Marshall who, when collared on the tryline, flung the ball blindly over his left shoulder. Scrum-half Nathan Fien was trailing in support, and touched down for the winning try. There were just 93 seconds left on the clock. And it was the first time New Zealand had been in front all night.

The Kiwis had upset Australia in the final of a major international tournament for the third time in five years (having won the 2005 Tri-Nations and the 2008 World Cup, although the Aussies beat them in the Final of the 2006 Tri-Nations).

Australia took the lead when Darren Lockyer slipped a clever kick along the turf. New Zealand fullback Lance Hohaia was caught moving in the wrong direction, and his former Warriors teammate Brent Tate pounced and scored. The conversion by Cameron Smith put the Australians ahead 6-nil. But twenty-one minutes into the action Australian back-rower Luke Lewis was helped off the pitch and was out of the game for good. Australia also lost Tate with a knee injury at half-time.

Just before the break a slick move, with a pass from Marshall that appeared forward, gave Kenny-Dowall a clear run for the line to even the scores. A long-range field-goal attempt by Marshall as the siren was about to sound failed. But there was still time for an all-in brawl precipitated by props Adam Blair and David Shillington.

Two mistakes by the Kiwis cost them dearly midway through the second half. Young Warriors second-rower Ben Matulino lost the ball in a tackle, and then Smith conceded a penalty for going high on Greg Bird. A couple of tackles later Slater ran off a Greg Bird pass to score. And with a 12-6 lead the Australians were in the box seat, until Marshall's late interventions.

FOUR NATIONS - FINAL

Saturday 13th November 2010

AUSTRALIA 12 NEW ZEALAND 16

AUSTRALIA: 1 Billy Slater (Melbourne Storm); 2 Brett Morris (St George Illawarra Dragons); 3 Brent Tate (New Zealand Warriors); 4 Willie Tonga (North Queensland Cowboys); 5 Lote Tuqiri (Wests Tigers); 6 Darren Lockyer (Brisbane Broncos) (C); 7 Cooper Cronk (Melbourne Storm); 8 Matt Scott (North Queensland Cowboys); 9 Cameron Smith (Melbourne Storm); 10 David Shillington (Canberra Raiders); 11 Luke Lewis (Penrith Panthers); 12 Sam Thaiday (Brisbane Broncos); 13 Paul Gallen (Cronulla Sharks). Subs (all used): 14 Tom Learoyd-Lahrs (Canberra Raiders); 16 Greg Bird (Gold Coast Titans); 17 Kurt Gidley (Newcastle Knights); 18 Nate Myles (Sydney Roosters).
Tries: Tate (3), Slater (58); **Goals:** Smith 2/2.
NEW ZEALAND: 1 Lance Hohaia (New Zealand Warriors); 2 Jason Nightingale (St George Illawarra Dragons); 3 Shaun Kenny-Dowall (Sydney Roosters); 12 Simon Mannering (New Zealand Warriors); 5 Sam Perrett (Sydney Roosters); 6 Benji Marshall (Wests Tigers) (C); 7 Nathan Fien (St George Illawarra Dragons); 17 Sam McKendry (Penrith Panthers); 9 Thomas Leuluai (Wigan Warriors); 10 Adam Blair (Melbourne Storm); 11 Bronson Harrison (Canberra Raiders); 15 Ben Matulino (New Zealand Warriors); 13 Jeremy Smith (St George Illawarra Dragons). Subs (all used): 8 Greg Eastwood (Leeds Rhinos); 14 Issac Luke (South Sydney Rabbitohs); 16 Frank-Paul Nuuausala (Sydney Roosters); 18 Sika Manu (Melbourne Storm).
Tries: Kenny-Dowall (36), Nightingale (70), Fien (79);
Goals: Marshall 2/3.
Rugby Leaguer & League Express Men of the Match:
Australia: Sam Thaiday; *New Zealand:* Benji Marshall.
Penalty count: 5-8; **Half-time:** 6-6;
Referee: Tony Archer (Australia).
Attendance: 36,299 *(at Suncorp Stadium, Brisbane).*

Four Nations heroes Nathan Fien and Benji Marshall celebrate

OTHER INTERNATIONALS
Wales on the up

ALITALIA EUROPEAN CUP

Wales were winners of the 2010 European Cup, sponsored by Italian airline Alitalia, shocking France in a decider in Albi to win a place in the 2011 Four Nations tournament, to be staged in the UK.

A penalty from Lloyd White sealed the win for Wales right at the death after skipper Gareth Thomas and North Wales youngster Rhys Williams scored tries. 'The win shows how far we've come in such a short time. It's our biggest achievement ever,' was Wales Rugby League's Executive Chairman Mark Rowley's reaction.

Wales opened their European Cup account with a 60-22 win in Glasgow, inflicting a record home defeat on Scotland with 24 points in the last 12 minutes. Warrington winger Rhys Williams and Crusaders fullback Elliott Kear both scored hat-tricks, while, on his comeback three years after retiring from the international game, Lee Briers masterminded operations.

The day before, France laid down a marker with four tries from Olivier Elima helping France to an impressive 58-24 win over a defiant Ireland in front of over 14,000 sun-baked spectators in Avignon. Dragons stand-off Tony Gigot's deft offloads caused problems throughout, while Kane Bentley's direct running out of dummy half kept the visitors on the back foot. Up front, Jamal Fakir made his presence felt at prop and new Dragons signing, loose forward Jason Baitieri, on international debut, was rewarded for an industrious display with a try on the hour, while Remi Casty was a constant threat.

The following weekend Wales didn't look so convincing as they edged a 31-30 win over Ireland in a tense match in Neath. Wales certainly didn't have it all their own way at The Gnoll and it took a late field goal from Lee Briers to give the home side a seven-point cushion going into the final five minutes. It was a score the Welsh needed as Ireland fought back, with a final Gregg McNally try leading to a tense final 120 seconds.

ALITALIA EUROPEAN CUP

Saturday 9th October 2010

FRANCE 58 IRELAND 24

FRANCE: 1 Cyril Stacul (Catalans Dragons); 2 Frederic Vaccari (Catalans Dragons); 3 Jean-Phillipe Baile (Catalans Dragons); 4 Teddy Sadaoui (Carcassonne); 5 Vincent Duport (Toulouse Olympique); 6 Tony Gigot (Catalans Dragons); 7 Maxime Greseque (Pia); 8 Jamal Fakir (Catalans Dragons); 9 Kane Bentley (Catalans Dragons); 10 Remi Casty (Catalans Dragons); 11 Olivier Elima (Catalans Dragons) (C); 12 Julien Touxagas (Catalans Dragons); 13 Jason Baitieri (Sydney Roosters). Subs (all used): 14 Andrew Bentley (Catalans Dragons); 15 Mathieu Griffi (Toulouse Olympique); 16 Michael Simon (Catalans Dragons); 17 Nicolas Munoz (Lezignan).
Tries: Casty (10), Sadaoui (15), Stacul (19), Elima (23, 55, 76, 78), Gigot (42), A Bentley (50), Baitieri (61); **Goals:** Greseque 4/4, Munoz 5/6.
IRELAND: 1 Gregg McNally (Oldham); 2 Tim Bergin (Sheffield Eagles); 3 Simon Grix (Warrington Wolves); 4 Jamie O'Callaghan (Harlequins); 5 John Gillam (Oldham); 6 Scott Grix (Huddersfield Giants) (C); 7 Liam Finn (Featherstone Rovers); 8 Michael Haley (Sheffield Eagles); 9 Bob Beswick (Halifax); 10 Brett McDermott (Barrow Raiders); 11 Sean Hesketh (Batley Bulldogs); 12 Luke Ambler (Leeds Rhinos); 13 Matthew Fox (Wakefield Trinity Wildcats). Subs (all used): 14 Brendan Guilfoyle (Treaty City Titans); 15 Joe Taylor (North Dublin Eagles); 16 Wayne Kerr (Oldham); 17 Matt Ashe (Oldham).
Tries: Hesketh (7), Gillam (28, 69), O'Callaghan (31), McNally (71); **Goals:** McNally 1/4, Finn 1/1.
Rugby Leaguer & League Express Men of the Match:
France: Olivier Elima; *Ireland:* Scott Grix.
Penalty count: 7-7; **Half-time:** 24-14; **Referee:** Phil Bentham (England); **Attendance:** 14,522 *(at Parc Des Sports, Avignon).*

Sunday 10th October 2010

SCOTLAND 22 WALES 60

SCOTLAND: 1 Rob Lunt (Doncaster); 2 Jamie Benn (Castleford Panthers); 3 Joe Wardle (Huddersfield Giants); 4 Kevin Henderson (Wakefield Trinity Wildcats); 5 Jon Steel (Featherstone Rovers); 6 Brendon Lindsay (Sheffield Eagles); 7 Danny Brough (Huddersfield Giants) (C); 8 Oliver Wilkes (Harlequins); 9 Ben Fisher (Hull Kingston Rovers); 10 Mitchell Stringer (Sheffield Eagles); 11 Alex Szostak (Sheffield Eagles); 12 Sam Barlow (Halifax); 13 Dale Ferguson (Wakefield Trinity Wildcats). Subs (all used): 14 Andrew Henderson (Sheffield Eagles); 15 Neil Lowe (Hunslet Hawks); 16 Paddy Coupar (Workington Town); 17 Jack Howieson (Sheffield Eagles).
Tries: Fisher (10, 55), A Henderson (34, 37); **Goals:** Brough 3/4.
WALES: 1 Elliot Kear (Crusaders); 2 Rhys Williams (Warrington Wolves); 3 Christiaan Roets (South Wales Scorpions); 4 Gareth Thomas (Crusaders); 5 Mark Lennon (Cronulla Sharks); 6 Lee Briers (Warrington Wolves) (C); 7 Danny Jones (Keighley Cougars); 8 Jordan James (Crusaders); 9 Lloyd White (Crusaders); 10 Jacob Emmitt (St Helens); 11 Chris Beasley (Central Queensland Comets); 12 Aled James (South Wales Scorpions); 13 Ian Webster (Central Queensland Comets). Subs (all used): 14 Ben Flower (Crusaders); 15 Gil Dudson (Crusaders); 16 Jordan Ross (York City Knights); 17 Neil Budworth (Mackay Cutters).
Tries: Williams (7, 42, 71), Kear (14, 19, 68), Lennon (22), White (25), Thomas (44), Emmitt (75), J James (79); **Goals:** Briers 8/11.
Rugby Leaguer & League Express Men of the Match:
Scotland: Danny Brough; *Wales:* Lee Briers.
Penalty count: 4-6; **Half-time:** 18-26; **Referee:** Thierry Alibert (France); **Attendance:** 787 *(at Old Anniesland, Glasgow).*

127

ALITALIA EUROPEAN CUP

Saturday 16th October 2010

FRANCE 26 SCOTLAND 12

FRANCE: 1 William Barthau (Catalans Dragons); 2 Frederic Vaccari (Catalans Dragons); 3 Jean-Phillipe Baile (Catalans Dragons); 4 Teddy Sadaoui (Carcassonne); 5 Cyril Stacul (Catalans Dragons); 6 Tony Gigot (Catalans Dragons); 7 Nicolas Munoz (Lezignan); 8 Michael Simon (Catalans Dragons); 9 Kane Bentley (Catalans Dragons); 10 Remi Casty (Catalans Dragons); 11 Olivier Elima (Catalans Dragons) (C); 12 Julien Touxagas (Catalans Dragons); 13 Jason Baitieri (Sydney Roosters). Subs (all used): 14 Andrew Bentley (Catalans Dragons); 15 Mathieu Griffi (Toulouse Olympique); 16 Sebastien Martins (Catalans Dragons); 17 Romaric Bemba (Carcassonne).
Tries: Vaccari (11), Gigot (34), Martins (48), Simon (65), K Bentley (75); **Goals:** Munoz 3/5.
On report: Munoz (56) – alleged dangerous tackle.
SCOTLAND: 1 Lee Paterson (Carpentras); 2 Dave Arnot (London Skolars); 3 Joe Wardle (Bradford Bulls); 4 Kevin Henderson (Wakefield Trinity Wildcats); 5 Jon Steel (Featherstone Rovers); 6 Brendon Lindsay (Sheffield Eagles); 7 Danny Brough (Huddersfield Giants) (C); 8 Oliver Wilkes (Harlequins); 9 Ben Fisher (Hull Kingston Rovers); 10 Mitchell Stringer (Sheffield Eagles); 11 Alex Szostak (Sheffield Eagles); 12 Sam Barlow (Halifax); 13 Dale Ferguson (Wakefield Trinity Wildcats). Subs (all used): 14 Andrew Henderson (Sheffield Eagles); 15 Paddy Coupar (Workington Town); 16 Neil Lowe (Hunslet Hawks); 17 Jack Howieson (Sheffield Eagles).
Tries: Szostak (42), Barlow (70); **Goals:** Brough 2/2.
Rugby Leaguer & League Express Men of the Match:
France: Tony Gigot; *Scotland:* Sam Barlow.
Penalty count: 11-9; **Half-time:** 10-0; **Referee:** Phil Bentham (England); **Attendance:** 6,721 *(at Stadium Municipal, Albi).*

Sunday 17th October 2010

WALES 31 IRELAND 30

WALES: 1 Andrew Gay (South Wales Scorpions); 2 Mark Lennon (Cronulla Sharks); 3 Gareth Thomas (Crusaders); 4 Christiaan Roets (South Wales Scorpions); 5 Rhys Williams (Warrington Wolves); 6 Lee Briers (Warrington Wolves) (C); 7 Danny Jones (Keighley Cougars); 8 Jordan James (Crusaders); 9 Lloyd White (Crusaders); 10 Jacob Emmitt (St Helens); 11 Chris Beasley (Central Queensland Comets); 12 Aled James (South Wales Scorpions); 13 Ian Webster (Central Queensland Comets). Subs (all used): 14 Ben Flower (Crusaders); 15 Ross Divorty (Featherstone Rovers); 16 Jordan Ross (York City Knights); 17 Neil Budworth (Mackay Cutters).
Tries: Lennon (4, 31), Webster (39), Williams (58, 72), Roets (68); **Goals:** Briers 0/2, White 3/4; **Field goal:** Briers (74).
IRELAND: 1 Gregg McNally (Oldham); 2 Tim Bergin (Sheffield Eagles); 3 James Haley (Halifax); 4 Jamie O'Callaghan (Harlequins); 5 John Gillam (Oldham); 6 Scott Grix (Huddersfield Giants) (C); 7 Liam Finn (Featherstone Rovers); 8 Ryan Boyle (Salford City Reds); 9 Bob Beswick (Halifax); 10 Brett McDermott (Barrow Raiders); 11 Simon Finnigan (Huddersfield Giants); 12 Luke Ambler (Leeds Rhinos); 13 Matthew Fox (Wakefield Trinity Wildcats). Subs (all used): 14 Sean Hesketh (Batley Bulldogs); 15 Wayne Kerr (Oldham); 16 Matt Ashe (Oldham); 17 Joe Taylor (North Dublin Eagles).
Tries: Bergin (17), McNally (20), Boyle (46), Ambler (63), McNally (77); **Goals:** McNally 5/5.
Rugby Leaguer & League Express Men of the Match:
Wales: Lloyd White; *Ireland:* Gregg McNally.
Penalty count: 4-3; **Half-time:** 14-12; **Referee:** Thierry Alibert (France); **Attendance:** 2,165 *(at The Gnoll, Neath).*

ALITALIA EUROPEAN CUP

Saturday 23rd October 2010

FRANCE 11 WALES 12

FRANCE: 1 Cyril Stacul (Catalans Dragons); 2 Frederic Vaccari (Catalans Dragons); 3 Jean-Phillipe Baile (Catalans Dragons); 4 Teddy Sadaoui (Carcassonne); 5 Quentin Nauroy (St Esteve-XIII Catalan); 6 Tony Gigot (Catalans Dragons); 7 Nicolas Munoz (Lezignan); 8 Jamal Fakir (Catalans Dragons); 9 Kane Bentley (Catalans Dragons); 10 Remi Casty (Catalans Dragons); 11 Olivier Elima (Catalans Dragons) (C); 12 Michael Simon (Catalans Dragons); 13 Jason Baitieri (Sydney Roosters). Subs (all used): 14 Sebastien Martins (Catalans Dragons); 15 Mathieu Griffi (Toulouse Olympique); 16 Andrew Bentley (Catalans Dragons); 17 Yoan Tisseyre (Toulouse Olympique).
Tries: Nauroy (18), Sadaoui (67); **Goals:** Munoz 1/2; **Field goal:** Gigot (75).
WALES: 1 Elliot Kear (Crusaders); 2 Rhys Williams (Warrington Wolves); 3 Christiaan Roets (South Wales Scorpions); 4 Gareth Thomas (Crusaders) (C); 5 Mark Lennon (Cronulla Sharks); 6 Ian Webster (Central Queensland Comets); 7 Danny Jones (Keighley Cougars); 8 Jordan James (Crusaders); 9 Lloyd White (Crusaders); 10 Jacob Emmitt (St Helens); 11 Chris Beasley (Central Queensland Comets); 12 Aled James (South Wales Scorpions); 13 Ben Flower (Crusaders). Subs (all used): 14 Jordan Ross (York City Knights); 15 Ross Divorty (Featherstone Rovers); 16 Gil Dudson (Crusaders); 17 Neil Budworth (Mackay Cutters).
Tries: Williams (46), Thomas (61); **Goals:** White 2/3.
Rugby Leaguer & League Express Men of the Match:
France: Remi Casty; *Wales:* Lloyd White.
Penalty count: 10-8; **Half-time:** 4-0; **Referee:** Phil Bentham (England); **Attendance:** 10,416 *(at Stadium Municipal, Albi).*

Sunday 24th October 2010

IRELAND 22 SCOTLAND 42

IRELAND: 1 Gregg McNally (Oldham); 2 Tim Bergin (Sheffield Eagles); 3 James Haley (Halifax); 4 Jamie O'Callaghan (Harlequins); 5 John Gillam (Oldham); 6 Scott Grix (Huddersfield Giants) (C); 7 Liam Finn (Featherstone Rovers); 8 Ryan Boyle (Salford City Reds); 9 Bob Beswick (Halifax); 10 Brett McDermott (Barrow Raiders); 11 Simon Finnigan (Huddersfield Giants); 12 Simon Grix (Warrington Wolves); 13 Luke Ambler (Leeds Rhinos). Subs (all used): 14 Joe Taylor (North Dublin Eagles); 15 Wayne Kerr (Oldham); 16 Matt Ashe (Oldham); 17 Matthew Fox (Wakefield Trinity Wildcats).
Tries: Gillam (5, 65), Scott Grix (15), Finn (38); **Goals:** McNally 3/4.
SCOTLAND: 1 Brett Carter (Workington Town); 2 Dave Arnot (London Skolars); 3 Rob Lunt (Doncaster); 4 Kevin Henderson (Wakefield Trinity Wildcats); 5 Joe Wardle (Bradford Bulls); 6 Brendon Lindsay (Sheffield Eagles); 7 Lee Paterson (Carpentras); 8 Oliver Wilkes (Harlequins) (C); 9 Ben Fisher (Hull Kingston Rovers); 10 Mitchell Stringer (Sheffield Eagles); 11 Alex Szostak (Sheffield Eagles); 12 Sam Barlow (Halifax); 13 Dale Ferguson (Wakefield Trinity Wildcats). Subs (all used): 14 Andrew Henderson (Sheffield Eagles); 15 Neil Lowe (Hunslet Hawks); 16 Paddy Coupar (Workington Town); 17 Jack Howieson (Sheffield Eagles).
Tries: Fisher (10), K Henderson (42), A Henderson (48), Ferguson (50, 75), Carter (55), Stringer (63), Wardle (80); **Goals:** Lindsay 1/1, Paterson 4/7.
Rugby Leaguer & League Express Men of the Match:
Ireland: Scott Grix; *Scotland:* Dale Ferguson.
Penalty count: 7-7; **Half-time:** 18-4; **Referee:** Thierry Alibert (France); **Attendance:** 684 *(at Tallaght Stadium, Dublin).*

The game was finally sealed with 70 seconds remaining when Ireland's Tim Bergin fumbled a pass on the wing, giving Wales possession for the rest of the match. They almost went over for a further try but the hard-working Jordan James was held up over the line. "We've used our get out of jail free card if I'm honest," said Wales coach Iestyn Harris.

France duly overcame a spirited Scotland 26-12 to lead the group and set up a final clash with Wales. The French missed the presence of Maxime Grésèque and Jamal Fakir, as well as Vincent Duport, out for six months with a knee injury. Michael Simon's 65th-minute touchdown, followed by Kane Bentley's try ten minutes later, proved decisive in a match which Scotland never allowed to run away from them.

On the final Sunday of the three-week tournament, Scotland beat Ireland 42-22 at the impressive Tallaght Stadium just outside Dublin after a second-half comeback. Steve McCormack's Scots trailed by 18-4 at half-time but after the turnaround produced a point-a-minute barrage that left the Irish stunned. There were two tries from Wakefield loose forward Dale Ferguson.

On the Saturday in Albi, a dramatic Lloyd White penalty goal three minutes from full time gave Wales, without talismanic Lee Briers, who injured a knee the week before, the Alitalia European Cup and a place in the 2011 Four Nations.

When Cyril Stacul's half break was converted by Teddy Sadaoui into a debut try for young winger Quentin Nauroy, after Mark Lennon had been denied at the other end, the French held the upper hand. But faced with only a 4-0 half-time deficit, Iestyn Harris's men began to swing the balance of the game in their favour at the restart. White produced a skidding kick in midfield, picked up and the ball went via the supporting Elliot Kear and Danny Jones to Rhys Williams, who went in at the corner, White converting splendidly from touch to give Wales a 6-4 lead.

The French conceded a second try just after the hour when Gareth Thomas, captaining the side in only his seventeenth game of Rugby League and his first in France since switching codes, had a simple run-in after a fine handling move, White just missing the conversion.

Tony Gigot put France back in contention when his high kick to the corner was missed by Rhys Williams under pressure from Nauroy, and Sadaoui put the ball over the line, Nicolas Munoz converting brilliantly from touch to level the scores at 10-apiece.

As the action and the crowd became more frantic, a White field-goal attempt was disallowed for obstruction by one of his own players.

A minute later, and with five left on the clock, following an Elima break downfield, Gigot appeared to have turned the game France's way with a coolly-taken one-pointer. But as play moved back into the French half, Jamal Fakir committed a crucial indiscretion and was penalised for a tackle on Christiaan Roets after the ball had gone. White stepped up to drive home the match-winning 32-metre penalty.

ALITALIA EUROPEAN CUP - FINAL TABLE								
	P	W	D	L	F	A	D	Pts
Wales	3	3	0	0	103	63	40	6
France	3	2	0	1	95	46	49	4
Scotland	3	1	0	2	76	108	-32	2
Ireland	3	0	0	3	74	131	-57	0

GILLETTE FUSION INTERNATIONAL

Under-strength France were never a threat to England at the Leigh Sports Village in June but the Gillette Fusion International gave new England coach Steve McNamara the chance to trial new combinations. Melbourne fullback Gareth Widdop, who had emigrated to Australia from Halifax as a teenager, produced some great link-ups with man of the match Sam Tomkins, Tomkins scoring a record-equalling four tries, all of them in the first half and including a brilliant spell of three in seven minutes just before the break.

Widdop was joined in jetting in from Australia by forward duo Sam Burgess and Gareth Ellis, who both showed how they had been taking the NRL by storm, and there was also an eye-catching performance from Chris Bridge at right centre that culminated in a deserved second-half try.

ENGLAND: 1 Gareth Widdop (Melbourne Storm); 2 Tom Briscoe (Hull FC); 3 Chris Bridge (Warrington Wolves); 4 Michael Shenton (Castleford Tigers); 5 Ryan Hall (Leeds Rhinos); 6 Kevin Brown (Huddersfield Giants); 7 Sam Tomkins (Wigan Warriors); 8 Jamie Peacock (Leeds Rhinos); 9 Kevin Sinfield (Leeds Rhinos) (C); 10 James Graham (St Helens); 11 Gareth Ellis (Wests Tigers); 12 Sam Burgess (South Sydney Rabbitohs); 13 Sean O'Loughlin (Wigan Warriors). Subs (all used): 14 James Roby (St Helens); 15 Adrian Morley (Warrington Wolves); 16 Joel Tomkins (Wigan Warriors); 17 Ben Westwood (Warrington Wolves). **Tries:** Widdop (2), Briscoe (6), S Tomkins (14, 31, 35, 38), Shenton (55, 78), Ellis (68, 75), Bridge (71); **Goals:** Sinfield 6/7, Widdop 2/4.
FRANCE: 1 Constant Villegas (Toulouse Olympique); 2 Nicolas Piquemal (Lezignan); 3 Cyrille Gossard (Catalans Dragons); 4 Sebastien Raguin (Catalans Dragons); 5 Frederic Vaccari (Catalans Dragons); 6 Tony Gigot (Catalans Dragons); 7 Nicolas Munoz (Lezignan); 8 David Ferriol (Catalans Dragons); 9 Gregory Mounis (Catalans Dragons); 10 Remi Casty (Catalans Dragons); 11 Olivier Elima (Catalans Dragons) (C); 12 Jamal Fakir (Catalans Dragons); 13 Andrew Bentley (Catalans Dragons). Subs (all used): 14 Julien Touxagas (Catalans Dragons); 15 Mathieu Griffi (Toulouse Olympique); 16 Michael Simon (Catalans Dragons); 17 William Barthau (Catalans Dragons).
Try: Bentley (18); **Goals:** Mounis 1/1.
Sin bin: Villegas (68) - professional foul.
Rugby Leaguer & League Express Men of the Match:
England: Sam Tomkins; *France:* Remi Casty.
Penalty count: 7-4; **Half-time:** 34-6; **Referee:** Leon Williamson (New Zealand); **Attendance:** 7,951 *(at Leigh Sports Village).*

Bobbie Goulding's French side had the game's first attack, following an early Sean O'Loughlin error when he tried to get a pass out of a tackle, but it petered out when Tony Gigot lost possession. England punished them with a try in the very next set. Kevin Brown's wide pass launched Burgess, whose terrific back-hand flick released Bridge down the right. Widdop supported on his left shoulder to score a try with his first touch in an England shirt.

His second touch created the next home try four minutes later, as Brown and Widdop linked at speed to send Tom Briscoe over in the right corner. Kevin Sinfield converted from the touchline to make it 12-0. Widdop was heavily involved in the third try on 14 minutes. After Burgess bumped David Ferriol with apparent ease, the Melbourne fullback accelerated through a gap, and quick hands from Bridge sent Sam Tomkins racing over under the posts.

But France then found a response, after a second O'Loughlin knock-on and penalty for interference, as Remi Casty's smart pass sent Andrew Bentley over by the posts. But the

French resistance was ended when Sam Tomkins virtually crawled over the line for his second try, and Widdop converted, with Sinfield having been replaced by James Roby at hooker.

Tomkins completed a first half hat-trick when he took brother Joel's smart offload and scampered over in the corner and his fourth try was the pick. The Wigan halfback started it by chipping over the defence on halfway for Widdop, who in Billy Slater style collected and kicked again immediately, allowing Tomkins to collect and beat three French defenders to score.

After the break it took another moment of Sam Tomkins brilliance to stir England, as he took an Adrian Morley offload, accelerated through a gap, and sent Michael Shenton over out wide. It took a French sin-binning to see the French defence crack again. Fullback Constant Villegas was the man in question, binned by Kiwi referee Leon Williamson after tripping Bridge, on his way to a spectacular try after breaking down the right and then side-stepping the Toulouse man. Seconds later Tomkins' pass sent Gareth Ellis over.

That prompted another spurt of scoring, as Bridge got the try his performance warranted as he took a pass from clubmate Ben Westwood to race over out wide.

Ellis then grabbed his second, attacking the French line and beating three defenders to score, while Shenton completed his own second-half double from Brown's pass in the closing stages.

THE GARRY PURDHAM MEMORIAL GAME

England struggled to a draw in their warm-up match the day before the Four Nations squad was finalised in a game played at Whitehaven's Recreation Ground in memory of Garry Purdham.

The England team was missing players from the Wigan, St Helens, Leeds and Huddersfield sides that contested the final weeks of the Super League play-offs and only six out of the 17 who wore an England jersey in Cumbria were selected the next day in Steve McNamara's final squad.

Harlequins' Tony Clubb went over from close range after running onto a short pass from Mickey Higham to open the scoring on 12 minutes. Ben Westwood added the extras. But Leeds Rhinos rookie Kyle Amor delighted the crowd when he made a strong charge at the line and stretched out to score. Garry's brother Rob Purdham added the extras to level things before Garreth Carvell forced his way over under the posts before the break, Westwood again converting.

Cumbria started the second half as they'd finished the first, fierce, committed and focussed, and were rewarded for their endeavour with a fairytale try from the only amateur in the team, John-Paul Brocklebank, from Garry's former amateur club Egremont Rangers. Gregg McNally converted to level the scores.

England responded and Chris Riley broke in centre field, only to be stopped just short of the line. But as Cumbria struggled to re-organise, Richie Myler squeezed himself

THE GARRY PURDHAM MEMORIAL GAME

Sunday 3rd October 2010

CUMBRIA 18 ENGLAND 18

CUMBRIA: 1 Gary Broadbent (Barrow Raiders); 2 Ade Gardner (St Helens); 3 Jason Mossop (Workington Town); 4 Scott McAvoy (Whitehaven); 5 Will Sharp (Harlequins); 13 Rob Purdham (Harlequins) (C); 7 Liam Campbell (Barrow Raiders); 8 Ewan Dowes (Hull FC); 9 Jack Pedley (Workington Town); 10 Kyle Amor (Leeds Rhinos/Whitehaven) *; 11 Brett McDermott (Barrow Raiders); 12 Spencer Miller (Whitehaven); 6 Oliver Wilkes (Harlequins). Subs (all used): 15 Howard Hill (Whitehaven); 14 Kris Coward (Workington Town); 21 Gregg McNally (Oldham); 17 Jamie Butler (Workington Town); 27 John-Paul Brocklebank (Egremont Rangers); 22 Aaron Low (Workington Town); 20 Neil Frazer (Workington Town).
Tries: Amor (17), Brocklebank (46), McAvoy (70);
Goals: Purdham 1/1, McNally 2/2.
ENGLAND: 1 Chris Riley (Warrington Wolves); 2 Peter Fox (Hull Kingston Rovers); 3 Michael Shenton (Castleford Tigers); 4 Tony Clubb (Harlequins); 5 Tom Briscoe (Hull FC); 6 Paul Sykes (Bradford Bulls); 7 Richard Myler (Warrington Wolves); 8 Andy Lynch (Bradford Bulls) (C); 9 Mick Higham (Warrington Wolves); 10 Louie McCarthy-Scarsbrook (Harlequins); 11 Joe Westerman (Castleford Tigers); 12 Ben Westwood (Warrington Wolves); 13 Jamie Langley (Bradford Bulls). Subs (all used): 14 Ryan Atkins (Warrington Wolves); 15 Garreth Carvell (Warrington Wolves); 16 Nick Scruton (Bradford Bulls); 17 Ben Harrison (Warrington Wolves); 18 Scott Murrell (Hull Kingston Rovers); 19 Jodie Broughton (Salford City Reds).
Tries: Clubb (12), Carvell (36), Myler (70);
Goals: Westwood 2/2, Myler 1/1.
Rugby Leaguer & League Express Men of the Match:
Cumbria: Rob Purdham; *England:* Ben Westwood.
Penalty count: 10-8; **Half-time:** 6-12; **Referee:** Phil Bentham;
Attendance: 5,250 *(at The Recreation Ground, Whitehaven).*

* Dual registered player

between two defenders and crossed for England's third score, which he converted himself.

The equalising score came on the 70th minute as Whitehaven's Scott McAvoy broke from half way and beat Chris Riley on the outside. The conversion from the touchline was required to level things up, and McNally duly obliged.

ANZAC TEST

Melbourne's latest field of dreams – the $270 million AAMI Park stadium – was packed to the rafters for its opening night. And although the action on the pitch never quite lived up to the spectacular surroundings, the fans came away contented as Australia accounted for the Kiwis in the dour struggle. It was Australia's ninth straight victory in the traditional mid-season confrontation between the Trans-Tasman neighbours.

It looked close on the scoreboard, but in reality the Australians never looked likely to lose the match after leading 6-nil at the break and 12-nil soon after play resumed in the second half.

New Zealand's coach Stephen Kearney succinctly summed up his

ANZAC TEST

Friday 7th May 2010

AUSTRALIA 12 NEW ZEALAND 8

AUSTRALIA: 1 Billy Slater (Melbourne Storm); 2 Brett Morris (St George Illawarra Dragons); 3 Greg Inglis (Melbourne Storm); 4 Jamie Lyon (Manly Sea Eagles); 5 Jarryd Hayne (Parramatta Eels); 6 Darren Lockyer (Brisbane Broncos) (C); 7 Cooper Cronk (Melbourne Storm); 8 Petero Civoniceva (Penrith Panthers); 9 Cameron Smith (Melbourne Storm); 10 David Shillington (Canberra Raiders); 11 Luke Lewis (Penrith Panthers); 12 Sam Thaiday (Brisbane Broncos); 13 Paul Gallen (Cronulla Sharks). Subs (all used): 14 Kurt Gidley (Newcastle Knights); 15 Josh Perry (Manly Sea Eagles); 16 Anthony Watmough (Manly Sea Eagles); 17 Michael Weyman (St George Illawarra Dragons). **Tries:** Morris (39, 47); **Goals:** Lyon 2/3.
NEW ZEALAND: 1 Lance Hohaia (New Zealand Warriors); 2 Sam Perrett (Sydney Roosters); 3 Junior Sa'u (Newcastle Knights); 4 Steve Matai (Manly Sea Eagles); 5 Jason Nightingale (St George Illawarra Dragons); 6 Benji Marshall (Wests Tigers) (C); 7 Kieran Foran (Manly Sea Eagles); 8 Frank-Paul Nuuausala (Sydney Roosters); 9 Issac Luke (South Sydney Rabbitohs); 10 Sam Rapira (New Zealand Warriors); 11 Bronson Harrison (Canberra Raiders); 12 Zeb Taia (Newcastle Knights); 13 Adam Blair (Melbourne Storm). Subs (all used): 14 Aaron Heremaia (New Zealand Warriors); 15 Sika Manu (Melbourne Storm); 16 Jared Waerea-Hargreaves (Sydney Roosters); 17 Ben Matulino (New Zealand Warriors). **Tries:** Nightingale (68), Sa'u (78); **Goals:** Luke 0/2.
On report: Matai (38) – alleged late tackle on Slater.
Rugby Leaguer & League Express Men of the Match:
Australia: Greg Inglis; *New Zealand:* Bronson Harrison.
Half-time: 6-0; **Referee:** Richard Silverwood (England); **Attendance:** 29,442 *(at AAMI Park, Melbourne).*

players efforts: "Very good, but not good enough! We hung in there well but we got little reward."

It was a tough, uncompromising first half played in driving rain. The Kiwis showed early spirit and when Australian winger Jarryd Hayne fumbled a bomb he set the scene for the ball to travel almost the length of the pitch. Eventually the attack broke down.

Some 14 minutes into the action Australian centre Greg Inglis split the Kiwis' defence with a long run but was grassed by fullback Lance Hohaia. From the following play-the-ball Hohaia was the saviour, scooping a rolling ball over the dead-ball line.

Twice in the first half the Kiwis had the Australians stuck close their own line, but the New Zealanders gave away stupid penalties. Penalties late in the half allowed Australia to sneak ahead at the break. Adam Blair was penalised and former Man of Steel Jamie Lyon, back in the Test side, potted a two-pointer. Then Steve Matai laid out Billy Slater with a late tackle and was placed on report. (Match officials later decided to take no action against him). Less than a minute after Matai's tackle, Darren Lockyer put in a clever, low kick for a speeding Brett Morris to beat everyone to the ball and score.

There was more to come. Early in the second half another silly penalty conceded by the Kiwis, this time by Ben Matulino, gave the Aussies a sniff. When the rampaging second-rower Sam Thaiday got caught close to the tryline he tossed an overhead pass to Morris, who was over for his eighth try in six Tests.

To their credit the Kiwis refused to surrender. After some long passes across the backline by Marshall and Hohaia, the Dragons' winger Jason Nightingale went over for New Zealand's first try. Newcastle's centre Junior Sa'u cut the deficit with a clever try. Sadly for the Kiwis, with less than two minutes remaining on the clock, it proved to be too little, too late.

However Australia's coach Tim Sheen still had a nervous final couple of minutes. With just 80 seconds left Sam Perrett dashed down the right flank, only to graze the touchline as he looked an outside chance of scoring in the corner.

Other Internationals

FOUR NATIONS - WARM-UP GAMES

Saturday 16th October 2010

NEW ZEALAND MAORI 18 ENGLAND 18

MAORI: 1 Kevin Locke (New Zealand Warriors); 2 Sandor Earl (Penrith Panthers); 3 Timana Tahu (Parramatta Eels); 4 Clinton Toopi (Gold Coast Titans) (C); 5 Kaine Manihera (Northern Pride); 6 Arana Taumata (North Queensland Cowboys); 7 Rangi Chase (Castleford Tigers); 8 James Tamou (North Queensland Cowboys); 9 Aaron Heremaia (New Zealand Warriors); 10 Russell Packer (New Zealand Warriors); 11 Weller Hauraki (Crusaders); 12 Justin Horo (Parramatta Eels); 13 Bodene Thompson (Gold Coast Titans). Subs (all used): 14 Jeremy Smith (Salford City Reds); 15 Kevin Proctor (Melbourne Storm); 16 Sam McKendry (Penrith Panthers); 17 Lewis Brown (New Zealand Warriors). **Tries:** Thompson (52), Heremaia (63), Taumata (70); **Goals:** Locke 3/4.
ENGLAND: 1 Gareth Widdop (Melbourne Storm); 2 Tom Briscoe (Hull FC); 3 Michael Shenton (Castleford Tigers); 4 Ryan Atkins (Warrington Wolves); 5 Ryan Hall (Leeds Rhinos); 6 Kevin Brown (Huddersfield Giants); 7 Sam Tomkins (Wigan Warriors); 8 Adrian Morley (Warrington Wolves) (C); 9 James Roby (St Helens); 10 Darrell Griffin (Huddersfield Giants); 11 Gareth Ellis (Wests Tigers); 12 Sam Burgess (South Sydney Rabbitohs); 13 Sean O'Loughlin (Wigan Warriors). Subs (all used): 14 Luke Robinson (Huddersfield Giants); 15 Eorl Crabtree (Huddersfield Giants); 16 Joel Tomkins (Wigan Warriors); 17 Ben Westwood (Warrington Wolves).
Tries: Atkins (21), S Tomkins (27), O'Loughlin (40); **Goals:** Widdop 3/3.
Rugby Leaguer & League Express Men of the Match:
Maori: Rangi Chase; *England:* Luke Robinson.
Penalty count: 8-6; **Half-time:** 0-18; **Referee:** Leon Williamson (New Zealand); **Attendance:** 11,650 *(at Mt Smart Stadium, Auckland).*

NEW ZEALAND 50 SAMOA 6

NEW ZEALAND: 1 Lance Hohaia (New Zealand Warriors); 2 Jason Nightingale (St George Illawarra Dragons); 3 Shaun Kenny-Dowall (Sydney Roosters); 4 Junior Sa'u (Newcastle Knights); 5 Manu Vatuvei (New Zealand Warriors); 6 Benji Marshall (Wests Tigers) (C); 7 Thomas Leuluai (Wigan Warriors); 8 Greg Eastwood (Leeds Rhinos); 9 Issac Luke (South Sydney Rabbitohs); 10 Adam Blair (Melbourne Storm); 11 Frank Pritchard (Penrith Panthers); 12 Bronson Harrison (Canberra Raiders); 13 Jeremy Smith (St George Illawarra Dragons). Subs (all used): 14 Nathan Fien (St George Illawarra Dragons); 15 Ben Matulino (New Zealand Warriors); 16 Simon Mannering (New Zealand Warriors); 17 Sika Manu (Melbourne Storm).
Tries: Kenny-Dowall (5, 22), Nightingale (35), Marshall (38), Fien (50), Leuluai (60), Vatuvei (61, 71), Hohaia (69), Pritchard (74);
Goals: Luke 3/5, Marshall 2/5.
SAMOA: 1 Quentin Togaga'e (Souths Logan Magpies); 2 Francis Meli (St Helens); 3 George Carmont (Wigan Warriors); 4 Frank Winterstein (Crusaders); 5 Willie Isa (Melbourne Storm); 6 Joseph Paulo (Penrith Panthers); 7 Pita Godinet (Auckland Vulcans); 8 Tony Puletua (St Helens) (C); 9 Masada Iosefa (Penrith Panthers); 10 Mark Taufua (Newcastle Knights); 11 Harrison Hansen (Wigan Warriors); 12 David Solomona (Warrington Wolves); 13 David Faiumu (Huddersfield Giants). Subs (all used): 14 Josh McGuire (Brisbane Broncos); 15 Ali Lauitiiti (Leeds Rhinos); 16 Terrence Seu Seu (Manly Sea Eagles); 17 Con Mika (Newcastle Knights).
Try: Godinet (78); **Goals:** Paulo 1/1.
Rugby Leaguer & League Express Men of the Match:
New Zealand: Benji Marshall; *Samoa:* George Carmont.
Penalty count: 0-4; **Half-time:** 16-0; **Referee:** Shane Rehm (New Zealand); **Attendance:** 11,650 *(at Mt Smart Stadium, Auckland).*

INTERNATIONAL FRIENDLY

Wednesday 6th October 2010

WALES 6 ITALY 13

WALES: 1 Andrew Gay (South Wales Scorpions); 2 Ashley Bateman (South Wales Scorpions); 3 Lewis Reece (South Wales Scorpions); 4 Gareth Thomas (Crusaders); 5 Lee Williams (South Wales Scorpions); 6 Danny Jones (Keighley Cougars); 7 Ian Watson (Swinton Lions) (C); 8 Gil Dudson (Crusaders); 9 Steve Parry (South Wales Scorpions); 10 Ben Flower (Crusaders); 11 Lewis Mills (Crusaders); 12 Jordan Ross (York City Knights); 13 Geraint Davies (South Wales Scorpions). Subs (all used): 14 Rhodri Lloyd (Crusaders); 15 Harri Greville (South Wales Scorpions); 16 Joe Burke (South Wales Scorpions); 17 Chris Davies (Crusaders); 18 Mark Wool (Leeds Rhinos); 19 Dafydd Carter (Crusaders); 20 Jack Pring (Crusaders).
Try: Thomas (9); **Goals:** Reece 1/1.
ITALY: 1 Dominic Nasso (Parramatta Eels); 2 Josh Mantellato (Newcastle Rebels); 3 Rob Quitadamo (XIII del Ducato); 4 Domenico Brunetta (Grifons Padova); 5 Christophe Caligari (Palau); 6 Ben Stewart (Windsor Wolves); 7 Rhys Lenarduzzi (Sydney Roosters); 8 Andrew Kaleopa (Cabramatta); 9 Raymond Nasso (Windsor Wolves); 10 Ryan Tramonte (Windsor Wolves); 11 Dean Vicelich (Leoni Veneti); 12 Rocky Trimarchi (Crusaders) (C); 13 Ben Falcone (Wests Tigers). Subs: 14 Alessandro Cuomo (XIII del Ducato) (not used); 15 Marcelo Segundo (XIII del Ducato); 16 Matt Sands (Grifons Padova); 17 Fabio Nannini (XIII del Ducato); 18 Jonathan Marcinczak (West Bowling); 19 Liam Zollo (Grifons Padova); 20 Mauro Fusaro (Leoni Veneti) (not used).
Tries: Caligari (34), Falcone (59); **Goals:** Mantellato 2/2; **Field goal:** Stewart (79).
Rugby Leaguer & League Express Men of the Match:
Wales: Andrew Gay; *Italy:* Christophe Caligari.
Penalty count: 5-3; **Half-time:** 6-6; **Referee:** Ben Thaler (England); **Attendance:** 2,971 *(at The Racecourse Ground, Wrexham).*

INTERNATIONAL FRIENDLY

Sunday 24th October 2010

SAMOA 22 TONGA 6

SAMOA: 1 Quentin Togaga'e (Souths Logan Magpies); 2 Francis Meli (St Helens); 3 George Carmont (Wigan Warriors); 4 Frank Winterstein (Crusaders); 5 Tanelu Pasene (Lions); 6 Ben Roberts (Canterbury Bulldogs); 7 Pita Godinet (Auckland Vulcans); 8 Tony Puletua (St Helens) (C); 9 Masada Iosefa (Penrith Panthers); 10 Mark Taufua (Newcastle Knights); 11 Harrison Hansen (Wigan Warriors); 12 David Solomona (Warrington Wolves); 13 Joseph Paulo (Penrith Panthers). Subs (all used): 14 Josh McGuire (Brisbane Broncos); 15 Ali Lauitiiti (Leeds Rhinos); 16 Terrence Seu Seu (Manly Sea Eagles); 17 Con Mika (Newcastle Knights).
Tries: Iosefa (34), Puletua (48), Togaga'e (62), Carmont (69);
Goals: Roberts 0/1, Godinet 3/4.
TONGA: 1 Etu Uasele (Wenthworthville Magpies); 2 Atelea Okati (Bombers); 3 Sione Lousi (New Zealand Warriors); 4 Sione Tonga (Junee); 5 Fetongi Tunauvai (Auckland Vulcans); 6 Feleti Mateo (Parramatta Eels) (C); 7 Eddie Paea (North Sydney Bears); 8 Mickey Paea (Canterbury Bulldogs); 9 Tevita Leo-Latu (Wakefield Trinity Wildcats); 10 Epalahame Lauaki (Hull FC); 11 Ukuma Ta'ai (New Zealand Warriors); 12 Richard Fa'aoso (Newcastle Knights); 13 Andrew Fifita (Wests Tigers). Subs (all used): 14 Alai Taufa'ao (Newcastle Knights); 15 Sam Moa (Hull FC); 16 Ronnie Alovilli (Gold Coast Titans); 17 Siosaia Vave (Cronulla Sharks).
Try: Fa'aoso (26); **Goals:** E Paea 1/1.
Rugby Leaguer & League Express Men of the Match:
Samoa: George Carmont; *Tonga:* Richard Fa'aoso.
Penalty count: 6-8; **Half-time:** 6-6; **Referee:** Richard Silverwood (England); **Attendance:** 11,308 *(at Parramatta Stadium).*

REPRESENTATIVE GAME

Sunday 26th September 2010

PAPUA NEW GUINEA 18 AUSTRALIAN PRIME MINISTER'S XIII 30

PAPUA NEW GUINEA: 1 Ryan Tongia (Gold Coast Titans); 2 Michael Mark (Hunslet Hawks); 3 Jessie Joe Parker (Port Moresby Vipers); 4 Larsen Marabe (Rabaul Gurias); 5 Elijah Riyong (Port Moresby Vipers); 6 Dion Aiye (Rabaul Gurias); 7 Benjamin John (Parkes Spacemen); 8 George Moni (Rabaul Gurias); 9 Paul Aiton (Cronulla Sharks) (C); 10 Rodney Pora (Rabaul Gurias); 11 Rodney Griffin (Northern Pride); 12 Sigfred Gande (Rabaul Gurias); 13 Glen Nami (Goroka Lahanis). Subs (all used): 14 Charlie Wabo (Hunslet Hawks); 15 Tony Dai (Goroka Lahanis); 16 Andrew Sam (Mendi Muruks); 17 Pidi Tongap (Rabaul Gurias); 18 Desmond Mok (Ipswich Jets); 19 Johnson Kuike (Port Moresby Rangers); 20 Joseph Pombo (Canterbury Bulls); 21 Nickson Kolo (Port Moresby Rangers).
Tries: Kolo 2, Nami; **Goals:** Tongia 3.
PRIME MINISTER'S XIII: 1 Matt Bowen (North Queensland Cowboys); 2 Akuila Uate (Newcastle Knights); 3 Blake Ferguson (Cronulla Sharks); 4 Willie Tonga (North Queensland Cowboys); 5 Tony Williams (Manly Sea Eagles); 6 James Maloney (New Zealand Warriors); 7 Chris Sandow (South Sydney Rabbitohs); 8 Luke Douglas (Cronulla Sharks); 9 Michael Ennis (Canterbury Bulldogs); 10 Tim Mannah (Parramatta Eels); 11 Matt Gillett (Brisbane Broncos); 12 Ben Smith (Parramatta Eels); 13 Corey Parker (Brisbane Broncos) (C). Subs (all used): 14 Anthony Watts (North Queensland Cowboys); 15 Dave Taylor (South Sydney Rabbitohs); 16 Kade Snowden (Cronulla Sharks), 17 Chris Bailey (Manly Sea Eagles); 18 Micheal Luck (New Zealand Warriors).
Tries: Smith, Uate, Sandow, Tonga, Snowden, Douglas; **Goals:** Parker 2, Maloney.
Rugby Leaguer & League Express Men of the Match:
Papua New Guinea: Rodney Griffin; *Prime Minister's XIII:* Akuila Uate.
Half-time: 0-4; **Referee:** Tony De Las Heras (Australia); **Attendance:** 10,586 *(at Lloyd Robson Oval, Port Moresby).*

RLEF EUROPEAN SHIELD (WEST)	RLEF EUROPEAN BOWL	22 September, Monselice
		Italy 1 Lebanon 16
26 June 2010	*4 June 2010*	
Czech Republic 4	Malta 30 Norway 20	*25 September, Padova*
Serbia 56	*at Victor Tedesco Stadium, Hamrun*	Italy 24 Lebanon 16
at RK Petrovice, Prague		*3 October, Tripoli*
3 July 2010		Lebanon 30 Pakistan 10
Serbia 40 Germany 14	**2010 - OTHER INTERNATIONALS**	
at FK Radnicki Stadium, Belgrade		*6 October, Tripoli*
	1 June, Apia	Lebanon 28 Palestine 0
17 July 2010	Samoa 4 Fiji 24	
Germany 96		**NORDIC CUP**
Czech Republic 0	*10 July, Prague*	
at Hochsper, Kaiserslautern	Czech Republic 16	*20 November,*
	Catalonia 66	*Gothenburg*
RLEF EUROPEAN SHIELD (EAST)		Sweden 20 Norway 20
	31 July, Pretoria	
	South Africa 6	**FRIENDLIES**
27 June 2010	GB Community Lions under-18s 36	
Russia 62 Ukraine 14		*16 October, Ipswich, Qld*
at Dinamo Stadium, Moscow	*22 August, Hunslet*	Ipswich Jets 26
	Great Britain Community	Papua New Guinea 50
31 July 2010	Lions 50 Jamaica 22	
Latvia 4 Russia 54		*16 October, Sydney*
at Upezhtsiems Stadium, Riga	**COLONIAL CUP**	Fiji 16
		Bundaberg Cup Select 22
18 September 2010	*9 September,*	
Ukraine 112 Latvia 0	*Kingston, Ontario*	*16 October, Tamworth,*
at Arsenal Stadium, Kiev	Canada 16 USA 22	*NSW*
		Cook Islands 26
		NSW Country Select 22

* In April it was announced the 2013 World Cup would involve 14 sides compared to the ten that took part in 2008. Wales and the Cook Islands were thought likely to be the two nations to join the ten sides that played in 2008 as the automatic qualifiers of the competition, to be held in the UK. Two nations would have to qualify, one from among Italy, Serbia, Russia and Lebanon, and one from America, Jamaica and South Africa.

SEASON DOWN UNDER
Seven up for supercoach

If ever there were any doubts about the genius of Wayne Bennett, the super coach certainly dispelled them in 2010, steering St George Illawarra Dragons to their first Premiership since the merger in 1999. It was also 31 years since the old St George club had won a grand final. And the Illawarra Steelers never managed to win even one.

This year's success came just four years after Bennett had engineered his sixth grand final success with the Brisbane Broncos. His harshest critics reckoned he would never make the podium with another club because the Broncos had the 'unfair' advantage of being able to draw on most of the young talent in Queensland.

When he took over from Huddersfield Giants mentor Nathan Brown at the start of 2009 he had to change the whole Dragons psyche. Their detractors labelled them chokers and the players were starting to believe the criticism.

"These guys have suffered a fair bit of pain here," said Bennett. "It's been deep. It was deeper than I thought it was, to the point where they questioned themselves...whether they were the problem. I assured them they weren't part of the problem but they were part of the solution."

And they found the solution against the Sydney Roosters in front of 82,334 fans at the Olympic stadium in Homebush on a wet October evening. There was plenty of controversy in the first half when a try to Saints centre Mark Gasnier was answered by tries to the Roosters' second-row pairing of Braith Anasta and Mitch Aubusson. But the 8-6 half-time lead was as good as it got for the Roosters.

Bennett had introduced Kiwi Test hooker Nathan Fien from the bench just before the break and he almost immediately had the Dragons on the front foot. And the likes of fullback Darius Boyd and winger Jason Nightingale relished the extra space. The Dragons ran in four unanswered tries in the second spell to score a one-sided 32-8 victory. Boyd won the Clive Churchill Medal as man of the match.

It wasn't a pretty victory, but typical of the tactics that had characterised the St George Illawarra displays all season. The critics moaned, but the Dragons' no-frills style of play won them 20 of their 27 matches, including the one that really counted.

At the other end of the NRL Ladder was Melbourne Storm, who had won the previous year's grand final. They were handed the wooden spoon, not because they couldn't win matches but because they had been found to have cheated on the salary cap for several years. In late April news of the scandal broke, rocking the whole Rugby League world. Between 2006 and 2010, the Storm had cheated to the extent of $3.17 million. There were two sets of books – one shown to the NRL salary cap auditor Ian Schubert, the other kept secret from any prying eyes.

The penalties were Draconian. The club was stripped of its 2007 and 2009 Premierships and the Minor Premierships of 2006, 2007 and 2008. It was also fined $500,000 and ordered to repay $1 million in prize-money. All competition points already earned in 2010 were forfeited and, although the Storm would continue to play each weekend until the end of the season they would not receive points for any victories. The club was allowed to continue as part of the competition to give its players the chance to represent at Test and Origin level.

Here is how the clubs fared in 2010:

ST GEORGE ILLAWARRA DRAGONS (Premiers)

In 2010 the Dragons at last threw off the tag of chokers – allegedly unable to handle the pressure of the play-offs. A year earlier they had finished as Minor Premiers then bowed out in the second week of the finals' series after losses to Parramatta and Brisbane. The previous year they had crashed out in the first weekend when beaten by Manly.

The Dragons had won their way through to the 2010 grand final thanks to a late field goal from stand-off Jamie Soward. That victory over Wests Tigers before a massive attendance of 71,212 was not without controversy. Eight minutes from full-time the match officials ignored a knee in the back from Kiwi Test man Jeremy Smith on the Tigers' dual international Lote Tuqiri. There was not even a penalty although Smith later pleaded guilty to a charge of dangerous contact with his knees. From the ensuing set of six tackles, the St George Illawarra side was able to establish good pitch position for Soward to snap his field goal. It was the first time the Dragons had been in front all night. But winning by one point was as good as winning by 20.

It had been an eventful season for the Dragons. They lost hooker Nathan Fien with a broken leg in the opening match, against Parramatta. But Fien shocked everyone by an early comeback and was one of the Dragons' best players in the grand final. He also earned himself a place in the New Zealand side for the Four Nations tournament.

Midway through the season the club's stocks were boosted by the return from French rugby union of their 'Prodigal Son' Mark Gasnier. Former Test winger Darius Boyd was a revelation at fullback, led the Dally M Medal voting for much of the year and was rewarded with the Clive Churchill Medal as the player of the match in the grand final. He earned a recall to the international arena in Australia's squad for the Four Nations. Also in the squad were winger Brett Morris and utility Dean Young. The latter provided a rare father-son international representation – his dad Craig Young had made 20 Test appearances in the late-1970s and early-1980s. And winger Jason Nightingale joined Fien and Smith in the Kiwis squad.

SYDNEY ROOSTERS (2nd)

The Sydney Roosters were eying a little bit of history when they reached the grand final. They were just one win away from becoming only the second club to go from wooden-spooners one year to Premiership-winners the next. The only time such a feat was achieved was when the Western Suburbs Magpies went from last in 1933 to beat Eastern Suburbs (the club now known as the Roosters) in the 1934 season finale. But in 1933 Wests were without their five best players who were en route to England for a Kangaroo tour.

As the October headlines showed, it wasn't to be. The Roosters led the Dragons 8-6 at the break but crumbled in the second half. But that didn't detract from the enormity of the feat by the boys from Bondi Junction who lifted under new coach Brian Smith.

Much of the momentum was provided by former 'bad boy' Todd Carney, back from the wilderness of 'bush' rugby in northern Queensland. Smith tried him first at fullback but then switched him to stand-off, where he immediately forged a great partnership with State of Origin scrum-half Mitchell Pearce. It was no co-incidence that, with plenty of quick ball, the former backpacker Shaun Kenny-Dowall ran riot in the centres, sharing top spot in the NRL tryscoring lists with Newcastle's Akuila Uate after touching down 21 times. Kenny-Dowall's great form earned him a recall to the Kiwi Test ranks after an absence of three years and won him the New Zealand Player of the Year award.

Carney and big forward Nate Myles also gained international status for the first time when chosen in Australia's squad for the Four Nations. Props Frank-Paul Nuuausala and Jared Waerea-Hargreaves and winger Sam Perrett were in the New Zealand squad with Kenny-Dowall for the Four Nations.

WESTS TIGERS (3rd)

So near, yet so far. Wests Tigers were back in the play-offs for the first time since they stunned the Rugby League world by winning the 2005 Premiership. And it was only two heartbreaking narrow losses that halted their roll to the grand final.

In the qualifying final against Sydney Roosters, the Tigers squandered a 15-2 lead midway through the second half. Then a controversial scrum win against the feed by Sydney Roosters gave their captain Braith Anasta the field position from which to snap a last-minute field goal that sent the game into 'golden point' extra time, where the Roosters centre Shaun Kenny-Dowall scored a 60-metre intercept try. No week off for the Tigers to rest their weary, injury-plagued bodies. That told against them in their preliminary final clash with the Dragons, who were never in front until stand-off Jamie Soward snapped a field goal with six minutes left on the clock to give his side a one-point victory.

Injuries told against Wests – especially the season-ending knee injury to exciting youngster Tim Moltzen and the one suffered by prop Todd Payten in a training mishap on the eve of the preliminary final.

But there were plenty of highlights. The consistent brilliance of stand-off Benji Marshall. The great form of captain Robbie Farah (second in the voting for the Dally M Medal), English Test forward Gareth Ellis, Liam Fulton (back from the Huddersfield Giants) and fellow forward Chris Heighington. There was also the triumphant return from rugby union of Lote Tuqiri, who scored with his first touch of the ball (against Manly in round one) and went on to score another 17 tries. He joined Farah and centre Chris Lawrence in Australia's Four Nations squad. Three youngsters – forwards Simon Dwyer and Andrew Fifita and scrum-half Robert Lui – came of age.

GOLD COAST TITANS (4th)

The Titans kept surprising the critics. Regularly written off, they knocked over more fancied opponents. Indeed they won six of their final seven games in the season proper to claim a place in the top four, giving them a home game in the play-offs.

Vital was the experience of the Titans veterans, halfback Scott Prince, prop Luke Bailey (who played for half the season with a broken foot), fullback Preston Campbell and centre/stand-off Mat Rogers. The controversial signing of 'enfant terrible' Greg Bird also added some starch to the Gold Coast line-up (and he was rewarded with a place in Australia's Four Nations squad), while young wingers Kevin 'Flash' Gordon and David Mead provided speed on the flanks. And what about Nathan Friend? The clever rake was regularly among the Gold Coast's best and averaged 43 tackles per match. Then, of course, there was the clever coaching of John Cartwright.

Rogers provided one of the great moments of the season when in Round 20 in July he snared a field goal for the Gold Coast's crucial 11-10 victory over St George Illawarra at Jubilee Oval. That sparked the Titans' great late-season surge.

Once in the finals series they ended the New Zealand Warriors' season with a solid 28-16 victory at Robina. But after a week's rest and with talk of them making the grand final for the first time, the Titans imploded. In what was their worst display of the season, they went down 32-6 to the Roosters in front of 44,787 fans at Suncorp Stadium. The Titans were still in the equation at half-time, trailing by just 12-6. However they couldn't contain the Roosters after the break.

Bird represented New South Wales and Country Origin during the year, Ashley Harrison turned out for Queensland and Anthony Laffranchi and Mark Minichiello played for City Origin.

At the end of the season, the evergreen Rogers decided to hang up his boots – and it won't be long before a few others follow him into retirement.

PENRITH PANTHERS (5th)

The Panthers were genuine Premiership threats for much of the season – even though they temporarily lost their way in July and August with five losses in six straight weeks. They claimed second spot on the final ladder after putting on a half-century of points in two of their last three outings in the season proper (thrashing South Sydney 54-18 and Cronulla 50-12).

But then everything went terribly wrong. Inspirational captain Petero Civoniceva was suspended for two matches after being sent off for a high tackle in the clash with Canterbury Bulldogs on the penultimate weekend of the home-and-away games. And his encouragement was sorely missed in the Panthers' 24-22 loss to Canberra in their qualifying final. He was back for the semi-final against Sydney Roosters – but his team was wracked with injuries. The Panthers were without Test second-rowers Trent Waterhouse and Frank Pritchard, and then lost two more internationals, Michael Jennings and Luke Lewis, in the first 25 minutes. The Panthers lost 34-12 and their season was over.

Civoniceva and Lewis pulled on Australian jerseys for the Four Nations, while young prop Sam McKendry and veteran back-rower Pritchard were in the Kiwi squad. Civoniceva, Lewis, Waterhouse and Jennings all made Origin appearances in 2010.

CANBERRA RAIDERS (6th)

The Raiders looked out of contention in early July, when they were among the cellar-dwellers in 13th place. But Canberra came home under a wet sail to win eight of the last nine home-and-away games, including an 18-16 last-round victory over the Broncos in Brisbane (a win that kept the Broncos out of the play-offs and ensured Canberra's presence).

The remarkable run had come on the back of some inspirational displays by captain Terry Campese and exciting creativity by the youngsters Josh Dugan, Jarrod Croker, Daniel Vidot and Josh McCrone who built on the solid foundations laid by the big boppers up front, not the least being David Shillington and Tom Learoyd-Lahrs.

Once in the finals series, Canberra shocked the second-placed Panthers 24-22 at Penrith. Then at home to Wests Tigers in the semi-finals they nearly pulled off another upset. As the clock wound down and trailing 24-22, the usually reliable Raiders goalkicker Croker took a simple attempt at a penalty goal that would have sent the match into 'golden point' extra time. But the ball drifted wide of the posts.

Shillington and Learoyd-Lahrs were rewarded with selection in Australia's Four Nations squad, while back-rower Bronson Harrison pulled on the Kiwi jersey for the tournament.

NEW ZEALAND WARRIORS (7th)

The vagaries of the NRL's play-off system cost the New Zealand Warriors dearly in 2010. After finishing 14th the previous season, the Auckland club leaped into fifth spot. But in the qualifying round they went down 28-16 to the fourth-placed Gold Coast Titans. And when Penrith (2nd) and Wests Tigers (3rd) got beaten, the Warriors suddenly found themselves unceremoniously bundled out of the finals' series after just one week.

The season provided a sad end to the career of veteran prop Steve Price, whose chronic foot injury sidelined him for the entire season. In June he announced his retirement 16 years after he made his senior debut (for the Canterbury Bulldogs) and with a total of 313 Premiership appearances, 15 Tests for Australia and a guest appearance for the New Zealand All Golds in their centenary match against the Northern Union.

He was sorely missed. But, in his absence, captain Simon Mannering lifted his game and several of the younger forwards came of age. Lewis Brown created mayhem on the edges of the rucks and was rewarded by being named New Zealand's International Rookie of the Year. The 21-year-old Russell Packer and Ben Matulino played with new-found maturity.

But the real star was that Kiwi folk-hero Manu Vatuvei who scored 20 tries in his 19 appearances. In doing so he took his career total to 78, beating Stacey Jones' previous club tryscoring record of 77.

Brent Tate, who will be in Cowboys colours next season, was chosen for Australia in the Four Nations. The Kiwis squad included five Warriors – Brown, Lance Hohaia, Mannering, Matulino and Vatuvei – while Sam Rapira and Aaron Heremaia played in the Anzac Test against the Australians. Former Eels and Storm scrum-half James Maloney and the ever-consistent Micheal Luck were chosen for the Prime Minister's XIII for the annual match against Papua New Guinea.

MANLY SEA EAGLES (8th)

The season started and finished disastrously for Manly. The Sea Eagles lost their clever fullback Brett Stewart in the opening round after he suffered a season-ending knee injury when tackling big Tigers winger Lote Tuqiri. And when they eventually snuck into the finals series in eighth place they were soundly thrashed 28-0 by the eventual Premiers, St George Illawarra, and departed in the first week for the second straight year.

But the Sea Eagles had only themselves to blame for the early exit. They would have been much higher on the NRL ladder had they not squandered so many big leads in the second half of several matches, including a 26-22 defeat by the Tigers after the Sea Eagles led 20-4 at the break in round one and 24-20 by Parramatta In round two, after the Eels had trailed 20-0 at half-time.

But the Sea Eagles did unearth some young stars, not the least centre Dean Whare, who scored a hat-trick of tries in his senior debut (against North Queensland) and was selected for the Junior Kiwis for their two 'Tests' against the Junior Kangaroos in October. Will Hopoate, son of the former Test player John, and utility Jamie Buhrer were others to impress when they broke into the senior ranks.

Prop Josh Perry and back-rower Anthony Watmough played for Australia in the Anzac Test. Steve Matai was in the Kiwis line-up and would have been there for the Four Nations but for a seven-match suspension for a late and high tackle on Canterbury hooker Michael Ennis in their final round encounter. But Watmough made the Australian squad.

For the record, hooker Matt Ballin, who was called into the Queensland side for Origin I when Cameron Smith dropped out through injury, made the most tackles during a season by any Manly player in the history of the club – 958.

SOUTH SYDNEY RABBITOHS (9th)

So much was expected of the Rabbitohs in 2010. Following the recruitment of boom England Test forward Sam Burgess and up-and-coming Broncos prop Dave Taylor, they could boast one of the most formidable packs in the competition. But, once again, they failed to live up to their reputation, missing out on the play-offs yet again.

They had looked certainties after handing out a 50-10 flogging to Wests Tigers at the Sydney Cricket Ground in May. And they were to snatch a 'golden point' victory over the same side late in the season. Mid-season, they were poised ready to pounce in fifth spot. Sadly for the Souths fans they lost eight of their final 12 matches in the season proper. They were still in with a faint chance with one round to play but couldn't halt the Dragons.

Injuries cost the Rabbitohs dearly. At various stages they were without Taylor, enigmatic stand-off John Sutton, Kiwi Test hooker Issac Luke and workhorse Luke Stuart for extended periods.

Souths will again offer their fans plenty of hope in 2011. Their 19-year-old centre Dylan Farrell scored a hat-trick of tries when he made his senior debut in the second encounter with the Tigers – his third touchdown providing the 'golden point' win – and he is certain to play a major role for the side next year. And the Rabbitohs' Toyota Cup (under-20s) side reached the grand final.

Luke made the Kiwis Four Nations squad after starring in the Anzac Test. And Burgess was a key player in England's side. The arrival in 2011 of 2009 *Rugby League World* Golden Boot winner Greg Inglis is also a mouthwatering prospect.

BRISBANE BRONCOS (10th)
What a bizarre season it was for the Broncos! They missed the play-offs for the first time in almost two decades. They suffered a body blow before the season started when they lost Test centre Justin Hodges with a torn Achilles tendon. They then opened the season disastrously, losing six of their first eight matches. But suddenly they hit full stride, winning nine of their next 12 encounters.

Just as it looked a finals spot beckoned they lost captain Darren Lockyer to a rib injury in their Round 22 win over the Cowboys and, without his inspirational on-field leadership, they crashed to defeat in their final four games, including a 36-4 walloping by the New Zealand Warriors.

But the Brisbane fans can see some positives in the season. They must have wondered how the Broncos were going to replace international fullback Karmichael Hunt, who defected to Australian Rules football at the end of 2009. Their fears would have been short-lived with the emergence of 22-year-old Josh Hoffman. Such was his form that he won the Paul Morgan Medal as the Broncos Player of the Year.

Another to shine was another 22-year-old, utility Matt Gillett who was named Dally M Rookie of the Year. Only international Israel Folau scored more tries for Brisbane than Gillett. He has been signed until the end of 2013. Other rookies, centre Gerard Beale (20) and prop Mitchell Dodds (21) were also impressive during the 2010 season. Beale was chosen in the Junior Kangaroos side that took on the Junior Kiwis in October, together with stand-off Corey Norman and second-rower Tariq Sims.

Sims has left for the Cowboys, but Test star Ben Hannant will be in Broncos colours next season. Lockyer captained Australia in the 2010 Anzac Test against the Kiwis and in the Four Nations tournament, with fellow Bronco Sam Thaiday as his teammate. Corey Parker was captain of the Prime Minister's XIII for the annual clash with Papua New Guinea. Gillett was in the same side.

NEWCASTLE KNIGHTS (11th)
Newcastle never really recovered from an off-field crisis that rocked the club before the season had opened. Danny Wicks and Chris Houston were charged by police with serious drug offences – and suddenly the Knights were without two of their hardest-working forwards. To add to the Knights woes, captain Kurt Gidley suffered a hamstring injury in the pre-season All Stars game that sidelined him for the first four rounds. And they managed to win just one of those four encounters. But, to their credit, the Knights were still in with a chance of making the final eight until losses in the final two rounds of the season proper.

There was plenty of excitement on the Newcastle wings. Fijian World Cup flier Akuila Uate scored 21 tries in his 24 appearances to share top billing in the NRL tryscoring lists with the Roosters Shaun Kenny-Dowall. And on the other flank Cooper Vuna, who later defected to rugby union, scored 16 in his 17 games.

Gidley's utility value saw him selected for Australia in the Trans-Tasman Test against the Kiwis and the Four Nations. He also captained New South Wales in the first two Origin encounters. Uate played for the Prime Minister's XIII in the clash with the Kumuls.

PARRAMATTA EELS (12th)
Before the season had kicked off the bookmakers had installed the Parramatta Eels as firm favourites to take out the 2010 Premiership. After all, they had come home

dramatically the previous year to reach the grand final, where they were no match for the Melbourne Storm, subsequently proved to have cheated on the salary cap and stripped of their title.

But the Eels failed miserably to justify their favouritism. They lost four of their first five matches and, despite a mid-season revival on the back of some scintillating displays by Jarryd Hayne, they eventually slumped to lose five of their last six games and miss the play-offs.

Coach Daniel Anderson was made the scapegoat and, even though he had steered the Eels to the 2009 grand final, he was shown the door. The players weren't consulted about his sacking and many were upset, which is something the new coach, Kiwis Test mentor Stephen Kearney, had to address before the start of the 2011 season.

It was sad way for Nathan Cayless, the Parramatta stalwart and the longest-serving captain in the history of the NRL, to end his illustrious career. The 32-year-old prop called it a day after 14 seasons and 258 senior appearances for the Eels, during which time he played 38 Tests for New Zealand and captained the Kiwis to their shock victory in the 2008 World Cup. Only teammate Nathan Hindmarsh and the great stand-off of the 1980s Brett Kenny played more games for Parramatta. Hindmarsh set a new club record of 283 appearances during the season and had the chance to join the '300 Club' in 2011.

Hayne played for Australia in the Anzac Test but missed the Four Nations through injury while prop Tim Mannah and second-rower Ben Smith were in the Prime Minister's XIII that played the Kumuls.

CANTERBURY BULLDOGS (13th)

What a slump. The Canterbury Bulldogs would have been Minor Premiers in 2009 except for being penalised two competition points for briefly having 14 men on the pitch in one match. They then reached the penultimate week of the play-offs. A year later and they were never in the hunt after losing nine of their first 13 matches. And things didn't get much better when they got back into a bit of form. In July they led the Roosters 30-18 but got run down 36-32.

But at least they sent champion scrum-half Brett Kimmorley into retirement and long-serving fullback Luke Patten off to Salford City with a rousing defeat of Manly in the final round. There were some positives. The enigmatic young half Ben Barba mesmerised many an opposition player and ended the season with the most tries for Canterbury – 15 in 21 appearances. And 2009 Dally M Rookie of the Year Jamal Idris continued from where he left off with a stirring season in which he broke into the NSW State of Origin ranks. Kimmorley and hooker Michael Ennis also wore the Blue for New South Wales, while prop Ben Hannant appeared in Queensland Origin strip.

Hannant is returning to Brisbane for 2011, but the Dogs will be boosted by the return of homesick Greg Eastwood from Leeds Rhinos, his Kiwi Four Nations teammate Frank Pritchard and the youngsters Trent Hodkinson (from Manly) and Kris Keating (Parramatta).

CRONULLA SHARKS (14th)

It was a wretched season for the Cronulla Sharks both on and off the pitch. The front-office was in turmoil and the chaos was reflected in the performances of the players. Coach Ricky Stuart didn't even wait for his planned departure at the end of the year, handing over to his assistant Shane Flanagan midway through the tumult.

It was hardly a decent way for captain Trent Barrett to finish his long career. But he retired with his head held high after 292 senior club appearances (45 with the Illawarra Steelers, 154 with St George Illawarra Dragons, 58 with Wigan Warriors and 35 with Cronulla Sharks). He also played 13 Tests for Australia and 11 Origin matches for New South Wales, captaining the Blues in his final appearance, in Origin III of 2010. Exciting Penrith 20-year-old Wade Graham has been signed as his replacement.

The problem that faced the Sharks in 2010 was their inability to score enough points. They managed just 354 – some 59 less than the nearest pauper, Parramatta.

The most positive aspect of the season was the consistency of loose forward Paul Gallen, who was rewarded with selection for Australia in the Anzac Test and the Four Nations. He finished fifth in the voting for the Dally M Medal as NRL Player of the Year. Gallen will be joined at Cronulla in 2011 by the Kiwis' No 13 Jeremy Smith.

Exciting 21-year-old threequarter Blake Ferguson and prop Luke Douglas, who has played 122 consecutive games since making his senior debut in 2006, were chosen for the Prime Minister's XIII for the annual clash with Papua New Guinea.

NORTH QUEENSLAND COWBOYS (15th)

Such was the extent of the disaster in Townsville, that the North Queensland Cowboys commissioned a thorough inquiry into the failed season. Chief executive Peter Parr was demoted to football manager and assistant coach Matt Parish and football manager Dean Lance departed. Test scrum-half Johnathan Thurston's role as captain was also said to be under review. The Cowboys won just five matches and would have ended up with another wooden spoon but for the penalties imposed on Melbourne Storm for their salary cap cheating.

Perhaps the only positive was the selection of 25-year-old prop Matt Scott in Australia's Four Nations squad. But there are high hopes for 2011 with the recruitment of former Test forward Dallas Johnson from Catalans Dragons and current international Brent Tate from the New Zealand Warriors, although Tate suffered a career-threatening injury in the Four Nations Final. Exciting Brisbane Broncos youngsters Antonio Winterstein and Tariq Sims, the latter named as NRL Toyota Cup Player of the Year, will also be great additions to the Cowboys squad.

MELBOURNE STORM (16th)

So much has been written about the Storm in 2010 that every Rugby League fan in the world is aware of their predicament. Their spot at the foot of the ladder was set in concrete as soon as the salary cap scandal broke. But it was testament to their personal pride that the players still gave a whole-hearted effort each and every weekend. Indeed in the first match after being told they would lose all Premiership points for the season they hammered the New Zealand Warriors 40-6.

All told they finished with 14 wins, the same number they had in the season proper last year when they 'won' the Premiership. All this while knowing that half of them would have to find new clubs for 2011. Among others, three went to Wigan – ex-Origin stand-off Brett Finch, former Australian Test back-rower Ryan Hoffman and Kiwis prop Jeff Lima – where they joined former Storm assistant coach Michael Maguire for 2011. The 2009 Golden Boot winner Greg Inglis was poised to leave at the end of the season. And former Four Nations prop Brett White joined Canberra Raiders.

However, the Storm were able to hold on to three of their international linchpins – fullback Billy Slater, scrum-half Cooper Cronk and hooker Cameron Smith.

ALL STARS GAME

Saturday 13th February 2010

NRL ALL STARS 12 NRL INDIGENOUS ALL STARS 16

NRL ALL STARS: 20 Jarryd Hayne (Parramatta Eels); 2 Israel Folau (Brisbane Broncos); 3 Michael Jennings (Penrith Panthers); 4 Matt Cooper (St George Illawarra Dragons); 5 Manu Vatuvei (New Zealand Warriors); 6 Darren Lockyer (Brisbane Broncos) (C); 7 Benji Marshall (Wests Tigers); 8 Adam Blair (Melbourne Storm); 9 Cameron Smith (Melbourne Storm); 10 Sam Burgess (South Sydney Rabbitohs); 11 Anthony Watmough (Manly Sea Eagles); 12 David Shillington (Canberra Raiders); 13 Luke O'Donnell (North Queensland Cowboys). Subs (all used): 1 Brett Finch (Melbourne Storm); 14 Kurt Gidley (Newcastle Knights); 15 Anthony Tupou (Cronulla Sharks); 16 Nate Myles (Sydney Roosters); 17 Robbie Farah (Wests Tigers); 18 Luke Bailey (Gold Coast Titans); 19 Josh Morris (Canterbury Bulldogs).
Tries: Morris (53), Marshall (59), Jennings (61).
NRL INDIGENOUS ALL STARS: 1 Preston Campbell (Gold Coast Titans) (C); 2 Nathan Merritt (South Sydney Rabbitohs); 3 Ty Williams (North Queensland Cowboys); 4 Beau Champion (South Sydney Rabbitohs); 5 Wendell Sailor (St George Illawarra Dragons); 6 Scott Prince (Gold Coast Titans); 7 Johnathan Thurston (North Queensland Cowboys); 8 George Rose (Manly Sea Eagles); 9 Ben Jones (Sydney Roosters); 10 Carl Webb (North Queensland Cowboys); 11 Cory Paterson (Newcastle Knights); 12 Tom Learoyd-Lahrs (Canberra Raiders); 13 Sam Thaiday (Brisbane Broncos). Subs (all used): 14 Jamie Soward (St George Illawarra Dragons); 15 Yileen Gordon (Canterbury Bulldogs); 16 Greg Bird (Cronulla Sharks); 17 Jharal Yow Yeh (Brisbane Broncos); 18 Travis Waddell (Canberra Raiders); 19 Joel Thompson (Canberra Raiders); 20 Blake Ferguson (Cronulla Sharks).
Tries: Sailor (2), Jones (32), Soward (74); **Goals:** Thurston 2.
Rugby Leaguer & League Express Men of the Match:
NRL All Stars: Sam Burgess; *NRL Indigenous All Stars:* Johnathan Thurston.
Preston Campbell Medal (Man of the Match, judged by fans):
Johnathan Thurston.
Half-time: 0-10; **Referees:** Shayne Hayne, Ashley Klein, Gavin Badger & Luke Phillips; **Attendance:** 26,687 *(at Skilled Park, Robina).*

NRL SCOREBOARD

FINAL NRL PREMIERSHIP TABLE

	P	W	D	L	B	F	A	Pts
St George Illawarra Dragons	24	17	0	7	2	518	299	38
Penrith Panthers	24	15	0	9	2	645	489	34
Wests Tigers	24	15	0	9	2	537	503	34
Gold Coast Titans	24	15	0	9	2	520	498	34
New Zealand Warriors	24	14	0	10	2	539	486	32
Sydney Roosters	24	14	0	10	2	559	510	32
Canberra Raiders	24	13	0	11	2	499	493	30
Manly Sea Eagles	24	12	0	12	2	545	510	28
South Sydney Rabbitohs	24	11	0	13	2	584	567	26
Brisbane Broncos	24	11	0	13	2	508	535	26
Newcastle Knights	24	10	0	14	2	499	569	24
Parramatta Eels	24	10	0	14	2	413	491	24
Canterbury Bulldogs	24	9	0	15	2	494	539	22
Cronulla Sharks	24	7	0	17	2	354	609	18
North Queensland Cowboys	24	5	0	19	2	425	667	14
Melbourne Storm *	24	14	0	10	2	489	363	0

* Melbourne Storm deducted all points for 2010

QUALIFYING FINALS

Friday 10th September 2010

GOLD COAST TITANS 28 ....NEW ZEALAND WARRIORS 16
Titans: Tries: Zillman (17, 32), Toopi (27), Rogers (35), Gordon (64);
Goals: Prince 4/6
Warriors: Tries: Heremaia (6), Moon (47), Vatuvei (59);
Goals: Maloney 2/3
Half-time: 22-6; Referees: Tony Archer & Gavin Badger; Attendance: 27,026

Saturday 11th September 2010

PENRITH PANTHERS 22 ....CANBERRA RAIDERS 24
Panthers: Tries: Gordon (8, 21), Earl (59, 67); Goals: Gordon 3/4
Raiders: Tries: Campese (3), Tilse (15), Harrison (33), Robinson (42);
Goals: Croker 4/4
Half-time: 12-18; Referees: Ben Cummins & Steve Lyons;
Attendance: 16,668

WESTS TIGERS 15.....................................SYDNEY ROOSTERS 19
(after golden point extra time)
Tigers: Tries: Tuqiri (28), Ryan (35), Ayshford (48); Goals: Marshall 1/3;
Field goal: Farah (53)
Roosters: Tries: Anasta (59), Pearce (74), Kenny-Dowall (100);
Goals: Carney 3/3; Field goal: Anasta (80)
Half-time: 10-2; Referees: Shayne Hayne & Matt Cecchin;
Attendance: 33,315 *(at Sydney Football Stadium)*

Sunday 12th September 2010

ST GEORGE ILLAWARRA DRAGONS 28 ....MANLY SEA EAGLES 0
Dragons: Tries: Hornby (8), Cooper (65, 68), Gasnier (71);
Goals: Soward 6/8
Half-time: 10-0; Referees: Jared Maxwell & Jason Robinson;
Attendance: 16,574 *(at Jubilee Oval)*

SEMI-FINALS

Friday 17th September 2010

CANBERRA RAIDERS 24 ....WESTS TIGERS 26
Raiders: Tries: Harrison (12), Monaghan (26), Thurling (56), Tongue (72);
Goals: Croker 4/4
Tigers: Tries: Heighington (6), Ellis (15), Tuqiri (20), Lawrence (48);
Goals: Marshall 5/5
Half-time: 12-18; Referees: Tony Archer & Jared Maxwell;
Attendance: 26,476

Saturday 18th September 2010

SYDNEY ROOSTERS 34 ....PENRITH PANTHERS 12
Roosters: Tries: Pearce (11), Anasta (32), Perrett (45, 77),
Minichiello (65), Carney (68); Goals: Carney 5/7
Panthers: Tries: Purtell (64), Graham (72); Goals: Gordon 2/2
Half-time: 12-0; Referees: Shayne Hayne & Ben Cummins;
Attendance: 23,459 *(at Sydney Football Stadium)*

PRELIMINARY FINALS

Friday 24th September 2010

GOLD COAST TITANS 6 ....SYDNEY ROOSTERS 32
Titans: Try: Zillman (18); Goals: Prince 1/1
Roosters: Tries: Perrett (10, 23), Conn (48), Anasta (62), Nuuausala (80);
Goals: Carney 6/6
Half-time: 6-12; Referees: Tony Archer & Jared Maxwell;
Attendance: 44,787 *(at Suncorp Stadium, Brisbane)*

Saturday 25th September 2010

ST GEORGE ILLAWARRA DRAGONS 13 ....WESTS TIGERS 12
Dragons: Tries: Smith (27), Nightingale (49); Goals: Soward 2/2;
Field goal: Soward (74)
Tigers: Tries: Tuqiri (16), Lui (35); Goals: Marshall 2/2
Half-time: 6-12; Referees: Shayne Hayne & Ben Cummins;
Attendance: 71,212 *(at ANZ Stadium, Sydney)*

GRAND FINAL

Sunday 3rd October 2010

ST GEORGE ILLAWARRA DRAGONS 32 SYDNEY ROOSTERS 8

DRAGONS: 1 Darius Boyd; 2 Brett Morris; 3 Mark Gasnier; 4 Matt
Cooper; 5 Jason Nightingale; 6 Jamie Soward; 7 Ben Hornby (C); 8
Neville Costigan; 9 Dean Young; 10 Michael Weyman; 11 Beau Scott; 12
Ben Creagh; 13 Jeremy Smith. Subs (all used): 14 Nathan Fien; 15 Trent
Merrin; 16 Matt Prior; 17 Jarrod Saffy.
Tries: Gasnier (8), Nightingale (46, 59), Young (61), Fien (70);
Goals: Soward 6/7.
ROOSTERS: 1 Anthony Minichiello; 5 Sam Perrett; 3 Kane Linnett; 4 Shaun
Kenny-Dowall; 2 BJ Leilua; 6 Todd Carney; 7 Mitchell Pearce; 8 Jason
Ryles; 9 Jake Friend; 20 Lopini Paea; 11 Nate Myles; 12 Mitchell Aubusson;
13 Braith Anasta (C). Subs (all used): 10 Frank-Paul Nuuausala; 14 Martin
Kennedy; 15 Jared Waerea-Hargreaves; 16 Daniel Conn.
Tries: Anasta (16), Aubusson (30); **Goals:** Carney 0/2.
On report: Conn (35) - alleged high tackle on Weyman.
Rugby Leaguer & League Express Men of the Match:
Dragons: Nathan Fien; *Roosters:* Todd Carney.
Clive Churchill Medal: Darius Boyd (St George Illawarra Dragons).
Half-time: 6-8; **Referees:** Tony Archer & Shayne Hayne;
Attendance: 82,334 *(at ANZ Stadium, Sydney)*.

TOP POINTSCORERS

		T	G	FG	Pts
Michael Gordon	Penrith Panthers	16	103	0	270
Todd Carney	Sydney Roosters	16	95	1	255
Benji Marshall	Wests Tigers	12	76	3	203
Jamie Soward	St George Illawarra Dragons	6	84	5	197
James Maloney	New Zealand Warriors	10	73	2	188

TOP TRYSCORERS

Shaun Kenny-Dowall	Sydney Roosters	21
Akuila Uate	Newcastle Knights	21
Israel Folau	Brisbane Broncos	20
Manu Vatuvei	New Zealand Warriors	20
Brett Morris	St George Illawarra Dragons	19

OTHER GRAND FINALS

TOYOTA CUP (Under-20s)
Sunday 3rd October 2010

NEW ZEALAND WARRIORS 42 ....SOUTH SYDNEY RABBITOHS 28
Warriors: Tries: Taylor 2, Fisiiahi, Likiliki, Niko, Seluni, Lousi; Goals: Johnson 7
Rabbitohs: Tries: Roberts, Vaivai, Peats, Judd, Tulemau; Goals: Reynolds 4
Half-time: 12-10; Referee: Gavin Reynolds *(at ANZ Stadium, Sydney)*

NEW SOUTH WALES CUP
Sunday 3rd October 2010

CANTERBURY BULLDOGS 24 ....WINDSOR WOLVES 12
Bulldogs: Tries: Reynolds 2, Cutler, Jack; Goals: Reynolds 4
Wolves: Tries: Sene Lefeo, Tangata-Toa; Goals: Trindall 2
Half-time: 16-0; Referee: David Munro *(at ANZ Stadium, Sydney)*

QUEENSLAND CUP
Saturday 18th September 2010

NORTHERN PRIDE 30 ....NORTHS DEVILS 20
Pride: Tries: Slyney, Griffin, Bani, Jensen, Underwood; Goals: Bird 5
Devils: Tries: Samoa 2, Mzembe, Gibb; Goals: Watene 2
Half-time: 18-6; Referee: Justin Davis;
Attendance: 6,300 *(at Suncorp Stadium, Brisbane)*

DALLY M AWARDS

Dally M Medal (Player of the Year): Todd Carney (Sydney Roosters)
Provan-Summons Medal (People's Choice): Todd Carney (Sydney Roosters)
Coach of the Year: Brian Smith (Sydney Roosters)
Captain of the Year: Braith Anasta (Sydney Roosters)
Rookie of the Year: Matt Gillett (Brisbane Broncos)
Representative Player of the Year: Billy Slater (Melbourne Storm)

Fullback: Darius Boyd (St George Illawarra Dragons)
Winger: Akuila Uate (Newcastle Knights)
Centre: Jamie Lyon (Manly Sea Eagles)
Stand-off: Todd Carney (Sydney Roosters)
Scrum half: Scott Prince (Gold Coast Titans)
Prop: David Shillington (Canberra Raiders)
Hooker: Robbie Farah (Wests Tigers)
Second-rower: Sam Thaiday (Brisbane Broncos)
Loose forward: Luke Lewis (Penrith Panthers)

Toyota Cup (Under-20s) Player of the Year: Tariq Sims (Brisbane Broncos)

141

Members of the Sydney media were adamant – this was going to be the year the Blues would halt Queensland's State of Origin dominance. The NSW newspaper readers and radio listeners believed the propaganda. So much so that the rush of money bet with the bookmakers for Origin I turned the Blues from rank outsiders on the Sunday before the clash into hot favourites when it came to kick-off three days later. How wrong they all were.

ORIGIN I

Beaten NSW coach Craig Bellamy couldn't believe the 28-24 defeat. Like every other New South Welshman he honestly believed he had the winning formula. Instead his players were left licking their wounds. "It seemed like Groundhog day," Bellamy noted.

Queensland captain Darren Lockyer was at his vintage best – but even his class act paled when compared with that of his halfback partner Johnathan Thurston, who explained the Maroons' victory simply: "It's a special bond we Queenslanders have. We never give up."

As the post mortem began, Allan Langer was calling JT the greatest scrum-half in Origin history. Any hopes for an expansive, razzle-dazzle game were drowned by the torrential rain that swept across Sydney in the days leading up to the clash.

There was lots of dropped ball brought on by the slippery conditions and some frightening defence. And that's how the first try was scored. Queensland's international Darius Boyd lost the ball on his own line and Jarryd Hayne dived on it to score for the Blues.

Thurston set up the reply. In the 15th minute he dragged a few defenders into him and flung the ball over the top of the centres for Boyd to have clear run at the line to touch down. And when Thurston booted the conversion from wide out on the left flank the scores were locked up at 6-all. The Blues went ahead 11 minutes before the interval after Lyon kicked a penalty goal from a controversial refereeing decision.

The critics reckoned the rain would nullify the genius of Slater. But six minutes before the break he pounced on a rolling ball from a Thurston kick and scored, to put the Maroons in front for the first time.

Another brilliant Slater run was thwarted by a tackle by Brett Morris on one side of the pitch. And when the ball spun across the field Hayne and Timana Tahu prevented what looked likely to be a certain try to Greg Inglis, holding him up over the line.

Young Bulldogs centre Jamal Idris made his Origin debut at the start of the second half, replacing the injured Matt Cooper, and made a strong 20-metre run with his first touch of the ball. Moments later David Shillington stood in a tackle and handed the ball on to a trailing Lockyer. The veteran was across the stripe in a split second.

When the Blues looked certain to reply Hayne threw a loose pass into touch when supports were waiting to score. Minutes later video referees Bill Harrigan and Paul Simpkins awarded a controversial try to NSW loose forward Anthony Watmough although there looked to be more than a hint of a knock-on from Trent Waterhouse in the lead-up.

Some wonderful passing saw Inglis in to score after handling twice. And Thurston was able to convert from near the left sideline to restore Queensland's eight-point lead. Another controversial video decision gave Sam Thaiday a try on the benefit of the doubt.

A try to Idris off a clever pass from Jamie Lyon in the closing minutes made the score more respectable for the Blues. And when Ben Creagh was awarded a try after looking to have knocked on the Blues finished even closer than they deserved.

ORIGIN II

There was a sense of panic when it came time for the Blues to name their side for the second encounter. Hayne was switched to fullback, creating the farcical situation of captain Kurt Gidley starting off the bench. There was a new combination in the halves – veteran Trent Barrett combining with the Roosters' talented young playmaker Mitchell Pearce. Test loose forward Paul Gallen, controversially overlooked for Origin I, was re-instated as was the evergreen Nathan Hindmarsh. But the whole mood in the Blues' camp wasn't helped when

Tahu walked out. The Parramatta dual international, who has both Aboriginal and Maori heritage, took offence at a racial comment by assistant coach Andrew Johns, who promptly tendered his resignation.

The newspaper headline writers had a wonderful time with the match reports of Queensland's 34-6 thumping of the Blues. 'Blue Murder' shouted one paper. 'New South Wails' roared another.

In a brutal, spiteful encounter the Blues had no answer to the brilliance of the Queensland stars. The Blues confusion began well before kick-off when the team bus left for the stadium without fullback Hayne and hooker Michael Ennis. Ironically, the pair's hastily-organised taxi fared better than the bus in the peak-hour traffic snarl and they arrived before the rest of the team.

Things then went from bad to worse. With less than three minutes on the clock, Thurston feigned to send a long ball to winger Boyd but held it short to set Inglis on his way to the line, bouncing off the gold-booted Hayne to score. The Maroons were in once more when Willie Tonga sent a pass that looked a trifle forward for Israel Folau to touch down.

The action exploded midway through the first half. Gallen was placed on report for a high tackle on Nate Myles. The following day he was charged by the NRL match review committee but, in making an early guilty plea, Gallen escaped suspension. Then Luke O'Donnell was very lucky to stay on the pitch after he speared Boyd into the pitch, precipitating an all-in brawl. He was placed on report, but how he was ever allowed to stay on the field was difficult to understand especially as in the brawl O'Donnell made a head-butt on big Dave Taylor and threw a solid punch. The following day O'Donnell pleaded guilty to a dangerous throw and was suspended for three matches.

Moments later Matt Cooper appeared to foul Folau but the Queenslanders stuck to the task ahead of them. A pass from Lockyer to Slater, who was across the stripe in the twinkling of an eyelid, was ruled forward even though the ball left the skipper's hands backwards. The Queenslanders eventually were rewarded when Boyd scored late in the half for the Maroons to go to the break with a 16-nil lead.

When play resumed for the second spell, Taylor made a couple of early bursts before the Maroon Marauders extended their lead. Hayne fumbled a bomb and Tonga was on hand to dive across the stripe. Folau scored again, then substitute Cooper Cronk danced through some woeful defence to extend the lead to 34-nil. Only the late consolation try to Brett White saved the Blues from a record thrashing.

ORIGIN III

Queenslanders never give up! Never was the adage as true as it was in the concluding match of the 2010 Origin series, at Homebush.

When NSW loose forward Greg Bird scored with 12 minutes remaining to give the Blues an 18-13 lead, it looked as if the home side had at last got the better of the wonderful Queensland line-up. But two tries in the final seven minutes of the encounter – to Slater and Tonga – enabled Queensland to snatch victory and crush the spirit of each of the Blues players. It was Queensland's record fifth straight series victory.

At least this time around, the Blues made a contest of the conflict, although there were early doubts. It was hardly a good start for the Blues when Gallen lost the ball in the second tackle after just 16 seconds. And then debutant Michael Gordon was trapped behind his own line. Blues centre Beau Scott was lucky not to have spent some time in the sin-bin when he hit Slater off the ball. Scott capitalised on his good fortune with two important tackles that cut off promising Queensland moves, the latter sending Inglis into touch.

Midway through the half there were quick hands along the Maroons' backline with the ball zipping through the fingertips of Inglis for Boyd to score wide out on the left flank. Thurston converted from the sideline for the Queenslanders to lead by six. A few moments later, with the Maroons attacking, the NSW tacklers fell off Myles as he strolled across the line off a pass from Cameron Smith.

Nevertheless, the Blues eventually got back into the equation. Gallen, who had been solid throughout the first half, surged across the stripe late in the session to help reduce the deficit to just six. Right on the siren Lockyer booted a field goal from 48 metres out to give the Queenslanders a seven-point lead at the break.

Immediately after the resumption the Blues were lucky when the referees missed a blatant obstruction. A couple of tackles later substitute Gidley skipped across the whitewash. Michael Gordon's conversion brought the shortfall back to just one point. The Blues pounded the Queensland line but the Maroons dug deep with some wonderful defence. Who said no one cared about a dead rubber? Midway through the half, Hayne made a break and sent a pass that should have put the Blues in front – but Brett Morris fumbled with the line at his mercy.

With some 16 minutes remaining, Slater pulled off one of the great try-saving tackles in Origin history. Anthony Watmough charged across the whitewash, but somehow Slater managed to get himself under the Sea Eagle to trap the ball on his chest – and well off the turf.

After a great Gidley break for the Blues, Thurston knocked down a pass from Scott to save what looked a certain try. But moments later Bird sped through to dive on the ball and put the New South Welshmen in front for the first time.

Then came the defining moment. NSW hooker Michael Ennis gave away a stupid penalty, laying into Shillington and starting an all-in brawl. The subsequent penalty gave the Maroons a great position to set up Slater's match-winning try.

It was the first time in 15 years that the Maroons had managed to win all three encounters.

ORIGIN I

Wednesday 26th May 2010

NEW SOUTH WALES 24 QUEENSLAND 28

NEW SOUTH WALES: 1 Kurt Gidley (Newcastle Knights) (C); 2 Brett Morris (St George Illawarra Dragons); 3 Matt Cooper (St George Illawarra Dragons); 4 Timana Tahu (Parramatta Eels); 5 Jarryd Hayne (Parramatta Eels); 6 Jamie Lyon (Manly Sea Eagles); 7 Brett Kimmorley (Canterbury Bulldogs); 8 Michael Weyman (St George Illawarra Dragons); 9 Michael Ennis (Canterbury Bulldogs); 10 Josh Perry (Manly Sea Eagles); 11 Trent Waterhouse (Penrith Panthers); 12 Ben Creagh (St George Illawarra Dragons); 13 Anthony Watmough (Manly Sea Eagles). Subs (all used): 14 Jamal Idris (Canterbury Bulldogs); 15 Tom Learoyd-Lahrs (Canberra Raiders); 16 Luke Lewis (Penrith Panthers); 17 Brett White (Melbourne Storm).
Tries: Hayne (7), Watmough (56), Idris (73), Creagh (79); **Goals:** Lyon 4/5.
QUEENSLAND: 1 Billy Slater (Melbourne Storm); 2 Darius Boyd (St George Illawarra Dragons); 3 Greg Inglis (Melbourne Storm); 4 Willie Tonga (North Queensland Cowboys); 5 Israel Folau (Brisbane Broncos); 6 Darren Lockyer (Brisbane Broncos) (C); 7 Johnathan Thurston (North Queensland Cowboys); 8 Matt Scott (North Queensland Cowboys); 9 Matt Ballin (Manly Sea Eagles); 10 Petero Civoniceva (Penrith Panthers); 11 Nate Myles (Sydney Roosters); 12 Sam Thaiday (Brisbane Broncos); 13 Ashley Harrison (Gold Coast Titans). Subs (all used): 14 Cooper Cronk (Melbourne Storm); 15 David Shillington (Canberra Raiders); 16 Neville Costigan (St George Illawarra Dragons); 17 Dave Taylor (South Sydney Rabbitohs).
Tries: Boyd (15), Slater (34), Lockyer (47), Inglis (61), Thaiday (67); **Goals:** Thurston 4/5.
Rugby Leaguer & League Express Men of the Match:
New South Wales: Anthony Watmough; *Queensland:* Johnathan Thurston.
Half-time: 8-12; **Referees:** Tony Archer & Shayne Hayne;
Attendance: 68,753 *(at ANZ Stadium, Sydney).*

ORIGIN II

Wednesday 16th June 2010

QUEENSLAND 34 NEW SOUTH WALES 6

QUEENSLAND: 1 Billy Slater (Melbourne Storm); 2 Darius Boyd (St George Illawarra Dragons); 3 Greg Inglis (Melbourne Storm); 4 Willie Tonga (North Queensland Cowboys); 5 Israel Folau (Brisbane Broncos); 6 Darren Lockyer (Brisbane Broncos) (C); 7 Johnathan Thurston (North Queensland Cowboys); 8 Matt Scott (North Queensland Cowboys); 9 Cameron Smith (Melbourne Storm); 10 David Shillington (Canberra Raiders); 11 Nate Myles (Sydney Roosters); 12 Sam Thaiday (Brisbane Broncos); 13 Ashley Harrison (Gold Coast Titans). Subs (all used): 14 Cooper Cronk (Melbourne Storm); 15 Ben Hannant (Canterbury Bulldogs); 16 Neville Costigan (St George Illawarra Dragons); 17 Dave Taylor (South Sydney Rabbitohs).
Tries: Inglis (3), Folau (11, 47), Boyd (34), Tonga (43), Cronk (64); **Goals:** Thurston 5/6.
NEW SOUTH WALES: 1 Jarryd Hayne (Parramatta Eels); 2 Brett Morris (St George Illawarra Dragons); 3 Matt Cooper (St George Illawarra Dragons); 4 Beau Scott (St George Illawarra Dragons); 5 Joel Monaghan (Canberra Raiders); 6 Trent Barrett (Cronulla Sharks); 7 Mitchell Pearce (Sydney Roosters); 8 Michael Weyman (St George Illawarra Dragons); 9 Michael Ennis (Canterbury Bulldogs); 10 Brett White (Melbourne Storm); 12 Ben Creagh (St George Illawarra Dragons); 13 Paul Gallen (Cronulla Sharks). Subs (all used): 11 Trent Waterhouse (Penrith Panthers); 14 Kurt Gidley (Newcastle Knights) (C); 16 Tom Learoyd-Lahrs (Canberra Raiders); 17 Luke O'Donnell (North Queensland Cowboys).
Try: White (78); **Goals:** Ennis 1/1.
On report: Gallen (23) – alleged high tackle on Myles;
O'Donnell (25) – alleged dangerous tackle on Boyd.
Rugby Leaguer & League Express Men of the Match:
Queensland: Darren Lockyer; *New South Wales:* Nathan Hindmarsh.
Half-time: 16-0; **Referees:** Tony Archer & Shayne Hayne;
Attendance: 52,452 *(at Suncorp Stadium, Brisbane).*

ORIGIN III

Wednesday 7th July 2010

NEW SOUTH WALES 18 QUEENSLAND 23

NEW SOUTH WALES: 1 Jarryd Hayne (Parramatta Eels); 2 Brett Morris (St George Illawarra Dragons); 3 Michael Jennings (Penrith Panthers); 4 Beau Scott (St George Illawarra Dragons); 5 Michael Gordon (Penrith Panthers); 6 Trent Barrett (Cronulla Sharks) (C); 7 Mitchell Pearce (Sydney Roosters); 8 Jason King (Manly Sea Eagles); 9 Michael Ennis (Canterbury Bulldogs); 10 Kade Snowden (Cronulla Sharks); 11 Luke Lewis (Penrith Panthers); 12 Paul Gallen (Cronulla Sharks); 13 Greg Bird (Gold Coast Titans). Subs (all used): 14 Kurt Gidley (Newcastle Knights); 15 Tom Learoyd-Lahrs (Canberra Raiders); 16 Tim Mannah (Parramatta Eels); 17 Anthony Watmough (Manly Sea Eagles).
Tries: Gallen (35), Gidley (47), Bird (68); **Goals:** Gordon 3/3.
QUEENSLAND: 1 Billy Slater (Melbourne Storm); 2 Darius Boyd (St George Illawarra Dragons); 3 Greg Inglis (Melbourne Storm); 4 Willie Tonga (North Queensland Cowboys); 5 Israel Folau (Brisbane Broncos); 6 Darren Lockyer (Brisbane Broncos) (C); 7 Johnathan Thurston (North Queensland Cowboys); 8 Matt Scott (North Queensland Cowboys); 9 Cameron Smith (Melbourne Storm); 10 Petero Civoniceva (Penrith Panthers); 11 Nate Myles (Sydney Roosters); 12 Sam Thaiday (Brisbane Broncos); 13 Ashley Harrison (Gold Coast Titans). Subs (all used): 14 Cooper Cronk (Melbourne Storm); 15 David Shillington (Canberra Raiders); 16 Neville Costigan (St George Illawarra Dragons); 17 Dave Taylor (South Sydney Rabbitohs).
Tries: Boyd (19), Myles (27), Slater (73), Tonga (79); **Goals:** Thurston 3/3, Folau 0/1;
Field goal: Lockyer (40).
Rugby Leaguer & League Express Men of the Match:
New South Wales: Paul Gallen; *Queensland:* Billy Slater.
Half-time: 6-13; **Referees:** Tony Archer & Shayne Hayne;
Attendance: 61,259 *(at ANZ Stadium, Sydney).*

Wally Lewis Medal (Man of the Series): Billy Slater (Queensland).

AUSTRALIA 12
NEW ZEALAND 16

ABOVE: New Zealand celebrate their dramatic Four Nations Final win over Australia

BELOW: Simon Mannering upended by Sam Thaiday, Nate Myles and Greg Bird

RUGBY LEAGUE
FOUR NATIONS
FINAL

Grounded Willie Tonga can only watch as Benji Marshall beats Brett Morris and Cooper Cronk on the way to setting up Nathan Fien's late winning try

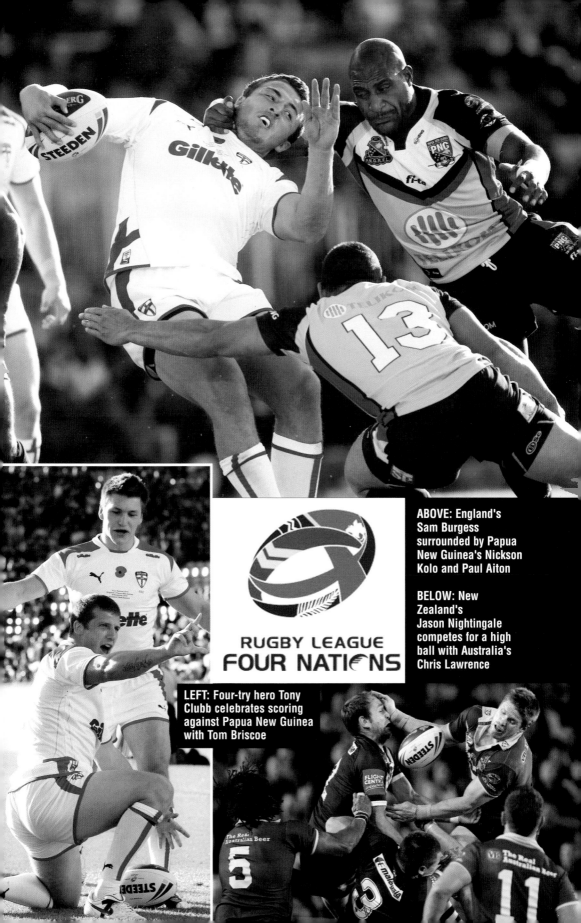

RUGBY LEAGUE FOUR NATIONS

ABOVE: England's Sam Burgess surrounded by Papua New Guinea's Nickson Kolo and Paul Aiton

BELOW: New Zealand's Jason Nightingale competes for a high ball with Australia's Chris Lawrence

LEFT: Four-try hero Tony Clubb celebrates scoring against Papua New Guinea with Tom Briscoe

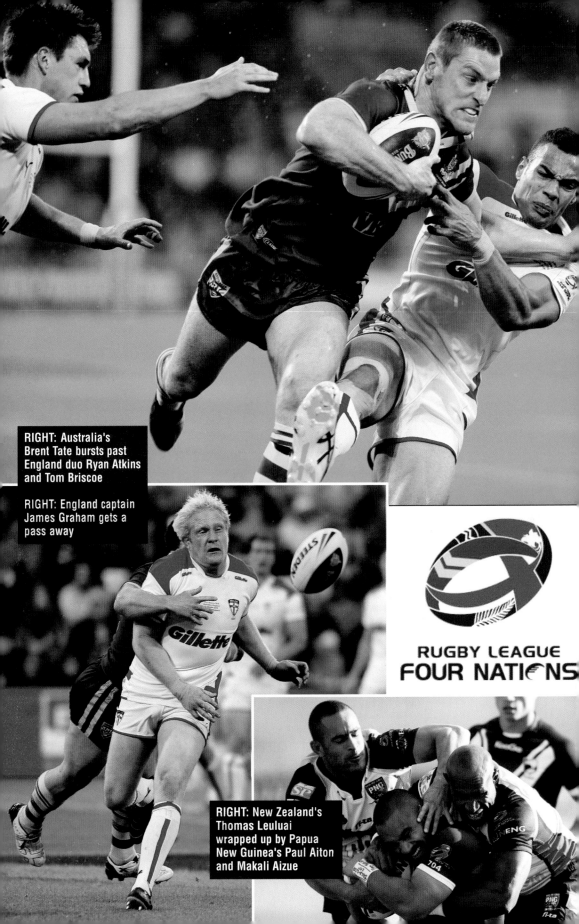

RIGHT: Australia's Brent Tate bursts past England duo Ryan Atkins and Tom Briscoe

RIGHT: England captain James Graham gets a pass away

RUGBY LEAGUE
FOUR NATIONS

RIGHT: New Zealand's Thomas Leuluai wrapped up by Papua New Guinea's Paul Aiton and Makali Aizue

HT: New Zealand's
un Kenny-Dowall
shes past England
rtet Ben Westwood,
in Brown, Sam Burgess
Darrell Griffin for a try

LEFT: Sam Tomkins
looks to escape the
New Zealand defence

RIGHT: Australia's Lote Tuqiri
looks for a way through
against Papua New Guinea

UGBY LEAGUE
UR NATIONS

RIGHT: Clinton Toopi leads the New Zealand Maori haka following his side's draw with England in a Four Nations warm-up game

BELOW: Eorl Crabtree offloads under heavy pressure from the Maori defence

ABOVE: John Paul Brocklebank dives over as Cumbria hold England in the Garry Purdham Memorial match

RIGHT: England's Gareth Ellis reaches out to score against France

RUGBY LEAGUE EUROPEAN CUP

Alitalia
Official Sponsor

ABOVE: Wales' Gareth Thomas makes a break against France

RIGHT: Lee Briers lifts the European Cup

BOVE: Ireland's Bob Beswick on the charge against Scotland

IGHT: Wales' Mark Lennon fends off Ireland's Liam Finn

RIGHT: Scotland's Oliver Wilkes catches France's Jason Baitieri high

RIGHT: France's Tony Gigot in action against Ireland in front of a packed house at Avignon

ABOVE: Wales' Lloyd White offloads against Scotland

STATE OF **ORIGIN**

ABOVE: New South Wales' Jarryd Hayne drives back Queensland's Johnathan Thurston and Ashley Harrison during Origin I

BELOW: Queensland celebrate winning their fifth successive Origin title

Harvey Norman
RUGBY LEAGUE
ALL STARS

ABOVE: Australia's Sam Thaiday fends off New Zealand's Issac Luke

RIGHT: Sam Burgess in action for the NRL All-Stars against the Indigenous All-Stars

ANZAC TEST

2010 DOMESTIC SEASON

egie Challenge Cup ● NRL Grand Final ● World Club Challenge ● Championship Grand Finals ● Academy & Reserves

Carnegie Challenge Cup Winners 10

FINAL

LEEDS RHINOS ....
WARRINGTON WOLVES 3

ABOVE: Warrington celebrate
retaining the Challenge Cup

BELOW: Louis Anderson crashes pas
Leeds' Brent Webb to score
Warrington's last try

ABOVE: No way past Ben Harrison
and Paul Wood for Kevin Sinfield

SEMI-FINALS

BOVE: Matt King races away for a Varrington try against Catalans

ELOW: Thomas Bosc lands atalans' winning field goal gainst Crusaders as time runs out

ABOVE: Leeds' Lee Smith and St Helens' Ade Gardner contest a high ball during a semi-final thriller

ROUND 5   QUARTER FINALS

Carnegie Challenge Cup

ABOVE: A jubilant Lee Smith celebrates his late winning try that sees Leeds home against Wigan

LEFT: Barrow jump for joy following their shock win over Castleford

ROUND 4

Dean Young and Jeremy Smith show off the NRL trophy to the Dragons' fans

BELOW: Mark Gasnier leaps high to claim the game's opening try

NRL

GRAND FINAL

ABOVE: Jason Nightingale shows his delight at scoring

BELOW: Braith Anasta pounces to claim the Roosters' first try

Gillette Fusion

RUGBY LEAGUE
WORLD CLUB CHALLENGE

ABOVE: Leeds' Ryan Hall dumped to the ground by the Melbourne defence

LEFT: Danny McGuire goes the length of the field to score

BELOW: Storm skipper Cameron Smith lifts the World Club Challenge trophy

The co-operative CHAMPIONSHIP GRAND FINAL

FEATHERSTONE ROVERS 22
HALIFAX 23

ABOVE: Halifax go wild after Ben Black's golden point field goal *(inset)*

LEFT: Zak Hardaker gets a pass away as he is tackled towards the touchline by Shad Royston

LEFT: David Larder and Graham Holroyd lead the Halifax celebrations

BATLEY BULLDOGS.....................
WIDNES VIKINGS ....

LEFT: Johnny Campbell goes past Kirk Netherton

NORTHERN RAIL CU

LEFT: John and Tommy Gallagher show off the Northern Rail Cup

CHAMPIONS! Hunslet celebrate winning the Championship 1 title with the Hawks fans

The co-operative CHAMPIONSHIP 1 GRAND FINAL

LEFT:
A jubilant Chris Thorman touches down for York

BELOW: Alan Reddecliff and Warren Ayres celebrate Warrington Wizards' Grand Final win over Huddersfield Underbank Rangers

ABOVE: Oldham's Lucas Onyango keeps York's Wayne Reittie at arms length as the City Knights grab the second promotion spot to the Championship

CONFERENCE NATIONAL GRAND FINAL

RIGHT: Graham Healey scores the Wizards' decisive late try

LEFT: Wigan show off the Valv[oline] Cup after defeating St Helens
BELOW: Jonny Walker collare[d] Maurie Fa'asavalu

Valvoline
VALVOLINE CUP WINNERS 2010

Valvoline
CUP
GRAND FINAL

RESERVES CHAMPIONSHIP - GRAND FINAL
RIGHT: Whitehaven celebrate their win over Featherstone
LEFT: Marc Jackson dives over for a try

NATIONAL CONFERENCE PREMIER DIVISION GRAND FINAL
LEFT: Leigh East's Gary Middlehurst goes acrobatic to score
RIGHT: Danny Kilshaw leads the celebrations following East's victory against Siddal

RUGBY LEAGUE CONFERENCE CHAMPIONS
St Albans Centurions

5
STATISTICAL REVIEW

SUPER LEAGUE PLAYERS
1996-2010

Super League Players 1996-2010

PLAYER	CLUB	YEAR	APP	TRIES	GOALS	FG	PTS
Carl Ablett	Leeds	2004,					
		2006-10	58(32)	15	0	0	60
	London	2005	3(2)	0	0	0	0
Darren Abram	Oldham	1996-97	25(2)	11	0	0	44
Darren Adams	Paris	1996	9(1)	1	0	0	4
Guy Adams	Huddersfield	1998	1(2)	0	0	0	0
Luke Adamson	Salford	2006-07,					
		2009-10	43(25)	6	0	0	24
Matt Adamson	Leeds	2002-04	54(8)	9	0	0	36
Phil Adamson	St Helens	1999	(1)	0	0	0	0
Toby Adamson	Salford	2010	(1)	0	0	0	0
Danny Addy	Bradford	2010	4(7)	1	5	0	14
Ade Adebisi	London	2004	(1)	0	0	0	0
Jamie Ainscough	Wigan	2002-03	30(2)	18	0	0	72
Shaun Ainscough	Wigan	2009-10	12	13	0	0	52
	Castleford	2010	7	4	0	0	16
Glen Air	London	1998-2001	57(13)	27	0	1	109
Makali Aizue	Hull KR	2007-09	18(32)	4	0	0	16
Darren Albert	St Helens	2002-05	105	77	0	0	308
Paul Alcock	Widnes	2003, 2005	1(7)	1	0	0	4
Neil Alexander	Salford	1998	(1)	0	0	0	0
Malcolm Alker	Salford	1997-2002, 2004-07, 2009-10	271(2)	40	0	1	161
Danny Allan	Leeds	2008-09	2(5)	0	0	0	0
Chris Allen	Castleford	1996	(1)	0	0	0	0
David Allen	Wigan	2003, 2005	6(15)	2	0	0	8
Gavin Allen	London	1996	10	0	0	0	0
John Allen	Workington	1996	20(1)	6	0	0	24
Ray Allen	London	1996	5(3)	3	0	0	12
Richard Allwood	Gateshead	1999	(4)	0	0	0	0
Sean Allwood	Gateshead	1999	3(17)	1	0	0	4
David Alstead	Warrington	2000-02	23(10)	3	0	0	12
Luke Ambler	Leeds	2010	1(8)	1	0	0	4
Asa Amone	Halifax	1996-97	32(7)	10	0	0	40
Kyle Amor	Leeds	2010	(3)	0	0	0	0
Grant Anderson	Castleford	1996-97	15(6)	3	0	0	12
Louis Anderson	Warrington	2008-10	73	11	0	0	44
Paul Anderson	St Helens	2005-06	48(5)	7	1	0	30
	Bradford	1997-2004	74(104)	30	0	0	120
	Halifax	1996	5(1)	1	0	0	4
Paul Anderson	Sheffield	1999	3(7)	1	0	0	4
	St Helens	1996-98	2(28)	4	1	0	18
Vinnie Anderson	Warrington	2007-10	57(19)	22	0	0	88
	St Helens	2005-06	28(14)	17	0	0	68
Phil Anderton	St Helens	2004	1	0	0	0	0
Eric Anselme	Leeds	2008	2(2)	2	0	0	8
	Halifax	1997	(2)	0	0	0	0
Mark Applegarth	Wakefield	2004-07	20(5)	3	0	0	12
Graham Appo	Warrington	2002-05	60(13)	35	80	0	300
	Huddersfield	2001	7	4	0	0	16
Anthony Armour	London	2005	11(7)	1	0	0	4
Colin Armstrong	Workington	1996	11(2)	1	0	0	4
Tom Armstrong	St Helens	2009-10	6(1)	4	0	0	16
Richard Armswood							
	Workington	1996	5(1)	1	0	0	4
Danny Arnold	Salford	2001-02	26(13)	13	0	0	52
	Huddersfield	1998-2000	55(7)	26	0	0	104
	Castleford	2000	(4)	0	0	0	0
	St Helens	1996-97	40(1)	33	0	0	132
Joe Arundel	Castleford	2008, 2010	5(4)	2	0	0	4
Craig Ashall	St Helens	2006	1	1	0	0	4
Chris Ashton	Wigan	2005-07	44(2)	25	2	0	104
Matty Ashurst	St Helens	2009-10	8(29)	5	0	0	20
Martin Aspinwall	Huddersfield	2006-10	72(8)	22	0	0	88
	Wigan	2001-05	85(13)	27	0	0	108
Mark Aston	Sheffield	1996-99	67(6)	6	243	6	516
Paul Atcheson	Widnes	2002-04	16(35)	4	0	0	16
	St Helens	1998-2000	58(4)	18	0	0	72
	Oldham	1996-97	40	21	0	0	84
David Atkins	Huddersfield	2001	26(1)	4	0	0	16
Ryan Atkins	Warrington	2010	29	11	0	0	44
	Wakefield	2006-09	86(2)	45	0	0	180
Brad Attwood	Halifax	2003	(3)	0	0	0	0
Warren Ayres	Salford	1999	2(9)	1	2	0	8
Jerome Azema	Paris	1997	(1)	0	0	0	0
Marcus Bai	Bradford	2006	24	9	0	0	36
	Leeds	2004-05	57	42	0	0	168
David Baildon	Hull	1998-99	26(2)	4	0	0	16
Jean-Phillipe Baile							
	Catalans	2008-10	34(5)	13	0	0	52
Andy Bailey	Hull	2004-05	2(8)	1	0	0	4
Julian Bailey	Huddersfield	2003-04	47	13	0	0	52
Phil Bailey	Wigan	2007-10	84(4)	13	0	0	52
Ryan Bailey	Leeds	2002-10	130(68)	8	0	0	32
Simon Baldwin	Salford	2004-06	20(29)	3	0	0	12
	Sheffield	1999	7(15)	2	0	0	8
	Halifax	1996-98	41(15)	16	0	1	65
Rob Ball	Wigan	1998-2000	3(4)	0	0	0	0
Paul Ballard	Celtic	2009	2	0	0	0	0
	Widnes	2005	3(1)	2	0	0	8
Darren Bamford	Salford	2005	2(1)	0	0	0	0
Michael Banks	Bradford	1998	(1)	0	0	0	0

PLAYER	CLUB	YEAR	APP	TRIES	GOALS	FG	PTS
Steve Bannister	Harlequins	2007	(6)	0	0	0	0
	St Helens	2006-07	(3)	0	0	0	0
Frederic Banquet	Paris	1996	16(2)	7	4	0	36
Lee Bardauskas	Castleford	1996-97	(2)	0	0	0	0
Craig Barker	Workington	1996	(2)	0	0	0	0
Dwayne Barker	Harlequins	2008	5(5)	1	0	0	4
	London	2004	3	1	0	0	4
	Hull	2003	(1)	0	0	0	0
Mark Barlow	Wakefield	2002	(1)	0	0	0	0
Danny Barnes	Halifax	1999	2	0	0	0	0
Richie Barnett	Salford	2007	7	4	0	0	16
	Warrington	2006-07	26(10)	15	0	0	60
	Hull	2004-05	21(5)	21	0	0	84
	Widnes	2005	4	2	0	0	8
Richie Barnett	Hull	2003-04	31(1)	17	0	0	68
	London	2001-02	31(4)	13	0	0	52
David Barnhill	Leeds	2000	20(8)	5	0	0	20
Trent Barrett	Wigan	2007-08	53(1)	22	0	4	92
Paul Barrow	Warrington	1996-97	1(10)	1	0	0	4
Scott Barrow	St Helens	1997-2000	9(13)	1	0	0	4
Steve Barrow	London	2000	2	0	0	0	0
	Hull	1998-99	4(17)	1	0	0	4
	Wigan	1996	(8)	3	0	0	12
William Barthau	Catalans	2010	6(1)	0	3	0	6
Ben Barton	Huddersfield	1998	1(6)	1	0	0	4
Danny Barton	Salford	2001	1	0	0	0	0
Wayne Bartrim	Castleford	2002-03	41(2)	9	157	0	350
Greg Barwick	London	1996-97	30(4)	21	110	2	306
David Bastian	Halifax	1996	(2)	0	0	0	0
Ashley Bateman	Celtic	2009	1	0	0	0	0
David Bates	Castleford	2001-02	(4)	0	0	0	0
	Warrington	2001	1(2)	0	0	0	0
Nathan Batty	Wakefield	2001	1(1)	0	0	0	0
Andreas Bauer	Hull KR	2007	10(2)	5	0	0	20
Russell Bawden	London	1996-97, 2002-04	50(49)	15	0	0	60
Neil Baxter	Salford	2001	1	0	0	0	0
Neil Baynes	Salford	1999-2002, 2004	84(19)	10	0	0	40
	Wigan	1996-98	(10)	1	0	0	4
Chris Beasley	Celtic	2009	15(5)	2	0	0	8
Chris Beattie	Catalans	2006	22(5)	3	0	0	12
Robbie Beazley	London	1997-99	48(15)	13	0	0	52
Robbie Beckett	Halifax	2002	27	15	0	0	60
Dean Bell	Leeds	1996	1	1	0	0	4
Ian Bell	Hull	2003	(1)	0	0	0	0
Mark Bell	Wigan	1998	22	12	0	0	48
Paul Bell	Leeds	2000	1	0	0	0	0
Steven Bell	Catalans	2009-10	43	14	0	0	56
Troy Bellamy	Paris	1997	5(10)	0	0	0	0
Adrian Belle	Huddersfield	1998	10(2)	0	0	0	0
	Oldham	1996	19	8	0	0	32
Jamie Benn	Castleford	1998, 2000	3(8)	1	15	0	34
Andy Bennett	Warrington	1996	6(5)	1	0	0	4
Mike Bennett	St Helens	2000-08	74(70)	15	0	0	60
Andrew Bentley	Catalans	2007-10	9(15)	1	0	0	4
John Bentley	Huddersfield	1999	13(4)	3	0	0	12
	Halifax	1996, 1998	22(3)	24	0	0	96
Kane Bentley	Catalans	2007-10	11(19)	5	0	0	20
Phil Bergman	Paris	1997	20(1)	14	0	0	56
Shaun Berrigan	Hull	2008-10	60(8)	12	0	0	48
Joe Berry	Huddersfield	1998-99	25(14)	3	0	0	12
David Berthezene	Salford	2007	9(1)	0	0	0	0
	Catalans	2006-07	5(14)	0	0	0	0
Colin Best	Hull	2003-04	57	34	0	0	136
Roger Best	London	1997-98	1(5)	1	0	0	4
Bob Beswick	Wigan	2004-05	5(14)	2	0	0	8
Monty Betham	Wakefield	2006	26	2	0	0	8
Mike Bethwaite	Workington	1996	17(3)	1	0	0	4
Denis Betts	Wigan	1998-2001	82(24)	33	0	0	132
Cliff Beverley	Salford	2004-05	47(1)	14	0	0	56
Kyle Bibb	Wakefield	2008-10	1(24)	0	0	0	0
	Harlequins	2010	(2)	0	0	0	0
	Hull KR	2009	(2)	0	0	0	0
Adam Bibey	Widnes	2004	(1)	0	0	0	0
Ricky Bibey	Wakefield	2007-09	32(25)	1	0	0	4
	St Helens	2004	4(14)	0	0	0	0
	Wigan	2001-03	5(29)	0	0	0	0
Chris Birchall	Halifax	2002-03	24(22)	4	0	0	16
	Bradford	2000	(1)	0	0	0	0
Deon Bird	Castleford	2006	17(6)	5	0	0	20
	Widnes	2003-04	39(6)	9	0	0	36
	Wakefield	2002	10(1)	1	0	0	4
	Hull	2000-02	37(22)	20	0	0	80
	Gateshead	1999	19(3)	13	0	0	52
	Paris	1996-97	30	12	2	0	52
Greg Bird	Catalans	2009	20(2)	5	3	0	26
Nathan Blacklock	Hull	2005-06	44(3)	33	0	0	132
Richie Blackmore	Leeds	1997-2000	63	25	0	0	100
Anthony Blackwood							
	Crusaders	2010	1	0	0	0	0
	Celtic	2009	25	5	0	0	20
Luke Blake	Wakefield	2009	(2)	0	0	0	0
Matthew Blake	Wakefield	2003-04	1(5)	0	0	0	0

PLAYER	CLUB	YEAR	APP	TRIES	GOALS	FG	PTS
Steve Blakeley	Salford	1997-2002	103(5)	26	241	2	588
	Warrington	2000	4(3)	1	9	0	22
Richard Blakeway	Castleford	2002-04	1(14)	0	0	0	0
Damien Blanch	Wakefield	2008-10	44(3)	31	0	0	124
	Castleford	2006	3(2)	0	0	0	0
Matt Blaymire	Wakefield	2007-10	85(3)	26	0	1	105
Ian Blease	Salford	1997	(1)	0	0	0	0
Jamie Bloem	Huddersfield	2003	18(4)	3	11	0	34
	Halifax	1998-2002	82(25)	25	100	2	302
Vea Bloomfield	Paris	1996	4(14)	3	0	0	12
Matty Blythe	Warrington	2007-10	6(13)	3	0	0	12
Ben Bolger	Harlequins	2010	4(11)	0	0	0	0
Pascal Bomati	Paris	1996	17(1)	10	0	0	40
Simon Booth	Hull	1998-99	15(9)	2	0	0	8
	St Helens	1996-97	10(4)	1	0	0	4
Steve Booth	Huddersfield	1998-99	16(4)	2	3	0	14
Alan Boothroyd	Halifax	1997	2(3)	0	0	0	0
Thomas Bosc	Catalans	2006-10	100(3)	30	288	3	699
John Boslem	Paris	1996	(5)	0	0	0	0
Liam Bostock	St Helens	2004	1	0	0	0	0
Liam Botham	Wigan	2005	5	0	0	0	0
	Leeds	2003-05	2(11)	4	0	0	16
	London	2004	6(2)	3	6	0	24
Frano Botica	Castleford	1996	21	5	84	2	190
Matthew Bottom	Leigh	2005	(1)	0	0	0	0
Hadj Boudebza	Paris	1996	(2)	0	0	0	0
David Boughton	Huddersfield	1999	26(1)	4	0	0	16
David Bouveng	Halifax	1997-99	66(2)	19	0	0	76
Tony Bowes	Huddersfield	1998	3(2)	0	0	0	0
Radney Bowker	London	2004	3	1	0	0	4
	St Helens	2001	(1)	0	0	0	0
David Boyle	Bradford	1999-2000	36(13)	15	0	1	61
Ryan Boyle	Salford	2010	20(2)	2	0	0	8
	Castleford	2006, 2008-09	(29)	2	0	0	8
Andy Bracek	Warrington	2005-08	7(49)	7	0	0	28
	St Helens	2004	(1)	0	0	0	0
David Bradbury	Hudds-Sheff	2000	21(2)	1	0	0	4
	Salford	1997-99	23(10)	6	0	0	24
	Oldham	1996-97	19(6)	9	0	0	36
John Braddish	St Helens	2001-02	1(1)	0	3	0	6
Graeme Bradley	Bradford	1996-98	62(1)	29	0	0	116
Nick Bradley-Qalilawa	Harlequins	2006	27	6	0	0	24
	London	2005	28	19	0	0	76
Darren Bradstreet	London	1999-2000	1(3)	0	0	0	0
Dominic Brambani	Castleford	2004	2(2)	0	0	0	0
Liam Bretherton	Wigan	1999	(5)	2	0	0	8
	Warrington	1997	(2)	0	0	0	0
Johnny Brewer	Halifax	1996	4(2)	2	0	0	8
Chris Bridge	Warrington	2005-10	90(12)	45	141	1	463
	Bradford	2003-04	2(14)	4	6	0	28
Lee Briers	Warrington	1997-2010	304(12)	106	773	61	2031
	St Helens	1997	3	0	11	0	22
Carl Briggs	Salford	1999	8(5)	3	0	1	13
	Halifax	1996	5(3)	1	0	0	4
Mike Briggs	Widnes	2002	1(2)	1	0	0	4
Shaun Briscoe	Hull KR	2008-10	70	22	0	0	88
	Hull	2004-07	83(9)	50	0	0	200
	Wigan	2002-03	23(5)	11	0	0	44
Tom Briscoe	Hull	2008-10	48(3)	28	0	0	112
Darren Britt	St Helens	2002-03	41	3	0	0	12
Gary Broadbent	Salford	1997-2002	117(2)	22	0	0	88
Paul Broadbent	Wakefield	2002	16(5)	0	0	0	0
	Hull	2000-01	40(9)	3	0	0	12
	Halifax	1999	26(1)	2	0	0	8
	Sheffield	1996-98	63(1)	6	0	0	24
Andrew Brocklehurst	Salford	2004-07	34(23)	5	0	0	20
	London	2004	12(6)	2	0	0	8
	Halifax	2001-03	37(8)	2	0	0	8
Justin Brooker	Wakefield	2001	25	9	0	0	36
	Bradford	2000	17(4)	11	0	0	44
Danny Brough	Huddersfield	2010	19(3)	5	22	2	66
	Wakefield	2008-10	50(1)	14	174	4	408
	Castleford	2006	10	1	31	2	68
	Hull	2005-06	25(12)	3	85	1	183
Jodie Broughton	Salford	2010	23	12	0	0	48
	Hull	2008-09	9(3)	6	0	0	24
Alex Brown	Huddersfield	2009	1	0	0	0	0
Darren Brown	Salford	1999-2001	47(9)	11	6	0	56
Gavin Brown	Leeds	1996-97	5(2)	1	2	0	8
Kevin Brown	Huddersfield	2006-10	113	32	0	1	129
	Wigan	2003-06	46(18)	27	0	0	108
Lee Brown	Hull	1999	(1)	0	0	0	0
Michael Brown	Huddersfield	2008	(1)	0	0	0	0
Michael Brown	London	1996	(2)	0	0	0	0
Todd Brown	Paris	1996	8(1)	2	0	0	8
Adrian Brunker	Wakefield	1999	17	6	0	0	24
Lamont Bryan	Harlequins	2008-10	9(14)	1	0	0	4
Justin Bryant	Paris	1996	4(1)	0	0	0	0
	London	1996	7(8)	1	0	0	4

PLAYER	CLUB	YEAR	APP	TRIES	GOALS	FG	PTS
Mark Bryant	Crusaders	2010	26(2)	1	0	0	4
	Celtic	2009	23(3)	0	0	0	0
Austin Buchanan	Wakefield	2005-06	6	2	0	0	8
	London	2003	3(1)	2	0	0	8
Danny Buderus	Leeds	2009-10	29(12)	8	0	0	32
Neil Budworth	Celtic	2009	8(19)	0	0	0	0
	Harlequins	2006	2(19)	0	0	0	0
	London	2002-05	59(11)	4	1	0	18
James Bunyan	Huddersfield	1998-99	8(7)	2	0	0	8
Andy Burgess	Salford	1997	3(12)	0	0	0	0
Luke Burgess	Leeds	2008-10	5(57)	6	0	0	24
	Harlequins	2007	(3)	0	0	0	0
Sam Burgess	Bradford	2006-09	46(34)	14	5	0	66
Mike Burnett	Hull	2008-10	13(21)	3	0	0	12
Darren Burns	Warrington	2002-04	66(6)	19	0	0	76
Gary Burns	Oldham	1996	6	1	0	0	4
Paul Burns	Workington	1996	5(2)	1	0	0	4
Rob Burrow	Leeds	2001-10	192(69)	112	120	4	692
Dean Busby	Warrington	1999-2002	34(34)	7	0	0	28
	Hull	1998	8(6)	0	0	0	0
	St Helens	1996-98	1(7)	0	0	0	0
Tom Bush	Leeds	2010	3(1)	1	0	0	4
Ikram Butt	London	1996	5(1)	0	0	0	0
Shane Byrne	Huddersfield	1998-99	1(5)	0	0	0	0
Todd Byrne	Hull	2008-09	20	4	0	0	16
Didier Cabestany	Paris	1996-97	20(6)	2	0	0	8
Joel Caine	Salford	2004	24	8	13	0	58
	London	2003	6	4	1	0	18
Mark Calderwood	Hull	2009-10	23	6	0	0	24
	Wigan	2006-08	64	23	0	0	92
	Leeds	2001-05	117(9)	88	0	0	352
Mike Callan	Warrington	2002	(4)	0	0	0	0
Matt Calland	Huddersfield	2003	2	0	0	0	0
	Hull	1999	1	0	0	0	0
	Bradford	1996-98	44(5)	24	0	0	96
Dean Callaway	London	1999-2000	26(24)	12	0	0	48
Laurent Cambres	Paris	1996	(1)	0	0	0	0
Chris Campbell	Warrington	2000	7(1)	2	0	0	8
Liam Campbell	Wakefield	2005	(1)	0	0	0	0
Logan Campbell	Hull	1998-99, 2001	70(13)	14	0	0	56
	Castleford	2000	14(2)	3	0	0	12
	Workington	1996	7(1)	1	0	0	4
Blake Cannova	Widnes	2002	(1)	0	0	0	0
Phil Cantillon	Widnes	2002-03	27(21)	18	0	0	72
	Leeds	1997	(1)	0	0	0	0
Daryl Cardiss	Warrington	2003-04	23(2)	3	4	0	20
	Halifax	1999-2003	91(8)	39	4	0	164
	Wigan	1996-98	12(6)	4	0	0	16
Dale Cardoza	Warrington	2002	5	1	0	0	4
	Halifax	2001	3	1	0	0	4
	Huddersfield	2000-01	20(9)	11	0	0	44
	Sheffield	1998-99	11(7)	3	0	0	12
Paul Carige	Salford	1999	24(1)	7	0	0	28
Dane Carlaw	Catalans	2008-10	58(15)	9	0	0	36
Keal Carlile	Huddersfield	2009	(1)	0	0	0	0
	Bradford	2008	(1)	0	0	0	0
Jim Carlton	Huddersfield	1997	3(11)	2	0	0	8
George Carmont	Wigan	2008-10	84	37	0	0	148
Brian Carney	Warrington	2009	4	2	0	0	8
	Wigan	2001-05	91(10)	42	1	0	170
	Hull	2000	13(3)	7	0	0	28
	Gateshead	1999	3(2)	2	0	0	8
Martin Carney	Warrington	1997	(1)	0	0	0	0
Paul Carr	Sheffield	1996-98	45(5)	15	0	0	60
Bernard Carroll	London	1996	2(1)	1	0	0	4
Mark Carroll	London	1998	15(3)	1	0	0	4
Tonie Carroll	Leeds	2001-02	42(2)	30	0	0	120
Darren Carter	Workington	1996	10(3)	0	1	0	2
Steve Carter	Widnes	2002	14(7)	4	0	0	16
John Cartwright	Salford	1997	9	0	0	0	0
Garreth Carvell	Warrington	2009-10	37(5)	5	0	0	20
	Hull	2001-08	69(83)	22	0	0	88
	Leeds	1997-2000	(4)	0	0	0	0
	Gateshead	1999	4(4)	1	0	0	4
Garen Casey	Salford	1999	13(5)	3	23	0	58
Ray Cashmere	Salford	2009-10	39(2)	4	0	0	16
Mick Cassidy	Widnes	2005	24	0	0	0	0
	Wigan	1996-2004	184(36)	30	0	0	120
Remi Casty	Catalans	2006-10	14(78)	6	0	0	24
Ned Catic	Castleford	2008	7(7)	3	0	0	12
	Wakefield	2006-07	17(29)	4	0	0	16
Chris Causey	Warrington	1997-99	(18)	1	0	0	4
Jason Cayless	St Helens	2006-09	62(9)	7	0	0	28
Arnaud Cervello	Paris	1996	4	4	0	0	16
Marshall Chalk	Celtic	2009	13	4	0	0	16
Gary Chambers	Warrington	1996-2000	65(28)	2	0	0	8
Pierre Chamorin	Paris	1996-97	27(3)	8	3	0	38
Alex Chan	Catalans	2006-08	59(11)	11	0	0	44
Jason Chan	Crusaders	2010	26	6	0	0	24
	Celtic	2009	17(6)	3	0	0	12
Joe Chandler	Leeds	2008	(1)	0	0	0	0
Chris Chapman	Leeds	1999	(1)	0	0	0	0
Damien Chapman	London	1998	6(2)	3	4	1	21

PLAYER	CLUB	YEAR	APP	TRIES	GOALS	FG	PTS
David Chapman	Castleford	1996-98	24(6)	8	0	0	32
Jaymes Chapman	Halifax	2002-03	5(8)	1	0	0	4
Richard Chapman	Sheffield	1996	1	2	0	0	8
Chris Charles	Salford	2004-06	59(16)	6	140	0	304
	Castleford	2001	1(4)	1	0	0	4
Olivier Charles	Catalans	2007	2	2	0	0	8
Josh Charnley	Wigan	2010	(1)	1	0	0	4
	Hull KR	2010	5	5	0	0	20
Rangi Chase	Castleford	2009-10	49(4)	17	0	1	69
Andy Cheetham	Huddersfield	1998-99	30	11	0	0	44
Kris Chesney	London	1998	1(2)	0	0	0	0
Chris Chester	Hull KR	2007-08	28(6)	4	0	0	16
	Hull	2002-06	67(25)	13	0	0	52
	Wigan	1999-2001	21(22)	5	0	0	20
	Halifax	1996-99	47(14)	16	15	1	95
Lee Chilton	Workington	1996	10(3)	6	0	0	24
Gary Christie	Bradford	1996-97	4(7)	1	0	0	4
Dean Clark	Leeds	1996	11(2)	3	0	0	12
Des Clark	St Helens	1999	4	0	0	0	0
	Halifax	1998-99	35(13)	6	0	0	24
Greg Clarke	Halifax	1997	1(1)	0	0	0	0
John Clarke	Oldham	1996-97	27(4)	5	0	0	20
Jon Clarke	Warrington	2001-10	215(11)	55	2	0	224
	London	2000-01	19(11)	2	0	0	8
	Wigan	1997-99	13(10)	3	0	0	12
Chris Clarkson	Leeds	2010	12(3)	5	0	0	20
Ryan Clayton	Castleford	2004, 2008-10	36(24)	5	0	0	20
	Salford	2006	3(8)	2	0	0	8
	Huddersfield	2005	4(6)	0	0	0	0
	Halifax	2000, 2002-03	28(12)	6	0	0	24
Gavin Clinch	Salford	2004	21(1)	1	0	1	5
	Halifax	1998-99, 2001-02	88(2)	26	45	5	199
	Hudds-Sheff	2000	18(2)	5	0	1	21
	Wigan	1999	10(2)	4	12	0	40
Joel Clinton	Hull KR	2010	22(3)	2	0	0	8
John Clough	Salford	2004-06	1(16)	0	0	0	0
Paul Clough	St Helens	2005-10	41(66)	13	0	0	52
Tony Clubb	Harlequins	2006-10	73(11)	19	0	0	76
Bradley Clyde	Leeds	2001	7(5)	1	0	0	4
Michael Coady	Leeds	2010	1	0	0	0	0
Evan Cochrane	London	1996	5(1)	1	0	0	4
Ben Cockayne	Hull KR	2007-10	65(20)	22	0	0	88
Liam Colbon	Hull KR	2009-10	38	14	0	0	56
	Wigan	2004-05, 2007-08	37(14)	14	0	0	56
Anthony Colella	Huddersfield	2003	5(1)	2	0	0	8
Liam Coleman	Leigh	2005	1(4)	0	0	0	0
Andy Coley	Wigan	2008-10	79(5)	7	0	0	28
	Salford	2001-02, 2004-07	112(34)	34	0	0	136
Richard Colley	Bradford	2004	1	0	0	0	0
Steve Collins	Hull	2000	28	17	0	0	68
	Gateshead	1999	20(4)	13	0	0	52
Wayne Collins	Leeds	1997	21	3	0	0	12
Aurelien Cologni	Catalans	2006	4(1)	3	0	0	12
Gary Connolly	Widnes	2005	20	4	1	0	18
	Wigan	1996-2002, 2004	168(10)	70	5	0	290
	Leeds	2003-04	27	6	0	0	24
Matt Cook	Hull KR	2010	5(12)	3	0	0	12
	Bradford	2005-09	11(52)	4	0	0	16
	Castleford	2008	2(1)	1	0	0	4
Mick Cook	Sheffield	1996	9(10)	2	0	0	8
Paul Cook	Huddersfield	1998-99	11(6)	2	13	0	34
	Bradford	1996-97	14(8)	7	38	1	105
Peter Cook	St Helens	2004	(1)	0	0	0	0
Paul Cooke	Wakefield	2010	16(1)	3	36	1	85
	Hull KR	2007-10	54(5)	8	76	2	186
	Hull	1999-2007	177(27)	32	333	4	798
Ben Cooper	Leigh	2005	25(1)	5	0	0	20
	Huddersfield	2000-01, 2003-04	28(12)	3	0	0	12
Michael Cooper	Warrington	2006-10	2(42)	4	0	0	16
	Castleford	2010	1(5)	2	0	0	8
Ged Corcoran	Halifax	2003	1(11)	0	0	0	0
Wayne Corcoran	Halifax	2003	4(2)	0	0	0	0
Josh Cordoba	Hull	2009	8	1	0	0	4
Mark Corvo	Salford	2002	7(5)	0	0	0	0
Brandon Costin	Huddersfield	2001, 2003-04	69	42	93	3	357
	Bradford	2002	20(1)	8	0	0	32
Wes Cotton	London	1997-98	12	3	0	0	12
Phil Coussons	Salford	1997	7(2)	3	0	0	12
Alex Couttet	Paris	1997	1	0	0	0	0
Nick Couttet	Paris	1997	1	0	0	0	0
Jamie Coventry	Castleford	1996	1	0	0	0	0
Jimmy Cowan	Oldham	1996-97	2(8)	0	0	0	0
Will Cowell	Warrington	1998-2000	6(8)	1	0	0	4
Neil Cowie	Wigan	1996-2001	116(27)	10	0	1	41
Mark Cox	London	2003	(3)	0	0	0	0
James Coyle	Wigan	2005	2(3)	1	0	0	4
Thomas Coyle	Wigan	2008	2(1)	0	0	0	0
Eorl Crabtree	Huddersfield	2001, 2003-10	72(120)	21	0	0	84
Andy Craig	Halifax	1999	13(7)	1	3	0	10
	Wigan	1996	5(5)	2	0	0	8
Owen Craigie	Widnes	2005	15	7	0	2	30
Scott Cram	London	1999-2002	65(7)	4	0	0	16
Steve Craven	Hull	1998-2003	53(42)	4	0	0	16
Nicky Crellin	Workington	1996	(2)	0	0	0	0
Jason Critchley	Wakefield	2000	7(1)	4	0	0	16
	Castleford	1997-98	27(3)	11	0	0	44
Jason Croker	Catalans	2007-09	56(2)	11	0	1	45
Martin Crompton	Salford	1998-2000	30(6)	11	6	2	58
	Oldham	1996-97	36(1)	16	0	3	67
Paul Crook	Widnes	2005	2(2)	0	5	1	11
Paul Crook	Oldham	1996	4(9)	0	3	0	6
Jason Crookes	Bradford	2009-10	6(1)	0	0	0	0
Lee Crooks	Castleford	1996-97	27(2)	2	14	0	36
Alan Cross	St Helens	1997	(2)	0	0	0	0
Steve Crossley	Bradford	2010	(7)	1	0	0	4
Garret Crossman	Hull KR	2008	8(18)	0	0	0	0
Steve Crouch	Castleford	2004	4(1)	2	0	0	8
Kevin Crouthers	Warrington	2001-03	12(1)	4	0	0	16
	London	2000	6(4)	1	0	0	4
	Wakefield	1999	4(4)	1	0	0	4
	Bradford	1997-98	3(9)	2	0	0	8
Matt Crowther	Hull	2001-03	48	20	166	0	412
	Hudds-Sheff	2000	10(4)	5	22	0	64
	Sheffield	1996-99	43(4)	22	10	0	108
Heath Cruckshank	Halifax	2003	19(1)	0	0	0	0
	St Helens	2001	1(12)	0	0	0	0
Leroy Cudjoe	Huddersfield	2008-10	65(1)	43	40	0	252
Paul Cullen	Warrington	1996	19	3	0	0	12
Francis Cummins	Leeds	1996-2005	217(13)	120	26	2	534
Keiron Cunningham	St Helens	1996-2010	357(24)	138	0	0	552
Liam Cunningham	Hull	2010	(1)	0	0	0	0
Andy Currier	Warrington	1996-97	(2)	1	0	0	4
Peter Cusack	Hull	2008-10	34(22)	3	0	0	12
Joe Dakuitoga	Sheffield	1996	6(3)	0	0	0	0
Matty Dale	Hull	2006, 2008	(7)	1	0	0	4
	Wakefield	2008	1(1)	0	0	0	0
Brett Dallas	Wigan	2000-06	156	89	0	0	356
Mark Dalle Cort	Celtic	2009	23	4	0	0	16
Paul Darbyshire	Warrington	1997	(6)	0	0	0	0
James Davey	Wakefield	2009-10	(7)	0	0	0	0
Maea David	Hull	1998	1	0	0	0	0
Paul Davidson	Halifax	2001-03	22(30)	10	0	0	40
	London	2000	6(10)	4	0	0	16
	St Helens	1998-99	27(16)	7	0	0	28
	Oldham	1996-97	17(18)	14	0	1	57
Ben Davies	Wigan	2010	(5)	0	0	0	0
Gareth Davies	Warrington	1996-97	1(6)	0	0	0	0
Geraint Davies	Celtic	2009	(7)	0	0	0	0
John Davies	Castleford	2010	(1)	0	0	0	0
Wes Davies	Wigan	1998-2001	22(22)	11	0	0	44
Brad Davis	Castleford	1997-2000, 2004, 2006	102(3)	31	43	10	220
	Wakefield	2001-03	51(12)	15	22	5	109
Matt Daylight	Hull	2000	17(1)	7	0	0	28
	Gateshead	1999	30	25	0	0	100
Michael De Vere	Huddersfield	2005-06	36	6	74	0	172
Paul Deacon	Wigan	2010	13(7)	1	0	0	4
	Bradford	1998-2009	258(43)	72	1029	23	2369
	Oldham	1997	(2)	0	0	0	0
Chris Dean	St Helens	2007-10	18(3)	9	0	0	36
Craig Dean	Halifax	1996-97	25(11)	12	1	1	51
Gareth Dean	London	2002	(4)	0	0	0	0
Yacine Dekkiche	Hudds-Sheff	2000	11(3)	3	0	0	12
Brett Delaney	Leeds	2010	24	9	0	0	36
Jason Demetriou	Wakefield	2004-10	174(3)	50	2	0	204
	Widnes	2002-03	47(1)	15	1	0	62
Martin Dermott	Warrington	1997	1	0	0	0	0
David Despin	Paris	1996	(1)	0	0	0	0
Fabien Devecchi	Paris	1996-97	17(10)	2	0	0	8
Paul Devlin	Widnes	2002-04	32	16	0	0	64
Stuart Dickens	Salford	2005	4(5)	0	4	0	8
Matt Diskin	Leeds	2001-10	195(37)	40	0	0	160
Andrew Dixon	St Helens	2009-10	14(11)	6	0	0	24
Kirk Dixon	Castleford	2008-10	65(1)	30	98	0	316
	Hull	2004-06	13(4)	7	4	0	36
Paul Dixon	Sheffield	1996-97	5(9)	1	0	0	4
Gareth Dobson	Castleford	1998-2000	(10)	0	0	0	0
Michael Dobson	Hull KR	2008-10	71	30	237	6	600
	Wigan	2006	14	5	61	0	142
	Catalans	2006	10	4	31	1	79
Michael Docherty	Hull	2000-01	(6)	0	0	0	0
Sid Domic	Hull	2006-07	39(4)	15	0	0	60
	Wakefield	2004-05	48	30	0	0	120
	Warrington	2002-03	41(4)	17	0	0	68
Scott Donald	Leeds	2006-10	131	77	0	0	308

PLAYER	CLUB	YEAR	APP	TRIES	GOALS	FG	PTS
James Donaldson							
	Bradford	2009-10	3(16)	2	0	0	8
Glen Donkin	Hull	2002-03	(10)	1	0	0	4
Stuart Donlan	Castleford	2008	20	8	0	0	32
	Huddersfield	2004-06	59(3)	15	0	0	60
	Halifax	2001-03	65(2)	22	0	0	88
Jason Donohue	Bradford	1996	(4)	0	0	0	0
Jeremy Donougher							
	Bradford	1996-99	40(21)	13	0	0	52
Justin Dooley	London	2000-01	37(18)	2	0	0	8
Dane Dorahy	Halifax	2003	20	7	45	0	118
	Wakefield	2000-01	16(2)	4	19	1	55
Luke Dorn	Harlequins	2006, 2009-10	61(1)	44	0	0	176
	Castleford	2008	25(1)	19	0	0	76
	Salford	2007	19(8)	11	0	0	44
	London	2005	28	23	0	0	92
Ewan Dowes	Hull	2003-10	167(33)	9	0	0	36
	Leeds	2001-03	1(9)	0	0	0	0
Adam Doyle	Warrington	1998	9(3)	4	0	0	16
Rod Doyle	Sheffield	1997-99	52(10)	10	0	0	40
Brad Drew	Huddersfield	2005-07, 2010	78(13)	18	13	1	99
	Wakefield	2008-09	27(9)	7	14	1	57
Damien Driscoll	Salford	2001	23(1)	1	0	0	4
Gil Dudson	Celtic	2009	(1)	0	0	0	0
Jason Duffy	Leigh	2005	3(1)	0	0	0	0
John Duffy	Leigh	2005	21	6	0	0	24
	Salford	2000	3(11)	0	1	1	3
	Warrington	1997-99	12(12)	0	0	0	0
Tony Duggan	Celtic	2009	4	3	0	0	12
Andrew Duncan	London	1997	2(4)	2	0	0	8
	Warrington	1997	(1)	0	0	0	0
Andrew Dunemann							
	Salford	2006	25	1	0	2	6
	Leeds	2003-05	76(4)	11	0	2	46
	Halifax	1999-2002	68	19	0	1	77
Matt Dunford	London	1997-98	18(20)	3	0	1	13
Vincent Duport	Catalans	2007-09	27(14)	11	0	0	44
Jamie Durbin	Widnes	2005	1	0	0	0	0
	Warrington	2003	(1)	0	0	0	0
James Durkin	Paris	1997	(5)	0	0	0	0
Bernard Dwyer	Bradford	1996-2000	65(10)	14	0	0	56
Luke Dyer	Crusaders	2010	23(1)	5	0	0	20
	Celtic	2009	21	6	0	0	24
	Hull KR	2007	26	13	0	0	52
	Castleford	2006	17(2)	5	0	0	20
Adam Dykes	Hull	2008	12	1	0	2	6
Jim Dymock	London	2001-04	94(1)	15	0	1	61
Leo Dynevor	London	1996	8(11)	5	7	0	34
Jason Eade	Paris	1997	9	4	0	0	16
Michael Eagar	Hull	2004-05	12	4	0	0	16
	Castleford	1999-2003	130(2)	60	0	0	240
	Warrington	1998	21	6	0	0	24
Kyle Eastmond	St Helens	2007-10	36(15)	30	113	3	349
Greg Eastwood	Leeds	2010	5(12)	1	0	0	4
Barry Eaton	Widnes	2002	25	2	49	4	110
	Castleford	2000	1(4)	0	3	0	6
Greg Ebrill	Salford	2002	15(6)	1	0	0	4
Cliff Eccles	Salford	1997-98	30(5)	1	0	0	4
Chris Eckersley	Warrington	1996	5	1	0	0	4
Steve Edmed	Sheffield	1997	15(1)	0	0	0	0
Mark Edmondson	Salford	2007	10(2)	0	0	0	0
	St Helens	1999-2005	27(75)	10	0	0	40
Diccon Edwards	Castleford	1996-97	10(5)	1	0	0	4
Grant Edwards	Castleford	2006	(2)	0	0	0	0
Max Edwards	Harlequins	2010	1	0	0	0	0
Peter Edwards	Salford	1997-98	35(2)	4	0	0	16
Shaun Edwards	London	1997-2000	32(8)	16	1	0	66
	Bradford	1998	8(2)	4	0	0	16
	Wigan	1996	17(3)	12	1	0	50
Danny Ekis	Halifax	2001	(1)	0	0	0	0
Abi Ekoku	Bradford	1997-98	21(4)	6	0	0	24
	Halifax	1996	15(1)	5	0	0	20
Shane Elford	Huddersfield	2007-08	26(1)	7	0	0	28
Olivier Elima	Catalans	2008-10	56(10)	30	0	0	120
	Wakefield	2003-07	40(47)	13	0	0	52
	Castleford	2002	(1)	1	0	0	4
Abderazak Elkhalouki							
	Paris	1997	(1)	0	0	0	0
Andy Ellis	Harlequins	2010	10(3)	3	0	0	12
Gareth Ellis	Leeds	2005-08	109	24	1	0	98
	Wakefield	1999-2004	86(17)	21	2	0	88
James Ellis	St Helens	2009	(2)	0	1	0	2
Danny Ellison	Castleford	1998-99	7(16)	6	0	0	24
	Wigan	1996-97	15(1)	13	0	0	52
Andrew Emelio	Widnes	2005	22(2)	8	0	0	32
Jacob Emmitt	St Helens	2008-10	1(16)	1	0	0	4
Patrick Entat	Paris	1996	22	2	0	0	8
Jason Erba	Sheffield	1997	1(4)	0	0	0	0
Ryan Esders	Harlequins	2009-10	9(11)	3	0	0	12
	Hull KR	2009	(1)	0	0	0	0

PLAYER	CLUB	YEAR	APP	TRIES	GOALS	FG	PTS
James Evans	Castleford	2009-10	26(1)	13	0	0	52
	Bradford	2007-08	43(5)	20	0	0	80
	Wakefield	2006	6	3	0	0	12
	Huddersfield	2004-06	51	22	0	0	88
Paul Evans	Paris	1997	18	8	0	0	32
Rhys Evans	Warrington	2010	(1)	0	0	0	0
Wayne Evans	London	2002	11(6)	2	0	0	8
Richie Eyres	Warrington	1997	2(5)	0	0	0	0
	Sheffield	1997	2(3)	0	0	0	0
Henry Fa'afili	Warrington	2004-07	90(1)	70	0	0	280
David Fa'alogo	Huddersfield	2010	12(5)	3	0	0	12
Sala Fa'alogo	Widnes	2004-05	8(15)	2	0	0	8
Richard Fa'aoso	Castleford	2006	10(15)	5	0	0	20
Maurie Fa'asavalu							
	St Helens	2004-10	5(137)	29	0	0	116
Bolouagi Fagborun							
	Huddersfield	2004-06	4(2)	1	0	0	4
Esene Faimalo	Salford	1997-99	23(25)	2	0	0	8
	Leeds	1996	3(3)	0	0	0	0
Joe Faimalo	Salford	1998-2000	23(47)	7	0	0	28
	Oldham	1996-97	37(5)	7	0	0	28
Karl Fairbank	Bradford	1996	17(2)	4	0	0	16
David Fairleigh	St Helens	2001	26(1)	8	0	0	32
David Faiumu	Huddersfield	2008-10	20(36)	7	0	0	28
Jamal Fakir	Catalans	2006-10	43(39)	10	0	0	40
Jim Fallon	Leeds	1996	10	5	0	0	20
Danny Farrar	Warrington	1998-2000	76	13	0	0	52
Andy Farrell	Wigan	1996-2004	230	77	1026	16	2376
Anthony Farrell	Widnes	2002-03	24(22)	4	1	0	18
	Leeds	1997-2001	99(23)	18	0	0	72
	Sheffield	1996	14(5)	5	0	0	20
Craig Farrell	Hull	2000-01	1(3)	0	0	0	0
Liam Farrell	Wigan	2010	9(11)	9	0	0	36
Abraham Fatnowna							
	London	1997-98	7(2)	2	0	0	8
	Workington	1996	5	2	0	0	8
Sione Faumuina	Castleford	2009	18	1	0	0	4
	Hull	2005	3	1	0	0	4
Vince Fawcett	Wakefield	1999	13(1)	2	0	0	8
	Warrington	1998	4(7)	1	0	0	4
	Oldham	1997	5	3	0	0	12
Danny Fearon	Huddersfield	2001	(1)	0	0	0	0
	Halifax	1999-2000	5(6)	0	0	0	0
Chris Feather	Castleford	2009	1(23)	0	0	0	0
	Bradford	2007-08	7(20)	1	0	0	4
	Leeds	2003-04, 2006	16(35)	6	0	0	24
	Wakefield	2001-02, 2004-05	29(32)	9	0	0	36
Dom Feaunati	Leigh	2005	4	1	0	0	4
	St Helens	2004	10(7)	7	0	0	28
Adel Fellous	Hull	2008	1(2)	0	0	0	0
	Catalans	2006-07	16(22)	4	0	0	16
Luke Felsch	Hull	2000-01	46(6)	7	0	0	28
	Gateshead	1999	28(1)	2	0	0	8
Leon Felton	Warrington	2002	4(2)	0	0	0	0
	St Helens	2001	1(1)	0	0	0	0
Dale Ferguson	Wakefield	2007-10	39(14)	10	0	0	40
Brett Ferres	Castleford	2009-10	41(2)	16	0	0	64
	Wakefield	2007-08	36(2)	6	5	0	34
	Bradford	2005-06	18(17)	11	2	0	48
David Ferriol	Catalans	2007-10	39(45)	6	0	0	24
Jason Ferris	Leigh	2005	4	1	0	0	4
Jamie Field	Wakefield	1999-2006	133(59)	19	0	0	76
	Huddersfield	1998	15(5)	0	0	0	0
	Leeds	1996-97	3(11)	0	0	0	0
Mark Field	Wakefield	2003-07	28(7)	3	0	0	12
Jamie Fielden	London	2003	(1)	0	0	0	0
	Huddersfield	1998-2000	4(8)	0	0	0	0
Stuart Fielden	Wigan	2006-10	103(24)	2	0	0	8
	Bradford	1998-2006	142(78)	41	0	0	164
Lafaele Filipo	Workington	1996	15(4)	3	0	0	12
Salesi Finau	Warrington	1996-97	16(15)	8	0	0	32
Vinny Finigan	Bradford	2010	4(1)	4	0	0	16
Liam Finn	Wakefield	2004	1(1)	0	1	1	2
	Halifax	2002-03	16(5)	2	30	1	69
Lee Finnerty	Halifax	2003	18(2)	5	2	0	24
Phil Finney	Warrington	1998	1	0	0	0	0
Simon Finnigan	Huddersfield	2009-10	22(5)	6	0	0	24
	Bradford	2008	14(13)	8	0	0	32
	Salford	2006-07	50	17	0	0	68
	Widnes	2003-05	51(19)	21	0	0	84
Matt Firth	Halifax	2000-01	12(2)	0	0	0	0
Andy Fisher	Warrington	1999-2000	31(8)	4	0	0	16
Ben Fisher	Hull KR	2007-10	70(29)	15	0	0	60
Craig Fitzgibbon	Hull	2010	21	5	7	0	34
Daniel Fitzhenry	Hull KR	2008-09	36(11)	14	0	0	56
Karl Fitzpatrick	Salford	2004-07, 2009-10	89(11)	33	2	0	136
Mark Flanagan	Wigan	2009	3(7)	1	0	0	4
Chris Flannery	St Helens	2007-10	76(3)	20	0	0	80
Darren Fleary	Leigh	2005	24	1	0	0	4
	Huddersfield	2003-04	43(8)	4	0	0	16
	Leeds	1997-2002	98(9)	3	0	0	12

PLAYER	CLUB	YEAR	APP	TRIES	GOALS	FG	PTS
Greg Fleming	London	1999-2001	64(1)	40	2	0	164
Adam Fletcher	Castleford	2006, 2008	16(7)	11	0	0	44
Bryan Fletcher	Wigan	2006-07	47(2)	14	0	0	56
Richard Fletcher	Castleford	2006	13(5)	3	4	0	20
	Hull	1999-2004	11(56)	5	0	0	20
Greg Florimo	Halifax	2000	26	6	4	0	32
	Wigan	1999	18(2)	7	1	0	30
Ben Flower	Crusaders	2010	1(10)	0	0	0	0
	Celtic	2009	2(15)	0	0	0	0
Jason Flowers	Salford	2004	6(1)	0	0	0	0
	Halifax	2002	24(4)	4	0	0	16
	Castleford	1996-2001	119(19)	33	0	1	133
Stuart Flowers	Castleford	1996	(3)	0	0	0	0
Adrian Flynn	Castleford	1996-97	19(2)	10	0	0	40
Wayne Flynn	Sheffield	1997	3(5)	0	0	0	0
Adam Fogerty	Warrington	1998	4	0	0	0	0
	St Helens	1996	13	1	0	0	4
Carl Forber	Leigh	2005	4	1	0	0	4
	St Helens	2004	1(1)	0	6	0	12
Paul Forber	Salford	1997-98	19(12)	4	0	0	16
Byron Ford	Hull KR	2007	13	6	0	0	24
James Ford	Castleford	2009	3(5)	1	0	0	4
Mike Ford	Castleford	1997-98	25(12)	5	0	3	23
	Warrington	1996	3	0	0	0	0
Jim Forshaw	Salford	1999	(1)	0	0	0	0
Mike Forshaw	Warrington	2004	20(1)	5	0	0	20
	Bradford	1997-2003	162(7)	32	0	0	128
	Leeds	1996	11(3)	5	0	0	20
Mark Forster	Warrington	1996-2000	102(1)	40	0	0	160
David Foster	Halifax	2000-01	4(9)	0	0	0	0
Jamie Foster	St Helens	2010	14	7	60	0	148
Peter Fox	Hull KR	2008-10	78	47	0	0	188
	Wakefield	2007	23	11	0	0	44
Nick Fozzard	St Helens	2004-08, 2010	100(25)	7	0	0	28
	Hull KR	2009	18(4)	1	0	0	4
	Warrington	2002-03	43(11)	2	0	0	8
	Huddersfield	1998-2000	24(8)	2	0	0	8
	Leeds	1996-97	6(16)	3	0	0	12
David Fraisse	Workington	1996	8	0	0	0	0
Daniel Frame	Widnes	2002-05	100(6)	24	0	0	96
Paul Franze	Castleford	2006	2(1)	0	0	0	0
Laurent Frayssinous	Catalans	2006	14(2)	3	32	0	76
Andrew Frew	Halifax	2003	17	5	0	0	20
	Wakefield	2002	21	8	0	0	32
	Huddersfield	2001	26	15	0	0	60
Dale Fritz	Castleford	1999-2003	120(4)	9	0	0	36
Gareth Frodsham	St Helens	2008-09	1(9)	0	0	0	0
Liam Fulton	Huddersfield	2009	12(3)	4	0	0	16
David Furner	Leeds	2003-04	45	8	23	0	78
	Wigan	2001-02	51(2)	21	13	0	110
David Furness	Castleford	1996	(1)	0	0	0	0
Matt Gafa	Harlequins	2006-09	81	26	16	0	136
Luke Gale	Harlequins	2009-10	30(12)	10	11	1	63
Ben Galea	Hull KR	2008-10	71(1)	16	0	0	64
Tommy Gallagher	Hull KR	2007	1(7)	0	0	0	0
	Widnes	2004	(6)	0	0	0	0
	London	2003	1(9)	1	0	0	4
Mark Gamson	Sheffield	1996	3	0	0	0	0
Jim Gannon	Hull KR	2007	7(16)	1	0	0	4
	Huddersfield	2003-06	79(14)	11	0	0	44
	Halifax	1999-2002	83(4)	14	0	0	56
Steve Garces	Salford	2001	(1)	0	0	0	0
Jean-Marc Garcia	Sheffield	1996-97	35(3)	22	0	0	88
Ade Gardner	St Helens	2002-10	203(12)	128	0	0	512
Matt Gardner	Harlequins	2009	6(3)	2	0	0	8
	Huddersfield	2006-07	22(3)	7	0	0	28
	Castleford	2004	1	1	0	0	4
Steve Gartland	Oldham	1996	1(1)	0	1	0	2
Daniel Gartner	Bradford	2001-03	74(1)	26	0	0	104
Dean Gaskell	Warrington	2002-05	58(1)	10	0	0	40
Lee Gaskell	St Helens	2010	1(2)	1	0	0	4
George Gatis	Huddersfield	2008	5(5)	1	0	0	4
Richard Gay	Castleford	1996-2002	94(16)	39	0	0	156
Andrew Gee	Warrington	2000-01	33(1)	4	0	0	16
Stanley Gene	Hull KR	2007-09	37(17)	9	0	0	36
	Bradford	2006	5(16)	8	0	0	32
	Huddersfield	2001, 2003-05	70(6)	27	0	0	108
	Hull	2000-01	5(23)	6	0	0	24
Steve Georgallis	Warrington	2001	5(1)	2	0	0	8
Luke George	Wakefield	2007-10	22(3)	17	0	0	68
Shaun Geritas	Warrington	1997	(5)	1	0	0	4
Anthony Gibbons	Leeds	1996	9(4)	2	0	1	9
David Gibbons	Leeds	1996	3(4)	2	0	0	8
Scott Gibbs	St Helens	1996	9	3	0	0	12
Ashley Gibson	Salford	2010	25(2)	10	0	0	40
	Leeds	2005-09	25(7)	13	9	0	70
Damian Gibson	Castleford	2003-04	40(3)	5	0	0	20
	Salford	2002	28	3	0	0	12
	Halifax	1998-2001	104(1)	39	0	0	156
	Leeds	1997	18	3	0	0	12
Matt Gidley	St Helens	2007-10	105	40	6	0	172
Tony Gigot	Catalans	2010	4(11)	0	2	0	4
Ian Gildart	Oldham	1996-97	31(7)	0	0	0	0
Chris Giles	Widnes	2003-04	35	12	0	0	48
	St Helens	2002	(1)	0	0	0	0
Peter Gill	London	1996-99	75(6)	20	0	0	80
Carl Gillespie	Halifax	1996-99	47(36)	13	0	0	52
Michael Gillett	London	2001-02	23(21)	12	2	0	52
Simon Gillies	Warrington	1999	28	6	0	0	24
Lee Gilmour	Huddersfield	2010	29	11	0	0	44
	St Helens	2004-09	149(3)	41	0	0	164
	Bradford	2001-03	44(31)	20	0	0	80
	Wigan	1997-2000	44(39)	22	0	0	88
Marc Glanville	Leeds	1998-99	43(3)	5	0	0	20
Eddie Glaze	Castleford	1996	1	0	0	0	0
Paul Gleadhill	Leeds	1996	4	0	0	0	0
Ben Gledhill	Wakefield	2010	(7)	0	0	0	0
Mark Gleeson	Warrington	2000-08	38(102)	12	0	0	48
Martin Gleeson	Wigan	2009-10	44(1)	19	0	0	76
	Warrington	2005-09	110(1)	44	0	0	176
	St Helens	2002-04	56(1)	25	0	0	100
	Huddersfield	1999-2001	47(9)	18	0	0	72
Sean Gleeson	Wakefield	2007-10	67(6)	20	0	0	80
	Wigan	2005-06	3(3)	0	0	0	0
Jon Goddard	Hull KR	2007	20	2	0	0	8
	Castleford	2000-01	(2)	0	0	0	0
Richard Goddard	Castleford	1996-97	11(3)	2	10	0	28
Brad Godden	Leeds	1998-99	47	15	0	0	60
Wayne Godwin	Bradford	2008-10	16(44)	9	0	0	36
	Hull	2007	3(13)	1	0	0	4
	Wigan	2005-06	9(38)	6	0	0	24
	Castleford	2001-04	30(33)	18	56	0	184
Jason Golden	Harlequins	2009-10	32(9)	3	0	0	12
	Wakefield	2007-08	26(5)	1	0	0	4
Marvin Golden	Widnes	2003	4	1	0	0	4
	London	2001	17(2)	1	0	0	4
	Halifax	2000	20(2)	5	0	0	20
	Leeds	1996-99	43(11)	19	0	0	76
Brett Goldspink	Halifax	2000-02	64(5)	2	0	0	8
	Wigan	1999	6(16)	1	0	0	4
	St Helens	1998	19(4)	2	0	0	8
	Oldham	1997	13(2)	0	0	0	0
Lee Gomersall	Hull KR	2008	1	0	0	0	0
Luke Goodwin	London	1998	9(2)	3	1	1	15
	Oldham	1997	16(4)	10	17	2	76
Aaron Gorrell	Catalans	2007-08	23	6	14	0	52
Andy Gorski	Salford	2001-02	(2)	0	0	0	0
Cyrille Gossard	Catalans	2006-10	52(21)	5	0	0	20
Bobbie Goulding	Salford	2001-02	31(1)	2	56	4	124
	Wakefield	2000	12	3	25	3	65
	Huddersfield	1998-99	27(1)	3	65	4	146
	St Helens	1996-98	42(2)	9	210	4	460
Darrell Goulding	Wigan	2005-10	56(20)	48	0	0	192
	Salford	2009	9	5	0	0	20
Mick Govin	Leigh	2005	5(6)	4	0	0	16
David Gower	Salford	2006-07	(16)	0	0	0	0
James Graham	St Helens	2003-10	104(63)	41	0	0	164
Nathan Graham	Bradford	1996-98	17(28)	4	0	1	17
Nick Graham	Wigan	2003	13(1)	2	0	0	8
Jon Grayshon	Harlequins	2007-09	10(32)	4	0	0	16
	Huddersfield	2003-06	7(43)	5	0	0	20
Brett Green	Gateshead	1999	10(2)	0	0	0	0
Toby Green	Huddersfield	2001	3(1)	1	0	0	4
Craig Greenhill	Castleford	2004	21(4)	1	0	0	4
	Hull	2002-03	56	3	2	0	16
Clint Greenshields	Catalans	2007-10	95	50	0	0	200
Brandon Greenwood	Halifax	1996	1	0	0	0	0
Gareth Greenwood	Huddersfield	2003	(1)	0	0	0	0
	Halifax	2002	1	0	0	0	0
Lee Greenwood	Huddersfield	2005	7	3	0	0	12
	London	2004-05	30(2)	19	0	0	76
	Halifax	2000-03	38(2)	17	0	0	68
	Sheffield	1999	1(1)	0	0	0	0
Maxime Greseque	Wakefield	2007	2(1)	0	0	0	0
Mathieu Griffi	Catalans	2006-08	1(25)	0	0	0	0
Darrell Griffin	Huddersfield	2007-10	47(54)	10	0	0	40
	Wakefield	2003-06	55(37)	9	3	0	42
Josh Griffin	Huddersfield	2009	2	0	0	0	0
Jonathan Griffiths	Paris	1996	(4)	1	0	0	4
Andrew Grima	Workington	1996	2(9)	2	0	0	8
Tony Grimaldi	Hull	2000-01	56(1)	14	0	0	56
	Gateshead	1999	27(2)	10	0	0	40
Danny Grimley	Sheffield	1996	4(1)	1	0	0	4
Scott Grix	Huddersfield	2010	6(10)	8	0	0	32
	Wakefield	2008-09	39(3)	18	0	0	72
Simon Grix	Warrington	2006-10	53(16)	21	0	0	84
	Halifax	2003	2(4)	0	0	0	0
Brett Grogan	Gateshead	1999	14(7)	3	0	0	12
Brent Grose	Warrington	2003-07	134(1)	55	0	0	220
David Guasch	Catalans	2010	1	0	0	0	0

PLAYER	CLUB	YEAR	APP	TRIES	GOALS	FG	PTS
Renaud Guigue	Catalans	2006	14(4)	3	0	0	12
Jerome Guisset	Catalans	2006-10	102(23)	9	0	0	36
	Wigan	2005	20(2)	3	0	0	12
	Warrington	2000-04	59(65)	21	0	0	84
Awen Guttenbeil	Castleford	2008	19	0	0	0	0
Reece Guy	Oldham	1996	3(4)	0	0	0	0
Tom Haberecht	Castleford	2008	2(2)	1	0	0	4
Gareth Haggerty	Harlequins	2008-09	8(28)	6	0	0	24
	Salford	2004-07	1(93)	15	0	0	60
	Widnes	2002	1(2)	1	0	0	4
Andy Haigh	St Helens	1996-98	20(16)	11	0	0	44
Michael Haley	Leeds	2008	(1)	0	0	0	0
Carl Hall	Leeds	1996	7(2)	3	0	0	12
Craig Hall	Hull	2007-10	59(9)	39	11	0	178
Glenn Hall	Bradford	2010	7(18)	2	0	0	8
Martin Hall	Halifax	1998	2(10)	0	0	0	0
	Hull	1999	7	0	0	0	0
	Castleford	1998	4	0	0	0	0
	Wigan	1996-97	31(5)	7	6	0	40
Ryan Hall	Leeds	2007-10	76(2)	67	0	0	268
Steve Hall	Widnes	2004	1	0	0	0	0
	London	2002-03	35(3)	10	0	0	40
	St Helens	1999-2001	36(22)	19	0	0	76
Graeme Hallas	Huddersfield	2001	1	0	0	0	0
	Hull	1998-99	30(10)	6	39	1	103
	Halifax	1996	11(4)	5	0	0	20
Dave Halley	Bradford	2007-10	63(12)	20	0	0	80
	Wakefield	2009	5	4	0	0	16
Danny Halliwell	Salford	2007	2(3)	0	0	0	0
	Leigh	2005	5	3	0	0	12
	Halifax	2000-01	17(8)	4	0	0	16
	Warrington	2002	9(1)	8	0	0	32
	Wakefield	2002	3	0	0	0	0
Colum Halpenny	Wakefield	2003-06	103(1)	36	0	0	144
	Halifax	2002	22	12	0	0	48
Jon Hamer	Bradford	1996	(1)	0	0	0	0
Andrew Hamilton	London	1997, 2003	1(20)	3	0	0	12
John Hamilton	St Helens	1998	3	0	0	0	0
Karle Hammond	Halifax	2002	10(2)	2	14	0	36
	Salford	2001	2(3)	1	0	0	4
	London	1999-2000	47	23	2	3	99
	St Helens	1996-98	58(8)	28	0	4	116
Rhys Hanbury	Crusaders	2010	17(1)	10	0	0	40
Anthony Hancock	Paris	1997	8(6)	1	0	0	4
Michael Hancock	Salford	2001-02	12(24)	7	0	0	28
Gareth Handford	Castleford	2001	7(2)	0	0	0	0
	Bradford	2000	1(1)	0	0	0	0
Paul Handforth	Castleford	2006	2(15)	2	1	0	10
	Wakefield	2000-04	17(44)	10	13	0	66
Paddy Handley	Leeds	1996	1(1)	2	0	0	8
Dean Hanger	Warrington	1999	7(11)	3	0	0	12
	Huddersfield	1998	20(1)	5	0	0	20
Josh Hannay	Celtic	2009	17	2	24	0	56
Harrison Hansen	Wigan	2004-10	89(59)	28	0	0	112
Lee Hansen	Wigan	1997	10(5)	0	0	0	0
Shontayne Hape	Bradford	2003-08	123(2)	79	0	0	316
Lionel Harbin	Wakefield	2001	(1)	0	0	0	0
Ian Hardman	Hull KR	2007	18	4	0	0	16
	St Helens	2003-07	32(11)	9	5	0	46
Jeff Hardy	Hudds-Sheff	2000	20(5)	6	0	1	25
	Sheffield	1999	22(4)	7	0	0	28
Spencer Hargrave							
	Castleford	1996-99	(6)	0	0	0	0
Bryn Hargreaves	St Helens	2007-10	53(44)	7	0	0	28
	Wigan	2004-06	16(12)	1	0	0	4
Lee Harland	Castleford	1996-2004	148(35)	20	0	0	80
Neil Harmon	Halifax	2003	13(3)	0	0	0	0
	Salford	2001	6(5)	0	0	0	0
	Bradford	1998-2000	15(13)	2	0	0	8
	Huddersfield	1998	12	1	0	0	4
	Leeds	1996	10	1	0	0	4
Ben Harris	Bradford	2005-07	70(4)	24	0	0	96
Iestyn Harris	Bradford	2004-08	109(11)	35	87	2	316
	Leeds	1997-2001	111(7)	57	490	6	1214
	Warrington	1996	16	4	63	2	144
Ben Harrison	Warrington	2007-10	52(31)	6	0	0	24
Karl Harrison	Hull	1999	26	2	0	0	8
	Halifax	1996-98	60(2)	2	0	0	8
Andrew Hart	London	2004	12(1)	2	0	0	8
Tim Hartley	Harlequins	2006	2	1	0	0	4
	Salford	2004-05	6(7)	5	0	0	20
Carlos Hassan	Bradford	1996	6(4)	2	0	0	8
Phil Hassan	Wakefield	2002	9(1)	0	0	0	0
	Halifax	2000-01	25(4)	3	0	0	12
	Salford	1998	15	2	0	0	8
	Leeds	1996-97	38(4)	12	0	0	48
Tom Haughey	Castleford	2006	1(3)	1	0	0	4
	London	2003-04	10(8)	1	0	0	4
	Wakefield	2001-02	5(12)	0	0	0	0
Simon Haughton	Wigan	1996-2002	63(46)	32	0	0	128
Solomon Haumono							
	Harlequins	2006	10(9)	6	0	0	24
	London	2005	24(5)	8	0	0	32
Weller Hauraki	Crusaders	2010	26(1)	11	0	0	44

PLAYER	CLUB	YEAR	APP	TRIES	GOALS	FG	PTS
Richie Hawkyard	Bradford	2007	1(2)	1	0	0	4
Andy Hay	Widnes	2003-04	50(2)	7	0	0	28
	Leeds	1997-2002	112(27)	43	0	0	172
	Sheffield	1996-97	17(3)	5	0	0	20
Adam Hayes	Hudds-Sheff	2000	2(1)	0	0	0	0
Joey Hayes	Salford	1999	9	2	0	0	8
	St Helens	1996-98	11(6)	7	0	0	28
James Haynes	Hull KR	2009	1	0	0	0	0
Mathew Head	Hull	2007	9(1)	1	0	1	5
Mitch Healey	Castleford	2001-03	68(1)	10	16	0	72
Daniel Heckenberg							
	Harlequins	2006-09	31(39)	4	0	0	16
Ricky Helliwell	Salford	1997-99	(2)	0	0	0	0
Tom Hemingway	Huddersfield	2005-09	7(7)	1	17	0	38
Bryan Henare	St Helens	2000-01	4(12)	1	0	0	4
Richard Henare	Warrington	1996-97	28(2)	24	0	0	96
Andrew Henderson							
	Castleford	2006, 2008	44(11)	4	0	0	16
Ian Henderson	Bradford	2005-07	33(37)	13	0	0	52
Kevin Henderson	Wakefield	2005-10	45(53)	8	0	0	32
	Leigh	2005	(1)	0	0	0	0
Mark Henry	Salford	2009-10	42	12	0	0	48
Brad Hepi	Castleford	1999, 2001	9(21)	3	0	0	12
	Salford	2000	1(3)	0	0	0	0
	Hull	1998	15(1)	3	0	0	12
Jon Hepworth	Castleford	2003-04	19(23)	7	8	0	44
	Leeds	2003	(1)	0	0	0	0
	London	2002	(2)	0	0	0	0
Ian Herron	Hull	2000	9	1	17	0	38
	Gateshead	1999	25	4	105	0	226
Jason Hetherington							
	London	2001-02	37	9	0	0	36
Gareth Hewitt	Salford	1999	2(1)	0	0	0	0
Andrew Hick	Hull	2000	9(9)	1	0	0	4
	Gateshead	1999	12(5)	2	0	0	8
Chris Hicks	Warrington	2008-10	72	56	120	0	464
Paul Hicks	Wakefield	1999	(1)	0	0	0	0
Darren Higgins	London	1998	5(6)	2	0	0	8
Iain Higgins	London	1997-98	1(7)	2	0	0	8
Liam Higgins	Castleford	2008-10	42(32)	2	0	0	8
	Hull	2003-06	1(34)	0	0	0	0
Mick Higham	Warrington	2009-10	12(27)	13	0	0	52
	Wigan	2006-08	61(28)	13	0	0	52
	St Helens	2001-05	43(56)	32	0	0	128
Chris Highton	Warrington	1997	1(1)	0	0	0	0
David Highton	London	2004-05	21(24)	2	0	0	8
	Salford	2002	4(5)	2	0	0	8
	Warrington	1998-2001	18(14)	2	0	0	8
Paul Highton	Salford	1998-2002,					
		2004-07	114(80)	14	0	0	56
	Halifax	1996-97	12(18)	2	0	0	8
Andy Hill	Huddersfield	1999	(4)	0	0	0	0
	Castleford	1999	4(4)	0	0	0	0
Chris Hill	Leigh	2005	(1)	0	0	0	0
Danny Hill	Wigan	2006-07	1(10)	0	0	0	0
	Hull KR	2007	2	0	0	0	0
	Hull	2004-06	4(6)	0	0	0	0
Howard Hill	Oldham	1996-97	22(18)	4	0	0	16
John Hill	St Helens	2003	(1)	0	0	0	0
	Halifax	2003	1(2)	0	0	0	0
	Warrington	2001-02	(4)	0	0	0	0
Scott Hill	Harlequins	2007-08	41(2)	13	0	0	52
Mark Hilton	Warrington	1996-2000,					
		2002-06	141(40)	7	0	0	28
Ian Hindmarsh	Catalans	2006	25	3	0	0	12
Brendan Hlad	Castleford	2008	(3)	0	0	0	0
Andy Hobson	Widnes	2004	5(13)	0	0	0	0
	Halifax	1998-2003	51(85)	8	0	0	32
Gareth Hock	Wigan	2003-09	98(37)	24	0	0	96
Tommy Hodgkinson							
	St Helens	2006	(1)	0	0	0	0
Andy Hodgson	Wakefield	1999	14(2)	2	1	0	10
	Bradford	1997-98	8(2)	4	0	0	16
Brett Hodgson	Huddersfield	2010	45	13	166	0	384
David Hodgson	Huddersfield	2008-10	66	46	0	0	184
	Salford	2005-07	81	30	47	0	214
	Wigan	2000-04	90(19)	43	0	0	172
	Halifax	1999	10(3)	5	0	0	20
Elliot Hodgson	Huddersfield	2009	1	0	0	0	0
Josh Hodgson	Hull KR	2010	6(14)	0	0	0	0
	Hull	2009	(2)	0	0	0	0
Darren Hogg	London	1996	(1)	0	0	0	0
Michael Hogue	Paris	1997	5(7)	0	0	0	0
Chris Holden	Warrington	1996-97	2(1)	0	0	0	0
Daniel Holdsworth							
	Salford	2010	19	5	46	1	113
Stephen Holgate	Halifax	2000	1(10)	0	0	0	0
	Hull	1999	1	0	0	0	0
	Wigan	1997-98	11(26)	2	0	0	8
	Workington	1996	19	3	0	0	12
Martyn Holland	Wakefield	2000-03	52(3)	6	0	0	24
Oliver Holmes	Castleford	2010	(4)	0	0	0	0
Tim Holmes	Widnes	2004-05	15(4)	0	0	0	0

Super League Players 1996-2010

PLAYER	CLUB	YEAR	APP	TRIES	GOALS	FG	PTS
Graham Holroyd	Huddersfield	2003	3(5)	0	0	0	0
	Salford	2000-02	40(11)	8	75	5	187
	Halifax	1999	24(2)	3	74	5	165
	Leeds	1996-98	40(26)	22	101	8	298
Dallas Hood	Wakefield	2003-04	18(9)	1	0	0	4
Jason Hooper	St Helens	2003-07	89(6)	35	30	0	200
Lee Hopkins	Harlequins	2006-07	44(3)	11	0	0	44
	London	2005	29	6	0	0	24
Sean Hoppe	St Helens	1999-2002	69(16)	32	0	0	128
Graeme Horne	Huddersfield	2010	12(8)	3	0	0	12
	Hull	2003-09	49(74)	24	0	0	96
Richard Horne	Hull	1999-2010	260(11)	96	12	6	414
John Hough	Warrington	1996-97	9	2	0	0	8
Danny Houghton	Hull	2007-10	34(45)	9	0	0	36
Sylvain Houles	Wakefield	2003, 2005	8(1)	1	0	0	4
	London	2001-02	17(10)	11	0	0	44
	Hudds-Sheff	2000	5(2)	1	0	0	4
Harvey Howard	Wigan	2001-02	25(27)	1	0	0	4
	Bradford	1998	4(2)	1	0	0	4
	Leeds	1996	8	0	0	0	0
Kim Howard	London	1997	4(5)	0	0	0	0
Stuart Howarth	Workington	1996	(2)	0	0	0	0
David Howell	Harlequins	2008-10	64	26	0	0	104
Phil Howlett	Bradford	1999	5(1)	2	0	0	8
Craig Huby	Castleford	2003-04, 2006, 2008-10	64(44)	18	37	0	146
Ryan Hudson	Castleford	2002-04, 2009-10	114(7)	29	0	0	116
	Huddersfield	1998-99, 2007-08	51(22)	10	0	0	40
	Wakefield	2000-01	42(9)	11	0	1	45
Adam Hughes	Widnes	2002-05	89(2)	45	51	0	282
	Halifax	2001	8(8)	8	0	0	32
	Wakefield	1999-2000	43(3)	21	34	0	152
	Leeds	1996-97	4(5)	4	0	0	16
Ian Hughes	Sheffield	1996	9(8)	4	0	0	16
Mark Hughes	Catalans	2006	23	9	0	0	36
Steffan Hughes	London	1999-2001	1(13)	1	0	0	4
David Hulme	Salford	1997-99	53(1)	5	0	0	20
	Leeds	1996	8(1)	2	0	0	8
Paul Hulme	Warrington	1996-97	23(1)	2	0	0	8
Gary Hulse	Widnes	2005	12(5)	2	0	0	8
	Warrington	2001-04	20(28)	8	0	1	33
Alan Hunte	Salford	2002	19(2)	9	0	0	36
	Warrington	1999-2001	83	49	0	0	196
	Hull	1998	21	7	0	0	28
	St Helens	1996-97	30(2)	28	0	0	112
Kieran Hyde	Wakefield	2010	1	1	0	0	4
Nick Hyde	Paris	1997	5(5)	1	0	0	4
Chaz I'Anson	Hull KR	2007-10	17(13)	3	0	0	12
Andy Ireland	Hull	1998-99	22(15)	0	0	0	0
	Bradford	1996	1	0	0	0	0
Kevin Iro	St Helens	1999-2001	76	39	0	0	156
	Leeds	1996	16	9	0	0	36
Andrew Isherwood	Wigan	1998-99	(5)	0	0	0	0
Olu Iwenofu	London	2000-01	2(1)	0	0	0	0
Chico Jackson	Hull	1999	(4)	0	0	0	0
Lee Jackson	Hull	2001-02	37(9)	12	1	0	50
	Leeds	1999-2000	28(24)	7	0	0	28
Michael Jackson	Sheffield	1998-99	17(17)	2	0	0	8
	Halifax	1996-97	27(6)	11	0	0	44
Paul Jackson	Castleford	2003-04, 2010	24(23)	1	0	0	4
	Huddersfield	1998, 2005-09	50(73)	4	0	0	16
	Wakefield	1999-2002	57(41)	2	0	0	8
Rob Jackson	Leigh	2005	20(3)	5	0	0	20
	London	2002-04	26(14)	9	0	0	36
Wayne Jackson	Halifax	1996-97	17(5)	2	0	0	8
Aled James	Celtic	2009	3(3)	0	0	0	0
	Widnes	2003	3	0	0	0	0
Andy James	Halifax	1996	(4)	0	0	0	0
Jordan James	Crusaders	2010	(14)	1	0	0	4
	Celtic	2009	17(4)	1	0	0	4
	Wigan	2006	2(4)	3	0	0	12
Matt James	Harlequins	2010	(2)	0	0	0	0
	Bradford	2006-09	1(23)	0	0	0	0
Pascal Jampy	Catalans	2006	4(7)	0	0	0	0
	Paris	1996-97	3(2)	0	0	0	0
Adam Janowski	Harlequins	2008	(1)	0	0	0	0
Ben Jeffries	Wakefield	2003-07, 2010	146(10)	67	27	6	328
	Bradford	2008-09	43(3)	13	0	0	52
Mick Jenkins	Hull	2000	24	2	0	0	8
	Gateshead	1999	16	3	0	0	12
Ed Jennings	London	1998-99	1(2)	0	0	0	0
Rod Jensen	Huddersfield	2007-08	26(3)	13	0	0	52
Anthony Jerram	Warrington	2007	(2)	0	0	0	0
Lee Jewitt	Salford	2007, 2009-10	9(32)	0	0	0	0
	Wigan	2005	(2)	0	0	0	0
Andrew Johns	Warrington	2005	3	1	12	1	29
Matthew Johns	Wigan	2001	24	3	0	1	13
Andy Johnson	Salford	2004-05	8(26)	7	0	0	28
	Castleford	2002-03	32(16)	11	0	0	44
	London	2000-01	24(21)	12	0	0	48
	Huddersfield	1999	5	1	0	0	4
	Wigan	1996-99	24(20)	19	0	0	76
Bruce Johnson	Widnes	2004-05	(4)	0	0	0	0
Dallas Johnson	Catalans	2010	26	1	0	0	4
Jason Johnson	St Helens	1997-99	2	0	0	0	0
Mark Johnson	Salford	1999-2000	22(9)	16	0	0	64
	Hull	1998	10(1)	4	0	0	16
	Workington	1996	12	4	0	0	16
Nick Johnson	London	2003	(1)	0	0	0	0
Paul Johnson	Wakefield	2010	12(3)	4	0	0	16
	Warrington	2007-09	37(9)	17	0	0	68
	Bradford	2004-06	46(8)	19	0	0	76
	Wigan	1996-2003	74(46)	54	0	0	216
Paul Johnson	St Helens	2000	(2)	0	0	0	0
Richard Johnson	Bradford	2008	(2)	0	0	0	0
Ben Jones	Harlequins	2010	(2)	0	0	0	0
Chris Jones	Leigh	2005	1(1)	0	0	0	0
Danny Jones	Halifax	2003	1	0	0	0	0
David Jones	Oldham	1997	14(1)	5	0	0	20
Mark Jones	Warrington	1996	8(11)	2	0	0	8
Phil Jones	Leigh	2005	16	8	31	0	94
	Wigan	1999-2001	14(7)	6	25	0	74
Stacey Jones	Catalans	2006-07	39	11	43	3	133
Stephen Jones	Huddersfield	2005	(1)	0	0	0	0
Stuart Jones	Castleford	2009-10	33(17)	6	0	0	24
	Huddersfield	2004-08	96(22)	17	0	0	68
	St Helens	2003	(18)	2	0	0	8
	Wigan	2002	5(3)	1	0	0	4
Ben Jones-Bishop	Harlequins	2010	17	10	0	0	40
	Leeds	2008-09	3(1)	0	0	0	0
Jamie Jones-Buchanan	Leeds	1999-2010	146(58)	42	0	0	168
Tim Jonkers	Wigan	2006	3(1)	0	0	0	0
	Salford	2004-06	5(11)	0	0	0	0
	St Helens	1999-2004	41(64)	12	0	0	48
Darren Jordan	Wakefield	2003	(1)	0	0	0	0
Phil Joseph	Huddersfield	2004	7(6)	0	0	0	0
Warren Jowitt	Hull	2003	(2)	0	0	0	0
	Salford	2001-02	17(4)	2	0	0	8
	Wakefield	2000	19(3)	8	0	0	32
	Bradford	1996-99	13(25)	5	0	0	20
Chris Joynt	St Helens	1996-2004	201(14)	68	0	0	272
Gregory Kacala	Paris	1996	7	1	0	0	4
Andy Kain	Castleford	2004, 2006	9(7)	3	10	0	32
Mal Kaufusi	London	2004	1(3)	0	0	0	0
Ben Kaye	Harlequins	2009-10	2(13)	0	0	0	0
	Leeds	2008	2(2)	1	0	0	4
Elliot Kear	Crusaders	2010	5	0	0	0	0
	Celtic	2009	3	0	0	0	0
Brett Kearney	Bradford	2010	23	11	0	0	44
Stephen Kearney	Hull	2005	22(2)	5	0	0	20
Damon Keating	Wakefield	2002	7(17)	1	0	0	4
Shaun Keating	London	1996	1(3)	0	0	0	0
Mark Keenan	Workington	1996	3(4)	1	0	0	4
Tony Kemp	Wakefield	1999-2000	15(5)	2	0	1	9
	Leeds	1996-98	23(2)	5	0	2	22
Damien Kennedy	London	2003	5(11)	1	0	0	4
Ian Kenny	St Helens	2004	(1)	0	0	0	0
Jason Kent	Leigh	2005	23	1	0	0	4
Shane Kenward	Wakefield	1999	28	6	0	0	24
	Salford	1998	1	0	0	0	0
Jason Keough	Paris	1997	2	1	0	0	4
Keiran Kerr	Widnes	2005	6	1	0	0	8
Martin Ketteridge	Halifax	1996	7(5)	0	0	0	0
Ronnie Kettlewell	Warrington	1996	(1)	0	0	0	0
Younes Khattabi	Catalans	2006-08	24(4)	10	0	0	40
David Kidwell	Warrington	2001-02	14(12)	9	0	0	36
Andrew King	London	2003	23(1)	15	0	0	60
Dave King	Huddersfield	1998-99	11(17)	2	0	0	8
James King	Leigh	2005	5(7)	0	0	0	0
Kevin King	Wakefield	2005	8(1)	2	0	0	8
	Castleford	2004	(1)	0	0	0	0
Matt King	Warrington	2008-10	73	39	0	0	156
Paul King	Wakefield	2010	9(9)	0	0	1	1
	Hull	1999-2009	136(93)	20	0	1	81
Andy Kirk	Wakefield	2005	6(3)	1	0	0	4
	Salford	2004	20	5	0	0	20
	Leeds	2001-02	4(4)	0	0	0	0
Ian Kirke	Leeds	2006-10	40(53)	7	0	0	28
John Kirkpatrick	London	2004-05	18(1)	5	0	0	20
	St Helens	2001-03	10(11)	10	0	0	40
	Halifax	2003	4	1	0	0	4
Danny Kirmond	Huddersfield	2008-10	12(22)	7	0	0	28
	Wakefield	2010	12(4)	1	0	0	4
Wayne Kitchin	Workington	1996	11(6)	3	17	1	47
Ian Knott	Leigh	2005	8(1)	2	0	0	8
	Wakefield	2002-03	34(5)	7	79	0	186
	Warrington	1996-2001	68(41)	24	18	0	132
Matt Knowles	Wigan	1996	(3)	0	0	0	0

PLAYER	CLUB	YEAR	APP	TRIES	GOALS	FG	PTS
Michael Knowles	Castleford	2006	(1)	0	0	0	0
Phil Knowles	Salford	1997	1	0	0	0	0
Simon Knox	Halifax	1999	(6)	0	0	0	0
	Salford	1998	1(1)	0	0	0	0
	Bradford	1996-98	9(19)	7	0	0	28
Toa Kohe-Love	Warrington	1996-2001, 2005-06	166(3)	90	0	0	360
	Bradford	2004	1(1)	0	0	0	0
	Hull	2002-03	42	19	0	0	76
Paul Koloi	Wigan	1997	1(2)	1	0	0	4
Craig Kopczak	Bradford	2006-10	9(65)	3	0	0	12
Michael Korkidas	Wakefield	2003-06, 2009-10	118(32)	14	0	0	56
	Huddersfield	2009	4(1)	1	0	0	4
	Castleford	2008	15(6)	1	0	0	4
	Salford	2007	26(1)	1	0	0	4
Olsi Krasniqi	Harlequins	2010	2(8)	1	0	0	4
David Krause	London	1996-97	22(1)	7	0	0	28
Ben Kusto	Huddersfield	2001	21(4)	9	0	1	37
Adrian Lam	Wigan	2001-04	105(2)	40	1	9	171
Mark Lane	Paris	1996	(2)	0	0	0	0
Allan Langer	Warrington	2000-01	47	13	4	0	60
Kevin Langer	London	1996	12(4)	2	0	0	8
Junior Langi	Salford	2005-06	27(7)	7	0	0	28
Chris Langley	Huddersfield	2000-01	18(1)	3	0	0	12
Gareth Langley	St Helens	2006	1	1	3	0	10
Jamie Langley	Bradford	2002-10	136(47)	31	0	0	124
Andy Last	Hull	1999-2005	16(10)	4	0	0	16
Sam Latus	Hull KR	2010	7	1	0	0	4
Epalahame Lauaki	Hull	2009-10	3(23)	3	0	0	12
Dale Laughton	Warrington	2002	15(1)	0	0	0	0
	Huddersfield	2000-01	36(2)	4	0	0	16
	Sheffield	1996-99	48(22)	5	0	0	20
Ali Lauitiiti	Leeds	2004-10	58(104)	54	0	0	216
Jason Laurence	Salford	1997	1	0	0	0	0
Graham Law	Wakefield	1999-2002	34(30)	6	40	0	104
Neil Law	Wakefield	1999-2002	83	39	0	0	156
	Sheffield	1998	1(1)	1	0	0	4
Dean Lawford	Widnes	2003-04	17(1)	5	2	4	28
	Halifax	2001	1(1)	0	0	0	0
	Leeds	1997-2000	15(8)	2	3	0	14
	Huddersfield	1999	6(1)	0	6	1	13
	Sheffield	1996	9(5)	2	1	1	11
Johnny Lawless	Halifax	2001-03	73(1)	10	0	0	40
	Hudds-Sheff	2000	19(6)	3	0	0	12
	Sheffield	1996-99	76(4)	11	0	0	44
Michael Lawrence	Huddersfield	2007-10	60(1)	18	0	0	72
Charlie Leaeno	Wakefield	2010	7(3)	2	0	0	8
Mark Leafa	Castleford	2008	5(9)	1	0	0	4
	Leigh	2005	28	2	0	0	8
Leroy Leapai	London	1996	2	0	0	0	0
Jim Leatham	Hull	1998-99	20(18)	4	0	0	16
	Leeds	1997	(1)	0	0	0	0
Andy Leathem	Warrington	1999	2(8)	0	0	0	0
	St Helens	1996-98	20(1)	1	0	0	4
Danny Lee	Gateshead	1999	16(2)	0	0	0	0
Jason Lee	Halifax	2001	10(1)	2	0	0	8
Mark Lee	Salford	1997-2000	25(11)	1	0	4	8
Robert Lee	Hull	1999	4(3)	0	0	0	0
Tommy Lee	Crusaders	2010	3(9)	0	0	0	0
	Hull	2005-09	44(27)	6	0	0	24
Matthew Leigh	Salford	2000	(6)	0	0	0	0
Chris Leikvoll	Warrington	2004-07	72(18)	4	0	0	16
Jim Lenihan	Huddersfield	1999	19(1)	10	0	0	40
Mark Lennon	Celtic	2009	10(3)	1	8	0	20
	Hull KR	2007	11(4)	5	7	0	34
	Castleford	2001-03	30(21)	10	21	0	82
Tevita Leo-Latu	Wakefield	2006-10	28(49)	10	0	0	40
Gary Lester	Hull	1998-99	46	17	0	0	68
Stuart Lester	Wigan	1997	1(3)	0	0	0	0
Heath L'Estrange	Bradford	2010	27	3	0	0	12
Afi Leuila	Oldham	1996-97	17(3)	2	0	0	8
Kylie Leuluai	Leeds	2007-10	87(21)	10	0	0	40
Phil Leuluai	Salford	2007, 2009-10	7(47)	3	0	0	12
Thomas Leuluai	Wigan	2007-10	119	36	0	0	144
	Harlequins	2006	15(2)	6	0	0	24
	London	2005	20	13	0	0	52
Simon Lewis	Castleford	2001	4	3	0	0	12
Paul Leyland	St Helens	2006	1	0	0	0	0
Jon Liddell	Leeds	2001	1	0	0	0	0
Jason Lidden	Castleford	1997	15(1)	7	0	0	28
Danny Lima	Wakefield	2007	(3)	0	0	0	0
	Salford	2006	7(2)	0	0	0	0
	Warrington	2004-06	15(47)	9	0	0	36
Craig Littler	St Helens	2006	1	1	0	0	4
Stuart Littler	Salford	1998-2002, 2004-07, 2009-10	217(30)	65	0	0	260
Peter Livett	Workington	1996	3(1)	0	0	0	0
Scott Logan	Wigan	2006	10(11)	0	0	0	0
	Hull	2001-03	27(20)	5	0	0	20

PLAYER	CLUB	YEAR	APP	TRIES	GOALS	FG	PTS
Jamahl Lolesi	Huddersfield	2007-10	75(9)	27	0	0	108
Filimone Lolohea	Harlequins	2006	3(6)	0	0	0	0
	London	2005	8(15)	0	0	0	0
David Lomax	Huddersfield	2000-01	45(9)	4	0	0	16
	Paris	1997	19(2)	1	0	0	4
Jonny Lomax	St Helens	2009-10	20(2)	9	26	0	88
Dave Long	London	1999	(1)	0	0	0	0
Karl Long	London	2003	(1)	0	0	0	0
	Widnes	2002	4	1	0	0	4
Sean Long	Hull	2010	15	5	0	0	20
	St Helens	1997-2009	253(8)	126	826	20	2176
	Wigan	1996-97	1(5)	0	0	0	0
Davide Longo	Bradford	1996	1(3)	0	0	0	0
Gary Lord	Oldham	1996-97	28(12)	3	0	0	12
Paul Loughlin	Huddersfield	1998-99	34(2)	4	4	0	24
	Bradford	1996-97	36(4)	15	8	0	76
Rhys Lovegrove	Hull KR	2007-10	29(39)	9	0	0	36
Karl Lovell	Hudds-Sheff	2000	14	5	0	0	20
	Sheffield	1999	22(4)	8	0	0	32
James Lowes	Bradford	1996-2003	205	84	2	2	342
Laurent Lucchese	Paris	1996	13(5)	2	0	0	8
Zebastian Luisi	Harlequins	2006-07	23(2)	4	0	0	16
	London	2004-05	21(1)	7	0	0	28
Shaun Lunt	Huddersfield	2009-10	24(19)	23	0	0	92
Peter Lupton	Crusaders	2010	22(6)	5	0	0	20
	Celtic	2009	16(4)	4	0	0	16
	Castleford	2006, 2008	40	11	0	0	44
	Hull	2003-06	19(26)	10	3	0	46
	London	2000-02	10(15)	2	2	0	12
Andy Lynch	Bradford	2005-10	132(29)	37	0	0	148
	Castleford	1999-2004	78(48)	15	0	0	60
Reece Lyne	Hull	2010	6	2	0	0	8
Jamie Lyon	St Helens	2005-06	54(1)	39	172	0	500
Duncan MacGillivray	Wakefield	2004-08	75(18)	6	0	0	24
Brad Mackay	Bradford	2000	24(2)	8	0	0	32
Graham Mackay	Hull	2002	27	18	24	0	120
	Bradford	2001	16(3)	12	1	0	50
	Leeds	2000	12(8)	10	2	0	44
Keiron Maddocks	Leigh	2005	1(3)	0	0	0	0
Steve Maden	Leigh	2005	23	9	0	0	36
	Warrington	2002	3	0	0	0	0
Mateaki Mafi	Warrington	1996-97	7(8)	7	0	0	28
Shaun Magennis	St Helens	2010	3(1)	3	0	0	12
Brendan Magnus	London	2000	3	1	0	0	4
Mark Maguire	London	1996-97	11(4)	7	13	0	54
Adam Maher	Hull	2000-03	88(4)	24	0	0	96
	Gateshead	1999	21(5)	3	0	0	12
Lee Maher	Leeds	1996	4(1)	0	0	0	0
Shaun Mahony	Paris	1997	5	0	0	0	0
Hutch Maiava	Hull	2007	(19)	1	0	0	4
David Maiden	Hull	2000-01	32(10)	11	0	0	44
	Gateshead	1999	5(16)	8	0	0	32
Craig Makin	Salford	1999-2001	24(20)	2	0	0	8
Brady Malam	Wigan	2000	5(20)	1	0	0	4
Dominic Maloney	Hull	2009	(2)	0	0	0	0
Francis Maloney	Castleford	1998-99, 2003-04	71(7)	24	33	3	165
	Salford	2001-02	45(1)	26	5	0	114
	Wakefield	2000	11	1	1	0	6
	Oldham	1996-97	39(2)	12	91	2	232
George Mann	Warrington	1997	14(5)	1	0	0	4
	Leeds	1996	11(4)	2	0	0	8
Dane Manning	Leeds	2009	(1)	0	0	0	0
Misili Manu	Widnes	2005	1	0	0	0	0
Willie Manu	Hull	2007-10	84(11)	16	0	0	64
	Castleford	2006	19(4)	9	0	0	36
Darren Mapp	Celtic	2009	9(2)	1	0	0	4
David March	Wakefield	1999-2007	164(23)	34	126	0	388
Paul March	Wakefield	1999-2001, 2007	42(31)	17	23	0	114
	Huddersfield	2003-06	71(19)	17	36	1	141
Nick Mardon	London	1997-98	14	2	0	0	8
Frankie Mariano	Hull KR	2010	(3)	0	0	0	0
Oliver Marns	Halifax	1996-2002	54(19)	23	0	0	92
Paul Marquet	Warrington	2002	23(2)	0	0	0	0
Iain Marsh	Salford	1998-2001	1(4)	0	0	0	0
Lee Marsh	Salford	2001-02	3(4)	0	0	0	0
Stefan Marsh	Wigan	2010	5	1	0	0	4
Richard Marshall	Leigh	2005	4(16)	1	0	0	4
	London	2002-03	33(11)	1	0	0	4
	Huddersfield	2000-01	35(14)	1	0	0	4
	Halifax	1996-99	38(34)	2	0	0	8
Jason Martin	Paris	1997	15(2)	3	0	0	12
Scott Martin	Salford	1997-99	32(18)	8	0	0	32
Tony Martin	Crusaders	2010	16(1)	5	0	0	20
	Wakefield	2008-09	33	10	33	0	106
	London	1996-97, 2001-03	97(1)	36	170	1	485
Mick Martindale	Halifax	1996	(4)	0	0	0	0
Sebastien Martins	Catalans	2006, 2009-10	(13)	2	0	0	8
Tommy Martyn	St Helens	1996-2003	125(20)	87	63	12	486

171

Super League Players 1996-2010

PLAYER	CLUB	YEAR	APP	TRIES	GOALS	FG	PTS
Dean Marwood	Workington	1996	9(6)	0	22	0	44
Martin Masella	Warrington	2001	10(14)	5	0	0	20
	Wakefield	2000	14(8)	4	0	0	16
	Leeds	1997-1999	59(5)	1	0	0	4
Colin Maskill	Castleford	1996	8	1	1	0	6
Keith Mason	Huddersfield	2006-10	93(5)	3	0	0	12
	Castleford	2006	(2)	0	0	0	0
	St Helens	2003-05	33(23)	4	0	0	16
	Wakefield	2000-01	5(17)	0	0	0	0
Nathan Massey	Castleford	2008-10	1(6)	0	0	0	0
Vila Matautia	St Helens	1996-2001	31(68)	9	0	0	36
Feleti Mateo	London	2005	4(10)	1	0	0	4
Barrie-Jon Mather							
	Castleford	1998, 2000-02	50(12)	21	0	0	84
Richard Mathers	Warrington	2002, 2009-10	42(3)	11	0	0	44
	Wigan	2008-09	23(1)	2	0	0	8
	Leeds	2002-06	85(2)	26	0	0	104
Jamie Mathiou	Leeds	1997-2001	31(82)	3	0	0	12
Terry Matterson	London	1996-98	46	15	90	6	246
Luke May	Harlequins	2009-10	(3)	0	0	0	0
Casey Mayberry	Halifax	2000	1(1)	0	0	0	0
Chris Maye	Halifax	2003	3(4)	0	0	0	0
Joe Mbu	Harlequins	2006-09	33(20)	3	0	0	12
	London	2003-05	29(19)	4	0	0	16
Danny McAllister	Gateshead	1999	3(3)	1	0	0	4
	Sheffield	1996-97	33(7)	10	0	0	40
John McAtee	St Helens	1996	2(1)	0	0	0	0
Nathan McAvoy	Bradford	1998-2002, 2007	83(31)	46	0	0	184
	Wigan	2006	15(2)	5	0	0	20
	Salford	1997-98, 2004-05	57(4)	18	0	0	72
Tyrone McCarthy	Warrington	2009-10	1(6)	2	0	0	8
Louie McCarthy-Scarsbrook							
	Harlequins	2006-10	41(50)	17	0	0	68
Dave McConnell	London	2003	(4)	0	0	0	0
	St Helens	2001-02	3(2)	4	0	0	16
Robbie McCormack							
	Wigan	1998	24	2	0	0	8
Steve McCurrie	Leigh	2005	7(3)	1	0	0	4
	Widnes	2002-04	55(22)	10	0	0	40
	Warrington	1998-2001	69(26)	31	0	0	124
Barrie McDermott							
	Leeds	1996-2005	163(69)	28	0	0	112
Brian McDermott	Bradford	1996-2002	138(32)	33	0	0	132
Ryan McDonald	Widnes	2002-03	6(4)	0	0	0	0
Wayne McDonald	Huddersfield	2005-06	11(23)	1	0	0	4
	Wigan	2005	(4)	0	0	0	0
	Leeds	2002-05	34(47)	14	0	0	56
	St Helens	2001	7(11)	4	0	0	16
	Hull	2000	5(8)	4	0	0	16
	Wakefield	1999	9(17)	8	0	0	32
Craig McDowell	Huddersfield	2003	(1)	0	0	0	0
	Warrington	2002	(1)	0	0	0	0
	Bradford	2000	(1)	0	0	0	0
Wes McGibbon	Halifax	1999	1	0	0	0	0
Jermaine McGillvary							
	Huddersfield	2010	5	7	0	0	28
Dean McGilvray	Salford	2009-10	14	4	0	0	16
	St Helens	2006-08	5(1)	1	0	0	4
Billy McGinty	Workington	1996	1	0	0	0	0
Ryan McGoldrick	Castleford	2006, 2008-10	104	23	10	0	112
Kevin McGuinness							
	Salford	2004-07	63(3)	11	0	0	44
Casey McGuire	Catalans	2007-10	87(4)	27	0	0	108
Danny McGuire	Leeds	2001-10	186(34)	171	0	2	686
Gary McGuirk	Workington	1996	(4)	0	0	0	0
Michael McIlorum							
	Wigan	2007-10	20(38)	5	0	0	20
Richard McKell	Castleford	1997-98	22(7)	2	0	0	8
Chris McKenna	Bradford	2006-07	40(7)	7	0	0	28
	Leeds	2003-05	65(4)	18	0	0	72
Phil McKenzie	Workington	1996	4	0	0	0	0
Chris McKinney	Oldham	1996-97	4(9)	2	0	0	8
Mark McLinden	Harlequins	2006-08	46(1)	20	0	1	81
	London	2005	22(3)	8	0	0	32
Shayne McMenemy							
	Hull	2003-07	80(8)	12	0	0	48
	Halifax	2001-03	63	11	0	0	44
Andy McNally	London	2004	5(3)	0	0	0	0
	Castleford	2001, 2003	2(5)	1	0	0	4
Steve McNamara	Huddersfield	2001, 2003	41(9)	3	134	1	281
	Wakefield	2000	15(2)	2	32	0	72
	Bradford	1996-99	90(3)	14	348	7	759
Paul McNicholas	Hull	2004-05	28(12)	4	0	0	16
Neil McPherson	Salford	1997	(1)	0	0	0	0
Duncan McRae	London	1996	11(2)	3	0	1	13
Paul McShane	Leeds	2009-10	3(9)	1	0	0	4
	Hull	2010	(4)	0	0	0	0
Derek McVey	St Helens	1996-97	28(4)	6	1	0	26
Dallas Mead	Warrington	1997	2	0	0	0	0

PLAYER	CLUB	YEAR	APP	TRIES	GOALS	FG	PTS
Robbie Mears	Leigh	2005	8(6)	0	0	0	0
	Leeds	2001	23	6	0	0	24
Paul Medley	Bradford	1996-98	6(35)	9	0	0	36
Francis Meli	St Helens	2006-10	119(1)	77	0	0	308
Vince Mellars	Crusaders	2010	23	11	0	0	44
Chris Melling	Harlequins	2007-10	75(11)	26	4	0	112
	Wigan	2004-05	8(2)	1	3	0	10
Paul Mellor	Castleford	2003-04	36(3)	18	0	0	72
Craig Menkins	Paris	1997	4(5)	0	0	0	0
Luke Menzies	Hull KR	2008	(1)	0	0	0	0
Steve Menzies	Bradford	2009-10	52(1)	24	1	0	98
Gary Mercer	Castleford	2002	(1)	0	0	0	0
	Leeds	1996-97, 2001	40(2)	9	0	0	36
	Warrington	2001	18	2	0	0	8
	Halifax	1998-2001	73(2)	16	0	0	64
Tony Mestrov	London	1996-97, 2001	59(8)	4	0	0	16
	Wigan	1998-2000	39(39)	3	0	0	12
Keiran Meyer	London	1996	4	1	0	0	4
Brad Meyers	Bradford	2005-06	40(11)	13	0	0	52
Gary Middlehurst	Widnes	2004	(2)	0	0	0	0
Simon Middleton	Castleford	1996-97	19(3)	8	0	0	32
Darryl Millard	Wakefield	2010	21	11	0	0	44
Shane Millard	Wigan	2007	19(6)	3	0	0	12
	Leeds	2006	6(21)	3	0	0	12
	Widnes	2003-05	69	23	0	0	92
	London	1998-2001	72(14)	11	1	0	46
David Mills	Harlequins	2006-07, 2010	25(32)	2	0	0	8
	Hull KR	2008-09	20(11)	1	0	0	4
	Widnes	2002-05	17(77)	8	0	0	32
Lewis Mills	Celtic	2009	(4)	0	0	0	0
Adam Milner	Castleford	2010	(4)	2	0	0	8
Lee Milner	Halifax	1999	(1)	0	0	0	0
John Minto	London	1996	13	4	0	0	16
Lee Mitchell	Warrington	2007-10	8(22)	3	0	0	12
Sam Moa	Hull	2009-10	(33)	1	0	0	4
Martin Moana	Salford	2004	6(3)	1	0	0	4
	Halifax	1996-2001, 2003	126(22)	62	0	1	249
	Wakefield	2002	19(2)	10	0	0	40
	Huddersfield	2001	3(3)	2	0	0	8
Adam Mogg	Catalans	2007-10	74	19	0	1	77
Steve Molloy	Huddersfield	2000-01	26(20)	3	0	0	12
	Sheffield	1998-99	32(17)	3	0	0	12
Chris Molyneux	Huddersfield	2000-01	1(18)	0	0	0	0
	Sheffield	1999	1(2)	0	0	0	0
Michael Monaghan							
	Warrington	2008-10	76(1)	15	0	2	62
Adrian Moore	Huddersfield	1998-99	1(4)	0	0	0	0
Danny Moore	London	2000	7	0	0	0	0
	Wigan	1998-99	49(3)	18	0	0	72
Jason Moore	Workington	1996	(5)	0	0	0	0
Richard Moore	Wakefield	2007-10	50(44)	8	0	0	32
	Leigh	2005	2(5)	0	0	0	0
	Bradford	2002-04	1(26)	0	0	0	0
	London	2002, 2004	5(9)	2	0	0	8
Scott Moore	St Helens	2004-07, 2010	25(18)	8	0	0	32
	Huddersfield	2009	23(2)	9	0	0	36
	Castleford	2008	11(5)	1	0	0	4
Dennis Moran	Wigan	2005-06	39	17	1	1	71
	London	2001-04	107(2)	74	2	5	305
Willie Morganson	Sheffield	1997-98	18(12)	5	3	0	26
Paul Moriarty	Halifax	1996	3(2)	0	0	0	0
Adrian Morley	Warrington	2007-10	93(1)	5	0	0	20
	Bradford	2005	2(4)	0	0	0	0
	Leeds	1996-2000	95(14)	25	0	0	100
Chris Morley	Salford	1999	3(5)	0	0	0	0
	Warrington	1998	2(8)	0	0	0	0
	St Helens	1996-97	21(16)	4	0	0	16
Glenn Morrison	Wakefield	2010	22(1)	7	0	0	28
	Bradford	2007-09	48(2)	19	0	0	76
Iain Morrison	Hull KR	2007	5(6)	1	0	0	4
	Huddersfield	2003-05	11(23)	0	0	0	0
	London	2001	(1)	0	0	0	0
Dale Morton	Wakefield	2009-10	13(3)	5	0	0	20
Gareth Morton	Hull KR	2007	7(4)	3	23	0	58
	Leeds	2001-02	1(1)	0	0	0	0
Lee Mossop	Wigan	2008-10	2(26)	1	0	0	4
	Huddersfield	2009	1(4)	1	0	0	4
Aaron Moule	Salford	2006-07	45	17	0	0	68
	Widnes	2004-05	29	12	0	0	48
Wilfried Moulinec	Paris	1996	1	0	0	0	0
Gregory Mounis	Catalans	2006-10	85(38)	16	16	0	96
Mark Moxon	Huddersfield	1998-2001	20(5)	1	0	0	5
Brett Mullins	Leeds	2001	5(3)	1	0	0	4
Damian Munro	Widnes	2002	8(2)	1	0	0	4
	Halifax	1996-97	9(6)	8	0	0	32
Matt Munro	Oldham	1996-97	26(5)	8	0	0	32
Craig Murdock	Salford	2000	(2)	0	0	0	0
	Hull	1998-99	21(6)	8	0	2	34
	Wigan	1996-98	18(17)	14	0	0	56

Super League Players 1996-2010

PLAYER	CLUB	YEAR	APP	TRIES	GOALS	FG	PTS
Aaron Murphy	Wakefield	2008-10	37(2)	10	0	0	40
Justin Murphy	Catalans	2006-08	59	49	0	0	196
	Widnes	2004	5	1	0	0	4
Doc Murray	Warrington	1997	(2)	0	0	0	0
	Wigan	1997	6(2)	0	0	0	0
Scott Murrell	Hull KR	2007-10	82(8)	17	17	1	103
	Leeds	2005	(1)	0	0	0	0
	London	2004	3(3)	2	0	0	8
David Mycoe	Sheffield	1996-97	12(13)	1	0	0	4
Richard Myler	Warrington	2010	20(1)	14	1	0	58
	Salford	2009	18	11	0	0	44
Rob Myler	Oldham	1996-97	19(2)	6	0	0	24
Stephen Myler	Salford	2006	4(8)	1	15	0	34
	Widnes	2003-05	35(14)	8	74	0	180
Vinny Myler	Salford	2004	(4)	0	0	0	0
	Bradford	2003	(1)	0	0	0	0
Matt Nable	London	1997	2(2)	1	0	0	4
Brad Nairn	Workington	1996	14	4	0	0	16
Frank Napoli	London	2000	14(6)	2	0	0	8
Carlo Napolitano	Salford	2000	(3)	1	0	0	4
Stephen Nash	Salford	2007, 2009	2(18)	1	0	0	4
	Widnes	2005	4(1)	0	0	0	0
Jim Naylor	Halifax	2000	7(6)	2	0	0	8
Scott Naylor	Salford	1997-98, 2004	30(1)	9	0	0	36
	Bradford	1999-2003	127(1)	51	0	0	204
Adam Neal	Salford	2010	4(2)	0	0	0	0
Mike Neal	Salford	1998	(1)	0	0	0	0
	Oldham	1996-97	6(4)	3	0	0	12
Jonathan Neill	Huddersfield	1998-99	20(11)	0	0	0	0
	St Helens	1996	1	0	0	0	0
Chris Nero	Bradford	2008-10	65(5)	24	0	0	96
	Huddersfield	2004-07	97(8)	38	0	0	152
Jason Netherton	Hull KR	2007-10	34(46)	4	0	0	16
	London	2003-04	6	0	0	0	0
	Halifax	2002	2(3)	0	0	0	0
	Leeds	2001	(3)	0	0	0	0
Kirk Netherton	Castleford	2009-10	5(23)	3	0	0	12
	Hull KR	2007-08	9(15)	2	0	0	8
Paul Newlove	Castleford	2004	5	1	0	0	4
	St Helens	1996-2003	162	106	0	0	424
Richard Newlove	Wakefield	2003	17(5)	8	0	0	32
Clint Newton	Hull KR	2008-10	74(1)	29	0	0	116
Terry Newton	Wakefield	2010	(2)	0	0	0	0
	Bradford	2006-09	83(6)	26	0	0	104
	Wigan	2000-05	157(9)	62	0	0	248
	Leeds	1996-1999	55(14)	4	0	0	16
Gene Ngamu	Huddersfield	1999-2000	29(2)	9	67	0	170
Danny Nicklas	Hull	2010	(3)	0	0	0	0
Sonny Nickle	St Helens	1999-2002	86(18)	14	0	0	56
	Bradford	1996-98	25(16)	9	0	0	36
Jason Nicol	Salford	2000-02	52(7)	11	0	0	44
Tawera Nikau	Warrington	2000-01	51	7	0	0	28
Rob Nolan	Hull	1998-99	20(11)	6	0	0	24
Paul Noone	Harlequins	2006	5(2)	0	0	0	0
	Warrington	2000-06	60(59)	12	20	0	88
Chris Norman	Halifax	2003	13(3)	2	0	0	8
Paul Norman	Oldham	1996	(1)	0	0	0	0
Andy Northey	St Helens	1996-97	8(17)	2	0	0	8
Danny Nutley	Castleford	2006	28	3	0	0	12
	Warrington	1998-2001	94(1)	3	0	0	12
Tony Nuttall	Oldham	1996-97	1(7)	0	0	0	0
Clinton O'Brien	Wakefield	2003	(2)	0	0	0	0
Sam Obst	Wakefield	2005-10	99(28)	40	7	0	174
Jamie O'Callaghan	Harlequins	2008-10	29(2)	6	0	0	24
Eamon O'Carroll	Wigan	2006-10	2(55)	2	0	0	8
Matt O'Connor	Paris	1997	11(4)	1	26	0	58
Terry O'Connor	Widnes	2005	25	2	0	0	8
	Wigan	1996-2004	177(45)	9	0	0	36
Jarrod O'Doherty	Huddersfield	2003	26	3	0	0	12
David O'Donnell	Paris	1997	21	3	0	0	12
Martin Offiah	Salford	2000-01	41	20	0	2	82
	London	1996-99	29(3)	21	0	0	84
	Wigan	1996	8	7	0	0	28
Mark O'Halloran	London	2004-05	34(3)	10	0	0	40
Ryan O'Hara	Crusaders	2010	24(1)	2	0	0	8
	Celtic	2009	27	3	0	0	12
Hefin O'Hare	Huddersfield	2001, 2003-05	72(10)	27	0	0	108
Hitro Okesene	Hull	1998	21(1)	0	0	0	0
Anderson Okiwe	Sheffield	1997	1	0	0	0	0
Tom Olbison	Bradford	2009-10	(7)	1	0	0	4
Jamie Olejnik	Paris	1997	11	8	0	0	32
Kevin O'Loughlin	Halifax	1997-98	2(4)	0	0	0	0
	St Helens	1997	(3)	0	0	0	0
Sean O'Loughlin	Wigan	2002-10	194(20)	42	2	2	174
Mark O'Meley	Hull	2010	21	4	0	0	16
Jules O'Neill	Widnes	2003-05	57(3)	14	158	7	379
	Wakefield	2005	10(2)	2	4	0	16
	Wigan	2002-03	29(1)	12	72	0	192
Julian O'Neill	Widnes	2002-05	57(39)	3	0	0	12
	Wakefield	2001	24(1)	2	0	0	8
	St Helens	1997-2000	95(8)	5	0	0	20
Mark O'Neill	Hull KR	2007	17	5	0	0	20
	Leeds	2006	1(8)	0	0	0	0
Steve O'Neill	Gateshead	1999	1(1)	0	0	0	0
Tom O'Reilly	Warrington	2001-02	8(6)	1	0	0	4
Matt Orford	Bradford	2010	12	3	31	2	76
Chris Orr	Huddersfield	1998	19(3)	2	0	0	8
Danny Orr	Harlequins	2007-10	90(4)	13	96	0	244
	Wigan	2004-06	66(2)	18	11	0	94
	Castleford	1997-2003	150(18)	65	279	3	821
Gareth Owen	Salford	2010	(3)	0	0	0	0
Nick Owen	Leigh	2005	8(1)	1	11	0	26
Richard Owen	Castleford	2008-10	47(3)	22	0	0	88
Iafeta Palea'aesina	Wigan	2006-10	55(77)	16	0	0	64
Jason Palmada	Workington	1996	12	2	0	0	8
Junior Paramore	Castleford	1996	5(5)	3	0	0	12
Paul Parker	Hull	1999-2002	23(18)	9	0	0	36
Rob Parker	Salford	2009-10	22(11)	2	0	0	8
	Warrington	2006-08	10(56)	6	0	0	24
	Bradford	2000, 2002-05	19(76)	14	0	0	56
	London	2001	9	1	0	0	4
Wayne Parker	Halifax	1996-97	12(1)	0	0	0	0
Ian Parry	Warrington	2001	(1)	0	0	0	0
Jules Parry	Paris	1996	10(2)	0	0	0	0
Regis Pastre-Courtine	Paris	1996	4(3)	4	0	0	16
Andrew Patmore	Oldham	1996	8(5)	3	0	0	12
Larne Patrick	Huddersfield	2009-10	8(27)	8	0	0	32
Henry Paul	Harlequins	2006-08	60(1)	8	94	2	222
	Bradford	1999-2001	81(5)	29	350	6	822
	Wigan	1996-98	60	37	23	0	194
Junior Paul	London	1996	3	1	0	0	4
Robbie Paul	Salford	2009	2(3)	2	0	0	8
	Huddersfield	2006-07	44(8)	7	0	0	28
	Bradford	1996-2005	198(31)	121	3	0	490
Jason Payne	Castleford	2006	1(1)	0	0	0	0
Danny Peacock	Bradford	1997-99	32(2)	15	0	0	60
Jamie Peacock	Leeds	2006-10	119(8)	16	0	0	64
	Bradford	1999-2005	163(25)	38	0	0	152
Martin Pearson	Wakefield	2001	21(1)	3	60	3	135
	Halifax	1997-98, 2000	55(6)	24	181	0	458
	Sheffield	1999	17(6)	9	36	2	110
Jacques Pech	Paris	1996	16	0	0	0	0
Mike Pechey	Warrington	1998	6(3)	2	0	0	8
Bill Peden	London	2003	21(3)	7	0	0	28
Adam Peek	Crusaders	2010	5(19)	1	0	0	4
	Celtic	2009	5(12)	3	0	0	12
Dimitri Pelo	Catalans	2007-10	79	37	0	0	148
Sean Penkywicz	Huddersfield	2004-05	21(11)	7	0	0	28
	Halifax	2000-03	29(27)	8	0	0	32
Julian Penni	Salford	1998-99	4	0	0	0	0
Kevin Penny	Harlequins	2010	5	3	0	0	12
	Warrington	2006-09	39(1)	26	0	0	104
Lee Penny	Warrington	1996-2003	140(5)	54	0	0	216
Paul Penrice	Workington	1996	11(2)	2	0	0	8
Chris Percival	Widnes	2002-03	26	6	0	0	24
Apollo Perelini	St Helens	1996-2000	103(16)	27	0	0	108
Mark Perrett	Halifax	1996-97	15(4)	4	0	0	16
Shane Perry	Catalans	2009	8(8)	1	0	0	4
Adam Peters	Paris	1997	16(3)	0	0	0	0
Dominic Peters	London	1998-2003	58(11)	12	0	0	48
Mike Peters	Warrington	2000	2(12)	1	0	0	4
	Halifax	2000	1	0	0	0	0
Willie Peters	Widnes	2004	9	3	0	2	14
	Wigan	2000	29	15	5	6	76
	Gateshead	1999	27	11	1	6	52
Matt Petersen	Wakefield	2008-09	14	3	0	0	12
Adrian Petrie	Workington	1996	(1)	0	0	0	0
Cameron Phelps	Wigan	2008-10	43(1)	14	4	0	64
Rowland Phillips	Workington	1996	22	1	0	0	4
Nathan Picchi	Leeds	1996	(1)	0	0	0	0
Ian Pickavance	Hull	1999	4(2)	2	0	0	8
	Huddersfield	1999	3(14)	0	0	0	0
	St Helens	1996-98	12(44)	6	0	0	24
James Pickering	Castleford	1999	1(19)	0	0	0	0
Steve Pickersgill	Warrington	2005-09	1(36)	0	0	0	0
Nick Pinkney	Salford	2000-02	64	29	0	0	116
	Halifax	1999	26(2)	13	0	0	52
	Sheffield	1997-98	33	10	0	0	40
Mikhail Piskunov	Paris	1996	1(1)	1	0	0	4
Darryl Pitt	London	1996	2(16)	4	0	1	17
Jay Pitts	Leeds	2009-10	5(5)	1	0	0	4
	Wakefield	2008-09	9(8)	2	0	0	8
Andy Platt	Salford	1997-98	20(3)	1	0	0	4
Michael Platt	Bradford	2007-10	76(3)	28	0	0	112
	Castleford	2006	26	7	0	0	28
	Salford	2001-02	3	1	0	0	4
Willie Poching	Leeds	2002-06	58(73)	44	0	0	176
	Wakefield	1999-2001	65(4)	20	0	0	80
Quentin Pongia	Wigan	2003-04	15(10)	0	0	0	0
Dan Potter	Widnes	2002-03	34(2)	6	0	0	24
	London	2001	1(3)	1	0	0	4

Super League Players 1996-2010

PLAYER	CLUB	YEAR	APP	TRIES	GOALS	FG	PTS
Craig Poucher	Hull	1999-2002	31(5)	5	0	0	20
Bryn Powell	Salford	2004	1(1)	0	0	0	0
Daio Powell	Sheffield	1999	13(1)	2	0	0	8
	Halifax	1997-98	30(3)	17	0	0	68
Daryl Powell	Leeds	1998-2000	49(30)	12	0	2	50
Karl Pratt	Bradford	2003-05	35(19)	18	0	0	72
	Leeds	1999-2002	62(12)	33	0	0	132
Paul Prescott	Wigan	2004-10	34(57)	1	0	0	4
Steve Prescott	Hull	1998-99, 2001-03	99	46	191	3	569
	Wakefield	2000	22(1)	3	13	0	38
	St Helens	1996-97	32	15	17	0	94
Lee Prest	Workington	1996	(1)	0	0	0	0
Gareth Price	Salford	2002	(2)	0	0	0	0
	London	2002	2(2)	3	0	0	12
	St Helens	1999	(11)	2	0	0	8
Gary Price	Wakefield	1999-2001	55(13)	11	0	0	44
Richard Price	Sheffield	1996	1(2)	0	0	0	0
Tony Priddle	Paris	1997	11(7)	3	0	0	12
Karl Pryce	Wigan	2009-10	11(2)	12	0	0	48
	Bradford	2003-06	28(19)	33	1	0	134
Leon Pryce	St Helens	2006-10	128(2)	63	0	0	252
	Bradford	1998-2005	159(29)	86	0	0	344
Waine Pryce	Wakefield	2007	10(2)	4	0	0	16
	Castleford	2000-06	97(12)	49	0	0	196
Tony Puletua	St Helens	2009-10	45(9)	26	0	0	104
Andrew Purcell	Castleford	2000	15(3)	3	0	0	12
	Hull	1999	27	4	0	0	16
Rob Purdham	Harlequins	2006-10	95(1)	16	129	1	323
	London	2002-05	53(15)	16	2	0	69
Luke Quigley	Catalans	2007	16(1)	1	0	0	4
Damien Quinn	Celtic	2009	20(1)	4	12	0	40
Scott Quinnell	Wigan	1996	6(3)	1	0	0	4
Florian Quintilla	Catalans	2008-09	1(4)	0	0	0	0
Lee Radford	Hull	1998, 2006-10	126(15)	16	1	0	66
	Bradford	1999-2005	79(65)	18	12	0	96
Kris Radlinski	Wigan	1996-2006	236(1)	134	1	0	538
Sebastien Raguin	Catalans	2007-10	65(10)	19	0	0	76
Adrian Rainey	Castleford	2002	4(7)	1	0	0	4
Andy Raleigh	Huddersfield	2006-10	69(39)	13	0	0	52
Jean-Luc Ramondou	Paris	1996	1(1)	1	0	0	4
Chad Randall	Harlequins	2006-10	116(2)	33	0	1	133
Craig Randall	Halifax	1999	8(11)	4	0	0	16
	Salford	1997-98	12(18)	4	0	0	16
Scott Ranson	Oldham	1996-97	19(2)	7	0	0	28
Aaron Raper	Castleford	1999-2001	48(4)	4	2	1	21
Stefan Ratchford	Salford	2007, 2009-10	40(4)	12	18	0	84
Mike Ratu	Hull KR	2010	5	1	0	0	4
	Leeds	2007, 2009	1(5)	1	0	0	4
Paul Rauhihi	Warrington	2006-09	67(20)	10	0	0	40
Ben Rauter	Wakefield	2001	15(6)	4	0	0	16
Gareth Raynor	Crusaders	2010	7	4	0	0	16
	Hull	2001-09	186	102	0	0	408
	Leeds	2000	(3)	0	0	0	0
Tony Rea	London	1996	22	4	0	0	16
Stuart Reardon	Bradford	2003-05, 2010	78(11)	37	0	0	148
	Warrington	2006-08	48	12	0	0	48
	Salford	2002	7(1)	3	0	0	12
Mark Reber	Wigan	1999-2000	9(9)	5	0	0	20
Alan Reddicliffe	Warrington	2001	1	0	0	0	0
Tahi Reihana	Bradford	1997-98	17(21)	0	0	0	0
Paul Reilly	Wakefield	2008	5(2)	1	0	0	4
	Huddersfield	1999-2001, 2003-07	150(8)	35	1	0	142
Robert Relf	Widnes	2002-04	68(2)	5	0	0	20
Steve Renouf	Wigan	2000-01	55	40	0	0	160
Steele Retchless	London	1998-2004	177(6)	13	0	0	52
Scott Rhodes	Hull	2000	2	0	0	0	0
Phillipe Ricard	Paris	1996-97	2	0	0	0	0
Andy Rice	Huddersfield	2000-01	2(13)	1	0	0	4
Basil Richards	Huddersfield	1998-99	28(17)	1	0	0	4
Craig Richards	Oldham	1996	1	0	0	0	0
Pat Richards	Wigan	2006-10	138	95	480	3	1343
Andy Richardson	Hudds-Sheff	2000	(2)	0	0	0	0
Sean Richardson	Widnes	2002	2(18)	1	0	0	4
	Wakefield	1999	5(1)	0	0	0	0
	Castleford	1996-97	3(8)	1	0	0	4
Mark Riddell	Wigan	2009-10	45(11)	5	2	0	24
Neil Rigby	St Helens	2006	(1)	0	0	0	0
Shane Rigon	Bradford	2001	14(11)	12	0	0	48
Craig Rika	Halifax	1996	2	0	0	0	0
Chris Riley	Warrington	2005-10	77(10)	51	0	0	204
Peter Riley	Workington	1996	7(5)	0	0	0	0
Julien Rinaldi	Wakefield	2002, 2010	6(7)	3	0	0	12
	Bradford	2009	(7)	1	0	0	4
	Harlequins	2007-08	4(43)	9	0	0	36
	Catalans	2006	16(6)	3	1	0	14
Dean Ripley	Castleford	2004	3(4)	1	0	0	4
Leroy Rivett	Warrington	2002	9	1	0	0	4
	Hudds-Sheff	2000	5(1)	1	0	0	4
	Leeds	1996-2000	39(15)	21	0	0	84

PLAYER	CLUB	YEAR	APP	TRIES	GOALS	FG	PTS
Jason Roach	Warrington	1998-99	29(7)	15	0	0	60
	Castleford	1997	7	4	0	0	16
Ben Roarty	Castleford	2006	11(6)	2	0	0	8
	Huddersfield	2003-05	52	5	0	0	20
Amos Roberts	Wigan	2009-10	43(1)	25	5	0	110
Mark Roberts	Wigan	2003	(3)	0	0	0	0
Robert Roberts	Huddersfield	2001	(1)	0	0	0	0
	Halifax	2000	(3)	0	0	0	0
	Hull	1999	24(2)	4	13	4	46
Chad Robinson	Harlequins	2009	13(1)	2	0	0	8
Craig Robinson	Wakefield	2005	(1)	0	0	0	0
Jason Robinson	Wigan	1996-2000	126(1)	87	0	1	349
Jeremy Robinson	Paris	1997	10(3)	1	21	0	46
John Robinson	Widnes	2003-04	7	1	0	0	4
Luke Robinson	Huddersfield	2008-10	79(1)	20	4	0	88
	Salford	2005-07	79	28	10	2	134
	Wigan	2002-04	17(25)	9	6	1	49
	Castleford	2004	9	4	3	0	22
Will Robinson	Hull	2000	22	4	0	0	16
	Gateshead	1999	28	9	0	0	36
James Roby	St Helens	2004-10	65(114)	51	0	0	204
Mike Roby	St Helens	2004	(1)	0	0	0	0
Carl Roden	Warrington	1997	1	0	0	0	0
Matt Rodwell	Warrington	2002	10	3	0	0	12
Darren Rogers	Castleford	1999-2004	162(1)	81	0	0	324
	Salford	1997-98	42	16	0	0	64
Jamie Rooney	Wakefield	2003-09	113(7)	60	314	21	889
	Castleford	2001	2(1)	0	6	0	12
Jonathan Roper	Castleford	2001	13	7	12	0	52
	Salford	2000	1(4)	1	3	0	10
	London	2000	4	0	0	0	0
	Warrington	1996-2000	75(8)	33	71	0	274
Scott Roskell	London	1996-97	30(2)	16	0	0	64
Steve Rosolen	London	1996-98	25(9)	10	0	0	40
Adam Ross	London	1996	(1)	0	0	0	0
Paul Round	Castleford	1996	(3)	0	0	0	0
Steve Rowlands	Widnes	2004-05	18(3)	2	15	0	38
	St Helens	2003	(1)	0	0	0	0
Paul Rowley	Leigh	2005	15(7)	3	0	0	12
	Huddersfield	2001	24	3	0	0	12
	Halifax	1996-2000	107(3)	27	1	3	113
Nigel Roy	London	2001-04	100	39	0	0	156
Nicky Royle	Widnes	2004	13	7	0	0	28
Chris Rudd	Warrington	1996-98	31(17)	10	16	0	72
Sean Rudder	Catalans	2006	22(1)	6	0	0	24
	Castleford	2004	9(3)	2	0	0	8
James Rushforth	Halifax	1997	(4)	0	0	0	0
Danny Russell	Huddersfield	1998-2000	50(13)	8	0	0	32
Ian Russell	Oldham	1997	1(3)	1	0	0	4
	Paris	1996	3	0	0	0	0
Richard Russell	Castleford	1996-98	37(4)	2	0	0	8
Robert Russell	Salford	1998-99	2(1)	0	1	0	2
Sean Rutgerson	Salford	2004-06	60(9)	4	0	0	16
Chris Ryan	London	1998-99	44(3)	17	10	0	88
Sean Ryan	Castleford	2004	11(5)	2	0	0	8
	Hull	2002-03	53	8	0	0	32
Justin Ryder	Wakefield	2004	19(3)	11	0	0	44
Jason Ryles	Catalans	2009	19(2)	2	0	0	8
Setaimata Sa	Catalans	2010	18(4)	5	0	0	20
Teddy Sadaoui	Catalans	2006	7	0	0	0	0
Matt Salter	London	1997-99	14(34)	4	0	0	0
Ben Sammut	Hull	2000	20	4	67	0	150
	Gateshead	1999	26(2)	6	17	0	58
Jarrod Sammut	Crusaders	2010	10(2)	5	0	0	20
Dean Sampson	Castleford	1996-2003	124(28)	24	0	0	96
Paul Sampson	London	2004	1(2)	1	0	0	4
	Wakefield	2000	17	8	0	0	32
Lee Sanderson	London	2004	1(5)	1	7	0	18
Jason Sands	Paris	1996-97	28	0	0	0	0
Mitchell Sargent	Castleford	2008-10	37(21)	6	0	0	24
Lokeni Savelio	Halifax	2000	2(11)	0	0	0	0
	Salford	1997-98	18(20)	0	0	0	0
Tom Saxton	Salford	2007	5	0	0	0	0
	Wakefield	2006	9(6)	2	0	0	8
	Hull	2005	19(8)	3	0	0	12
	Castleford	2002-04	37(12)	11	0	0	44
Jonathan Scales	Halifax	2000	1	0	0	0	0
	Bradford	1996-98	46(4)	24	0	0	96
Andrew Schick	Castleford	1996-98	45(13)	10	0	0	40
Clinton Schifcofske	Crusaders	2010	20	3	54	0	120
Garry Schofield	Huddersfield	1998	(2)	0	0	0	0
Gary Schubert	Workington	1996	(1)	0	0	0	0
Matt Schultz	Hull	1998-99	23(9)	2	0	0	8
	Leeds	1996	2(4)	0	0	0	0
John Schuster	Halifax	1996-97	31	9	127	3	293
Nick Scruton	Bradford	2009-10	42(6)	2	0	0	8
	Leeds	2002, 2004-08	11(53)	3	0	0	12
	Hull	2004	2(16)	3	0	0	12
Danny Sculthorpe	Huddersfield	2009	5(8)	0	0	0	0
	Wakefield	2007-09	14(28)	1	0	0	4
	Castleford	2006	18(1)	4	0	1	17
	Wigan	2002-05	13(49)	7	0	0	28

PLAYER	CLUB	YEAR	APP	TRIES	GOALS	FG	PTS
Paul Sculthorpe	St Helens	1998-2008	223(4)	94	356	7	1095
	Warrington	1996-97	40	6	0	0	24
Mick Seaby	London	1997	3(2)	1	0	0	4
Danny Seal	Halifax	1996-99	8(17)	3	0	0	12
Matt Seers	Wakefield	2003	11(1)	2	0	0	8
Anthony Seibold	London	1999-2000	33(19)	5	0	0	20
Keith Senior	Leeds	1999-2010	305(2)	155	0	0	620
	Sheffield	1996-99	90(2)	40	0	0	160
Fili Seru	Hull	1998-99	37(1)	13	0	0	52
Anthony Seuseu	Halifax	2003	1(11)	1	0	0	4
Jerry Seuseu	Wigan	2005-06	29(9)	1	0	0	4
Will Sharp	Harlequins	2008-10	65(1)	19	0	0	76
Darren Shaw	Salford	2002	5(9)	1	0	0	4
	London	1996, 2002	22(8)	3	0	0	12
	Castleford	2000-01	50(6)	1	0	0	4
	Sheffield	1998-99	51(1)	3	0	1	13
Mick Shaw	Halifax	1999	5	1	0	0	4
	Leeds	1996	12(2)	7	0	0	28
Phil Shead	Paris	1996	3(2)	0	0	0	0
Richard Sheil	St Helens	1997	(1)	0	0	0	0
Kelly Shelford	Warrington	1996-97	25(3)	4	0	2	18
Michael Shenton	Castleford	2004, 2006, 2008-10	97(2)	46	0	0	184
Ryan Sheridan	Castleford	2004	2	0	0	0	0
	Widnes	2003	14(3)	2	0	0	8
	Leeds	1997-2002	123(7)	46	0	1	185
	Sheffield	1996	9(3)	5	0	1	21
Rikki Sheriffe	Bradford	2009-10	51	14	0	0	56
	Harlequins	2006-08	35(1)	16	0	0	64
	Halifax	2003	6(1)	3	0	0	12
Ian Sherratt	Oldham	1996	5(3)	1	0	0	4
Brent Sherwin	Catalans	2010	12	1	0	1	5
	Castleford	2008-10	48(1)	4	0	3	19
Peter Shiels	St Helens	2001-02	44(3)	11	0	0	44
Gary Shillabeer	Huddersfield	1999	(2)	0	0	0	0
Mark Shipway	Salford	2004-05	30(12)	3	0	0	12
Ian Sibbit	Salford	2005-07, 2009-10	64(17)	11	0	0	44
	Warrington	1999-2001, 2003-04	63(18)	24	0	0	96
Mark Sibson	Huddersfield	1999	2	2	0	0	8
Adam Sidlow	Salford	2009-10	15(26)	6	0	0	24
Jon Simms	St Helens	2002	(1)	0	0	0	0
Craig Simon	Hull	2000	23(2)	8	0	0	32
	Gateshead	1999	25(4)	6	0	0	24
Michael Simon	Catalans	2010	(9)	0	0	0	0
Darren Simpson	Huddersfield	1998-99	17(1)	5	0	0	20
Robbie Simpson	London	1999	6(7)	0	0	0	0
Kevin Sinfield	Leeds	1997-2010	294(25)	51	1001	19	2225
Matt Sing	Hull	2007-08	41	14	0	0	56
Wayne Sing	Paris	1997	18(1)	2	0	0	8
Fata Sini	Salford	1997	22	7	0	0	28
John Skandalis	Huddersfield	2007-08	37(5)	4	0	0	16
Dylan Skee	Harlequins	2008-09	(3)	0	0	0	0
Ben Skerrett	Castleford	2003	(1)	0	0	0	0
Kelvin Skerrett	Halifax	1997-99	31(6)	2	0	0	8
	Wigan	1996	1(8)	0	0	0	0
Troy Slattery	Wakefield	2002-03	33(5)	4	0	0	16
	Huddersfield	1999	3	1	0	0	4
Mick Slicker	Huddersfield	2001, 2003-05	17(48)	2	0	0	8
	Sheffield	1999	(3)	1	0	0	4
	Halifax	1997	2(5)	0	0	0	0
Ian Smales	Castleford	1996-97	10(8)	5	0	0	20
Aaron Smith	Castleford	2006	(2)	0	0	0	0
	Bradford	2003-04	12(1)	3	0	0	12
Andy Smith	Harlequins	2007	6(3)	3	0	0	12
	Bradford	2004-06	9(9)	4	0	0	16
	Salford	2005	4	1	0	0	4
Byron Smith	Castleford	2004	(9)	0	0	0	0
	Halifax	2003	6(1)	0	0	0	0
Chris Smith	Hull	2001-02	12	3	0	0	12
	St Helens	1998-2000	62(9)	26	0	0	104
	Castleford	1996-97	36(1)	12	0	0	48
Craig Smith	Wigan	2002-04	77(3)	10	0	0	40
Damien Smith	St Helens	1998	21(1)	8	0	0	32
Danny Smith	Paris	1996	10(2)	1	15	0	34
	London	1996	2(1)	1	0	0	4
Darren Smith	St Helens	2003	25(1)	14	0	0	56
Gary Smith	Castleford	2001	(1)	0	0	0	0
Hudson Smith	Bradford	2000	8(22)	2	0	0	8
	Salford	1999	23(2)	5	0	0	20
James Smith	Salford	2000	23(3)	6	0	0	24
Jamie Smith	Hull	1998-99	24(6)	6	12	0	48
	Workington	1996	5(3)	0	1	0	2
Jason Smith	Hull	2001-04	61(3)	17	0	1	69
Jeremy Smith	Salford	2009-10	27(17)	2	0	0	8
Kris Smith	London	2001	(1)	0	0	0	0
	Halifax	2001	(1)	0	0	0	0
Lee Smith	Leeds	2005-10	104(5)	54	34	1	285
Leigh Smith	Workington	1996	9	4	0	0	16
Mark Smith	Widnes	2005	12(15)	4	0	0	16
	Wigan	1999-2004	35(77)	8	0	0	32
Martyn Smith	Harlequins	2010	(2)	0	0	0	0

PLAYER	CLUB	YEAR	APP	TRIES	GOALS	FG	PTS
Matty Smith	St Helens	2006-08, 2010	17(2)	3	10	1	33
	Salford	2010	22(3)	8	4	1	41
	Celtic	2009	15(1)	3	2	1	17
Michael Smith	Hull KR	2007	(3)	1	0	0	4
	Castleford	1998, 2001-04	86(33)	32	0	0	128
	Hull	1999	12(6)	3	0	0	12
Paul Smith	Huddersfield	2004-06	52(17)	13	0	0	52
Paul Smith	Warrington	2001	1	0	0	0	0
	Castleford	1997-2000	6(37)	3	0	0	12
Paul Smith	London	1997	7(1)	2	0	0	8
Peter Smith	Oldham	1996	2	0	0	0	0
Richard Smith	Wakefield	2001	8(1)	1	0	0	4
	Salford	1997	(1)	1	0	0	4
Tim Smith	Wigan	2008-09	13(8)	2	0	0	8
Tony Smith	Hull	2001-03	43(5)	26	0	0	104
	Wigan	1997-2000	66(5)	46	0	0	184
	Castleford	1996-97	18(2)	10	0	0	40
Tony Smith	Workington	1996	9	1	0	0	4
Tyrone Smith	Harlequins	2006-07	49(1)	13	0	0	52
	London	2005	20(4)	11	0	0	44
Rob Smyth	Leigh	2005	15(1)	4	0	0	16
	Warrington	2000-03	65	35	20	0	180
	London	1998-2000	32(2)	9	15	0	66
	Wigan	1996	11(5)	16	0	0	64
Marc Sneyd	Salford	2010	4(2)	0	0	0	0
Steve Snitch	Castleford	2010	20(5)	7	0	0	28
	Wakefield	2002-05, 2009	33(55)	9	0	0	36
	Huddersfield	2006-08	24(35)	12	0	0	48
Bright Sodje	Wakefield	2000	15	4	0	0	16
	Sheffield	1996-99	54	34	0	0	136
Iosia Soliola	St Helens	2010	5(1)	0	0	0	0
David Solomona	Warrington	2010	4(23)	9	0	0	36
	Bradford	2007-09	44(9)	19	0	0	76
	Wakefield	2004-06	73(3)	26	0	0	104
Alfred Songoro	Wakefield	1999	8(5)	4	0	0	16
Romain Sort	Paris	1997	(1)	0	0	0	0
Paul Southern	Salford	1997-2002	79(33)	6	13	0	50
	St Helens	2002	1(1)	0	0	0	0
Cain Southernwood	Bradford	2010	2	0	0	0	0
Roy Southernwood	Wakefield	1999	1	0	0	0	0
	Halifax	1996	2	0	0	0	0
Jason Southwell	Huddersfield	2004	(1)	0	0	0	0
Waisale Sovatabua	Wakefield	2001-03	44(3)	19	0	0	76
	Hudds-Sheff	2000	23(1)	8	0	0	32
	Sheffield	1996-99	56(17)	19	0	1	77
Yusef Sozi	London	2000-01	(5)	0	0	0	0
Scott Spaven	Hull KR	2010	(2)	0	0	0	0
Andy Speak	Castleford	2001	4(4)	0	0	0	0
	Wakefield	2000	6(5)	2	0	0	8
	Leeds	1999	4	1	0	0	4
Tim Spears	Castleford	2003	(3)	0	0	0	0
Ady Spencer	London	1996-99	8(36)	5	0	0	20
Jack Spencer	Salford	2009-10	(3)	0	0	0	0
Rob Spicer	Wakefield	2002-05	28(18)	4	0	0	16
Stuart Spruce	Widnes	2002-03	45(4)	19	0	0	76
	Bradford	1996-2001	107(2)	57	0	0	228
Lee St Hilaire	Castleford	1997	4(2)	0	0	0	0
Marcus St Hilaire	Bradford	2006-07	34(1)	12	0	0	48
	Huddersfield	2003-05	72(2)	30	0	0	120
	Leeds	1996-2002	59(33)	31	0	0	124
Cyril Stacul	Catalans	2007-10	39(1)	11	0	0	44
Dylan Stainton	Workington	1996	2(3)	0	0	0	0
Mark Stamper	Workington	1996	(1)	0	0	0	0
John Stankevitch	Widnes	2005	17(5)	0	0	0	0
	St Helens	2000-04	74(40)	25	0	0	100
Gareth Stanley	Bradford	2000	1	1	0	0	4
Craig Stapleton	Salford	2009	24	2	0	0	8
	Leigh	2005	27(1)	4	0	0	16
Graham Steadman	Castleford	1996-97	11(17)	5	0	0	20
Jon Steel	Hull KR	2007-08	18	6	0	0	24
Jamie Stenhouse	Warrington	2000-01	9(3)	3	0	0	12
Gareth Stephens	Sheffield	1997-99	23(6)	2	0	0	8
David Stephenson	Hull	1998	11(7)	3	0	0	12
	Oldham	1997	10(8)	2	0	0	8
Francis Stephenson	London	2002-05	42(34)	5	0	0	20
	Wigan	2001	2(9)	0	0	0	0
	Wakefield	1999-2000	50(1)	6	0	0	24
Paul Sterling	Leeds	1997-2000	79(12)	50	0	0	200
Paul Stevens	Oldham	1996	2(1)	0	0	0	0
	London	1996	(1)	0	0	0	0
Warren Stevens	Leigh	2005	4(14)	1	0	0	4
	Warrington	1996-99, 2002-05	17(66)	1	0	0	4
	Salford	2001	(8)	0	0	0	0

175

Super League Players 1996-2010

PLAYER	CLUB	YEAR	APP	TRIES	GOALS	FG	PTS
Anthony Stewart	Harlequins	2006	4	0	0	0	0
	Salford	2004-06	51(2)	15	0	0	60
	St Helens	1997-2003	93(23)	44	0	0	176
Troy Stone	Widnes	2002	18(6)	1	0	0	4
	Huddersfield	2001	12(1)	1	0	0	4
James Stosic	Wakefield	2009	8(10)	1	0	0	4
Lynton Stott	Wakefield	1999	21	4	6	1	29
	Sheffield	1996-98	40(4)	15	0	0	60
Mitchell Stringer	Salford	2005-06	12(4)	0	0	0	0
	London	2004-05	10(19)	0	0	0	0
Graham Strutton	London	1996	9(1)	2	0	0	8
Matt Sturm	Leigh	2005	8(19)	3	0	0	12
	Warrington	2002-04	1(18)	0	0	0	0
	Huddersfield	1998-99	46	8	0	0	32
Anthony Sullivan	St Helens	1996-2001	137(2)	105	0	0	420
Michael Sullivan	Warrington	2006-07	21(16)	8	1	0	34
Phil Sumner	Warrington	1996	(5)	0	0	0	0
Simon Svabic	Salford	1998-2000	13(5)	3	19	0	50
Luke Swain	Salford	2009-10	54	3	0	0	12
Richard Swain	Hull	2004-07	89	5	0	0	20
Anthony Swann	Warrington	2001	3	1	0	0	4
Logan Swann	Warrington	2005-06	49(1)	17	0	0	68
	Bradford	2004	25	6	0	0	24
Willie Swann	Warrington	1996-97	25(2)	6	0	0	24
Nathan Sykes	Castleford	1996-2004	158(52)	3	0	0	12
Paul Sykes	Bradford	1999-2002, 2008-10	81(4)	29	60	2	238
	Harlequins	2006-07	31(2)	15	47	1	155
	London	2001-05	95(1)	26	220	3	547
Wayne Sykes	London	1999	(2)	0	0	0	0
Semi Tadulala	Bradford	2008-09	49	30	0	0	120
	Wakefield	2004-07	85	36	0	0	144
Whetu Taewa	Sheffield	1997-98	33(7)	8	0	0	32
Alan Tait	Leeds	1996	3(3)	1	0	0	4
Willie Talau	Salford	2009-10	22	4	0	0	16
	St Helens	2003-08	130(1)	50	0	0	200
	Wigan	1997	3	1	0	0	4
Ian Talbot	Wakefield	1999	9(5)	2	31	0	70
Albert Talipeau	Wakefield	2004	2(3)	0	0	0	0
Gael Tallec	Halifax	2000	5(19)	3	0	0	12
	Castleford	1998-99	19(21)	3	0	0	12
	Wigan	1996-97	8(12)	3	0	0	12
Joe Tamani	Bradford	1996	11(3)	4	0	0	16
Ryan Tandy	Hull KR	2007	8(4)	2	0	0	8
Andrew Tangata-Toa	Huddersfield	1999	15	2	0	0	8
David Tangata-Toa	Celtic	2009	1(18)	4	0	0	16
	Hull KR	2007	(17)	3	0	0	12
Jordan Tansey	Hull	2009-10	30	9	0	0	36
	Leeds	2006-08	18(32)	19	3	0	82
Kris Tassell	Wakefield	2002	24	10	0	0	40
	Salford	2000-01	35(10)	12	0	0	48
Shem Tatupu	Wigan	1996	(3)	0	0	0	0
Tony Tatupu	Wakefield	2000-01	20	2	0	0	8
	Warrington	1997	21(1)	6	0	0	24
James Taylor	Leigh	2005	(4)	0	0	0	0
Joe Taylor	Paris	1997	9(5)	2	0	0	8
Lawrence Taylor	Sheffield	1996	(1)	0	0	0	0
Scott Taylor	Hull KR	2009-10	(4)	0	0	0	0
Frederic Teixido	Sheffield	1999	(4)	0	0	0	0
	Paris	1996-97	2(3)	1	0	0	4
Lionel Teixido	Catalans	2006-07	11(13)	3	0	0	12
Karl Temata	Harlequins	2006-10	80(13)	4	0	0	16
	London	2005	1(2)	1	0	0	4
Jason Temu	Hull	1998	13(2)	1	0	0	4
	Oldham	1996-97	25(3)	1	0	0	4
Paul Terry	London	1997	(1)	0	0	0	0
Anthony Thackeray	Castleford	2008	3(6)	0	0	0	0
	Hull	2007	2	0	0	0	0
Jamie Thackray	Crusaders	2010	1(16)	2	0	0	8
	Hull	2005-06, 2008-09	37(45)	6	0	0	24
	Leeds	2006-07	5(27)	7	0	0	28
	Castleford	2003-04	7(11)	3	0	0	12
	Halifax	2000-02	10(38)	3	0	0	12
Adam Thaler	Castleford	2002	(1)	0	0	0	0
Gareth Thomas	Crusaders	2010	10(1)	2	0	0	8
Giles Thomas	London	1997-99	1(2)	0	0	0	0
Steve Thomas	London	2004	4(2)	0	0	0	0
	Warrington	2001	2	0	0	0	0
Alex Thompson	Warrington	2009	(1)	1	0	0	4
Alex Thompson	Sheffield	1997	4(11)	0	0	0	0
Bobby Thompson	Salford	1999	28	5	2	0	24
Jordan Thompson	Castleford	2009-10	10(6)	4	0	0	16
Sam Thompson	Harlequins	2009	(2)	0	0	0	0
	St Helens	2008	(5)	0	0	0	0
Chris Thorman	Hull	2009	19(2)	1	0	0	4
	Huddersfield	2000-01, 2005-08	126(20)	51	320	3	847
	London	2003	26(1)	7	81	1	191
	Sheffield	1999	5(13)	2	8	1	25
Tony Thorniley	Warrington	1997	(5)	0	0	0	0
Andy Thornley	Salford	2009	(1)	1	0	0	4
Danny Tickle	Hull	2007-10	102	24	319	1	735
	Wigan	2002-06	94(36)	35	201	2	544
	Halifax	2000-02	25(17)	10	91	2	224
Kris Tickle	Warrington	2001	(1)	0	0	0	0
John Timu	London	1998-2000	57(3)	11	0	0	44
Kerrod Toby	London	1997	2(2)	0	0	0	0
Tulsen Tollett	London	1996-2001	105(5)	38	49	1	251
Joel Tomkins	Wigan	2005-10	71(36)	38	0	0	152
Sam Tomkins	Wigan	2009-10	49(5)	27	2	1	113
Glen Tomlinson	Wakefield	1999-2000	41(5)	8	0	0	32
	Hull	1998	5	1	0	0	4
	Bradford	1996-97	27(13)	12	0	0	48
Ian Tonks	Castleford	1996-2001	32(50)	11	13	0	70
Motu Tony	Hull	2005-09	76(20)	25	0	0	100
	Castleford	2004	8(1)	1	0	0	4
Mark Tookey	Harlequins	2006	12(14)	1	0	0	4
	London	2005	13(14)	5	0	0	20
	Castleford	2004	2(8)	1	0	0	4
Clinton Toopi	Leeds	2006-08	40(3)	9	0	0	36
David Tootill	Harlequins	2008	(4)	0	0	0	0
Paul Topping	Oldham	1996-97	23(10)	1	19	0	42
Patrick Torreilles	Paris	1996	9(1)	1	25	0	54
Albert Torrens	Huddersfield	2006	7	5	0	0	20
Mat Toshack	London	1998-2004	120(21)	24	0	0	96
Julien Touxagas	Catalans	2006-10	14(43)	4	0	0	16
Darren Treacy	Salford	2002	24(1)	6	1	0	26
Dean Treister	Hull	2003	16(1)	3	0	0	12
Rocky Trimarchi	Crusaders	2010	16(8)	0	0	0	0
Steve Trindall	London	2003-05	40(20)	3	0	0	12
Shane Tronc	Wakefield	2010	8(3)	2	0	0	8
George Truelove	Wakefield	2002	2	1	0	0	4
	London	2000	5	1	0	0	4
Va'aiga Tuigamala	Wigan	1996	21	10	3	0	46
Fereti Tuilagi	St Helens	1999-2000	43(15)	21	0	0	84
	Halifax	1996-98	55(3)	27	0	0	108
Sateki Tuipulotu	Leeds	1996	3(2)	1	2	0	8
Tame Tupou	Bradford	2007-08	10(7)	8	0	0	32
Neil Turley	Leigh	2005	6(3)	2	20	1	49
Darren Turner	Huddersfield	2000-01, 2003-04	42(13)	13	0	0	52
	Sheffield	1996-99	41(29)	15	0	0	60
Ian Turner	Paris	1996	1(1)	1	0	0	4
Jordan Turner	Hull	2010	22	7	0	0	28
	Salford	2006-07, 2009	22(10)	4	1	0	18
Chris Tuson	Wigan	2008, 2010	3(12)	2	0	0	8
	Castleford	2010	3(5)	0	0	0	0
Gregory Tutard	Paris	1996	1(1)	0	0	0	0
Brendon Tuuta	Warrington	1998	18(2)	4	0	0	16
	Castleford	1996-97	41(1)	3	0	0	12
Steve Tyrer	Salford	2010	20	6	9	0	42
	Celtic	2009	8	2	5	0	18
	St Helens	2006-08	17(3)	12	42	0	132
Mike Umaga	Halifax	1996-97	38(1)	16	5	0	74
Kava Utoikamanu	Paris	1996	6(3)	0	0	0	0
Frederic Vaccari	Catalans	2010	14	6	0	0	24
David Vaealiki	Wigan	2005-07	67(1)	17	0	0	68
Joe Vagana	Bradford	2001-08	176(44)	17	0	0	68
Nigel Vagana	Warrington	1997	20	17	0	0	68
Tevita Vaikona	Bradford	1998-2004	145(2)	89	0	0	356
Lesley Vainikolo	Bradford	2002-07	132(4)	136	1	0	546
Eric Van Brussell	Paris	1996	2	0	0	0	0
Jace Van Dijk	Celtic	2009	19	1	1	0	6
Richard Varkulis	Warrington	2004	4(1)	3	0	0	12
Marcus Vassilakopoulos	Sheffield	1997-99	15(11)	3	10	2	34
	Leeds	1996-97	1(3)	0	0	0	0
Phil Veivers	Huddersfield	1998	7(6)	1	0	0	4
	St Helens	1996	(1)	1	0	0	4
Michael Vella	Hull KR	2007-10	87(5)	11	0	0	44
Bruno Verges	Catalans	2006	25	6	0	0	24
Eric Vergniol	Paris	1996	14(1)	6	0	0	24
Gray Viane	Salford	2007	9	2	0	0	8
	Castleford	2006	20(7)	14	0	0	56
	Widnes	2005	20	13	0	0	52
	St Helens	2004	4	1	0	0	4
Adrian Vowles	Castleford	1997-2001, 2003	125(1)	29	1	1	119
	Wakefield	2002-03	24(3)	6	1	0	26
	Leeds	2002	14(3)	2	0	0	8
Michael Wainwright	Castleford	2008-10	70	22	0	0	88
	Wakefield	2004-05	21(10)	8	0	0	32
Mike Wainwright	Salford	2000-02, 2007	75(3)	9	0	0	36
	Warrington	1996-99, 2003-07	168(14)	23	0	0	92
Adam Walker	Huddersfield	2010	(1)	0	0	0	0
Ben Walker	Leeds	2002	23(1)	8	100	0	232
Chev Walker	Hull KR	2008-09	24(7)	5	0	0	20
	Leeds	1999-2006	142(19)	77	0	0	308

PLAYER	CLUB	YEAR	APP	TRIES	GOALS	FG	PTS
Chris Walker	Catalans	2010	11	6	2	0	28
Jonathan Walker	Castleford	2010	(7)	0	0	0	0
Jonny Walker	Wigan	2010	(1)	0	0	0	0
Matt Walker	Huddersfield	2001	3(6)	0	0	0	0
Anthony Wall	Paris	1997	9	3	3	0	18
Mark Wallace	Workington	1996	14(1)	3	0	0	12
Joe Walsh	Huddersfield	2009	1(1)	1	0	0	4
	Harlequins	2007-08	1(4)	0	0	0	0
Kerrod Walters	Gateshead	1999	10(12)	2	1	0	10
Kevin Walters	Warrington	2001	1	0	0	0	0
Jason Walton	Salford	2009	(5)	0	0	0	0
Barry Ward	St Helens	2002-03	20(30)	4	0	0	16
Danny Ward	Harlequins	2008-10	65(7)	4	0	0	16
	Hull KR	2007	11(9)	0	0	0	0
	Castleford	2006	18(7)	2	0	0	8
	Leeds	1999-2005	70(48)	9	0	1	37
Joe Wardle	Bradford	2010	1(1)	0	0	0	0
Phil Waring	Salford	1997-99	6(8)	2	0	0	8
Brett Warton	London	1999-2001	49(7)	14	133	0	322
Kyle Warren	Castleford	2002	13(14)	3	0	0	12
Danny Washbrook							
	Hull	2005-10	88(17)	10	0	0	40
Adam Watene	Wakefield	2006-08	45(8)	5	0	0	20
	Bradford	2006	(4)	0	0	0	0
Frank Watene	Wakefield	1999-2001	24(37)	6	0	0	24
Kallum Watkins	Leeds	2008-10	15(6)	7	0	0	28
Dave Watson	Sheffield	1998-99	41(4)	4	0	0	16
Ian Watson	Salford	1997, 2002	24(17)	8	3	5	43
	Workington	1996	4(1)	1	15	0	34
Kris Watson	Warrington	1996	11(2)	2	0	0	8
Brad Watts	Widnes	2005	6	3	0	0	12
Liam Watts	Hull KR	2008, 2010	13(16)	3	0	0	12
Michael Watts	Warrington	2002	3	0	0	0	0
Brent Webb	Leeds	2007-10	96(1)	58	0	0	232
Jason Webber	Salford	2000	25(1)	10	0	0	40
Ian Webster	St Helens	2006	1	0	0	0	0
Jake Webster	Hull KR	2008-10	60(1)	21	7	0	98
James Webster	Hull	2008	1	0	0	0	0
	Hull KR	2007-08	36	2	0	2	10
Pat Weisner	Hull KR	2007	(2)	0	0	0	0
	Harlequins	2006	10(6)	3	0	0	12
Taylor Welch	Warrington	2008	1	0	0	0	0
Kris Welham	Hull KR	2007-10	62(2)	33	0	0	132
Paul Wellens	St Helens	1998-2010	308(23)	149	34	1	665
Jon Wells	Harlequins	2006-09	66	10	0	0	40
	London	2004-05	42(2)	19	0	0	76
	Wakefield	2003	22(1)	1	0	0	4
	Castleford	1996-2002	114(14)	49	0	0	196
Dwayne West	St Helens	2000-02	8(16)	6	0	0	24
	Wigan	1999	1(1)	0	0	0	0
Joe Westerman	Castleford	2008-10	68(7)	29	151	0	418
Craig Weston	Widnes	2002, 2004	23(9)	2	1	2	12
	Huddersfield	1998-99	46(1)	15	15	0	90
Ben Westwood	Warrington	2002-10	200(6)	70	52	0	384
	Wakefield	1999-2002	31(7)	8	1	0	34
Andrew Whalley	Workington	1996	(2)	0	0	0	0
Paul Whatuira	Huddersfield	2008-10	59	23	0	0	92
Scott Wheeldon	Hull KR	2009-10	21(25)	4	0	0	16
	Hull	2006-08	2(60)	4	0	0	16
Gary Wheeler	St Helens	2008-10	17(5)	8	3	0	38
Matt Whitaker	Castleford	2006	8(2)	0	0	0	0
	Widnes	2004-05	10(20)	9	0	0	36
	Huddersfield	2003-04	3(14)	0	0	0	0
David White	Wakefield	2000	(1)	0	0	0	0
Josh White	Salford	1998	18(3)	5	5	1	31
	London	1997	14(2)	8	0	1	33
Lloyd White	Crusaders	2010	1(5)	0	0	0	0
	Celtic	2009	6	1	0	0	4
Paul White	Salford	2009	1	1	0	0	4
	Wakefield	2006-07	24(12)	12	0	0	48
	Huddersfield	2003-05	11(32)	17	16	0	100
Elliott Whitehead	Bradford	2009-10	27(6)	9	0	0	36
Richard Whiting	Hull	2004-10	98(31)	41	8	2	182
Danny Whittle	Warrington	1998	(2)	0	0	0	0
David Whittle	St Helens	2002	1(2)	0	0	0	0
	Warrington	2001	1(2)	0	0	0	0
Jon Whittle	Wakefield	2006	8(2)	3	0	0	12
	Widnes	2005	13	2	0	0	8
	Wigan	2003	1	0	0	0	0
Dean Widders	Castleford	2009-10	20(14)	15	0	0	60
Stephen Wild	Huddersfield	2006-10	116(2)	33	0	0	132
	Wigan	2001-05	67(20)	24	0	0	96
Matthew Wildie	Wakefield	2010	1	0	0	0	0
Oliver Wilkes	Harlequins	2010	20(7)	0	0	0	0
	Wakefield	2008-09	41(13)	6	0	0	24
	Wigan	2006	1(5)	0	0	0	0
	Leigh	2005	13(1)	1	0	0	4
	Huddersfield	2000-01	1(6)	0	0	0	0
	Sheffield	1998	(1)	0	0	0	0
Jon Wilkin	St Helens	2003-10	149(25)	55	0	1	221
Alex Wilkinson	Hull	2003-04	11(4)	1	0	0	4
	Huddersfield	2003	8	4	0	0	16
	London	2002	5(1)	0	0	0	0
	Bradford	2000-01	3(3)	1	0	0	4
Bart Williams	London	1998	5(3)	1	0	0	4
Daley Williams	Salford	2006-07	9(2)	4	0	0	16
Danny Williams	Harlequins	2006	9(13)	4	0	0	16
	London	2005	1(16)	0	0	0	0
Danny Williams	Leeds	2006, 2008	13(2)	7	0	0	28
	Hull	2008	3	0	0	0	0
Dave Williams	Harlequins	2008-10	1(7)	0	0	0	0
Desi Williams	Wigan	2004	2	0	0	0	0
Jonny Williams	London	2004	(4)	0	0	0	0
Rhys Williams	Warrington	2010	1(1)	1	0	0	4
Luke Williamson	Harlequins	2009-10	39	6	0	0	24
John Wilshere	Salford	2006-07,					
		2009	72(2)	32	142	0	412
	Leigh	2005	26	8	6	0	44
	Warrington	2004	5	2	0	0	8
Craig Wilson	Hull	2000	2(16)	1	0	1	5
	Gateshead	1999	17(11)	5	0	1	21
George Wilson	Paris	1996	7(2)	3	0	0	12
John Wilson	Catalans	2006-08	69	23	0	0	92
Richard Wilson	Hull	1998-99	(13)	0	0	0	0
Scott Wilson	Warrington	1998-99	23(2)	6	0	0	24
Johan Windley	Hull	1999	2(2)	1	0	0	4
Paul Wingfield	Warrington	1997	5(3)	6	1	0	26
Frank Winterstein	Crusaders	2010	13(14)	3	0	0	12
	Wakefield	2009	(5)	0	0	0	0
Lincoln Withers	Crusaders	2010	27	3	0	0	12
	Celtic	2009	21	6	0	0	24
Michael Withers	Wigan	2007	6(1)	1	0	0	4
	Bradford	1999-2006	156(6)	94	15	4	410
Michael Witt	Crusaders	2010	15	6	35	1	95
Jeff Wittenberg	Huddersfield	1998	18(1)	1	0	0	4
	Bradford	1997	8(9)	4	0	0	16
Kyle Wood	Castleford	2010	1(4)	0	0	0	0
Martin Wood	Sheffield	1997-98	24(11)	4	18	2	54
Nathan Wood	Warrington	2002-05	90	38	0	3	155
	Wakefield	2002	11	2	0	0	8
Paul Wood	Warrington	2000-10	94(128)	33	0	0	132
Phil Wood	Widnes	2004	2(1)	0	0	0	0
Darren Woods	Widnes	2005	(1)	0	0	0	0
David Woods	Halifax	2002	18(2)	8	0	0	32
Simon Worrall	Leeds	2008-09	5(16)	1	0	0	4
Michael Worrincy	Bradford	2009-10	12(34)	12	0	0	48
	Harlequins	2006-08	20(12)	10	0	0	40
Rob Worrincy	Castleford	2004	1	0	0	0	0
Troy Wozniak	Widnes	2004	13(7)	1	0	0	4
Matthew Wray	Wakefield	2002-03	13(3)	2	0	0	8
David Wrench	Wakefield	2002-06	28(52)	6	0	0	24
	Leeds	1999-2001	7(17)	0	0	0	0
Craig Wright	Castleford	2000	1(9)	0	0	0	0
Nigel Wright	Huddersfield	1999	4(6)	1	0	0	4
	Wigan	1996-97	5(5)	2	0	1	9
Ricky Wright	Sheffield	1997-99	2(13)	0	0	0	0
Vincent Wulf	Paris	1996	13(4)	4	0	0	16
Andrew Wynyard	London	1999-2000	34(6)	4	0	0	16
Bagdad Yaha	Paris	1996	4(4)	2	4	0	16
Malakai Yasa	Sheffield	1996	1(3)	0	0	0	0
Kirk Yeaman	Hull	2001-10	191(17)	103	0	0	412
Grant Young	London	1998-99	22(2)	2	0	0	8
Nick Youngquest	Crusaders	2010	26(1)	9	0	0	36
Ronel Zenon	Paris	1996	(4)	0	0	0	0
Nick Zisti	Bradford	1999	6(1)	0	0	0	0
Freddie Zitter	Catalans	2006	1	0	0	0	0

Super League Players 1996-2010

NEW FACES - Players making their Super League debuts in 2010

PLAYER	CLUB	DEBUT vs	ROUND	DATE
Toby Adamson	Salford	Huddersfield (a)	26	22/8/10
Danny Addy	Bradford	Leeds (h)	15	23/5/10
		(first team debut: Dewsbury (a), CCR4, 18/4/10)		
Luke Ambler	Leeds	Wigan (a)	8	26/3/10
Kyle Amor	Leeds	Hull KR (h)	7	19/3/10
William Barthau	Catalans	Harlequins (a)	2	14/2/10
Ben Bolger	Harlequins	Wakefield (h)	3	30/1/10
Tom Bush	Leeds	Harlequins (h)	5	5/3/10
Josh Charnley	Wigan	Hull KR (a)	26	22/8/10
	Hull KR	Leeds (h)	21	9/7/10
Chris Clarkson	Leeds	Hull KR (h)	7	19/3/10
Joel Clinton	Hull KR	Castleford (a)	4	27/2/10
Michael Coady	Leeds	Hull KR (h)	7	19/3/10
Steve Crossley	Bradford	Crusaders (a)	17	13/6/10
Liam Cunningham	Hull	Catalans (a)	14	15/5/10
Ben Davies	Wigan	Crusaders (a)	15	22/5/10
John Davies	Castleford	Catalans (a)	6	13/3/10
Brett Delaney	Leeds	Crusaders (a)	4	29/1/10
Greg Eastwood	Leeds	Crusaders (a)	4	29/1/10
Max Edwards	Harlequins	Leeds (a)	5	5/3/10
Andy Ellis	Harlequins	Crusaders (h)	16	6/6/10
Rhys Evans	Warrington	Harlequins (a)	27	3/9/10
David Fa'alogo	Huddersfield	Bradford (h)	1	5/2/10
Liam Farrell	Wigan	Wakefield (h)	10	5/4/10
Vinny Finigan	Bradford	Salford (h)	22	18/7/10
Craig Fitzgibbon	Hull	St Helens (a)	1	6/2/10
Jamie Foster	St Helens	Leeds (h)	12	24/4/10
		(first team debut: Toulouse (a), CCR4, 17/4/10)		
Lee Gaskell	St Helens	Catalans (h)	21	9/7/10
Tony Gigot	Catalans	Crusaders (a)	7	19/3/10
Ben Gledhill	Wakefield	Hull KR (a)	6	12/3/10
David Guasch	Catalans	Crusaders (a)	7	19/3/10
Glenn Hall	Bradford	Huddersfield (a)	1	5/2/10
Rhys Hanbury	Crusaders	Wakefield (a)	11	11/4/10
Weller Hauraki	Crusaders	Wigan (a)	1	5/2/10
Daniel Holdsworth	Salford	Hull KR (a)	1	7/2/10
Oliver Holmes	Castleford	Huddersfield (a)	11	9/4/10
Kieran Hyde	Wakefield	St Helens (h)	23	25/7/10
Dallas Johnson	Catalans	Wakefield (a)	1	7/2/10
Paul Johnson	St Helens	Huddersfield (h)	17	11/6/10
Ben Jones	Harlequins	St Helens (h)	11	10/4/10
Brett Kearney	Bradford	Huddersfield (a)	1	5/2/10
Olsi Krasniqi	Harlequins	Crusaders (h)	16	6/6/10
Sam Latus	Hull KR	Huddersfield (a)	19	25/6/10
Charlie Leaeno	Wakefield	Wigan (h)	17	13/6/10
Heath L'Estrange	Bradford	Huddersfield (a)	1	5/2/10
Reece Lyne	Hull	Salford (a)	8	27/3/10
Shaun Magennis	St Helens	Hull (a)	16	4/6/10
Frankie Mariano	Hull KR	Bradford (h)	23	24/7/10
		(first team debut: Sheffield (h), CCR5, 10/5/09)		
Stefan Marsh	Wigan	Huddersfield (MM)	13	2/5/10
Jermaine McGillvary	Huddersfield	Bradford (a)	16	6/6/10
Vince Mellars	Crusaders	Leeds (h)	4	29/1/10
Darryl Millard	Wakefield	Harlequins (a)	3	30/1/10
Adam Milner	Castleford	Huddersfield (h)	20	4/7/10
Adam Neal	Salford	Bradford (a)	22	18/7/10
Danny Nicklas	Hull	Wakefield (h)	12	23/4/10
Mark O'Meley	Hull	St Helens (a)	1	6/2/10
Matt Orford	Bradford	Huddersfield (a)	1	5/2/10
Gareth Owen	Salford	Hull KR (h)	25	15/8/10
Setaimata Sa	Catalans	Wakefield (a)	1	7/2/10
Jarrod Sammut	Crusaders	Bradford (MM)	13	1/5/10
Clinton Schifcofske	Crusaders	Bradford (a)	10	5/4/10
Michael Simon	Catalans	Huddersfield (a)	9	2/4/10
Martyn Smith	Harlequins	Hull (a)	4	26/2/10
Marc Sneyd	Salford	Warrington (h)	16	4/6/10
Iosia Soliola	St Helens	Hull (h)	1	6/2/10
Cain Southernwood	Bradford	Warrington (a)	18	19/6/10
Scott Spaven	Hull KR	Bradford (a)	12	25/4/10
Gareth Thomas	Crusaders	Catalans (h)	7	19/3/10
Rocky Trimarchi	Crusaders	Leeds (h)	4	29/1/10
Shane Tronc	Wakefield	Harlequins (a)	3	30/1/10
Frederic Vaccari	Catalans	Huddersfield (a)	9	2/4/10
Adam Walker	Huddersfield	Salford (a)	10	5/4/10
Chris Walker	Catalans	Wakefield (a)	1	7/2/10
Jonathan Walker	Castleford	Wigan (a)	16	6/6/10
Jonny Walker	Wigan	Harlequins (h)	12	23/4/10
Joe Wardle	Bradford	Huddersfield (h)	16	6/6/10
		(first team debut: Warrington (h), CCQF, 30/5/10)		
Matthew Wildie	Wakefield	Huddersfield (a)	24	1/8/10
Rhys Williams	Warrington	Crusaders (h)	5	7/3/10
Michael Witt	Crusaders	Leeds (h)	4	29/1/10
Kyle Wood	Castleford	Hull (h)	15	23/5/10
Nick Youngquest	Crusaders	Leeds (h)	4	29/1/10

OLD FACES - Players making their debuts for new clubs in 2010

PLAYER	CLUB	DEBUT vs	ROUND	DATE
Shaun Ainscough	Castleford	Hull KR (h)	4	27/2/10
Ryan Atkins	Warrington	Harlequins (h)	1	7/2/10
Kyle Bibb	Harlequins	Leeds (a)	5	5/3/10
Ryan Boyle	Salford	Hull KR (a)	1	7/2/10
Danny Brough	Huddersfield	St Helens (h)	8	28/3/10
Jodie Broughton	Salford	Hull KR (a)	1	7/2/10
Matt Cook	Hull KR	Salford (h)	1	7/2/10
Paul Cooke	Wakefield	Salford (h)	7	21/3/10
Michael Cooper	Castleford	Catalans (a)	6	13/3/10
Paul Deacon	Wigan	Crusaders (h)	1	5/2/10
Brad Drew	Huddersfield	Crusaders (a) (D2)	12	25/4/10
Nick Fozzard	St Helens	Hull (h) (D2)	1	6/2/10
Ashley Gibson	Salford	Hull KR (a)	1	7/2/10
Lee Gilmour	Huddersfield	Bradford (h)	1	5/2/10
Scott Grix	Huddersfield	Bradford (h)	1	5/2/10
Josh Hodgson	Hull KR	Wakefield (h)	6	12/3/10
Graeme Horne	Huddersfield	Bradford (h)	1	5/2/10
Paul Jackson	Castleford	Leeds (a) (D2)	1	7/2/10
Matt James	Harlequins	Wakefield (h)	3	30/1/10
Ben Jeffries	Wakefield	Harlequins (a) (D2)	3	30/1/10
Paul Johnson	Wakefield	Catalans (h)	1	7/2/10
Ben Jones-Bishop	Harlequins	Wakefield (h)	3	30/1/10
Paul King	Wakefield	Catalans (h)	1	7/2/10
Danny Kirmond	Wakefield	Warrington (a)	8	26/3/10
Tommy Lee	Crusaders	Leeds (h)	4	29/1/10
Sean Long	Hull	St Helens (a)	1	6/2/10
Tony Martin	Crusaders	St Helens (a)	6	12/3/10
Paul McShane	Hull	Wakefield (h)	12	23/4/10
David Mills	Harlequins	Castleford (h) (D2)	14	16/5/10
Scott Moore	St Helens	Hull (h) (D2)	1	6/2/10
Glenn Morrison	Wakefield	Harlequins (a)	3	30/1/10
Richard Myler	Warrington	Harlequins (h)	1	7/2/10
Terry Newton	Wakefield	Harlequins (a)	3	30/1/10
Kevin Penny	Harlequins	St Helens (h)	11	10/4/10
Mike Ratu	Hull KR	Huddersfield (h)	3	21/2/10
Gareth Raynor	Crusaders	Leeds (h)	4	29/1/10
Stuart Reardon	Bradford	Huddersfield (a) (D2)	1	5/2/10
Julien Rinaldi	Wakefield	Catalans (a) (D2)	18	19/6/10
Brent Sherwin	Catalans	Salford (h)	15	22/5/10
Lee Smith	Leeds	Bradford (h) (D2)	9	1/4/10
Matty Smith	St Helens	Warrington (h) (D2)	QPO	10/9/10
	Salford	Hull KR (a)	1	7/2/10
Steve Snitch	Castleford	Leeds (a)	1	5/2/10
David Solomona	Warrington	Harlequins (h)	1	7/2/10
Jamie Thackray	Crusaders	Leeds (h)	4	29/1/10
Jordan Turner	Hull	Harlequins (a)	4	26/2/10
Chris Tuson	Castleford	Crusaders (h)	8	26/3/10
Steve Tyrer	Salford	Hull KR (a)	1	7/2/10
Oliver Wilkes	Harlequins	Wakefield (h)	3	30/1/10
Frank Winterstein	Crusaders	Leeds (h)	4	29/1/10

SUPER LEAGUE XV
Club by Club

26 December 2009 - 26-16 win at Castleford in Boxing Day clash at the Jungle.

7 January 2010 - Geoff Evans appointed Head of Physical Performance.

17 January 2010 - 12-10 defeat by Leeds in Matt Diskin testimonial match at Headingley.

28 January 2010 - Matt Orford makes debut in 18-16 friendly win at Hull KR.

1 February 2010 - Andy Lynch appointed captain for 2010.

5 February 2010 - 24-12 round 1 defeat at Huddersfield.

14 February 2010 - 38-6 home hammering in round two by St Helens.

19 February 2010 - 41-22 round 3 home win over Castleford opens Bulls' account.

26 February 2010 - 7-0 win at Salford.

5 March 2010 - Matt Orford scores two tries in 22-20 home win over unbeaten Wigan after trailing 20-0 at half-time.

1 April 2010 - young Wakefield halfback Cain Southernwood signs three-and-a-half year deal; Kieran Hyde moves the other way.

1 April 2010 - Leeds come back from 20-6 down to snatch 20-20 Easter Thursday draw at Headingley.

18 April 2010 - 50-0 win at Dewsbury in fourth round of Challenge Cup.

21 April 2010 - Steve McNamara appointed coach of England, part-time until the end of the season.

22 April 2010 - youngster Danny Addy signs dual-registration deal with the Rams.

27 April 2010 - prop Nick Scruton found not guilty of high tackle on Joel Clinton in 40-4 home thrashing of Hull KR.

1 May 2010 - 19-0 defeat to Crusaders at Murrayfield ends five-match unbeaten run.

7 May 2010 - 58-16 home win over Leigh to make Challenge Cup quarter-finals.

15 May 2010 - 29-10 comeback win over Wakefield at Belle Vue.

23 May 2010 - Orford and Kearney miss 26-12 derby defeat at hands of Leeds.

30 May 2010 - 26-22 Challenge Cup quarter final-defeat to Warrington at Odsal.

4 June 2010 - Paul Sykes has one match ban for dangerous throw overturned by RFL.

6 June 2010 - 52-6 hammering inflicted by Giants at Odsal in absence of Orford and Kearney.

KEY DATES - BRADFORD BULLS

8 June 2010 - James Donaldson ruptures ACL and medial ligaments, out for six months.

8 June 2010 - Michael Platt suspended for two games for dangerous tackle on David Hodgson in drubbing by Giants.

8 June 2010 - Andy Lynch set to miss four games following knee surgery.

13 June 2010 - 44-20 away defeat by Crusaders as losing run extends to four.

16 June 2010 - Matt Orford requires shoulder surgery and is out for the season.

17 June 2010 - Paul Sykes agrees three-year contract extension to 2013.

19 June 2010 - Nick Scruton suffers knee injury in 40-28 home loss against Warrington.

13 July 2010 - Paul Sykes banned for two games for dangerous tackle in 35-18 defeat to Harlequins.

13 July 2010 - coach Steve McNamara released with immediate effect to take up full-time role with England. Assistant Lee St Hilaire takes over to end of season.

16 July 2010 - Mick Potter appointed head coach on two-year contract from 2011.

2 August 2010 - Chris Nero turns down new contract offer.

5 August 2010 - Jamie Langley signs new three-year contract until end of 2013 season.

16 August 2010 - Vinny Finigan signs first full-time contract on one-year deal.

22 August 2010 - 12-game losing streak ends with 38-28 home defeat of Wakefield.

25 August 2010 - Chev Walker signs on one-year deal from Hull KR after missing SLXV with broken leg.

26 August 2010 - 20-16 defeat to Wigan in Carnegie Floodlit 9s final. Dave Halley to miss start of SLXVI after damaging knee ligaments.

30 August 2010 - Wigan Warriors winger Shaun Ainscough joins on one-year contract.

31 August 2010 - New Zealand Warriors release utility back Patrick Ah Van to take up one-year deal with Bulls.

3 September 2010 - prop forward Bryn Hargreaves from St Helens joins on two-year deal.

3 September 2010 - season ends with 34-12 round 27 defeat at Wigan.

8 September 2010 - Olivier Elima signs from Catalans Dragons on two-year contract.

11 September 2010 - Ian Sibbit joins from Salford on two-year deal.

14 September 2010 - Joe Wardle turns down contract offer.

16 September 2010 - former Hull FC and Crusaders winger Gareth Raynor signs one-year contract.

18 September 2010 - Shad Royston joins from Halifax on one-year contract.

21 September 2010 - Elliott Whitehead signs new improved contract to end of 2013 season.

23 September 2010 - England Academy hooker Adam O'Brien signs new three-year contract to end of 2013.

23 September 2010 - Steve Menzies signs for Catalans.

26 September 2010 - former player, Great Britain international Terry Newton found dead at his home near Wigan.

28 September 2010 - Jason Crookes, Steve Crossley and Danny Addy all sign new two-year contracts.

29 September 2010 - undisclosed fee received from Huddersfield for Joe Wardle.

6 October 2010 - Francis Cummins joins as assistant coach on one-year contract.

19 October 2010 - Matt Diskin joins from Leeds on three-year deal.

27 October 2010 - Matt Orford requests release from remaining two years of contract.

29 October 2010 - Canberra Raiders halfback Marc Herbert signs one-year deal.

CLUB RECORDS

Highest score:
98-6 v Toulouse, 19/4/2008
Highest score against:
18-75 v Leeds, 14/9/31
Record attendance:
69,429 v Huddersfield, 14/3/53

MATCH RECORDS

Tries:
6 Eric Batten v Leeds, 15/9/45
Trevor Foster v Wakefield, 10/4/48
Steve McGowan v Barrow, 8/11/92
Lesley Vainikolo v Hull, 2/9/2005
Goals:
15 Iestyn Harris v Toulouse, 15/4/2008
Points:
36 John Woods v Swinton, 13/10/85

SEASON RECORDS

Tries: 63 Jack McLean 1951-52
Goals: 213 *(inc 5fg)* Henry Paul 2001
Points: 457 Henry Paul 2001

CAREER RECORDS

Tries: 261 Jack McLean 1950-56
Goals:
1,165 *(inc 25fg)* Paul Deacon 1998-2009
Points: 2,605 Paul Deacon 1998-2009
Appearances:
588 Keith Mumby 1973-90; 1992-93

BRADFORD BULLS

DATE	FIXTURE	RESULT	SCORERS	LGE	ATT
5/2/10	Huddersfield (a)	L24-12	t:Reardon(2),Sheriffe	10th	9,774
14/2/10	St Helens (h)	L6-38	t:Orford g:Orford	14th	10,165
19/2/10	Castleford (h)	W41-22	t:Scruton,Sheriffe,Whitehead,Kearney(2),Halley,Sykes g:Orford(6)		
			fg:Orford	10th	8,019
26/2/10	Salford (a)	W0-7	t:Menzies g:Orford fg:Sykes	8th	3,806
5/3/10	Wigan (h)	W22-20	t:Kearney,Orford(2),Hall g:Orford(3)	7th	9,244
13/3/10	Warrington (a)	L33-8	t:Lynch,Sykes	8th	10,434
19/3/10	Hull (a)	L18-6	t:Reardon g:Sykes	9th	14,466
26/3/10	Harlequins (h)	W19-12	t:Platt,Kearney,Menzies g:Orford(3) fg:Orford	8th	7,153
1/4/10	Leeds (a)	D20-20	t:Nero(2),Halley,Menzies g:Orford(2)	7th	17,244
5/4/10	Crusaders (h)	W20-16	t:Halley,Nero,Hall,Platt g:Orford(2)	7th	7,853
10/4/10	Catalans (a) ●	W14-36	t:Lynch,Kearney,Sheriffe(3),Menzies g:Orford(5),Sykes	5th	8,884
18/4/10	Dewsbury (a) (CCR4)	W0-50	t:Whitehead,Scruton,Hall(2),Kearney(2),Godwin,L'Estrange,Addy		
			g:Orford(5),Addy(2)	N/A	3,995
25/4/10	Hull KR (h)	W40-4	t:Lynch,Whitehead,Sheriffe(2),Kearney(2) g:Orford(8)	5th	9,234
1/5/10	Crusaders (MM) ●●	L0-19		5th	N/A
7/5/10	Leigh (h) (CCR5)	W58-16	t:Nero(3),Sykes,Menzies(2),Kearney,Worrincy,Godwin,Hall		
			g:Sykes(8),Hall	N/A	4,250
14/5/10	Wakefield (a)	W10-29	t:Nero,Menzies(2),Godwin,L'Estrange g:Sykes(4) fg:Sykes	4th	5,381
23/5/10	Leeds (h)	L12-26	t:Whitehead,Platt g:Sykes(2)	6th	13,269
30/5/10	Warrington (h) (CCQF)	L22-26	t:Sheriffe,Halley,Nero,Menzies g:Sykes(3)	N/A	7,092
6/6/10	Huddersfield (h)	L6-52	t:Menzies g:Sykes	7th	8,156
13/6/10	Crusaders (a)	L44-20	t:Nero,Halley,Worrincy,Whitehead g:Sykes(2)	7th	2,979
19/6/10	Warrington (h)	L28-40	t:L'Estrange,Nero,Menzies,Halley,Kearney g:Sykes(4)	8th	8,128
27/6/10	Castleford (a)	L28-22	t:Whitehead,Menzies,Kearney,Platt g:Sykes(3)	8th	5,482
4/7/10	Hull (h)	L22-28	t:Nero(2),Kearney,Addy g:Sykes(2)	9th	8,411
9/7/10	Harlequins (a)	L35-18	t:Whitehead,Sykes,Crossley g:Sykes(3)	10th	3,152
18/7/10	Salford (h)	L26-30	t:Menzies,Finigan(2),Reardon,Whitehead g:Addy(3)	10th	6,382
24/7/10	Hull KR (a)	L49-24	t:Reardon,Finigan(2),Kopczak,L'Estrange g:Addy(2)	11th	7,854
1/8/10	Catalans (h)	L22-24	t:Lynch,Olbison,Menzies,Platt g:Sykes(3)	11th	6,217
13/8/10	St Helens (a)	L60-12	t:Sheriffe,Worrincy g:Sykes(2)	11th	9,032
22/8/10	Wakefield (h)	W38-28	t:Kearney,Lynch,Godwin(2),Whitehead,Menzies g:Sykes(7)	10th	7,437
3/9/10	Wigan (a)	L34-12	t:Kopczak,Lynch g:Sykes,Menzies	10th	17,058

● Played at Stade Aime Giral
●● Played at Murrayfield, Edinburgh

		APP		TRIES		GOALS		FG		PTS	
	D.O.B.	ALL	SL	ALL	SL	ALL	SL	ALL	SL	ALL	SL
Danny Addy	15/1/91	4(8)	4(7)	2	1	7	5	0	0	22	14
Jason Crookes	21/4/90	5	4	0	0	0	0	0	0	0	0
Steve Crossley	28/11/89	(7)	(7)	1	1	0	0	0	0	4	4
James Donaldson	14/9/91	4(10)	3(9)	0	0	0	0	0	0	0	0
Vinny Finigan	4/8/89	4(1)	4(1)	4	4	0	0	0	0	16	16
Wayne Godwin	13/3/82	7(23)	6(21)	5	3	0	0	0	0	20	12
Glenn Hall	21/3/81	10(18)	7(18)	5	2	1	0	0	0	22	8
Dave Halley	12/10/86	26	23	6	5	0	0	0	0	24	20
Brett Kearney	29/9/83	25	23	14	11	0	0	0	0	56	44
Craig Kopczak	20/12/86	5(24)	5(21)	2	2	0	0	0	0	8	8
Jamie Langley	21/12/83	20	19	0	0	0	0	0	0	0	0
Heath L'Estrange	21/5/85	29(1)	27	4	3	0	0	0	0	16	12
Andy Lynch	20/10/79	27	25	6	6	0	0	0	0	24	24
Steve Menzies	4/12/73	30	27	15	12	1	1	0	0	62	50
Chris Nero	14/2/81	26	24	12	8	0	0	0	0	48	32
Tom Olbison	20/3/91	(7)	(6)	1	1	0	0	0	0	4	4
Matt Orford	22/4/78	14	12	3	3	36	31	2	2	86	76
Michael Platt	23/3/84	20(1)	18	5	5	0	0	0	0	20	20
Stuart Reardon	13/10/81	17	16	5	5	0	0	0	0	20	20
Nick Scruton	24/12/84	23(1)	20(1)	2	1	0	0	0	0	8	4
Rikki Sheriffe	5/5/84	27	24	9	8	0	0	0	0	36	32
Cain Southernwood	4/5/92	2	2	0	0	0	0	0	0	0	0
Paul Sykes	11/8/81	27	25	4	3	48	37	2	2	114	88
Joe Wardle	22/9/91	1(2)	1(1)	0	0	0	0	0	0	0	0
Elliott Whitehead	4/9/89	27(2)	24(2)	9	8	0	0	0	0	36	32
Michael Worrincy	16/2/86	10(15)	8(14)	3	2	0	0	0	0	12	8

Brett Kearney

LEAGUE RECORD
P27-W9-D1-L17
(10th, SL)
F528, A728, Diff-200
19 points.

CHALLENGE CUP
Quarter Finalists

ATTENDANCES
Best - v Leeds (SL - 13,269)
Worst - v Leigh (CC - 4,250)
Total (SL only) - 109,668
Average (SL only) - 8,436
(Down by 1,241 on 2009)

26 December 2009 - 26-16 defeat by Bradford in Boxing Day clash at the Jungle.

16 January 2010 - 14-12 friendly win over Catalans Dragons in Perpignan. Coach Terry Matterson loses finger in training ground accident.

27 January 2010 - 28-10 home defeat by Huddersfield Giants in last warm-up.

5 February 2010 - 18-unanswered second-half points produces 24-10 win over Leeds at Headingley.

13 February 2010 - Dean Widders to undergo surgery on knee injured in 28-16 home defeat to Warrington.

22 February 2010 - Richard Owen out for season after with broken leg suffered in 41-22 defeat at Bradford.

24 February 2010 - Wigan winger Shaun Ainscough joins on one-month loan deal.

27 February 2010 - Shaun Ainscough scores hat-trick in controversial 24-20 defeat to Hull KR. Brett Ferres injures shoulder which requires surgery.

2 March 2010 - Jordan Thompson and John Davies join York City Knights on dual contract.

5 March 2010 - Paul Jackson sustains groin injury in 42-22 defeat at Hull FC.

10 March 2010 - prop Mike Cooper signed on month's loan from Warrington.

13 March 2010 - 20-16 win over Catalans in snowbound Perpignan.

21 March 2010 - Jordan Thompson makes debut in 36-22 home defeat by Wigan.

24 March 2010 - Wigan reserve back-rower Chris Tuson is third loan signing of season.

26 March 2010 - Shaun Ainscough's loan deal extended until end of season.

31 March 2010 - prop Nathan Massey joins Keighley on dual registration.

9 April 2010 - Rangi Chase and Joe Westerman dropped as 'disciplinary measure' before 24-0 defeat at Huddersfield.

15 April 2010 - Warrington recall Mike Cooper from loan spell.

17 April 2010 - 34-28 home defeat to Barrow Raiders in Challenge Cup fourth round.

21 April 2010 - Shaun Ainscough recalled from loan spell by Wigan.

25 April 2010 - 30-12 home win over Salford.

27 April 2010 - Chris Tuson's loan spell extended on week-to-week basis.

KEY DATES - CASTLEFORD TIGERS

2 May 2010 - 34-18 win over Catalans at Murrayfield.

16 May 2010 - Brett Ferres returns in 40-24 away loss to Harlequins; Chris Tuson suffers head injury.

20 May 2010 - Brent Sherwin completes transfer to Catalans Dragons; Kyle Wood arrives from Huddersfield on month loan deal.

23 May 2010 - 34-26 defeat by Hull FC at The Jungle.

6 June 2010 - 38-22 defeat at Wigan.

15 June 2010 - Joe Arundel makes season debut in Tuesday night 24-20 home victory over Catalans.

20 June 2010 - Dean Widders scores hat-trick in 28-22 away win at Salford.

24 June 2010 - Kyle Wood loan deal extended by a month.

29 June 2010 - £40,000 fine for homophobic chants during 22-16 win over Crusaders at The Jungle on March 26.

4 July 2010 - 44-18 home win over Giants is fourth on a row.

5 July 2010 - fullback Richard Owen signs new two-year deal.

9 July 2010 - three fans banned until at least end of season following allegations of obscene chanting.

13 July 2010 - Warrington fullback Richard Mathers joins on three-year deal from 2011.

20 July 2010 - Danny Orr signs 12-month playing and coaching contract for 2011.

22 July 2010 - centre Joe Arundel agrees new two-year deal; Michael Shenton to join St Helens.

25 July 2010 - Wakefield Trinity Wildcats rule out possible ground-sharing deal at Glasshoughton.

22 August 2010 - 40-28 home win over Harlequins puts Tigers in eighth spot.

4 September 2010 - 40-30 last-round defeat at St Helens means Crusaders snatch eighth place.

9 September 2010 - winger Nick Youngquest signs from Crusaders on two-year deal.

10 September 2010 - £40,000 fine imposed in June for misconduct halved by RFL appeals tribunal.

14 September 2010 - Michael Wainwright, Liam Higgins and Ryan Clayton, released.

16 September 2010 - props Nick Fozzard, one year, and Jacob Emmitt, two years join from St Helens.

28 October 2010 - Joe Westerman transferred to Hull FC for a six-figure transfer fee.

8 November 2010 - James Evans announces retirement due to injury.

14 November 2010 - Tigers in talks with Canberra centre Joel Monaghan.

CLUB RECORDS
Highest score: 106-0 v Rochdale, 9/9/2007 **Highest score against:** 12-76 v Leeds, 14/8/2009 **Record attendance:** 25,449 v Hunslet, 9/3/35
MATCH RECORDS
Tries: 5 Derek Foster v Hunslet, 10/11/72 John Joyner v Millom, 16/9/73 Steve Fenton v Dewsbury, 27/1/78 Ian French v Hunslet, 9/2/86 St John Ellis v Whitehaven, 10/12/89 **Goals:** 17 Sammy Lloyd v Millom, 16/9/73 **Points:** 43 Sammy Lloyd v Millom, 16/9/73
SEASON RECORDS
Tries: 40 St John Ellis 1993-94 **Goals:** 158 Sammy Lloyd 1976-77 **Points:** 334 Bob Beardmore 1983-84
CAREER RECORDS
Tries: 206 Alan Hardisty 1958-71 **Goals:** 875 Albert Lunn 1951-63 **Points:** 1,870 Albert Lunn 1951-63 **Appearances:** 613 John Joyner 1973-92

CASTLEFORD TIGERS

DATE	FIXTURE	RESULT	SCORERS	LGE	ATT
5/2/10	Leeds (a)	W10-24	t:Evans,Westerman,Sherwin,Widders g:Huby,Westerman(3)	7th	15,875
13/2/10	Warrington (h)	L16-28	t:Evans(2),Westerman g:Westerman(2)	8th	7,569
19/2/10	Bradford (a)	L41-22	t:Shenton,Owen,Snitch,Hudson g:Westerman(3)	9th	8,019
27/2/10	Hull KR (h)	L20-24	t:Wainwright,Ainscough(3) g:Westerman(2)	11th	6,855
5/3/10	Hull (a)	L42-22	t:Hudson,Ainscough,Chase,Evans g:Huby(2),Dixon	11th	13,352
13/3/10	Catalans (a)	W16-20	t:Cooper,Chase,Jones,Wainwright g:Westerman(2)	10th	6,810
21/3/10	Wigan (h)	L22-36	t:Shenton(2),Wainwright,Cooper g:Westerman(3)	11th	8,493
26/3/10	Crusaders (h)	W22-16	t:Dixon,McGoldrick,Westerman,Thompson g:Westerman(3)	10th	5,299
2/4/10	Wakefield (a)	L19-6	t:Thompson g:Westerman	10th	8,337
5/4/10	St Helens (h)	L18-52	t:Huby,Clayton,Westerman,Shenton g:Westerman	11th	6,879
9/4/10	Huddersfield (a)	L24-0		11th	5,932
18/4/10	Barrow (h) (CCR4)	L28-34	t:Thompson,Westerman(2),Sargent,Dixon g:Westerman(4)	N/A	5,285
25/4/10	Salford (h)	W30-12	t:McGoldrick,Sargent,Thompson,Jones g:Westerman(7)	10th	5,025
2/5/10	Catalans (MM) ●	W34-18	t:Wainwright,McGoldrick(2),Sherwin(2),Evans g:Westerman(5)	11th	N/A
16/5/10	Harlequins (a)	L40-24	t:Westerman,Ferres,Higgins,Snitch g:Westerman(4)	10th	2,941
23/5/10	Hull (h)	L26-34	t:Jones,Arundel,Wainwright,Chase,Wainwright g:Westerman(3)	10th	7,996
6/6/10	Wigan (a)	L38-22	t:Jackson,Jones,Ferres,Huby g:Westerman(3)	10th	14,047
15/6/10	Catalans (h)	W24-20	t:Snitch(2),Wainwright(2) g:Westerman(4)	10th	4,209
20/6/10	Salford (h)	W22-28	t:Widders(3),Huby,Ferres g:Westerman(4)	10th	3,130
27/6/10	Bradford (h)	W28-22	t:Shenton(3),Ferres,Dixon g:Westerman,Dixon(3)	10th	5,482
4/7/10	Huddersfield (h)	W44-18	t:Huby(2),Chase(2),Snitch,McGoldrick,Dixon g:Westerman(6),Dixon(2)	8th	5,925
11/7/10	Warrington (a)	L54-30	t:Dixon,Westerman(2),Wainwright,Clayton,Snitch g:Westerman(3)	9th	10,577
18/7/10	Wakefield (h)	W40-16	t:Dixon(2),Wainwright,Widders(2),McGoldrick,Hudson g:Westerman(5),Dixon	8th	8,517
25/7/10	Crusaders (a) ●●	L30-24	t:Westerman,Widders,Shenton,Chase g:Westerman(4)	8th	1,495
1/8/10	Hull KR (a)	L28-26	t:Ferres,Arundel,Chase,Jones g:Westerman(5)	8th	8,104
13/8/10	Leeds (h)	L6-38	t:Snitch g:Westerman	9th	7,901
22/8/10	Harlequins (h)	W40-28	t:McGoldrick,Shenton,Hudson,Dixon,Huby,Milner,Sargent g:Westerman(6)	8th	5,862
4/9/10	St Helens (a)	L40-30	t:McGoldrick,Milner,Widders(2),Shenton,Hudson g:Westerman,Dixon(2)	9th	13,978

● Played at Murrayfield, Edinburgh
●● Played at The Gnoll, Neath

		APP		TRIES		GOALS		FG		PTS	
	D.O.B.	ALL	SL	ALL	SL	ALL	SL	ALL	SL	ALL	SL
Shaun Ainscough	27/11/89	7	7	4	4	0	0	0	0	16	16
Joe Arundel	22/8/91	5(4)	5(3)	2	2	0	0	0	0	8	8
Rangi Chase	11/4/86	26	25	7	7	0	0	0	0	28	28
Ryan Clayton	22/11/82	14(5)	13(5)	2	2	0	0	0	0	8	8
Michael Cooper	15/9/88	1(5)	1(5)	2	2	0	0	0	0	8	8
John Davies	8/1/91	(1)	(1)	0	0	0	0	0	0	0	0
Kirk Dixon	19/7/84	19(1)	18(1)	8	7	9	9	0	0	50	46
James Evans	5/11/78	9	8	5	5	0	0	0	0	20	20
Brett Ferres	17/4/86	18	18	5	5	0	0	0	0	20	20
Liam Higgins	19/7/83	13(11)	13(11)	1	1	0	0	0	0	4	4
Oliver Holmes	7/8/92	(5)	(4)	0	0	0	0	0	0	0	0
Craig Huby	21/5/86	21(6)	20(6)	6	6	3	3	0	0	30	30
Ryan Hudson	20/11/79	26(2)	26(1)	5	5	0	0	0	0	20	20
Paul Jackson	29/9/78	18(2)	17(2)	1	1	0	0	0	0	4	4
Stuart Jones	7/12/81	14(13)	13(13)	5	5	0	0	0	0	20	20
Nathan Massey	11/7/89	(2)	(2)	0	0	0	0	0	0	0	0
Ryan McGoldrick	12/1/81	27	26	8	8	0	0	0	0	32	32
Adam Milner	19/12/91	(4)	(4)	2	2	0	0	0	0	8	8
Kirk Netherton	10/5/85	2(2)	1(2)	0	0	0	0	0	0	0	0
Richard Owen	25/4/90	3	3	1	1	0	0	0	0	4	4
Mitchell Sargent	2/7/79	10(16)	10(15)	3	2	0	0	0	0	12	8
Michael Shenton	22/7/86	22	22	10	10	0	0	0	0	40	40
Brent Sherwin	20/3/78	11(1)	11(1)	3	3	0	0	0	0	12	12
Steve Snitch	22/3/83	21(5)	20(5)	7	7	0	0	0	0	28	28
Jordan Thompson	4/9/91	10(5)	9(5)	4	3	0	0	0	0	16	12
Chris Tuson	25/2/90	3(5)	3(5)	0	0	0	0	0	0	0	0
Michael Wainwright	4/11/80	26	25	10	10	0	0	0	0	40	40
Jonathan Walker	20/2/91	(7)	(7)	0	0	0	0	0	0	0	0
Joe Westerman	15/11/89	26	25	10	8	86	82	0	0	212	196
Dean Widders	25/10/79	12(4)	12(4)	9	9	0	0	0	0	36	36
Kyle Wood	18/6/89	1(4)	1(4)	0	0	0	0	0	0	0	0

Joe Westerman

LEAGUE RECORD
P27-W11-D0-L16
(9th, SL)
F648, A766, Diff-118
22 points.

CHALLENGE CUP
Round Four

ATTENDANCES
Best - v Wakefield (SL - 8,517)
Worst - v Catalans (SL - 4,209)
Total (SL only) - 86,012
Average (SL only) - 6,616
(Down by 874 on 2009)

25 November 2009 - out-of-contract 2009 captain Greg Bird escapes jail after his conviction for reckless wounding is quashed in a Sydney court.

7 December 2009 - Greg Bird joins Gold Coast Titans for 2010.

14 December 2009 - winger Chris Walker signs from Gold Coast Titans on two-year contract.

16 January 2010 - 14-12 defeat to Castleford Tigers in pre-season trial in Perpignan.

22 January 2010 - Thomas Bosc appointed new captain for 2010 season.

5 February 2010 - Thomas Bosc damages ankle in training days before SLXV kick-off.

7 February 2010 - five Dragons players arrested in Leeds after 28-20 round one defeat to Wakefield at Belle Vue.

9 February 2010 - Remi Casty handed one-match ban for high tackle on Wakefield forward Paul Johnson.

14 February 2010 - David Ferriol sent off for punching in 16-4 win defeat at Harlequins and escapes with fine.

20 February 2010 - acting captain Olivier Elima banned for one game after being sent off for high tackle on Jonny Lomax during 42-12 home defeat to St Helens.

5 March 2010 - 24-12 round 5 win at Salford is first of the season.

15 March 2010 - Clint Greenshields breaks leg in 20-16 home defeat by Castleford Tigers

22 March 2010 - Adam Mogg released with 18 months remaining on contract and joins Canberra.

30 March 2010 - Chris Walker suspended for two games for challenge on winger Liam Colbon in round 8, 16-10 win over Hull KR. Thomas Bosc makes first appearance of season.

13 April 2010 - Chris Walker dropped for Challenge Cup fourth-round tie against Salford for unspecified disciplinary measure.

25 April 2010 - Dragons sink to bottom of table after 40-6 defeat at Warrington.

2 May 2010 - 34-18 defeat by Castleford at Murrayfield.

9 May 2010 - last-minute Thomas Bosc field goal secures 35-34 round five Challenge Cup win at Crusaders.

18 May 2010 - David Ferriol suspended for one match for punching Danny Washbrook in 28-14 home defeat by Hull FC. Jean-Philippe Baile breaks arm.

20 May 2010 - Brent Sherwin signs from Castleford Tigers for rest of season.

KEY DATES - CATALANS DRAGONS

22 May 2010 - 22-14 home defeat by Salford despite Thomas Bosc's 14-point tally.

25 May 2010 - Gregory Mounis suspended for two games for dangerous tackle in loss to Salford.

27 May 2010 - head coach Kevin Walters announces his departure at end of the season.

29 May 2010 - 74-12 win at Batley in Challenge Cup quarter-final.

6 June 2010 - 24-6 away defeat to Hull Kingston Rovers.

15 June 2010 - 24-20 Tuesday-night reverse at Castleford is ninth consecutive defeat.

19 June 2010 - Clint Greenshields scores on return in 30-23 home win over Wakefield.

23 June 2010 - move to appoint John Kear as coach falls through after dispute with Wakefield over compensation.

1 July 2010 - Roosters assistant Trent Robinson signs three-year deal as head coach.

4 July 2010 - 34-16 home defeat by Wigan.

8 July 2010 - David Ferriol signs new two-year contract.

14 July 2010 - Dimitri Pelo and Setaimata Sa dropped for home game against Crusaders as disciplinary measure.

17 July 2010 - 26-22 home defeat to Crusaders.

22 July 2010 - disciplinary ban on Pelo and Sa lifted.

24 July 2010 - Sa returns in 29-28 home defeat of second-placed Warrington.

8 August 2010 - 54-12 defeat to Warrington in Cup semi-final at Widnes.

13 August 2010 - Newcastle scrum-half Scott Dureau signs two-year deal.

19 August 2010 - Dimitri Pelo joins rugby union club Montpellier after deal agreed for compensation.

20 August 2010 - Dimitri Pelo and Setaimata Sa receive suspended sentences at Leeds Crown Court for affray after round one loss at Wakefield.

23 August 2010 - former Bradford hooker Ian Henderson joins on three-year contract from NZ Warriors.

29 August 2010 - Dane Carlaw signs new 12-month contract. Olivier Elima leaves for Bradford.

31 August 2010 - Dallas Johnson released 12 months into three-year contract to join North Queensland.

31 August 2010 - Paris-born, former Australian Schoolboys international Jason Baitieri joins on two-year contract.

4 September 2010 - 26-12 home defeat by Huddersfield ensures wooden spoon.

7 September 2010 - Tonga World Cup captain Lopini Paea joins on two-year contract from Sydney Roosters.

13 September 2010 - Wakefield winger Damien Blanch joins on two-year contract.

14 September 2010 - Manly Sea Eagles' Ben Farrar signs two-year contract.

23 September 2010 - Steve Menzies signs 12-month contract.

2 November 2010 - Jerome Guisset retires and takes up coaching role.

CLUB RECORDS

Highest score:
74-12 v Batley, 29/5/2010
Highest score against:
12-60 v Leeds, 15/9/2006
Record attendance: 18,150 v Warrington
(in Barcelona), 20//6/2009

MATCH RECORDS

Tries:
4 Justin Murphy v Warrington, 13/9/2008
Goals:
11 Thomas Bosc v Featherstone, 31/3/2007
11 Thomas Bosc v Batley, 29/5/2010
Points:
26 Thomas Bosc v Featherstone,
31/3/2007

SEASON RECORDS

Tries: 27 Justin Murphy 2006
Goals: 124 *(inc 1fg)* Thomas Bosc 2008
Points: 275 Thomas Bosc 2008

CAREER RECORDS

Tries: 55 Clint Greenshields 2005-10
Goals:
346 *(inc 5fg)* Thomas Bosc 2006-10
Points: 825 Thomas Bosc 2006-10
Appearances:
139 Jerome Guisset 2006-09

CATALANS DRAGONS

DATE	FIXTURE	RESULT	SCORERS	LGE	ATT
7/2/10	Wakefield (a)	L28-20	t:Pelo,Elima,Martins,Walker g:Walker(2)	9th	5,818
14/2/10	Harlequins (a)	L16-4	t:Greenshields	12th	2,330
20/2/10	St Helens (h)	L12-42	t:Sa,Walker(2)	14th	7,825
26/2/10	Wigan (a)	L58-0		14th	12,001
5/3/10	Salford (a)	W12-24	t:Walker(2),Greenshields,Sa,Raguin g:Mounis(2)	12th	3,022
13/3/10	Castleford (h)	L16-20	t:Walker,Fakir,McGuire g:Mounis(2)	13th	6,810
19/3/10	Crusaders (a)	L14-6	t:Elima g:Mounis	13th	6,124
27/3/10	Hull KR (h)	W16-10	t:Bell,Carlaw,Gossard g:Bosc(2)	13th	6,620
2/4/10	Huddersfield (a)	L48-6	t:Pelo g:Barthau	13th	5,296
5/4/10	Leeds (h) ●	L24-34	t:Guisset,Johnson,Touxagas,K Bentley g:Bosc(4)	13th	8,230
10/4/10	Bradford (h) ●	L14-36	t:Vaccari,Bell,Mounis g:Bosc	13th	8,884
18/4/10	Salford (h) (CCR4)	W30-8	t:Guisset,Vaccari(2),Bell,McGuire,Casty g:Bosc(2),Mounis	N/A	5,238
25/4/10	Warrington (a)	L40-6	t:Ferriol g:Mounis	14th	9,619
2/5/10	Castleford (MM) ●●	L34-18	t:Vaccari,Elima,Mounis,Baile g:Mounis	14th	N/A
9/5/10	Crusaders (a) (CCR5)	W34-35	t:Sa(3),Bell,Bosc,Carlaw g:Bosc(5) fg:Bosc	N/A	1,817
15/5/10	Hull (h)	L14-28	t:Pelo,Raguin,Bell g:Bosc	14th	6,512
22/5/10	Salford (h)	L14-22	t:Bosc(2) g:Bosc(3)	14th	5,115
29/5/10	Batley (a) (CCQF)	W12-74	t:Guisset,Fakir(2),Casty,Carlaw,Vaccari,Elima(2),Raguin,Bell,Ferriol, A Bentley,Gigot g:Bosc(11)	N/A	2,132
6/6/10	Hull KR (a)	L24-6	t:Raguin g:Bosc	14th	7,102
15/6/10	Castleford (a)	L24-20	t:McGuire,Raguin,Vaccari(2) g:Barthau(2)	14th	4,209
19/6/10	Wakefield (h)	W30-23	t:Pelo,Raguin,Greenshields,Sa,Elima g:Bosc(5)	14th	5,055
25/6/10	Hull (a)	L10-8	t:McGuire g:Bosc(2)	14th	11,466
4/7/10	Wigan (h)	L16-34	t:Greenshields(2),Stacul g:Bosc(2)	14th	7,612
9/7/10	St Helens (a)	W20-30	t:Carlaw,Greenshields,McGuire,Sherwin g:Bosc(5)	14th	8,432
17/7/10	Crusaders (h)	L22-26	t:Greenshields(2),Casty g:Bosc(5)	14th	6,208
24/7/10	Warrington (h) ●	W29-28	t:Vaccari,Carlaw,Bell,Stacul,Casty g:Bosc(4) fg:Sherwin	14th	7,852
1/8/10	Bradford (h)	W22-24	t:Sa,Raguin,Bell,Elima g:Bosc(4)	13th	6,217
8/8/10	Warrington (CCSF) ●●●	L12-54	t:Greenshields(2) g:Bosc(2)	N/A	12,265
14/8/10	Harlequins (h)	L12-16	t:Carlaw,Raguin g:Bosc(2)	14th	6,152
20/8/10	Leeds (a)	L52-6	t:McGuire g:Bosc	14th	15,154
4/9/10	Huddersfield (h)	L12-26	t:Sa,Vaccari g:Gigot(2)	14th	5,708

● Played at Stade Aime Giral
●● Played at Murrayfield, Edinburgh
●●● Played at Stobart Stadium, Widnes

		APP		TRIES		GOALS		FG		PTS	
	D.O.B.	ALL	SL	ALL	SL	ALL	SL	ALL	SL	ALL	SL
Jean-Phillipe Baile	7/6/87	7	5	1	1	0	0	0	0	4	4
William Barthau	30/1/90	6(1)	6(1)	0	0	3	3	0	0	6	6
Steven Bell	28/5/76	26	22	8	5	0	0	0	0	32	20
Andrew Bentley	13/5/85	(9)	(8)	1	0	0	0	0	0	4	0
Kane Bentley	16/4/87	10(6)	8(5)	1	1	0	0	0	0	4	4
Thomas Bosc	5/8/83	22	18	3	2	62	42	1	0	137	92
Dane Carlaw	21/2/80	23(7)	21(5)	6	4	0	0	0	0	24	16
Remi Casty	5/2/85	10(15)	9(12)	4	2	0	0	0	0	16	8
Olivier Elima	19/5/83	26	22	7	5	0	0	0	0	28	20
Jamal Fakir	30/8/82	6(16)	5(14)	3	1	0	0	0	0	12	4
David Ferriol	24/4/79	21(2)	18(1)	2	1	0	0	0	0	8	4
Tony Gigot	27/12/90	4(13)	4(11)	0	0	2	2	0	0	8	4
Cyrille Gossard	7/2/82	13(8)	12(7)	1	1	0	0	0	0	4	4
Clint Greenshields	11/1/82	13	12	11	9	0	0	0	0	44	36
David Guasch	3/1/90	1	1	0	0	0	0	0	0	0	0
Jerome Guisset	29/8/78	19(7)	16(6)	3	1	0	0	0	0	12	4
Dallas Johnson	26/11/82	28	26	1	1	0	0	0	0	4	4
Sebastien Martins	18/11/84	(9)	(8)	1	1	0	0	0	0	4	4
Casey McGuire	24/1/80	25	22	6	5	0	0	0	0	24	20
Adam Mogg	31/7/77	4	4	0	0	0	0	0	0	0	0
Gregory Mounis	18/1/85	18(9)	15(9)	2	2	8	7	0	0	24	22
Dimitri Pelo	17/4/85	20	17	4	4	0	0	0	0	16	16
Sebastien Raguin	14/2/79	24(3)	20(3)	8	7	0	0	0	0	32	28
Setaimata Sa	14/9/87	21(4)	18(4)	8	5	0	0	0	0	32	20
Brent Sherwin	20/3/78	14	12	1	1	0	0	1	1	5	5
Michael Simon	2/4/87	(10)	(9)	0	0	0	0	0	0	0	0
Cyril Stacul	12/10/84	11(1)	11(1)	2	2	0	0	0	0	8	8
Julien Touxagas	12/2/84	2(3)	2(3)	1	1	0	0	0	0	4	4
Frederic Vaccari	7/11/87	17	14	9	6	0	0	0	0	36	24
Chris Walker	27/2/80	12	11	6	6	2	2	0	0	28	28

Dane Carlaw

LEAGUE RECORD
P27-W6-D0-L21
(14th, SL)
F409, A747, Diff-338
12 points.

CHALLENGE CUP
Semi-Finalists

ATTENDANCES
Best - v Bradford (SL - 8,884)
Worst - v Wakefield (SL - 5,055)
Total (SL only) - 88,583
Average (SL only) - 6,814
(Down by 2,290 on 2009)

2 December 2009 - released Hull FC halfback Tommy Lee joins on 12-month deal as Brian Noble's first signing.

15 December 2009 - Crusaders RL confirm move from south Wales to Racecourse Ground after being taken over by Wrexham FC.

21 December 2009 - Frank Winterstein, from Wakefield and Nick Youngquest from Gateshead join on one-year contracts.

29 December 2009 - Tony Martin and Michael Witt sign two-year contracts.

14 January 2010 - Jon Wells testimonial match at Rosslyn Park postponed with Crusaders unable to travel due to snow.

15 January 2010 - New Zealand threequarter Vince Mellars joins from rugby union side Crusaders on one-year deal.

15 January 2010 - Jamie Thackray, released by Hull FC, signs one-year deal.

17 January 2010 - Australian utility player Rocky Trimarchi joins from Wests Tigers on one-year contract.

21 January 2010 - Gareth Raynor signs one-year deal to become third former Hull FC player to join Crusaders.

26 January 2010 - Ryan O'Hara appointed new captain.

29 January 2010 - 34-6 defeat to Leeds in season, round four opener at sold-out Racecourse Ground.

31 January 2010 - Weller Hauraki, released by Parramatta, arrives on one-year contract.

5 February 2010 - 38-6 defeat at Wigan in round one proper.

12 February 2010 - Vince Mellars scores hat-trick in 36-16 defeat of Salford at the Willows.

21 February 2010 - 18-16 home success over Hull FC.

5 March 2010 - 35-year-old Gareth Thomas signs from Cardiff rugby union on contract to end of season, with option for one more year.

19 March 2010 - Gareth Thomas concussed in first tackle of debut, a 14-6 home to Catalans, and leaves field before half-time.

26 March 2010 - Tommy Lee breaks leg in training.

1 April 2010 - veteran Australian fullback Clinton Schifcofske signs contract to end of 2010 after spell in rugby union.

1 April 2010 - Easter Thursday game with Quins in Neath is postponed because of waterlogged pitch.

KEY DATES - CRUSADERS

9 April 2010 - utility back Rhys Hanbury from Wests Tigers arrives on contract to end of 2010.

14 April 2010 - Gareth Raynor pleads guilty at Hull Crown Court to 14 counts of fraud and counterfeiting.

28 April 2010 - Australian utility back Jarrod Sammut joins on two-and-a-half-year deal.

1 May 2010 - 19-0 win over Bradford at Murrayfield.

9 May 2010 - 35-34 home defeat to Catalans means Challenge Cup fifth round exit.

16 May 2010 - 54-10 defeat by Hull KR in east Yorkshire is heaviest of season.

19 May 2010 - Crusaders release Gareth Raynor following jailing for fraud.

22 May 2010 - 46-26 home defeat to Wigan marred by Jarrod Sammut cheekbone fracture.

2 June 2010 - 20-year-old wing or fullback Jamie Murphy signs on 18-month deal from South Wales Scorpions.

6 June 2010 - 50-22 thrashing by Harlequins at the Stoop is fourth straight defeat. Michael Witt damages knee ligaments.

13 June 2010 - Rhys Hanbury stars in 44-20 home victory over Bradford.

18 June 2010 - Michael Witt to miss the rest of season with damaged knee ligaments.

20 June 2010 - 32-26 win at Leeds courtesy of Vince Mellars' second try two minutes from time.

4 July 2010 - Gareth Thomas suffers recurrence of groin injury in 30-10 home defeat by Warrington.

17 July 2010 - 26-22 win over Catalans in Perpignan.

6 August 2010 - 16-12 win over Harlequins in re-arranged game in Neath is fourth win in a row.

13 August 2010 - coach Brian Noble to face RFL investigation after confronting match official James Child in final minutes of 18-16 defeat at Hull FC.

24 August 2010 - out-for-the-season Gareth Thomas signs new one-year contract.

4 September 2010 - thrilling 30-24 home win over Hull KR assures last play-off spot.

11 September 2010 - 18-12 away defeat by Huddersfield in Elimination Play-off.

8 November 2010 - Iestyn Harris appointed head coach following Brian Noble's resignation.

9 November 2010 - Stuart Reardon joins on 12-month contract.

9 November 2010 - Vince Mellars signs new three-year contract to end of 2013.

10 November 2010 - Peter Lupton and Frank Winterstein sign new two-year contracts.

CLUB RECORDS
Highest score: 84-10 v Hunslet, 11/8/2007 **Highest score against:** 0-68 v Leeds, 2/8/2009 **Record attendance:** 10,334 v Leeds, 29/1/2010

MATCH RECORDS
Tries: 4 Tony Duggan v Lokomotiv Moscow, 12/3/2006 Carl de Chenu v London Skolars, 14/4/2006 Craig Richards v Blackpool, 9/4/2007 Damien Quinn v Swinton, 28/4/2007 Paul Ballard v London Skolars, 7/7/2007 **Goals:** 12 Damien Quinn v St Albans, 26/2/2006 **Points:** 32 Damien Quinn v St Albans, 26/2/2006

SEASON RECORDS
Tries: 40 Tony Duggan 2007 **Goals:** 96 Mark Lennon 2008 **Points:** 252 Damien Quinn 2007

CAREER RECORDS
Tries: 101 Tony Duggan 2006-09 **Goals:** 190 Damien Quinn 2006-09 **Points:** 612 Damien Quinn 2006-09 **Appearances:** 112 Damien Quinn 2006-09

CRUSADERS

DATE	FIXTURE	RESULT	SCORERS	LGE	ATT
29/1/10	Leeds (h)	L6-34	t:Raynor g:Witt	N/A	10,334
5/2/10	Wigan (a)	L38-6	t:Dyer g:Witt	13th	13,680
12/2/10	Salford (a)	W16-36	t:Mellars(3),Winterstein,Witt,Thackray,Raynor g:Witt(4)	10th	3,421
21/2/10	Hull (h)	W18-16	t:Youngquest(2),Witt g:Witt(3)	8th	6,794
7/3/10	Warrington (a)	L46-12	t:Bryant,Withers g:Witt(2)	10th	11,113
12/3/10	St Helens (a)	L37-30	t:Mellars,Thackray,Raynor,Withers,Dyer g:Witt(5)	11th	8,507
19/3/10	Catalans (h)	W14-6	t:Chan,Lupton g:Witt(3)	10th	6,124
26/3/10	Castleford (a)	L22-16	t:Mellars,Chan,Hauraki g:Witt(2)	11th	5,299
5/4/10	Bradford (a)	L20-16	t:Hauraki,Mellars g:Witt(4)	10th	7,853
11/4/10	Wakefield (a)	W10-20	t:Thomas,Witt,Youngquest,Mellars g:Witt(2)	10th	4,671
18/4/10	York (a) (CCR4)	W8-58	t:Hanbury(2),Youngquest,Thackray,Chan(2),White(2),Flower,Thomas g:Witt(9)	N/A	719
25/4/10	Huddersfield (h)	L10-38	t:Hauraki,Dyer g:Witt	11th	4,127
1/5/10	Bradford (MM) ●	W0-19	t:Witt(2),Sammut g:Witt(3) fg:Witt	10th	N/A
9/5/10	Catalans (h) (CCR5)	L34-35	t:Schifcofske,Mellars,Winterstein,Lupton,Sammut,Youngquest g:Witt(2),Schifcofske(3)	N/A	1,817
16/5/10	Hull KR (a)	L54-10	t:Raynor,Sammut g:Witt	11th	7,273
22/5/10	Wigan (h)	L26-46	t:Youngquest,Hanbury,Chan,Witt,Lupton g:Witt(3)	11th	6,075
6/6/10	Harlequins (a)	L50-22	t:Schifcofske,Chan,Lupton,Hanbury g:Schifcofske(3)	11th	2,381
13/6/10	Bradford (h)	W44-20	t:Thomas,Mellars,Hauraki(2),Martin,Youngquest,Withers g:Schifcofske(8)	11th	2,979
20/6/10	Leeds (a)	W26-32	t:Mellars(2),Peek,Hauraki(2) g:Schifcofske(6)	11th	14,371
27/6/10	Wakefield (h)	L0-41		11th	2,837
4/7/10	Warrington (h)	L10-30	t:Youngquest,Hanbury g:Schifcofske	11th	5,197
11/7/10	Huddersfield (a)	L30-12	t:Sammut,Hauraki g:Schifcofske(2)	11th	5,339
17/7/10	Catalans (a)	W22-26	t:Hauraki,Chan,Hanbury,Lupton g:Schifcofske(5)	11th	6,208
25/7/10	Castleford (h) ●●	W30-24	t:Hanbury,James,Hauraki,Martin,Sammut g:Schifcofske(5)	10th	1,495
1/8/10	Salford (h)	W60-16	t:Youngquest(3),Hanbury,Schifcofske(2),Martin(2),O'Hara,Hauraki,Winterstein g:Schifcofske(8)	9th	2,412
6/8/10	Harlequins (h) ●●	W16-12	t:Hanbury(2),Chan g:Schifcofske(2)	8th	1,122
13/8/10	Hull (a)	L18-16	t:Dyer,Lupton g:Schifcofske(4)	8th	11,762
21/8/10	St Helens (h)	L10-36	t:Mellars,Winterstein g:Schifcofske	9th	5,436
4/9/10	Hull KR (h)	W30-24	t:O'Hara,Martin,Hanbury,Sammut,Dyer g:Schifcofske(5)	8th	5,137
11/9/10	Huddersfield (a) (EPO)	L18-12	t:Hanbury g:Schifcofske(4)	N/A	5,869

● Played at Murrayfield, Edinburgh
●● Played at The Gnoll, Neath

		APP		TRIES		GOALS		FG		PTS	
	D.O.B.	ALL	SL	ALL	SL	ALL	SL	ALL	SL	ALL	SL
Anthony Blackwood	13/9/82	1	1	0	0	0	0	0	0	0	0
Mark Bryant	10/4/81	28(2)	26(2)	1	1	0	0	0	0	4	4
Jason Chan	26/1/84	28	26	8	6	0	0	0	0	32	24
Gil Dudson	16/6/90	(1)	0	0	0	0	0	0	0	0	0
Luke Dyer	15/8/81	25(1)	23(1)	5	5	0	0	0	0	20	20
Ben Flower	19/10/87	1(12)	1(10)	1	0	0	0	0	0	4	0
Rhys Hanbury	27/8/85	19(1)	17(1)	12	10	0	0	0	0	48	40
Weller Hauraki	18/2/85	27(1)	26(1)	11	11	0	0	0	0	44	44
Jordan James	24/5/80	(14)	(14)	1	1	0	0	0	0	4	4
Elliot Kear	29/11/88	5(1)	5	0	0	0	0	0	0	0	0
Tommy Lee	1/2/88	3(9)	3(9)	0	0	0	0	0	0	0	0
Peter Lupton	7/3/82	23(7)	22(6)	6	5	0	0	0	0	24	20
Tony Martin	7/10/78	16(1)	16(1)	5	5	0	0	0	0	20	20
Vince Mellars	27/1/84	24	23	12	11	0	0	0	0	48	44
Ryan O'Hara	18/8/80	25(1)	24(1)	2	2	0	0	0	0	8	8
Adam Peek	5/2/77	5(19)	5(19)	1	1	0	0	0	0	4	4
Gareth Raynor	24/2/78	7	7	4	4	0	0	0	0	16	16
Jarrod Sammut	15/2/87	11(2)	10(2)	6	5	0	0	0	0	24	20
Clinton Schifcofske	10/11/75	22	20	4	3	57	54	0	0	130	120
Jamie Thackray	30/9/79	2(17)	1(16)	3	2	0	0	0	0	12	8
Gareth Thomas	25/7/74	12(1)	10(1)	3	2	0	0	0	0	12	8
Rocky Trimarchi	7/1/86	18(8)	16(8)	0	0	0	0	0	0	0	0
Lloyd White	9/10/88	1(6)	1(5)	2	0	0	0	0	0	8	0
Frank Winterstein	17/12/86	14(15)	13(14)	4	3	0	0	0	0	16	12
Lincoln Withers	7/5/81	29	27	3	3	0	0	0	0	12	12
Michael Witt	1/1/84	17	15	6	6	46	35	1	1	117	95
Nick Youngquest	28/7/83	28(1)	26(1)	11	9	0	0	0	0	44	36

Clinton Schifcofske

LEAGUE RECORD
P27-W12-D0-L15
(8th, SL/Elimination Play-Off)
F547, A732, Diff-185
24 points.

CHALLENGE CUP
Round Five

ATTENDANCES
Best - v Leeds (SL - 10,334)
Worst - v Harlequins (SL - 1,122)
Total (SL only) - 60,069
Average (SL only) - 4,621
(Up by 1,018 on 2009,
Celtic Crusaders)

12 January 2010 - captain Rob Purdham suffers shoulder injury during pre-season training camp at Army barracks in Kent.

12 January 2010 - Australian forward Chad Robinson released half way through two-year contract because of persistent knee injury.

13 January 2010 - Luke Gale signs new three-year contract until end of 2012.

14 January 2010 - Jon Wells Testimonial game at Rosslyn Park cancelled as Crusaders unable to travel due to frost and snow.

19 January 2010 - Chad Randall to be captain in injury absence of Rob Purdham.

2 February 2010 - Louie McCarthy-Scarsbrook suspended for one match after fight with Richard Moore during opening (round 3) game, an 18-10 home defeat to Wakefield.

7 February 2010 - 58-0, round 1 defeat at Warrington.

10 February 2010 - Ryan Esders wins appeal against severity of one-match suspension for dangerous throw on Richie Mathers.

14 February 2010 - Will Sharp scores all three tries in 16-4 win over Catalans. Luke Gale breaks jaw.

21 February 2010 - 34-10 defeat to Melbourne Storm in Gillette World Club Challenge warm-up.

2 March 2010 - prop Matt James has two-year contract cancelled by mutual consent.

3 March 2010 - prop Kyle Bibb arrives on month's loan from Wakefield.

5 March 2010 - 62-4 hammering at Leeds.

20 March 2010 - Jon Wells announces retirement after failing to recover from neck injury.

1 April 2010 - Easter Thursday game against Crusaders in Neath postponed because of waterlogged pitch.

5 April 2010 - Rob Purdham makes comeback in 52-12 home Easter Monday defeat by Hull KR.

7 April 2010 - Warrington Wolves winger Kevin Penny arrives on month's loan.

10 April 2010 - 32-24 home defeat to St Helens.

17 April 2010 - Luke Dorn makes first appearance of season in 23-16 home, round 4 Challenge Cup win over Wakefield.

KEY DATES - HARLEQUINS

23 April 2010 - stunning 38-26 victory at leaders Wigan, after trailing 24-6 at half-time. Ben Jones-Bishop sustains depressed fracture of skull.

27 April 2010 - Rob Purdham escapes with fine after being found guilty of chicken-wing tackle on Sam Tomkins.

1 May 2010 - 25-8 win over Hull FC at Murrayfield.

6 May 2010 - loan spell of winger Kevin Penny extended on week-by-week basis.

9 May 2010 - 30-10 home to defeat to St Helens in round five of Challenge Cup.

14 May 2010 - David Mills makes one-month loan move from Hull KR.

16 May 2010 - 40-24 home victory against Castleford Tigers.

23 May 2010 - 54-12 defeat at Wakefield.

3 June 2010 - Rob Purdham granted compassionate leave following death of brother in Cumbria shooting.

4 June 2010 - Kevin Penny recalled by Warrington.

6 June 2010 - Luke Dorn scores four tries in 50-22 home thrashing of Crusaders.

12 June 2010 - 42-22 home defeat by Leeds.

20 June 2010 - Rob Purdham returns in 42-6 thumping by Hull KR at Craven Park.

28 June 2010 - Tony Clubb signs new four-year deal to end of 2014.

8 July 2010 - Brian McDermott rules himself out of running to be new Bradford coach.

16 July 2010 - Luke Williamson to retire at end of season.

20 July 2010 - Danny Orr to return to Castleford for 2011 season.

11 August 2010 - Will Sharp signs for Hull FC.

17 August 2010 - Brian McDermott to rejoin Leeds Rhinos as assistant coach at end of season for family reasons after four years in charge.

3 September 2010 - 36-22 home defeat to Warrington means 13th-place finish.

9 September 2010 - Jason Golden signs new two-year deal.

10 September 2010 - assistant Rob Powell appointed acting head coach.

13 September 2010 - Lamont Bryan and Omari Caro sign two-year contracts; Dave Williams one year.

14 September 2010 - Luke Dorn signs new three-year deal to end of 2013 season.

24 September 2010 - David Howell, three years, and Olsi Krasniqi, two years, sign new contracts.

27 September 2010 - Ben Bolger signs new two-year contract.

30 September 2010 - Danny Ward signs new 12-month contract; Jamie O'Callaghan new three-year deal.

4 October 2010 - Karl Temata signs new 12-month contract.

5 October 2010 - general manager Paul Blanchard becomes chief executive.

13 October 2010 - Sydney Roosters' Nick Kouparitsas signs on one-year deal.

21 October 2010 - Manly forward Chris Bailey signs for 2011 season.

8 November 2010 - Luke Ambler signs on season-long loan from Leeds.

CLUB RECORDS

Highest score: 82-0 v Highfield, 12/11/95
82-2 v Barrow, 20/5/2006
Highest score against:
12-74 v Bradford, 9/6/99
Record attendance:
15,013 v Wakefield, 15/2/81

MATCH RECORDS

Tries:
5 Martin Offiah v Whitehaven, 14/3/99
Goals:
13 Rob Purdham v Barrow, 20/5/2006
Points:
34 Rob Purdham v Barrow, 20/5/2006

SEASON RECORDS

Tries: 43 Mark Johnson 1993-94
Goals: 159 John Gallagher 1993-94
Points: 384 John Gallagher 1993-94

CAREER RECORDS

Tries: 86 Scott Roskell 1992-97
Goals: 309 Steve Diamond 1981-84
Points: 772 Paul Sykes 2001-07
Appearances:
202 Steele Retchless 1998-2004

HARLEQUINS

DATE	FIXTURE	RESULT	SCORERS	LGE	ATT
30/1/10	Wakefield (h)	L10-18	t:Jones-Bishop(2) g:Orr	N/A	3,688
7/2/10	Warrington (a)	L58-0		14th	11,678
14/2/10	Catalans (h)	W16-4	t:Sharp(3) g:Orr(2)	11th	2,330
26/2/10	Hull (a)	L28-4	t:Clubb	12th	13,965
5/3/10	Leeds (a)	L62-4	t:O'Callaghan	13th	12,684
14/3/10	Salford (h)	L22-26	t:Orr,Temata,Bryan,Jones-Bishop g:Orr(3)	14th	2,395
20/3/10	Huddersfield (h)	L18-32	t:Randall,Melling,Clubb g:Orr(3)	14th	2,624
26/3/10	Bradford (a)	L19-12	t:Melling,Orr g:Orr,Gale	14th	7,153
5/4/10	Hull KR (h)	L12-52	t:Orr,Williamson g:Orr(2)	14th	2,819
10/4/10	St Helens (h)	L24-32	t:Jones-Bishop,Penny,Williamson,Clubb g:Orr(4)	14th	5,220
17/4/10	Wakefield (h) (CCR4)	W23-16	t:Jones-Bishop,Clubb(2),Howell g:Orr(3) fg:Gale	N/A	2,355
23/4/10	Wigan (a)	W26-38	t:Howell,Dorn(2),Sharp,Purdham,Randall g:Orr(7)	13th	18,605
1/5/10	Hull (MM) ●	W25-8	t:Randall,Sharp,Dorn,Penny,Gale g:Orr(2) fg:Randall	12th	N/A
9/5/10	St Helens (h) (CCR5)	L10-30	t:Howell,Gale g:Orr	N/A	3,381
16/5/10	Castleford (h)	W40-24	t:Melling,Penny,Randall(2),Williamson,Orr,Howell g:Orr(4),Gale(2)	12th	2,941
23/5/10	Wakefield (a)	L54-12	t:Clubb,Dorn g:Orr(2)	13th	4,371
6/6/10	Crusaders (h)	W50-22	t:Dorn(4),Melling,Gale,Howell,Krasniqi g:Gale(6),Orr(3)	12th	2,381
12/6/10	Leeds (h)	L22-42	t:Dorn(2),Howell,Gale g:Orr(2),Melling	12th	4,117
20/6/10	Hull KR (a)	L42-6	t:Ward g:Orr	13th	7,612
26/6/10	Wigan (h)	L12-36	t:O'Callaghan,Jones-Bishop g:Orr(2)	13th	5,084
2/7/10	Salford (a)	L17-14	t:Purdham,Jones-Bishop(2) g:Orr	13th	2,672
9/7/10	Bradford (h)	W35-18	t:Dorn,Ellis,Jones-Bishop(2),Melling g:Orr(7) fg:Gale	12th	3,152
18/7/10	St Helens (a)	L32-18	t:Golden,O'Callaghan,Esders g:Orr(3)	13th	10,399
25/7/10	Huddersfield (a)	L40-4	t:Dorn	13th	5,336
31/7/10	Hull (h)	L18-42	t:Dorn,Sharp,McCarthy-Scarsbrook g:Purdham(3)	14th	3,982
6/8/10	Crusaders (a) ●●	L16-12	t:O'Callaghan,Jones-Bishop g:Purdham(2)	14th	1,122
14/8/10	Catalans (a)	W12-16	t:Clubb,Dorn,Ellis g:Purdham(2)	12th	6,152
22/8/10	Castleford (a)	L40-28	t:Howell,Sharp,O'Callaghan,Gale,Dorn g:Purdham(4)	12th	5,862
3/9/10	Warrington (h)	L22-36	t:Ellis,Dorn(3) g:Purdham(3)	13th	3,211

● Played at Murrayfield, Edinburgh
●● Played at The Gnoll, Neath

		APP		TRIES		GOALS		FG		PTS	
	D.O.B.	ALL	SL	ALL	SL	ALL	SL	ALL	SL	ALL	SL
Kyle Bibb	25/1/88	(2)	(2)	0	0	0	0	0	0	0	0
Ben Bolger	13/9/89	4(11)	4(11)	0	0	0	0	0	0	0	0
Lamont Bryan	12/4/88	3(11)	2(11)	1	1	0	0	0	0	4	4
Tony Clubb	12/6/87	29	27	7	5	0	0	0	0	28	20
Luke Dorn	2/7/82	17(2)	16(1)	18	18	0	0	0	0	72	72
Max Edwards	29/11/90	1	1	0	0	0	0	0	0	0	0
Andy Ellis	15/12/84	10(3)	10(3)	3	3	0	0	0	0	12	12
Ryan Esders	20/10/86	5(9)	5(7)	1	1	0	0	0	0	4	4
Luke Gale	22/6/88	21(2)	19(2)	5	4	9	9	2	1	40	35
Jason Golden	6/11/85	16(1)	16(1)	1	1	0	0	0	0	4	4
David Howell	18/11/83	23	21	7	5	0	0	0	0	28	20
Matt James	26/3/87	(2)	(2)	0	0	0	0	0	0	0	0
Ben Jones	18/10/88	(3)	(2)	0	0	0	0	0	0	0	0
Ben Jones-Bishop	24/8/88	18	17	11	10	0	0	0	0	44	40
Ben Kaye	19/12/88	(1)	(1)	0	0	0	0	0	0	0	0
Olsi Krasniqi	26/6/92	2(8)	2(8)	1	1	0	0	0	0	4	4
Luke May	23/8/89	(2)	(2)	0	0	0	0	0	0	0	0
Louie McCarthy-Scarsbrook	14/1/86	17(9)	15(9)	1	1	0	0	0	0	4	4
Chris Melling	21/9/84	26(2)	24(2)	5	5	1	1	0	0	22	22
David Mills	1/6/81	1(12)	1(12)	0	0	0	0	0	0	0	0
Jamie O'Callaghan	21/9/90	22(1)	22(1)	5	5	0	0	0	0	20	20
Danny Orr	17/5/78	23(2)	21(2)	4	4	56	52	0	0	128	120
Kevin Penny	3/10/87	5	5	3	3	0	0	0	0	12	12
Rob Purdham	14/4/80	17	15	2	2	12	12	0	0	32	32
Chad Randall	30/12/80	20	18	5	5	0	0	1	1	21	21
Will Sharp	12/5/86	29	27	7	7	0	0	0	0	28	28
Martyn Smith	27/2/92	(2)	(2)	0	0	0	0	0	0	0	0
Karl Temata	12/7/78	9(4)	8(3)	1	1	0	0	0	0	4	4
Danny Ward	15/6/80	22(4)	20(4)	1	1	0	0	0	0	4	4
Oliver Wilkes	2/5/80	20(9)	20(7)	0	0	0	0	0	0	0	0
Dave Williams	29/1/87	1(6)	1(5)	0	0	0	0	0	0	0	0
Luke Williamson	2/6/78	20	18	3	3	0	0	0	0	12	12

Luke Dorn

LEAGUE RECORD
P27-W7-D0-L20
(13th, SL)
F494, A838, Diff-344
14 points.

CHALLENGE CUP
Round Five

ATTENDANCES
Best - v St Helens (SL - 5,220)
Worst - v Catalans (SL - 2,330)
Total (SL only) - 43,944
Average (SL only) - 3,380
(Down by 56 on 2009)

8 October 2009 - Wakefield utility back Scott Grix joins on two-year deal.

22 November 2009 - former Castleford back-rower Jamie Cording signs on part-time contract.

30 November 2009 - released Hull FC utility player Graeme Horne signs one-year deal.

30 November 2009 - released South Sydney back-rower David Fa'alogo arrives on three-year contract.

27 January 2010 - 28-10 win at Castleford in pre-season warm-up.

3 February 2010 - Larne Patrick signs two-year contract extension to end of 2012.

5 February 2010 - Keith Mason tears pectoral muscle in first minute of 24-12 opening-round win at home to Bradford.

9 February 2010 - Andy Raleigh found guilty of late tackle on Matt Orford but escapes punishment.

12 February 2010 - Brett Hodgson misses 14-6 defeat at Hull FC with back injury.

21 February 2010 - Brett Hodgson back for 30-0 hammering of Hull KR at Craven Park.

23 February 2010 - Leroy Cudjoe signs two-year contract extension to end of 2012.

28 February 2010 - Brett Hodgson damages ankle ligaments in 14-10 home defeat to Warrington.

6 March 2010 - 52-0 drubbing of Wakefield in televised game at Belle Vue.

10 March 2010 - Luke Robinson signs contract extension until end of 2012 season.

14 March 2010 - Michael Lawrence suffers ankle ligament injury in 26-20 home win over Leeds Rhinos.

24 March 2010 - Danny Brough signs from Wakefield on contract to end of 2014 season. Danny Kirmond moves the other way on loan.

28 March 2010 - Danny Brough makes debut in 24-6 home defeat to St Helens. Stephen Wild suffers knee injury.

1 April 2010 - teenage prop Adam Walker signs two-year deal until end of 2012 season

5 April 2010 - shock 30-18 Easter Monday defeat at Salford.

15 April 2010 - Andy Raleigh signs new three-year contract to end of 2013 season.

18 April 2010 - 40-12 home win over Hull KR in Challenge Cup fourth round.

24 April 2010 - Brett Hodgson rejects one-year contract offer and will join Warrington at end of season.

KEY DATES - HUDDERSFIELD GIANTS

25 April 2010 - Shaun Lunt out for two months with Achilles injury sustained in warm-up before 38-10 win at Crusaders. Brett Hodgson missing with thigh strain.

29 April 2010 - coach Nathan Brown linked with return to Australia.

2 May 2010 - 28-10 defeat to Wigan at Murrayfield.

4 May 2010 - David Fa'alogo damages hamstring in training.

7 May 2010 - assistant coach Paul Anderson signs two-year contract extension to end of 2012.

8 May 2010 - Brett Hodgson makes early return in 60-4 thrashing by Warrington at Galpharm in Challenge Cup fifth round.

11 May 2010 - coach Nathan Brown to leave at end of season and return to Australia for family reasons.

16 May 2010 - David Hodgson's hat-trick unable to prevent 38-30 loss to Wigan at the Galpharm.

18 May 2010 - Gregg McNally goes to Oldham on one-month's loan deal.

20 May 2010 - assistant coach Paul Anderson linked with head-coach position.

20 May 2010 - Kyle Wood goes on one-month loan deal to Castleford.

23 May 2010 - Scott Grix and Lee Gilmour sin-binned in 36-20 defeat at Warrington.

6 June 2010 - Jermaine McGillvary scores twice on debut in 52-6 rout of Bradford at Odsal.

11 June 2010 - 30-22 away defeat by St Helens compounded by David Fa'alogo hamstring injury and Eorl Crabtree ankle ligament damage.

14 June 2010 - Kevin Brown commits to Giants until end of 2015 season.

20 June 2010 - Brad Drew returns in fight back from 18-0 down to 32-18 home victory over Hull FC.

26 June 2010 - Paul Whatuira granted early release from contract on compassionate grounds.

11 July 2010 - Nathan Brown announces he will remain as coach until end of 2011 season.

21 July 2010 - former Australia international Luke O'Donnell signs from North Queensland Cowboys on four-year deal from 2011.

30 July 2010 - Giants linked with Willie Mason.

31 July 2010 - Josh Griffin, on dual registration with Batley, signs new one-year contract.

1 August 2010 - Larne Patrick breaks jaw and fractures eye socket in 58–6 home win over Wakefield.

12 August 2010 - Stephen Wild to join Salford City Reds.

15 August 2010 - Leroy Cudjoe scores late winner in 18-16 victory at Wigan.

17 August 2010 - Keith Mason given three-match ban for part in fight at Wigan, Darrell Griffin suspended for one game.

31 August 2010 - Danny Kirmond recalled from loan spell at Wakefield.

4 September 2010 - 26-12 win in Perpignan secures fifth spot.

11 September 2010 - 18-12 home win over Crusaders in Elimination Play-off.

18 September 2010 - late length-of-the-field interception try from Leroy Cudjoe seals 34-22 Preliminary Semi-final win at Warrington.

24 September 2010 - 42-22 Qualifying Semi-final defeat at St Helens.

29 September 2010 - Joe Wardle transferred for undisclosed fee from Bradford on a three-year deal.

1 October 2010 - Graeme Horne signs new 12-month contract.

13 October 2010 - Australian Paul Watson appointed new strength and conditioning coach for 2011.

CLUB RECORDS

Highest score:
142-4 v Blackpool Gladiators, 26/11/94
Highest score against:
12-94 v Castleford, 18/9/88
Record attendance:
32,912 v Wigan, 4/3/50 *(Fartown)*
15,629 v Leeds, 10/2/2008
(Galpharm Stadium)

MATCH RECORDS

Tries:
10 Lionel Cooper v Keighley, 17/11/51
Goals:
18 Major Holland v Swinton Park, 28/2/14
Points:
39 Major Holland v Swinton Park, 28/2/14

SEASON RECORDS

Tries: 80 Albert Rosenfeld 1913-14
Goals: 147 Ben Gronow 1919-20
Points: 332 Pat Devery 1952-53

CAREER RECORDS

Tries: 420 Lionel Cooper 1947-55
Goals: 958 Frank Dyson 1949-63
Points: 2,072 Frank Dyson 1949-63
Appearances: 485 Douglas Clark 1909-29

HUDDERSFIELD GIANTS

DATE	FIXTURE	RESULT	SCORERS	LGE	ATT
5/2/10	Bradford (h)	W24-12	t:Cudjoe(2),Lunt,Fa'alogo g:B Hodgson(4)	8th	9,774
12/2/10	Hull (a)	L14-6	t:Grix g:Cudjoe	7th	14,520
21/2/10	Hull KR (a)	W0-30	t:Lunt,D Hodgson(3),Patrick,Cudjoe g:B Hodgson(3)	5th	7,575
28/2/10	Warrington (h)	L10-14	t:Brown,Whatuira g:B Hodgson	6th	8,567
6/3/10	Wakefield (a)	W0-52	t:Fa'alogo,Whatuira,Aspinwall,Cudjoe,Grix(2),Gilmour,D Hodgson,Patrick,Lunt g:Cudjoe(6)	4th	5,237
14/3/10	Leeds (h)	W26-20	t:Lunt,Gilmour,Patrick,Aspinwall g:Cudjoe(5)	3rd	10,116
20/3/10	Harlequins (a)	W18-32	t:Gilmour,Cudjoe(3),Crabtree,Horne g:B Hodgson(4)	3rd	2,624
28/3/10	St Helens (h)	L6-24	t:Grix g:B Hodgson	4th	9,648
2/4/10	Catalans (h)	W48-6	t:Faiumu,Gilmour,Brough(2),D Hodgson(2),Brown,Cudjoe,B Hodgson g:B Hodgson(6)	3rd	5,296
5/4/10	Salford (a)	L30-18	t:D Hodgson,Patrick,Cudjoe,Whatuira g:Brough	4th	4,014
9/4/10	Castleford (a)	W24-0	t:D Hodgson(3),Lolesi g:B Hodgson(4)	4th	5,932
18/4/10	Hull KR (h) (CCR4)	W40-12	t:Lolesi,Fa'alogo(2),Robinson,D Hodgson,Brough,Aspinwall g:B Hodgson(6)	N/A	7,241
25/4/10	Crusaders (a)	W10-38	t:Brown,D Hodgson(3),Cudjoe,Grix,Drew g:Brough(5)	4th	4,127
2/5/10	Wigan (MM) ●	L10-28	t:Gilmour,Crabtree g:Brough	4th	N/A
8/5/10	Warrington (h) (CCR5)	L4-60	t:Aspinwall	N/A	6,641
16/5/10	Wigan (h)	L30-38	t:Cudjoe,D Hodgson(3),Whatuira,Crabtree g:B Hodgson(3)	5th	8,390
23/5/10	Warrington (a)	L36-20	t:Robinson,Cudjoe(2),Lolesi g:B Hodgson(2)	7th	11,087
6/6/10	Bradford (a)	W6-52	t:Gilmour,D Hodgson(2),McGillvary(2),Cudjoe,Robinson,B Hodgson,Griffin g:B Hodgson(8)	6th	8,156
11/6/10	St Helens (a)	L30-22	t:Faiumu,Gilmour,Grix,Cudjoe g:B Hodgson(3)	6th	9,034
20/6/10	Hull (h)	W32-18	t:D Hodgson,Brown,Cudjoe,Lolesi,Lunt g:B Hodgson(6)	6th	7,939
25/6/10	Hull KR (h)	D16-16	t:Lawrence,Brown g:B Hodgson(4)	6th	6,304
4/7/10	Castleford (a)	L44-18	t:Cudjoe,Lolesi,Lunt(2) g:B Hodgson	6th	5,925
11/7/10	Crusaders (h)	W30-12	t:Lunt,Wild,McGillvary(2),Lawrence,Brown g:B Hodgson(2),Brough	6th	5,339
16/7/10	Leeds (a)	L21-20	t:Lunt,D Hodgson(2),Patrick g:Brough,Cudjoe	6th	15,070
25/7/10	Harlequins (a)	W40-4	t:McGillvary(2),Brown,Finnigan,Lawrence,Grix,D Hodgson,Brough g:Brough(4)	6th	5,336
1/8/10	Wakefield (h)	W58-6	t:D Hodgson,Gilmour,Griffin,Lunt,McGillvary,Cudjoe(2),Grix,Brough,Horne g:Brough(9)	6th	6,055
15/8/10	Wigan (a)	W16-18	t:Cudjoe(2),Robinson g:B Hodgson(3)	6th	13,619
22/8/10	Salford (h)	W52-4	t:Brough,Wild,Fa'alogo,Faiumu(2),Brown,Patrick,Horne,Gilmour g:B Hodgson(8)	6th	6,697
4/9/10	Catalans (a)	W12-26	t:Wild,D Hodgson,Lunt,Cudjoe,Robinson g:B Hodgson(3)	5th	5,708
11/9/10	Crusaders (h) (EPO)	W18-12	t:Robinson,Patrick,Cudjoe g:B Hodgson(3)	N/A	5,869
18/9/10	Warrington (a) (PSF)	W22-34	t:Wild,Kirmond,Gilmour,Brown,Cudjoe g:B Hodgson(6) fg:Brough(2)	N/A	8,050
24/9/10	St Helens (a) (QSF)	L42-22	t:Lunt,Lawrence(2),Gilmour g:B Hodgson(3)	N/A	13,510

● Played at Murrayfield, Edinburgh

	D.O.B.	APP		TRIES		GOALS		FG		PTS	
		ALL	SL	ALL	SL	ALL	SL	ALL	SL	ALL	SL
Martin Aspinwall	21/10/81	9(4)	8(3)	4	2	0	0	0	0	16	8
Danny Brough	15/1/83	21(3)	19(3)	6	5	22	22	2	2	70	66
Kevin Brown	2/10/84	31	29	9	9	0	0	0	0	36	36
Eorl Crabtree	2/10/82	8(20)	8(18)	3	3	0	0	0	0	12	12
Leroy Cudjoe	7/4/88	30	28	24	24	13	13	0	0	122	122
Brad Drew	25/8/75	4(5)	4(5)	1	1	0	0	0	0	4	4
David Fa'alogo	4/9/80	13(5)	12(5)	5	3	0	0	0	0	20	12
David Faiumu	30/4/83	13(19)	12(18)	4	4	0	0	0	0	16	16
Simon Finnigan	8/12/81	3(4)	3(4)	1	1	0	0	0	0	4	4
Lee Gilmour	12/3/78	31	29	11	11	0	0	0	0	44	44
Darrell Griffin	19/6/81	25(5)	23(5)	2	2	0	0	0	0	8	8
Scott Grix	1/5/84	6(11)	6(10)	8	8	0	0	0	0	32	32
Brett Hodgson	12/2/78	23	21	2	2	84	78	0	0	176	164
David Hodgson	8/8/81	32	30	25	24	0	0	0	0	100	96
Graeme Horne	22/3/85	12(9)	12(8)	3	3	0	0	0	0	12	12
Danny Kirmond	11/11/85	1(2)	1(2)	1	1	0	0	0	0	4	4
Michael Lawrence	12/4/90	26	26	5	5	0	0	0	0	20	20
Jamahl Lolesi	20/3/81	17	15	5	4	0	0	0	0	20	16
Shaun Lunt	15/4/86	18(9)	18(8)	12	12	0	0	0	0	48	48
Keith Mason	20/1/82	17	15	0	0	0	0	0	0	0	0
Jermaine McGillvary	16/5/88	5	5	7	7	0	0	0	0	28	28
Larne Patrick	3/11/88	2(22)	2(22)	7	7	0	0	0	0	28	28
Andy Raleigh	17/3/81	10(8)	9(7)	0	0	0	0	0	0	0	0
Luke Robinson	25/7/84	28(1)	26(1)	6	5	0	0	0	0	24	20
Adam Walker	20/2/91	(1)	(1)	0	0	0	0	0	0	0	0
Paul Whatuira	31/7/81	12	10	4	4	0	0	0	0	16	16
Stephen Wild	26/4/81	19	19	4	4	0	0	0	0	16	16

Leroy Cudjoe

LEAGUE RECORD
P27-W16-D1-L10
(5th, SL/Qualifying Semi-Final)
F758, A439, Diff+319
33 points.

CHALLENGE CUP
Round Five

ATTENDANCES
Best - v Leeds (SL - 10,116)
Worst - v Catalans (SL - 5,296)
Total (SL, inc play-offs) - 101,262
Average (SL, inc play-offs) - 7,233
(Down by 408 on 2009)

26 December 2009 - winger Gareth Raynor leaves by mutual consent with 12 months left on contract.

11 January 2010 - Sean Long confirmed as captain for 2010.

17 January 2010 - 28-16 home victory over Hull KR in Richard Horne Testimonial match in front of 16,000-plus crowd at KC Stadium.

6 February 2010 - Sean Long stars in 32-12, round 1 win at fog-bound St Helens.

12 February 2010 - Sean Long suffers hamstring injury in 14-6 home win over Huddersfield.

21 February 2010 - Sean Long misses 18-16 defeat at Crusaders.

5 March 2010 - 42-22 home win over Castleford makes it four wins from five as Hull go joint top.

12 March 2010 - Sean Long returns in 48-24 defeat at Wigan.

27 March 2010 - Reece Lyne scores try on debut in 27-20 defeat at Salford.

1 April 2010 - Richard Agar signs new two-year contract to remain as head coach until end of 2012.

2 April 2010 - 18-14 win at Craven Park in Good Friday derby.

5 April 2010 - Sean Long suffers ankle injury in Easter Monday 29-10 round 10 defeat to Warrington at the KC Stadium.

11 April 2010 - Shaun Berrigan suffers broken collarbone in 46-30 defeat at Leeds.

17 April 2010 - 48-24 home defeat by Leeds in Challenge Cup round four.

20 April 2010 - Kirk Yeaman signs new three-year contract to end of 2013.

21 April 2010 - Leeds Rhinos hooker Paul McShane arrives on month's loan.

23 April 2010 - 12-8 home win over Wakefield.

1 May 2010 - 25-8 defeat to Harlequins in round 13 at Murrayfield. Knee injury sidelines Richard Horne and Epalahame Lauaki suffers calf strain.

5 May 2010 - assistant coach Dennis Moore granted release from 12-month contract for personal reasons.

12 May 2010 - Willie Manu signs new two-year contract to end of 2012.

15 May 2010 - 28-14 victory over Catalans in Perpignan.

18 May 2010 - former Hull KR scrum-half James Webster joins coaching staff.

21 May 2010 - Paul McShane's loan deal extended on weekly basis.

KEY DATES - HULL F.C.

23 May 2010 - 34-26 triumph away at Castleford.

4 June 2010 - last-minute Danny Tickle field goal clinches 27-26 home comeback win over Saints.

8 June 2010 - Danny Houghton signs new two-year contract to end 2012. Paul McShane's loan spell ends.

11 June 2010 - Shaun Berrigan and Epalahame Lauaki return in 34-12 home victory over Salford.

18 June 2010 - Danny Tickle signs new three-year contract to end of 2013.

20 June 2010 - 32-18 defeat by Huddersfield at the Galpharm having led 18-nil.

25 June 2010 - Craig Fitzgibbon signs new one-year contract.

25 June 2010 - captain Sean Long ruled out for eight weeks with dislocated elbow in 10-8 home win over Catalans.

3 July 2010 - teenage winger Reece Lyne signs deal until end of 2013 season.

15 July 2010 - 80th-minute Tom Briscoe tackle earns 20-16 win in home derby. Richard Whiting breaks arm and returning Mark Calderwood damages hamstring.

20 July 2010 - Danny Tickle banned for one match for part in derby brawl. Sam Moa also found guilty of fighting but escapes with fine. Jordan Tansey cautioned.

20 July 2010 - Willie Manu trains with initial England train-on squad.

23 July 2010 - Ben Crooks, son of former Hull and Great Britain forward Lee, signs two-year contract.

9 August 2010 - Craig Hall not offered new deal.

11 August 2010 - Harlequins winger Will Sharp signs on two-year contract.

17 August 2010 - James Webster to stay on as assistant coach on one-year deal for 2011.

2 September 2010 - Lee Radford signs new two-year contract to end of 2012 season.

4 September 2010 - Lee Radford sent off in 10th minute of 18-14 home defeat by Leeds, meaning sixth-place finish.

8 September 2010 - one-match ban for Lee Radford overturned on appeal.

11 September 2010 - 21-4 home defeat to Hull KR in Elimination Play-off.

27 September 2010 - Craig Hall leaves for Hull KR.

6 October 2010 - Mark Calderwood released.

19 October 2010 - Ewan Dowes signs new one–year contract.

28 October 2010 - Joe Westerman signs four-year deal from Castleford for a six-figure transfer fee.

CLUB RECORDS

Highest score: 88-0 v Sheffield, 2/3/2003
Highest score against:
16-74 v St Helens, 18/7/99
Record attendance:
28,798 v Leeds, 7/3/36 *(The Boulevard)*
23,004 v Hull KR, 2/9/2007 *(KC Stadium)*

MATCH RECORDS

Tries: 7 Clive Sullivan v Doncaster, 15/4/68
Goals: 14 Jim Kennedy v Rochdale, 7/4/21
Sammy Lloyd v Oldham, 10/9/78
Matt Crowther v Sheffield, 2/3/2003
Points: 36 Jim Kennedy v Keighley, 29/1/21

SEASON RECORDS

Tries: 52 Jack Harrison 1914-15
Goals: 170 Sammy Lloyd 1978-79
Points: 369 Sammy Lloyd 1978-79

CAREER RECORDS

Tries: 250 Clive Sullivan 1961-74; 1981-85
Goals: 687 Joe Oliver 1928-37; 1943-45
Points: 1,842 Joe Oliver 1928-37; 1943-45
Appearances: 500 Edward Rogers 1906-25

HULL F.C.

DATE	FIXTURE	RESULT	SCORERS	LGE	ATT
6/2/10	St Helens (a)	W12-32	t:Manu,Lauaki,Long,Briscoe,Yeaman g:Tickle(4),Fitzgibbon(2)	4th	12,142
12/2/10	Huddersfield (h)	W14-6	t:Tickle,Hall g:Tickle(3)	4th	14,520
21/2/10	Crusaders (a)	L18-16	t:Radford,Briscoe,Yeaman g:Fitzgibbon(2)	6th	6,794
26/2/10	Harlequins (h)	W28-4	t:Fitzgibbon,Yeaman,Hall,Tickle,Horne g:Tickle(3),Fitzgibbon	3rd	13,965
5/3/10	Castleford (h)	W42-22	t:Yeaman,Manu,Horne(2),Cusack,Hall,Fitzgibbon g:Tickle(6),Fitzgibbon	3rd	13,352
12/3/10	Wigan (a)	L48-24	t:Whiting,Hall,Long,Horne g:Tickle(4)	5th	15,045
19/3/10	Bradford (h)	W18-6	t:Tansey(2),Radford g:Tickle(3)	5th	14,466
27/3/10	Salford (a)	L27-20	t:Long,Yeaman,Lauaki,Lyne g:Tickle(2)	5th	3,535
2/4/10	Hull KR (a)	W14-18	t:Briscoe,Fitzgibbon,Tansey g:Tickle(3)	5th	10,089
5/4/10	Warrington (h)	L10-29	t:Hall,Manu g:Whiting	5th	14,131
11/4/10	Leeds (a)	L46-30	t:Briscoe(4),Hall,Turner g:Whiting(2),Hall	6th	16,896
17/4/10	Leeds (h) (CCR4)	L24-48	t:Briscoe,Tansey,Whiting(2),Turner g:Tickle,Fitzgibbon	N/A	15,109
23/4/10	Wakefield (h)	W12-8	t:Whiting(2) g:Hall(2)	6th	11,160
1/5/10	Harlequins (MM) ●	L25-8	t:Houghton,Briscoe	6th	N/A
15/5/10	Catalans (a)	W14-28	t:Briscoe,Fitzgibbon,O'Meley,Whiting,Tansey g:Tickle(4)	6th	6,512
23/5/10	Castleford (a)	W26-34	t:Yeaman,Tansey,Long,Briscoe,Fitzgibbon,O'Meley g:Tickle(5)	4th	7,996
4/6/10	St Helens (h)	W27-26	t:Briscoe,Turner,Houghton,Manu,Tickle g:Tickle(3) fg:Tickle	4th	13,300
11/6/10	Salford (h)	W34-12	t:Hall(2),Long,Whiting,Tansey,Turner g:Tickle(5)	4th	11,397
20/6/10	Huddersfield (a)	L32-18	t:Turner,Manu,Yeaman g:Tickle(3)	4th	7,939
25/6/10	Catalans (h)	W10-8	t:Turner,Whiting g:Tickle	4th	11,466
4/7/10	Bradford (a)	W22-28	t:Briscoe,Tansey,Tickle,Yeaman,Hall g:Tickle(4)	4th	8,411
10/7/10	Wakefield (h)	L29-6	t:Turner g:Tickle	4th	5,366
15/7/10	Hull KR (h)	W20-16	t:Houghton,Manu,Berrigan g:Tickle(4)	4th	20,079
23/7/10	Wigan (h)	L0-46		5th	12,694
31/7/10	Harlequins (a)	W18-42	t:O'Meley(2),Yeaman,Houghton,Turner,Moa,Tansey g:Tickle(7)	4th	3,982
13/8/10	Crusaders (h)	W18-16	t:Lyne g:Tickle(7)	4th	11,762
20/8/10	Warrington (a)	L36-18	t:Briscoe,Lauaki,Radford g:Tickle(3)	5th	10,042
4/9/10	Leeds (h)	L14-18	t:Briscoe,Washbrook g:Tickle(2),Fitzgibbon	6th	16,208
11/9/10	Hull KR (h) (EPO)	L4-21	t:Briscoe	N/A	17,699

● Played at Murrayfield, Edinburgh

		APP		TRIES		GOALS		FG		PTS	
	D.O.B.	ALL	SL	ALL	SL	ALL	SL	ALL	SL	ALL	SL
Shaun Berrigan	4/11/78	19(4)	19(4)	1	1	0	0	0	0	4	4
Tom Briscoe	19/3/90	27	26	16	15	0	0	0	0	64	60
Mike Burnett	6/10/88	4(4)	4(4)	0	0	0	0	0	0	0	0
Mark Calderwood	25/10/81	4	4	0	0	0	0	0	0	0	0
Liam Cunningham	28/10/89	(1)	(1)	0	0	0	0	0	0	0	0
Peter Cusack	27/1/77	8(17)	8(16)	1	1	0	0	0	0	4	4
Ewan Dowes	4/3/81	14(12)	14(11)	0	0	0	0	0	0	0	0
Craig Fitzgibbon	16/6/77	22	21	5	5	8	7	0	0	36	34
Craig Hall	21/2/88	17(4)	16(4)	9	9	3	3	0	0	42	42
Richard Horne	16/7/82	14(1)	13(1)	4	4	0	0	0	0	16	16
Danny Houghton	25/9/88	18(10)	17(10)	4	4	0	0	0	0	16	16
Epalahame Lauaki	27/1/84	3(21)	3(20)	3	3	0	0	0	0	12	12
Sean Long	24/9/76	15	15	5	5	0	0	0	0	20	20
Reece Lyne	2/12/92	6	6	2	2	0	0	0	0	8	8
Willie Manu	20/3/80	27	26	6	6	0	0	0	0	24	24
Paul McShane	19/11/89	(4)	(4)	0	0	0	0	0	0	0	0
Sam Moa	14/6/86	(19)	(19)	1	1	0	0	0	0	4	4
Danny Nicklas	29/6/91	(3)	(3)	0	0	0	0	0	0	0	0
Mark O'Meley	22/5/81	22	21	4	4	0	0	0	0	16	16
Lee Radford	26/3/79	19(8)	18(8)	3	3	0	0	0	0	12	12
Jordan Tansey	9/9/86	25	24	9	8	0	0	0	0	36	32
Danny Tickle	10/3/83	23	22	4	4	78	77	1	1	173	171
Jordan Turner	9/1/89	22(1)	22	8	7	0	0	0	0	32	28
Danny Washbrook	18/9/85	19(2)	18(2)	1	1	0	0	0	0	4	4
Richard Whiting	20/12/84	22(1)	21(1)	8	6	3	3	0	0	38	30
Kirk Yeaman	15/9/83	27	26	9	9	0	0	0	0	36	36

Tom Briscoe

LEAGUE RECORD
P27-W16-D0-L11
(6th, SL/Elimination Play-Off)
F569, A584, Diff-15
32 points.

CHALLENGE CUP
Round Four

ATTENDANCES
Best - v Hull KR (SL - 20,079)
Worst - v Wakefield (SL - 11,160)
Total (SL, inc play-offs) - 196,199
Average (SL, inc play-offs) - 14,014
(Up by 788 on 2009)

17 January 2010 - 28-16 defeat to Hull FC at KC Stadium in Richard Horne Testimonial match.

28 January 2010 - 18-16 home defeat to Bradford in final friendly.

7 February 2010 - Peter Fox scores two tries in the opening seven minutes of 30-12, round 1 home win over Salford.

21 February 2010 - new recruit Joel Clinton unveiled before 30-0 home hammering by Huddersfield after arriving on three-year contract.

27 February 2010 - Joel Clinton makes debut in 24-20 win at Castleford.

7 March 2010 - Liam Colbon scores hat-trick in 28-24 home win over St Helens.

12 March 2010 - 31-18 home defeat to Wakefield after leading 18-6 half-time.

19 March 2010 - Paul Cooke released and joins Wakefield.

19 March 2010 - stunning 17-10 victory at Leeds is first at Headingley since 1985.

26 March 2010 - Liam Colbon undergoes surgery after breaking jaw in 16-10 defeat by Catalans Dragons in Perpignan.

2 April 2010 - 18-14 Good Friday derby defeat at Craven Park.

5 April 2010 - Kris Welham scores four tries in 52-12 Easter Monday win at Harlequins.

11 April 2010 - Peter Fox scores twice in 36-16 home win over Warrington.

18 April 2010 - 40-12 defeat at Huddersfield in Challenge Cup fourth round.

25 April 2010 - 40-4 hammering at Bradford.

2 May 2010 - 54-0 humbling by St Helens at Murrayfield.

4 May 2010 - chairman Neil Hudgell apologises to supporters for slump in form and backs coach Justin Morgan.

4 May 2010 - Michael Dobson pledges future commitment to club. Liam Watts signs contract extension to end 2012.

13 May 2010 - Rhys Lovegrove signs two-year contract extension to end of 2012.

16 May 2010 - Michael Dobson scores hat-trick in 54-10 rout of Crusaders at Craven Park to end three-game losing run.

21 May 2010 - 68-12 annihilation at St Helens.

2 June 2010 - Chaz l'Anson loaned to Widnes on monthly basis.

KEY DATES - HULL KINGSTON ROVERS

6 June 2010 - 24-6 home win over Catalans. Jake Webster sustains hip injury.

11 June 2010 - Clint Newton sin-binning pivotal in 35-16 defeat at Warrington.

15 June 2010 - Jake Webster set to miss the rest of season after being told he needs hip surgery.

18 June 2010 - Chaz l'Anson sustains season-ending knee injury for Widnes.

20 June 2010 - Michael Dobson amasses 22 points in 42-6 home win over Harlequins.

22 June 2010 - Jake Webster signs new two-year contract.

24 June 2010 - Ben Galea agrees new one-year deal to end of 2011.

2 July 2010 - coach Justin Morgan holds talks with Melbourne stand-off Brett Finch.

2 July 2010 - Chev Walker's future in doubt after being ruled out for season.

5 July 2010 - Michael Ratu to miss rest of season with shoulder injury suffered in 16-16 draw with Huddersfield.

19 July 2010 - 19-year-old Josh Charnley makes debut in 25-6 home win over Leeds after joining on one-month loan from Wigan.

20 July 2010 - Ben Cockayne suspended for two games after brawl in 20-16 Hull derby defeat at KC Stadium. Liam Watts escapes with fine and Jason Netherton with caution.

6 August 2010 - Wigan agree to extend centre Josh Charnley's loan to end of regular season.

19 August 2010 - Wigan Warriors recall Josh Charnley from loan spell.

25 August 2010 - Chev Walker signs for Bradford Bulls.

1 September 2010 - Liam Colbon signs new contract for 2011.

3 September 2010 - former Australia forward Willie Mason signs on two-year deal.

4 September 2010 - 30-24, round 27 defeat at Crusaders means seventh-place finish.

6 September 2010 - Chaz l'Anson signs for Widnes Vikings.

11 September 2010 - 21-4 defeat of Hull FC in Elimination Play-off at KC Stadium.

17 September 2010 - 42-18 Preliminary Semi-final defeat at Wigan ends season.

27 September 2010 - Craig Hall signs from Hull FC on two-year deal.

6 October 2010 - Scott Wheeldon signs new two-year contract to end of 2012.

CLUB RECORDS

Highest score:
100-6 v Nottingham City, 19/8/90
Highest score against:
8-76 v Halifax, 20/10/91
Record attendance:
27,670 v Hull FC, 3/4/53 *(Boothferry Park)*
10,089 v Hull FC, 2/4/2010 *(Craven Park)*

MATCH RECORDS

Tries: 11 George West
v Brookland Rovers, 4/3/1905
Goals:
14 Alf Carmichael v Merthyr, 8/10/1910
Mike Fletcher v Whitehaven, 18/3/90
Colin Armstrong v Nottingham City, 19/8/90
Damien Couturier v Halifax, 23/4/2006
Points: 53 George West
v Brookland Rovers, 4/3/1905

SEASON RECORDS

Tries: 45 Gary Prohm 1984-85
Goals: 199 Mike Fletcher 1989-90
Points: 450 Mike Fletcher 1989-90

CAREER RECORDS

Tries: 207 Roger Millward 1966-80
Goals: 1,268 Mike Fletcher 1987-98
Points: 2,760 Mike Fletcher 1987-98
Appearances: 489 Mike Smith 1975-91

HULL KINGSTON ROVERS

DATE	FIXTURE	RESULT	SCORERS	LGE	ATT
7/2/10	Salford (h)	W30-12	t:Fox(2),Webster,Dobson,Newton g:Dobson(5)	5th	9,123
12/2/10	Wigan (a)	L32-6	t:Fisher g:Dobson	9th	12,429
21/2/10	Huddersfield (h)	L0-30		11th	7,575
27/2/10	Castleford (a)	W20-24	t:Murrell,Dobson,Cockayne,Watts g:Dobson(4)	9th	6,855
7/3/10	St Helens (h)	W28-24	t:Galea,Colbon(3),Fisher g:Dobson(4)	8th	8,202
12/3/10	Wakefield (h)	L18-31	t:Colbon,Webster,Murrell g:Dobson(3)	9th	8,004
19/3/10	Leeds (h)	W10-17	t:Colbon,Fox,Briscoe g:Dobson(2) fg:Dobson	7th	15,201
27/3/10	Catalans (a)	L16-10	t:Webster,Welham g:Dobson	7th	6,620
2/4/10	Hull (h)	L14-18	t:Cockayne,Welham g:Dobson(3)	8th	10,089
5/4/10	Harlequins (a)	W12-52	t:Galea(2),Cook,Dobson,Welham(4),Lovegrove g:Dobson(8)	8th	2,819
11/4/10	Warrington (h)	W36-16	t:Welham,Cockayne,Briscoe,Fox(2),Cook g:Dobson(6)	7th	8,452
18/4/10	Huddersfield (a) (CCR4)	L40-12	t:Webster,Briscoe g:Dobson(2)	N/A	7,241
25/4/10	Bradford (a)	L40-4	t:Cockayne	7th	9,234
2/5/10	St Helens (MM) ●	L0-54		9th	N/A
16/5/10	Crusaders (h)	W54-10	t:Newton(2),Cockayne,Dobson(3),Watts,Fox,Welham g:Dobson(9)	8th	7,273
21/5/10	St Helens (a)	L68-12	t:Welham,Newton g:Dobson(2)	9th	9,375
6/6/10	Catalans (h)	W24-6	t:Galea,Welham,Murrell,Dobson g:Dobson(4)	8th	7,102
11/6/10	Warrington (a)	L35-16	t:Welham,Ratu,Fisher g:Dobson(2)	8th	9,216
20/6/10	Harlequins (h)	W42-6	t:Newton(2),Dobson(2),Briscoe,Wheeldon,Clinton g:Dobson(7)	7th	7,612
25/6/10	Huddersfield (a)	D16-16	t:Murrell,Newton g:Dobson(4)	7th	6,304
4/7/10	Wakefield (a)	W14-46	t:Dobson,Newton,Welham,Fox(2),Wheeldon(2) g:Dobson(9)	7th	6,218
9/7/10	Leeds (h)	W25-6	t:Galea,Fisher,Fox,Cockayne g:Dobson(4) fg:Dobson	7th	8,406
15/7/10	Hull (a)	L20-16	t:Charnley,Newton,Watts g:Dobson(2)	7th	20,079
24/7/10	Bradford (h)	W49-24	t:Fox(3),Latus,Clinton,Newton(2),Briscoe(2) g:Dobson(6) fg:Dobson	7th	7,854
1/8/10	Castleford (h)	W28-26	t:Charnley(3),Briscoe g:Dobson(6)	7th	8,104
15/8/10	Salford (a)	W18-44	t:Colbon,Newton(2),Charnley,Murrell,Dobson,Briscoe(2) g:Dobson(6)	7th	4,111
22/8/10	Wigan (h)	L18-38	t:Murrell,Cook,Lovegrove g:Dobson(3)	7th	9,250
4/9/10	Crusaders (a)	L30-24	t:Fox,Briscoe,Welham,Galea g:Dobson(4)	7th	5,137
11/9/10	Hull (a) (EPO)	W4-21	t:Fox,Fisher,Welham g:Dobson(4) fg:Murrell	N/A	17,699
17/9/10	Wigan (a) (PSF)	L42-18	t:Fox(2),Cockayne g:Dobson(3)	N/A	11,133

● Played at Murrayfield, Edinburgh

		APP		TRIES		GOALS		FG		PTS	
	D.O.B.	ALL	SL	ALL	SL	ALL	SL	ALL	SL	ALL	SL
Shaun Briscoe	23/2/83	27	26	10	9	0	0	0	0	40	36
Josh Charnley	26/6/91	5	5	5	5	0	0	0	0	20	20
Joel Clinton	8/12/81	23(3)	22(3)	2	2	0	0	0	0	8	8
Ben Cockayne	20/7/83	24(2)	23(2)	7	7	0	0	0	0	28	28
Liam Colbon	30/9/84	14	14	6	6	0	0	0	0	24	24
Matt Cook	14/11/86	5(13)	5(12)	3	3	0	0	0	0	12	12
Paul Cooke	17/4/81	3	3	0	0	0	0	0	0	0	0
Michael Dobson	29/5/86	30	29	11	11	114	112	3	3	275	271
Ben Fisher	4/2/81	15(13)	15(12)	5	5	0	0	0	0	20	20
Peter Fox	5/11/83	30	29	16	16	0	0	0	0	64	64
Ben Galea	16/8/78	23	22	6	6	0	0	0	0	24	24
Josh Hodgson	31/10/89	6(14)	6(14)	0	0	0	0	0	0	0	0
Chaz I'Anson	30/11/86	8	7	0	0	0	0	0	0	0	0
Sam Latus	21/10/89	7	7	1	1	0	0	0	0	4	4
Rhys Lovegrove	11/3/87	14(16)	14(15)	2	2	0	0	0	0	8	8
Frankie Mariano	10/5/87	(3)	(3)	0	0	0	0	0	0	0	0
Scott Murrell	5/9/85	29(1)	28(1)	6	6	0	0	1	1	25	25
Jason Netherton	5/10/82	13(13)	12(13)	0	0	0	0	0	0	0	0
Clint Newton	18/6/81	30	29	13	13	0	0	0	0	52	52
Mike Ratu	16/10/87	5	5	1	1	0	0	0	0	4	4
Scott Spaven	6/3/90	(2)	(2)	0	0	0	0	0	0	0	0
Scott Taylor	27/2/91	(3)	(3)	0	0	0	0	0	0	0	0
Michael Vella	19/2/78	24(3)	23(3)	0	0	0	0	0	0	0	0
Liam Watts	8/7/90	13(14)	13(13)	3	3	0	0	0	0	12	12
Jake Webster	29/10/83	15	14	4	3	0	0	0	0	16	12
Kris Welham	12/5/87	23	22	14	14	0	0	0	0	56	56
Scott Wheeldon	23/2/86	4(20)	4(20)	3	3	0	0	0	0	12	12

Peter Fox

LEAGUE RECORD
P27-W14-D1-L12
(7th, SL/Preliminary Semi-Final)
F653, A632, Diff+21
29 points.

CHALLENGE CUP
Round Four

ATTENDANCES
Best - v Hull (SL - 10,089)
Worst - v Catalans (SL - 7,102)
Total (SL only) - 107,046
Average (SL only) - 8,234
(Down by 267 on 2009)

195

17 December 2009 - back-row forward Joe Chandler joins Oldham.

18 December 2009 - Jodie Broughton joins Salford City Reds.

26 December 2009 - Brent Webb scores two tries in 32-12 Boxing Day win over Wakefield at snowy Headingley.

14 January 2010 - Carl Ablett signs new four-year contract to end of 2014 season.

18 January 2010 - 12-10 win over Bradford Bulls in Matt Diskin testimonial match at Headingley.

29 January 2010 - 34-6 win over Crusaders at the Racecourse Ground in snowy round four opener.

2 February 2010 - Ryan Hall signs new four-year contract to end of 2013.

5 February 2010 - rested Jamie Peacock returns in shock 24-10 defeat to Castleford at Headingley. Carl Ablett suffers ankle injury.

14 February 2010 - 28-18 defeat to Wakefield is first Super League loss at Belle Vue.

19 February 2010 - Scott Donald dislocates shoulder in 22-10 home win over Salford.

28 February 2010 - Kevin Sinfield suffers leg injury in second consecutive World Club Challenge defeat, by 18-10 to Melbourne at Elland Road.

5 March 2010 - Greg Eastwood out for 10 weeks with a wrist fracture sustained in 62-4 home thrashing of Harlequins.

10 March 2010 - Keith Senior fined £1,000, half suspended, by RFL for criticising referee Richard Silverwood after Gillette World Club Challenge.

14 March 2010 - Kallum Watkins out for season after rupturing anterior cruciate ligament in Leeds' 26-20 defeat at Huddersfield.

19 March 2010 - Jamie Peacock ruptures foot ligaments in 17-10 home defeat by Hull KR.

26 March 2010 - 24-4 defeat at Wigan leaves Leeds outside play-off spots.

31 March 2010 - Lee Smith signs three-and-a-half-year contract after short-lived move to London Wasps.

1 April 2010 - two Lee Smith tries complete comeback from 20-6 down to 20-all draw at home to Bradford. Kevin Sinfield makes first appearance since WCC.

5 April 2010 - Carl Ablett returns in 34-24 Easter Monday win over Catalans in Perpignan.

11 April 2010 - Lee Smith to face two charges of illegal use of the knees after the Rhinos' 46-30 round 11 home win over Hull FC.

13 April 2010 - Lee Smith found guilty of one charge of illegal use of the knees but escapes with a warning.

17 April 2010 - Carl Ablett stars in 48-24 win at Hull FC in Challenge Cup round four.

KEY DATES - LEEDS RHINOS

21 April 2010 - hooker Paul McShane goes to Hull FC on month's loan.

24 April 2010 - 41-20 defeat at St Helens

1 May 2010 - Rob Burrow suffers knee injury as late Danny Buderus try secures 34-30 comeback win over Wakefield in Edinburgh.

18 May 2010 - Brent Webb gets two-match suspension for high tackle on Mickey Higham during 26-16 home win over Warrington. Jamie Peacock sprains knee ligaments.

23 May 2010 - Danny McGuire scores hat-trick as Scott Donald returns in 26-12 win at Bradford.

24 May 2010 - Brian McClennan agrees one-year contract extension until end of 2011 season.

29 May 2010 - Lee Smith scores only try of game, two minutes from time, to defeat Wigan 12-10 in home Challenge Cup quarter-final.

4 June 2010 - Brent Webb returns in 28-22 win over Wakefield at Headingley.

10 June 2010 - Paul McShane recalled from loan spell at Hull FC.

12 June 2010 - Paul McShane scores try in 42-22 win over Harlequins at the Stoop. Matt Diskin suffers groin injury.

19 June 2010 - Brent Webb suffers ankle ligament damage in training.

20 June 2010 - 32-26 home defeat to Crusaders ends seven-game winning run.

30 June 2010 - Keith Senior, Ryan Bailey, Kylie Leuluai, Scott Donald, Ali Lauitiiti, Danny Buderus and Matt Diskin all sign one-year deals for 2011.

6 July 2010 - Luke Ambler and Chris Clarkson sign new contracts to end of 2012 season.

9 July 2010 - Rob Burrow returns after two-month lay-off with knee injury in 25-6 defeat at Hull KR.

12 July 2010 - assistant coaches Francis Cummins and Willie Poching to leave at end of season.

29 July 2010 - Greg Eastwood, on a three-year deal at start of season, put on transfer list at own request with a £100,000 price tag.

3 August 2010 - Carl Ablett handed three-match ban for late challenge on Sam Tomkins during 26-12 home defeat by Wigan, and loses appeal.

7 August 2010 - Danny McGuire try settles classic Challenge Cup semi-final with St Helens 32-28 in Rhinos' favour.

13 August 2010 - Jamie Peacock sidelined for season with knee injury in 38-6 win at Castleford. Luke Burgess breaks jaw.

17 August 2010 - Brian McDermott to return as assistant coach to Brian McClennan.

19 August 2010 - Scott Donald to retire at the end of season and return home to Australia.

25 August 2010 - Kallum Watkins makes return from long-term knee injury in Carnegie Nines.

28 August 2010 - Jamie Jones-Buchanan suffers foot injury in 30-6 defeat by Warrington at Wembley.

4 September 2010 - 18-14 win at Hull FC secures fourth-place finish.

12 September 2010 - late Kevin Sinfield field goal wins Qualifying Play-off at Wigan, 27-26.

13 September 2010 - knee injury rules Danny McGuire out until 2011.

15 September 2010 - Danny Buderus one-match ban for spear tackle in Wigan win reduced to fine on appeal.

25 September 2010 - 26-6 Qualifying Semi-final defeat by Wigan at Headingley ends season.

26 September 2010 - former player, Great Britain international Terry Newton found dead at his home near Wigan.

8 October 2010 - Greg Eastwood joins Canterbury Bulldogs after undisclosed compensation agreed.

12 October 2010 - Newcastle Knights prop Ben Cross signed on two-year deal.

15 October 2010 - Featherstone winger Zak Hardaker signs five-year contract.

25 October 2010 - Brian McClennan steps down from head coach position; Brian McDermott steps up.

CLUB RECORDS
Highest score: 106-10 v Swinton, 11/2/2001
Highest score against: 6-74 v Wigan, 20/5/92
Record attendance: 40,175 v Bradford, 21/5/47

MATCH RECORDS
Tries: 8 Fred Webster v Coventry, 12/4/13 Eric Harris v Bradford, 14/9/31
Goals: 17 Iestyn Harris v Swinton, 11/2/2001
Points: 42 Iestyn Harris v Huddersfield, 16/7/99

SEASON RECORDS
Tries: 63 Eric Harris 1935-36
Goals: 166 Lewis Jones 1956-57
Points: 431 Lewis Jones 1956-57

CAREER RECORDS
Tries: 391 Eric Harris 1930-39
Goals: 1,244 Lewis Jones 1952-64
Points: 2,920 Lewis Jones 1952-64
Appearances: 625 John Holmes 1968-89

LEEDS RHINOS

DATE	FIXTURE	RESULT	SCORERS	LGE	ATT
29/1/10	Crusaders (a)	W6-34	t:Donald,McGuire,Lauitiiti(2),Sinfield,Delaney g:Sinfield(5)	N/A	10,334
5/2/10	Castleford (h)	L10-24	t:McGuire,Delaney g:Sinfield	6th	15,875
14/2/10	Wakefield (a)	L28-18	t:McGuire,Donald(2) g:Burrow,Sinfield(2)	6th	9,783
19/2/10	Salford (h)	W22-10	t:Senior(2),Webb,Kirke g:Sinfield(3)	7th	12,700
28/2/10	Melbourne (WCC) ●	L10-18	t:McGuire g:Sinfield,Burrow(2)	N/A	27,697
5/3/10	Harlequins (h)	W62-4	t:Webb(2),Hall(2),Buderus(2),Lauitiiti(2),McGuire,Watkins,Senior,Bush g:Burrow(5)	5th	12,684
14/3/10	Huddersfield (a)	L26-20	t:Burrow,McGuire,Hall g:Burrow(4)	7th	10,116
19/3/10	Hull KR (h)	L10-17	t:Jones-Buchanan,Senior g:Burrow	8th	15,201
26/3/10	Wigan (a)	L24-4	t:Hall	9th	17,883
1/4/10	Bradford (h)	D20-20	t:Smith(2),Delaney,Sinfield g:Sinfield(2)	9th	17,244
5/4/10	Catalans (a) ●●	W24-34	t:Lauitiiti,Jones-Buchanan,Senior,McGuire(2),Delaney g:Sinfield(5)	9th	8,230
11/4/10	Hull (h)	W46-30	t:Senior(2),Hall(2),Lauitiiti,Burrow,Jones-Buchanan,McGuire g:Sinfield(7)	9th	16,896
17/4/10	Hull (h) (CCR4)	W24-48	t:Ablett,Webb(2),Kirke,Hall(4) g:Sinfield(8)	N/A	15,109
24/4/10	St Helens (a)	L41-20	t:Smith,Delaney,Hall,Burrow g:Sinfield(2)	9th	11,048
1/5/10	Wakefield (MM) ●●●	W34-30	t:Hall(3),Webb,Clarkson,Buderus g:Sinfield(5)	7th	N/A
7/5/10	Blackpool (h) (CCR5)	W70-22	t:Webb(5),Hall,Lauitiiti,Delaney,Coady(3),Eastwood g:Sinfield(11)	N/A	5,316
14/5/10	Warrington (h)	W26-16	t:Ablett,Hall,Webb,McGuire g:Sinfield(5)	7th	16,733
23/5/10	Bradford (a)	W12-26	t:McGuire(3),Senior,Delaney g:Sinfield(3)	5th	13,269
29/5/10	Wigan (h) (CCQF)	W12-10	t:Smith g:Sinfield(4)	N/A	9,242
4/6/10	Wakefield (h)	W28-22	t:McGuire,Jones-Buchanan,Donald,Buderus g:Sinfield(6)	5th	13,869
12/6/10	Harlequins (a)	W22-42	t:Smith(3),McShane,Webb,Ambler,Ablett g:Smith(7)	5th	4,117
20/6/10	Crusaders (h)	L26-32	t:Hall,Smith,Donald,Delaney g:Sinfield(5)	5th	14,371
27/6/10	Warrington (a)	W30-37	t:Senior,Eastwood,Donald,Buderus,Hall,McGuire g:Sinfield(6) fg:Sinfield	5th	10,442
3/7/10	St Helens (h)	W28-24	t:Clarkson,Delaney,McGuire(2),Hall g:Sinfield(4)	5th	17,200
9/7/10	Hull KR (a)	L25-6	t:Hall g:Sinfield	5th	8,406
16/7/10	Huddersfield (h)	W21-20	t:Clarkson,Hall,McGuire g:Sinfield(4) fg:Sinfield	5th	15,070
25/7/10	Salford (h)	W22-31	t:Kirke,Hall(2),Sinfield,Donald g:Sinfield(5) fg:Sinfield	4th	4,651
30/7/10	Wigan (h)	L12-26	t:Clarkson,Senior g:Sinfield(2)	5th	16,622
7/8/10	St Helens (CCSF) ●●●●	W32-28	t:Hall(2),McGuire(2),Webb g:Sinfield(6)	N/A	15,267
13/8/10	Castleford (a)	W6-38	t:Clarkson,McGuire,Burrow,Lauitiiti,Hall(2),Donald g:Smith(5)	5th	7,901
20/8/10	Catalans (h)	W52-6	t:McGuire(3),Hall(3),Burrow,Smith,Delaney g:Sinfield(8)	4th	15,154
28/8/10	Warrington (CCF) ●●●●●	L6-30	t:Smith g:Sinfield	N/A	85,217
4/9/10	Hull (a)	W14-18	t:Donald,McGuire(2) g:Sinfield(3)	4th	16,208
12/9/10	Wigan (a) (QPO)	W26-27	t:Buderus,Hall,McGuire,Donald g:Sinfield(5) fg:Sinfield	N/A	12,117
25/9/10	Wigan (h) (QSF)	L6-26	t:Sinfield g:Sinfield	N/A	13,692

● Played at Elland Road, Leeds
●● Played at Stade Aime Giral
●●● Played at Murrayfield, Edinburgh
●●●● Played at Galpharm Stadium, Huddersfield
●●●●● Played at Wembley Stadium

		APP		TRIES		GOALS		FG		PTS	
	D.O.B.	ALL	SL	ALL	SL	ALL	SL	ALL	SL	ALL	SL
Carl Ablett	19/12/85	17(4)	15(3)	3	2	0	0	0	0	12	8
Luke Ambler	18/12/89	2(8)	1(8)	1	1	0	0	0	0	4	4
Kyle Amor	26/5/87	(3)	(3)	0	0	0	0	0	0	0	0
Ryan Bailey	11/11/83	23(6)	19(5)	0	0	0	0	0	0	0	0
Danny Buderus	6/2/78	24(7)	20(5)	6	6	0	0	0	0	24	24
Luke Burgess	20/2/87	2(16)	1(14)	0	0	0	0	0	0	0	0
Rob Burrow	26/9/82	21(3)	17(3)	5	5	15	13	0	0	50	46
Tom Bush	25/1/90	3(1)	3(1)	1	1	0	0	0	0	4	4
Chris Clarkson	7/4/90	15(4)	12(3)	5	5	0	0	0	0	20	20
Michael Coady	15/4/87	2	1	3	0	0	0	0	0	12	0
Brett Delaney	26/10/85	30	24	10	9	0	0	0	0	40	36
Matt Diskin	27/1/82	10(17)	8(14)	0	0	0	0	0	0	0	0
Scott Donald	14/2/80	19	18	10	10	0	0	0	0	40	40
Greg Eastwood	10/3/87	5(17)	5(12)	2	1	0	0	0	0	8	4
Ryan Hall	27/11/87	33	27	31	24	0	0	0	0	124	96
Jamie Jones-Buchanan	1/8/81	29(2)	24(2)	4	4	0	0	0	0	16	16
Ian Kirke	26/12/80	18(13)	15(11)	3	2	0	0	0	0	12	8
Ali Lauitiiti	13/7/79	2(19)	2(17)	8	7	0	0	0	0	32	28
Kylie Leuluai	29/3/78	26(3)	22(1)	0	0	0	0	0	0	0	0
Danny McGuire	6/12/82	32	27	27	24	0	0	0	0	108	96
Paul McShane	19/11/89	2(7)	2(7)	1	1	0	0	0	0	4	4
Jamie Peacock	14/12/77	17(5)	15(2)	0	0	0	0	0	0	0	0
Jay Pitts	9/12/89	6(4)	5(4)	0	0	0	0	0	0	0	0
Keith Senior	24/4/76	33(1)	27(1)	10	10	0	0	0	0	40	40
Kevin Sinfield	12/9/80	29	23	4	4	121	90	4	4	262	200
Lee Smith	8/8/86	23	18	10	8	12	12	0	0	64	56
Kallum Watkins	12/3/91	6	5	1	1	0	0	0	0	4	4
Brent Webb	8/11/80	26	21	14	6	0	0	0	0	56	24

Danny McGuire

LEAGUE RECORD
P27-W17-D1-L9
(4th, SL/Qualifying Semi-Final)
F725, A561, Diff+164
35 points.

CHALLENGE CUP
Runners-Up

ATTENDANCES
Best - v Bradford (SL - 17,244)
Worst - v Blackpool (CC - 5,316)
Total (SL, inc play-offs) - 213,311
Average (SL, inc play-offs) - 15,237
(Down by 75 on 2009)

197

20 November 2009 - Canterbury Bulldogs goalkicking utility player Daniel Holdsworth signed for engage Super League XV.

4 December 2009 - prop Steve Nash joins Leigh.

18 December 2009 - Leeds Rhinos threequarter Jodie Broughton joins on a two-year contract.

17 January 2010 - 50-12 demolition of derby rivals Swinton in pre-season trial match at the Willows.

24 January 2010 - Karl Fitzpatrick sent off in Reds' 36-0 warm-up win over Widnes Vikings but escapes ban.

7 February 2010 - 30-12 round 1 defeat at Hull KR.

12 February 2010 - 36-16 home defeat to Crusaders.

19 February 2010 - 22-10 defeat at Leeds.

23 February 2010 - Stuart Littler avoids suspension after being cited for high tackle.

26 February 2010 - 7-0 home defeat to Bradford.

5 March 2010 - 24-12 defeat to winless Catalans at the Willows.

14 March 2010 - 26-22 round 6 win at Harlequins is first of season.

16 March 2010 - Jeremy Smith gets two-match ban for striking Danny Orr with his forearm during the Reds' 26-22 win over Harlequins.

21 March 2010 - 36-6 hammering at Wakefield.

27 March 2010 - Rob Parker breaks hand in 27-20 home win over Hull FC.

5 April 2010 - shock 30-18 Easter Monday win over Huddersfield at the Willows.

11 April 2010 - leaders Wigan made to work hard for 18-4 win at the Willows.

25 April 2010 - Ray Cashmere sidelined indefinitely after rib injury in 30-12 defeat at Castleford.

1 May 2010 - 68-16 humbling by Warrington at Murrayfield.

15 May 2010 - Matty Smith scores hat-trick as St Helens defeated 42-34 at the Willows.

22 May 2010 - 22-14 triumph over Catalans in Perpignan.

25 May 2010 - Adam Neal signs one month loan deal from Warrington.

1 June 2010 - Adam Neal signs permanent deal to end of 2011.

KEY DATES - SALFORD CITY REDS

1 June 2010 - Daniel Holdsworth signs contract until end 2011.

4 June 2010 - Daniel Holdsworth misses 27-10 home defeat to Warrington with torn calf muscle.

11 June 2010 - 34-12 away defeat by Hull KR.

20 June 2010 - Daniel Holdsworth returns and stars as Reds lose 28-22 at home to Castleford.

29 June 2010 - Ashley Gibson signs new two-year contract.

12 July 2010 - Phil Leuluai joins French champions Lezignan for 2011.

12 July 2010 - on-loan-for-the-season St Helens halfback Matty Smith agrees permanent new two-year contract.

27 July 2010 - Canterbury Bulldogs fullback Luke Patten signs three-year deal from 2011.

30 July 2010 - Daniel Holdsworth out for season after deciding to undergo shoulder surgery.

5 August 2010 - Chris Nero signs from Bradford for three years and Vinnie Anderson for two years from Warrington.

10 August 2010 - Malcolm Alker to stay on in assistant coaching capacity in 2011.

12 August 2010 - Huddersfield loose forward Stephen Wild signs three–year deal from 2011.

13 August 2010 - Wakefield Trinity Wildcats hooker Tevita Leo-Latu signs two-year deal. Jodie Broughton signs new three-year contract.

1 September 2010 - Wigan pair Iafeta Palea'aesina joins on three-year contract and Phil Bailey signs two-year deal.

5 September 2010 - Stuart Littler scores final try in his last game, a 16-12 home win over Wakefield.

6 September 2010 - Sean Gleeson joins from Wakefield on two-year deal.

11 September 2010 - Steve Tyrer leaves for Widnes Vikings.

CLUB RECORDS

Highest score:
100-12 v Gateshead, 23/3/2003
Highest score against:
16-96 v Bradford, 25/6/2000
Record attendance:
26,470 v Warrington, 13/2/37

MATCH RECORDS

Tries:
6 Frank Miles v Lees, 5/3/1898
Ernest Bone v Goole, 29/3/1902
Jack Hilton v Leigh, 7/10/39
Goals:
14 Steve Blakeley v Gateshead, 23/3/2003
Points:
39 Jim Lomas v Liverpool City, 2/2/1907

SEASON RECORDS

Tries: 46 Keith Fielding 1973-74
Goals: 221 David Watkins 1972-73
Points: 493 David Watkins 1972-73

CAREER RECORDS

Tries: 297 Maurice Richards 1969-83
Goals: 1,241 David Watkins 1967-79
Points: 2,907 David Watkins 1967-79
Appearances:
498 Maurice Richards 1969-83

SALFORD CITY REDS

DATE	FIXTURE	RESULT	SCORERS	LGE	ATT
7/2/10	Hull KR (a)	L30-12	t:M Smith,Broughton g:Ratchford(2)	11th	9,123
12/2/10	Crusaders (h)	L16-36	t:Holdsworth,M Smith,Fitzpatrick g:Ratchford(2)	13th	3,421
19/2/10	Leeds (a)	L22-10	t:Gibson,Talau g:Ratchford	13th	12,700
26/2/10	Bradford (h)	L0-7		13th	3,806
5/3/10	Catalans (h)	L12-24	t:Talau,Gibson g:Ratchford(2)	14th	3,022
14/3/10	Harlequins (a)	W22-26	t:Fitzpatrick,Tyrer(3),Broughton g:Holdsworth(3)	12th	2,395
21/3/10	Wakefield (a)	L36-6	t:Littler g:Ratchford	12th	4,883
27/3/10	Hull (h)	W27-20	t:Sidlow,Fitzpatrick(2),Broughton(2) g:Holdsworth(3) fg:Holdsworth	12th	3,535
2/4/10	Warrington (a)	L32-2	g:Holdsworth	12th	11,467
5/4/10	Huddersfield (h)	W30-18	t:Sidlow,Gibson,Holdsworth,Tyrer g:Holdsworth(7)	12th	4,014
11/4/10	Wigan (h)	L4-18	t:Gibson	12th	6,618
18/4/10	Catalans (a) (CCR4)	L30-8	t:Broughton(2)	N/A	5,238
25/4/10	Castleford (a)	L30-12	t:Gibson,Henry g:Holdsworth(2)	12th	5,025
1/5/10	Warrington (MM) ●	L16-68	t:Ratchford(2),M Smith g:Holdsworth(2)	13th	N/A
15/5/10	St Helens (h)	W42-34	t:M Smith(3),Holdsworth,Gibson(2),Broughton,Boyle g:Holdsworth(5)	13th	5,685
22/5/10	Catalans (a)	W14-24	t:Littler,Fitzpatrick,Leuluai g:Holdsworth(5)	12th	5,115
4/6/10	Warrington (h)	L10-27	t:Henry,Broughton g:Tyrer	13th	6,093
11/6/10	Hull (a)	L34-12	t:Fitzpatrick,Sidlow g:M Smith(2)	13th	11,397
20/6/10	Castleford (h)	L22-28	t:Fitzpatrick,Littler,Broughton,Sibbit g:Holdsworth(3)	12th	3,130
25/6/10	St Helens (a)	L58-34	t:Boyle,Sidlow(2),Henry,Gibson,Holdsworth g:Holdsworth(5)	12th	7,728
2/7/10	Harlequins (h)	W17-14	t:Swain,M Smith g:Holdsworth(4) fg:M Smith	12th	2,672
9/7/10	Wigan (a)	L60-10	t:Holdsworth,Broughton g:Holdsworth	13th	12,221
18/7/10	Bradford (a)	W26-30	t:Broughton(2),Tyrer,Littler,Fitzpatrick g:Holdsworth(5)	12th	6,382
25/7/10	Leeds (h)	L22-31	t:Broughton,Gibson(2),Cashmere g:Tyrer(3)	12th	4,651
1/8/10	Crusaders (a)	L60-16	t:Ratchford,Cashmere,Fitzpatrick g:M Smith(2)	12th	2,412
15/8/10	Hull KR (h)	L18-44	t:Parker,Cashmere,M Smith g:Tyrer(3)	13th	4,111
22/8/10	Huddersfield (a)	L52-4	t:Broughton	13th	6,697
5/9/10	Wakefield (h)	W16-12	t:Tyrer,Cashmere,Littler g:Tyrer(2)	12th	3,401

● Played at Murrayfield, Edinburgh

	D.O.B.	APP ALL	SL	TRIES ALL	SL	GOALS ALL	SL	FG ALL	SL	PTS ALL	SL
Luke Adamson	17/11/87	13(7)	12(7)	0	0	0	0	0	0	0	0
Toby Adamson	28/5/90	(1)	(1)	0	0	0	0	0	0	0	0
Malcolm Alker	4/11/78	25	24	0	0	0	0	0	0	0	0
Ryan Boyle	17/10/87	21(2)	20(2)	2	2	0	0	0	0	8	8
Jodie Broughton	9/1/88	24	23	14	12	0	0	0	0	56	48
Ray Cashmere	12/1/80	14(1)	13(1)	4	4	0	0	0	0	16	16
Karl Fitzpatrick	13/9/80	25	24	9	9	0	0	0	0	36	36
Ashley Gibson	25/9/86	26(2)	25(2)	10	10	0	0	0	0	40	40
Mark Henry	19/4/81	21	20	3	3	0	0	0	0	12	12
Daniel Holdsworth	27/4/84	20	19	5	5	46	46	1	1	113	113
Lee Jewitt	14/2/87	5(8)	5(7)	0	0	0	0	0	0	0	0
Phil Leuluai	16/7/77	3(19)	3(19)	1	1	0	0	0	0	4	4
Stuart Littler	19/2/79	17(9)	17(8)	5	5	0	0	0	0	20	20
Dean McGilvray	24/4/88	2	2	0	0	0	0	0	0	0	0
Adam Neal	21/5/90	4(2)	4(2)	0	0	0	0	0	0	0	0
Gareth Owen	3/7/92	(3)	(3)	0	0	0	0	0	0	0	0
Rob Parker	5/9/81	7(11)	7(11)	1	1	0	0	0	0	4	4
Stefan Ratchford	19/7/88	14(4)	13(4)	3	3	8	8	0	0	28	28
Ian Sibbit	15/10/80	17(4)	17(3)	1	1	0	0	0	0	4	4
Adam Sidlow	25/10/87	10(15)	9(15)	5	5	0	0	0	0	20	20
Jeremy Smith	18/7/81	4(16)	4(16)	0	0	0	0	0	0	0	0
Matty Smith	23/7/87	22(4)	22(3)	8	8	4	4	1	1	41	41
Marc Sneyd	9/2/91	4(2)	4(2)	0	0	0	0	0	0	0	0
Jack Spencer	21/12/90	(2)	(2)	0	0	0	0	0	0	0	0
Luke Swain	24/2/82	28	27	1	1	0	0	0	0	4	4
Willie Talau	25/1/76	18	17	2	2	0	0	0	0	8	8
Steve Tyrer	16/3/89	20	20	6	6	9	9	0	0	42	42

Daniel Holdsworth

LEAGUE RECORD
P27-W8-D0-L19
(12th, SL)
F448, A857, Diff-409
16 points.

CHALLENGE CUP
Round Four

ATTENDANCES
Best - v Wigan (SL - 6,618)
Worst - v Harlequins (SL - 2,672)
Total (SL only) - 54,159
Average (SL only) - 4,166
(Down by 224 on 2009)

2 December 2009 - Kyle Eastmond signs new two-year contract.

2 December 2009 - Chris Dean to be dual registered with Widnes Vikings for 2010.

15 December 2009 - Saints announce 2010 will be final season at Knowsley Road.

27 December 2009 - ice and snow lead to postponement of home friendly with Wigan.

17 January 2010 - Mike Bennett Testimonial game against Barrow called off because of snow.

19 January 2010 - Sia Soliola makes try-scoring debut in 42-26 pre-season friendly win at Widnes.

22 January 2010 - 38-18 victory over Halifax in Mike Bennett's re-arranged testimonial match at Knowsley Road.

6 February 2010 - Sean Long stars for Hull FC in 32-12 round 1 win at fogbound Knowsley Road. Ade Gardner suffers rib injury and Sia Soliola an ankle problem.

14 February 2010 - Paul Wellens scores four tries in 38-6 round 2 win at Bradford Bulls.

26 February 2010 - Keiron Cunningham scores trademark try in 500th career appearance, a 22-16 home comeback win over Wakefield.

12 March 2010 - Ade Gardner, Jon Wilkin and Chris Flannery return from injury in 37-30 home win over Crusaders.

19 March 2010 - Paul Wellens tears quad in 28-18 home win over Warrington Wolves.

24 March 2010 - Sia Soliola out until September after rupturing knee ligament in training days after making only his second Saints appearance at Warrington.

28 March 2010 - Francis Meli gets two tries in 24-6 win at Huddersfield.

2 April 2010 - 18-10 home defeat by Wigan.

5 April 2010 - 52-18 win at Castleford.

24 April 2010 - Paul Wellens returns from injury in 41-20 home win over Leeds Rhinos.

2 May 2010 - 54-0 thrashing of Hull KR at Murrayfield.

4 May 2010 - head coach Mick Potter confirms he will leave at season's end.

9 May 2010 - 30-10 win at Harlequins in fifth round of Challenge Cup.

15 May 2010 - 42-34 away defeat to Salford City Reds.

21 May 2010 - Ade Gardner scores four tries in 68-12 romp over Hull KR.

KEY DATES - ST HELENS

29 May 2010 - Kyle Eastmond suffers ankle ligament damage in 32-12 Challenge Cup home quarter-final defeat of Barrow.

4 June 2010 - 26-6 lead ends in 27-26 defeat by Hull at KC Stadium.

11 June 2010 - Paul Johnson makes debut in 30-22 home triumph over Huddersfield.

15 June 2010 - Australian international Josh Perry signs three-year contract from 2011 season.

20 June 2010 - 26-24 derby win at Wigan.

3 July 2010 - Kyle Eastmond goes off with ankle injury and Leon Pryce a back problem in 28-24 defeat at Leeds.

12 July 2010 - halfback Matty Smith joins loan club Salford on permanent deal for 2011.

16 July 2010 - Mick Potter confirmed as new Bradford Bulls head coach for 2011.

16 July 2010 - Maurie Fa'asavalu returns to rugby union with Harlequins.

18 July 2010 - Saints to play their home matches at Widnes in 2011 while new ground is being built.

22 July 2010 - Wests Tigers assistant Royce Simmons to succeed head coach Mick Potter on two-year contract.

3 August 2010 - England international centre Michael Shenton signs from Castleford on three-year contract.

7 August 2010 - 32-28 Challenge Cup semi-final defeat by Leeds.

31 August 2010 - assistant coach Kieron Purtill signs new two-year contract.

3 September 2010 - Bryn Hargreaves signs for Bradford.

3 September 2010 - Louie McCarthy-Scarsbrook signs from Harlequins on four-year contract from 2011.

4 September 2010 - last-second Keiron Cunningham try secures second spot in 40-30 home win over Castleford.

6 September 2010 - Leon Pryce ruled out of play-offs for neck surgery.

8 September 2010 - Matty Smith recalled from loan at Salford for play-off clash with Warrington.

10 September 2010 - 28-12 home Qualifying Play-off win over Warrington.

16 September 2010 - props Nick Fozzard and Jacob Emmitt join Castleford.

19 September 2010 - Saints choose Huddersfield over Wigan as Qualifying Semi-final opponents.

24 September 2010 - Kyle Eastmond damages ankle in 42-22 home win over Huddersfield in Qualifying Semi-final.

27 September 2010 - Kyle Eastmond ruled out of Super League Grand Final.

2 October 2010 - 22-10 defeat by Wigan in Grand Final as Saints finish runners-up for fourth consecutive year.

5 October 2010 - Jonny Lomax signs three-year deal; Paul Clough and Jamie Foster two-year contracts.

8 October 2010 - prop Paul Johnson moves to Wakefield.

23 October 2010 - Michael Shenton suffers ankle ligament damage in 24-10 England defeat by New Zealand.

CLUB RECORDS

Highest score:
112-0 v Carlisle, 14/9/86
Highest score against:
6-78 v Warrington, 12 April 1909
Record attendance:
35,695 v Wigan, 26/12/49

MATCH RECORDS

Tries: 6 Alf Ellaby v Barrow, 5/3/32
Steve Llewellyn v Castleford, 3/3/56
Steve Llewellyn v Liverpool, 20/8/56
Tom van Vollenhoven v Wakefield, 21/12/57
Tom van Vollenhoven v Blackpool, 23/4/62
Frank Myler v Maryport, 1/9/69
Shane Cooper v Hull, 17/2/88
Goals: 16 Paul Loughlin v Carlisle, 14/9/86
Points:
40 Paul Loughlin v Carlisle, 14/9/86

SEASON RECORDS

Tries 62 Tom van Vollenhoven 1958-59
Goals: 214 Kel Coslett 1971-72
Points: 452 Kel Coslett 1971-72

CAREER RECORDS

Tries: 392 Tom van Vollenhoven 1957-68
Goals: 1,639 Kel Coslett 1962-76
Points: 3,413 Kel Coslett 1962-76
Appearances: 531 Kel Coslett 1962-76

ST HELENS

DATE	FIXTURE	RESULT	SCORERS	LGE	ATT
6/2/10	Hull (h)	L12-32	t:Gidley,Flannery g:Eastmond(2)	12th	12,142
14/2/10	Bradford (a)	W6-38	t:Wilkin,Wellens(4),Eastmond g:Eastmond(7)	5th	10,165
20/2/10	Catalans (a)	W12-42	t:Lomax(2),Meli(2),Gidley(2),Fa'asavalu,Eastmond g:Eastmond(5)	4th	7,825
26/2/10	Wakefield (h)	W22-16	t:Lomax,Eastmond,Cunningham,Meli g:Eastmond(3)	4th	10,717
7/3/10	Hull KR (a)	L28-24	t:Wheeler,Eastmond,Moore,Meli,Dean g:Eastmond(2)	6th	8,202
12/3/10	Crusaders (h)	W37-30	t:Roby,Eastmond,Meli,Dean,Moore,Pryce g:Eastmond(6) fg:Eastmond	4th	8,507
19/3/10	Warrington (h)	W28-18	t:Eastmond,Wilkin,Gardner(2) g:Eastmond(6)	4th	17,500
28/3/10	Huddersfield (a)	W6-24	t:Meli(2),Graham,Eastmond g:Eastmond(4)	3rd	9,648
2/4/10	Wigan (h)	L10-18	t:Gardner,Puletua g:Eastmond	4th	17,500
5/4/10	Castleford (a)	W18-52	t:Eastmond(2),Meli(2),Fa'asavalu,Roby(2),Puletua,Pryce g:Eastmond(8)	3rd	6,879
10/4/10	Harlequins (a)	W24-32	t:Dixon(2),Eastmond,Roby(2) g:Eastmond(6)	3rd	5,220
17/4/10	Toulouse (h) (CCR4)	W56-16	t:Dean,Flannery(2),Wheeler(2),Fa'asavalu(2),Gardner,Dixon,Puletua g:Foster(8)	N/A	4,043
24/4/10	Leeds (h)	W41-20	t:Moore,Puletua,Roby(2),Flannery,Ashurst g:Foster(8) fg:Eastmond	3rd	11,048
2/5/10	Hull KR (MM) ●	W0-54	t:Wellens,Eastmond,Armstrong,Clough,Flannery,Roby,Graham,Ashurst,Foster,Gardner(2) g:Eastmond(3),Foster(2)	3rd	N/A
9/5/10	Harlequins (a) (CCR5)	W10-30	t:Cunningham,Gardner,Meli(2),Pryce g:Eastmond(5)	N/A	3,381
15/5/10	Salford (a)	L42-34	t:Graham(2),Eastmond,Wellens,Gardner,Moore g:Eastmond(5)	3rd	5,685
21/5/10	Hull KR (h)	W68-12	t:Gardner(4),Puletua,Flannery,Emmitt,Moore,Eastmond,Gidley,Lomax,Roby,Dixon g:Eastmond(5),Lomax(3)	3rd	9,375
29/5/10	Barrow (h) (CCQF)	W32-12	t:Clough(2),Lomax(2),Roby,Gidley g:Eastmond,Lomax(3)	N/A	4,972
4/6/10	Hull (a)	L27-26	t:Meli(4),Cunningham g:Lomax(3)	3rd	13,300
11/6/10	Huddersfield (h)	W30-22	t:Gidley,Wheeler,Puletua,Fozzard,Dixon g:Foster(5)	3rd	9,034
20/6/10	Wigan (a)	W24-26	t:Pryce,Meli,Roby,Wellens,Foster g:Foster(3)	3rd	20,498
25/6/10	Salford (h)	W58-34	t:Gardner,Puletua,Wellens(4),Pryce(2),Flannery,Ashurst g:Lomax(9)	3rd	7,728
3/7/10	Leeds (a)	L28-24	t:Flannery(2),Lomax,Pryce g:Lomax(4)	3rd	17,200
9/7/10	Catalans (h)	L20-30	t:Wellens,Meli(2),Gaskell g:Lomax(2)	3rd	8,432
18/7/10	Harlequins (h)	W32-18	t:Magennis,Meli(2),Wellens(2),Dean g:Lomax(4)	3rd	10,399
25/7/10	Wakefield (a)	W6-50	t:Pryce,Gardner,Puletua(2),Wilkin(2),Magennis(2),Meli g:Foster(7)	3rd	5,217
31/7/10	Warrington (a)	W24-26	t:Ashurst,Foster(2),Meli,Roby g:Foster(3)	3rd	12,863
7/8/10	Leeds (CCSF) ●●	L32-28	t:Wellens,Cunningham,Meli,Gidley,Graham g:Foster(4)	N/A	15,267
13/8/10	Bradford (h)	W60-12	t:Gardner,Moore,Wilkin(2),Foster(2),Roby,Eastmond,Lomax,Ashurst,Puletua g:Foster(8)	3rd	9,032
21/8/10	Crusaders (a)	W10-36	t:Eastmond,Wellens,Gardner,Foster,Roby,Lomax,Puletua g:Foster(4)	2nd	5,436
4/9/10	Castleford (a)	W40-30	t:Wellens,Graham,Flannery,Meli,Puletua,Gidley,Cunningham g:Foster(6)	2nd	13,978
10/9/10	Warrington (h) (QPO)	W28-10	t:Wellens,Cunningham,Graham,Flannery g:Foster(6)	N/A	14,632
24/9/10	Huddersfield (h) (QSF)	W42-22	t:Hargreaves(2),Wellens(2),Puletua,Meli,Cunningham g:Foster(7)	N/A	13,510
2/10/10	Wigan (GF) ●●●	L10-22	t:Dixon,Meli g:Foster	N/A	71,526

● Played at Murrayfield, Edinburgh
●● Played at Galpharm Stadium, Huddersfield
●●● Played at Old Trafford, Manchester

			APP		TRIES		GOALS		FG		PTS	
	D.O.B.		ALL	SL	ALL	SL	ALL	SL	ALL	SL	ALL	SL
Tom Armstrong	12/9/89		1	1	1	1	0	0	0	0	4	4
Matty Ashurst	1/11/89		6(18)	4(16)	5	5	0	0	0	0	20	20
Paul Clough	27/9/87		21(10)	18(9)	3	1	0	0	0	0	12	4
Keiron Cunningham	28/10/76		20(8)	17(7)	7	5	0	0	0	0	28	20
Chris Dean	17/1/88		10(1)	9(1)	4	3	0	0	0	0	16	12
Andrew Dixon	28/2/90		9(10)	8(8)	6	5	0	0	0	0	24	20
Kyle Eastmond	17/7/89		23	20	15	15	69	63	2	2	200	188
Jacob Emmitt	4/10/88		(13)	(11)	1	1	0	0	0	0	4	4
Maurie Fa'asavalu	12/1/80		(13)	(12)	4	2	0	0	0	0	16	8
Chris Flannery	5/6/80		28	24	11	9	0	0	0	0	44	36
Jamie Foster	27/7/90		16	14	7	7	72	60	0	0	172	148
Nick Fozzard	22/7/77		9(10)	8(8)	1	1	0	0	0	0	4	4
Ade Gardner	24/6/83		22(1)	19(1)	16	14	0	0	0	0	64	56
Lee Gaskell	28/10/90		1(2)	1(2)	1	1	0	0	0	0	4	4
Matt Gidley	1/7/77		27	24	8	6	0	0	0	0	32	24
James Graham	10/9/85		31(1)	28(1)	7	6	0	0	0	0	28	24
Bryn Hargreaves	14/11/85		21(12)	17(12)	2	2	0	0	0	0	8	8
Paul Johnson	13/3/88		(2)	(2)	0	0	0	0	0	0	0	0
Jonny Lomax	4/9/90		16	15	9	7	28	25	0	0	92	78
Shaun Magennis	2/12/89		4(1)	3(1)	3	3	0	0	0	0	12	12
Francis Meli	20/8/80		25	23	26	23	0	0	0	0	104	92
Scott Moore	23/1/88		20(9)	17(8)	6	6	0	0	0	0	24	24
Leon Pryce	9/10/81		25	22	8	7	0	0	0	0	32	28
Tony Puletua	25/6/79		23(8)	21(6)	13	12	0	0	0	0	52	48
James Roby	22/11/85		18(15)	16(13)	14	13	0	0	0	0	56	52
Matty Smith	23/7/87		3	3	0	0	0	0	0	0	0	0
Iosia Soliola	4/8/86		5(1)	5(1)	0	0	0	0	0	0	0	0
Paul Wellens	27/2/80		26	24	20	19	0	0	0	0	80	76
Gary Wheeler	30/9/89		12(1)	10(1)	4	2	0	0	0	0	16	8
Jon Wilkin	11/1/83		20	19	6	6	0	0	0	0	24	24

Keiron Cunningham

LEAGUE RECORD
P27-W20-D0-L7
(2nd, SL/Grand Final Runners-Up)
F946, A547, Diff+399
40 points.

CHALLENGE CUP
Semi-Finalists

ATTENDANCES
Best - v Warrington/Wigan
(SL - 17,500)
Worst - v Toulouse (CC - 4,043)
Total (SL, inc play-offs) - 173,534
Average (SL, inc play-offs) - 11,569
(Up by 542 on 2009)

19 November 2009 - NZ-born prop James Stosic given until end of month to acquire Macedonian passport or be released.

23 November 2009 - coach John Kear issues statement playing down links with England coaching vacancy.

30 November 2009 - James Stosic released.

7 December 2009 - released Hull FC prop Paul King signs on 12-month contract.

14 December 2009 - Paul Johnson, released by Warrington Wolves, signs 12-month contract.

26 December 2009 - Damien Blanch breaks hand in 32-12 Boxing Day defeat by Leeds at snowy Headingley.

10 January 2010 - friendly at Featherstone is postponed due to snow.

17 January 2010 - three tries in final nine minutes snatch Wigan a 40-38 friendly victory at Belle Vue.

27 January 2010 - Wildcats avoid winding-up order by paying off outstanding tax bill.

2 February 2010 - Richard Moore suspended for one match after fight with Louie McCarthy-Scarsbrook during opening (round 3) game, 18-10 win at Harlequins.

7 February 2010 - Paul Johnson suffers head injury minutes after coming off bench for debut in 28-20 home win over Catalans. Remi Casty gets one-match ban.

14 February 2010 - Danny Brough inspires 28-18 home win over Leeds Rhinos.

19 February 2010 - hooker Terry Newton admits taking human growth hormone - the first sportsman to be caught.

22 February 2010 - Terry Newton's contract is cancelled with immediate effect.

26 February 2010 - 22-16 defeat at St Helens is first of season.

3 March 2010 - prop Kyle Bibb goes to Harlequins on month's loan.

6 March 2010 - Damien Blanch plays first game of season in 52-0 hammering by Huddersfield in televised Belle Vue clash.

9 March 2010 - former Castleford prop Ben Gledhill signs on two-year contract.

12 March 2010 - Shane Tronc scores twice in 31-18 win at Hull KR.

19 March 2010 - Hull KR stand-off Paul Cooke joins on contract to end of season.

21 March 2010 - Paul Cooke debuts in 36-6 home defeat of Salford.

24 March 2010 - Danny Brough signed by Huddersfield, with Danny Kirmond coming to Belle Vue on loan.

26 March 2010 - Danny Kirmond makes debut in 32-16 defeat at Warrington.

1 April 2010 - 20-year-old Bradford utility back Kieran Hyde signs two-and-a-half-year contract, with halfback Cain Southernwood moving the other way.

2 April 2010 - Ben Jeffries back for first game since leg injury in round 5 in 19-6 win over Castleford in Good Friday derby.

KEY DATES - WAKEFIELD T WILDCATS

5 April 2010 - Paul King makes debut in 54-14 Easter Monday hiding at Wigan.

11 April 2010 - Glenn Morrison breaks thumb in 20-10 home defeat to Crusaders.

16 April 2010 - Shane Tronc released six months into two-year contract for family reasons and joins Brisbane Broncos.

17 April 2010 - 23-16 Challenge Cup round four exit at Harlequins.

23 April 2010 - Darryl Millard damages knee ligaments in 12-8 defeat at Hull FC.

1 May 2010 - Danny Buderus try three minutes from time steals 34-30 win for Leeds at Murrayfield.

6 May 2010 - 18-year-old Wath Brow centre Karl Olstrum signs full-time contract.

14 May 2010 - 29-10 home defeat by Bradford signals sixth straight defeat.

20 May 2010 - Samoan prop forward Charlie Leaeno signs performance-based contract until end of 2011 season.

23 May 2010 - Ben Jeffries returns in 54-12 demolition of Harlequins at Belle Vue.

4 June 2010 - late Glenn Morrison sin-binning in late 28-22 defeat at Leeds.

6 June 2010 - John Kear linked with Catalans coaching role.

10 June 2010 - Glenn Morrison extends contract until end of 2011 season.

11 June 2010 - Kyle Bibb joins Whitehaven on month's loan.

13 June 2010 - 48-6 hammering by Wigan at Belle Vue.

14 June 2010 - captain Jason Demetriou told his contract will not be renewed at end of season.

17 June 2010 - one-month loan deal agreed with Villeneuve for French hooker Julian Rinaldi.

19 June 2010 - 22-10 second-half lead conceded in 30-23 loss away at Dragons.

23 June 2010 - talks break down over compensation payment from Dragons, keeping John Kear at Wakefield.

27 June 2010 - Darryl Millard returns in 41-0 thrashing of Crusaders in delayed-by-traffic kick-off in Wrexham.

9 July 2010 - Julien Rinaldi signs deal to end of season.

22 July 2010 - Luke George (shoulder), Dale Morton (knee) both out for season.

25 July 2010 - Wildcats rule out ground-share with Castleford Tigers at Glasshoughton.

13 August 2010 - Tevita Leo-Latu signs for Salford for 2011.

31 August 2010 - Danny Kirmond recalled early from loan spell by Huddersfield.

3 September 2010 - chairman Ted Richardson offers to hand over control of club in a bid to attract new investment.

5 September 2010 - 16-12 last-round defeat at Salford means 11th-placed finish.

6 September 2010 - Sean Gleeson signs for Salford.

9 September 2010 - Paul Cooke released at the end of short-term contract.

10 September 2010 - HM Revenue serve winding-up order on club.

13 September 2010 - Damien Blanch signs for Catalans Dragons.

19 September 2010 - Julien Rinaldi signs contract for 2011.

22 September 2010 - Jeremy Smith joins from Salford and Frankie Mariano from Hull KR on 12-month contracts.

23 September 2010 - PNG centre Jessie Joe Parker signs two-year contract.

24 September 2010 - Warrington winger Kevin Penny joins on two-year deal.

25 September 2010 - Tommy Lee joins from Crusaders on two-year contract.

26 September 2010 - former player, Great Britain international Terry Newton found dead at his home near Wigan.

8 October 2010 - St Helens reserve prop Paul Johnson joins on a two-year deal.

22 October 2010 - outline planning permission granted for new stadium.

25 October 2010 - former RFL chairman Sir Rodney Walker donates £164,000 to clear HMRC debt.

28 October 2010 - Motu Tony signs for 2011.

CLUB RECORDS

Highest score:
90-12 v Highfield, 27/10/92
Highest score against:
0-86 v Castleford, 17/4/95
Record attendance:
30,676 v Huddersfield, 26/2/21

MATCH RECORDS

Tries:
7 Fred Smith v Keighley, 25/4/59
Keith Slater v Hunslet, 6/2/71
Goals:
13 Mark Conway v Highfield, 27/10/92
Points:
36 Jamie Rooney v Chorley, 27/2/2004

SEASON RECORDS

Tries: 38 Fred Smith 1959-60
David Smith 1973-74
Goals: 163 Neil Fox 1961-62
Points: 407 Neil Fox 1961-62

CAREER RECORDS

Tries: 272 by Neil Fox 1956-69; 1970-74
Goals: 1,836 by Neil Fox 1956-69; 1970-74
Points: 4,488 by Neil Fox 1956-69; 1970-74
Appearances:
605 Harry Wilkinson 1930-49

WAKEFIELD T WILDCATS

DATE	FIXTURE	RESULT	SCORERS	LGE	ATT
30/1/10	Harlequins (a)	W10-18	t:Millard,Jeffries,Murphy g:Brough(3)	N/A	3,688
7/2/10	Catalans (h)	W28-20	t:Ferguson,George,Morton(2),Morrison g:Brough(4)	1st	5,818
14/2/10	Leeds (h)	W28-18	t:Gleeson,Jeffries,Brough,Millard g:Brough(6)	1st	9,783
26/2/10	St Helens (a)	L22-16	t:Morton,Millard(2) g:Brough(2)	5th	10,717
6/3/10	Huddersfield (h)	L0-52		9th	5,237
12/3/10	Hull KR (a)	W18-31	t:Tronc(2),Obst,Blaymire,Millard g:Obst(2),Brough(3) fg:Blaymire	6th	8,004
21/3/10	Salford (h)	W36-6	t:Millard,Leo-Latu,Morrison,Ferguson,Murphy,Obst,Blanch g:Obst(4)	6th	4,883
26/3/10	Warrington (a)	L32-16	t:Murphy,Korkidas,Obst g:Cooke(2)	6th	10,723
2/4/10	Castleford (h)	W19-6	t:Obst,Morton,Leo-Latu g:Cooke(3) fg:Cooke	6th	8,337
5/4/10	Wigan (a)	L54-14	t:Blanch,Blaymire(2) g:Cooke	6th	14,615
11/4/10	Crusaders (h)	L10-20	t:Blanch,George g:Cooke	8th	4,671
17/4/10	Harlequins (a) (CCR4)	L23-16	t:Blanch,Kirmond,George g:Cooke(2)	N/A	2,355
23/4/10	Hull (a)	L12-8	t:Millard,Blanch	8th	11,160
1/5/10	Leeds (MM) ●	L34-30	t:Jeffries,Blanch(2),Johnson,Leo-Latu g:Jeffries(5)	8th	N/A
14/5/10	Bradford (h)	L10-29	t:Murphy,Johnson g:Cooke	9th	5,381
23/5/10	Harlequins (h)	W54-12	t:George(2),Gleeson(2),Obst(2),Henderson,Blanch,Demetriou,Cooke g:Cooke(7)	8th	4,371
4/6/10	Leeds (a)	L28-22	t:Morrison,Obst,Murphy,Demetriou g:Cooke(3)	9th	13,869
13/6/10	Wigan (h)	L6-48	t:Blanch g:Cooke	9th	6,947
19/6/10	Catalans (a)	L30-23	t:Blanch,Cooke,Blaymire,Rinaldi g:Cooke(3) fg:King	9th	5,055
27/6/10	Crusaders (a)	W0-41	t:Jeffries,Millard,Demetriou,Leaeno,Johnson,Blanch(2) g:Cooke(6) fg:Jeffries	9th	2,837
4/7/10	Hull KR (h)	L14-46	t:Millard,Moore,Johnson g:Cooke	10th	6,218
10/7/10	Hull (h)	W29-6	t:Cooke,Rinaldi,Leaeno,Millard,Demetriou g:Cooke(4) fg:Jeffries	8th	5,366
18/7/10	Castleford (a)	L40-16	t:Morrison(2),Blaymire g:Cooke(2)	9th	8,517
25/7/10	St Helens (h)	L6-50	t:Hyde g:Cooke	9th	5,217
1/8/10	Huddersfield (a)	L58-6	t:Gleeson g:Jeffries	10th	6,055
15/8/10	Warrington (h)	L18-36	t:Blanch,Jeffries,Morrison,Leo-Latu g:Jeffries	10th	5,562
22/8/10	Bradford (a)	L38-28	t:Kirmond,Millard,Obst,Morrison,Gleeson g:Jeffries(4)	11th	7,437
5/9/10	Salford (a)	L16-12	t:Leo-Latu,Gleeson g:Jeffries(2)	11th	3,401

● Played at Murrayfield, Edinburgh

		APP		TRIES		GOALS		FG		PTS	
	D.O.B.	ALL	SL	ALL	SL	ALL	SL	ALL	SL	ALL	SL
Kyle Bibb	25/1/88	(2)	(2)	0	0	0	0	0	0	0	0
Damien Blanch	24/5/83	21(1)	20(1)	13	12	0	0	0	0	52	48
Matt Blaymire	10/6/82	16(2)	16(2)	5	5	0	0	1	1	21	21
Danny Brough	15/1/83	6	6	1	1	18	18	0	0	40	40
Paul Cooke	17/4/81	17(1)	16(1)	3	3	38	36	1	1	89	85
James Davey	21/8/89	1(6)	(6)	0	0	0	0	0	0	0	0
Jason Demetriou	13/1/76	26(1)	25(1)	4	4	0	0	0	0	16	16
Dale Ferguson	13/4/88	12(5)	11(5)	2	2	0	0	0	0	8	8
Luke George	30/10/87	12	11	5	4	0	0	0	0	20	16
Ben Gledhill	18/9/89	(8)	(7)	0	0	0	0	0	0	0	0
Sean Gleeson	29/11/87	19(1)	18(1)	6	6	0	0	0	0	24	24
Kevin Henderson	1/10/81	6(17)	6(17)	1	1	0	0	0	0	4	4
Kieran Hyde	10/10/89	1	1	1	1	0	0	0	0	4	4
Ben Jeffries	4/9/80	19(3)	18(3)	5	5	13	13	2	2	48	48
Paul Johnson	25/11/78	13(3)	12(3)	4	4	0	0	0	0	16	16
Paul King	28/6/79	10(9)	9(9)	0	0	0	0	1	1	1	1
Danny Kirmond	11/11/85	13(4)	12(4)	2	1	0	0	0	0	8	4
Michael Korkidas	12/1/81	16(12)	16(11)	1	1	0	0	0	0	4	4
Charlie Leaeno	15/2/86	7(3)	7(3)	2	2	0	0	0	0	8	8
Tevita Leo-Latu	3/7/81	19(5)	19(5)	5	5	0	0	0	0	20	20
Darryl Millard	20/2/85	21(1)	21	11	11	0	0	0	0	44	44
Richard Moore	2/2/81	15(12)	14(12)	1	1	0	0	0	0	4	4
Glenn Morrison	28/5/76	22(1)	22(1)	7	7	0	0	0	0	28	28
Dale Morton	31/10/90	11(2)	11(2)	4	4	0	0	0	0	16	16
Aaron Murphy	26/11/88	26	25	5	5	0	0	0	0	20	20
Terry Newton	7/11/78	(2)	(2)	0	0	0	0	0	0	0	0
Sam Obst	26/11/80	20(4)	20(3)	8	8	6	6	0	0	44	44
Julien Rinaldi	27/4/79	6(4)	6(4)	2	2	0	0	0	0	8	8
Shane Tronc	19/1/82	8(3)	8(3)	2	2	0	0	0	0	8	8
Matthew Wildie	25/10/90	1	1	0	0	0	0	0	0	0	0

Damien Blanch

LEAGUE RECORD
P27-W9-D0-L18
(11th, SL)
F539, A741, Diff-202
18 points.

CHALLENGE CUP
Round Four

ATTENDANCES
Best - v Leeds (SL - 9,783)
Worst - v Harlequins (SL - 4,371)
Total (SL only) - 77,791
Average (SL only) - 5,984
(Up by 93 on 2009)

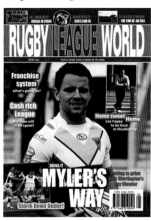

KEY DATES - WARRINGTON WOLVES

20 April 2010 - Simon Grix, Mickey Higham and Rhys Williams agree two-year contract extensions until November 2012; Paul Wood and Lee Briers agree further one-year contracts.

27 April 2010 - reigning Man of Steel Brett Hodgson signs two-year deal from 2011.

6 May 2010 - Kevin Penny loan spell at Harlequins extended on week-by-week basis.

8 May 2010 - Richie Myler suffers knee injury as Chris Bridge scores five tries in round five 60-4 Carnegie Challenge Cup win at Huddersfield.

15 May 2010 - 26-16 defeat by Leeds at Headingley.

23 May 2010 - second position consolidated as Chris Hicks scores brace in 36-20 win over Huddersfield.

27 May 2010 - David Solomona pens one-year contract extension until end of 2011.

30 May 2010 - 26-22 victory over Bradford Bulls in Challenge Cup quarter-final at Odsal.

4 June 2010 - 27-10 win away at Salford is third on the bounce.

11 June 2010 - Lee Briers' 19-point haul ensures 35-16 victory over Hull KR at Halliwell-Jones Stadium.

15 June 2010 - Michael Monaghan signs new two-year contract to end of 2013 season.

17 June 2010 - Richie Mathers confirms departure at end of season after refusing 12-month contract offer.

19 June 2010 - 40-28 defeat of Bradford at Odsal.

27 June 2010 - Chris Bridge suffers shoulder injury in 37-30 home defeat by Leeds.

29 June 2010 - Mike Cooper signs new two–year contract.

14 July 2010 - Chris Hicks signs new one-year contract.

16 July 2010 - 23-16 win at Wigan is first ever game televised in 3D.

22 July 2010 - Tyrone McCarthy and Lee Mitchell, on dual registration at Leigh, sign new one-year contracts.

8 August 2010 - 54-10 rout of Catalans Dragons in Challenge Cup semi-final.

28 August 2010 - Chris Hicks scores hat-trick, Lee Briers wins Lance Todd Trophy as Warrington retain Carnegie Challenge Cup with 30-6 victory over Leeds.

7 January 2010 - Andrew Johns joins Wolves on pre-season warm-weather training camp in Tenerife.

17 January 2010 - Richie Myler scores four tries in 60-16 friendly win at Leigh.

28 January 2010 - 20-12 defeat to Wigan in Paul Wood testimonial match at Halliwell Jones Stadium.

7 February 2010 - Chris Riley scores five tries in 58-0 home, round one thrashing of Harlequins.

11 February 2010 - Matty Blythe, Lee Mitchell and Tyrone McCarthy go to Leigh on dual registration.

13 February 2010 - Lee Briers stars in comeback 28-16 win at Castleford.

16 February 2010 - Garreth Carvell banned for one match for leading with elbow, reduced to fine on appeal.

20 February 2010 - Lee Briers suffers ankle injury in 22-20 home, round three defeat to Wigan.

28 February 2010 - two Matt King tries set up 14-10 win at Huddersfield.

10 March 2010 - prop Mike Cooper goes to Castleford on month's loan.

19 March 2010 - 28-18 defeat at St Helens.

7 April 2010 - Kevin Penny joins Harlequins on month's loan.

9 April 2010 - Vinnie Anderson breaks toe in weight training

11 April 2010 - Garreth Carvell breaks leg in 36-16 defeat at Hull KR.

15 April 2010 - Mike Cooper recalled from loan spell with Castleford.

20 April 2010 - coach Tony Smith agrees two-year contract extension until November 2013.

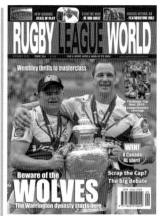

3 September 2010 - 36-22 win at Harlequins leaves Wolves one point short on points difference on second-placed St Helens.

10 September 2010 - 28-12 Qualifying Play-off defeat at St Helens.

18 September 2010 - 34-22 home Preliminary Semi-final defeat by Huddersfield ends season.

3 November 2010 - Matty Blythe signs contract for 2011.

4 November 2010 - Chris Riley signs two-year contract extension to end of 2013.

CLUB RECORDS
Highest score: 84-1 v York, 27/2/2000
Highest score against:
12-84 v Bradford, 9/9/2001
Record attendance:
34,404 v Wigan, 22/1/49 *(Wilderspool)*
14,206 v Wakefield, 21/2/2004
(Halliwell Jones Stadium)

MATCH RECORDS
Tries:
7 Brian Bevan v Leigh, 29/3/48
Brian Bevan v Bramley, 22/4/53
Goals:
14 Harold Palin v Liverpool City, 13/9/50
Lee Briers v York, 27/2/2000
Points:
40 Lee Briers v York, 27/2/2000

SEASON RECORDS
Tries: 66 Brian Bevan 1952-53
Goals: 170 Steve Hesford 1978-79
Points: 363 Harry Bath 1952-53

CAREER RECORDS
Tries: 740 Brian Bevan 1945-62
Goals: 1,159 Steve Hesford 1975-85
Points: 2,416 Steve Hesford 1975-85
Appearances: 620 Brian Bevan 1945-62

WARRINGTON WOLVES

DATE	FIXTURE	RESULT	SCORERS	LGE	ATT
7/2/10	Harlequins (h)	W58-0	t:Carvell,Mathers,Monaghan,Bridge,Riley(5),Myler,Grix g:Briers(7)	2nd	11,678
13/2/10	Castleford (a)	W16-28	t:Grix,Riley,Briers,Myler(2) g:Briers,Bridge(3)	2nd	7,569
20/2/10	Wigan (h)	L20-22	t:Myler,Riley,Solomona,L Anderson g:Briers(2)	3rd	13,024
28/2/10	Huddersfield (a)	W10-14	t:King(2),Hicks g:Myler	2nd	8,567
7/3/10	Crusaders (h)	W46-12	t:King(2),Grix,Westwood(2),Monaghan,Hicks,Solomona g:Bridge(7)	2nd	11,113
13/3/10	Bradford (h)	W33-8	t:Myler,Atkins(2),King(2),Monaghan g:Bridge(4) fg:Monaghan	2nd	10,434
19/3/10	St Helens (a)	L28-18	t:Grix,King,Harrison,Hicks g:Bridge	2nd	17,500
26/3/10	Wakefield (h)	W32-16	t:Riley(3),Bridge,Atkins(2) g:Bridge(2)	2nd	10,723
2/4/10	Salford (h)	W32-2	t:Hicks(2),Atkins,Riley(2),Mathers,Solomona g:Bridge(2)	2nd	11,467
5/4/10	Hull (a)	W10-29	t:Hicks(3),Myler,Monaghan g:Briers(3),Hicks fg:Briers	2nd	14,131
11/4/10	Hull KR (a)	L36-16	t:Mathers,King,Riley g:Westwood(2)	2nd	8,452
18/4/10	Featherstone (h) (CCR4)	W48-24	t:Grix,Riley(2),Myler(3),V Anderson,Solomona(2) g:Westwood(4),Bridge(2)	N/A	7,754
25/4/10	Catalans (h)	W40-6	t:Mathers(2),Briers,Myler,Riley,Cooper,Higham g:Westwood(6)	2nd	9,619
1/5/10	Salford (MM) ●	W16-68	t:Monaghan,Hicks(2),Atkins,Williams,Briers,Riley,V Anderson,Myler(2), Bridge,Solomona g:Westwood(6),Briers,Bridge(3)	2nd	N/A
8/5/10	Huddersfield (a) (CCR5)	W4-60	t:Atkins,Bridge(5),Myler,Hicks(3),Riley,Higham g:Westwood(4),Briers(2)	N/A	6,641
14/5/10	Leeds (a)	L26-16	t:King,Grix,Harrison g:Bridge(2)	2nd	16,733
23/5/10	Huddersfield (h)	W36-20	t:Morley,Bridge,Riley,Hicks(2),King,Wood g:Bridge(4)	2nd	11,087
30/5/10	Bradford (a) (CCQF)	W22-26	t:Briers,Atkins,V Anderson,Hicks(2) g:Bridge(3)	N/A	7,092
4/6/10	Salford (a)	W10-27	t:Hicks,Mathers(2),Higham,Solomona g:Bridge(3) fg:Briers	2nd	6,093
11/6/10	Hull KR (h)	W35-16	t:Briers(2),L Anderson,Atkins,Monaghan,King g:Briers(5) fg:Briers	2nd	9,216
19/6/10	Bradford (a)	W28-40	t:Riley(2),King,Briers,Higham(2),Atkins g:Briers(6)	2nd	8,128
27/6/10	Leeds (h)	L30-37	t:King(2),Hicks(2),Atkins,Riley g:Briers(3)	2nd	10,442
4/7/10	Crusaders (a)	W10-30	t:Hicks(2),Solomona,Higham,Riley(2) g:Briers(2),Westwood	2nd	5,197
11/7/10	Castleford (h)	W54-30	t:Riley,Myler(3),Morley,Atkins,Mathers,Hicks,Solomona g:Westwood(9)	2nd	10,577
16/7/10	Wigan (a)	W16-23	t:Hicks,Myler,Atkins,Westwood g:Westwood(3) fg:Briers	2nd	22,701
24/7/10	Catalans (a) ●●	L29-28	t:Hicks(2),Clarke,V Anderson,Briers g:Westwood(4)	2nd	7,852
31/7/10	St Helens (h)	L24-26	t:Wood,Clarke,Westwood(2) g:Westwood(4)	2nd	12,863
8/8/10	Catalans (CCSF) ●●●	W12-54	t:Harrison,L Anderson(3),King,Riley,Briers,Myler,Clarke g:Westwood(7),Briers,Myler	N/A	12,265
15/8/10	Wakefield (a)	W18-36	t:Hicks,King(3),Riley,Blythe,Briers g:Westwood(3),Briers	2nd	5,562
20/8/10	Hull (h)	W36-18	t:Riley(2),Clarke,Westwood,Morley,Myler g:Westwood(6)	3rd	10,042
28/8/10	Leeds (CCF) ●●●●	W6-30	t:Atkins(2),Hicks(3),L Anderson g:Westwood(3)	N/A	85,217
3/9/10	Harlequins (a)	W22-36	t:Clarke,Solomona(2),Cooper,Bridge(2) g:Bridge(6)	3rd	3,211
10/9/10	St Helens (a) (QPO)	L28-12	t:King(2),Bridge	N/A	14,632
18/9/10	Huddersfield (h) (PSF)	L22-34	t:Higham(2),Hicks(2) g:Westwood(3)	N/A	8,050

● Played at Murrayfield, Edinburgh
●● Played at Stade Aime Giral
●●● Played at Stobart Stadium, Widnes
●●●● Played at Wembley Stadium

		APP		TRIES		GOALS		FG		PTS	
	D.O.B.	ALL	SL	ALL	SL	ALL	SL	ALL	SL	ALL	SL
Louis Anderson	27/6/85	31	27	6	2	0	0	0	0	24	8
Vinnie Anderson	14/2/79	7(16)	7(12)	4	2	0	0	0	0	16	8
Ryan Atkins	7/10/85	34	29	15	11	0	0	0	0	60	44
Matty Blythe	20/11/88	1	1	1	1	0	0	0	0	4	4
Chris Bridge	5/7/84	19(4)	16(4)	12	7	44	39	0	0	136	106
Lee Briers	14/6/78	23	19	10	8	34	31	4	4	112	98
Garreth Carvell	21/4/80	19(4)	17(4)	1	1	0	0	0	0	4	4
Jon Clarke	4/4/79	7(3)	5(3)	5	4	0	0	0	0	20	16
Michael Cooper	15/9/88	1(13)	1(11)	2	2	0	0	0	0	8	8
Rhys Evans	30/10/92	(1)	(1)	0	0	0	0	0	0	0	0
Simon Grix	28/9/85	20(5)	17(5)	6	5	0	0	0	0	24	20
Ben Harrison	24/2/88	29(3)	25(2)	3	2	0	0	0	0	12	8
Chris Hicks	19/3/77	28	24	32	24	1	1	0	0	130	98
Mick Higham	18/9/80	4(22)	3(19)	8	7	0	0	0	0	32	28
Matt King	22/8/80	31	26	20	19	0	0	0	0	80	76
Richard Mathers	24/10/83	29	24	8	8	0	0	0	0	32	32
Tyrone McCarthy	21/4/88	(3)	(3)	0	0	0	0	0	0	0	0
Lee Mitchell	8/9/88	(6)	(5)	0	0	0	0	0	0	0	0
Michael Monaghan	13/5/80	30	26	6	6	0	0	1	1	25	25
Adrian Morley	10/5/77	31	26	3	3	0	0	0	0	12	12
Richard Myler	21/5/90	22(2)	20(1)	19	14	2	1	0	0	80	58
Chris Riley	22/2/88	33(1)	29	29	25	0	0	0	0	116	100
David Solomona	26/1/78	5(27)	4(23)	11	9	0	0	0	0	44	36
Ben Westwood	25/7/81	30	25	6	6	65	47	0	0	154	118
Rhys Williams	8/12/89	2(1)	1(1)	1	1	0	0	0	0	4	4
Paul Wood	10/10/81	6(24)	5(21)	2	2	0	0	0	0	8	8

Ryan Atkins

LEAGUE RECORD
P27-W20-D0-L7
(3rd, SL/Preliminary Semi-Final)
F885, A488, Diff+397
40 points.

CHALLENGE CUP
Winners

ATTENDANCES
Best - v Wigan (SL - 13,024)
Worst - v Featherstone (CC - 7,754)
Total (SL, inc play-offs) - 150,335
Average (SL, inc play-offs) - 10,738
(Up by 1,510 on 2009)

1 December 2009 - Kris Radlinski appointed rugby general manager.

7 December 2009 - Phil Bailey agrees new contract for 2010.

27 December 2009 - friendly derby clash at ice-bound St Helens called off on safety grounds.

12 January 2010 - Michael Maguire scraps captaincy and appoints leadership team of Thomas Leuluai, Sean O'Loughlin, Andy Coley, Phil Bailey and George Carmont.

17 January 2010 - three tries in the final nine minutes snatch 40-38 friendly victory at Wakefield.

28 January 2010 - 20-12 win at Warrington in Paul Wood testimonial match.

5 February 2010 - Shaun Ainscough and Liam Farrell join Widnes on dual registration deal; Ben Davies on loan.

5 February 2010 - 38-6 home defeat of Crusaders in round 1.

12 February 2010 - Cameron Phelps suffers ankle injury in 32-6 home win over Hull KR in round 2.

20 February 2010 - Warriors top the table after gripping 22-20 win at Warrington.

24 February 2010 - Shaun Ainscough goes to Castleford on one-month loan deal.

26 February 2010 - Pat Richards scores five tries in 58-0 home hammering of Catalans.

5 March 2010 - 20-0 half-time lead is wasted in 22-20 defeat at Bradford.

12 March 2010 - Harrison Hansen damages shoulder in 48-24 home win over Hull FC.

21 March 2010 - Amos Roberts hat-trick in 36-22 win at Castleford.

24 March 2010 - reserve back-rower Chris Tuson starts loan spell at Castleford.

26 March 2010 - Castleford extend Shaun Ainscough loan until end of season.

29 March 2010 - Lee Mossop signs new contract until end of 2014.

2 April 2010 - 18-10 win at St Helens in last Good Friday derby at Knowsley Road.

5 April 2010 - Amos Roberts ruptures knee ligament in collision with post during 54–14 home Easter Monday win over Wakefield.

17 April 2010 - 50-34 win over Sheffield at Bramall Lane in Challenge Cup fourth round.

21 April 2010 - Shaun Ainscough recalled from loan spell at Castleford.

23 April 2010 - shock 38-24 home defeat to Harlequins after leading 24-6 at half-time.

27 April 2010 - Chris Tuson's loan spell at Castleford extended on week-to-week basis.

29 April 2010 - Shaun Ainscough re-joins Widnes on dual registration.

2 May 2010 - 28-10 win over Huddersfield at Murrayfield.

KEY DATES - WIGAN WARRIORS

8 May 2010 - 64-10 win at Widnes in fifth round of Challenge Cup.

16 May 2010 - 38-30 win at Huddersfield moves Warriors four points clear at top.

19 May 2010 - Shaun Ainscough banned for three games for fighting in reserve match.

20 May 2010 - Lee Mossop sidelined for five weeks following shoulder dislocation in win over Huddersfield.

22 May 2010 - Karl Pryce scores four tries in 46-26 away win over Crusaders.

29 May 2010 - Lee Smith try two minutes from time spells 12-10 defeat in Challenge Cup quarter-final.

2 June 2010 - Andy Coley gets one-match ban for dangerous throw in Challenge Cup loss against Leeds.

3 June 2010 - chief executive Mick Hogan announces immediate departure to Sale rugby union club.

6 June 2010 - Darrell Goulding scores hat-trick in 38-22 defeat of Castleford.

13 June 2010 - 48-6 win over Wakefield at Belle Vue. Sean O'Loughlin suffers quad strain.

20 June 2010 - Sean O'Loughlin absent as Warriors succumb to 26-24 derby defeat against Saints.

26 June 2010 - Darrell Goulding signs new contract to end of 2011 season.

30 June 2010 - Mark Riddell to leave at end of season for family reasons.

6 July 2010 - Andy Coley gets two-match ban after being sent off for high tackle on Jamal Fakir in 34-16 away win over Catalans.

8 July 2010 - centre Josh Charnley joins Hull KR on one-month loan.

16 July 2010 - 23-16 home defeat by Warrington Wolves.

19 July 2010 - assistant coach Shaun Wane takes charge as Michael Maguire goes to Australia to be with his gravely ill father.

19 July 2010 - Melbourne Storm trio sign Ryan Hoffman (one year), Brett Finch (two) and Jeff Lima (three) for next season.

30 July 2010 - Michael Maguire still absent for 26-12 win at Leeds.

6 August 2010 - Josh Charnley's loan at Hull KR extended to the end of regular season.

10 August 2010 - Lee Mossop to miss rest of season with recurrence of shoulder injury in under-20s.

15 August 2010 - 18-16 home defeat to Huddersfield delays minor premiership.

17 August 2010 - Stuart Fielden banned for one game for fighting in Huddersfield defeat.

19 August 2010 - Josh Charnley recalled from loan spell at Hull KR.

22 August 2010 - Charnley scores try as League Leaders Shield secured with 38-18 defeat of Hull KR at Craven Park. Harrison Hansen to miss rest of season with recurrence of shoulder injury.

25 August 2010 - Shaun Ainscough player of the tournament as reserve team wins Carnegie Nines.

30 August 2010 - winger Shaun Ainscough joins Bradford.

31 August 2010 - Iafeta Palea'aesina and Phil Bailey to be released at season end and sign for Salford.

3 September 2010 - Pat Richards equals Andy Farrell's Super League points record of 388 and beats Kris Radlinski's club record of 28 tries in 34-12 home victory over Bradford.

7 September 2010 - Stuart Fielden signs new two-year deal; Andy Coley signs 12 months, with option for 2012.

12 September 2010 - home 27-26 Qualifying Play-off defeat by Leeds.

17 September 2010 - 42-18 home Preliminary Semi-final win over Hull KR.

25 September 2010 - 26-6 Qualifying Semi-final win over Leeds at Headingley.

26 September 2010 - former player, Great Britain international Terry Newton found dead at his home near Wigan.

2 October 2010 - 22-10 Grand Final win over St Helens at Old Trafford. Pat Richards ends season with club record 462 points.

4 November 2010 - George Carmont signs new one–year contract.

CLUB RECORDS

Highest score:
116-0 v Flimby & Fothergill, 14/2/25
Highest score against:
0-75 v St Helens, 26/6/2005
Record attendance:
47,747 v St Helens, 27/3/59 *(Central Park)*
25,004 v St Helens, 25/3/2005
(JJB Stadium)

MATCH RECORDS

Tries: 10 Martin Offiah v Leeds, 10/5/92
Shaun Edwards v Swinton, 29/9/92
Goals: 22 Jim Sullivan
v Flimby & Fothergill, 14/2/25
Points: 44 Jim Sullivan
v Flimby & Fothergill, 14/2/25

SEASON RECORDS

Tries: 62 Johnny Ring 1925-26
Goals: 186 Frano Botica 1994-95
Points: 462 Pat Richards 2010

CAREER RECORDS

Tries: 478 Billy Boston 1953-68
Goals: 2,317 Jim Sullivan 1921-46
Points: 4,883 Jim Sullivan 1921-46
Appearances: 774 Jim Sullivan 1921-46

WIGAN WARRIORS

DATE	FIXTURE	RESULT	SCORERS	LGE	ATT
5/2/10	Crusaders (h)	W38-6	t:Roberts(2),Coley,Gleeson,Richards,Phelps,Mossop g:Richards(5)	3rd	13,680
12/2/10	Hull KR (h)	W32-6	t:Roberts(2),Gleeson,O'Loughlin,Richards,J Tomkins g:Richards(4)	3rd	12,429
20/2/10	Warrington (a)	W20-22	t:Roberts(2),Goulding,J Tomkins g:Richards(3)	1st	13,024
26/2/10	Catalans (h)	W58-0	t:Richards(5),O'Loughlin,Goulding,Leuluai,Carmont(2) g:Richards(9)	1st	12,001
5/3/10	Bradford (a)	L22-20	t:Goulding,Hansen,S Tomkins,Richards g:Richards(2)	1st	9,244
12/3/10	Hull (h)	W48-24	t:Richards,Goulding(2),Gleeson,Roberts,S Tomkins(2),Phelps g:Richards(8)	1st	15,045
21/3/10	Castleford (a)	W22-36	t:Roberts(3),Phelps,Richards,J Tomkins(2) g:Richards(4)	1st	8,493
26/3/10	Leeds (h)	W24-4	t:Carmont,Goulding(2),J Tomkins g:Richards(4)	1st	17,883
2/4/10	St Helens (a)	W10-18	t:Goulding,Palea'aesina g:Richards(5)	1st	17,500
5/4/10	Wakefield (h)	W54-14	t:Roberts(2),Richards(3),J Tomkins,Goulding(3),Farrell g:Richards(7)	1st	14,615
11/4/10	Salford (a)	W4-18	t:Deacon,Richards(2) g:Richards(3)	1st	6,618
17/4/10	Sheffield (a) (CCR4)	W34-50	t:Richards,Gleeson,Carmont,Palea'aesina,O'Loughlin,S Tomkins(3),Coley g:Richards(7)	N/A	2,950
23/4/10	Harlequins (h)	L26-38	t:Farrell(2),Phelps,J Tomkins g:Richards(5)	1st	18,605
2/5/10	Huddersfield (MM) ●	W10-28	t:Goulding,S Tomkins,Pryce,Carmont,Leuluai g:Richards,Riddell,S Tomkins(2)	1st	N/A
8/5/10	Widnes (a) (CCR5)	W10-64	t:Pryce(3),Leuluai,J Tomkins(2),Gleeson(2),O'Loughlin,S Tomkins(3) g:S Tomkins(2),Riddell(6)	N/A	5,504
16/5/10	Huddersfield (a)	W30-38	t:J Tomkins(2),Carmont,Goulding(2),Coley g:Richards(7)	1st	8,390
22/5/10	Crusaders (a)	W26-46	t:O'Loughlin,Pryce(4),Gleeson(2),Richards g:Richards(7)	1st	6,075
29/5/10	Leeds (a) (CCQF)	L12-10	g:Richards(5)	N/A	9,242
6/6/10	Castleford (h)	W38-22	t:Goulding(3),Leuluai,Tuson,O'Loughlin(2) g:Richards(5)	1st	14,047
13/6/10	Wakefield (a)	W6-48	t:Pryce(3),O'Loughlin,Farrell,Richards(2),Roberts,S Tomkins g:Richards(6)	1st	6,947
20/6/10	St Helens (h)	L24-26	t:Pryce,Leuluai,McIlorum,Gleeson g:Richards(4)	1st	20,498
26/6/10	Harlequins (a)	W12-36	t:S Tomkins,Goulding,McIlorum,Richards(2),Farrell g:Richards(6)	1st	5,084
4/7/10	Catalans (a)	W16-34	t:Richards,Riddell,Leuluai,Coley,Gleeson,Goulding g:Richards(5)	1st	7,612
9/7/10	Salford (h)	W60-10	t:S Tomkins(2),Goulding(3),Gleeson,J Tomkins,Carmont,O'Loughlin,Hansen g:Richards(10)	1st	12,221
16/7/10	Warrington (h)	L16-23	t:Riddell,Tuson,Richards g:Richards(2)	1st	22,701
23/7/10	Hull (a)	W0-46	t:Richards(3),Farrell(2),Goulding,S Tomkins(2) g:Richards(7)	1st	12,694
30/7/10	Leeds (a)	W12-26	t:Leuluai,Carmont,Hansen,Gleeson g:Richards(5)	1st	16,622
15/8/10	Huddersfield (h)	L16-18	t:Pryce,J Tomkins,S Tomkins g:Richards(2)	1st	13,619
22/8/10	Hull KR (a)	W18-38	t:Richards(2),Marsh,S Tomkins,J Tomkins,Charnley g:Richards(7)	1st	9,250
3/9/10	Bradford (h)	W34-12	t:Carmont,Palea'aesina,Richards(2),J Tomkins,Goulding(2) g:Richards(3)	1st	17,058
12/9/10	Leeds (h) (QPO)	L26-27	t:S Tomkins(2),Farrell,Richards g:Richards(5)	N/A	12,117
17/9/10	Hull KR (h) (PSF)	W42-18	t:Richards,Farrell,Goulding(2),Leuluai,Gleeson,J Tomkins g:Richards(7)	N/A	11,133
25/9/10	Leeds (a) (QSF)	W6-26	t:Goulding,J Tomkins,Carmont,Gleeson g:Richards(5)	N/A	13,692
2/10/10	St Helens (GF) ●●	W10-22	t:Gleeson(2),Goulding,S Tomkins g:Richards(2),Riddell	N/A	71,526

● Played at Murrayfield, Edinburgh
●● Played at Old Trafford, Manchester

		APP		TRIES		GOALS		FG		PTS	
	D.O.B.	ALL	SL	ALL	SL	ALL	SL	ALL	SL	ALL	SL
Shaun Ainscough	27/11/89	1	1	0	0	0	0	0	0	0	0
Phil Bailey	25/5/80	15(4)	13(4)	0	0	0	0	0	0	0	0
George Carmont	30/6/78	31	28	10	9	0	0	0	0	40	36
Josh Charnley	26/6/91	(1)	(1)	1	1	0	0	0	0	4	4
Andy Coley	7/7/78	26(2)	24(1)	4	3	0	0	0	0	16	12
Ben Davies	2/11/89	(5)	(5)	0	0	0	0	0	0	0	0
Paul Deacon	13/2/79	13(7)	13(7)	1	1	0	0	0	0	4	4
Liam Farrell	2/7/90	10(13)	9(11)	9	9	0	0	0	0	36	36
Stuart Fielden	14/9/79	30(2)	27(2)	0	0	0	0	0	0	0	0
Martin Gleeson	28/5/80	28(1)	25(1)	16	13	0	0	0	0	64	52
Darrell Goulding	3/3/88	26	24	29	29	0	0	0	0	116	116
Harrison Hansen	26/10/85	13(3)	13(3)	3	3	0	0	0	0	12	12
Thomas Leuluai	22/6/85	31	29	8	7	0	0	0	0	32	28
Stefan Marsh	3/9/90	5	5	1	1	0	0	0	0	4	4
Michael McIlorum	10/1/88	11(9)	10(7)	2	2	0	0	0	0	8	8
Lee Mossop	17/1/89	3(15)	2(14)	1	1	0	0	0	0	4	4
Eamon O'Carroll	13/6/87	(12)	(11)	0	0	0	0	0	0	0	0
Sean O'Loughlin	24/11/82	30(1)	27(1)	9	7	0	0	0	0	36	28
Iafeta Palea'aesina	10/2/82	(21)	(20)	3	2	0	0	0	0	12	8
Cameron Phelps	11/2/85	7	6	4	4	0	0	0	0	16	16
Paul Prescott	1/1/86	11(17)	10(15)	0	0	0	0	0	0	0	0
Karl Pryce	27/7/86	9	7	13	10	0	0	0	0	52	40
Pat Richards	27/2/82	34	31	32	31	167	155	0	0	462	434
Mark Riddell	9/12/80	22(9)	20(8)	2	2	8	2	0	0	24	12
Amos Roberts	2/11/80	15(1)	14(1)	13	13	0	0	0	0	52	52
Joel Tomkins	21/3/87	34	31	17	15	0	0	0	0	68	60
Sam Tomkins	23/3/89	34	31	21	15	4	2	0	0	92	64
Chris Tuson	25/2/90	3(11)	3(11)	2	2	0	0	0	0	8	8
Jonny Walker	26/3/88	(1)	(1)	0	0	0	0	0	0	0	0

Pat Richards

LEAGUE RECORD
P27-W22-D0-L5
(1st, SL/Grand Final Winners,
Champions)
F922, A411, Diff+511
44 points.

CHALLENGE CUP
Quarter Finalists

ATTENDANCES
Best - v Warrington (SL - 22,701)
Worst - v Hull KR (PSF - 11,133)
Total (SL, inc play-offs) - 227,652
Average (SL, inc play-offs) - 15,177
(Up by 1,482 on 2009)

SUPER LEAGUE XV
Round by Round

ROUND 4

Friday 29th January 2010

CRUSADERS 6 LEEDS RHINOS 34

CRUSADERS: 2 Nick Youngquest (D); 14 Luke Dyer; 13 Rocky Trimarchi (D); 4 Vince Mellars (D); 5 Gareth Raynor (D); 6 Michael Witt (D); 9 Lincoln Withers; 8 Ryan O'Hara (C); 15 Tommy Lee (D); 10 Mark Bryant; 12 Jason Chan; 17 Adam Peek; 16 Frank Winterstein (D). Subs (all used): 18 Jamie Thackray (D); 19 Jordan James; 21 Lloyd White; 23 Peter Lupton.
Try: Raynor (28); **Goals:** Witt 1/2.
RHINOS: 23 Kallum Watkins; 2 Scott Donald; 3 Brett Delaney (D); 4 Keith Senior; 5 Ryan Hall; 6 Danny McGuire; 7 Rob Burrow; 8 Kylie Leuluai; 9 Danny Buderus; 16 Ryan Bailey; 11 Jamie Jones-Buchanan; 18 Carl Ablett; 13 Kevin Sinfield (C). Subs (all used): 12 Ali Lauitiiti; 14 Matt Diskin; 15 Greg Eastwood (D); 17 Ian Kirke.
Tries: Donald (19), McGuire (65), Lauitiiti (67, 79), Sinfield (71), Delaney (75); **Goals:** Sinfield 5/6.
Rugby Leaguer & League Express Men of the Match: *Crusaders:* Jason Chan; *Rhinos:* Brett Delaney.
Penalty count: 9-4; **Half-time:** 6-6;
Referee: Ben Thaler; **Attendance:** 10,334.

ROUND 3

Saturday 30th January 2010

HARLEQUINS 10 WAKEFIELD TRINITY WILDCATS 18

HARLEQUINS: 26 Ben Jones-Bishop (D); 1 Chris Melling; 3 Tony Clubb; 4 David Howell; 5 Will Sharp; 21 Luke Gale; 7 Danny Orr; 14 Oliver Wilkes (D); 9 Chad Randall (C); 10 Louie McCarthy-Scarsbrook; 11 Luke Williamson; 18 Ryan Esders; 16 Jason Golden. Subs (all used): 22 Jamie O'Callaghan; 19 Matt James (D); 17 Danny Ward; 28 Ben Bolger (D).
Tries: Jones-Bishop (18, 45); **Goals:** Orr 1/2.
WILDCATS: 18 Aaron Murphy; 5 Luke George; 3 Sean Gleeson; 4 Darryl Millard (D); 23 Dale Morton; 14 Sam Obst; 7 Danny Brough; 10 Michael Korkidas; 20 Tevita Leo-Latu; 8 Shane Tronc (D); 11 Dale Ferguson; 17 Kevin Henderson; 12 Glenn Morrison (D). Subs (all used): 6 Ben Jeffries (D2); 9 Terry Newton (D); 13 Jason Demetriou (C); 25 Richard Moore.
Tries: Millard (13), Jeffries (37), Murphy (56);
Goals: Brough 3/4.
Rugby Leaguer & League Express Men of the Match: *Harlequins:* Ben Jones-Bishop; *Wildcats:* Ben Jeffries.
Penalty count: 9-10; **Half-time:** 4-12;
Referee: Ian Smith; **Attendance:** 3,688.

ROUND 1

Friday 5th February 2010

HUDDERSFIELD GIANTS 24 BRADFORD BULLS 12

GIANTS: 1 Brett Hodgson (C); 2 Leroy Cudjoe; 3 Jamahl Lolesi; 19 Michael Lawrence; 5 David Hodgson; 6 Kevin Brown; 7 Luke Robinson; 16 Darrell Griffin; 9 Shaun Lunt; 10 Keith Mason; 11 Lee Gilmour (D); 33 Graeme Horne (D); 20 David Faiumu. Subs (all used): 8 Eorl Crabtree; 21 Scott Grix (D); 12 David Fa'alogo (D); 15 Andy Raleigh.
Tries: Cudjoe (7, 16), Lunt (23), Fa'alogo (44);
Goals: B Hodgson 4/5.
Sin bin: Robinson (48) - holding down;
Gilmour (63) - obstruction.
On report: Raleigh (63) - alleged late tackle.
BULLS: 1 Dave Halley; 2 Rikki Sheriffe; 3 Paul Sykes; 4 Chris Nero; 5 Stuart Reardon (D2); 6 Brett Kearney (D); 7 Matt Orford (D); 8 Nick Scruton; 9 Heath L'Estrange (D); 10 Andy Lynch (C); 13 Jamie Langley; 12 Glenn Hall (D); 11 Steve Menzies. Subs (all used): 14 Wayne Godwin; 16 Michael Worrincy; 18 Craig Kopczak; 22 James Donaldson.
Tries: Reardon (34, 65), Sheriffe (38);
Goals: Sykes 0/2, Orford 0/1.
Rugby Leaguer & League Express Men of the Match: *Giants:* Brett Hodgson; *Bulls:* Jamie Langley.
Penalty count: 9-13; **Half-time:** 16-8;
Referee: Steve Ganson; **Attendance:** 9,774.

LEEDS RHINOS 10 CASTLEFORD TIGERS 24

RHINOS: 1 Brent Webb; 2 Scott Donald; 3 Brett Delaney; 4 Keith Senior; 5 Ryan Hall; 6 Danny McGuire; 7 Rob Burrow; 16 Ryan Bailey; 9 Danny Buderus; 10 Jamie Peacock; 11 Jamie Jones-Buchanan; 18 Carl Ablett; 13 Kevin Sinfield (C). Subs (all used): 15 Greg Eastwood; 19 Luke Burgess; 12 Ali Lauitiiti; 14 Matt Diskin.
Tries: McGuire (23), Delaney (38); **Goals:** Sinfield 1/2.
TIGERS: 23 Ryan McGoldrick; 1 Richard Owen; 3 Michael Shenton; 4 James Evans; 5 Michael Wainwright; 6 Rangi Chase; 7 Brent Sherwin; 16 Paul Jackson (D2); 9 Ryan Hudson (C); 15 Liam Higgins; 11 Brett Ferres; 12 Steve Snitch (D); 13 Joe Westerman. Subs (all used): 10 Craig Huby; 8 Mitchell Sargent; 14 Stuart Jones; 25 Dean Widders.
Tries: Evans (34), Westerman (52), Sherwin (57), Widders (78); **Goals:** Huby 1/1, Westerman 3/3.
Rugby Leaguer & League Express Men of the Match: *Rhinos:* Jamie Jones-Buchanan; *Tigers:* Rangi Chase.
Penalty count: 7-6; **Half time:** 10-6;
Referee: Ian Smith; **Attendance:** 15,875.

WIGAN WARRIORS 38 CRUSADERS 6

WARRIORS: 1 Cameron Phelps; 2 Amos Roberts; 3 Martin Gleeson; 4 George Carmont; 5 Pat Richards; 6 Sam Tomkins; 7 Thomas Leuluai; 8 Stuart Fielden; 9 Mark Riddell; 14 Paul Prescott; 11 Harrison Hansen; 12 Joel Tomkins; 13 Sean O'Loughlin (C). Subs (all used): 10 Andy Coley; 17 Iafeta Palea'aesina; 19 Paul Deacon (D); 23 Lee Mossop.
Tries: Roberts (15, 56), Coley (22), Gleeson (29), Richards (34), Phelps (51), Mossop (65);
Goals: Richards 5/7.
CRUSADERS: 2 Nick Youngquest; 14 Luke Dyer; 13 Rocky Trimarchi; 4 Vince Mellars; 5 Gareth Raynor; 6 Michael Witt; 9 Lincoln Withers; 8 Ryan O'Hara (C); 15 Tommy Lee; 18 Jamie Thackray; 12 Jason Chan; 11 Weller Hauraki (D); 16 Frank Winterstein. Subs (all used): 10 Mark Bryant; 17 Adam Peek; 19 Jordan James; 23 Peter Lupton.
Try: Dyer (38); **Goals:** Witt 1/1.
Rugby Leaguer & League Express Men of the Match: *Warriors:* Cameron Phelps; *Crusaders:* Michael Witt.
Penalty count: 9-8; **Half-time:** 20-6;
Referee: James Child; **Attendance:** 13,680.

Saturday 6th February 2010

ST HELENS 12 HULL FC 32

SAINTS: 1 Paul Wellens; 2 Ade Gardner; 3 Matt Gidley; 4 Iosia Soliola (D); 21 Gary Wheeler; 6 Leon Pryce; 7 Kyle Eastmond; 10 James Graham; 9 Keiron Cunningham (C); 8 Nick Fozzard (D2); 11 Tony Puletua; 12 Jon Wilkin; 13 Chris Flannery. Subs (all used): 14 James Roby; 16 Scott Moore (D2); 17 Paul Clough; 23 Maurie Fa'asavalu.
Tries: Gidley (64), Flannery (69); **Goals:** Eastmond 2/2.
HULL: 1 Jordan Tansey; 24 Craig Hall; 21 Richard Whiting; 4 Kirk Yeaman; 3 Tom Briscoe; 6 Richard Horne; 7 Sean Long (C) (D); 10 Mark O'Meley (D); 9 Shaun Berrigan; 11 Lee Radford; 16 Willie Manu; 12 Danny Tickle; 13 Craig Fitzgibbon (D). Subs (all used): 8 Ewan Dowes; 15 Epalahame Lauaki; 17 Peter Cusack; 20 Danny Houghton.
Tries: Manu (26), Lauaki (37), Long (42), Briscoe (56), Yeaman (76); **Goals:** Tickle 4/4, Fitzgibbon 2/2.
Sin bin: Tansey (63) - professional foul.
Rugby Leaguer & League Express Men of the Match: *Saints:* Kyle Eastmond; *Hull:* Sean Long.
Penalty count: 9-6; **Half-time:** 0-12;
Referee: Ben Thaler; **Attendance:** 12,142.

Sunday 7th February 2010

HULL KINGSTON ROVERS 30 SALFORD CITY REDS 12

ROVERS: 1 Shaun Briscoe; 2 Peter Fox; 3 Kris Welham; 28 Ben Cockayne; 5 Liam Colbon; 4 Jake Webster; 7 Michael Dobson; 8 Rhys Lovegrove; 9 Scott Murrell; 10 Scott Wheeldon; 11 Clint Newton; 14 Matt Cook (D); 6 Paul Cooke. Subs (all used): 20 Michael Vella (C); 22 Liam Watts; 17 Ben Fisher; 16 Jason Netherton.
Tries: Fox (2, 6), Webster (36), Dobson (54), Newton (61); **Goals:** Dobson 5/5.
CITY REDS: 1 Karl Fitzpatrick; 2 Jodie Broughton (D); 5 Ashley Gibson; 20 Steve Tyrer (D); 24 Dean McGilvray; 6 Stefan Ratchford; 14 Matty Smith (D); 8 Ray Cashmere; 9 Malcolm Alker (C); 10 Rob Parker; 12 Luke Adamson; 13 Luke Swain; 21 Daniel Holdsworth (D). Subs (all used): 7 Jeremy Smith; 11 Ian Sibbit; 16 Phil Leuluai; 19 Ryan Boyle (D).
Tries: M Smith (20), Broughton (64);
Goals: Ratchford 2/2.
Rugby Leaguer & League Express Men of the Match: *Rovers:* Michael Dobson; *City Reds:* Matty Smith.
Penalty count: 10-8; **Half-time:** 18-6;
Referee: Richard Silverwood; **Attendance:** 9,123.

WARRINGTON WOLVES 58 HARLEQUINS 0

WOLVES: 1 Richard Mathers; 2 Chris Riley; 4 Chris Bridge; 23 Ryan Atkins (D); 3 Matt King; 6 Lee Briers; 7 Richard Myler (D); 8 Adrian Morley (C); 9 Michael Monaghan; 10 Garreth Carvell; 11 Louis Anderson; 12 Ben Westwood; 13 Ben Harrison. Subs (all used): 14 Mick Higham; 16 Paul Wood; 17 Simon Grix; 26 David Solomona (D).
Tries: Carvell (4), Mathers (9), Monaghan (26), Bridge (38), Riley (40, 48, 51, 53, 64), Myler (56), Grix (68); **Goals:** Briers 7/11.
HARLEQUINS: 22 Jamie O'Callaghan; 1 Chris Melling; 3 Tony Clubb; 4 David Howell; 5 Will Sharp; 7 Danny Orr; 21 Luke Gale; 24 Dave Williams; 9 Chad Randall (C); 14 Oliver Wilkes; 11 Luke Williamson; 18 Ryan Esders; 16 Jason Golden. Subs (all used): 15 Ben Kaye; 19 Matt James; 25 Lamont Bryan; 28 Ben Bolger.
Sin bin: Randall (22) - delaying restart.
Rugby Leaguer & League Express Men of the Match: *Wolves:* Ben Harrison; *Harlequins:* Oliver Wilkes.
Penalty count: 10-7; **Half-time:** 28-0;
Referee: Thierry Alibert; **Attendance:** 11,678.

WAKEFIELD TRINITY WILDCATS 28 CATALANS DRAGONS 20

WILDCATS: 18 Aaron Murphy; 23 Dale Morton; 3 Sean Gleeson; 4 Darryl Millard; 5 Luke George; 6 Ben Jeffries; 7 Danny Brough; 8 Shane Tronc; 20 Tevita Leo-Latu; 10 Michael Korkidas; 11 Dale Ferguson; 12 Glenn Morrison; 13 Jason Demetriou (C). Subs (all used): 14 Sam Obst; 16 Paul Johnson (D); 19 Paul King (D); 17 Kevin Henderson.
Tries: Ferguson (3), George (30), Morton (51, 68), Morrison (53); **Goals:** Brough 4/6.
DRAGONS: 23 Chris Walker (D); 2 Steven Bell; 4 Setaimata Sa (D); 15 Jean-Phillipe Baile; 5 Dimitri Pelo; 6 Adam Mogg; 9 Casey McGuire; 8 David Ferriol; 12 Gregory Mounis; 10 Jerome Guisset; 11 Olivier Elima (C); 17 Cyrille Gossard; 13 Dallas Johnson (D). Subs (all used): 3 Sebastien Raguin; 20 Kane Bentley; 21 Sebastien Martins; 24 Remi Casty.
Tries: Pelo (12), Elima (22), Martins (43), Walker (78);
Goals: Walker 2/4.
Sin bin: Johnson (35) - interference.
Rugby Leaguer & League Express Men of the Match: *Wildcats:* Ben Jeffries; *Dragons:* Casey McGuire.
Penalty count: 11-9; **Half-time:** 10-10;
Referee: Phil Bentham; **Attendance:** 5,818.

ROUND 2

Friday 12th February 2010

HULL FC 14 HUDDERSFIELD GIANTS 6

HULL: 1 Jordan Tansey; 24 Craig Hall; 21 Richard Whiting; 4 Kirk Yeaman; 3 Tom Briscoe; 6 Richard Horne; 7 Sean Long (C); 10 Mark O'Meley; 9 Shaun Berrigan; 11 Lee Radford; 12 Danny Tickle; 16 Willie Manu; 13 Craig Fitzgibbon. Subs (all used): 8 Ewan Dowes; 15 Epalahame Lauaki; 17 Peter Cusack; 20 Danny Houghton.
Tries: Tickle (7), Hall (26); **Goals:** Tickle 3/3.
GIANTS: 2 Leroy Cudjoe; 3 Jamahl Lolesi; 19 Michael Lawrence; 4 Paul Whatuira; 5 David Hodgson; 6 Kevin Brown; 7 Luke Robinson; 16 Darrell Griffin; 9 Shaun Lunt; 15 Andy Raleigh (C); 11 Lee Gilmour; 33 Graeme Horne; 20 David Faiumu. Subs (all used): 8 Eorl Crabtree; 21 Scott Grix; 12 David Fa'alogo; 23 Larne Patrick.
Try: Grix (45); **Goals:** Cudjoe 1/1.
Rugby Leaguer & League Express Men of the Match: *Hull:* Danny Tickle; *Giants:* Luke Robinson.
Penalty count: 9-7; **Half-time:** 12-0;
Referee: Thierry Alibert; **Attendance:** 14,520.

SALFORD CITY REDS 16 CRUSADERS 36

CITY REDS: 1 Karl Fitzpatrick; 2 Jodie Broughton; 20 Steve Tyrer; 5 Ashley Gibson; 24 Dean McGilvray; 6 Stefan Ratchford; 14 Matty Smith; 8 Ray Cashmere; 9 Malcolm Alker (C); 10 Rob Parker; 12 Luke Adamson; 13 Luke Swain; 21 Daniel Holdsworth. Subs (all used): 16 Phil Leuluai; 7 Jeremy Smith; 19 Ryan Boyle; 11 Ian Sibbit.
Tries: Holdsworth (7), M Smith (29), Fitzpatrick (74);
Goals: Ratchford 2/3.
Sin bin: Holdsworth (58) - holding down.
CRUSADERS: 22 Elliot Kear; 2 Nick Youngquest; 14 Luke Dyer; 4 Vince Mellars; 5 Gareth Raynor; 23 Peter Lupton; 6 Michael Witt; 8 Ryan O'Hara (C); 9 Lincoln Withers; 10 Mark Bryant; 12 Jason Chan; 16 Frank Winterstein; 13 Rocky Trimarchi. Subs (all used): 18 Jamie Thackray; 17 Adam Peek; 11 Weller Hauraki; 20 Ben Flower.
Tries: Mellars (5, 13, 42), Winterstein (10), Witt (48), Thackray (59), Raynor (78); **Goals:** Witt 4/7.
Rugby Leaguer & League Express Men of the Match: *City Reds:* Daniel Holdsworth; *Crusaders:* Michael Witt.
Penalty count: 6-5; **Half-time:** 12-14;
Referee: Steve Ganson; **Attendance:** 3,421.

WIGAN WARRIORS 32 HULL KINGSTON ROVERS 6

WARRIORS: 1 Cameron Phelps; 2 Amos Roberts; 3 Martin Gleeson; 4 George Carmont (C); 5 Pat Richards; 6 Sam Tomkins; 7 Thomas Leuluai; 8 Stuart Fielden; 9 Mark Riddell; 10 Andy Coley; 11 Harrison Hansen; 12 Joel Tomkins; 13 Sean O'Loughlin. Subs (all used): 14 Paul Prescott; 17 Iafeta Palea'aesina; 19 Paul Deacon; 23 Lee Mossop.
Tries: Roberts (3, 77), Gleeson (7), O'Loughlin (49), Richards (55), J Tomkins (69); **Goals:** Richards 4/6.
ROVERS: 1 Shaun Briscoe; 2 Peter Fox; 3 Kris Welham; 28 Ben Cockayne; 5 Liam Colbon; 4 Jake Webster; 7 Michael Dobson; 8 Rhys Lovegrove; 9 Scott Murrell; 10 Scott Wheeldon; 11 Clint Newton; 14 Matt Cook; 6 Paul Cooke. Subs (all used): 20 Michael Vella (C); 22 Liam Watts; 17 Ben Fisher; 16 Jason Netherton.
Try: Fisher (35); **Goals:** Dobson 1/1.
Rugby Leaguer & League Express Men of the Match: *Warriors:* Amos Roberts; *Rovers:* Clint Newton.
Penalty count: 6-7; **Half-time:** 10-6;
Referee: Ian Smith; **Attendance:** 12,429.

Saturday 13th February 2010

CASTLEFORD TIGERS 16 WARRINGTON WOLVES 28

TIGERS: 23 Ryan McGoldrick; 1 Richard Owen; 3 Michael Shenton; 4 James Evans; 5 Michael Wainwright; 6 Rangi Chase; 7 Brent Sherwin; 16 Paul Jackson; 9 Ryan Hudson (C); 10 Craig Huby; 11 Brett Ferres; 12 Steve Snitch; 13 Joe Westerman. Subs (all used): 8 Mitchell Sargent; 14 Stuart Jones; 15 Liam Higgins; 25 Dean Widders.
Tries: Evans (11, 51), Westerman (20);
Goals: Westerman 2/5.
WOLVES: 1 Richard Mathers; 2 Chris Riley; 4 Chris Bridge; 23 Ryan Atkins; 3 Matt King; 6 Lee Briers; 7 Richard Myler; 8 Adrian Morley (C); 9 Michael Monaghan; 10 Garreth Carvell; 11 Louis Anderson; 12 Ben Westwood; 13 Ben Harrison. Subs (all used): 14 Mick Higham; 17 Simon Grix; 16 Paul Wood; 27 Vinnie Anderson.
Tries: Grix (29), Riley (35), Briers (53), Myler (60, 74);
Goals: Briers 1/2, Bridge 3/4.
Rugby Leaguer & League Express Men of the Match: *Tigers:* James Evans; *Wolves:* Lee Briers.
Penalty count: 13-10; **Half-time:** 10-10;
Referee: Ben Thaler; **Attendance:** 7,569.

Sunday 14th February 2010

HARLEQUINS 16 CATALANS DRAGONS 4

HARLEQUINS: 26 Ben Jones-Bishop; 22 Jamie O'Callaghan; 3 Tony Clubb; 4 David Howell; 5 Will Sharp; 7 Danny Orr; 21 Luke Gale; 17 Danny Ward; 9 Chad Randall (C); 14 Oliver Wilkes; 11 Luke Williamson; 16 Jason Golden; 18 Ryan Esders. Subs: 10 Louie McCarthy-Scarsbrook; 19 Matt James (not used); 1 Chris Melling; 28 Ben Bolger.
Tries: Sharp (11, 39, 46); **Goals:** Orr 2/4.
DRAGONS: 1 Clint Greenshields; 2 Steven Bell; 23 Chris Walker; 4 Setaimata Sa; 5 Dimitri Pelo; 6 Adam Mogg; 16 William Barthau (D); 8 David Ferriol; 9 Casey McGuire; 10 Jerome Guisset; 11 Olivier Elima (C); 17 Cyrille Gossard; 13 Dallas Johnson. Subs (all used): 3 Sebastien Raguin; 12 Gregory Mounis; 18 Dane Carlaw; 22 Jamal Fakir.
Try: Greenshields (25); **Goals:** Barthau 0/1.
Dismissal: Ferriol (65) - punching.
Rugby Leaguer & League Express Men of the Match: *Harlequins:* Will Sharp; *Dragons:* Clint Greenshields.
Penalty count: 5-4; **Half-time:** 8-4;
Referee: Richard Silverwood; **Attendance:** 2,330.

BRADFORD BULLS 6 ST HELENS 38

BULLS: 1 Dave Halley; 2 Rikki Sheriffe; 3 Paul Sykes; 4 Chris Nero; 5 Stuart Reardon; 6 Brett Kearney; 7 Matt Orford; 8 Nick Scruton; 9 Heath L'Estrange; 10 Andy Lynch (C); 13 Jamie Langley; 20 Elliott Whitehead; 11 Steve Menzies. Subs (all used): 14 Wayne Godwin; 16 Michael Worrincy; 18 Craig Kopczak; 12 Glenn Hall.
Try: Orford (80); **Goals:** Orford 1/1.
SAINTS: 1 Paul Wellens (C); 24 Jonny Lomax; 3 Matt Gidley; 21 Gary Wheeler; 5 Francis Meli; 6 Leon Pryce; 7 Kyle Eastmond; 8 Nick Fozzard; 16 Scott Moore; 10 James Graham; 13 Chris Flannery; 12 Jon Wilkin; 11 Tony Puletua. Subs (all used): 14 James Roby; 17 Paul Clough; 23 Maurie Fa'asavalu; 15 Bryn Hargreaves.
Tries: Wilkin (11), Wellens (19, 28, 68, 72), Eastmond (47); **Goals:** Eastmond 7/7.
Rugby Leaguer & League Express Men of the Match: *Bulls:* Glenn Hall; *Saints:* Paul Wellens.
Penalty count: 8-7; **Half-time:** 0-20;
Referee: Phil Bentham; **Attendance:** 10,165.

WAKEFIELD TRINITY WILDCATS 28 LEEDS RHINOS 18

WILDCATS: 18 Aaron Murphy; 23 Dale Morton; 3 Sean Gleeson; 4 Darryl Millard; 5 Luke George; 6 Ben Jeffries; 7 Danny Brough; 8 Shane Tronc; 14 Sam Obst; 10 Michael Korkidas; 12 Glenn Morrison; 13 Jason Demetriou (C); 20 Tevita Leo-Latu. Subs (all used): 9 Terry Newton; 11 Dale Ferguson; 25 Richard Moore; 17 Kevin Henderson.
Tries: Gleeson (10), Jeffries (31), Brough (42), Millard (55); **Goals:** Brough 6/8.
RHINOS: 1 Brent Webb; 2 Scott Donald; 23 Kallum Watkins; 4 Keith Senior; 5 Ryan Hall; 6 Danny McGuire; 7 Rob Burrow; 8 Kylie Leuluai; 9 Danny Buderus; 10 Jamie Peacock; 11 Jamie Jones-Buchanan; 15 Greg Eastwood; 13 Kevin Sinfield (C). Subs (all used): 14 Matt Diskin; 17 Ian Kirke; 12 Ali Lauitiiti; 16 Ryan Bailey.
Tries: McGuire (34), Donald (59, 65);
Goals: Burrow 1/1, Sinfield 2/2.
Sin bin: Sinfield (51) - interference.
Rugby Leaguer & League Express Men of the Match: *Wildcats:* Danny Brough; *Rhinos:* Danny Buderus.
Penalty count: 17-7; **Half-time:** 14-6;
Referee: James Child; **Attendance:** 9,783.

ROUND 3

Friday 19th February 2010

BRADFORD BULLS 41 CASTLEFORD TIGERS 22

BULLS: 1 Dave Halley; 2 Rikki Sheriffe; 3 Paul Sykes; 4 Chris Nero; 5 Stuart Reardon; 6 Brett Kearney; 7 Matt Orford; 8 Nick Scruton; 9 Heath L'Estrange; 10 Andy Lynch (C); 13 Jamie Langley; 20 Elliott Whitehead; 11 Steve Menzies. Subs (all used): 14 Wayne Godwin; 16 Michael Worrincy; 18 Craig Kopczak; 12 Glenn Hall.
Tries: Scruton (4), Sheriffe (6), Whitehead (23), Kearney (28, 65), Halley (59), Sykes (79);
Goals: Orford 6/7; **Field goal:** Orford (40).
TIGERS: 23 Ryan McGoldrick; 1 Richard Owen; 3 Michael Shenton; 4 James Evans; 5 Michael Wainwright; 12 Steve Snitch; 6 Rangi Chase; 16 Paul Jackson; 9 Ryan Hudson (C); 15 Liam Higgins; 11 Brett Ferres; 14 Stuart Jones; 13 Joe Westerman. Subs (all used): 8 Mitchell Sargent; 10 Craig Huby; 19 Kirk Netherton; 17 Ryan Clayton.
Tries: Shenton (19), Owen (32), Snitch (70), Hudson (75); **Goals:** Westerman 3/3, McGoldrick 0/1.
Rugby Leaguer & League Express Men of the Match: *Bulls:* Brett Kearney; *Tigers:* Ryan McGoldrick.
Penalty count: 9-9; **Half-time:** 25-12;
Referee: Thierry Alibert; **Attendance:** 8,019.

LEEDS RHINOS 22 SALFORD CITY REDS 10

RHINOS: 1 Brent Webb; 2 Scott Donald; 23 Kallum Watkins; 4 Keith Senior; 5 Ryan Hall; 6 Danny McGuire; 7 Rob Burrow; 8 Kylie Leuluai; 14 Matt Diskin; 10 Jamie Peacock; 11 Jamie Jones-Buchanan; 17 Ian Kirke; 13 Kevin Sinfield (C). Subs (all used): 15 Greg Eastwood; 16 Ryan Bailey; 9 Danny Buderus; 12 Ali Lauitiiti.
Tries: Senior (6, 66), Webb (45), Kirke (79);
Goals: Sinfield 3/4.
CITY REDS: 1 Karl Fitzpatrick; 2 Jodie Broughton; 3 Mark Henry; 4 Willie Talau; 5 Ashley Gibson; 6 Stefan Ratchford; 14 Matty Smith; 19 Ryan Boyle; 9 Malcolm Alker (C); 10 Rob Parker; 11 Ian Sibbit; 12 Luke Adamson; 13 Luke Swain. Subs (all used): 16 Phil Leuluai; 17 Adam Sidlow; 15 Stuart Littler; 7 Jeremy Smith.
Tries: Gibson (31), Talau (51); **Goals:** Ratchford 1/2.
Rugby Leaguer & League Express Men of the Match: *Rhinos:* Jamie Jones-Buchanan; *City Reds:* Luke Swain.
Penalty count: 6-5; **Half time:** 6-4;
Referee: Phil Bentham; **Attendance:** 12,700.

Saturday 20th February 2010

CATALANS DRAGONS 12 ST HELENS 42

DRAGONS: 1 Clint Greenshields; 26 Cyril Stacul; 23 Chris Walker; 4 Setaimata Sa; 5 Dimitri Pelo; 6 Adam Mogg; 16 William Barthau; 8 David Ferriol; 9 Casey McGuire; 18 Dane Carlaw; 11 Olivier Elima (C); 17 Cyrille Gossard; 13 Dallas Johnson. Subs (all used): 3 Sebastien Raguin; 12 Gregory Mounis; 22 Jamal Fakir; 24 Remi Casty.
Tries: Sa (2), Walker (9, 75); **Goals:** Barthau 0/3.
Dismissal: Elima (24) - high tackle on Lomax.
SAINTS: 1 Paul Wellens (C); 24 Jonny Lomax; 3 Matt Gidley; 21 Gary Wheeler; 5 Francis Meli; 6 Leon Pryce; 7 Kyle Eastmond; 8 Nick Fozzard; 16 Scott Moore; 10 James Graham; 11 Tony Puletua; 17 Paul Clough; 12 Jon Wilkin. Subs (all used): 23 Maurie Fa'asavalu; 14 James Roby; 15 Bryn Hargreaves; 18 Matty Ashurst.
Tries: Lomax (14, 24), Meli (30, 50), Gidley (37, 59), Fa'asavalu (45), Eastmond (49); **Goals:** Eastmond 5/8.
Rugby Leaguer & League Express Men of the Match: *Dragons:* Clint Greenshields; *Saints:* Matt Gidley.
Penalty count: 8-8; **Half-time:** 8-18;
Referee: Steve Ganson; **Attendance:** 7,825.

WARRINGTON WOLVES 20 WIGAN WARRIORS 22

WOLVES: 1 Richard Mathers; 2 Chris Riley; 4 Chris Bridge; 23 Ryan Atkins; 3 Matt King; 6 Lee Briers; 7 Richard Myler; 8 Adrian Morley (C); 9 Michael Monaghan; 10 Garreth Carvell; 11 Louis Anderson; 12 Ben Westwood; 13 Ben Harrison. Subs (all used): 14 Mick Higham; 16 Paul Wood; 17 Simon Grix; 26 David Solomona.
Tries: Myler (18), Riley (28), Solomona (37), L Anderson (73); **Goals:** Briers 2/3, Bridge 0/1.
WARRIORS: 2 Amos Roberts; 24 Darrell Goulding; 3 Martin Gleeson; 4 George Carmont; 5 Pat Richards; 6 Sam Tomkins; 19 Paul Deacon; 8 Stuart Fielden; 7 Thomas Leuluai; 10 Andy Coley (C); 11 Harrison Hansen; 12 Joel Tomkins; 13 Sean O'Loughlin. Subs (all used): 14 Paul Prescott; 16 Phil Bailey; 17 Iafeta Palea'aesina; 23 Lee Mossop.
Tries: Roberts (9, 56), Goulding (59), J Tomkins (68);
Goals: Richards 3/5.
Rugby Leaguer & League Express Men of the Match: *Wolves:* David Solomona; *Warriors:* Andy Coley.
Penalty count: 10-9; **Half-time:** 16-4;
Referee: Richard Silverwood; **Attendance:** 13,024.

Sunday 21st February 2010

CRUSADERS 18 HULL FC 16

CRUSADERS: 22 Elliot Kear; 2 Nick Youngquest; 14 Luke Dyer; 4 Vince Mellars; 5 Gareth Raynor; 15 Tommy Lee; 6 Michael Witt; 8 Ryan O'Hara (C); 9 Lincoln Withers; 10 Mark Bryant; 11 Weller Hauraki; 12 Jason Chan; 13 Rocky Trimarchi. Subs (all used): 17 Adam Peek; 16 Frank Winterstein; 18 Jamie Thackray; 23 Peter Lupton.
Tries: Youngquest (12, 70), Witt (27); **Goals:** Witt 3/3.
HULL: 1 Jordan Tansey; 24 Craig Hall; 21 Richard Whiting; 4 Kirk Yeaman; 3 Tom Briscoe; 14 Danny Washbrook; 6 Richard Horne; 10 Mark O'Meley; 9 Shaun Berrigan; 11 Lee Radford; 22 Mike Burnett; 16 Willie Manu; 13 Craig Fitzgibbon (C). Subs (all used): 8 Ewan Dowes; 15 Epalahame Lauaki; 17 Peter Cusack; 20 Danny Houghton.
Tries: Radford (15), Briscoe (17), Yeaman (61);
Goals: Fitzgibbon 2/3.
On report: Lauaki (55) - alleged use of the elbow.
Rugby Leaguer & League Express Men of the Match: *Crusaders:* Michael Witt; *Hull:* Jordan Tansey.
Penalty count: 8-7; **Half-time:** 12-12;
Referee: Ian Smith; **Attendance:** 6,794.

HULL KINGSTON ROVERS 0 HUDDERSFIELD GIANTS 30

ROVERS: 28 Ben Cockayne; 2 Peter Fox; 15 Mike Ratu (D); 3 Kris Welham; 5 Liam Colbon; 4 Jake Webster; 7 Michael Dobson; 8 Rhys Lovegrove; 9 Scott Murrell; 20 Michael Vella (C); 11 Clint Newton; 16 Jason Netherton; 6 Paul Cooke. Subs (all used): 22 Liam Watts; 10 Scott Wheeldon; 14 Matt Cook; 17 Ben Fisher.
GIANTS: 1 Brett Hodgson (C); 2 Leroy Cudjoe; 3 Jamahl Lolesi; 19 Michael Lawrence; 5 David Hodgson; 6 Kevin Brown; 7 Luke Robinson; 16 Darrell Griffin; 9 Shaun Lunt; 15 Andy Raleigh; 11 Lee Gilmour; 33 Graeme Horne; 20 David Faiumu. Subs (all used): 8 Eorl Crabtree; 12 David Fa'alogo; 21 Scott Grix; 23 Larne Patrick.
Tries: Lunt (9), D Hodgson (22, 54, 74), Patrick (28), Cudjoe (78); **Goals:** B Hodgson 3/6.
Rugby Leaguer & League Express Men of the Match: *Rovers:* Jake Webster; *Giants:* Brett Hodgson.
Penalty count: 7-3; **Half-time:** 0-18;
Referee: Ben Thaler; **Attendance:** 7,575.

ROUND 4

Friday 26th February 2010

HULL FC 28 HARLEQUINS 4

HULL: 21 Richard Whiting; 2 Mark Calderwood; 24 Craig Hall; 4 Kirk Yeaman; 3 Tom Briscoe; 19 Jordan Turner (D); 6 Richard Horne; 11 Lee Radford; 9 Shaun Berrigan; 10 Mark O'Meley; 16 Willie Manu; 12 Danny Tickle; 13 Craig Fitzgibbon (C). Subs (all used): 20 Danny Houghton; 17 Peter Cusack; 8 Ewan Dowes; 15 Epalahame Lauaki.
Tries: Fitzgibbon (9), Yeaman (21), Hall (44), Tickle (49), Horne (67); **Goals:** Tickle 3/4, Fitzgibbon 1/1.
HARLEQUINS: 26 Ben Jones-Bishop; 22 Jamie O'Callaghan; 3 Tony Clubb; 4 David Howell; 5 Will Sharp; 1 Chris Melling; 7 Danny Orr; 10 Louie McCarthy-Scarsbrook; 9 Chad Randall (C); 14 Oliver Wilkes; 11 Luke Williamson; 18 Ryan Esders; 16 Jason Golden. Subs (all used): 8 Karl Temata; 17 Danny Ward; 28 Ben Bolger; 29 Martyn Smith (D).
Try: Clubb (62); **Goals:** Orr 0/1.
Rugby Leaguer & League Express Men of the Match: *Hull:* Richard Whiting; *Harlequins:* Will Sharp.
Penalty count: 5-2; **Half-time:** 12-0;
Referee: Steve Ganson; **Attendance:** 13,965.

SALFORD CITY REDS 0 BRADFORD BULLS 7

CITY REDS: 1 Karl Fitzpatrick; 2 Jodie Broughton; 3 Mark Henry; 4 Willie Talau; 5 Ashley Gibson; 6 Stefan Ratchford; 21 Daniel Holdsworth; 19 Ryan Boyle; 9 Malcolm Alker (C); 10 Rob Parker; 11 Ian Sibbit; 12 Luke Adamson; 13 Luke Swain. Subs (all used): 16 Phil Leuluai; 17 Adam Sidlow; 15 Stuart Littler; 7 Jeremy Smith.
BULLS: 1 Dave Halley; 2 Rikki Sheriffe; 3 Paul Sykes; 4 Chris Nero; 5 Stuart Reardon; 6 Brett Kearney; 7 Matt Orford; 8 Nick Scruton; 9 Heath L'Estrange; 10 Andy Lynch (C); 13 Jamie Langley; 20 Elliott Whitehead; 11 Steve Menzies. Subs (all used): 14 Wayne Godwin; 22 James Donaldson; 18 Craig Kopczak; 12 Glenn Hall.
Try: Menzies (23); **Goals:** Orford 1/2;
Field goal: Sykes (78).
Rugby Leaguer & League Express Men of the Match: *City Reds:* Stefan Ratchford; *Bulls:* Matt Orford.
Penalty count: 8-6; **Half-time:** 0-4;
Referee: James Child; **Attendance:** 3,806.

ST HELENS 22 WAKEFIELD TRINITY WILDCATS 16

SAINTS: 1 Paul Wellens; 24 Jonny Lomax; 3 Matt Gidley; 21 Gary Wheeler; 5 Francis Meli; 6 Leon Pryce; 7 Kyle Eastmond; 10 James Graham; 16 Scott Moore; 8 Nick Fozzard; 11 Tony Puletua; 17 Paul Clough; 14 James Roby. Subs (all used): 9 Keiron Cunningham (C); 15 Bryn Hargreaves; 18 Matty Ashurst; 23 Maurie Fa'asavalu.
Tries: Lomax (28), Eastmond (43), Cunningham (50), Meli (56); **Goals:** Eastmond 3/5.
WILDCATS: 1 Matt Blaymire; 18 Aaron Murphy; 4 Darryl Millard; 3 Sean Gleeson; 23 Dale Morton; 6 Ben Jeffries; 7 Danny Brough; 8 Shane Tronc; 14 Sam Obst; 10 Michael Korkidas; 12 Glenn Morrison; 13 Jason Demetriou (C); 20 Tevita Leo-Latu. Subs (all used): 11 Dale Ferguson; 17 Kevin Henderson; 24 James Davey; 25 Richard Moore.
Tries: Morton (16), Millard (18, 64);
Goals: Brough 2/2, Obst 0/1.
Rugby Leaguer & League Express Men of the Match: *Saints:* James Graham; *Wildcats:* Glenn Morrison.
Penalty count: 10-7; **Half-time:** 6-12;
Referee: Thierry Alibert; **Attendance:** 10,717.

WIGAN WARRIORS 58 CATALANS DRAGONS 0

WARRIORS: 2 Amos Roberts; 24 Darrell Goulding; 3 Martin Gleeson; 4 George Carmont; 5 Pat Richards; 6 Sam Tomkins; 7 Thomas Leuluai; 8 Stuart Fielden; 9 Mark Riddell; 10 Andy Coley; 16 Phil Bailey; 12 Joel Tomkins; 13 Sean O'Loughlin (C). Subs (all used): 14 Paul Prescott; 19 Paul Deacon; 21 Eamon O'Carroll; 23 Lee Mossop.
Tries: Richards (9, 15, 20, 37, 75), O'Loughlin (26), Goulding (29), Leuluai (58), Carmont (62, 71);
Goals: Richards 9/10.
DRAGONS: 1 Clint Greenshields; 26 Cyril Stacul; 23 Chris Walker; 4 Setaimata Sa; 5 Dimitri Pelo; 6 Adam Mogg; 16 William Barthau; 8 David Ferriol; 9 Casey McGuire; 18 Dane Carlaw; 3 Sebastien Raguin; 17 Cyrille Gossard; 13 Dallas Johnson. Subs (all used): 10 Jerome Guisset (C); 12 Gregory Mounis; 22 Jamal Fakir; 24 Remi Casty.
Rugby Leaguer & League Express Men of the Match: *Warriors:* Pat Richards; *Dragons:* Casey McGuire.
Penalty count: 5-1; **Half-time:** 36-0;
Referee: Ben Thaler; **Attendance:** 12,001.

Saturday 27th February 2010

CASTLEFORD TIGERS 20 HULL KINGSTON ROVERS 24

TIGERS: 23 Ryan McGoldrick; 27 Shaun Ainscough (D); 3 Michael Shenton; 4 James Evans; 5 Michael Wainwright; 6 Rangi Chase; 7 Brent Sherwin; 16 Paul Jackson; 9 Ryan Hudson (C); 8 Mitchell Sargent; 11 Brett Ferres; 12 Steve Snitch; 13 Joe Westerman. Subs: 10 Craig Huby; 14 Stuart Jones; 15 Liam Higgins; 21 Jordan Thompson (not used).
Tries: Wainwright (3), Ainscough (9, 47, 52);
Goals: Westerman 2/4.
ROVERS: 1 Shaun Briscoe; 2 Peter Fox; 3 Kris Welham; 4 Jake Webster; 28 Ben Cockayne; 19 Chaz I'Anson; 7 Michael Dobson; 8 Rhys Lovegrove; 9 Scott Murrell; 30 Joel Clinton (D); 11 Clint Newton; 14 Matt Cook; 20 Michael Vella (C). Subs (all used): 17 Ben Fisher; 22 Liam Watts; 16 Jason Netherton; 10 Scott Wheeldon.
Tries: Murrell (22), Dobson (29), Cockayne (65), Watts (73); **Goals:** Dobson 4/4.
Rugby Leaguer & League Express Men of the Match: *Tigers:* Shaun Ainscough; *Rovers:* Michael Dobson.
Penalty count: 5-5; **Half-time:** 10-12;
Referee: Phil Bentham; **Attendance:** 6,855.

Sunday 28th February 2010

HUDDERSFIELD GIANTS 10 WARRINGTON WOLVES 14

GIANTS: 1 Brett Hodgson (C); 2 Leroy Cudjoe; 19 Michael Lawrence; 4 Paul Whatuira; 5 David Hodgson; 6 Kevin Brown; 7 Luke Robinson; 16 Darrell Griffin; 20 David Faiumu; 15 Andy Raleigh; 11 Lee Gilmour; 12 David Fa'alogo; 22 Martin Aspinwall. Subs (all used): 8 Eorl Crabtree; 9 Shaun Lunt; 23 Larne Patrick; 33 Graeme Horne.
Tries: Brown (12), Whatuira (18); **Goals:** B Hodgson 1/2.
On report: Lawrence (57) - alleged spear tackle on Grix.
WOLVES: 1 Richard Mathers; 5 Chris Hicks; 3 Matt King; 23 Ryan Atkins; 2 Chris Riley; 17 Simon Grix; 7 Richard Myler; 8 Adrian Morley (C); 9 Michael Monaghan; 10 Garreth Carvell; 11 Louis Anderson; 12 Ben Westwood; 13 Ben Harrison. Subs (all used): 14 Mick Higham; 16 Paul Wood; 26 David Solomona; 27 Vinnie Anderson.
Tries: King (3, 30), Hicks (65); **Goals:** Myler 1/3.
Rugby Leaguer & League Express Men of the Match:
Giants: Kevin Brown; *Wolves:* Matt King.
Penalty count: 8-9; **Half-time:** 10-10;
Referee: Ian Smith; **Attendance:** 8,567.

ROUND 5

Friday 5th March 2010

BRADFORD BULLS 22 WIGAN WARRIORS 20

BULLS: 1 Dave Halley; 19 Jason Crookes; 3 Paul Sykes; 4 Chris Nero; 5 Stuart Reardon; 6 Brett Kearney; 7 Matt Orford; 8 Nick Scruton; 9 Heath L'Estrange; 10 Andy Lynch (C); 13 Jamie Langley; 20 Elliott Whitehead; 11 Steve Menzies. Subs (all used): 14 Wayne Godwin; 16 Michael Worrincy; 18 Craig Kopczak; 12 Glenn Hall.
Tries: Kearney (46), Orford (48, 72), Hall (78);
Goals: Orford 3/4.
WARRIORS: 2 Amos Roberts; 24 Darrell Goulding; 3 Martin Gleeson; 4 George Carmont; 5 Pat Richards; 6 Sam Tomkins; 7 Thomas Leuluai; 8 Stuart Fielden; 9 Mark Riddell; 10 Andy Coley; 11 Harrison Hansen; 12 Joel Tomkins; 13 Sean O'Loughlin (C). Subs (all used): 16 Phil Bailey; 19 Paul Deacon; 21 Eamon O'Carroll; 17 Iafeta Palea'aesina.
Tries: Goulding (4), Hansen (25), S Tomkins (36), Richards (39); **Goals:** Richards 2/4.
Rugby Leaguer & League Express Men of the Match:
Bulls: Matt Orford; *Warriors:* Amos Roberts.
Penalty count: 4-6; **Half-time:** 0-20;
Referee: Phil Bentham; **Attendance:** 9,244.

HULL FC 42 CASTLEFORD TIGERS 22

HULL: 1 Jordan Tansey; 2 Mark Calderwood; 24 Craig Hall; 4 Kirk Yeaman; 3 Tom Briscoe; 19 Jordan Turner; 6 Richard Horne; 10 Mark O'Meley; 9 Shaun Berrigan; 8 Ewan Dowes; 12 Danny Tickle; 16 Willie Manu; 13 Craig Fitzgibbon (C). Subs (all used): 15 Epalahame Lauaki; 17 Peter Cusack; 21 Richard Whiting; 23 Sam Moa.
Tries: Yeaman (11), Manu (22), Horne (47, 54), Cusack (52), Hall (58), Fitzgibbon (79);
Goals: Tickle 6/6, Fitzgibbon 1/1.
TIGERS: 23 Ryan McGoldrick; 27 Shaun Ainscough; 3 Michael Shenton; 4 James Evans; 5 Michael Wainwright; 6 Rangi Chase; 7 Brent Sherwin; 16 Paul Jackson; 9 Ryan Hudson (C); 8 Mitchell Sargent; 10 Craig Huby; 12 Steve Snitch; 17 Ryan Clayton. Subs (all used): 2 Kirk Dixon; 14 Stuart Jones; 15 Liam Higgins; 18 Nathan Massey.
Tries: Hudson (17), Ainscough (28), Chase (65), Evans (73); **Goals:** Huby 2/3, Dixon 1/1.
Rugby Leaguer & League Express Men of the Match:
Hull: Richard Horne; *Tigers:* James Evans.
Penalty count: 9-9; **Half-time:** 12-12;
Referee: Richard Silverwood; **Attendance:** 13,352.

LEEDS RHINOS 62 HARLEQUINS 4

RHINOS: 1 Brent Webb; 5 Ryan Hall; 23 Kallum Watkins; 4 Keith Senior; 26 Tom Bush (D); 6 Danny McGuire; 7 Rob Burrow; 16 Ryan Bailey; 14 Matt Diskin; 10 Jamie Peacock (C); 15 Greg Eastwood; 20 Jay Pitts; 11 Jamie Jones-Buchanan. Subs (all used): 12 Ali Lauitiiti; 19 Luke Burgess; 8 Kylie Leuluai; 9 Danny Buderus.
Tries: Webb (4, 28), Hall (35, 70), Buderus (45, 50), Lauitiiti (59, 72), McGuire (62), Watkins (67), Senior (76), Bush (79); **Goals:** Burrow 7/12.
HARLEQUINS: 26 Ben Jones-Bishop; 22 Jamie O'Callaghan; 3 Tony Clubb; 4 David Howell; 5 Will Sharp; 1 Chris Melling; 31 Max Edwards (D); 14 Oliver Wilkes; 9 Chad Randall (C); 17 Danny Ward; 11 Luke Williamson; 28 Ben Bolger; 16 Jason Golden. Subs (all used): 10 Louie McCarthy-Scarsbrook; 29 Martyn Smith; 25 Lamont Bryan; 34 Kyle Bibb (D).
Try: O'Callaghan (8); **Goals:** Melling 0/1.
Rugby Leaguer & League Express Men of the Match:
Rhinos: Danny McGuire; *Harlequins:* Will Sharp.
Penalty count: 14-2; **Half-time:** 14-4;
Referee: Thierry Alibert; **Attendance:** 12,684.

SALFORD CITY REDS 12 CATALANS DRAGONS 24

CITY REDS: 1 Karl Fitzpatrick; 2 Jodie Broughton; 3 Mark Henry; 4 Willie Talau; 5 Ashley Gibson; 6 Stefan Ratchford; 21 Daniel Holdsworth; 19 Ryan Boyle; 9 Malcolm Alker (C); 10 Rob Parker; 11 Ian Sibbit; 12 Luke Adamson; 13 Luke Swain. Subs (all used): 7 Jeremy Smith; 15 Stuart Littler; 16 Phil Leuluai; 17 Adam Sidlow.
Tries: Talau (19), Gibson (40); **Goals:** Ratchford 2/2.
DRAGONS: 1 Clint Greenshields; 2 Steven Bell; 3 Sebastien Raguin; 23 Chris Walker; 5 Dimitri Pelo; 4 Setaimata Sa; 9 Casey McGuire; 8 David Ferriol; 20 Kane Bentley; 18 Dane Carlaw; 17 Cyrille Gossard; 11 Olivier Elima (C); 13 Dallas Johnson. Subs (all used): 10 Jerome Guisset; 12 Gregory Mounis; 21 Sebastien Martins; 22 Jamal Fakir.
Tries: Walker (27, 31), Greenshields (51), Sa (59), Raguin (69); **Goals:** Walker 0/2, Mounis 2/3.
Rugby Leaguer & League Express Men of the Match:
City Reds: Stefan Ratchford; *Dragons:* Setaimata Sa.
Penalty count: 4-5; **Half-time:** 12-8;
Referee: Steve Ganson; **Attendance:** 3,022.

Saturday 6th March 2010

WAKEFIELD TRINITY WILDCATS 0 HUDDERSFIELD GIANTS 52

WILDCATS: 1 Matt Blaymire; 18 Aaron Murphy; 4 Darryl Millard; 3 Sean Gleeson; 23 Dale Morton; 6 Ben Jeffries; 7 Danny Brough; 8 Shane Tronc; 20 Tevita Leo-Latu; 10 Michael Korkidas; 12 Glenn Morrison; 11 Dale Ferguson; 13 Jason Demetriou (C). Subs (all used): 2 Damien Blanch; 25 Richard Moore; 14 Sam Obst; 17 Kevin Henderson.
GIANTS: 2 Leroy Cudjoe; 19 Michael Lawrence; 3 Jamahl Lolesi; 4 Paul Whatuira; 5 David Hodgson; 6 Kevin Brown; 7 Luke Robinson; 16 Darrell Griffin; 9 Shaun Lunt; 15 Andy Raleigh (C); 11 Lee Gilmour; 12 David Fa'alogo; 22 Martin Aspinwall. Subs (all used): 8 Eorl Crabtree; 20 David Faiumu; 21 Scott Grix; 23 Larne Patrick.
Tries: Fa'alogo (6), Whatuira (8), Aspinwall (12), Cudjoe (23), Grix (32, 68), Gilmour (45), D Hodgson (62), Patrick (73), Lunt (78); **Goals:** Cudjoe 6/10.
Rugby Leaguer & League Express Men of the Match:
Wildcats: Sam Obst; *Giants:* Paul Whatuira.
Penalty count: 6-3; **Half-time:** 0-26;
Referee: Ben Thaler; **Attendance:** 5,237.

Sunday 7th March 2010

HULL KINGSTON ROVERS 28 ST HELENS 24

ROVERS: 1 Shaun Briscoe; 2 Peter Fox; 3 Kris Welham; 4 Jake Webster; 5 Liam Colbon; 19 Chaz l'Anson; 7 Michael Dobson; 20 Michael Vella (C); 9 Scott Murrell; 30 Joel Clinton; 11 Clint Newton; 8 Rhys Lovegrove; 13 Ben Galea. Subs (all used): 16 Jason Netherton; 17 Ben Fisher; 22 Liam Watts; 28 Ben Cockayne.
Tries: Galea (14), Colbon (21, 23, 47), Fisher (78);
Goals: Dobson 4/5.
SAINTS: 1 Paul Wellens; 24 Jonny Lomax; 19 Chris Dean; 21 Gary Wheeler; 5 Francis Meli; 6 Leon Pryce; 7 Kyle Eastmond; 10 James Graham; 16 Scott Moore; 8 Nick Fozzard; 11 Tony Puletua; 17 Paul Clough; 14 James Roby. Subs (all used): 23 Maurie Fa'asavalu; 9 Keiron Cunningham (C); 15 Bryn Hargreaves; 22 Andrew Dixon.
Tries: Wheeler (8), Eastmond (27), Moore (36), Meli (38), Dean (57); **Goals:** Eastmond 2/5.
Rugby Leaguer & League Express Men of the Match:
Rovers: Rhys Lovegrove; *Saints:* Kyle Eastmond.
Penalty count: 8-3; **Half-time:** 16-20;
Referee: Ian Smith; **Attendance:** 8,202.

WARRINGTON WOLVES 46 CRUSADERS 12

WOLVES: 2 Chris Riley; 5 Chris Hicks; 4 Chris Bridge; 23 Ryan Atkins; 3 Matt King; 17 Simon Grix; 9 Michael Monaghan; 8 Adrian Morley (C); 14 Mick Higham; 10 Garreth Carvell; 11 Louis Anderson; 12 Ben Westwood; 13 Ben Harrison. Subs (all used): 16 Paul Wood; 26 David Solomona; 27 Vinnie Anderson; 29 Rhys Williams (D).
Tries: King (13, 38), Grix (22), Westwood (39, 44), Monaghan (58), Hicks (68), Solomona (77);
Goals: Bridge 7/8.
CRUSADERS: 22 Elliot Kear; 2 Nick Youngquest; 14 Luke Dyer; 4 Vince Mellars; 5 Gareth Raynor; 23 Peter Lupton; 6 Michael Witt; 8 Ryan O'Hara (C); 9 Lincoln Withers; 10 Mark Bryant; 12 Jason Chan; 11 Weller Hauraki; 13 Rocky Trimarchi. Subs (all used): 21 Lloyd White; 17 Adam Peek; 16 Frank Winterstein; 18 Jamie Thackray.
Tries: Bryant (7), Withers (16); **Goals:** Witt 2/2.
Rugby Leaguer & League Express Men of the Match:
Wolves: Matt King; *Crusaders:* Elliot Kear.
Penalty count: 11-1; **Half-time:** 24-12;
Referee: James Child; **Attendance:** 11,113.

ROUND 6

Friday 12th March 2010

HULL KINGSTON ROVERS 18 WAKEFIELD TRINITY WILDCATS 31

ROVERS: 1 Shaun Briscoe; 2 Peter Fox; 3 Kris Welham; 4 Jake Webster; 5 Liam Colbon; 9 Scott Murrell; 7 Michael Dobson; 30 Joel Clinton; 21 Josh Hodgson (D); 20 Michael Vella (C); 11 Clint Newton; 8 Rhys Lovegrove; 13 Ben Galea. Subs (all used): 17 Ben Fisher; 10 Scott Wheeldon; 22 Liam Watts; 28 Ben Cockayne.
Tries: Colbon (4), Webster (19), Murrell (24);
Goals: Dobson 3/4.
WILDCATS: 1 Matt Blaymire; 23 Dale Morton; 3 Sean Gleeson; 4 Darryl Millard; 18 Aaron Murphy; 14 Sam Obst; 7 Danny Brough; 8 Shane Tronc; 20 Tevita Leo-Latu; 25 Richard Moore; 11 Dale Ferguson; 13 Jason Demetriou (C); 12 Glenn Morrison. Subs (all used): 10 Michael Korkidas; 17 Kevin Henderson; 24 James Davey; 31 Ben Gledhill (D).
Tries: Tronc (9, 73), Obst (45), Blaymire (47), Millard (61); **Goals:** Obst 2/2, Brough 3/3;
Field goal: Blaymire (67).
Sin bin: Brough (39) - professional foul.
Rugby Leaguer & League Express Men of the Match:
Rovers: Jake Webster; *Wildcats:* Sam Obst.
Penalty count: 5-8; **Half-time:** 18-6;
Referee: James Child; **Attendance:** 8,004.

ST HELENS 37 CRUSADERS 30

SAINTS: 7 Kyle Eastmond; 2 Ade Gardner; 19 Chris Dean; 21 Gary Wheeler; 5 Francis Meli; 6 Leon Pryce; 14 James Roby; 10 James Graham; 9 Keiron Cunningham (C); 15 Bryn Hargreaves; 13 Chris Flannery; 12 Jon Wilkin; 17 Paul Clough. Subs (all used): 8 Nick Fozzard; 16 Scott Moore; 18 Matty Ashurst; 23 Maurie Fa'asavalu.
Tries: Roby (5), Eastmond (11), Meli (25), Dean (35), Moore (47), Pryce (55); **Goals:** Eastmond 6/6;
Field goal: Eastmond (77).
CRUSADERS: 2 Nick Youngquest; 24 Anthony Blackwood; 14 Luke Dyer; 4 Vince Mellars; 5 Gareth Raynor; 23 Peter Lupton; 6 Michael Witt; 8 Ryan O'Hara (C); 9 Lincoln Withers; 10 Mark Bryant; 12 Jason Chan; 11 Weller Hauraki; 13 Rocky Trimarchi. Subs (all used): 3 Tony Martin (D); 17 Adam Peek; 16 Frank Winterstein; 18 Jamie Thackray.
Tries: Mellars (17), Thackray (45), Raynor (57), Withers (69), Dyer (73); **Goals:** Witt 5/5.
Rugby Leaguer & League Express Men of the Match:
Saints: Leon Pryce; *Crusaders:* Michael Witt.
Penalty count: 11-3; **Half-time:** 24-6;
Referee: Phil Bentham; **Attendance:** 8,507.

WIGAN WARRIORS 48 HULL FC 24

WARRIORS: 1 Cameron Phelps; 2 Amos Roberts; 3 Martin Gleeson; 24 Darrell Goulding; 5 Pat Richards; 6 Sam Tomkins; 7 Thomas Leuluai; 8 Stuart Fielden; 9 Mark Riddell; 10 Andy Coley; 11 Harrison Hansen; 12 Joel Tomkins; 13 Sean O'Loughlin (C). Subs (all used): 14 Paul Prescott; 16 Phil Bailey; 21 Eamon O'Carroll; 23 Lee Mossop.
Tries: Richards (15), Goulding (20, 47), Gleeson (33), Roberts (39), S Tomkins (55, 63), Phelps (71);
Goals: Richards 8/9.
HULL: 1 Jordan Tansey; 24 Craig Hall; 21 Richard Whiting; 4 Kirk Yeaman; 3 Tom Briscoe; 6 Richard Horne; 7 Sean Long (C); 10 Mark O'Meley; 9 Shaun Berrigan; 8 Ewan Dowes; 12 Danny Tickle; 16 Willie Manu; 13 Craig Fitzgibbon. Subs (all used): 15 Epalahame Lauaki; 17 Peter Cusack; 11 Lee Radford; 20 Danny Houghton.
Tries: Whiting (24), Hall (67), Long (75), Horne (78);
Goals: Tickle 4/4.
Rugby Leaguer & League Express Men of the Match:
Warriors: Sean O'Loughlin; *Hull:* Craig Fitzgibbon.
Penalty count: 10-8; **Half-time:** 24-6;
Referee: Thierry Alibert; **Attendance:** 15,045.

Saturday 13th March 2010

WARRINGTON WOLVES 33 BRADFORD BULLS 8

WOLVES: 2 Chris Riley; 5 Chris Hicks; 4 Chris Bridge; 23 Ryan Atkins; 3 Matt King; 17 Simon Grix; 7 Richard Myler; 8 Adrian Morley (C); 9 Michael Monaghan; 10 Garreth Carvell; 11 Louis Anderson; 12 Ben Westwood; 13 Ben Harrison. Subs (all used): 16 Paul Wood; 14 Mick Higham; 26 David Solomona; 27 Vinnie Anderson.
Tries: Myler (32), Atkins (51, 63), King (61, 78), Monaghan (68); **Goals:** Bridge 4/6;
Field goal: Monaghan (74).
BULLS: 1 Dave Halley; 2 Rikki Sheriffe; 3 Paul Sykes; 4 Chris Nero; 5 Stuart Reardon; 6 Brett Kearney; 7 Matt Orford; 8 Nick Scruton; 9 Heath L'Estrange; 10 Andy Lynch (C); 20 Elliott Whitehead; 12 Glenn Hall; 11 Steve Menzies. Subs (all used): 14 Wayne Godwin; 18 Craig Kopczak; 16 Michael Worrincy; 22 James Donaldson.
Tries: Lynch (24), Sykes (38);
Goals: Orford 0/2, Sykes 0/1.
Rugby Leaguer & League Express Men of the Match:
Wolves: Adrian Morley; *Bulls:* Heath L'Estrange.
Penalty count: 7-6; **Half-time:** 6-8;
Referee: Steve Ganson; **Attendance:** 10,434.

CATALANS DRAGONS 16 CASTLEFORD TIGERS 20

DRAGONS: 1 Clint Greenshields; 2 Steven Bell; 3 Sebastien Raguin; 23 Chris Walker; 26 Cyril Stacul; 4 Setaimata Sa; 9 Casey McGuire; 8 David Ferriol; 20 Kane Bentley; 18 Dane Carlaw; 11 Olivier Elima (C); 17 Cyrille Gossard; 13 Dallas Johnson. Subs (all used): 10 Jerome Guisset; 12 Gregory Mounis; 22 Jamal Fakir; 24 Remi Casty.
Tries: Walker (15), Fakir (35), McGuire (60);
Goals: Walker 0/1, Mounis 2/2.
TIGERS: 23 Ryan McGoldrick; 5 Michael Wainwright; 3 Michael Shenton; 2 Kirk Dixon; 27 Shaun Ainscough; 6 Rangi Chase; 7 Brent Sherwin; 15 Liam Higgins; 9 Ryan Hudson (C); 10 Craig Huby; 17 Ryan Clayton; 12 Steve Snitch; 13 Joe Westerman. Subs (all used): 14 Stuart Jones; 8 Mitchell Sargent; 29 Michael Cooper (D); 22 John Davies (D).
Tries: Cooper (39), Chase (47), Jones (55), Wainwright (64); **Goals:** Westerman 2/4.
Rugby Leaguer & League Express Men of the Match:
Dragons: Chris Walker; *Tigers:* Rangi Chase.
Penalty count: 6-7; **Half-time:** 10-6;
Referee: Ian Smith; **Attendance:** 6,810.

Sunday 14th March 2010

HARLEQUINS 22 SALFORD CITY REDS 26

HARLEQUINS: 26 Ben Jones-Bishop; 22 Jamie O'Callaghan; 3 Tony Clubb; 4 David Howell; 5 Will Sharp; 1 Chris Melling; 7 Danny Orr; 17 Danny Ward; 9 Chad Randall (C); 10 Louie McCarthy-Scarsbrook; 11 Luke Williamson; 28 Ben Bolger; 16 Jason Golden. Subs (all

used): 34 Kyle Bibb; 14 Oliver Wilkes; 25 Lamont Bryan; 8 Karl Temata.
Tries: Orr (30), Temata (32), Bryan (48), Jones-Bishop (79); **Goals:** Orr 3/4.
CITY REDS: 1 Karl Fitzpatrick; 2 Jodie Broughton; 3 Mark Henry; 5 Ashley Gibson; 20 Steve Tyrer; 21 Daniel Holdsworth; 14 Matty Smith; 10 Rob Parker; 9 Malcolm Alker (C); 19 Ryan Boyle; 15 Stuart Littler; 12 Luke Adamson; 13 Luke Swain. Subs (all used): 16 Phil Leuluai; 7 Jeremy Smith; 18 Lee Jewitt; 17 Adam Sidlow.
Tries: Fitzpatrick (11), Tyrer (52, 60, 77), Broughton (75); **Goals:** Holdsworth 3/5.
Sin bin: J Smith (39) - late tackle on Orr.
Rugby Leaguer & League Express Men of the Match: *Harlequins:* Danny Orr; *City Reds:* Steve Tyrer.
Penalty count: 3-2; **Half-time:** 12-4;
Referee: Ben Thaler; **Attendance:** 2,395.

HUDDERSFIELD GIANTS 26 LEEDS RHINOS 20

GIANTS: 2 Leroy Cudjoe; 3 Jamahl Lolesi; 19 Michael Lawrence; 13 Stephen Wild; 5 David Hodgson; 6 Kevin Brown; 7 Luke Robinson; 16 Darrell Griffin; 9 Shaun Lunt; 15 Andy Raleigh (C); 11 Lee Gilmour; 12 David Fa'alogo; 22 Martin Aspinwall. Subs (all used): 8 Eorl Crabtree; 20 David Faiumu; 21 Scott Grix; 23 Larne Patrick.
Tries: Lunt (11), Gilmour (14), Patrick (48), Aspinwall (63); **Goals:** Cudjoe 5/5.
Sin bin: Raleigh (44) - fighting.
RHINOS: 1 Brent Webb; 5 Ryan Hall; 3 Brett Delaney; 4 Keith Senior; 23 Kallum Watkins; 6 Danny McGuire; 7 Rob Burrow; 16 Ryan Bailey; 9 Danny Buderus; 8 Kylie Leuluai; 10 Jamie Peacock (C); 17 Ian Kirke; 11 Jamie Jones-Buchanan. Subs (all used): 12 Ali Lauitiiti; 14 Matt Diskin; 19 Luke Burgess; 20 Jay Pitts.
Tries: Burrow (28), McGuire (37), Hall (39);
Goals: Burrow 4/4.
Sin bin: Lauitiiti (44) - fighting.
Rugby Leaguer & League Express Men of the Match: *Giants:* David Fa'alogo; *Rhinos:* Jamie Peacock.
Penalty count: 10-8; **Half-time:** 12-18;
Referee: Richard Silverwood; **Attendance:** 10,116.

ROUND 7

Friday 19th March 2010

CRUSADERS 14 CATALANS DRAGONS 6

CRUSADERS: 22 Elliot Kear; 1 Gareth Thomas (D); 3 Tony Martin; 4 Vince Mellars; 14 Luke Dyer; 23 Peter Lupton; 6 Michael Witt; 8 Ryan O'Hara (C); 9 Lincoln Withers; 10 Mark Bryant; 11 Weller Hauraki; 12 Jason Chan; 13 Rocky Trimarchi. Subs (all used): 2 Nick Youngquest; 16 Frank Winterstein; 18 Jamie Thackray; 20 Ben Flower.
Tries: Chan (8), Lupton (69); **Goals:** Witt 3/3.
DRAGONS: 14 David Guasch (D); 2 Steven Bell; 3 Sebastien Raguin; 5 Dimitri Pelo; 26 Cyril Stacul; 4 Setaimata Sa; 9 Casey McGuire; 8 David Ferriol; 20 Kane Bentley; 18 Dane Carlaw; 11 Olivier Elima (C); 17 Cyrille Gossard; 13 Dallas Johnson. Subs (all used): 10 Jerome Guisset; 12 Gregory Mounis; 22 Jamal Fakir; 25 Tony Gigot (D).
Try: Elima (48); **Goals:** Mounis 1/1.
Rugby Leaguer & League Express Men of the Match: *Crusaders:* Peter Lupton; *Dragons:* Dimitri Pelo.
Penalty count: 9-7; **Half-time:** 8-0;
Referee: Thierry Alibert; **Attendance:** 6,124.

HULL FC 18 BRADFORD BULLS 6

HULL: 1 Jordan Tansey; 2 Mark Calderwood; 21 Richard Whiting; 4 Kirk Yeaman; 3 Tom Briscoe; 19 Jordan Turner; 7 Sean Long (C); 10 Mark O'Meley; 9 Shaun Berrigan; 11 Lee Radford; 12 Danny Tickle; 16 Willie Manu; 13 Craig Fitzgibbon. Subs (all used): 15 Epalahame Lauaki; 17 Peter Cusack; 8 Ewan Dowes; 20 Danny Houghton.
Tries: Tansey (40, 46), Radford (70); **Goals:** Tickle 3/3.
BULLS: 1 Dave Halley; 2 Rikki Sheriffe; 15 Michael Platt; 4 Chris Nero; 5 Stuart Reardon; 3 Paul Sykes; 6 Brett Kearney; 8 Nick Scruton; 9 Heath L'Estrange; 10 Andy Lynch (C); 13 Jamie Langley; 20 Elliott Whitehead; 11 Steve Menzies. Subs (all used): 14 Wayne Godwin; 22 James Donaldson; 18 Craig Kopczak; 12 Glenn Hall.
Try: Reardon (79); **Goals:** Sykes 1/1, Godwin 0/1.
Rugby Leaguer & League Express Men of the Match: *Hull:* Jordan Turner; *Bulls:* Brett Kearney.
Penalty count: 5-4; **Half-time:** 6-2;
Referee: Ben Thaler; **Attendance:** 14,466.

LEEDS RHINOS 10 HULL KINGSTON ROVERS 17

RHINOS: 1 Brent Webb; 22 Michael Coady (D); 3 Brett Delaney; 4 Keith Senior; 27 Chris Clarkson (D); 6 Danny McGuire; 7 Rob Burrow; 8 Kylie Leuluai; 14 Matt Diskin; 10 Jamie Peacock (C); 20 Jay Pitts; 17 Ian Kirke; 11 Jamie Jones-Buchanan. Subs (all used): 12 Ali Lauitiiti; 19 Luke Burgess; 21 Kyle Amor (D); 25 Paul McShane.
Tries: Jones-Buchanan (1), Senior (47);
Goals: Burrow 1/2.
ROVERS: 1 Shaun Briscoe; 2 Peter Fox; 4 Jake Webster; 3 Kris Welham; 5 Liam Colbon; 9 Scott Murrell; 7 Michael Dobson; 20 Michael Vella (C); 21 Josh Hodgson; 30 Joel Clinton; 8 Rhys Lovegrove; 11 Clint Newton; 13 Ben Galea. Subs (all used): 16 Jason Netherton; 17 Ben Fisher; 10 Scott Wheeldon; 22 Liam Watts.
Tries: Colbon (22), Fox (26), Briscoe (35);
Goals: Dobson 2/4; **Field goal:** Dobson (77).
Rugby Leaguer & League Express Men of the Match: *Rhinos:* Danny McGuire; *Rovers:* Ben Galea.
Penalty count: 7-5; **Half-time:** 6-16;
Referee: Steve Ganson; **Attendance:** 15,201.

ST HELENS 28 WARRINGTON WOLVES 18

SAINTS: 1 Paul Wellens; 2 Ade Gardner; 3 Matt Gidley; 19 Chris Dean; 5 Francis Meli; 6 Leon Pryce; 7 Kyle Eastmond; 10 James Graham; 9 Keiron Cunningham (C); 11 Tony Puletua; 13 Chris Flannery; 4 Iosia Soliola; 12 Jon Wilkin. Subs (all used): 14 James Roby; 17 Paul Clough; 15 Bryn Hargreaves; 23 Maurie Fa'asavalu.
Tries: Eastmond (7), Wilkin (37), Gardner (47, 67);
Goals: Eastmond 6/6.
WOLVES: 1 Richard Mathers; 5 Chris Hicks; 3 Matt King; 23 Ryan Atkins; 2 Chris Riley; 17 Simon Grix; 7 Richard Myler; 8 Adrian Morley (C); 9 Michael Monaghan; 10 Garreth Carvell; 11 Louis Anderson; 12 Ben Westwood; 13 Ben Harrison. Subs (all used): 16 Paul Wood; 14 Mick Higham; 26 David Solomona; 4 Chris Bridge.
Tries: Grix (31), King (55), Harrison (59), Hicks (62);
Goals: Myler 0/1, Bridge 1/3.
Rugby Leaguer & League Express Men of the Match: *Saints:* Kyle Eastmond; *Wolves:* Michael Monaghan.
Penalty count: 9-12; **Half-time:** 12-4;
Referee: Richard Silverwood; **Attendance:** 17,500.

Saturday 20th March 2010

HARLEQUINS 18 HUDDERSFIELD GIANTS 32

HARLEQUINS: 26 Ben Jones-Bishop; 5 Will Sharp; 3 Tony Clubb; 4 David Howell; 22 Jamie O'Callaghan; 1 Chris Melling; 7 Danny Orr; 14 Oliver Wilkes; 9 Chad Randall (C); 17 Danny Ward; 11 Luke Williamson; 28 Ben Bolger; 16 Jason Golden. Subs: 25 Lamont Bryan; 24 Dave Williams; 34 Kyle Bibb (not used); 10 Louie McCarthy-Scarsbrook.
Tries: Randall (40), Melling (61), Clubb (65);
Goals: Orr 3/3.
GIANTS: 1 Brett Hodgson (C); 2 Leroy Cudjoe; 13 Stephen Wild; 11 Lee Gilmour; 5 David Hodgson; 6 Kevin Brown; 7 Luke Robinson; 16 Darrell Griffin; 9 Shaun Lunt; 15 Andy Raleigh; 33 Graeme Horne; 12 David Fa'alogo; 22 Martin Aspinwall. Subs (all used): 8 Eorl Crabtree; 23 Larne Patrick; 21 Scott Grix; 20 David Faiumu.
Tries: Gilmour (3), Cudjoe (6, 35, 45), Crabtree (50), Horne (57); **Goals:** B Hodgson 4/7.
Rugby Leaguer & League Express Men of the Match: *Harlequins:* Ben Jones-Bishop; *Giants:* Leroy Cudjoe.
Penalty count: 4-8; **Half-time:** 6-14;
Referee: Phil Bentham; **Attendance:** 2,624.

Sunday 21st March 2010

CASTLEFORD TIGERS 22 WIGAN WARRIORS 36

TIGERS: 23 Ryan McGoldrick; 21 Jordan Thompson; 3 Michael Shenton; 2 Kirk Dixon; 5 Michael Wainwright; 13 Joe Westerman; 6 Rangi Chase; 15 Liam Higgins; 9 Ryan Hudson (C); 10 Craig Huby; 12 Steve Snitch; 14 Stuart Jones; 17 Ryan Clayton. Subs (all used): 7 Brent Sherwin; 8 Mitchell Sargent; 18 Nathan Massey; 29 Michael Cooper.
Tries: Shenton (18, 26), Wainwright (63), Cooper (78);
Goals: Westerman 3/5.
Sin bin: Chase (61) - punching.
WARRIORS: 1 Cameron Phelps; 2 Amos Roberts; 3 Martin Gleeson; 4 George Carmont; 5 Pat Richards; 6 Sam Tomkins; 7 Thomas Leuluai; 8 Stuart Fielden; 9 Mark Riddell; 10 Andy Coley; 16 Phil Bailey; 12 Joel Tomkins; 13 Sean O'Loughlin (C). Subs (all used): 14 Paul Prescott; 21 Eamon O'Carroll; 23 Lee Mossop; 29 Chris Tuson.
Tries: Roberts (13, 46, 72), Phelps (16), Richards (29), J Tomkins (44, 51); **Goals:** Richards 4/8.
Rugby Leaguer & League Express Men of the Match: *Tigers:* Ryan Hudson; *Warriors:* Amos Roberts.
Penalty count: 12-9; **Half-time:** 12-14;
Referee: James Child; **Attendance:** 8,493.

WAKEFIELD TRINITY WILDCATS 36
SALFORD CITY REDS 6

WILDCATS: 1 Matt Blaymire; 2 Damien Blanch; 3 Sean Gleeson; 4 Darryl Millard; 18 Aaron Murphy; 13 Jason Demetriou (C); 14 Sam Obst; 8 Shane Tronc; 20 Tevita Leo-Latu; 25 Richard Moore; 11 Dale Ferguson; 17 Kevin Henderson; 12 Glenn Morrison. Subs (all used): 10 Michael Korkidas; 21 Paul Cooke (D); 24 James Davey; 31 Ben Gledhill.
Tries: Millard (6), Leo-Latu (10), Morrison (13), Ferguson (18), Murphy (24), Obst (53), Blanch (69);
Goals: Obst 4/7.
CITY REDS: 1 Karl Fitzpatrick; 20 Steve Tyrer; 3 Mark Henry; 5 Ashley Gibson; 2 Jodie Broughton; 21 Daniel Holdsworth; 14 Matty Smith; 19 Ryan Boyle; 9 Malcolm Alker (C); 10 Rob Parker; 15 Stuart Littler; 12 Luke Adamson; 13 Luke Swain. Subs (all used): 8 Ray Cashmere; 17 Adam Sidlow; 18 Lee Jewitt; 6 Stefan Ratchford.
Try: Littler (60); **Goals:** Ratchford 1/1.
Rugby Leaguer & League Express Men of the Match: *Wildcats:* Sam Obst; *City Reds:* Luke Swain.
Penalty count: 7-7; **Half-time:** 28-0;
Referee: Gareth Hewer; **Attendance:** 4,883.

ROUND 8

Friday 26th March 2010

BRADFORD BULLS 19 HARLEQUINS 12

BULLS: 6 Brett Kearney; 2 Rikki Sheriffe; 15 Michael Platt; 4 Chris Nero; 5 Stuart Reardon; 3 Paul Sykes; 7 Matt Orford; 8 Nick Scruton; 9 Heath L'Estrange; 10 Andy Lynch (C); 13 Jamie Langley; 20 Elliott Whitehead; 11 Steve Menzies. Subs (all used): 14 Wayne Godwin; 22 James Donaldson; 18 Craig Kopczak; 12 Glenn Hall.
Tries: Platt (14), Kearney (35), Menzies (52);
Goals: Orford 3/4; **Field goal:** Orford (78).
HARLEQUINS: 26 Ben Jones-Bishop; 5 Will Sharp; 3 Tony Clubb; 4 David Howell; 22 Jamie O'Callaghan; 21 Luke Gale; 9 Chad Randall (C); 14 Oliver Wilkes; 7 Danny Orr; 17 Danny Ward; 11 Luke Williamson; 1 Chris Melling; 16 Jason Golden. Subs (all used): 25 Lamont Bryan; 24 Dave Williams; 28 Ben Bolger; 10 Louie McCarthy-Scarsbrook.
Tries: Melling (13), Orr (63); **Goals:** Orr 1/1, Gale 1/1.
Rugby Leaguer & League Express Men of the Match: *Bulls:* Brett Kearney; *Harlequins:* Chad Randall.
Penalty count: 8-8; **Half-time:** 10-6;
Referee: Richard Silverwood; **Attendance:** 7,153.

CASTLEFORD TIGERS 22 CRUSADERS 16

TIGERS: 23 Ryan McGoldrick; 21 Jordan Thompson; 3 Michael Shenton; 2 Kirk Dixon; 27 Shaun Ainscough; 6 Rangi Chase; 7 Brent Sherwin; 15 Liam Higgins; 9 Ryan Hudson (C); 8 Mitchell Sargent; 14 Stuart Jones; 12 Steve Snitch; 13 Joe Westerman. Subs (all used): 17 Ryan Clayton; 29 Michael Cooper; 30 Chris Tuson (D); 16 Paul Jackson.
Tries: Dixon (16), McGoldrick (30), Westerman (38), Thompson (72); **Goals:** Westerman 3/5.
CRUSADERS: 22 Elliot Kear; 2 Nick Youngquest; 3 Tony Martin; 4 Vince Mellars; 14 Luke Dyer; 6 Michael Witt; 23 Peter Lupton; 8 Ryan O'Hara (C); 9 Lincoln Withers; 10 Mark Bryant; 11 Weller Hauraki; 12 Jason Chan; 13 Rocky Trimarchi. Subs (all used): 1 Gareth Thomas; 16 Frank Winterstein; 17 Adam Peek; 18 Jamie Thackray.
Tries: Mellars (25), Chan (53), Hauraki (74);
Goals: Witt 2/3.
Rugby Leaguer & League Express Men of the Match: *Tigers:* Rangi Chase; *Crusaders:* Weller Hauraki.
Penalty count: 8-12; **Half-time:** 16-6;
Referee: Ian Smith; **Attendance:** 5,299.

WARRINGTON WOLVES 32
WAKEFIELD TRINITY WILDCATS 16

WOLVES: 1 Richard Mathers; 5 Chris Hicks; 3 Matt King; 23 Ryan Atkins; 2 Chris Riley; 17 Simon Grix; 7 Richard Myler; 8 Adrian Morley (C); 9 Michael Monaghan; 10 Garreth Carvell; 11 Louis Anderson; 12 Ben Westwood; 4 Chris Bridge. Subs (all used): 13 Ben Harrison; 14 Mick Higham; 16 Paul Wood; 26 David Solomona.
Tries: Riley (4, 27, 45), Bridge (12), Atkins (40, 50);
Goals: Bridge 4/6.
WILDCATS: 1 Matt Blaymire; 2 Damien Blanch; 3 Sean Gleeson; 4 Darryl Millard; 18 Aaron Murphy; 21 Paul Cooke; 14 Sam Obst; 8 Shane Tronc; 20 Tevita Leo-Latu; 25 Richard Moore; 11 Dale Ferguson; 13 Jason Demetriou (C); 12 Glenn Morrison. Subs (all used): 10 Michael Korkidas; 17 Kevin Henderson; 31 Ben Gledhill; 32 Danny Kirmond (D).
Tries: Murphy (18), Korkidas (37), Obst (63);
Goals: Cooke 2/3.
Rugby Leaguer & League Express Men of the Match: *Wolves:* Chris Bridge; *Wildcats:* Kevin Henderson.
Penalty count: 7-5; **Half-time:** 22-10;
Referee: Phil Bentham; **Attendance:** 10,723.

WIGAN WARRIORS 24 LEEDS RHINOS 4

WARRIORS: 2 Amos Roberts; 24 Darrell Goulding; 3 Martin Gleeson; 4 George Carmont; 5 Pat Richards; 6 Sam Tomkins; 7 Thomas Leuluai; 8 Stuart Fielden; 9 Mark Riddell; 10 Andy Coley; 16 Phil Bailey (C); 12 Joel Tomkins; 13 Sean O'Loughlin. Subs (all used): 14 Paul Prescott; 15 Michael Mcllorum; 21 Eamon O'Carroll; 23 Lee Mossop.
Tries: Carmont (33), Goulding (50, 64), J Tomkins (62);
Goals: Richards 4/5.
On report: J Tomkins (74) - alleged use of the knee.
RHINOS: 1 Brent Webb; 5 Ryan Hall; 27 Chris Clarkson; 4 Keith Senior (C); 26 Tom Bush; 6 Danny McGuire; 7 Rob Burrow; 19 Luke Burgess; 14 Matt Diskin; 16 Ryan Bailey; 20 Jay Pitts; 17 Ian Kirke; 11 Jamie Jones-Buchanan. Subs (all used): 9 Danny Buderus; 12 Ali Lauitiiti; 21 Kyle Amor; 24 Luke Ambler (D).
Try: Hall (46); **Goals:** Burrow 0/1.
On report: Bailey (80) - alleged dangerous tackle.
Rugby Leaguer & League Express Men of the Match: *Warriors:* Sean O'Loughlin; *Rhinos:* Rob Burrow.
Penalty count: 8-8; **Half-time:** 6-0;
Referee: Steve Ganson; **Attendance:** 17,883.

Saturday 27th March 2010

SALFORD CITY REDS 27 HULL FC 20

CITY REDS: 1 Karl Fitzpatrick; 2 Jodie Broughton; 3 Mark Henry; 4 Willie Talau; 20 Steve Tyrer; 14 Matty Smith; 21 Daniel Holdsworth; 8 Ray Cashmere; 9 Malcolm Alker (C); 19 Ryan Boyle; 17 Adam Sidlow; 12 Luke Adamson; 13 Luke Swain. Subs (all used): 15 Stuart Littler; 10 Rob Parker; 18 Lee Jewitt; 5 Ashley Gibson.
Tries: Sidlow (3), Fitzpatrick (19, 54), Broughton (44, 62); **Goals:** Holdsworth 3/5; **Field goal:** Holdsworth (80).
HULL: 1 Jordan Tansey; 25 Reece Lyne (D); 21 Richard Whiting; 4 Kirk Yeaman; 3 Tom Briscoe; 19 Jordan Turner; 7 Sean Long (C); 10 Mark O'Meley; 9 Shaun Berrigan; 11 Lee Radford; 16 Willie Manu; 12 Danny Tickle; 13 Craig Fitzgibbon. Subs (all used): 8 Ewan Dowes; 15 Epalahame Lauaki; 20 Danny Houghton; 23 Sam Moa.
Tries: Long (14), Yeaman (26), Lauaki (38), Lyne (58);
Goals: Tickle 2/4.
Rugby Leaguer & League Express Men of the Match: *City Reds:* Daniel Holdsworth; *Hull:* Danny Houghton.
Penalty count: 13-9; **Half-time:** 12-16;
Referee: James Child; **Attendance:** 3,535.

Catalans' Chris Walker leaves Hull KR duo Clint Newton and Rhys Lovegrove trailing

CATALANS DRAGONS 16 HULL KINGSTON ROVERS 10

DRAGONS: 23 Chris Walker; 2 Steven Bell; 3 Sebastien Raguin; 5 Dimitri Pelo; 26 Cyril Stacul; 4 Setaimata Sa; 7 Thomas Bosc; 8 David Ferriol; 9 Casey McGuire; 18 Dane Carlaw; 11 Olivier Elima (C); 17 Cyrille Gossard; 13 Dallas Johnson. Subs (all used): 10 Jerome Guisset; 12 Gregory Mounis; 21 Sebastien Martins; 25 Tony Gigot.
Tries: Bell (32), Carlaw (49), Gossard (64);
Goals: Bosc 2/3.
On report: Walker (76) - alleged high tackle on Colbon.
ROVERS: 1 Shaun Briscoe; 2 Peter Fox; 4 Jake Webster; 3 Kris Welham; 5 Liam Colbon; 9 Scott Murrell; 7 Michael Dobson; 20 Michael Vella (C); 21 Josh Hodgson; 30 Joel Clinton; 11 Clint Newton; 14 Matt Cook; 13 Ben Galea. Subs (all used): 16 Jason Netherton; 17 Ben Fisher; 8 Rhys Lovegrove; 10 Scott Wheeldon.
Tries: Webster (73), Welham (75); **Goals:** Dobson 1/2.
Rugby Leaguer & League Express Men of the Match: *Dragons:* Chris Walker; *Rovers:* Jake Webster.
Penalty count: 5-8; **Half-time:** 6-0;
Referee: Ben Thaler; **Attendance:** 6,620.

Sunday 28th March 2010

HUDDERSFIELD GIANTS 6 ST HELENS 24

GIANTS: 1 Brett Hodgson (C); 3 Jamahl Lolesi; 13 Stephen Wild; 4 Paul Whatuira; 5 David Hodgson; 6 Kevin Brown; 7 Luke Robinson; 16 Darrell Griffin; 9 Shaun Lunt; 15 Andy Raleigh; 11 Lee Gilmour; 23 Larne Patrick; 20 David Faiumu. Subs (all used): 8 Eorl Crabtree; 34 Danny Brough (D); 21 Scott Grix; 22 Martin Aspinwall.
Try: Grix (48); **Goals:** B Hodgson 1/1.
SAINTS: 7 Kyle Eastmond; 2 Ade Gardner; 3 Matt Gidley; 21 Gary Wheeler; 5 Francis Meli; 6 Leon Pryce; 16 Scott Moore; 10 James Graham; 9 Keiron Cunningham (C); 11 Tony Puletua; 13 Chris Flannery; 17 Paul Clough; 12 Jon Wilkin. Subs (all used): 23 Maurie Fa'asavalu; 15 Bryn Hargreaves; 14 James Roby; 22 Andrew Dixon.
Tries: Meli (6, 16), Graham (67), Eastmond (78);
Goals: Eastmond 4/5.
Rugby Leaguer & League Express Men of the Match: *Giants:* Andy Raleigh; *Saints:* Keiron Cunningham.
Penalty count: 8-10; **Half-time:** 0-10;
Referee: Thierry Alibert; **Attendance:** 9,648.

ROUND 9

Thursday 1st April 2010

LEEDS RHINOS 20 BRADFORD BULLS 20

RHINOS: 1 Brent Webb; 28 Lee Smith (D2); 3 Brett Delaney; 4 Keith Senior; 5 Ryan Hall; 6 Danny McGuire; 7 Rob Burrow; 8 Kylie Leuluai; 14 Matt Diskin; 16 Ryan Bailey; 17 Ian Kirke; 11 Jamie Jones-Buchanan; 13 Kevin Sinfield (C). Subs (all used): 24 Luke Ambler; 19 Luke Burgess; 9 Danny Buderus; 12 Ali Lauitiiti.
Tries: Smith (33, 75), Delaney (66), Sinfield (71);
Goals: Sinfield 2/4.
Sin bin: Buderus (57) - professional foul.
BULLS: 6 Brett Kearney; 1 Dave Halley; 15 Michael Platt; 4 Chris Nero; 5 Stuart Reardon; 3 Paul Sykes; 7 Matt Orford; 10 Andy Lynch (C); 9 Heath L'Estrange; 8 Nick Scruton; 20 Elliott Whitehead; 13 Jamie Langley; 11 Steve Menzies. Subs (all used): 12 Glenn Hall; 14 Wayne Godwin; 22 James Donaldson; 18 Craig Kopczak.
Tries: Nero (3, 52), Halley (11), Menzies (24);
Goals: Orford 2/5.
Rugby Leaguer & League Express Men of the Match: *Rhinos:* Lee Smith; *Bulls:* Andy Lynch.
Penalty count: 9-7; **Half time:** 6-16;
Referee: Phil Bentham; **Attendance:** 17,244.

Friday 2nd April 2010

HULL KINGSTON ROVERS 14 HULL FC 18

ROVERS: 1 Shaun Briscoe; 2 Peter Fox; 3 Kris Welham; 4 Jake Webster; 28 Ben Cockayne; 19 Chaz I'Anson; 7 Michael Dobson; 20 Michael Vella (C); 9 Scott Murrell; 30 Joel Clinton; 11 Clint Newton; 16 Jason Netherton; 13 Ben Galea. Subs (all used): 21 Josh Hodgson; 8 Rhys Lovegrove; 22 Liam Watts; 10 Scott Wheeldon.
Tries: Cockayne (3), Welham (20); **Goals:** Dobson 3/3.
On report: Newton (78) - alleged late tackle on Tansey.
HULL: 1 Jordan Tansey; 24 Craig Hall; 21 Richard Whiting; 4 Kirk Yeaman; 3 Tom Briscoe; 6 Richard Horne; 7 Sean Long (C); 10 Mark O'Meley; 9 Shaun Berrigan; 17 Peter Cusack; 12 Danny Tickle; 16 Willie Manu; 13 Craig Fitzgibbon. Subs (all used): 11 Lee Radford; 15 Epalahame Lauaki; 8 Ewan Dowes; 20 Danny Houghton.
Tries: Briscoe (16), Fitzgibbon (24), Tansey (60);
Goals: Tickle 3/4.
Rugby Leaguer & League Express Men of the Match: *Rovers:* Michael Vella; *Hull:* Richard Whiting.
Penalty count: 14-9; **Half-time:** 14-12;
Referee: Richard Silverwood; **Attendance:** 10,089.

ST HELENS 10 WIGAN WARRIORS 18

SAINTS: 6 Leon Pryce; 2 Ade Gardner; 3 Matt Gidley; 19 Chris Dean; 5 Francis Meli; 12 Jon Wilkin; 7 Kyle Eastmond; 10 James Graham; 9 Keiron Cunningham (C); 11 Tony Puletua; 13 Chris Flannery; 17 Paul Clough; 16 Scott Moore. Subs (all used): 14 James Roby; 15 Bryn Hargreaves; 22 Andrew Dixon; 23 Maurie Fa'asavalu.
Tries: Gardner (47), Puletua (56); **Goals:** Eastmond 1/2.
WARRIORS: 2 Amos Roberts; 24 Darrell Goulding; 3 Martin Gleeson; 4 George Carmont; 5 Pat Richards; 6 Sam Tomkins; 7 Thomas Leuluai; 8 Stuart Fielden; 15 Michael McIlorum; 14 Paul Prescott; 16 Phil Bailey; 12 Joel Tomkins; 13 Sean O'Loughlin (C). Subs (all used): 17 Iafeta Palea'aesina; 19 Paul Deacon; 21 Eamon O'Carroll; 23 Lee Mossop.
Tries: Goulding (29), Palea'aesina (34);
Goals: Richards 5/5.
Sin bin: Roberts (46) - delaying restart.
Rugby Leaguer & League Express Men of the Match: *Saints:* Jon Wilkin; *Warriors:* Sean O'Loughlin.
Penalty count: 14-14; **Half-time:** 0-14;
Referee: Ben Thaler; **Attendance:** 17,500.

WARRINGTON WOLVES 32 SALFORD CITY REDS 2

WOLVES: 1 Richard Mathers; 5 Chris Hicks; 3 Matt King; 23 Ryan Atkins; 2 Chris Riley; 17 Simon Grix; 7 Richard Myler; 8 Adrian Morley (C); 9 Michael Monaghan; 16 Paul Wood; 11 Louis Anderson; 12 Ben Westwood; 4 Chris Bridge. Subs (all used): 10 Garreth Carvell; 13 Ben Harrison; 14 Mick Higham; 26 David Solomona.
Tries: Hicks (11, 77), Atkins (36), Riley (51, 80), Mathers (60), Solomona (70); **Goals:** Bridge 2/7.
CITY REDS: 1 Karl Fitzpatrick; 20 Steve Tyrer; 3 Mark Henry; 4 Willie Talau; 2 Daniel Holdsworth; 14 Matty Smith; 8 Ray Cashmere; 9 Malcolm Alker (C); 19 Ryan Boyle; 11 Ian Sibbit; 17 Adam Sidlow; 13 Luke Swain. Subs (all used): 5 Ashley Gibson; 15 Stuart Littler; 16 Phil Leuluai; 18 Lee Jewitt.
Goals: Holdsworth 1/2.
Rugby Leaguer & League Express Men of the Match: *Wolves:* Louis Anderson; *City Reds:* Ray Cashmere.
Penalty count: 7-8; **Half-time:** 10-2;
Referee: Thierry Alibert; **Attendance:** 11,467.

HUDDERSFIELD GIANTS 48 CATALANS DRAGONS 6

GIANTS: 1 Brett Hodgson (C); 5 David Hodgson; 4 Paul Whatuira; 3 Jamahl Lolesi; 2 Leroy Cudjoe; 6 Kevin Brown; 34 Danny Brough; 10 Keith Mason; 7 Luke Robinson; 15 Andy Raleigh; 11 Lee Gilmour; 22 Martin Aspinwall; 20 David Faiumu. Subs (all used): 16 Darrell Griffin; 9 Shaun Lunt; 33 Graeme Horne; 8 Eorl Crabtree.
Tries: Faiumu (5), Gilmour (11), Brough (23, 60), D Hodgson (28, 66), Brown (33), Cudjoe (52), B Hodgson (78); **Goals:** B Hodgson 6/9.
DRAGONS: 5 Dimitri Pelo; 28 Frederic Vaccari (D); 19 Julien Touxagas; 25 Tony Gigot; 2 Steven Bell; 16 William Barthau; 7 Thomas Bosc; 22 Jamal Fakir; 9 Casey McGuire; 10 Jerome Guisset (C); 18 Dane Carlaw; 12 Gregory Mounis; 13 Dallas Johnson. Subs (all used): 20 Kane Bentley; 21 Sebastien Martins; 27 Michael Simon (D); 29 Andrew Bentley.
Try: Pelo (49); **Goals:** Barthau 1/1.
Rugby Leaguer & League Express Men of the Match: *Giants:* Danny Brough; *Dragons:* Dimitri Pelo.
Penalty count: 2-3; **Half-time:** 26-0;
Referee: Steve Ganson; **Attendance:** 5,296.

WAKEFIELD TRINITY WILDCATS 19
CASTLEFORD TIGERS 6

WILDCATS: 1 Matt Blaymire; 2 Damien Blanch; 18 Aaron Murphy; 4 Darryl Millard; 23 Dale Morton; 21 Paul Cooke; 6 Ben Jeffries; 10 Michael Korkidas; 14 Sam Obst; 25 Richard Moore; 17 Kevin Henderson; 13 Jason Demetriou (C); 12 Glenn Morrison. Subs (all used): 19 Paul King; 20 Tevita Leo-Latu; 8 Shane Tronc; 32 Danny Kirmond.
Tries: Obst (13), Morton (45), Leo-Latu (50);
Goals: Cooke 3/4; **Field goal:** Cooke (71).
TIGERS: 23 Ryan McGoldrick; 21 Jordan Thompson; 3 Michael Shenton; 2 Kirk Dixon; 27 Shaun Ainscough; 6 Rangi Chase; 7 Brent Sherwin; 16 Paul Jackson; 14 Stuart Jones; 10 Craig Huby; 30 Chris Tuson; 12 Steve Snitch; 13 Joe Westerman. Subs (all used): 9 Ryan Hudson (C); 15 Liam Higgins; 17 Ryan Clayton; 29 Michael Cooper.
Try: Thompson (22); **Goals:** Westerman 1/1.
Rugby Leaguer & League Express Men of the Match:
Wildcats: Sam Obst; *Tigers:* Rangi Chase.
Penalty count: 9-4; **Half-time:** 6-6;
Referee: James Child; **Attendance:** 8,337.

ROUND 10

Monday 5th April 2010

HARLEQUINS 12 HULL KINGSTON ROVERS 52

HARLEQUINS: 26 Ben Jones-Bishop; 22 Jamie O'Callaghan; 3 Tony Clubb; 13 Rob Purdham (C); 5 Will Sharp; 21 Luke Gale; 9 Chad Randall; 14 Oliver Wilkes; 7 Danny Orr; 17 Danny Ward; 11 Luke Williamson; 1 Chris Melling; 16 Jason Golden. Subs (all used): 10 Louie McCarthy-Scarsbrook; 24 Dave Williams; 25 Lamont Bryan; 28 Ben Bolger.
Tries: Orr (52), Williamson (68); **Goals:** Orr 2/2.
ROVERS: 1 Shaun Briscoe; 2 Peter Fox; 4 Jake Webster; 3 Kris Welham; 28 Ben Cockayne; 19 Chaz I'Anson; 7 Michael Dobson; 8 Rhys Lovegrove; 17 Ben Fisher; 20 Michael Vella (C); 11 Clint Newton; 14 Matt Cook; 13 Ben Galea. Subs (all used): 16 Jason Netherton; 22 Liam Watts; 30 Joel Clinton; 9 Scott Murrell.
Tries: Galea (4, 58), Cook (9), Dobson (12), Welham (31, 45, 72, 76), Lovegrove (78); **Goals:** Dobson 8/9.
Rugby Leaguer & League Express Men of the Match:
Harlequins: Rob Purdham; *Rovers:* Kris Welham.
Penalty count: 7-8; **Half-time:** 0-22;
Referee: Thierry Alibert; **Attendance:** 2,819.

BRADFORD BULLS 20 CRUSADERS 16

BULLS: 6 Brett Kearney; 2 Rikki Sheriffe; 15 Michael Platt; 4 Chris Nero; 1 Dave Halley; 3 Paul Sykes; 7 Matt Orford; 8 Nick Scruton; 9 Heath L'Estrange; 10 Andy Lynch (C); 20 Elliott Whitehead; 13 Jamie Langley; 11 Steve Menzies. Subs (all used): 14 Wayne Godwin; 22 James Donaldson; 16 Michael Worrincy; 12 Glenn Hall.
Tries: Halley (4), Nero (30), Hall (35), Platt (72);
Goals: Orford 2/4, Sykes 0/1.
CRUSADERS: 26 Clinton Schifcofske (D); 1 Gareth Thomas; 14 Luke Dyer; 4 Vince Mellars; 2 Nick Youngquest; 6 Michael Witt; 3 Tony Martin; 8 Ryan O'Hara (C); 9 Lincoln Withers; 10 Mark Bryant; 11 Weller Hauraki; 12 Jason Chan; 13 Rocky Trimarchi. Subs (all used): 23 Peter Lupton; 16 Frank Winterstein; 17 Adam Peek; 18 Jamie Thackray.
Tries: Hauraki (9), Mellars (23); **Goals:** Witt 4/5.
Rugby Leaguer & League Express Men of the Match:
Bulls: Jamie Langley; *Crusaders:* Weller Hauraki.
Penalty count: 9-10; **Half-time:** 14-12;
Referee: James Child; **Attendance:** 7,853.

SALFORD CITY REDS 30 HUDDERSFIELD GIANTS 18

CITY REDS: 1 Karl Fitzpatrick; 3 Mark Henry; 4 Willie Talau; 5 Ashley Gibson; 20 Steve Tyrer; 6 Stefan Ratchford; 21 Daniel Holdsworth; 8 Ray Cashmere; 9 Malcolm Alker (C); 19 Ryan Boyle; 17 Adam Sidlow; 11 Ian Sibbit; 13 Luke Swain. Subs (all used): 14 Matty Smith; 15 Stuart Littler; 16 Phil Leuluai; 18 Lee Jewitt.
Tries: Sidlow (5), Gibson (34), Holdsworth (41), Tyrer (62); **Goals:** Holdsworth 7/7.
GIANTS: 2 Leroy Cudjoe; 3 Jamahl Lolesi; 19 Michael Lawrence; 4 Paul Whatuira; 5 David Hodgson; 6 Kevin Brown; 34 Danny Brough; 15 Andy Raleigh (C); 9 Shaun Lunt; 23 Larne Patrick; 33 Graeme Horne; 22 Martin Aspinwall; 21 Scott Grix. Subs (all used): 7 Luke Robinson; 16 Darrell Griffin; 20 David Faiumu; 30 Adam Walker (D).
Tries: D Hodgson (59), Patrick (67), Cudjoe (72), Whatuira (78); **Goals:** Brough 1/4.
Rugby Leaguer & League Express Men of the Match:
City Reds: Daniel Holdsworth; *Giants:* Kevin Brown.
Penalty count: 8-8; **Half-time:** 16-0;
Referee: Ian Smith; **Attendance:** 4,014.

WIGAN WARRIORS 54
WAKEFIELD TRINITY WILDCATS 14

WARRIORS: 2 Amos Roberts; 24 Darrell Goulding; 3 Martin Gleeson; 16 Phil Bailey; 5 Pat Richards; 6 Sam Tomkins; 7 Thomas Leuluai; 8 Stuart Fielden; 15 Michael McIlorum; 10 Andy Coley; 23 Lee Mossop; 12 Joel Tomkins; 13 Sean O'Loughlin (C). Subs (all used): 14 Paul Prescott; 19 Paul Deacon; 21 Eamon O'Carroll; 25 Liam Farrell (D).
Tries: Roberts (3, 33), Richards (4, 16, 75), J Tomkins (24), Goulding (39, 43, 79), Farrell (64);
Goals: Richards 7/10.
WILDCATS: 1 Matt Blaymire; 2 Damien Blanch; 18 Aaron Murphy; 4 Darryl Millard; 23 Dale Morton; 21 Paul Cooke; 6 Ben Jeffries; 10 Michael Korkidas; 14 Sam Obst; 25 Richard Moore; 11 Dale Ferguson; 32 Danny Kirmond; 20 Tevita Leo-Latu. Subs (all used): 8 Shane Tronc; 12 Glenn Morrison (C); 17 Kevin Henderson; 19 Paul King.
Tries: Blanch (46), Blaymire (52, 56); **Goals:** Cooke 1/3.
Sin bin: Millard (78) - interference.
Rugby Leaguer & League Express Men of the Match:
Warriors: Pat Richards; *Wildcats:* Matt Blaymire.
Penalty count: 9-6; **Half-time:** 32-0;
Referee: Richard Silverwood; **Attendance:** 14,615.

HULL FC 10 WARRINGTON WOLVES 29

HULL: 1 Jordan Tansey; 21 Richard Whiting; 19 Jordan Turner; 4 Kirk Yeaman; 24 Craig Hall; 14 Danny Washbrook; 7 Sean Long (C); 17 Peter Cusack; 9 Shaun Berrigan; 10 Mark O'Meley; 16 Willie Manu; 22 Mike Burnett; 11 Lee Radford. Subs: 20 Danny Houghton; 8 Ewan Dowes; 25 Reece Lyne (not used); 23 Sam Moa.
Tries: Hall (16), Manu (28); **Goals:** Whiting 1/2.
WOLVES: 1 Richard Mathers; 5 Chris Hicks; 3 Matt King; 23 Ryan Atkins; 2 Chris Riley; 6 Lee Briers; 7 Richard Myler; 8 Adrian Morley (C); 9 Michael Monaghan; 10 Garreth Carvell; 11 Louis Anderson; 17 Simon Grix; 13 Ben Harrison. Subs (all used): 16 Paul Wood; 26 David Solomona; 4 Chris Bridge; 14 Mick Higham.
Tries: Hicks (3, 32, 75), Myler (49), Monaghan (70);
Goals: Briers 3/4, Hicks 1/1; **Field goal:** Briers (73).
Rugby Leaguer & League Express Men of the Match:
Hull: Shaun Berrigan; *Wolves:* Chris Hicks.
Penalty count: 3-3; **Half-time:** 10-10;
Referee: Steve Ganson; **Attendance:** 14,131.

CASTLEFORD TIGERS 18 ST HELENS 52

TIGERS: 23 Ryan McGoldrick; 27 Shaun Ainscough; 17 Ryan Clayton; 3 Michael Shenton; 5 Michael Wainwright; 6 Rangi Chase; 7 Brent Sherwin; 8 Mitchell Sargent; 9 Ryan Hudson (C); 16 Paul Jackson; 14 Stuart Jones; 30 Chris Tuson; 13 Joe Westerman. Subs (all used): 10 Craig Huby; 15 Liam Higgins; 19 Kirk Netherton; 29 Michael Cooper.
Tries: Huby (21), Clayton (23), Westerman (50), Shenton (80); **Goals:** Westerman 1/4.
SAINTS: 6 Leon Pryce; 2 Ade Gardner; 3 Matt Gidley; 19 Chris Dean; 5 Francis Meli; 12 Jon Wilkin; 7 Kyle Eastmond; 10 James Graham; 9 Keiron Cunningham (C); 8 Nick Fozzard; 18 Matty Ashurst; 13 Chris Flannery; 11 Tony Puletua. Subs (all used): 14 James Roby; 15 Bryn Hargreaves; 16 Scott Moore; 23 Maurie Fa'asavalu.
Tries: Eastmond (8, 60), Meli (11, 46), Fa'asavalu (37), Roby (43, 73), Puletua (63), Pryce (68);
Goals: Eastmond 8/9.
Rugby Leaguer & League Express Men of the Match:
Tigers: Joe Westerman; *Saints:* James Roby.
Penalty count: 8-13; **Half-time:** 10-16;
Referee: Phil Bentham; **Attendance:** 6,879.

CATALANS DRAGONS 24 LEEDS RHINOS 34

DRAGONS: 5 Dimitri Pelo; 2 Steven Bell; 18 Dane Carlaw; 19 Julien Touxagas; 28 Frederic Vaccari; 9 Casey McGuire; 7 Thomas Bosc; 8 David Ferriol; 20 Kane Bentley; 10 Jerome Guisset (C); 22 Jamal Fakir; 12 Gregory Mounis; 13 Dallas Johnson. Subs (all used): 21 Sebastien Martins; 25 Tony Gigot; 26 Cyril Stacul; 29 Andrew Bentley.
Tries: Guisset (8), Johnson (37), Touxagas (55), K Bentley (69); **Goals:** Bosc 4/4.
RHINOS: 1 Brent Webb; 28 Lee Smith; 4 Keith Senior; 3 Brett Delaney; 5 Ryan Hall; 13 Kevin Sinfield (C); 6 Danny McGuire; 8 Kylie Leuluai; 14 Matt Diskin; 16 Ryan Bailey; 11 Jamie Jones-Buchanan; 12 Ali Lauitiiti; 18 Carl Ablett. Subs (all used): 7 Rob Burrow; 17 Ian Kirke; 19 Luke Burgess; 24 Luke Ambler.
Tries: Lauitiiti (11), Jones-Buchanan (14), Senior (21), McGuire (22, 76), Delaney (34); **Goals:** Sinfield 5/7.
Sin bin: Leuluai (53) - late tackle on Pelo.
Rugby Leaguer & League Express Men of the Match:
Dragons: Thomas Bosc; *Rhinos:* Brett Delaney.
Penalty count: 7-7; **Half-time:** 12-26; **Referee:** Ben Thaler; **Attendance:** 8,230 *(at Stade Aime Giral).*

ROUND 11

Friday 9th April 2010

HUDDERSFIELD GIANTS 24 CASTLEFORD TIGERS 0

GIANTS: 1 Brett Hodgson (C); 3 Jamahl Lolesi; 19 Michael Lawrence; 4 Paul Whatuira; 5 David Hodgson; 6 Kevin Brown; 34 Danny Brough; 16 Darrell Griffin; 7 Luke Robinson; 10 Keith Mason; 11 Lee Gilmour; 12 David Fa'alogo; 22 Martin Aspinwall. Subs (all used): 8 Eorl Crabtree; 20 David Faiumu; 21 Scott Grix; 15 Andy Raleigh.
Tries: D Hodgson (14, 46, 65), Lolesi (68);
Goals: B Hodgson 4/4.
TIGERS: 21 Jordan Thompson; 27 Shaun Ainscough; 3 Michael Shenton; 17 Ryan Clayton; 5 Michael Wainwright; 23 Ryan McGoldrick; 19 Kirk Netherton; 16 Paul Jackson; 9 Ryan Hudson (C); 10 Craig Huby; 29 Michael Cooper; 12 Steve Snitch; 14 Stuart Jones. Subs (all used): 8 Mitchell Sargent; 15 Liam Higgins; 26 Oliver Holmes (D); 30 Chris Tuson.
Rugby Leaguer & League Express Men of the Match:
Giants: David Hodgson; *Tigers:* Ryan Hudson.
Penalty count: 5-11; **Half-time:** 6-0;
Referee: Steve Ganson; **Attendance:** 5,932.

Saturday 10th April 2010

HARLEQUINS 24 ST HELENS 32

HARLEQUINS: 26 Ben Jones-Bishop; 35 Kevin Penny (D); 3 Tony Clubb; 13 Rob Purdham (C); 5 Will Sharp; 21 Luke Gale; 9 Chad Randall; 10 Louie McCarthy-Scarsbrook; 7 Danny Orr; 17 Danny Ward; 11 Luke Williamson; 16 Jason Golden; 1 Chris Melling. Subs (all used): 14 Oliver Wilkes; 27 Ben Jones (D); 25 Lamont Bryan; 18 Ryan Esders.
Tries: Jones-Bishop (12), Penny (52), Williamson (56), Clubb (78); **Goals:** Orr 4/4.
SAINTS: 6 Leon Pryce; 2 Ade Gardner; 19 Chris Dean; 21 Gary Wheeler; 5 Francis Meli; 12 Jon Wilkin; 7 Kyle Eastmond; 10 James Graham; 14 James Roby; 11 Tony Puletua; 22 Andrew Dixon; 13 Chris Flannery; 17 Paul Clough. Subs (all used): 15 Bryn Hargreaves; 9 Keiron Cunningham (C); 23 Maurie Fa'asavalu; 18 Matty Ashurst.
Tries: Dixon (19, 47), Eastmond (45), Roby (61, 72);
Goals: Eastmond 6/6.
Rugby Leaguer & League Express Men of the Match:
Harlequins: Chad Randall; *Saints:* Kyle Eastmond.
Penalty count: 7-11; **Half-time:** 6-6;
Referee: James Child; **Attendance:** 5,220.

CATALANS DRAGONS 14 BRADFORD BULLS 36

DRAGONS: 23 Chris Walker; 28 Frederic Vaccari; 2 Steven Bell; 15 Jean-Phillipe Baile; 5 Dimitri Pelo; 9 Casey McGuire; 7 Thomas Bosc; 8 David Ferriol; 20 Kane Bentley; 10 Jerome Guisset (C); 18 Dane Carlaw; 4 Setaimata Sa; 13 Dallas Johnson. Subs (all used): 24 Remi Casty; 12 Gregory Mounis; 21 Sebastien Martins; 25 Tony Gigot.
Tries: Vaccari (28), Bell (47), Mounis (66);
Goals: Bosc 1/3.
BULLS: 6 Brett Kearney; 2 Rikki Sheriffe; 15 Michael Platt; 4 Chris Nero; 1 Dave Halley; 3 Paul Sykes; 7 Matt Orford; 8 Nick Scruton; 9 Heath L'Estrange; 10 Andy Lynch (C); 20 Elliott Whitehead; 13 Jamie Langley; 11 Steve Menzies. Subs (all used): 14 Wayne Godwin; 12 Glenn Hall; 22 James Donaldson; 18 Craig Kopczak.
Tries: Lynch (5), Kearney (24), Sheriffe (40, 77, 80), Menzies (61); **Goals:** Orford 5/7, Sykes 1/1.
Sin bin: Orford (57) - interference.
Rugby Leaguer & League Express Men of the Match:
Dragons: Sebastien Martins; *Bulls:* Steve Menzies.
Penalty count: 12-7; **Half-time:** 4-20; **Referee:** Richard Silverwood; **Attendance:** 8,884 *(at Stade Aime Giral).*

Sunday 11th April 2010

HULL KINGSTON ROVERS 36
WARRINGTON WOLVES 16

ROVERS: 1 Shaun Briscoe; 2 Peter Fox; 3 Kris Welham; 4 Jake Webster; 28 Ben Cockayne; 19 Chaz I'Anson; 7 Michael Dobson; 20 Michael Vella (C); 9 Scott Murrell; 30 Joel Clinton; 11 Clint Newton; 16 Jason Netherton; 13 Ben Galea. Subs (all used): 8 Rhys Lovegrove; 14 Matt Cook; 21 Josh Hodgson; 22 Liam Watts.
Tries: Welham (18), Cockayne (27), Briscoe (31), Fox (58, 68), Cook (65); **Goals:** Dobson 6/7.
WOLVES: 1 Richard Mathers; 5 Chris Hicks; 3 Matt King; 23 Ryan Atkins; 2 Chris Riley; 17 Simon Grix; 7 Richard Myler; 8 Adrian Morley (C); 14 Mick Higham; 10 Garreth Carvell; 11 Louis Anderson; 12 Ben Westwood; 13 Ben Harrison. Subs (all used): 4 Chris Bridge; 16 Paul Wood; 19 Lee Mitchell; 26 David Solomona.
Tries: Mathers (9), King (39), Riley (54);
Goals: Westwood 2/3.
Sin bin: Bridge (76) - holding down.
On report: Solomona (51) - alleged dangerous tackle.
Rugby Leaguer & League Express Men of the Match:
Rovers: Peter Fox; *Wolves:* Ben Westwood.
Penalty count: 13-7; **Half-time:** 16-12;
Referee: Ian Smith; **Attendance:** 8,452.

LEEDS RHINOS 46 HULL FC 30

RHINOS: 1 Brent Webb; 28 Lee Smith; 3 Brett Delaney; 4 Keith Senior; 5 Ryan Hall; 6 Danny McGuire; 7 Rob Burrow; 8 Kylie Leuluai; 9 Danny Buderus; 16 Ryan Bailey; 11 Jamie Jones-Buchanan; 12 Ali Lauitiiti; 13 Kevin Sinfield (C). Subs (all used): 17 Ian Kirke; 18 Carl Ablett; 19 Luke Burgess; 14 Matt Diskin.
Tries: Senior (5, 57), Hall (17, 25), Lauitiiti (49), Burrow (59), Jones-Buchanan (65), McGuire (70);
Goals: Sinfield 7/8.
On report: Bailey (76) - alleged high tackle on Lauaki.
HULL: 1 Jordan Tansey; 21 Richard Whiting; 24 Craig Hall; 4 Kirk Yeaman; 3 Tom Briscoe; 19 Jordan Turner; 14 Danny Washbrook; 17 Peter Cusack; 9 Shaun Berrigan; 10 Mark O'Meley; 16 Willie Manu; 15 Epalahame Lauaki; 11 Lee Radford (C). Subs (all used): 20 Danny Houghton; 8 Ewan Dowes; 23 Sam Moa; 22 Mike Burnett.
Tries: Briscoe (29, 33, 45, 78), Hall (74), Turner (80);
Goals: Whiting 2/5, Hall 1/1.
Rugby Leaguer & League Express Men of the Match:
Rhinos: Kevin Sinfield; *Hull:* Kirk Yeaman.
Penalty count: 4-6; **Half time:** 16-10;
Referee: Phil Bentham; **Attendance:** 16,896.

SALFORD CITY REDS 4 WIGAN WARRIORS 18

CITY REDS: 1 Karl Fitzpatrick; 3 Mark Henry; 4 Willie Talau; 5 Ashley Gibson; 20 Steve Tyrer; 6 Stefan Ratchford; 21 Daniel Holdsworth; 8 Ray Cashmere; 9 Malcolm Alker (C); 18 Lee Jewitt; 17 Adam Sidlow; 12 Luke Adamson; 13 Luke Swain. Subs (all used): 11 Ian Sibbit; 14 Matty Smith; 15 Stuart Littler; 16 Phil Leuluai.
Try: Gibson (40); **Goals:** Holdsworth 0/1.

WARRIORS: 1 Cameron Phelps; 24 Darrell Goulding; 3 Martin Gleeson; 4 George Carmont; 5 Pat Richards; 6 Sam Tomkins; 19 Paul Deacon; 10 Andy Coley (C); 9 Mark Riddell; 14 Paul Prescott; 16 Phil Bailey; 12 Joel Tomkins; 13 Sean O'Loughlin. Subs (all used): 17 Iafeta Palea'aesina; 21 Eamon O'Carroll; 23 Lee Mossop; 15 Michael McIlorum.
Tries: Deacon (28), Richards (49, 60);
Goals: Richards 3/5.
Rugby Leaguer & League Express Men of the Match: *City Reds:* Daniel Holdsworth; *Warriors:* Pat Richards.
Penalty count: 11-8; **Half-time:** 4-6;
Referee: Thierry Alibert; **Attendance:** 6,618.

WAKEFIELD TRINITY WILDCATS 10 CRUSADERS 20

WILDCATS: 1 Matt Blaymire; 2 Damien Blanch; 18 Aaron Murphy; 4 Darryl Millard; 5 Luke George; 6 Ben Jeffries; 14 Sam Obst; 25 Richard Moore; 20 Tevita Leo-Latu; 10 Michael Korkidas; 13 Jason Demetriou (C); 12 Glenn Morrison; 21 Paul Cooke. Subs (all used): 19 Paul King; 17 Kevin Henderson; 8 Shane Tronc; 32 Danny Kirmond.
Tries: Blanch (15), George (27); **Goals:** Cooke 1/2.
CRUSADERS: 26 Clinton Schifcofske; 1 Gareth Thomas; 12 Jason Chan; 4 Vince Mellars; 2 Nick Youngquest; 23 Peter Lupton; 6 Michael Witt; 8 Ryan O'Hara (C); 9 Lincoln Withers; 10 Mark Bryant; 11 Weller Hauraki; 16 Frank Winterstein; 13 Rocky Trimarchi. Subs (all used): 20 Ben Flower; 17 Adam Peek; 18 Jamie Thackray; 27 Rhys Hanbury (D).
Tries: Thomas (6), Witt (18), Youngquest (54), Mellars (68); **Goals:** Witt 2/4.
Rugby Leaguer & League Express Men of the Match: *Wildcats:* Glenn Morrison; *Crusaders:* Michael Witt.
Penalty count: 10-3; **Half-time:** 10-10;
Referee: Gareth Hewer; **Attendance:** 4,671.

ROUND 12

Friday 23rd April 2010

HULL FC 12 WAKEFIELD TRINITY WILDCATS 8

HULL: 1 Jordan Tansey; 21 Richard Whiting; 19 Jordan Turner; 24 Craig Hall; 3 Tom Briscoe; 14 Danny Washbrook; 6 Richard Horne; 8 Ewan Dowes; 20 Danny Houghton; 10 Mark O'Meley (C); 22 Mike Burnett; 15 Epalahame Lauaki; 16 Willie Manu. Subs (all used): 32 Paul McShane (D); 30 Danny Nicklas (D); 23 Sam Moa; 17 Peter Cusack.
Tries: Whiting (22, 38); **Goals:** Hall 2/2.
WILDCATS: 18 Aaron Murphy; 5 Luke George; 3 Sean Gleeson; 4 Darryl Millard; 2 Damien Blanch; 21 Paul Cooke; 6 Ben Jeffries; 25 Richard Moore; 20 Tevita Leo-Latu; 19 Paul King; 16 Paul Johnson; 13 Jason Demetriou (C); 32 Danny Kirmond. Subs (all used): 10 Michael Korkidas; 11 Dale Ferguson; 14 Sam Obst; 15 Kyle Bibb.
Tries: Millard (11), Blanch (79, no attempt at goal);
Goals: Cooke 0/1.
On report: Bibb (75) - alleged dangerous tackle.
Rugby Leaguer & League Express Men of the Match: *Hull:* Richard Whiting; *Wildcats:* Paul Johnson.
Penalty count: 11-9; **Half-time:** 12-4;
Referee: Ian Smith; **Attendance:** 11,160.

WIGAN WARRIORS 26 HARLEQUINS 38

WARRIORS: 1 Cameron Phelps; 22 Shaun Ainscough; 16 Phil Bailey (C); 4 George Carmont; 5 Pat Richards; 13 Sean O'Loughlin; 6 Sam Tomkins; 8 Stuart Fielden; 9 Mark Riddell; 14 Paul Prescott; 25 Liam Farrell; 12 Joel Tomkins; 23 Lee Mossop. Subs (all used): 15 Michael McIlorum; 17 Iafeta Palea'aesina; 21 Eamon O'Carroll; 32 Jonny Walker (D).
Tries: Farrell (14, 38), Phelps (18), J Tomkins (31);
Goals: Richards 5/5.
HARLEQUINS: 26 Ben Jones-Bishop; 35 Kevin Penny; 3 Tony Clubb; 4 David Howell; 5 Will Sharp; 6 Luke Dorn; 9 Chad Randall; 17 Danny Ward; 7 Danny Orr; 10 Louie McCarthy-Scarsbrook; 11 Luke Williamson; 13 Rob Purdham (C); 1 Chris Melling. Subs (all used): 8 Karl Temata; 14 Oliver Wilkes; 21 Luke Gale; 25 Lamont Bryan.
Tries: Howell (8), Dorn (42, 52), Sharp (64), Purdham (69), Randall (78); **Goals:** Orr 7/7.
Rugby Leaguer & League Express Men of the Match: *Warriors:* Liam Farrell; *Harlequins:* Danny Orr.
Penalty count: 9-6; **Half-time:** 24-6;
Referee: Phil Bentham; **Attendance:** 18,605.

Saturday 24th April 2010

ST HELENS 41 LEEDS RHINOS 20

SAINTS: 1 Paul Wellens; 2 Ade Gardner; 21 Gary Wheeler; 13 Chris Flannery; 30 Jamie Foster; 16 Scott Moore; 7 Kyle Eastmond; 10 James Graham; 9 Keiron Cunningham (C); 15 Bryn Hargreaves; 17 Paul Clough; 22 Andrew Dixon; 11 Tony Puletua. Subs (all used): 8 Nick Fozzard; 14 James Roby; 18 Matty Ashurst; 23 Maurie Fa'asavalu.
Tries: Moore (16), Puletua (22), Roby (37, 71), Flannery (48), Ashurst (67); **Goals:** Foster 8/8;
Field goal: Eastmond (52).
RHINOS: 28 Lee Smith; 5 Ryan Hall; 3 Brett Delaney; 4 Keith Senior; 26 Tom Bush; 6 Danny McGuire; 7 Rob Burrow; 8 Kylie Leuluai; 14 Matt Diskin; 16 Ryan Bailey; 11 Jamie Jones-Buchanan; 17 Ian Kirke; 13 Kevin Sinfield (C). Subs (all used): 9 Danny Buderus; 10 Jamie Peacock; 19 Luke Burgess; 24 Luke Ambler.
Tries: Smith (1), Delaney (56), Hall (60), Burrow (77);
Goals: Sinfield 2/4.
Rugby Leaguer & League Express Men of the Match: *Saints:* James Roby; *Rhinos:* Brett Delaney.
Penalty count: 12-12; **Half-time:** 20-6;
Referee: Richard Silverwood; **Attendance:** 11,048.

Sunday 25th April 2010

BRADFORD BULLS 40 HULL KINGSTON ROVERS 4

BULLS: 6 Brett Kearney; 2 Rikki Sheriffe; 15 Michael Platt; 4 Chris Nero; 1 Dave Halley; 3 Paul Sykes; 7 Matt Orford; 8 Nick Scruton; 9 Heath L'Estrange; 10 Andy Lynch (C); 20 Elliott Whitehead; 22 James Donaldson; 11 Steve Menzies. Subs (all used): 14 Wayne Godwin; 16 Michael Worrincy; 18 Craig Kopczak; 12 Glenn Hall.
Tries: Lynch (8), Whitehead (12), Sheriffe (63, 67), Kearney (71, 79); **Goals:** Orford 8/8.
ROVERS: 1 Shaun Briscoe; 2 Peter Fox; 4 Jake Webster; 3 Kris Welham; 28 Ben Cockayne; 19 Chaz I'Anson; 7 Michael Dobson; 20 Michael Vella (C); 17 Ben Fisher; 30 Joel Clinton; 11 Clint Newton; 16 Jason Netherton; 9 Scott Murrell. Subs (all used): 22 Liam Watts; 8 Rhys Lovegrove; 23 Scott Spaven (D); 14 Matt Cook.
Try: Cockayne (77); **Goals:** Dobson 0/1.
Dismissal: Webster (73) - high tackle on Menzies.
Rugby Leaguer & League Express Men of the Match: *Bulls:* Brett Kearney; *Rovers:* Ben Cockayne.
Penalty count: 14-9; **Half-time:** 12-0;
Referee: James Child; **Attendance:** 9,234.

CRUSADERS 10 HUDDERSFIELD GIANTS 38

CRUSADERS: 26 Clinton Schifcofske; 1 Gareth Thomas; 14 Luke Dyer; 4 Vince Mellars; 2 Nick Youngquest; 6 Michael Witt; 23 Peter Lupton; 8 Ryan O'Hara (C); 9 Lincoln Withers; 10 Mark Bryant; 11 Weller Hauraki; 12 Jason Chan; 16 Frank Winterstein. Subs (all used): 18 Jamie Thackray; 17 Adam Peek; 20 Ben Flower; 21 Lloyd White.
Tries: Hauraki (24), Dyer (56); **Goals:** Witt 1/2.
GIANTS: 2 Leroy Cudjoe; 3 Jamahl Lolesi; 19 Michael Lawrence; 4 Paul Whatuira; 5 David Hodgson; 6 Kevin Brown (C); 34 Danny Brough; 10 Keith Mason; 33 Graeme Horne; 16 Darrell Griffin; 11 Lee Gilmour; 12 David Fa'alogo; 20 David Faiumu. Subs (all used): 8 Eorl Crabtree; 23 Larne Patrick; 21 Scott Grix; 18 Brad Drew (D2).
Tries: Brown (3), D Hodgson (9, 72, 78), Cudjoe (38), Grix (45), Drew (64); **Goals:** Brough 5/7.
Rugby Leaguer & League Express Men of the Match: *Crusaders:* Jamie Thackray; *Giants:* Kevin Brown.
Penalty count: 6-3; **Half-time:** 6-18;
Referee: Phil Bentham; **Attendance:** 4,127.

WARRINGTON WOLVES 40 CATALANS DRAGONS 6

WOLVES: 1 Richard Mathers; 2 Chris Riley; 4 Chris Bridge; 23 Ryan Atkins; 3 Matt King; 6 Lee Briers; 7 Richard Myler; 8 Adrian Morley (C); 9 Michael Monaghan; 16 Paul Wood; 11 Louis Anderson; 12 Ben Westwood; 13 Ben Harrison. Subs (all used): 14 Mick Higham; 18 Michael Cooper; 26 David Solomona; 27 Vinnie Anderson.
Tries: Mathers (4, 30), Briers (14), Myler (23), Riley (39), Cooper (53), Higham (74); **Goals:** Westwood 6/7.
Sin bin: Riley (29) - fighting.
DRAGONS: 5 Dimitri Pelo; 2 Steven Bell; 3 Sebastien Raguin; 15 Jean-Phillipe Baile; 28 Frederic Vaccari; 7 Thomas Bosc (C); 9 Casey McGuire; 8 David Ferriol; 25 Tony Gigot; 10 Jerome Guisset; 11 Olivier Elima; 12 Gregory Mounis; 13 Dallas Johnson. Subs (all used): 4 Setaimata Sa; 17 Cyrille Gossard; 18 Dane Carlaw; 24 Remi Casty.
Try: Ferriol (65); **Goals:** Mounis 1/1.
Sin bin: Baile (29) - fighting.
Rugby Leaguer & League Express Men of the Match: *Wolves:* Richard Mathers; *Dragons:* Thomas Bosc.
Penalty count: 15-8; **Half-time:** 28-0;
Referee: Thierry Alibert; **Attendance:** 9,619.

CASTLEFORD TIGERS 30 SALFORD CITY REDS 12

TIGERS: 21 Jordan Thompson; 2 Kirk Dixon; 4 James Evans; 23 Ryan McGoldrick; 5 Michael Wainwright; 6 Rangi Chase; 7 Brent Sherwin; 8 Mitchell Sargent; 9 Ryan Hudson (C); 16 Paul Jackson; 10 Craig Huby; 14 Stuart Jones; 13 Joe Westerman. Subs (all used): 12 Steve Snitch; 15 Liam Higgins; 17 Ryan Clayton; 30 Chris Tuson.
Tries: McGoldrick (7), Sargent (54), Thompson (64), Jones (78); **Goals:** Westerman 7/7.
CITY REDS: 1 Karl Fitzpatrick; 20 Steve Tyrer; 3 Mark Henry; 4 Willie Talau; 5 Ashley Gibson; 6 Stefan Ratchford; 21 Daniel Holdsworth; 8 Ray Cashmere; 9 Malcolm Alker (C); 19 Ryan Boyle; 17 Adam Sidlow; 12 Luke Adamson; 13 Luke Swain. Subs (all used): 14 Matty Smith; 15 Stuart Littler; 16 Phil Leuluai; 18 Lee Jewitt.
Tries: Gibson (39), Henry (62); **Goals:** Holdsworth 2/2.
Rugby Leaguer & League Express Men of the Match: *Tigers:* Jordan Thompson; *City Reds:* Ashley Gibson.
Penalty count: 11-6; **Half-time:** 10-6;
Referee: Ben Thaler; **Attendance:** 5,025.

ROUND 13 - MURRAYFIELD MAGIC

Saturday 1st May 2010

BRADFORD BULLS 0 CRUSADERS 19

BULLS: 6 Brett Kearney; 2 Rikki Sheriffe; 19 Jason Crookes; 4 Chris Nero; 1 Dave Halley; 3 Paul Sykes; 7 Matt Orford; 8 Nick Scruton; 9 Heath L'Estrange; 10 Andy Lynch (C); 20 Elliott Whitehead; 22 James Donaldson; 11 Steve Menzies. Subs (all used): 14 Wayne Godwin; 16 Michael Worrincy; 12 Glenn Hall; 18 Craig Kopczak.
CRUSADERS: 26 Clinton Schifcofske; 1 Gareth Thomas; 4 Vince Mellars; 27 Rhys Hanbury; 2 Nick Youngquest; 6 Michael Witt; 23 Peter Lupton; 8 Ryan O'Hara (C); 9 Lincoln Withers; 10 Mark Bryant; 11 Weller Hauraki; 12 Jason Chan; 13 Rocky Trimarchi. Subs (all used): 7 Jarrod Sammut (D); 17 Adam Peek; 18 Jamie Thackray; 16 Frank Winterstein.
Tries: Witt (23, 39), Sammut (71); **Goals:** Witt 3/3;
Field goal: Witt (37).
Rugby Leaguer & League Express Men of the Match: *Bulls:* Steve Menzies; *Crusaders:* Michael Witt.
Penalty count: 9-5; **Half-time:** 0-13;
Referee: Richard Silverwood.

HARLEQUINS 25 HULL FC 8

HARLEQUINS: 6 Luke Dorn; 5 Will Sharp; 3 Tony Clubb; 4 David Howell; 35 Kevin Penny; 9 Chad Randall; 21 Luke Gale; 17 Danny Ward; 7 Danny Orr; 10 Louie McCarthy-Scarsbrook; 13 Rob Purdham (C); 8 Karl Temata; 1 Chris Melling. Subs (all used): 27 Ben Jones; 24 Dave Williams; 18 Ryan Esders; 14 Oliver Wilkes.
Tries: Randall (7), Sharp (15), Dorn (26), Penny (51), Gale (77); **Goals:** Orr 2/5; **Field goal:** Randall (40).
HULL: 1 Jordan Tansey; 21 Richard Whiting; 24 Craig Hall; 4 Kirk Yeaman; 3 Tom Briscoe; 19 Jordan Turner; 6 Richard Horne; 8 Ewan Dowes; 20 Danny Houghton; 10 Mark O'Meley (C); 16 Willie Manu; 22 Mike Burnett; 14 Danny Washbrook. Subs (all used): 23 Sam Moa; 11 Lee Radford; 15 Epalahame Lauaki; 32 Paul McShane.
Tries: Houghton (57), Briscoe (75); **Goals:** Hall 0/2.
Rugby Leaguer & League Express Men of the Match: *Harlequins:* Chad Randall; *Hull:* Willie Manu.
Penalty count: 5-13; **Half-time:** 15-0;
Referee: Gareth Hewer.

SALFORD CITY REDS 16 WARRINGTON WOLVES 68

CITY REDS: 1 Karl Fitzpatrick; 5 Ashley Gibson; 6 Stefan Ratchford; 4 Willie Talau; 20 Steve Tyrer; 14 Matty Smith; 21 Daniel Holdsworth; 11 Ian Sibbit; 9 Malcolm Alker (C); 19 Ryan Boyle; 15 Stuart Littler; 12 Luke Adamson; 13 Luke Swain. Subs (all used): 7 Jeremy Smith; 16 Phil Leuluai; 17 Adam Sidlow; 25 Jack Spencer.
Tries: Ratchford (11, 79), M Smith (33);
Goals: Holdsworth 2/3.
WOLVES: 2 Chris Riley; 5 Chris Hicks; 4 Chris Bridge; 23 Ryan Atkins; 29 Rhys Williams; 6 Lee Briers; 7 Richard Myler; 8 Adrian Morley (C); 9 Michael Monaghan; 13 Ben Harrison; 11 Louis Anderson; 12 Ben Westwood; 17 Simon Grix. Subs (all used): 18 Michael Cooper; 22 Tyrone McCarthy; 26 David Solomona; 27 Vinnie Anderson.
Tries: Monaghan (2), Hicks (7, 20), Atkins (23), Williams (26), Briers (37), Riley (40), V Anderson (45), Myler (52, 71), Bridge (67), Solomona (76);
Goals: Westwood 6/8, Briers 1/1, Bridge 3/3.
Rugby Leaguer & League Express Men of the Match: *City Reds:* Stefan Ratchford; *Wolves:* Lee Briers.
Penalty count: 3-12; **Half-time:** 12-38;
Referee: James Child.

LEEDS RHINOS 34 WAKEFIELD TRINITY WILDCATS 30

RHINOS: 1 Brent Webb; 28 Lee Smith; 3 Brett Delaney; 4 Keith Senior; 5 Ryan Hall; 6 Danny McGuire; 7 Rob Burrow; 16 Ryan Bailey; 9 Danny Buderus; 10 Jamie Peacock; 11 Jamie Jones-Buchanan; 17 Ian Kirke; 13 Kevin Sinfield (C). Subs (all used): 27 Chris Clarkson; 19 Luke Burgess; 14 Matt Diskin; 24 Luke Ambler.
Tries: Hall (20, 40, 63), Webb (25), Clarkson (46), Buderus (77); **Goals:** Sinfield 5/6.
WILDCATS: 18 Aaron Murphy; 2 Damien Blanch; 3 Sean Gleeson; 13 Jason Demetriou (C); 5 Luke George; 6 Ben Jeffries; 14 Sam Obst; 10 Michael Korkidas; 20 Tevita Leo-Latu; 19 Paul King; 11 Dale Ferguson; 16 Paul Johnson; 17 Kevin Henderson. Subs (all used): 25 Richard Moore; 15 Kyle Bibb; 23 Dale Morton; 24 James Davey.
Tries: Jeffries (7), Blanch (12, 35), Johnson (31), Leo-Latu (37); **Goals:** Jeffries 5/6.
Rugby Leaguer & League Express Men of the Match: *Rhinos:* Chris Clarkson; *Wildcats:* Ben Jeffries.
Penalty count: 12-8; **Half time:** 16-28;
Referee: Thierry Alibert.

Attendance: 26,642 *(at Murrayfield, Edinburgh)*.

Sunday 2nd May 2010

CASTLEFORD TIGERS 34 CATALANS DRAGONS 18

TIGERS: 23 Ryan McGoldrick; 5 Michael Wainwright; 4 James Evans; 21 Jordan Thompson; 2 Kirk Dixon; 6 Rangi Chase; 7 Brent Sherwin; 8 Mitchell Sargent; 9 Ryan Hudson (C); 16 Paul Jackson; 10 Craig Huby; 14 Stuart Jones; 13 Joe Westerman. Subs (all used): 12 Steve Snitch; 15 Liam Higgins; 26 Oliver Holmes; 30 Chris Tuson.
Tries: Wainwright (9), McGoldrick (16, 76), Sherwin (34, 79), Evans (46); **Goals:** Westerman 5/7.
DRAGONS: 5 Dimitri Pelo; 2 Steven Bell; 3 Sebastien Raguin; 4 Setaimata Sa; 28 Frederic Vaccari; 7 Thomas Bosc (C); 9 Casey McGuire; 18 Dane Carlaw; 15 Jean-Phillipe Baile; 10 Jerome Guisset; 11 Olivier Elima; 12 Gregory Mounis; 13 Dallas Johnson. Subs (all used): 19 Julien Touxagas; 20 Kane Bentley; 21 Sebastien Martins; 24 Remi Casty.
Tries: Vaccari (16), Elima (30), Mounis (50), Baile (66);
Goals: Mounis 1/4.
Rugby Leaguer & League Express Men of the Match: *Tigers:* Brent Sherwin; *Dragons:* Jean-Phillipe Baile.
Penalty count: 5-8; **Half-time:** 16-10; **Referee:** Ian Smith.

HUDDERSFIELD GIANTS 10 WIGAN WARRIORS 28

GIANTS: 2 Leroy Cudjoe; 21 Scott Grix; 19 Michael Lawrence; 4 Paul Whatuira; 5 David Hodgson; 6 Kevin Brown (C); 34 Danny Brough; 8 Eorl Crabtree; 7 Luke Robinson; 10 Keith Mason; 11 Lee Gilmour; 33 Graeme Horne; 22 Martin Aspinwall. Subs (all used): 15 Andy Raleigh; 18 Brad Drew; 20 David Faiumu; 23 Larne Patrick.
Tries: Gilmour (15), Crabtree (72); **Goals:** Brough 1/2.
WARRIORS: 5 Pat Richards; 24 Darrell Goulding; 27 Stefan Marsh (D); 4 George Carmont; 20 Karl Pryce; 6 Sam Tomkins; 7 Thomas Leuluai; 8 Stuart Fielden; 15 Michael McIlorum; 10 Andy Coley; 16 Phil Bailey; 12 Joel Tomkins; 13 Sean O'Loughlin (C). Subs (all used): 9 Mark Riddell; 17 Iafeta Palea'aesina; 21 Eamon O'Carroll; 25 Liam Farrell.
Tries: Goulding (20), S Tomkins (46), Pryce (49), Carmont (54), Leuluai (65);
Goals: Richards 1/2, Riddell 1/1, S Tomkins 2/2.
Rugby Leaguer & League Express Men of the Match: *Giants:* Eorl Crabtree; *Warriors:* Sam Tomkins.
Penalty count: 6-7; **Half-time:** 4-4; **Referee:** Ben Thaler.

HULL KINGSTON ROVERS 0 ST HELENS 54

ROVERS: 1 Shaun Briscoe; 2 Peter Fox; 15 Mike Ratu; 4 Jake Webster; 28 Ben Cockayne; 19 Chaz I'Anson; 7 Michael Dobson; 8 Rhys Lovegrove; 9 Scott Murrell; 30 Joel Clinton; 11 Clint Newton; 16 Jason Netherton; 20 Michael Vella (C). Subs (all used): 14 Matt Cook; 22 Liam Watts; 17 Ben Fisher; 10 Scott Wheeldon.
SAINTS: 1 Paul Wellens; 2 Ade Gardner; 26 Tom Armstrong; 13 Chris Flannery; 30 Jamie Foster; 6 Leon Pryce; 7 Kyle Eastmond; 10 James Graham; 14 James Roby; 15 Bryn Hargreaves; 22 Andrew Dixon; 17 Paul Clough; 11 Tony Puletua. Subs (all used): 9 Keiron Cunningham (C); 8 Nick Fozzard; 18 Matty Ashurst; 16 Scott Moore.
Tries: Wellens (3), Eastmond (7), Armstrong (20), Clough (26), Flannery (35), Roby (38), Graham (46), Ashurst (51), Foster (54), Gardner (74, 76);
Goals: Eastmond 3/5, Foster 2/6.
Rugby Leaguer & League Express Men of the Match: *Rovers:* Jake Webster; *Saints:* Leon Pryce.
Penalty count: 3-4; **Half-time:** 0-30;
Referee: Phil Bentham.

Attendance: 25,401 *(at Murrayfield, Edinburgh).*

ROUND 14

Friday 14th May 2010

LEEDS RHINOS 26 WARRINGTON WOLVES 16

RHINOS: 1 Brent Webb; 28 Lee Smith; 3 Brett Delaney; 4 Keith Senior; 5 Ryan Hall; 13 Kevin Sinfield (C); 6 Danny McGuire; 8 Kylie Leuluai; 9 Danny Buderus; 10 Jamie Peacock; 11 Jamie Jones-Buchanan; 17 Ian Kirke; 27 Chris Clarkson. Subs (all used): 16 Ryan Bailey; 18 Carl Ablett; 15 Greg Eastwood; 14 Matt Diskin.
Tries: Ablett (18), Hall (28), Webb (44), McGuire (62);
Goals: Sinfield 5/5.
WOLVES: 1 Richard Mathers; 5 Chris Hicks; 4 Chris Bridge; 3 Matt King; 2 Chris Riley; 17 Simon Grix; 6 Lee Briers; 8 Adrian Morley (C); 14 Mick Higham; 13 Ben Harrison; 11 Louis Anderson; 12 Ben Westwood; 23 Ryan Atkins. Subs (all used): 16 Paul Wood; 27 Vinnie Anderson; 18 Michael Cooper; 26 David Solomona.
Tries: King (13), Grix (69), Harrison (73);
Goals: Bridge 2/3.
Sin bin: Hicks (58) - professional foul.
Rugby Leaguer & League Express Men of the Match: *Rhinos:* Ryan Bailey; *Wolves:* Ben Harrison.
Penalty count: 11-10; **Half-time:** 12-6;
Referee: Ben Thaler; **Attendance:** 16,733.

WAKEFIELD TRINITY WILDCATS 10 BRADFORD BULLS 29

WILDCATS: 18 Aaron Murphy; 5 Luke George; 3 Sean Gleeson; 13 Jason Demetriou (C); 2 Damien Blanch; 21 Paul Cooke; 14 Sam Obst; 10 Michael Korkidas; 20 Tevita Leo-Latu; 19 Paul King; 16 Paul Johnson; 11 Dale Ferguson; 32 Danny Kirmond. Subs (all used): 23 Dale Morton; 25 Richard Moore; 31 Ben Gledhill; 17 Kevin Henderson.
Tries: Murphy (10), Johnson (16); **Goals:** Cooke 1/2.
BULLS: 1 Dave Halley; 2 Rikki Sheriffe; 15 Michael Platt; 4 Chris Nero; 5 Stuart Reardon; 3 Paul Sykes; 6 Brett Kearney; 8 Nick Scruton; 9 Heath L'Estrange; 10 Andy Lynch (C); 20 Elliott Whitehead; 16 Michael Worrincy; 11 Steve Menzies. Subs (all used): 14 Wayne Godwin; 22 James Donaldson; 12 Glenn Hall; 18 Craig Kopczak.
Tries: Nero (39), Menzies (42, 46), Godwin (75), L'Estrange (79); **Goals:** Sykes 4/6; **Field goal:** Sykes (63).
Rugby Leaguer & League Express Men of the Match: *Wildcats:* Paul King; *Bulls:* Wayne Godwin.
Penalty count: 8-8; **Half-time:** 10-4;
Referee: Ian Smith; **Attendance:** 5,381.

Saturday 15th May 2010

SALFORD CITY REDS 42 ST HELENS 34

CITY REDS: 1 Karl Fitzpatrick; 2 Jodie Broughton; 3 Mark Henry; 4 Willie Talau; 5 Ashley Gibson; 14 Matty Smith; 21 Daniel Holdsworth; 19 Ryan Boyle; 9 Malcolm Alker (C); 18 Lee Jewitt; 11 Ian Sibbit; 15 Stuart Littler; 13 Luke Swain. Subs (all used): 7 Jeremy Smith; 17 Adam Sidlow; 16 Phil Leuluai; 6 Stefan Ratchford.
Tries: M Smith (2, 27, 47), Holdsworth (12), Gibson (18, 55), Broughton (68), Boyle (74); **Goals:** Holdsworth 5/8.
SAINTS: 1 Paul Wellens; 2 Ade Gardner; 3 Matt Gidley; 30 Jamie Foster; 24 Jonny Lomax; 6 Leon Pryce; 7 Kyle Eastmond; 10 James Graham; 9 Keiron Cunningham (C); 15 Bryn Hargreaves; 22 Andrew Dixon; 17 Paul Clough; 11 Tony Puletua. Subs (all used): 8 Nick Fozzard; 14 James Roby; 16 Scott Moore; 18 Matty Ashurst.
Tries: Graham (16, 61), Eastmond (22), Wellens (39), Gardner (53), Moore (71); **Goals:** Eastmond 5/6.
Rugby Leaguer & League Express Men of the Match: *City Reds:* Matty Smith; *Saints:* James Graham.
Penalty count: 7-12; **Half-time:** 22-18;
Referee: Thierry Alibert; **Attendance:** 5,685.

CATALANS DRAGONS 14 HULL FC 28

DRAGONS: 5 Dimitri Pelo; 2 Steven Bell; 3 Sebastien Raguin; 4 Setaimata Sa; 28 Frederic Vaccari; 25 Tony Gigot; 7 Thomas Bosc (C); 8 David Ferriol; 15 Jean-Phillipe Baile; 10 Jerome Guisset; 11 Olivier Elima; 12 Gregory Mounis; 13 Dallas Johnson. Subs (all used): 20 Kane Bentley; 18 Dane Carlaw; 22 Jamal Fakir; 24 Remi Casty.
Tries: Pelo (21), Raguin (69), Bell (80); **Goals:** Bosc 1/3.
Sin bin: Ferriol (15) - fighting.
HULL: 1 Jordan Tansey; 21 Richard Whiting; 19 Jordan Turner; 4 Kirk Yeaman; 3 Tom Briscoe; 14 Danny Washbrook; 7 Sean Long (C); 10 Mark O'Meley; 20 Danny Houghton; 8 Ewan Dowes; 11 Lee Radford; 12 Danny Tickle; 13 Craig Fitzgibbon. Subs (all used): 22 Mike Burnett; 23 Sam Moa; 31 Liam Cunningham (D); 32 Paul McShane.
Tries: Briscoe (7), Fitzgibbon (16), O'Meley (28), Whiting (35), Tansey (65); **Goals:** Tickle 4/5.
Sin bin: Yeaman (15) - fighting.
Rugby Leaguer & League Express Men of the Match: *Dragons:* Dimitri Pelo; *Hull:* Mark O'Meley.
Penalty count: 15-9; **Half-time:** 4-22;
Referee: James Child; **Attendance:** 6,512.

Sunday 16th May 2010

HARLEQUINS 40 CASTLEFORD TIGERS 24

HARLEQUINS: 6 Luke Dorn; 35 Kevin Penny; 3 Tony Clubb; 4 David Howell; 5 Will Sharp; 21 Luke Gale; 9 Chad Randall; 10 Louie McCarthy-Scarsbrook; 7 Danny Orr; 8 Karl Temata; 13 Rob Purdham (C); 11 Luke Williamson; 1 Chris Melling. Subs (all used): 14 Oliver Wilkes; 36 David Mills (D2); 18 Ryan Esders; 23 Luke May.
Tries: Melling (2), Penny (9), Randall (31, 70), Williamson (72), Orr (75), Howell (78);
Goals: Orr 4/5, Gale 2/2.
TIGERS: 23 Ryan McGoldrick; 21 Jordan Thompson; 4 James Evans; 11 Brett Ferres; 5 Michael Wainwright; 6 Rangi Chase; 7 Brent Sherwin; 10 Craig Huby; 9 Ryan Hudson (C); 15 Liam Higgins; 14 Stuart Jones; 17 Ryan Clayton; 13 Joe Westerman. Subs (all used): 12 Steve Snitch; 26 Oliver Holmes; 30 Chris Tuson; 25 Dean Widders.
Tries: Westerman (18), Ferres (38), Higgins (40), Snitch (55); **Goals:** Westerman 4/4.
Rugby Leaguer & League Express Men of the Match: *Harlequins:* Danny Orr; *Tigers:* Rangi Chase.
Penalty count: 6-8; **Half-time:** 16-18;
Referee: Ian Smith; **Attendance:** 2,941.

HUDDERSFIELD GIANTS 30 WIGAN WARRIORS 38

GIANTS: 1 Brett Hodgson (C); 2 Leroy Cudjoe; 3 Jamahl Lolesi; 4 Paul Whatuira; 5 David Hodgson; 6 Kevin Brown; 34 Danny Brough; 8 Eorl Crabtree; 7 Luke Robinson; 10 Keith Mason; 11 Lee Gilmour; 13 Stephen Wild; 20 David Faiumu. Subs (all used): 9 Shaun Lunt; 15 Andy Raleigh; 22 Martin Aspinwall; 16 Darrell Griffin.
Tries: Cudjoe (8), D Hodgson (17, 37, 64), Whatuira (27), Crabtree (60); **Goals:** B Hodgson 3/6.
On report: Mason (20) - alleged late tackle on Leuluai.
WARRIORS: 5 Pat Richards; 24 Darrell Goulding; 27 Stefan Marsh; 4 George Carmont; 20 Karl Pryce; 6 Sam Tomkins; 7 Thomas Leuluai; 8 Stuart Fielden; 15 Michael McIlorum; 10 Andy Coley; 16 Phil Bailey; 12 Joel Tomkins; 13 Sean O'Loughlin (C). Subs (all used): 9 Mark Riddell; 14 Paul Prescott; 21 Eamon O'Carroll; 23 Lee Mossop.
Tries: J Tomkins (2, 45), Carmont (12), Goulding (39, 68), Coley (48); **Goals:** Richards 7/8.
Sin bin: J Tomkins (26) - holding down; Coley (53) - holding down.
Rugby Leaguer & League Express Men of the Match: *Giants:* David Hodgson; *Warriors:* Stuart Fielden.
Penalty count: 10-12; **Half-time:** 20-18;
Referee: Richard Silverwood; **Attendance:** 8,390.

HULL KINGSTON ROVERS 54 CRUSADERS 10

ROVERS: 1 Shaun Briscoe; 2 Peter Fox; 11 Clint Newton; 3 Kris Welham; 28 Ben Cockayne; 9 Scott Murrell; 7 Michael Dobson; 20 Michael Vella (C); 21 Josh Hodgson; 30 Joel Clinton; 13 Ben Galea; 16 Jason Netherton; 22 Liam Watts. Subs (all used): 10 Scott Wheeldon; 17 Ben Fisher; 8 Rhys Lovegrove; 14 Matt Cook.
Tries: Newton (6, 53), Cockayne (8), Dobson (13, 28, 34), Watts (65), Fox (77), Welham (79);
Goals: Dobson 9/9.
CRUSADERS: 26 Clinton Schifcofske; 1 Gareth Thomas; 4 Vince Mellars; 27 Rhys Hanbury; 5 Gareth Raynor; 6 Michael Witt; 7 Jarrod Sammut; 8 Ryan O'Hara (C); 9 Lincoln Withers; 10 Mark Bryant; 11 Weller Hauraki; 12 Jason Chan; 13 Rocky Trimarchi. Subs (all used): 16 Frank Winterstein; 17 Adam Peek; 20 Ben Flower; 23 Peter Lupton.
Tries: Raynor (24), Sammut (61); **Goals:** Witt 1/2.
Rugby Leaguer & League Express Men of the Match: *Rovers:* Michael Dobson; *Crusaders:* Lincoln Withers.
Penalty count: 11-9; **Half-time:** 30-4;
Referee: Phil Bentham; **Attendance:** 7,273.

ROUND 15

Friday 21st May 2010

ST HELENS 68 HULL KINGSTON ROVERS 12

SAINTS: 24 Jonny Lomax; 2 Ade Gardner; 3 Matt Gidley; 13 Chris Flannery; 30 Jamie Foster; 6 Leon Pryce; 7 Kyle Eastmond; 10 James Graham; 9 Keiron Cunningham (C); 15 Bryn Hargreaves; 17 Paul Clough; 22 Andrew Dixon; 14 James Roby. Subs (all used): 11 Tony Puletua; 16 Scott Moore; 18 Matty Ashurst; 25 Jacob Emmitt.
Tries: Gardner (4, 19, 46, 61), Puletua (21), Flannery (29), Emmitt (36), Moore (43), Eastmond (50), Gidley (58), Lomax (71), Roby (74), Dixon (78);
Goals: Eastmond 5/9, Foster 0/1, Lomax 3/3.
ROVERS: 1 Shaun Briscoe; 2 Peter Fox; 11 Clint Newton; 3 Kris Welham; 28 Ben Cockayne; 9 Scott Murrell; 7 Michael Dobson; 20 Michael Vella (C); 21 Josh Hodgson; 30 Joel Clinton; 16 Jason Netherton; 13 Ben Galea; 22 Liam Watts. Subs (all used): 8 Rhys Lovegrove; 10 Scott Wheeldon; 14 Matt Cook; 17 Ben Fisher.
Tries: Welham (10), Newton (54); **Goals:** Dobson 2/2.
Sin bin: Cockayne (32) - late tackle on Eastmond; Fisher (33) - interference.
Rugby Leaguer & League Express Men of the Match: *Saints:* James Roby; *Rovers:* Clint Newton.
Penalty count: 12-5; **Half-time:** 26-6;
Referee: James Child; **Attendance:** 9,375.

Saturday 22nd May 2010

CRUSADERS 26 WIGAN WARRIORS 46

CRUSADERS: 26 Clinton Schifcofske (C); 1 Gareth Thomas; 4 Vince Mellars; 27 Rhys Hanbury; 2 Nick Youngquest; 6 Michael Witt; 7 Jarrod Sammut; 8 Ryan O'Hara; 9 Lincoln Withers; 20 Ben Flower; 11 Weller Hauraki; 12 Jason Chan; 13 Rocky Trimarchi. Subs (all used): 18 Jamie Thackray; 17 Adam Peek; 10 Mark Bryant; 23 Peter Lupton.
Tries: Youngquest (28), Hanbury (42), Chan (62), Witt (71), Lupton (75); **Goals:** Witt 3/5.
WARRIORS: 5 Pat Richards; 24 Darrell Goulding; 3 Martin Gleeson; 4 George Carmont; 20 Karl Pryce; 6 Sam Tomkins; 7 Thomas Leuluai; 8 Stuart Fielden; 9 Mark Riddell; 10 Andy Coley; 16 Phil Bailey; 12 Joel Tomkins; 13 Sean O'Loughlin (C). Subs (all used): 15 Michael McIlorum; 25 Liam Farrell; 26 Ben Davies (D); 17 Iafeta Palea'aesina.
Tries: O'Loughlin (3), Pryce (6, 10, 21, 68), Gleeson (13, 79), Richards (52); **Goals:** Richards 7/8.
Rugby Leaguer & League Express Men of the Match: *Crusaders:* Jarrod Sammut; *Warriors:* Pat Richards.
Penalty count: 10-8; **Half-time:** 4-28;
Referee: Thierry Alibert; **Attendance:** 6,075.

CATALANS DRAGONS 14 SALFORD CITY REDS 22

DRAGONS: 5 Dimitri Pelo; 2 Steven Bell; 3 Sebastien Raguin; 4 Setaimata Sa; 28 Frederic Vaccari; 30 Brent Sherwin (D); 7 Thomas Bosc (C); 24 Remi Casty; 20 Kane Bentley; 10 Jerome Guisset; 11 Olivier Elima; 12 Gregory Mounis; 13 Dallas Johnson. Subs (all used): 29 Andrew Bentley; 18 Dane Carlaw; 22 Jamal Fakir; 25 Tony Gigot.
Tries: Bosc (58, 71); **Goals:** Bosc 3/3.
Dismissal: Mounis (75) - dangerous tackle.
CITY REDS: 1 Karl Fitzpatrick; 5 Ashley Gibson; 3 Mark Henry; 4 Willie Talau; 2 Jodie Broughton; 21 Daniel Holdsworth; 14 Matty Smith; 19 Ryan Boyle; 9 Malcolm Alker (C); 18 Lee Jewitt; 11 Ian Sibbit; 15 Stuart Littler; 13 Luke Swain. Subs (all used): 6 Stefan Ratchford; 7 Jeremy Smith; 16 Phil Leuluai; 17 Adam Sidlow.
Tries: Littler (4), Fitzpatrick (7), Leuluai (45);
Goals: Holdsworth 5/5.
Rugby Leaguer & League Express Men of the Match: *Dragons:* Thomas Bosc; *City Reds:* Daniel Holdsworth.
Penalty count: 11-11; **Half-time:** 2-12;
Referee: Phil Bentham; **Attendance:** 5,115.

Sunday 23rd May 2010

WARRINGTON WOLVES 36 HUDDERSFIELD GIANTS 20

WOLVES: 1 Richard Mathers; 5 Chris Hicks; 3 Matt King; 23 Ryan Atkins; 2 Chris Riley; 6 Lee Briers; 4 Chris Bridge; 8 Adrian Morley (C); 9 Michael Monaghan; 13 Ben Harrison; 11 Louis Anderson; 12 Ben Westwood; 17 Simon Grix. Subs (all used): 16 Paul Wood; 26 David Solomona; 19 Lee Mitchell; 27 Vinnie Anderson.
Tries: Morley (5), Bridge (20), Riley (23), Hicks (33, 47), King (56), Wood (70); **Goals:** Bridge 4/7.
Sin bin: Riley (1) - interference.
GIANTS: 1 Brett Hodgson (C); 2 Leroy Cudjoe; 3 Jamahl Lolesi; 19 Michael Lawrence; 5 David Hodgson; 6 Kevin Brown; 21 Scott Grix; 8 Eorl Crabtree; 7 Luke Robinson; 10 Keith Mason; 11 Lee Gilmour; 13 Stephen Wild; 20 David Faiumu. Subs (all used): 15 Andy Raleigh; 16 Darrell Griffin; 22 Martin Aspinwall; 9 Shaun Lunt.
Tries: Robinson (2), Cudjoe (26, 68), Lolesi (62);
Goals: B Hodgson 2/4.
Sin bin: Gilmour (54) - interference.
Rugby Leaguer & League Express Men of the Match: *Wolves:* Adrian Morley; *Giants:* Luke Robinson.
Penalty count: 12-7; **Half-time:** 20-10;
Referee: Ian Smith; **Attendance:** 11,087.

Huddersfield's David Hodgson upended by Bradford's Heath L'Estrange and Michael Platt

CASTLEFORD TIGERS 26 HULL FC 34

TIGERS: 23 Ryan McGoldrick; 5 Michael Wainwright; 3 Michael Shenton; 11 Brett Ferres; 32 Joe Arundel; 25 Dean Widders; 6 Rangi Chase; 15 Liam Higgins; 9 Ryan Hudson (C); 10 Craig Huby; 14 Stuart Jones; 12 Steve Snitch; 13 Joe Westerman. Subs (all used): 8 Mitchell Sargent; 17 Ryan Clayton; 30 Chris Tuson; 33 Kyle Wood (D).
Tries: Jones (18), Arundel (32), Wainwright (39), Chase (78), Wainwright (79); **Goals:** Westerman 3/6.
HULL: 1 Jordan Tansey; 21 Richard Whiting; 19 Jordan Turner; 4 Kirk Yeaman; 3 Tom Briscoe; 14 Danny Washbrook; 7 Sean Long (C); 8 Ewan Dowes; 20 Danny Houghton; 10 Mark O'Meley; 11 Lee Radford; 12 Danny Tickle; 13 Craig Fitzgibbon. Subs (all used): 22 Mike Burnett; 24 Craig Hall; 23 Sam Moa; 32 Paul McShane.
Tries: Yeaman (9), Tansey (12), Long (43), Briscoe (53), Fitzgibbon (63), O'Meley (73); **Goals:** Tickle 5/7.
Sin bin: Dowes (71) - late tackle.
Rugby Leaguer & League Express Men of the Match:
Tigers: Michael Wainwright; *Hull:* Sean Long.
Penalty count: 11-14; **Half-time:** 16-10;
Referee: Ben Thaler; **Attendance:** 7,996.

WAKEFIELD TRINITY WILDCATS 54 HARLEQUINS 12

WILDCATS: 18 Aaron Murphy; 2 Damien Blanch; 3 Sean Gleeson; 13 Jason Demetriou (C); 5 Luke George; 21 Paul Cooke; 14 Sam Obst; 25 Richard Moore; 20 Tevita Leo-Latu; 19 Paul King; 16 Paul Johnson; 11 Dale Ferguson; 32 Danny Kirmond. Subs (all used): 1 Matt Blaymire; 10 Michael Korkidas; 24 James Davey; 17 Kevin Henderson.
Tries: George (16, 72), Gleeson (19, 66), Obst (26, 70), Henderson (43), Blanch (51), Demetriou (58), Cooke (76); **Goals:** Cooke 7/10.
HARLEQUINS: 6 Luke Dorn; 35 Kevin Penny; 3 Tony Clubb; 4 David Howell; 5 Will Sharp; 21 Luke Gale; 22 Jamie O'Callaghan; 10 Louie McCarthy-Scarsbrook; 7 Danny Orr; 8 Karl Temata; 11 Luke Williamson; 13 Rob Purdham (C); 1 Chris Melling. Subs: 14 Oliver Wilkes; 36 David Mills; 23 Luke May (not used); 18 Ryan Esders.
Tries: Clubb (32), Dorn (80); **Goals:** Orr 2/2.
Rugby Leaguer & League Express Men of the Match:
Wildcats: Sam Obst; *Harlequins:* Luke Dorn.
Penalty count: 6-1; **Half-time:** 18-6;
Referee: Gareth Hewer; **Attendance:** 4,371.

BRADFORD BULLS 12 LEEDS RHINOS 26

BULLS: 1 Dave Halley; 2 Rikki Sheriffe; 15 Michael Platt; 4 Chris Nero; 5 Stuart Reardon; 3 Paul Sykes; 9 Heath L'Estrange; 8 Nick Scruton; 14 Wayne Godwin; 10 Andy Lynch (C); 20 Elliott Whitehead; 22 James Donaldson; 11 Steve Menzies. Subs (all used): 32 Danny Addy; 12 Glenn Hall; 16 Michael Worrincy; 18 Craig Kopczak.
Tries: Whitehead (4), Platt (20); **Goals:** Sykes 2/3.

RHINOS: 28 Lee Smith; 2 Scott Donald; 3 Brett Delaney; 4 Keith Senior; 5 Ryan Hall; 13 Kevin Sinfield (C); 6 Danny McGuire; 8 Kylie Leuluai; 9 Danny Buderus; 16 Ryan Bailey; 18 Carl Ablett; 17 Ian Kirke; 11 Jamie Jones-Buchanan. Subs (all used): 15 Greg Eastwood; 20 Jay Pitts; 14 Matt Diskin; 19 Luke Burgess.
Tries: McGuire (15, 28, 61), Senior (35), Delaney (42);
Goals: Sinfield 3/5.
Rugby Leaguer & League Express Men of the Match:
Bulls: Paul Sykes; *Rhinos:* Danny McGuire.
Penalty count: 8-7; **Half-time:** 12-14;
Referee: Richard Silverwood; **Attendance:** 13,269.

ROUND 16

Friday 4th June 2010

HULL FC 27 ST HELENS 26

HULL: 1 Jordan Tansey; 21 Richard Whiting; 19 Jordan Turner; 4 Kirk Yeaman; 3 Tom Briscoe; 14 Danny Washbrook; 7 Sean Long (C); 8 Ewan Dowes; 20 Danny Houghton; 10 Mark O'Meley; 16 Willie Manu; 12 Danny Tickle; 13 Craig Fitzgibbon. Subs: 11 Lee Radford; 23 Sam Moa; 17 Peter Cusack; 24 Craig Hall (not used).
Tries: Briscoe (10), Turner (47), Houghton (54), Manu (62), Tickle (68); **Goals:** Tickle 3/5;
Field goal: Tickle (79).
SAINTS: 1 Paul Wellens; 24 Jonny Lomax; 3 Matt Gidley; 13 Chris Flannery; 5 Francis Meli; 6 Leon Pryce; 16 Scott Moore; 10 James Graham; 9 Keiron Cunningham (C); 15 Bryn Hargreaves; 22 Andrew Dixon; 17 Paul Clough; 14 James Roby. Subs (all used): 8 Nick Fozzard; 18 Matty Ashurst; 28 Shaun Magennis (D); 21 Gary Wheeler.
Tries: Meli (17, 20, 38, 44), Cunningham (24);
Goals: Lomax 3/5.
Rugby Leaguer & League Express Men of the Match:
Hull: Danny Houghton; *Saints:* James Graham.
Penalty count: 8-8; **Half-time:** 6-22;
Referee: Phil Bentham; **Attendance:** 13,300.

LEEDS RHINOS 28 WAKEFIELD TRINITY WILDCATS 22

RHINOS: 1 Brent Webb; 2 Scott Donald; 3 Brett Delaney; 28 Lee Smith; 5 Ryan Hall; 13 Kevin Sinfield (C); 6 Danny McGuire; 8 Kylie Leuluai; 9 Danny Buderus; 17 Ian Kirke; 18 Carl Ablett; 20 Jay Pitts; 11 Jamie Jones-Buchanan. Subs (all used): 10 Jamie Peacock; 15 Greg Eastwood; 4 Keith Senior; 14 Matt Diskin.
Tries: McGuire (13), Jones-Buchanan (26), Donald (39), Buderus (75); **Goals:** Sinfield 6/6.
WILDCATS: 18 Aaron Murphy; 2 Damien Blanch; 3 Sean Gleeson; 13 Jason Demetriou (C); 5 Luke George; 21 Paul Cooke; 14 Sam Obst; 25 Richard Moore; 20 Tevita Leo-Latu; 19 Paul King; 16 Paul Johnson; 12 Glenn Morrison;

32 Danny Kirmond. Subs (all used): 10 Michael Korkidas; 17 Kevin Henderson; 6 Ben Jeffries; 1 Matt Blaymire.
Tries: Morrison (2), Obst (8), Murphy (50), Demetriou (77); **Goals:** Cooke 3/5.
Sin bin: Morrison (71) - obstruction.
Rugby Leaguer & League Express Men of the Match:
Rhinos: Kylie Leuluai; *Wildcats:* Kevin Henderson.
Penalty count: 9-8; **Half-time:** 18-14;
Referee: Ian Smith; **Attendance:** 13,869.

SALFORD CITY REDS 10 WARRINGTON WOLVES 27

CITY REDS: 3 Mark Henry; 20 Steve Tyrer; 5 Ashley Gibson; 4 Willie Talau; 2 Jodie Broughton; 14 Matty Smith; 7 Jeremy Smith; 19 Ryan Boyle; 9 Malcolm Alker (C); 18 Lee Jewitt; 11 Ian Sibbit; 15 Stuart Littler; 13 Luke Swain. Subs (all used): 16 Phil Leuluai; 17 Adam Sidlow; 12 Luke Adamson; 26 Marc Sneyd (D).
Tries: Henry (28), Broughton (53); **Goals:** Tyrer 1/2.
WOLVES: 1 Richard Mathers; 5 Chris Hicks; 3 Matt King; 23 Ryan Atkins; 2 Chris Riley; 4 Chris Bridge; 6 Lee Briers; 8 Adrian Morley (C); 9 Michael Monaghan; 13 Ben Harrison; 11 Louis Anderson; 27 Vinnie Anderson; 17 Simon Grix. Subs (all used): 14 Mick Higham; 19 Lee Mitchell; 18 Michael Cooper; 26 David Solomona.
Tries: Hicks (17), Mathers (25, 32), Higham (76), Solomona (79); **Goals:** Bridge 3/6; **Field goal:** Briers (63).
Rugby Leaguer & League Express Men of the Match:
City Reds: Luke Swain; *Wolves:* Vinnie Anderson.
Penalty count: 4-8; **Half-time:** 6-16;
Referee: Ben Thaler; **Attendance:** 6,093.

Sunday 6th June 2010

BRADFORD BULLS 6 HUDDERSFIELD GIANTS 52

BULLS: 1 Dave Halley; 2 Rikki Sheriffe; 15 Michael Platt; 4 Chris Nero; 5 Stuart Reardon; 3 Paul Sykes; 9 Heath L'Estrange; 8 Nick Scruton; 14 Wayne Godwin; 10 Andy Lynch (C); 20 Elliott Whitehead; 12 Glenn Hall; 11 Steve Menzies. Subs (all used): 29 Joe Wardle; 16 Michael Worrincy; 32 Danny Addy; 18 Craig Kopczak.
Try: Menzies (69); **Goals:** Sykes 1/1.
GIANTS: 1 Brett Hodgson (C); 27 Jermaine McGillvary (D); 2 Leroy Cudjoe; 19 Michael Lawrence; 5 David Hodgson; 6 Kevin Brown; 34 Danny Brough; 8 Eorl Crabtree; 7 Luke Robinson; 10 Keith Mason; 11 Lee Gilmour; 13 Stephen Wild; 20 David Faiumu. Subs (all used): 23 Larne Patrick; 16 Darrell Griffin; 12 David Fa'alogo; 9 Shaun Lunt.
Tries: Gilmour (6), D Hodgson (15, 77), McGillvary (19, 29), Cudjoe (21), Robinson (55), B Hodgson (62), Griffin (72); **Goals:** B Hodgson 8/9.
Rugby Leaguer & League Express Men of the Match:
Bulls: Steve Menzies; *Giants:* Brett Hodgson.
Penalty count: 7-7; **Half-time:** 0-28;
Referee: James Child; **Attendance:** 8,156.

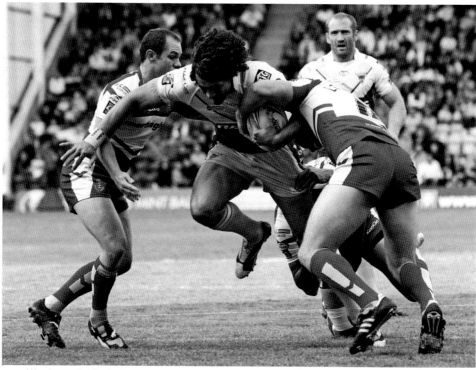

Warrington's Vinnie Anderson takes the ball forward against Hull KR as Ben Fisher moves in

HULL KINGSTON ROVERS 24 CATALANS DRAGONS 6

ROVERS: 1 Shaun Briscoe; 2 Peter Fox; 4 Jake Webster; 3 Kris Welham; 28 Ben Cockayne; 9 Scott Murrell; 7 Michael Dobson; 20 Michael Vella (C); 21 Josh Hodgson; 30 Joel Clinton; 13 Ben Galea; 11 Clint Newton; 22 Liam Watts. Subs (all used): 17 Ben Fisher; 16 Jason Netherton; 8 Rhys Lovegrove; 10 Scott Wheeldon.
Tries: Galea (2), Welham (19), Murrell (51), Dobson (77); **Goals:** Dobson 4/4.
DRAGONS: 5 Dimitri Pelo; 2 Steven Bell; 3 Sebastien Raguin; 4 Setaimata Sa; 28 Frederic Vaccari; 7 Thomas Bosc (C); 30 Brent Sherwin; 8 David Ferriol; 12 Gregory Mounis; 10 Jerome Guisset; 11 Olivier Elima; 18 Dane Carlaw; 13 Dallas Johnson. Subs (all used): 22 Jamal Fakir; 24 Remi Casty; 25 Tony Gigot; 29 Andrew Bentley.
Try: Raguin (56); **Goals:** Bosc 1/1.
Rugby Leaguer & League Express Men of the Match:
Rovers: Scott Murrell; *Dragons:* Thomas Bosc.
Penalty count: 4-10; **Half-time:** 12-0;
Referee: Ian Smith; **Attendance:** 7,102.

WIGAN WARRIORS 38 CASTLEFORD TIGERS 22

WARRIORS: 5 Pat Richards; 24 Darrell Goulding; 3 Martin Gleeson; 4 George Carmont; 20 Karl Pryce; 6 Sam Tomkins; 7 Thomas Leuluai; 8 Stuart Fielden; 15 Michael McIlorum; 14 Paul Prescott; 16 Phil Bailey; 12 Joel Tomkins; 13 Sean O'Loughlin (C). Subs (all used): 9 Mark Riddell; 17 Iafeta Palea'aesina; 25 Liam Farrell; 29 Chris Tuson.
Tries: Goulding (11, 49, 60), Leuluai (23), Tuson (31), O'Loughlin (62, 71); **Goals:** Richards 5/7.
TIGERS: 23 Ryan McGoldrick; 2 Kirk Dixon; 3 Michael Shenton; 11 Brett Ferres; 5 Michael Wainwright; 25 Dean Widders; 33 Kyle Wood; 15 Liam Higgins; 9 Ryan Hudson (C); 16 Paul Jackson; 10 Craig Huby; 17 Ryan Clayton; 13 Joe Westerman. Subs (all used): 8 Mitchell Sargent; 14 Stuart Jones; 21 Jordan Thompson; 31 Jonathan Walker (D).
Tries: Jackson (6), Jones (36), Ferres (44), Huby (77); **Goals:** Westerman 3/4.
Sin bin: Jones (68) - interference.
Rugby Leaguer & League Express Men of the Match:
Warriors: Sean O'Loughlin; *Tigers:* Craig Huby.
Penalty count: 10-10; **Half-time:** 16-12;
Referee: Thierry Alibert; **Attendance:** 14,047.

HARLEQUINS 50 CRUSADERS 22

HARLEQUINS: 6 Luke Dorn; 22 Jamie O'Callaghan; 3 Tony Clubb; 4 David Howell; 5 Will Sharp; 21 Luke Gale; 9 Chad Randall (C); 10 Louie McCarthy-Scarsbrook; 7 Danny Orr; 14 Oliver Wilkes; 11 Luke Williamson; 8 Karl Temata; 1 Chris Melling. Subs (all used): 17 Danny Ward; 18 Ryan Esders; 20 Andy Ellis (D); 33 Olsi Krasniqi (D).

Tries: Dorn (10, 25, 60, 65), Melling (14), Gale (46), Howell (50), Krasniqi (72); **Goals:** Gale 6/6, Orr 3/3.
CRUSADERS: 26 Clinton Schifcofske (C); 1 Gareth Thomas; 14 Luke Dyer; 4 Vince Mellars; 2 Nick Youngquest; 6 Michael Witt; 27 Rhys Hanbury; 8 Ryan O'Hara; 9 Lincoln Withers; 10 Mark Bryant; 12 Jason Chan; 11 Weller Hauraki; 23 Peter Lupton. Subs (all used): 16 Frank Winterstein; 17 Adam Peek; 19 Jordan James; 20 Ben Flower.
Tries: Schifcofske (38), Chan (56), Lupton (73), Hanbury (76); **Goals:** Schifcofske 3/4.
Rugby Leaguer & League Express Men of the Match:
Harlequins: Luke Dorn; *Crusaders:* Clinton Schifcofske.
Penalty count: 9-6; **Half-time:** 20-6;
Referee: Ben Thaler; **Attendance:** 2,381.

ROUND 17

Friday 11th June 2010

HULL FC 34 SALFORD CITY REDS 12

HULL: 1 Jordan Tansey; 21 Richard Whiting; 19 Jordan Turner; 4 Kirk Yeaman; 24 Craig Hall; 14 Danny Washbrook; 7 Sean Long (C); 17 Peter Cusack; 20 Danny Houghton; 8 Ewan Dowes; 16 Willie Manu; 12 Danny Tickle; 13 Craig Fitzgibbon. Subs (all used): 9 Shaun Berrigan; 15 Epalahame Lauaki; 23 Sam Moa; 11 Lee Radford.
Tries: Hall (16, 78), Long (20), Whiting (29), Tansey (47), Turner (61); **Goals:** Tickle 5/6.
Sin bin: Houghton (8) - holding down.
CITY REDS: 1 Karl Fitzpatrick; 2 Jodie Broughton; 3 Mark Henry; 4 Willie Talau; 5 Ashley Gibson; 7 Jeremy Smith; 14 Matty Smith; 18 Lee Jewitt; 9 Malcolm Alker (C); 19 Ryan Boyle; 11 Ian Sibbit; 15 Stuart Littler; 13 Luke Swain. Subs (all used): 16 Phil Leuluai; 17 Adam Sidlow; 12 Luke Adamson; 26 Marc Sneyd.
Tries: Fitzpatrick (23), Sidlow (26); **Goals:** M Smith 2/2.
Rugby Leaguer & League Express Men of the Match:
Hull: Jordan Tansey; *City Reds:* Adam Sidlow.
Penalty count: 8-7; **Half-time:** 18-12;
Referee: Phil Bentham; **Attendance:** 11,397.

ST HELENS 30 HUDDERSFIELD GIANTS 22

SAINTS: 1 Paul Wellens; 30 Jamie Foster; 3 Matt Gidley; 21 Gary Wheeler; 5 Francis Meli; 6 Leon Pryce; 16 Scott Moore; 8 Nick Fozzard; 9 Keiron Cunningham (C); 15 Bryn Hargreaves; 17 Paul Clough; 13 Chris Flannery; 11 Tony Puletua. Subs (all used): 18 Matty Ashurst; 22 Andrew Dixon; 25 Jacob Emmitt; 33 Paul Johnson (D).
Tries: Gidley (10), Wheeler (14), Puletua (22), Fozzard (46), Dixon (72); **Goals:** Foster 5/6.

On report:
Meli (65) - alleged dangerous challenge on McGillvary.
GIANTS: 1 Brett Hodgson (C); 27 Jermaine McGillvary; 2 Leroy Cudjoe; 19 Michael Lawrence; 5 David Hodgson; 34 Danny Brough; 7 Luke Robinson; 16 Darrell Griffin; 9 Shaun Lunt; 10 Keith Mason; 11 Lee Gilmour; 13 Stephen Wild; 20 David Faiumu. Subs (all used): 23 Larne Patrick; 21 Scott Grix; 12 David Fa'alogo; 8 Eorl Crabtree.
Tries: Faiumu (18), Gilmour (35), Grix (38), Cudjoe (62); **Goals:** B Hodgson 3/4.
Rugby Leaguer & League Express Men of the Match:
Saints: Keiron Cunningham; *Giants:* Shaun Lunt.
Penalty count: 8-9; **Half-time:** 16-16;
Referee: Ben Thaler; **Attendance:** 9,034.

WARRINGTON WOLVES 35
HULL KINGSTON ROVERS 16

WOLVES: 1 Richard Mathers; 5 Chris Hicks; 3 Matt King; 23 Ryan Atkins; 2 Chris Riley; 17 Simon Grix; 6 Lee Briers; 16 Paul Wood; 9 Michael Monaghan (C); 13 Ben Harrison; 11 Louis Anderson; 27 Vinnie Anderson; 26 David Solomona. Subs (all used): 14 Mick Higham; 18 Michael Cooper; 19 Lee Mitchell; 22 Tyrone McCarthy.
Tries: Briers (23, 57), L Anderson (54), Atkins (59), Monaghan (72), King (78); **Goals:** Briers 5/6.
Field goal: Briers (70).
ROVERS: 1 Shaun Briscoe; 2 Peter Fox; 15 Mike Ratu; 3 Kris Welham; 28 Ben Cockayne; 9 Scott Murrell; 7 Michael Dobson; 20 Michael Vella (C); 17 Ben Fisher; 16 Jason Netherton; 11 Clint Newton; 13 Ben Galea; 22 Liam Watts. Subs (all used): 30 Joel Clinton; 21 Josh Hodgson; 10 Scott Wheeldon; 8 Rhys Lovegrove.
Tries: Welham (16), Ratu (69), Fisher (76); **Goals:** Dobson 2/3.
Sin bin: Newton (53) - high tackle on Monaghan.
Rugby Leaguer & League Express Men of the Match:
Wolves: Ben Harrison; *Rovers:* Shaun Briscoe.
Penalty count: 10-7; **Half-time:** 6-4;
Referee: Ian Smith; **Attendance:** 9,216.

Saturday 12th June 2010

HARLEQUINS 22 LEEDS RHINOS 42

HARLEQUINS: 6 Luke Dorn; 22 Jamie O'Callaghan; 3 Tony Clubb; 4 David Howell; 5 Will Sharp; 21 Luke Gale; 9 Chad Randall (C); 14 Oliver Wilkes; 7 Danny Orr; 10 Louie McCarthy-Scarsbrook; 11 Luke Williamson; 8 Karl Temata; 1 Chris Melling. Subs (all used): 20 Andy Ellis; 33 Olsi Krasniqi; 17 Danny Ward; 18 Ryan Esders.
Tries: Dorn (32, 43), Howell (66), Gale (68);
Goals: Orr 2/4, Melling 1/1.
RHINOS: 1 Brent Webb; 2 Scott Donald; 3 Brent Delaney; 4 Keith Senior (C); 28 Lee Smith; 18 Carl Ablett; 25 Paul McShane; 8 Kyle Leuluai; 9 Danny

Buderus; 24 Luke Ambler; 17 Ian Kirke; 20 Jay Pitts; 27 Chris Clarkson. Subs (all used): 14 Matt Diskin; 21 Kyle Amor; 15 Greg Eastwood; 26 Tom Bush.
Tries: Smith (11, 53, 77), McShane (15), Webb (26), Ambler (46), Ablett (56); **Goals:** Smith 7/8.
Rugby Leaguer & League Express Men of the Match: *Harlequins:* David Howell; *Rhinos:* Lee Smith.
Penalty count: 10-9; **Half-time:** 6-16;
Referee: James Child; **Attendance:** 4,117.

Sunday 13th June 2010

WAKEFIELD TRINITY WILDCATS 6
WIGAN WARRIORS 48

WILDCATS: 1 Matt Blaymire; 2 Damien Blanch; 18 Aaron Murphy; 13 Jason Demetriou (C); 5 Luke George; 12 Glenn Morrison; 21 Paul Cooke; 10 Michael Korkidas; 14 Sam Obst; 19 Paul King; 16 Paul Johnson; 17 Kevin Henderson; 32 Danny Kirmond. Subs (all used): 35 Charlie Leaeno (D); 11 Dale Ferguson; 24 James Davey; 25 Richard Moore.
Try: Blanch (54); **Goals:** Cooke 1/1.
Sin bin: Ferguson (58) - interference.
WARRIORS: 5 Pat Richards; 2 Amos Roberts; 3 Martin Gleeson; 4 George Carmont; 20 Karl Pryce; 6 Sam Tomkins; 7 Thomas Leuluai; 8 Stuart Fielden; 15 Michael Mcllorum; 10 Andy Coley (C); 16 Phil Bailey; 12 Joel Tomkins; 13 Sean O'Loughlin. Subs (all used): 9 Mark Riddell; 14 Paul Prescott; 17 Iafeta Palea'aesina; 25 Liam Farrell.
Tries: Pryce (2, 35, 47), O'Loughlin (8), Farrell (17), Richards (56, 69), Roberts (62), S Tomkins (71);
Goals: Richards 6/9.
Sin bin: Bailey (21) - interference.
Rugby Leaguer & League Express Men of the Match: *Wildcats:* Jason Demetriou; *Warriors:* Sam Tomkins.
Penalty count: 10-10; **Half-time:** 0-20;
Referee: Ian Smith; **Attendance:** 6,947.

CRUSADERS 44 BRADFORD BULLS 20

CRUSADERS: 26 Clinton Schifcofske (C); 1 Gareth Thomas; 3 Tony Martin; 4 Vince Mellars; 2 Nick Youngquest; 23 Peter Lupton; 27 Rhys Hanbury; 8 Ryan O'Hara; 9 Lincoln Withers; 10 Mark Bryant; 11 Weller Hauraki; 12 Jason Chan; 13 Rocky Trimarchi. Subs (all used): 16 Frank Winterstein; 17 Adam Peek; 14 Luke Dyer; 20 Ben Flower.
Tries: Thomas (3), Mellars (13), Hauraki (19, 68), Martin (46), Youngquest (72), Withers (76);
Goals: Schifcofske 8/8.
BULLS: 1 Dave Halley; 2 Rikki Sheriffe; 29 Joe Wardle; 4 Chris Nero; 5 Stuart Reardon; 3 Paul Sykes; 6 Brett Kearney; 8 Nick Scruton; 9 Heath L'Estrange; 12 Glenn Hall; 20 Elliott Whitehead; 16 Michael Worrincy; 11 Steve Menzies (C). Subs (all used): 14 Wayne Godwin; 32 Danny Addy; 18 Craig Kopczak; 23 Steve Crossley (D).
Tries: Nero (26), Halley (32), Worrincy (42), Whitehead (79); **Goals:** Sykes 2/4.
Rugby Leaguer & League Express Men of the Match: *Crusaders:* Rhys Hanbury; *Bulls:* Brett Kearney.
Penalty count: 6-8; **Half-time:** 20-10;
Referee: Phil Bentham; **Attendance:** 2,979.

Tuesday 15th June 2010

CASTLEFORD TIGERS 24 CATALANS DRAGONS 20

TIGERS: 21 Jordan Thompson; 2 Kirk Dixon; 3 Michael Shenton; 11 Brett Ferres; 5 Michael Wainwright; 25 Dean Widders; 6 Rangi Chase; 16 Paul Jackson; 9 Ryan Hudson (C); 15 Liam Higgins; 10 Craig Huby; 14 Stuart Jones; 13 Joe Westerman. Subs (all used): 12 Steve Snitch; 33 Kyle Wood; 32 Joe Arundel; 8 Mitchell Sargent.
Tries: Snitch (18, 27), Wainwright (59, 74);
Goals: Westerman 4/4.
DRAGONS: 16 William Barthau; 2 Steven Bell; 3 Sebastien Raguin; 17 Cyrille Gossard; 28 Frederic Vaccari; 4 Setaimata Sa; 30 Brent Sherwin; 8 David Ferriol; 9 Casey McGuire; 10 Jerome Guisset; 11 Olivier Elima (C); 18 Dane Carlaw; 13 Dallas Johnson. Subs (all used): 12 Gregory Mounis; 22 Jamal Fakir; 24 Remi Casty; 29 Andrew Bentley.
Tries: McGuire (4), Raguin (34), Vaccari (54, 80);
Goals: Barthau 2/4.
Rugby Leaguer & League Express Men of the Match: *Tigers:* Michael Wainwright; *Dragons:* Dallas Johnson.
Penalty count: 5-4; **Half-time:** 12-10;
Referee: Richard Silverwood; **Attendance:** 4,209.

ROUND 18

Saturday 19th June 2010

BRADFORD BULLS 28 WARRINGTON WOLVES 40

BULLS: 6 Brett Kearney; 2 Rikki Sheriffe; 11 Steve Menzies (C); 4 Chris Nero; 1 Dave Halley; 3 Paul Sykes; 31 Cain Southernwood (D); 8 Nick Scruton; 9 Heath L'Estrange; 12 Glenn Hall; 20 Elliott Whitehead; 16 Michael Worrincy; 14 Wayne Godwin. Subs (all used): 24 Tom Olbison; 32 Danny Addy; 23 Steve Crossley; 18 Craig Kopczak.
Tries: L'Estrange (21), Nero (27), Menzies (44), Halley (50), Kearney (61); **Goals:** Sykes 4/5.
WOLVES: 2 Chris Riley; 5 Chris Hicks; 4 Chris Bridge; 23 Ryan Atkins; 3 Matt King; 6 Lee Briers; 17 Simon Grix; 8 Adrian Morley (C); 9 Michael Monaghan; 16 Paul Wood; 11 Louis Anderson; 12 Ben Westwood; 13 Ben Harrison. Subs (all used): 26 David Solomona; 18 Michael Cooper; 10 Garreth Carvell; 14 Mick Higham.
Tries: Riley (9, 57), King (14), Briers (32), Higham (38, 73), Atkins (59); **Goals:** Briers 6/7.
Rugby Leaguer & League Express Men of the Match: *Bulls:* Heath L'Estrange; *Wolves:* Mick Higham.
Penalty count: 11-7; **Half-time:** 10-22;
Referee: Ian Smith; **Attendance:** 8,128.

CATALANS DRAGONS 30
WAKEFIELD TRINITY WILDCATS 23

DRAGONS: 1 Clint Greenshields; 2 Steven Bell; 3 Sebastien Raguin; 4 Setaimata Sa; 5 Dimitri Pelo; 7 Thomas Bosc (C); 30 Brent Sherwin; 8 David Ferriol; 9 Casey McGuire; 10 Jerome Guisset; 11 Olivier Elima; 12 Gregory Mounis; 13 Dallas Johnson. Subs: 17 Cyrille Gossard; 18 Dane Carlaw; 24 Remi Casty; 28 Frederic Vaccari (not used).
Tries: Pelo (13), Raguin (35), Greenshields (51), Sa (69), Elima (73); **Goals:** Bosc 5/6.
WILDCATS: 1 Matt Blaymire; 2 Damien Blanch; 13 Jason Demetriou (C); 18 Aaron Murphy; 5 Luke George; 21 Paul Cooke; 6 Ben Jeffries; 19 Paul King; 14 Sam Obst; 10 Michael Korkidas; 17 Kevin Henderson; 16 Paul Johnson; 12 Glenn Morrison. Subs (all used): 25 Richard Moore; 32 Danny Kirmond; 35 Charlie Leaeno; 36 Julien Rinaldi (D2).
Tries: Blanch (6), Cooke (21), Blaymire (23), Rinaldi (44); **Goals:** Cooke 3/4; **Field goal:** King (65).
Rugby Leaguer & League Express Men of the Match: *Dragons:* Clint Greenshields; *Wildcats:* Paul Cooke.
Penalty count: 7-10; **Half-time:** 10-18;
Referee: Ben Thaler; **Attendance:** 5,055.

Sunday 20th June 2010

HUDDERSFIELD GIANTS 32 HULL FC 18

GIANTS: 1 Brett Hodgson (C); 2 Leroy Cudjoe; 3 Jamahl Lolesi; 19 Michael Lawrence; 5 David Hodgson; 6 Kevin Brown; 34 Danny Brough; 16 Darrell Griffin; 7 Luke Robinson; 10 Keith Mason; 11 Lee Gilmour; 13 Stephen Wild; 9 Shaun Lunt. Subs (all used): 18 Brad Drew; 23 Larne Patrick; 20 David Faiumu; 33 Graeme Horne.
Tries: D Hodgson (36), Brown (45), Cudjoe (54), Lolesi (68), Lunt (72); **Goals:** B Hodgson 6/6.
HULL: 1 Jordan Tansey; 21 Richard Whiting; 19 Jordan Turner; 4 Kirk Yeaman; 3 Tom Briscoe; 14 Danny Washbrook; 7 Sean Long (C); 8 Ewan Dowes; 20 Danny Houghton; 17 Peter Cusack; 12 Danny Tickle; 16 Willie Manu; 13 Craig Fitzgibbon. Subs (all used): 11 Lee Radford; 23 Sam Moa; 15 Epalahame Lauaki; 9 Shaun Berrigan.
Tries: Turner (8), Manu (22), Yeaman (27);
Goals: Tickle 3/3.
Rugby Leaguer & League Express Men of the Match: *Giants:* Brett Hodgson; *Hull:* Danny Houghton.
Penalty count: 13-7; **Half-time:** 6-18;
Referee: James Child; **Attendance:** 7,939.

HULL KINGSTON ROVERS 42 HARLEQUINS 6

ROVERS: 1 Shaun Briscoe; 2 Peter Fox; 3 Kris Welham; 15 Mike Ratu; 28 Ben Cockayne; 9 Scott Murrell; 7 Michael Dobson; 20 Michael Vella (C); 17 Ben Fisher; 30 Joel Clinton; 11 Clint Newton; 13 Ben Galea; 22 Liam Watts. Subs (all used): 8 Rhys Lovegrove; 24 Scott Taylor; 10 Scott Wheeldon; 21 Josh Hodgson.
Tries: Newton (16, 21), Dobson (27, 44), Briscoe (48), Wheeldon (58), Clinton (74); **Goals:** Dobson 7/7.
HARLEQUINS: 6 Luke Dorn; 22 Jamie O'Callaghan; 3 Tony Clubb; 4 David Howell; 5 Will Sharp; 13 Rob Purdham (C); 9 Chad Randall; 17 Danny Ward; 7 Danny Orr; 14 Oliver Wilkes; 8 Karl Temata; 1 Chris Melling; 25 Lamont Bryan. Subs (all used): 36 David Mills; 20 Andy Ellis; 33 Olsi Krasniqi; 28 Ben Bolger.
Try: Ward (62); **Goals:** Orr 1/1.
Rugby Leaguer & League Express Men of the Match: *Rovers:* Michael Dobson; *Harlequins:* Lamont Bryan.
Penalty count: 6-4; **Half-time:** 18-0;
Referee: Richard Silverwood; **Attendance:** 7,612.

LEEDS RHINOS 26 CRUSADERS 32

RHINOS: 28 Lee Smith; 2 Scott Donald; 3 Brett Delaney; 4 Keith Senior; 5 Ryan Hall; 13 Kevin Sinfield (C); 6 Danny McGuire; 8 Kylie Leuluai; 9 Danny Buderus; 10 Jamie Peacock; 15 Greg Eastwood; 18 Carl Ablett; 27 Chris Clarkson. Subs (all used): 16 Ryan Bailey; 11 Jamie Jones-Buchanan; 17 Ian Kirke; 25 Paul McShane.
Tries: Hall (3), Smith (52), Donald (55), Delaney (74);
Goals: Sinfield 5/5.
CRUSADERS: 26 Clinton Schifcofske (C); 2 Nick Youngquest; 3 Tony Martin; 4 Vince Mellars; 14 Luke Dyer; 23 Peter Lupton; 27 Rhys Hanbury; 8 Ryan O'Hara; 9 Lincoln Withers; 10 Mark Bryant; 11 Weller Hauraki; 12 Jason Chan; 16 Frank Winterstein. Subs (all used): 17 Adam Peek; 20 Ben Flower; 19 Jordan James; 21 Lloyd White.
Tries: Mellars (27, 76), Peek (33), Hauraki (46, 69);
Goals: Schifcofske 6/6.
On report: Dangerous tackle (57) on Leuluai.
Rugby Leaguer & League Express Men of the Match: *Rhinos:* Ryan Hall; *Crusaders:* Rhys Hanbury.
Penalty count: 9-7; **Half-time:** 8-12;
Referee: Robert Hicks; **Attendance:** 14,371.

SALFORD CITY REDS 22 CASTLEFORD TIGERS 28

CITY REDS: 1 Karl Fitzpatrick; 2 Jodie Broughton; 4 Willie Talau; 5 Ashley Gibson; 20 Steve Tyrer; 14 Matty Smith; 21 Daniel Holdsworth; 19 Ryan Boyle; 9 Malcolm Alker (C); 17 Adam Sidlow; 11 Ian Sibbit; 15 Stuart Littler; 13 Luke Swain. Subs (all used): 16 Phil Leuluai; 12 Luke Adamson; 7 Jeremy Smith; 10 Rob Parker.
Tries: Fitzpatrick (24), Littler (42), Broughton (46), Sibbit (57); **Goals:** Holdsworth 3/4.
TIGERS: 23 Ryan McGoldrick; 2 Kirk Dixon; 32 Joe Arundel; 11 Brett Ferres; 5 Michael Wainwright; 25 Dean Widders; 6 Rangi Chase; 15 Liam Higgins; 9 Ryan Hudson (C); 16 Paul Jackson; 10 Craig Huby; 12 Steve Snitch; 13 Joe Westerman. Subs (all used): 8 Mitchell Sargent; 14 Stuart Jones; 21 Jordan Thompson; 33 Kyle Wood.
Tries: Widders (2, 5, 28), Huby (16), Ferres (74);
Goals: Westerman 4/6.
Rugby Leaguer & League Express Men of the Match: *City Reds:* Daniel Holdsworth; *Tigers:* Dean Widders.
Penalty count: 4-5; **Half-time:** 6-22;
Referee: Steve Ganson; **Attendance:** 3,130.

WIGAN WARRIORS 24 ST HELENS 26

WARRIORS: 5 Pat Richards; 2 Amos Roberts; 3 Martin Gleeson; 4 George Carmont; 20 Karl Pryce; 6 Sam Tomkins; 7 Thomas Leuluai; 8 Stuart Fielden; 15 Michael Mcllorum; 10 Andy Coley; 16 Phil Bailey (C); 12 Joel Tomkins; 25 Liam Farrell. Subs (all used): 9 Mark Riddell; 14 Paul Prescott; 17 Iafeta Palea'aesina; 29 Chris Tuson.
Tries: Pryce (40), Leuluai (42), Mcllorum (73), Gleeson (76); **Goals:** Richards 4/5.
SAINTS: 1 Paul Wellens; 30 Jamie Foster; 3 Matt Gidley; 13 Chris Flannery; 5 Francis Meli; 6 Leon Pryce; 16 Scott Moore; 10 James Graham; 9 Keiron Cunningham (C); 15 Bryn Hargreaves; 17 Paul Clough; 22 Andrew Dixon; 11 Tony Puletua. Subs (all used): 18 Matty Ashurst; 8 Nick Fozzard; 33 Paul Johnson; 14 James Roby.
Tries: Pryce (15), Meli (26), Roby (30), Wellens (53), Foster (67); **Goals:** Foster 3/5.
Rugby Leaguer & League Express Men of the Match: *Warriors:* Thomas Leuluai; *Saints:* James Roby.
Penalty count: 9-8; **Half-time:** 6-16;
Referee: Phil Bentham; **Attendance:** 20,498.

ROUND 19

Friday 25th June 2010

HUDDERSFIELD GIANTS 16
HULL KINGSTON ROVERS 16

GIANTS: 1 Brett Hodgson (C); 2 Leroy Cudjoe; 3 Jamahl Lolesi; 19 Michael Lawrence; 5 David Hodgson; 6 Kevin Brown; 34 Danny Brough; 16 Darrell Griffin; 7 Luke Robinson; 10 Keith Mason; 11 Lee Gilmour; 14 Simon Finnigan; 13 Stephen Wild. Subs (all used): 18 Brad Drew; 23 Larne Patrick; 20 David Faiumu; 33 Graeme Horne.
Tries: Lawrence (28), Brown (49); **Goals:** B Hodgson 4/4.
ROVERS: 28 Ben Cockayne; 2 Peter Fox; 3 Kris Welham; 15 Mike Ratu; 29 Sam Latus (D); 9 Scott Murrell; 7 Michael Dobson; 20 Michael Vella (C); 17 Ben Fisher; 30 Joel Clinton; 11 Clint Newton; 13 Ben Galea; 22 Liam Watts. Subs (all used): 8 Rhys Lovegrove; 10 Scott Wheeldon; 21 Josh Hodgson; 24 Scott Taylor.
Tries: Murrell (15), Newton (23); **Goals:** Dobson 4/4.
Rugby Leaguer & League Express Men of the Match: *Giants:* Kevin Brown; *Rovers:* Clint Newton.
Penalty count: 6-5; **Half-time:** 6-12;
Referee: Phil Bentham; **Attendance:** 6,304.

HULL FC 10 CATALANS DRAGONS 8

HULL: 1 Jordan Tansey; 21 Richard Whiting; 19 Jordan Turner; 4 Kirk Yeaman; 3 Tom Briscoe; 14 Danny Washbrook; 7 Sean Long (C); 8 Ewan Dowes; 20 Danny Houghton; 17 Peter Cusack; 16 Willie Manu; 12 Danny Tickle; 11 Lee Radford. Subs (all used): 23 Sam Moa; 15 Epalahame Lauaki; 9 Shaun Berrigan; 24 Craig Hall.
Tries: Turner (11), Whiting (23); **Goals:** Tickle 1/3.
DRAGONS: 1 Clint Greenshields; 18 Dane Carlaw; 3 Sebastien Raguin; 4 Setaimata Sa; 28 Frederic Vaccari; 7 Thomas Bosc (C); 30 Brent Sherwin; 8 David Ferriol; 9 Casey McGuire; 10 Jerome Guisset; 11 Olivier Elima; 12 Gregory Mounis; 13 Dallas Johnson. Subs (all used): 17 Cyrille Gossard; 22 Jamal Fakir; 24 Remi Casty; 27 Michael Simon.
Try: McGuire (19); **Goals:** Bosc 2/2.
Rugby Leaguer & League Express Men of the Match: *Hull:* Danny Houghton; *Dragons:* Frederic Vaccari.
Penalty count: 11-9; **Half-time:** 8-8;
Referee: Thierry Alibert; **Attendance:** 11,466.

ST HELENS 58 SALFORD CITY REDS 34

SAINTS: 1 Paul Wellens; 24 Jonny Lomax; 3 Matt Gidley; 19 Chris Dean; 2 Ade Gardner; 6 Leon Pryce; 16 Scott Moore; 15 Bryn Hargreaves; 9 Keiron Cunningham (C); 11 Tony Puletua; 17 Paul Clough; 13 Chris Flannery; 14 James Roby. Subs (all used): 8 Nick Fozzard; 10 James Graham; 18 Matty Ashurst; 22 Andrew Dixon.
Tries: Gardner (6), Puletua (23), Wellens (25, 32, 57, 70), Pryce (29, 79), Flannery (48), Ashurst (73); **Goals:** Lomax 9/10.
CITY REDS: 1 Karl Fitzpatrick; 20 Steve Tyrer; 5 Ashley Gibson; 3 Mark Henry; 2 Jodie Broughton; 14 Matty Smith; 21 Daniel Holdsworth; 19 Ryan Boyle; 9 Malcolm Alker (C); 16 Phil Leuluai; 11 Ian Sibbit; 15 Stuart Littler; 13 Luke Swain. Subs (all used): 6 Stefan Ratchford; 7 Jeremy Smith; 10 Rob Parker; 17 Adam Sidlow.
Tries: Boyle (11), Sidlow (19, 39), Henry (51), Gibson (60), Holdsworth (76); **Goals:** Holdsworth 5/6.
Rugby Leaguer & League Express Men of the Match: *Saints:* Paul Wellens; *City Reds:* Matty Smith.
Penalty count: 7-8; **Half-time:** 28-16;
Referee: Ian Smith; **Attendance:** 7,728.

Saturday 26th June 2010

HARLEQUINS 12 WIGAN WARRIORS 36

HARLEQUINS: 26 Ben Jones-Bishop; 22 Jamie

O'Callaghan; 3 Tony Clubb; 4 David Howell; 5 Will Sharp; 6 Luke Dorn; 9 Chad Randall; 17 Danny Ward; 7 Danny Orr; 8 Karl Temata; 14 Oliver Wilkes; 13 Rob Purdham (C); 25 Lamont Bryan. Subs (all used): 10 Louie McCarthy-Scarsbrook; 28 Ben Bolger; 36 David Mills; 20 Andy Ellis.
Tries: O'Callaghan (53), Jones-Bishop (62);
Goals: Orr 2/2.
WARRIORS: 6 Sam Tomkins; 24 Darrell Goulding; 3 Martin Gleeson; 4 George Carmont; 5 Pat Richards; 19 Paul Deacon; 7 Thomas Leuluai (C); 8 Stuart Fielden; 15 Michael Mcllorum; 14 Paul Prescott; 29 Chris Tuson; 12 Joel Tomkins; 25 Liam Farrell. Subs (all used): 9 Mark Riddell; 16 Phil Bailey; 23 Lee Mossop; 26 Ben Davies.
Tries: S Tomkins (6), Goulding (49), Mcllorum (58), Richards (67, 69), Farrell (77); **Goals:** Richards 6/7.
Sin bin: J Tomkins (40) - dissent.
Rugby Leaguer & League Express Men of the Match:
Harlequins: Jamie O'Callaghan; *Warriors:* Sam Tomkins.
Penalty count: 7-7; **Half-time:** 0-8;
Referee: Steve Ganson; **Attendance:** 5,084.

Sunday 27th June 2010

CRUSADERS 0 WAKEFIELD TRINITY WILDCATS 41

CRUSADERS: 26 Clinton Schifcofske (C); 14 Luke Dyer; 3 Tony Martin; 12 Jason Chan; 2 Nick Youngquest; 23 Peter Lupton; 27 Rhys Hanbury; 8 Ryan O'Hara; 9 Lincoln Withers; 10 Mark Bryant; 11 Weller Hauraki; 16 Frank Winterstein; 13 Rocky Trimarchi. Subs (all used): 17 Adam Peek; 19 Jordan James; 20 Ben Flower; 21 Lloyd White.
WILDCATS: 1 Matt Blaymire; 2 Damien Blanch; 4 Darryl Millard; 18 Aaron Murphy; 23 Dale Morton; 21 Paul Cooke; 6 Ben Jeffries; 25 Richard Moore; 14 Sam Obst; 35 Charlie Leaeno; 32 Danny Kirmond; 12 Glenn Morrison; 13 Jason Demetriou (C). Subs (all used): 19 Paul King; 10 Michael Korkidas; 16 Paul Johnson; 36 Julien Rinaldi.
Tries: Jeffries (7), Millard (11), Demetriou (38), Leaeno (42), Johnson (66), Blanch (73, 77);
Goals: Cooke 6/7; **Field goal:** Jeffries (33).
Rugby Leaguer & League Express Men of the Match:
Crusaders: Jason Chan; *Wildcats:* Ben Jeffries.
Penalty count: 8-8; **Half-time:** 0-19;
Referee: Richard Silverwood; **Attendance:** 2,837.

CASTLEFORD TIGERS 28 BRADFORD BULLS 22

TIGERS: 23 Ryan McGoldrick; 2 Kirk Dixon; 3 Michael Shenton; 32 Joe Arundel; 5 Michael Wainwright; 25 Dean Widders; 6 Rangi Chase; 15 Liam Higgins; 9 Ryan Hudson (C); 10 Craig Huby; 11 Brett Ferres; 12 Steve Snitch; 13 Joe Westerman. Subs (all used): 8 Mitchell Sargent; 14 Stuart Jones; 16 Paul Jackson; 33 Kyle Wood.
Tries: Shenton (8, 75, 78), Ferres (16), Dixon (66);
Goals: Westerman 1/5, Dixon 3/3.
Sin bin: Ferres (30) - punching.
BULLS: 6 Brett Kearney; 2 Rikki Sheriffe; 15 Michael Platt; 4 Chris Nero; 1 Dave Halley; 3 Paul Sykes; 31 Cain Southernwood; 10 Andy Lynch (C); 9 Heath L'Estrange; 12 Glenn Hall; 20 Elliott Whitehead; 13 Jamie Langley; 11 Steve Menzies. Subs (all used): 18 Craig Kopczak; 16 Michael Worrincy; 14 Wayne Godwin; 32 Danny Addy.
Tries: Whitehead (6), Menzies (28), Kearney (62), Platt (80); **Goals:** Sykes 3/5.
Rugby Leaguer & League Express Men of the Match:
Tigers: Michael Shenton; *Bulls:* Brett Kearney.
Penalty count: 11-11; **Half-time:** 8-10;
Referee: Ben Thaler; **Attendance:** 5,482.

WARRINGTON WOLVES 30 LEEDS RHINOS 37

WOLVES: 1 Richard Mathers; 5 Chris Hicks; 3 Matt King; 23 Ryan Atkins; 2 Chris Riley; 4 Chris Bridge; 6 Lee Briers; 8 Adrian Morley (C); 9 Michael Monaghan; 13 Ben Harrison; 11 Louis Anderson; 12 Ben Westwood; 17 Simon Grix. Subs (all used): 14 Mick Higham; 16 Paul Wood; 26 David Solomona; 27 Vinnie Anderson.
Tries: King (6, 45), Hicks (20, 36), Atkins (26), Riley (61); **Goals:** Briers 3/7.
RHINOS: 28 Lee Smith; 2 Scott Donald; 3 Brett Delaney; 4 Keith Senior; 5 Ryan Hall; 13 Kevin Sinfield (C); 6 Danny McGuire; 16 Ryan Bailey; 9 Danny Buderus; 10 Jamie Peacock; 11 Jamie Jones-Buchanan; 15 Greg Eastwood; 18 Carl Ablett. Subs (all used): 17 Ian Kirke; 20 Jay Pitts; 24 Luke Ambler; 25 Paul McShane.
Tries: Senior (14), Eastwood (31), Donald (42), Buderus (49), Hall (52), McGuire (66);
Goals: Sinfield 6/6; **Field goal:** Sinfield (75).
Rugby Leaguer & League Express Men of the Match:
Wolves: Adrian Morley; *Rhinos:* Jamie Peacock.
Penalty count: 8-10; **Half-time:** 20-12;
Referee: James Child; **Attendance:** 10,442.

ROUND 20

Friday 2nd July 2010

SALFORD CITY REDS 17 HARLEQUINS 14

CITY REDS: 1 Karl Fitzpatrick; 2 Jodie Broughton; 3 Mark Henry; 5 Ashley Gibson; 20 Steve Tyrer; 14 Matty Smith; 21 Daniel Holdsworth; 19 Ryan Boyle; 9 Malcolm Alker (C); 16 Phil Leuluai; 11 Ian Sibbit; 15 Stuart Littler; 13 Luke Swain. Subs (all used); 7 Jeremy Smith; 17 Adam Sidlow; 12 Luke Adamson; 10 Rob Parker.
Tries: Swain (10), M Smith (22); **Goals:** Holdsworth 4/5;
Field goal: M Smith (73).
HARLEQUINS: 6 Luke Dorn; 5 Will Sharp; 3 Tony Clubb; 26 Ben Jones-Bishop; 22 Jamie O'Callaghan; 21 Luke Gale; 9 Chad Randall; 17 Danny Ward; 20 Andy Ellis; 8 Karl Temata; 13 Rob Purdham (C); 1 Chris Melling; 14 Oliver Wilkes. Subs (all used): 10 Louie McCarthy-Scarsbrook; 36 David Mills; 7 Danny Orr; 16 Jason Golden.
Tries: Purdham (15), Jones-Bishop (58, 74);
Goals: Orr 1/3.
Rugby Leaguer & League Express Men of the Match:
City Reds: Daniel Holdsworth; *Harlequins:* Tony Clubb.
Penalty count: 7-9; **Half-time:** 14-4;
Referee: Phil Bentham; **Attendance:** 2,672.

Saturday 3rd July 2010

LEEDS RHINOS 28 ST HELENS 24

RHINOS: 28 Lee Smith; 2 Scott Donald; 3 Brett Delaney; 4 Keith Senior; 5 Ryan Hall; 13 Kevin Sinfield (C); 6 Danny McGuire; 16 Ryan Bailey; 9 Danny Buderus; 10 Jamie Peacock; 11 Jamie Jones-Buchanan; 18 Carl Ablett; 27 Chris Clarkson. Subs (all used): 24 Luke Ambler; 15 Greg Eastwood; 17 Ian Kirke; 25 Paul McShane.
Tries: Clarkson (10), Delaney (22), McGuire (24, 63), Hall (67); **Goals:** Sinfield 4/6.
SAINTS: 1 Paul Wellens (C); 24 Jonny Lomax; 3 Matt Gidley; 13 Chris Flannery; 2 Ade Gardner; 6 Leon Pryce; 7 Kyle Eastmond; 10 James Graham; 14 James Roby; 15 Bryn Hargreaves; 17 Paul Clough; 22 Andrew Dixon; 16 Scott Moore. Subs (all used): 19 Chris Dean; 8 Nick Fozzard; 18 Matty Ashurst; 25 Jacob Emmitt.
Tries: Flannery (2, 38), Lomax (34), Pryce (52);
Goals: Lomax 4/5.
Rugby Leaguer & League Express Men of the Match:
Rhinos: Kevin Sinfield; *Saints:* James Roby.
Penalty count: 5-4; **Half time:** 16-16;
Referee: Richard Silverwood; **Attendance:** 17,200.

Sunday 4th July 2010

BRADFORD BULLS 22 HULL FC 28

BULLS: 6 Brett Kearney; 2 Rikki Sheriffe; 15 Michael Platt; 4 Chris Nero; 5 Stuart Reardon; 3 Paul Sykes; 9 Heath L'Estrange; 10 Andy Lynch (C); 14 Wayne Godwin; 12 Glenn Hall; 13 Jamie Langley; 16 Michael Worrincy; 11 Steve Menzies. Subs (all used): 20 Elliott Whitehead; 32 Danny Addy; 23 Steve Crossley; 18 Craig Kopczak.
Tries: Nero (17, 48), Kearney (43), Addy (58);
Goals: Sykes 3/4.
HULL: 1 Jordan Tansey; 21 Richard Whiting; 19 Jordan Turner; 4 Kirk Yeaman; 3 Tom Briscoe; 14 Danny Washbrook; 9 Shaun Berrigan; 8 Ewan Dowes; 20 Danny Houghton; 17 Peter Cusack; 16 Willie Manu; 12 Danny Tickle; 13 Craig Fitzgibbon (C). Subs: 22 Mike Burnett (not used); 15 Epalahame Lauaki; 11 Lee Radford; 24 Craig Hall.
Tries: Briscoe (14), Tansey (28), Tickle (31), Yeaman (39), Hall (67); **Goals:** Tickle 4/5.
Rugby Leaguer & League Express Men of the Match:
Bulls: Danny Addy; *Hull:* Jordan Tansey.
Penalty count: 7-3; **Half-time:** 6-22;
Referee: Ian Smith; **Attendance:** 8,411.

CRUSADERS 10 WARRINGTON WOLVES 30

CRUSADERS: 26 Clinton Schifcofske (C); 14 Luke Dyer; 1 Gareth Thomas; 3 Tony Martin; 2 Nick Youngquest; 23 Peter Lupton; 27 Rhys Hanbury; 8 Ryan O'Hara; 21 Lloyd White; 10 Mark Bryant; 11 Weller Hauraki; 16 Frank Winterstein; 13 Rocky Trimarchi. Subs (all used): 17 Adam Peek; 18 Jamie Thackray; 20 Ben Flower; 7 Jarrod Sammut.
Tries: Youngquest (14), Hanbury (71);
Goals: Schifcofske 1/2.
WOLVES: 1 Richard Mathers; 5 Chris Hicks; 3 Matt King; 23 Ryan Atkins; 2 Chris Riley; 6 Lee Briers; 7 Richard Myler; 16 Paul Wood; 9 Michael Monaghan (C); 13 Ben Harrison; 11 Louis Anderson; 12 Ben Westwood; 27 Vinnie Anderson. Subs (all used): 14 Mick Higham; 17 Simon Grix; 26 David Solomona; 10 Garreth Carvell.
Tries: Hicks (2, 22), Solomona (34), Higham (49), Riley (55, 80); **Goals:** Briers 2/5, Westwood 1/1.
Rugby Leaguer & League Express Men of the Match:
Crusaders: Jarrod Sammut; *Wolves:* Chris Riley.
Penalty count: 3-6; **Half-time:** 4-14;
Referee: Steve Ganson; **Attendance:** 5,197.

CASTLEFORD TIGERS 44 HUDDERSFIELD GIANTS 18

TIGERS: 23 Ryan McGoldrick; 2 Kirk Dixon; 11 Brett Ferres; 3 Michael Shenton; 5 Michael Wainwright; 25 Dean Widders; 6 Rangi Chase; 10 Craig Huby; 9 Ryan Hudson (C); 16 Paul Jackson; 12 Steve Snitch; 17 Ryan Clayton; 13 Joe Westerman. Subs (all used): 8 Mitchell Sargent; 28 Adam Milner (D); 21 Jordan Thompson; 31 Jonathan Walker.
Tries: Huby (16, 50), Chase (18, 80), Snitch (40), McGoldrick (42), Dixon (69);
Goals: Westerman 6/6, Dixon 2/2.
GIANTS: 1 Brett Hodgson (C); 2 Leroy Cudjoe; 3 Jamahl Lolesi; 19 Michael Lawrence; 5 David Hodgson; 6 Kevin Brown; 7 Luke Robinson; 16 Darrell Griffin; 18 Brad Drew; 10 Keith Mason; 11 Lee Gilmour; 14 Simon Finnigan; 9 Shaun Lunt. Subs (all used): 34 Danny Brough; 23 Larne Patrick; 20 David Faiumu; 33 Graeme Horne.
Tries: Cudjoe (2), Lolesi (8), Lunt (23, 73);
Goals: B Hodgson 1/4.
Rugby Leaguer & League Express Men of the Match:
Tigers: Rangi Chase; *Giants:* Kevin Brown.
Penalty count: 9-9; **Half-time:** 18-14;
Referee: Thierry Alibert; **Attendance:** 5,925.

WAKEFIELD TRINITY WILDCATS 14 HULL KINGSTON ROVERS 46

WILDCATS: 1 Matt Blaymire; 2 Damien Blanch; 18 Aaron Murphy; 4 Darryl Millard; 23 Dale Morton; 21 Paul Cooke; 6 Ben Jeffries; 25 Richard Moore; 36 Julien Rinaldi; 35 Charlie Leaeno; 32 Danny Kirmond; 12 Glenn Morrison; 13 Jason Demetriou (C). Subs (all used): 10 Michael Korkidas; 19 Paul King; 16 Paul Johnson; 20 Tevita Leo-Latu.
Tries: Millard (27), Moore (51), Johnson (58);
Goals: Cooke 1/3.
Sin bin: Korkidas (73) - late challenge on Dobson.
ROVERS: 28 Ben Cockayne; 2 Peter Fox; 11 Clint Newton; 3 Kris Welham; 29 Sam Latus; 9 Scott Murrell; 7 Michael Dobson; 30 Joel Clinton; 17 Ben Fisher; 10 Scott Wheeldon; 8 Rhys Lovegrove; 13 Ben Galea; 22 Liam Watts. Subs (all used): 20 Michael Vella (C); 24 Scott Taylor; 21 Josh Hodgson; 14 Matt Cook.
Tries: Dobson (4), Newton (22), Welham (38), Fox (46, 48), Wheeldon (76, 78); **Goals:** Dobson 9/10.
Sin bin: Lovegrove (73) - retaliation.
Rugby Leaguer & League Express Men of the Match:
Wildcats: Glenn Morrison; *Rovers:* Ben Galea.
Penalty count: 8-12; **Half-time:** 4-16;
Referee: Ben Thaler; **Attendance:** 6,218.

CATALANS DRAGONS 16 WIGAN WARRIORS 34

DRAGONS: 1 Clint Greenshields; 28 Frederic Vaccari; 18 Dane Carlaw; 3 Sebastien Raguin; 26 Cyril Stacul; 7 Thomas Bosc (C); 30 Brent Sherwin; 24 Remi Casty; 9 Casey McGuire; 10 Jerome Guisset; 11 Olivier Elima; 17 Cyrille Gossard; 13 Dallas Johnson. Subs (all used): 16 William Barthau; 22 Jamal Fakir; 27 Michael Simon; 29 Andrew Bentley.
Tries: Greenshields (56, 74), Stacul (77); **Goals:** Bosc 2/3.
WARRIORS: 6 Sam Tomkins; 24 Darrell Goulding; 3 Martin Gleeson; 4 George Carmont (C); 5 Pat Richards; 19 Paul Deacon; 7 Thomas Leuluai; 10 Andy Coley; 15 Michael Mcllorum; 14 Paul Prescott; 29 Chris Tuson; 12 Joel Tomkins; 25 Liam Farrell. Subs (all used): 8 Stuart Fielden; 9 Mark Riddell; 11 Harrison Hansen; 23 Lee Mossop.
Tries: Richards (14), Riddell (30), Leuluai (44), Coley (47), Gleeson (54), Goulding (60); **Goals:** Richards 5/7.
Dismissal: Coley (64) - high tackle on Fakir.
Rugby Leaguer & League Express Men of the Match:
Dragons: Clint Greenshields; *Warriors:* Sam Tomkins.
Penalty count: 10-11; **Half-time:** 0-14;
Referee: James Child; **Attendance:** 7,612.

ROUND 21

Friday 9th July 2010

HARLEQUINS 35 BRADFORD BULLS 18

HARLEQUINS: 6 Luke Dorn; 22 Jamie O'Callaghan; 3 Tony Clubb; 26 Ben Jones-Bishop; 5 Will Sharp; 7 Danny Orr (C); 21 Luke Gale; 17 Danny Ward; 20 Andy Ellis; 10 Louie McCarthy-Scarsbrook; 16 Jason Golden; 1 Chris Melling; 14 Oliver Wilkes. Subs (all used): 28 Ben Bolger; 25 Lamont Bryan; 36 David Mills; 33 Olsi Krasniqi.
Tries: Dorn (6), Ellis (9), Jones-Bishop (17, 57), Melling (69); **Goals:** Orr 7/8; **Field goal:** Gale (40).
BULLS: 6 Brett Kearney; 2 Rikki Sheriffe; 15 Michael Platt; 4 Chris Nero; 1 Dave Halley; 32 Danny Addy; 3 Paul Sykes; 10 Andy Lynch (C); 9 Heath L'Estrange; 18 Craig Kopczak; 20 Elliott Whitehead; 13 Jamie Langley; 11 Steve Menzies. Subs (all used): 14 Wayne Godwin; 12 Glenn Hall; 23 Steve Crossley; 16 Michael Worrincy.
Tries: Whitehead (21), Sykes (50), Crossley (75);
Goals: Sykes 3/3.
Sin bin: Menzies (63) - dissent.
Rugby Leaguer & League Express Men of the Match:
Harlequins: Ben Jones-Bishop; *Bulls:* Andy Lynch.
Penalty count: 9-9; **Half-time:** 21-6;
Referee: Richard Silverwood; **Attendance:** 3,152.

HULL KINGSTON ROVERS 25 LEEDS RHINOS 6

ROVERS: 1 Shaun Briscoe; 2 Peter Fox; 32 Josh Charnley (D); 28 Ben Cockayne; 29 Sam Latus; 9 Scott Murrell; 7 Michael Dobson; 20 Michael Vella (C); 17 Ben Fisher; 30 Joel Clinton; 11 Clint Newton; 13 Ben Galea; 22 Liam Watts. Subs (all used): 8 Rhys Lovegrove; 14 Matt Cook; 16 Jason Netherton; 21 Josh Hodgson.
Tries: Galea (7), Fisher (18), Fox (38), Cockayne (72);
Goals: Dobson 4/4; **Field goal:** Dobson (67).
RHINOS: 28 Lee Smith; 2 Scott Donald; 3 Brett Delaney; 4 Keith Senior; 5 Ryan Hall; 13 Kevin Sinfield (C); 6 Danny McGuire; 16 Ryan Bailey; 25 Paul McShane; 10 Jamie Peacock; 18 Carl Ablett; 11 Jamie Jones-Buchanan; 27 Chris Clarkson. Subs (all used): 17 Ian Kirke; 24 Luke Ambler; 20 Jay Pitts; 7 Rob Burrow.
Try: Hall (51); **Goals:** Sinfield 1/1.
Rugby Leaguer & League Express Men of the Match:
Rovers: Michael Vella; *Rhinos:* Luke Ambler.
Penalty count: 10-6; **Half-time:** 18-0;
Referee: Thierry Alibert; **Attendance:** 8,406.

ST HELENS 20 CATALANS DRAGONS 30

SAINTS: 1 Paul Wellens (C); 24 Jonny Lomax; 3 Matt Gidley; 19 Chris Dean; 5 Francis Meli; 32 Lee Gaskell (D); 12 Jon Wilkin; 10 James Graham; 14 James Roby; 8 Nick Fozzard; 18 Matty Ashurst; 13 Chris Flannery; 17 Paul Clough. Subs (all used): 2 Ade Gardner; 11 Tony Puletua; 15 Bryn Hargreaves; 16 Scott Moore.
Tries: Wellens (6), Meli (27, 59), Gaskell (50);
Goals: Lomax 2/4.
DRAGONS: 1 Clint Greenshields; 2 Steven Bell; 3 Sebastien Raguin; 18 Dane Carlaw; 26 Cyril Stacul; 7 Thomas Bosc (C); 30 Brent Sherwin; 24 Remi Casty; 9 Casey McGuire; 10 Jerome Guisset; 17 Cyrille Gossard; 12 Gregory Mounis; 13 Dallas Johnson. Subs (all used):

Kevin Sinfield kicks a last-gasp field goal to take Leeds to victory against Huddersfield

22 Jamal Fakir; 25 Tony Gigot; 27 Michael Simon; 29 Andrew Bentley.
Tries: Carlaw (9), Greenshields (33, 39), McGuire (37), Sherwin (54); **Goals:** Bosc 5/5.
Rugby Leaguer & League Express Men of the Match: *Saints:* Lee Gaskell; *Dragons:* Clint Greenshields.
Penalty count: 3-5; **Half-time:** 10-24;
Referee: Ian Smith; **Attendance:** 8,432.

WIGAN WARRIORS 60 SALFORD CITY REDS 10

WARRIORS: 6 Sam Tomkins; 24 Darrell Goulding; 3 Martin Gleeson; 4 George Carmont; 5 Pat Richards; 19 Paul Deacon; 7 Thomas Leuluai; 8 Stuart Fielden; 9 Mark Riddell; 14 Paul Prescott; 11 Harrison Hansen; 12 Joel Tomkins; 29 Chris Tuson. Subs (all used): 2 Amos Roberts; 25 Liam Farrell; 13 Sean O'Loughlin (C); 23 Lee Mossop.
Tries: S Tomkins (6, 43), Goulding (9, 57, 75), Gleeson (19), J Tomkins (34), Carmont (37), O'Loughlin (49), Hansen (62); **Goals:** Richards 10/10.
CITY REDS: 1 Karl Fitzpatrick; 2 Jodie Broughton; 3 Mark Henry; 5 Ashley Gibson; 20 Steve Tyrer; 14 Matty Smith; 21 Daniel Holdsworth; 19 Ryan Boyle; 9 Malcolm Alker (C); 16 Phil Leuluai; 13 Luke Adamson; 10 Rob Parker. Subs (all used): 7 Jeremy Smith; 17 Adam Sidlow; 12 Luke Adamson; 10 Rob Parker.
Tries: Holdsworth (47), Broughton (65);
Goals: Holdsworth 1/2.
Dismissal: Boyle (21) - high tackle on Fielden.
Rugby Leaguer & League Express Men of the Match: *Warriors:* Sam Tomkins; *City Reds:* Daniel Holdsworth.
Penalty count: 5-4; **Half-time:** 30-0;
Referee: Ben Thaler; **Attendance:** 12,221.

Saturday 10th July 2010

WAKEFIELD TRINITY WILDCATS 29 HULL FC 6

WILDCATS: 1 Matt Blaymire; 3 Sean Gleeson; 18 Aaron Murphy; 4 Darryl Millard; 23 Dale Morton; 21 Paul Cooke; 6 Ben Jeffries; 35 Charlie Leaeno; 36 Julien Rinaldi; 25 Richard Moore; 13 Jason Demetriou (C); 16 Paul Johnson; 12 Glenn Morrison. Subs (all used): 10 Michael Korkidas; 19 Paul King; 17 Kevin Henderson; 20 Tevita Leo-Latu.
Tries: Cooke (16), Rinaldi (29), Leaeno (53), Millard (71), Demetriou (79);
Goals: Cooke 4/5, Jeffries 0/1; **Field goal:** Jeffries (57).
HULL: 1 Jordan Tansey; 21 Richard Whiting; 19 Jordan Turner; 4 Kirk Yeaman; 3 Tom Briscoe; 14 Danny Washbrook; 9 Shaun Berrigan; 8 Ewan Dowes; 20 Danny Houghton; 17 Peter Cusack; 16 Willie Manu; 12 Danny Tickle; 13 Craig Fitzgibbon (C). Subs (all used): 11 Lee Radford; 15 Epalahame Lauaki; 24 Craig Hall; 6 Richard Horne.

Try: Turner (11); **Goals:** Tickle 1/1.
Rugby Leaguer & League Express Men of the Match: *Wildcats:* Julien Rinaldi; *Hull:* Tom Briscoe.
Penalty count: 12-6; **Half-time:** 12-6;
Referee: Steve Ganson; **Attendance:** 5,366.

Sunday 11th July 2010

HUDDERSFIELD GIANTS 30 CRUSADERS 12

GIANTS: 1 Brett Hodgson (C); 27 Jermaine McGillvary; 2 Leroy Cudjoe; 19 Michael Lawrence; 5 David Hodgson; 6 Kevin Brown; 7 Luke Robinson; 16 Darrell Griffin; 18 Brad Drew; 33 Graeme Horne; 11 Lee Gilmour; 9 Shaun Lunt; 13 Stephen Wild. Subs (all used): 8 Eorl Crabtree; 20 David Faiumu; 23 Larne Patrick; 34 Danny Brough.
Tries: Lunt (21), Wild (32), McGillvary (34, 80), Lawrence (44), Brown (73);
Goals: B Hodgson 2/3, Brough 1/3.
CRUSADERS: 26 Clinton Schifcofske (C); 14 Luke Dyer; 3 Tony Martin; 4 Vince Mellars; 2 Nick Youngquest; 7 Jarrod Sammut; 27 Rhys Hanbury; 10 Mark Bryant; 9 Lincoln Withers; 17 Adam Peek; 16 Frank Winterstein; 11 Weller Hauraki; 23 Peter Lupton. Subs (all used): 15 Tommy Lee; 19 Jordan James; 18 Jamie Thackray; 14 Rocky Trimarchi.
Tries: Sammut (27), Hauraki (59); **Goals:** Schifcofske 2/2.
Rugby Leaguer & League Express Men of the Match: *Giants:* Shaun Lunt; *Crusaders:* Luke Dyer.
Penalty count: 11-12; **Half-time:** 16-6;
Referee: James Child; **Attendance:** 5,339.

WARRINGTON WOLVES 54 CASTLEFORD TIGERS 30

WOLVES: 1 Richard Mathers; 5 Chris Hicks; 3 Matt King; 23 Ryan Atkins; 2 Chris Riley; 17 Simon Grix; 7 Richard Myler; 8 Adrian Morley (C); 9 Michael Monaghan; 10 Garreth Carvell; 11 Louis Anderson; 12 Ben Westwood; 26 David Solomona. Subs (all used): 16 Paul Wood; 18 Michael Cooper; 27 Vinnie Anderson; 15 Jon Clarke.
Tries: Riley (2), Myler (21, 40, 74), Morley (26), Atkins (31), Mathers (49), Hicks (53), Solomona (71);
Goals: Westwood 9/9.
TIGERS: 23 Ryan McGoldrick; 2 Kirk Dixon; 11 Brett Ferres; 21 Jordan Thompson; 5 Michael Wainwright; 25 Dean Widders; 6 Rangi Chase; 10 Craig Huby; 9 Ryan Hudson (C); 16 Paul Jackson; 12 Steve Snitch; 17 Ryan Clayton; 13 Joe Westerman. Subs (all used): 8 Mitchell Sargent; 28 Adam Milner; 14 Stuart Jones; 31 Jonathan Walker.
Tries: Dixon (9), Westerman (47, 66), Wainwright (58), Clayton (63), Snitch (79); **Goals:** Westerman 3/6.
Rugby Leaguer & League Express Men of the Match: *Wolves:* Michael Monaghan; *Tigers:* Rangi Chase.
Penalty count: 6-5; **Half-time:** 30-4;
Referee: Phil Bentham; **Attendance:** 10,577.

ROUND 22

Thursday 15th July 2010

HULL FC 20 HULL KINGSTON ROVERS 16

HULL: 21 Richard Whiting; 2 Mark Calderwood; 19 Jordan Turner; 4 Kirk Yeaman; 3 Tom Briscoe; 1 Jordan Tansey; 6 Richard Horne; 8 Ewan Dowes; 20 Danny Houghton; 11 Lee Radford (C); 16 Willie Manu; 12 Danny Tickle; 14 Danny Washbrook. Subs (all used): 17 Peter Cusack; 15 Epalahame Lauaki; 23 Sam Moa; 9 Shaun Berrigan.
Tries: Houghton (9), Manu (56), Berrigan (64);
Goals: Tickle 4/5.
Sin bin: Calderwood (68) - fighting.
ROVERS: 1 Shaun Briscoe (C); 2 Peter Fox; 32 Josh Charnley; 28 Ben Cockayne; 29 Sam Latus; 9 Scott Murrell; 7 Michael Dobson; 10 Scott Wheeldon; 17 Ben Fisher; 30 Joel Clinton; 11 Clint Newton; 13 Ben Galea; 22 Liam Watts. Subs (all used): 14 Matt Cook; 16 Jason Netherton; 21 Josh Hodgson; 8 Rhys Lovegrove.
Tries: Charnley (17), Newton (41), Watts (72);
Goals: Dobson 2/3.
Sin bin: Cockayne (68) - fighting.
Rugby Leaguer & League Express Men of the Match: *Hull:* Danny Houghton; *Rovers:* Peter Fox.
Penalty count: 4-4; **Half-time:** 10-6;
Referee: Phil Bentham; **Attendance:** 20,079.

Friday 16th July 2010

LEEDS RHINOS 21 HUDDERSFIELD GIANTS 20

RHINOS: 28 Lee Smith; 2 Scott Donald; 3 Brett Delaney; 4 Keith Senior; 5 Ryan Hall; 13 Kevin Sinfield (C); 6 Danny McGuire; 8 Kylie Leuluai; 9 Danny Buderus; 10 Jamie Peacock; 18 Carl Ablett; 11 Jamie Jones-Buchanan; 27 Chris Clarkson. Subs (all used): 17 Ian Kirke; 12 Ali Lauititi; 25 Paul McShane; 19 Luke Burgess.
Tries: Clarkson (14), Hall (52), McGuire (76);
Goals: Sinfield 4/4; **Field goal:** Sinfield (80).
GIANTS: 21 Scott Grix; 2 Leroy Cudjoe; 19 Michael Lawrence; 11 Lee Gilmour; 5 David Hodgson; 6 Kevin Brown (C); 7 Luke Robinson; 8 Eorl Crabtree; 34 Danny Brough; 16 Darrell Griffin; 14 Simon Finnigan; 13 Stephen Wild; 20 David Faiumu. Subs (all used): 23 Larne Patrick; 9 Shaun Lunt; 33 Graeme Horne; 18 Brad Drew.
Tries: Lunt (24), D Hodgson (42, 45), Patrick (73);
Goals: Brough 1/3, Cudjoe 1/1.
Sin bin: Griffin (9) - late tackle on McGuire.
Rugby Leaguer & League Express Men of the Match: *Rhinos:* Danny Buderus; *Giants:* Luke Robinson.
Penalty count: 6-8; **Half-time:** 6-4;
Referee: Ben Thaler; **Attendance:** 15,070.

Hull KR's Shaun Briscoe dives over for a try against Bradford

WIGAN WARRIORS 16 WARRINGTON WOLVES 23

WARRIORS: 2 Amos Roberts; 24 Darrell Goulding; 3 Martin Gleeson; 4 George Carmont; 5 Pat Richards; 6 Sam Tomkins; 7 Thomas Leuluai; 8 Stuart Fielden; 9 Mark Riddell; 14 Paul Prescott; 11 Harrison Hansen; 12 Joel Tomkins; 13 Sean O'Loughlin (C). Subs (all used): 19 Paul Deacon; 25 Liam Farrell; 29 Chris Tuson; 23 Lee Mossop. **Tries:** Riddell (10), Tuson (50), Richards (61); **Goals:** Richards 2/4.
WOLVES: 1 Richard Mathers; 5 Chris Hicks; 3 Matt King; 23 Ryan Atkins; 2 Chris Riley; 6 Lee Briers; 7 Richard Myler; 8 Adrian Morley (C); 9 Michael Monaghan; 10 Garreth Carvell; 11 Louis Anderson; 12 Ben Westwood; 13 Ben Harrison. Subs: 16 Paul Wood; 17 Simon Grix; 26 David Solomona; 15 Jon Clarke (not used). **Tries:** Hicks (26), Myler (30), Atkins (44), Westwood (70); **Goals:** Westwood 3/4; **Field goal:** Briers (76).
Rugby Leaguer & League Express Men of the Match: *Warriors:* Mark Riddell; *Wolves:* Ben Westwood.
Penalty count: 6-8; **Half-time:** 6-10;
Referee: Richard Silverwood; **Attendance:** 22,701.

Saturday 17th July 2010

CATALANS DRAGONS 22 CRUSADERS 26

DRAGONS: 1 Clint Greenshields; 2 Steven Bell; 3 Sebastien Raguin; 12 Dane Carlaw; 26 Cyril Stacul; 7 Thomas Bosc (C); 30 Brent Sherwin; 24 Remi Casty; 9 Casey McGuire; 10 Jerome Guisset; 11 Olivier Elima; 12 Gregory Mounis; 13 Dallas Johnson. Subs (all used): 17 Cyrille Gossard; 22 Jamal Fakir; 25 Tony Gigot; 27 Michael Simon.
Tries: Greenshields (18, 32), Casty (53); **Goals:** Bosc 5/5.
CRUSADERS: 26 Clinton Schifcofske (C); 14 Luke Dyer; 3 Tony Martin; 4 Vince Mellars; 2 Nick Youngquest; 7 Jarrod Sammut; 27 Rhys Hanbury; 10 Mark Bryant; 9 Lincoln Withers; 15 Tommy Lee; 16 Frank Winterstein; 19 Jordan James.
Tries: Hauraki (6), Chan (40), Hanbury (42), Lupton (74); **Goals:** Schifcofske 5/5.
Rugby Leaguer & League Express Men of the Match: *Dragons:* Thomas Bosc; *Crusaders:* Rhys Hanbury.
Penalty count: 10-5; **Half-time:** 12-12;
Referee: Thierry Alibert; **Attendance:** 6,208.

Sunday 18th July 2010

BRADFORD BULLS 26 SALFORD CITY REDS 30

BULLS: 33 Vinny Finigan (D); 2 Rikki Sheriffe; 15 Michael Platt; 4 Chris Nero; 5 Stuart Reardon; 6 Brett Kearney; 32 Danny Addy; 10 Andy Lynch (C); 9 Heath L'Estrange; 18 Craig Kopczak; 20 Elliott Whitehead; 13 Jamie Langley;

11 Steve Menzies. Subs (all used): 14 Wayne Godwin; 16 Michael Worrincy; 23 Steve Crossley; 12 Glenn Hall. **Tries:** Menzies (14), Finigan (35, 72), Reardon (67), Whitehead (69); **Goals:** Addy 3/5.
CITY REDS: 1 Karl Fitzpatrick; 2 Jodie Broughton; 3 Mark Henry; 5 Ashley Gibson; 20 Steve Tyrer; 14 Matty Smith; 21 Daniel Holdsworth; 8 Ray Cashmere; 9 Malcolm Alker (C); 22 Adam Neal (D); 11 Ian Sibbit; 15 Stuart Littler; 13 Luke Swain. Subs (all used): 7 Jeremy Smith; 17 Adam Sidlow; 10 Rob Parker; 12 Luke Adamson.
Tries: Broughton (2, 53), Tyrer (6), Littler (26), Fitzpatrick (47); **Goals:** Holdsworth 5/5.
Rugby Leaguer & League Express Men of the Match: *Bulls:* Vinny Finigan; *City Reds:* Karl Fitzpatrick.
Penalty count: 8-4; **Half-time:** 10-18;
Referee: Ian Smith; **Attendance:** 6,382.

ST HELENS 32 HARLEQUINS 18

SAINTS: 1 Paul Wellens (C); 24 Jonny Lomax; 3 Matt Gidley; 19 Chris Dean; 5 Francis Meli; 6 Leon Pryce; 16 Scott Moore; 10 James Graham; 14 James Roby; 15 Bryn Hargreaves; 12 Jon Wilkin; 17 Paul Clough; 28 Shaun Magennis. Subs (all used): 11 Tony Puletua; 18 Matty Ashurst; 32 Lee Gaskell; 25 Jacob Emmitt.
Tries: Magennis (9), Meli (23, 36), Wellens (32, 76), Dean (67); **Goals:** Lomax 4/6.
HARLEQUINS: 6 Luke Dorn; 22 Jamie O'Callaghan; 3 Tony Clubb; 26 Ben Jones-Bishop; 5 Will Sharp; 7 Danny Orr (C); 21 Luke Gale; 17 Danny Ward; 20 Andy Ellis; 10 Louie McCarthy-Scarsbrook; 1 Chris Melling; 16 Jason Golden; 14 Oliver Wilkes. Subs (all used): 18 Ryan Esders; 33 Olsi Krasniqi; 28 Ben Bolger; 36 David Mills.
Tries: Golden (13), O'Callaghan (50), Esders (60); **Goals:** Orr 3/3.
Rugby Leaguer & League Express Men of the Match: *Saints:* Leon Pryce; *Harlequins:* Luke Gale.
Penalty count: 4-6; **Half-time:** 20-6;
Referee: Steve Ganson; **Attendance:** 10,399.

**CASTLEFORD TIGERS 40
WAKEFIELD TRINITY WILDCATS 16**

TIGERS: 23 Ryan McGoldrick; 2 Kirk Dixon; 3 Michael Shenton; 11 Brett Ferres; 5 Michael Wainwright; 25 Dean Widders; 6 Rangi Chase; 10 Craig Huby; 9 Ryan Hudson (C); 16 Paul Jackson; 12 Steve Snitch; 17 Ryan Clayton; 13 Joe Westerman. Subs (all used): 8 Mitchell Sargent; 15 Liam Higgins; 14 Stuart Jones; 21 Jordan Thompson.
Tries: Dixon (11, 43), Wainwright (52), Widders (59, 64), McGoldrick (73), Hudson (79);
Goals: Westerman 5/7, Dixon 1/1.
WILDCATS: 1 Matt Blaymire; 3 Sean Gleeson; 18 Aaron Murphy; 4 Darryl Millard; 2 Damien Blanch; 21 Paul Cooke; 6 Ben Jeffries; 35 Charlie Leaeno; 36 Julien Rinaldi; 25 Richard Moore; 13 Jason Demetriou; 16 Paul Johnson; 12 Glenn Morrison. Subs (all used): 10

Michael Korkidas; 17 Kevin Henderson; 19 Paul King; 20 Tevita Leo-Latu.
Tries: Morrison (8, 55), Blaymire (34); **Goals:** Cooke 2/3.
Sin bin: Gleeson (31) - professional foul.
Rugby Leaguer & League Express Men of the Match: *Tigers:* Dean Widders; *Wildcats:* Glenn Morrison.
Penalty count: 13-8; **Half-time:** 6-10;
Referee: James Child; **Attendance:** 8,517.

ROUND 23

Friday 23rd July 2010

HULL FC 0 WIGAN WARRIORS 46

HULL: 1 Jordan Tansey; 24 Craig Hall; 19 Jordan Turner; 4 Kirk Yeaman; 3 Tom Briscoe; 9 Shaun Berrigan; 6 Richard Horne; 8 Ewan Dowes; 20 Danny Houghton; 11 Lee Radford (C); 16 Willie Manu; 15 Epalahame Lauaki; 14 Danny Washbrook. Subs (all used): 23 Sam Moa; 17 Peter Cusack; 22 Mike Burnett; 30 Danny Nicklas.
WARRIORS: 6 Sam Tomkins; 24 Darrell Goulding; 3 Martin Gleeson; 4 George Carmont; 5 Pat Richards; 19 Paul Deacon; 7 Thomas Leuluai; 10 Andy Coley; 9 Mark Riddell; 14 Paul Prescott; 25 Liam Farrell; 12 Joel Tomkins; 13 Sean O'Loughlin (C). Subs (all used): 8 Stuart Fielden; 11 Harrison Hansen; 17 Iafeta Palea'aesina.
Tries: Richards (12, 54, 72), Farrell (14, 64), Goulding (35), S Tomkins (38, 43); **Goals:** Richards 7/8.
Rugby Leaguer & League Express Men of the Match: *Hull:* Lee Radford; *Warriors:* Pat Richards.
Penalty count: 6-9; **Half-time:** 0-22;
Referee: Richard Silverwood; **Attendance:** 12,694.

Saturday 24th July 2010

HULL KINGSTON ROVERS 49 BRADFORD BULLS 24

ROVERS: 1 Shaun Briscoe (C); 2 Peter Fox; 32 Josh Charnley; 5 Liam Colbon; 29 Sam Latus; 9 Scott Murrell; 7 Michael Dobson; 30 Joel Clinton; 17 Ben Fisher; 8 Rhys Lovegrove; 11 Clint Newton; 13 Ben Galea; 22 Liam Watts. Subs (all used): 10 Scott Wheeldon; 16 Jason Netherton; 23 Scott Spaven; 26 Frankie Mariano.
Tries: Fox (5, 50, 64), Latus (16), Clinton (22), Newton (30, 42), Briscoe (56, 76); **Goals:** Dobson 6/9;
Field goal: Dobson (71).
BULLS: 1 Dave Halley; 33 Vinny Finigan; 15 Michael Platt; 4 Chris Nero; 5 Stuart Reardon; 11 Steve Menzies; 32 Danny Addy; 10 Andy Lynch (C); 9 Heath L'Estrange; 18 Craig Kopczak; 20 Elliott Whitehead; 16 Michael Worrincy; 13 Jamie Langley. Subs (all used): 23 Steve Crossley; 14 Wayne Godwin; 12 Glenn Hall; 24 Tom Olbison.
Tries: Reardon (27), Finigan (38, 68), Kopczak (59), L'Estrange (61); **Goals:** Addy 2/5.

Rugby Leaguer & League Express Men of the Match: *Rovers:* Clint Newton; *Bulls:* Heath L'Estrange.
Penalty count: 4-4; **Half-time:** 20-8;
Referee: Thierry Alibert; **Attendance:** 7,854.

CATALANS DRAGONS 29 WARRINGTON WOLVES 28

DRAGONS: 26 Cyril Stacul; 2 Steven Bell; 3 Sebastien Raguin; 18 Dane Carlaw; 28 Frederic Vaccari; 7 Thomas Bosc (C); 30 Brent Sherwin; 24 Remi Casty; 9 Casey McGuire; 22 Jamal Fakir; 11 Olivier Elima; 12 Gregory Mounis; 13 Dallas Johnson. Subs (all used): 4 Setaimata Sa; 10 Jerome Guisset; 19 Julien Touxagas; 27 Michael Simon.
Tries: Vaccari (7), Carlaw (29), Bell (34), Stacul (42), Casty (46); **Goals:** Bosc 4/5; **Field goal:** Sherwin (63).
WOLVES: 1 Richard Mathers; 5 Chris Hicks; 17 Simon Grix; 23 Ryan Atkins; 2 Chris Riley; 6 Lee Briers; 7 Richard Myler; 8 Adrian Morley (C); 9 Michael Monaghan; 13 Ben Harrison; 27 Vinnie Anderson; 12 Ben Westwood; 26 David Solomona. Subs (all used): 10 Garreth Carvell; 15 Jon Clarke; 18 Michael Cooper; 22 Tyrone McCarthy.
Tries: Hicks (11, 38), Clarke (40), V Anderson (54), Briers (76); **Goals:** Westwood 4/5.
Rugby Leaguer & League Express Men of the Match: *Dragons:* Brent Sherwin; *Wolves:* David Solomona.
Penalty count: 10-7; **Half-time:** 16-16; **Referee:** Ian Smith; **Attendance:** 7,852 *(at Stade Aime Giral).*

Sunday 25th July 2010

CRUSADERS 30 CASTLEFORD TIGERS 24

CRUSADERS: 26 Clinton Schifcofske (C); 14 Luke Dyer; 3 Tony Martin; 4 Vince Mellars; 2 Nick Youngquest; 27 Rhys Hanbury; 7 Jarrod Sammut; 17 Adam Peek; 9 Lincoln Withers; 10 Mark Bryant; 11 Weller Hauraki; 12 Jason Chan; 23 Peter Lupton. Subs (all used): 15 Tommy Lee; 19 Jordan James; 16 Frank Winterstein; 13 Rocky Trimarchi.
Tries: Hanbury (32), James (36), Hauraki (47), Martin (73), Sammut (76); **Goals:** Schifcofske 5/5.
TIGERS: 23 Ryan McGoldrick; 2 Kirk Dixon; 3 Michael Shenton; 11 Brett Ferres; 5 Michael Wainwright; 25 Dean Widders; 6 Rangi Chase; 10 Craig Huby; 9 Ryan Hudson (C); 16 Paul Jackson; 12 Steve Snitch; 17 Ryan Clayton; 13 Joe Westerman. Subs (all used): 8 Mitchell Sargent; 14 Stuart Jones; 15 Liam Higgins; 21 Jordan Thompson.
Tries: Westerman (16), Widders (24), Shenton (57), Chase (60); **Goals:** Westerman 4/5.
Rugby Leaguer & League Express Men of the Match: *Crusaders:* Jarrod Sammut; *Tigers:* Joe Westerman.
Penalty count: 7-6; **Half-time:** 12-12; **Referee:** Steve Ganson; **Attendance:** 1,495 *(at The Gnoll, Neath).*

HUDDERSFIELD GIANTS 40 HARLEQUINS 4

GIANTS: 21 Scott Grix; 27 Jermaine McGillvary; 2 Leroy Cudjoe; 19 Michael Lawrence; 5 David Hodgson; 6 Kevin Brown (C); 34 Danny Brough; 16 Darrell Griffin; 18 Brad Drew; 33 Graeme Horne; 11 Lee Gilmour; 13 Stephen Wild; 9 Shaun Lunt. Subs (all used): 8 Eorl Crabtree; 14 Simon Finnigan; 20 David Faiumu; 23 Larne Patrick.
Tries: McGillvary (4, 75), Brown (25), Finnigan (44), Lawrence (47), Grix (51), D Hodgson (55), Brough (62); **Goals:** Brough 4/7, Cudjoe 0/1.
HARLEQUINS: 26 Ben Jones-Bishop; 22 Jamie O'Callaghan; 3 Tony Clubb; 13 Rob Purdham (C); 5 Will Sharp; 7 Danny Orr; 21 Luke Gale; 17 Danny Ward; 20 Andy Ellis; 14 Oliver Wilkes; 1 Chris Melling; 16 Jason Golden; 18 Ryan Esders. Subs (all used): 36 David Mills; 33 Olsi Krasniqi; 28 Ben Bolger; 6 Luke Dorn.
Try: Dorn (40); **Goals:** Purdham 0/1.
Rugby Leaguer & League Express Men of the Match: *Giants:* Kevin Brown; *Harlequins:* Will Sharp.
Penalty count: 6-5; **Half-time:** 8-4;
Referee: James Child; **Attendance:** 5,336.

SALFORD CITY REDS 22 LEEDS RHINOS 31

CITY REDS: 1 Karl Fitzpatrick; 2 Jodie Broughton; 3 Mark Henry; 5 Ashley Gibson; 20 Steve Tyrer; 26 Marc Sneyd; 14 Matty Smith; 8 Ray Cashmere; 9 Malcolm Alker (C); 19 Ryan Boyle; 15 Stuart Littler; 17 Adam Sidlow; 13 Luke Swain. Subs (all used): 7 Jeremy Smith; 22 Adam Neal; 10 Rob Parker; 12 Luke Adamson.
Tries: Broughton (3), Gibson (18, 79), Cashmere (66); **Goals:** Tyrer 3/5.
RHINOS: 1 Brent Webb; 2 Scott Donald; 3 Brett Delaney; 28 Lee Smith; 5 Ryan Hall; 13 Kevin Sinfield (C); 6 Danny McGuire; 8 Kylie Leuluai; 9 Danny Buderus; 16 Ryan Bailey; 17 Ian Kirke; 11 Jamie Jones-Buchanan; 27 Chris Clarkson. Subs (all used): 18 Carl Ablett; 12 Ali Lauitiiti; 25 Paul McShane; 19 Luke Burgess.
Tries: Kirke (9), Hall (53, 72), Sinfield (58), Donald (63); **Goals:** Sinfield 5/7; **Field goal:** Sinfield (69).
Rugby Leaguer & League Express Men of the Match: *City Reds:* Matty Smith; *Rhinos:* Kevin Sinfield.
Penalty count: 7-6; **Half-time:** 10-4;
Referee: Phil Bentham; **Attendance:** 4,651.

WAKEFIELD TRINITY WILDCATS 6 ST HELENS 50

WILDCATS: 33 Kieran Hyde (D); 3 Sean Gleeson; 13 Jason Demetriou (C); 4 Darryl Millard; 2 Damien Blanch; 21 Paul Cooke; 14 Sam Obst; 35 Charlie Leaeno; 36 Julien Rinaldi; 10 Michael Korkidas; 12 Glenn Morrison; 32 Danny Kirmond; 20 Tevita Leo-Latu. Subs (all used): 6 Ben Jeffries; 25 Richard Moore; 31 Ben Gledhill; 17 Kevin Henderson.
Try: Hyde (8); **Goals:** Cooke 1/1.
SAINTS: 1 Paul Wellens (C); 2 Ade Gardner; 5 Francis Meli; 3 Matt Gidley; 30 Jamie Foster; 6 Leon Pryce; 16 Scott Moore; 10 James Graham; 14 James Roby; 15 Bryn Hargreaves; 12 Jon Wilkin; 18 Matty Ashurst; 28 Shaun Magennis. Subs (all used): 11 Tony Puletua; 25 Jacob Emmitt; 17 Paul Clough; 32 Lee Gaskell.
Tries: Pryce (13), Gardner (26), Puletua (30, 72), Wilkin (47, 63), Magennis (57, 66), Meli (77);
Goals: Foster 7/9.
Rugby Leaguer & League Express Men of the Match: *Wildcats:* Tevita Leo-Latu; *Saints:* Leon Pryce.
Penalty count: 8-7; **Half-time:** 6-16;
Referee: Ben Thaler; **Attendance:** 5,217.

ROUND 24

Friday 30th July 2010

LEEDS RHINOS 12 WIGAN WARRIORS 26

RHINOS: 1 Brent Webb; 2 Scott Donald; 3 Brett Delaney; 4 Keith Senior; 5 Ryan Hall; 13 Kevin Sinfield (C); 6 Danny McGuire; 8 Kylie Leuluai; 9 Danny Buderus; 10 Jamie Peacock; 11 Jamie Jones-Buchanan; 18 Carl Ablett; 27 Chris Clarkson. Subs (all used): 16 Ryan Bailey; 12 Ali Lauitiiti; 19 Luke Burgess; 7 Rob Burrow.
Tries: Clarkson (39), Senior (47); **Goals:** Sinfield 2/2.
On report: Ablett (18) – alleged high tackle on S Tomkins; Bailey (24) – alleged use of the knee.
WARRIORS: 6 Sam Tomkins; 24 Darrell Goulding; 3 Martin Gleeson; 4 George Carmont; 5 Pat Richards; 19 Paul Deacon; 7 Thomas Leuluai; 8 Stuart Fielden; 9 Mark Riddell; 10 Andy Coley; 11 Harrison Hansen; 12 Joel Tomkins; 13 Sean O'Loughlin (C). Subs (all used): 17 Iafeta Palea'aesina; 25 Liam Farrell; 29 Chris Tuson; 26 Ben Davies.
Tries: Leuluai (8), Carmont (26), Hansen (61), Gleeson (69); **Goals:** Richards 5/6.
Sin bin: Coley (42) – late tackle on Burrow.
Rugby Leaguer & League Express Men of the Match: *Rhinos:* Rob Burrow; *Warriors:* Paul Deacon.
Penalty count: 10-13; **Half time:** 6-12;
Referee: Steve Ganson; **Attendance:** 16,622.

Saturday 31st July 2010

HARLEQUINS 18 HULL FC 42

HARLEQUINS: 26 Ben Jones-Bishop; 5 Will Sharp; 3 Tony Clubb; 4 David Howell; 22 Jamie O'Callaghan; 6 Luke Dorn; 21 Luke Gale; 17 Danny Ward; 20 Andy Ellis; 14 Oliver Wilkes; 16 Jason Golden; 13 Rob Purdham (C); 1 Chris Melling. Subs (all used): 10 Louie McCarthy-Scarsbrook; 24 Dave Williams; 33 Olsi Krasniqi; 36 David Mills.
Tries: Dorn (54), Sharp (65), McCarthy-Scarsbrook (72); **Goals:** Purdham 3/3.
HULL: 1 Jordan Tansey; 25 Reece Lyne; 19 Jordan Turner; 3 Tom Briscoe; 4 Kirk Yeaman; 14 Danny Washbrook; 9 Shaun Berrigan; 11 Lee Radford; 20 Danny Houghton; 10 Mark O'Meley; 16 Willie Manu; 12 Danny Tickle; 13 Craig Fitzgibbon (C). Subs (all used): 15 Epalahame Lauaki; 23 Sam Moa; 17 Peter Cusack; 30 Danny Nicklas.
Tries: O'Meley (10, 78), Yeaman (16), Houghton (24), Turner (27), Moa (31), Tansey (75); **Goals:** Tickle 7/7.
Rugby Leaguer & League Express Men of the Match: *Harlequins:* Will Sharp; *Hull:* Sam Moa.
Penalty count: 7-5; **Half-time:** 0-30;
Referee: Ian Smith; **Attendance:** 3,982.

WARRINGTON WOLVES 24 ST HELENS 26

WOLVES: 1 Richard Mathers; 5 Chris Hicks; 3 Matt King; 23 Ryan Atkins; 2 Chris Riley; 6 Lee Briers; 7 Richard Myler; 8 Adrian Morley (C); 9 Michael Monaghan; 10 Garreth Carvell; 11 Louis Anderson; 12 Ben Westwood; 13 Ben Harrison. Subs (all used): 15 Jon Clarke; 16 Paul Wood; 26 David Solomona; 27 Vinnie Anderson.
Tries: Wood (23), Clarke (28), Westwood (52, 72);
Goals: Westwood 4/5.
SAINTS: 1 Paul Wellens; 30 Jamie Foster; 13 Chris Flannery; 5 Francis Meli; 2 Ade Gardner; 6 Leon Pryce; 16 Scott Moore; 10 James Graham; 14 James Roby; 15 Bryn Hargreaves; 12 Jon Wilkin; 18 Matty Ashurst; 28 Shaun Magennis. Subs (all used): 9 Keiron Cunningham (C); 11 Tony Puletua; 17 Paul Clough; 25 Jacob Emmitt.
Tries: Ashurst (9), Foster (19, 65), Meli (32), Roby (55);
Goals: Foster 3/5.
Rugby Leaguer & League Express Men of the Match: *Wolves:* Ben Westwood; *Saints:* Paul Wellens.
Penalty count: 13-6; **Half-time:** 14-16;
Referee: Thierry Alibert; **Attendance:** 12,863.

Sunday 1st August 2010

BRADFORD BULLS 22 CATALANS DRAGONS 24

BULLS: 1 Dave Halley; 33 Vinny Finigan; 15 Michael Platt; 4 Chris Nero; 2 Rikki Sheriffe; 11 Steve Menzies; 3 Paul Sykes; 10 Andy Lynch (C); 9 Heath L'Estrange; 18 Craig Kopczak; 20 Elliott Whitehead; 13 Jamie Langley; 14 Wayne Godwin. Subs (all used): 16 Michael Worrincy; 24 Tom Olbison; 23 Steve Crossley; 12 Glenn Hall.
Tries: Lynch (23), Olbison (43), Menzies (48), Platt (60);
Goals: Sykes 3/4.
Sin bin: Worrincy (35) – interference.
DRAGONS: 5 Dimitri Pelo; 2 Steven Bell; 3 Sebastien Raguin; 18 Dane Carlaw; 23 Chris Walker; 7 Thomas Bosc (C); 30 Brent Sherwin; 24 Remi Casty; 20 Kane Bentley; 22 Jamal Fakir; 11 Olivier Elima; 12 Gregory Mounis; 4 Setaimata Sa. Subs (all used): 8 David Ferriol; 25 Tony Gigot; 27 Michael Simon; 17 Cyrille Gossard.
Tries: Sa (2), Raguin (10), Bell (40), Elima (68);
Goals: Bosc 4/5.
Rugby Leaguer & League Express Men of the Match: *Bulls:* Jamie Langley; *Dragons:* Gregory Mounis.
Penalty count: 14-16; **Half-time:** 6-16;
Referee: James Child; **Attendance:** 6,217.

CRUSADERS 60 SALFORD CITY REDS 16

CRUSADERS: 26 Clinton Schifcofske (C); 14 Luke Dyer; 3 Tony Martin; 12 Jason Chan; 2 Nick Youngquest; 7 Jarrod Sammut; 27 Rhys Hanbury; 17 Adam Peek; 9 Lincoln Withers; 10 Mark Bryant; 11 Weller Hauraki; 16 Frank Winterstein; 23 Peter Lupton. Subs (all used): 15 Tommy Lee; 19 Jordan James; 8 Ryan O'Hara; 13 Rocky Trimarchi.
Tries: Youngquest (3, 10, 59), Hanbury (12), Schifcofske (19, 63), Martin (34, 65), O'Hara (38), Hauraki (55), Winterstein (69); **Goals:** Schifcofske 8/11.
CITY REDS: 1 Karl Fitzpatrick; 2 Jodie Broughton; 3 Mark Henry; 4 Willie Talau; 5 Ashley Gibson; 6 Stefan Ratchford; 14 Matty Smith; 8 Ray Cashmere; 9 Malcolm Alker (C); 19 Ryan Boyle; 15 Stuart Littler; 12 Luke Adamson; 13 Luke Swain. Subs (all used): 7 Jeremy Smith; 17 Adam Sidlow; 10 Rob Parker; 22 Adam Neal.
Tries: Ratchford (5), Cashmere (74), Fitzpatrick (80);
Goals: M Smith 2/3.
Dismissal: J Smith (71) - dissent.
Rugby Leaguer & League Express Men of the Match: *Crusaders:* Clinton Schifcofske; *City Reds:* Stuart Littler.
Penalty count: 7-2; **Half-time:** 32-6;
Referee: Ben Thaler; **Attendance:** 2,412.

HUDDERSFIELD GIANTS 58
WAKEFIELD TRINITY WILDCATS 6

GIANTS: 21 Scott Grix; 27 Jermaine McGillvary; 2 Leroy Cudjoe; 19 Michael Lawrence; 5 David Hodgson; 6 Kevin Brown (C); 18 Brad Drew; 8 Eorl Crabtree; 34 Danny Brough; 16 Darrell Griffin; 11 Lee Gilmour; 9 Shaun Lunt; 13 Stephen Wild. Subs (all used): 20 David Faiumu; 23 Larne Patrick; 14 Simon Finnigan; 33 Graeme Horne.
Tries: D Hodgson (7), Gilmour (12), Griffin (18), Lunt (24), McGillvary (35), Cudjoe (38, 58), Grix (63), Brough (70), Horne (76); **Goals:** Brough 9/10.
WILDCATS: 1 Matt Blaymire; 3 Sean Gleeson; 13 Jason Demetriou (C); 4 Darryl Millard; 2 Damien Blanch; 26 Matthew Wildie (D); 6 Ben Jeffries; 35 Charlie Leaeno; 36 Julien Rinaldi; 10 Michael Korkidas; 16 Paul Johnson; 32 Danny Kirmond; 12 Glenn Morrison. Subs (all used): 17 Kevin Henderson; 20 Tevita Leo-Latu; 25 Richard Moore; 31 Ben Gledhill.
Try: Gleeson (50); **Goals:** Jeffries 1/1.
Rugby Leaguer & League Express Men of the Match: *Giants:* Kevin Brown; *Wildcats:* Charlie Leaeno.
Penalty count: 7-5; **Half-time:** 36-0;
Referee: Richard Silverwood; **Attendance:** 6,055.

HULL KINGSTON ROVERS 28 CASTLEFORD TIGERS 26

ROVERS: 1 Shaun Briscoe (C); 2 Peter Fox; 32 Josh Charnley; 5 Liam Colbon; 29 Sam Latus; 9 Scott Murrell; 7 Michael Dobson; 30 Joel Clinton; 17 Ben Fisher; 8 Rhys Lovegrove; 11 Clint Newton; 13 Ben Galea; 22 Liam Watts. Subs (all used): 10 Scott Wheeldon; 16 Jason Netherton; 21 Josh Hodgson; 26 Frankie Mariano.
Tries: Charnley (6, 22, 70), Briscoe (17);
Goals: Dobson 6/6.
TIGERS: 23 Ryan McGoldrick; 2 Kirk Dixon; 3 Michael Shenton; 32 Joe Arundel; 5 Michael Wainwright; 25 Dean Widders; 6 Rangi Chase; 10 Craig Huby; 9 Ryan Hudson (C); 8 Mitchell Sargent; 11 Brett Ferres; 17 Ryan Clayton; 13 Joe Westerman. Subs (all used): 12 Steve Snitch; 14 Stuart Jones; 26 Oliver Holmes; 31 Jonathan Walker.
Tries: Ferres (11), Arundel (31), Chase (44), Jones (60);
Goals: Westerman 5/6.
Rugby Leaguer & League Express Men of the Match: *Rovers:* Josh Charnley; *Tigers:* Rangi Chase.
Penalty count: 11-5; **Half-time:** 18-12;
Referee: Phil Bentham; **Attendance:** 8,104.

ROUND 9

Friday 6th August 2010

CRUSADERS 16 HARLEQUINS 12

CRUSADERS: 26 Clinton Schifcofske (C); 14 Luke Dyer; 3 Tony Martin; 12 Jason Chan; 2 Nick Youngquest; 27 Rhys Hanbury; 7 Jarrod Sammut; 8 Ryan O'Hara; 9 Lincoln Withers; 10 Mark Bryant; 11 Weller Hauraki; 16 Frank Winterstein; 23 Peter Lupton. Subs (all used): 15 Tommy Lee; 19 Jordan James; 18 Jamie Thackray; 13 Rocky Trimarchi.
Tries: Hanbury (18, 76), Chan (73);
Goals: Schifcofske 2/3.
HARLEQUINS: 26 Ben Jones-Bishop; 5 Will Sharp; 3 Tony Clubb; 4 David Howell; 22 Jamie O'Callaghan; 6 Luke Dorn; 7 Danny Orr; 17 Danny Ward; 20 Andy Ellis; 14 Oliver Wilkes; 16 Jason Golden; 13 Rob Purdham (C); 10 Louie McCarthy-Scarsbrook. Subs (all used): 21 Luke Gale; 1 Chris Melling; 36 David Mills; 33 Olsi Krasniqi.
Tries: O'Callaghan (13), Jones-Bishop (32);
Goals: Orr 2/3.
Rugby Leaguer & League Express Men of the Match: *Crusaders:* Jason Chan; *Harlequins:* Luke Dorn.
Penalty count: 5-5; **Half-time:** 4-10; **Referee:** Ben Thaler; **Attendance:** 1,122 *(at The Gnoll, Neath).*

ROUND 25

Friday 13th August 2010

CASTLEFORD TIGERS 6 LEEDS RHINOS 38

TIGERS: 23 Ryan McGoldrick; 2 Kirk Dixon; 3 Michael

Shenton; 32 Joe Arundel; 5 Michael Wainwright; 13 Joe Westerman; 6 Rangi Chase; 10 Craig Huby; 9 Ryan Hudson (C); 8 Mitchell Sargent; 12 Steve Snitch; 17 Ryan Clayton; 11 Brett Ferres. Subs (all used): 25 Dean Widders; 15 Liam Higgins; 14 Stuart Jones; 31 Jonathan Walker.
Try: Snitch (72); **Goals:** Westerman 1/1.
RHINOS: 1 Brent Webb; 2 Scott Donald; 4 Keith Senior; 28 Lee Smith; 5 Ryan Hall; 6 Danny McGuire; 7 Rob Burrow; 8 Kylie Leuluai; 14 Matt Diskin; 10 Jamie Peacock (C); 17 Ian Kirke; 15 Greg Eastwood; 27 Chris Clarkson. Subs (all used): 19 Luke Burgess; 11 Jamie Jones-Buchanan; 12 Ali Lauitiiti; 25 Paul McShane.
Tries: Clarkson (15), McGuire (20), Burrow (28), Lauitiiti (50), Hall (54, 76), Donald (60); **Goals:** Smith 5/7.
On report: Lauitiiti (46) - alleged high tackle.
Rugby Leaguer & League Express Men of the Match: *Tigers:* Brett Ferres; *Rhinos:* Danny McGuire.
Penalty count: 9-5; **Half time:** 0-18;
Referee: Richard Silverwood; **Attendance:** 7,901.

HULL FC 18 CRUSADERS 16

HULL: 1 Jordan Tansey; 25 Reece Lyne; 19 Jordan Turner; 4 Kirk Yeaman; 3 Tom Briscoe; 14 Danny Washbrook; 9 Shaun Berrigan; 10 Mark O'Meley; 20 Danny Houghton; 11 Lee Radford; 16 Willie Manu; 12 Danny Tickle; 13 Craig Fitzgibbon (C). Subs (all used): 8 Ewan Dowes; 17 Peter Cusack; 15 Epalahame Lauaki; 23 Sam Moa.
Try: Lyne (27); **Goals:** Tickle 7/7.
Dismissal:
Tansey (75) - dangerous tackle on Schifcofske.
CRUSADERS: 26 Clinton Schifcofske (C); 14 Luke Dyer; 3 Tony Martin; 12 Jason Chan; 2 Nick Youngquest; 7 Jarrod Sammut; 27 Rhys Hanbury; 8 Ryan O'Hara; 9 Lincoln Withers; 10 Mark Bryant; 16 Frank Winterstein; 11 Weller Hauraki; 23 Peter Lupton. Subs (all used): 15 Tommy Lee; 19 Jordan James; 17 Adam Peek; 13 Rocky Trimarchi.
Tries: Dyer (14), Lupton (76); **Goals:** Schifcofske 4/4.
Rugby Leaguer & League Express Men of the Match: *Hull:* Danny Tickle; *Crusaders:* Clinton Schifcofske.
Penalty count: 11-11; **Half-time:** 12-8;
Referee: James Child; **Attendance:** 11,762.

ST HELENS 60 BRADFORD BULLS 12

SAINTS: 1 Paul Wellens; 30 Jamie Foster; 3 Matt Gidley; 5 Francis Meli; 2 Ade Gardner; 16 Scott Moore; 7 Kyle Eastmond; 10 James Graham; 14 James Roby; 11 Tony Puletua; 13 Chris Flannery; 12 Jon Wilkin; 24 Jonny Lomax. Subs (all used): 9 Keiron Cunningham (C); 15 Bryn Hargreaves; 18 Matty Ashurst; 25 Jacob Emmitt.
Tries: Gardner (4), Moore (6), Wilkin (11, 65), Foster (19, 77), Roby (25), Eastmond (39), Lomax (52), Ashurst (55), Puletua (60); **Goals:** Foster 8/11.
BULLS: 1 Dave Halley; 2 Rikki Sheriffe; 15 Michael Platt; 11 Steve Menzies; 19 Jason Crookes; 6 Brett Kearney; 3 Paul Sykes; 18 Craig Kopczak; 9 Heath L'Estrange; 10 Andy Lynch (C); 20 Elliott Whitehead; 16 Michael Worrincy; 13 Jamie Langley. Subs (all used): 8 Nick Scruton; 14 Wayne Godwin; 24 Tom Olbison; 33 Vinny Finigan.
Tries: Sheriffe (73), Worrincy (74); **Goals:** Sykes 2/2.
Rugby Leaguer & League Express Men of the Match: *Saints:* Jamie Foster; *Bulls:* Rikki Sheriffe.
Penalty count: 9-6; **Half-time:** 32-0;
Referee: Thierry Alibert; **Attendance:** 9,032.

Saturday 14th August 2010

CATALANS DRAGONS 12 HARLEQUINS 16

DRAGONS: 1 Clint Greenshields; 2 Steven Bell; 3 Sebastien Raguin; 18 Dane Carlaw; 23 Chris Walker; 7 Thomas Bosc (C); 16 William Barthau; 24 Remi Casty; 20 Kane Bentley; 8 David Ferriol; 11 Olivier Elima; 12 Gregory Mounis; 13 Dallas Johnson. Subs (all used): 4 Setaimata Sa; 17 Cyrille Gossard; 25 Tony Gigot; 27 Michael Simon.
Tries: Carlaw (43), Raguin (47); **Goals:** Bosc 2/2.
HARLEQUINS: 1 Chris Melling; 22 Jamie O'Callaghan; 3 Tony Clubb; 4 David Howell; 5 Will Sharp; 6 Luke Dorn; 21 Luke Gale; 10 Louie McCarthy-Scarsbrook; 20 Andy Ellis; 17 Danny Ward; 13 Rob Purdham (C); 11 Luke Williamson; 33 Olsi Krasniqi. Subs: 14 Oliver Wilkes; 28 Ben Bolger (not used); 25 Lamont Bryan; 36 David Mills.
Tries: Clubb (6), Dorn (12), Ellis (74);
Goals: Purdham 2/3.
Sin bin: Gale (77) - late tackle.
Rugby Leaguer & League Express Men of the Match: *Dragons:* Clint Greenshields; *Harlequins:* Luke Dorn.
Penalty count: 9-4; **Half-time:** 0-10;
Referee: Robert Hicks; **Attendance:** 6,152.

Sunday 15th August 2010

SALFORD CITY REDS 18 HULL KINGSTON ROVERS 44

CITY REDS: 1 Karl Fitzpatrick; 2 Jodie Broughton; 4 Willie Talau; 5 Ashley Gibson; 20 Steve Tyrer; 6 Stefan Ratchford; 26 Marc Sneyd; 8 Ray Cashmere; 14 Matty Smith; 22 Adam Neal; 15 Stuart Littler (C); 17 Adam Sidlow; 13 Luke Swain. Subs (all used): 28 Gareth Owen (D); 10 Rob Parker; 25 Jack Spencer; 16 Phil Leuluai.
Tries: Parker (36), Cashmere (64), M Smith (68);
Goals: Tyrer 3/3.
On report: Cashmere (57) - alleged dangerous tackle.
ROVERS: 1 Shaun Briscoe; 2 Peter Fox; 32 Josh Charnley; 28 Ben Cockayne; 5 Liam Colbon; 9 Scott Murrell; 7 Michael Dobson; 20 Michael Vella (C); 17 Ben Fisher; 16 Jason Netherton; 11 Clint Newton; 13 Ben Galea; 22 Liam Watts. Subs (all used): 10 Scott Wheeldon; 8 Rhys Lovegrove; 26 Frankie Mariano; 21 Josh Hodgson.
Tries: Colbon (2), Newton (28, 52), Charnley (45), Murrell (48), Dobson (54), Briscoe (58, 73);
Goals: Dobson 6/8.
Rugby Leaguer & League Express Men of the Match: *City Reds:* Matty Smith; *Rovers:* Michael Dobson.
Penalty count: 6-12; **Half-time:** 6-12;
Referee: Ian Smith; **Attendance:** 4,111.

WAKEFIELD TRINITY WILDCATS 18 WARRINGTON WOLVES 36

WILDCATS: 18 Aaron Murphy; 32 Danny Kirmond; 16 Paul Johnson; 4 Darryl Millard; 2 Damien Blanch; 21 Paul Cooke; 6 Ben Jeffries; 35 Charlie Leaeno; 14 Sam Obst; 10 Michael Korkidas; 13 Jason Demetriou (C); 12 Glenn Morrison; 20 Tevita Leo-Latu. Subs (all used): 17 Kevin Henderson; 19 Paul King; 25 Richard Moore; 36 Julien Rinaldi.
Tries: Blanch (27), Jeffries (39), Morrison (60), Leo-Latu (70); **Goals:** Cooke 0/1, Jeffries 1/3.
WOLVES: 2 Chris Riley; 5 Chris Hicks; 20 Matty Blythe; 23 Ryan Atkins; 3 Matt King; 6 Lee Briers; 7 Richard Myler; 8 Adrian Morley (C); 15 Jon Clarke; 10 Garreth Carvell; 11 Louis Anderson; 12 Ben Westwood; 13 Ben Harrison. Subs (all used): 16 Paul Wood; 14 Mick Higham; 18 Michael Cooper; 27 Vinnie Anderson.
Tries: Hicks (7), King (15, 23, 48), Riley (32), Blythe (41), Briers (63); **Goals:** Westwood 3/6, Briers 1/1.
Rugby Leaguer & League Express Men of the Match: *Wildcats:* Danny Kirmond; *Wolves:* Lee Briers.
Penalty count: 5-6; **Half-time:** 10-18;
Referee: Ben Thaler; **Attendance:** 5,562.

WIGAN WARRIORS 16 HUDDERSFIELD GIANTS 18

WARRIORS: 6 Sam Tomkins; 20 Karl Pryce; 27 Stefan Marsh; 4 George Carmont; 5 Pat Richards; 19 Paul Deacon; 7 Thomas Leuluai (C); 8 Stuart Fielden; 9 Mark Riddell; 10 Andy Coley; 11 Harrison Hansen; 12 Joel Tomkins; 13 Sean O'Loughlin. Subs (all used): 17 Iafeta Palea'aesina; 25 Liam Farrell; 29 Chris Tuson; 26 Ben Davies.
Tries: Pryce (4), J Tomkins (35), S Tomkins (65);
Goals: Richards 2/3.
Sin bin: Fielden (16) - fighting.
GIANTS: 1 Brett Hodgson (C); 5 David Hodgson; 2 Leroy Cudjoe; 33 Graeme Horne; 19 Michael Lawrence; 6 Kevin Brown; 7 Luke Robinson; 16 Darrell Griffin; 34 Danny Brough; 10 Keith Mason; 11 Lee Gilmour; 12 David Fa'alogo; 13 Stephen Wild. Subs (all used): 20 David Faiumu; 8 Eorl Crabtree; 14 Simon Finnigan; 9 Shaun Lunt.
Tries: Cudjoe (55, 71), Robinson (60);
Goals: B Hodgson 3/3.
Sin bin: Brown (15) - obstruction; Mason (16) - fighting.
Rugby Leaguer & League Express Men of the Match: *Warriors:* Sam Tomkins; *Giants:* Leroy Cudjoe.
Penalty count: 7-4; **Half-time:** 10-0;
Referee: Phil Bentham; **Attendance:** 13,619.

ROUND 26

Friday 20th August 2010

LEEDS RHINOS 52 CATALANS DRAGONS 6

RHINOS: 1 Brent Webb; 28 Lee Smith; 4 Keith Senior; 3 Brett Delaney; 5 Ryan Hall; 6 Danny McGuire; 7 Rob Burrow; 8 Kylie Leuluai; 9 Danny Buderus; 16 Ryan Bailey; 27 Chris Clarkson; 11 Jamie Jones-Buchanan; 13 Kevin Sinfield (C). Subs (all used): 15 Greg Eastwood; 17 Ian Kirke; 12 Ali Lauitiiti; 14 Matt Diskin.
Tries: McGuire (3, 36, 62), Hall (12, 19, 48), Burrow (16), Smith (38), Delaney (56); **Goals:** Sinfield 8/9.
DRAGONS: 26 Cyril Stacul; 2 Steven Bell; 18 Dane Carlaw; 23 Chris Walker; 28 Frederic Vaccari; 7 Thomas Bosc (C); 30 Brent Sherwin; 8 David Ferriol; 9 Casey McGuire; 24 Remi Casty; 11 Olivier Elima; 17 Cyrille Gossard; 13 Dallas Johnson. Subs (all used): 4 Setaimata Sa; 19 Julien Touxagas; 20 Kane Bentley; 25 Tony Gigot.
Try: McGuire (27); **Goals:** Bosc 1/1.
Sin bin: Ferriol (79) - late tackle on Smith.
On report:
Johnson (18) - alleged dangerous tackle on Clarkson.
Rugby Leaguer & League Express Men of the Match: *Rhinos:* Danny McGuire; *Dragons:* Casey McGuire.
Penalty count: 15-6; **Half-time:** 34-6;
Referee: James Child; **Attendance:** 15,154.

WARRINGTON WOLVES 36 HULL FC 18

WOLVES: 1 Richard Mathers; 5 Chris Hicks; 3 Matt King; 23 Ryan Atkins; 2 Chris Riley; 7 Richard Myler; 9 Michael Monaghan; 8 Adrian Morley (C); 15 Jon Clarke; 13 Ben Harrison; 11 Louis Anderson; 12 Ben Westwood; 27 Vinnie Anderson. Subs (all used): 16 Paul Wood; 14 Mick Higham; 26 David Solomona; 18 Michael Cooper.
Tries: Riley (21, 39), Clarke (57), Westwood (63), Morley (68), Myler (71); **Goals:** Westwood 6/6.
HULL: 24 Craig Hall; 25 Reece Lyne; 19 Jordan Turner; 4 Kirk Yeaman; 3 Tom Briscoe; 14 Danny Washbrook; 9 Shaun Berrigan; 11 Lee Radford; 20 Danny Houghton; 10 Mark O'Meley; 16 Willie Manu; 12 Danny Tickle; 13 Craig Fitzgibbon (C). Subs (all used): 23 Sam Moa; 17 Peter Cusack; 8 Ewan Dowes; 15 Epalahame Lauaki.
Tries: Briscoe (9), Lauaki (36), Radford (66);
Goals: Tickle 3/3.
Sin bin: Tickle (55) – holding down.
Rugby Leaguer & League Express Men of the Match: *Wolves:* Ben Westwood; *Hull:* Shaun Berrigan.
Penalty count: 9-3; **Half-time:** 12-12;
Referee: Ian Smith; **Attendance:** 10,042.

Saturday 21st August 2010

CRUSADERS 10 ST HELENS 36

CRUSADERS: 26 Clinton Schifcofske (C); 14 Luke Dyer; 3 Tony Martin; 4 Vince Mellars; 2 Nick Youngquest; 23 Peter Lupton; 27 Rhys Hanbury; 8 Ryan O'Hara; 9 Lincoln Withers; 10 Mark Bryant; 16 Frank Winterstein; 12 Jason Chan; 11 Weller Hauraki. Subs (all used): 15 Tommy Lee; 19 Jordan James; 18 Jamie Thackray; 13 Rocky Trimarchi.
Tries: Mellars (3), Winterstein (20);
Goals: Schifcofske 1/2.
SAINTS: 1 Paul Wellens; 30 Jamie Foster; 3 Matt Gidley; 5 Francis Meli; 2 Ade Gardner; 24 Jonny Lomax; 7 Kyle Eastmond; 10 James Graham; 14 James Roby; 15 Bryn Hargreaves; 13 Chris Flannery; 12 Jon Wilkin; 16 Scott Moore. Subs (all used): 9 Keiron Cunningham (C); 11 Tony Puletua; 18 Matty Ashurst; 25 Jacob Emmitt.
Tries: Eastmond (13), Wellens (15), Gardner (30), Foster (56), Roby (65), Lomax (71), Puletua (74);
Goals: Foster 4/7.
Rugby Leaguer & League Express Men of the Match: *Crusaders:* Clinton Schifcofske; *Saints:* James Roby.
Penalty count: 7-8; **Half-time:** 10-14;
Referee: Richard Silverwood; **Attendance:** 5,436.

Sunday 22nd August 2010

BRADFORD BULLS 38 WAKEFIELD TRINITY WILDCATS 28

BULLS: 1 Dave Halley; 2 Rikki Sheriffe; 3 Paul Sykes; 15 Michael Platt; 19 Jason Crookes; 6 Brett Kearney; 32 Danny Addy; 8 Nick Scruton; 9 Heath L'Estrange; 10 Andy Lynch (C); 16 Michael Worrincy; 13 Jamie Langley; 11 Steve Menzies. Subs (all used): 14 Wayne Godwin; 24 Tom Olbison; 18 Craig Kopczak; 20 Elliott Whitehead.
Tries: Kearney (14), Lynch (26), Godwin (36, 40), Whitehead (49), Menzies (62); **Goals:** Sykes 7/7.
WILDCATS: 18 Aaron Murphy; 32 Danny Kirmond; 16 Paul Johnson; 4 Darryl Millard; 2 Damien Blanch; 6 Ben Jeffries; 14 Sam Obst; 19 Paul King; 36 Julien Rinaldi; 10 Michael Korkidas; 13 Jason Demetriou (C); 12 Glenn Morrison; 20 Tevita Leo-Latu. Subs (all used): 3 Sean Gleeson; 35 Charlie Leaeno; 11 Dale Ferguson; 25 Richard Moore.
Tries: Kirmond (3), Millard (12), Obst (54), Morrison (56), Gleeson (66); **Goals:** Jeffries 4/5.
Rugby Leaguer & League Express Men of the Match: *Bulls:* Wayne Godwin; *Wildcats:* Glenn Morrison.
Penalty count: 7-10; **Half-time:** 26-12;
Referee: Robert Hicks; **Attendance:** 7,437.

HUDDERSFIELD GIANTS 52 SALFORD CITY REDS 4

GIANTS: 1 Brett Hodgson (C); 2 Leroy Cudjoe; 19 Michael Lawrence; 11 Lee Gilmour; 5 David Hodgson; 6 Kevin Brown; 7 Luke Robinson; 8 Eorl Crabtree; 34 Danny Brough; 33 Graeme Horne; 9 Shaun Lunt; 12 David Fa'alogo; 13 Stephen Wild. Subs (all used): 14 Simon Finnigan; 15 Andy Raleigh; 20 David Faiumu; 23 Larne Patrick.
Tries: Brough (4), Wild (25), Fa'alogo (32), Faiumu (43, 65), Brown (46), Patrick (49), Horne (67), Gilmour (72); **Goals:** B Hodgson 8/9.
CITY REDS: 6 Stefan Ratchford; 2 Jodie Broughton; 5 Ashley Gibson; 15 Stuart Littler (C); 20 Steve Tyrer; 26 Marc Sneyd; 14 Matty Smith; 8 Ray Cashmere; 7 Jeremy Smith; 22 Adam Neal; 11 Ian Sibbit; 17 Adam Sidlow; 13 Luke Swain. Subs (all used): 10 Rob Parker; 16 Phil Leuluai; 28 Gareth Owen; 29 Toby Adamson (D).
Try: Broughton (80); **Goals:** Tyrer 0/1.
Rugby Leaguer & League Express Men of the Match: *Giants:* Kevin Brown; *City Reds:* Marc Sneyd.
Penalty count: 10-5; **Half-time:** 16-0;
Referee: Thierry Alibert; **Attendance:** 6,697.

HULL KINGSTON ROVERS 18 WIGAN WARRIORS 38

ROVERS: 1 Shaun Briscoe; 2 Peter Fox; 29 Sam Latus; 28 Ben Cockayne; 5 Liam Colbon; 9 Scott Murrell; 7 Michael Dobson; 20 Michael Vella (C); 17 Ben Fisher; 8 Rhys Lovegrove; 11 Clint Newton; 16 Jason Netherton; 22 Liam Watts. Subs (all used): 10 Scott Wheeldon; 30 Joel Clinton; 21 Josh Hodgson; 14 Matt Cook.
Tries: Murrell (42), Cook (46), Lovegrove (49);
Goals: Dobson 3/3.
WARRIORS: 6 Sam Tomkins; 2 Amos Roberts; 24 Darrell Goulding; 27 Stefan Marsh; 5 Pat Richards; 19 Paul Deacon; 7 Thomas Leuluai; 11 Harrison Hansen; 9 Mark Riddell; 10 Andy Coley; 12 Joel Tomkins; 25 Liam Farrell; 13 Sean O'Loughlin (C). Subs (all used): 17 Iafeta Palea'aesina; 26 Ben Davies; 29 Chris Tuson; 31 Josh Charnley (D).
Tries: Richards (5, 70), Marsh (25), S Tomkins (62), J Tomkins (76), Charnley (78); **Goals:** Richards 7/8.
Rugby Leaguer & League Express Men of the Match: *Rovers:* Rhys Lovegrove; *Warriors:* Pat Richards.
Penalty count: 8-3; **Half-time:** 0-14;
Referee: Ben Thaler; **Attendance:** 9,250.

CASTLEFORD TIGERS 40 HARLEQUINS 28

TIGERS: 23 Ryan McGoldrick; 2 Kirk Dixon; 3 Michael Shenton; 11 Brett Ferres; 5 Michael Wainwright; 25 Dean Widders; 6 Rangi Chase; 8 Mitchell Sargent; 9 Ryan Hudson (C); 15 Liam Higgins; 12 Steve Snitch; 14 Stuart Jones; 13 Joe Westerman. Subs (all used): 10 Craig Huby; 28 Adam Milner; 31 Jonathan Walker; 32 Joe Arundel.
Tries: McGoldrick (18), Shenton (23), Hudson (31), Dixon (43), Huby (47), Milner (60), Sargent (75);
Goals: Westerman 6/7.

Salford's Marc Sneyd wrongfoots Wakefield's Richard Moore and Jason Demetriou

HARLEQUINS: 1 Chris Melling; 22 Jamie O'Callaghan; 3 Tony Clubb; 4 David Howell; 5 Will Sharp; 21 Luke Gale; 6 Luke Dorn; 17 Danny Ward; 20 Andy Ellis; 14 Oliver Wilkes; 13 Rob Purdham (C); 11 Luke Williamson; 16 Jason Golden. Subs (all used): 10 Louie McCarthy-Scarsbrook; 36 David Mills; 7 Danny Orr; 25 Lamont Bryan.
Tries: Howell (12), Sharp (45), O'Callaghan (68), Gale (70), Dorn (78); **Goals:** Purdham 4/5.
Rugby Leaguer & League Express Men of the Match: *Tigers:* Mitchell Sargent; *Harlequins:* Luke Dorn.
Penalty count: 5-6; **Half-time:** 18-6;
Referee: Phil Bentham; **Attendance:** 5,862.

ROUND 27

Friday 3rd September 2010

HARLEQUINS 22 WARRINGTON WOLVES 36

HARLEQUINS: 1 Chris Melling; 5 Will Sharp; 3 Tony Clubb; 4 David Howell; 22 Jamie O'Callaghan; 6 Luke Dorn; 21 Luke Gale; 17 Danny Ward; 20 Andy Ellis; 14 Oliver Wilkes; 11 Luke Williamson; 13 Rob Purdham (C); 33 Olsi Krasniqi. Subs (all used): 10 Louie McCarthy-Scarsbrook; 36 David Mills; 24 Luke May; 28 Ben Bolger.
Tries: Ellis (5), Dorn (7, 47, 75);
Goals: Purdham 3/3, Williamson 0/1.
WOLVES: 1 Richard Mathers; 5 Chris Hicks; 4 Chris Bridge; 23 Ryan Atkins; 2 Chris Riley; 7 Richard Myler; 9 Michael Monaghan (C); 18 Michael Cooper; 15 Jon Clarke; 10 Garreth Carvell; 26 David Solomona; 27 Vinnie Anderson; 3 Ben Harrison. Subs (all used): 14 Mick Higham; 19 Lee Mitchell; 31 Rhys Evans (D); 16 Paul Wood.
Tries: Clarke (12), Solomona (18, 55), Cooper (37), Bridge (40, 60); **Goals:** Bridge 6/6.
Rugby Leaguer & League Express Men of the Match: *Harlequins:* Luke Dorn; *Wolves:* Chris Bridge.
Penalty count: 6-5; **Half-time:** 12-24;
Referee: Thierry Alibert; **Attendance:** 3,211.

WIGAN WARRIORS 34 BRADFORD BULLS 12

WARRIORS: 6 Sam Tomkins; 24 Darrell Goulding; 27 Stefan Marsh; 4 George Carmont; 5 Pat Richards; 19 Paul Deacon; 7 Thomas Leuluai; 8 Stuart Fielden; 9 Mark Riddell; 10 Andy Coley; 25 Liam Farrell; 12 Joel Tomkins (C); 13 Sean O'Loughlin. Subs (all used): 17 Iafeta Palea'aesina; 14 Paul Prescott; 29 Chris Tuson; 3 Martin Gleeson.
Tries: Carmont (16), Palea'aesina (27), Richards (33, 41), J Tomkins (39), Goulding (67, 77); **Goals:** Richards 3/7.
BULLS: 15 Michael Platt; 2 Rikki Sheriffe; 3 Paul Sykes; 11 Steve Menzies; 33 Vinny Finigan; 6 Brett Kearney; 9 Heath L'Estrange; 8 Nick Scruton; 14 Wayne Godwin; 10 Andy Lynch (C); 16 Michael Worrincy; 20 Elliott Whitehead; 13 Jamie Langley. Subs (all used): 12 Glenn Hall; 24 Tom Olbison; 18 Craig Kopczak; 32 Danny Addy.
Tries: Kopczak (75), Lynch (79);
Goals: Sykes 1/1, Menzies 1/1.

Rugby Leaguer & League Express Men of the Match: *Warriors:* Pat Richards; *Bulls:* Andy Lynch.
Penalty count: 8-12; **Half-time:** 20-0;
Referee: James Child; **Attendance:** 17,058.

Saturday 4th September 2010

HULL FC 14 LEEDS RHINOS 18

HULL: 24 Craig Hall; 3 Tom Briscoe; 9 Shaun Berrigan; 4 Kirk Yeaman; 25 Reece Lyne; 6 Richard Horne; 7 Sean Long (C); 11 Lee Radford; 20 Danny Houghton; 10 Mark O'Meley; 16 Willie Manu; 12 Danny Tickle; 13 Craig Fitzgibbon. Subs: 23 Sam Moa; 14 Danny Washbrook; 17 Peter Cusack; 19 Jordan Turner (not used).
Tries: Briscoe (23), Washbrook (33);
Goals: Tickle 2/2, Fitzgibbon 1/1.
Dismissal: Radford (10) - punching.
RHINOS: 1 Brent Webb; 5 Ryan Hall; 3 Brett Delaney; 28 Lee Smith; 2 Scott Donald; 6 Danny McGuire; 7 Rob Burrow; 8 Kylie Leuluai; 9 Danny Buderus; 16 Ryan Bailey; 18 Carl Ablett; 4 Keith Senior; 13 Kevin Sinfield (C). Subs (all used): 14 Matt Diskin; 15 Greg Eastwood; 17 Ian Kirke; 12 Ali Lauitiiti.
Tries: Donald (44), McGuire (64, 70); **Goals:** Sinfield 3/3.
Rugby Leaguer & League Express Men of the Match: *Hull:* Craig Fitzgibbon; *Rhinos:* Danny McGuire.
Penalty count: 9-6; **Half-time:** 12-0;
Referee: Ian Smith; **Attendance:** 16,208.

CATALANS DRAGONS 12 HUDDERSFIELD GIANTS 26

DRAGONS: 1 Clint Greenshields; 28 Frederic Vaccari; 3 Sebastien Raguin; 18 Dane Carlaw; 26 Cyril Stacul; 30 Brent Sherwin; 25 Tony Gigot; 24 Remi Casty; 9 Casey McGuire; 22 Jamal Fakir; 11 Olivier Elima (C); 4 Setaimata Sa; 13 Dallas Johnson. Subs (all used): 21 Sebastien Martins; 17 Cyrille Gossard; 29 Andrew Bentley; 27 Michael Simon.
Tries: Sa (52), Vaccari (66); **Goals:** Gigot 2/2.
GIANTS: 1 Brett Hodgson (C); 2 Leroy Cudjoe; 11 Lee Gilmour; 19 Michael Lawrence; 5 David Hodgson; 6 Kevin Brown; 7 Luke Robinson; 8 Eorl Crabtree; 34 Danny Brough; 16 Darrell Griffin; 9 Shaun Lunt; 12 David Fa'alogo; 13 Stephen Wild. Subs (all used): 15 Andy Raleigh; 20 David Faiumu; 23 Larne Patrick; 33 Graeme Horne.
Tries: Wild (30), D Hodgson (38), Lunt (42), Cudjoe (48), Robinson (64); **Goals:** B Hodgson 3/5.
Rugby Leaguer & League Express Men of the Match: *Dragons:* Casey McGuire; *Giants:* Luke Robinson.
Penalty count: 4-4; **Half-time:** 0-10;
Referee: Richard Silverwood; **Attendance:** 5,708.

CRUSADERS 30 HULL KINGSTON ROVERS 24

CRUSADERS: 26 Clinton Schifcofske (C); 14 Luke Dyer; 3 Tony Martin; 4 Vince Mellars; 2 Nick Youngquest; 7 Jarrod Sammut; 27 Rhys Hanbury; 8 Ryan O'Hara; 9 Lincoln Withers; 10 Mark Bryant; 12 Jason Chan; 11 Weller Hauraki; 23 Peter Lupton. Subs (all used): 16 Frank Winterstein; 15 Tommy Lee; 19 Jordan James; 17 Adam Peek.
Tries: O'Hara (5), Martin (25), Hanbury (49), Sammut (53), Dyer (78); **Goals:** Schifcofske 5/6.

ROVERS: 1 Shaun Briscoe; 2 Peter Fox; 3 Kris Welham; 28 Ben Cockayne; 5 Liam Colbon; 9 Scott Murrell; 7 Michael Dobson; 20 Michael Vella (C); 17 Ben Fisher; 30 Joel Clinton; 11 Clint Newton; 13 Ben Galea; 8 Rhys Lovegrove. Subs (all used): 16 Jason Netherton; 22 Liam Watts; 10 Scott Wheeldon; 21 Josh Hodgson.
Tries: Fox (10), Briscoe (43), Welham (47), Galea (67); **Goals:** Dobson 4/4.
Rugby Leaguer & League Express Men of the Match: *Crusaders:* Jarrod Sammut; *Rovers:* Ben Galea.
Penalty count: 8-8; **Half-time:** 12-6;
Referee: Robert Hicks; **Attendance:** 5,137.

ST HELENS 40 CASTLEFORD TIGERS 30

SAINTS: 1 Paul Wellens; 30 Jamie Foster; 3 Matt Gidley; 5 Francis Meli; 2 Ade Gardner; 24 Jonny Lomax; 7 Kyle Eastmond; 10 James Graham; 9 Keiron Cunningham (C); 11 Tony Puletua; 13 Chris Flannery; 12 Jon Wilkin; 14 James Roby. Subs (all used): 4 Iosia Soliola; 15 Bryn Hargreaves; 16 Scott Moore; 17 Paul Clough.
Tries: Wellens (3), Graham (8), Flannery (39), Meli (52), Puletua (55), Gidley (78), Cunningham (80);
Goals: Foster 6/7.
TIGERS: 23 Ryan McGoldrick; 2 Kirk Dixon; 3 Michael Shenton; 11 Brett Ferres; 5 Michael Wainwright; 25 Dean Widders; 6 Rangi Chase; 8 Mitchell Sargent; 9 Ryan Hudson (C); 15 Liam Higgins; 14 Stuart Jones; 12 Steve Snitch; 13 Joe Westerman. Subs (all used): 10 Craig Huby; 28 Adam Milner; 31 Jonathan Walker; 32 Joe Arundel.
Tries: McGoldrick (14), Milner (44), Widders (59, 77), Shenton (72), Hudson (74);
Goals: Westerman 1/3, Dixon 2/3.
Rugby Leaguer & League Express Men of the Match: *Saints:* Keiron Cunningham; *Tigers:* Dean Widders.
Penalty count: 5-7; **Half-time:** 18-4;
Referee: Ben Thaler; **Attendance:** 13,978.

Sunday 5th September 2010

SALFORD CITY REDS 16 WAKEFIELD TRINITY WILDCATS 12

CITY REDS: 6 Stefan Ratchford; 2 Jodie Broughton; 5 Ashley Gibson; 4 Willie Talau; 20 Steve Tyrer; 26 Marc Sneyd; 14 Matty Smith; 8 Ray Cashmere; 7 Jeremy Smith; 22 Adam Neal; 11 Ian Sibbit; 15 Stuart Littler (C); 13 Luke Swain. Subs (all used): 10 Rob Parker; 18 Lee Jewitt; 16 Phil Leuluai; 28 Gareth Owen.
Tries: Tyrer (49), Cashmere (59), Littler (73);
Goals: Tyrer 2/3.
WILDCATS: 1 Matt Blaymire; 2 Damien Blanch; 3 Sean Gleeson; 4 Darryl Millard; 18 Aaron Murphy; 6 Ben Jeffries; 14 Sam Obst; 19 Paul King; 20 Tevita Leo-Latu; 25 Richard Moore; 11 Dale Ferguson; 13 Jason Demetriou (C); 12 Glenn Morrison. Subs (all used): 10 Michael Korkidas; 17 Kevin Henderson; 31 Ben Gledhill; 36 Julien Rinaldi.
Tries: Leo-Latu (42), Gleeson (78); **Goals:** Jeffries 2/2.
Rugby Leaguer & League Express Men of the Match: *City Reds:* Stefan Ratchford; *Wildcats:* Tevita Leo-Latu.
Penalty count: 5-2; **Half-time:** 0-0;
Referee: Gareth Hewer; **Attendance:** 3,401.

PLAY-OFFS

QUALIFYING PLAY-OFF

Friday 10th September 2010

ST HELENS 28 WARRINGTON WOLVES 12

SAINTS: 1 Paul Wellens; 30 Jamie Foster; 3 Matt Gidley; 5 Francis Meli; 2 Ade Gardner; 12 Jon Wilkin; 34 Matty Smith (D2); 10 James Graham; 9 Keiron Cunningham (C); 15 Bryn Hargreaves; 4 Iosia Soliola; 13 Chris Flannery; 11 Tony Puletua. Subs (all used): 14 James Roby; 17 Paul Clough; 22 Andrew Dixon; 25 Jacob Emmitt.
Tries: Wellens (14), Cunningham (21), Graham (35), Flannery (57); **Goals:** Foster 6/8.
WOLVES: 1 Richard Mathers; 3 Matt King; 4 Chris Bridge; 23 Ryan Atkins; 2 Chris Riley; 6 Lee Briers; 9 Michael Monaghan; 8 Adrian Morley (C); 15 Jon Clarke; 10 Garreth Carvell; 11 Louis Anderson; 12 Ben Westwood; 13 Ben Harrison. Subs (all used): 7 Richard Myler; 16 Paul Wood; 26 David Solomona; 18 Michael Cooper.
Tries: King (3, 6), Bridge (62);
Goals: Westwood 0/2, Bridge 0/1.
Rugby Leaguer & League Express Men of the Match: *Saints:* Matty Smith; *Wolves:* Matt King.
Penalty count: 9-6; **Half-time:** 18-8;
Referee: Richard Silverwood; **Attendance:** 14,632.

ELIMINATION PLAY-OFFS

Saturday 11th September 2010

HUDDERSFIELD GIANTS 18 CRUSADERS 12

GIANTS: 1 Brett Hodgson (C); 2 Leroy Cudjoe; 19 Michael Lawrence; 11 Lee Gilmour; 5 David Hodgson; 6 Kevin Brown; 7 Luke Robinson; 16 Darrell Griffin; 34 Danny Brough; 33 Graeme Horne; 9 Shaun Lunt; 12 David Fa'alogo; 13 Stephen Wild. Subs (all used): 8 Eorl Crabtree; 17 Danny Kirmond; 20 David Faiumu; 23 Larne Patrick.
Tries: Robinson (44), Patrick (72), Cudjoe (77);
Goals: B Hodgson 3/3.
CRUSADERS: 26 Clinton Schifcofske (C); 14 Luke Dyer; 3 Tony Martin; 4 Vince Mellars; 2 Nick Youngquest; 7 Jarrod Sammut; 27 Rhys Hanbury; 8 Ryan O'Hara; 9 Lincoln Withers; 10 Mark Bryant; 11 Weller Hauraki; 12 Jason Chan; 23 Peter Lupton. Subs (all used): 15 Tommy Lee; 16 Frank Winterstein; 13 Rocky Trimarchi; 19 Jordan James.
Try: Hanbury (37); **Goals:** Schifcofske 4/4.
Sin bin: James (69) - delaying restart.
Rugby Leaguer & League Express Men of the Match: *Giants:* Luke Robinson; *Crusaders:* Clinton Schifcofske.
Penalty count: 5-3; **Half-time:** 0-8;
Referee: Richard Silverwood; **Attendance:** 5,869.

HULL FC 4 HULL KINGSTON ROVERS 21

HULL: 24 Craig Hall; 25 Reece Lyne; 19 Jordan Turner; 9 Shaun Berrigan; 3 Tom Briscoe; 6 Richard Horne; 7 Sean Long (C); 11 Lee Radford; 20 Danny Houghton; 10 Mark O'Meley; 16 Willie Manu; 12 Danny Tickle; 13 Craig Fitzgibbon. Subs (all used): 14 Danny Washbrook; 15 Epalahame Lauaki; 17 Peter Cusack; 23 Sam Moa.
Try: Briscoe (51); **Goals:** Tickle 0/1.
On report: Alleged biting (38) on Murrell.
ROVERS: 1 Shaun Briscoe; 2 Peter Fox; 28 Ben Cockayne; 3 Kris Welham; 5 Liam Colbon; 9 Scott Murrell; 7 Michael Dobson; 20 Michael Vella (C); 17 Ben Fisher; 30 Joel Clinton; 11 Clint Newton; 13 Ben Galea; 16 Jason Netherton. Subs (all used): 8 Rhys Lovegrove; 10 Scott Wheeldon; 14 Matt Cook; 21 Josh Hodgson.
Tries: Fox (10), Fisher (29), Welham (75);
Goals: Dobson 4/4; **Field goal:** Murrell (77).
Rugby Leaguer & League Express Men of the Match: *Hull:* Tom Briscoe; *Rovers:* Scott Murrell.
Penalty count: 8-6; **Half-time:** 0-12;
Referee: Phil Bentham; **Attendance:** 17,699.

QUALIFYING PLAY-OFF

Sunday 12th September 2010

WIGAN WARRIORS 26 LEEDS RHINOS 27

WARRIORS: 6 Sam Tomkins; 24 Darrell Goulding; 3 Martin Gleeson; 4 George Carmont; 5 Pat Richards; 19 Paul Deacon; 7 Thomas Leuluai; 8 Stuart Fielden; 9 Mark Riddell; 10 Andy Coley (C); 25 Liam Farrell; 12 Joel Tomkins; 13 Sean O'Loughlin. Subs (all used): 11 Harrison Hansen; 14 Paul Prescott; 29 Chris Tuson; 15 Michael McIlorum.
Tries: S Tomkins (3, 5), Farrell (48), Richards (65);
Goals: Richards 5/8.
RHINOS: 1 Brent Webb; 5 Ryan Hall; 3 Brett Delaney; 4 Keith Senior; 2 Scott Donald; 6 Danny McGuire; 7 Rob Burrow; 8 Kylie Leuluai; 9 Danny Buderus; 16 Ryan Bailey; 18 Carl Ablett; 17 Ian Kirke; 13 Kevin Sinfield (C). Subs (all used): 14 Matt Diskin; 15 Greg Eastwood; 27 Chris Clarkson; 12 Ali Lauitiiti.
Tries: Buderus (23), Hall (27), McGuire (43), Donald (62); **Goals:** Sinfield 5/5; **Field goal:** Sinfield (76).
On report:
Buderus (30) - alleged dangerous tackle on Prescott.
Rugby Leaguer & League Express Men of the Match: *Warriors:* Sam Tomkins; *Rhinos:* Greg Eastwood.
Penalty count: 10-6; **Half-time:** 14-14;
Referee: Thierry Alibert; **Attendance:** 12,117.

Huddersfield's Lee Gilmour beats Warrington's Richard Mathers to the ball for a crucial try

PRELIMINARY SEMI-FINALS

Friday 17th September 2010

WIGAN WARRIORS 42 HULL KINGSTON ROVERS 18

WARRIORS: 6 Sam Tomkins; 24 Darrell Goulding; 3 Martin Gleeson; 4 George Carmont; 5 Pat Richards; 13 Sean O'Loughlin; 7 Thomas Leuluai (C); 8 Stuart Fielden; 9 Mark Riddell; 10 Andy Coley; 12 Joel Tomkins; 11 Harrison Hansen; 25 Liam Farrell. Subs (all used): 17 Iafeta Palea'aesina; 14 Paul Prescott; 29 Chris Tuson; 15 Michael McIlorum.
Tries: Richards (4), Farrell (14), Goulding (23, 37), Leuluai (52), Gleeson (55), J Tomkins (69);
Goals: Richards 7/7.
ROVERS: 1 Shaun Briscoe; 2 Peter Fox; 3 Kris Welham; 28 Ben Cockayne; 5 Liam Colbon; 9 Scott Murrell; 7 Michael Dobson; 20 Michael Vella (C); 17 Ben Fisher; 30 Joel Clinton; 11 Clint Newton; 13 Ben Galea; 16 Jason Netherton. Subs (all used): 8 Rhys Lovegrove; 10 Scott Wheeldon; 14 Matt Cook; 21 Josh Hodgson.
Tries: Fox (7, 67), Cockayne (9); **Goals:** Dobson 3/4.
Rugby Leaguer & League Express Men of the Match: *Warriors:* Sam Tomkins; *Rovers:* Peter Fox.
Penalty count: 11-12; **Half-time:** 24-14;
Referee: Richard Silverwood; **Attendance:** 11,133.

Saturday 18th September 2010

WARRINGTON WOLVES 22 HUDDERSFIELD GIANTS 34

WOLVES: 1 Richard Mathers; 3 Chris Hicks; 3 Matt King; 23 Ryan Atkins; 2 Chris Riley; 6 Lee Briers; 9 Michael Monaghan; 8 Adrian Morley (C); 15 Jon Clarke; 10 Garreth Carvell; 11 Louis Anderson; 12 Ben Westwood; 27 Vinnie Anderson. Subs (all used): 14 Mick Higham; 16 Paul Wood; 26 David Solomona; 4 Chris Bridge.
Tries: Higham (44, 65), Hicks (58, 73);
Goals: Westwood 3/4.
GIANTS: 1 Brett Hodgson (C); 2 Leroy Cudjoe; 19 Michael Lawrence; 11 Lee Gilmour; 5 David Hodgson; 6 Kevin Brown; 7 Luke Robinson; 10 Keith Mason; 34 Danny Brough; 33 Graeme Horne; 17 Danny Kirmond; 12 David Fa'alogo; 13 Stephen Wild. Subs (all used): 8 Eorl Crabtree; 9 Shaun Lunt; 20 David Faiumu; 23 Larne Patrick.
Tries: Wild (2), Kirmond (13), Gilmour (20), Brown (33), Cudjoe (79); **Goals:** B Hodgson 6/8;
Field goals: Brough (40, 76).
Rugby Leaguer & League Express Men of the Match: *Wolves:* Mick Higham; *Giants:* Danny Brough.
Penalty count: 5-5; **Half-time:** 0-23;
Referee: Phil Bentham; **Attendance:** 8,050.

QUALIFYING SEMI-FINALS

Friday 24th September 2010

ST HELENS 42 HUDDERSFIELD GIANTS 22

SAINTS: 1 Paul Wellens; 30 Jamie Foster; 3 Matt Gidley; 4 Iosia Soliola; 5 Francis Meli; 34 Matty Smith; 7 Kyle Eastmond; 10 James Graham; 9 Keiron Cunningham (C); 15 Bryn Hargreaves; 12 Jon Wilkin; 13 Chris Flannery; 11 Tony Puletua. Subs (all used): 14 James Roby; 17 Paul Clough; 22 Andrew Dixon; 25 Jacob Emmitt.
Tries: Hargreaves (6, 12), Wellens (36, 55), Puletua (62), Meli (68), Cunningham (74); **Goals:** Foster 7/7.
GIANTS: 1 Brett Hodgson (C); 2 Leroy Cudjoe; 19 Michael Lawrence; 11 Lee Gilmour; 5 David Hodgson; 6 Kevin Brown; 7 Luke Robinson; 16 Darrell Griffin; 34 Danny Brough; 10 Keith Mason; 9 Shaun Lunt; 12 David Fa'alogo; 13 Stephen Wild. Subs (all used): 8 Eorl Crabtree; 17 Danny Kirmond; 20 David Faiumu; 23 Larne Patrick.
Tries: Lunt (22), Lawrence (27, 40), Gilmour (48);
Goals: B Hodgson 3/4.
Rugby Leaguer & League Express Men of the Match: *Saints:* Keiron Cunningham; *Giants:* Brett Hodgson.
Penalty count: 7-8; **Half-time:** 18-16;
Referee: Phil Bentham; **Attendance:** 13,510.

Saturday 25th September 2010

LEEDS RHINOS 6 WIGAN WARRIORS 26

RHINOS: 1 Brent Webb; 2 Scott Donald; 4 Keith Senior; 3 Brett Delaney; 5 Ryan Hall; 13 Kevin Sinfield (C); 7 Rob Burrow; 8 Kylie Leuluai; 9 Danny Buderus; 16 Ryan Bailey; 18 Carl Ablett; 17 Ian Kirke; 11 Jamie Jones-Buchanan. Subs (all used): 15 Greg Eastwood; 12 Ali Lauitiiti; 27 Chris Clarkson; 14 Matt Diskin.
Try: Sinfield (17); **Goals:** Sinfield 1/1.
WARRIORS: 6 Sam Tomkins; 24 Darrell Goulding; 3 Martin Gleeson; 4 George Carmont; 5 Pat Richards; 19 Paul Deacon; 7 Thomas Leuluai; 8 Stuart Fielden; 9 Mark Riddell; 10 Andy Coley (C); 11 Harrison Hansen; 12 Joel Tomkins; 13 Sean O'Loughlin. Subs (all used): 9 Mark Riddell; 17 Iafeta Palea'aesina; 14 Paul Prescott.
Tries: Goulding (35), J Tomkins (42), Carmont (45), Gleeson (79); **Goals:** Richards 5/5.
Rugby Leaguer & League Express Men of the Match: *Rhinos:* Brent Webb; *Warriors:* George Carmont.
Penalty count: 6-9; **Half-time:** 6-8;
Referee: Richard Silverwood; **Attendance:** 13,692.

GRAND FINAL

Saturday 2nd October 2010

ST HELENS 10 WIGAN WARRIORS 22

SAINTS: 1 Paul Wellens; 30 Jamie Foster; 3 Matt Gidley; 5 Francis Meli; 2 Jonny Lomax; 12 Jon Wilkin; 34 Matty Smith; 10 James Graham; 9 Keiron Cunningham (C); 15 Bryn Hargreaves; 4 Iosia Soliola; 13 Chris Flannery; 11 Tony Puletua. Subs (all used): 17 Paul Clough; 14 James Roby; 22 Andrew Dixon; 25 Jacob Emmitt.
Tries: Dixon (28), Meli (74); **Goals:** Foster 1/2.
WARRIORS: 6 Sam Tomkins; 24 Darrell Goulding; 3 Martin Gleeson; 4 George Carmont; 5 Pat Richards; 19 Paul Deacon; 7 Thomas Leuluai; 8 Stuart Fielden; 9 Mark Riddell; 17 Iafeta Palea'aesina; 25 Liam Farrell; 14 Paul Prescott.
Tries: Gleeson (4, 16), Goulding (20), S Tomkins (53);
Goals: Richards 2/3, Riddell 1/3, S Tomkins 0/1.
Rugby Leaguer & League Express Men of the Match: *Saints:* Tony Puletua; *Warriors:* Thomas Leuluai.
Penalty count: 6-11; **Half time:** 6-16;
Referee: Richard Silverwood;
Attendance: 71,526 *(at Old Trafford, Manchester)*.

Wigan's Thomas Leuluai halted by St Helens duo Jon Wilkin and Tony Puletua during the
Super League Grand Final

SUPER LEAGUE XV
Opta Analysis

SUPER LEAGUE XV
TOP PERFORMERS

TACKLES
Dallas Johnson	Catalans	1106
Malcolm Alker	Salford	964
Heath L'Estrange	Bradford	944
Luke Swain	Salford	910
Danny Houghton	Hull FC	843
Lincoln Withers	Crusaders	831
Craig Fitzgibbon	Hull FC	829
Rhys Lovegrove	Hull KR	787
Sean O'Loughlin	Wigan	783
Ryan Hudson	Castleford	773

TACKLES MADE *(% success)*
Liam Farrell	Wigan	99.04
Martin Aspinwall	Huddersfield	98.18
Eorl Crabtree	Huddersfield	98.15
Nick Fozzard	St Helens	97.95
Paul Clough	St Helens	97.82
Jacob Emmitt	St Helens	97.50
Luke Adamson	Salford	97.44
Sean O'Loughlin	Wigan	97.39
Stephen Wild	Huddersfield	97.00
Jon Wilkin	St Helens	97.00

OFFLOADS
Andy Lynch	Bradford	75
David Faiumu	Huddersfield	69
Leon Pryce	St Helens	64
Keith Senior	Leeds	61
Will Sharp	Harlequins	53
Paul Wood	Warrington	53
Steve Menzies	Bradford	50
Tony Clubb	Harlequins	47
James Roby	St Helens	46
David Solomona	Warrington	46

CLEAN BREAKS
David Hodgson	Huddersfield	25
Danny McGuire	Leeds	25
Pat Richards	Wigan	25
Sam Tomkins	Wigan	23
Kevin Brown	Huddersfield	22
Chris Riley	Warrington	21
Matt King	Warrington	20
Darrell Goulding	Wigan	19
Ryan Hall	Leeds	19
Peter Fox	Hull KR	18

TRY ASSISTS
Rangi Chase	Castleford	31
Michael Dobson	Hull KR	30
Leon Pryce	St Helens	23
Kevin Brown	Huddersfield	20
Danny McGuire	Leeds	18
Sam Tomkins	Wigan	18
Lee Briers	Warrington	17
Sean O'Loughlin	Wigan	16
Brett Hodgson	Huddersfield	15
Luke Robinson	Huddersfield	15

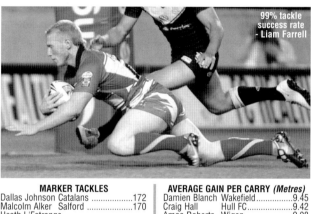

99% tackle success rate
- Liam Farrell

MARKER TACKLES
Dallas Johnson	Catalans	172
Malcolm Alker	Salford	170
Heath L'Estrange	Bradford	163
Joel Tomkins	Wigan	134
Glenn Morrison	Wakefield	122
Luke Swain	Salford	122
Lincoln Withers	Crusaders	121
Ryan Hudson	Castleford	118
Ben Fisher	Hull KR	117
Sean O'Loughlin	Wigan	116

METRES
James Graham	St Helens	4036
James Roby	St Helens	3749
Pat Richards	Wigan	3670
Nick Youngquest	Crusaders	3347
Ryan McGoldrick	Castleford	3189
Peter Fox	Hull KR	3100
Andy Lynch	Bradford	3074
David Hodgson	Huddersfield	3073
Rhys Lovegrove	Hull KR	3029
Rangi Chase	Castleford	3006

CARRIES
Rangi Chase	Castleford	653
James Graham	St Helens	598
James Roby	St Helens	529
Ryan McGoldrick	Castleford	511
Andy Lynch	Bradford	506
Danny McGuire	Leeds	489
Pat Richards	Wigan	444
Kevin Brown	Huddersfield	428
Will Sharp	Harlequins	420
Thomas Leuluai	Wigan	419

*All statistics in Opta Analysis include
Super League regular season games only*

AVERAGE GAIN PER CARRY *(Metres)*
Damien Blanch	Wakefield	9.45
Craig Hall	Hull FC	9.42
Amos Roberts	Wigan	9.08
Peter Fox	Hull KR	8.71
Pat Richards	Wigan	8.41
Tom Briscoe	Hull FC	8.34
Matt King	Warrington	8.34
Nick Youngquest	Crusaders	8.31
Larne Patrick	Huddersfield	8.28
Darrell Goulding	Wigan	8.21

TACKLE BUSTS
Sam Tomkins	Wigan	103
Rangi Chase	Castleford	102
Willie Manu	Hull FC	99
James Roby	St Helens	84
Matt King	Warrington	79
Ryan Hall	Leeds	78
Pat Richards	Wigan	74
Stuart Fielden	Wigan	73
Peter Fox	Hull KR	73
Leon Pryce	St Helens	72

40/20s
Michael Dobson	Hull KR	5
Matty Smith	St Helens/Salford	4
Michael Monaghan	Warrington	3
Scott Murrell	Hull KR	3
Casey McGuire	Catalans	2
Brent Sherwin	Catalans/Castleford	2
Jordan Tansey	Hull FC	2
Marc Sneyd	Salford	2
Leon Pryce	St Helens	2
Sam Obst	Wakefield	2

PENALTIES CONCEDED
Joel Tomkins	Wigan	33
Heath L'Estrange	Bradford	28
Jon Wilkin	St Helens	26
Olivier Elima	Catalans	25
David Howell	Harlequins	24
Stuart Littler	Salford	24
Glenn Morrison	Wakefield	24
Adam Sidlow	Salford	24
Andy Coley	Wigan	23
Liam Watts	Hull KR	23

St Helens' Leon Pryce crashes over the Salford tryline to score. Saints scored 169 tries in 2010, the most in Super League XV

SUPER LEAGUE XV AVERAGES PER MATCH

TACKLES	OFFLOADS	METRES	ERRORS
Salford City Reds 324.0	Leeds Rhinos 17.2	St Helens....................1372.7	Harlequins.....................14.8
Huddersfield Giants.....319.6	Warrington Wolves 16.1	Warrington Wolves 1362.3	Warrington Wolves 14.7
Catalans Dragons 318.3	Harlequins.....................15.0	Leeds Rhinos 1357.3	Leeds Rhinos 14.1
Harlequins....................314.3	St Helens......................13.7	Wigan Warriors 1350.3	Wakefield T Wildcats.....13.9
Hull Kingston Rovers ..313.2	Bradford Bulls 13.0	Huddersfield Giants....1322.4	Huddersfield Giants........13.3
Crusaders 309.1	Hull FC 12.9	Wakefield T Wildcats..1282.9	Catalans Dragons 13.1
Hull FC 306.5	Salford City Reds 12.8	Hull FC 1272.9	Bradford Bulls 12.8
Wakefield T Wildcats...300.9	Crusaders 12.0	Hull Kingston Rovers 1267.7	Salford City Reds 12.8
Bradford Bulls 298.1	Huddersfield Giants.......10.9	Crusaders 1235.4	Crusaders 11.8
Wigan Warriors 293.8	Wakefield T Wildcats.....10.7	Castleford Tigers 1234.6	Castleford Tigers 11.7
Leeds Rhinos 293.0	Catalans Dragons 10.6	Bradford Bulls 1198.1	Hull FC 11.6
Castleford Tigers..........291.4	Wigan Warriors 9.4	Harlequins..................1182.0	Hull Kingston Rovers 11.6
Warrington Wolves 289.9	Castleford Tigers 9.1	Catalans Dragons 1158.5	St Helens.......................11.6
St Helens......................287.7	Hull Kingston Rovers 7.5	Salford City Reds 1080.4	Wigan Warriors..............11.4

MISSED TACKLES	CLEAN BREAKS	CARRIES	KICKS IN GENERAL PLAY
Harlequins......................31.3	Warrington Wolves 6.2	St Helens......................213.7	Hull Kingston Rovers 20.6
Hull Kingston Rovers 29.3	Wigan Warriors 6.0	Leeds Rhinos 213.3	Salford City Reds 20.4
Wakefield T Wildcats.....25.9	Huddersfield Giants.........5.9	Huddersfield Giants.....206.2	Huddersfield Giants........20.0
Catalans Dragons 24.5	Leeds Rhinos 5.7	Bradford Bulls 204.3	Catalans Dragons 19.7
Castleford Tigers...........24.1	St Helens........................5.4	Wigan Warriors 201.3	Hull FC 19.6
Warrington Wolves 23.6	Hull Kingston Rovers 5.0	Warrington Wolves 200.0	Crusaders 19.2
Bradford Bulls 23.4	Hull FC 4.5	Hull FC 198.0	Castleford Tigers 18.9
Crusaders 23.0	Harlequins.......................4.5	Crusaders 197.7	Wigan Warriors..............18.6
Leeds Rhinos 22.2	Salford City Reds 4.0	Harlequins...................197.7	Wakefield T Wildcats......18.5
Hull FC 20.3	Crusaders 4.0	Salford City Reds 197.4	Bradford Bulls 18.2
Salford City Reds 20.2	Catalans Dragons 3.9	Castleford Tigers 197.1	St Helens.......................17.9
Huddersfield Giants.......17.5	Bradford Bulls 3.9	Wakefield T Wildcats....196.1	Harlequins.....................17.7
St Helens.......................17.3	Wakefield T Wildcats.......3.8	Catalans Dragons 195.8	Warrington Wolves 17.0
Wigan Warriors..............14.7	Castleford Tigers.............3.3	Hull Kingston Rovers ..190.4	Leeds Rhinos 16.9

SUPER LEAGUE XV TRIES SCORED/CONCEDED

TOTAL TRIES SCORED	TOTAL TRIES CONCEDED	SCORED FROM KICKS	CONCEDED FROM KICKS
St Helens 169	Salford City Reds 154	Castleford Tigers 29	Catalans Dragons..............29
Warrington Wolves..........162	Harlequins 148	Warrington Wolves............29	Castleford Tigers 28
Wigan Warriors 161	Castleford Tigers 136	Wigan Warriors 26	Crusaders.........................21
Huddersfield Giants 139	Catalans Dragons 132	Huddersfield Giants 24	Salford City Reds 21
Leeds Rhinos 126	Wakefield T Wildcats 131	St Helens 19	Wakefield T Wildcats 21
Castleford Tigers 115	Bradford Bulls 128	Hull Kingston Rovers 17	Bradford Bulls 19
Hull Kingston Rovers 110	Crusaders 127	Wakefield T Wildcats 17	Hull FC 18
Hull FC 97	Hull Kingston Rovers 113	Catalans Dragons..............16	Hull Kingston Rovers 18
Wakefield T Wildcats 97	Hull FC 102	Salford City Reds 16	Leeds Rhinos 18
Bradford Bulls 94	St Helens 98	Crusaders.........................15	Harlequins.........................17
Crusaders..........................94	Leeds Rhinos 96	Harlequins 15	St Helens 17
Harlequins 86	Warrington Wolves............88	Bradford Bulls 14	Huddersfield Giants 14
Salford City Reds 78	Wigan Warriors 75	Hull FC 14	Warrington Wolves............14
Catalans Dragons 74	Huddersfield Giants 74	Leeds Rhinos 14	Wigan Warriors 10

SUPER LEAGUE XV TRIES SCORED/CONCEDED

TRIES SCORED FROM OWN HALF
Huddersfield Giants	22
Warrington Wolves	22
Wigan Warriors	22
Hull Kingston Rovers	21
Harlequins	18
Leeds Rhinos	16
Wakefield T Wildcats	15
Salford City Reds	14
St Helens	13
Castleford Tigers	12
Hull FC	12
Crusaders	11
Bradford Bulls	9
Catalans Dragons	3

TRIES CONCEDED FROM OVER 50M
Bradford Bulls	26
Wakefield T Wildcats	26
Castleford Tigers	18
Harlequins	18
Salford City Reds	17
Catalans Dragons	16
Hull FC	14
Hull Kingston Rovers	14
Crusaders	13
Warrington Wolves	12
Huddersfield Giants	9
Leeds Rhinos	9
St Helens	9
Wigan Warriors	9

TRIES SCORED FROM UNDER 10M
St Helens	88
Warrington Wolves	87
Wigan Warriors	69
Castleford Tigers	61
Huddersfield Giants	53
Leeds Rhinos	53
Bradford Bulls	49
Wakefield T Wildcats	49
Hull FC	46
Crusaders	45
Hull Kingston Rovers	44
Catalans Dragons	37
Harlequins	34
Salford City Reds	33

TRIES CONCEDED FROM UNDER 10M
Salford City Reds	89
Catalans Dragons	60
Castleford Tigers	59
Wakefield T Wildcats	57
St Helens	55
Bradford Bulls	54
Crusaders	54
Harlequins	54
Leeds Rhinos	54
Hull Kingston Rovers	48
Hull FC	43
Wigan Warriors	43
Huddersfield Giants	39
Warrington Wolves	39

TOTAL PENALTIES AWARDED
Warrington Wolves	241
Wigan Warriors	235
Bradford Bulls	230
Wakefield T Wildcats	227
Castleford Tigers	222
St Helens	222
Hull FC	218
Hull Kingston Rovers	218
Leeds Rhinos	217
Catalans Dragons	211
Crusaders	198
Huddersfield Giants	195
Salford City Reds	172
Harlequins	168

TOTAL PENALTIES CONCEDED
Wigan Warriors	227
Hull FC	226
Bradford Bulls	220
Salford City Reds	220
Crusaders	219
Leeds Rhinos	217
Castleford Tigers	214
St Helens	214
Catalans Dragons	213
Huddersfield Giants	208
Wakefield T Wildcats	207
Harlequins	203
Warrington Wolves	196
Hull Kingston Rovers	190

FOUL PLAY - AWARDED
Catalans Dragons	50
Huddersfield Giants	43
Wigan Warriors	42
Hull FC	41
Harlequins	40
St Helens	40
Crusaders	35
Bradford Bulls	34
Castleford Tigers	33
Hull Kingston Rovers	33
Leeds Rhinos	31
Warrington Wolves	31
Salford City Reds	30
Wakefield T Wildcats	25

FOUL PLAY - CONCEDED
Catalans Dragons	48
Hull Kingston Rovers	47
Salford City Reds	45
Crusaders	43
Hull FC	43
Castleford Tigers	39
St Helens	37
Wakefield T Wildcats	36
Huddersfield Giants	33
Leeds Rhinos	33
Wigan Warriors	33
Warrington Wolves	29
Bradford Bulls	25
Harlequins	20

OFFSIDE - AWARDED
Hull Kingston Rovers	30
Bradford Bulls	29
Castleford Tigers	27
Hull FC	26
St Helens	24
Leeds Rhinos	23
Warrington Wolves	23
Wakefield T Wildcats	22
Huddersfield Giants	20
Crusaders	19
Salford City Reds	19
Wigan Warriors	17
Catalans Dragons	16
Harlequins	10

OFFSIDE - CONCEDED
Leeds Rhinos	30
St Helens	30
Wigan Warriors	28
Bradford Bulls	27
Wakefield T Wildcats	27
Castleford Tigers	26
Huddersfield Giants	23
Hull Kingston Rovers	21
Salford City Reds	20
Harlequins	18
Warrington Wolves	17
Hull FC	14
Crusaders	13
Catalans Dragons	11

SUPER LEAGUE XV PENALTIES

INTERFERENCE - AWARDED
Wakefield T Wildcats	98
Warrington Wolves	98
Wigan Warriors	91
Castleford Tigers	86
Leeds Rhinos	83
Hull FC	79
Bradford Bulls	77
Catalans Dragons	71
Hull Kingston Rovers	71
St Helens	69
Salford City Reds	65
Crusaders	62
Huddersfield Giants	55
Harlequins	52

INTERFERENCE - CONCEDED
Hull FC	91
Crusaders	87
Harlequins	84
Catalans Dragons	79
Wigan Warriors	79
Salford City Reds	75
Bradford Bulls	74
Castleford Tigers	74
Huddersfield Giants	74
Wakefield T Wildcats	74
St Helens	70
Warrington Wolves	69
Leeds Rhinos	64
Hull Kingston Rovers	63

OBSTRUCTION - AWARDED
St Helens	16
Warrington Wolves	16
Bradford Bulls	14
Huddersfield Giants	13
Castleford Tigers	12
Crusaders	11
Leeds Rhinos	11
Catalans Dragons	10
Wigan Warriors	10
Harlequins	9
Hull FC	9
Hull Kingston Rovers	9
Salford City Reds	8
Wakefield T Wildcats	5

OBSTRUCTION - CONCEDED
Bradford Bulls	15
St Helens	14
Wakefield T Wildcats	14
Castleford Tigers	13
Salford City Reds	13
Hull Kingston Rovers	12
Catalans Dragons	10
Crusaders	10
Huddersfield Giants	10
Leeds Rhinos	10
Hull FC	9
Harlequins	8
Wigan Warriors	8
Warrington Wolves	7

BALL STEALING - AWARDED
Wakefield T Wildcats	21
Bradford Bulls	20
Hull FC	20
Warrington Wolves	17
Crusaders	16
Hull Kingston Rovers	16
Catalans Dragons	15
Huddersfield Giants	15
Castleford Tigers	13
Harlequins	12
Leeds Rhinos	12
St Helens	11
Salford City Reds	10
Wigan Warriors	8

BALL STEALING - CONCEDED
Harlequins	22
Warrington Wolves	22
Leeds Rhinos	21
St Helens	20
Bradford Bulls	19
Hull FC	16
Wigan Warriors	15
Hull Kingston Rovers	14
Huddersfield Giants	12
Catalans Dragons	11
Crusaders	9
Salford City Reds	9
Wakefield T Wildcats	9
Castleford Tigers	7

OFFSIDE MARKERS - AWARDED
Wigan Warriors	23
Bradford Bulls	22
Leeds Rhinos	22
Hull Kingston Rovers	19
Wakefield T Wildcats	19
Warrington Wolves	19
Castleford Tigers	17
Catalans Dragons	17
St Helens	17
Hull FC	15
Crusaders	14
Huddersfield Giants	14
Harlequins	7
Salford City Reds	6

OFFSIDE MARKERS - CONCEDED
Castleford Tigers	22
Huddersfield Giants	22
Salford City Reds	21
Warrington Wolves	21
Bradford Bulls	19
Wigan Warriors	19
Hull FC	18
Harlequins	16
Leeds Rhinos	16
Wakefield T Wildcats	14
St Helens	13
Crusaders	12
Catalans Dragons	11
Hull Kingston Rovers	7

NOT PLAYING BALL CORRECTLY - AWARDED
Hull FC	6
Bradford Bulls	4
Castleford Tigers	3
Salford City Reds	3
St Helens	3
Wakefield T Wildcats	3
Catalans Dragons	2
Harlequins	2
Huddersfield Giants	2
Leeds Rhinos	2
Warrington Wolves	2
Wigan Warriors	2
Hull Kingston Rovers	1
Crusaders	0

NOT PLAYING BALL CORRECTLY - CONCEDED
Bradford Bulls	4
Catalans Dragons	4
Crusaders	4
Huddersfield Giants	4
Hull FC	4
Castleford Tigers	3
Harlequins	3
Leeds Rhinos	3
St Helens	2
Wakefield T Wildcats	2
Wigan Warriors	2
Hull Kingston Rovers	0
Salford City Reds	0
Warrington Wolves	0

DISSENT - AWARDED
Wakefield T Wildcats	10
Harlequins	9
Crusaders	8
Hull Kingston Rovers	7
Salford City Reds	6
Catalans Dragons	5
Castleford Tigers	4
Wigan Warriors	4
Leeds Rhinos	3
St Helens	3
Warrington Wolves	2
Bradford Bulls	1
Huddersfield Giants	1
Hull FC	1

DISSENT - CONCEDED
Hull FC	9
Bradford Bulls	7
Catalans Dragons	7
Leeds Rhinos	7
Crusaders	6
Warrington Wolves	5
Harlequins	4
Wigan Warriors	4
Hull Kingston Rovers	3
Salford City Reds	3
Wakefield T Wildcats	3
Castleford Tigers	2
Huddersfield Giants	2
St Helens	2

BRADFORD BULLS

Andy Lynch

Heath
L'Estrange

MARKER TACKLES
Heath L'Estrange	163
Jamie Langley	108
Wayne Godwin	100
Elliott Whitehead	92
Michael Worrincy	85

METRES
Andy Lynch	3074
Jamie Langley	2539
Brett Kearney	2320
Rikki Sheriffe	1986
Nick Scruton	1948

CARRIES
Andy Lynch	506
Heath L'Estrange	401
Brett Kearney	380
Jamie Langley	378
Paul Sykes	323

TACKLES
Heath L'Estrange	944
Andy Lynch	682
Jamie Langley	638
Steve Menzies	626
Elliott Whitehead	563

CLEAN BREAKS
Brett Kearney	16
Steve Menzies	10
Chris Nero	10
Paul Sykes	10
Rikki Sheriffe	9

TACKLE BUSTS
Brett Kearney	51
Rikki Sheriffe	43
Andy Lynch	41
Chris Nero	34
Paul Sykes	34

OFFLOADS
Andy Lynch	75
Steve Menzies	50
Michael Platt	31
Dave Halley	26
Brett Kearney	20

TRY ASSISTS
Paul Sykes	13
Heath L'Estrange	11
Steve Menzies	8
Matt Orford	8
Brett Kearney	6

TOTAL OPTA INDEX
Andy Lynch	15981
Heath L'Estrange	13773
Brett Kearney	13157
Jamie Langley	12170
Paul Sykes	11938

CASTLEFORD TIGERS

Rangi Chase

Craig Huby

MARKER TACKLES
Ryan Hudson	118
Joe Westerman	110
Stuart Jones	87
Steve Snitch	84
Paul Jackson	67

METRES
Ryan McGoldrick	3189
Rangi Chase	3006
Craig Huby	2482
Steve Snitch	2188
Michael Wainwright	2128

CARRIES
Rangi Chase	653
Ryan McGoldrick	511
Craig Huby	413
Steve Snitch	323
Michael Wainwright	314

TACKLES
Ryan Hudson	773
Joe Westerman	723
Craig Huby	678
Steve Snitch	624
Stuart Jones	620

CLEAN BREAKS
Rangi Chase	10
Kirk Dixon	7
Brett Ferres	7
Michael Shenton	6
Dean Widders	6

TACKLE BUSTS
Rangi Chase	102
Joe Westerman	44
Steve Snitch	40
Ryan McGoldrick	31
Stuart Jones	30

OFFLOADS
Craig Huby	46
Rangi Chase	38
Mitchell Sargent	24
Joe Westerman	18
Ryan McGoldrick	14

TRY ASSISTS
Rangi Chase	31
Ryan Hudson	12
Ryan McGoldrick	11
Brent Sherwin	9
Brett Ferres	4

TOTAL OPTA INDEX
Rangi Chase	22313
Craig Huby	13002
Ryan Hudson	11991
Joe Westerman	11248
Ryan McGoldrick	11184

CATALANS DRAGONS

Casey
McGuire

Dallas
Johnson

TACKLES
Dallas Johnson 1106
Olivier Elima 676
Gregory Mounis.............618
Dane Carlaw 586
Jerome Guisset 527

OFFLOADS
Olivier Elima 32
David Ferriol 31
Setaimata Sa 31
Clint Greenshields 15
Remi Casty 14

CLEAN BREAKS
Clint Greenshields 13
Dane Carlaw 9
Olivier Elima 9
Sebastien Raguin...............9
Chris Walker 9

TRY ASSISTS
Thomas Bosc....................15
Olivier Elima 6
Casey McGuire 5
Brent Sherwin 5
Clint Greenshields 4

MARKER TACKLES
Dallas Johnson 172
Olivier Elima 77
Dane Carlaw 72
Jerome Guisset 71
David Ferriol 57

METRES
Dallas Johnson 2085
Olivier Elima 1989
Casey McGuire 1904
Jerome Guisset 1903
Dane Carlaw 1794

TACKLE BUSTS
Clint Greenshields 48
Steven Bell.......................42
Dimitri Pelo......................41
Sebastien Raguin.............30
Chris Walker 26

CARRIES
Dallas Johnson 412
Casey McGuire 399
Olivier Elima 294
Jerome Guisset 291
David Ferriol 274

TOTAL OPTA INDEX
Dallas Johnson 16184
Casey McGuire 12754
Brent Sherwin 12669
Dane Carlaw 10859
Olivier Elima 10425

CRUSADERS

Jason
Chan

Lincoln
Withers

TACKLES
Lincoln Withers 831
Mark Bryant....................720
Weller Hauraki 669
Ryan O'Hara 661
Jason Chan 653

OFFLOADS
Clinton Schifcofske 42
Weller Hauraki 36
Adam Peek 22
Mark Bryant.....................19
Ryan O'Hara 18

CLEAN BREAKS
Jarrod Sammut 14
Rhys Hanbury 11
Nick Youngquest 9
Weller Hauraki 8
Vince Mellars....................7

TRY ASSISTS
Rhys Hanbury 8
Lincoln Withers 8
Michael Witt 8
Jarrod Sammut 7
Weller Hauraki 5

MARKER TACKLES
Lincoln Withers 121
Ryan O'Hara 113
Mark Bryant....................108
Peter Lupton 106
Jason Chan 87

METRES
Nick Youngquest 3347
Clinton Schifcofske 2992
Jason Chan 2265
Weller Hauraki 2144
Mark Bryant..................2120

TACKLE BUSTS
Clinton Schifcofske 65
Jason Chan 58
Weller Hauraki 48
Rhys Hanbury 36
Nick Youngquest 36

CARRIES
Nick Youngquest 403
Clinton Schifcofske 394
Lincoln Withers 379
Mark Bryant....................345
Weller Hauraki 342

TOTAL OPTA INDEX
Lincoln Withers 13642
Jason Chan 13331
Weller Hauraki 12147
Mark Bryant...............11948
Ryan O'Hara 11649

HARLEQUINS

Danny Ward

MARKER TACKLES
Danny Ward	106
Chris Melling	93
Oliver Wilkes	92
Louie McCarthy-Scarsbrook	89
Jason Golden	80

METRES
Tony Clubb	2568
Jamie O'Callaghan	2516
Will Sharp	2490
Oliver Wilkes	2308
Danny Ward	2281

CARRIES
Will Sharp	420
Tony Clubb	383
Danny Ward	374
Jamie O'Callaghan	348
Louie McCarthy-Scarsbrook	342

Louie McCarthy-Scarsbrook

TACKLES
Oliver Wilkes	724
Chris Melling	708
Danny Ward	693
Louie McCarthy-Scarsbrook	618
Jason Golden	540

CLEAN BREAKS
Luke Dorn	16
Tony Clubb	10
David Howell	10
Ben Jones-Bishop	9
Chris Melling	8

OFFLOADS
Will Sharp	53
Tony Clubb	47
Danny Ward	28
Oliver Wilkes	25
David Howell	24

TRY ASSISTS
Chad Randall	11
Luke Gale	10
Tony Clubb	9
Luke Dorn	8
Danny Orr	5

TACKLE BUSTS
Will Sharp	61
Tony Clubb	57
Ben Jones-Bishop	48
Louie McCarthy-Scarsbrook	39
Luke Gale	32

TOTAL OPTA INDEX
Danny Ward	11362
Louie McCarthy-Scarsbrook	11360
Tony Clubb	11357
Chad Randall	10716
Will Sharp	10408

HUDDERSFIELD GIANTS

Danny Brough

MARKER TACKLES
Michael Lawrence	81
David Faiumu	80
Shaun Lunt	75
Lee Gilmour	72
Luke Robinson	71

METRES
David Hodgson	3073
Leroy Cudjoe	2608
Darrell Griffin	2343
Eorl Crabtree	2340
David Faiumu	2124

CARRIES
Kevin Brown	428
Luke Robinson	399
David Hodgson	371
Leroy Cudjoe	368
Darrell Griffin	349

Kevin Brown

TACKLES
Lee Gilmour	699
Luke Robinson	652
David Faiumu	631
Shaun Lunt	626
Michael Lawrence	554

CLEAN BREAKS
David Hodgson	25
Kevin Brown	22
Leroy Cudjoe	14
Shaun Lunt	10
Luke Robinson	9

OFFLOADS
David Faiumu	69
Leroy Cudjoe	37
Eorl Crabtree	31
Kevin Brown	25
David Fa'alogo	19

TRY ASSISTS
Kevin Brown	20
Brett Hodgson	15
Luke Robinson	15
Danny Brough	13
Leroy Cudjoe	4

TACKLE BUSTS
David Hodgson	55
Kevin Brown	54
Shaun Lunt	51
David Faiumu	49
Brett Hodgson	48

TOTAL OPTA INDEX
Danny Brough	16200
(includes Wakefield total)	
Kevin Brown	16089
David Hodgson	14650
Leroy Cudjoe	13963
Luke Robinson	13534

HULL F.C.

Danny Houghton

Craig Fitzgibbon

TACKLES
Danny Houghton	843
Craig Fitzgibbon	829
Ewan Dowes	649
Danny Tickle	598
Lee Radford	596

OFFLOADS
Danny Tickle	33
Kirk Yeaman	33
Sam Moa	32
Tom Briscoe	29
Willie Manu	29

CLEAN BREAKS
Tom Briscoe	15
Jordan Tansey	12
Craig Hall	11
Kirk Yeaman	11
Richard Horne	10

TRY ASSISTS
Jordan Tansey	9
Richard Horne	8
Craig Fitzgibbon	6
Sean Long	6
Danny Houghton	5

MARKER TACKLES
Craig Fitzgibbon	111
Danny Houghton	111
Ewan Dowes	92
Lee Radford	91
Mark O'Meley	71

METRES
Mark O'Meley	2424
Tom Briscoe	2274
Craig Fitzgibbon	2218
Lee Radford	2132
Jordan Tansey	2069

CARRIES
Craig Fitzgibbon	376
Mark O'Meley	348
Jordan Tansey	336
Lee Radford	331
Kirk Yeaman	321

TACKLE BUSTS
Willie Manu	99
Epalahame Lauaki	60
Jordan Tansey	55
Tom Briscoe	50
Kirk Yeaman	42

TOTAL OPTA INDEX
Craig Fitzgibbon	14195
Danny Houghton	13424
Jordan Tansey	13177
Willie Manu	12029
Ewan Dowes	11235

HULL KINGSTON ROVERS

Clint Newton

Michael Dobson

TACKLES
Rhys Lovegrove	787
Clint Newton	726
Ben Fisher	713
Liam Watts	633
Scott Murrell	568

OFFLOADS
Clint Newton	37
Liam Watts	25
Ben Cockayne	15
Rhys Lovegrove	12
Scott Murrell	12

CLEAN BREAKS
Peter Fox	18
Kris Welham	14
Clint Newton	13
Jake Webster	12
Michael Dobson	10

TRY ASSISTS
Michael Dobson	30
Scott Murrell	7
Liam Watts	6
Kris Welham	6
Ben Galea	5

MARKER TACKLES
Ben Fisher	117
Rhys Lovegrove	115
Clint Newton	90
Scott Murrell	84
Liam Watts	82

METRES
Peter Fox	3100
Rhys Lovegrove	3029
Michael Vella	2549
Clint Newton	2470
Joel Clinton	2230

CARRIES
Rhys Lovegrove	408
Michael Dobson	387
Michael Vella	370
Peter Fox	350
Clint Newton	337

TACKLE BUSTS
Peter Fox	73
Clint Newton	51
Ben Cockayne	39
Ben Galea	36
Rhys Lovegrove	35

TOTAL OPTA INDEX
Michael Dobson	20751
Clint Newton	14342
Rhys Lovegrove	12551
Peter Fox	12215
Scott Murrell	11380

LEEDS RHINOS

Danny McGuire

Kevin Sinfield

MARKER TACKLES
Kevin Sinfield....................92
Keith Senior......................91
Jamie Jones-Buchanan 81
Danny Buderus 80
Ian Kirke 79

METRES
Danny McGuire 2858
Ryan Hall 2811
Jamie Peacock..............2594
Keith Senior 2235
Jamie Jones-Buchanan..2183

CARRIES
Danny McGuire 489
Kevin Sinfield.................371
Jamie Peacock...............347
Ryan Hall 345
Brent Webb 333

TACKLES
Jamie Jones-Buchanan ..637
Kevin Sinfield.................585
Danny Buderus 576
Ian Kirke 522
Jamie Peacock...............514

CLEAN BREAKS
Danny McGuire 25
Ryan Hall 19
Keith Senior.....................13
Brett Delaney 9
Lee Smith 9

TACKLE BUSTS
Ryan Hall 78
Danny McGuire 60
Brent Webb 52
Keith Senior......................50
Greg Eastwood 38

OFFLOADS
Keith Senior......................61
Kevin Sinfield....................42
Jamie Peacock..................35
Ali Lauititi 34
Jamie Jones-Buchanan 33

TRY ASSISTS
Danny McGuire 18
Brent Webb 13
Kevin Sinfield.....................9
Rob Burrow 7
Keith Senior.......................7

TOTAL OPTA INDEX
Danny McGuire 18821
Kevin Sinfield..............17258
Keith Senior...............12629
Ryan Hall 11744
Jamie Jones-Buchanan..11210

SALFORD CITY REDS

Luke Swain

Malcolm Alker

MARKER TACKLES
Malcolm Alker 170
Luke Swain 122
Luke Adamson................108
Stuart Littler 68
Adam Sidlow 62

METRES
Jodie Broughton 2509
Luke Swain 2288
Adam Sidlow 1922
Phil Leuluai 1697
Stuart Littler 1662

CARRIES
Luke Swain 418
Daniel Holdsworth 318
Jodie Broughton 309
Stuart Littler 308
Adam Sidlow 308

TACKLES
Malcolm Alker 964
Luke Swain 910
Luke Adamson................647
Stuart Littler 577
Adam Sidlow 568

CLEAN BREAKS
Jodie Broughton 14
Ashley Gibson 13
Karl Fitzpatrick.................11
Steve Tyrer 10
Stefan Ratchford 9

TACKLE BUSTS
Mark Henry 48
Ashley Gibson 43
Jodie Broughton 39
Luke Adamson..................32
Stefan Ratchford 32

OFFLOADS
Adam Sidlow 40
Ray Cashmere 39
Phil Leuluai 31
Luke Swain 25
Ashley Gibson 23

TRY ASSISTS
Daniel Holdsworth 14
Matty Smith.......................7
Ashley Gibson 6
Malcolm Alker 5
Jeremy Smith 4

TOTAL OPTA INDEX
Luke Swain 14257
Malcolm Alker 13634
Matty Smith...............12715
Daniel Holdsworth 12137
Jodie Broughton 11207

ST HELENS

James Graham

James Roby

TACKLES
James Roby	752
James Graham	615
Scott Moore	608
Paul Clough	583
Bryn Hargreaves	510

OFFLOADS
Leon Pryce	64
James Roby	46
Matt Gidley	29
Tony Puletua	29
James Graham	27

CLEAN BREAKS
James Roby	17
Kyle Eastmond	16
Leon Pryce	16
Francis Meli	12
Paul Wellens	12

TRY ASSISTS
Leon Pryce	23
Keiron Cunningham	11
Scott Moore	10
Kyle Eastmond	9
Jon Wilkin	9

METRES
James Graham	4036
James Roby	3749
Tony Puletua	2340
Paul Clough	2197
Leon Pryce	2036

TACKLE BUSTS
James Roby	84
Leon Pryce	72
Kyle Eastmond	59
Paul Wellens	52
Tony Puletua	45

MARKER TACKLES
James Roby	105
Scott Moore	77
Chris Flannery	69
Paul Clough	66
Bryn Hargreaves	60

CARRIES
James Graham	598
James Roby	529
Leon Pryce	328
Tony Puletua	326
Scott Moore	315

TOTAL OPTA INDEX
James Roby	20553
James Graham	16561
Kyle Eastmond	15138
Leon Pryce	14651
Paul Wellens	12020

WAKEFIELD T WILDCATS

Glenn Morrison

Sam Obst

TACKLES
Glenn Morrison	740
Jason Demetriou	588
Kevin Henderson	578
Sam Obst	564
Michael Korkidas	508

OFFLOADS
Richard Moore	33
Paul King	32
Shane Tronc	31
Glenn Morrison	25
Tevita Leo-Latu	21

CLEAN BREAKS
Damien Blanch	14
Ben Jeffries	13
Aaron Murphy	7
Sam Obst	7
Sean Gleeson	6

TRY ASSISTS
Ben Jeffries	13
Danny Brough	7
Paul Cooke	7
Sam Obst	7
Jason Demetriou	4

METRES
Michael Korkidas	2954
Jason Demetriou	2526
Damien Blanch	2182
Richard Moore	2057
Glenn Morrison	1968

TACKLE BUSTS
Jason Demetriou	66
Kevin Henderson	55
Sam Obst	50
Glenn Morrison	38
Tevita Leo-Latu	34

MARKER TACKLES
Glenn Morrison	122
Jason Demetriou	88
Kevin Henderson	82
Sam Obst	82
Richard Moore	63

CARRIES
Michael Korkidas	382
Jason Demetriou	365
Ben Jeffries	331
Glenn Morrison	322
Kevin Henderson	283

TOTAL OPTA INDEX
Sam Obst	12878
Glenn Morrison	12270
Jason Demetriou	12030
Michael Korkidas	11329
Kevin Henderson	10955

WARRINGTON WOLVES

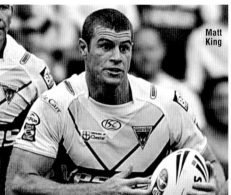

Matt King

Michael Monaghan

MARKER TACKLES
Ben Harrison	109
Michael Monaghan	109
Ben Westwood	109
Paul Wood	101
Mick Higham	93

METRES
Adrian Morley	2993
Matt King	2813
Paul Wood	2663
Ryan Atkins	2421
Chris Riley	2294

CARRIES
Paul Wood	381
Adrian Morley	373
Richard Mathers	339
Matt King	335
Ben Harrison	328

TACKLES
Michael Monaghan	695
Adrian Morley	673
Ben Westwood	642
Ben Harrison	636
Paul Wood	581

CLEAN BREAKS
Chris Riley	21
Matt King	20
Richard Myler	17
Chris Hicks	16
Chris Bridge	12

TACKLE BUSTS
Matt King	79
Ryan Atkins	64
Chris Riley	57
Paul Wood	46
Ben Westwood	41

OFFLOADS
Paul Wood	53
David Solomona	46
Ryan Atkins	38
Ben Harrison	36
Ben Westwood	34

TRY ASSISTS
Lee Briers	17
Chris Bridge	14
Ryan Atkins	13
Matt King	12
Richard Myler	12

TOTAL OPTA INDEX
Matt King	14191
Michael Monaghan	13781
Adrian Morley	13175
Paul Wood	12527
Lee Briers	12159

WIGAN WARRIORS

Pat Richards

Sam Tomkins

MARKER TACKLES
Joel Tomkins	134
Sean O'Loughlin	116
Stuart Fielden	89
Andy Coley	78
Liam Farrell	77

METRES
Pat Richards	3670
Sam Tomkins	2580
Joel Tomkins	2577
Stuart Fielden	2543
Darrell Goulding	1926

CARRIES
Pat Richards	444
Thomas Leuluai	419
Joel Tomkins	400
Sam Tomkins	400
Stuart Fielden	358

TACKLES
Sean O'Loughlin	783
Joel Tomkins	749
Stuart Fielden	607
Andy Coley	523
Mark Riddell	521

CLEAN BREAKS
Pat Richards	25
Sam Tomkins	23
Darrell Goulding	19
Amos Roberts	15
George Carmont	12

TACKLE BUSTS
Sam Tomkins	103
Pat Richards	74
Stuart Fielden	73
Joel Tomkins	64
Amos Roberts	50

OFFLOADS
Joel Tomkins	45
Stuart Fielden	23
Martin Gleeson	22
Amos Roberts	20
Sam Tomkins	17

TRY ASSISTS
Sam Tomkins	18
Sean O'Loughlin	16
Paul Deacon	14
Pat Richards	11
George Carmont	10

TOTAL OPTA INDEX
Pat Richards	19480
Sam Tomkins	19464
Joel Tomkins	14950
Thomas Leuluai	14483
Sean O'Loughlin	13405

CHAMPIONSHIP 2010
Club by Club

BARROW RAIDERS

DATE	FIXTURE	RESULT	SCORERS	LGE	ATT
7/2/10	Blackpool (h) (NRC)	W34-8	t:Halliwell,Young,Campbell(2),Catic,Bracek g:Knowles(3),Fletcher(2)	3rd(P1)	1,474
14/2/10	Widnes (a) (NRC)	L22-20	t:Nixon,Harrison,Mossop g:Rooney(4)	6th(P1)	3,432
17/2/10	Doncaster (a) (NRC)	W0-60	t:Henderson,Nixon(2),Knowles,Catic(3),Luisi,Rooney,Mossop g:Rooney(8),Knowles(2)	4th(P1)	285
25/2/10	Leigh (a)	D20-20	t:Rooney,Ballard,Halliwell,Young g:Rooney(2)	5th	2,203
7/3/10	Hunslet Warriors (h) (CCR3)	W62-10	t:Campbell,Ballard(2),Henderson,Catic(2),Larkin,Ostler,McDermott,Mossop(2) g:Rooney(6),Fletcher,Knowles(2)	N/A	1,330
10/3/10	Keighley (h) (NRC)	W62-18	t:Harrison(3),Knowles,Roberts,Ballard,Larkin(2),Rooney,Mossop,McDermott g:Rooney(9)	2nd(P1)	1,277
20/3/10	Featherstone (h)	L6-20	t:McGillvary g:Rooney	8th	1,998
27/3/10	Toulouse (a)	W16-48	t:James,Harrison(2),Luisi,Campbell(3),Ballard,Blackwood g:Rooney(6)	6th	1,500
1/4/10	Whitehaven (a)	W8-19	t:Ballard,Ostler(2) g:Rooney(3) fg:Rooney	5th	1,382
5/4/10	Sheffield (h)	W50-4	t:Luisi,Harrison,Blackwood,McGillvary,Rooney,Ballard,James,Noone,Knowles g:Rooney(7)	5th	1,854
10/4/10	Batley (h)	W56-10	t:Catic,Harrison(2),James,McGillvary(3),Henderson,Roberts,Ballard g:Rooney(8)	4th	1,725
18/4/10	Castleford (a) (CCR4)	W28-34	t:Rooney(2),McGillvary(2),Ballard,Catic g:Rooney(5)	N/A	5,285
24/4/10	Dewsbury (h)	W34-24	t:Mossop,Catic,Blackwood,Harrison,Campbell,Broadbent g:Rooney(3),Ballard(2)	4th	1,715
3/5/10	Keighley (a)	W10-40	t:Rooney(2),Campbell(2),Mossop,Bracek,Ballard g:Rooney(6)	3rd	1,047
9/5/10	Hunslet (h) (CCR5)	W42-24	t:Mossop,Campbell(2),Catic,Ballard,Knowles,Luisi g:Rooney(7)	N/A	2,241
16/5/10	Halifax (a)	L46-24	t:Ballard,Fletcher,Catic,Young g:Rooney(4)	4th	2,175
29/5/10	St Helens (a) (CCQF)	L32-12	t:Catic(2) g:Rooney(2)	N/A	4,972
3/6/10	Widnes (a) (NRCQF)	L26-12	t:Catic(2) g:Rooney(2)	N/A	1,718
8/6/10	Whitehaven (h)	W30-0	t:Ballard,McDermott,Rooney,Ostler,Bracek g:Rooney(5)	4th	1,920
13/6/10	Widnes (a)	W20-24	t:Knowles(2),Catic g:Rooney(6)	4th	2,958
24/6/10	Sheffield (a)	W26-36	t:Ostler,Harrison,Ballard,Young,Bauer,Catic,Mossop g:Rooney(4)	4th	848
3/7/10	Leigh (h)	W34-24	t:Rooney(2),Broadbent,Ballard,McGillvary,McDermott g:Rooney(5)	3rd	2,078
11/7/10	Batley (a)	L34-16	t:Ballard,Catic,Luisi g:Ballard(2)	4th	802
22/7/10	Halifax (h)	L34-42	t:Rooney,Carlile,Knowles,Ostler,Bauer,Harrison g:Rooney(5)	4th	1,707
31/7/10	Toulouse (h)	W42-6	t:Coyle(2),Rooney,Catic(2),Noone,Ballard g:Rooney(7)	4th	1,440
7/8/10	Keighley (h)	W54-0	t:Ballard(2),Catic(2),Ostler,Harrison(2),Rooney,Carlile,Blackwood g:Rooney(7)	3rd	1,404
15/8/10	Dewsbury (a)	L35-6	t:Coyle g:Rooney	4th	1,227
18/8/10	Widnes (h)	L14-32	t:Ballard(2),Rooney g:Rooney	4th	1,796
22/8/10	Featherstone (a)	L72-20	t:Campbell,Bauer,Bracek g:Ballard(2)	4th	2,073
5/9/10	Widnes (h) (EPO)	W38-0	t:Catic,Harrison,Campbell(2),Coyle,Ballard,James g:Rooney(4),Ballard	N/A	2,434
10/9/10	Sheffield (h) (ESF)	L14-21	t:Coyle,Ostler g:Rooney(3)	N/A	2,231

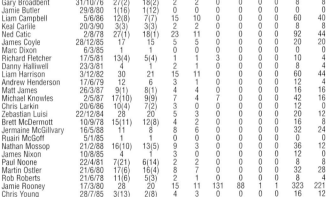

		APP		TRIES		GOALS		FG		PTS	
	D.O.B.	ALL	Ch	ALL	Ch	ALL	Ch	ALL	Ch	ALL	Ch
Andy Ballard	10/5/86	29	21	22	17	7	7	0	0	102	82
Andreas Bauer	26/9/82	13(1)	11(1)	3	3	0	0	0	0	12	12
Nick Beech	22/1/85	2	2	0	0	0	0	0	0	0	0
Anthony Blackwood	13/9/82	12	11	4	4	0	0	0	0	16	16
Andy Bracek	21/3/84	23(7)	17(4)	4	3	0	0	0	0	16	12
Gary Broadbent	31/10/76	27(2)	18(2)	2	2	0	0	0	0	8	8
Jamie Butler	29/8/80	1(16)	1(12)	0	0	0	0	0	0	0	0
Liam Campbell	5/6/86	12(8)	7(7)	15	10	0	0	0	0	60	40
Keal Carlile	20/3/90	3(3)	3(3)	2	2	0	0	0	0	8	8
Ned Catic	2/8/78	27(1)	18(1)	23	11	0	0	0	0	92	44
James Coyle	28/12/85	17	15	5	5	0	0	0	0	20	20
Marc Dixon	6/3/85	1	1	0	0	0	0	0	0	0	0
Richard Fletcher	17/5/81	13(4)	5(4)	1	1	3	0	0	0	10	4
Danny Halliwell	23/3/81	4	1	2	1	0	0	0	0	8	4
Liam Harrison	3/12/82	30	21	15	11	0	0	0	0	60	44
Andrew Henderson	17/6/79	12	6	3	1	0	0	0	0	12	4
Matt James	26/3/87	9(1)	8(1)	4	4	0	0	0	0	16	16
Michael Knowles	2/5/87	17(10)	9(9)	7	4	7	0	0	0	42	16
Chris Larkin	20/6/86	10(4)	7(2)	3	0	0	0	0	0	12	0
Zebastian Luisi	22/12/84	28	20	5	3	0	0	0	0	20	12
Brett McDermott	10/9/78	15(11)	12(8)	4	2	0	0	0	0	16	8
Jermaine McGillvary	16/5/88	11	8	8	6	0	0	0	0	32	24
Ruairi McGoff	5/1/85	1	1	0	0	0	0	0	0	0	0
Nathan Mossop	21/2/88	16(10)	13(5)	9	3	0	0	0	0	36	12
James Nixon	10/8/85	4	1	3	0	0	0	0	0	12	0
Paul Noone	22/4/81	7(21)	6(14)	2	2	0	0	0	0	8	8
Martin Ostler	21/6/80	17(6)	16(4)	8	7	0	0	0	0	32	28
Rob Roberts	21/6/78	11(6)	5(3)	2	1	0	0	0	0	8	4
Jamie Rooney	17/3/80	28	20	15	11	131	88	1	1	323	221
Chris Young	28/7/85	3(13)	2(8)	4	3	0	0	0	0	16	12

Jamie Rooney

LEAGUE RECORD
P20-W12-D1-L7-BP1
(4th, Championship/
Elimination Semi-Final)
F607, A449, Diff+158
39 points.

CHALLENGE CUP
Quarter Finalists

NORTHERN RAIL CUP
Quarter Finalists/3rd, Pool 1

ATTENDANCES
Best - v Widnes (EPO - 2,434)
Worst - v Keighley (NRC - 1,277)
Total (excluding Challenge Cup) - 25,053
Average (excluding
Challenge Cup) - 1,790
(Down by 416 on 2009)

CLUB RECORDS
MATCH RECORDS
Highest score: 138-0 v Nottingham City, 27/11/94 **Highest score against:** 0-90 v Leeds, 11/2/90 **Record attendance:** 21,651 v Salford, 15/4/38
Tries: 6 Val Cumberbatch v Batley, 21/11/36; Jim Thornburrow v Maryport, 19/2/38; Steve Rowan v Nottingham City, 15/11/92
Goals: 17 Darren Carter v Nottingham City, 27/11/94 **Points:** 42 Darren Carter v Nottingham City, 27/11/94
SEASON RECORDS
Tries: 50 Jim Lewthwaite 1956-57 **Goals:** 135 Joe Ball 1956-57 **Points:** 323 Jamie Rooney 2010
CAREER RECORDS
Tries: 352 Jim Lewthwaite 1943-57 **Goals:** 741 Willie Horne 1943-59 **Points:** 1,818 Willie Horne 1943-59 **Appearances:** 500 Jim Lewthwaite 1943-57

BATLEY BULLDOGS

DATE	FIXTURE	RESULT	SCORERS	LGE	ATT
7/2/10	Widnes (h) (NRC)	D30-30	t:Preece,Campbell(2),Martin,Greenwood g:Moore(5)	6th(P1)	1,004
10/2/10	Whitehaven (a) (NRC)	W26-34	t:Campbell(2),Handforth(2),Moore g:Moore(7)	3rd(P1)	888
14/2/10	Swinton (h) (NRC)	W46-10	t:Preece(3),T Gallagher,Campbell(2),Simpson,Lindsay,Greenwood g:Moore(5)	3rd(P1)	507
28/2/10	Featherstone (a)	L36-10	t:Walton,Campbell g:Moore	10th	1,353
7/3/10	Leeds Met University (h) (CCR3)	W70-6	t:Toohey,Barlow,Kilroy,Buttery,Tootill,J Gallagher,Campbell(2),Moore(2),Greenwood(2) g:Moore(11)	N/A	502
11/3/10	Halifax (h)	L24-34	t:Preece,Lindsay,Campbell(2) g:Moore(4)	10th	1,837
17/3/10	Gateshead (a) (NRC)	W4-100	t:Moore(2),Buttery,Wood(2),Tootill(2),Walton(2),Barlow,Campbell(3),Hesketh,Preece(2),Potter g:Moore(16)	1st(P1)	237
25/3/10	Keighley (a)	W12-22	t:Buttery,Barlow,Hesketh,Maun g:Moore(2),Handforth	8th	1,336
2/4/10	Dewsbury (h)	W22-8	t:Buttery,Preece(2),Lythe g:Handforth(3)	6th	1,484
5/4/10	Leigh (a)	L26-4	t:Martin	6th	2,246
10/4/10	Barrow (a)	L56-10	t:Walton,Brown g:Handforth	7th	1,725
18/4/10	Siddal (a) (CCR4) ●	W2-34	t:T Gallagher,Brown,Barlow,Moore,Handforth,Walton g:Handforth(2),Moore(3)	N/A	1,926
25/4/10	Widnes (h)	L24-32	t:Hesketh,Walton(2),Brown,Greenwood g:Moore(2)	7th	1,146
1/5/10	Toulouse (a)	L20-12	t:Toohey,Lythe g:Handforth(2)	8th	1,100
12/5/10	Sheffield (a)	L22-12	t:Moore,Tootill g:Moore(2)	8th	1,170
16/5/10	Whitehaven (h)	W54-6	t:Maun(3),Campbell(4),Buttery,Handforth,Smith g:Moore(7)	8th	666
19/5/10	Swinton (a) (CCR5) ▲	W6-58	t:Maun,Moore,Martin,Campbell(2),J Gallagher,Greenwood(2),Potter,Tootill,Hesketh g:Moore(7)	N/A	636
23/5/10	Widnes (a)	W16-35	t:Barlow(2),Handforth,Maun,Campbell g:Moore(7) fg:Handforth	7th	2,780
29/5/10	Catalans (h) (CCQF)	L12-74	t:Walton,Lythe g:Moore(2)	N/A	2,132
6/6/10	Sheffield (h) (NRCQF)	W26-16	t:Hesketh,Potter,Campbell,Lindsay g:Moore(5)	N/A	708
13/6/10	Leigh (h)	W32-12	t:Griffin,Govin,Moore,Brown,Lythe g:Moore(6)	7th	938
17/6/10	Leigh (a) (NRCSF)	W4-25	t:Maun(2),Hesketh,Lythe g:Moore(4) fg:Moore	N/A	2,058
22/6/10	Toulouse (a)	L40-42	t:Griffin,Maun(2),Toohey,Walton,Campbell,Govin g:Moore(6)	6th	689
4/7/10	Sheffield (h)	L12-20	t:Hesketh,Brown g:Hesketh(2)	8th	747
11/7/10	Barrow (h)	W34-16	t:Griffin,T Gallagher(5),Campbell g:Preece(2),Hesketh	8th	802
18/7/10	Widnes (NRCF) ●●	W25-24	t:Walton,Hesketh,Brown(2) g:Moore(4) fg:Moore	N/A	8,138
25/7/10	Dewsbury (a)	L36-16	t:Griffin,Toohey,Handforth g:Moore(2)	8th	1,935
1/8/10	Keighley (h)	W56-4	t:Griffin,Walton(2),Campbell(3),Moore,Preece(2),Greenwood,Lythe g:Moore(6)	6th	952
8/8/10	Featherstone (h)	L26-34	t:Lindsay,J Gallagher,Maun,Moore,Walton g:Moore(3)	7th	1,422
15/8/10	Halifax (a)	L30-22	t:Campbell,Lythe,Moore g:Moore(3)	7th	4,795
22/8/10	Whitehaven (a)	L26-12	t:Campbell,Hesketh g:Handforth,Moore	7th	706

● Played at The Shay, Halifax   ●● Played at Bloomfield Road, Blackpool
▲ *Challenge Cup Round Five: Batley were drawn at Halifax, who were disqualified for fielding an illegible player at Swinton in Round Four*

		APP		TRIES		GOALS		FG		PTS	
	D.O.B.	ALL	Ch	ALL	Ch	ALL	Ch	ALL	Ch	ALL	Ch
Mark Barlow	16/2/84	14(1)	6(1)	6	3	0	0	0	0	24	12
Alex Brown	28/8/87	13	9	7	4	0	0	0	0	28	16
Chris Buttery	23/12/85	16(8)	10(4)	5	3	0	0	0	0	20	12
John Campbell	17/7/87	29	18	30	16	0	0	0	0	120	64
John Gallagher	25/9/85	19(6)	11(4)	3	1	0	0	0	0	12	4
Tommy Gallagher	10/9/83	9(12)	6(8)	7	5	0	0	0	0	28	20
Mick Govin	5/11/84	2(8)	2(5)	2	2	0	0	0	0	8	8
Lee Greenwood	28/9/80	25(1)	17	8	2	0	0	0	0	32	8
Josh Griffin	9/5/90	14	13	5	5	0	0	0	0	20	20
Paul Handforth	6/10/81	27	17	6	3	10	8	1	1	45	29
Sean Hesketh	17/8/86	30	20	9	4	3	3	0	0	42	22
Eddie Kilroy	1/5/89	2	0	1	0	0	0	0	0	4	0
Ashley Lindsay	31/7/83	21(8)	14(5)	4	2	0	0	0	0	16	8
Kris Lythe	29/3/83	31	20	7	5	0	0	0	0	28	20
James Martin	11/11/87	(23)	(16)	3	1	0	0	0	0	12	4
Danny Maun	5/1/81	26	16	11	8	0	0	0	0	44	32
Gareth Moore	3/6/89	26(1)	16	12	5	121	52	2	0	292	124
Craig Potter	17/12/80	9(14)	5(9)	3	0	0	0	0	0	12	0
Ian Preece	13/6/85	17	12	11	5	2	2	0	0	48	24
Jon Simpson	16/7/83	1	0	1	0	0	0	0	0	4	0
Byron Smith	5/3/84	27	18	1	1	0	0	0	0	4	4
Mark Toohey	16/6/82	15(4)	10(1)	4	3	0	0	0	0	16	12
David Tootill	22/5/86	1(28)	(19)	5	1	0	0	0	0	20	4
Jason Walton	13/6/90	25(3)	17(1)	13	8	0	0	0	0	52	32
Kyle Wood	18/6/89	4(6)	3(6)	2	0	0	0	0	0	8	0

Gareth Moore

LEAGUE RECORD
P20-W7-D0-L13-BP8
(7th, Championship)
F479, A488, Diff-9
29 points.

CHALLENGE CUP
Quarter Finalists

NORTHERN RAIL CUP
Winners/1st, Pool 1

ATTENDANCES
Best - v Catalans (CC - 2,132)
Worst - v Leeds Met Uni (CC - 502)
Total (excluding Challenge Cup) - 12,902
Average (excluding Challenge Cup) - 992
(Up by 136 on 2009)

CLUB RECORDS MATCH RECORDS
Highest score: 100-4 v Gateshead, 17/3/2010   Highest score against: 9-78 v Wakefield, 26/8/67   Record attendance: 23,989 v Leeds, 14/3/25
Tries: 5 Joe Oakland v Bramley, 19/12/1908; Tommy Brannan v Swinton, 17/1/20; Jim Wale v Bramley, 4/12/26; Jim Wale v Cottingham, 12/2/27;
Tommy Oldroyd v Highfield, 6/3/94; Ben Feehan v Halifax, 10/8/2008; Jermaine McGillvary v Whitehaven, 24/5/2009; Tommy Gallagher v Barrow, 11/7/2010
Goals: 16 Gareth Moore v Gateshead, 17/3/2010   Points: 40 Gareth Moore v Gateshead, 17/3/2010

SEASON RECORDS CAREER RECORDS
Tries: 30 John Campbell 2010   Goals: 144 Barry Eaton 2004   Points: 308 Richard Price 1997
Tries: 142 Craig Lingard 1998-2008   Goals: 463 Wharton 'Wattie' Davies 1897-1912   Points: 1,297 Wharton 'Wattie' Davies 1897-1912
Appearances: 421 Wharton 'Wattie' Davies 1897-1912

DEWSBURY RAMS

DATE	FIXTURE	RESULT	SCORERS	LGE	ATT
31/1/10	London Skolars (h) (NRC)	W50-4	t:Spicer,Lunt(2),Emmett,Powell,Turner,Watson,Robinson,Haynes,Bostock g:P Walker,Brambani(2),Turner(2)	N/A	887
7/2/10	Halifax (a) (NRC)	L24-0		4th(P2)	2,141
14/2/10	Rochdale (a) (NRC)	W12-48	t:P Walker,Brambani,Turner(3),Bostock,Spurr,Menzies,Faal g:P Walker(6)	3rd(P2)	575
28/2/10	Toulouse (a)	L26-22	t:Emmett,Bostock,Turner(2) g:P Walker(3)	7th	1,200
3/3/10	Leigh (h) (NRC)	L22-44	t:Sanderson,P Walker,Woodhead,Smith g:P Walker(3)	5th(P2)	888
7/3/10	Drighlington (a) (CCR3) ●	W10-42	t:Lockwood,Haynes,Spurr,Hayes,Faal,Stenchion,Robinson g:P Walker(7)	N/A	1,222
14/3/10	Featherstone (h)	L10-40	t:Stenchion,Lunt g:P Walker	9th	1,313
19/3/10	Sheffield (a) ●●	L22-10	t:P Walker,Sanderson g:P Walker	9th	835
28/3/10	Widnes (h)	L30-36	t:Spurr(3),Powell,P Walker g:P Walker(5)	9th	1,499
2/4/10	Batley (a)	L22-8	t:Powell,Emmett	10th	1,484
5/4/10	Keighley (h)	L10-42	t:Wandless,Turner g:P Walker	10th	1,025
11/4/10	Whitehaven (h)	L12-20	t:Powell,Lingard,Robinson	10th	850
18/4/10	Bradford (h) (CCR4)	L0-50		N/A	3,995
24/4/10	Barrow (a)	L34-24	t:Faal(2),Robinson(2) g:P Walker(4)	10th	1,715
29/4/10	Leigh (h)	L14-30	t:Brambani,Bostock g:P Walker(2)	10th	1,151
20/5/10	Sheffield (h)	L20-22	t:Barber,Lockwood,Bostock,Powell g:P Walker(2)	10th	1,066
30/5/10	Featherstone (a)	L36-32	t:Blake(2),Powell,Turner(2),England g:Barber(4)	10th	1,665
6/6/10	Halifax (a)	L28-8	t:Powell g:Barber(2)	10th	1,851
13/6/10	Keighley (a)	W16-20	t:Spicer,Faal,P Walker,Bostock g:Brambani(2)	9th	971
27/6/10	Halifax (h)	W37-30	t:Spicer(2),Blake,Stenchion,England,Powell g:Brambani(6) fg:Brambani	9th	1,030
3/7/10	Toulouse (h)	L12-36	t:Lingard,P Walker g:Brambani(2)	9th	864
11/7/10	Widnes (a)	L27-26	t:Fox(2),P Walker,Brambani,Bretherton g:Brambani(3)	9th	2,715
25/7/10	Batley (h)	W36-16	t:Brambani(2),Craven(2),Stenchion,Powell g:Brambani(6)	9th	1,935
1/8/10	Leigh (a)	W6-30	t:Barber,Powell(2),P Walker,Craven g:Brambani(2),P Walker(3)	9th	1,682
8/8/10	Whitehaven (a)	W10-48	t:Hirst(2),Brambani(2),Craven,Spicer,Robinson,Buchanan g:P Walker(8)	9th	504
15/8/10	Barrow (h)	W35-6	t:Craven,P Walker,Stenchion,Spicer,Powell(2) g:P Walker(5) fg:Brambani	9th	1,227

● Played at Tetley's Stadium
●● Played at Don Valley Stadium

	D.O.B.	APP ALL	APP Ch	TRIES ALL	TRIES Ch	GOALS ALL	GOALS Ch	FG ALL	FG Ch	PTS ALL	PTS Ch
Danny Addy	15/1/91	2	2	0	0	0	0	0	0	0	0
Ed Barber	26/4/90	9(3)	9(2)	2	2	6	6	0	0	20	20
Luke Blake	10/8/89	15(7)	14(5)	3	3	0	0	0	0	12	12
Andrew Bostock	25/2/85	19	14	6	4	0	0	0	0	24	16
Dominic Brambani	10/5/85	24	19	7	6	23	21	2	2	76	68
Alex Bretherton	5/12/82	8(2)	8(2)	1	1	0	0	0	0	4	4
Austin Buchanan	22/5/84	6(1)	6(1)	1	1	0	0	0	0	4	4
James Craven	14/10/88	7	7	5	5	0	0	0	0	20	20
Liam Crawley	18/4/87	1		0	0	0	0	0	0	0	0
Mike Emmett	13/5/87	12(10)	8(9)	3	2	0	0	0	0	12	8
Anthony England	19/10/86	13(7)	9(7)	2	2	0	0	0	0	8	8
Ayden Faal	12/12/86	17(1)	14(1)	5	3	0	0	0	0	20	12
Matthew Fox	27/3/88	1(1)	1(1)	2	2	0	0	0	0	8	8
Adam Hayes	30/11/81	8	3	1	0	0	0	0	0	4	0
James Haynes	22/3/89	13	7	2	0	0	0	0	0	8	0
Keegan Hirst	13/12/88	21(3)	15(3)	2	2	0	0	0	0	8	8
Paul Hughes	28/12/84	1(3)	(2)	0	0	0	0	0	0	0	0
Lee Lingard	21/10/83	7(1)	7	2	2	0	0	0	0	8	8
James Lockwood	21/3/86	19(4)	17(3)	2	1	0	0	0	0	8	4
Rob Lunt	8/2/85	4(2)	3	3	1	0	0	0	0	12	4
Allister McMaster	8/10/89	(2)	(1)	0	0	0	0	0	0	0	0
Luke Menzies	29/6/88	(3)	(2)	1	0	0	0	0	0	4	0
Andrew Moody	15/5/84	1(1)	(1)	0	0	0	0	0	0	0	0
Bryn Powell	5/9/79	25	20	13	12	0	0	0	0	52	48
Adam Robinson	8/4/87	5(16)	4(12)	6	4	0	0	0	0	24	16
Stewart Sanderson	10/4/85	11	8	2	1	0	0	0	0	8	4
Ryan Smith	25/10/88	1(4)	(1)	1	0	0	0	0	0	4	0
Rob Spicer	22/9/84	14	11	6	5	0	0	0	0	24	20
Chris Spurr	7/7/80	10	5	5	3	0	0	0	0	20	12
Luke Stenchion	15/2/86	5(16)	4(14)	5	4	0	0	0	0	20	16
Josh Tonks	14/8/91	(5)	(5)	0	0	0	0	0	0	0	0
Scott Turner	15/4/88	24	18	9	5	2	0	0	0	40	20
James Walker	15/4/77	6(6)	5(5)	0	0	0	0	0	0	0	0
Pat Walker	24/3/86	26	20	9	7	53	36	0	0	142	100
Tom Wandless	27/12/86	2(2)	2(1)	1	1	0	0	0	0	4	4
Scott Watson	16/3/88	(2)		1	0	0	0	0	0	4	0
Martin Woodhead	23/3/88	1	1	0	0	0	0	0	0	4	0

Bryn Powell

LEAGUE RECORD
P20-W6-D0-L14-BP8
(9th, Championship)
F444, A505, Diff-61
26 points.

CHALLENGE CUP
Round Four

NORTHERN RAIL CUP
7th, Pool 2

ATTENDANCES
Best - v Bradford (CC - 3,995)
Worst - v Whitehaven (Ch - 850)
Total (excluding Challenge Cup) - 13,735
Average (excluding
Challenge Cup) - 1,145
(Down by 118 on 2009, Ch1)

CLUB RECORDS
MATCH RECORDS
Highest score: 90-5 v Blackpool, 4/4/93 Highest score against: 0-82 v Widnes, 30/11/86 Record attendance: 26,584 v Halifax, 30/10/20
Tries: 8 Dai Thomas v Liverpool, 13/4/1907
Goals: 13 Greg Pearce v Blackpool Borough, 4/4/93; Francis Maloney v Hunslet, 25/3/2007 Points: 32 Les Holliday v Barrow, 11/9/94
SEASON RECORDS Tries: 40 Dai Thomas 1906-07 Goals: 169 Barry Eaton 2000 Points: 394 Barry Eaton 2000
CAREER RECORDS Tries: 144 Joe Lyman 1913-31 Goals: 863 Nigel Stephenson 1967-78; 1984-86 Points: 2,082 Nigel Stephenson 1967-78; 1984-86
Appearances: 454 Joe Lyman 1913-31

FEATHERSTONE ROVERS

DATE	FIXTURE	RESULT	SCORERS	LGE	ATT
7/2/10	Sheffield (h) (NRC)	D18-18	t:Welham(3),Steel g:Briggs	7th(P2)	1,175
14/2/10	Leigh (a) (NRC)	L36-6	t:Finn g:Briggs	8th(P2)	1,729
23/2/10	Rochdale (h) (NRC)	W56-10	t:Steel(2),Grayshon(2),Dobek,Divorty,Marabe(2),Hardman,Briggs,Parker g:Briggs(5),Dobek	7th(P2)	777
28/2/10	Batley (h)	W36-10	t:Hardman(2),Dale,Welham,Steel(2) g:Briggs(6)	2nd	1,353
4/3/10	Hunslet (a) (NRC)	W0-68	t:Parker(2),Allan,Hardaker(3),Dobek,Saxton,Divorty,Williamson,Marabe,Lee g:Dobek(10)	3rd(P2)	513
7/3/10	Workington (h) (CCR3)	W74-0	t:Welham,Parker(3),Grayshon(2),Saxton(3),Hardman,Steel,Kain,Finn g:Briggs(2),Finn(5)	N/A	1,215
14/3/10	Dewsbury (a)	W10-40	t:Hardman,Parker,Finn,Welham,Kain(3) g:Briggs(5),Finn	2nd	1,313
20/3/10	Barrow (a)	W6-20	t:Steel,Finn g:Briggs(6)	1st	1,998
28/3/10	Whitehaven (h)	W54-18	t:Dickens,Parker(3),Welham(2),Briggs(3),Finn g:Briggs(7)	1st	1,551
2/4/10	Halifax (h)	W44-4	t:Grayshon,Dickens,Hardman,Briggs,Steel,Finn,Spears g:Briggs(8)	1st	2,353
11/4/10	Sheffield (a)	W16-40	t:Parker,Grayshon,Kain(2),Welham,Manning,Morrison g:Briggs(6)	1st	2,871
18/4/10	Warrington (a) (CCR4)	L48-24	t:Parker(2),Hardaker,Dickens g:Briggs(4)	N/A	7,754
22/4/10	Keighley (h)	W76-12	t:Coady,Briggs(2),Finn(4),Hardman,Hardaker(2),Morrison,Kain,Manning g:Finn(3),Briggs(9)	1st	2,171
30/4/10	Widnes (a)	W8-9	t:Parker,Kain fg:Finn	1st	3,448
6/5/10	Toulouse (h)	L24-26	t:Hardman(2),Hardaker(2) g:Briggs(4)	1st	2,223
18/5/10	Leigh (a)	W16-24	t:Grayshon(2),Welham,Parker g:Briggs(4)	1st	2,425
22/5/10	Toulouse (a)	W28-34	t:Briggs,Kain(2),Saxton,Dale(2) g:Briggs(5)	1st	1,328
30/5/10	Dewsbury (h)	W36-32	t:Briggs(2),Coady,Finn,Divorty,Parker g:Briggs(5),Finn	1st	1,665
10/6/10	Halifax (a)	W16-26	t:Welham(2),Field,Parker,Divorty g:Briggs(3)	1st	2,135
27/6/10	Widnes (h)	W30-22	t:Dale,Hardaker,Finn,Grayshon,Briggs g:Briggs(5)	1st	1,776
4/7/10	Keighley (a)	W6-24	t:Briggs(2),Kain,Hardaker g:Briggs(4)	1st	1,185
8/7/10	Leigh (h)	W34-26	t:Hardaker,Briggs,Finn,Manning,Smeaton(2) g:Briggs(5)	1st	1,632
25/7/10	Whitehaven (a)	W0-48	t:Hardaker(2),Finn,Dickens,Smeaton(2),Briggs,Kain,Tonks,Hardman g:Briggs(2),Finn(2)	1st	825
1/8/10	Sheffield (h)	L30-32	t:Briggs,Hardaker(2),Steel,Spears,Welham g:Finn,Briggs(2)	1st	2,381
8/8/10	Batley (a)	W26-34	t:Hardaker(3),Dale,Dickens,Divorty g:Finn(5)	1st	1,422
22/8/10	Barrow (h)	W72-20	t:Hardaker(2),Saxton,Divorty,Spears,Kain,Dale(2),Welham,Tonks,Kaye,Smeaton, Finn g:Finn(2),Briggs(8)	1st	2,073
9/9/10	Halifax (h) (QSF)	W46-16	t:Dickens,Welham,Saxton,Manning,Briggs(3),Finn g:Briggs(7)	N/A	2,553
26/9/10	Halifax (GF) ●	L22-23 *(aet)*	t:Briggs,Hardaker(2),Dale g:Briggs(3)	N/A	9,443

● Played at Halliwell Jones Stadium, Warrington

	D.O.B.	APP		TRIES		GOALS		FG		PTS	
		ALL	Ch	ALL	Ch	ALL	Ch	ALL	Ch	ALL	Ch
Danny Allan	9/4/89	4(2)	1(2)	1	0	0	0	0	0	4	0
Kyle Briggs	7/12/87	26	21	20	19	117	104	0	0	314	284
Thomas Carr	16/7/91	1	0	0	0	0	0	0	0	0	0
Michael Coady	15/4/87	6(1)	5	2	2	0	0	0	0	8	8
Matty Dale	10/10/86	26(1)	22	8	8	0	0	0	0	32	32
Stuart Dickens	23/3/80	27	22	6	5	0	0	0	0	24	20
Ross Divorty	27/11/88	1(26)	(21)	6	4	0	0	0	0	24	16
Aaron Dobek	10/9/87	2(2)	(1)	2	0	11	0	0	0	30	0
Jamie Field	12/12/76	17(3)	14(3)	1	1	0	0	0	0	4	4
Liam Finn	2/11/83	27	22	16	14	24	15	1	1	113	87
Jon Grayshon	10/5/83	16(7)	13(6)	9	5	0	0	0	0	36	20
Zak Hardaker	17/10/91	14	12	22	18	0	0	0	0	88	72
Ian Hardman	8/12/84	27	22	10	8	0	0	0	0	40	32
Andy Kain	1/9/85	5(21)	3(19)	13	12	0	0	0	0	52	48
Ben Kaye	19/12/88	20	17	1	1	0	0	0	0	4	4
Jack Lee	1/11/88	4(5)	3(2)	1	0	0	0	0	0	4	0
Tom Lynch	6/11/86	(1)	0	0	0	0	0	0	0	0	0
Dane Manning	15/4/89	6(17)	2(17)	4	4	0	0	0	0	16	16
Larsen Marabe	9/6/86	2	0	3	0	0	0	0	0	12	0
Iain Morrison	6/5/83	9(8)	5(7)	2	2	0	0	0	0	8	8
Jessie Joe Parker	22/8/85	14(1)	11	17	9	0	0	0	0	68	36
Tom Saxton	3/10/83	21(1)	11	7	3	0	0	0	0	28	12
Jode Sheriffe	4/7/87	1(5)	(3)	0	0	0	0	0	0	0	0
Sam Smeaton	26/10/88	12	10	5	5	0	0	0	0	20	20
Tim Spears	27/7/84	12(7)	10(6)	3	3	0	0	0	0	12	12
Jon Steel	14/3/80	16	11	9	5	0	0	0	0	36	20
Duane Straugheir	29/9/89	2	2	0	0	0	0	0	0	0	0
Tony Tonks	27/4/85	23(3)	22	2	2	0	0	0	0	8	8
Liam Welham	11/11/88	23	19	15	11	0	0	0	0	60	44
Gareth Williamson	8/6/90	(1)	0	1	0	0	0	0	0	4	0

Kyle Briggs

LEAGUE RECORD
P20-W18-D0-L2-BP2
(1st, Championship/
Grand Final Runners-Up)
F735, A334, Diff+401
56 points.

CHALLENGE CUP
Round Four

NORTHERN RAIL CUP
5th, Pool 2

ATTENDANCES
Best - v Halifax (QSF - 2,553)
Worst - v Rochdale (NRC - 777)
Total (excluding Challenge Cup) - 23,683
Average (excluding
Challenge Cup) - 1,822
(Up by 68 on 2009)

CLUB RECORDS Highest score: 96-0 v Castleford Lock Lane, 8/2/2004 Highest score against: 14-80 v Bradford, 3/4/2005 Record attendance: 17,531 v St Helens, 21/3/59
MATCH RECORDS Tries: 6 Mike Smith v Doncaster, 13/4/68; Chris Bibb v Keighley, 17/9/89
Goals: 13 Mark Knapper v Keighley, 17/9/89 Points: 40 Martin Pearson v Whitehaven, 26/11/95
SEASON RECORDS Tries: 48 Paul Newlove 1992-93 Goals: 165 (inc 9 fg) Jamie Rooney 2002 Points: 429 Jamie Rooney 2002
CAREER RECORDS Tries: 162 Don Fox 1953-66 Goals: 1,210 Steve Quinn 1975-88 Points: 2,654 Steve Quinn 1975-88 Appearances: 440 Jim Denton 1921-34

HALIFAX

DATE	FIXTURE	RESULT	SCORERS	LGE	ATT
7/2/10	Dewsbury (h) (NRC)	W24-0	t:Haley(2),Nash,Paterson,Royston g:Paterson(2)	3rd(P2)	2,141
14/2/10	London Skolars (a) (NRC)	W0-68	t:Penkywicz(2),Worrincy(4),Tamghart,Bowman,Beswick(2),Watene,Goddard,Haley g:Paterson(8)	2nd(P2)	416
17/2/10	Sheffield (a) (NRC) ●	L13-6	t:Goddard g:Paterson	2nd(P2)	851
28/2/10	Sheffield (h)	W32-26	t:Worrincy,Royston(3),Penkywicz g:Paterson(6)	3rd	2,139
7/3/10	Ovenden (a) (CCR3) ●●	W10-88	t:Branighan(4),White(2),Royston(3),Worrincy,Watene,Bowman,Roberts(2), Penkywicz,Goddard g:Paterson(12)	N/A	2,319
11/3/10	Batley (a)	W24-34	t:Maloney(2),Wrench,Branighan(2),Royston g:Paterson(5)	3rd	1,837
18/3/10	Widnes (a)	W28-30	t:Worrincy,White,Paterson,Royston,Penkywicz g:Paterson(3),Branighan(2)	2nd	3,286
21/3/10	Hunslet (h) (NRC)	L36-42	t:Nash(2),Bowman,Worrincy,Watene,Branighan g:Paterson(6)	6th(P2)	1,771
28/3/10	Leigh (h)	L10-48	t:Royston,Beswick g:Paterson	4th	3,071
2/4/10	Featherstone (a)	L44-4	t:Paterson	4th	2,353
5/4/10	Toulouse (h)	W50-6	t:Royston(3),Paterson(2),Haley(2),Worrincy,Watene g:Paterson(7)	4th	1,725
8/4/10	Keighley (h)	W40-20	t:Haley,Gene,Worrincy,Penkywicz,Nash,Bannister,Paterson g:Paterson(6)	3rd	2,522
16/4/10	Swinton (a) (CCR4) ▲	W4-56	t:Branighan(2),Royston(2),Tamghart,Roberts,Black(2),Penkywicz,Bannister g:Paterson(8)	N/A	633
25/4/10	Whitehaven (a)	W10-28	t:Royston(2),Black(2),Tamghart g:Paterson(4)	3rd	1,140
16/5/10	Barrow (h)	W46-24	t:Bannister,Royston,Gene,Worrincy,Goddard,Beswick,Branighan,White g:Paterson(7)	3rd	2,175
23/5/10	Keighley (a)	W32-46	t:Paterson(2),White,Goddard,Gleeson,Beswick,Penkywicz,Branighan g:Paterson(7)	3rd	1,602
30/5/10	Leigh (a)	W40-46	t:Black(2),Nash,Royston,Worrincy(3),White g:Paterson(7)	3rd	2,536
6/6/10	Dewsbury (h)	W28-8	t:Gene,Black(2),Bannister,Goddard g:Paterson(4)	3rd	1,851
10/6/10	Featherstone (h)	L16-26	t:Branighan,White,Black g:Paterson(2)	3rd	2,135
27/6/10	Dewsbury (a)	L37-30	t:Worrincy(2),Bannister,Royston,Larder g:Branighan(5)	3rd	1,030
11/7/10	Whitehaven (h)	W66-16	t:Paterson,Worrincy(4),Bowman,Royston(2),Bannister,Black,Barlow,Beswick g:Paterson(9)	3rd	1,970
22/7/10	Barrow (a)	W34-42	t:Goddard(2),Nash,Wrench,Barlow,Royston,Worrincy g:Paterson(7)	3rd	1,707
29/7/10	Widnes (h)	W30-16	t:Penkywicz(3),Royston,Branighan g:Paterson(5)	2nd	2,707
8/8/10	Sheffield (a)	W24-38	t:Paterson,Maloney,Black,Larder,Royston,Penkywicz,Nash g:Paterson(5)	2nd	1,473
15/8/10	Batley (h)	W30-22	t:Goddard,Penkywicz,Royston,Paterson(2) g:Paterson(4),Branighan	2nd	4,795
21/8/10	Toulouse (a)	W24-38	t:Wrench,Royston(2),Worrincy,Holroyd,Penkywicz,White g:Paterson(5)	2nd	902
9/9/10	Featherstone (a) (QSF)	L46-16	t:Penkywicz,Royston,Worrincy g:Paterson(2)	N/A	2,553
16/9/10	Sheffield (h) (FE) ●●●	W42-16	t:Penkywicz,Black,Barlow,Aizue,Paterson,Royston,Worrincy,Royston g:Paterson(7)	N/A	1,490
26/9/10	Featherstone (GF) ●●●	W22-23 *(aet)*	t:Worrincy,Black,Branighan,Bannister g:Paterson(3) fg:Black		9,443

● Played at Don Valley Stadium   ●● Played at The Shay   ●●● Played at Halliwell Jones Stadium, Warrington
▲ *Halifax were disqualified from the Challenge Cup for fielding an illegible player at Swinton in Round Four*

		APP		TRIES		GOALS		FG		PTS	
	D.O.B.	ALL	Ch	ALL	Ch	ALL	Ch	ALL	Ch	ALL	Ch
Makali Aizue	30/12/77	8(6)	7(5)	1	1	0	0	0	0	4	4
Steve Bannister	10/10/87	19(6)	14(5)	7	6	0	0	0	0	28	24
Sam Barlow	7/3/88	5(1)	5(1)	3	3	0	0	0	0	12	12
Bob Beswick	8/12/84	21(5)	16(4)	6	4	0	0	0	0	24	16
Ben Black	29/4/81	22(4)	18(4)	13	11	0	0	1	1	53	45
Anthony Bowman	18/3/92	9(4)	6(2)	4	1	0	0	0	0	16	4
Luke Branighan	29/6/81	24	18	14	7	8	8	0	0	72	44
Neil Cherryholme	20/12/86	14(1)	9(1)	0	0	0	0	0	0	0	0
Stanley Gene	11/5/74	10(1)	8(1)	3	3	0	0	0	0	12	12
Mark Gleeson	16/6/82	3(7)	2(5)	1	1	0	0	0	0	4	4
Jon Goddard	21/6/82	22(2)	17(1)	9	6	0	0	0	0	36	24
James Haley	2/7/85	13(1)	7(1)	6	3	0	0	0	0	24	12
Graham Holroyd	25/10/75	6(2)	6(2)	1	1	0	0	0	0	4	4
David Larder	5/6/76	21	20	2	2	0	0	0	0	8	8
Dominic Maloney	12/3/87	9(11)	8(10)	3	3	0	0	0	0	12	12
Dylan Nash	28/12/86	17(4)	15(3)	7	4	0	0	0	0	28	16
Michael Ostick	23/1/88	13(3)	12(3)	0	0	0	0	0	0	0	0
Lee Paterson	20/7/82	28	22	13	12	143	106	0	0	338	260
Sean Penkywicz	18/5/82	15(10)	12(8)	16	12	0	0	0	0	64	48
Mark Roberts	9/11/82	3(3)	(2)	3	0	0	0	0	0	12	0
Shad Royston	29/11/82	27(1)	23	30	24	0	0	0	0	120	96
Adam Rudd	29/7/86	1	1	0	0	0	0	0	0	0	0
Said Tamghart	13/5/80	2(15)	2(11)	3	1	0	0	0	0	12	4
Frank Watene	15/2/77	3(26)	3(20)	4	1	0	0	0	0	16	4
Paul White	7/12/82	16(2)	12(2)	8	6	0	0	0	0	32	24
Rob Worrincy	9/7/85	26	20	25	19	0	0	0	0	100	76
David Wrench	3/1/79	20(1)	16(1)	3	3	0	0	0	0	12	12

Shad Royston

LEAGUE RECORD
P20-W16-D0-L4-BP2
(2nd, Championship/
Grand Final Winners, Champions)
F684, A509, Diff+175
50 points.

CHALLENGE CUP
Round Four

NORTHERN RAIL CUP
6th, Pool 2

ATTENDANCES
Best - v Batley (Ch - 4,795)
Worst - v Sheffield (FE - 1,490)
Total (excluding Challenge Cup) - 30,492
Average (excluding
Challenge Cup) - 2,345
(Up by 15 on 2009)

CLUB RECORDS	
	Highest score: 88-6 v Workington, 2/3/2008; 88-10 v Ovenden, 7/3/2010 **Highest score against:** 6-88 v Hull KR, 23/4/2006
	Record attendance: 29,153 v Wigan, 21/3/59
MATCH RECORDS	**Tries:** 8 Keith Williams v Dewsbury, 9/11/57 **Goals:** 14 Bruce Burton v Hunslet, 27/8/72 **Points:** 32 John Schuster v Doncaster, 9/10/94
SEASON RECORDS	**Tries:** 48 Johnny Freeman 1956-57 **Goals:** 156 Graham Holroyd 2008 **Points:** 362 John Schuster 1994-95
CAREER RECORDS	**Tries:** 290 Johnny Freeman 1954-67 **Goals:** 1,028 Ronnie James 1961-71 **Points:** 2,191 Ronnie James 1961-71 **Appearances:** 482 Stan Kielty 1946-58

KEIGHLEY COUGARS

DATE	FIXTURE	RESULT	SCORERS	LGE	ATT
31/1/10	Blackpool (a) (NRC)	W22-24	t:Rawlins,Belcher,Haythornthwaite,Duffy g:D Jones(4)	N/A	468
7/2/10	Whitehaven (h) (NRC)	W17-16	t:Haythornthwaite,Belcher g:D Jones(4) fg:D Jones	1st(P1)	750
14/2/10	Workington (h) (NRC)	W38-10	t:Belcher,Sagar(2),Presley(3),Rawlins g:D Jones(3),Belcher(2)	1st(P1)	654
28/2/10	Widnes (a)	L72-10	t:Duffy,Moss g:D Jones	11th	2,777
6/3/10	Toulouse (h) (CCR3)	L26-35	t:Benjafield,Burton,Presley,G Rayner,Shickell g:D Jones(3)	N/A	543
10/3/10	Barrow (a) (NRC)	L62-18	t:Presley,D Jones,G Rayner g:D Jones(3)	3rd(P1)	1,277
14/3/10	Leigh (h)	L12-34	t:Benjafield,G Rayner g:D Jones(2)	11th	1,115
20/3/10	Toulouse (a)	L34-26	t:Pursglove,Duffy,D Jones,Baines,Feather g:D Jones(3)	11th	1,829
25/3/10	Batley (h)	L12-22	t:Burton,D Jones g:D Jones(2)	11th	1,336
2/4/10	Sheffield (h)	D16-16	t:Shickell,Duffy g:D Jones(4)	11th	927
5/4/10	Dewsbury (a)	W10-42	t:D Jones,Cartledge,Shickell,G Rayner,Nicholson,Williams(2) g:D Jones(7)	11th	1,025
8/4/10	Halifax (a)	L40-20	t:Presley,Burton,Shickell,Haythornthwaite g:D Jones(2)	11th	2,522
22/4/10	Featherstone (a)	L76-12	t:Duffy,D Jones g:D Jones(2)	11th	2,171
3/5/10	Barrow (h)	L10-40	t:Duffy,Williams g:D Jones	11th	1,047
9/5/10	Whitehaven (a)	W12-22	t:Williams,Duffy,Pursglove(2) g:D Jones(3)	11th	900
23/5/10	Halifax (h)	L32-46	t:Benjafield,D Jones,Law,Hutchinson,Presley g:D Jones(6)	11th	1,602
27/5/10	Sheffield (a)	W24-25	t:D Jones,Hutchinson,Sheldrake g:D Jones(6) fg:D Jones	11th	1,271
6/6/10	York (h) (NRCQF)	W32-6	t:Sheldrake,Wray,Williams(2),Shickell g:D Jones(6)	N/A	712
13/6/10	Dewsbury (h)	L16-20	t:Rawlins,Feather g:D Jones(4)	11th	971
20/6/10	Widnes (h) (NRCSF)	L18-48	t:Wray,Eaton,Cartledge g:D Jones(3)	N/A	1,686
27/6/10	Leigh (a)	L36-18	t:Hutchinson,Benjafield,Duffy(2) g:D Jones	11th	1,265
4/7/10	Featherstone (h)	L6-24	t:Rawlins g:D Jones	11th	1,185
24/7/10	Toulouse (h)	W27-26	t:Burton(2),Rawlins,Hutchinson,Duffy g:D Jones(3) fg:D Jones	11th	736
1/8/10	Batley (a)	L56-4	t:Duffy	11th	952
7/8/10	Barrow (a)	L54-0		11th	1,404
15/8/10	Whitehaven (h)	L28-29	t:Baines(2),Cartledge,Duffy,Hutchinson g:D Jones(4)	11th	739
22/8/10	Widnes (h)	L24-32	t:Duffy,Hutchinson,Rawlins,Burton g:D Jones(4)	11th	1,173

		APP		TRIES		GOALS		FG		PTS	
	D.O.B.	ALL	Ch	ALL	Ch	ALL	Ch	ALL	Ch	ALL	Ch
Chris Baines	25/9/84	23(1)	19	3	3	0	0	0	0	12	12
Dan Belcher	30/12/88	6	3	3	0	2	0	0	0	16	0
Ryan Benjafield	3/8/82	15(11)	14(5)	4	3	0	0	0	0	16	12
Tom Burton	5/11/87	19	14	6	5	0	0	0	0	24	20
Will Cartledge	11/9/79	18(5)	15(5)	3	2	0	0	0	0	12	8
Sam Crowther	21/10/86	2	1	0	0	0	0	0	0	0	0
Gavin Duffy	9/4/87	25	20	13	12	0	0	0	0	52	48
Barry Eaton	30/9/73	1(1)	1	1	0	0	0	0	0	4	0
James Feather	15/4/84	23(4)	17(3)	2	2	0	0	0	0	8	8
Tom Hall	24/8/89	1	0	0	0	0	0	0	0	0	0
James Haythornthwaite	19/10/90	3(17)	2(13)	3	1	0	0	0	0	12	4
Luke Helliwell	1/3/88	1(1)	1(1)	0	0	0	0	0	0	0	0
Carl Hughes	30/11/82	9(5)	7(4)	0	0	0	0	0	0	0	0
James Hutchinson	27/11/85	14	12	6	6	0	0	0	0	24	24
Danny Jones	6/3/86	26	19	7	6	82	56	3	2	195	138
Richard Jones	7/7/89	4(1)	1(1)	0	0	0	0	0	0	0	0
Scott Law	19/2/85	13(5)	7(5)	1	1	0	0	0	0	4	4
Richard Lopag	13/9/89	1(1)	1(1)	0	0	0	0	0	0	0	0
Nathan Massey	11/7/89	(1)	(1)	0	0	0	0	0	0	0	0
Craig Moss	4/8/84	19	13	1	1	0	0	0	0	4	4
Greg Nicholson	24/9/85	11(6)	9(5)	1	1	0	0	0	0	4	4
Jon Presley	8/7/84	23	17	7	2	0	0	0	0	28	8
Oliver Pursglove	18/1/86	21(1)	16(1)	3	3	0	0	0	0	12	12
Brendan Rawlins	28/1/82	1(22)	1(16)	6	4	0	0	0	0	24	16
George Rayner	19/9/80	12	8	4	2	0	0	0	0	16	8
Luke Rayner	8/11/87	1	0	0	0	0	0	0	0	0	0
Ben Sagar	19/12/89	3	1	2	0	0	0	0	0	8	0
Tom Sheldrake	3/9/88	11(1)	9(1)	2	1	0	0	0	0	8	4
Jamie Shepherd	14/8/90	1(2)	(2)	0	0	0	0	0	0	0	0
Andy Shickell	9/5/81	22(4)	17(2)	5	3	0	0	0	0	20	12
Daley Williams	15/5/86	17	11	6	4	0	0	0	0	24	16
Jamaine Wray	15/3/84	5(19)	4(14)	2	0	0	0	0	0	8	0

Gavin Duffy

LEAGUE RECORD
P20-W4-D1-L15-BP5
(11th, Championship)
F362, A703, Diff-341
10 points. *(9 points deducted for entering administration)*

CHALLENGE CUP
Round Three

NORTHERN RAIL CUP
Semi-Finalists/4th, Pool 1

ATTENDANCES
Best - v Widnes (NRCSF - 1,686)
Worst - v Toulouse (CC - 543)
Total (excluding Challenge Cup) - 14,633
Average (excluding Challenge Cup) - 1,045
(Up by 129 on 2009, Ch1)

CLUB RECORDS **MATCH RECORDS**	**Highest score:** 104-4 v Highfield, 23/4/95 **Highest score against:** 2-92 v Leigh, 30/4/86 **Record attendance:** 14,500 v Halifax, 3/3/51
	Tries: 6 Jason Critchley v Widnes, 18/8/96
	Goals: 15 John Wasyliw v Nottingham City, 1/11/92; Martyn Wood v Lancashire Lynx, 1/5/2000 **Points:** 36 John Wasyliw v Nottingham City, 1/11/92
SEASON RECORDS	**Tries:** 45 Nick Pinkney 1994-95 **Goals:** 187 John Wasyliw 1992-93 **Points:** 490 John Wasyliw 1992-93
CAREER RECORDS	**Tries:** 155 Sam Stacey 1904-1920 **Goals:** 967 Brian Jefferson 1965-77 **Points:** 2,116 Brian Jefferson 1965-77
	Appearances: 372 Hartley Tempest 1902-1915; David McGoun 1925-38

LEIGH CENTURIONS

DATE	FIXTURE	RESULT	SCORERS	LGE	ATT
31/1/10	Oldham (h) (NRC)	W24-12	t:Maden(2),McConnell,Goulden,Cunniffe g:Nanyn(2)	N/A	1,627
7/2/10	York (a) (NRC)	L13-12	t:Alstead,McConnell g:Nanyn(2)	1st(P2)	911
14/2/10	Featherstone (h) (NRC)	W36-6	t:Hill,Leuluai,Alstead,Nanyn(2),Mitchell g:Hartley(6)	1st(P2)	1,729
25/2/10	Barrow (h)	D20-20	t:Donlan(2),Alstead g:Hartley(3),Nanyn	6th	2,203
3/3/10	Dewsbury (a) (NRC)	W22-44	t:Maden,Duffy(2),Blythe,Emmitt,McCarthy,Hill,Armitstead g:Nanyn(6)	2nd(P2)	888
7/3/10	Wath Brow (h) (CCR3)	W52-4	t:Goulden(2),Alstead(4),Stanton,Nanyn(2),Hill g:Nanyn(6)	N/A	1,370
14/3/10	Keighley (a)	W12-34	t:Ridyard,Nanyn(2),Taylor,Paul,Maden g:Nanyn(5)	4th	1,115
21/3/10	Whitehaven (h)	W44-12	t:Paul,McCarthy,Ridyard,Nanyn,Emmitt,Alstead,Maden,Blythe g:Nanyn(5),Ridyard	3rd	1,891
28/3/10	Halifax (a)	W10-48	t:Ridyard,Mitchell(2),Emmitt,Donlan,Nanyn,Blythe,Paul g:Nanyn(6),Ridyard(2)	2nd	3,071
2/4/10	Toulouse (a)	W6-36	t:Leuluai,McConnell,Armitstead,Stanton,Donlan,Higson g:Nanyn(6)	2nd	1,100
5/4/10	Batley (h)	W26-4	t:Blythe(3),Hill,Duffy g:Nanyn,Paul(2)	1st	2,246
17/4/10	Limoux (a) (CCR4)	W20-32	t:Alstead,Stanton,Nanyn(2),Morrison,Hill g:Nanyn(4)	N/A	2,000
25/4/10	Sheffield (h)	W36-20	t:Donlan(2),Paul,Hill,McConnell,Blythe g:Nanyn(6)	2nd	1,878
29/4/10	Dewsbury (a)	W14-30	t:Armitstead,Goulden,Emmitt(2),Ridyard g:Nanyn(5)	2nd	1,151
7/5/10	Bradford (a) (CCR5)	L58-16	t:Ridyard,Donlan,Armitstead g:Nanyn(2)	N/A	4,250
13/5/10	Widnes (h)	W30-16	t:McConnell(2),Nanyn(2),Emmitt g:Nanyn(5)	1st	3,392
18/5/10	Featherstone (a)	L16-24	t:Goulden,Hill,Nanyn g:Nanyn(2)	2nd	2,425
23/5/10	Whitehaven (a)	W8-12	t:Ridyard,Paul g:Nanyn(2)	2nd	1,100
30/5/10	Halifax (a)	L40-46	t:Maden(2),Goulden,Donlan,Morrison,Ridyard,Armitstead g:Nanyn(6)	2nd	2,536
6/6/10	Hunslet (a) (NRCQF)	W6-42	t:Taylor,Nicholson,Nanyn(2),Morrison,Alstead,Emmitt g:Nanyn(7)	N/A	770
13/6/10	Batley (a)	L32-12	t:Mort,Maden g:Nanyn,Mort	2nd	938
17/6/10	Batley (h) (NRCSF)	L4-25	t:Maden	N/A	2,058
27/6/10	Keighley (h)	W36-18	t:Donlan,Alstead,Armitstead,Blythe(2),Ridyard,Duffy g:Nanyn(4)	2nd	1,265
3/7/10	Barrow (a)	L34-24	t:Morrison,Mitchell,McCarthy,Ridyard g:Nanyn(4)	2nd	2,078
8/7/10	Featherstone (a)	L34-26	t:Ridyard,Mitchell,Emmitt,Blythe,Goulden g:Ridyard(3)	2nd	1,632
25/7/10	Widnes (a)	W18-38	t:Donlan(2),Stanton,Nanyn(2),Duffy g:Nanyn(7)	2nd	3,356
1/8/10	Dewsbury (h)	L6-30	t:McConnell g:Stanton	3rd	1,682
14/8/10	Toulouse (h)	W38-16	t:Hill,Maden(2),Leuluai,Mitchell,Donlan,Ridyard g:Duffy,Ridyard(4)	3rd	1,922
19/8/10	Sheffield (a)	L29-28	t:Nanyn(2),Mitchell,Duffy,Bibey g:Nanyn(4)	3rd	1,243
2/9/10	Sheffield (h) (EPO)	L24-26	t:Armitstead,Smith,Nanyn,Nash g:Nanyn(4)	N/A	1,516

		APP		TRIES		GOALS		FG		PTS	
	D.O.B.	ALL	Ch	ALL	Ch	ALL	Ch	ALL	Ch	ALL	Ch
Andy Ainscough	24/4/90	(2)	0	0	0	0	0	0	0	0	0
David Alstead	18/2/82	17(3)	10(3)	11	3	0	0	0	0	44	12
Dave Armitstead	15/1/84	13(15)	8(11)	7	5	0	0	0	0	28	20
Ricky Bibey	22/9/81	20(3)	16(3)	1	1	0	0	0	0	4	4
Matty Blythe	20/11/88	19	17	10	9	0	0	0	0	40	36
Craig Briscoe	8/12/92	(1)	(1)	0	0	0	0	0	0	0	0
Dale Cunniffe	25/3/87	(1)	0	1	0	0	0	0	0	4	0
Stuart Donlan	29/8/78	28	20	12	11	0	0	0	0	48	44
John Duffy	2/7/80	15(12)	11(10)	6	4	1	1	0	0	26	18
Jamie Durbin	7/9/84	1(1)	1	0	0	0	0	0	0	0	0
Jacob Emmitt	4/10/88	6(7)	4(5)	8	6	0	0	0	0	32	24
Tommy Goulden	30/6/81	21(6)	14(4)	7	4	0	0	0	0	28	16
Tim Hartley	2/1/86	4(1)	1	0	0	9	3	0	0	18	6
Adam Higson	19/5/87	9(4)	7(1)	1	1	0	0	0	0	4	4
Chris Hill	3/11/87	22(7)	16(5)	8	4	0	0	0	0	32	16
Macgraff Leuluai	9/2/90	15(10)	7(9)	3	2	0	0	0	0	12	8
Steve Maden	13/9/82	30	21	11	7	0	0	0	0	44	28
Tyrone McCarthy	21/4/88	8(6)	7(4)	3	2	0	0	0	0	12	8
Dave McConnell	25/3/81	21(7)	15(4)	7	5	0	0	0	0	28	20
Danny Meekin	16/3/89	(3)	0	0	0	0	0	0	0	0	0
Lee Mitchell	8/9/88	10(4)	7(4)	7	6	0	0	0	0	28	24
Mike Morrison	9/9/87	6(13)	3(10)	4	2	0	0	0	0	16	8
Ian Mort	21/6/88	2(1)	1	1	1	1	1	0	0	6	6
Mick Nanyn	3/6/82	27	19	20	12	103	74	0	0	286	196
Stephen Nash	14/1/86	2(3)	2(3)	1	1	0	0	0	0	4	4
Anthony Nicholson	28/11/90	(2)	(1)	1	0	0	0	0	0	4	0
Robbie Paul	3/2/76	27	19	5	5	2	2	0	0	24	24
Martyn Ridyard	25/7/86	22(5)	16(3)	11	10	10	10	0	0	64	60
Paul Smith	17/5/77	3(2)	3(2)	1	1	0	0	0	0	4	4
Nicky Stanton	18/3/89	13(1)	8(1)	4	2	1	1	0	0	18	10
James Taylor	11/9/84	29	20	2	1	0	0	0	0	8	4

Mick Nanyn

LEAGUE RECORD
P20-W12-D1-L7-BP5
(3rd, Championship/
Elimination Play-Off)
F580, A403, Diff+177
43 points.

CHALLENGE CUP
Round Five

NORTHERN RAIL CUP
Semi-Finalists/2nd, Pool 2

ATTENDANCES
Best - v Widnes (Ch - 3,392)
Worst - v Keighley (Ch - 1,265)
Total (excluding Challenge Cup) - 28,370
Average (excluding
Challenge Cup) - 2,026
(Up by 109 on 2009)

CLUB RECORDS
MATCH RECORDS
Highest score: 92-2 v Keighley, 30/4/86 Highest score against: 4-94 v Workington, 26/2/95 **Record attendance:** 31,326 v St Helens, 14/3/53
Tries: 6 Jack Wood v York, 4/10/47; Neil Turley v Workington, 31/1/2001
Goals: 15 Mick Stacey v Doncaster, 28/3/76 **Points:** 42 Neil Turley v Chorley, 4/4/2004

SEASON RECORDS
CAREER RECORDS
Tries: 55 Neil Turley 2001 **Goals:** 187 Neil Turley 2004 **Points:** 468 Neil Turley 2004
Tries: 189 Mick Martyn 1954-67 **Goals:** 1,043 Jimmy Ledgard 1948-58 **Points:** 2,492 John Woods 1976-85; 1990-92
Appearances: 503 Albert Worrall 1920-38

SHEFFIELD EAGLES

DATE	FIXTURE	RESULT	SCORERS	LGE	ATT
7/2/10	Featherstone (a) (NRC)	D18-18	t:Stringer,Rowe,Cook g:Woodcock(3)	6th(P2)	1,175
14/2/10	York (h) (NRC) ●	W40-10	t:Stringer(3),McDonald,Ropati,Hirst,Cook(2) g:Woodcock(4)	5th(P2)	814
17/2/10	Halifax (h) (NRC) ●	W13-6	t:Ropati,Howieson g:Woodcock(2) fg:Cook	1st(P2)	851
22/2/10	Oldham (a) (NRC) ●●	W22-24	t:Barlow(2),Coleman,Green g:Coleman(4)	1st(P2)	340
28/2/10	Halifax (a)	L32-26	t:Cook,Thackeray,Yere(2) g:Stringer(3),Ropati(2)	8th	2,139
7/3/10	Thatto Heath (h) (CCR3) ●	W54-0	t:Stringer,Cook(2),Yere,Green,Hirst,Taulapapa(2),Lindsay,Brooks g:Stringer(5),Ropati(2)	N/A	502
14/3/10	Widnes (h) ●	L30-44	t:Stringer,Ropati(2),Yere,Cook g:Stringer(4),Lindsay	8th	1,085
19/3/10	Dewsbury (h) ●	W22-10	t:Stringer,Ropati(2),McDonald g:Stringer(2),Ropati	6th	835
2/4/10	Keighley (a)	D16-16	t:Szostak,Barlow,Cook g:Stringer,Lindsay	7th	927
5/4/10	Barrow (a)	L50-4	t:Stringer	7th	1,854
11/4/10	Featherstone (h)	L16-40	t:Taulapapa,Cook,McDonald g:Lindsay,Stringer	9th	2,871
17/4/10	Wigan (h) (CCR4)	L34-50	t:Yere,Barnett(3),Rowe,Lindsay g:Stringer(5)	N/A	2,950
25/4/10	Leigh (a)	L36-20	t:Barnett,Ropati,Groom,Exton g:Stringer(2)	9th	1,878
3/5/10	Whitehaven (h)	W64-24	t:Yere,Szostak,Brooks,Rowe(3),Ropati(2),Groom,Cook(2),Thackeray g:Ropati(4),Lindsay(4)	7th	1,301
12/5/10	Batley (h)	W22-12	t:Thackeray,Cook,Mills,Rowe(2) g:Lindsay,Ropati(2)	7th	1,170
15/5/10	Toulouse (h)	W38-24	t:Ropati,Groom,Barnett,Rowe,Cook(3) g:Stringer(4),Lindsay	6th	979
20/5/10	Dewsbury (a)	W20-22	t:Cook(2),Stringer,McDonald g:Stringer(3)	6th	1,066
27/5/10	Keighley (h)	L24-25	t:Hirst,Yere,Exton,Barlow,Lindsay g:Stringer,Lindsay	5th	1,271
6/6/10	Batley (a) (NRCQF)	L26-16	t:McDonald,Cook,Mills g:Lindsay(2)	N/A	708
13/6/10	Whitehaven (a)	W14-24	t:Green,Yere(2),Cook,Lindsay g:Bergin(2)	5th	860
24/6/10	Barrow (h)	L26-36	t:Stringer,Taulapapa(2),Exton g:Bergin(5)	5th	848
4/7/10	Batley (h)	W12-20	t:Hepworth,Taulapapa,Brooks g:Bergin(4)	5th	747
10/7/10	Toulouse (a)	W24-34	t:Brown,Brooks,Ropati,Bergin(2),Szostak g:Bergin(5)	5th	2,214
1/8/10	Featherstone (a)	W30-32	t:Yere(3),Lindsay,Bergin,Ropati g:Brown,Bergin(3)	5th	2,381
8/8/10	Halifax (h)	L24-38	t:Yere(2),Green,Ropati(2) g:Brown(2)	5th	1,473
12/8/10	Widnes (a)	L30-10	t:Bergin,Taulapapa g:Brown	6th	2,659
19/8/10	Leigh (h)	W29-28	t:Taulapapa(3),Bergin,Cook g:Brown(4) fg:Brown	6th	1,243
2/9/10	Leigh (a) (EPO)	W24-26	t:Bergin(2),Hirst,Yere(2),Szostak g:Brown	N/A	1,516
10/9/10	Barrow (a) (ESF)	W14-21	t:Lindsay,Rowe,Cook g:Brown(4) fg:Brown	N/A	2,231
16/9/10	Halifax (a) (FE)	L42-16	t:Mills,Rowe,Ropati g:Brown(2)	N/A	1,490

● Played at Don Valley Stadium
●● Played at Park Lane, Sedgley Park

		APP		TRIES		GOALS		FG		PTS	
	D.O.B.	ALL	Ch	ALL	Ch	ALL	Ch	ALL	Ch	ALL	Ch
Sam Barlow	7/3/88	1(14)	(9)	4	2	0	0	0	0	16	8
Richie Barnett	26/4/81	11	7	5	2	0	0	0	0	20	8
Tim Bergin	29/7/85	15	13	7	7	19	19	0	0	66	66
Matty Brooks	9/10/86	6(9)	4(8)	4	3	0	0	0	0	16	12
Simon Brown	23/6/89	8	8	1	1	15	15	2	2	36	36
Mike Burnett	6/10/88	2(1)	2(1)	0	0	0	0	0	0	0	0
John Coleman	22/6/86	1	0	1	0	4	0	0	0	12	0
Craig Cook	26/5/83	30	23	20	14	0	0	1	0	81	56
Ged Corcoran	28/3/83	5(11)	3(8)	0	0	0	0	0	0	0	0
Jamie Cottle	20/5/90	1	1	0	0	0	0	0	0	0	0
Trevor Exton	8/11/81	16(12)	12(10)	3	3	0	0	0	0	12	12
Peter Green	2/12/81	24(3)	19(3)	4	2	0	0	0	0	16	8
Aaron Groom	23/6/87	6(3)	5(1)	3	3	0	0	0	0	12	12
Michael Haley	19/9/87	6(13)	4(10)	0	0	0	0	0	0	0	0
Corey Hanson	11/8/92	(1)	(1)	0	0	0	0	0	0	0	0
Andrew Henderson	17/6/79	(7)	(7)	0	0	0	0	0	0	0	0
Ryan Hepworth	16/1/81	11(11)	9(9)	1	1	0	0	0	0	4	4
Joe Hirst	21/4/87	17(8)	14(7)	4	2	0	0	0	0	16	8
Jack Howieson	28/7/81	12(1)	8(1)	1	0	0	0	0	0	4	0
Kyle Kesik	3/6/89	(1)	0	0	0	0	0	0	0	0	0
Brendon Lindsay	21/9/77	29	23	6	4	12	10	0	0	48	36
Dane McDonald	14/7/87	18(2)	11(2)	5	3	0	0	0	0	20	12
Danny Mills	10/8/82	14	13	3	2	0	0	0	0	12	8
Jason Mossop	12/9/85	6(3)	3(1)	0	0	0	0	0	0	0	0
Tangi Ropati	15/11/84	27	21	15	13	11	9	0	0	82	70
Alex Rowe	11/3/85	(18)	(13)	10	8	0	0	0	0	40	32
Mitchell Stringer	1/11/83	27	21	10	5	31	21	0	0	102	62
Alex Szostak	4/3/86	23(1)	19(1)	4	4	0	0	0	0	16	16
Misi Taulapapa	25/1/82	26	21	10	8	0	0	0	0	40	32
Ashley Thackeray	6/11/87	15	9	3	3	0	0	0	0	12	12
Jonny Woodcock	8/12/81	6(1)	3	0	0	9	0	0	0	18	0
Menzie Yere	24/10/83	27	23	16	14	0	0	0	0	64	56

Brendon Lindsay

LEAGUE RECORD
P20-W10-D1-L9-BP3
(6th, Championship/
Final Eliminator)
F503, A545, Diff-42
35 points.

CHALLENGE CUP
Round Four

NORTHERN RAIL CUP
Quarter Finalists/1st, Pool 2

ATTENDANCES
Best - v Wigan (CC - 2,950)
Worst - v Thatto Heath (CC - 502)
Total (excluding Challenge Cup) - 14,741
Average (excluding
Challenge Cup) - 1,228
(Up by 138 on 2009)

CLUB RECORDS	Highest score: 98-4 v London Skolars, 3/8/2003 Highest score against: 0-88 v Hull, 2/3/2003 Record attendance: 10,603 v Bradford, 16/8/97
MATCH RECORDS	Tries: 5 Daryl Powell v Mansfield, 2/1/89 Goals: 13 Gavin Brown v London Skolars, 3/8/2003 Points: 32 Roy Rafferty v Fulham, 21/9/86
SEASON RECORDS	Tries: 30 Iva Ropati 1991-92 Goals: 148 Mark Aston 1988-89 Points: 307 Mark Aston 1988-89
CAREER RECORDS	Tries: 114 Daryl Powell 1984-95 Goals: 986 Mark Aston 1986-2004 Points: 2,142 Mark Aston 1986-2004 Appearances: 389 Mark Aston 1986-2004

TOULOUSE OLYMPIQUE

DATE	FIXTURE	RESULT	SCORERS	LGE	ATT
28/2/10	Dewsbury (h)	W26-22	t:Bromley(2),Duport,Tisseyre,Planas g:N Wynn(3)	4th	1,200
6/3/10	Keighley (a) (CCR3)	W26-35	t:Planas(2),Bienes,Tisseyre,N Wynn,Bromley g:N Wynn(5) fg:N Wynn	N/A	543
13/3/10	Whitehaven (a)	L34-20	t:Bromley,Maria,Ormeno,Planas g:N Wynn(2)	6th	1,181
20/3/10	Keighley (h)	W34-26	t:Bienes,Gay(2),Bromley,Planas,Larroyer g:N Wynn(5)	5th	1,829
27/3/10	Barrow (h)	L16-48	t:Maria,Gay,Larroyer g:N Wynn(2)	5th	1,500
2/4/10	Leigh (h)	L6-36	t:Pelo g:N Wynn	8th	1,100
5/4/10	Halifax (a)	L50-6	t:Bromley g:N Wynn	8th	1,725
10/4/10	Widnes (a)	W36-42	t:Griffi,Duport(3),N Wynn(2),Payan g:N Wynn(7)	6th	2,793
17/4/10	St Helens (a) (CCR4)	L56-16	t:Duport,Mendes Varela,Mitchell g:N Wynn(2)	N/A	4,043
1/5/10	Batley (h)	W20-12	t:Mendes Varela(2),Griffi g:N Wynn(4)	6th	1,100
6/5/10	Featherstone (a)	W24-26	t:Tisseyre,Planas,Mitchell,Bromley,Duport g:N Wynn(3)	6th	2,223
15/5/10	Sheffield (a)	L38-24	t:Houles,Duport,Bromley,Griffi g:N Wynn(4)	7th	979
22/5/10	Featherstone (h)	L28-34	t:Planas,Mitchell,Bienes,Tisseyre,Bromley g:N Wynn(4)	8th	1,328
22/6/10	Batley (a)	W40-42	t:Maria,Mitchell,Mendes Varela(2),Larroyer(2),Bromley,Gigord g:N Wynn(5)	8th	689
26/6/10	Whitehaven (h)	W34-12	t:Bromley(2),N Wynn,Mitchell,Anselme,Pelo g:N Wynn(5)	6th	1,071
3/7/10	Dewsbury (a)	W12-36	t:Mitchell(3),Bromley(2),N Wynn g:N Wynn(6)	6th	864
10/7/10	Sheffield (h)	L24-34	t:Maria,Houles,Ormeno,Pelo g:N Wynn(4)	7th	2,214
24/7/10	Keighley (a)	W27-26	t:Gigot,Payan,N Wynn,Mendes Varela g:N Wynn(5)	6th	736
31/7/10	Barrow (a)	L42-6	t:Maria g:N Wynn	7th	1,440
7/8/10	Widnes (h)	L30-44	t:Mendes Varela(2),Maria(2),Anselme g:N Wynn(5)	8th	987
14/8/10	Leigh (a)	L38-16	t:Payan(2),Anselme g:N Wynn(2)	8th	1,922
21/8/10	Halifax (h)	L24-38	t:Payan,Bromley,Pelo,N Wynn g:N Wynn(4)	8th	902

		APP		TRIES		GOALS		FG		PTS	
	D.O.B.	ALL	Ch	ALL	Ch	ALL	Ch	ALL	Ch	ALL	Ch
Eric Anselme	20/5/79	22	20	3	3	0	0	0	0	12	12
William Barthau	30/1/90	1	1	0	0	0	0	0	0	0	0
Clement Bienes	21/1/90	14	12	3	2	0	0	0	0	12	8
Rory Bromley	1/5/84	21	19	15	14	0	0	0	0	60	56
Vincent Duport	15/12/87	13	11	7	6	0	0	0	0	28	24
Nicolas Faure	30/5/84	1(5)	1(5)	0	0	0	0	0	0	0	0
Cedric Gay	12/3/82	4(2)	4(2)	3	3	0	0	0	0	12	12
Yohann Gigord	4/1/89	5(6)	4(6)	1	1	0	0	0	0	4	4
Tony Gigot	27/12/90	(1)	(1)	1	1	0	0	0	0	4	4
Jerome Gout	13/5/86	2(9)	2(8)	0	0	0	0	0	0	0	0
Mathieu Griffi	2/3/83	9(6)	9(5)	3	3	0	0	0	0	12	12
Maxime Herold	9/9/89	(2)	(2)	0	0	0	0	0	0	0	0
Sylvain Houles	3/8/81	16(3)	15(2)	2	2	0	0	0	0	8	8
Kevin Larroyer	19/6/89	3(16)	3(14)	4	4	0	0	0	0	16	16
Antoni Maria	21/3/87	20(2)	19(1)	7	7	0	0	0	0	28	28
Romain Mencarini	4/8/89	5(9)	5(8)	0	0	0	0	0	0	0	0
Carlos Mendes Varela	28/12/84	18	16	8	7	0	0	0	0	32	28
Martin Mitchell	21/10/85	11(1)	10(1)	8	7	0	0	0	0	32	28
Andrei Olari	4/11/88	3	3	0	0	0	0	0	0	0	0
Bruno Ormeno	3/12/82	11(1)	11	2	2	0	0	0	0	8	8
Sebastien Payan	12/7/86	11	10	5	5	0	0	0	0	20	20
Teli Pelo	22/7/84	3(9)	2(9)	4	4	0	0	0	0	16	16
Sebastien Planas	5/5/84	22	20	7	5	0	0	0	0	28	20
Yoan Tisseyre	8/5/89	17(4)	15(4)	4	3	0	0	0	0	16	12
Remi Vignau	13/11/91	(2)	(2)	0	0	0	0	0	0	0	0
Constant Villegas	21/10/86	4(1)	4(1)	0	0	0	0	0	0	0	0
Simon Worrall	10/10/84	3(4)	2(4)	0	0	0	0	0	0	0	0
Brendan Worth	18/7/84	17(1)	15(1)	0	0	0	0	0	0	0	0
Nathan Wynn	10/1/86	22	20	7	6	80	73	1	0	189	170
Tim Wynn	19/7/85	8(4)	7(4)	0	0	0	0	0	0	0	0

Rory Bromley

LEAGUE RECORD
P20-W8-D0-L12-BP3
(8th, Championship)
F486, A649, Diff-163
27 points.

CHALLENGE CUP
Round Four

NORTHERN RAIL CUP
Not entered

ATTENDANCES
Best - v Sheffield (Ch - 2,214)
Worst - v Halifax (Ch - 902)
Total (excluding Challenge Cup) - 13,231
Average (excluding
Challenge Cup) - 1,323
(Down by 1,049 on 2009)

CLUB RECORDS
MATCH RECORDS

Highest score: 60-22 v Batley, 13/4/2009 Highest score against: 0-70 v Widnes, 12/3/2009 Record attendance: 3,507 v Leigh, 20/4/2009
Tries: 3 Nathan Wynn v Batley, 13/4/2009; Vincent Duport v Widnes, 10/4/2010; Martin Mitchell v Dewsbury, 3/7/2010
Goals: 8 Nathan Wynn v Doncaster, 26/4/2009; Nathan Wynn v Batley, 13 April 2009
Points: 22 Nathan Wynn v Batley, 13/4/2009; Nathan Wynn v Widnes, 10/4/2010

SEASON RECORDS

Tries: 15 Rory Bromley 2010 Goals: 81 (inc 1 fg) Nathan Wynn 2010 Points: 189 Nathan Wynn 2010

CAREER RECORDS

Tries: 27 Rory Bromley 2009-10 Goals: 158 (inc 1 fg) Nathan Wynn 2009-10 Points: 363 Nathan Wynn 2009-10 Appearances: 42 Antoni Maria 2009-10

WHITEHAVEN

DATE	FIXTURE	RESULT	SCORERS	LGE	ATT
7/2/10	Keighley (a) (NRC)	L17-16	t:Mattinson,Calvert,S Miller g:Rudd(2)	7th(P1)	750
10/2/10	Batley (h) (NRC)	L26-34	t:Skee,Thornley,R Jackson(2),Eilbeck g:Rudd(3)	7th(P1)	888
14/2/10	Doncaster (h) (NRC)	W54-10	t:Eilbeck(3),S Miller(2),R Fox,Benson,Farrer,Calvert,Amor g:Skee(6),M Jackson	4th(P1)	808
21/2/10	Workington (a) (NRC)	L22-14	t:Mattinson,Calvert g:Rudd(3)	6th(P1)	736
5/3/10	Leigh Miners Rangers (a) (CCR3) ●	W20-40	t:Calvert,Mattinson,M Jackson,R Fox,Farrer,Sice,D Miller g:Rudd(6)	N/A	491
13/3/10	Toulouse (h)	W34-20	t:Skee,Rudd,Sice(2),R Fox,Mort g:Rudd(5)	5th	1,181
21/3/10	Leigh (a)	L44-12	t:Skee,McAvoy g:Rudd(2)	7th	1,891
28/3/10	Featherstone (a)	L54-18	t:R Fox,Eilbeck,Sice g:Rudd(3)	10th	1,551
1/4/10	Barrow (h)	L8-19	t:Rudd g:Rudd(2)	9th	1,382
5/4/10	Widnes (a)	L48-18	t:Joe,Mort,Dawes g:McNally(2),Govin	9th	3,033
11/4/10	Dewsbury (a)	W12-20	t:Rudd,Mattinson,Thornley g:Rudd(4)	8th	850
18/4/10	Blackpool (a) (CCR4)	L24-18	t:Rudd,D Miller,Philip g:Rudd(3)	N/A	471
25/4/10	Halifax (h)	L10-28	t:Smith,Rudd g:Rudd	8th	1,140
3/5/10	Sheffield (a)	L64-24	t:M Jackson,Calvert(2),R Jackson g:Rudd(4)	9th	1,301
9/5/10	Keighley (h)	L12-22	t:Veivers,Wilton g:Rudd(2)	9th	900
16/5/10	Batley (a)	L54-6	t:Mattinson g:Rudd	9th	666
23/5/10	Leigh (h)	L8-12	t:Johnson g:Rudd(2)	9th	1,100
8/6/10	Barrow (a)	L30-0		9th	1,920
13/6/10	Sheffield (h)	L14-24	t:Eilbeck,Calvert(2) g:Rudd	10th	860
26/6/10	Toulouse (a)	L34-12	t:Calvert,Barker g:Rudd(2)	10th	1,071
1/7/10	Widnes (h)	L4-40	t:Eilbeck	10th	1,518
11/7/10	Halifax (a)	L66-16	t:Rossi,Mattinson,Bower g:Rudd(2)	10th	1,970
25/7/10	Featherstone (h)	L0-48		10th	825
8/8/10	Dewsbury (h)	L10-48	t:Skee,Mattinson g:Skee	10th	504
15/8/10	Keighley (a)	W28-29	t:Hamzat,Skee,D Miller,Ackerley,S Miller g:Skee(4) fg:Barker	10th	739
22/8/10	Batley (h)	W26-12	t:McAvoy,Amor,Hamzat,S Miller,Crellin g:Skee(3)	10th	706

● Played at Leigh Sports Village

		APP		TRIES		GOALS		FG		PTS	
	D.O.B.	ALL	Ch	ALL	Ch	ALL	Ch	ALL	Ch	ALL	Ch
Shane Ackerley	19/11/91	2	2	1	1	0	0	0	0	4	4
Kyle Amor	26/5/87	14(6)	11(4)	2	1	0	0	0	0	8	4
Daniel Barker	1/12/88	13(5)	9(4)	1	1	0	0	1	1	5	5
Craig Benson	19/8/85	8	3	1	0	0	0	0	0	4	0
Kyle Bibb	25/1/88	1(3)	1(3)	0	0	0	0	0	0	0	0
Danny Bower	18/7/91	(4)	(4)	1	1	0	0	0	0	4	4
Craig Calvert	10/2/84	20	14	9	5	0	0	0	0	36	20
Brad Crellin	2/7/89	(2)	(2)	1	1	0	0	0	0	4	4
Tyrone Dalton	7/1/89	4(1)	4(1)	0	0	0	0	0	0	0	0
Mike Darby	14/10/87	2(1)	2	0	0	0	0	0	0	0	0
Stephen Dawes	14/1/85	5(1)	3(1)	1	1	0	0	0	0	4	4
Derry Eilbeck	1/6/84	21	16	7	3	0	0	0	0	28	12
Richard Farrer	25/11/85	2(6)	2(2)	2	0	0	0	0	0	8	0
David Ford	29/5/87	1(3)	(1)	0	0	0	0	0	0	0	0
Reece Fox	1/5/89	8(4)	4(4)	4	2	0	0	0	0	16	8
Steve Fox	13/2/92	3(2)	3(2)	0	0	0	0	0	0	0	0
Scott George	21/11/90	1	0	0	0	0	0	0	0	0	0
Andy Gorski	31/3/81	2(2)	2(2)	0	0	0	0	0	0	0	0
Mick Govin	5/11/84	3(3)	2(2)	0	0	1	1	0	0	2	2
Loz Hamzat	26/10/90	6	6	2	2	0	0	0	0	8	8
Howard Hill	16/1/75	18(5)	13(5)	0	0	0	0	0	0	0	0
Marc Jackson	21/8/79	7(8)	3(6)	2	1	1	0	0	0	10	4
Rob Jackson	4/9/81	21	16	3	1	0	0	0	0	12	4
Leroy Joe	31/12/74	17(3)	15(3)	1	1	0	0	0	0	4	4
Paul Johnson	13/3/88	6	6	1	1	0	0	0	0	4	4
Stefan Marsh	3/9/90	1	1	0	0	0	0	0	0	0	0
Graeme Mattinson	24/4/85	26	20	7	4	0	0	0	0	28	16
Scott McAvoy	9/4/86	10	10	2	2	0	0	0	0	8	8
Ryan McDonald	24/2/78	2(3)	1(1)	0	0	0	0	0	0	0	0
Gregg McNally	2/1/91	3	3	0	0	2	2	0	0	4	4
Dexter Miller	3/6/82	13(2)	8(1)	3	1	0	0	0	0	12	4
Spencer Miller	27/2/80	18(1)	13	5	2	0	0	0	0	20	8
Ian Mort	21/6/88	4	4	2	2	0	0	0	0	8	8
Tom Philip	25/6/83	2(1)	1(1)	1	0	0	0	0	0	4	0
Jay Rossi	26/6/93	4	4	1	1	0	0	0	0	4	4
Carl Rudd	10/10/82	21	15	5	4	48	31	0	0	116	78
Marc Shackley	14/1/89	2(3)	2(3)	0	0	0	0	0	0	0	0
Carl Sice	13/4/80	2(9)	1(6)	4	3	0	0	0	0	16	12
Dylan Skee	13/1/86	15	12	5	4	14	8	0	0	48	32
Chris Smith	21/1/90	(10)	(9)	1	1	0	0	0	0	4	4
Andy Thornley	1/3/89	15(9)	13(6)	2	1	0	0	0	0	8	4
Motu Tony	29/5/81	5	5	0	0	0	0	0	0	0	0
Josh Veivers	9/12/89	8	8	1	1	0	0	0	0	4	4
Kurt Wilton	26/6/89	2(7)	2(7)	1	1	0	0	0	0	4	4

Graeme Mattinson

LEAGUE RECORD
P20-W4-D0-L16-BP4
(10th, Championship)
F281, A707, Diff-426
16 points.

CHALLENGE CUP
Round Four

NORTHERN RAIL CUP
7th, Pool 1

ATTENDANCES
Best - v Widnes (Ch - 1,518)
Worst - v Dewsbury (Ch - 504)
Total (excluding Challenge Cup) - 11,812
Average (excluding Challenge Cup) - 984
(Down by 615 on 2009)

CLUB RECORDS	**Highest score:** 86-6 v Highfield, 25/1/95 **Highest score against:** 8-106 v Wigan, 12/5/2008 **Record attendance:** 18,500 v Wakefield, 19/3/60
MATCH RECORDS	**Tries:** 6 Vince Gribbin v Doncaster, 18/11/84 **Goals:** 13 Lee Anderson v Highfield, 25/1/95 **Points:** 32 Mick Nanyn v Batley, 22/8/2004
SEASON RECORDS	**Tries:** 34 Mike Pechey 1994-95 **Goals:** 141 John McKeown 1956-57 **Points:** 398 Mick Nanyn 2004
CAREER RECORDS	**Tries:** 248 David Seeds 1993-2007 **Goals:** 1,050 John McKeown 1948-61 **Points:** 2,133 John McKeown 1948-61
	Appearances: 417 John McKeown 1948-61

WIDNES VIKINGS

DATE	FIXTURE	RESULT	SCORERS	LGE	ATT
2/2/10	Gateshead (h) (NRC)	W50-6	t:Thackeray,Ford(4),Pickersgill,Gardner,Dean(2),Grady,Allen g:Yates,Grady(2)	N/A	2,200
7/2/10	Batley (a) (NRC)	D30-30	t:Doran,Kavanagh(2),Ainscough(2),Thackeray g:Grady(3)	2nd(P1)	1,004
14/2/10	Barrow (h) (NRC)	W22-20	t:Farrell,Houghton,Coyle,Ainscough g:Grady(3)	2nd(P1)	3,432
21/2/10	Swinton (a) (NRC)	W12-36	t:Kohe-Love(2),Gardner,Grady,Ainscough,M Smith,Thackeray g:Grady(4)	1st(P1)	816
28/2/10	Keighley (h)	W72-10	t:Grady(3),Gardner,Thompson(3),Allen,Farrell,Coyle,Varkulis,Thackeray,Yates g:Grady(10)	1st	2,777
9/3/10	Wigan St Judes (h) (CCR3)	W64-12	t:Allen(2),Thackeray,Doran,Yates,Houghton,Grady,Hulme(2),Varkulis(2),Coyle g:Grady(8)	N/A	1,622
14/3/10	Sheffield (a) ●	W30-44	t:G Haggerty,Gannon(2),Gardner(2),Thackeray,Webster g:Grady(8)	1st	1,085
18/3/10	Halifax (h)	L28-30	t:Coyle(2),Doran,Farrell,Varkulis g:Grady(4)	4th	3,286
28/3/10	Dewsbury (a)	W30-36	t:Thackeray(3),Webster,Grady,C Gerrard g:Grady(6)	3rd	1,499
5/4/10	Whitehaven (h)	W48-18	t:Thackeray,Ford,Doran,C Gerrard,Kohe-Love,Gardner,Hulme,Grady,Flynn g:Grady(6)	3rd	3,033
10/4/10	Toulouse (h)	L38-42	t:Davies,Strong,Flynn,Thackeray(3),Coyle g:Grady(5)	5th	2,793
22/4/10	Lezignan (h) (CCR4)	W44-24	t:Coyle,Thackeray,Gardner,C Gerrard,Yates(3),Kavanagh g:Grady(6)	N/A	1,349
25/4/10	Batley (a)	W24-32	t:Grady,Ford,C Gerrard,Flynn(2) g:Grady(6)	5th	1,146
30/4/10	Featherstone (h)	L8-9	t:Gardner,Flynn	5th	3,448
8/5/10	Wigan (h) (CCR5)	L10-64	t:Gardner(2) g:Grady	N/A	5,504
13/5/10	Leigh (a)	L30-16	t:Ainscough,Netherton,Flynn g:Grady(2)	5th	3,392
23/5/10	Batley (h)	L16-35	t:Kavanagh,Thackeray(2) g:Grady(2)	5th	2,780
3/6/10	Barrow (h) (NRCQF)	W26-12	t:Grady,Netherton(2),Gaskell(2),Kohe-Love g:Grady	N/A	1,718
13/6/10	Barrow (h)	L20-24	t:Varkulis(2),Gannon(2) g:Grady(2)	6th	2,958
20/6/10	Keighley (a) (NRCSF)	W18-48	t:Thackeray(3),Allen,Flynn,Ainscough,M Smith,Houghton g:Grady(8)	N/A	1,686
27/6/10	Featherstone (a)	L30-22	t:C Gerrard,Gardner,Allen,Ainscough g:Grady(3)	7th	1,776
1/7/10	Whitehaven (a)	W4-40	t:Allen(2),Grady(2),Netherton,Doran,Varkulis g:Grady(4),Craven(2)	7th	1,518
11/7/10	Dewsbury (h) ●●	W27-26	t:Davies,Thackeray,C Gerrard,M Smith,Grady g:Grady(3) fg:Coyle	6th	2,715
18/7/10	Batley (NRCF) ●●	L25-24	t:Davies,Thackeray,Flynn,C Gerrard g:Grady(4)	N/A	8,138
25/7/10	Leigh (a)	L18-38	t:Marsh,K Haggerty,Ainscough g:Craven(3)	7th	3,356
29/7/10	Halifax (a)	L30-16	t:Kavanagh,Flynn,Gaskell g:Craven(2)	8th	2,707
7/8/10	Toulouse (a)	W30-44	t:Craven,M Smith,Marsh(2),Flynn,Thackeray,Gaskell,Gardner g:Craven(6)	6th	987
12/8/10	Sheffield (h)	W30-10	t:Gaskell,C Gerrard(2),Thackeray,Craven g:Craven(5)	5th	2,659
18/8/10	Barrow (a)	W14-32	t:K Haggerty,Varkulis(3),Thackeray,Flynn g:Thackeray,K Haggerty(2),Craven	5th	1,796
22/8/10	Keighley (a)	W24-32	t:Craven(3),Coyle,Brown,Pickersgill g:Craven(4)	5th	1,173
5/9/10	Barrow (a) (EPO)	L38-0		N/A	2,434

● Played at Don Valley Stadium   ●● Played at Bloomfield Road, Blackpool

		APP		TRIES		GOALS		FG		PTS	
	D.O.B.	ALL	Ch	ALL	Ch	ALL	Ch	ALL	Ch	ALL	Ch
Shaun Ainscough	27/11/89	9(1)	4(1)	8	3	0	0	0	0	32	12
Dave Allen	15/9/85	16(1)	9(1)	8	4	0	0	0	0	32	16
Alex Brown	28/4/93	1	1	1	0	0	0	0	0	4	4
Thomas Coyle	10/5/88	9(11)	6(8)	8	5	0	0	1	1	33	21
Danny Craven	21/11/91	7(1)	7(1)	5	5	23	23	0	0	66	66
Ben Davies	2/11/89	6(11)	5(8)	3	2	0	0	0	0	12	8
Chris Dean	17/1/88	1	0	2	0	0	0	0	0	8	0
Lee Doran	23/3/81	29	20	5	3	0	0	0	0	20	12
Liam Farrell	2/7/90	5(1)	3	3	2	0	0	0	0	12	8
Paddy Flynn	11/12/87	25	19	11	9	0	0	0	0	44	36
James Ford	29/9/82	12	5	6	2	0	0	0	0	24	8
Jim Gannon	16/6/77	27	20	4	4	0	0	0	0	16	16
Matt Gardner	24/8/84	29	19	12	7	0	0	0	0	48	28
Dean Gaskell	12/4/83	12(1)	9(1)	5	3	0	0	0	0	20	12
Alex Gerrard	5/11/91	(2)	(1)	0	0	0	0	0	0	0	0
Chris Gerrard	1/10/89	21(7)	15(3)	9	7	0	0	0	0	36	28
Shane Grady	13/12/89	24(2)	14(2)	13	9	101	61	0	0	254	158
Gareth Haggerty	8/9/81	7(1)	3(1)	1	1	0	0	0	0	4	4
Kurt Haggerty	8/1/89	8(1)	8(1)	2	2	2	2	0	0	12	12
Daniel Heckenberg	27/10/79	7(2)	7(2)	0	0	0	0	0	0	0	0
David Houghton	2/11/89	1(22)	(14)	3	0	0	0	0	0	12	0
Danny Hulme	15/2/91	(6)	(3)	3	1	0	0	0	0	12	4
Chaz I'Anson	30/11/86	1	0	0	0	0	0	0	0	0	0
Jordan James	24/5/80	4(2)	4(1)	0	0	0	0	0	0	0	0
Ben Kavanagh	4/3/88	15(16)	10(11)	5	2	0	0	0	0	20	8
Tom Kelly	26/1/92	1(7)	1(7)	0	0	0	0	0	0	0	0
Toa Kohe-Love	2/12/76	13	7	4	1	0	0	0	0	16	4
Chris Lunt	18/12/90	(1)	(1)	0	0	0	0	0	0	0	0
Stefan Marsh	3/9/90	3	3	3	3	0	0	0	0	12	12
Kirk Netherton	10/5/85	11(3)	8(3)	4	2	0	0	0	0	16	8
Steve Pickersgill	28/11/85	3(6)	1(5)	2	1	0	0	0	0	8	4
Greg Scott	21/6/91	1	1	0	0	0	0	0	0	0	0
Jack Smith	16/12/91	(1)	0	0	0	0	0	0	0	0	0
Mark Smith	18/8/81	19(3)	13(2)	4	2	0	0	0	0	16	8
Matthew Strong	17/2/87	4(4)	2(2)	1	1	0	0	0	0	4	4
Anthony Thackeray	19/2/86	30	20	24	15	1	1	0	0	98	62
Dean Thompson	22/11/88	2(1)	1(1)	3	3	0	0	0	0	12	12
Richard Varkulis	21/5/82	17(5)	14(3)	10	8	0	0	0	0	40	32
James Webster	11/7/79	13	7	2	2	0	0	0	0	8	8
Scott Yates	8/9/88	10(2)	7(1)	5	1	1	0	0	0	22	4

Shane Grady

LEAGUE RECORD
P20-W11-D0-L9-BP5
(5th, Championship)
Elimination Play-Off)
F619, A488, Diff+131
38 points.

CHALLENGE CUP
Round Five

NORTHERN RAIL CUP
Runners-Up/2nd, Pool 1

ATTENDANCES
Best - v Wigan (CC - 5,504)
Worst - v Lezignan (CC - 1,349)
Total (excluding Challenge Cup) - 37,155
Average (excluding
Challenge Cup) - 2,858
(Down by 554 on 2009)

CLUB RECORDS MATCH RECORDS	Highest score: 90-4 v Doncaster, 10/6/2007 Highest score against: 24-74 v Bradford, 7/8/2005 Record attendance: 24,205 v St Helens, 16/2/61 Tries: 7 Phil Cantillon v York, 18/2/2001
SEASON RECORDS CAREER RECORDS	Goals: 14 Mark Hewitt v Oldham, 25/7/99; Tim Hartley v Saddleworth, 7/3/2009 Points: 38 Gavin Dodd v Doncaster, 10/6/2007 Tries: 58 Martin Offiah 1988-89 Goals: 161 Mick Nanyn 2007 Points: 434 Mick Nanyn 2007 Tries: 234 Mal Aspey 1964-80 Goals: 1,083 Ray Dutton 1966-78 Points: 2,195 Ray Dutton 1966-78 Appearances: 591 Keith Elwell 1970-86

CHAMPIONSHIP 2010
Round by Round

ROUND 1

Thursday 25th February 2010

LEIGH CENTURIONS 20 BARROW RAIDERS 20

CENTURIONS: 1 Stuart Donlan; 3 David Alstead; 36 Matty Blythe; 4 Mick Nanyn; 2 Steve Maden; 6 Tim Hartley; 7 Robbie Paul; 8 Chris Hill; 9 John Duffy; 35 Jacob Emmitt; 11 James Taylor; 34 Lee Mitchell; 37 Tyrone McCarthy. Subs (all used): 14 Tommy Goulden; 15 Dave McConnell; 13 Dave Armitstead; 12 Macgraff Leuluai.
Tries: Donlan (13, 72), Alstead (18);
Goals: Hartley 3/3, Nanyn 1/2.
RAIDERS: 1 Gary Broadbent; 2 Andy Ballard; 20 Danny Halliwell; 4 Liam Harrison; 5 James Nixon; 6 Jamie Rooney; 7 James Coyle; 8 Andy Bracek; 9 Andrew Henderson; 15 Rob Roberts; 12 Ned Catic; 24 Richard Fletcher; 13 Zebastian Luisi. Subs (all used): 10 Chris Young; 16 Brett McDermott; 17 Paul Noone; 19 Nathan Mossop.
Tries: Rooney (7), Ballard (43), Halliwell (53), Young (54); **Goals:** Rooney 2/5.
Rugby Leaguer & League Express Men of the Match: *Centurions:* Chris Hill; *Raiders:* Chris Young.
Penalty count: 8-8; **Half-time:** 12-6;
Referee: Gareth Hewer; **Attendance:** 2,203.

Sunday 28th February 2010

FEATHERSTONE ROVERS 36 BATLEY BULLDOGS 10

ROVERS: 1 Ian Hardman; 5 Jon Steel; 21 Michael Coady; 4 Liam Welham; 2 Tom Saxton; 6 Kyle Briggs; 9 Liam Finn; 17 Tony Tonks; 22 Jack Lee; 10 Stuart Dickens; 12 Jon Grayshon; 11 Matty Dale; 13 Jamie Field. Subs (all used): 8 Iain Morrison; 19 Ross Divorty; 7 Andy Kain; 16 Dane Manning.
Tries: Hardman (3, 79), Dale (11), Welham (31), Steel (35, 66); **Goals:** Briggs 6/6.
BULLDOGS: 5 John Campbell; 1 Ian Preece; 3 Mark Barlow; 4 Danny Maun; 2 Lee Greenwood; 6 Paul Handforth; 7 Gareth Moore; 8 Byron Smith; 9 Kris Lythe; 10 Sean Hesketh; 17 Craig Potter; 23 Chris Buttery; 12 Mark Toohey. Subs (all used): 13 Ashley Lindsay; 26 Jason Walton; 21 James Martin; 20 David Tootill.
Tries: Walton (41), Campbell (75); **Goals:** Moore 1/2.
Rugby Leaguer & League Express Men of the Match: *Rovers:* Liam Finn; *Bulldogs:* Paul Handforth.
Penalty count: 13-11; **Half time:** 24-0;
Referee: Robert Hicks; **Attendance:** 1,353.

HALIFAX 32 SHEFFIELD EAGLES 26

HALIFAX: 4 Shad Royston; 2 Lee Paterson; 3 Jon Goddard; 5 James Haley; 23 Rob Worrincy; 6 Luke Branighan; 7 Ben Black; 8 Makali Aizue; 9 Sean Penkywicz; 16 Said Tamghart; 11 David Larder; 12 Stanley Gene; 13 Bob Beswick. Subs (all used): 14 Mark Gleeson; 19 Dominic Maloney; 17 Frank Watene; 22 David Wrench.
Tries: Worrincy (30), Royston (37, 56, 59), Penkywicz (76); **Goals:** Paterson 6/6.
EAGLES: 5 Ashley Thackeray; 24 Misi Taulapapa; 3 Menzie Yere; 23 Tangi Ropati; 27 Richie Barnett; 6 Brendon Lindsay; 21 Dane McDonald; 8 Jack Howieson; 9 Craig Cook; 10 Mitchell Stringer; 11 Alex Szostak; 12 Ged Corcoran; 19 Joe Hirst. Subs (all used): 13 Peter Green; 16 Trevor Exton; 15 Sam Barlow; 22 Ryan Hepworth.
Tries: Cook (14), Thackeray (16), Yere (41, 52);
Goals: Stringer 3/3, Ropati 2/2.
Rugby Leaguer & League Express Men of the Match: *Halifax:* Shad Royston; *Eagles:* Menzie Yere.
Penalty count: 8-10; **Half-time:** 12-12;
Referee: Jamie Leahy; **Attendance:** 2,139.

TOULOUSE OLYMPIQUE 26 DEWSBURY RAMS 22

OLYMPIQUE: 1 Rory Bromley; 2 Sebastien Payan; 3 Sebastien Planas; 4 Vincent Duport; 5 Carlos Mendes Varela; 16 Sylvain Houles; 7 Nathan Wynn; 8 Brendan Worth; 9 Martin Mitchell; 11 Tim Wynn; 14 Antoni Maria; 18 Yoan Tisseyre; 13 Eric Anselme. Subs (all used): 10 Mathieu Griffi; 15 Jerome Gout; 17 Cedric Gay; 19 Romain Mencarini.
Tries: Bromley (2, 67), Duport (18), Tisseyre (48), Planas (74); **Goals:** N Wynn 3/5.
RAMS: 2 James Haynes; 15 Bryn Powell; 26 Ayden Faal; 10 Scott Turner; 18 Chris Spurr; 13 Pat Walker; 8 Dominic Brambani; 23 Keegan Hirst; 9 Mike Emmett; 24 Anthony England; 21 Andrew Bostock; 19 Adam Hayes; 4 Rob Lunt. Subs (all used): 11 Adam Robinson; 14 Luke Stenchion; 25 James Lockwood; 36 Paul Hughes.
Tries: Emmett (12), Bostock (25), Turner (43, 52);
Goals: P Walker 3/4.
Rugby Leaguer & League Express Men of the Match: *Olympique:* Rory Bromley; *Rams:* Dominic Brambani.
Penalty count: 7-7; **Half-time:** 10-12;
Referee: Peter Brooke; **Attendance:** 1,200.

WIDNES VIKINGS 72 KEIGHLEY COUGARS 10

VIKINGS: 18 Scott Yates; 3 Richard Varkulis; 22 Dean Thompson; 15 Shane Grady; 19 Matt Gardner; 6 Anthony Thackeray; 7 James Webster; 17 Ben Kavanagh; 9 Mark Smith; 10 Jim Gannon; 27 Liam Farrell; 11 Lee Doran; 12 Dave Allen. Subs (all used): 14 Thomas Coyle; 13 Chris Gerrard; 31 Ben Davies; 23 David Houghton.
Tries: Grady (4, 39, 45), Gardner (9), Thompson (21, 47, 55), Allen (26), Farrell (30), Coyle (66), Varkulis (71), Thackeray (75), Yates (77); **Goals:** Grady 10/13.
COUGARS: 1 George Rayner; 2 Craig Moss; 3 Tom Burton; 12 Oliver Pursglove; 5 Gavin Duffy; 6 Jon Presley; 7 Danny Jones; 8 Andy Shickell; 9 James Feather; 16 Brendan Rawlins; 11 Will Cartledge; 21 Richard Jones; 13 Carl Hughes. Subs (all used): 14 Jamaine Wray; 18 James Haythornthwaite; 10 Scott Law; 17 Ryan Benjafield.
Tries: Duffy (34), Moss (63); **Goals:** D Jones 1/2.
Rugby Leaguer & League Express Men of the Match: *Vikings:* Shane Grady; *Cougars:* Jon Presley.
Penalty count: 14-9; **Half-time:** 34-6;
Referee: Ronnie Laughton (replaced by Chris Dean, half-time); **Attendance:** 2,777.

ROUND 2

Thursday 11th March 2010

BATLEY BULLDOGS 24 HALIFAX 34

BULLDOGS: 5 John Campbell; 1 Ian Preece; 12 Mark Toohey; 4 Danny Maun; 2 Lee Greenwood; 6 Paul Handforth; 7 Gareth Moore; 17 Craig Potter; 9 Kris Lythe; 10 Sean Hesketh; 23 Chris Buttery; 26 Jason Walton; 13 Ashley Lindsay. Subs (all used): 25 Kyle Wood; 11 Tommy Gallagher; 20 David Tootill; 21 James Martin.
Tries: Preece (5), Lindsay (52), Campbell (68, 74);
Goals: Moore 4/4.
HALIFAX: 4 Shad Royston; 2 Lee Paterson; 3 Jon Goddard; 5 James Haley; 23 Rob Worrincy; 6 Luke Branighan; 7 Ben Black; 8 Makali Aizue; 9 Sean Penkywicz; 19 Dominic Maloney; 11 David Larder; 22 David Wrench; 12 Stanley Gene. Subs (all used): 13 Bob Beswick; 14 Mark Gleeson; 16 Said Tamghart; 17 Frank Watene.
Tries: Maloney (8, 16), Wrench (25), Branighan (35, 45), Royston (39); **Goals:** Paterson 5/7.
Sin bin: Wrench (59) - interference.
Rugby Leaguer & League Express Men of the Match: *Bulldogs:* Gareth Moore; *Halifax:* Ben Black.
Penalty count: 15-11; **Half-time:** 6-30;
Referee: Ronnie Laughton; **Attendance:** 1,837.

Saturday 13th March 2010

WHITEHAVEN 34 TOULOUSE OLYMPIQUE 20

WHITEHAVEN: 31 Ian Mort; 29 Stephen Dawes; 3 Rob Jackson; 19 Dexter Miller; 2 Craig Calvert; 6 Carl Rudd; 14 Dylan Skee; 8 Marc Jackson; 9 Graeme Mattinson; 33 Kyle Amor; 12 Spencer Miller; 11 Howard Hill; 13 Mick Govin. Subs (all used): 30 Carl Sice; 22 Richard Farrer; 15 Reece Fox; 17 Andy Thornley.
Tries: Skee (7), Rudd (36), Sice (43, 45), R Fox (73), Mort (75); **Goals:** Rudd 5/6.
OLYMPIQUE: 1 Rory Bromley; 20 Bruno Ormeno; 3 Sebastien Planas; 4 Vincent Duport; 5 Carlos Mendes Varela; 16 Sylvain Houles; 7 Nathan Wynn; 8 Brendan Worth; 17 Cedric Gay; 11 Tim Wynn; 18 Yoan Tisseyre; 14 Antoni Maria; 13 Eric Anselme. Subs (all used): 15 Jerome Gout; 21 Nicolas Faure; 12 Simon Worrall; 33 Kevin Larroyer.
Tries: Bromley (3), Maria (20), Ormeno (24), Planas (39); **Goals:** N Wynn 2/4.
Dismissal: Duport (52) - dangerous tackle on S Miller.
Rugby Leaguer & League Express Men of the Match: *Whitehaven:* Carl Sice; *Olympique:* Sylvain Houles.
Penalty count: 15-9; **Half-time:** 10-20;
Referee: Jamie Leahy; **Attendance:** 1,181.

Sunday 14th March 2010

DEWSBURY RAMS 10 FEATHERSTONE ROVERS 40

RAMS: 2 James Haynes; 15 Bryn Powell; 26 Ayden Faal; 18 Chris Spurr; 10 Scott Turner; 8 Dominic Brambani; 13 Pat Walker; 33 James Walker; 9 Mike Emmett; 24 Anthony England; 25 James Lockwood; 21 Andrew Bostock; 4 Rob Lunt. Subs (all used): 14 Luke Stenchion; 11 Adam Robinson; 37 Luke Blake; 23 Keegan Hirst.
Tries: Stenchion (17), Lunt (75); **Goals:** P Walker 1/2.
Sin bin: England (68) – late tackle on Finn.
ROVERS: 1 Ian Hardman; 5 Jon Steel; 15 Jessie Joe Parker; 4 Liam Welham; 2 Tom Saxton; 6 Kyle Briggs; 9 Liam Finn; 17 Tony Tonks; 31 Ben Kaye; 10 Stuart Dickens; 12 Jon Grayshon; 11 Matty Dale; 13 Jamie Field. Subs (all used): 8 Iain Morrison; 19 Ross Divorty; 7 Andy Kain; 22 Jack Lee.
Tries: Hardman (5), Parker (10), Finn (13), Welham (24), Kain (41, 56, 71); **Goals:** Briggs 5/6, Finn 1/1.
Sin bin: Welham (73) – holding down.
Rugby Leaguer & League Express Men of the Match: *Rams:* Bryn Powell; *Rovers:* Andy Kain.
Penalty count: 11-9; **Half-time:** 6-22;
Referee: Gareth Hewer; **Attendance:** 1,313.

KEIGHLEY COUGARS 12 LEIGH CENTURIONS 34

COUGARS: 1 George Rayner; 2 Craig Moss; 3 Tom Burton; 4 Daley Williams; 5 Gavin Duffy; 6 Jon Presley; 7 Danny Jones; 8 Andy Shickell; 9 James Feather; 19 Sam Crowther; 23 Chris Baines; 12 Oliver Pursglove; 13 Carl Hughes. Subs (all used): 14 Jamaine Wray; 18 James Haythornthwaite; 11 Will Cartledge; 17 Ryan Benjafield.
Tries: Benjafield (24), G Rayner (72); **Goals:** D Jones 2/2.
CENTURIONS: 1 Stuart Donlan; 2 Steve Maden; 25 Matty Blythe; 4 Mick Nanyn; 3 David Alstead; 22 Martyn Ridyard; 7 Robbie Paul; 8 Chris Hill; 9 John Duffy; 16 Mike Morrison; 14 Tommy Goulden; 11 James Taylor; 26 Lee Mitchell. Subs (all used): 10 Ricky Bibey; 27 Jacob Emmitt; 12 Macgraff Leuluai; 13 Dave Armitstead.
Tries: Ridyard (5), Nanyn (18, 79), Taylor (35), Paul (49), Maden (58); **Goals:** Nanyn 5/6.
Rugby Leaguer & League Express Men of the Match: *Cougars:* George Rayner; *Centurions:* Dave Armitstead.
Penalty count: 6-5; **Half-time:** 6-18;
Referee: Robert Hicks; **Attendance:** 1,115.

SHEFFIELD EAGLES 30 WIDNES VIKINGS 44

EAGLES: 5 Ashley Thackeray; 27 Richie Barnett; 3 Menzie Yere; 23 Tangi Ropati; 24 Misi Taulapapa; 6 Brendon Lindsay; 21 Dane McDonald; 8 Jack Howieson; 9 Craig Cook; 10 Mitchell Stringer; 11 Alex Szostak; 13 Peter Green; 19 Joe Hirst. Subs (all used): 12 Ged Corcoran; 15 Sam Barlow; 16 Trevor Exton; 22 Ryan Hepworth.
Tries: Stringer (16), Ropati (25, 76), Yere (46), Cook (50); **Goals:** Stringer 4/5, Lindsay 1/2.
Sin bin: Ropati (4) – holding down;
Taulapapa (67) - fighting.
VIKINGS: 18 Scott Yates; 5 Paddy Flynn; 3 Richard Varkulis; 15 Shane Grady; 19 Matt Gardner; 6 Anthony Thackeray; 7 James Webster; 16 Gareth Haggerty; 9 Mark Smith; 10 Jim Gannon; 27 Liam Farrell; 11 Lee Doran; 12 Dave Allen. Subs (all used): 14 Thomas Coyle; 17 Ben Kavanagh; 23 David Houghton; 31 Ben Davies.
Tries: G Haggerty (10), Gannon (21, 59), Gardner (37, 71), Thackeray (62), Webster (74); **Goals:** Grady 8/8.
Sin bin: M Smith (67) - fighting.
On report:
G Haggerty (56) – alleged late tackle on Barlow.
Rugby Leaguer & League Express Men of the Match: *Eagles:* Craig Cook; *Vikings:* James Webster.
Penalty count: 13-7; **Half-time:** 14-18; **Referee:** Warren Turley; **Attendance:** 1,085 *(at Don Valley Stadium).*

ROUND 3

Thursday 18th March 2010

WIDNES VIKINGS 28 HALIFAX 30

VIKINGS: 18 Scott Yates; 5 Paddy Flynn; 15 Shane Grady; 3 Richard Varkulis; 19 Matt Gardner; 6 Anthony Thackeray; 7 James Webster; 16 Gareth Haggerty; 14 Thomas Coyle; 10 Jim Gannon; 11 Lee Doran; 27 Liam Farrell; 12 Dave Allen. Subs (all used): 17 Ben Kavanagh; 21 Matthew Strong; 28 Ben Davies; 23 David Houghton.
Tries: Coyle (3, 52), Doran (39), Farrell (61), Varkulis (79); **Goals:** Grady 4/6.
HALIFAX: 4 Shad Royston; 20 Paul White; 2 Lee Paterson; 3 Jon Goddard; 23 Rob Worrincy; 6 Luke Branighan; 7 Ben Black; 8 Makali Aizue; 9 Sean Penkywicz; 19 Dominic Maloney; 11 David Larder; 22 David Wrench; 12 Stanley Gene. Subs (all used): 14 Mark Gleeson; 21 Anthony Bowman; 16 Said Tamghart; 17 Frank Watene.
Tries: Worrincy (21), White (28), Paterson (32), Royston (71), Penkywicz (77);
Goals: Paterson 3/4, Branighan 2/2.
Rugby Leaguer & League Express Men of the Match: *Vikings:* Lee Doran; *Halifax:* Luke Branighan.
Penalty count: 9-11; **Half-time:** 10-16;
Referee: Robert Hicks; **Attendance:** 3,286.

Friday 19th March 2010

SHEFFIELD EAGLES 22 DEWSBURY RAMS 10

EAGLES: 1 Jonny Woodcock; 5 Ashley Thackeray; 3 Menzie Yere; 23 Tangi Ropati; 24 Misi Taulapapa; 6 Brendon Lindsay; 21 Dane McDonald; 18 Michael Haley; 9 Craig Cook; 10 Mitchell Stringer; 11 Alex Szostak; 13 Peter Green; 19 Joe Hirst. Subs (all used): 20 Matty Brooks; 15 Sam Barlow; 16 Trevor Exton; 32 Mike Burnett.
Tries: Stringer (21), Ropati (32, 73), McDonald (45);
Goals: Stringer 2/2, Lindsay 0/1, Ropati 1/2.
Sin bin: Taulapapa (65) - fighting.
RAMS: 2 James Haynes; 15 Bryn Powell; 26 Ayden Faal; 10 Scott Turner; 3 Stewart Sanderson; 8 Dominic Brambani; 13 Pat Walker; 24 Anthony England; 37 Luke Blake; 33 James Walker; 25 James Lockwood; 21 Andrew Bostock; 4 Rob Lunt. Subs (all used): 14 Luke Stenchion; 11 Adam Robinson; 36 Paul Hughes; 6 Ryan Smith.
Tries: P Walker (18), Sanderson (36);
Goals: P Walker 1/2.
Sin bin: Bostock (43) - late tackle on Lindsay;
Robinson (65) - fighting.
Rugby Leaguer & League Express Men of the Match: *Eagles:* Tangi Ropati; *Rams:* Pat Walker.
Penalty count: 11-6; **Half-time:** 12-10; **Referee:** Jamie Leahy; **Attendance:** 835 *(at Don Valley Stadium).*

Saturday 20th March 2010

BARROW RAIDERS 6 FEATHERSTONE ROVERS 20

RAIDERS: 1 Gary Broadbent; 21 Chris Larkin; 3 Anthony Blackwood; 4 Liam Harrison; 25 Jermaine McGillvary; 13 Zebastian Luisi; 6 Jamie Rooney; 8 Andy Bracek; 9 Andrew Henderson; 15 Rob Roberts; 11 Michael Knowles; 12 Ned Catic; 24 Richard Fletcher. Subs (all used): 14 Martin Ostler; 19 Nathan Mossop; 16 Brett McDermott; 31 Matt James.
Try: McGillvary (78); **Goals:** Rooney 1/1.
ROVERS: 1 Ian Hardman; 5 Jon Steel; 15 Jessie Joe Parker; 4 Liam Welham; 2 Tom Saxton; 6 Kyle Briggs; 9 Liam Finn; 10 Stuart Dickens; 31 Ben Kaye; 17 Tony Tonks; 12 Jon Grayshon; 11 Matty Dale; 13 Jamie Field. Subs (all used): 16 Dane Manning; 19 Ross Divorty; 22 Jack Lee; 7 Andy Kain.
Tries: Steel (17), Finn (73); **Goals:** Briggs 6/6.
Rugby Leaguer & League Express Men of the Match: *Raiders:* Gary Broadbent; *Rovers:* Kyle Briggs.
Penalty count: 9-10; **Half-time:** 0-8;
Referee: Ian Smith; **Attendance:** 1,998.

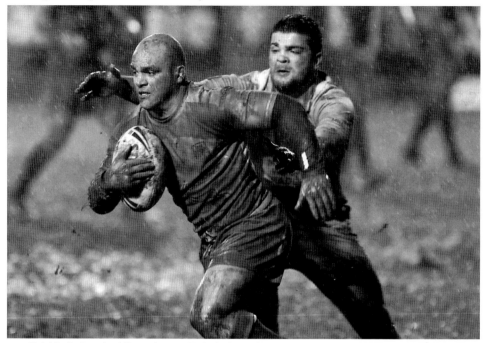

Keighley's Jamaine Wray takes on Batley's Jason Walton in the mud and rain at Cougar Park

TOULOUSE OLYMPIQUE 34 KEIGHLEY COUGARS 26

OLYMPIQUE: 1 Rory Bromley; 22 Clement Bienes; 3 Sebastien Planas; 4 Vincent Duport; 5 Carlos Mendes Varela; 16 Sylvain Houles; 7 Nathan Wynn; 8 Brendan Worth; 17 Cedric Gay; 15 Jerome Gout; 31 Kevin Larroyer; 14 Antoni Maria; 13 Eric Anselme. Subs (all used): 11 Tim Wynn; 12 Simon Worrall; 18 Yoan Tisseyre; 19 Romain Mencarini.
Tries: Bienes (3), Gay (10, 39), Bromley (42), Planas (54), Larroyer (77); **Goals:** N Wynn 5/7.
Dismissal: Worth (20) - head-butt on Shickell.
COUGARS: 1 George Rayner; 2 Craig Moss; 3 Tom Burton; 4 Daley Williams; 5 Gavin Duffy; 6 Jon Presley; 7 Danny Jones; 8 Andy Shickell; 9 James Feather; 17 Ryan Benjafield; 23 Chris Baines; 12 Oliver Pursglove; 13 Carl Hughes. Subs (all used): 14 Jamaine Wray; 18 James Haythornthwaite; 11 Will Cartledge; 16 Brendan Rawlins.
Tries: Pursglove (37), Duffy (63), D Jones (69), Baines (74), Feather (80); **Goals:** D Jones 3/5.
Sin bin: Benjafield (66) - late tackle on Bromley.
Rugby Leaguer & League Express Men of the Match: *Olympique:* Rory Bromley; *Cougars:* Danny Jones.
Penalty count: 7-7; **Half-time:** 14-4;
Referee: Warren Turley; **Attendance:** 1,829.

Sunday 21st March 2010

LEIGH CENTURIONS 44 WHITEHAVEN 12

CENTURIONS: 1 Stuart Donlan; 2 Steve Maden; 36 Matty Blythe; 4 Mick Nanyn; 3 David Alstead; 22 Martyn Ridyard; 7 Robbie Paul; 8 Chris Hill; 15 Dave McConnell; 13 Dave Armitstead; 11 James Taylor; 12 Macgraff Leuluai; 37 Tyrone McCarthy. Subs (all used): 14 Tommy Goulden; 9 John Duffy; 10 Ricky Bibey; 35 Jacob Emmitt.
Tries: Paul (18), McCarthy (30), Ridyard (42), Nanyn (50), Emmitt (57), Alstead (62), Maden (74), Blythe (80); **Goals:** Nanyn 5/7, Ridyard 1/1.
WHITEHAVEN: 1 Craig Benson; 29 Stephen Dawes; 4 Scott McAvoy; 3 Rob Jackson; 2 Craig Calvert; 6 Carl Rudd; 14 Dylan Skee; 24 Ryan McDonald; 9 Graeme Mattinson; 8 Marc Jackson; 15 Reece Fox; 11 Howard Hill; 17 Andy Thornley. Subs (all used): 30 Carl Sice; 19 Dexter Miller; 22 Richard Farrer; 28 Tyrone Dalton.
Tries: Skee (67), McAvoy (70); **Goals:** Rudd 2/2.
Rugby Leaguer & League Express Men of the Match: *Centurions:* Ricky Bibey; *Whitehaven:* Graeme Mattinson.
Penalty count: 15-9; **Half-time:** 12-0;
Referee: Peter Brooke; **Attendance:** 1,891.

ROUND 4

Thursday 25th March 2010

KEIGHLEY COUGARS 12 BATLEY BULLDOGS 22

COUGARS: 1 George Rayner; 2 Craig Moss; 3 Tom Burton; 4 Daley Williams; 5 Gavin Duffy; 6 Jon Presley; 7 Danny Jones; 8 Andy Shickell; 9 James Feather; 17 Ryan Benjafield; 23 Chris Baines; 12 Oliver Pursglove; 13 Carl Hughes. Subs (all used): 11 Will Cartledge; 14 Jamaine Wray; 15 Greg Nicholson; 18 James Haythornthwaite.
Tries: Burton (29), D Jones (40); **Goals:** D Jones 2/3.
BULLDOGS: 1 Ian Preece; 2 Lee Greenwood; 12 Mark Toohey; 4 Danny Maun; 3 Mark Barlow; 6 Paul Handforth; 7 Gareth Moore; 8 Byron Smith; 9 Kris Lythe; 10 Sean Hesketh; 23 Chris Buttery; 26 Jason Walton; 11 Tommy Gallagher. Subs (all used): 17 Craig Potter; 21 James Martin; 25 Kyle Wood; 31 John Gallagher.
Tries: Buttery (12), Barlow (37), Hesketh (67), Maun (73); **Goals:** Moore 2/3, Handforth 1/1.
Rugby Leaguer & League Express Men of the Match: *Cougars:* Andy Shickell; *Bulldogs:* Paul Handforth.
Penalty count: 11-6; **Half-time:** 12-10;
Referee: Jamie Leahy; **Attendance:** 1,336.

Saturday 27th March 2010

TOULOUSE OLYMPIQUE 16 BARROW RAIDERS 48

OLYMPIQUE: 1 Rory Bromley; 22 Clement Bienes; 3 Sebastien Planas; 4 Vincent Duport; 5 Carlos Mendes Varela; 6 Constant Villegas; 7 Nathan Wynn; 8 Brendan Worth; 17 Cedric Gay; 15 Jerome Gout; 18 Yoan Tisseyre; 13 Eric Anselme; 16 Sylvain Houles. Subs (all used): 14 Antoni Maria; 33 Kevin Larroyer; 21 Nicolas Faure; 12 Simon Worrall.
Tries: Maria (17), Gay (28), Larroyer (39); **Goals:** N Wynn 2/4.
RAIDERS: 1 Gary Broadbent; 2 Andy Ballard; 3 Anthony Blackwood; 4 Liam Harrison; 25 Jermaine McGillvary; 6 Jamie Rooney; 7 James Coyle; 15 Rob Roberts; 9 Andrew Henderson; 16 Brett McDermott; 14 Martin Ostler; 31 Matt James; 13 Zebastian Luisi. Subs (all used): 8 Andy Bracek; 10 Chris Young; 11 Michael Knowles; 18 Liam Campbell.
Tries: James (21), Harrison (24, 56), Luisi (31), Campbell (50, 52, 66), Ballard (68), Blackwood (73); **Goals:** Rooney 6/9.
Rugby Leaguer & League Express Men of the Match: *Olympique:* Nathan Wynn; *Raiders:* Liam Campbell.
Penalty count: 7-6; **Half-time:** 16-16;
Referee: Gareth Hewer; **Attendance:** 1,500.

Sunday 28th March 2010

DEWSBURY RAMS 30 WIDNES VIKINGS 36

RAMS: 2 James Haynes; 15 Bryn Powell; 18 Chris Spurr; 10 Scott Turner; 3 Stewart Sanderson; 8 Dominic Brambani; 13 Pat Walker; 23 Keegan Hirst; 9 Mike Emmett; 24 Anthony England; 25 James Lockwood; 21 Andrew Bostock; 26 Ayden Faal. Subs (all used): 14 Luke Stenchion; 11 Adam Robinson; 37 Luke Blake; 7 Tom Wandless.
Tries: Spurr (5, 47, 67), Powell (27), P Walker (38); **Goals:** P Walker 5/7.
VIKINGS: 18 Scott Yates; 5 Paddy Flynn; 4 Toa Kohe-Love; 15 Shane Grady; 19 Matt Gardner; 6 Anthony Thackeray; 7 James Webster; 28 Ben Davies; 9 Mark Smith; 10 Jim Gannon; 11 Lee Doran; 3 Richard Varkulis; 13 Chris Gerrard. Subs (all used): 14 Thomas Coyle; 17 Ben Kavanagh; 21 Matthew Strong; 23 David Houghton.
Tries: Thackeray (13, 72, 77), Webster (16), Grady (33), C Gerrard (58); **Goals:** Grady 6/7.
Rugby Leaguer & League Express Men of the Match: *Rams:* Adam Robinson; *Vikings:* Anthony Thackeray.
Penalty count: 11-6; **Half-time:** 14-16;
Referee: Ronnie Laughton; **Attendance:** 1,499.

FEATHERSTONE ROVERS 54 WHITEHAVEN 18

ROVERS: 1 Ian Hardman; 5 Jon Steel; 15 Jessie Joe Parker; 4 Liam Welham; 2 Tom Saxton; 6 Kyle Briggs; 9 Liam Finn; 10 Stuart Dickens; 7 Andy Kain; 17 Tony Tonks; 12 Jon Grayshon; 11 Matty Dale; 13 Jamie Field. Subs (all used): 19 Ross Divorty; 8 Iain Morrison; 27 Aaron Dobek; 16 Dane Manning.
Tries: Dickens (1), Parker (8, 32, 46), Welham (14, 23), Briggs (35, 50, 57), Finn (53); **Goals:** Briggs 7/10.
WHITEHAVEN: 28 Ian Mort; 29 Stephen Dawes; 4 Scott McAvoy; 3 Rob Jackson; 5 Derry Eilbeck; 6 Carl Rudd; 25 Gregg McNally; 17 Andy Thornley; 9 Graeme Mattinson; 11 Howard Hill; 15 Reece Fox; 23 Steve Fox; 7 Leroy Joe. Subs (all used): 30 Carl Sice; 24 Ryan McDonald; 13 Mick Govin; 16 Andy Gorski.
Tries: R Fox (11), Eilbeck (24), Sice (42); **Goals:** Rudd 3/3.
Rugby Leaguer & League Express Men of the Match: *Rovers:* Kyle Briggs; *Whitehaven:* Ryan McDonald.
Penalty count: 6-2; **Half-time:** 32-12;
Referee: Warren Turley; **Attendance:** 1,551.

HALIFAX 10 LEIGH CENTURIONS 48

HALIFAX: 4 Shad Royston; 5 James Haley; 3 Jon Goddard; 2 Lee Paterson; 23 Rob Worrincy; 9 Sean Penkywicz; 7 Ben Black; 8 Makali Aizue; 13 Bob Beswick; 22 David Wrench; 11 David Larder; 24 Steve Bannister; 12 Stanley Gene. Subs (all used): 15 Mark Roberts; 17 Frank Watene; 19 Dominic Maloney; 20 Paul White.
Tries: Royston (36), Beswick (66); **Goals:** Paterson 1/2.
Sin bin: Penkywicz (68) - dissent.
CENTURIONS: 1 Stuart Donlan; 2 Steve Maden; 25 Matty Blythe; 4 Mick Nanyn; 3 David Alstead; 22 Martyn Ridyard; 7 Robbie Paul; 8 Chris Hill; 15 Dave McConnell; 10 Ricky Bibey; 11 James Taylor; 14 Tommy Goulden; 28 Tyrone McCarthy. Subs (all used): 9 John Duffy; 13 Dave Armitstead; 26 Lee Mitchell; 27 Jacob Emmitt.
Tries: Ridyard (29), Mitchell (31, 71), Emmitt (38), Donlan (53), Nanyn (57), Blythe (73), Paul (75); **Goals:** Nanyn 6/7, Ridyard 2/2.
Rugby Leaguer & League Express Men of the Match: *Halifax:* Shad Royston; *Centurions:* James Taylor.
Penalty count: 9-8; **Half-time:** 4-20;
Referee: Matthew Thomasson; **Attendance:** 3,071.

ROUND 5

Thursday 1st April 2010

WHITEHAVEN 8 BARROW RAIDERS 19

WHITEHAVEN: 31 Ian Mort; 5 Derry Eilbeck; 3 Rob Jackson; 4 Scott McAvoy; 2 Craig Calvert; 6 Carl Rudd; 25 Gregg McNally; 22 Richard Farrer; 9 Graeme Mattinson; 33 Kyle Amor; 12 Spencer Miller; 11 Howard Hill; 7 Leroy Joe. Subs (all used): 13 Mick Govin; 8 Marc Jackson; 15 Reece Fox; 16 Andy Gorski.
Try: Rudd (7); **Goals:** Rudd 2/2.
RAIDERS: 1 Gary Broadbent; 2 Andy Ballard; 3 Anthony Blackwood; 4 Liam Harrison; 25 Jermaine McGillvary; 7 James Coyle; 6 Jamie Rooney; 16 Brett McDermott; 9 Andrew Henderson; 8 Andy Bracek; 14 Martin Ostler; 31 Matt James; 13 Zebastian Luisi. Subs (all used): 18 Liam Campbell; 11 Michael Knowles; 17 Paul Noone; 21 Chris Larkin.
Tries: Ballard (17), Ostler (62, 71); **Goals:** Rooney 3/5; **Field goal:** Rooney (74).
Rugby Leaguer & League Express Men of the Match: *Whitehaven:* Graeme Mattinson; *Raiders:* Zebastian Luisi.
Penalty count: 8-9; **Half-time:** 8-6;
Referee: Robert Hicks; **Attendance:** 1,382.

Friday 2nd April 2010

BATLEY BULLDOGS 22 DEWSBURY RAMS 8

BULLDOGS: 5 John Campbell; 1 Ian Preece; 12 Mark Toohey; 4 Danny Maun; 2 Lee Greenwood; 6 Paul Handforth; 25 Kyle Wood; 8 Byron Smith; 9 Kris Lythe; 10 Sean Hesketh; 23 Chris Buttery; 26 Jason Walton; 11 Tommy Gallagher. Subs (all used): 14 John Gallagher; 17 Craig Potter; 20 David Tootill; 13 Ashley Lindsay.
Tries: Buttery (6), Preece (32, 55), Lythe (67);
Goals: Handforth 3/5.
RAMS: 10 Scott Turner; 15 Bryn Powell; 18 Chris Spurr; 26 Ayden Faal; 3 Stewart Sanderson; 8 Dominic Brambani; 13 Pat Walker; 33 James Walker; 9 Mike Emmett; 23 Keegan Hirst; 25 James Lockwood; 21 Andrew Bostock; 19 Adam Hayes. Subs: 14 Luke Stenchion; 11 Adam Robinson; 37 Luke Blake; 7 Tom Wandless (not used).
Tries: Powell (39), Emmett (72); **Goals:** P Walker 0/2.
Rugby Leaguer & League Express Men of the Match: *Bulldogs:* Ian Preece; *Rams:* Adam Hayes.
Penalty count: 12-8; **Half-time:** 10-4;
Referee: Warren Turley; **Attendance:** 1,484.

FEATHERSTONE ROVERS 44 HALIFAX 4

ROVERS: 1 Ian Hardman; 5 Jon Steel; 15 Jessie Joe Parker; 4 Liam Welham; 2 Tom Saxton; 6 Kyle Briggs; 9 Liam Finn; 17 Tony Tonks; 22 Jack Lee; 10 Stuart Dickens; 12 Jon Grayshon; 8 Iain Morrison; 11 Matty Dale. Subs (all used): 7 Andy Kain; 19 Ross Divorty; 16 Dane Manning; 18 Tim Spears.
Tries: Grayshon (13), Dickens (44), Hardman (48), Briggs (57), Steel (65), Finn (77), Spears (80);
Goals: Briggs 8/9.
HALIFAX: 4 Shad Royston; 20 Paul White; 2 Lee Paterson; 5 James Haley; 23 Rob Worrincy; 21 Anthony Bowman; 7 Ben Black; 19 Dominic Maloney; 9 Sean Penkywicz; 25 Michael Ostick; 11 David Larder; 3 Jon Goddard; 24 Steve Bannister. Subs (all used): 13 Bob Beswick; 8 Makali Aizue; 16 Said Tamghart; 17 Frank Watene.
Try: Paterson (72); **Goals:** Paterson 0/1.
Rugby Leaguer & League Express Men of the Match: *Rovers:* Kyle Briggs; *Halifax:* Anthony Bowman.
Penalty count: 7-6; **Half-time:** 8-0;
Referee: Gareth Hewer; **Attendance:** 2,353.

KEIGHLEY COUGARS 16 SHEFFIELD EAGLES 16

COUGARS: 1 George Rayner; 2 Craig Moss; 3 Tom Burton; 4 Daley Williams; 5 Gavin Duffy; 6 Jon Presley; 7 Danny Jones; 8 Andy Shickell; 9 James Feather; 17 Ryan Benjafield; 23 Chris Baines; 11 Will Cartledge; 13 Carl Hughes. Subs (all used): 14 Jamaine Wray; 18 James Haythornthwaite; 16 Brendan Rawlins; 32 Nathan Massey.
Tries: Shickell (55), Duffy (60); **Goals:** D Jones 4/4.
EAGLES: 1 Jonny Woodcock; 5 Ashley Thackeray; 3 Menzie Yere; 23 Tangi Ropati; 24 Misi Taulapapa; 6 Brendon Lindsay; 20 Matty Brooks; 12 Ged Corcoran; 9 Craig Cook; 10 Mitchell Stringer; 11 Alex Szostak; 13 Peter Green; 19 Joe Hirst. Subs (all used): 17 Alex Rowe; 16 Trevor Exton; 21 Dane McDonald; 15 Sam Barlow.
Tries: Szostak (6), Barlow (37), Cook (71);
Goals: Stringer 1/2, Lindsay 1/1.
Rugby Leaguer & League Express Men of the Match: *Cougars:* Jamaine Wray; *Eagles:* Brendon Lindsay.
Penalty count: 9-9; **Half-time:** 2-10;
Referee: Matthew Thomasson; **Attendance:** 927.

TOULOUSE OLYMPIQUE 6 LEIGH CENTURIONS 36

OLYMPIQUE: 1 Rory Bromley; 22 Clement Bienes; 3 Sebastien Planas; 4 Vincent Duport; 20 Bruno Ormeno; 16 Sylvain Houles; 7 Nathan Wynn; 21 Nicolas Faure; 12 Simon Worrall; 11 Tim Wynn; 14 Antoni Maria; 18 Yoan Tisseyre; 13 Eric Anselme. Subs (all used): 9 Martin Mitchell; 10 Mathieu Griffi; 23 Kevin Larroyer; 25 Teli Pelo.
Try: Pelo (77); **Goals:** N Wynn 1/1.
CENTURIONS: 1 Stuart Donlan; 2 Steve Maden; 3 David Alstead; 4 Mick Nanyn; 5 Nicky Stanton; 22 Martyn Ridyard; 7 Robbie Paul; 8 Chris Hill; 15 Dave McConnell; 10 Ricky Bibey; 11 James Taylor; 12 Macgraff Leuluai; 14 Tommy Goulden. Subs (all used): 9 John Duffy; 13 Dave Armitstead; 16 Mike Morrison; 18 Adam Higson.
Tries: Leuluai (19), McConnell (33), Armitstead (39), Stanton (47), Donlan (52), Higson (69);
Goals: Nanyn 6/6.
Rugby Leaguer & League Express Men of the Match: *Olympique:* Rory Bromley; *Centurions:* John Duffy.
Penalty count: 6-10; **Half-time:** 0-18;
Referee: Craig Halloran; **Attendance:** 1,100.

ROUND 6

Monday 5th April 2010

BARROW RAIDERS 50 SHEFFIELD EAGLES 4

RAIDERS: 1 Gary Broadbent; 2 Andy Ballard; 3 Anthony Blackwood; 4 Liam Harrison; 25 Jermaine McGillvary; 6 Jamie Rooney; 7 James Coyle; 31 Matt James; 9 Andrew Henderson; 8 Andy Bracek; 14 Martin Ostler; 11 Michael Knowles; 13 Zebastian Luisi. Subs (all used): 17 Paul Noone; 15 Rob Roberts; 18 Liam Campbell; 12 Ned Catic.
Tries: Luisi (10), Harrison (24), Blackwood (33), McGillvary (35), Rooney (39), Ballard (51), James (58), Noone (62), Knowles (66); **Goals:** Rooney 7/9.
EAGLES: 1 Jonny Woodcock; 24 Misi Taulapapa; 23 Tangi Ropati; 3 Menzie Yere; 5 Ashley Thackeray; 6 Brendon Lindsay; 20 Matty Brooks; 12 Ged Corcoran; 9 Craig Cook; 10 Mitchell Stringer; 11 Alex Szostak; 13 Peter Green; 19 Joe Hirst. Subs (all used): 18 Michael Haley; 16 Trevor Exton; 21 Dane McDonald; 15 Sam Barlow.
Try: Stringer (14); **Goals:** Stringer 0/1.
Rugby Leaguer & League Express Men of the Match: *Raiders:* Jamie Rooney; *Eagles:* Brendon Lindsay.
Penalty count: 8-4; **Half-time:** 28-4;
Referee: Ronnie Laughton; **Attendance:** 1,854.

DEWSBURY RAMS 10 KEIGHLEY COUGARS 42

RAMS: 2 James Haynes; 3 Stewart Sanderson; 10 Scott Turner; 18 Chris Spurr; 15 Bryn Powell; 13 Pat Walker; 7 Tom Wandless; 33 James Walker; 9 Mike Emmett; 23 Keegan Hirst; 25 James Lockwood; 19 Adam Hayes; 26 Ayden Faal. Subs (all used): 14 Luke Stenchion; 24 Anthony England; 37 Luke Blake; 11 Adam Robinson.
Tries: Wandless (35), Turner (46); **Goals:** P Walker 1/2.
COUGARS: 1 George Rayner; 2 Craig Moss; 3 Tom Burton; 4 Daley Williams; 5 Gavin Duffy; 6 Jon Presley; 7 Danny Jones; 8 Andy Shickell; 14 Jamaine Wray; 17 Ryan Benjafield; 23 Chris Baines; 11 Will Cartledge; 13 Carl Hughes. Subs (all used): 9 James Feather; 18 James Haythornthwaite; 15 Greg Nicholson; 16 Brendan Rawlins.
Tries: D Jones (21), Cartledge (28), Shickell (42), G Rayner (55), Nicholson (67), Williams (73, 78);
Goals: D Jones 7/8.
Rugby Leaguer & League Express Men of the Match: *Rams:* Tom Wandless; *Cougars:* Danny Jones.
Penalty count: 7-7; **Half-time:** 6-14;
Referee: Craig Halloran; **Attendance:** 1,025.

WIDNES VIKINGS 48 WHITEHAVEN 18

VIKINGS: 1 James Ford; 5 Paddy Flynn; 4 Toa Kohe-Love; 15 Shane Grady; 19 Matt Gardner; 13 Chris Gerrard; 6 Anthony Thackeray; 28 Ben Davies; 9 Mark Smith; 10 Jim Gannon; 3 Richard Varkulis; 21 Matthew Strong; 11 Lee Doran. Subs (all used): 17 Ben Kavanagh; 18 Scott Yates; 24 Danny Hulme; 22 Dean Thompson.
Tries: Thackeray (6), Ford (10), Doran (13), C Gerrard (16), Kohe-Love (19), Gardner (23), Hulme (44), Grady (65), Flynn (71); **Goals:** Grady 6/9.
Sin bin: Davies (1) - late tackle.
WHITEHAVEN: 28 Ian Mort; 5 Derry Eilbeck; 3 Rob Jackson; 23 Steve Fox; 2 Craig Calvert; 13 Mick Govin; 25 Gregg McNally; 22 Richard Farrer; 30 Carl Sice; 33 Kyle Amor; 15 Reece Fox; 16 Andy Gorski; 9 Graeme Mattinson. Subs (all used): 17 Andy Thornley; 7 Leroy Joe; 32 Marc Shackley; 29 Stephen Dawes.
Tries: Joe (33), Mort (76), Dawes (79);
Goals: McNally 2/3, Govin 1/1.
Sin bin: R Fox (21) - holding down.
Rugby Leaguer & League Express Men of the Match: *Vikings:* Matt Gardner; *Whitehaven:* Gregg McNally.
Penalty count: 7-7; **Half-time:** 30-8;
Referee: Jamie Leahy; **Attendance:** 3,033.

HALIFAX 50 TOULOUSE OLYMPIQUE 6

HALIFAX: 4 Shad Royston; 2 Lee Paterson; 3 Jon Goddard; 18 Dylan Nash; 23 Rob Worrincy; 21 Anthony Bowman; 7 Ben Black; 25 Michael Ostick; 9 Sean Penkywicz; 10 Neil Cherryholme; 11 David Larder; 24 Steve Bannister; 13 Bob Beswick. Subs (all used): 5 James Haley; 15 Mark Roberts; 16 Said Tamghart; 17 Frank Watene.
Tries: Royston (1, 12, 41), Paterson (33, 75), Haley (57, 69), Worrincy (64), Watene (79);
Goals: Paterson 7/9.
OLYMPIQUE: 1 Rory Bromley; 22 Clement Bienes; 3 Sebastien Planas; 4 Vincent Duport; 2 Sebastien Payan; 6 Constant Villegas; 7 Nathan Wynn; 8 Brendan Worth; 23 Yohann Gigord; 31 Teli Pelo; 14 Antoni Maria; 12 Simon Worrall; 13 Eric Anselme. Subs (all used): 19 Romain Mencarini; 10 Mathieu Griffi; 33 Kevin Larroyer; 18 Yoan Tisseyre.
Try: Bromley (29); **Goals:** N Wynn 1/1.
Rugby Leaguer & League Express Men of the Match: *Halifax:* Shad Royston; *Olympique:* Nathan Wynn.
Penalty count: 7-7; **Half-time:** 16-6;
Referee: Peter Brooke; **Attendance:** 1,725.

LEIGH CENTURIONS 26 BATLEY BULLDOGS 4

CENTURIONS: 1 Stuart Donlan; 3 David Alstead; 35 Matty Blythe; 4 Mick Nanyn; 2 Steve Maden; 22 Martin Ridyard; 7 Robbie Paul; 8 Chris Hill; 15 Dave McConnell; 10 Ricky Bibey; 14 Tommy Goulden; 11 James Taylor; 37 Tyrone McCarthy. Subs (all used): 13 Dave Armitstead; 9 John Duffy; 16 Mike Morrison; 36 Lee Mitchell.
Tries: Blythe (2, 18, 33), Hill (63), Duffy (65);
Goals: Nanyn 1/3, Paul 2/2.
BULLDOGS: 5 John Campbell; 3 Mark Barlow; 22 Josh Griffin; 4 Danny Maun; 1 Ian Preece; 6 Paul Handforth; 25 Kyle Wood; 8 Byron Smith; 9 Kris Lythe; 10 Sean Hesketh; 23 Chris Buttery; 26 Jason Walton; 11 Tommy Gallagher. Subs (all used): 13 Ashley Lindsay; 20 David Tootill; 21 James Martin; 31 John Gallagher.
Try: Martin (36); **Goals:** Handforth 0/1.
Sin bin: Tootill (76) - high tackle.
Rugby Leaguer & League Express Men of the Match: *Centurions:* Matty Blythe; *Bulldogs:* Jason Walton.
Penalty count: 13-8; **Half-time:** 14-4;
Referee: Gareth Hewer; **Attendance:** 2,246.

ROUND 7

Thursday 8th April 2010

HALIFAX 40 KEIGHLEY COUGARS 20

HALIFAX: 4 Shad Royston; 2 Lee Paterson; 3 Jon Goddard; 5 James Haley; 23 Rob Worrincy; 21 Anthony Bowman; 7 Ben Black; 25 Michael Ostick; 9 Sean Penkywicz; 19 Dominic Maloney; 11 David Larder; 12 Stanley Gene; 13 Bob Beswick. Subs (all used): 16 Said Tamghart; 17 Frank Watene; 18 Dylan Nash; 24 Steve Bannister.
Tries: Haley (13), Gene (34), Worrincy (36), Penkywicz (51), Nash (60), Bannister (69), Paterson (74); **Goals:** Paterson 6/7.
COUGARS: 1 George Rayner; 2 Craig Moss; 3 Tom Burton; 4 Daley Williams; 5 Gavin Duffy; 6 Jon Presley; 7 Danny Jones; 8 Andy Shickell; 14 Jamaine Wray; 17 Ryan Benjafield; 23 Chris Baines; 11 Will Cartledge; 22 Ben Sagar. Subs (all used): 9 James Feather; 15 Greg Nicholson; 16 Brendan Rawlins; 18 James Haythornthwaite.
Tries: Presley (11), Burton (47), Shickell (54), Haythornthwaite (79); **Goals:** D Jones 2/5.
Rugby Leaguer & League Express Men of the Match: *Halifax:* Ben Black; *Cougars:* Danny Jones.
Penalty count: 7-5; **Half-time:** 16-6;
Referee: Robert Hicks; **Attendance:** 2,522.

Saturday 10th April 2010

WIDNES VIKINGS 38 TOULOUSE OLYMPIQUE 42

VIKINGS: 18 Scott Yates; 5 Paddy Flynn; 4 Toa Kohe-Love; 15 Shane Grady; 19 Matt Gardner; 13 Chris Gerrard; 6 Anthony Thackeray; 28 Ben Davies; 9 Mark Smith; 10 Jim Gannon; 3 Richard Varkulis; 21 Matthew Strong; 11 Lee Doran. Subs (all used): 17 Ben Kavanagh; 31 Jordan James; 14 Thomas Coyle; 23 David Houghton.
Tries: Davies (8), Strong (17), Flynn (58), Thackeray (64, 70, 78), Coyle (76); **Goals:** Grady 5/7.
OLYMPIQUE: 1 Rory Bromley; 5 Carlos Mendes Varela; 3 Sebastien Planas; 4 Vincent Duport; 2 Sebastien Payan; 22 Clement Bienes; 7 Nathan Wynn; 8 Brendan Worth; 9 Martin Mitchell; 10 Mathieu Griffi; 18 Yoan Tisseyre; 14 Antoni Maria; 13 Eric Anselme. Subs (all used): 19 Romain Mencarini; 25 Kevin Larroyer; 21 Nicolas Faure; 12 Simon Worrall.
Tries: Griffi (5), Duport (11, 34, 49), N Wynn (28, 56), Payan (38); **Goals:** N Wynn 7/7.
Rugby Leaguer & League Express Men of the Match: *Vikings:* Anthony Thackeray; *Olympique:* Nathan Wynn.
Penalty count: 11-6; **Half-time:** 12-30;
Referee: Matthew Thomasson; **Attendance:** 2,793.

BARROW RAIDERS 56 BATLEY BULLDOGS 10

RAIDERS: 1 Gary Broadbent; 2 Andy Ballard; 3 Anthony Blackwood; 4 Liam Harrison; 25 Jermaine McGillvary; 7 James Coyle; 6 Jamie Rooney; 31 Matt James; 9 Andrew Henderson; 8 Andy Bracek; 14 Martin Ostler; 11 Michael Knowles; 12 Ned Catic. Subs (all used): 17 Paul Noone; 15 Rob Roberts; 18 Liam Campbell; 21 Chris Larkin.
Tries: Catic (2), Harrison (6, 48), James (15), McGillvary (24, 34, 76), Henderson (30), Roberts (44), Ballard (68); **Goals:** Rooney 8/10.
BULLDOGS: 5 John Campbell; 2 Lee Greenwood; 26 Jason Walton; 22 Josh Griffin; 24 Alex Brown; 6 Paul Handforth; 25 Kyle Wood; 8 Byron Smith; 9 Kris Lythe; 10 Sean Hesketh; 23 Chris Buttery; 17 Craig Potter; 11 Tommy Gallagher. Subs (all used): 14 John Gallagher; 13 Ashley Lindsay; 21 James Martin; 20 David Tootill.
Tries: Walton (18), Brown (52); **Goals:** Handforth 1/2.
Sin bin: J Gallagher (43) - obstruction.
Rugby Leaguer & League Express Men of the Match: *Raiders:* Jermaine McGillvary; *Bulldogs:* Paul Handforth.
Penalty count: 8-4; **Half-time:** 32-4;
Referee: Craig Halloran; **Attendance:** 1,725.

Sunday 11th April 2010

DEWSBURY RAMS 12 WHITEHAVEN 20

RAMS: 1 Lee Lingard; 15 Bryn Powell; 26 Ayden Faal; 10 Scott Turner; 3 Stewart Sanderson; 8 Dominic Brambani; 7 Tom Wandless; 24 Anthony England; 9 Mike Emmett; 23 Keegan Hirst; 25 James Lockwood; 21 Andrew Bostock; 13 Pat Walker. Subs (all used): 14 Luke Stenchion; 37 Luke Blake; 11 Adam Robinson; 41 Andrew Moody.
Tries: Powell (28), Lingard (43), Robinson (65);
Goals: P Walker 0/3.

WHITEHAVEN: 31 Josh Veivers; 5 Derry Eilbeck; 3 Rob Jackson; 27 Stefan Marsh; 2 Craig Calvert; 6 Carl Rudd; 14 Dylan Skee; 8 Marc Jackson; 9 Graeme Mattinson; 33 Kyle Amor; 12 Spencer Miller; 15 Reece Fox; 7 Leroy Joe. Subs (all used): 30 Carl Sice; 32 Daniel Barker; 17 Andy Thornley; 28 Marc Shackley.
Tries: Rudd (8), Mattinson (15), Thornley (39);
Goals: Rudd 4/4.
Rugby Leaguer & League Express Men of the Match:
Rams: Adam Robinson; *Whitehaven:* Daniel Barker.
Penalty count: 4-4; **Half-time:** 4-18;
Referee: Peter Brooke; **Attendance:** 850.

SHEFFIELD EAGLES 16 FEATHERSTONE ROVERS 40

EAGLES: 24 Misi Taulapapa; 27 Richie Barnett; 3 Menzie Yere; 23 Tangi Ropati; 5 Ashley Thackeray; 6 Brendon Lindsay; 21 Dane McDonald; 8 Jack Howieson; 9 Craig Cook; 10 Mitchell Stringer; 11 Alex Szostak; 16 Trevor Exton; 19 Joe Hirst. Subs (all used): 25 Jason Mossop; 13 Peter Green; 12 Ged Corcoran; 15 Sam Barlow.
Tries: Taulapapa (20), Cook (61), McDonald (74);
Goals: Lindsay 1/1, Stringer 1/2.
ROVERS: 1 Ian Hardman; 21 Michael Coady; 15 Jesse Joe Parker; 4 Liam Welham; 2 Tom Saxton; 6 Kyle Briggs; 9 Liam Finn; 10 Stuart Dickens; 22 Jack Lee; 17 Tony Tonks; 12 Jon Grayshon; 8 Iain Morrison; 11 Matty Dale. Subs (all used): 7 Andy Kain; 16 Dane Manning; 19 Ross Divorty; 18 Tim Spears.
Tries: Parker (13), Grayshon (27), Kain (39, 54, pen), Welham (59), Manning (69), Morrison (80);
Goals: Briggs 6/7.
Rugby Leaguer & League Express Men of the Match:
Eagles: Craig Cook; *Rovers:* Kyle Briggs.
Penalty count: 9-9; **Half-time:** 6-16;
Referee: Jamie Leahy; **Attendance:** 2,871.

ROUND 11

Thursday 22nd April 2010

FEATHERSTONE ROVERS 76 KEIGHLEY COUGARS 12

ROVERS: 1 Ian Hardman; 2 Tom Saxton; 21 Michael Coady; 15 Jessie Joe Parker; 26 Zak Hardaker; 6 Kyle Briggs; 9 Liam Finn; 10 Stuart Dickens; 31 Ben Kaye; 17 Tony Tonks; 12 Jon Grayshon; 13 Jamie Field; 11 Matty Dale. Subs (all used): 7 Andy Kain; 8 Iain Morrison; 16 Dane Manning; 14 Danny Allan.
Tries: Coady (2), Briggs (10, 58), Finn (25, 27, 65, 76), Hardman (34), Hardaker (44, 74), Morrison (55), Kain (62), Manning (63); **Goals:** Finn 3/3, Briggs 9/10.
COUGARS: 1 George Rayner; 2 Craig Moss; 3 Tom Burton; 18 James Haythornthwaite; 5 Gavin Duffy; 6 Jon Presley; 7 Danny Jones; 8 Andy Shickell; 14 Jamaine Wray; 17 Ryan Benjafield; 23 Chris Baines; 11 Will Cartledge; 13 Carl Hughes. Subs (all used): 9 James Feather; 15 Greg Nicholson; 16 Brendan Rawlins; 12 Oliver Pursglove.
Tries: Duffy (50), D Jones (70); **Goals:** D Jones 2/2.
Rugby Leaguer & League Express Men of the Match:
Rovers: Kyle Briggs; *Cougars:* Jon Presley.
Penalty count: 8-6; **Half-time:** 30-0;
Referee: Gareth Hewer; **Attendance:** 2,171.

ROUND 8

Saturday 24th April 2010

BARROW RAIDERS 34 DEWSBURY RAMS 24

RAIDERS: 1 Gary Broadbent; 2 Andy Ballard; 3 Anthony Blackwood; 4 Liam Harrison; 25 Jermaine McGillvary; 6 Jamie Rooney; 7 James Coyle; 8 Andy Bracek; 19 Nathan Mossop; 31 Matt James; 14 Martin Ostler; 12 Ned Catic; 13 Zebastian Luisi. Subs (all used): 17 Paul Noone; 16 Brett McDermott; 18 Liam Campbell; 11 Michael Knowles.
Tries: Mossop (7), Catic (12), Blackwood (15), Harrison (40), Campbell (56), Broadbent (75);
Goals: Rooney 3/4, Ballard 2/2.
Sin bin: McDermott (33) – fighting.
RAMS: 1 Lee Lingard; 15 Bryn Powell; 26 Ayden Faal; 10 Scott Turner; 2 James Haynes; 13 Pat Walker; 8 Dominic Brambani; 14 Luke Stenchion; 37 Luke Blake; 23 Keegan Hirst; 25 James Lockwood; 21 Andrew Bostock; 35 Danny Addy. Subs (all used): 11 Adam Robinson; 30 Luke Menzies; 40 Ed Barber; 33 James Walker.
Tries: Faal (23, 72), Robinson (33, 54);
Goals: P Walker 4/4, Brambani 0/1.
Sin bin: J Walker (33) – fighting.
Rugby Leaguer & League Express Men of the Match:
Raiders: Gary Broadbent; *Rams:* Dominic Brambani.
Penalty count: 6-9; **Half-time:** 22-12;
Referee: Matthew Thomasson; **Attendance:** 1,715.

Sunday 25th April 2010

BATLEY BULLDOGS 24 WIDNES VIKINGS 32

BULLDOGS: 5 John Campbell; 2 Lee Greenwood; 22 Josh Griffin; 4 Danny Maun; 24 Alex Brown; 6 Paul Handforth; 7 Gareth Moore; 8 Byron Smith; 9 Kris Lythe; 10 Sean Hesketh; 23 Chris Buttery; 26 Jason Walton; 12 Mark Toohey. Subs (all used): 13 Ashley Lindsay; 25 Kyle Wood; 20 David Tootill; 21 James Martin.
Tries: Hesketh (42), Walton (45, 50), Brown (64), Greenwood (79); **Goals:** Moore 2/5.
VIKINGS: 1 James Ford; 5 Paddy Flynn; 4 Toa Kohe-Love; 19 Matt Gardner; 18 Scott Yates; 6 Anthony Thackeray; 7 James Webster; 10 Jim Gannon; 13 Chris Gerrard; 31 Jordan James; 15 Shane Grady; 17 Ben Kavanagh; 11 Lee Doran. Subs (all used): 24 Danny Hulme; 23 David Houghton; 28 Ben Davies; 32 Tom Kelly.
Tries: Grady (3), Ford (5), C Gerrard (8), Flynn (40, 61);
Goals: Grady 6/7.
Rugby Leaguer & League Express Men of the Match:
Bulldogs: Sean Hesketh; *Vikings:* Shane Grady.
Penalty count: 10-6; **Half-time:** 0-24;
Referee: Craig Halloran; **Attendance:** 1,146.

LEIGH CENTURIONS 36 SHEFFIELD EAGLES 20

CENTURIONS: 1 Stuart Donlan; 2 Steve Maden; 25 Matty Blythe; 4 Mick Nanyn; 3 David Alstead; 22 Martyn Ridyard; 7 Robbie Paul; 10 Ricky Bibey; 9 John Duffy; 8 Chris Hill; 11 James Taylor; 14 Tommy Goulden; 26 Lee Mitchell. Subs (all used): 15 Dave McConnell; 12 Macgraff Leuluai; 13 Dave Armitstead; 27 Jacob Emmitt.
Tries: Donlan (17, 31), Paul (23), Hill (26), McConnell (63), Blythe (70); **Goals:** Nanyn 6/6.
Dismissal: Alstead (33) – high tackle on Green.
EAGLES: 24 Misi Taulapapa; 27 Richie Barnett; 3 Menzie Yere; 23 Tangi Ropati; 5 Ashley Thackeray; 6 Brendon Lindsay; 21 Dane McDonald; 10 Mitchell Stringer; 9 Craig Cook; 8 Jack Howieson; 11 Alex Szostak; 13 Peter Green; 16 Trevor Exton. Subs (all used): 7 Aaron Groom; 15 Sam Barlow; 19 Joe Hirst; 17 Alex Rowe.
Tries: Barnett (9), Ropati (36), Groom (42), Exton (45);
Goals: Stringer 2/4.
Rugby Leaguer & League Express Men of the Match:
Centurions: Robbie Paul; *Eagles:* Trevor Exton.
Penalty count: 11-12; **Half-time:** 24-10;
Referee: Robert Hicks; **Attendance:** 1,878.

WHITEHAVEN 10 HALIFAX 28

WHITEHAVEN: 31 Josh Veivers; 5 Derry Eilbeck; 3 Rob Jackson; 32 Mike Darby; 2 Craig Calvert; 6 Carl Rudd; 14 Dylan Skee; 17 Andy Thornley; 9 Graeme Mattinson; 33 Kyle Amor; 16 Andy Gorski; 26 Daniel Barker; 7 Leroy Joe. Subs (all used): 21 Chris Smith; 8 Marc Jackson; 11 Howard Hill; 28 Tom Philip.
Tries: Smith (31), Rudd (70); **Goals:** Rudd 1/2.
Sin bin: M Jackson (38) - punching.
HALIFAX: 4 Shad Royston; 20 Paul White; 2 Lee Paterson; 18 Dylan Nash; 23 Rob Worrincy; 6 Luke Branighan; 7 Ben Black; 16 Said Tamghart; 9 Sean Penkywicz; 19 Dominic Maloney; 24 Steve Bannister; 22 David Wrench; 21 Anthony Bowman. Subs (all used): 8 Makali Aizue; 13 Bob Beswick; 17 Frank Watene; 25 Michael Ostick.
Tries: Royston (10, 35), Black (26, 57), Tamghart (54);
Goals: Paterson 4/6.
Rugby Leaguer & League Express Men of the Match:
Whitehaven: Graeme Mattinson; *Halifax:* Shad Royston.
Penalty count: 11-7; **Half-time:** 6-18;
Referee: Ronnie Laughton; **Attendance:** 1,140.

ROUND 9

Thursday 29th April 2010

DEWSBURY RAMS 14 LEIGH CENTURIONS 30

RAMS: 1 Lee Lingard; 15 Bryn Powell; 26 Ayden Faal; 10 Scott Turner; 2 James Haynes; 13 Pat Walker; 8 Dominic Brambani; 14 Luke Stenchion; 37 Luke Blake; 23 Keegan Hirst; 21 Andrew Bostock; 11 Adam Robinson; 35 Danny Addy. Subs (all used): 25 James Lockwood; 30 Luke Menzies; 33 James Walker; 40 Ed Barber.
Tries: Brambani (24), Bostock (59); **Goals:** P Walker 3/3.
CENTURIONS: 1 Stuart Donlan; 2 Steve Maden; 4 Mick Nanyn; 25 Matty Blythe; 18 Adam Higson; 22 Martyn Ridyard; 7 Robbie Paul; 10 Ricky Bibey; 9 John Duffy; 8 Chris Hill; 14 Tommy Goulden; 11 James Taylor; 13 Dave Armitstead. Subs (all used): 5 Nicky Stanton; 12 Macgraff Leuluai; 15 Dave McConnell; 27 Jacob Emmitt.
Tries: Armitstead (16), Goulden (32), Emmitt (38, 49), Ridyard (78); **Goals:** Nanyn 5/5.
Rugby Leaguer & League Express Men of the Match:
Rams: Andrew Bostock; *Centurions:* Jacob Emmitt.
Penalty count: 10-7; **Half-time:** 8-18;
Referee: Robert Hicks; **Attendance:** 1,151.

Friday 30th April 2010

WIDNES VIKINGS 8 FEATHERSTONE ROVERS 9

VIKINGS: 1 James Ford; 26 Shaun Ainscough; 4 Toa Kohe-Love; 19 Matt Gardner; 5 Paddy Flynn; 6 Anthony Thackeray; 7 James Webster; 31 Jordan James; 32 Kirk Netherton; 10 Jim Gannon; 11 Lee Doran; 15 Shane Grady; 13 Chris Gerrard. Subs (all used): 3 Richard Varkulis; 12 Dave Allen; 17 Ben Kavanagh; 28 Ben Davies.
Tries: Gardner (44), Flynn (57); **Goals:** Grady 0/2.
ROVERS: 1 Ian Hardman; 2 Tom Saxton; 4 Liam Welham; 15 Jessie Joe Parker; 26 Zak Hardaker; 6 Kyle Briggs; 9 Liam Finn; 10 Stuart Dickens; 31 Ben Kaye; 17 Tony Tonks; 16 Dane Manning; 13 Jamie Field; 11 Matty Dale. Subs (all used): 7 Andy Kain; 14 Danny Allan; 8 Iain Morrison; 19 Ross Divorty.
Tries: Parker (3), Kain (27); **Goals:** Briggs 0/3;
Field goal: Finn (79).
Rugby Leaguer & League Express Men of the Match:
Vikings: Lee Doran; *Rovers:* Andy Kain.
Penalty count: 13-9; **Half-time:** 0-8;
Referee: Jamie Leahy; **Attendance:** 3,448.

Saturday 1st May 2010

TOULOUSE OLYMPIQUE 20 BATLEY BULLDOGS 12

OLYMPIQUE: 1 Rory Bromley; 24 Andrei Olari; 3 Sebastien Planas; 20 Bruno Ormeno; 5 Carlos Mendes Varela; 16 Sylvain Houles; 7 Nathan Wynn; 8 Brendan Worth; 9 Martin Mitchell; 10 Mathieu Griffi; 14 Antoni Maria; 18 Yoan Tisseyre; 13 Eric Anselme. Subs (all used): 11 Tim Wynn; 23 Kevin Larroyer; 25 Teli Pelo; 31 Yohann Gigord.
Tries: Mendes Varela (35, 38), Griffi (71);
Goals: N Wynn 4/4.
BULLDOGS: 5 John Campbell; 2 Lee Greenwood; 4 Danny Maun; 12 Mark Toohey; 24 Alex Brown; 6 Paul Handforth; 7 Gareth Moore; 8 Byron Smith; 9 Kris Lythe; 10 Sean Hesketh; 23 Chris Buttery; 17 Craig Potter; 13 Ashley Lindsay. Subs (all used): 3 Mark Barlow; 25 Kyle Wood; 20 David Tootill; 21 James Martin.
Tries: Toohey (50), Lythe (60); **Goals:** Handforth 2/4.
Rugby Leaguer & League Express Men of the Match:
Olympique: Yoan Tisseyre; *Bulldogs:* Ashley Lindsay.
Penalty count: 3-9; **Half-time:** 14-4;
Referee: Ronnie Laughton; **Attendance:** 1,100.

Monday 3rd May 2010

KEIGHLEY COUGARS 10 BARROW RAIDERS 40

COUGARS: 2 Craig Moss; 5 Gavin Duffy; 23 Chris Baines; 4 Daley Williams; 31 James Hutchinson; 18 James Haythornthwaite; 7 Danny Jones; 8 Andy Shickell; 9 James Feather; 17 Ryan Benjafield; 11 Will Cartledge; 12 Oliver Pursglove; 15 Greg Nicholson. Subs (all used): 25 Jamie Shepherd; 16 Brendan Rawlins; 10 Scott Law; 33 Tom Sheldrake.
Tries: Duffy (38), Williams (44); **Goals:** D Jones 1/2.
Sin bin: Nicholson (25) - interference.
RAIDERS: 1 Gary Broadbent; 2 Andy Ballard; 3 Anthony Blackwood; 4 Liam Harrison; 21 Chris Larkin; 6 Jamie Rooney; 18 Liam Campbell; 8 Andy Bracek; 19 Nathan Mossop; 31 Matt James; 14 Martin Ostler; 12 Ned Catic; 13 Zebastian Luisi. Subs (all used): 16 Brett McDermott; 11 Michael Knowles; 17 Paul Noone; 15 Rob Roberts.
Tries: Rooney (10, 24), Campbell (19, 30), Mossop (27), Bracek (47), Ballard (51); **Goals:** Rooney 6/7.
Rugby Leaguer & League Express Men of the Match:
Cougars: Andy Shickell; *Raiders:* Jamie Rooney.
Penalty count: 9-9; **Half-time:** 6-30;
Referee: Craig Halloran; **Attendance:** 1,047.

SHEFFIELD EAGLES 64 WHITEHAVEN 24

EAGLES: 24 Misi Taulapapa; 2 Danny Mills; 3 Menzie Yere; 23 Tangi Ropati; 5 Ashley Thackeray; 6 Brendon Lindsay; 7 Aaron Groom; 22 Ryan Hepworth; 9 Craig Cook; 16 Trevor Exton; 11 Alex Szostak; 13 Peter Green; 21 Dane McDonald. Subs (all used): 19 Joe Hirst; 17 Alex Rowe; 20 Matty Brooks; 12 Ged Corcoran.
Tries: Yere (3), Szostak (15), Brooks (39), Rowe (45, 47, 72), Ropati (55, 65), Groom (58), Cook (74, 80), Thackeray (77); **Goals:** Ropati 4/7, Lindsay 4/5.
WHITEHAVEN: 31 Josh Veivers; 5 Derry Eilbeck; 32 Mike Darby; 3 Rob Jackson; 2 Craig Calvert; 6 Carl Rudd; 14 Dylan Skee; 17 Andy Thornley; 9 Graeme Mattinson; 33 Kyle Amor; 12 Spencer Miller; 26 Daniel Barker; 7 Leroy Joe. Subs (all used): 21 Chris Smith; 8 Marc Jackson; 11 Howard Hill; 15 Reece Fox.
Tries: M Jackson (21), Calvert (33, 43), R Jackson (52);
Goals: Rudd 4/4.
Rugby Leaguer & League Express Men of the Match:
Eagles: Misi Taulapapa; *Whitehaven:* Graeme Mattinson.
Penalty count: 8-2; **Half-time:** 14-12;
Referee: Matthew Thomasson; **Attendance:** 1,301.

ROUND 8

Thursday 6th May 2010

FEATHERSTONE ROVERS 24 TOULOUSE OLYMPIQUE 26

ROVERS: 1 Ian Hardman; 26 Zak Hardaker; 15 Jessie Joe Parker; 14 Danny Allan; 2 Tom Saxton; 6 Kyle Briggs; 9 Liam Finn; 17 Tony Tonks; 31 Ben Kaye; 10 Stuart Dickens; 11 Matty Dale; 16 Dane Manning; 13 Jamie Field. Subs (all used): 7 Andy Kain; 19 Ross Divorty; 8 Iain Morrison; 18 Tim Spears.
Tries: Hardman (6, 35), Hardaker (9, 43);
Goals: Briggs 4/6.
On report: Morrison (72) - alleged use of the forearm.
OLYMPIQUE: 1 Rory Bromley; 24 Andrei Olari; 3 Sebastien Planas; 4 Vincent Duport; 5 Carlos Mendes Varela; 16 Sylvain Houles; 7 Nathan Wynn; 8 Brendan Worth; 9 Martin Mitchell; 10 Mathieu Griffi; 18 Yoan Tisseyre; 14 Antoni Maria; 13 Eric Anselme. Subs (all used): 11 Tim Wynn; 23 Kevin Larroyer; 25 Teli Pelo; 31 Yohann Gigord.
Tries: Tisseyre (2), Planas (16), Mitchell (48), Bromley (51), Duport (78); **Goals:** N Wynn 3/5.
On report: Larroyer (31) - alleged dangerous tackle.
Rugby Leaguer & League Express Men of the Match:
Rovers: Ian Hardman; *Olympique:* Rory Bromley.
Penalty count: 14-11; **Half-time:** 18-10;
Referee: Warren Turley; **Attendance:** 2,223.

ROUND 10

Sunday 9th May 2010

WHITEHAVEN 12 KEIGHLEY COUGARS 22

WHITEHAVEN: 31 Josh Veivers; 5 Derry Eilbeck; 3 Rob Jackson; 28 Tom Philip; 2 Craig Calvert; 6 Carl Rudd; 7 Leroy Joe; 17 Andy Thornley; 9 Graeme Mattinson; 33 Kyle Amor; 12 Spencer Miller; 26 Daniel Barker; 32 Kurt

The Toulouse defence can't stop Sheffield's Alex Rowe from scoring

Wilton. Subs (all used): 30 Carl Sice; 8 Marc Jackson; 15 Reece Fox; 11 Howard Hill.
Tries: Veivers (15), Wilton (18); **Goals:** Rudd 2/2.
COUGARS: 2 Craig Moss; 5 Gavin Duffy; 33 Tom Sheldrake; 4 Daley Williams; 31 James Hutchinson; 6 Jon Presley; 7 Danny Jones; 8 Andy Shickell; 9 James Feather; 17 Ryan Benjafield; 23 Chris Baines; 12 Oliver Pursglove; 15 Greg Nicholson. Subs (all used): 14 Jamaine Wray; 16 Brendan Rawlins; 11 Will Cartledge; 25 Jamie Shepherd.
Tries: Williams (23), Duffy (46), Pursglove (65, 72); **Goals:** D Jones 3/4.
Rugby Leaguer & League Express Men of the Match: *Whitehaven:* Graeme Mattinson; *Cougars:* Danny Jones.
Penalty count: 6-2; **Half-time:** 12-6;
Referee: Jamie Leahy; **Attendance:** 900.

Wednesday 12th May 2010

SHEFFIELD EAGLES 22 BATLEY BULLDOGS 12

EAGLES: 24 Misi Taulapapa; 2 Danny Mills; 3 Menzie Yere; 23 Tangi Ropati; 5 Ashley Thackeray; 6 Brendon Lindsay; 7 Aaron Groom; 22 Ryan Hepworth; 9 Craig Cook; 16 Trevor Exton; 11 Alex Szostak; 13 Peter Green; 21 Dane McDonald. Subs (all used): 19 Joe Hirst; 17 Alex Rowe; 20 Matty Brooks; 12 Ged Corcoran.
Tries: Thackeray (44), Mills (49), Rowe (75, 78);
Goals: Lindsay 1/2, Ropati 2/2.
BULLDOGS: 5 John Campbell; 2 Lee Greenwood; 4 Danny Maun; 12 Mark Toohey; 24 Alex Brown; 6 Paul Handforth; 7 Gareth Moore; 8 Byron Smith; 9 Kris Lythe; 10 Sean Hesketh; 26 Jason Walton; 14 John Gallagher; 13 Ashley Lindsay. Subs (all used): 25 Kyle Wood; 17 Craig Potter; 21 James Martin; 20 David Tootill.
Tries: Moore (4), Tootill (23); **Goals:** Moore 2/2.
Rugby Leaguer & League Express Men of the Match: *Eagles:* Ryan Hepworth; *Bulldogs:* Gareth Moore.
Penalty count: 8-2; **Half-time:** 0-12;
Referee: Matthew Thomasson; **Attendance:** 1,170.

ROUND 11

Thursday 13th May 2010

LEIGH CENTURIONS 30 WIDNES VIKINGS 16

CENTURIONS: 1 Stuart Donlan; 2 Steve Maden; 25 Matty Blythe; 4 Mick Nanyn; 5 Nicky Stanton; 22 Martyn Ridyard; 7 Robbie Paul; 10 Ricky Bibey; 15 Dave McConnell; 27 Jacob Emmitt; 14 Tommy Goulden; 11 James Taylor; 13 Dave Armitstead. Subs (all used): 8 Chris Hill; 9 John Duffy; 16 Mike Morrison; 3 David Alstead.
Tries: McConnell (3, 9), Nanyn (24, 38), Emmitt (61);
Goals: Nanyn 5/6.
VIKINGS: 1 James Ford; 5 Paddy Flynn; 4 Toa Kohe-

Love; 19 Matt Gardner; 26 Shaun Ainscough; 6 Anthony Thackeray; 7 James Webster; 10 Jim Gannon; 32 Kirk Netherton; 31 Jordan James; 11 Lee Doran; 15 Shane Grady; 13 Chris Gerrard. Subs (all used): 2 Dean Gaskell; 3 Richard Varkulis; 17 Ben Kavanagh; 28 Ben Davies.
Tries: Ainscough (36), Netherton (48), Flynn (54);
Goals: Grady 2/3.
Rugby Leaguer & League Express Men of the Match: *Centurions:* Martyn Ridyard; *Vikings:* Kirk Netherton.
Penalty count: 4-4; **Half-time:** 24-4;
Referee: Gareth Hewer; **Attendance:** 3,392.

Saturday 15th May 2010

SHEFFIELD EAGLES 38 TOULOUSE OLYMPIQUE 24

EAGLES: 24 Misi Taulapapa; 27 Richie Barnett; 3 Menzie Yere; 23 Tangi Ropati; 26 Tim Bergin; 6 Brendon Lindsay; 7 Aaron Groom; 18 Michael Haley; 9 Craig Cook; 10 Mitchell Stringer; 11 Alex Szostak; 13 Peter Green; 21 Dane McDonald. Subs (all used): 20 Matty Brooks; 16 Trevor Exton; 22 Ryan Hepworth; 17 Alex Rowe.
Tries: Ropati (6), Groom (16), Barnett (21), Rowe (47), Cook (60, 67, 77); **Goals:** Stringer 4/5, Lindsay 1/2.
OLYMPIQUE: 1 Rory Bromley; 24 Andrei Olari; 3 Sebastien Planas; 4 Vincent Duport; 5 Carlos Mendes Varela; 16 Sylvain Houles; 7 Nathan Wynn; 8 Brendan Worth; 9 Martin Mitchell; 10 Mathieu Griffi; 14 Antoni Maria; 18 Yoan Tisseyre; 13 Eric Anselme. Subs (all used): 11 Tim Wynn; 25 Teli Pelo; 23 Kevin Larroyer; 6 Constant Villegas.
Tries: Houles (13), Duport (36), Bromley (43), Griffi (65); **Goals:** N Wynn 4/5.
Rugby Leaguer & League Express Men of the Match: *Eagles:* Matty Brooks; *Olympique:* Nathan Wynn.
Penalty count: 5-5; **Half-time:** 16-12;
Referee: Craig Halloran; **Attendance:** 979.

Sunday 16th May 2010

BATLEY BULLDOGS 54 WHITEHAVEN 6

BULLDOGS: 5 John Campbell; 3 Mark Barlow; 22 Josh Griffin; 4 Danny Maun; 2 Lee Greenwood; 6 Paul Handforth; 7 Gareth Moore; 8 Byron Smith; 9 Kris Lythe; 10 Sean Hesketh; 26 Jason Walton; 31 John Gallagher; 13 Ashley Lindsay. Subs (all used): 25 Kyle Wood; 23 Chris Buttery; 11 Tommy Gallagher; 20 David Tootill.
Tries: Maun (10, 22, 67), Campbell (13, 35, 63, 75), Buttery (28), Handforth (32), Smith (54);
Goals: Moore 7/10.
WHITEHAVEN: 31 Josh Veivers; 1 Craig Benson; 5 Derry Eilbeck; 3 Rob Jackson; 2 Craig Calvert; 6 Carl Rudd; 34 Motu Tony; 17 Andy Thornley; 9 Graeme Mattinson; 32 Paul Johnson; 12 Spencer Miller; 11 Howard Hill; 7 Leroy Joe. Subs (all used): 21 Chris Smith; 33 Kyle Amor; 8 Marc Jackson; 26 Daniel Barker.
Try: Mattinson (5); **Goals:** Rudd 1/1.

Rugby Leaguer & League Express Men of the Match: *Bulldogs:* Sean Hesketh; *Whitehaven:* Daniel Barker.
Penalty count: 11-4; **Half-time:** 30-6;
Referee: Tim Roby; **Attendance:** 666.

HALIFAX 46 BARROW RAIDERS 24

HALIFAX: 4 Shad Royston; 20 Paul White; 2 Lee Paterson; 7 Ben Black; 17 Frank Watene; 9 Sean Penkywicz; 22 David Wrench; 11 David Larder; 24 Steve Bannister; 12 Stanley Gene. Subs (all used): 3 Jon Goddard; 13 Bob Beswick; 16 Said Tamghart; 8 Makali Aizue.
Tries: Bannister (2), Royston (21), Gene (25), Worricny (55), Goddard (57), Beswick (62), Branighan (78), White (80); **Goals:** Paterson 7/9.
RAIDERS: 1 Gary Broadbent; 2 Andy Ballard; 12 Ned Catic; 4 Liam Harrison; 25 Jermaine McGillvary; 6 Jamie Rooney; 18 Liam Campbell; 8 Andy Bracek; 19 Nathan Mossop; 15 Rob Roberts; 11 Michael Knowles; 24 Richard Fletcher; 13 Zebastian Luisi. Subs (all used): 10 Chris Young; 16 Brett McDermott; 17 Paul Noone; 23 Jamie Butler.
Tries: Ballard (10), Fletcher (15), Catic (69), Young (74);
Goals: Rooney 4/5.
Rugby Leaguer & League Express Men of the Match: *Halifax:* Luke Branighan; *Raiders:* Ned Catic.
Penalty count: 11-13; **Half-time:** 20-12;
Referee: Robert Hicks; **Attendance:** 2,175.

ROUND 10

Tuesday 18th May 2010

LEIGH CENTURIONS 16 FEATHERSTONE ROVERS 24

CENTURIONS: 1 Stuart Donlan; 2 Steve Maden; 25 Matty Blythe; 4 Mick Nanyn; 5 Nicky Stanton; 22 Martyn Ridyard; 7 Robbie Paul; 8 Chris Hill; 15 Dave McConnell; 10 Ricky Bibey; 14 Tommy Goulden; 11 James Taylor; 13 Dave Armitstead. Subs (all used): 16 Mike Morrison; 9 John Duffy; 12 Macgraff Leuluai; 3 David Alstead.
Tries: Goulden (29), Hill (49), Nanyn (78);
Goals: Nanyn 2/4.
ROVERS: 1 Ian Hardman; 5 Jon Steel; 15 Jessie Joe Parker; 4 Liam Welham; 2 Tom Saxton; 6 Kyle Briggs; 9 Liam Finn; 17 Tony Tonks; 31 Ben Kaye; 10 Stuart Dickens; 12 Jon Grayshon; 8 Iain Morrison; 11 Matty Dale. Subs (all used): 19 Ross Divorty; 16 Dane Manning; 18 Tim Spears; 7 Andy Kain.
Tries: Grayshon (6, 60), Welham (43), Parker (70);
Goals: Briggs 4/5.
Rugby Leaguer & League Express Men of the Match: *Centurions:* Chris Hill; *Rovers:* Liam Finn.
Penalty count: 11-9; **Half-time:** 4-8;
Referee: Robert Hicks; **Attendance:** 2,425.

Whitehaven's Leroy Joe gets to grips with Leigh's Steve Maden

ROUND 12

Thursday 20th May 2010

DEWSBURY RAMS 20 SHEFFIELD EAGLES 22

RAMS: 1 Lee Lingard; 15 Bryn Powell; 17 Alex Bretherton; 10 Scott Turner; 16 Austin Buchanan; 40 Ed Barber; 8 Dominic Brambani; 11 Adam Robinson; 37 Luke Blake; 23 Keegan Hirst; 20 Rob Spicer; 21 Andrew Bostock; 13 Pat Walker. Subs (all used): 9 Mike Emmett; 33 James Walker; 26 Ayden Faal; 25 James Lockwood.
Tries: Barber (22), Lockwood (38), Bostock (42), Powell (74); **Goals:** P Walker 2/4.
EAGLES: 24 Misi Taulapapa; 27 Richie Barnett; 3 Menzie Yere; 23 Tangi Ropati; 26 Tim Bergin; 6 Brendon Lindsay; 7 Aaron Groom; 10 Mitchell Stringer; 9 Craig Cook; 18 Michael Haley; 16 Trevor Exton; 13 Peter Green; 21 Dane McDonald. Subs (all used): 22 Ryan Hepworth; 20 Matty Brooks; 17 Alex Rowe; 15 Sam Barlow.
Tries: Cook (8, 52), Stringer (12), McDonald (27);
Goals: Stringer 3/5.
Rugby Leaguer & League Express Men of the Match: *Rams:* Rob Spicer; *Eagles:* Mitchell Stringer.
Penalty count: 10-9; **Half-time:** 10-14; **Referee:** Ronnie Laughton; **Attendance:** 1,066.

Saturday 22nd May 2010

TOULOUSE OLYMPIQUE 28 FEATHERSTONE ROVERS 34

OLYMPIQUE: 1 Rory Bromley; 22 Clement Bienes; 3 Sebastien Planas; 6 Constant Villegas; 5 Carlos Mendes Varela; 16 Sylvain Houles; 7 Nathan Wynn; 8 Brendan Worth; 9 Martin Mitchell; 10 Mathieu Griffi; 11 Tim Wynn; 14 Antoni Maria; 13 Eric Anselme. Subs (all used): 18 Yoan Tisseyre; 19 Romain Mencarini; 21 Nicolas Faure; 23 Kevin Larroyer.
Tries: Planas (10), Mitchell (27), Bienes (41), Tisseyre (54), Bromley (59); **Goals:** N Wynn 4/5.
Sin bin: Bromley (37) - holding down.
ROVERS: 1 Ian Hardman; 2 Tom Saxton; 4 Liam Welham; 21 Michael Coady; 5 Jon Steel; 6 Kyle Briggs; 31 Ben Kaye; 17 Tony Tonks; 9 Liam Finn; 10 Stuart Dickens; 8 Iain Morrison; 12 Jon Grayshon; 11 Matty Dale. Subs (all used): 18 Tim Spears; 7 Andy Kain; 13 Jamie Field; 19 Ross Divorty.
Tries: Briggs (35), Kain (37, 39), Saxton (46), Dale (69, 76); **Goals:** Briggs 5/6.
Rugby Leaguer & League Express Men of the Match: *Olympique:* Nathan Wynn; *Rovers:* Iain Morrison.
Penalty count: 7-7; **Half-time:** 10-18;
Referee: Matthew Thomasson; **Attendance:** 1,328.

Sunday 23rd May 2010

KEIGHLEY COUGARS 32 HALIFAX 46

COUGARS: 2 Craig Moss; 5 Gavin Duffy; 33 Tom Sheldrake; 4 Daley Williams; 31 James Hutchinson; 6 Jon Presley; 7 Danny Jones; 10 Scott Law; 9 James Feather; 17 Ryan Benjafield; 23 Chris Baines; 12 Oliver Pursglove; 15 Greg Nicholson. Subs (all used): 14 Jamaine Wray; 18 James Haythornthwaite; 11 Will Cartledge; 21 Richard Jones.
Tries: Benjafield (6), D Jones (20), Law (52), Hutchinson (56), Presley (73); **Goals:** D Jones 6/8.
HALIFAX: 4 Shad Royston; 20 Paul White; 2 Lee Paterson; 3 Jon Goddard; 5 James Haley; 6 Luke Branighan; 21 Anthony Bowman; 17 Frank Watene; 9 Sean Penkywicz; 22 David Wrench; 11 David Larder; 24 Steve Bannister; 13 Bob Beswick. Subs (all used): 14 Mark Gleeson; 16 Said Tamghart; 18 Dylan Nash; 25 Michael Ostick.
Tries: Paterson (3, 18), White (26), Goddard (32), Gleeson (38), Beswick (45), Penkywicz (78), Branighan (79); **Goals:** Paterson 7/8.
Rugby Leaguer & League Express Men of the Match: *Cougars:* Jon Presley; *Halifax:* David Larder.
Penalty count: 12-8; **Half-time:** 14-28;
Referee: Warren Turley; **Attendance:** 1,602.

WHITEHAVEN 8 LEIGH CENTURIONS 12

WHITEHAVEN: 31 Josh Veivers; 5 Derry Eilbeck; 3 Rob Jackson; 34 Motu Tony; 2 Craig Calvert; 6 Carl Rudd; 14 Dylan Skee; 17 Andy Thornley; 9 Graeme Mattinson; 28 Paul Johnson; 12 Spencer Miller; 11 Howard Hill; 7 Leroy Joe. Subs (all used): 21 Chris Smith; 33 Kyle Amor; 32 Marc Shackley; 26 Daniel Barker.
Try: Johnson (19); **Goals:** Rudd 2/3.
CENTURIONS: 1 Stuart Donlan; 2 Steve Maden; 18 Adam Higson; 4 Mick Nanyn; 5 Nicky Stanton; 22 Martyn Ridyard; 7 Robbie Paul; 8 Chris Hill; 9 John Duffy; 10 Ricky Bibey; 11 James Taylor; 14 Tommy Goulden; 12 Macgraff Leuluai. Subs (all used): 15 Dave McConnell; 16 Mike Morrison; 13 Dave Armitstead; 17 Stephen Nash.
Tries: Ridyard (6), Paul (60); **Goals:** Nanyn 2/2.
Dismissal: Duffy (62) - entering the field of play without permission.
Rugby Leaguer & League Express Men of the Match: *Whitehaven:* Paul Johnson; *Centurions:* Ricky Bibey.
Penalty count: 7-11; **Half-time:** 8-6;
Referee: Phil Halloran; **Attendance:** 1,100.

WIDNES VIKINGS 16 BATLEY BULLDOGS 35

VIKINGS: 15 Shane Grady; 2 Dean Gaskell; 4 Toa Kohe-Love; 19 Matt Gardner; 5 Paddy Flynn; 6 Anthony Thackeray; 13 Chris Gerrard; 29 Jordan James; 32 Kirk

Netherton; 10 Jim Gannon; 17 Ben Kavanagh; 12 Dave Allen; 11 Lee Doran. Subs (all used): 30 Daniel Heckenberg; 23 David Houghton; 3 Richard Varkulis; 24 Danny Hulme.
Tries: Kavanagh (53), Thackeray (62, 71);
Goals: Grady 2/3.
BULLDOGS: 5 John Campbell; 3 Mark Barlow; 22 Josh Griffin; 4 Danny Maun; 2 Lee Greenwood; 6 Paul Handforth; 7 Gareth Moore; 8 Byron Smith; 9 Kris Lythe; 10 Sean Hesketh; 26 Jason Walton; 14 John Gallagher; 13 Ashley Lindsay. Subs (all used): 21 James Martin; 23 Chris Buttery; 11 Tommy Gallagher; 20 David Tootill.
Tries: Barlow (16, 33), Handforth (30), Maun (49), Campbell (69); **Goals:** Moore 7/7;
Field goal: Handforth (78).
Rugby Leaguer & League Express Men of the Match: *Vikings:* Dave Allen; *Bulldogs:* Paul Handforth.
Penalty count: 7-7; **Half-time:** 0-20;
Referee: Robert Hicks; **Attendance:** 2,780.

ROUND 13

Thursday 27th May 2010

SHEFFIELD EAGLES 24 KEIGHLEY COUGARS 25

EAGLES: 24 Misi Taulapapa; 27 Richie Barnett; 3 Menzie Yere; 23 Tangi Ropati; 2 Danny Mills; 6 Brendon Lindsay; 7 Aaron Groom; 18 Michael Haley; 9 Craig Cook; 10 Mitchell Stringer; 13 Peter Green; 16 Trevor Exton; 19 Joe Hirst. Subs (all used): 20 Matty Brooks; 15 Sam Barlow; 17 Alex Rowe; 22 Ryan Hepworth.
Tries: Hirst (8), Yere (12), Exton (49), Barlow (52), Lindsay (55); **Goals:** Stringer 1/4, Lindsay 1/1.
COUGARS: 2 Craig Moss; 5 Gavin Duffy; 33 Tom Sheldrake; 4 Daley Williams; 31 James Hutchinson; 6 Jon Presley; 7 Danny Jones; 10 Scott Law; 9 James Feather; 17 Ryan Benjafield; 23 Chris Baines; 12 Oliver Pursglove; 11 Will Cartledge. Subs (all used): 14 Jamaine Wray; 13 Carl Hughes; 16 Brendan Rawlins; 8 Andy Shickell.
Tries: D Jones (23), Hutchinson (27), Sheldrake (32);
Goals: D Jones 6/6; **Field goal:** D Jones (80).
Rugby Leaguer & League Express Men of the Match: *Eagles:* Michael Haley; *Cougars:* Danny Jones.
Penalty count: 7-7; **Half-time:** 8-20;
Referee: Thierry Alibert; **Attendance:** 1,271.

Sunday 30th May 2010

FEATHERSTONE ROVERS 36 DEWSBURY RAMS 32

ROVERS: 1 Ian Hardman; 21 Michael Coady; 15 Jessie Joe Parker; 4 Liam Welham; 2 Tom Saxton; 6 Kyle

Briggs; 9 Liam Finn; 17 Tony Tonks; 31 Ben Kaye; 10 Stuart Dickens; 12 Jon Grayshon; 8 Iain Morrison; 11 Matty Dale. Subs (all used): 7 Andy Kain; 18 Tim Spears; 16 Dane Manning; 19 Ross Divorty.
Tries: Briggs (8, 76), Coady (11), Finn (19), Divorty (45), Parker (48); **Goals:** Briggs 5/5, Finn 1/1.
RAMS: 16 Austin Buchanan; 15 Bryn Powell; 26 Ayden Faal; 17 Alex Bretherton; 10 Scott Turner; 40 Ed Barber; 8 Dominic Brambani; 14 Luke Stenchion; 37 Luke Blake; 25 James Lockwood; 20 Rob Spicer; 21 Andrew Bostock; 13 Pat Walker. Subs (all used): 9 Mike Emmett; 33 James Walker; 24 Anthony England; 23 Keegan Hirst.
Tries: Blake (16, 62), Powell (25), Turner (34, 58), England (53); **Goals:** Barber 4/6.
Rugby Leaguer & League Express Men of the Match: *Rovers:* Tom Saxton; *Rams:* Dominic Brambani.
Penalty count: 8-6; **Half-time:** 18-16;
Referee: Gareth Hewer; **Attendance:** 1,665.

LEIGH CENTURIONS 40 HALIFAX 46

CENTURIONS: 1 Stuart Donlan; 2 Steve Maden; 25 Matty Blythe; 4 Mick Nanyn; 18 Adam Higson; 22 Martyn Ridyard; 9 John Duffy; 17 Stephen Nash; 15 Dave McConnell; 10 Ricky Bibey; 11 James Taylor; 14 Tommy Goulden; 13 Dave Armitstead. Subs (all used): 8 Chris Hill; 16 Mike Morrison; 12 Macgraff Leuluai; 3 David Alstead.
Tries: Maden (16, 56), Goulden (28), Donlan (38), Morrison (46), Ridyard (74), Armitstead (80);
Goals: Nanyn 6/7.
HALIFAX: 4 Shad Royston; 20 Paul White; 3 Jon Goddard; 2 Lee Paterson; 23 Rob Worrincy; 6 Luke Branighan; 7 Ben Black; 25 Michael Ostick; 14 Mark Gleeson; 22 David Wrench; 12 Stanley Gene; 24 Steve Bannister; 13 Bob Beswick. Subs (all used): 9 Sean Penkywicz; 16 Said Tamghart; 17 Frank Watene; 18 Dylan Nash.
Tries: Black (10, 61), Nash (23), Royston (32), Worrincy (35, 63, 70), White (43); **Goals:** Paterson 7/8.
Rugby Leaguer & League Express Men of the Match: *Centurions:* Martyn Ridyard; *Halifax:* Luke Branighan.
Penalty count: 12-5; **Half-time:** 18-24;
Referee: Ben Thaler; **Attendance:** 2,536.

ROUND 10

Sunday 6th June 2010

HALIFAX 28 DEWSBURY RAMS 8

HALIFAX: 4 Shad Royston; 2 Lee Paterson; 3 Jon Goddard; 5 James Haley; 23 Rob Worrincy; 6 Luke Branighan; 7 Ben Black; 11 David Larder; 13 Bob Beswick; 25 Michael Ostick; 18 Dylan Nash; 24 Steve Bannister; 12 Stanley Gene. Subs (all used): 14 Mark Gleeson; 16 Said Tamghart; 17 Frank Watene; 20 Paul White.
Tries: Gene (7), Black (45, 62), Bannister (54), Goddard (76); **Goals:** Paterson 4/5.
Sin bin: Royston (38) – interference.
RAMS: 3 Stewart Sanderson; 15 Bryn Powell; 17 Alex Bretherton; 26 Ayden Faal; 10 Scott Turner; 40 Ed Barber; 8 Dominic Brambani; 25 James Lockwood; 37 Luke Blake; 33 James Walker; 20 Rob Spicer; 21 Andrew Bostock; 13 Pat Walker. Subs (all used): 9 Mike Emmett; 16 Austin Buchanan; 23 Keegan Hirst; 24 Anthony England.
Try: Powell (22); **Goals:** Barber 2/2.
Rugby Leaguer & League Express Men of the Match: *Halifax:* Ben Black; *Rams:* Rob Spicer.
Penalty count: 6-12; **Half-time:** 6-8;
Referee: Craig Halloran; **Attendance:** 1,851.

ROUND 13

Tuesday 8th June 2010

BARROW RAIDERS 30 WHITEHAVEN 0

RAIDERS: 1 Gary Broadbent; 2 Andy Ballard; 12 Ned Catic; 4 Liam Harrison; 32 Andreas Bauer; 6 Jamie Rooney; 18 Liam Campbell; 16 Brett McDermott; 19 Nathan Mossop; 15 Rob Roberts; 11 Michael Knowles; 14 Martin Ostler; 13 Zebastian Luisi. Subs (all used): 8 Andy Bracek; 10 Chris Young; 17 Paul Noone; 24 Richard Fletcher.
Tries: Ballard (35), McDermott (47), Rooney (58), Ostler (60), Bracek (76); **Goals:** Rooney 5/5.
WHITEHAVEN: 31 Josh Veivers; 5 Derry Eilbeck; 3 Rob Jackson; 34 Motu Tony; 2 Craig Calvert; 6 Carl Rudd; 14 Dylan Skee; 33 Kyle Amor; 9 Graeme Mattinson; 17 Andy Thornley; 12 Spencer Miller; 11 Howard Hill; 7 Leroy Joe. Subs (all used): 10 David Ford; 26 Daniel Barker; 21 Chris Smith; 25 Kurt Wilton.
Rugby Leaguer & League Express Men of the Match: *Raiders:* Ned Catic; *Whitehaven:* Carl Rudd.
Penalty count: 9-3; **Half-time:** 6-0;
Referee: Robert Hicks; **Attendance:** 1,920.

ROUND 14

Thursday 10th June 2010

HALIFAX 16 FEATHERSTONE ROVERS 26

HALIFAX: 4 Shad Royston; 23 Rob Worrincy; 2 Lee Paterson; 3 Jon Goddard; 20 Paul White; 6 Luke Branighan; 7 Ben Black; 8 Makali Aizue; 14 Mark Gleeson; 25 Michael Ostick; 18 Dylan Nash; 24 Steve Bannister; 13 Bob Beswick. Subs (all used): 9 Sean Penkywicz; 12 Stanley Gene; 17 Frank Watene; 19 Dominic Maloney.
Tries: Branighan (39), White (63), Black (76);
Goals: Paterson 2/3.
ROVERS: 1 Ian Hardman; 15 Jessie Joe Parker; 3 Sam Smeaton; 4 Liam Welham; 2 Tom Saxton; 6 Kyle Briggs; 9 Liam Finn; 10 Stuart Dickens; 31 Ben Kaye; 17 Tony Tonks; 13 Jamie Field; 18 Tim Spears; 11 Matty Dale. Subs (all used): 7 Andy Kain; 16 Dane Manning; 8 Iain Morrison; 19 Ross Divorty.
Tries: Welham (5, 57), Field (31), Parker (37), Divorty (45); **Goals:** Briggs 3/5.
Rugby Leaguer & League Express Men of the Match: *Halifax:* Luke Branighan; *Rovers:* Ross Divorty.
Penalty count: 13-10; **Half-time:** 6-14;
Referee: Matthew Thomasson; **Attendance:** 2,135.

Sunday 13th June 2010

BATLEY BULLDOGS 32 LEIGH CENTURIONS 12

BULLDOGS: 5 John Campbell; 24 Alex Brown; 22 Josh Griffin; 4 Danny Maun; 2 Lee Greenwood; 6 Paul Handforth; 7 Gareth Moore; 8 Byron Smith; 9 Kris Lythe; 10 Sean Hesketh; 26 Jason Walton; 31 John Gallagher; 13 Ashley Lindsay. Subs (all used): 33 Mick Govin; 17 Craig Potter; 23 Chris Buttery; 20 David Tootill.
Tries: Griffin (17), Govin (27), Moore (40), Brown (65), Lythe (73); **Goals:** Moore 6/6.
CENTURIONS: 20 Ian Mort; 3 David Alstead; 2 Steve Maden; 18 Adam Higson; 4 Mick Nanyn; 9 John Duffy; 21 Jamie Durbin; 8 Chris Hill; 15 Dave McConnell; 17 Stephen Nash; 14 Tommy Goulden; 12 Macgraff Leuluai; 13 Dave Armitstead. Subs (all used): 36 Craig Briscoe; 39 Anthony Nicholson; 16 Mike Morrison; 40 Paul Smith.
Tries: Mort (15), Maden (77);
Goals: Nanyn 1/1, Mort 1/1.
Rugby Leaguer & League Express Men of the Match: *Bulldogs:* Gareth Moore; *Centurions:* Anthony Nicholson.
Penalty count: 10-6; **Half-time:** 18-6;
Referee: Gareth Hewer; **Attendance:** 938.

KEIGHLEY COUGARS 16 DEWSBURY RAMS 20

COUGARS: 2 Craig Moss; 5 Gavin Duffy; 33 Tom Sheldrake; 4 Daley Williams; 31 James Hutchinson; 6 Jon Presley; 7 Danny Jones; 10 Scott Law; 9 James Feather; 17 Ryan Benjafield; 23 Chris Baines; 12 Oliver Pursglove; 11 Will Cartledge. Subs (all used): 14 Jamaine Wray; 18 James Haythornthwaite; 16 Brendan Rawlins; 8 Andy Shickell.
Tries: Rawlins (39), Feather (79); **Goals:** D Jones 4/4.
Sin bin: D Jones (26) - dissent.
RAMS: 1 Lee Lingard; 15 Bryn Powell; 26 Ayden Faal; 10 Scott Turner; 3 Stewart Sanderson; 13 Pat Walker; 8 Dominic Brambani; 25 James Lockwood; 37 Luke Blake; 14 Luke Stenchion; 20 Rob Spicer; 21 Andrew Bostock; 40 Ed Barber. Subs (all used): 11 Adam Robinson; 24 Anthony England; 9 Mike Emmett; 17 Alex Bretherton.
Tries: Spicer (19), Faal (28), P Walker (61), Bostock (64); **Goals:** Brambani 2/3, Barber 0/1.
Rugby Leaguer & League Express Men of the Match: *Cougars:* Andy Shickell; *Rams:* Dominic Brambani.
Penalty count: 9-4; **Half-time:** 10-8;
Referee: Dave Merrick; **Attendance:** 971.

WHITEHAVEN 14 SHEFFIELD EAGLES 24

WHITEHAVEN: 31 Josh Veivers; 5 Derry Eilbeck; 3 Rob Jackson; 19 Dexter Miller; 2 Craig Calvert; 6 Carl Rudd; 34 Motu Tony; 17 Andy Thornley; 9 Graeme Mattinson; 28 Kyle Bibb; 12 Spencer Miller; 26 Daniel Barker; 7 Leroy Joe. Subs (all used): 30 Carl Sice; 8 Marc Jackson; 25 Kurt Wilton; 11 Howard Hill.
Tries: Eilbeck (29), Calvert (56, 69); **Goals:** Rudd 1/3.
Sin bin: Sice (36) - professional foul.
EAGLES: 24 Misi Taulapapa; 23 Tangi Ropati; 3 Menzie Yere; 25 Jason Mossop; 26 Tim Bergin; 6 Brendon Lindsay; 20 Matty Brooks; 22 Ryan Hepworth; 9 Craig Cook; 10 Mitchell Stringer; 16 Trevor Exton; 32 Mike Burnett; 21 Dane McDonald. Subs (all used): 13 Peter Green; 12 Ged Corcoran; 18 Michael Haley; 19 Joe Hirst.
Tries: Green (42), Yere (47, 64), Cook (76), Lindsay (79); **Goals:** Lindsay 0/2, Bergin 2/3.
Rugby Leaguer & League Express Men of the Match: *Whitehaven:* Daniel Barker; *Eagles:* Brendon Lindsay.
Penalty count: 5-10; **Half-time:** 4-0;
Referee: Peter Brooke; **Attendance:** 860.

WIDNES VIKINGS 20 BARROW RAIDERS 24

VIKINGS: 1 James Ford; 2 Dean Gaskell; 3 Richard Varkulis; 19 Matt Gardner; 5 Paddy Flynn; 6 Anthony Thackeray; 9 Mark Smith; 10 Jim Gannon; 32 Kirk Netherton; 28 Ben Davies; 15 Shane Grady; 17 Ben Kavanagh; 11 Lee Doran. Subs (all used): 31 Tom Kelly; 33 Chris Lunt; 26 Shaun Ainscough; 23 David Houghton.
Tries: Varkulis (36, 68), Gannon (60, 78);
Goals: Grady 2/3, Thackeray 0/1.
RAIDERS: 1 Gary Broadbent; 2 Andy Ballard; 12 Ned Catic; 4 Liam Harrison; 32 Andreas Bauer; 6 Jamie Rooney; 18 Liam Campbell; 16 Brett McDermott; 19 Nathan Mossop; 8 Andy Bracek; 11 Michael Knowles; 14 Martin Ostler; 13 Zebastian Luisi. Subs (all used): 24 Richard Fletcher; 10 Chris Young; 17 Paul Noone; 23 Jamie Butler.
Tries: Knowles (3, 12), Catic (23); **Goals:** Rooney 6/6.
Rugby Leaguer & League Express Men of the Match: *Vikings:* Richard Varkulis; *Raiders:* Jamie Rooney.
Penalty count: 11-9; **Half-time:** 4-22;
Referee: Robert Hicks; **Attendance:** 2,958.

ROUND 13

Tuesday 22nd June 2010

BATLEY BULLDOGS 40 TOULOUSE OLYMPIQUE 42

BULLDOGS: 5 John Campbell; 2 Lee Greenwood; 22 Josh Griffin; 4 Danny Maun; 1 Ian Preece; 6 Paul Handforth; 7 Gareth Moore; 17 Craig Potter; 9 Kris Lythe; 10 Sean Hesketh; 26 Jason Walton; 12 Mark Toohey; 13 Ashley Lindsay. Subs (all used): 33 Mick Govin; 11 Tommy Gallagher; 21 James Martin; 20 David Tootill.
Tries: Griffin (8), Maun (17, 58), Toohey (25), Walton (34), Campbell (48), Govin (66); **Goals:** Moore 6/7.
OLYMPIQUE: 1 Rory Bromley; 5 Carlos Mendes Varela; 3 Sebastien Planas; 20 Bruno Ormeno; 2 Sebastien Payan; 6 Constant Villegas; 7 Nathan Wynn; 11 Tim Wynn; 9 Martin Mitchell; 10 Mathieu Griffi; 14 Antoni Maria; 18 Yoan Tisseyre; 13 Eric Anselme. Subs (all used): 25 Teli Pelo; 19 Romain Mencarini; 23 Kevin Larroyer; 26 Yohann Gigord.
Tries: Maria (5), Mitchell (12), Mendes Varela (31, 75), Larroyer (37, 40), Bromley (55), Gigord (71);
Goals: N Wynn 5/8.
On report: Griffi (66) - alleged high tackle.
Rugby Leaguer & League Express Men of the Match: *Bulldogs:* Danny Maun; *Olympique:* Kevin Larroyer.
Penalty count: 8-9; **Half-time:** 24-26;
Referee: Matthew Thomasson; **Attendance:** 689.

ROUND 15

Thursday 24th June 2010

SHEFFIELD EAGLES 26 BARROW RAIDERS 36

EAGLES: 24 Misi Taulapapa; 2 Danny Mills; 3 Menzie Yere; 25 Jason Mossop; 26 Tim Bergin; 6 Brendon Lindsay; 21 Dane McDonald; 22 Ryan Hepworth; 9 Craig Cook; 10 Mitchell Stringer; 13 Peter Green; 32 Mike Burnett; 16 Trevor Exton. Subs (all used): 20 Matty Brooks; 11 Alex Szostak; 19 Joe Hirst; 12 Ged Corcoran.
Tries: Stringer (5), Taulapapa (40, 48), Exton (80);
Goals: Bergin 5/5.
RAIDERS: 1 Gary Broadbent; 2 Andy Ballard; 12 Ned Catic; 4 Liam Harrison; 32 Andreas Bauer; 6 Jamie Rooney; 18 Liam Campbell; 8 Andy Bracek; 19 Nathan Mossop; 16 Brett McDermott; 11 Michael Knowles; 14 Martin Ostler; 13 Zebastian Luisi. Subs (all used): 10 Chris Young; 17 Paul Noone; 23 Jamie Butler; 24 Richard Fletcher.
Tries: Ostler (23), Harrison (29), Ballard (38), Young (44), Bauer (68), Catic (75), Mossop (78);
Goals: Rooney 4/7.
Rugby Leaguer & League Express Men of the Match: *Eagles:* Ryan Hepworth; *Raiders:* Jamie Rooney.
Penalty count: 10-10; **Half-time:** 14-14;
Referee: Gareth Hewer; **Attendance:** 848.

Saturday 26th June 2010

TOULOUSE OLYMPIQUE 34 WHITEHAVEN 12

OLYMPIQUE: 1 Rory Bromley; 5 Carlos Mendes Varela; 3 Sebastien Planas; 20 Bruno Ormeno; 2 Sebastien Payan; 16 Sylvain Houles; 7 Nathan Wynn; 10 Mathieu Griffi; 9 Martin Mitchell; 11 Tim Wynn; 18 Yoan Tisseyre; 14 Antoni Maria; 13 Eric Anselme. Subs (all used): 19 Romain Mencarini; 23 Kevin Larroyer; 31 Yohann Gigord; 25 Teli Pelo.
Tries: Bromley (34, 58), N Wynn (46), Mitchell (62), Anselme (65), Pelo (77); **Goals:** N Wynn 5/7.
WHITEHAVEN: 34 Motu Tony; 2 Craig Calvert; 3 Rob Jackson; 4 Scott McAvoy; 5 Derry Eilbeck; 6 Carl Rudd; 14 Dylan Skee; 32 Paul Johnson; 9 Graeme Mattinson; 17 Andy Thornley; 19 Dexter Miller; 11 Howard Hill; 26 Daniel Barker. Subs (all used): 7 Leroy Joe; 28 Kyle Bibb; 33 Kyle Amor; 25 Kurt Wilton.
Tries: Calvert (4), Barker (56); **Goals:** Rudd 2/3.
Rugby Leaguer & League Express Men of the Match: *Olympique:* Rory Bromley; *Whitehaven:* Carl Rudd.
Penalty count: 9-4; **Half-time:** 4-8;
Referee: Tim Roby; **Attendance:** 1,071.

Sunday 27th June 2010

DEWSBURY RAMS 37 HALIFAX 30

RAMS: 42 James Craven; 15 Bryn Powell; 26 Ayden Faal; 10 Scott Turner; 3 Stewart Sanderson; 13 Pat Walker; 8 Dominic Brambani; 25 James Lockwood; 37 Luke Blake; 23 Keegan Hirst; 20 Rob Spicer; 21 Andrew Bostock; 9 Mike Emmett. Subs (all used): 24 Anthony England; 17 Alex Bretherton; 14 Luke Stenchion; 11 Adam Robinson.
Tries: Spicer (5, 22), Blake (26), Stenchion (49), England (55), Powell (77); **Goals:** Brambani 6/7;
Field goal: Brambani (78).
HALIFAX: 4 Shad Royston; 20 Paul White; 3 Jon Goddard; 18 Dylan Nash; 23 Rob Worrincy; 6 Luke Branighan; 26 Graham Holroyd; 19 Dominic Maloney; 13 Bob Beswick; 10 Neil Cherryholme; 11 David Larder; 24 Steve Bannister; 22 David Wrench. Subs (all used): 7 Ben Black; 8 Makali Aizue; 17 Frank Watene; 25 Michael Ostick.
Tries: Worrincy (9, 15), Bannister (14), Royston (28), Larder (60); **Goals:** Branighan 5/6.
Rugby Leaguer & League Express Men of the Match: *Rams:* Rob Spicer; *Halifax:* Luke Branighan.
Penalty count: 8-7; **Half-time:** 18-22;
Referee: Robert Hicks; **Attendance:** 1,030.

Championship 2010 - Round by Round

FEATHERSTONE ROVERS 30 WIDNES VIKINGS 22

ROVERS: 1 Ian Hardman; 26 Zak Hardaker; 3 Sam Smeaton; 4 Liam Welham; 2 Tom Saxton; 6 Kyle Briggs; 9 Liam Finn; 17 Tony Tonks; 31 Ben Kaye; 10 Stuart Dickens; 13 Jamie Field; 18 Tim Spears; 11 Matty Dale. Subs (all used): 7 Andy Kain; 12 Jon Grayshon; 16 Dane Manning; 19 Ross Divorty.
Tries: Dale (6), Hardaker (9), Finn (57), Grayshon (67), Briggs (79); **Goals:** Briggs 5/6.
Sin bin: Manning (39) – professional foul.
VIKINGS: 5 Paddy Flynn; 26 Shaun Ainscough; 3 Richard Varkulis; 19 Matt Gardner; 2 Dean Gaskell; 6 Anthony Thackeray; 9 Mark Smith; 10 Jim Gannon; 32 Kirk Netherton; 17 Ben Kavanagh; 15 Shane Grady; 12 Dave Allen; 11 Lee Doran. Subs (all used): 13 Chris Gerrard; 23 David Houghton; 31 Tom Kelly; 34 Kurt Haggerty.
Tries: C Gerrard (41), Gardner (47), Allen (72), Ainscough (75); **Goals:** Grady 3/4.
Rugby Leaguer & League Express Men of the Match: *Rovers:* Tom Saxton; *Vikings:* Kurt Haggerty.
Penalty count: 13-7; **Half-time:** 10-0;
Referee: Jamie Leahy; **Attendance:** 1,776.

LEIGH CENTURIONS 36 KEIGHLEY COUGARS 18

CENTURIONS: 1 Stuart Donlan; 2 Steve Maden; 25 Matty Blythe; 4 Mick Nanyn; 3 David Alstead; 22 Martyn Ridyard; 7 Robbie Paul; 27 Jacob Emmitt; 9 John Duffy; 10 Ricky Bibey; 11 James Taylor; 12 Macgraff Leuluai; 28 Tyrone McCarthy. Subs (all used): 26 Lee Mitchell; 8 Chris Hill; 13 Dave Armitstead; 36 Paul Smith.
Tries: Donlan (15), Alstead (19), Armitstead (32), Blythe (36, 51), Ridyard (54), Duffy (60); **Goals:** Nanyn 4/7.
COUGARS: 20 Dan Belcher; 5 Gavin Duffy; 33 Tom Sheldrake; 3 Tom Burton; 31 James Hutchinson; 6 Jon Presley; 7 Danny Jones; 8 Andy Shickell; 9 James Feather; 17 Ryan Benjafield; 23 Chris Baines; 12 Oliver Pursglove; 11 Will Cartledge. Subs (all used): 14 Jamaine Wray; 15 Greg Nicholson; 10 Scott Law; 16 Brendan Rawlins.
Tries: Hutchinson (11), Benjafield (47), Duffy (78, 80); **Goals:** D Jones 1/4.
Rugby Leaguer & League Express Men of the Match: *Centurions:* Matty Blythe; *Cougars:* Ryan Benjafield.
Penalty count: 11-9; **Half-time:** 20-4;
Referee: Mohammed Drizza; **Attendance:** 1,265.

ROUND 16

Thursday 1st July 2010

WHITEHAVEN 4 WIDNES VIKINGS 40

WHITEHAVEN: 5 Derry Eilbeck; 25 Loz Hamzat; 3 Rob Jackson; 4 Scott McAvoy; 2 Craig Calvert; 6 Carl Rudd; 7 Leroy Joe; 33 Kyle Amor; 9 Graeme Mattinson; 28 Paul Johnson; 11 Howard Hill; 19 Dexter Miller; 26 Daniel Barker. Subs (all used): 21 Chris Smith; 17 Andy Thornley; 32 Kyle Bibb; 31 Danny Bower.
Try: Eilbeck (39); **Goals:** Rudd 0/1.
VIKINGS: 5 Paddy Flynn; 19 Matt Gardner; 15 Shane Grady; 34 Kurt Haggerty; 3 Richard Varkulis; 6 Anthony Thackeray; 14 Thomas Coyle; 30 Daniel Heckenberg; 9 Mark Smith; 10 Jim Gannon; 11 Lee Doran; 12 Dave Allen; 13 Chris Gerrard. Subs (all used): 17 Ben Kavanagh; 23 David Houghton; 32 Kirk Netherton; 33 Danny Craven.
Tries: Allen (9, 20), Grady (17, 62), Netherton (43), Doran (49), Varkulis (66); **Goals:** Grady 4/5, Craven 2/2.
Rugby Leaguer & League Express Men of the Match: *Whitehaven:* Loz Hamzat; *Vikings:* Dave Allen.
Penalty count: 7-10; **Half-time:** 4-18;
Referee: Robert Hicks; **Attendance:** 1,518.

Saturday 3rd July 2010

DEWSBURY RAMS 12 TOULOUSE OLYMPIQUE 36

RAMS: 1 Lee Lingard; 15 Bryn Powell; 26 Ayden Faal; 20 Rob Spicer; 42 James Craven; 13 Pat Walker; 8 Dominic Brambani; 23 Keegan Hirst; 37 Luke Blake; 25 James Lockwood; 21 Andrew Bostock; 11 Adam Robinson; 9 Mike Emmett. Subs (all used): 24 Anthony England; 14 Luke Stenchion; 27 Allister McMaster; 33 James Walker.
Tries: Lingard (57), P Walker (68); **Goals:** Brambani 2/2.
OLYMPIQUE: 1 Rory Bromley; 2 Sebastien Payan; 3 Sebastien Planas; 20 Bruno Ormeno; 22 Clement Bienes; 16 Sylvain Houles; 7 Nathan Wynn; 19 Romain Mencarini; 9 Martin Mitchell; 11 Tim Wynn; 14 Antoni Maria; 18 Yoan Tisseyre; 13 Eric Anselme. Subs (all used): 8 Brendan Worth; 25 Teli Pelo; 23 Kevin Larroyer; 26 Yohann Gigord.
Tries: Mitchell (40, 41, 45), Bromley (55, 75), N Wynn (77); **Goals:** N Wynn 6/6.
Rugby Leaguer & League Express Men of the Match: *Rams:* Dominic Brambani; *Olympique:* Rory Bromley.
Penalty count: 6-2; **Half-time:** 0-6;
Referee: Ronnie Laughton; **Attendance:** 864.

BARROW RAIDERS 34 LEIGH CENTURIONS 24

RAIDERS: 1 Gary Broadbent; 2 Andy Ballard; 32 Andreas Bauer; 4 Liam Harrison; 25 Jermaine McGillvary; 6 Jamie Rooney; 18 Liam Campbell; 8 Andy Bracek; 19 Nathan Mossop; 10 Chris Young; 12 Ned Catic; 14 Martin Ostler; 13 Zebastian Luisi. Subs (all used): 11 Michael Knowles; 16 Brett McDermott; 17 Paul Noone; 23 Jamie Butler.
Tries: Rooney (7, 57), Broadbent (18), Ballard (21), McGillvary (37), McDermott (43); **Goals:** Rooney 5/6.
CENTURIONS: 1 Stuart Donlan; 2 Steve Maden; 25 Matty Blythe; 4 Mick Nanyn; 5 Nicky Stanton; 22 Martyn Ridyard; 7 Robbie Paul; 16 Mike Morrison; 15 Dave McConnell; 10 Ricky Bibey; 11 James Taylor; 26 Lee Mitchell; 28 Tyrone McCarthy. Subs (all used): 9 John Duffy; 12 Macgraff Leuluai; 8 Chris Hill; 13 Dave Armitstead.
Tries: Morrison (12), Mitchell (50), McCarthy (68), Ridyard (72); **Goals:** Nanyn 4/4.
Rugby Leaguer & League Express Men of the Match: *Raiders:* Zebastian Luisi; *Centurions:* Ricky Bibey.
Penalty count: 7-6; **Half-time:** 22-6;
Referee: Craig Halloran; **Attendance:** 2,078.

Sunday 4th July 2010

BATLEY BULLDOGS 12 SHEFFIELD EAGLES 20

BULLDOGS: 5 John Campbell; 24 Alex Brown; 22 Josh Griffin; 12 Mark Toohey; 2 Lee Greenwood; 33 Mick Govin; 7 Gareth Moore; 8 Byron Smith; 9 Kris Lythe; 10 Sean Hesketh; 23 Chris Buttery; 31 John Gallagher; 13 Ashley Lindsay. Subs: 1 Ian Preece (not used); 21 James Martin; 11 Tommy Gallagher; 20 David Tootill.
Tries: Hesketh (55), Brown (67); **Goals:** Hesketh 2/2.
Sin bin: Lindsay (45) - dissent.
EAGLES: 24 Misi Taulapapa; 26 Tim Bergin; 3 Menzie Yere; 25 Jason Mossop; 2 Danny Mills; 6 Brendon Lindsay; 20 Matty Brooks; 22 Ryan Hepworth; 9 Craig Cook; 10 Mitchell Stringer; 13 Peter Green; 11 Alex Szostak; 16 Trevor Exton. Subs (all used): 17 Alex Rowe; 12 Ged Corcoran; 18 Michael Haley; 19 Joe Hirst.
Tries: Hepworth (14), Taulapapa (20), Brooks (40);
Goals: Bergin 4/4.
Dismissal: Yere (66) - dangerous tackle.
Rugby Leaguer & League Express Men of the Match: *Bulldogs:* Tommy Gallagher; *Eagles:* Matty Brooks.
Penalty count: 8-11; **Half-time:** 0-18;
Referee: Jamie Leahy; **Attendance:** 747.

KEIGHLEY COUGARS 6 FEATHERSTONE ROVERS 24

COUGARS: 20 Dan Belcher; 5 Gavin Duffy; 23 Chris Baines; 3 Tom Burton; 31 James Hutchinson; 6 Jon Presley; 7 Danny Jones; 8 Andy Shickell; 9 James Feather; 17 Ryan Benjafield; 11 Will Cartledge; 12 Oliver Pursglove; 15 Greg Nicholson. Subs (all used): 14 Jamaine Wray; 13 Carl Hughes; 10 Scott Law; 16 Brendan Rawlins.
Try: Rawlins (45); **Goals:** D Jones 1/2.
ROVERS: 1 Ian Hardman; 26 Zak Hardaker; 3 Sam Smeaton; 32 Duane Straugheir; 5 Jon Steel; 6 Kyle Briggs; 9 Liam Finn; 17 Tony Tonks; 31 Ben Kaye; 10 Stuart Dickens; 12 Jon Grayshon; 18 Tim Spears; 11 Matty Dale. Subs (all used): 19 Ross Divorty; 23 Jode Sheriffe; 7 Andy Kain; 13 Jamie Field.
Tries: Briggs (38, 65), Kain (56), Hardaker (75);
Goals: Briggs 4/4.
Rugby Leaguer & League Express Men of the Match: *Cougars:* Brendan Rawlins; *Rovers:* Andy Kain.
Penalty count: 10-6; **Half-time:** 2-6;
Referee: Gareth Hewer; **Attendance:** 1,185.

ROUND 17

Thursday 8th July 2010

FEATHERSTONE ROVERS 34 LEIGH CENTURIONS 26

ROVERS: 1 Ian Hardman; 26 Zak Hardaker; 3 Sam Smeaton; 4 Liam Welham; 5 Jon Steel; 6 Kyle Briggs; 9 Liam Finn; 17 Tony Tonks; 31 Ben Kaye; 10 Stuart Dickens; 12 Jon Grayshon; 18 Tim Spears; 11 Matty Dale. Subs (all used): 19 Ross Divorty; 23 Jode Sheriffe; 7 Andy Kain; 16 Dane Manning.
Tries: Hardaker (6), Briggs (10), Finn (20), Manning (38), Smeaton (47, 55); **Goals:** Briggs 5/6.
CENTURIONS: 1 Stuart Donlan; 2 Steve Maden; 25 Matty Blythe; 12 Macgraff Leuluai; 5 Nicky Stanton; 22 Martyn Ridyard; 7 Robbie Paul; 27 Jacob Emmitt; 15 Dave McConnell; 10 Ricky Bibey; 11 James Taylor; 26 Lee Mitchell; 13 Dave Armitstead. Subs (all used): 9 John Duffy; 14 Tommy Goulden; 28 Tyrone McCarthy; 8 Chris Hill.
Tries: Ridyard (25), Mitchell (30), Emmitt (35), Blythe (65), Goulden (71); **Goals:** Ridyard 3/5.
Sin bin: Maden (69) - dissent.
Rugby Leaguer & League Express Men of the Match: *Rovers:* Sam Smeaton; *Centurions:* John Duffy.
Penalty count: 11-5; **Half-time:** 24-16;
Referee: Jamie Leahy; **Attendance:** 1,632.

Saturday 10th July 2010

TOULOUSE OLYMPIQUE 24 SHEFFIELD EAGLES 34

OLYMPIQUE: 1 Rory Bromley; 22 Clement Bienes; 20 Bruno Ormeno; 3 Sebastien Planas; 5 Carlos Mendes Varela; 16 Sylvain Houles; 7 Nathan Wynn; 8 Brendan Worth; 26 Yohann Gigord; 19 Romain Mencarini; 14 Antoni Maria; 18 Yoan Tisseyre; 13 Eric Anselme. Subs (all used): 25 Teli Pelo; 15 Jerome Gout; 23 Kevin Larroyer; 17 Cedric Gay.
Tries: Maria (2), Houles (30), Ormeno (75), Pelo (78);
Goals: N Wynn 4/4.
EAGLES: 24 Misi Taulapapa; 2 Danny Mills; 3 Menzie Yere; 23 Tangi Ropati; 26 Tim Bergin; 6 Brendon Lindsay; 29 Simon Brown; 22 Ryan Hepworth; 9 Craig Cook; 10 Mitchell Stringer; 11 Alex Szostak; 13 Peter Green; 16 Trevor Exton. Subs (all used): 12 Ged Corcoran; 18 Michael Haley; 19 Joe Hirst; 20 Matty Brooks.
Tries: Brown (7), Brooks (27), Ropati (38), Bergin (56, 63), Szostak (70); **Goals:** Bergin 5/6.
Rugby Leaguer & League Express Men of the Match: *Olympique:* Rory Bromley; *Eagles:* Tim Bergin.
Penalty count: 7-7; **Half-time:** 12-18;
Referee: Robert Hicks; **Attendance:** 2,214.

Sunday 11th July 2010

BATLEY BULLDOGS 34 BARROW RAIDERS 16

BULLDOGS: 5 John Campbell; 24 Alex Brown; 22 Josh Griffin; 4 Danny Maun; 2 Lee Greenwood; 11 Tommy Gallagher; 1 Ian Preece; 8 Byron Smith; 9 Kris Lythe; 10 Sean Hesketh; 26 Jason Walton; 31 John Gallagher; 13 Ashley Lindsay. Subs (all used): 23 Chris Buttery; 17 Craig Potter; 21 James Martin; 20 David Tootill.
Tries: Griffin (5), T Gallagher (9, 35, 40, 49, 77), Campbell (13); **Goals:** Preece 2/4, Hesketh 1/3.
RAIDERS: 1 Gary Broadbent; 2 Andy Ballard; 32 Andreas Bauer; 4 Liam Harrison; 33 Nick Beech; 13 Zebastian Luisi; 7 James Coyle; 8 Andy Bracek; 19 Nathan Mossop; 10 Chris Young; 17 Paul Noone; 14 Martin Ostler; 12 Ned Catic. Subs (all used): 11 Michael Knowles; 16 Brett McDermott; 23 Jamie Butler; 30 Keal Carlile.
Tries: Ballard (18), Catic (47), Luisi (63);
Goals: Ballard 2/3.
Sin bin: Catic (35) - holding down.
Rugby Leaguer & League Express Men of the Match: *Bulldogs:* Tommy Gallagher; *Raiders:* Zebastian Luisi.
Penalty count: 3-6; **Half-time:** 26-4;
Referee: Ronnie Laughton; **Attendance:** 802.

HALIFAX 66 WHITEHAVEN 16

HALIFAX: 4 Shad Royston; 2 Lee Paterson; 3 Jon Goddard; 18 Dylan Nash; 23 Rob Worrincy; 6 Luke Branighan; 26 Graham Holroyd; 10 Neil Cherryholme; 13 Bob Beswick; 19 Dominic Maloney; 11 David Larder; 22 David Wrench; 21 Anthony Bowman. Subs (all used): 7 Ben Black; 17 Frank Watene; 24 Steve Bannister; 27 Sam Barlow.
Tries: Paterson (4), Worrincy (15, 60, 75, 78), Bowman (22), Royston (26, 73), Bannister (30), Black (36), Barlow (45), Beswick (69); **Goals:** Paterson 9/12.
WHITEHAVEN: 5 Derry Eilbeck; 36 Jay Rossi; 3 Rob Jackson; 4 Scott McAvoy; 37 Loz Hamzat; 6 Carl Rudd; 34 Tyrone Dalton; 33 Kyle Amor; 9 Graeme Mattinson; 25 Paul Johnson; 11 Howard Hill; 43 Kurt Wilton; 7 Leroy Joe. Subs (all used): 21 Chris Smith; 40 Kyle Bibb; 29 Danny Bower; 17 Andy Thornley.
Tries: Rossi (6), Mattinson (11), Bower (57);
Goals: Rudd 2/3.
Sin bin: Bibb (69) - ball steal.
Rugby Leaguer & League Express Men of the Match: *Halifax:* Rob Worrincy; *Whitehaven:* Kurt Wilton.
Penalty count: 13-7; **Half-time:** 30-10;
Referee: Mohammed Drizza; **Attendance:** 1,970.

WIDNES VIKINGS 27 DEWSBURY RAMS 26

VIKINGS: 5 Paddy Flynn; 3 Richard Varkulis; 19 Matt Gardner; 15 Shane Grady; 2 Dean Gaskell; 6 Anthony Thackeray; 14 Thomas Coyle; 10 Jim Gannon; 32 Kirk Netherton; 28 Ben Davies, 34 Kurt Haggerty; 12 Dave Allen; 11 Lee Doran. Subs (all used): 9 Mark Smith; 13 Chris Gerrard; 17 Ben Kavanagh; 30 Daniel Heckenberg.
Tries: Davies (10), Thackeray (43), C Gerrard (52), M Smith (64), Grady (79); **Goals:** Grady 3/5;
Field goal: Coyle (60).
RAMS: 1 Lee Lingard; 15 Bryn Powell; 32 Matthew Fox; 17 Alex Bretherton; 42 James Craven; 13 Pat Walker; 8 Dominic Brambani; 23 Keegan Hirst; 37 Luke Blake; 25 James Lockwood; 20 Rob Spicer; 11 Adam Robinson; 40 Ed Barber. Subs (all used): 9 Mike Emmett; 14 Luke Stenchion; 24 Anthony England; 31 Josh Tonks.
Tries: Fox (21, 71), P Walker (31), Brambani (69), Bretherton (76); **Goals:** Brambani 3/5.
Rugby Leaguer & League Express Men of the Match: *Vikings:* Chris Gerrard; *Rams:* Dominic Brambani.
Penalty count: 11-9; **Half-time:** 6-10;
Referee: Gareth Hewer; **Attendance:** 2,715.

ROUND 18

Thursday 22nd July 2010

BARROW RAIDERS 34 HALIFAX 42

RAIDERS: 1 Gary Broadbent; 2 Andy Ballard; 3 Anthony Blackwood; 4 Liam Harrison; 32 Andreas Bauer; 6 Jamie Rooney; 7 James Coyle; 16 Brett McDermott; 19 Nathan Mossop; 8 Andy Bracek; 12 Ned Catic; 17 Paul Noone; 13 Zebastian Luisi. Subs (all used): 11 Michael Knowles; 30 Keal Carlile; 14 Martin Ostler; 23 Jamie Butler.
Tries: Rooney (45), Carlile (49), Knowles (52), Ostler (55), Bauer (70), Harrison (75); **Goals:** Rooney 5/6.
HALIFAX: 4 Shad Royston; 23 Rob Worrincy; 18 Dylan Nash; 3 Jon Goddard; 2 Lee Paterson; 6 Luke Branighan; 7 Ben Black; 10 Neil Cherryholme; 13 Bob Beswick; 25 Michael Ostick; 11 David Larder; 22 David Wrench; 27 Sam Barlow. Subs (all used): 9 Sean Penkywicz; 21 Anthony Bowman; 19 Dominic Maloney; 17 Frank Watene.
Tries: Goddard (14, 27), Nash (23), Wrench (30), Barlow (47), Royston (67), Worrincy (79);
Goals: Paterson 7/7.
Rugby Leaguer & League Express Men of the Match: *Raiders:* Gary Broadbent; *Halifax:* Rob Worrincy.
Penalty count: 11-3; **Half-time:** 0-24;
Referee: Ronnie Laughton; **Attendance:** 1,707.

Saturday 24th July 2010

KEIGHLEY COUGARS 27 TOULOUSE OLYMPIQUE 26

COUGARS: 20 Dan Belcher; 5 Gavin Duffy; 23 Chris Baines; 3 Tom Burton; 31 James Hutchinson; 6 Jon Presley; 7 Danny Jones; 8 Andy Shickell; 9 James Feather; 17 Ryan Benjafield; 11 Will Cartledge; 12 Oliver Pursglove; 15 Greg Nicholson. Subs (all used): 14

Widnes' Dave Allen gets a pass away under heavy pressure from Dewsbury's James Lockwood

Jamaine Wray; 13 Carl Hughes; 10 Scott Law; 16 Brendan Rawlins.
Tries: Burton (2, 26), Rawlins (31), Hutchinson (69), Duffy (75); **Goals:** D Jones 3/6; **Field goal:** D Jones (79).
Sin bin: D Jones (57) – dissent.
OLYMPIQUE: 1 Rory Bromley; 5 Carlos Mendes Varela; 4 Vincent Duport; 3 Sebastien Planas; 2 Sebastien Payan; 16 Sylvain Houles; 7 Nathan Wynn; 8 Brendan Worth; 17 Cedric Gay; 19 Romain Mencarini; 14 Antoni Maria; 23 Kevin Larroyer; 13 Eric Anselme. Subs (all used): 25 Teli Pelo; 15 Jerome Gout; 31 Maxime Herold; 32 Tony Gigot.
Tries: Gigot (21), Payan (36), N Wynn (45), Mendes Varela (57); **Goals:** N Wynn 5/5.
Rugby Leaguer & League Express Men of the Match: *Cougars:* Danny Jones; *Olympique:* Nathan Wynn.
Penalty count: 11-7; **Half-time:** 18-12;
Referee: Craig Halloran; **Attendance:** 736.

Sunday 25th July 2010

DEWSBURY RAMS 36 BATLEY BULLDOGS 16

RAMS: 42 James Craven; 15 Bryn Powell; 17 Alex Bretherton; 10 Scott Turner; 16 Austin Buchanan; 13 Pat Walker; 8 Dominic Brambani; 23 Keegan Hirst; 37 Luke Blake; 24 Anthony England; 20 Rob Spicer; 25 James Lockwood; 40 Ed Barber. Subs: 14 Luke Stenchion; 9 Mike Emmett; 31 Josh Tonks; 34 Danny Flowers (not used).
Tries: Brambani (26, 37), Craven (39, 79), Stenchion (44), Powell (53); **Goals:** Brambani 6/9.
BULLDOGS: 5 John Campbell; 24 Alex Brown; 22 Josh Griffin; 12 Mark Toohey; 1 Ian Preece; 6 Paul Handforth; 7 Gareth Moore; 8 Byron Smith; 9 Kris Lythe; 10 Sean Hesketh; 26 Jason Walton; 23 Chris Buttery; 13 Ashley Lindsay. Subs (all used): 33 Mick Govin; 11 Tommy Gallagher; 17 Craig Potter; 20 David Tootill.
Tries: Griffin (20), Toohey (30), Handforth (76);
Goals: Moore 2/3.
Rugby Leaguer & League Express Men of the Match: *Rams:* Dominic Brambani; *Bulldogs:* Jason Walton.
Penalty count: 14-11; **Half-time:** 16-10;
Referee: Mohammed Drizza; **Attendance:** 1,935.

WHITEHAVEN 0 FEATHERSTONE ROVERS 48

WHITEHAVEN: 1 Craig Benson; 5 Derry Eilbeck; 19 Dexter Miller; 4 Scott McAvoy; 25 Loz Hamzat; 14 Dylan Skee; 27 Tyrone Dalton; 33 Kyle Amor; 9 Graeme Mattinson; 28 Paul Johnson; 12 Spencer Miller; 11 Howard Hill; 26 Daniel Barker. Subs (all used): 7 Leroy Joe; 17 Andy Thornley; 31 Danny Bower; 32 Kurt Wilton.
ROVERS: 1 Ian Hardman; 26 Zak Hardaker; 3 Sam Smeaton; 4 Liam Welham; 32 Duane Straugheir; 6 Kyle Briggs; 9 Liam Finn; 17 Tony Tonks; 31 Ben Kaye; 10 Stuart Dickens; 12 Jon Grayshon; 18 Tim Spears; 11 Matty Dale. Subs (all used): 19 Ross Divorty; 13 Jamie

Field; 16 Dane Manning; 7 Andy Kain.
Tries: Hardaker (2, 19), Finn (15), Dickens (26), Smeaton (31, 79), Briggs (38), Kain (47), Tonks (57), Hardman (75); **Goals:** Briggs 2/5, Finn 2/5.
Rugby Leaguer & League Express Men of the Match: *Whitehaven:* Graeme Mattinson; *Rovers:* Liam Finn.
Penalty count: 4-13; **Half-time:** 0-30;
Referee: Warren Turley; **Attendance:** 825.

WIDNES VIKINGS 18 LEIGH CENTURIONS 38

VIKINGS: 33 Danny Craven; 26 Shaun Ainscough; 34 Kurt Haggerty; 35 Stefan Marsh; 5 Paddy Flynn; 6 Anthony Thackeray; 14 Thomas Coyle; 16 Gareth Haggerty; 32 Kirk Netherton; 10 Jim Gannon; 11 Lee Doran; 12 Dave Allen; 13 Chris Gerrard. Subs (all used): 28 Ben Davies; 8 Steve Pickersgill; 9 Mark Smith; 17 Ben Kavanagh.
Tries: Marsh (22), K Haggerty (31), Ainscough (39);
Goals: Craven 3/3.
CENTURIONS: 1 Stuart Donlan; 5 Nicky Stanton; 2 Steve Maden; 4 Mick Nanyn; 25 Matty Blythe; 22 Martyn Ridyard; 7 Robbie Paul; 10 Ricky Bibey; 15 Dave McConnell; 8 Chris Hill; 14 Tommy Goulden; 11 James Taylor; 37 Paul Smith. Subs (all used): 9 John Duffy; 12 Macgraff Leuluai; 16 Mike Morrison; 17 Stephen Nash.
Tries: Donlan (5, 49), Stanton (11), Nanyn (26, 79), Duffy (69); **Goals:** Nanyn 7/7.
Rugby Leaguer & League Express Men of the Match: *Vikings:* Stefan Marsh; *Centurions:* Mick Nanyn.
Penalty count: 11-12; **Half-time:** 18-18;
Referee: Tim Roby; **Attendance:** 3,356.

ROUND 19

Thursday 29th July 2010

HALIFAX 30 WIDNES VIKINGS 16

HALIFAX: 4 Shad Royston; 2 Lee Paterson; 3 Jon Goddard; 18 Dylan Nash; 23 Rob Worrincy; 6 Luke Branighan; 7 Ben Black; 25 Michael Ostick; 13 Bob Beswick; 10 Neil Cherryholme; 11 David Larder; 22 David Wrench; 27 Sam Barlow. Subs (all used): 9 Sean Penkywicz; 17 Frank Watene; 19 Dominic Maloney; 24 Steve Bannister.
Tries: Penkywicz (29, 58, 75), Royston (32), Branighan (48); **Goals:** Paterson 5/6.
Sin bin: Nash (78) – fighting; Barlow (78) – fighting.
VIKINGS: 33 Danny Craven; 2 Dean Gaskell; 35 Stefan Marsh; 19 Matt Gardner; 5 Paddy Flynn; 13 Chris Gerrard; 14 Thomas Coyle; 30 Daniel Heckenberg; 9 Mark Smith; 10 Jim Gannon; 34 Kurt Haggerty; 12 Dave Allen; 17 Ben Kavanagh. Subs (all used): 8 Steve Pickersgill; 23 David Houghton; 31 Tom Kelly; 32 Kirk Netherton.
Tries: Kavanagh (13), Flynn (20), Gaskell (72);

Goals: Craven 2/3.
Sin bin: Gaskell (78) – fighting.
Rugby Leaguer & League Express Men of the Match: *Halifax:* Sean Penkywicz; *Vikings:* Danny Craven.
Penalty count: 12-10; **Half-time:** 12-12;
Referee: Mohammed Drizza; **Attendance:** 2,707.

Saturday 31st July 2010

BARROW RAIDERS 42 TOULOUSE OLYMPIQUE 6

RAIDERS: 2 Andy Ballard; 33 Nick Beech; 12 Ned Catic; 4 Liam Harrison; 21 Chris Larkin; 6 Jamie Rooney; 7 James Coyle; 8 Andy Bracek; 30 Keal Carlile; 16 Brett McDermott; 11 Michael Knowles; 14 Martin Ostler; 13 Zebastian Luisi. Subs (all used): 17 Paul Noone; 10 Chris Young; 19 Nathan Mossop; 23 Jamie Butler.
Tries: Coyle (11, 67), Rooney (21), Catic (40, 74), Noone (53), Ballard (79); **Goals:** Rooney 7/7.
OLYMPIQUE: 22 Clement Bienes; 2 Sebastien Payan; 3 Sebastien Planas; 4 Vincent Duport; 20 Bruno Ormeno; 31 William Barthau; 7 Nathan Wynn; 8 Brendan Worth; 26 Yohann Gigord; 19 Romain Mencarini; 14 Antoni Maria; 23 Kevin Larroyer; 13 Eric Anselme. Subs (all used): 15 Jerome Gout; 10 Mathieu Griffi; 16 Sylvain Houles; 18 Yoan Tisseyre.
Try: Maria (28); **Goals:** N Wynn 1/1.
Rugby Leaguer & League Express Men of the Match: *Raiders:* Ned Catic; *Olympique:* Brendan Worth.
Penalty count: 11-6; **Half-time:** 18-6;
Referee: Warren Turley; **Attendance:** 1,440.

Sunday 1st August 2010

BATLEY BULLDOGS 56 KEIGHLEY COUGARS 4

BULLDOGS: 1 Ian Preece; 5 John Campbell; 22 Josh Griffin; 26 Jason Walton; 2 Lee Greenwood; 6 Paul Handforth; 7 Gareth Moore; 8 Byron Smith; 9 Kris Lythe; 10 Sean Hesketh; 31 John Gallagher; 11 Tommy Gallagher; 13 Ashley Lindsay. Subs (all used): 33 Mick Govin; 17 Craig Potter; 21 James Martin; 20 David Tootill.
Tries: Griffin (25), Walton (28, 64), Campbell (36, 39, 45), Moore (51), Preece (60, 76), Greenwood (72), Lythe (79); **Goals:** Moore 6/11.
COUGARS: 5 Gavin Duffy; 33 Tom Sheldrake; 3 Tom Burton; 23 Chris Baines; 31 James Hutchinson; 6 Jon Presley; 7 Danny Jones; 8 Andy Shickell; 9 James Feather; 10 Scott Law; 15 Greg Nicholson; 12 Oliver Pursglove; 11 Will Cartledge. Subs (all used): 13 Carl Hughes; 18 James Haythornthwaite; 16 Brendan Rawlins; 34 Richard Lopag.
Try: Duffy (62); **Goals:** D Jones 0/1.
Rugby Leaguer & League Express Men of the Match: *Bulldogs:* Ian Preece; *Cougars:* Brendan Rawlins.
Penalty count: 7-6; **Half-time:** 18-0;
Referee: Gareth Hewer; **Attendance:** 952.

FEATHERSTONE ROVERS 30 SHEFFIELD EAGLES 32

ROVERS: 1 Ian Hardman; 26 Zak Hardaker; 3 Sam Smeaton; 4 Liam Welham; 5 Jon Steel; 6 Kyle Briggs; 9 Liam Finn; 17 Tony Tonks; 7 Andy Kain; 10 Stuart Dickens; 11 Matty Dale; 18 Tim Spears; 13 Jamie Field. Subs (all used): 19 Ross Divorty; 23 Jode Sheriffe; 12 Jon Grayshon; 16 Dane Manning.
Tries: Briggs (26), Hardaker (37, 69), Steel (49), Spears (69), Welham (78); **Goals:** Finn 1/1, Briggs 2/5.
EAGLES: 24 Misi Taulapapa; 2 Danny Mills; 3 Menzie Yere; 23 Tangi Ropati; 26 Tim Bergin; 6 Brendon Lindsay; 29 Simon Brown; 22 Ryan Hepworth; 9 Craig Cook; 10 Mitchell Stringer; 11 Alex Szostak; 13 Peter Green; 19 Joe Hirst. Subs (all used): 31 Corey Hanson; 17 Alex Rowe; 18 Michael Haley; 34 Andrew Henderson.
Tries: Yere (9, 13, 56), Lindsay (32), Bergin (42), Ropati (58); **Goals:** Brown 1/1, Bergin 3/5.
Rugby Leaguer & League Express Men of the Match: *Rovers:* Liam Finn; *Eagles:* Simon Brown.
Penalty count: 6-5; **Half-time:** 12-14;
Referee: Robert Hicks; **Attendance:** 2,381.

LEIGH CENTURIONS 6 DEWSBURY RAMS 30

CENTURIONS: 1 Stuart Donlan; 2 Steve Maden; 25 Matty Blythe; 4 Mick Nanyn; 5 Nicky Stanton; 22 Martyn Ridyard; 7 Robbie Paul; 8 Chris Hill; 15 Dave McConnell; 10 Ricky Bibey; 14 Tommy Goulden; 37 Paul Smith; 11 James Taylor. Subs (all used): 9 John Duffy; 26 Lee Mitchell; 12 Macgraff Leuluai; 28 Tyrone McCarthy.
Try: McConnell (59); **Goals:** Stanton 1/1.
RAMS: 42 James Craven; 15 Bryn Powell; 17 Alex Bretherton; 10 Scott Turner; 16 Austin Buchanan; 13 Pat Walker; 8 Dominic Brambani; 23 Keegan Hirst; 37 Luke Blake; 24 Anthony England; 20 Rob Spicer; 25 James Lockwood; 40 Ed Barber. Subs (all used): 9 Mike Emmett; 31 Josh Tonks; 32 Matthew Fox; 14 Luke Stenchion.
Tries: Barber (14), Powell (32, 49), P Walker (35), Craven (74); **Goals:** Brambani 2/4, P Walker 3/3.
Rugby Leaguer & League Express Men of the Match: *Centurions:* Chris Hill; *Rams:* Dominic Brambani.
Penalty count: 4-7; **Half-time:** 0-16;
Referee: Ronnie Laughton; **Attendance:** 1,682.

ROUND 20

Saturday 7th August 2010

BARROW RAIDERS 54 KEIGHLEY COUGARS 0

RAIDERS: 1 Gary Broadbent; 2 Andy Ballard; 3 Anthony Blackwood; 4 Liam Harrison; 21 Chris Larkin; 6 Jamie Rooney; 7 James Coyle; 8 Andy Bracek; 30 Keal Carlile; 16 Brett McDermott; 14 Martin Ostler; 12 Ned Catic; 13 Zebastian Luisi. Subs (all used): 32 Andreas Bauer; 19 Nathan Mossop; 17 Paul Noone; 23 Jamie Butler.
Tries: Ballard (12, 31), Catic (15, 22), Ostler (17), Harrison (29, 34), Rooney (69), Carlile (71), Blackwood (79); **Goals:** Rooney 7/10.
COUGARS: 5 Gavin Duffy; 34 Richard Lopag; 23 Chris Baines; 33 Tom Sheldrake; 31 James Hutchinson; 6 Jon Presley; 9 James Feather; 8 Andy Shickell; 14 Jamaine Wray; 10 Scott Law; 11 Will Cartledge; 12 Oliver Pursglove; 15 Greg Nicholson. Subs (all used): 18 James Haythornthwaite; 32 Luke Helliwell; 16 Brendan Rawlins; 17 Ryan Benjafield.
Sin bin: Shickell (71) - dissent.
Rugby Leaguer & League Express Men of the Match: *Raiders:* Ned Catic; *Cougars:* Tom Sheldrake.
Penalty count: 9-6; **Half-time:** 36-0;
Referee: Jamie Leahy; **Attendance:** 1,404.

TOULOUSE OLYMPIQUE 30 WIDNES VIKINGS 44

OLYMPIQUE: 1 Rory Bromley; 5 Carlos Mendes Varela; 3 Sebastien Planas; 20 Bruno Ormeno; 22 Clement Bienes; 16 Sylvain Houles; 7 Nathan Wynn; 8 Brendan Worth; 9 Martin Mitchell; 19 Romain Mencarini; 14 Antoni Maria; 18 Yoan Tisseyre; 13 Eric Anselme. Subs (all used): 10 Mathieu Griffi; 15 Jerome Gout; 23 Kevin Larroyer; 31 Maxime Herold.
Tries: Mendes Varela (4, 55), Maria (52, 62), Anselme (60); **Goals:** N Wynn 5/6.
VIKINGS: 33 Danny Craven; 2 Dean Gaskell; 35 Stefan Marsh; 19 Matt Gardner; 5 Paddy Flynn; 13 Chris Gerrard; 6 Anthony Thackeray; 30 Daniel Heckenberg; 9 Mark Smith; 10 Jim Gannon; 11 Lee Doran; 34 Kurt Haggerty; 17 Ben Kavanagh. Subs (all used): 16 Gareth Haggerty; 14 Thomas Coyle; 15 Shane Grady; 28 Ben Davies.
Tries: Craven (9), M Smith (12), Marsh (24, 43), Flynn (29), Thackeray (38), Gaskell (40), Gardner (77); **Goals:** Craven 6/8.
Rugby Leaguer & League Express Men of the Match: *Olympique:* Nathan Wynn; *Vikings:* Anthony Thackeray.
Penalty count: 7-4; **Half-time:** 8-32;
Referee: Matthew Thomasson; **Attendance:** 987.

Sunday 8th August 2010

BATLEY BULLDOGS 26 FEATHERSTONE ROVERS 34

BULLDOGS: 1 Ian Preece; 5 John Campbell; 22 Josh Griffin; 4 Danny Maun; 2 Lee Greenwood; 33 Mick Govin; 7 Gareth Moore; 8 Byron Smith; 9 Kris Lythe; 10 Sean Hesketh; 26 Jason Walton; 31 John Gallagher; 13 Ashley Lindsay. Subs (all used): 11 Tommy Gallagher; 17 Craig Potter; 21 James Martin; 20 David Tootill.
Tries: Lindsay (20), J Gallagher (30), Maun (38), Moore (55), Walton (67); **Goals:** Moore 3/5.
ROVERS: 1 Ian Hardman; 26 Zak Hardaker; 3 Sam Smeaton; 4 Liam Welham; 5 Jon Steel; 7 Andy Kain; 9 Liam Finn; 17 Tony Tonks; 31 Ben Kaye; 10 Stuart Dickens; 13 Jamie Field; 18 Tim Spears; 11 Matty Dale. Subs (all used): 19 Ross Divorty; 16 Dane Manning; 12 Jon Grayshon; 2 Tom Saxton.
Tries: Hardaker (7, 34, 79), Dale (40), Dickens (50), Divorty (75); **Goals:** Finn 5/6.
Rugby Leaguer & League Express Men of the Match: *Bulldogs:* Mick Govin; *Rovers:* Liam Finn.
Penalty count: 9-9; **Half-time:** 16-18;
Referee: Ronnie Laughton; **Attendance:** 1,422.

Featherstone's Matty Dale tackled by Batley's Josh Griffin

SHEFFIELD EAGLES 24 HALIFAX 38

EAGLES: 24 Misi Taulapapa; 2 Danny Mills; 3 Menzie Yere; 23 Tangi Ropati; 26 Tim Bergin; 6 Brendon Lindsay; 29 Simon Brown; 22 Ryan Hepworth; 9 Craig Cook; 10 Mitchell Stringer; 11 Alex Szostak; 13 Peter Green; 19 Joe Hirst. Subs (all used): 17 Alex Rowe; 18 Michael Haley; 16 Trevor Exton; 34 Andrew Henderson.
Tries: Yere (2, 19), Green (50), Ropati (67, 71); **Goals:** Bergin 0/2, Brown 2/3.
HALIFAX: 4 Shad Royston; 2 Lee Paterson; 3 Jon Goddard; 18 Dylan Nash; 20 Paul White; 6 Luke Branighan; 7 Ben Black; 10 Neil Cherryholme; 13 Bob Beswick; 25 Michael Ostick; 28 Adam Rudd; 24 Steve Bannister; 11 David Larder. Subs (all used): 9 Sean Penkywicz; 17 Frank Watene; 19 Dominic Maloney; 26 Graham Holroyd.
Tries: Paterson (15), Maloney (29), Black (34), Larder (54), Royston (59), Penkywicz (65), Nash (75); **Goals:** Paterson 5/7.
Rugby Leaguer & League Express Men of the Match: *Eagles:* Tangi Ropati; *Halifax:* David Larder.
Penalty count: 6-5; **Half-time:** 8-16;
Referee: Gareth Hewer; **Attendance:** 1,473.

WHITEHAVEN 10 DEWSBURY RAMS 48

WHITEHAVEN: 5 Derry Eilbeck; 25 Loz Hamzat; 19 Dexter Miller; 4 Scott McAvoy; 31 Jay Rossi; 27 Tyrone Dalton; 14 Dylan Skee; 20 Marc Shackley; 9 Graeme Mattinson; 17 Andy Thornley; 12 Spencer Miller; 11 Howard Hill; 7 Leroy Joe. Subs (all used): 32 Brad Crellin; 23 Steve Fox; 18 Danny Bower; 28 Kurt Wilton.
Tries: Skee (32), Mattinson (46); **Goals:** Skee 1/2.
RAMS: 42 James Craven; 15 Bryn Powell; 17 Alex Bretherton; 10 Scott Turner; 16 Austin Buchanan; 13 Pat Walker; 8 Dominic Brambani; 23 Keegan Hirst; 37 Luke Blake; 24 Anthony England; 20 Rob Spicer; 25 James Lockwood; 40 Ed Barber. Subs (all used): 14 Luke Stenchion; 9 Mike Emmett; 31 Josh Tonks; 11 Adam Robinson.
Tries: Hirst (13, 70), Brambani (25, 74), Craven (38), Spicer (40), Robinson (43), Buchanan (64); **Goals:** P Walker 8/8.
Rugby Leaguer & League Express Men of the Match: *Whitehaven:* Graeme Mattinson; *Rams:* Dominic Brambani.
Penalty count: 14-13; **Half-time:** 4-24;
Referee: Mohammed Drizza; **Attendance:** 504.

ROUND 21

Thursday 12th August 2010

WIDNES VIKINGS 30 SHEFFIELD EAGLES 10

VIKINGS: 33 Danny Craven; 2 Dean Gaskell; 3 Richard Varkulis; 19 Matt Gardner; 5 Paddy Flynn; 13 Chris Gerrard; 6 Anthony Thackeray; 10 Jim Gannon; 9 Mark Smith; 30 Daniel Heckenberg; 11 Lee Doran; 34 Kurt Haggerty; 17 Ben Kavanagh. Subs (all used): 14 Thomas Coyle; 23 David Houghton; 8 Steve Pickersgill; 31 Tom Kelly.
Tries: Gaskell (11), C Gerrard (21, 77), Thackeray (43), Craven (66); **Goals:** Craven 5/5.
EAGLES: 24 Misi Taulapapa; 2 Danny Mills; 3 Menzie Yere; 23 Tangi Ropati; 26 Tim Bergin; 6 Brendon Lindsay; 29 Simon Brown; 22 Ryan Hepworth; 9 Craig Cook; 10 Mitchell Stringer; 11 Alex Szostak; 13 Peter Green; 19 Joe Hirst. Subs (all used): 8 Jack Howieson; 16 Trevor Exton; 34 Andrew Henderson; 17 Alex Rowe.
Tries: Bergin (35), Taulapapa (61); **Goals:** Brown 1/2.
Rugby Leaguer & League Express Men of the Match: *Vikings:* Danny Craven; *Eagles:* Menzie Yere.
Penalty count: 7-6; **Half-time:** 12-4;
Referee: Ronnie Laughton; **Attendance:** 2,659.

Saturday 14th August 2010

LEIGH CENTURIONS 38 TOULOUSE OLYMPIQUE 16

CENTURIONS: 1 Stuart Donlan; 2 Steve Maden; 18 Adam Higson; 12 Macgraff Leuluai; 3 David Alstead; 9 John Duffy; 7 Robbie Paul; 8 Chris Hill; 15 Dave McConnell; 10 Ricky Bibey; 11 James Taylor; 14 Tommy Goulden; 26 Lee Mitchell. Subs (all used): 22 Martyn Ridyard; 13 Dave Armitstead; 16 Mike Morrison; 28 Tyrone McCarthy.
Tries: Hill (17), Maden (30, 44), Leuluai (32), Mitchell (39), Donlan (50), Ridyard (66);
Goals: Duffy 1/1, Ridyard 4/6.
OLYMPIQUE: 22 Clement Bienes; 2 Sebastien Payan; 3 Sebastien Planas; 20 Bruno Ormeno; 5 Carlos Mendes Varela; 1 Rory Bromley; 7 Nathan Wynn; 8 Brendan Worth; 26 Yohann Gigord; 10 Mathieu Griffi; 14 Antoni Maria; 18 Yoan Tisseyre; 13 Eric Anselme. Subs (all used): 15 Jerome Gout; 19 Romain Mencarini; 16 Sylvain Houles; 33 Remi Vignau.
Tries: Payan (7, 60), Anselme (58); **Goals:** N Wynn 2/3.
Rugby Leaguer & League Express Men of the Match: *Centurions:* Martyn Ridyard; *Olympique:* Eric Anselme.
Penalty count: 11-7; **Half-time:** 22-4;
Referee: Greg Dolan; **Attendance:** 1,922.

Sunday 15th August 2010

DEWSBURY RAMS 35 BARROW RAIDERS 6

RAMS: 42 James Craven; 15 Bryn Powell; 17 Alex Bretherton; 10 Scott Turner; 16 Austin Buchanan; 13 Pat Walker; 8 Dominic Brambani; 23 Keegan Hirst; 37 Luke Blake; 24 Anthony England; 20 Rob Spicer; 25 James Lockwood; 40 Ed Barber. Subs (all used): 14 Luke Stenchion; 9 Mike Emmett; 31 Josh Tonks; 11 Adam Robinson.
Tries: Craven (4), P Walker (23), Stenchion (36), Spicer (41), Powell (46, 67); **Goals:** P Walker 5/7;
Field goal: Brambani (75).
RAIDERS: 1 Gary Broadbent; 2 Andy Ballard; 3 Anthony Blackwood; 4 Liam Harrison; 32 Andreas Bauer; 7 James Coyle; 6 Jamie Rooney; 8 Andy Bracek; 30 Keal Carlile; 16 Brett McDermott; 14 Martin Ostler; 12 Ned Catic; 13 Zebastian Luisi. Subs (all used): 19 Nathan Mossop; 17 Paul Noone; 23 James Butler; 10 Chris Young.
Try: Coyle (59); **Goals:** Rooney 1/1.
Rugby Leaguer & League Express Men of the Match: *Rams:* Dominic Brambani; *Raiders:* Brett McDermott.
Penalty count: 9-6; **Half-time:** 18-0;
Referee: Gareth Hewer; **Attendance:** 1,227.

HALIFAX 30 BATLEY BULLDOGS 22

HALIFAX: 4 Shad Royston; 2 Lee Paterson; 3 Jon Goddard; 18 Dylan Nash; 20 Paul White; 6 Luke Branighan; 7 Ben Black; 19 Dominic Maloney; 13 Bob Beswick; 25 Michael Ostick; 24 Steve Bannister; 22 David Wrench; 11 David Larder. Subs (all used): 9 Sean Penkywicz; 10 Neil Cherryholme; 17 Frank Watene; 26 Graham Holroyd.
Tries: Goddard (18), Penkywicz (29), Royston (41), Paterson (51, 66); **Goals:** Paterson 4/5, Branighan 1/1.
Sin bin: Black (58) - fighting.
BULLDOGS: 1 Ian Preece; 5 John Campbell; 22 Josh Griffin; 4 Danny Maun; 24 Alex Brown; 6 Paul Handforth; 7 Gareth Moore; 8 Byron Smith; 9 Kris Lythe; 10 Sean Hesketh; 26 Jason Walton; 31 John Gallagher; 13 Ashley Lindsay. Subs (all used): 11 Tommy Gallagher; 12 Mark Toohey; 20 David Tootill; 21 James Martin.
Tries: Campbell (37, 56), Lythe (44), Moore (76);
Goals: Moore 3/5.
Sin bin: Moore (58) - fighting.
Rugby Leaguer & League Express Men of the Match: *Halifax:* David Larder; *Bulldogs:* Paul Handforth.
Penalty count: 8-5; **Half-time:** 10-4;
Referee: Jamie Leahy; **Attendance:** 4,795.

KEIGHLEY COUGARS 28 WHITEHAVEN 29

COUGARS: 33 Tom Sheldrake; 5 Gavin Duffy; 23 Chris Baines; 3 Tom Burton; 31 James Hutchinson; 32 Barry Eaton; 7 Danny Jones; 8 Andy Shickell; 9 James Feather; 10 Scott Law; 11 Will Cartledge; 12 Oliver Pursglove; 15 Greg Nicholson. Subs (all used): 14 Jamaine Wray; 18 James Haythornthwaite; 17 Ryan Benjafield; 16 Brendan Rawlins.

Widnes' Alex Brown leaves Keighley's Tom Sheldrake grounded on the way to a try

Tries: Baines (23, 63), Cartledge (44), Duffy (50), Hutchinson (67); **Goals:** D Jones 4/5.
WHITEHAVEN: 37 Shane Ackerley; 36 Jay Rossi; 19 Dexter Miller; 4 Scott McAvoy; 34 Loz Hamzat; 14 Dylan Skee; 40 Tyrone Dalton; 17 Andy Thornley; 9 Graeme Mattinson; 43 Marc Shackley; 26 Daniel Barker; 12 Spencer Miller; 7 Leroy Joe. Subs (all used): 21 Chris Smith; 23 Steve Fox; 11 Howard Hill; 25 Kurt Wilton.
Tries: Hamzat (7), Skee (10), D Miller (13), Ackerley (18), S Miller (31); **Goals:** Skee 4/6;
Field goal: Barker (70).
Rugby Leaguer & League Express Men of the Match:
Cougars: Danny Jones; *Whitehaven:* Scott McAvoy.
Penalty count: 4-3; **Half-time:** 4-28;
Referee: Craig Halloran; **Attendance:** 739.

ROUND 10

Wednesday 18th August 2010

BARROW RAIDERS 14 WIDNES VIKINGS 32

RAIDERS: 1 Gary Broadbent; 2 Andy Ballard; 3 Anthony Blackwood; 4 Liam Harrison; 32 Andreas Bauer; 7 James Coyle; 6 Jamie Rooney; 16 Brett McDermott; 19 Nathan Mossop; 8 Andy Bracek; 17 Paul Noone; 12 Ned Catic; 13 Zebastian Luisi. Subs (all used): 30 Keal Carlile; 23 Jamie Butler; 14 Martin Ostler; 11 Michael Knowles.
Tries: Ballard (63, 80), Rooney (78); **Goals:** Rooney 1/3.
Sin bin: McDermott (6) - fighting.
VIKINGS: 33 Danny Craven; 5 Paddy Flynn; 3 Richard Varkulis; 19 Matt Gardner; 2 Dean Gaskell; 13 Chris Gerrard; 6 Anthony Thackeray; 30 Daniel Heckenberg; 9 Mark Smith; 10 Jim Gannon; 11 Lee Doran; 34 Kurt Haggerty; 17 Ben Kavanagh. Subs (all used): 14 Thomas Coyle; 8 Steve Pickersgill; 23 David Houghton; 31 Tom Kelly.
Tries: K Haggerty (18), Varkulis (22, 24, 51), Thackeray (47), Flynn (72);
Goals: Thackeray 1/3, K Haggerty 2/3, Craven 1/1.
Sin bin: Doran (6) - fighting.
Rugby Leaguer & League Express Men of the Match:
Raiders: Gary Broadbent; *Vikings:* Anthony Thackeray.
Penalty count: 9-12; **Half-time:** 0-16;
Referee: Warren Turley; **Attendance:** 1,796.

ROUND 22

Thursday 19th August 2010

SHEFFIELD EAGLES 29 LEIGH CENTURIONS 28

EAGLES: 24 Misi Taulapapa; 2 Danny Mills; 3 Menzie Yere; 23 Tangi Ropati; 26 Tim Bergin; 6 Brendon Lindsay; 29 Simon Brown; 8 Jack Howieson; 9 Craig Cook; 10 Mitchell Stringer; 19 Joe Hirst; 11 Alex Szostak; 13 Peter Green. Subs (all used): 16 Trevor Exton; 22 Ryan

Hepworth; 18 Michael Haley; 34 Andrew Henderson.
Tries: Taulapapa (14, 36, 39), Bergin (25), Cook (67); **Goals:** Brown 4/5; **Field goal:** Brown (78).
CENTURIONS: 1 Stuart Donlan; 2 Steve Maden; 25 Matty Blythe; 4 Mick Nanyn; 18 Adam Higson; 9 John Duffy; 7 Robbie Paul; 8 Chris Hill; 15 Dave McConnell; 10 Ricky Bibey; 11 James Taylor; 28 Tyrone McCarthy; 26 Lee Mitchell. Subs (all used): 22 Martyn Ridyard; 13 Dave Armitstead; 16 Mike Morrison; 14 Tommy Goulden.
Tries: Nanyn (5, 59), Mitchell (21), Duffy (47), Bibey (80); **Goals:** Nanyn 4/5.
Rugby Leaguer & League Express Men of the Match:
Eagles: Misi Taulapapa; *Centurions:* John Duffy.
Penalty count: 6-5; **Half-time:** 22-10;
Referee: Gareth Hewer; **Attendance:** 1,243.

Saturday 21st August 2010

TOULOUSE OLYMPIQUE 24 HALIFAX 38

OLYMPIQUE: 22 Clement Bienes; 2 Sebastien Payan; 3 Sebastien Planas; 20 Bruno Ormeno; 5 Carlos Mendes Varela; 1 Rory Bromley; 7 Nathan Wynn; 25 Teli Pelo; 13 Eric Anselme; 10 Mathieu Griffi; 14 Antoni Maria; 18 Yoan Tisseyre; 16 Sylvain Houles. Subs (all used): 21 Nicolas Faure; 15 Jerome Gout; 26 Yohann Gigord; 33 Remi Vignau.
Tries: Payan (28), Bromley (43), Pelo (51), N Wynn (56); **Goals:** N Wynn 4/4.
HALIFAX: 4 Shad Royston; 20 Paul White; 2 Lee Paterson; 18 Dylan Nash; 23 Rob Worrincy; 6 Luke Branighan; 26 Graham Holroyd; 25 Michael Ostick; 9 Sean Penkywicz; 10 Neil Cherryholme; 22 David Wrench; 24 Steve Bannister; 11 David Larder. Subs (all used): 17 Frank Watene; 16 Said Tamghart; 19 Dominic Maloney; 7 Ben Black.
Tries: Wrench (8), Royston (15, 25), Worrincy (21), Holroyd (37), Penkywicz (73), White (79);
Goals: Paterson 5/8.
Sin bin: Larder (72) - holding down.
Rugby Leaguer & League Express Men of the Match:
Olympique: Rory Bromley; *Halifax:* Luke Branighan.
Penalty count: 7-7; **Half-time:** 6-26;
Referee: Mohammed Drizza; **Attendance:** 902.

Sunday 22nd August 2010

FEATHERSTONE ROVERS 72 BARROW RAIDERS 20

ROVERS: 1 Ian Hardman; 2 Tom Saxton; 3 Sam Smeaton; 4 Liam Welham; 26 Zak Hardaker; 6 Kyle Briggs; 9 Liam Finn; 17 Tony Tonks; 31 Ben Kaye; 10 Stuart Dickens; 18 Tim Spears; 13 Jamie Field; 11 Matty Dale. Subs (all used): 7 Andy Kain; 16 Dane Manning; 12 Jon Grayshon; 19 Ross Divorty.
Tries: Hardaker (4, 9), Saxton (15), Divorty (17), Spears (20), Kain (35), Dale (38, 51), Welham (43), Tonks (61), Kaye (63), Smeaton (75), Finn (78);
Goals: Finn 2/2, Briggs 8/11.

RAIDERS: 2 Andy Ballard; 33 Marc Dixon; 32 Andreas Bauer; 4 Liam Harrison; 21 Chris Larkin; 7 James Coyle; 18 Liam Campbell; 23 Jamie Butler; 19 Nathan Mossop; 22 Ruairi McGoff; 11 Michael Knowles; 17 Paul Noone; 24 Richard Fletcher. Subs: 8 Andy Bracek; 14 Martin Ostler; 1 Gary Broadbent (not used); 16 Brett McDermott.
Tries: Campbell (28, 59), Bauer (73), Bracek (80);
Goals: Ballard 2/4.
Rugby Leaguer & League Express Men of the Match:
Rovers: Tony Tonks; *Raiders:* Liam Campbell.
Penalty count: 6-2; **Half-time:** 38-6;
Referee: Craig Halloran; **Attendance:** 2,073.

KEIGHLEY COUGARS 24 WIDNES VIKINGS 32

COUGARS: 33 Tom Sheldrake; 5 Gavin Duffy; 3 Tom Burton; 12 Oliver Pursglove; 31 James Hutchinson; 34 Luke Helliwell; 7 Danny Jones; 8 Andy Shickell; 9 James Feather; 10 Scott Law; 11 Will Cartledge; 23 Chris Baines; 15 Greg Nicholson. Subs (all used): 14 Jamaine Wray; 18 James Haythornthwaite; 17 Ryan Benjafield; 16 Brendan Rawlins.
Tries: Duffy (6), Hutchinson (21), Rawlins (68), Burton (70); **Goals:** D Jones 4/5.
VIKINGS: 33 Danny Craven; 1 Alex Brown; 3 Richard Varkulis; 4 Greg Scott; 2 Dean Gaskell; 13 Chris Gerrard; 6 Anthony Thackeray; 30 Daniel Heckenberg; 32 Kirk Netherton; 10 Jim Gannon; 11 Lee Doran; 31 Tom Kelly; 17 Ben Kavanagh. Subs (all used): 14 Thomas Coyle; 8 Steve Pickersgill; 15 Shane Grady; 16 Alex Gerrard.
Tries: Craven (31, 54, 57), Coyle (34), Brown (43), Pickersgill (60); **Goals:** Craven 4/6.
Rugby Leaguer & League Express Men of the Match:
Cougars: Luke Helliwell; *Vikings:* Danny Craven.
Penalty count: 9-11; **Half-time:** 12-10;
Referee: Jamie Leahy; **Attendance:** 1,173.

WHITEHAVEN 26 BATLEY BULLDOGS 12

WHITEHAVEN: 31 Shane Ackerley; 25 Loz Hamzat; 19 Dexter Miller; 4 Scott McAvoy; 27 Jay Rossi; 7 Leroy Joe; 14 Dylan Skee; 17 Andy Thornley; 9 Graeme Mattinson; 11 Howard Hill; 12 Spencer Miller; 23 Steve Fox; 26 Daniel Barker. Subs (all used): 21 Chris Smith; 28 Brad Crellin; 33 Kyle Amor; 32 Kurt Wilton.
Tries: McAvoy (7), Amor (17), Hamzat (26), S Miller (36), Crellin (67); **Goals:** Skee 3/5.
BULLDOGS: 1 Ian Preece; 5 John Campbell; 3 Mark Barlow; 4 Danny Maun; 2 Lee Greenwood; 6 Paul Handforth; 7 Gareth Moore; 8 Byron Smith; 9 Kris Lythe; 10 Sean Hesketh; 26 Jason Walton; 31 John Gallagher; 13 Ashley Lindsay. Subs (all used): 33 Mick Govin; 17 Craig Potter; 21 James Martin; 20 David Tootill.
Tries: Campbell (54), Hesketh (62);
Goals: Handforth 1/1, Moore 1/1.
Rugby Leaguer & League Express Men of the Match:
Whitehaven: Leroy Joe; *Bulldogs:* Kris Lythe.
Penalty count: 2-8; **Half-time:** 22-0;
Referee: Matthew Thomasson; **Attendance:** 706.

Barrow's Andreas Bauer and Andy Ballard halt the progress of Widnes' Kurt Haggerty

PLAY-OFFS

ELIMINATION PLAY-OFFS

Thursday 2nd September 2010

LEIGH CENTURIONS 24 SHEFFIELD EAGLES 26

CENTURIONS: 1 Stuart Donlan; 2 Steve Maden; 25 Matty Blythe; 4 Mick Nanyn; 18 Adam Higson; 9 John Duffy; 7 Robbie Paul; 8 Chris Hill; 15 Dave McConnell; 16 Mike Morrison; 37 Paul Smith; 11 James Taylor; 13 Dave Armitstead. Subs (all used): 10 Ricky Bibey; 17 Stephen Nash; 22 Martyn Ridyard; 28 Tyrone McCarthy.
Tries: Armitstead (9), Smith (32), Nanyn (39), Nash (53); **Goals:** Nanyn 4/4.
Sin bin: Hill (3) – late tackle.
EAGLES: 24 Misi Taulapapa; 2 Danny Mills; 3 Menzie Yere; 23 Tangi Ropati; 26 Tim Bergin; 6 Brendon Lindsay; 29 Simon Brown; 8 Jack Howieson; 9 Craig Cook; 10 Mitchell Stringer; 11 Alex Szostak; 13 Peter Green; 19 Joe Hirst. Subs (all used): 34 Andrew Henderson; 18 Michael Haley; 22 Ryan Hepworth; 16 Trevor Exton.
Tries: Bergin (4, 78), Hirst (14), Yere (35, 42), Szostak (60, pen); **Goals:** Brown 1/6.
Rugby Leaguer & League Express Men of the Match:
Centurions: Chris Hill; *Eagles:* Menzie Yere.
Penalty count: 4-3; **Half-time:** 18-12;
Referee: Robert Hicks; **Attendance:** 1,516.

Sunday 5th September 2010

BARROW RAIDERS 38 WIDNES VIKINGS 0

RAIDERS: 13 Zebastian Luisi; 2 Andy Ballard; 32 Andreas Bauer; 4 Liam Harrison; 21 Chris Larkin; 7 James Coyle; 6 Jamie Rooney; 16 Brett McDermott; 19 Nathan Mossop; 31 Matt James; 14 Martin Ostler; 12 Ned Catic; 17 Paul Noone. Subs (all used): 18 Liam Campbell; 23 Jamie Butler; 24 Richard Fletcher; 8 Andy Bracek.
Tries: Catic (17), Harrison (22), Campbell (35, 79), Coyle (47), Ballard (60), James (68);
Goals: Rooney 4/5, Ballard 1/2.
VIKINGS: 33 Danny Craven; 5 Paddy Flynn; 3 Richard Varkulis; 19 Matt Gardner; 18 Scott Yates; 6 Anthony Thackeray; 14 Thomas Coyle; 8 Steve Pickersgill; 9 Mark Smith; 30 Daniel Heckenberg; 11 Lee Doran; 34 Kurt Haggerty; 13 Chris Gerrard. Subs (all used): 32 Kirk Netherton; 17 Ben Kavanagh; 23 David Houghton; 31 Tom Kelly.
Rugby Leaguer & League Express Men of the Match:
Raiders: Martin Ostler; *Vikings:* Mark Smith.
Penalty count: 9-10; **Half-time:** 18-0;
Referee: Ronnie Laughton; **Attendance:** 2,434.

QUALIFYING SEMI-FINAL

Thursday 9th September 2010

FEATHERSTONE ROVERS 46 HALIFAX 16

ROVERS: 1 Ian Hardman; 26 Zak Hardaker; 3 Sam Smeaton; 4 Liam Welham; 2 Tom Saxton; 6 Kyle Briggs; 9 Liam Finn; 17 Tony Tonks; 31 Ben Kaye; 10 Stuart Dickens; 13 Jamie Field; 18 Tim Spears; 11 Matty Dale. Subs (all used): 19 Ross Divorty; 16 Dane Manning; 12 Jon Grayshon; 7 Andy Kain.
Tries: Dickens (11), Welham (15), Saxton (18), Manning (30), Briggs (36, 72, 79), Finn (65); **Goals:** Briggs 7/8.
HALIFAX: 4 Shad Royston; 2 Lee Paterson; 24 Steve Bannister; 18 Dylan Nash; 23 Rob Worricy; 6 Luke Branighan; 26 Graham Holroyd; 17 Frank Watene; 9 Sean Penkywicz; 25 Michael Ostick; 11 David Larder; 22 David Wrench; 27 Sam Barlow. Subs (all used): 7 Ben Black; 8 Makali Aizue; 16 Said Tamghart; 19 Dominic Maloney.
Tries: Penkywicz (6), Royston (22), Worricy (33);
Goals: Paterson 2/3.
Rugby Leaguer & League Express Men of the Match:
Rovers: Kyle Briggs; *Halifax:* Ben Black.
Penalty count: 7-6; **Half-time:** 28-16;
Referee: Robert Hicks; **Attendance:** 2,553.

ELIMINATION SEMI-FINAL

Friday 10th September 2010

BARROW RAIDERS 14 SHEFFIELD EAGLES 21

RAIDERS: 13 Zebastian Luisi; 2 Andy Ballard; 32 Andreas Bauer; 12 Ned Catic; 21 Chris Larkin; 6 Jamie Rooney; 7 James Coyle; 16 Brett McDermott; 19 Nathan Mossop; 31 Matt James; 14 Martin Ostler; 24 Richard Fletcher; 17 Paul Noone. Subs (all used): 1 Gary Broadbent; 11 Michael Knowles; 23 Jamie Butler; 18 Liam Campbell.
Tries: Coyle (37), Ostler (59); **Goals:** Rooney 3/4.
EAGLES: 23 Tangi Ropati; 26 Tim Bergin; 3 Menzie Yere; 19 Joe Hirst; 2 Danny Mills; 6 Brendon Lindsay; 29 Simon Brown; 8 Jack Howieson; 9 Craig Cook; 10 Mitchell Stringer; 11 Alex Szostak; 13 Peter Green; 16 Trevor Exton. Subs (all used): 34 Andrew Henderson; 18 Michael Haley; 22 Ryan Hepworth; 17 Alex Rowe.
Tries: Lindsay (32), Rowe (70), Cook (74);
Goals: Brown 4/4; **Field goal:** Brown (77).
Rugby Leaguer & League Express Men of the Match:
Raiders: Gary Broadbent; *Eagles:* Simon Brown.
Penalty count: 5-4; **Half-time:** 8-8;
Referee: Gareth Hewer; **Attendance:** 2,231.

FINAL ELIMINATOR

Thursday 16th September 2010

HALIFAX 42 SHEFFIELD EAGLES 16

HALIFAX: 4 Shad Royston; 20 Paul White; 2 Lee Paterson; 18 Dylan Nash; 23 Rob Worricy; 26 Graham Holroyd; 7 Ben Black; 10 Neil Cherryholme; 13 Bob Beswick; 8 Makali Aizue; 22 David Wrench; 11 David Larder; 27 Sam Barlow. Subs (all used): 9 Sean Penkywicz; 17 Frank Watene; 19 Dominic Maloney; 24 Steve Bannister.
Tries: Penkywicz (27), Black (31), Barlow (35), Aizue (39), Paterson (42), Worricy (49), Royston (55);
Goals: Paterson 7/7.
EAGLES: 33 Jamie Cottle; 2 Danny Mills; 3 Menzie Yere; 23 Tangi Ropati; 26 Tim Bergin; 6 Brendon Lindsay; 29 Simon Brown; 8 Jack Howieson; 9 Craig Cook; 10 Mitchell Stringer; 11 Alex Szostak; 19 Joe Hirst; 16 Trevor Exton. Subs (all used): 17 Alex Rowe; 18 Michael Haley; 22 Ryan Hepworth; 34 Andrew Henderson.
Tries: Mills (23), Rowe (46), Ropati (78);
Goals: Brown 2/2, Bergin 0/1.
Rugby Leaguer & League Express Men of the Match:
Halifax: Graham Holroyd; *Eagles:* Trevor Exton.
Penalty count: 8-6; **Half-time:** 24-6;
Referee: Robert Hicks; **Attendance:** 1,490.

GRAND FINAL

Sunday 26th September 2010

FEATHERSTONE ROVERS 22 HALIFAX 23
(after golden point extra time)

ROVERS: 1 Ian Hardman; 26 Zak Hardaker; 3 Sam Smeaton; 4 Liam Welham; 2 Tom Saxton; 6 Kyle Briggs; 9 Liam Finn; 17 Tony Tonks; 31 Ben Kaye; 10 Stuart Dickens; 13 Jamie Field; 11 Matty Dale. Subs (all used): 19 Ross Divorty; 16 Dane Manning; 12 Jon Grayshon; 7 Andy Kain.
Tries: Briggs (28), Hardaker (30, 52), Dale (45);
Goals: Briggs 3/4.
HALIFAX: 4 Shad Royston; 2 Lee Paterson; 6 Luke Branighan; 18 Dylan Nash; 23 Rob Worricy; 26 Graham Holroyd; 7 Ben Black; 10 Neil Cherryholme; 13 Bob Beswick; 8 Makali Aizue; 11 David Larder; 22 David Wrench; 27 Sam Barlow. Subs (all used): 9 Sean Penkywicz; 17 Frank Watene; 19 Dominic Maloney; 24 Steve Bannister.
Tries: Worricy (20), Black (58), Branighan (60), Bannister (75); **Goals:** Paterson 3/4.
Field goal: Black (82).
On report: Barlow (35) - alleged high tackle on Divorty.
Rugby Leaguer & League Express Men of the Match:
Rovers: Tom Saxton; *Halifax:* Ben Black.
Penalty count: 6-3; **Half-time:** 12-4; **Full-time:** 22-22;
Referee: Robert Hicks; **Attendance:** 9,443.
(at Halliwell Jones Stadium, Warrington).

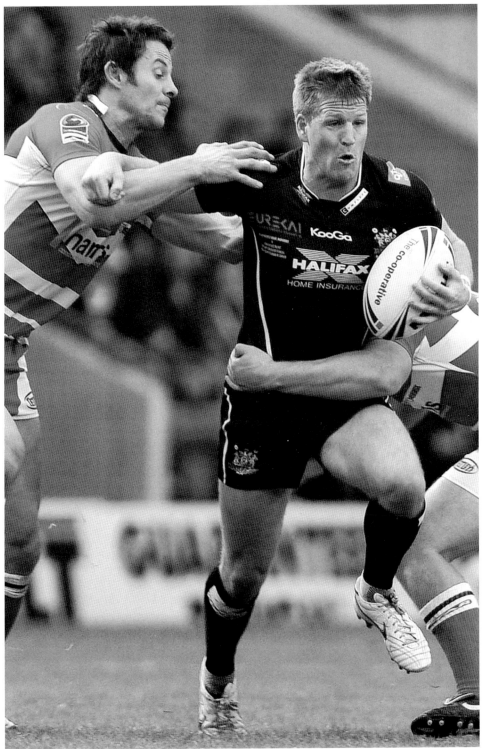

Halifax's Championship Grand Final hero Ben Black takes on Featherstone's Jamie Field

CHAMPIONSHIP ONE 2010
Club by Club

BLACKPOOL PANTHERS

DATE	FIXTURE	RESULT	SCORERS	LGE	ATT
31/1/10	Keighley (h) (NRC)	L22-24	t:Woodcock,Munro,Ainscough,Ratcliffe g:Hemingway(3)	N/A	468
7/2/10	Barrow (a) (NRC)	L34-8	t:Munro(2)	9th(P1)	1,474
14/2/10	Gateshead (h) (NRC)	W74-6	t:Ainscough(2),Keavney(3),Munro(2),Haggerty,Clough,Ballard(2),Hemingway, Leather,Forber g:Hemingway(9)	5th(P1)	194
7/3/10	Royal Navy (a) (CCR3)	W16-50	t:Hobson(2),Mayberry(3),McCully,Munro,Leather,Svabic g:Hemingway(7)	N/A	250
12/3/10	Rochdale (h)	W36-14	t:Keavney,Holland,Clough,Ballard(2),Mayberry,Alcock g:Hemingway(4)	5th	352
24/3/10	Doncaster (a) (NRC)	W20-40	t:Clough,Hemingway,Woodcock(2),Munro(2),Boland,Keavney g:Forber(2),Leather(2)	5th(P1)	192
28/3/10	Swinton (h)	W54-6	t:Halliwell(2),Mayberry(2),Ainscough,Leather,Keavney,Hobson,Munro(2) g:Hemingway(7)	4th	385
2/4/10	London Skolars (a)	W18-42	t:Ballard,Leigh,Forber(2),Ratcliffe(2),Leather,Alcock g:Leather(5)	3rd	323
5/4/10	York (h)	W27-14	t:Ballard,Munro,Llewellyn(3) g:Leather(3) fg:Leather	2nd	405
11/4/10	Workington (a)	W12-32	t:Munro(2),Ballard,McCully,Forber,Halliwell g:Leather(4)	2nd	521
18/4/10	Whitehaven (h) (CCR4)	W24-18	t:Ainscough(3),Leather,Keavney g:Leather(2)	N/A	471
23/4/10	Doncaster (h)	W48-12	t:Ballard,Haggerty,Forber,Charnley(2),Halliwell(2),McCully,Munro g:Charnley(6)	2nd	253
3/5/10	South Wales (a)	W24-28	t:Munro,Charnley,McCully,Llewellyn,Hemingway g:Charnley(4)	2nd	623
7/5/10	Leeds (a) (CCR5)	L70-22	t:Ainscough,Clough,Munro,Ratcliffe g:Hemingway(3)	N/A	5,316
16/5/10	Gateshead (h)	W132-0	t:Haggerty(2),Charnley(2),Ballard(2),Halliwell,Ainscough(2),Munro(2),Clough(2), Hemingway,Mayberry(2),Leather,Anderson,Thomas,Keavney(2),McCully g:Hemingway(22)	2nd	253
30/5/10	York (a)	L24-22	t:Mayberry,Leather,McCully,Munro g:Hemingway(3)	3rd	535
6/6/10	Oldham (a)	L40-26	t:Woodcock,Munro(2),Hemingway,Haggerty g:Hemingway(3)	3rd	923
13/6/10	Workington (h)	W24-10	t:Ainscough,Halliwell,Clough,Hemingway g:Hemingway(4)	3rd	248
20/6/10	Hunslet (a)	L28-12	t:Mayberry,Ainscough g:Hemingway(2)	3rd	584
27/6/10	Swinton (a)	W6-28	t:Clough,McCully,Ainscough,Woodcock,Thompson g:Hemingway(4)	3rd	387
3/7/10	South Wales (h)	W44-24	t:Clough(2),Hemingway,Woodcock,McCully,Mayberry(2),Ainscough g:Hemingway(6)	3rd	266
11/7/10	Doncaster (a)	W18-46	t:Forber,Miller,Thompson,Mayberry(2),Munro,Ainscough,Hemingway g:Hemingway(7)	3rd	485
25/7/10	Oldham (h)	L22-24	t:Mayberry(2),Munro,Halliwell g:Hemingway(3)	3rd	780
31/7/10	London Skolars (h)	W54-40	t:Mayberry,Ainscough(2),Clough,Forber(2),McCully,Hobson,Vaughan g:Hemingway(9)	5th	289
8/8/10	Gateshead (a)	W10-78	t:Hemingway,Vaughan(3),Forber(3),Clough(3),Thompson(2),Keavney,Woodcock g:Hemingway(11)	5th	554
15/8/10	Hunslet (h)	L24-30	t:Mayberry(2),Munro,Alcock g:Hemingway(3)	5th	497
22/8/10	Rochdale (a)	W16-26	t:Halliwell,Anderson,Thompson,Forber,Clough g:Hemingway(3)	4th	592
5/9/10	Workington (h) (EPO)	W36-26	t:Clough,Ainscough,Keavney,McCully,Munro,Halliwell g:Hemingway(6)	N/A	308
12/9/10	Rochdale (h) (ESF)	W34-26	t:McCully,Ainscough,Mayberry(2),Forber,Halliwell g:Hemingway(5)	N/A	453
19/9/10	York (a) (FE)	L38-18	t:Forber,Anderson,McCully g:Hemingway(3)	N/A	673

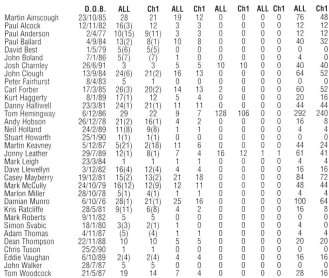

		APP		TRIES		GOALS		FG		PTS	
	D.O.B.	ALL	Ch1	ALL	Ch1	ALL	Ch1	ALL	Ch1	ALL	Ch1
Martin Ainscough	23/10/85	28	21	19	12	0	0	0	0	76	48
Paul Alcock	12/11/82	16(3)	12	3	3	0	0	0	0	12	12
Paul Anderson	2/4/77	10(15)	9(11)	3	3	0	0	0	0	12	12
Paul Ballard	4/9/84	13(2)	8(1)	10	8	0	0	0	0	40	32
David Best	1/5/79	5(6)	5(5)	0	0	0	0	0	0	0	0
John Boland	7/1/86	5(7)	(7)	1	0	0	0	0	0	4	0
Josh Charnley	26/6/91	3	3	5	5	10	10	0	0	40	40
John Clough	13/9/84	24(6)	21(2)	16	13	0	0	0	0	64	52
Peter Fairhurst	8/4/83	5	1	0	0	0	0	0	0	0	0
Carl Forber	17/3/85	26(3)	20(2)	14	13	2	0	0	0	60	52
Kurt Haggerty	8/1/89	17(1)	12	5	4	0	0	0	0	20	16
Danny Halliwell	23/3/81	24(1)	21(1)	11	11	0	0	0	0	44	44
Tom Hemingway	6/12/86	29	22	9	7	128	106	0	0	292	240
Andy Hobson	26/12/78	21(2)	16(1)	4	2	0	0	0	0	16	8
Neil Holland	24/2/89	11(8)	9(8)	1	1	0	0	0	0	4	4
Stuart Howarth	25/1/90	1(1)	1(1)	0	0	0	0	0	0	0	0
Martin Keavney	5/12/87	5(21)	2(18)	11	6	0	0	0	0	44	24
Jonny Leather	29/7/89	12(1)	8(1)	7	4	16	12	1	1	61	41
Mark Leigh	23/3/84	1	1	1	1	0	0	0	0	4	4
Dave Llewellyn	3/12/82	16(4)	12(4)	4	4	0	0	0	0	16	16
Casey Mayberry	19/12/81	15(3)	13(2)	21	18	0	0	0	0	84	72
Mark McCully	24/10/79	16(12)	12(9)	12	11	0	0	0	0	48	44
Marlon Miller	28/10/78	5(1)	4(1)	1	1	0	0	0	0	4	4
Damian Munro	6/10/76	28(1)	21(1)	25	16	0	0	0	0	100	64
Kris Ratcliffe	28/5/81	9(11)	6(8)	4	2	0	0	0	0	16	8
Mark Roberts	9/11/82	5	5	0	0	0	0	0	0	0	0
Simon Svabic	18/1/80	3(3)	2(1)	1	0	0	0	0	0	4	0
Adam Thomas	4/11/87	(5)	(4)	1	1	0	0	0	0	4	4
Dean Thompson	22/11/88	10	10	5	5	0	0	0	0	20	20
Chris Tuson	25/2/90	1	1	0	0	0	0	0	0	0	0
Eddie Vaughan	6/10/89	2(4)	2(4)	4	4	0	0	0	0	16	16
John Walker	28/7/87	5	5	0	0	0	0	0	0	0	0
Tom Woodcock	21/5/87	19	14	7	4	0	0	0	0	28	16

Damian Munro

LEAGUE RECORD
P20-W15-D0-L5-BP3
(4th, Championship 1/
Final Eliminator)
F805, A370, Diff+435
38 points. *(10 points deducted for operational rules breach)*

CHALLENGE CUP
Round Five

NORTHERN RAIL CUP
5th, Pool 1

ATTENDANCES
Best - v Oldham (Ch1 - 780)
Worst - v Gateshead (NRC - 194)
Total (excluding Challenge Cup) - 5,151
Average (excluding Challenge Cup) - 368
(Down by 134 on 2009)

CLUB RECORDS	**Highest score:** 132-0 v Gateshead, 16/5/2010 **Highest score against:** 6-86 v Workington, 15/7/2007 **Record attendance:** 1,124 v Leigh, 10/2/2006
MATCH RECORDS	**Tries:** 4 Dave Llewellyn v Rochdale 8/6/2008 **Goals:** 22 Tom Hemingway v Gateshead, 16/5/2010 **Points:** 48 Tom Hemingway v Gateshead, 16/5/2010
SEASON RECORDS	**Tries:** 25 Damian Munro 2010 **Goals:** 128 Tom Hemingway 2010 **Points:** 292 Tom Hemingway 2010
CAREER RECORDS	**Tries:** 49 Damian Munro 2008-10 **Goals:** 128 Tom Hemingway 2010 **Points:** 302 Jonny Leather 2008-10 **Appearances:** 89 Eddie Kilgannon 2005-08

DONCASTER

DONCASTER RUGBY LEAGUE CLUB

DATE	FIXTURE	RESULT	SCORERS	LGE	ATT
7/2/10	Swinton (a) (NRC)	L30-20	t:Wilson,Osborne,Leaf,Gomersall g:Fawcett(2)	8th(P1)	380
14/2/10	Whitehaven (a) (NRC)	L54-10	t:Edwards,Wilson g:Fawcett	9th(P1)	808
17/2/10	Barrow (h) (NRC)	L0-60		9th(P1)	285
28/2/10	Rochdale (a)	L56-24	t:Edwards(2),Ely(2) g:Edwards(3),Steen	10th	412
6/3/10	Siddal (h) (CCR3)	L0-26		N/A	561
14/3/10	South Wales (h)	L8-18	t:Gomersall,Wilson	9th	296
21/3/10	Swinton (a)	L36-30	t:Shaw,Allan,Griffiths,Cooper,Gomersall(2) g:S Brown(3)	9th	323
24/3/10	Blackpool (h) (NRC)	L20-40	t:Osborne,P Brown,Ellery,King g:S Brown,Stanley	9th(P1)	192
28/3/10	York (h)	W40-24	t:Griffiths,Allan(2),Collins,King,Leaf,Ely,Kesik g:S Brown(4)	9th	532
2/4/10	Hunslet (a)	L54-12	t:Gomersall,Ellery g:S Brown(2)	9th	539
5/4/10	London Skolars (h)	W38-28	t:Bates(2),Ellery,Gomersall,Henry,Lawton,S Brown g:S Brown(5)	7th	380
11/4/10	Gateshead (a)	W28-32	t:Henry(2),Griffiths(2),Steen,Ely g:S Brown(4)	5th	579
23/4/10	Blackpool (a)	L48-12	t:Griffiths,Hughes g:S Brown(2)	7th	253
3/5/10	Oldham (h)	L26-46	t:Wilson,Griffiths,Ely,Colton g:S Brown(5)	8th	730
16/5/10	Workington (a)	L34-20	t:Butterfield,Leaf(2),Spurr g:S Brown(2)	9th	410
23/5/10	Swinton (h)	W16-0	t:Kesik,Griffiths,Leaf(2)	8th	430
30/5/10	Hunslet (h)	L20-30	t:Lunt(2),Colton,Crawley g:S Brown(2)	9th	550
13/6/10	Oldham (a)	L28-18	t:Ely,Spurr,Lunt g:S Brown(3)	9th	740
26/6/10	Rochdale (h)	W30-20	t:Henry,Spurr,Ely,Lunt(2) g:S Brown(5)	9th	578
4/7/10	York (a)	L32-16	t:Lunt,Leaf,Spurr g:S Brown(2)	9th	735
11/7/10	Blackpool (h)	L18-46	t:Colton,Ellery,Ely g:Dobek(3)	9th	485
25/7/10	London Skolars (a)	W26-38	t:Watson,Leaf(2),Steen,Spurr,Hughes,Fawcett g:Dobek(5)	9th	290
1/8/10	Gateshead (h)	W66-0	t:Watson,Henry(3),Colton(2),Lunt(3),Butterfield,Dobek,Fawcett g:Dobek(9)	9th	525
8/8/10	South Wales (a)	L22-8	t:Lunt g:Dobek(2)	9th	492
22/8/10	Workington (h)	W46-12	t:Lunt(2),Fawcett,Ely,Colton,Jones,Hughes(2) g:Kesik(2),Henry(5)	9th	1,127

		APP		TRIES		GOALS		FG		PTS	
	D.O.B.	ALL	Ch1	ALL	Ch1	ALL	Ch1	ALL	Ch1	ALL	Ch1
Danny Allan	9/4/89	6	5	3	3	0	0	0	0	12	12
Nathan Anderson	26/9/86	1(1)	1	0	0	0	0	0	0	0	0
Jake Bassinder	15/7/90	2(5)	1(3)	0	0	0	0	0	0	0	0
David Bates	23/10/80	10(2)	5(2)	2	2	0	0	0	0	8	8
Jamie Bovill	21/3/83	9(2)	8(1)	0	0	0	0	0	0	0	0
Liam Brown	10/9/88	8(1)	3(1)	0	0	0	0	0	0	0	0
Paul Brown	23/2/83	3(8)	1(5)	1	0	0	0	0	0	4	0
Simon Brown	23/6/89	16	14	1	1	40	39	0	0	84	82
Gareth Burns	18/2/83	(1)	0	0	0	0	0	0	0	0	0
Michael Butterfield	5/12/84	7	7	2	2	0	0	0	0	8	8
Matt Carbutt	3/10/85	8(4)	8(4)	0	0	0	0	0	0	0	0
Ben Collins	7/7/89	6(2)	4(1)	1	1	0	0	0	0	4	4
Dean Colton	18/2/83	11	11	6	6	0	0	0	0	24	24
Nick Cooper	2/5/83	2	1	1	1	0	0	0	0	4	4
Liam Crawley	18/4/87	11(1)	11(1)	1	1	0	0	0	0	4	4
Aaron Dobek	10/9/87	4(2)	4(2)	1	1	19	19	0	0	42	42
Grant Edwards	22/3/87	4	1	3	2	3	3	0	0	18	14
Gary Ellery	29/6/85	9(7)	8(6)	4	3	0	0	0	0	16	12
Jack Ely	3/12/89	7(16)	3(16)	9	9	0	0	0	0	36	36
Craig Fawcett	8/11/85	16	13	3	3	3	0	0	0	18	12
Lee Gomersall	14/11/86	16(3)	12(3)	6	5	0	0	0	0	24	20
Tommy Griffiths	8/12/86	15(2)	11(2)	7	7	0	0	0	0	28	28
Aaron Henry	5/4/85	12	11	7	7	5	5	0	0	38	38
Scott Howlett	23/2/92	2(4)	(2)	0	0	0	0	0	0	0	0
Paul Hughes	28/12/84	6(7)	6(7)	4	4	0	0	0	0	16	16
Scott Johnson	16/7/88	(2)	(2)	0	0	0	0	0	0	0	0
Ben Jones	18/10/88	5(1)	5(1)	1	1	0	0	0	0	4	4
Kyle Kesik	3/6/89	15(3)	14(3)	2	2	2	2	0	0	12	12
Gary King	27/10/87	5(1)	4	2	1	0	0	0	0	8	4
Craig Lawton	17/2/81	9	8	1	1	0	0	0	0	4	4
Shaun Leaf	10/2/84	18(1)	15(1)	9	8	0	0	0	0	36	32
Rob Lunt	8/2/85	13	13	12	12	0	0	0	0	48	48
Jarryn Osborne	27/1/85	5	1	2	0	0	0	0	0	8	0
Paul Shaw	11/7/89	4(9)	2(6)	1	1	0	0	0	0	4	4
Chris Spurr	7/7/80	11	11	5	5	0	0	0	0	20	20
Danny Stanley	15/8/86	3(9)	1(8)	0	0	1	0	0	0	2	0
Ryan Steen	26/6/89	24	20	2	2	1	1	0	0	10	10
Mark Ward	20/12/88	(2)	(1)	0	0	0	0	0	0	0	0
Scott Watson	16/3/88	7(1)	7(1)	2	2	0	0	0	0	8	8
Scott Wilson	21/9/88	12(1)	9(1)	4	2	0	0	0	0	16	8
John Winter	21/3/88	3(2)	1	0	0	0	0	0	0	0	0

Jack Ely

LEAGUE RECORD
P20-W8-D0-L12-BP4
(9th, Championship 1)
F518, A588, Diff-70
28 points.

CHALLENGE CUP
Round Three

NORTHERN RAIL CUP
9th, Pool 1

ATTENDANCES
Best - v Workington (Ch1 - 1,127)
Worst - v Blackpool (NRC - 192)
Total (excluding Challenge Cup) - 6,110
Average (excluding Challenge Cup) - 509
(Down by 196 on 2009, Ch)

CLUB RECORDS **MATCH RECORDS**	Highest score: 96-0 v Highfield, 20/3/94 **Highest score against:** 4-90 v Widnes, 10/6/2007 **Record attendance:** 10,000 v Bradford, 16/2/52
	Tries: 6 Kane Epati v Oldham, 30/7/2006 **Goals:** 12 Tony Zelei v Nottingham City, 1/9/91; Robert Turner v Highfield, 20/3/94
	Points: 32 Tony Zelei v Nottingham City, 1/9/91
SEASON RECORDS **CAREER RECORDS**	Tries: 30 Luke Gale 2008 **Goals:** 129 Jonny Woodcock 2002 **Points:** 306 Jonny Woodcock 2002
	Tries: 112 Mark Roache 1985-97 **Goals:** 850 David Noble 1976-77; 1980-89; 1992 **Points:** 1,751 David Noble 1976-77; 1980-89; 1992
	Appearances: 327 Audley Pennant 1980-83; 1985-97

GATESHEAD THUNDER

DATE	FIXTURE	RESULT	SCORERS	LGE	ATT
2/2/10	Widnes (a) (NRC)	L50-6	t:Peers g:Neighbour	N/A	2,200
7/2/10	Workington (h) (NRC)	L12-26	t:Wilson,Ryan Clarke,J Brown	10th(P1)	404
14/2/10	Blackpool (a) (NRC)	L74-6	t:Cakacaka g:Ryan Clarke	10th(P1)	194
28/2/10	Hunslet (a)	L40-12	t:Duffy,J Brown g:Ryan Clarke(2)	11th	481
7/3/10	York (h) (CCR3)	L12-44	t:Peers,Atkinson,Neighbour	N/A	336
17/3/10	Batley (h) (NRC)	L4-100	t:M Brown	10th(P1)	237
21/3/10	London Skolars (h)	W24-18	t:Atkinson(3),Neighbour,Wilson g:Ryan Clarke,Neighbour	11th	356
28/3/10	Workington (a)	L44-0		11th	413
2/4/10	York (a)	L72-14	t:M Barron,Bate,M Brown g:Neighbour	11th	686
11/4/10	Doncaster (h)	L28-32	t:Ryan Clarke,Wilson,Aderiye,Bate,Neighbour g:Neighbour(4)	11th	579
24/4/10	Oldham (a) ●	L64-10	t:Wilson,Duffy g:Neighbour	11th	413
3/5/10	Rochdale (a)	L50-12	t:M Barron,Young g:Neighbour(2)	11th	604
8/5/10	South Wales (h)	L8-50	t:J Brown,Wilson	11th	258
16/5/10	Blackpool (a)	L132-0		11th	253
23/5/10	Workington (h)	L24-42	t:Aderiye,Garside,Young,Duffy g:Ryan Clarke(4)	11th	286
30/5/10	Rochdale (h)	L6-64	t:Aderiye g:Ryan Clarke	11th	265
6/6/10	Swinton (h)	L12-34	t:Peers,Neighbour g:Ryan Clarke,N Scott	11th	353
26/6/10	York (h)	L12-60	t:Garside(2) g:N Scott(2)	11th	346
4/7/10	Oldham (h)	L10-68	t:Bate,Neighbour g:N Scott	11th	433
11/7/10	South Wales (a)	L70-16	t:Bate,Aderiye,M Brown g:Ryan Clarke(2)	11th	480
25/7/10	Hunslet (h)	L16-86	t:M Brown,Wilson,Ryan Clarke g:Ryan Clarke(2)	11th	401
1/8/10	Doncaster (a)	L66-0		11th	525
8/8/10	Blackpool (h)	L10-78	t:Garside,M Barron g:Ryan Clarke	11th	554
15/8/10	London Skolars (a)	L68-22	t:Neighbour,Rhys Clarke,J Brown,Payne g:Ryan Clarke(3)	11th	288
22/8/10	Swinton (a)	L94-0		11th	331

● Played at Park Lane, Sedgley Park

	D.O.B.	APP ALL	APP Ch1	TRIES ALL	TRIES Ch1	GOALS ALL	GOALS Ch1	FG ALL	FG Ch1	PTS ALL	PTS Ch1
Ade Aderiye	26/2/85	16(4)	15(4)	4	4	0	0	0	0	16	16
Jimmy Atkinson	31/1/84	8(1)	7	4	3	0	0	0	0	16	12
Gareth Barron	31/5/82	1(7)	1(6)	0	0	0	0	0	0	0	0
Matt Barron	17/11/86	17(4)	14(2)	3	3	0	0	0	0	12	12
Will Bate	6/12/89	16(7)	12(6)	4	4	0	0	0	0	16	16
Gary Bates	8/9/91	(1)	(1)	0	0	0	0	0	0	0	0
Joe Brown	24/4/87	19	16	4	3	0	0	0	0	16	12
Michael Brown	9/9/86	17(1)	12(1)	4	3	0	0	0	0	16	12
Tabua Cakacaka	8/3/77	4(5)	2(4)	1	0	0	0	0	0	4	0
David Cash	20/12/89	4(9)	2(7)	0	0	0	0	0	0	0	0
Rhys Clarke	12/3/91	18	17	1	1	0	0	0	0	4	4
Ryan Clarke	8/9/85	25	20	3	2	18	17	0	0	48	42
Liam Duffy	17/8/85	16	12	3	3	0	0	0	0	12	12
Jason Elliott	5/5/87	6(2)	3(2)	0	0	0	0	0	0	0	0
Matt Garside	1/10/90	11(1)	11	4	4	0	0	0	0	16	16
James Hall	16/12/88	1(2)	1(2)	0	0	0	0	0	0	0	0
Rob Harvey	26/1/87	1	0	0	0	0	0	0	0	0	0
Richie Humphries	20/6/89	13(3)	8(3)	0	0	0	0	0	0	0	0
Richard Lopag	13/9/89	3	0	0	0	0	0	0	0	0	0
Crawford Matthews	23/11/91	1	0	0	0	0	0	0	0	0	0
Kevin Neighbour	10/7/83	22	17	6	5	10	9	0	0	44	38
Dan O'Sullivan	30/7/89	10(4)	8(4)	0	0	0	0	0	0	0	0
Chris Parker	9/9/78	14(10)	9(10)	0	0	0	0	0	0	0	0
Jason Payne	20/1/88	11(3)	11(3)	1	1	0	0	0	0	4	4
Robin Peers	18/1/82	16	13	3	1	0	0	0	0	12	4
Jonny Scott	13/3/87	(3)	(1)	0	0	0	0	0	0	0	0
Nigel Scott	27/3/88	5	5	0	0	4	4	0	0	8	8
Jonny Shields	30/12/92	1	1	0	0	0	0	0	0	0	0
Josh Stoker	26/7/92	13(1)	13(1)	0	0	0	0	0	0	0	0
Mark Walker	14/12/73	(3)	(1)	0	0	0	0	0	0	0	0
Phil Wall	17/1/84	2(1)	1	0	0	0	0	0	0	0	0
Luke Watson	18/7/85	(1)	0	0	0	0	0	0	0	0	0
Stephen Welton	15/3/91	10(12)	8(10)	0	0	0	0	0	0	0	0
Tom Wilson	4/10/88	17(1)	14	6	5	0	0	0	0	24	20
Reece Young	29/1/91	6(13)	6(11)	2	2	0	0	0	0	8	8

Ryan Clarke

LEAGUE RECORD
P20-W1-D0-L19-BP1
(11th, Championship 1)
F236, A1232, Diff-996
-2 points. *(6 points deducted for entering administration)*

CHALLENGE CUP
Round Three

NORTHERN RAIL CUP
10th, Pool 1

ATTENDANCES
Best - v Doncaster (Ch1 - 579)
Worst - v Batley (NRC - 237)
Total (excluding Challenge Cup) - 4,472
Average (excluding Challenge Cup) - 373
(Down by 306 on 2009, Ch)

CLUB RECORDS	**Highest score:** 66-6 v Wakefield, 5/9/99 **Highest score against:** 0-132 v Blackpool Panthers, 16/5/2010 **Record attendance:** 6,631 v Bradford, 16/5/99
MATCH RECORDS	**Tries:** 5 Andy Walker v London Skolars, 22/6/03 **Goals:** 11 Ian Herron v Wakefield, 5/9/99 **Points:** 26 Ian Herron v Wakefield, 5/9/99
SEASON RECORDS	**Tries:** 25 Matt Daylight 1999 **Goals:** 129 (inc 1 fg) Dan Russell 2008 **Points:** 293 Dan Russell 2008
CAREER RECORDS	**Tries:** 74 Kevin Neighbour 2001-06; 2008-10 **Goals:** 151 Paul Thorman 2001-04 **Points:** 387 Paul Thorman 2001-04 **Appearances:** 203 Kevin Neighbour 2001-06; 2008-10

HUNSLET HAWKS

DATE	FIXTURE	RESULT	SCORERS	LGE	ATT
7/2/10	London Skolars (a) (NRC)	W12-60	t:Houston,McHugh(4),P March,R Kelly,Chapman,Clayton,Sullivan,Larvin g:McHugh(8)	2nd(P2)	328
14/2/10	Oldham (h) (NRC)	W28-14	t:McHugh,Mark,Lowe,Chapman,Haughey(2) g:McHugh(2)	4th(P2)	519
28/2/10	Gateshead (h)	W40-12	t:McHugh,Kain(2),Dooler,D March,P March,Mark g:McHugh(6)	2nd	481
4/3/10	Featherstone (h) (NRC)	L0-68		7th(P2)	513
6/3/10	Leigh East (a) (CCR3) ●	W14-30	t:Dooler,P March,Mark(2),Robinson g:McHugh(5)	N/A	694
12/3/10	Oldham (h)	L16-29	t:McHugh,Clayton,Oakes g:McHugh(2)	7th	521
21/3/10	Halifax (a) (NRC)	W36-42	t:Knight,Larvin,Lowe,Wabo,Houston,Chapman,Mark g:Knight(4),Robinson,Sheldrake(2)	4th(P2)	1,771
28/3/10	Rochdale (h)	W44-8	t:Haughey,Clayton(3),Knight,Kain,Pryce,Grimshaw g:Knight(6)	5th	514
2/4/10	Doncaster (h)	W54-12	t:P March,McHugh(3),Mark,Kain,Pryce(2),Haughey,Knight g:Knight(7)	4th	539
5/4/10	South Wales (a)	W12-42	t:Chapman,Kain(2),P March,Grimshaw,Mark,D March,Lowe g:Knight(5)	1st	798
11/4/10	Swinton (h)	W46-12	t:McHugh,Lowe(2),Grimshaw,Haughey,Wabo,Chapman,D March g:D March(7)	1st	546
18/4/10	Oldham (h) (CCR4)	W42-12	t:D March,Mark(2),Lowe,Chapman,McHugh,Knight g:Knight(5),McHugh(2)	N/A	509
25/4/10	London Skolars (a)	W8-46	t:Clayton,Mark(2),Grimshaw(2),P March,McHugh,Oakes(2) g:Knight(5)	1st	372
3/5/10	Workington (a)	W16-30	t:Chapman,Houston,P March,Larvin,D March g:D March(5)	1st	578
9/5/10	Barrow (a) (CCR5)	L42-24	t:Haughey,Helme,Pryce,Lowe,Mark g:D March(2)	N/A	2,241
16/5/10	York (a)	W10-46	t:P March,Pryce,Haughey,Grimshaw,D March(2),McHugh,Clayton g:McHugh(6),D March	3rd	1,002
23/5/10	Oldham (a)	W4-60	t:Pryce(3),Kain,McHugh(3),Grimshaw,Mark,D March,Woodcock g:McHugh(8)	1st	1,004
30/5/10	Doncaster (h)	W20-30	t:Pryce,Mark(2),Grimshaw,McHugh,P March(2) g:D March	1st	550
6/6/10	Leigh (h) (NRCQF)	L6-42	t:McHugh g:D March	N/A	770
13/6/10	Rochdale (h)	L28-22	t:Haughey,P March,Lowe,Wabo g:Grimshaw(3)	2nd	814
20/6/10	Blackpool (h)	W28-12	t:Haigh,Chapman,McHugh,D March g:D March(6)	1st	584
27/6/10	London Skolars (h)	W60-16	t:McHugh(4),Pryce(4),Larvin,P March,Grimshaw,D March g:D March(3),Knight(3)	1st	309
4/7/10	Swinton (a)	W10-58	t:Pryce(2),Kain(3),Haughey,Haigh,Dooler,Grimshaw,Wabo,D March g:Knight(3),D March(4)	1st	386
11/7/10	York (h)	W34-18	t:Pryce,Woodcock,Haughey(2),P March,Chapman g:Knight(2),D March(3)	1st	537
25/7/10	Gateshead (a)	W16-86	t:Pryce(6),Chapman,Houston,P March,Wabo,Rayner(2),Haughey,Kain,Knight,Mark g:D March(11)	1st	401
5/8/10	Workington (h)	W24-14	t:P March,McHugh(3) g:D March(4)	1st	537
15/8/10	Blackpool (a)	W24-30	t:P March,Clayton,Haughey,D March,Knight g:D March(5)	1st	497
22/8/10	South Wales (h)	W32-24	t:Clayton,McHugh,Dooler,Woodcock,Houston g:D March(6)	1st	785

● Played at Leigh Sports Village

		APP		TRIES		GOALS		FG		PTS	
	D.O.B.	ALL	Ch1	ALL	Ch1	ALL	Ch1	ALL	Ch1	ALL	Ch1
Steve Brook	6/4/87	(1)	0	0	0	0	0	0	0	0	0
Corey Challenger	1/3/90	1	0	0	0	0	0	0	0	0	0
Richard Chapman	5/9/75	13(6)	8(6)	10	6	0	0	0	0	40	24
David Clayton	23/9/88	22(1)	17(1)	9	8	0	0	0	0	36	32
Danny Cook	14/10/81	1	0	0	0	0	0	0	0	0	0
Russ Dale	20/7/89	(1)	0	0	0	0	0	0	0	0	0
Steve Dooler	31/12/77	21(1)	16(1)	4	3	0	0	0	0	16	12
Gareth Firm	26/11/88	(2)	0	0	0	0	0	0	0	0	0
Danny Grimshaw	25/2/86	24	19	10	10	3	3	0	0	46	46
Luke Haigh	24/7/87	12(7)	11(4)	2	2	0	0	0	0	8	8
Tom Haughey	30/1/82	24(2)	18(2)	13	10	0	0	0	0	52	40
Joe Helme	1/4/84	6(6)	5(4)	1	0	0	0	0	0	4	0
James Houston	28/12/82	26	19	5	3	0	0	0	0	20	12
Stuart Kain	18/9/85	23	18	11	11	0	0	0	0	44	44
Michael Kelly	23/5/89	1(2)	(1)	0	0	0	0	0	0	0	0
Rob Kelly	1/3/86	5(2)	1(2)	1	0	0	0	0	0	4	0
Richard Knight	6/10/85	11(5)	7(5)	6	4	40	31	0	0	104	78
Nathan Larvin	25/7/85	6	2	4	2	0	0	0	0	16	8
Neil Lowe	20/12/78	(25)	(17)	8	4	0	0	0	0	32	16
David March	25/7/79	23	17	12	11	59	56	0	0	166	156
Paul March	25/7/79	27	20	16	14	0	0	0	0	64	56
Michael Mark	14/12/88	20	13	16	9	0	0	0	0	64	36
Wayne McHugh	1/2/80	20	15	28	21	39	22	0	0	190	128
John Oakes	12/2/88	22(1)	15(1)	3	3	0	0	0	0	12	12
Waine Pryce	3/10/81	20	18	22	21	0	0	0	0	88	84
George Rayner	19/9/80	1(1)	1(1)	2	2	0	0	0	0	8	8
Darren Robinson	28/5/79	3(5)	1(3)	1	0	1	0	0	0	6	0
Nigel Scott	27/3/88	1	0	0	0	0	0	0	0	0	0
Tom Sheldrake	3/9/88	1	0	0	0	2	0	0	0	4	0
Nicko Slain	19/4/83	1	0	0	0	0	0	0	0	0	0
Louis Stead	17/2/91	(1)	(1)	0	0	0	0	0	0	0	0
Adam Sullivan	14/11/82	23	16	1	0	0	0	0	0	4	0
Charlie Wabo	19/9/83	4(17)	3(12)	5	4	0	0	0	0	20	16
Jake Wilson	23/3/89	1(1)	0	0	0	0	0	0	0	0	0
Scott Woodcock	15/11/83	(24)	(19)	3	3	0	0	0	0	12	12
Stuart Young	7/5/88	1(1)	0	0	0	0	0	0	0	0	0

Paul March

LEAGUE RECORD
P20-W18-D0-L2-BP1
(Champions/1st, Championship 1)
F828, A305, Diff+523
55 points.

CHALLENGE CUP
Round Five

NORTHERN RAIL CUP
Quarter Finalists/4th, Pool 2

ATTENDANCES
Best - v South Wales (Ch1 - 785)
Worst - v London Skolars (Ch1 - 309)
Total (excluding Challenge Cup) - 7,155
Average (excluding Challenge Cup) - 550
(Down by 105 on 2009)

CLUB RECORDS Highest score: 82-0 v Highfield, 21/1/96 **Highest score against:** 0-82 v Bradford, 2/3/2003 **Record attendance:** 24,700 v Wigan, 15/3/24
MATCH RECORDS Tries: 7 George Dennis v Bradford, 20/1/34 **Goals:** 12 Billy Langton v Keighley, 18/8/59 **Points:** 30 Simon Wilson v Highfield, 21/1/96
SEASON RECORDS Tries: 34 Alan Snowden 1956-57 **Goals:** 181 Billy Langton 1958-59 **Points:** 380 Billy Langton 1958-59
CAREER RECORDS Tries: 154 Fred Williamson 1943-55 **Goals:** 1,044 Billy Langton 1955-66 **Points:** Billy Langton 1955-66 **Appearances:** 579 Geoff Gunney 1951-73

LONDON SKOLARS

DATE	FIXTURE	RESULT	SCORERS	LGE	ATT
31/1/10	Dewsbury (a) (NRC)	L50-4	t:Junor	N/A	887
7/2/10	Hunslet (h) (NRC)	L12-60	t:M Thomas,Quinn g:P Thorman(2)	9th(P2)	328
14/2/10	Halifax (h) (NRC)	L0-68		10th(P2)	416
28/2/10	York (a)	L36-8	t:Cook,M Thomas	9th	811
7/3/10	Limoux (h) (CCR3)	L16-42	t:Honor,Cunningham,M Thomas g:P Thorman(2)	N/A	376
10/3/10	York (a) (NRC)	L34-12	t:Montgomerie,Ball g:Boston(2)	10th(P2)	439
14/3/10	Swinton (h)	L16-52	t:Obuchowski,Roach,Welsh g:P Thorman(2)	10th	276
21/3/10	Gateshead (a)	L24-18	t:Cunningham,Isles,M Thomas g:P Thorman(3)	10th	356
28/3/10	South Wales (a)	L48-6	t:Carter g:P Thorman	10th	625
2/4/10	Blackpool (h)	L18-42	t:P Thorman,Isles,Adebisi g:P Thorman(3)	10th	323
5/4/10	Doncaster (a)	L38-28	t:Aggrey,Adebisi(2),May(2) g:P Thorman(4)	10th	380
11/4/10	Rochdale (h)	L68-10	t:Arnot,Adebisi g:P Thorman	10th	359
25/4/10	Hunslet (a)	L8-46	t:Welsh,Aggrey	10th	372
9/5/10	Workington (h)	L28-44	t:Boston(2),O'Callaghan,Adebisi,M Thomas g:P Thorman(4)	10th	258
16/5/10	Oldham (a)	L46-12	t:D Williams(2),Adebisi	10th	747
23/5/10	South Wales (h)	L22-70	t:N Thorman,Boston,Cook,Aggrey g:P Thorman(3)	10th	358
30/5/10	Swinton (a)	L56-28	t:Prescott,Honor(2),Paxton,Hodson g:Prescott,P Thorman(3)	10th	277
12/6/10	York (h) ●	L12-44	t:Adebisi,P Thorman g:P Thorman(2)	10th	1,350
27/6/10	Hunslet (a)	L60-16	t:Adebisi(3) g:P Thorman(2)	10th	309
4/7/10	Rochdale (h)	W28-26	t:Jy-Mel Coleman,M Thomas,Paxton(2),Gee g:P Thorman(4)	10th	372
11/7/10	Workington (a)	L38-34	t:Gee(2),Cook,Jy-Mel Coleman(2),M Thomas g:P Thorman(5)	10th	411
25/7/10	Doncaster (a)	L26-38	t:Adebisi,Jy-Mel Coleman,Purslow,P Thorman,Junor g:P Thorman(3)	10th	290
31/7/10	Blackpool (a)	L54-40	t:Gee(3),Jy-Mel Coleman(2),Paxton,Bloom,Adebisi g:P Thorman(4)	10th	289
15/8/10	Gateshead (h)	W68-22	t:Gee(3),N Thorman,Bloom,Aggrey(2),Purslow,M Thomas(2),Jy-Mel Coleman, Paxton,Adebisi g:Jy-Mel Coleman(8)	10th	288
27/8/10	Oldham (h)	L18-48	t:Aggrey,N Thorman,Purslow g:P Thorman(3)	10th	1,375

● Played at Twickenham Stoop

		APP		**TRIES**		**GOALS**		**FG**		**PTS**	
	D.O.B.	ALL	Ch1	ALL	Ch1	ALL	Ch1	ALL	Ch1	ALL	Ch1
Ade Adebisi	7/1/86	16(1)	14(1)	13	13	0	0	0	0	52	52
Austen Aggrey	12/5/79	10(8)	9(8)	6	6	0	0	0	0	24	24
Guy Aldam	3/9/89	1	1	0	0	0	0	0	0	0	0
Dave Arnot	27/6/88	10(1)	8(1)	1	1	0	0	0	0	4	4
Stephen Ball	15/3/89	19(4)	14(4)	1	0	0	0	0	0	4	0
Oliver Bloom	16/4/86	9(5)	8(5)	2	2	0	0	0	0	8	8
Jamie Boston	5/1/88	12(1)	11(1)	3	3	2	2	0	0	16	12
Lamont Bryan	12/4/88	3(1)	2	0	0	0	0	0	0	0	0
Matt Carter	26/1/89	5(7)	3(5)	1	1	0	0	0	0	4	4
Cariern Clement-Pascall	28/9/90	1(3)	1(3)	0	0	0	0	0	0	0	0
Jermaine Coleman	17/6/82	2	1	0	0	0	0	0	0	0	0
Jy-Mel Coleman	13/10/88	9	9	7	7	8	8	0	0	44	44
Jason Cook	10/6/89	13(1)	10	3	3	0	0	0	0	12	12
Curtis Cunningham	16/12/86	8	4	2	1	0	0	0	0	8	4
Sam Gee	28/2/87	10	10	9	9	0	0	0	0	36	36
Kris Hodson	4/9/87	1(2)	1(2)	1	1	0	0	0	0	4	4
Gareth Honor	1/10/81	10(10)	9(10)	3	2	0	0	0	0	12	8
Chad Isles	7/2/87	13(1)	9	2	2	0	0	0	0	8	8
Olu Iwenofu	28/9/81	12(1)	11(1)	0	0	0	0	0	0	0	0
Ben Jones	8/10/88	2(1)	1(1)	0	0	0	0	0	0	0	0
Smokie Junor	15/4/90	10(3)	8(1)	2	1	0	0	0	0	8	4
Ben Kaye	19/12/88	(1)	(1)	0	0	0	0	0	0	0	0
Luke May	23/8/89	10	7	2	2	0	0	0	0	8	8
Nathan McLoughlin	18/1/84	1(1)	(1)	0	0	0	0	0	0	0	0
Rob Montgomerie	15/1/87	1(2)	(1)	1	0	0	0	0	0	4	0
Jaroslaw Obuchowski	20/9/90	2(2)	1(1)	1	1	0	0	0	0	4	4
Jamie O'Callaghan	21/9/90	1	1	1	1	0	0	0	0	4	4
Jarryn Osborne	27/1/85	1	1	0	0	0	0	0	0	0	0
John Paxton	20/4/85	11	11	5	5	0	0	0	0	20	20
Liam Prescott	31/8/88	13(3)	11(3)	1	1	1	1	0	0	6	6
Oliver Purslow	17/9/87	14(9)	10(9)	3	3	0	0	0	0	12	12
Aran Quinn	21/6/86	(7)	(4)	1	0	0	0	0	0	4	0
Liam Roach	24/5/89	6(3)	4(2)	1	1	0	0	0	0	4	4
James Simon	20/1/87	7(8)	6(6)	0	0	0	0	0	0	0	0
Aaron Small	28/10/91	(1)	0	0	0	0	0	0	0	0	0
Michael Sykes	10/12/86	6(4)	6(4)	0	0	0	0	0	0	0	0
Matt Thomas	8/1/80	19(2)	15(1)	9	7	0	0	0	0	36	28
Rob Thomas	9/10/90	2	2	0	0	0	0	0	0	0	0
Neil Thorman	4/6/84	10	10	3	3	0	0	0	0	12	12
Paul Thorman	28/9/82	23(1)	19(1)	3	3	51	47	0	0	114	106
Josh Welsh	20/3/86	9(3)	5(2)	2	2	0	0	0	0	8	8
Dave Williams	29/1/87	7	4	2	2	0	0	0	0	8	8
Tony Williams	4/5/84	6(3)	3(2)	0	0	0	0	0	0	0	0

Stephen Ball

LEAGUE RECORD
P20-W2-D0-L18-BP4
(10th, Championship 1)
F444, A900, Diff-456
10 points.

CHALLENGE CUP
Round Three

NORTHERN RAIL CUP
10th, Pool 2

ATTENDANCES
Best - v Oldham (Ch1 - 1,375)
Worst - v Workington (Ch1 - 258)
Total (excluding Challenge Cup) - 6,006
Average (excluding Challenge Cup) - 501
(Up by 89 on 2009)

CLUB RECORDS **MATCH RECORDS**	Highest score: 70-28 v St Albans, 19/3/2006 **Highest score against:** 4-98 v Sheffield, 3/8/2003 **Record attendance:** 1,427 v Keighley, 29/8/2008 **Tries:** 5 Mark Cantoni v Gateshead, 27/6/2004
	Goals: 10 Jake Johnstone v Gateshead, 24/8/2003 **Points:** 20 Jake Johnstone v Gateshead, 24/8/2003; Mark Cantoni v Gateshead, 27/6/2004
SEASON RECORDS	**Tries:** 20 Mark Cantoni 2004 **Goals:** 79 Paul Thorman 2008 **Points:** 170 Paul Thorman 2008
CAREER RECORDS	**Tries:** 47 Austen Aggrey 2004-10 **Goals:** 223 (inc 2 fg) Paul Thorman 2007-10 **Points:** 488 Paul Thorman 2007-10 **Appearances:** 174 Gareth Honor 2003-10

OLDHAM

DATE	FIXTURE	RESULT	SCORERS	LGE	ATT
31/1/10	Leigh (a) (NRC)	L24-12	t:Littler,Gillam,Fogerty	N/A	1,627
8/2/10	Rochdale (h) (NRC) ●	W22-14	t:Ellison,Chandler,Onyango g:Ashe(4),O'Connor	6th(P2)	540
14/2/10	Hunslet (a) (NRC)	L28-14	t:Fogerty(2) g:Ashe(3)	6th(P2)	519
22/2/10	Sheffield (h) (NRC) ●	L22-24	t:O'Connor,Brocklehurst,N Roden,Onyango g:Ashe(3)	8th(P2)	340
28/2/10	Swinton (a)	W20-38	t:O'Connor,Onyango(3),M Roden,Kerr,Chandler g:Ashe(5)	4th	627
7/3/10	Blackwood (h) (CCR3) ●	W80-6	t:Chandler(3),Brocklehurst(3),O'Connor(2),Murtza(2),Onyango,Ashe(2),Ellison, Fogerty g:Ashe(10)	N/A	455
12/3/10	Hunslet (h)	W16-29	t:Ashe(2),Chandler,Reilly,Onyango g:Ashe(4) fg:N Roden	1st	521
2/4/10	Rochdale (a)	W16-22	t:Ashe,Sutton,Fogerty,Brocklehurst g:Ashe(3)	5th	1,412
5/4/10	Workington (h) ●	W16-14	t:Onyango,Fogerty(2) g:Ashe(2)	3rd	658
11/4/10	South Wales (a)	W16-22	t:Onyango,Whitmore,Fogerty,Boults g:O'Connor(3)	3rd	625
18/4/10	Hunslet (a) (CCR4)	L42-12	t:Brocklehurst,O'Connor g:Ashe(2)	N/A	509
24/4/10	Gateshead (h) ●	W64-10	t:Clarke,Gillam(4),O'Connor(2),Chandler,Ashe,Onyango,N Roden,Fogerty g:Ashe(8)	3rd	413
3/5/10	Doncaster (a)	W26-46	t:Boults,Ashe,Chandler,Fogerty,Clarke,Gillam,Heaton,Ellison g:Ashe(7)	3rd	730
9/5/10	York (h)	L28-34	t:Kerr,Gillam,Onyango,O'Connor(2),Fogerty g:Ashe(2)	1st	1,110
16/5/10	London Skolars (h)	W46-12	t:Onyango(2),M Roden,O'Connor,Whitmore,Heaton,Robinson,Gillam g:Ashe(7)	1st	747
23/5/10	Hunslet (h)	L4-60	t:Onyango	2nd	1,004
30/5/10	Workington (a)	W16-28	t:Boults,Ellison,Fogerty(2),O'Connor g:Ashe(4)	2nd	581
6/6/10	Blackpool (h)	W40-26	t:Onyango,St Hilaire,Chandler,McNally,Ellison,O'Connor g:McNally(7),O'Connor	1st	923
13/6/10	Doncaster (h)	W28-18	t:Onyango,Fogerty,Bentley,Chandler,Gillam g:McNally(4)	1st	740
4/7/10	Gateshead (a)	W10-68	t:Fogerty(3),O'Connor(2),Onyango,Whitmore(2),Clarke,Heaton,Kerr,Ellison g:Ashe,McNally(9)	2nd	433
11/7/10	Swinton (a)	W42-30	t:Clarke,St Hilaire,Gillam(2),N Roden,Kerr,Heaton,McNally g:McNally(5)	2nd	841
25/7/10	Blackpool (a)	W22-24	t:St Hilaire,O'Connor(3),Fogerty g:McNally(2)	2nd	780
1/8/10	South Wales (h)	L24-42	t:Onyango,McNally,Ashe,Heaton g:McNally(3),Ashe	2nd	908
8/8/10	York (a)	W18-33	t:Gillam(2),N Roden,O'Connor,Onyango g:Ashe(6) fg:N Roden	2nd	770
15/8/10	Rochdale (h)	W44-14	t:Boults(3),McNally(2),Gillam,Ellison,Kerr g:McNally(6)	2nd	1,005
27/8/10	London Skolars (a)	W18-48	t:Bentley,O'Connor,Gillam(2),Heaton,Clarke,McNally(2) g:Ashe(6),McNally(2)	2nd	1,375
12/9/10	York (h) (QSF)	W41-32	t:Chandler(2),Whitmore,Kerr,Bentley,Clarke g:McNally(8) fg:McNally	N/A	1,275
26/9/10	York (GF) ●●	L4-25	t:Fogerty	N/A	N/A

● Played at Park Lane, Sedgley Park
●● Played at Halliwell Jones Stadium, Warrington

	D.O.B.	APP		TRIES		GOALS		FG		PTS	
		ALL	Ch1	ALL	Ch1	ALL	Ch1	ALL	Ch1	ALL	Ch1
Matt Ashe	4/9/85	20(2)	14(2)	8	6	78	56	0	0	188	136
Valu Bentley	9/10/82	15(1)	13(1)	3	3	0	0	0	0	12	12
Jason Boults	7/9/83	23(3)	17(3)	6	6	0	0	0	0	24	24
Mark Brocklehurst	27/9/86	7(2)	4(2)	6	1	0	0	0	0	24	4
Joe Chandler	2/11/88	28	22	12	8	0	0	0	0	48	32
Chris Clarke	29/3/89	18(4)	13(4)	6	6	0	0	0	0	24	24
Dave Ellison	2/4/82	8(20)	4(18)	7	5	0	0	0	0	28	20
Mick Fogerty	19/2/81	28	22	19	15	0	0	0	0	76	60
John Gillam	15/10/84	19	17	16	15	0	0	0	0	64	60
Ben Heaton	12/3/90	14(13)	10(11)	6	6	0	0	0	0	24	24
Ian Hodson	23/10/81	9(3)	9(3)	0	0	0	0	0	0	0	0
Jamie I'Anson	19/6/87	(4)	(3)	0	0	0	0	0	0	0	0
Wayne Kerr	18/3/84	21(6)	19(2)	6	6	0	0	0	0	24	24
Craig Littler	4/9/85	3	0	1	0	0	0	0	0	4	0
Scott Mansfield	16/12/90	(4)	(4)	0	0	0	0	0	0	0	0
Gregg McNally	2/1/91	12	12	7	7	46	46	1	1	121	121
Ben Mellor	13/12/88	(3)	0	0	0	0	0	0	0	0	0
Saqib Murtza	18/11/85	(5)	(1)	2	0	0	0	0	0	8	0
Paul O'Connor	3/6/84	28	22	19	15	5	4	0	0	86	68
Lucas Onyango	12/4/81	28	22	19	16	0	0	0	0	76	64
Paul Reilly	10/5/76	4(2)	4(2)	1	1	0	0	0	0	4	4
Craig Robinson	30/7/85	4(9)	3(7)	1	1	0	0	0	0	4	4
Martin Roden	26/12/79	28	22	2	2	0	0	0	0	8	8
Neil Roden	9/4/80	21	15	4	3	0	0	2	2	18	14
Marcus St Hilaire	26/1/77	21	17	3	3	0	0	0	0	12	12
Luke Sutton	25/2/86	(9)	(9)	1	1	0	0	0	0	4	4
John Walker	28/7/87	2	2	0	0	0	0	0	0	0	0
Danny Whitmore	22/12/88	3(22)	3(16)	5	5	0	0	0	0	20	20

Mick Fogerty

LEAGUE RECORD
P20-W17-D0-L3-BP1
(2nd, Championship 1/
Grand Final Runners-Up)
F694, A438, Diff+256
52 points.

CHALLENGE CUP
Round Four

NORTHERN RAIL CUP
8th, Pool 2

ATTENDANCES
Best - v York (QSF - 1,275)
Worst - v Sheffield (NRC - 340)
Total (excluding Challenge Cup) - 10,504
Average (excluding Challenge Cup) - 808
(Down by 175 on 2009)

CLUB RECORDS
MATCH RECORDS Highest score: 80-6 v Blackwood, 7/3/2010 Highest score against: 0-84 v Widnes, 25/7/99 Record attendance: 28,000 v Huddersfield, 24/2/12
Tries: 7 James Miller v Barry, 31/10/1908
Goals: 14 Bernard Ganley v Liverpool City, 4/4/59 Points: 34 Andy Ballard v London Skolars, 2/5/2009; Chris Baines v Hunslet, 20/9/2009
SEASON RECORDS Tries: 49 Reg Farrar 1921-22 Goals: 200 Bernard Ganley 1957-58 Points: 412 Bernard Ganley 1957-58
CAREER RECORDS Tries: 174 Alan Davies 1950-61 Goals: 1,358 Bernard Ganley 1951-61 Points: 2,761 Bernard Ganley 1951-61 Appearances: 627 Joe Ferguson 1899-1923

ROCHDALE HORNETS

DATE	FIXTURE	RESULT	SCORERS	LGE	ATT
8/2/10	Oldham (a) (NRC) ●	L22-14	t:Smith,Samuel,Fagborun g:Roper	9th(P2)	540
14/2/10	Dewsbury (h) (NRC)	L12-48	t:Roper,Samuel g:Roper(2)	9th(P2)	575
17/2/10	York (h) (NRC)	L12-36	t:Bostock,Hatton g:Ashall,Hatton	9th(P2)	362
23/2/10	Featherstone (a) (NRC)	L56-10	t:Gorton,Corcoran g:Hatton	9th(P2)	777
28/2/10	Doncaster (h)	W56-24	t:Samuel,Donoghue(2),English,Johnson,Fagborun,Wood,Raftrey,Gorton(2),Roper g:Roper(6)	1st	412
7/3/10	Lezignan (h) (CCR3)	L22-32	t:Saywell(3),English,Ashall g:Ashall	N/A	398
12/3/10	Blackpool (a)	L36-14	t:Fagborun,Corcoran,Donoghue g:Roper	8th	352
21/3/10	Workington (h)	W32-24	t:Donoghue,Johnson,McGovern,Gorton,Wood g:McGovern(6)	5th	421
28/3/10	Hunslet (a)	L44-8	t:Johnson,Reid	7th	514
2/4/10	Oldham (h)	L16-22	t:Johnson,Hayes,Wood g:Hough(2)	7th	1,412
11/4/10	London Skolars (h)	W68-10	t:Hough(2),Bowman,Samuel,Ashall,English(3),Powell,Hayes,Johnson,Smith, Gorton g:Hough(8)	7th	359
25/4/10	York (a)	L36-34	t:Samuel,Bowman,Hough,Ashall,English,Wood g:Crook(5)	6th	987
3/5/10	Gateshead (h)	W50-12	t:Ashall,English(3),Gorton,Smith,Reid,Roper,Wood,Johnson g:Crook(5)	4th	604
8/5/10	Swinton (a)	W22-33	t:Samuel,Gorton,Bloomfield(2),Hough,Johnson g:Crook(4) fg:Roper	4th	470
23/5/10	York (h)	W44-34	t:Fagborun,Smith(2),Cookson,Crook,Wood,Bloomfield g:Crook(8)	4th	472
30/5/10	Gateshead (a)	W6-64	t:English(3),Ashall(3),Reid,Powell,Bloomfield,Saywell,Crook,Smith g:Crook(8)	4th	265
13/6/10	Hunslet (h)	W28-22	t:Samuel,English,Gorton,Saywell,Crook g:Crook(3) fg:Crook,Ashall	4th	814
20/6/10	South Wales (a)	L30-25	t:Johnson,Powell,Reid,Gorton,Saywell g:Crook(2) fg:Crook	4th	522
26/6/10	Doncaster (a)	L30-20	t:Samuel,Saywell,Johnson,Cookson g:Crook(2)	4th	578
4/7/10	London Skolars (a)	L28-26	t:Bloomfield(2),Roper,Wood,Saywell g:Crook(3)	5th	372
25/7/10	South Wales (h)	W46-14	t:Gorton,Cookson,Reid(3),Smith,Donoghue,Bloomfield g:Crook(3),Roper(4)	5th	471
1/8/10	Workington (a)	L18-12	t:Saywell,Crook g:Crook(2)	4th	434
8/8/10	Swinton (h)	W24-16	t:Smith,Gorton,Donoghue g:Crook(6)	3rd	502
15/8/10	Oldham (a)	L44-14	t:Fagborun(2),Ashall g:Crook	4th	1,005
22/8/10	Blackpool (h)	L16-26	t:Smith,Ashall g:Roper(4)	5th	592
5/9/10	South Wales (h) (EPO)	W60-26	t:English,Bowman,Crook(2),Ashall(2),Bloomfield(2),Cookson,Hayes g:Crook(10)	N/A	375
12/9/10	Blackpool (a) (ESF)	L34-26	t:Samuel,Crook,Wood,Gorton g:Crook(5)	N/A	453

● Played at Park Lane, Sedgley Park

		APP		TRIES		GOALS		FG		PTS	
	D.O.B.	ALL	Ch1	ALL	Ch1	ALL	Ch1	ALL	Ch1	ALL	Ch1
Craig Ashall	26/9/85	23(1)	20(1)	11	10	2	0	1	1	49	41
Dale Blackmore	29/1/91	(2)	(2)	0	0	0	0	0	0	0	0
Dale Bloomfield	24/10/87	12(4)	11(4)	9	9	0	0	0	0	36	36
Liam Bostock	1/12/84	2(1)	0	1	0	0	0	0	0	4	0
Adam Bowman	12/11/87	13(6)	13(5)	3	3	0	0	0	0	12	12
Semisi Cocka	14/3/79	4(10)	4(8)	0	0	0	0	0	0	0	0
John Cookson	12/12/84	4(20)	4(17)	4	4	0	0	0	0	16	16
Wayne Corcoran	10/7/85	2(3)	(2)	2	1	0	0	0	0	8	4
Paul Crook	28/8/86	14(3)	14(2)	7	7	67	67	2	2	164	164
Dayne Donoghue	22/9/88	12(1)	9(1)	6	6	0	0	0	0	24	24
Jay Duffy	16/4/87	1(1)	0	0	0	0	0	0	0	0	0
Wayne English	8/3/80	24	20	14	13	0	0	0	0	56	52
Bolu Fagborun	28/3/86	13	11	6	5	0	0	0	0	24	20
Peter Fairhurst	8/4/83	7(1)	7(1)	0	0	0	0	0	0	0	0
Danny Fleming	8/7/92	(1)	(1)	0	0	0	0	0	0	0	0
Dean Gorton	16/1/84	22(1)	20(1)	12	11	0	0	0	0	48	44
Dean Hatton	27/12/87	1(1)	0	1	0	2	0	0	0	8	0
Gareth Hayes	15/6/85	14(9)	11(8)	3	3	0	0	0	0	12	12
Mark Hobson	14/1/87	4(2)	1(2)	0	0	0	0	0	0	0	0
Andy Hore	17/10/88	(2)	0	0	0	0	0	0	0	0	0
Chris Hough	30/8/81	6(10)	4(9)	4	4	10	10	0	0	36	36
Craig Johnson	17/4/87	17	12	9	9	0	0	0	0	36	36
Liam McGovern	6/10/84	3	3	1	1	6	6	0	0	16	16
Ryan McPaul	27/4/90	3	0	0	0	0	0	0	0	0	0
Michael Ostick	23/1/88	5(2)	2(1)	0	0	0	0	0	0	0	0
Ryan Powell	3/2/88	13(10)	9(10)	3	3	0	0	0	0	12	12
Paul Raftrey	26/1/78	13(4)	10(3)	1	1	0	0	0	0	4	4
Damien Reid	14/3/84	19	18	7	7	0	0	0	0	28	28
Steve Roper	10/11/86	21(1)	18	4	3	18	15	1	1	53	43
Danny Samuel	8/8/85	22(1)	18(1)	9	7	0	0	0	0	36	28
Andy Saywell	1/1/79	13	12	9	6	0	0	0	0	36	24
Danny Smith	20/1/87	22(3)	18(3)	9	8	0	0	0	0	36	32
Andy Taylor	29/6/90	1(1)	(1)	0	0	0	0	0	0	0	0
Craig Tunstead	13/10/87	(3)	(2)	0	0	0	0	0	0	0	0
Adam Wayne	19/4/90	1	0	0	0	0	0	0	0	0	0
Phil Wood	25/10/83	20(4)	17(3)	8	8	0	0	0	0	32	32

Craig Ashall

LEAGUE RECORD
P20-W10-D0-L10-BP7
(5th, Championship 1/
Elimination Semi-Final)
F630, A498, Diff+132
37 points.

CHALLENGE CUP
Round Three

NORTHERN RAIL CUP
9th, Pool 2

ATTENDANCES
Best - v Oldham (Ch1 - 1,412)
Worst - v London Skolars (Ch1 - 359)
Total (excluding Challenge Cup) - 7,371
Average (excluding Challenge Cup) - 567
(Down by 70 on 2009)

CLUB RECORDS **Highest score:** 120-4 v Illingworth, 13/3/2005 **Highest score against:** 0-106 v Castleford, 9/9/2007 **Record attendance:** 26,664 v Oldham, 25/3/22
MATCH RECORDS **Tries:** 5 Jack Corsi v Barrow, 31/12/21; Jack Corsi v Broughton Moor, 25/2/22; Jack Williams v St Helens, 4/4/33; Norman Brelsford v Whitehaven, 3/9/73; Marlon Billy v York, 8/4/2001 **Goals:** 18 Lee Birdseye v Illingworth, 13/3/2005 **Points:** 44 Lee Birdseye v Illingworth, 13/3/2005
SEASON RECORDS **Tries:** 31 Marlon Billy 2001 **Goals:** 150 Martin Strett 1994-95 **Points:** 350 Mick Nanyn 2003
CAREER RECORDS **Tries:** 103 Jack Williams 1931-37 **Goals:** 741 Walter Gowers 1922-36 **Points:** 1,497 Walter Gowers 1922-36 **Appearances:** 456 Walter Gowers 1922-36

SOUTH WALES SCORPIONS

DATE	FIXTURE	RESULT	SCORERS	LGE	ATT
28/2/10	Workington (h)	W22-20	t:A James,Parry,Williams(2) g:White(3)	5th	565
14/3/10	Doncaster (a)	W8-18	t:Gay,Parry,D James g:A James(3)	2nd	296
21/3/10	York (a)	L25-24	t:Mills,Dudson,Richards,Parry g:White(4)	2nd	663
28/3/10	London Skolars (h)	W48-6	t:Parry,Wildbore,Flower,White(2),Roets,Phillips,Dudson g:White(7),Wildbore	1st	625
5/4/10	Hunslet (h)	L12-42	t:Roets,Parry g:Wildbore,White	5th	798
11/4/10	Oldham (h)	L16-22	t:Parry,Roets,Richards g:White(2)	4th	625
25/4/10	Swinton (a)	L20-14	t:Dudson,A James,Gay g:A James	5th	308
3/5/10	Blackpool (h)	L24-28	t:Richards(2),Parry,Murphy g:White(3),Wildbore	6th	623
8/5/10	Gateshead (a)	W8-50	t:Williams,Mills,Gay(2),Dallimore(2),Kear,Roets,Wildbore g:White(4),Murphy(3)	6th	258
23/5/10	London Skolars (a)	W22-70	t:Dudson(2),Bateman(2),White(2),Dallimore(2),Williams,Parry,Murphy,D James g:White(7),Wildbore(4)	5th	358
13/6/10	Swinton (h)	L12-16	t:Parry,A James g:Wildbore(2)	7th	890
20/6/10	Rochdale (h)	W30-25	t:Parry,Roets,Mills,Wildbore,Cunningham g:Wildbore(5)	7th	522
27/6/10	Workington (a)	L38-24	t:Wildbore,Parry,Gay,A James g:Wildbore(4)	8th	307
3/7/10	Blackpool (a)	L44-24	t:Bateman,Parry(2),Gay g:Wildbore(4)	8th	266
11/7/10	Gateshead (h)	W70-16	t:Kear(3),D James,Parry(3),Richards,Reece(2),Pope,Cunningham g:Reece(11)	7th	480
25/7/10	Rochdale (a)	L46-14	t:Williams,Murphy g:A James,White(2)	7th	471
1/8/10	Oldham (a)	W24-42	t:White(3),Parry,Gay,Bromilow g:White(7),Wildbore(2)	7th	908
8/8/10	Doncaster (h)	W22-8	t:Wildbore,Bateman,Mills,Williams g:White,Wildbore(2)	6th	492
15/8/10	York (h)	L16-18	t:Gay,Roach g:White(4)	6th	689
22/8/10	Hunslet (a)	L32-24	t:Kear,Parry,Gay,Mills g:A James(2),Murphy(2)	6th	785
5/9/10	Rochdale (a) (EPO)	L60-26	t:Parry,Murphy(2),Mills,A James g:A James(3)	N/A	375

		APP		TRIES		GOALS		FG		PTS	
	D.O.B.	ALL	Ch1	ALL	Ch1	ALL	Ch1	ALL	Ch1	ALL	Ch1
Ashley Bateman	11/2/90	21	21	4	4	0	0	0	0	16	16
Anthony Blackwood	13/9/82	1	1	0	0	0	0	0	0	0	0
Casey Bromilow	12/2/84	7(2)	7(2)	1	1	0	0	0	0	4	4
Joe Burke	18/5/90	2(9)	2(9)	0	0	0	0	0	0	0	0
Curtis Cunningham	16/12/86	2(4)	2(4)	2	2	0	0	0	0	8	8
Neil Dallimore	24/2/81	6(13)	6(13)	4	4	0	0	0	0	16	16
Geraint Davies	7/3/86	11(1)	11(1)	0	0	0	0	0	0	0	0
Gareth Dean	31/3/81	(1)	(1)	0	0	0	0	0	0	0	0
Gil Dudson	16/6/90	16	16	5	5	0	0	0	0	20	20
Ben Flower	19/10/87	3(1)	3(1)	1	1	0	0	0	0	4	4
Andrew Gay	5/10/89	21	21	9	9	0	0	0	0	36	36
Harri Greville	28/11/90	(8)	(8)	0	0	0	0	0	0	0	0
Matt Hutchings	18/10/80	(2)	(2)	0	0	0	0	0	0	0	0
Aled James	17/2/82	17	17	5	5	10	10	0	0	40	40
David James	1/9/85	8(2)	8(2)	3	3	0	0	0	0	12	12
Jordan James	24/5/80	2	2	0	0	0	0	0	0	0	0
Elliot Kear	29/11/88	13	13	5	5	0	0	0	0	20	20
Joe McLocklan	2/10/86	(5)	(5)	0	0	0	0	0	0	0	0
Lewis Mills	30/3/89	21	21	6	6	0	0	0	0	24	24
Jamie Murphy	29/12/89	13(3)	13(3)	5	5	5	5	0	0	30	30
Shaun Owens	29/11/88	3(2)	3(2)	0	0	0	0	0	0	0	0
Steve Parry	19/10/88	13(7)	13(7)	19	19	0	0	0	0	76	76
Barrie Phillips	27/5/86	8(11)	8(11)	1	1	0	0	0	0	4	4
Alan Pope	1/4/85	(2)	(2)	1	1	0	0	0	0	4	4
Lewis Reece	17/6/91	3	3	2	2	11	11	0	0	30	30
Craig Richards	10/10/78	15	15	5	5	0	0	0	0	20	20
Liam Roach	24/5/89	5(6)	5(6)	1	1	0	0	0	0	4	4
Christiaan Roets	5/9/80	19(1)	19(1)	5	5	0	0	0	0	20	20
Sam Studley	12/10/89	(1)	(1)	0	0	0	0	0	0	0	0
Jamie Thackray	30/9/79	(1)	(1)	0	0	0	0	0	0	0	0
Lloyd White	9/10/88	12(1)	12(1)	7	7	45	45	0	0	118	118
Loz Wildbore	23/9/84	16	16	5	5	26	26	0	0	72	72
Lee Williams	19/2/88	15(1)	15(1)	6	6	0	0	0	0	24	24

Steve Parry

LEAGUE RECORD
P20-W9-D0-L11-BP7
(6th, Championship 1/
Elimination Play-Off)
F576, A468, Diff+108
34 points.

CHALLENGE CUP
Not entered

NORTHERN RAIL CUP
Not entered

ATTENDANCES
Best - v Swinton (Ch1 - 890)
Worst - v Gateshead (Ch1 - 480)
Total (Championship 1 only) - 6,309
Average (Championship 1 only) - 631

CLUB RECORDS	**Highest score:** 70-22 v London Skolars, 23/5/2010; 70-16 v Gateshead, 11/7/2010 **Highest score against:** 60-26 v Rochdale, 5/9/2010 **Record attendance:** 890 v Swinton, 13/6/2010
MATCH RECORDS	**Tries:** 3 Elliot Kear v Gateshead, 11/7/2010; Steve Parry v Gateshead, 11/7/2010; Lloyd White v Oldham, 1/8/2010 **Goals:** 11 Lewis Reece v Gateshead, 11/7/2010 **Points:** 30 Lewis Reece v Gateshead, 11/7/2010
SEASON RECORDS	**Tries:** 19 Steve Parry 2010 **Goals:** 45 Lloyd White 2010 **Points:** 118 Lloyd White 2010
CAREER RECORDS	**Tries:** 19 Steve Parry 2010 **Goals:** 45 Lloyd White 2010 **Points:** 118 Lloyd White 2010 **Appearances:** 21 Ashley Bateman 2010; Andrew Gay 2010; Lewis Mills 2010

SWINTON LIONS

DATE	FIXTURE	RESULT	SCORERS	LGE	ATT
7/2/10	Doncaster (h) (NRC)	W30-20	t:P Smith,Isherwood,Foxen,Joseph,Holroyd g:Dodd(5)	5th(P1)	380
14/2/10	Batley (a) (NRC)	L46-10	t:P Smith,Foxen g:Holroyd	8th(P1)	507
17/2/10	Workington (a) (NRC)	W18-19	t:Hulse,Dodd,Sneyd g:Dodd(3) fg:Holroyd	4th(P1)	286
21/2/10	Widnes (h) (NRC)	L12-36	t:R Hawkyard,Dodd g:Dodd(2)	7th(P1)	816
28/2/10	Oldham (h)	L20-38	t:D Hull,Wingfield,Joseph,Grundy g:Dodd(2)	8th	627
5/3/10	Warrington Wizards (a) (CCR3) ●	W22-34	t:D Hull(2),Foxen(2),Wilson,Dodd g:Dodd(5)	N/A	430
14/3/10	London Skolars (a)	W16-52	t:Isherwood,R Hawkyard,Dodd(2),Wingfield,Reay(3),Foxen,Sneyd g:Dodd(6)	6th	276
21/3/10	Doncaster (h)	W36-30	t:Isherwood,R Hawkyard,Stewart,Reay,Wingfield,Wilson g:Dodd(6)	4th	323
28/3/10	Blackpool (a)	L54-6	t:Wilson g:Dodd	8th	385
11/4/10	Hunslet (a)	L46-12	t:P Smith,Isherwood g:Sneyd(2)	9th	546
16/4/10	Halifax (h) (CCR4) ▲	L4-56	t:Hamilton	N/A	633
25/4/10	South Wales (h)	W20-14	t:Holroyd,Wilson(2) g:Holroyd(4)	9th	308
3/5/10	York (a)	W30-36	t:R Hawkyard,Reay,P Smith(2),Stewart,Isherwood,Corcoran g:Holroyd(4)	7th	670
8/5/10	Rochdale (h)	L22-33	t:R Hawkyard,Wilson,Joseph,Foxen g:Holroyd(3)	7th	470
19/5/10	Batley (h) (CCR5)	L6-58	t:Joseph g:Holroyd	N/A	636
23/5/10	Doncaster (a)	L16-0		9th	430
30/5/10	London Skolars (h)	W56-28	t:Flooks,Foxen(3),D Hawkyard,Watson,Johnson,Isherwood,Cherryholme,Joseph g:Dodd(8)	8th	277
6/6/10	Gateshead (a)	W12-34	t:Wingfield,Wilson,Flooks,Heaton,Rigby,Foxen g:Flooks(5)	8th	353
13/6/10	South Wales (a)	W12-16	t:Wingfield,Dodd,Foxen g:Dodd(2)	6th	890
20/6/10	Workington (h)	D30-30	t:D Hawkyard,Joseph,Hulse,Watson,Dodd g:Dodd(5)	6th	287
27/6/10	Blackpool (h)	L6-28	t:Reay g:Dodd	7th	387
4/7/10	Hunslet (h)	L10-58	t:Foxen,Joseph g:Dodd	7th	386
11/7/10	Oldham (a)	L42-30	t:Foxen,Joseph(2),D Hawkyard,Burkinshaw g:Dodd(5)	8th	841
1/8/10	York (h)	L42-48	t:Cunniffe,Dodd(2),R Hawkyard,Hurst(2),Foxen,Joseph g:Dodd(5)	8th	431
8/8/10	Rochdale (a)	L24-16	t:Harvey(2),Dodd g:Dodd(2)	8th	502
15/8/10	Workington (a)	W22-32	t:R Hawkyard,Cunniffe,Mullally,Joseph,Foxen g:Dodd(6)	8th	501
22/8/10	Gateshead (h)	W94-0	t:Hurst(3),Cunniffe,Johnson,Wingfield,Harvey(2),Mullally,Joseph(4),Dodd(2),Foxen,D Hawkyard(2) g:Dodd(11)	8th	331

● Played at Wilderspool   ▲ *Swinton were reinstated into the Challenge Cup after Halifax were disqualified for fielding an illegible player*

		APP		TRIES		GOALS		FG		PTS	
	D.O.B.	ALL	Ch1	ALL	Ch1	ALL	Ch1	ALL	Ch1	ALL	Ch1
Andy Ainscough	24/4/90	1(7)	1(7)	0	0	0	0	0	0	0	0
Darren Bamford	8/8/86	2(1)	(1)	0	0	0	0	0	0	0	0
Simon Burkinshaw	27/2/85	6	6	1	1	0	0	0	0	4	4
Neil Cherryholme	20/12/86	8	8	1	1	0	0	0	0	4	4
Wayne Corcoran	10/7/85	1(2)	1(2)	1	1	0	0	0	0	4	4
Dale Cunniffe	25/3/87	5	5	3	3	0	0	0	0	12	12
Gavin Dodd	28/2/81	22	18	12	9	76	61	0	0	200	158
Joe Fitzpatrick	22/10/85	(4)	(4)	0	0	0	0	0	0	0	0
Richard Flooks	8/8/86	7	7	2	2	5	5	0	0	18	18
Rob Foxen	12/12/87	18(6)	13(4)	16	12	0	0	0	0	64	48
Mick Govin	5/11/84	3	2	0	0	0	0	0	0	0	0
Tommy Grundy	17/4/85	8(1)	4(1)	1	1	0	0	0	0	4	4
Barry Hamilton	25/2/86	9	5	1	0	0	0	0	0	4	0
Craig Harvey	12/3/88	5	5	4	4	0	0	0	0	16	16
Darren Hawkyard	14/10/84	10(1)	10(1)	5	5	0	0	0	0	20	20
Richie Hawkyard	21/1/86	19	15	7	6	0	0	0	0	28	24
Danny Heaton	19/4/81	6(3)	5(2)	1	1	0	0	0	0	4	4
Graham Holroyd	25/10/75	10(2)	6(1)	2	0	13	11	1	0	35	26
Chris Hull	4/12/86	11(5)	8(2)	0	0	0	0	0	0	0	0
Dave Hull	3/11/85	6	2	3	1	0	0	0	0	12	4
Gary Hulse	20/1/81	4(16)	2(13)	2	1	0	0	0	0	8	4
Alex Hurst	17/3/90	6	6	5	5	0	0	0	0	20	20
Andrew Isherwood	23/11/79	14(8)	11(4)	6	5	0	0	0	0	24	20
Bruce Johnson	26/1/84	4(7)	3(3)	2	2	0	0	0	0	8	8
Phil Joseph	10/1/85	19(1)	15(1)	15	13	0	0	0	0	60	52
Alex McClurg	28/8/89	3	3	0	0	0	0	0	0	0	0
Danny Meekin	16/3/89	3(6)	3(6)	0	0	0	0	0	0	0	0
Anthony Mullally	28/6/91	6	6	2	2	0	0	0	0	8	8
Saqib Murtza	18/11/85	1	1	0	0	0	0	0	0	0	0
Dave Newton	22/12/81	8(7)	5(6)	0	0	0	0	0	0	0	0
Sam Reay	23/5/84	20	14	6	6	0	0	0	0	24	24
Neil Rigby	5/2/86	13(5)	10(3)	1	1	0	0	0	0	4	4
Ian Sinfield	7/4/77	(1)	(1)	0	0	0	0	0	0	0	0
Aaron Smith	10/9/82	5(1)	1	0	0	0	0	0	0	0	0
Paul Smith	17/5/77	9(3)	3(2)	5	3	0	0	0	0	20	12
Carl Sneyd	11/4/87	7	4	2	1	2	2	0	0	12	8
Paul Southern	18/3/76	4	3	0	0	0	0	0	0	0	0
Anthony Stewart	5/3/79	15(1)	12	2	2	0	0	0	0	8	8
Chris Tyrer	10/10/85	1(2)	(1)	0	0	0	0	0	0	0	0
Ian Watson	27/10/76	26	19	2	2	0	0	0	0	8	8
Dana Wilson	22/5/83	12(11)	6(11)	7	6	0	0	0	0	28	24
Lee Wingfield	9/6/81	14(7)	12(4)	6	6	0	0	0	0	24	24

Phil Joseph

LEAGUE RECORD
P20-W9-D1-L10-BP4
(8th, Championship 1)
F570, A581, Diff-11
33 points.

CHALLENGE CUP
Round Five

NORTHERN RAIL CUP
8th, Pool 1

ATTENDANCES
Best - v Widnes (NRC - 816)
Worst - v London Skolars (Ch1 - 277)
Total (excluding Challenge Cup) - 5,023
Average (excluding Challenge Cup) - 419
(Down by 100 on 2009)

CLUB RECORDS MATCH RECORDS	Highest score: 94-0 v Gateshead, 22/8/2010 Highest score against: 10-106 v Leeds, 11/2/2001 Record attendance: 26,891 v Wigan, 12/2/64

Tries: 6 Mark Riley v Prescot, 11/8/96 **Goals:** 12 Ken Gowers v Liverpool City, 3/10/59
Points: 30 Greg Pearce v Prescot, 11/8/96; Mick Nanyn v York, 25/3/2001; Gavin Dodd v Gateshead, 22/8/2010

SEASON RECORDS
Tries: 42 John Stopford 1963-64 **Goals:** 128 Albert Blan 1960-61 **Points:** 310 Lee Marsh 2005
CAREER RECORDS
Tries: 197 Frank Evans 1921-31 **Goals:** 970 Ken Gowers 1954-73 **Points:** 2,105 Ken Gowers 1954-73 **Appearances:** 601 Ken Gowers 1954-73

WORKINGTON TOWN

DATE	FIXTURE	RESULT	SCORERS	LGE	ATT
7/2/10	Gateshead (a) (NRC)	W12-26	t:Pedley,Beattie,Backhouse(2),Marshall g:Kaighan(3)	4th(P1)	404
14/2/10	Keighley (a) (NRC)	L38-10	t:J Finch,Beattie g:Kaighan	7th(P1)	654
17/2/10	Swinton (h) (NRC)	L18-19	t:Low,Kaighan g:Kaighan(5)	8th(P1)	286
21/2/10	Whitehaven (h) (NRC)	W22-14	t:Kaighan(2),Frazer g:Kaighan(5)	5th(P1)	736
28/2/10	South Wales (a)	L22-20	t:Low,Frazer,Marshall,Beattie g:Kaighan(2)	6th	565
7/3/10	Featherstone (a) (CCR3)	L74-0		N/A	1,215
14/3/10	York (h)	W32-22	t:Kaighan,Stack,L Finch,King,Frazer g:Kaighan(6)	4th	466
21/3/10	Rochdale (a)	L32-24	t:Pedley,Backhouse(2),Beattie g:Kaighan(4)	6th	421
28/3/10	Gateshead (h)	W44-0	t:Low(2),Campbell,Marshall,Carter,Backhouse,Coward,Stack g:Kaighan(6)	2nd	413
5/4/10	Oldham (a) ●	L16-14	t:Kaighan,Whitehead,Frazer g:Kaighan	6th	658
11/4/10	Blackpool (h)	L12-32	t:Low,McGoff g:Kaighan(2)	8th	521
3/5/10	Hunslet (h)	L16-30	t:Low(2),Kaighan g:Kaighan(2)	9th	578
9/5/10	London Skolars (a)	W28-44	t:McDonald,Kaighan,Marshall(3),Robinson,Stack(2) g:Kaighan(6)	8th	372
16/5/10	Doncaster (h)	W34-20	t:Whitehead,Stack,McKenna,L Finch,Dutton,Frazer g:Kaighan,Holt(4)	7th	410
23/5/10	Gateshead (a)	W24-42	t:Backhouse(2),Low,Carter,Marshall,Kaighan(2),Beattie g:Holt(4),Kaighan	6th	286
30/5/10	Oldham (h)	L16-28	t:Beattie,Stack,Marshall g:Holt,Kaighan	7th	581
13/6/10	Blackpool (a)	L24-10	t:Carter(2) g:Kaighan	8th	248
20/6/10	Swinton (a)	D30-30	t:Holt,Kaighan,Stack(2),Pedley g:Holt(5)	8th	287
27/6/10	South Wales (h)	W38-24	t:Coward,Marshall,Kaighan,Carter,Low,Coupar g:Holt(7)	6th	307
11/7/10	London Skolars (h)	W38-34	t:Kaighan,Miller(2),Coupar,Low(2),Robinson g:Holt(5)	6th	411
25/7/10	York (a)	L18-14	t:Pedley,Stack g:Holt(3)	6th	612
1/8/10	Rochdale (h)	W18-12	t:Frazer,Pedley,Low g:Holt(3)	6th	434
5/8/10	Hunslet (a)	L24-14	t:Kaighan,Robinson g:Holt(3)	7th	537
15/8/10	Swinton (h)	L22-32	t:Beattie,Miller,Stack g:Holt(5)	7th	501
22/8/10	Doncaster (a)	L46-12	t:Coupar,Whitehead g:Holt(2)	7th	1,127
5/9/10	Blackpool (a) (EPO)	L36-26	t:Pedley,Stack(2),Miller g:Holt(4),Kaighan	N/A	308

● Played at Park Lane, Sedgley Park

		APP		TRIES		GOALS		FG		PTS	
	D.O.B.	ALL	Ch1	ALL	Ch1	ALL	Ch1	ALL	Ch1	ALL	Ch1
Mike Backhouse	14/6/82	23	18	7	5	0	0	0	0	28	20
Andrew Beattie	12/1/81	23	18	7	5	0	0	0	0	28	20
Dean Bragg	14/1/82	(2)	(1)	0	0	0	0	0	0	0	0
Scott Burgess	18/2/86	(3)	(1)	0	0	0	0	0	0	0	0
Jamie Butler	29/8/80	(4)	(4)	0	0	0	0	0	0	0	0
Ryan Campbell	23/9/81	4(4)	2(4)	1	1	0	0	0	0	4	4
Brett Carter	9/7/88	20	16	5	5	0	0	0	0	20	20
Paddy Coupar	26/6/86	23(2)	20	3	3	0	0	0	0	12	12
Kris Coward	1/10/81	24	20	2	2	0	0	0	0	8	8
Lee Dutton	3/11/80	11	9	1	1	0	0	0	0	4	4
James Finch	9/7/83	1(6)	(3)	1	0	0	0	0	0	4	0
Liam Finch	19/3/85	16	11	2	2	0	0	0	0	8	8
Neil Frazer	7/3/76	23	20	6	5	0	0	0	0	24	20
Phil Hewitt	10/12/78	6(1)	5(1)	0	0	0	0	0	0	0	0
Darren Holt	21/9/76	11(1)	11(1)	1	1	46	46	0	0	96	96
Matthew Johnson	18/3/82	(5)	(5)	0	0	0	0	0	0	0	0
Scott Kaighan	11/11/88	26	21	13	10	48	34	0	0	148	108
Darren King	9/3/82	3	3	1	1	0	0	0	0	4	4
John Lebbon	30/12/84	7(2)	5(2)	0	0	0	0	0	0	0	0
Aaron Low	5/5/88	26	21	12	11	0	0	0	0	48	44
Jamie Marshall	17/7/78	7(10)	6(7)	9	8	0	0	0	0	36	32
Keiron McAvoy	4/9/92	(1)	(1)	0	0	0	0	0	0	0	0
Ryan McDonald	24/2/78	3(10)	3(10)	1	1	0	0	0	0	4	4
Ruairi McGoff	5/1/85	8(5)	5(4)	1	1	0	0	0	0	4	4
Joe McKenna	21/8/87	2(12)	2(10)	1	1	0	0	0	0	4	4
Elliot Miller	14/9/90	4	4	4	4	0	0	0	0	16	16
Jason Mossop	12/9/85	2	2	0	0	0	0	0	0	0	0
Jack Pedley	9/11/89	10(6)	7(6)	6	5	0	0	0	0	24	20
Stewart Rhodes	16/1/72	5(5)	5(4)	0	0	0	0	0	0	0	0
James Robinson	4/3/79	(21)	(18)	3	3	0	0	0	0	12	12
Jarrad Stack	13/2/88	24	19	12	12	0	0	0	0	48	48
Mike Whitehead	25/8/78	25	20	3	3	0	0	0	0	12	12
Martyn Wilson	22/10/82	1(4)	(2)	0	0	0	0	0	0	0	0

Jarrad Stack

LEAGUE RECORD
P20-W8-D1-L11-BP7
(7th, Championship 1/
Elimination Play-Off)
F494, A498, Diff-4
33 points.

CHALLENGE CUP
Round Three

NORTHERN RAIL CUP
6th, Pool 1

ATTENDANCES
Best - v Whitehaven (NRC - 736)
Worst - v Swinton (NRC - 286)
Total (excluding Challenge Cup) - 5,644
Average (excluding Challenge Cup) - 470
(Down by 4 on 2009)

CLUB RECORDS
MATCH RECORDS — Highest score: 94-4 v Leigh, 26/2/95 Highest score against: 0-92 v Bradford, 14/2/99 Record attendance: 17,741 v Wigan, 3/3/65
Tries: 7 Ike Southward v Blackpool, 17/9/55 Goals: 13 Dean Marwood v Highfield, 1/11/92; Dean Marwood v Leigh, 26/2/95;
Wayne Kitchin v Thatto Heath, 26/1/97; Carl Forber v Blackpool Panthers, 15/7/2007
Points: 42 Dean Marwood v Highfield, 1/11/92; Dean Marwood v Leigh, 26/2/95

SEASON RECORDS — Tries: 49 Johnny Lawrenson 1951-52 Goals: 186 Lyn Hopkins 1981-82 Points: 438 Lyn Hopkins 1981-82
CAREER RECORDS — Tries: 274 Ike Southward 1952-59; 1960-68 Goals: 809 Iain MacCorquodale 1972-80 Points: 1,800 Iain MacCorquodale 1972-80
Appearances: 419 Paul Charlton 1961-69; 1975-80

YORK CITY KNIGHTS

DATE	FIXTURE	RESULT	SCORERS	LGE	ATT
7/2/10	Leigh (h) (NRC)	W13-12	t:Mitchell(2) g:Waterman(2) fg:Thorman	5th(P2)	911
14/2/10	Sheffield (a) (NRC) ●	L40-10	t:Reittie,Waterman g:Waterman	7th(P2)	814
17/2/10	Rochdale (a) (NRC)	W12-36	t:Waterman(3),Schofield,Waller(2),Clough g:Waterman(4)	5th(P2)	362
28/2/10	London Skolars (h)	W36-8	t:Waller,Waterman(2),Ratcliffe,Stamp,Schofield g:Waterman(6)	3rd	811
7/3/10	Gateshead (a) (CCR3)	W12-44	t:Bromilow(2),Waterman(2),McLocklan,Reittie,Hill,Blakeway g:Waterman(6)	N/A	336
10/3/10	London Skolars (h) (NRC)	W34-12	t:Schofield,Bromilow(2),Applegarth,Duckworth,Waterman g:Waterman(5)	3rd(P2)	439
14/3/10	Workington (a)	L32-22	t:Ratcliffe,Waterman(2),McLocklan g:Waterman(3)	3rd	466
21/3/10	South Wales (h)	W25-24	t:McLocklan,Waller,Ratcliffe,Bromilow g:Waterman(4) fg:Thorman	1st	663
28/3/10	Doncaster (a)	L40-24	t:McLocklan,Waterman,Wilson(2),Ratcliffe g:Waterman(2)	3rd	532
2/4/10	Gateshead (h)	W72-14	t:Schofield(3),McLocklan,Ratcliffe(3),Hill,Tuffour,Blakeway,Lineham,Peacock g:Waterman(12)	1st	686
5/4/10	Blackpool (a)	L27-14	t:Tuffour(2),McLocklan g:Waterman	4th	405
18/4/10	Crusaders (h) (CCR4)	L8-58	t:Schofield,Tuffour	N/A	719
25/4/10	Rochdale (h)	W36-34	t:Lineham,Wilson,Lee,Peacock,Blakeway,Hardbottle g:Waterman(6)	4th	987
3/5/10	Swinton (h)	L30-36	t:Stearman,Wilson,Waller,Ratcliffe g:Waterman(7)	5th	670
9/5/10	Oldham (a)	W28-34	t:Ratcliffe,Tuffour(2),Lewis,Waterman,Lineham g:Waterman(5)	5th	1,110
16/5/10	Hunslet (h)	L10-46	t:Waterman,Stamp g:Waterman	5th	1,002
23/5/10	Rochdale (a)	L44-34	t:Waterman(2),Lee,Waller(2),Tuffour g:Waterman(4),McLocklan	7th	472
30/5/10	Blackpool (h)	W24-22	t:Mitchell,Waterman,Lee,Lineham g:Waterman(4)	5th	535
6/6/10	Keighley (a) (NRCQF)	L32-6	t:Duckworth g:Waterman	N/A	712
12/6/10	London Skolars (a) ●●	W12-44	t:Waterman,Tuffour(2),Lee(2),Ratcliffe(2),Wilson g:Waterman(6)	5th	1,350
26/6/10	Gateshead (a)	W12-60	t:Lineham(2),Lee(2),Waterman(3),Stearman,Ratcliffe,Duckworth,Wilson g:Waterman(8)	5th	346
4/7/10	Doncaster (h)	W32-16	t:Waterman,Lineham(3),Lee,Wilson,Mitchell g:Ratcliffe(2)	4th	735
11/7/10	Hunslet (a)	L34-18	t:Thorman,Lee,Hardbottle g:Ratcliffe(3)	4th	537
25/7/10	Workington (h)	W18-14	t:Mitchell,Lewis,Lee g:Ratcliffe(3)	4th	612
1/8/10	Swinton (a)	W42-48	t:Thorman,Duckworth,Esders(3),Lee,Allan,Lineham(2) g:Ratcliffe(6)	3rd	431
8/8/10	Oldham (h)	L18-33	t:Reittie(2),Stearman g:Ratcliffe(3)	4th	770
15/8/10	South Wales (h)	W16-18	t:Duckworth,Thorman,Lee g:Waterman,Ratcliffe(2)	3rd	689
12/9/10	Oldham (a) (QSF)	L41-32	t:Bell,Esders(2),Waterman(2),Thorman g:Waterman(4)	N/A	1,275
19/9/10	Blackpool (h) (FE)	W38-18	t:Waterman,Benson,Ratcliffe(2),Wilson,Thorman g:Waterman(7)	N/A	673
26/9/10	Oldham (GF) ●●●	W4-25	t:Reittie,Haynes,Thorman,Lewis g:Waterman(2),Thorman(2) fg:Thorman	N/A	N/A

● Played at Don Valley Stadium   ●● Played at Twickenham Stoop   ●●● Played at Halliwell Jones Stadium, Warrington

		APP		TRIES		GOALS		FG		PTS	
	D.O.B.	ALL	Ch1	ALL	Ch1	ALL	Ch1	ALL	Ch1	ALL	Ch1
Danny Allan	9/4/89	5	4	1	1	0	0	0	0	4	4
Mark Applegarth	10/12/84	10(3)	7(2)	1	0	0	0	0	0	4	0
Carl Barrow	29/6/81	(4)	0	0	0	0	0	0	0	0	0
Ian Bell	28/1/83	1	1	1	1	0	0	0	0	4	4
Alex Benson	22/5/85	14(6)	10(5)	1	1	0	0	0	0	4	4
Richard Blakeway	22/7/83	14(1)	9(1)	3	2	0	0	0	0	12	8
Casey Bromilow	12/2/84	8(3)	4(3)	5	1	0	0	0	0	20	4
Davey Burns	22/6/86	1	1	0	0	0	0	0	0	0	0
Chris Clough	20/1/87	1(12)	(9)	1	0	0	0	0	0	4	0
Jy-Mel Coleman	13/10/88	(1)	(1)	0	0	0	0	0	0	0	0
John Davies	8/1/91	(1)	(1)	0	0	0	0	0	0	0	0
Callum Dinsdale	8/8/83	2(4)	2(4)	0	0	0	0	0	0	0	0
Matty Duckworth	26/7/89	13(2)	11(2)	5	3	0	0	0	0	20	12
Mike Embleton	17/10/81	1	0	0	0	0	0	0	0	0	0
Ryan Esders	20/10/86	5(1)	5(1)	5	5	0	0	0	0	20	20
Mark Falkingham	27/6/87	(2)	(1)	0	0	0	0	0	0	0	0
Jon Fallon	11/5/87	10(2)	7(2)	0	0	0	0	0	0	0	0
Nathan Freer	21/5/89	22(3)	19(2)	0	0	0	0	0	0	0	0
Luke Hardbottle	17/9/88	14(7)	13(5)	2	2	0	0	0	0	8	8
James Haynes	22/3/89	5(1)	5(1)	1	1	0	0	0	0	4	4
Luke Helliwell	1/3/88	(1)	0	0	0	0	0	0	0	0	0
Danny Hill	31/10/84	7(1)	3	2	1	0	0	0	0	8	4
Jack Lee	1/11/88	18	17	12	12	0	0	0	0	48	48
Steve Lewis	22/10/86	9(8)	6(8)	3	3	0	0	0	0	12	12
Tom Lineham	21/9/91	18	15	11	11	0	0	0	0	44	44
Joe McLocklan	2/10/86	16(1)	11	6	5	1	1	0	0	26	22
Mike Mitchell	7/4/85	19(1)	13(1)	5	3	0	0	0	0	20	12
Ben Parkinson	26/10/89	(1)	(1)	0	0	0	0	0	0	0	0
Kris Peacock	11/2/87	4(1)	3	2	2	0	0	0	0	8	8
Danny Ratcliffe	14/3/87	29	23	14	14	19	19	0	0	94	94
Wayne Reittie	21/1/88	16	12	5	3	0	0	0	0	20	12
Jordan Ross	25/10/84	25(2)	20(1)	0	0	0	0	0	0	0	0
Jonathan Schofield	17/4/90	6	3	7	4	0	0	0	0	28	16
Ed Smith	12/11/92	(2)	(2)	0	0	0	0	0	0	0	0
Paul Stamp	25/1/89	11(8)	9(5)	2	2	0	0	0	0	8	8
Tom Stancliffe	26/9/90	1	0	0	0	0	0	0	0	0	0
Jack Stearman	30/1/88	2(16)	1(16)	3	3	0	0	0	0	12	12
Chris Thorman	26/9/80	20	14	6	6	2	2	3	2	31	30
Dennis Tuffour	17/2/89	11	9	9	8	0	0	0	0	36	32
Brett Waller	3/7/87	(16)	(11)	7	5	0	0	0	0	28	20
Lee Waterman	13/4/87	26(1)	19(1)	25	18	102	83	0	0	304	238
Chris Williams	28/6/90	3(6)	2(5)	0	0	0	0	0	0	0	0
Danny Wilson	3/6/82	22	19	8	8	0	0	0	0	32	32
Scott Woods	10/12/90	2(1)	2(1)	0	0	0	0	0	0	0	0

Lee Waterman

LEAGUE RECORD
P20-W12-D0-L8-BP3
(3rd, Championship 1/
Grand Final Winners)
F617, A534, Diff+83
39 points.

CHALLENGE CUP
Round Four

NORTHERN RAIL CUP
Quarter Finalists/3rd, Pool 2

ATTENDANCES
Best - v Hunslet (Ch1 - 1,002)
Worst - v London Skolars (NRC - 439)
Total (excluding Challenge Cup) - 9,494
Average (excluding Challenge Cup) - 730
(Down by 366 on 2009)

CLUB RECORDS	Highest score: 84-0 v Nottingham City, 4/10/92 Highest score against: 0-98 v Rochdale, 8/4/2001 Record attendance: 14,689 v Swinton, 10/2/34
MATCH RECORDS	Tries: 7 Brad Davis v Highfield, 17/9/95 Goals: 13 Jamie Benn v Oldham, 29/8/99 Points: 30 Jamie Benn v Oldham, 29/8/99
SEASON RECORDS	Tries: 35 John Crossley 1980-81 Goals: 178 (inc 4 fg) Danny Brough 2004 Points: 412 Danny Brough 2004
CAREER RECORDS	Tries: 167 Peter Foster 1955-67 Goals: 1,060 Vic Yorke 1954-67 Points: 2,159 Vic Yorke 1954-67 Appearances: 449 Willie Hargreaves 1952-65

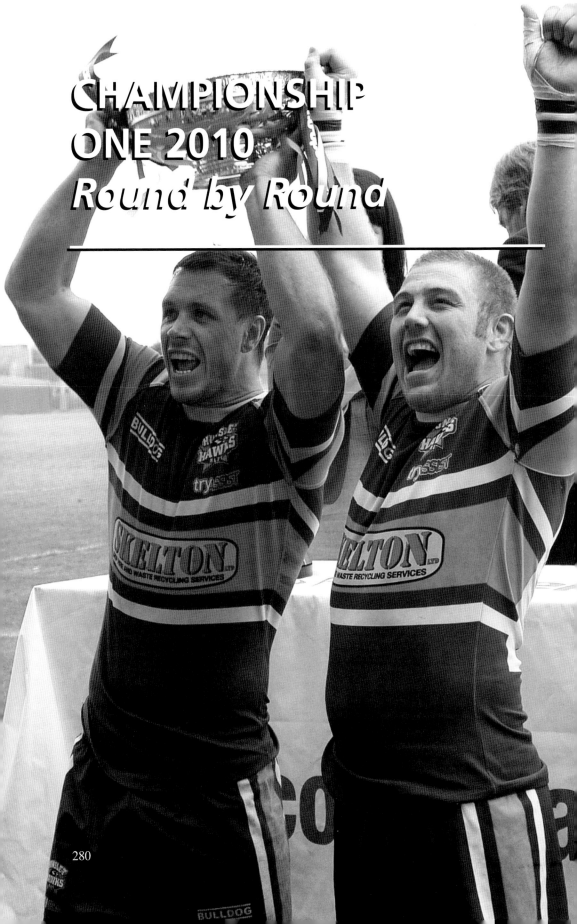

CHAMPIONSHIP ONE 2010
Round by Round

ROUND 1

Sunday 28th February 2010

**SOUTH WALES SCORPIONS 22
WORKINGTON TOWN 20**

SCORPIONS: 15 Andrew Gay; 1 Craig Richards; 32 Anthony Blackwood; 3 Lee Williams; 5 Ashley Bateman; 33 Lloyd White; 6 Loz Wildbore; 35 Jordan James; 9 Shaun Owens; 10 Gil Dudson; 22 Ben Flower; 8 Lewis Mills; 13 Aled James. Subs (all used): 7 Steve Parry; 11 Christiaan Roets; 12 Neil Dallimore; 17 Barrie Phillips.
Tries: A James (3), Parry (28), Williams (35, 47);
Goals: White 3/6.
TOWN: 5 Brett Carter; 2 Mike Backhouse; 3 Andrew Beattie; 15 Aaron Low; 17 Neil Frazer; 6 Liam Finch; 7 Scott Kaighan; 31 Ruairi McGoff; 9 Jack Pedley; 8 Lee Dutton; 11 Mike Whitehead; 12 Jarrad Stack; 21 Paddy Coupar. Subs (all used): 14 Jamie Marshall; 24 Dean Bragg; 4 James Finch; 20 James Robinson.
Tries: Low (50), Frazer (54), Marshall (60), Beattie (65);
Goals: Kaighan 2/4.
Rugby Leaguer & League Express Men of the Match:
Scorpions: Steve Parry; *Town:* Brett Carter.
Penalty count: 10-11; **Half-time:** 16-0;
Referee: Warren Turley; **Attendance:** 565.

ROCHDALE HORNETS 56 DONCASTER 24

HORNETS: 32 Wayne English; 1 Craig Johnson; 3 Dean Gorton; 22 Damien Reid; 5 Bolu Fagborun; 29 Ryan Powell; 7 Steve Roper; 17 Michael Ostick; 9 Phil Wood; 8 Paul Raftrey; 16 Danny Samuel; 13 Craig Ashall; 15 Dayne Donoghue. Subs (all used): 28 Chris Hough; 23 Wayne Corcoran; 12 Danny Smith; 10 Gareth Hayes.
Tries: Samuel (6), Donoghue (17, 20), English (24), Johnson (31), Fagborun (35), Wood (51), Raftrey (60), Gorton (63, 67), Roper (74); **Goals:** Roper 6/11.
DONCASTER: 1 Tommy Griffiths; 17 Jarryn Osborne; 2 Aaron Henry; 3 Lee Gomersall; 5 Ben Collins; 13 Grant Edwards; 7 Craig Fawcett; 10 David Bates; 20 Jack Ely; 24 Jamie Bovill; 32 Nathan Anderson; 11 Liam Brown; 12 Ryan Steen. Subs (all used): 9 Paul Brown; 4 Shaun Leaf; 8 Scott Johnson; 16 Paul Shaw.
Tries: Edwards (38, 47), Ely (44, 80);
Goals: Edwards 3/3, Steen 1/1.
Sin bin: Gomersall (23) – holding down.
Rugby Leaguer & League Express Men of the Match:
Hornets: Dayne Donoghue; *Doncaster:* Grant Edwards.
Penalty count: 8-17; **Half-time:** 30-6;
Referee: Matthew Thomasson; **Attendance:** 412.

SWINTON LIONS 20 OLDHAM 38

LIONS: 24 Gavin Dodd; 23 Rob Foxen; 3 Sam Reay; 27 Anthony Stewart; 5 Dave Hull; 7 Ian Watson; 20 Chris Hull; 17 Andrew Isherwood; 13 Aaron Smith; 26 Dave Newton; 11 Tommy Grundy; 12 Paul Smith; 19 Neil Rigby. Subs (all used): 14 Gary Hulse; 10 Danny Heaton; 15 Lee Wingfield; 9 Phil Joseph.
Tries: D Hull (15), Wingfield (35), Joseph (37), Grundy (44); **Goals:** Dodd 2/4.
Dismissal: Watson (80) - fighting.
Sin bin: Isherwood (74) - dissent.
OLDHAM: 1 Paul O'Connor; 2 Lucas Onyango; 24 Marcus St Hilaire; 4 Mick Fogerty; 20 Mark Brocklehurst; 6 Neil Roden; 7 Matt Ashe; 8 Jason Boults; 9 Martin Roden; 16 Wayne Kerr; 19 Ben Heaton; 13 Joe Chandler; 21 Valu Bentley. Subs (all used): 10 Dave Ellison; 15 Craig Robinson; 11 Saqib Murtza; 17 Danny Whitmore.
Tries: O'Connor (11), Onyango (20, 32, 51), M Roden (54), Kerr (70), Chandler (74); **Goals:** Ashe 5/9.
Dismissal: Kerr (80) - fighting.
Rugby Leaguer & League Express Men of the Match:
Lions: Gary Hulse; *Oldham:* Neil Roden.
Penalty count: 12-11; **Half-time:** 14-16;
Referee: Craig Halloran; **Attendance:** 627.

YORK CITY KNIGHTS 36 LONDON SKOLARS 8

CITY KNIGHTS: 1 Danny Ratcliffe; 2 Wayne Reittie; 3 Mike Mitchell; 4 Lee Waterman; 28 Danny Wilson; 6 Chris Thorman; 7 Jonathan Schofield; 17 Nathan Freer; 9 Joe McLocklan; 10 Alex Benson; 11 Jordan Ross; 15 Luke Hardbottle; 13 Richard Blakeway. Subs (all used): 8 Mark Applegarth; 12 Chris Clough; 32 Paul Stamp; 25 Brett Waller.
Tries: Waller (29), Waterman (35, 80), Ratcliffe (38), Stamp (60), Schofield (64); **Goals:** Waterman 6/6.
SKOLARS: 22 Curtis Cunningham; 31 Ade Adebisi; 4 Jason Cook; 14 Luke May; 23 Olu Iwenofu; 6 Jermaine Coleman; 7 Paul Thorman; 18 James Simon; 9 Gareth Honor; 20 Dave Williams; 11 Oliver Purslow; 3 Matt Thomas; 17 Chad Isles. Subs (all used): 8 Liam Roach; 12 Matt Carter; 1 Josh Welsh; 13 Stephen Ball.
Tries: Cook (2), M Thomas (46); **Goals:** P Thorman 0/2.
Rugby Leaguer & League Express Men of the Match:
City Knights: Lee Waterman; *Skolars:* Matt Carter.
Penalty count: 12-7; **Half-time:** 18-4;
Referee: Tim Roby; **Attendance:** 811.

HUNSLET HAWKS 40 GATESHEAD THUNDER 12

HAWKS: 29 Stuart Kain; 2 Michael Mark; 21 Wayne McHugh; 4 David Clayton; 5 John Oakes; 6 Danny Grimshaw; 7 Paul March; 15 Adam Sullivan; 9 Richard Chapman; 3 James Houston; 11 Rob Kelly; 12 Steve Dooler; 13 David March. Subs (all used): 8 Scott Woodcock; 33 Tom Haughey; 16 Neil Lowe; 18 Charlie Wabo.
Tries: McHugh (24), Kain (26, 45), Dooler (38), D March (55), P March (73), Mark (76); **Goals:** McHugh 6/7.
THUNDER: 28 Jason Elliott; 2 Robin Peers; 1 Kevin Neighbour; 4 Michael Brown; 5 Joe Brown; 6 Liam Duffy; 14 Will Bate; 17 Chris Parker; 9 Ryan Clarke; 10 Tabua Cakacaka; 30 Richie Humphries; 3 Tom Wilson; 32 Ade Aderiye. Subs (all used): 18 Stephen Welton; 26 David Cash; 33 Reece Young; 13 Matt Barron.
Tries: Duffy (47), J Brown (67); **Goals:** Ryan Clarke 2/2.
Rugby Leaguer & League Express Men of the Match:
Hawks: Stuart Kain; *Thunder:* Liam Duffy.
Penalty count: 10-7; **Half-time:** 16-0;
Referee: Clint Sharrad; **Attendance:** 481.

ROUND 2

Friday 12th March 2010

BLACKPOOL PANTHERS 36 ROCHDALE HORNETS 14

PANTHERS: 1 Jonny Leather; 24 Paul Ballard; 3 Casey Mayberry; 22 Dave Llewellyn; 5 Tom Woodcock; 6 Carl Forber; 7 Tom Hemingway; 17 Kris Ratcliffe; 14 Martin Keavney; 10 Andy Hobson; 32 Chris Tuson; 12 Paul Alcock; 11 Kurt Haggerty. Subs (all used): 9 John Clough; 15 Paul Anderson; 4 Mark McCully; 34 Neil Holland.
Tries: Keavney (9), Holland (24), Clough (28), Ballard (50, 53), Mayberry (55), Alcock (76);
Goals: Hemingway 4/7.
HORNETS: 32 Wayne English; 5 Bolu Fagborun; 3 Dean Gorton; 22 Damien Reid; 2 Andy Saywell; 29 Ryan Powell; 7 Steve Roper; 8 Paul Raftrey; 9 Phil Wood; 17 Michael Ostick; 4 Adam Bowman; 16 Danny Samuel; 15 Dayne Donoghue. Subs (all used): 10 Gareth Hayes; 23 Wayne Corcoran; 11 Mark Hobson; 18 John Cookson.
Tries: Fagborun (18), Corcoran (45), Donoghue (70);
Goals: Roper 1/2, Corcoran 0/1.
Sin bin: Roper (61) - holding down.
Rugby Leaguer & League Express Men of the Match:
Panthers: Carl Forber; *Hornets:* Dayne Donoghue.
Penalty count: 9-8; **Half-time:** 18-4;
Referee: Peter Brooke; **Attendance:** 352.

HUNSLET HAWKS 16 OLDHAM 29

HAWKS: 29 Stuart Kain; 26 Waine Pryce; 21 Wayne McHugh; 4 David Clayton; 5 John Oakes; 6 Danny Grimshaw; 7 Paul March; 15 Adam Sullivan; 19 Darren Robinson; 3 James Houston; 12 Steve Dooler; 33 Tom Haughey; 13 David March. Subs (all used): 8 Scott Woodcock; 11 Rob Kelly; 16 Neil Lowe; 30 Richard Knight.
Tries: McHugh (6), Clayton (30), Oakes (50);
Goals: McHugh 2/3.
Dismissal: Robinson (79) - dissent.
OLDHAM: 1 Paul O'Connor; 2 Lucas Onyango; 24 Marcus St Hilaire; 4 Mick Fogerty; 22 Paul Reilly; 6 Neil Roden; 7 Matt Ashe; 8 Jason Boults; 9 Martin Roden; 16 Wayne Kerr; 19 Ben Heaton; 13 Joe Chandler; 21 Valu Bentley. Subs (all used): 25 Scott Mansfield; 10 Dave Ellison; 27 Jamie I'Anson; 15 Craig Robinson.
Tries: Ashe (10, 54), Chandler (20), Reilly (26), Onyango (58); **Goals:** Ashe 4/6; **Field goal:** N Roden (77).
Sin bin: M Roden (34) - interference;
Fogerty (45) - interference.
Rugby Leaguer & League Express Men of the Match:
Hawks: Wayne McHugh; *Oldham:* Matt Ashe.
Penalty count: 11-11; **Half-time:** 10-16;
Referee: Chris Leatherbarrow; **Attendance:** 521.

Sunday 14th March 2010

DONCASTER 8 SOUTH WALES SCORPIONS 18

DONCASTER: 1 Tommy Griffiths; 22 Scott Wilson; 3 Lee Gomersall; 4 Shaun Leaf; 26 Gary King; 6 Simon Brown; 32 Kyle Kesik; 24 Jamie Bovill; 20 Jack Ely; 10 David Bates; 23 Craig Lawton; 12 Ryan Steen; 34 Danny Allan. Subs (all used): 9 Paul Brown; 8 Scott Johnson; 21 Scott Howlett; 19 Gary Ellery.
Tries: Gomersall (27), Wilson (71); **Goals:** S Brown 0/2.
SCORPIONS: 2 David James; 1 Craig Richards; 11 Christiaan Roets; 3 Lee Williams; 5 Ashley Bateman; 6 Loz Wildbore; 15 Andrew Gay; 35 Jordan James; 9 Shaun Owens; 10 Gil Dudson; 8 Lewis Mills; 22 Ben Flower; 13 Aled James. Subs (all used): 7 Steve Parry; 17 Barrie Phillips; 29 Harri Greville; 14 Jamie Murphy.
Tries: Gay (10), Parry (48), D James (51);
Goals: A James 3/4.
Rugby Leaguer & League Express Men of the Match:
Doncaster: Jamie Bovill; *Scorpions:* Andrew Gay.
Penalty count: 8-6; **Half-time:** 4-8;
Referee: Dave Merrick; **Attendance:** 296.

LONDON SKOLARS 16 SWINTON LIONS 52

SKOLARS: 22 Curtis Cunningham; 33 Jaroslaw Obuchowski; 2 Dave Arnot; 14 Luke May; 23 Olu Iwenofu; 9 Gareth Honor; 7 Paul Thorman; 10 Tony Williams; 1 Josh Welsh; 20 Dave Williams; 3 Matt Thomas; 12 Matt Carter; 11 Oliver Purslow. Subs (all used): 37 Nathan McLoughlin; 18 James Simon; 8 Liam Roach; 19 Liam Prescott.
Tries: Obuchowski (15), Roach (46), Welsh (49);
Goals: P Thorman 2/3.
LIONS: 24 Gavin Dodd; 3 Sam Reay; 27 Anthony Stewart; 4 Carl Sneyd; 23 Rob Foxen; 6 Graham Holroyd; 1 Richie Hawkyard; 16 Dana Wilson; 22 Alex McClurg; 26 Dave Newton; 17 Andrew Isherwood; 15 Lee Wingfield; 19 Neil Rigby. Subs (all used): 14 Gary Hulse; 21 Chris Tyrer; 20 Chris Hull; 2 Darren Bamford.
Tries: Isherwood (5), R Hawkyard (10), Dodd (13, 42), Wingfield (19), Reay (26, 38, 77), Foxen (33), Sneyd (66); **Goals:** Dodd 6/10.
Rugby Leaguer & League Express Men of the Match:
Skolars: Oliver Purslow; *Lions:* Lee Wingfield.
Penalty count: 6-8; **Half-time:** 4-36;
Referee: Greg Dolan; **Attendance:** 276.

WORKINGTON TOWN 32 YORK CITY KNIGHTS 22

TOWN: 5 Brett Carter; 2 Mike Backhouse; 3 Andrew Beattie; 15 Aaron Low; 17 Neil Frazer; 6 Liam Finch; 7 Scott Kaighan; 8 Lee Dutton; 13 Darren King; 10 Kris Coward; 11 Mike Whitehead; 12 Jarrad Stack; 21 Paddy Coupar. Subs (all used): 14 Jamie Marshall; 19 Joe McKenna; 4 James Finch; 31 Ruairi McGoff.
Tries: Kaighan (13), Stack (16), L Finch (21), King (29), Frazer (34); **Goals:** Kaighan 6/8.
CITY KNIGHTS: 1 Danny Ratcliffe; 2 Wayne Reittie; 3 Mike Mitchell; 4 Lee Waterman; 26 Steve Lewis; 6 Chris Thorman; 27 Casey Bromilow; 36 Jon Fallon; 9 Joe McLocklan; 10 Alex Benson; 11 Jordan Ross; 35 Danny Hill; 13 Richard Blakeway. Subs (all used): 32 Paul Stamp; 8 Mark Applegarth; 25 Brett Waller; 17 Nathan Freer.
Tries: Ratcliffe (38), Waterman (43, 48), McLocklan (57); **Goals:** Waterman 3/4.
Sin bin: Waller (79) – dissent.
Rugby Leaguer & League Express Men of the Match:
Town: Neil Frazer; *City Knights:* Brett Waller.
Penalty count: 10-9; **Half-time:** 30-6;
Referee: Matthew Kidd; **Attendance:** 466.

ROUND 3

Sunday 21st March 2010

GATESHEAD THUNDER 24 LONDON SKOLARS 18

THUNDER: 1 Kevin Neighbour; 5 Joe Brown; 3 Tom Wilson; 31 Matt Garside; 29 Jimmy Atkinson; 6 Liam Duffy; 9 Ryan Clarke; 17 Chris Parker; 14 Will Bate; 18 Stephen Welton; 30 Richie Humphries; 32 Ade Aderiye; 13 Matt Barron. Subs (all used): 33 Reece Young; 10 Tabua Cakacaka; 24 Mark Walker; 34 Josh Stoker.
Tries: Atkinson (3, 45, 78), Neighbour (19), Wilson (70);
Goals: Ryan Clarke 1/2, Neighbour 1/3.
SKOLARS: 22 Curtis Cunningham; 31 Ade Adebisi; 17 Chad Isles; 14 Luke May; 23 Olu Iwenofu; 9 Gareth Honor; 7 Paul Thorman; 10 Tony Williams; 19 Liam Prescott; 8 Liam Roach; 3 Matt Thomas; 13 Stephen Ball; 11 Oliver Purslow. Subs (all used): 12 Matt Carter; 5 Austen Aggrey; 2 Dave Arnot; 18 James Simon.
Tries: Cunningham (5), Isles (50), M Thomas (59);
Goals: P Thorman 3/5.
Rugby Leaguer & League Express Men of the Match:
Thunder: Jimmy Atkinson; *Skolars:* Gareth Honor.
Penalty count: 7-6; **Half-time:** 10-6;
Referee: Chris Leatherbarrow; **Attendance:** 356.

ROCHDALE HORNETS 32 WORKINGTON TOWN 24

HORNETS: 32 Wayne English; 1 Craig Johnson; 3 Dean Gorton; 22 Damien Reid; 5 Bolu Fagborun; 33 Liam McGovern; 7 Steve Roper; 10 Gareth Hayes; 9 Phil Wood; 8 Paul Raftrey; 16 Danny Samuel; 13 Craig Ashall; 15 Dayne Donoghue. Subs (all used): 17 Michael Ostick; 18 John Cookson; 29 Ryan Powell; 12 Danny Smith.
Tries: Donoghue (4), Johnson (11), McGovern (18), Gorton (37), Wood (45); **Goals:** McGovern 6/6.
TOWN: 1 John Lebbon; 17 Neil Frazer; 15 Aaron Low; 3 Andrew Beattie; 2 Mike Backhouse; 6 Liam Finch; 7 Scott Kaighan; 8 Lee Dutton; 13 Darren King; 10 Kris Coward; 11 Mike Whitehead; 12 Jarrad Stack; 21 Paddy Coupar. Subs (all used): 9 Jack Pedley; 20 James Robinson; 31 Ruairi McGoff; 32 Jamie Butler.
Tries: Pedley (27), Backhouse (52, 65), Beattie (77);
Goals: Kaighan 4/4.
Rugby Leaguer & League Express Men of the Match:
Hornets: Liam McGovern; *Town:* Kris Coward.
Penalty count: 7-5; **Half-time:** 24-6;
Referee: Craig Halloran; **Attendance:** 421.

SWINTON LIONS 36 DONCASTER 30

LIONS: 24 Gavin Dodd; 3 Sam Reay; 27 Anthony Stewart; 4 Carl Sneyd; 5 Dave Hull; 1 Richie Hawkyard; 7 Ian Watson; 16 Dana Wilson; 22 Alex McClurg; 26 Dave Newton; 17 Andrew Isherwood; 19 Neil Rigby; 9 Phil Joseph. Subs (all used): 15 Lee Wingfield; 11 Tommy Grundy; 14 Gary Hulse; 6 Graham Holroyd.
Tries: Isherwood (12), R Hawkyard (35), Stewart (46), Reay (50), Wingfield (52), Wilson (66); **Goals:** Dodd 6/6.
DONCASTER: 1 Tommy Griffiths; 22 Scott Wilson; 3 Lee Gomersall; 4 Shaun Leaf; 31 Nick Cooper; 32 Danny Allan; 6 Simon Brown; 10 David Bates; 32 Kyle Kesik; 24 Jamie Bovill; 23 Craig Lawton; 12 Ryan Steen; 20 Jack Ely. Subs (all used): 5 Ben Collins; 19 Gary Ellery; 16 Paul Shaw; 11 Liam Brown.
Tries: Shaw (24), Allan (26), Griffiths (56), Cooper (60), Gomersall (73, 78); **Goals:** S Brown 3/6.
Rugby Leaguer & League Express Men of the Match:
Lions: Phil Joseph; *Doncaster:* Tommy Griffiths.
Penalty count: 13-7; **Half-time:** 12-12;
Referee: Clint Sharrad; **Attendance:** 323.

**YORK CITY KNIGHTS 25
SOUTH WALES SCORPIONS 24**

CITY KNIGHTS: 1 Danny Ratcliffe; 2 Wayne Reittie; 26 Steve Lewis; 4 Lee Waterman; 5 Tom Lineham; 6 Chris Thorman; 27 Casey Bromilow; 8 Mark Applegarth; 32 Paul Stamp; 17 Nathan Freer; 11 Jordan Ross; 35 Danny Hill; 9 Joe McLocklan. Subs (all used): 13 Richard Blakeway; 15 Luke Hardbottle; 25 Brett Waller; 36 Jon Fallon.
Tries: McLocklan (16), Waller (28), Ratcliffe (52), Bromilow (67); **Goals:** Waterman 4/4;
Field goal: Thorman (79).
Sin bin: Bromilow (13) – holding down.

SCORPIONS: 15 Andrew Gay; 2 David James; 3 Lee Williams; 5 Ashley Bateman; 1 Craig Richards; 6 Loz Wildbore; 33 Lloyd White; 8 Lewis Mills; 9 Shaun Owens; 10 Gill Dudson; 11 Christiaan Roets; 12 Neil Dallimore; 13 Aled James. Subs (all used): 7 Steve Parry; 17 Barrie Phillips; 29 Harri Greville; 14 Jamie Murphy.
Tries: Mills (3), Dudson (43), Richards (45), Parry (75); **Goals:** White 4/4.
Rugby Leaguer & League Express Men of the Match: *City Knights:* Jordan Ross; *Scorpions:* Lloyd White.
Penalty count: 12-9; **Half-time:** 12-6;
Referee: Matthew Thomasson; **Attendance:** 663.

ROUND 4

Sunday 28th March 2010

SOUTH WALES SCORPIONS 48 LONDON SKOLARS 6

SCORPIONS: 14 Jamie Murphy; 2 David James; 5 Ashley Bateman; 3 Lee Williams; 1 Craig Richards; 6 Loz Wildbore; 15 Andrew Gay; 10 Gil Dudson; 7 Steve Parry; 8 Lewis Mills; 33 Lloyd White; 11 Christiaan Roets; 13 Aled James. Subs (all used): 22 Ben Flower; 18 Matt Hutchings; 12 Neil Dallimore; 17 Barrie Phillips.
Tries: Parry (2), Wildbore (6), Flower (25), White (37, 65), Roets (46), Phillips (53), Dudson (78); **Goals:** White 7/7, Wildbore 1/1.
SKOLARS: 22 Curtis Cunningham; 2 Dave Arnot; 14 Luke May; 17 Chad Isles; 23 Olu Iwenofu; 9 Gareth Honor; 7 Paul Thorman; 8 Liam Roach; 19 Liam Prescott; 18 James Simon; 13 Stephen Ball; 3 Matt Thomas; 11 Oliver Purslow. Subs (all used): 34 Aran Quinn; 1 Josh Welsh; 5 Austen Aggrey; 12 Matt Carter.
Try: Carter (75); **Goals:** P Thorman 1/1.
Rugby Leaguer & League Express Men of the Match: *Scorpions:* Lloyd White; *Skolars:* Olu Iwenofu.
Penalty count: 10-8; **Half-time:** 24-0;
Referee: Tim Roby; **Attendance:** 625.

BLACKPOOL PANTHERS 54 SWINTON LIONS 6

PANTHERS: 1 Jonny Leather; 2 Damian Munro; 3 Casey Mayberry; 18 Martin Ainscough; 5 Tom Woodcock; 6 Carl Forber; 7 Tom Hemingway; 34 Neil Holland; 9 John Clough; 10 Andy Hobson; 32 John Walker; 27 Danny Halliwell; 11 Kurt Haggerty. Subs (all used): 14 Martin Keavney; 15 Paul Anderson; 4 Mark McCully; 24 Paul Ballard.
Tries: Halliwell (3, 73), Mayberry (13, 55), Ainscough (16), Leather (19), Keavney (22), Hobson (50), Munro (58, 79); **Goals:** Hemingway 7/11.
LIONS: 24 Gavin Dodd; 3 Sam Reay; 27 Anthony Stewart; 4 Carl Sneyd; 23 Rob Foxen; 1 Richie Hawkyard; 7 Ian Watson; 16 Dana Wilson; 22 Alex McClurg; 10 Danny Heaton; 11 Tommy Grundy; 17 Andrew Isherwood; 12 Paul Smith. Subs (all used): 14 Gary Hulse; 19 Neil Rigby; 15 Lee Wingfield; 28 Ian Sinfield.
Try: Wilson (69); **Goals:** Dodd 1/1.
Rugby Leaguer & League Express Men of the Match: *Panthers:* Tom Hemingway; *Lions:* Sam Reay.
Penalty count: 13-4; **Half-time:** 28-0;
Referee: Matthew Kidd; **Attendance:** 385.

DONCASTER 40 YORK CITY KNIGHTS 24

DONCASTER: 1 Tommy Griffiths; 5 Ben Collins; 4 Shaun Leaf; 3 Lee Gomersall; 26 Gary King; 33 Danny Allan; 6 Simon Brown; 19 Gary Ellery; 32 Kyle Kesik; 24 Jamie Bovill; 12 Ryan Steen; 23 Craig Lawton; 11 Liam Brown. Subs (all used): 16 Paul Shaw; 15 Danny Stanley; 9 Paul Brown; 20 Jack Ely.
Tries: Griffiths (11), Allan (14, 68), Collins (20), King (42), Leaf (46), Ely (56), Kesik (61); **Goals:** S Brown 4/9.
CITY KNIGHTS: 1 Danny Ratcliffe; 28 Danny Wilson; 26 Steve Lewis; 4 Lee Waterman; 2 Wayne Reittie; 6 Chris Thorman; 27 Casey Bromilow; 8 Mark Applegarth; 32 Paul Stamp; 17 Nathan Freer; 11 Jordan Ross; 13 Richard Blakeway; 9 Joe McLocklan. Subs (all used): 29 John Davies; 25 Brett Waller; 12 Chris Clough; 36 Jon Fallon.
Tries: McLocklan (5), Waterman (17), Wilson (25, 37), Ratcliffe (75); **Goals:** Waterman 2/5.
Sin bin: McLocklan (80) – foul play.
On report: Alleged biting (9).
Rugby Leaguer & League Express Men of the Match: *Doncaster:* Craig Lawton; *City Knights:* Danny Wilson.
Penalty count: 6-10; **Half-time:** 14-18;
Referee: Greg Dolan; **Attendance:** 532.

WORKINGTON TOWN 44 GATESHEAD THUNDER 0

TOWN: 5 Brett Carter; 2 Mike Backhouse; 3 Andrew Beattie; 15 Aaron Low; 14 Jamie Marshall; 6 Liam Finch; 7 Scott Kaighan; 8 Lee Dutton; 9 Jack Pedley; 10 Kris Coward; 11 Mike Whitehead; 12 Jarrad Stack; 22 Ryan Campbell. Subs (all used): 18 Martyn Wilson; 19 Joe McKenna; 26 Ruairi McGoff; 32 Jamie Butler.
Tries: Low (7, 36), Campbell (13), Marshall (26), Carter (39), Backhouse (42), Coward (62), Stack (77);
Goals: Kaighan 6/8.
THUNDER: 1 Kevin Neighbour; 29 Jimmy Atkinson; 3 Tom Wilson; 4 Michael Brown; 5 Joe Brown; 14 Will Bate; 9 Ryan Clarke; 18 Stephen Welton; 33 Reece Young; 17 Chris Parker; 32 Ade Aderiye; 31 Matt Garside; 13 Matt Barron. Subs (all used): 28 Jason Elliott; 10 Tabua Cakacaka; 26 David Cash; 30 Richie Humphries.
Rugby Leaguer & League Express Men of the Match: *Town:* Jarrad Stack; *Thunder:* Ryan Clarke.
Penalty count: 10-7; **Half-time:** 26-0;
Referee: Clint Sharrad; **Attendance:** 413.

HUNSLET HAWKS 44 ROCHDALE HORNETS 8

HAWKS: 29 Stuart Kain; 2 Michael Mark; 5 John Oakes; 4 David Clayton; 26 Waine Pryce; 6 Danny Grimshaw; 7 Paul March; 15 Adam Sullivan; 9 Richard Chapman; 3 James Houston; 30 Richard Knight; 12 Steve Dooler; 33 Tom Haughey. Subs (all used): 8 Scott Woodcock; 16 Neil Lowe; 18 Charlie Wabo; 20 Joe Helme.
Tries: Haughey (2), Clayton (7, 49, 65), Knight (19), Kain (34), Pryce (60), Grimshaw (71); **Goals:** Knight 6/9.
HORNETS: 32 Wayne English; 1 Craig Johnson; 4 Adam Bowman; 22 Damien Reid; 5 Bolu Fagborun; 15 Dayne Donoghue; 33 Liam McGovern; 8 Paul Raftrey; 9 Phil Wood; 10 Gareth Hayes; 16 Danny Samuel; 13 Craig Ashall; 12 Danny Smith. Subs (all used): 3 Dean Gorton; 11 Mark Hobson; 18 John Cookson; 20 Semisi Cocka.
Tries: Johnson (14), Reid (52); **Goals:** McGovern 0/2.
Rugby Leaguer & League Express Men of the Match: *Hawks:* David Clayton; *Hornets:* Craig Johnson.
Penalty count: 5-2; **Half-time:** 22-4;
Referee: Robert Hicks; **Attendance:** 514.

ROUND 5

Friday 2nd April 2010

LONDON SKOLARS 18 BLACKPOOL PANTHERS 42

SKOLARS: 1 Josh Welsh; 4 Jason Cook; 14 Luke May; 17 Chad Isles; 30 Ade Adebisi; 9 Gareth Honor; 7 Paul Thorman; 39 Rob Thomas; 19 Liam Prescott; 18 James Simon; 3 Matt Thomas; 5 Austen Aggrey; 11 Oliver Purslow. Subs (all used): 13 Stephen Ball; 10 Tony Williams; 34 Aran Quinn; 23 Olu Iwenofu.
Tries: P Thorman (3), Isles (17), Adebisi (80);
Goals: P Thorman 3/4.
Sin bin: Williams (27) - late tackle.
PANTHERS: 24 Paul Ballard; 2 Damian Munro; 22 Dave Llewellyn; 18 Martin Ainscough; 25 Mark Leigh; 11 Kurt Haggerty; 6 Carl Forber; 21 Peter Fairhurst; 9 John Clough; 17 Kris Ratcliffe; 27 Danny Halliwell; 12 Paul Alcock; 4 Mark McCully. Subs (all used): 14 Martin Keavney; 15 Paul Anderson; 1 Jonny Leather; 23 John Boland.
Tries: Ballard (11), Leigh (25), Forber (48, 77), Ratcliffe (51, 62), Leather (70), Alcock (75);
Goals: Halliwell 0/2, Leather 5/6.
Sin bin: Clough (17) – late tackle.
Rugby Leaguer & League Express Men of the Match: *Skolars:* Paul Thorman; *Panthers:* Jonny Leather.
Penalty count: 10-12; **Half-time:** 14-8;
Referee: Greg Dolan; **Attendance:** 323.

ROCHDALE HORNETS 16 OLDHAM 22

HORNETS: 1 Craig Johnson; 4 Adam Bowman; 2 Andy Saywell; 3 Dean Gorton; 22 Damien Reid; 33 Liam McGovern; 29 Ryan Powell; 10 Gareth Hayes; 28 Chris Hough; 8 Paul Raftrey; 16 Danny Samuel; 12 Danny Smith; 13 Craig Ashall. Subs (all used): 34 Danny Fleming; 18 John Cookson; 9 Phil Wood; 6 Dale Bloomfield.
Tries: Johnson (34), Hayes (43), Wood (56);
Goals: Hough 2/3.
OLDHAM: 1 Paul O'Connor; 2 Lucas Onyango; 24 Marcus St Hilaire; 4 Mick Fogerty; 20 Mark Brocklehurst; 6 Neil Roden; 7 Matt Ashe; 8 Jason Boults; 9 Martin Roden; 10 Dave Ellison; 19 Ben Heaton; 13 Joe Chandler; 21 Valu Bentley. Subs (all used): 16 Wayne Kerr; 15 Craig Robinson; 25 Scott Mansfield; 14 Luke Sutton.
Tries: Ashe (5), Sutton (19), Fogerty (22), Brocklehurst (68); **Goals:** Ashe 3/5.
Rugby Leaguer & League Express Men of the Match: *Hornets:* Craig Johnson; *Oldham:* Neil Roden.
Penalty count: 9-8; **Half-time:** 4-18;
Referee: Dave Merrick; **Attendance:** 1,412.

YORK CITY KNIGHTS 72 GATESHEAD THUNDER 14

CITY KNIGHTS: 1 Danny Ratcliffe; 29 Dennis Tuffour; 18 Matty Duckworth; 4 Lee Waterman; 5 Tom Lineham; 9 Joe McLocklan; 7 Jonathan Schofield; 36 Jon Fallon; 32 Paul Stamp; 17 Nathan Freer; 19 Kris Peacock; 35 Danny Hill; 13 Richard Blakeway. Subs (all used): 33 Mark Falkingham; 34 Jy-Mel Coleman; 12 Chris Clough; 10 Alex Benson.
Tries: Schofield (6, 40, 47), McLocklan (16), Ratcliffe (27, 56, 73), Hill (30), Tuffour (43), Blakeway (53), Lineham (66), Peacock (69); **Goals:** Waterman 12/12.
Dismissal: Fallon (63) – fighting.
Sin bin: Hill (63) – fighting.
THUNDER: 1 Kevin Neighbour; 15 Dan O'Sullivan; 3 Tom Wilson; 4 Michael Brown; 28 Jason Elliott; 6 Liam Duffy; 9 Ryan Clarke; 17 Chris Parker; 14 Will Bate; 10 Tabua Cakacaka; 12 Rhys Clarke; 30 Richie Humphries; 13 Matt Barron. Subs (all used): 33 Reece Young; 18 Stephen Welton; 26 David Cash; 11 Jonny Scott.
Tries: M Barron (10), Bate (13), M Brown (78);
Goals: Neighbour 1/3.
Sin bin: Ryan Clarke (40) – professional foul; Cakacaka (63) – fighting.
Rugby Leaguer & League Express Men of the Match: *City Knights:* Lee Waterman; *Thunder:* Will Bate.
Penalty count: 10-10; **Half-time:** 30-8;
Referee: Matthew Kidd; **Attendance:** 686.

HUNSLET HAWKS 54 DONCASTER 12

HAWKS: 29 Stuart Kain; 2 Michael Mark; 5 John Oakes; 21 Wayne McHugh; 26 Waine Pryce; 6 Danny Grimshaw; 7 Paul March; 20 Joe Helme; 31 Luke Haigh; 3 James Houston; 30 Richard Knight; 12 Steve Dooler; 33 Tom Haughey. Subs (all used): 8 Scott Woodcock; 16 Neil Lowe; 18 Charlie Wabo; 4 David Clayton.
Tries: P March (7), McHugh (12, 22, 40), Mark (15), Kain (35), Pryce (42, 52), Haughey (67), Knight (73);
Goals: Knight 7/10.
DONCASTER: 1 Tommy Griffiths; 5 Ben Collins; 3 Lee Gomersall; 4 Shaun Leaf; 26 Gary King; 31 Danny Allan; 6 Simon Brown; 19 Gary Ellery; 32 Kyle Kesik; 24 Jamie Bovill; 12 Ryan Steen; 23 Craig Lawton; 11 Liam Brown. Subs (all used): 9 Paul Brown; 15 Danny Stanley; 16 Paul Shaw; 20 Jack Ely.
Tries: Gomersall (56), Ellery (70); **Goals:** S Brown 2/2.
Rugby Leaguer & League Express Men of the Match: *Hawks:* Wayne McHugh; *Doncaster:* Simon Brown.
Penalty count: 7-7; **Half-time:** 34-0;
Referee: Chris Leatherbarrow; **Attendance:** 539.

ROUND 6

Monday 5th April 2010

SOUTH WALES SCORPIONS 12 HUNSLET HAWKS 42

SCORPIONS: 14 Jamie Murphy; 1 Craig Richards; 5 Ashley Bateman; 3 Lee Williams; 2 David James; 6 Loz Wildbore; 15 Andrew Gay; 10 Gil Dudson; 33 Lloyd White; 8 Lewis Mills; 22 Ben Flower; 11 Christiaan Roets; 17 Barrie Phillips. Subs (all used): 7 Steve Parry; 16 Joe Burke; 12 Neil Dallimore; 29 Harri Greville.
Tries: Roets (29), Parry (46);
Goals: Wildbore 1/1, White 1/1.
HAWKS: 29 Stuart Kain; 2 Michael Mark; 4 David Clayton; 21 Wayne McHugh; 26 Waine Pryce; 6 Danny Grimshaw; 7 Paul March; 15 Adam Sullivan; 9 Richard Chapman; 3 James Houston; 33 Tom Haughey; 30 Richard Knight; 13 David March. Subs (all used): 31 Luke Haigh; 12 Steve Dooler; 16 Neil Lowe; 8 Scott Woodcock.
Tries: Chapman (5), Kain (21, 68), P March (34), Grimshaw (53), Mark (58), D March (65), Lowe (74);
Goals: Knight 5/6, McHugh 0/2.
Rugby Leaguer & League Express Men of the Match: *Scorpions:* Christiaan Roets; *Hawks:* Stuart Kain.
Penalty count: 6-5; **Half-time:** 6-16;
Referee: Matthew Kidd; **Attendance:** 798.

BLACKPOOL PANTHERS 27 YORK CITY KNIGHTS 14

PANTHERS: 1 Jonny Leather; 2 Damian Munro; 18 Martin Ainscough; 22 Dave Llewellyn; 24 Paul Ballard; 6 Carl Forber; 7 Tom Hemingway; 34 Neil Holland; 9 John Clough; 10 Andy Hobson; 32 John Walker; 27 Danny Halliwell; 11 Kurt Haggerty. Subs (all used): 14 Martin Keavney; 15 Paul Anderson; 4 Mark McCully; 17 Kris Ratcliffe.
Tries: Ballard (27), Munro (47), Llewellyn (57, 66, 69);
Goals: Hemingway 0/2, Leather 3/3;
Field goal: Leather (79).
CITY KNIGHTS: 1 Danny Ratcliffe; 29 Dennis Tuffour; 3 Mike Mitchell; 4 Lee Waterman; 5 Tom Lineham; 9 Joe McLocklan; 7 Jonathan Schofield; 8 Mark Applegarth; 32 Paul Stamp; 17 Nathan Freer; 11 Jordan Ross; 19 Kris Peacock; 13 Richard Blakeway. Subs (all used): 27 Casey Bromilow; 15 Luke Hardbottle; 12 Chris Clough; 10 Alex Benson.
Tries: Tuffour (39, 63), McLocklan (78);
Goals: Waterman 1/3.
Rugby Leaguer & League Express Men of the Match: *Panthers:* Jonny Leather; *City Knights:* Joe McLocklan.
Penalty count: 8-10; **Half-time:** 4-6;
Referee: Clint Sharrad; **Attendance:** 405.

DONCASTER 38 LONDON SKOLARS 28

DONCASTER: 2 Aaron Henry; 18 John Winter; 3 Lee Gomersall; 4 Shaun Leaf; 26 Gary King; 34 Danny Allan; 6 Simon Brown; 10 David Bates; 32 Kyle Kesik; 19 Gary Ellery; 23 Craig Lawton; 12 Ryan Steen; 14 Jake Bassinder. Subs (all used): 15 Danny Stanley; 33 Mark Ward; 9 Paul Brown; 1 Tommy Griffiths.
Tries: Bates (2, 18), Ellery (10), Gomersall (15), Henry (25), Lawton (34), S Brown (70); **Goals:** S Brown 5/7.
SKOLARS: 1 Josh Welsh; 30 Ade Adebisi; 14 Luke May; 4 Jason Cook; 23 Olu Iwenofu; 9 Gareth Honor; 7 Paul Thorman; 8 Liam Roach; 19 Liam Prescott; 18 James Simon; 3 Matt Thomas; 5 Austen Aggrey; 39 Jamie Boston. Subs (all used): 37 Oliver Bloom; 12 Matt Carter; 13 Stephen Ball; 10 Tony Williams.
Tries: Aggrey (4), Adebisi (54, 75), May (63, 79);
Goals: P Thorman 4/5.
Rugby Leaguer & League Express Men of the Match: *Doncaster:* Craig Lawton; *Skolars:* Ade Adebisi.
Penalty count: 12-8; **Half-time:** 32-6;
Referee: Dave Merrick; **Attendance:** 380.

OLDHAM 16 WORKINGTON TOWN 14

OLDHAM: 1 Paul O'Connor; 2 Lucas Onyango; 24 Marcus St Hilaire; 4 Mick Fogerty; 20 Mark Brocklehurst; 6 Neil Roden; 7 Matt Ashe; 8 Jason Boults; 9 Martin Roden; 10 Dave Ellison; 19 Ben Heaton; 13 Joe Chandler; 21 Valu Bentley. Subs (all used): 14 Luke Sutton; 15 Craig Robinson; 16 Wayne Kerr; 22 Paul Reilly.
Tries: Onyango (4), Fogerty (12, 67); **Goals:** Ashe 2/3.
TOWN: 5 Brett Carter; 2 Mike Backhouse; 3 Andrew Beattie; 15 Aaron Low; 17 Neil Frazer; 6 Liam Finch; 7 Scott Kaighan; 8 Lee Dutton; 9 Jack Pedley; 10 Kris Coward; 11 Mike Whitehead; 19 Joe McKenna; 21 Paddy Coupar. Subs (all used): 14 Jamie Marshall; 18 Martyn Wilson; 26 Ruairi McGoff; 32 Jamie Butler.
Tries: Kaighan (59), Whitehead (62), Frazer (79);
Goals: Kaighan 1/3.
Sin bin: L Finch (9) - collision with referee.
Rugby Leaguer & League Express Men of the Match: *Oldham:* Matt Ashe; *Town:* Jamie Marshall.
Penalty count: 7-5; **Half-time:** 10-0; **Referee:** Tim Roby;
Attendance: 658 *(at Park Lane, Sedgley Park)*.

ROUND 7

Sunday 11th April 2010

SOUTH WALES SCORPIONS 16 OLDHAM 22

SCORPIONS: 14 Jamie Murphy; 1 Craig Richards; 3 Lee Williams; 5 Ashley Bateman; 2 David James; 6 Loz Wildbore; 15 Andrew Gay; 8 Lewis Mills; 7 Steve Parry; 16 Joe Burke; 11 Christiaan Roets; 13 Aled James; 33 Lloyd White. Subs (all used): 21 Sam Studley; 29 Harri Greville; 12 Neil Dallimore; 17 Barrie Phillips.
Tries: Parry (24), Roets (62), Richards (72);
Goals: White 2/3.
OLDHAM: 1 Paul O'Connor; 2 Lucas Onyango; 24 Marcus St Hilaire; 4 Mick Fogerty; 20 Mark Brocklehurst; 6 Neil Roden; 17 Danny Whitmore; 8 Jason Boults; 9 Martin Roden; 10 Dave Ellison; 19 Ben Heaton; 13 Joe Chandler; 21 Valu Bentley. Subs (all used): 14 Luke Sutton; 18 Chris Clarke; 22 Paul Reilly; 27 Jamie I'Anson.
Tries: Onyango (11), Whitmore (29), Fogerty (32), Boults (54); **Goals:** O'Connor 3/4.
Rugby Leaguer & League Express Men of the Match: *Scorpions:* Christiaan Roets; *Oldham:* Neil Roden.
Penalty count: 7-3; **Half-time:** 6-16;
Referee: Greg Dolan; **Attendance:** 625.

GATESHEAD THUNDER 28 DONCASTER 32

THUNDER: 4 Michael Brown; 15 Dan O'Sullivan; 1 Kevin Neighbour; 3 Tom Wilson; 2 Robin Peers; 6 Liam Duffy; 9 Ryan Clarke; 17 Chris Parker; 14 Will Bate; 18 Stephen Welton; 12 Rhys Clarke; 32 Ade Aderiye; 13 Matt Barron. Subs (all used): 33 Reece Young; 25 Gareth Barron; 26 David Cash; 10 Tabua Cakacaka.
Tries: Ryan Clarke (29), Wilson (48), Aderiye (49), Bate (52), Neighbour (58); **Goals:** Neighbour 4/5.
DONCASTER: 1 Tommy Griffiths; 2 Aaron Henry; 3 Lee Gomersall; 4 Shaun Leaf; 22 Scott Wilson; 6 Simon Brown; 32 Kyle Kesik; 10 David Bates; 9 Paul Brown; 19 Gary Ellery; 23 Craig Lawton; 12 Ryan Steen; 27 Matt Carbutt. Subs (all used): 20 Jack Ely; 15 Danny Stanley; 16 Paul Shaw; 21 Scott Howlett.
Tries: Henry (6, 11), Griffiths (19, 37), Steen (21), Ely (43); **Goals:** S Brown 4/6.
Rugby Leaguer & League Express Men of the Match: *Thunder:* Gareth Barron; *Doncaster:* Aaron Henry.
Penalty count: 4-5; **Half-time:** 6-26;
Referee: Chris Leatherbarrow; **Attendance:** 579.

ROCHDALE HORNETS 68 LONDON SKOLARS 10

HORNETS: 32 Wayne English; 5 Bolu Fagborun; 4 Adam Bowman; 3 Dean Gorton; 1 Craig Johnson; 28 Chris Hough; 29 Ryan Powell; 8 Paul Raftrey; 9 Phil Wood; 10 Gareth Hayes; 16 Danny Samuel; 12 Danny Smith; 13 Craig Ashall. Subs (all used): 18 John Cookson; 20 Semisi Cocka; 27 Craig Tunstead; 6 Dale Bloomfield.
Tries: Hough (2, 6), Bowman (16), Samuel (23), Ashall (30), English (32, 55, 79), Powell (50), Hayes (53), Johnson (58), Smith (69), Gorton (74);
Goals: Hough 8/13.
SKOLARS: 1 Josh Welsh; 30 Ade Adebisi; 17 Chad Isles; 2 Dave Arnot; 23 Olu Iwenofu; 9 Gareth Honor; 7 Paul Thorman; 10 Tony Williams; 19 Liam Prescott; 8 Liam Roach; 5 Austen Aggrey; 33 Oliver Bloom; 11 Oliver Purslow. Subs (all used): 12 Matt Carter; 25 Smokie Junor; 31 Jaroslaw Obuchowski; 32 Aran Quinn.
Tries: Arnot (10), Adebisi (25); **Goals:** P Thorman 1/2.
Rugby Leaguer & League Express Men of the Match: *Hornets:* Chris Hough; *Skolars:* Ade Adebisi.
Penalty count: 6-6; **Half-time:** 30-10; **Referee:** Clint Sharrad (replaced by Dave Sharpe, 14); **Attendance:** 359.

WORKINGTON TOWN 12 BLACKPOOL PANTHERS 32

TOWN: 1 John Lebbon; 2 Mike Backhouse; 3 Andrew Beattie; 15 Aaron Low; 17 Neil Frazer; 6 Liam Finch; 7 Scott Kaighan; 26 Ruairi McGoff; 13 Darren King; 10 Kris Coward; 11 Mike Whitehead; 12 Jarrad Stack; 21 Paddy Coupar. Subs (all used): 19 Joe McKenna; 20 James Robinson; 22 Ryan Campbell; 32 Jamie Butler.
Tries: Low (65), McGoff (74); **Goals:** Kaighan 2/3.
PANTHERS: 1 Jonny Leather; 2 Damian Munro; 18 Martin Ainscough; 22 Dave Llewellyn; 24 Paul Ballard; 6 Carl Forber; 7 Tom Hemingway; 34 Neil Holland; 9 John Clough; 10 Andy Hobson; 4 Mark McCully; 27 Danny Halliwell; 11 Kurt Haggerty. Subs (all used): 14 Martin Keavney; 15 Paul Anderson; 17 Kris Ratcliffe; 23 John Boland.
Tries: Munro (26, 34), Ballard (29), McCully (32), Forber (41), Halliwell (51); **Goals:** Leather 4/6.
Rugby Leaguer & League Express Men of the Match: *Town:* Darren King; *Panthers:* Tom Hemingway.
Penalty count: 8-12; **Half-time:** 2-20;
Referee: Warren Turley; **Attendance:** 521.

HUNSLET HAWKS 46 SWINTON LIONS 12

HAWKS: 29 Stuart Kain; 26 Waine Pryce; 4 David Clayton; 21 Wayne McHugh; 5 John Oakes; 6 Danny Grimshaw; 7 Paul March; 15 Adam Sullivan; 9 Richard Chapman; 3 James Houston; 12 Steve Dooler; 33 Tom Haughey; 13 David March. Subs (all used): 8 Scott Woodcock; 16 Neil Lowe; 18 Charlie Wabo; 31 Luke Haigh.
Tries: McHugh (7), Lowe (22, 78), Grimshaw (27), Haughey (33), Wabo (38), Chapman (55), D March (69);
Goals: D March 7/8.
LIONS: 1 Richie Hawkyard; 3 Sam Reay; 27 Anthony Stewart; 4 Carl Sneyd; 25 Barry Hamilton; 6 Graham Holroyd; 7 Ian Watson; 16 Dana Wilson; 14 Gary Hulse; 8 Paul Southern; 15 Lee Wingfield; 12 Paul Smith; 19 Neil Rigby. Subs (all used): 20 Chris Hull; 26 Dave Newton; 17 Andrew Isherwood; 23 Rob Foxen.
Tries: P Smith (30), Isherwood (45); **Goals:** Sneyd 2/2.
Rugby Leaguer & League Express Men of the Match: *Hawks:* David March; *Lions:* Richie Hawkyard.
Penalty count: 10-12; **Half-time:** 28-6;
Referee: Ronnie Laughton; **Attendance:** 546.

ROUND 8

Friday 23rd April 2010

BLACKPOOL PANTHERS 48 DONCASTER 12

PANTHERS: 1 Jonny Leather; 24 Paul Ballard; 18 Martin Ainscough; 31 Josh Charnley; 2 Damian Munro; 6 Carl Forber; 7 Tom Hemingway; 17 Kris Ratcliffe; 9 John Clough; 10 Andy Hobson; 27 Danny Halliwell; 12 Paul Alcock; 11 Kurt Haggerty. Subs (all used): 14 Martin Keavney; 15 Paul Anderson; 4 Mark McCully; 34 Neil Holland.
Tries: Ballard (11), Haggerty (26), Forber (30), Charnley (55, 79), Halliwell (62, 70), McCully (65), Munro (67); **Goals:** Charnley 6/9.
DONCASTER: 1 Tommy Griffiths; 22 Scott Wilson; 12 Ryan Steen; 3 Lee Gomersall; 5 Ben Collins; 34 Rob Lunt; 6 Simon Brown; 24 Jamie Bovill; 32 Kyle Kesik; 19 Gary Ellery; 23 Craig Lawton; 16 Paul Shaw; 27 Matt Carbutt. Subs (all used): 14 Jake Bassinder; 28 Paul Hughes; 10 David Bates; 20 Jack Ely.
Tries: Griffiths (18), Hughes (46); **Goals:** S Brown 2/2.
Rugby Leaguer & League Express Men of the Match: *Panthers:* Josh Charnley; *Doncaster:* Simon Brown.
Penalty count: 5-11; **Half-time:** 14-6;
Referee: Matthew Kidd; **Attendance:** 253.

Saturday 24th April 2010

OLDHAM 64 GATESHEAD THUNDER 10

OLDHAM: 1 Paul O'Connor; 2 Lucas Onyango; 24 Marcus St Hilaire; 4 Mick Fogerty; 5 John Gillam; 6 Neil Roden; 7 Matt Ashe; 10 Dave Ellison; 9 Martin Roden; 16 Wayne Kerr; 15 Craig Robinson; 13 Joe Chandler; 18 Chris Clarke. Subs (all used): 14 Luke Sutton; 17 Danny Whitmore; 27 Jamie I'Anson; 26 Ian Hodson.
Tries: Clarke (4), Gillam (9, 31, 50, 66), O'Connor (25, 57), Chandler (35), Ashe (60), Onyango (70), N Roden (71), Fogerty (80); **Goals:** Ashe 8/12.
THUNDER: 4 Michael Brown; 2 Robin Peers; 3 Tom Wilson; 1 Kevin Neighbour; 5 Joe Brown; 6 Liam Duffy; 9 Ryan Clarke; 13 Matt Barron; 14 Will Bate; 17 Chris Parker; 12 Rhys Clarke; 30 Richie Humphries; 32 Ade Aderiye. Subs (all used): 33 Reece Young; 18 Stephen Welton; 26 David Cash; 25 Gareth Barron.
Tries: Wilson (63), Duffy (75); **Goals:** Neighbour 1/2.
Rugby Leaguer & League Express Men of the Match: *Oldham:* Neil Roden; *Thunder:* Ryan Clarke.
Penalty count: 6-7; **Half-time:** 28-0;
Referee: Chris Leatherbarrow; **Attendance:** 413 *(at Park Lane, Sedgley Park).*

Sunday 25th April 2010

LONDON SKOLARS 8 HUNSLET HAWKS 46

SKOLARS: 1 Josh Welsh; 23 Olu Iwenofu; 14 Luke May; 2 Dave Arnot; 25 Smokie Junor; 37 Jarryn Osborne; 7 Paul Thorman; 11 Oliver Purslow; 19 Liam Prescott; 12 Matt Carter; 5 Austen Aggrey; 13 Stephen Ball; 24 Jamie Boston. Subs (all used): 9 Gareth Honor; 39 Oliver Bloom; 36 Rob Montgomerie; 33 Aran Quinn.
Tries: Welsh (8), Aggrey (30); **Goals:** P Thorman 0/2.
HAWKS: 29 Stuart Kain; 5 John Oakes; 4 David Clayton; 21 Wayne McHugh; 2 Michael Mark; 6 Danny Grimshaw; 7 Paul March; 15 Adam Sullivan; 9 Richard Chapman; 20 Joe Helme; 30 Richard Knight; 10 Tom Haughey; 13 David March. Subs (all used): 19 Darren Robinson; 16 Neil Lowe; 8 Scott Woodcock; 18 Charlie Wabo.
Tries: Clayton (2), Mark (14, 24), Grimshaw (19, 45), P March (27), McHugh (33), Oakes (52, 56);
Goals: Knight 5/9.
Rugby Leaguer & League Express Men of the Match: *Skolars:* Liam Prescott; *Hawks:* Paul March.
Penalty count: 7-8; **Half-time:** 8-34;
Referee: Greg Dolan; **Attendance:** 372.

SWINTON LIONS 20 SOUTH WALES SCORPIONS 14

LIONS: 1 Richie Hawkyard; 25 Barry Hamilton; 27 Anthony Stewart; 3 Sam Reay; 24 Gavin Dodd; 6 Graham Holroyd; 20 Chris Hull; 8 Paul Southern; 7 Ian Watson; 31 Neil Cherryholme; 17 Andrew Isherwood; 15 Lee Wingfield; 9 Phil Joseph. Subs (all used): 14 Gary Hulse; 16 Dana Wilson; 26 Dave Newton; 23 Rob Foxen.
Tries: Holroyd (7), Wilson (27, 53); **Goals:** Holroyd 4/4.
SCORPIONS: 14 Jamie Murphy; 31 Elliot Kear; 20 Geraint Davies; 5 Ashley Bateman; 1 Craig Richards; 13 Aled James; 15 Andrew Gay; 10 Gil Dudson; 7 Steve Parry; 16 Joe Burke; 11 Christiaan Roets; 8 Lewis Mills; 6 Loz Wildbore. Subs (all used): 29 Harri Greville; 12 Neil Dallimore; 9 Shaun Owens; 3 Lee Williams.
Tries: Dudson (29), A James (37), Gay (75);
Goals: A James 1/2, Murphy 0/1.
On report: Alleged late tackle (67) on Watson.
Rugby Leaguer & League Express Men of the Match: *Lions:* Richie Hawkyard; *Scorpions:* Elliot Kear.
Penalty count: 10-8; **Half-time:** 12-10;
Referee: Jamie Leahy; **Attendance:** 308.

YORK CITY KNIGHTS 36 ROCHDALE HORNETS 34

CITY KNIGHTS: 1 Danny Ratcliffe; 2 Wayne Reittie; 28 Danny Wilson; 4 Lee Waterman; 5 Tom Lineham; 6 Chris Thorman; 9 Joe McLocklan; 8 Mark Applegarth; 32 Paul Stamp; 17 Nathan Freer; 19 Kris Peacock; 13 Richard Blakeway; 33 Jack Lee. Subs (all used): 11 Jordan Ross; 15 Luke Hardbottle; 26 Steve Lewis; 30 Jack Stearman.
Tries: Lineham (6), Wilson (15), Lee (28), Peacock (34), Blakeway (44), Hardbottle (57); **Goals:** Waterman 6/6.
HORNETS: 32 Wayne English; 3 Dean Gorton; 12 Danny Smith; 13 Craig Ashall; 1 Craig Johnson; 6 Dale Bloomfield; 29 Ryan Powell; 16 Danny Samuel; 9 Phil Wood; 8 Paul Raftrey; 4 Adam Bowman; 10 Gareth Hayes; 28 Chris Hough. Subs (all used): 20 Semisi Cocka; 18 John Cookson; 27 Craig Tunstead; 24 Paul Crook.
Tries: Samuel (23), Bowman (36), Hough (49), Ashall (51), English (69), Wood (78);
Goals: Hough 0/1, Crook 5/5.
Rugby Leaguer & League Express Men of the Match: *City Knights:* Mark Applegarth; *Hornets:* Craig Ashall.
Penalty count: 10-5; **Half-time:** 24-10;
Referee: Dave Merrick; **Attendance:** 987.

ROUND 9

Monday 3rd May 2010

WORKINGTON TOWN 16 HUNSLET HAWKS 30

TOWN: 5 Brett Carter; 2 Mike Backhouse; 3 Andrew Beattie; 15 Aaron Low; 17 Neil Frazer; 6 Liam Finch; 7 Scott Kaighan; 8 Lee Dutton; 14 Jamie Marshall; 10 Kris Coward; 11 Mike Whitehead; 12 Jarrad Stack; 21 Paddy Coupar. Subs (all used): 19 Joe McKenna; 20 James Robinson; 16 Scott Burgess; 32 Ryan McDonald.
Tries: Low (34, 57), Kaighan (38); **Goals:** Kaighan 2/3.
HAWKS: 1 Nathan Larvin; 2 Michael Mark; 4 David Clayton; 5 John Oakes; 26 Waine Pryce; 6 Danny Grimshaw; 7 Paul March; 3 James Houston; 9 Richard Chapman; 15 Adam Sullivan; 10 Tom Haughey; 12 Steve Dooler; 13 David March. Subs (all used): 16 Neil Lowe; 8 Scott Woodcock; 14 Luke Haigh; 30 Richard Knight.
Tries: Chapman (3), Houston (5), P March (28), Larvin (45), D March (69); **Goals:** D March 5/5.
Rugby Leaguer & League Express Men of the Match: *Town:* Brett Carter; *Hawks:* David March.
Penalty count: 8-12; **Half-time:** 12-18;
Referee: Dave Merrick; **Attendance:** 578.

DONCASTER 26 OLDHAM 46

DONCASTER: 1 Tommy Griffiths; 30 Dean Colton; 34 Rob Lunt; 25 Chris Spurr; 22 Scott Wilson; 6 Simon Brown; 7 Craig Fawcett; 24 Jamie Bovill; 32 Kyle Kesik; 19 Gary Ellery; 23 Craig Lawton; 12 Ryan Steen; 27 Matt Carbutt. Subs (all used): 29 Liam Crawley; 28 Paul Hughes; 20 Jack Ely; 10 David Bates.
Tries: Wilson (12), Griffiths (32), Ely (70), Colton (72);
Goals: S Brown 5/5.
OLDHAM: 1 Paul O'Connor; 2 Lucas Onyango; 22 Paul Reilly; 4 Mick Fogerty; 5 John Gillam; 6 Neil Roden; 7 Matt Ashe; 8 Jason Boults; 9 Martin Roden; 16 Wayne Kerr; 15 Craig Robinson; 13 Joe Chandler; 18 Chris Clarke. Subs (all used): 10 Dave Ellison; 14 Luke Sutton; 19 Ben Heaton; 17 Danny Whitmore.
Tries: Boults (6), Ashe (22), Chandler (44), Fogerty (54), Clarke (61), Gillam (64), Heaton (67), Ellison (77);
Goals: Ashe 7/8.
Rugby Leaguer & League Express Men of the Match: *Doncaster:* Dean Colton; *Oldham:* Chris Clarke.
Penalty count: 7-7; **Half-time:** 14-12;
Referee: Greg Dolan; **Attendance:** 730.

ROCHDALE HORNETS 50 GATESHEAD THUNDER 12

HORNETS: 1 Craig Johnson; 32 Wayne English; 3 Dean Gorton; 22 Damien Reid; 6 Dale Bloomfield; 24 Paul Crook; 7 Steve Roper; 10 Gareth Hayes; 9 Phil Wood; 20 Semisi Cocka; 16 Danny Samuel; 12 Danny Smith; 13 Craig Ashall. Subs (all used): 8 Paul Raftrey; 18 John Cookson; 4 Adam Bowman; 28 Chris Hough.
Tries: Ashall (6), English (11, 39, 69), Gorton (25), Smith (35), Reid (43), Roper (57), Wood (63), Johnson (76); **Goals:** Crook 5/10.
THUNDER: 5 Joe Brown; 2 Robin Peers; 4 Michael Brown; 1 Kevin Neighbour; 29 Jimmy Atkinson; 6 Liam Duffy; 12 Rhys Clarke; 17 Chris Parker; 9 Ryan Clarke; 13 Matt Barron; 26 David Cash; 32 Ade Aderiye; 21 James Hall. Subs (all used): 33 Reece Young; 10 Tabua Cakacaka; 25 Gareth Barron; 8 Jason Payne.
Tries: M Barron (3), Young (52); **Goals:** Neighbour 2/2.
Rugby Leaguer & League Express Men of the Match: *Hornets:* Wayne English; *Thunder:* Reece Young.
Penalty count: 12-9; **Half-time:** 22-6;
Referee: Matthew Kidd; **Attendance:** 604.

SOUTH WALES SCORPIONS 24 BLACKPOOL PANTHERS 28

SCORPIONS: 31 Elliot Kear; 14 Jamie Murphy; 3 Lee Williams; 5 Ashley Bateman; 1 Craig Richards; 6 Loz Wildbore; 15 Andrew Gay; 10 Gil Dudson; 7 Steve Parry; 8 Lewis Mills; 33 Lloyd White; 11 Christiaan Roets; 13 Aled James. Subs (all used): 9 Shaun Owens; 24 Liam Roach; 12 Neil Dallimore; 17 Barrie Phillips.
Tries: Richards (4, 25), Parry (57), Murphy (61);
Goals: White 3/5, Wildbore 1/1.
PANTHERS: 24 Paul Ballard; 2 Damian Munro; 3 Casey Mayberry; 22 Dave Llewellyn; 31 Josh Charnley; 6 Carl Forber; 7 Tom Hemingway; 34 Neil Holland; 9 John Clough; 10 Andy Hobson; 32 John Walker; 27 Danny Halliwell; 11 Kurt Haggerty. Subs (all used): 14 Martin Keavney; 15 Paul Anderson; 4 Mark McCully; 17 Kris Ratcliffe.
Tries: Munro (14), Charnley (17), McCully (46), Llewellyn (67), Hemingway (69); **Goals:** Charnley 4/5.
Sin bin: Holland (3) - high tackle, (76) - use of the forearm; Hobson (50) - high tackle.

Championship One 2010 - Round by Round

Rugby Leaguer & League Express Men of the Match: *Scorpions:* Craig Richards; *Panthers:* Josh Charnley.
Penalty count: 11-5; **Half-time:** 12-10;
Referee: Peter Brooke; **Attendance:** 623.

YORK CITY KNIGHTS 30 SWINTON LIONS 36

CITY KNIGHTS: 1 Danny Ratcliffe; 2 Wayne Reittie; 28 Danny Wilson; 4 Lee Waterman; 5 Tom Lineham; 9 Joe McLocklan; 27 Casey Bromilow; 36 Jon Fallon; 33 Jack Lee; 30 Jack Stearman; 11 Jordan Ross; 8 Mark Applegarth; 13 Richard Blakeway. Subs (all used): 15 Luke Hardbottle; 17 Nathan Freer; 25 Brett Waller; 26 Steve Lewis.
Tries: Stearman (2), Wilson (32), Waller (45), Ratcliffe (58); **Goals:** Waterman 7/8.
LIONS: 1 Richie Hawkyard; 25 Barry Hamilton; 27 Anthony Stewart; 3 Sam Reay; 24 Gavin Dodd; 6 Graham Holroyd; 29 Mick Govin; 8 Paul Southern; 7 Ian Watson; 31 Neil Cherryholme; 15 Lee Wingfield; 17 Andrew Isherwood; 9 Phil Joseph. Subs (all used): 23 Rob Foxen; 26 Dave Newton; 12 Paul Smith; 30 Wayne Corcoran.
Tries: R Hawkyard (9), Reay (20), P Smith (52, 73), Stewart (63), Isherwood (70), Corcoran (79);
Goals: Holroyd 4/7.
Sin bin: Stewart (36) – foul play.
Rugby Leaguer & League Express Men of the Match: *City Knights:* Lee Waterman; *Lions:* Paul Smith.
Penalty count: 14-7; **Half-time:** 18-10;
Referee: Chris Leatherbarrow; **Attendance:** 670.

ROUND 10

Saturday 8th May 2010

SWINTON LIONS 22 ROCHDALE HORNETS 33

LIONS: 1 Richie Hawkyard; 25 Barry Hamilton; 11 Tommy Grundy; 3 Sam Reay; 24 Gavin Dodd; 6 Graham Holroyd; 29 Mick Govin; 16 Dana Wilson; 7 Ian Watson; 31 Neil Cherryholme; 23 Rob Foxen; 17 Andrew Isherwood; 9 Phil Joseph. Subs (all used): 30 Wayne Corcoran; 26 Dave Newton; 15 Lee Wingfield; 12 Paul Smith.
Tries: R Hawkyard (14), Wilson (19), Joseph (23), Foxen (56); **Goals:** Holroyd 3/5.
HORNETS: 32 Wayne English; 1 Craig Johnson; 22 Damien Reid; 3 Dean Gorton; 6 Dale Bloomfield; 24 Paul Crook; 7 Steve Roper; 10 Gareth Hayes; 9 Phil Wood; 20 Semisi Cocka; 16 Danny Samuel; 12 Danny Smith; 13 Craig Ashall. Subs (all used): 8 Paul Raftrey; 18 John Cookson; 29 Ryan Powell; 28 Chris Hough.
Tries: Samuel (1), Gorton (12), Bloomfield (33, 73), Hough (37), Johnson (78); **Goals:** Crook 4/6;
Field goal: Roper (68).
Rugby Leaguer & League Express Men of the Match: *Lions:* Richie Hawkyard; *Hornets:* Paul Crook.
Penalty count: 6-10; **Half-time:** 16-20;
Referee: Greg Dolan; **Attendance:** 470.

GATESHEAD THUNDER 8
SOUTH WALES SCORPIONS 50

THUNDER: 4 Michael Brown; 5 Joe Brown; 1 Kevin Neighbour; 3 Tom Wilson; 34 Josh Stoker; 12 Rhys Clarke; 9 Ryan Clarke; 17 Chris Parker; 33 Reece Young; 18 Stephen Welton; 30 Richie Humphries; 32 Ade Aderiye; 13 Matt Barron. Subs (all used): 28 Jason Elliott; 25 Gareth Barron; 8 Jason Payne; 21 James Hall.
Tries: J Brown (38), Wilson (54); **Goals:** Neighbour 0/2.
SCORPIONS: 31 Elliot Kear; 14 Jamie Murphy; 3 Lee Williams; 5 Ashley Bateman; 1 Craig Richards; 6 Loz Wildbore; 15 Andrew Gay; 10 Gil Dudson; 7 Steve Parry; 8 Lewis Mills; 33 Lloyd White; 11 Christiaan Roets; 13 Aled James. Subs (all used): 20 Geraint Davies; 24 Liam Roach; 12 Neil Dallimore; 17 Barrie Phillips.
Tries: Williams (12), Mills (21), Gay (30, 78), Dallimore (48, 57), Kear (62), Roets (67), Wildbore (72);
Goals: White 4/6, Murphy 3/3.
Rugby Leaguer & League Express Men of the Match: *Thunder:* Reece Young; *Scorpions:* Neil Dallimore.
Penalty count: 2-11; **Half-time:** 4-18;
Referee: Craig Halloran; **Attendance:** 258.

Sunday 9th May 2010

LONDON SKOLARS 28 WORKINGTON TOWN 44

SKOLARS: 30 Ade Adebisi; 23 Olu Iwenofu; 21 Jamie O'Callaghan; 33 John Paxton; 25 Smokie Junor; 17 Chad Isles; 7 Paul Thorman; 38 Rob Thomas; 19 Liam Prescott; 37 Guy Aldam; 13 Stephen Ball; 12 Matt Carter; 24 Jamie Boston. Subs (all used): 5 Austen Aggrey; 3 Matt Thomas; 11 Oliver Purslow; 39 Oliver Bloom.
Tries: Boston (2, 35), O'Callaghan (15), Adebisi (58), M Thomas (64); **Goals:** P Thorman 4/5.
TOWN: 5 Brett Carter; 1 John Lebbon; 3 Andrew Beattie; 15 Aaron Low; 17 Neil Frazer; 6 Liam Finch; 7 Scott Kaighan; 8 Lee Dutton; 14 Jamie Marshall; 10 Kris Coward; 11 Mike Whitehead; 12 Jarrad Stack; 21 Paddy Coupar. Subs (all used): 19 Joe McKenna; 20 James Robinson; 23 Phil Hewitt; 32 Ryan McDonald.
Tries: McDonald (15), Kaighan (23), Marshall (27, 71, 75), Robinson (40), Stack (46, 55); **Goals:** Kaighan 6/9.
Rugby Leaguer & League Express Men of the Match: *Skolars:* Jamie Boston; *Town:* Jarrad Stack.
Penalty count: 10-12; **Half-time:** 18-22;
Referee: Matthew Kidd; **Attendance:** 258.

OLDHAM 28 YORK CITY KNIGHTS 34

OLDHAM: 1 Paul O'Connor; 2 Lucas Onyango; 19 Ben Heaton; 4 Mick Fogerty; 5 John Gillam; 17 Danny Whitmore; 7 Matt Ashe; 8 Jason Boults; 9 Martin Roden; 16 Wayne Kerr; 15 Craig Robinson; 13 Joe Chandler; 18 Chris Clarke. Subs (all used): 10 Dave Ellison; 14 Luke Sutton; 25 Scott Mansfield; 26 Ian Hodson.
Tries: Kerr (7), Gillam (16), Onyango (32), O'Connor (43, 66), Fogerty (55); **Goals:** Ashe 2/6.
Dismissal: Kerr (53) - high tackle on Tuffour.
CITY KNIGHTS: 1 Danny Ratcliffe; 29 Dennis Tuffour; 28 Danny Wilson; 4 Lee Waterman; 5 Tom Lineham; 9 Joe McLocklan; 32 Paul Stamp; 8 Mark Applegarth; 33 Jack Lee; 36 Jon Fallon; 11 Jordan Ross; 26 Steve Lewis; 13 Richard Blakeway. Subs (all used): 25 Brett Waller; 15 Luke Hardbottle; 30 Jack Stearman; 18 Matty Duckworth.
Tries: Ratcliffe (4), Tuffour (18, 79), Lewis (27), Waterman (30), Lineham (61);
Goals: Waterman 5/5, McLocklan 0/1.
On report: Waller (68) - alleged late tackle on Ellison.
Rugby Leaguer & League Express Men of the Match: *Oldham:* Paul O'Connor; *City Knights:* Dennis Tuffour.
Penalty count: 14-8; **Half-time:** 16-24;
Referee: Peter Brooke; **Attendance:** 1,110.

ROUND 11

Sunday 16th May 2010

BLACKPOOL PANTHERS 132 GATESHEAD THUNDER 0

PANTHERS: 24 Paul Ballard; 31 Josh Charnley; 1 Jonny Leather; 18 Martin Ainscough; 2 Damian Munro; 6 Carl Forber; 7 Tom Hemingway; 15 Paul Anderson; 14 Martin Keavney; 10 Andy Hobson; 4 Mark McCully; 27 Danny Halliwell; 11 Kurt Haggerty. Subs (all used): 9 John Clough; 19 Adam Thomas; 3 Casey Mayberry; 17 Kris Ratcliffe.
Tries: Haggerty (5, 14), Charnley (10, 22), Ballard (17, 57), Halliwell (25), Ainscough (31, 68), Munro (33, 39), Clough (35, 43), Hemingway (41), Mayberry (46, 73), Leather (48), Anderson (53), Thomas (60), Keavney (63, 66), McCully (71);
Goals: Hemingway 22/22.
THUNDER: 28 Jason Elliott; 15 Dan O'Sullivan; 36 Jonny Shields; 34 Josh Stoker; 29 Jimmy Atkinson; 12 Rhys Clarke; 9 Ryan Clarke; 18 Stephen Welton; 33 Reece Young; 17 Chris Parker; 30 Richie Humphries; 32 Ade Aderiye; 20 Phil Wall. Subs (all used): 14 Will Bate; 8 Jason Payne; 21 James Hall; 35 Gary Bates.
Rugby Leaguer & League Express Men of the Match: *Panthers:* Kurt Haggerty; *Thunder:* Josh Stoker.
Penalty count: 7-4; **Half-time:** 60-0;
Referee: Matthew Thomasson; **Attendance:** 253.

OLDHAM 46 LONDON SKOLARS 12

OLDHAM: 1 Paul O'Connor; 2 Lucas Onyango; 22 Paul Reilly; 4 Mick Fogerty; 5 John Gillam; 17 Danny Whitmore; 7 Matt Ashe; 8 Jason Boults; 9 Martin Roden; 16 Wayne Kerr; 26 Ian Hodson; 13 Joe Chandler; 18 Chris Clarke. Subs (all used): 10 Dave Ellison; 15 Craig Robinson; 19 Ben Heaton; 25 Scott Mansfield.
Tries: Onyango (10, 76), M Roden (14), O'Connor (24), Whitmore (37), Heaton (51), Robinson (54), Gillam (79);
Goals: Ashe 7/8.
SKOLARS: 30 Ade Adebisi; 23 Olu Iwenofu; 33 John Paxton; 24 Lamont Bryan; 2 Dave Arnot; 17 Chad Isles; 7 Paul Thorman; 38 Michael Sykes; 19 Liam Prescott; 20 Dave Williams; 13 Stephen Ball; 3 Matt Thomas; 34 Jamie Boston. Subs (all used): 5 Austen Aggrey; 9 Gareth Honor; 11 Oliver Purslow; 37 Oliver Bloom.
Tries: D Williams (33, 44), Adebisi (66);
Goals: P Thorman 0/3.
Rugby Leaguer & League Express Men of the Match: *Oldham:* Danny Whitmore; *Skolars:* Ade Adebisi.
Penalty count: 11-10; **Half-time:** 24-4;
Referee: Greg Dolan; **Attendance:** 747.

WORKINGTON TOWN 34 DONCASTER 20

TOWN: 5 Brett Carter; 2 Mike Backhouse; 3 Andrew Beattie; 15 Aaron Low; 17 Neil Frazer; 6 Liam Finch; 7 Scott Kaighan; 8 Lee Dutton; 14 Jamie Marshall; 10 Kris Coward; 11 Mike Whitehead; 12 Jarrad Stack; 21 Paddy Coupar. Subs (all used): 19 Joe McKenna; 20 James Robinson; 31 Darren Holt; 32 Ryan McDonald.
Tries: Whitehead (15), Stack (24), McKenna (35), L Finch (52), Dutton (66), Frazer (76);
Goals: Kaighan 1/3, Holt 4/4.
DONCASTER: 31 Michael Butterfield; 30 Dean Colton; 4 Shaun Leaf; 25 Chris Spurr; 22 Scott Wilson; 6 Simon Brown; 7 Craig Fawcett; 29 Liam Crawley; 32 Kyle Kesik; 16 Paul Shaw; 27 Matt Carbutt; 12 Ryan Steen; 34 Rob Lunt. Subs (all used): 28 Paul Hughes; 20 Jack Ely; 15 Danny Stanley; 14 Jake Bassinder.
Tries: Butterfield (45), Leaf (49, 57), Spurr (66);
Goals: S Brown 2/4.
Rugby Leaguer & League Express Men of the Match: *Town:* Darren Holt; *Doncaster:* Rob Lunt.
Penalty count: 9-3; **Half-time:** 16-0;
Referee: Chris Leatherbarrow; **Attendance:** 410.

YORK CITY KNIGHTS 10 HUNSLET HAWKS 46

CITY KNIGHTS: 1 Danny Ratcliffe; 29 Dennis Tuffour; 28 Danny Wilson; 4 Lee Waterman; 5 Tom Lineham; 9 Joe McLocklan; 32 Paul Stamp; 8 Mark Applegarth; 33 Jack Lee; 36 Jon Fallon; 18 Matty Duckworth; 26 Steve Lewis; 13 Richard Blakeway. Subs (all used): 25 Brett Waller; 27 Casey Bromilow; 30 Jack Stearman; 12 Chris Clough.
Tries: Waterman (9), Stamp (39); **Goals:** Waterman 1/2.
Dismissal: Clough (59) - tripping.
Sin bin: Stearman (39) - late tackle.
HAWKS: 29 Stuart Kain; 5 John Oakes; 4 David Clayton; 21 Wayne McHugh; 26 Waine Pryce; 6 Danny Grimshaw; 7 Paul March; 15 Adam Sullivan; 9 Richard Chapman; 3 James Houston; 12 Steve Dooler; 10 Tom Haughey; 13 David March. Subs (all used): 14 Luke Haigh; 18 Charlie Wabo; 16 Neil Lowe; 8 Scott Woodcock.
Tries: P March (7), Pryce (12), Haughey (20), Grimshaw (40), D March (45, 60), McHugh (54), Clayton (79); **Goals:** McHugh 6/7, D March 1/1.
Rugby Leaguer & League Express Men of the Match: *City Knights:* Paul Stamp; *Hawks:* Danny Grimshaw.
Penalty count: 10-10; **Half-time:** 10-22;
Referee: Dave Merrick; **Attendance:** 1,002.

ROUND 12

Sunday 23rd May 2010

DONCASTER 16 SWINTON LIONS 0

DONCASTER: 1 Tommy Griffiths; 30 Dean Colton; 25 Chris Spurr; 4 Shaun Leaf; 22 Scott Wilson; 6 Simon Brown; 7 Craig Fawcett; 29 Liam Crawley; 32 Kyle Kesik; 15 Danny Stanley; 27 Matt Carbutt; 12 Ryan Steen; 34 Rob Lunt. Subs (all used): 20 Jack Ely; 14 Jake Bassinder; 3 Lee Gomersall; 28 Paul Hughes.
Tries: Kesik (2), Griffiths (9), Leaf (47, 53);
Goals: S Brown 0/4.
LIONS: 24 Gavin Dodd; 25 Barry Hamilton; 11 Tommy Grundy; 20 Chris Hull; 23 Rob Foxen; 6 Graham Holroyd; 7 Ian Watson; 16 Dana Wilson; 30 Wayne Corcoran; 31 Neil Cherryholme; 15 Lee Wingfield; 28 Saqib Murtza; 19 Neil Rigby. Subs (all used): 14 Gary Hulse; 18 Bruce Johnson; 10 Danny Heaton; 17 Andrew Isherwood.
Rugby Leaguer & League Express Men of the Match: *Doncaster:* Shaun Leaf; *Lions:* Gary Hulse.
Penalty count: 14-8; **Half-time:** 8-0;
Referee: Jamie Leahy; **Attendance:** 430.

GATESHEAD THUNDER 24 WORKINGTON TOWN 42

THUNDER: 34 Josh Stoker; 5 Joe Brown; 31 Matt Garside; 3 Tom Wilson; 29 Jimmy Atkinson; 6 Liam Duffy; 9 Ryan Clarke; 8 Jason Payne; 14 Will Bate; 18 Stephen Welton; 12 Rhys Clarke; 30 Richie Humphries; 32 Ade Aderiye. Subs (all used): 16 Dan O'Sullivan; 17 Chris Parker; 26 David Cash; 33 Reece Young.
Tries: Aderiye (25), Garside (62), Young (68), Duffy (74); **Goals:** Ryan Clarke 4/4.
TOWN: 5 Brett Carter; 2 Mike Backhouse; 3 Andrew Beattie; 15 Aaron Low; 17 Neil Frazer; 6 Liam Finch; 7 Scott Kaighan; 32 Ryan McDonald; 31 Darren Holt; 10 Kris Coward; 11 Mike Whitehead; 12 Jarrad Stack; 21 Paddy Coupar. Subs (all used): 14 Jamie Marshall; 25 Stewart Rhodes; 1 John Lebbon; 20 James Robinson.
Tries: Backhouse (3, 7), Low (19), Carter (28), Marshall (31), Kaighan (56, 65), Beattie (59);
Goals: Holt 4/7, Kaighan 1/1.
Rugby Leaguer & League Express Men of the Match: *Thunder:* Ryan Clarke; *Town:* Jarrad Stack.
Penalty count: 5-8; **Half-time:** 6-24;
Referee: Greg Dolan; **Attendance:** 286.

LONDON SKOLARS 22 SOUTH WALES SCORPIONS 70

SKOLARS: 31 Neil Thorman; 23 Olu Iwenofu; 24 Lamont Bryan; 4 Jason Cook; 30 Ade Adebisi; 17 Chad Isles; 7 Paul Thorman; 11 Oliver Purslow; 19 Liam Prescott; 20 Dave Williams; 13 Stephen Ball; 3 Matt Thomas; 32 Sam Gee. Subs (all used): 5 Austen Aggrey; 9 Gareth Honor; 34 Jamie Boston; 37 Kris Hodson.
Tries: N Thorman (10), Boston (34), Cook (35), Aggrey (80); **Goals:** P Thorman 3/4.
SCORPIONS: 31 Elliot Kear; 14 Jamie Murphy; 3 Lee Williams; 5 Ashley Bateman; 22 Curtis Cunningham; 6 Loz Wildbore; 15 Andrew Gay; 10 Gil Dudson; 7 Steve Parry; 8 Lewis Mills; 33 Lloyd White; 11 Christiaan Roets; 20 Geraint Davies. Subs (all used): 12 Neil Dallimore; 17 Barrie Phillips; 2 David James; 16 Joe Burke.
Tries: Dudson (5, 14), Bateman (16, 40), White (19, 24), Dallimore (27, 68), Williams (56), Parry (60), Murphy (63), D James (75); **Goals:** White 7/8, Wildbore 4/4.
Rugby Leaguer & League Express Men of the Match: *Skolars:* Jason Cook; *Scorpions:* Lloyd White.
Penalty count: 10-10; **Half-time:** 16-40;
Referee: Matthew Kidd; **Attendance:** 358.

OLDHAM 4 HUNSLET HAWKS 60

OLDHAM: 1 Paul O'Connor; 2 Lucas Onyango; 22 Paul Reilly; 4 Mick Fogerty; 5 John Gillam; 28 Gregg McNally; 7 Matt Ashe; 8 Jason Boults; 9 Martin Roden; 16 Wayne Kerr; 26 Ian Hodson; 13 Joe Chandler; 18 Chris Clarke. Subs (all used): 10 Dave Ellison; 15 Craig Robinson; 17 Danny Whitmore; 19 Ben Heaton.
Try: Onyango (12); **Goals:** Ashe 0/1.
HAWKS: 29 Stuart Kain; 26 Waine Pryce; 4 David Clayton; 21 Wayne McHugh; 2 Michael Mark; 6 Danny Grimshaw; 7 Paul March; 15 Adam Sullivan; 14 Luke Haigh; 3 James Houston; 12 Steve Dooler; 10 Tom Haughey; 13 David March. Subs (all used): 8 Scott Woodcock; 16 Neil Lowe; 19 Darren Robinson; 20 Joe Helme.
Tries: Pryce (5, 20, 43), Kain (25), McHugh (27, 72, 79), Grimshaw (36), Mark (39), D March (54), Woodcock (61); **Goals:** McHugh 8/12.
Rugby Leaguer & League Express Men of the Match: *Oldham:* Ian Hodson; *Hawks:* Neil Lowe.
Penalty count: 4-9; **Half-time:** 4-32;
Referee: Clint Sharrad; **Attendance:** 1,004.

ROCHDALE HORNETS 44 YORK CITY KNIGHTS 34

HORNETS: 32 Wayne English; 5 Bolu Fagborun; 4 Adam Bowman; 22 Damien Reid; 6 Dale Bloomfield; 24 Paul Crook; 7 Steve Roper; 8 Paul Raftrey; 29 Ryan Powell; 20 Semisi Cocka; 3 Dean Gorton; 12 Danny Smith; 18

John Cookson. Subs (all used): 10 Gareth Hayes; 16 Danny Samuel; 9 Phil Wood; 13 Craig Ashall.
Tries: Fagborun (8), Smith (15, 48), Cookson (18), Crook (40), Wood (45), Bloomfield (68);
Goals: Crook 8/8.
CITY KNIGHTS: 1 Danny Ratcliffe; 29 Dennis Tuffour; 28 Danny Wilson; 4 Lee Waterman; 5 Tom Lineham; 9 Joe McLocklan; 32 Paul Stamp; 36 Jon Fallon; 33 Jack Lee; 17 Nathan Freer; 11 Jordan Ross; 18 Matty Duckworth; 26 Steve Lewis. Subs (all used): 20 Chris Williams; 30 Jack Stearman; 12 Chris Clough; 25 Brett Waller.
Tries: Waterman (4, 55), Lee (21), Waller (26, 74), Tuffour (31); **Goals:** Waterman 4/5, McLocklan 1/1.
Rugby Leaguer & League Express Men of the Match: *Hornets:* Wayne English; *City Knights:* Lee Waterman.
Penalty count: 7-10; **Half-time:** 26-22;
Referee: Chris Leatherbarrow; **Attendance:** 472.

ROUND 13

Sunday 30th May 2010

DONCASTER 20 HUNSLET HAWKS 30

DONCASTER: 31 Michael Butterfield; 30 Dean Colton; 25 Chris Spurr; 4 Shaun Leaf; 22 Scott Wilson; 6 Simon Brown; 7 Craig Fawcett; 29 Liam Crawley; 32 Kyle Kesik; 27 Matt Carbutt; 33 Scott Watson; 12 Ryan Steen; 34 Rob Lunt. Subs (all used): 28 Paul Hughes; 20 Jack Ely; 16 Paul Shaw; 3 Lee Gomersall.
Tries: Lunt (6, 79), Colton (31), Crawley (71);
Goals: S Brown 2/4.
HAWKS: 29 Stuart Kain; 2 Michael Mark; 5 John Oakes; 21 Wayne McHugh; 26 Waine Pryce; 6 Danny Grimshaw; 7 Paul March; 15 Adam Sullivan; 14 Luke Haigh; 3 James Houston; 12 Steve Dooler; 10 Tom Haughey; 13 David March. Subs (all used): 8 Scott Woodcock; 18 Charlie Wabo; 19 Darren Robinson; 20 Joe Helme.
Tries: Pryce (14), Mark (18, 37), Grimshaw (23), McHugh (39), P March (49, 50);
Goals: D March 1/1, McHugh 0/4, Robinson 0/2.
Sin bin: Wabo (73) - holding down;
P March (79) - interference.
Rugby Leaguer & League Express Men of the Match: *Doncaster:* Rob Lunt; *Hawks:* Danny Grimshaw.
Penalty count: 8-5; **Half-time:** 8-20;
Referee: Dave Merrick; **Attendance:** 550.

GATESHEAD THUNDER 6 ROCHDALE HORNETS 64

THUNDER: 34 Josh Stoker; 5 Joe Brown; 31 Matt Garside; 3 Tom Wilson; 29 Jimmy Atkinson; 6 Liam Duffy; 9 Ryan Clarke; 8 Jason Payne; 14 Will Bate; 18 Stephen Welton; 12 Rhys Clarke; 30 Richie Humphries; 32 Ade Aderiye. Subs (all used): 16 Dan O'Sullivan; 17 Chris Parker; 26 David Cash; 33 Reece Young.
Try: Aderiye (11); **Goals:** Ryan Clarke 1/1.
HORNETS: 32 Wayne English; 5 Bolu Fagborun; 4 Adam Bowman; 22 Damien Reid; 2 Andy Saywell; 24 Paul Crook; 7 Steve Roper; 8 Paul Raftrey; 9 Phil Wood; 20 Semisi Cocka; 11 Mark Hobson; 12 Danny Smith; 13 Craig Ashall. Subs (all used): 18 John Cookson; 29 Ryan Powell; 28 Chris Hough; 6 Dale Bloomfield.
Tries: English (4, 39, 53), Ashall (19, 21, 79), Reid (27), Powell (31), Bloomfield (44), Saywell (49), Crook (64), Smith (75); **Goals:** Crook 8/12.
Rugby Leaguer & League Express Men of the Match: *Thunder:* Ryan Clarke; *Hornets:* Wayne English.
Penalty count: 4-7; **Half-time:** 6-32;
Referee: Warren Turley; **Attendance:** 265.

SWINTON LIONS 56 LONDON SKOLARS 28

LIONS: 24 Gavin Dodd; 38 Richard Flooks; 37 Simon Burkinshaw; 3 Sam Reay; 23 Rob Foxen; 20 Chris Hull; 7 Ian Watson; 10 Danny Heaton; 9 Phil Joseph; 31 Neil Cherryholme; 19 Neil Rigby; 15 Lee Wingfield; 36 Darren Hawkyard. Subs (all used): 17 Andrew Isherwood; 16 Dana Wilson; 18 Bruce Johnson; 14 Gary Hulse.
Tries: Flooks (11), Foxen (15, 56, 67), D Hawkyard (25), Watson (29), Johnson (33), Isherwood (60), Cherryholme (78), Joseph (80); **Goals:** Dodd 8/10.
SKOLARS: 31 Neil Thorman; 2 Dave Arnot; 17 Chad Isles; 39 John Paxton; 30 Ade Adebisi; 33 Jy-Mel Coleman; 19 Liam Prescott; 38 Michael Sykes; 32 Sam Gee; 11 Oliver Purslow; 13 Stephen Ball; 3 Matt Thomas; 34 Jamie Boston. Subs (all used): 5 Austen Aggrey; 37 Kris Hodson; 9 Gareth Honor; 7 Paul Thorman.
Tries: Prescott (6), Honor (41, 63), Paxton (55), Hodson (72); **Goals:** Prescott 1/1, P Thorman 3/4.
Rugby Leaguer & League Express Men of the Match: *Lions:* Rob Foxen; *Skolars:* Gareth Honor.
Penalty count: 10-9; **Half-time:** 28-6;
Referee: Peter Brooke; **Attendance:** 277.

WORKINGTON TOWN 16 OLDHAM 28

TOWN: 5 Brett Carter; 2 Mike Backhouse; 3 Andrew Beattie; 15 Aaron Low; 17 Neil Frazer; 6 Liam Finch; 7 Scott Kaighan; 32 Ryan McDonald; 31 Darren Holt; 10 Kris Coward; 11 Mike Whitehead; 12 Jarrad Stack; 21 Paddy Coupar. Subs (all used): 14 Jamie Marshall; 20 James Robinson; 25 Stewart Rhodes; 22 Ryan Campbell.
Tries: Beattie (3), Stack (24), Marshall (70);
Goals: Holt 1/2, Kaighan 1/2.
OLDHAM: 1 Paul O'Connor; 2 Lucas Onyango; 24 Marcus St Hilaire; 4 Mick Fogerty; 5 John Gillam; 28 Gregg McNally; 7 Matt Ashe; 8 Jason Boults; 9 Martin Roden; 16 Wayne Kerr; 26 Ian Hodson; 13 Joe Chandler; 18 Chris Clarke. Subs (all used): 10 Dave Ellison; 14 Luke Sutton; 19 Ben Heaton; 17 Danny Whitmore.
Tries: Boults (31), Ellison (35), Fogerty (39, 63), O'Connor (66); **Goals:** Ashe 4/5.
Rugby Leaguer & League Express Men of the Match: *Town:* Mike Whitehead; *Oldham:* Danny Whitmore.
Penalty count: 12-14; **Half-time:** 10-18;
Referee: Matthew Kidd; **Attendance:** 581.

YORK CITY KNIGHTS 24 BLACKPOOL PANTHERS 22

CITY KNIGHTS: 28 Danny Wilson; 29 Dennis Tuffour; 3 Mike Mitchell; 4 Lee Waterman; 5 Tom Lineham; 6 Chris Thorman; 1 Danny Ratcliffe; 36 Jon Fallon; 33 Jack Lee; 17 Nathan Freer; 11 Jordan Ross; 18 Matty Duckworth; 15 Luke Hardbottle. Subs (all used): 20 Chris Williams; 10 Alex Benson; 25 Brett Waller; 30 Jack Stearman.
Tries: Mitchell (7), Waterman (18), Lee (51), Lineham (79); **Goals:** Waterman 4/6.
PANTHERS: 1 Jonny Leather; 2 Damian Munro; 3 Casey Mayberry; 18 Martin Ainscough; 24 Paul Ballard; 6 Carl Forber; 7 Tom Hemingway; 28 Neil Holland; 9 John Clough; 10 Andy Hobson; 32 John Walker; 27 Danny Halliwell; 11 Kurt Haggerty. Subs (all used): 14 Martin Keavney; 4 Mark McCully; 15 Paul Anderson; 31 Stuart Howarth.
Tries: Mayberry (12), Leather (46), McCully (57), Munro (77); **Goals:** Hemingway 3/4.
Sin bin: Anderson (34) – high tackle.
Rugby Leaguer & League Express Men of the Match: *City Knights:* Tom Lineham; *Panthers:* Casey Mayberry.
Penalty count: 17-8; **Half-time:** 14-6;
Referee: Chris Leatherbarrow; **Attendance:** 535.

ROUND 3

Sunday 6th June 2010

OLDHAM 40 BLACKPOOL PANTHERS 26

OLDHAM: 1 Paul O'Connor; 2 Lucas Onyango; 24 Marcus St Hilaire; 4 Mick Fogerty; 5 John Gillam; 6 Neil Roden; 28 Gregg McNally; 8 Jason Boults; 9 Martin Roden; 16 Wayne Kerr; 27 Ian Hodson; 13 Joe Chandler; 18 Chris Clarke. Subs (all used): 10 Dave Ellison; 14 Luke Sutton; 19 Ben Heaton; 17 Danny Whitmore.
Tries: Onyango (32), St Hilaire (37), Chandler (43), McNally (45), Ellison (49), O'Connor (65);
Goals: McNally 7/8, O'Connor 1/1.
PANTHERS: 1 Jonny Leather; 5 Tom Woodcock; 3 Casey Mayberry; 18 Martin Ainscough; 2 Damian Munro; 31 Stuart Howarth; 7 Tom Hemingway; 28 Neil Holland; 9 John Clough; 10 Andy Hobson; 32 John Walker; 12 Paul Alcock; 11 Kurt Haggerty. Subs (all used): 14 Martin Keavney; 4 Mark McCully; 27 Danny Halliwell; 17 Kris Ratcliffe.
Tries: Woodcock (8), Munro (30, 40), Hemingway (60), Haggerty (63); **Goals:** Hemingway 3/6.
Rugby Leaguer & League Express Men of the Match: *Oldham:* Gregg McNally; *Panthers:* Tom Hemingway.
Penalty count: 10-11; **Half-time:** 16-14;
Referee: Tim Roby; **Attendance:** 923.

ROUND 6

Sunday 6th June 2010

GATESHEAD THUNDER 12 SWINTON LIONS 34

THUNDER: 34 Josh Stoker; 5 Joe Brown; 1 Kevin Neighbour; 3 Tom Wilson; 2 Robin Peers; 6 Liam Duffy; 35 Nigel Scott; 8 Jason Payne; 9 Ryan Clarke; 13 Matt Barron; 12 Rhys Clarke; 32 Ade Aderiye; 31 Matt Garside. Subs (all used): 14 Will Bate; 16 Dan O'Sullivan; 18 Stephen Welton; 25 Gareth Barron.
Tries: Peers (54), Neighbour (77);
Goals: Ryan Clarke 1/2, N Scott 1/1.
LIONS: 28 Alex Hurst; 38 Richard Flooks; 37 Simon Burkinshaw; 3 Sam Reay; 23 Rob Foxen; 20 Chris Hull; 7 Ian Watson; 10 Danny Heaton; 9 Phil Joseph; 31 Neil Cherryholme; 17 Andrew Isherwood; 15 Lee Wingfield; 36 Darren Hawkyard. Subs (all used): 14 Gary Hulse; 19 Neil Rigby; 16 Dana Wilson; 26 Dave Newton.
Tries: Wingfield (10), Wilson (23), Flooks (48), Heaton (61), Rigby (66), Foxen (70); **Goals:** Flooks 5/6.
Rugby Leaguer & League Express Men of the Match: *Thunder:* Jason Payne; *Lions:* Richard Flooks.
Penalty count: 16-4; **Half-time:** 2-12;
Referee: Clint Sharrad; **Attendance:** 353.

ROUND 14

Saturday 12th June 2010

LONDON SKOLARS 12 YORK CITY KNIGHTS 44

SKOLARS: 31 Neil Thorman; 5 Austen Aggrey; 39 John Paxton; 32 Sam Gee; 30 Ade Adebisi; 33 Jy-Mel Coleman; 7 Paul Thorman; 38 Michael Sykes; 9 Gareth Honor; 11 Oliver Purslow; 13 Stephen Ball; 37 Kris Hodson; 34 Jamie Boston. Subs (all used): 18 James Simon; 28 Ben Jones; 19 Liam Prescott; 16 Oliver Bloom.
Tries: Adebisi (17), P Thorman (55);
Goals: P Thorman 2/2.
CITY KNIGHTS: 28 Danny Wilson; 29 Dennis Tuffour; 3 Mike Mitchell; 4 Lee Waterman; 5 Tom Lineham; 33 Jack Lee; 1 Danny Ratcliffe; 17 Nathan Freer; 20 Chris Williams; 10 Alex Benson; 11 Jordan Ross; 18 Matty Duckworth; 15 Luke Hardbottle. Subs (all used): 27 Casey Bromilow; 25 Brett Waller; 26 Steve Lewis; 30 Jack Stearman.
Tries: Waterman (5), Tuffour (8, 20), Lee (12, 42), Ratcliffe (45, 79), Wilson (63); **Goals:** Waterman 6/8.
Rugby Leaguer & League Express Men of the Match: *Skolars:* Ade Adebisi; *City Knights:* Dennis Tuffour.
Penalty count: 8-5; **Half-time:** 6-20; **Referee:** Jamie Leahy; **Attendance:** 1,350 *(at Twickenham Stoop).*

Sunday 13th June 2010

BLACKPOOL PANTHERS 24 WORKINGTON TOWN 10

PANTHERS: 2 Damian Munro; 20 Marlon Miller; 22 Dave Llewellyn; 18 Martin Ainscough; 5 Tom Woodcock; 6 Carl Forber; 7 Tom Hemingway; 15 Paul Anderson; 9 John Clough; 17 Kris Ratcliffe; 27 Danny Halliwell; 4 Mark McCully; 11 Kurt Haggerty. Subs (all used): 14 Martin Keavney; 23 John Boland; 19 Adam Thomas; 16 Simon Svabic.
Tries: Ainscough (4), Halliwell (44), Clough (69), Hemingway (79); **Goals:** Hemingway 4/4.
TOWN: 1 John Lebbon; 2 Mike Backhouse; 3 Andrew Beattie; 15 Aaron Low; 17 Neil Frazer; 5 Brett Carter; 7 Scott Kaighan; 10 Kris Coward; 23 Phil Hewitt; 11 Mike Whitehead; 22 Ryan Campbell; 12 Jarrad Stack; 21 Paddy Coupar. Subs (all used): 14 Jamie Marshall; 20 James Robinson; 25 Stewart Rhodes; 31 Matthew Johnson.
Tries: Carter (16, 26); **Goals:** Kaighan 1/2.
Rugby Leaguer & League Express Men of the Match: *Panthers:* Tom Hemingway; *Town:* Brett Carter.
Penalty count: 8-7; **Half-time:** 6-10;
Referee: Clint Sharrad; **Attendance:** 248.

OLDHAM 28 DONCASTER 18

OLDHAM: 1 Paul O'Connor; 2 Lucas Onyango; 24 Marcus St Hilaire; 4 Mick Fogerty; 5 John Gillam; 6 Neil Roden; 28 Gregg McNally; 18 Chris Clarke; 9 Martin Roden; 16 Wayne Kerr; 19 Ben Heaton; 13 Joe Chandler; 27 Ian Hodson. Subs (all used): 8 Jason Boults; 10 Dave Ellison; 21 Valu Bentley; 17 Danny Whitmore.
Tries: Onyango (13), Fogerty (15), Bentley (38), Chandler (41), Gillam (48); **Goals:** McNally 4/5.
Sin bin: N Roden (68) - dissent.
On report: Fogerty (68) - alleged punching.
DONCASTER: 1 Tommy Griffiths; 30 Dean Colton; 4 Shaun Leaf; 25 Chris Spurr; 2 Aaron Henry; 6 Simon Brown; 7 Craig Fawcett; 24 Jamie Bovill; 28 Paul Hughes; 29 Liam Crawley; 27 Matt Carbutt; 12 Ryan Steen; 34 Rob Lunt. Subs (all used): 32 Kyle Kesik; 15 Danny Stanley; 33 Scott Watson; 20 Jack Ely.
Tries: Ely (35), Spurr (55), Lunt (71); **Goals:** S Brown 3/3.
On report: Kesik (68) - alleged high tackle on McNally.
Rugby Leaguer & League Express Men of the Match: *Oldham:* Mick Fogerty; *Doncaster:* Rob Lunt.
Penalty count: 9-14; **Half-time:** 16-6;
Referee: Chris Leatherbarrow; **Attendance:** 740.

ROCHDALE HORNETS 28 HUNSLET HAWKS 22

HORNETS: 32 Wayne English; 5 Bolu Fagborun; 3 Dean Gorton; 22 Damien Reid; 2 Andy Saywell; 24 Paul Crook; 7 Steve Roper; 8 Paul Raftrey; 9 Phil Wood; 10 Gareth Hayes; 16 Danny Samuel; 4 Adam Bowman; 13 Craig Ashall. Subs (all used): 18 John Cookson; 20 Semisi Cocka; 29 Ryan Powell; 12 Danny Smith.
Tries: Samuel (23), English (38), Gorton (45), Saywell (50), Crook (56); **Goals:** Crook 3/5;
Field goals: Crook (72), Ashall (77).
Sin bin: Raftrey (10) - dissent, (71) - obstruction.
HAWKS: 29 Stuart Kain; 2 Michael Mark; 5 John Oakes; 4 David Clayton; 26 Waine Pryce; 6 Danny Grimshaw; 7 Paul March; 15 Adam Sullivan; 14 Luke Haigh; 3 James Houston; 12 Steve Dooler; 18 Charlie Wabo; 10 Tom Haughey. Subs (all used): 16 Neil Lowe; 8 Scott Woodcock; 9 Richard Chapman; 32 Michael Kelly.
Tries: Haughey (13), P March (19), Lowe (29), Wabo (40); **Goals:** Grimshaw 3/4.
Rugby Leaguer & League Express Men of the Match: *Hornets:* Andy Saywell; *Hawks:* Waine Pryce.
Penalty count: 10-14; **Half-time:** 10-22;
Referee: Mohammed Drizza; **Attendance:** 814.

SOUTH WALES SCORPIONS 12 SWINTON LIONS 16

SCORPIONS: 14 Jamie Murphy; 31 Elliot Kear; 17 Barrie Phillips; 5 Ashley Bateman; 1 Craig Richards; 6 Loz Wildbore; 15 Andrew Gay; 10 Gil Dudson; 7 Steve Parry; 8 Lewis Mills; 20 Geraint Davies; 11 Christiaan Roets; 13 Aled James. Subs (all used): 16 Joe Burke; 24 Liam Roach; 12 Neil Dallimore; 34 Curtis Cunningham.
Tries: Parry (6), A James (68); **Goals:** Wildbore 2/4.
LIONS: 24 Gavin Dodd; 38 Richard Flooks; 37 Simon Burkinshaw; 3 Sam Reay; 23 Rob Foxen; 20 Chris Hull; 7 Ian Watson; 31 Neil Cherryholme; 9 Phil Joseph; 10 Danny Heaton; 17 Andrew Isherwood; 15 Lee Wingfield; 19 Neil Rigby. Subs (all used): 14 Gary Hulse; 36 Darren Hawkyard; 26 Dave Newton; 33 Danny Meekin.
Tries: Wingfield (18), Dodd (54), Foxen (73);
Goals: Dodd 2/3, Flooks 0/1.
Rugby Leaguer & League Express Men of the Match: *Scorpions:* Aled James; *Lions:* Gavin Dodd.
Penalty count: 6-10; **Half-time:** 6-6;
Referee: Greg Dolan; **Attendance:** 890.

ROUND 5

Sunday 20th June 2010

SWINTON LIONS 30 WORKINGTON TOWN 30

LIONS: 1 Richie Hawkyard; 38 Richard Flooks; 37 Simon Burkinshaw; 3 Sam Reay; 24 Gavin Dodd; 20 Chris Hull; 7 Ian Watson; 10 Danny Heaton; 9 Phil Joseph; 31 Neil Cherryholme; 17 Andrew Isherwood; 36 Darren Hawkyard; 19 Neil Rigby. Subs (all used): 14 Gary Hulse;

16 Dana Wilson; 33 Danny Meekin; 32 Andy Ainscough.
Tries: D Hawkyard (10), Joseph (22), Hulse (50), Watson (55), Dodd (76); **Goals:** Dodd 5/6.
TOWN: 5 Brett Carter; 2 Mike Backhouse; 3 Andrew Beattie; 15 Aaron Low; 17 Neil Frazer; 31 Darren Holt; 7 Scott Kaighan; 26 Ruairi McGoff; 23 Phil Hewitt; 10 Kris Coward; 11 Mike Whitehead; 12 Jarrad Stack; 21 Paddy Coupar. Subs (all used): 9 Jack Pedley; 20 James Robinson; 25 Stewart Rhodes; 22 Ryan Campbell.
Tries: Holt (14), Kaighan (30), Stack (35, 71), Pedley (65); **Goals:** Holt 5/7.
Rugby Leaguer & League Express Men of the Match: *Lions:* Phil Joseph; *Town:* Jack Pedley.
Penalty count: 9-8; **Half-time:** 10-18;
Referee: Matthew Kidd; **Attendance:** 287.

ROUND 10

Sunday 20th June 2010

HUNSLET HAWKS 28 BLACKPOOL PANTHERS 12

HAWKS: 29 Stuart Kain; 26 Waine Pryce; 21 Wayne McHugh; 4 David Clayton; 5 John Oakes; 6 Danny Grimshaw; 7 Paul March; 15 Adam Sullivan; 14 Luke Haigh; 3 James Houston; 12 Steve Dooler; 10 Tom Haughey; 13 David March. Subs (all used): 8 Scott Woodcock; 9 Richard Chapman; 18 Charlie Wabo; 20 Joe Helme.
Tries: Haigh (13), Chapman (29), McHugh (36), D March (69); **Goals:** D March 6/6.
PANTHERS: 2 Damian Munro; 20 Marlon Miller; 3 Casey Mayberry; 18 Martin Ainscough; 5 Tom Woodcock; 6 Carl Forber; 7 Tom Hemingway; 8 David Best; 9 John Clough; 28 Neil Holland; 27 Danny Halliwell; 12 Paul Alcock; 11 Kurt Haggerty. Subs (all used): 14 Martin Keavney; 15 Paul Anderson; 17 Kris Ratcliffe; 22 Dave Llewellyn.
Tries: Mayberry (47), Ainscough (77);
Goals: Hemingway 2/2.
Rugby Leaguer & League Express Men of the Match: *Hawks:* David March; *Panthers:* Casey Mayberry.
Penalty count: 12-5; **Half-time:** 20-0;
Referee: Craig Halloran; **Attendance:** 584.

ROUND 11

Sunday 20th June 2010

SOUTH WALES SCORPIONS 30 ROCHDALE HORNETS 25

SCORPIONS: 1 Craig Richards; 19 Lewis Reece; 13 Aled James; 11 Christiaan Roets; 5 Ashley Bateman; 6 Loz Wildbore; 15 Andrew Gay; 8 Lewis Mills; 7 Steve Parry; 24 Liam Roach; 20 Geraint Davies; 12 Neil Dallimore; 17 Barrie Phillips. Subs (all used): 16 Joe Burke; 29 Harri Greville; 18 Matt Hutchings; 34 Curtis Cunningham.
Tries: Parry (31), Roets (36), Mills (45), Wildbore (53), Cunningham (70); **Goals:** Wildbore 5/5.
HORNETS: 32 Wayne English; 5 Bolu Fagborun; 1 Craig Johnson; 22 Damien Reid; 2 Andy Saywell; 24 Paul Crook; 7 Steve Roper; 18 John Cookson; 29 Ryan Powell; 16 Danny Samuel; 3 Dean Gorton; 12 Danny Smith; 13 Craig Ashall. Subs (all used): 10 Gareth Hayes; 6 Dale Bloomfield; 9 Phil Wood; 20 Semisi Cocka.
Tries: Johnson (12), Powell (15), Reid (58), Gorton (61), Saywell (72); **Goals:** Crook 2/3, Ashall 0/2;
Field goal: Crook (39).
Rugby Leaguer & League Express Men of the Match: *Scorpions:* Loz Wildbore; *Hornets:* Paul Crook.
Penalty count: 7-8; **Half-time:** 12-13;
Referee: Warren Turley; **Attendance:** 522.

ROUND 15

Saturday 26th June 2010

DONCASTER 30 ROCHDALE HORNETS 20

DONCASTER: 31 Michael Butterfield; 2 Aaron Henry; 25 Chris Spurr; 4 Shaun Leaf; 30 Dean Colton; 6 Simon Brown; 7 Craig Fawcett; 29 Liam Crawley; 28 Paul Hughes; 27 Matt Carbutt; 33 Scott Watson; 12 Ryan Steen; 34 Rob Lunt. Subs (all used): 20 Jack Ely; 19 Gary Ellery; 15 Danny Stanley; 35 Aaron Dobek.
Tries: Henry (6), Spurr (12), Ely (47), Lunt (53, 60);
Goals: S Brown 5/6.
HORNETS: 32 Wayne English; 1 Craig Johnson; 3 Dean Gorton; 22 Damien Reid; 2 Andy Saywell; 24 Paul Crook; 7 Steve Roper; 10 Gareth Hayes; 29 Ryan Powell; 18 John Cookson; 16 Danny Samuel; 12 Danny Smith; 13 Craig Ashall. Subs (all used): 8 Paul Raftrey; 4 Adam Bowman; 20 Semisi Cocka; 28 Chris Hough.
Tries: Samuel (22), Saywell (37), Johnson (74), Cookson (78); **Goals:** Crook 2/4.
Rugby Leaguer & League Express Men of the Match: *Doncaster:* Simon Brown; *Hornets:* Wayne English.
Penalty count: 7-8; **Half-time:** 12-10;
Referee: Clint Sharrad; **Attendance:** 578.

GATESHEAD THUNDER 12 YORK CITY KNIGHTS 60

THUNDER: 34 Josh Stoker; 5 Joe Brown; 1 Kevin Neighbour; 3 Tom Wilson; 2 Robin Peers; 9 Ryan Clarke; 35 Nigel Scott; 8 Jason Payne; 26 David Cash; 13 Matt Barron; 12 Rhys Clarke; 32 Ade Aderiye; 31 Matt Garside. Subs (all used): 14 Will Bate; 17 Chris Parker; 18 Stephen Welton; 4 Michael Brown.
Tries: Garside (42, 77); **Goals:** N Scott 2/2.
CITY KNIGHTS: 28 Danny Wilson; 29 Dennis Tuffour; 3 Mike Mitchell; 4 Lee Waterman; 5 Tom Lineham; 33 Jack Lee; 1 Danny Ratcliffe; 17 Nathan Freer; 20 Chris Williams; 36 Davey Burns; 18 Matty Duckworth; 11 Jordan Ross; 15 Luke Hardbottle. Subs (all used): 27 Scott Woods; 10 Alex Benson; 31 Ed Smith; 30 Jack Stearman.
Tries: Lineham (4, 20), Lee (9, 74), Waterman (26, 59, 70), Stearman (29), Ratcliffe (39), Duckworth (45), Wilson (67); **Goals:** Waterman 8/11.
Rugby Leaguer & League Express Men of the Match: *Thunder:* Matt Garside; *City Knights:* Lee Waterman.
Penalty count: 4-7; **Half-time:** 0-34;
Referee: Greg Dolan; **Attendance:** 346.

Sunday 27th June 2010

SWINTON LIONS 6 BLACKPOOL PANTHERS 28

LIONS: 24 Gavin Dodd; 38 Richard Flooks; 37 Simon Burkinshaw; 28 Alex Hurst; 3 Sam Reay; 20 Chris Hull; 7 Ian Watson; 33 Danny Meekin; 1 Richie Hawkyard; 26 Dave Newton; 36 Darren Hawkyard; 17 Andrew Isherwood; 9 Phil Joseph. Subs (all used): 14 Gary Hulse; 16 Dana Wilson; 19 Neil Rigby; 32 Andy Ainscough.
Try: Reay (73); **Goals:** Dodd 1/1.
Sin bin: Joseph (7) - fighting.
PANTHERS: 18 Martin Ainscough; 5 Tom Woodcock; 22 Dave Llewellyn; 34 Dean Thompson; 2 Damian Munro; 16 Simon Svabic; 7 Tom Hemingway; 8 David Best; 9 John Clough; 15 Paul Anderson; 27 Danny Halliwell; 12 Paul Alcock; 4 Mark McCully. Subs (all used): 6 Carl Forber; 14 Martin Keavney; 17 Kris Ratcliffe; 23 John Boland.
Tries: Clough (12), McCully (26), Ainscough (34), Woodcock (57), Thompson (69); **Goals:** Hemingway 4/5.
Sin bin: Best (7) - fighting, (63) - dissent.
Rugby Leaguer & League Express Men of the Match: *Lions:* Andrew Isherwood; *Panthers:* Simon Svabic.
Penalty count: 7-7; **Half-time:** 0-18;
Referee: Matthew Thomasson; **Attendance:** 387.

WORKINGTON TOWN 38 SOUTH WALES SCORPIONS 24

TOWN: 5 Brett Carter; 2 Mike Backhouse; 3 Andrew Beattie; 15 Aaron Low; 17 Neil Frazer; 31 Darren Holt; 7 Scott Kaighan; 26 Ruairi McGoff; 9 Jack Pedley; 10 Kris Coward; 11 Mike Whitehead; 12 Jarrad Stack; 21 Paddy Coupar. Subs (all used): 14 Jamie Marshall; 20 James Robinson; 27 Matthew Johnson; 32 Ryan McDonald.
Tries: Coward (18), Marshall (36), Kaighan (47), Carter (52), Low (64), Coupar (76); **Goals:** Holt 7/8.
SCORPIONS: 19 Lewis Reece; 5 Ashley Bateman; 13 Aled James; 11 Christiaan Roets; 22 Curtis Cunningham; 15 Andrew Gay; 6 Loz Wildbore; 8 Lewis Mills; 7 Steve Parry; 12 Neil Dallimore; 24 Liam Roach; 17 Barrie Phillips; 20 Geraint Davies. Subs (all used): 34 Jamie Thackray; 37 Casey Bromilow; 16 Joe Burke; 2 David James.
Tries: Wildbore (32), Parry (55), Gay (67), A James (73); **Goals:** Wildbore 4/4.
Rugby Leaguer & League Express Men of the Match: *Town:* Paddy Coupar; *Scorpions:* Andrew Gay.
Penalty count: 10-8; **Half-time:** 16-6;
Referee: Peter Brooke; **Attendance:** 307.

HUNSLET HAWKS 60 LONDON SKOLARS 16

HAWKS: 1 Nathan Larvin; 26 Waine Pryce; 21 Wayne McHugh; 4 David Clayton; 2 Michael Mark; 6 Danny Grimshaw; 7 Paul March; 15 Adam Sullivan; 14 Luke Haigh; 3 James Houston; 30 Richard Knight; 18 Charlie Wabo; 13 David March. Subs (all used): 8 Scott Woodcock; 9 Richard Chapman; 10 Tom Haughey; 16 Neil Lowe.
Tries: McHugh (2, 45, 51, 71), Pryce (10, 26, 40, 80), Larvin (20), P March (38), Grimshaw (56), D March (73); **Goals:** D March 3/6, Knight 3/6.
SKOLARS: 31 Neil Thorman; 5 Austen Aggrey; 34 John Paxton; 32 Sam Gee; 23 Olu Iwenofu; 33 Jy-Mel Coleman; 7 Paul Thorman; 38 Michael Sykes; 9 Gareth Honor; 28 Ben Jones; 16 Oliver Bloom; 3 Matt Thomas; 19 Liam Prescott. Subs (all used): 18 James Simon; 11 Oliver Purslow; 13 Stephen Ball; 30 Ade Adebisi.
Tries: Adebisi (41, 47, 61); **Goals:** P Thorman 2/3.
Rugby Leaguer & League Express Men of the Match: *Hawks:* Waine Pryce; *Skolars:* Ade Adebisi.
Penalty count: 6-8; **Half-time:** 30-0;
Referee: Dave Merrick; **Attendance:** 309.

ROUND 16

Saturday 3rd July 2010

BLACKPOOL PANTHERS 44 SOUTH WALES SCORPIONS 24

PANTHERS: 18 Martin Ainscough; 5 Tom Woodcock; 34 Dean Thompson; 22 Dave Llewellyn; 2 Damian Munro; 16 Simon Svabic; 7 Tom Hemingway; 8 David Best; 9 John Clough; 15 Paul Anderson; 27 Danny Halliwell; 12 Paul Alcock; 4 Mark McCully. Subs (all used): 23 John Boland; 3 Casey Mayberry; 6 Carl Forber; 17 Kris Ratcliffe.
Tries: Clough (2, 78), Hemingway (39), Woodcock (43), McCully (48), Mayberry (53, 64), Ainscough (59);
Goals: Hemingway 6/8.
SCORPIONS: 31 Elliot Kear; 1 Craig Richards; 11 Christiaan Roets; 5 Ashley Bateman; 2 David James; 6 Loz Wildbore; 15 Andrew Gay; 8 Lewis Mills; 7 Steve Parry; 10 Gil Dudson; 12 Neil Dallimore; 20 Geraint Davies; 17 Barrie Phillips. Subs (all used): 16 Joe Burke; 37 Casey Bromilow; 29 Harri Greville; 24 Liam Roach.
Tries: Bateman (12), Parry (20, 72), Gay (25);
Goals: Wildbore 4/5.
Rugby Leaguer & League Express Men of the Match: *Panthers:* Tom Woodcock; *Scorpions:* Lewis Mills.
Penalty count: 4-5; **Half-time:** 10-16;
Referee: Dave Merrick; **Attendance:** 266.

Sunday 4th July 2010

GATESHEAD THUNDER 10 OLDHAM 68

THUNDER: 34 Josh Stoker; 29 Jimmy Atkinson; 1 Kevin Neighbour; 4 Michael Brown; 2 Robin Peers; 6 Liam Duffy; 35 Nigel Scott; 8 Jason Payne; 9 Ryan Clarke; 18 Stephen Welton; 12 Rhys Clarke; 3 Tom Wilson; 5 Joe Brown. Subs (all used): 14 Will Bate; 15 Dan O'Sullivan; 17 Chris Parker; 32 Ade Aderiye.
Tries: Bate (38), Neighbour (69); **Goals:** N Scott 1/2.
OLDHAM: 1 Paul O'Connor; 2 Lucas Onyango; 24 Marcus St Hilaire; 4 Mick Fogerty; 5 John Gillam; 7 Matt Ashe; 28 Gregg McNally; 8 Jason Boults; 9 Martin Roden; 16 Wayne Kerr; 27 Ian Hodson; 13 Joe Chandler; 18 Chris Clarke. Subs (all used): 10 Dave Ellison; 15 Craig Robinson; 19 Ben Heaton; 17 Danny Whitmore.
Tries: Fogerty (15, 22, 74), O'Connor (25, 63), Onyango (30), Whitmore (34, 77), Clarke (51), Heaton (55), Kerr (59), Ellison (80); **Goals:** Ashe 1/2, McNally 9/10.
Sin bin: O'Connor (43) - dissent.
Rugby Leaguer & League Express Men of the Match: *Thunder:* Will Bate; *Oldham:* Gregg McNally.
Penalty count: 13-7; **Half-time:** 6-28;
Referee: Matthew Kidd; **Attendance:** 433.

LONDON SKOLARS 28 ROCHDALE HORNETS 26

SKOLARS: 31 Neil Thorman; 2 Dave Arnot; 37 John Paxton; 4 Jason Cook; 25 Smokie Junor; 34 Jy-Mel Coleman; 7 Paul Thorman; 13 Stephen Ball; 32 Sam Gee; 5 Austen Aggrey; 3 Matt Thomas; 16 Oliver Bloom; 26 Jamie Boston. Subs (all used): 9 Gareth Honor; 11 Oliver Purslow; 39 Cariern Clement-Pascall; 38 Michael Sykes.
Tries: Jy-Mel Coleman (10), M Thomas (17), Paxton (23, 49), Gee (80); **Goals:** P Thorman 4/5.
HORNETS: 32 Wayne English; 6 Dale Bloomfield; 3 Dean Gorton; 22 Damien Reid; 2 Andy Saywell; 24 Paul Crook; 7 Steve Roper; 4 Adam Bowman; 9 Phil Wood; 36 Peter Fairhurst; 12 Danny Smith; 13 Craig Ashall; 29 Ryan Powell. Subs (all used): 18 John Cookson; 10 Gareth Hayes; 25 Dale Blackmore; 26 Andy Taylor.
Tries: Bloomfield (38, 72), Roper (44), Wood (65), Saywell (70); **Goals:** Crook 3/6.
Dismissal: Saywell (80) - dissent.
Sin bin: Roper (51) - dissent.
Rugby Leaguer & League Express Men of the Match: *Skolars:* John Paxton; *Hornets:* Paul Crook.
Penalty count: 9-9; **Half-time:** 18-4;
Referee: Chris Leatherbarrow; **Attendance:** 372.

SWINTON LIONS 10 HUNSLET HAWKS 58

LIONS: 1 Richie Hawkyard; 24 Gavin Dodd; 3 Sam Reay; 36 Darren Hawkyard; 38 Richard Flooks; 14 Gary Hulse; 7 Ian Watson; 31 Anthony Mullally; 9 Phil Joseph; 26 Dave Newton; 32 Andy Ainscough; 27 Anthony Stewart; 19 Neil Rigby. Subs (all used): 23 Rob Foxen; 16 Dana Wilson; 17 Andrew Isherwood; 33 Danny Meekin.
Tries: Foxen (29), Joseph (80); **Goals:** Dodd 1/2.
Sin bin: D Hawkyard (23) - holding down.
HAWKS: 29 Stuart Kain; 5 John Oakes; 21 Wayne McHugh; 10 Tom Haughey; 26 Waine Pryce; 6 Danny Grimshaw; 7 Paul March; 20 Joe Helme; 14 Luke Haigh; 3 James Houston; 12 Steve Dooler; 30 Richard Knight; 13 David March. Subs (all used): 18 Charlie Wabo; 9 Richard Chapman; 8 Scott Woodcock; 16 Neil Lowe.
Tries: Pryce (3, 44), Kain (18, 37, 68), Haughey (24), Haigh (47), Dooler (50), Grimshaw (56), Wabo (60), D March (71); **Goals:** Knight 3/5, D March 4/6.
Rugby Leaguer & League Express Men of the Match: *Lions:* Phil Joseph; *Hawks:* Tom Haughey.
Penalty count: 7-17; **Half-time:** 4-20;
Referee: Warren Turley; **Attendance:** 386.

YORK CITY KNIGHTS 32 DONCASTER 16

CITY KNIGHTS: 28 Danny Wilson; 29 Dennis Tuffour; 3 Mike Mitchell; 4 Lee Waterman; 5 Tom Lineham; 27 James Haynes; 1 Danny Ratcliffe; 10 Alex Benson; 33 Jack Lee; 17 Nathan Freer; 11 Jordan Ross; 18 Matty Duckworth; 15 Luke Hardbottle. Subs (all used): 31 Ed Smith; 20 Chris Williams; 12 Chris Clough; 30 Jack Stearman.
Tries: Waterman (23), Lineham (28, 52, 78), Lee (38), Wilson (54), Mitchell (63);
Goals: Waterman 0/1, Ratcliffe 2/5, Tuffour 0/2.
Sin bin: Hardbottle (42) - late tackle;
Lineham (58) - fighting.
DONCASTER: 31 Michael Butterfield; 2 Aaron Henry; 25 Chris Spurr; 4 Shaun Leaf; 22 Scott Wilson; 6 Simon Brown; 7 Craig Fawcett; 19 Gary Ellery; 28 Paul Hughes; 29 Liam Crawley; 33 Scott Watson; 12 Ryan Steen; 34 Rob Lunt. Subs (all used): 20 Jack Ely; 1 Tommy Griffiths; 35 Aaron Dobek; 36 Ben Jones.
Tries: Lunt (15), Leaf (36), Spurr (66);
Goals: S Brown 2/2, Spurr 0/1.
Sin bin: S Brown (58) - fighting.
Rugby Leaguer & League Express Men of the Match: *City Knights:* Danny Ratcliffe; *Doncaster:* Liam Crawley.
Penalty count: 16-8; **Half-time:** 14-12;
Referee: Tim Roby; **Attendance:** 735.

ROUND 17

Sunday 11th July 2010

SOUTH WALES SCORPIONS 70 GATESHEAD THUNDER 16

SCORPIONS: 31 Elliot Kear; 1 Craig Richards; 5 Ashley

Hunslet's Waine Pryce dives past Danny Ratcliffe to score against York

Bateman; 19 Lewis Reece; 2 David James; 37 Casey Bromilow; 15 Andrew Gay; 8 Lewis Mills; 7 Steve Parry; 12 Neil Dallimore; 20 Geraint Davies; 17 Barrie Phillips; 11 Christiaan Roets. Subs (all used): 16 Joe Burke; 23 Alan Pope; 9 Joe McLocklan; 34 Curtis Cunningham.
Tries: Kear (5, 17, 25), D James (11),
Parry (20, 61, 63), Richards (28), Reece (34, 37),
Pope (46), Cunningham (74); **Goals:** Reece 11/12.
THUNDER: 34 Josh Stoker; 2 Robin Peers; 1 Kevin Neighbour; 4 Michael Brown; 15 Dan O'Sullivan; 9 Ryan Clarke; 6 Liam Duffy; 8 Jason Payne; 14 Will Bate; 13 Matt Barron; 31 Matt Garside; 12 Rhys Clarke; 5 Joe Brown. Subs (all used): 18 Stephen Welton; 32 Ade Aderiye; 33 Reece Young; 17 Chris Parker.
Tries: Bate (58), Aderiye (78), M Brown (80);
Goals: Ryan Clarke 2/3.
Rugby Leaguer & League Express Men of the Match:
Scorpions: Lewis Reece; *Thunder:* Ade Aderiye.
Penalty count: 5-6; **Half-time:** 46-0;
Referee: Chris Leatherbarrow; **Attendance:** 480.

WORKINGTON TOWN 38 LONDON SKOLARS 34

TOWN: 5 Brett Carter; 29 Elliot Miller; 3 Andrew Beattie; 15 Aaron Low; 17 Neil Frazer; 27 Darren Holt; 7 Scott Kaighan; 25 Stewart Rhodes; 14 Jamie Marshall; 10 Kris Coward; 26 Ruairi McGoff; 12 Jarrad Stack; 21 Paddy Coupar. Subs (all used): 9 Jack Pedley; 20 James Robinson; 31 Keiron McAvoy; 28 Ryan McDonald.
Tries: Kaighan (17), Miller (19, 63), Coupar (24),
Low (27, 37), Robinson (31); **Goals:** Holt 5/7.
SKOLARS: 31 Neil Thorman; 2 Dave Arnot; 37 John Paxton; 4 Jason Cook; 25 Smokie Junor; 34 Jy-Mel Coleman; 7 Paul Thorman; 38 Michael Sykes; 32 Sam Gee; 13 Stephen Ball; 16 Oliver Bloom; 3 Matt Thomas; 26 Jamie Boston. Subs (all used): 11 Oliver Purslow; 9 Gareth Honor; 18 James Simon; 33 Cariern Clement-Pascall.
Tries: Gee (3, 14), Cook (44), Jy-Mel Coleman (57, 60), M Thomas (67); **Goals:** P Thorman 5/6.
Rugby Leaguer & League Express Men of the Match:
Town: Ryan McDonald; *Skolars:* Sam Gee.
Penalty count: 8-10; **Half-time:** 34-12;
Referee: Craig Halloran; **Attendance:** 411.

DONCASTER 18 BLACKPOOL PANTHERS 46

DONCASTER: 1 Tommy Griffiths; 2 Aaron Henry; 3 Lee Gomersall; 31 Michael Butterfield; 30 Dean Colton; 35 Aaron Dobek; 7 Craig Fawcett; 19 Gary Ellery; 28 Paul Hughes; 29 Liam Crawley; 12 Ryan Steen; 36 Ben Jones; 34 Rob Lunt. Subs (all used): 24 Jamie Bovill; 20 Jack Ely; 32 Kyle Kesik; 22 Scott Wilson.
Tries: Colton (46), Ellery (49), Ely (56); **Goals:** Dobek 3/3.
PANTHERS: 18 Martin Ainscough; 20 Marlon Miller; 3 Casey Mayberry; 34 Dean Thompson; 5 Tom Woodcock; 6 Carl Forber; 7 Tom Hemingway; 8 David Best; 9 John Clough; 17 Kris Ratcliffe; 27 Danny Halliwell; 2 Dave

Llewellyn; 4 Mark McCully. Subs (all used): 28 Neil Holland; 23 John Boland; 2 Damian Munro; 19 Adam Thomas.
Tries: Forber (1), Miller (14), Thompson (26),
Mayberry (29, 53), Munro (60), Ainscough (65),
Hemingway (74); **Goals:** Hemingway 7/8.
Sin bin: Forber (54) - interference.
Rugby Leaguer & League Express Men of the Match:
Doncaster: Aaron Dobek; *Panthers:* Martin Ainscough.
Penalty count: 11-5; **Half-time:** 0-24;
Referee: Dave Merrick; **Attendance:** 485.

OLDHAM 42 SWINTON LIONS 30

OLDHAM: 1 Paul O'Connor; 2 Lucas Onyango; 24 Marcus St Hilaire; 4 Mick Fogerty; 5 John Gillam; 6 Neil Roden; 28 Gregg McNally; 18 Chris Clarke; 9 Martin Roden; 16 Wayne Kerr; 27 Ian Hodson; 13 Joe Chandler; 21 Valu Bentley. Subs (all used): 8 Jason Boults; 10 Dave Ellison; 17 Danny Whitmore; 19 Ben Heaton.
Tries: Clarke (10), St Hilaire (15), Gillam (36, 54),
N Roden (42), Kerr (62), Heaton (72), McNally (80);
Goals: McNally 5/8.
LIONS: 1 Richie Hawkyard; 38 Richard Flooks; 37 Simon Burkinshaw; 24 Gavin Dodd; 23 Rob Foxen; 34 Craig Harvey; 7 Ian Watson; 33 Danny Meekin; 9 Phil Joseph; 31 Anthony Mullally; 36 Darren Hawkyard; 15 Lee Wingfield; 39 Dale Cunniffe. Subs (all used): 14 Gary Hulse; 16 Dana Wilson; 18 Bruce Johnson; 32 Andy Ainscough.
Tries: Foxen (17), Joseph (31, 74), D Hawkyard (50),
Burkinshaw (67); **Goals:** Dodd 5/5.
Sin bin: Cunniffe (4) - late tackle;
Hulse (32) - interference.
Rugby Leaguer & League Express Men of the Match:
Oldham: Neil Roden; *Lions:* Phil Joseph.
Penalty count: 12-11; **Half-time:** 16-12;
Referee: Peter Brooke; **Attendance:** 841.

HUNSLET HAWKS 34 YORK CITY KNIGHTS 18

HAWKS: 29 Stuart Kain; 26 Waine Pryce; 10 Tom Haughey; 4 David Clayton; 5 John Oakes; 6 Danny Grimshaw; 7 Paul March; 15 Adam Sullivan; 14 Luke Haigh; 3 James Houston; 12 Steve Dooler; 30 Richard Knight; 13 David March. Subs (all used): 8 Scott Woodcock; 9 Richard Chapman; 16 Neil Lowe; 18 Charlie Wabo.
Tries: Pryce (13), Woodcock (22), Haughey (30, 38),
P March (65), Chapman (76);
Goals: Knight 2/3, D March 3/3.
CITY KNIGHTS: 2 Wayne Reittie; 28 Danny Wilson; 3 Mike Mitchell; 34 Danny Allan; 5 Tom Lineham; 6 Chris Thorman; 1 Danny Ratcliffe; 17 Nathan Freer; 33 Jack Lee; 10 Alex Benson; 11 Jordan Ross; 18 Matty Duckworth; 15 Luke Hardbottle. Subs (all used): 12 Chris Clough; 20 Chris Williams; 25 Brett Waller; 30 Jack Stearman.

Tries: Thorman (9), Lee (33), Hardbottle (61);
Goals: Ratcliffe 3/3.
Rugby Leaguer & League Express Men of the Match:
Hawks: Paul March; *City Knights:* Chris Thorman.
Penalty count: 9-6; **Half-time:** 22-12;
Referee: Clint Sharrad; **Attendance:** 537.

ROUND 18

Sunday 25th July 2010

BLACKPOOL PANTHERS 22 OLDHAM 24

PANTHERS: 18 Martin Ainscough; 5 Tom Woodcock; 3 Casey Mayberry; 34 Dean Thompson; 2 Damian Munro; 6 Carl Forber; 7 Tom Hemingway; 17 Kris Ratcliffe; 9 John Clough; 28 Neil Holland; 27 Danny Halliwell; 12 Paul Alcock; 4 Mark McCully. Subs (all used): 8 David Best; 10 Andy Hobson; 19 Adam Thomas; 22 Dave Llewellyn.
Tries: Mayberry (15, 45), Munro (58), Halliwell (72);
Goals: Hemingway 3/4.
OLDHAM: 1 Paul O'Connor; 2 Lucas Onyango; 24 Marcus St Hilaire; 4 Mick Fogerty; 5 John Gillam; 6 Neil Roden; 28 Gregg McNally; 8 Jason Boults; 9 Martin Roden; 16 Wayne Kerr; 27 Ian Hodson; 13 Joe Chandler; 21 Valu Bentley. Subs (all used): 10 Dave Ellison; 14 Luke Sutton; 17 Danny Whitmore; 19 Ben Heaton.
Tries: St Hilaire (8), O'Connor (25, 30, 51), Fogerty (79);
Goals: McNally 2/5.
Rugby Leaguer & League Express Men of the Match:
Panthers: John Clough; *Oldham:* Paul O'Connor.
Penalty count: 8-11; **Half-time:** 6-14;
Referee: Clint Sharrad; **Attendance:** 780.

GATESHEAD THUNDER 16 HUNSLET HAWKS 86

THUNDER: 34 Josh Stoker; 15 Dan O'Sullivan; 1 Kevin Neighbour; 4 Michael Brown; 2 Robin Peers; 6 Liam Duffy; 9 Ryan Clarke; 8 Jason Payne; 33 Reece Young; 13 Matt Baron; 12 Rhys Clarke; 3 Tom Wilson; 5 Joe Brown. Subs (all used): 14 Will Bate; 17 Chris Parker; 18 Stephen Welton; 32 Ade Aderiye.
Tries: M Brown (15), Wilson (59), Ryan Clarke (80);
Goals: Ryan Clarke 2/3.
Sin bin: Parker (37) - interference.
HAWKS: 29 Stuart Kain; 2 Michael Mark; 5 John Oakes; 4 David Clayton; 26 Waine Pryce; 6 Danny Grimshaw; 7 Paul March; 20 Joe Helme; 9 Richard Chapman; 3 James Houston; 18 Charlie Wabo; 10 Tom Haughey; 13 David March. Subs (all used): 31 Louis Stead; 30 Richard Knight; 16 Neil Lowe; 32 George Rayner.
Tries: Pryce (3, 54, 57, 62, 69, 76), Chapman (16),
Houston (29), P March (31), Wabo (38),
Rayner (41, 63), Haughey (51), Kain (56), Knight (75),
Mark (78); **Goals:** D March 11/13, Knight 0/3.
Rugby Leaguer & League Express Men of the Match:
Thunder: Ryan Clarke; *Hawks:* Waine Pryce.

Penalty count: 4-11; **Half time:** 6-28;
Referee: Gareth Hewer; **Attendance:** 401.

LONDON SKOLARS 26 DONCASTER 38

SKOLARS: 31 Neil Thorman; 30 Ade Adebisi; 37 John Paxton; 4 Jason Cook; 25 Smokie Junor; 34 Jy-Mel Coleman; 7 Paul Thorman; 13 Stephen Ball; 32 Sam Gee; 5 Austen Aggrey; 16 Oliver Bloom; 33 Cariern Clement-Pascall; 26 Jamie Boston. Subs (all used): 19 Liam Prescott; 9 Gareth Honor; 38 Michael Sykes; 11 Oliver Purslow.
Tries: Adebisi (30), Jy-Mel Coleman (44), Purslow (49), P Thorman (63), Junor (66); **Goals:** P Thorman 3/5.
DONCASTER: 31 Michael Butterfield; 30 Dean Colton; 4 Shaun Leaf; 25 Chris Spurr; 2 Aaron Henry; 35 Aaron Dobek; 7 Craig Fawcett; 36 Ben Jones; 28 Paul Hughes; 29 Liam Crawley; 33 Scott Watson; 12 Ryan Steen; 34 Rob Lunt. Subs (all used): 20 Jack Ely; 32 Kyle Kesik; 3 Lee Gomersall; 27 Matt Carbutt.
Tries: Watson (21), Leaf (25, 34), Steen (38), Spurr (42), Hughes (55), Fawcett (58); **Goals:** Dobek 5/7.
Rugby Leaguer & League Express Men of the Match:
Skolars: Jy-Mel Coleman; Doncaster: Shaun Leaf.
Penalty count: 10-5; **Half-time:** 4-20;
Referee: Matthew Kidd; **Attendance:** 290.

ROCHDALE HORNETS 46 SOUTH WALES SCORPIONS 14

HORNETS: 32 Wayne English; 6 Dale Bloomfield; 3 Dean Gorton; 22 Damien Reid; 2 Andy Saywell; 24 Paul Crook; 7 Steve Roper; 16 Danny Samuel; 9 Phil Wood; 36 Peter Fairhurst; 15 Dayne Donoghue; 12 Danny Smith; 13 Craig Ashall. Subs (all used): 18 John Cookson; 29 Ryan Powell; 4 Adam Bowman; 28 Chris Hough.
Tries: Gorton (2), Cookson (25), Reid (30, 43, 75), Smith (35), Donoghue (51), Bloomfield (70);
Goals: Crook 3/4, Roper 4/5.
SCORPIONS: 31 Elliot Kear; 2 David James; 3 Lee Williams; 5 Ashley Bateman; 1 Craig Richards; 15 Andrew Gay; 37 Casey Bromilow; 8 Lewis Mills; 7 Steve Parry; 10 Gil Dudson; 17 Barrie Phillips; 13 Aled James; 20 Geraint Davies. Subs (all used): 12 Neil Dallimore; 14 Jamie Murphy; 33 Lloyd White; 38 Gareth Dean.
Tries: Williams (6), Murphy (40);
Goals: A James 1/1, White 2/2.
Rugby Leaguer & League Express Men of the Match:
Hornets: Damien Reid; Scorpions: Lloyd White.
Penalty count: 9-9; **Half-time:** 24-14;
Referee: Matthew Thomasson; **Attendance:** 471.

YORK CITY KNIGHTS 18 WORKINGTON TOWN 14

CITY KNIGHTS: 31 James Haynes; 28 Danny Wilson; 3 Mike Mitchell; 34 Danny Allan; 5 Tom Lineham; 6 Chris Thorman; 1 Danny Ratcliffe; 36 Callum Dinsdale; 33 Jack Lee; 17 Nathan Freer; 18 Matty Duckworth; 11 Jordan Hoss; 15 Luke Hardbottle. Subs (all used): 20 Chris Williams; 26 Steve Lewis; 30 Jack Stearman; 12 Chris Clough.
Tries: Mitchell (58), Lewis (68), Lee (77);
Goals: Ratcliffe 3/3.
TOWN: 5 Brett Carter; 2 Mike Backhouse; 17 Neil Frazer; 15 Aaron Low; 14 Jamie Marshall; 27 Darren Holt; 7 Scott Kaighan; 10 Kris Coward; 9 Jack Pedley; 25 Stewart Rhodes; 11 Mike Whitehead; 12 Jarrad Stack; 21 Paddy Coupar. Subs (all used): 20 James Robinson; 28 Ryan McDonald; 19 Joe McKenna; 29 Matthew Johnson.
Tries: Pedley (6), Stack (70); **Goals:** Holt 3/4.
Sin bin: Whitehead (62) - late tackle on Wilson.
Rugby Leaguer & League Express Men of the Match:
City Knights: Nathan Freer; Town: Jarrad Stack.
Penalty count: 14-6; **Half-time:** 0-8;
Referee: Dave Merrick; **Attendance:** 612.

ROUND 19

Saturday 31st July 2010

BLACKPOOL PANTHERS 54 LONDON SKOLARS 40

PANTHERS: 18 Martin Ainscough; 20 Marlon Miller; 3 Casey Mayberry; 22 Dave Llewellyn; 2 Damian Munro; 6 Carl Forber; 7 Tom Hemingway; 15 Paul Anderson; 9 John Clough; 10 Andy Hobson; 27 Danny Halliwell; 4 Mark McCully; 32 Mark Roberts. Subs (all used): 14 Martin Keavney; 28 Neil Holland; 23 John Boland; 31 Eddie Vaughan.
Tries: Mayberry (9), Ainscough (11, 22), Clough (14), Forber (18, 80), McCully (37), Hobson (47), Vaughan (50); **Goals:** Hemingway 9/9.
SKOLARS: 31 Neil Thorman; 30 Ade Adebisi; 37 John Paxton; 4 Jason Cook; 25 Smokie Junor; 33 Jy-Mel Coleman; 7 Paul Thorman; 32 Sam Gee; 13 Stephen Ball; 3 Matt Thomas; 16 Oliver Bloom; 26 Jamie Boston. Subs (all used): 5 Austen Aggrey; 11 Oliver Purslow; 18 James Simon; 9 Gareth Honor.
Tries: Gee (4, 66, 75), Jy-Mel Coleman (29, 58), Paxton (34), Bloom (42), Adebisi (71); **Goals:** P Thorman 4/8.
Rugby Leaguer & League Express Men of the Match:
Panthers: Casey Mayberry; Skolars: Sam Gee.
Penalty count: 7-10; **Half-time:** 36-16;
Referee: Greg Dolan; **Attendance:** 289.

Sunday 1st August 2010

DONCASTER 66 GATESHEAD THUNDER 0

DONCASTER: 31 Michael Butterfield; 30 Dean Colton; 3 Lee Gomersall; 25 Chris Spurr; 2 Aaron Henry; 35 Aaron Dobek; 7 Craig Fawcett; 36 Ben Jones; 32 Kyle Kesik; 29 Liam Crawley; 33 Scott Watson; 12 Ryan Steen; 34 Rob

Oldham's Chris Clarke grounded against South Wales

Lunt. Subs (all used): 28 Paul Hughes; 20 Jack Ely; 27 Matt Carbutt; 19 Gary Ellery.
Tries: Watson (4), Henry (12, 54, 71), Colton (30, 62), Lunt (34, 46, 49), Butterfield (52), Dobek (60), Fawcett (64); **Goals:** Dobek 9/12.
THUNDER: 34 Josh Stoker; 2 Robin Peers; 3 Tom Wilson; 1 Kevin Neighbour; 4 Michael Brown; 35 Nigel Scott; 9 Ryan Clarke; 8 Jason Payne; 33 Reece Young; 13 Matt Barron; 12 Rhys Clarke; 31 Matt Garside; 5 Joe Brown. Subs (all used): 18 Stephen Welton; 14 Will Bate; 17 Chris Parker; 32 Ade Aderiye.
Rugby Leaguer & League Express Men of the Match:
Doncaster: Craig Fawcett; Thunder: Joe Brown.
Penalty count: 3-5; **Half-time:** 20-0;
Referee: Chris Leatherbarrow; **Attendance:** 525.

OLDHAM 24 SOUTH WALES SCORPIONS 42

OLDHAM: 1 Paul O'Connor; 2 Lucas Onyango; 24 Marcus St Hilaire; 4 Mick Fogerty; 5 John Gillam; 7 Matt Ashe; 28 Gregg McNally; 8 Jason Boults; 9 Martin Roden; 16 Wayne Kerr; 27 Ian Hodson; 13 Joe Chandler; 21 Valu Bentley. Subs (all used): 10 Dave Ellison; 18 Chris Clarke; 17 Danny Whitmore; 19 Ben Heaton.
Tries: Onyango (31), McNally (39), Ashe (56), Heaton (79); **Goals:** McNally 3/3, Ashe 1/1.
SCORPIONS: 31 Elliot Kear; 14 Jamie Murphy; 3 Lee Williams; 5 Ashley Bateman; 11 Christiaan Roets; 15 Andrew Gay; 37 Casey Bromilow; 10 Gil Dudson; 33 Lloyd White; 20 Geraint Davies; 6 Loz Wildbore; 8 Lewis Mills; 13 Aled James. Subs (all used): 12 Neil Dallimore; 17 Barrie Phillips; 7 Steve Parry; 24 Liam Roach.
Tries: White (2, 26, 63), Parry (36), Gay (45), Bromilow (51); **Goals:** White 7/7, Wildbore 2/2.
On report: Alleged dangerous tackle (59).
Rugby Leaguer & League Express Men of the Match:
Oldham: Gregg McNally; Scorpions: Lloyd White.
Penalty count: 10-9; **Half-time:** 12-18;
Referee: Craig Halloran; **Attendance:** 908.

SWINTON LIONS 42 YORK CITY KNIGHTS 48

LIONS: 1 Richie Hawkyard; 28 Alex Hurst; 27 Anthony Stewart; 24 Gavin Dodd; 23 Rob Foxen; 34 Craig Harvey; 7 Ian Watson; 31 Anthony Mullally; 9 Phil Joseph; 33 Danny Meekin; 36 Darren Hawkyard; 39 Dale Cunniffe; 19 Neil Rigby. Subs (all used): 14 Gary Hulse; 16 Dana Wilson; 40 Joe Fitzpatrick; 32 Andy Ainscough.
Tries: Cunniffe (8), Dodd (21, 47), R Hawkyard (26), Hurst (45, 77), Foxen (62), Joseph (75); **Goals:** Dodd 5/9.
Sin bin: Watson (44) - fighting; Harvey (69) - dissent.
CITY KNIGHTS: 31 James Haynes; 28 Danny Wilson; 3 Mike Mitchell; 34 Danny Allan; 5 Tom Lineham; 6 Chris Thorman; 1 Danny Ratcliffe; 17 Nathan Freer; 33 Jack Lee; 36 Callum Dinsdale; 11 Jordan Ross; 18 Matty Duckworth; 15 Luke Hardbottle. Subs (all used): 10 Alex Benson; 29 Ryan Esders; 26 Steve Lewis; 30 Jack Stearman.
Tries: Thorman (1), Duckworth (17), Esders (30, 38, 57), Lee (41), Allan (50), Lineham (54, 65);
Goals: Ratcliffe 6/10.
Dismissal: Ross (44) - fighting.
Sin bin: Esders (44) - fighting.

Rugby Leaguer & League Express Men of the Match:
Lions: Craig Harvey; City Knights: Jack Lee.
Penalty count: 4-12; **Half-time:** 16-22;
Referee: Dave Merrick; **Attendance:** 431.

WORKINGTON TOWN 18 ROCHDALE HORNETS 12

TOWN: 5 Brett Carter; 2 Mike Backhouse; 29 Jason Mossop; 15 Aaron Low; 17 Neil Frazer; 27 Darren Holt; 7 Scott Kaighan; 25 Stewart Rhodes; 23 Phil Hewitt; 10 Kris Coward; 11 Mike Whitehead; 12 Jarrad Stack; 21 Paddy Coupar. Subs (all used): 9 Jack Pedley; 20 James Robinson; 19 Joe McKenna; 28 Ryan McDonald.
Tries: Frazer (5), Pedley (29), Low (66); **Goals:** Holt 3/4.
On report: Pedley (32) - alleged late tackle.
HORNETS: 32 Wayne English; 2 Andy Saywell; 22 Damien Reid; 6 Dale Bloomfield; 24 Paul Crook; 7 Steve Roper; 36 Peter Fairhurst; 9 Phil Wood; 16 Danny Samuel; 12 Danny Smith; 15 Dayne Donoghue; 13 Craig Ashall. Subs (all used): 18 John Cookson; 4 Adam Bowman; 29 Ryan Powell; 28 Chris Hough.
Tries: Saywell (45), Crook (50); **Goals:** Crook 2/3.
Rugby Leaguer & League Express Men of the Match:
Town: Jarrad Stack; Hornets: Craig Ashall.
Penalty count: 10-11; **Half-time:** 14-2;
Referee: Clint Sharrad; **Attendance:** 434.

ROUND 20

Thursday 5th August 2010

HUNSLET HAWKS 24 WORKINGTON TOWN 14

HAWKS: 29 Stuart Kain; 5 John Oakes; 21 Wayne McHugh; 4 David Clayton; 26 Waine Pryce; 6 Danny Grimshaw; 7 Paul March; 15 Adam Sullivan; 14 Luke Haigh; 3 James Houston; 10 Tom Haughey; 12 Steve Dooler; 13 David March. Subs (all used): 8 Scott Woodcock; 9 Richard Chapman; 16 Neil Lowe; 18 Charlie Wabo.
Tries: P March (6), McHugh (24, 56, 80);
Goals: D March 4/4.
Sin bin: Chapman (72) - fighting.
TOWN: 5 Brett Carter; 2 Mike Backhouse; 29 Elliot Miller; 15 Aaron Low; 17 Neil Frazer; 27 Darren Holt; 7 Scott Kaighan; 25 Stewart Rhodes; 9 Jack Pedley; 10 Kris Coward; 11 Mike Whitehead; 12 Jarrad Stack; 21 Paddy Coupar. Subs (all used): 1 John Lebbon; 19 Joe McKenna; 20 James Robinson; 28 Ryan McDonald.
Tries: Kaighan (29), Robinson (47); **Goals:** Holt 3/4.
Sin bin: Stack (72) - fighting.
Rugby Leaguer & League Express Men of the Match:
Hawks: Wayne McHugh; Town: Darren Holt.
Penalty count: 13-7; **Half-time:** 12-8;
Referee: Tim Roby; **Attendance:** 537.

Sunday 8th August 2010

SOUTH WALES SCORPIONS 22 DONCASTER 8

SCORPIONS: 31 Elliot Kear; 14 Jamie Murphy; 11

Christiaan Roets; 3 Lee Williams; 5 Ashley Bateman; 37 Casey Bromilow; 15 Andrew Gay; 20 Geraint Davies; 33 Lloyd White; 10 Gil Dudson; 6 Loz Wildbore; 8 Lewis Mills; 13 Aled James. Subs (all used): 24 Liam Roach; 12 Neil Dallimore; 9 Joe McLocklan; 17 Barrie Phillips.
Tries: Wildbore (3), Bateman (30), Mills (33), Williams (44); **Goals:** White 1/2, Wildbore 2/3.
DONCASTER: 4 Shaun Leaf; 2 Aaron Henry; 25 Chris Spurr; 3 Lee Gomersall; 30 Dean Colton; 35 Aaron Dobek; 7 Craig Fawcett; 36 Ben Jones; 32 Kyle Kesik; 29 Liam Crawley; 33 Scott Watson; 12 Ryan Steen; 34 Rob Lunt. Subs (all used): 20 Jack Ely; 28 Paul Hughes; 19 Gary Ellery; 27 Matt Carbutt.
Try: Lunt (17); **Goals:** Dobek 2/2.
Rugby Leaguer & League Express Men of the Match: *Scorpions:* Christiaan Roets; *Doncaster:* Rob Lunt.
Penalty count: 10-11; **Half-time:** 16-8;
Referee: Matthew Kidd; **Attendance:** 492.

GATESHEAD THUNDER 10 BLACKPOOL PANTHERS 78

THUNDER: 1 Kevin Neighbour; 15 Dan O'Sullivan; 31 Matt Garside; 5 Joe Brown; 2 Robin Peers; 35 Nigel Scott; 14 Will Bate; 8 Jason Payne; 9 Ryan Clarke; 25 Gareth Barron; 12 Rhys Clarke; 32 Ade Aderiye; 34 Josh Stoker. Subs (all used): 30 Richie Humphries; 17 Chris Parker; 13 Matt Barron; 33 Reece Young.
Tries: Garside (26), M Barron (48);
Goals: Ryan Clarke 1/2.
PANTHERS: 31 Eddie Vaughan; 2 Damian Munro; 18 Martin Ainscough; 34 Dean Thompson; 5 Tom Woodcock; 6 Carl Forber; 7 Tom Hemingway; 8 David Best; 9 John Clough; 10 Andy Hobson; 12 Paul Alcock; 27 Danny Halliwell; 32 Mark Roberts. Subs (all used): 14 Martin Keavney; 15 Paul Anderson; 22 Dave Llewellyn; 20 Marlon Miller.
Tries: Hemingway (1), Vaughan (4, 13, 45), Forber (10, 67, 79), Clough (22, 54, 70), Thompson (34, 41), Keavney (36), Woodcock (72); **Goals:** Hemingway 11/14.
Rugby Leaguer & League Express Men of the Match: *Thunder:* Kevin Neighbour; *Panthers:* Eddie Vaughan.
Penalty count: 5-9; **Half-time:** 4-40;
Referee: Warren Turley; **Attendance:** 554.

ROCHDALE HORNETS 24 SWINTON LIONS 16

HORNETS: 32 Wayne English; 1 Craig Johnson; 12 Danny Smith; 3 Dean Gorton; 2 Andy Saywell; 24 Paul Crook; 7 Steve Roper; 36 Peter Fairhurst; 9 Phil Wood; 10 Gareth Hayes; 13 Craig Ashall; 4 Adam Bowman; 15 Dayne Donoghue. Subs (all used): 18 John Cookson; 20 Semisi Cocka; 28 Chris Hough; 29 Ryan Powell.
Tries: Smith (22), Gorton (27), Donoghue (55);
Goals: Crook 6/8.
LIONS: 1 Richie Hawkyard; 28 Alex Hurst; 27 Anthony Stewart; 24 Gavin Dodd; 23 Rob Foxen; 34 Craig Harvey; 7 Ian Watson; 31 Anthony Mullally; 9 Phil Joseph; 18 Bruce Johnson; 36 Darren Hawkyard; 39 Dale Cunniffe; 15 Lee Wingfield. Subs (all used): 32 Andy Ainscough; 16 Dana Wilson; 33 Danny Meekin; 40 Joe Fitzpatrick.
Tries: Harvey (9, 68), Dodd (35); **Goals:** Dodd 2/5.
Rugby Leaguer & League Express Men of the Match: *Hornets:* Paul Crook; *Lions:* Richie Hawkyard.
Penalty count: 11-8; **Half-time:** 12-10;
Referee: Craig Halloran; **Attendance:** 502.

YORK CITY KNIGHTS 18 OLDHAM 33

CITY KNIGHTS: 1 Danny Ratcliffe; 28 Danny Wilson; 3 Mike Mitchell; 29 Ryan Esders; 2 Wayne Reittie; 6 Chris Thorman; 27 Scott Woods; 10 Alex Benson; 33 Jack Lee; 17 Nathan Freer; 15 Luke Hardbottle; 11 Jordan Ross; 34 Danny Allan. Subs (all used): 4 Lee Waterman; 35 Ben Parkinson; 30 Jack Stearman; 18 Matty Duckworth.
Tries: Reittie (13, 73), Stearman (29); **Goals:** Ratcliffe 3/4.
OLDHAM: 1 Paul O'Connor; 2 Lucas Onyango; 24 Marcus St Hilaire; 4 Mick Fogerty; 5 John Gillam; 6 Neil Roden; 7 Matt Ashe; 8 Jason Boults; 9 Martin Roden; 16 Wayne Kerr; 19 Ben Heaton; 13 Joe Chandler; 21 Valu Bentley. Subs (all used): 10 Dave Ellison; 18 Chris Clarke; 17 Danny Whitmore; 27 Ian Hodson.
Tries: Gillam (5, 65), N Roden (26), O'Connor (32), Onyango (60); **Goals:** Ashe 6/6;
Field goal: N Roden (70).
Rugby Leaguer & League Express Men of the Match: *City Knights:* Chris Thorman; *Oldham:* Neil Roden.
Penalty count: 12-6; **Half-time:** 14-18;
Referee: Peter Brooke; **Attendance:** 770.

ROUND 21

Sunday 15th August 2010

SOUTH WALES SCORPIONS 16 YORK CITY KNIGHTS 18

SCORPIONS: 31 Elliot Kear; 14 Jamie Murphy; 11 Christiaan Roets; 3 Lee Williams; 5 Ashley Bateman; 37 Casey Bromilow; 15 Andrew Gay; 24 Liam Roach; 33 Lloyd White; 10 Gil Dudson; 20 Geraint Davies; 8 Lewis Mills; 13 Aled James. Subs (all used): 7 Steve Parry; 12 Neil Dallimore; 9 Joe McLocklan; 16 Joe Burke.
Tries: Gay (33), Roach (60); **Goals:** White 4/5.
CITY KNIGHTS: 1 Danny Ratcliffe; 2 Wayne Reittie; 29 Ryan Esders; 4 Lee Waterman; 28 Danny Wilson; 6 Chris Thorman; 27 Scott Woods; 17 Nathan Freer; 33 Jack Lee; 10 Alex Benson; 11 Jordan Ross; 18 Matty Duckworth; 15 Luke Hardbottle. Subs (all used): 3 Mike Mitchell; 32 Paul Stamp; 30 Jack Stearman; 36 Callum Dinsdale.
Tries: Duckworth (3), Thorman (37), Lee (67);
Goals: Waterman 1/3, Ratcliffe 2/2.
Rugby Leaguer & League Express Men of the Match: *Scorpions:* Andrew Gay; *City Knights:* Chris Thorman.
Penalty count: 8-8; **Half-time:** 8-10;
Referee: Chris Leatherbarrow; **Attendance:** 689.

LONDON SKOLARS 68 GATESHEAD THUNDER 22

SKOLARS: 31 Neil Thorman; 25 Smokie Junor; 34 John Paxton; 4 Jason Cook; 30 Ade Adebisi; 33 Jy-Mel Coleman; 7 Paul Thorman; 13 Stephen Ball; 32 Sam Gee; 18 James Simon; 3 Matt Thomas; 16 Oliver Bloom; 26 Jamie Boston. Subs (all used): 5 Austen Aggrey; 38 Michael Sykes; 11 Oliver Purslow; 9 Gareth Honor.
Tries: Gee (1, 11, 74), N Thorman (20), Bloom (27), Aggrey (29, 71), Purslow (50), M Thomas (53, 80), Jy-Mel Coleman (57), Paxton (60), Adebisi (64);
Goals: P Thorman 0/3, Jy-Mel Coleman 8/10.
THUNDER: 34 Josh Stoker; 2 Robin Peers; 1 Kevin Neighbour; 5 Joe Brown; 15 Dan O'Sullivan; 14 Will Bate; 9 Ryan Clarke; 8 Jason Payne; 33 Reece Young; 13 Matt Barron; 31 Matt Garside; 12 Rhys Clarke; 32 Ade Aderiye. Subs: 26 David Cash (not used); 17 Chris Parker; 18 Stephen Welton; 25 Gareth Barron.
Tries: Neighbour (17), Rhys Clarke (40), J Brown (68), Payne (77); **Goals:** Ryan Clarke 3/4.
Rugby Leaguer & League Express Men of the Match: *Skolars:* Sam Gee; *Thunder:* Jason Payne.
Penalty count: 6-10; **Half-time:** 24-12; **Referee:** Dave Merrick (replaced by Liam Todd, half-time);
Attendance: 288.

BLACKPOOL PANTHERS 24 HUNSLET HAWKS 30

PANTHERS: 31 Eddie Vaughan; 34 Dean Thompson; 3 Casey Mayberry; 18 Martin Ainscough; 2 Damian Munro; 6 Carl Forber; 7 Tom Hemingway; 28 Neil Holland; 9 John Clough; 10 Andy Hobson; 27 Danny Halliwell; 12 Paul Alcock; 32 Mark Roberts. Subs (all used): 14 Martin Keavney; 15 Paul Anderson; 4 Mark McCully; 8 David Best.
Tries: Mayberry (34, 71), Munro (53), Alcock (80);
Goals: Hemingway 4/4.
HAWKS: 29 Stuart Kain; 26 Waine Pryce; 4 David Clayton; 21 Wayne McHugh; 2 Michael Mark; 6 Danny Grimshaw; 7 Paul March; 15 Adam Sullivan; 14 Luke Haigh; 3 James Houston; 12 Steve Dooler; 10 Tom Haughey; 13 David March. Subs (all used): 18 Charlie Wabo; 16 Neil Lowe; 30 Richard Knight; 8 Scott Woodcock.
Tries: P March (12), Clayton (39), Haughey (43), D March (60), Knight (77); **Goals:** D March 5/7.
Rugby Leaguer & League Express Men of the Match: *Panthers:* Eddie Vaughan; *Hawks:* Tom Haughey.
Penalty count: 6-9; **Half-time:** 6-14;
Referee: Clint Sharrad; **Attendance:** 497.

OLDHAM 44 ROCHDALE HORNETS 14

OLDHAM: 1 Paul O'Connor; 2 Lucas Onyango; 19 Ben Heaton; 4 Mick Fogerty; 5 John Gillam; 6 Neil Roden; 28 Gregg McNally; 8 Jason Boults; 9 Martin Roden; 16 Wayne Kerr; 14 John Walker; 13 Joe Chandler; 21 Valu Bentley. Subs (all used): 10 Dave Ellison; 18 Chris Clarke; 17 Danny Whitmore; 20 Mark Brocklehurst.
Tries: Boults (11, 25, 60), McNally (14, 17), Gillam (38), Ellison (68), Kerr (71); **Goals:** McNally 6/9.
HORNETS: 32 Wayne English; 6 Dale Bloomfield; 3 Dean Gorton; 22 Damien Reid; 5 Bolu Fagborun; 24 Paul Crook; 7 Steve Roper; 36 Peter Fairhurst; 13 Craig Ashall; 10 Gareth Hayes; 15 Dayne Donoghue; 12 Danny Smith; 16 Danny Samuel. Subs (all used): 18 John Cookson; 20 Semisi Cocka; 4 Adam Bowman; 29 Ryan Powell.
Tries: Fagborun (21, 44), Ashall (35); **Goals:** Crook 1/3.
Rugby Leaguer & League Express Men of the Match: *Oldham:* Jason Boults; *Hornets:* Craig Ashall.
Penalty count: 13-9; **Half-time:** 26-10;
Referee: Matthew Kidd; **Attendance:** 1,005.

WORKINGTON TOWN 22 SWINTON LIONS 32

TOWN: 29 Elliot Miller; 2 Mike Backhouse; 3 Andrew Beattie; 15 Aaron Low; 17 Neil Frazer; 27 Darren Holt; 7 Scott Kaighan; 8 Lee Dutton; 23 Phil Hewitt; 10 Kris Coward; 11 Mike Whitehead; 12 Jarrad Stack; 21 Paddy Coupar. Subs (all used): 4 James Finch; 20 James Robinson; 9 Jack Pedley; 28 Ryan McDonald.
Tries: Beattie (22), Miller (25), Stack (54);
Goals: Holt 5/6.
LIONS: 1 Richie Hawkyard; 23 Rob Foxen; 24 Gavin Dodd; 27 Anthony Stewart; 28 Alex Hurst; 34 Craig Harvey; 7 Ian Watson; 31 Anthony Mullally; 9 Phil Joseph; 18 Bruce Johnson; 39 Dale Cunniffe; 36 Darren Hawkyard; 15 Lee Wingfield. Subs (all used): 32 Andy Ainscough; 16 Dana Wilson; 40 Joe Fitzpatrick; 33 Danny Meekin.
Tries: R Hawkyard (12), Cunniffe (16), Mullally (36), Joseph (39), Foxen (76); **Goals:** Dodd 6/8.
Rugby Leaguer & League Express Men of the Match: *Town:* Elliot Miller; *Lions:* Richie Hawkyard.
Penalty count: 15-10; **Half-time:** 14-22;
Referee: Warren Turley; **Attendance:** 501.

ROUND 22

Sunday 22nd August 2010

DONCASTER 46 WORKINGTON TOWN 12

DONCASTER: 2 Aaron Henry; 30 Dean Colton; 3 Lee Gomersall; 4 Shaun Leaf; 25 Chris Spurr; 7 Craig Fawcett; 28 Paul Hughes; 36 Ben Jones; 32 Kyle Kesik; 29 Liam Crawley; 33 Scott Watson; 12 Ryan Steen; 34 Rob Lunt. Subs (all used): 20 Jack Ely; 15 Danny Stanley; 19 Gary Ellery; 27 Matt Carbutt.
Tries: Lunt (2, 20), Fawcett (8), Ely (38), Colton (39), Jones (53), Hughes (62, 73); **Goals:** Kesik 2/2, Henry 5/6.
TOWN: 1 John Lebbon; 2 Mike Backhouse; 3 Andrew Beattie; 15 Aaron Low; 17 Neil Frazer; 27 Darren Holt; 7 Scott Kaighan; 25 Stewart Rhodes; 23 Phil Hewitt; 10 Kris Coward; 11 Mike Whitehead; 19 Joe McKenna; 21 Paddy Coupar. Subs (all used): 9 Jack Pedley; 20 James Robinson; 29 Matthew Johnson; 28 Ryan McDonald.
Tries: Coupar (47), Whitehead (77); **Goals:** Holt 2/2.
Rugby Leaguer & League Express Men of the Match: *Doncaster:* Paul Hughes; *Town:* Scott Kaighan.
Penalty count: 10-8; **Half-time:** 28-0;
Referee: Greg Dolan; **Attendance:** 1,127.

ROCHDALE HORNETS 16 BLACKPOOL PANTHERS 26

HORNETS: 6 Dale Bloomfield; 5 Bolu Fagborun; 3 Dean Gorton; 22 Damien Reid; 1 Craig Johnson; 28 Chris Hough; 7 Steve Roper; 4 Adam Bowman; 9 Phil Wood; 18 John Cookson; 16 Danny Samuel; 12 Danny Smith; 13 Craig Ashall. Subs (all used): 10 Gareth Hayes; 36 Peter Fairhurst; 15 Dayne Donoghue; 24 Paul Crook.
Tries: Smith (11), Ashall (34); **Goals:** Roper 4/5.
PANTHERS: 18 Martin Ainscough; 2 Damian Munro; 3 Casey Mayberry; 34 Dean Thompson; 5 Tom Woodcock; 6 Carl Forber; 7 Tom Hemingway; 15 Paul Anderson; 9 John Clough; 10 Andy Hobson; 4 Mark McCully; 27 Danny Halliwell; 32 Mark Roberts. Subs (all used): 14 Martin Keavney; 8 David Best; 28 Neil Holland; 31 Eddie Vaughan.
Tries: Halliwell (2), Anderson (8), Thompson (37), Forber (67), Clough (80);
Goals: Hemingway 3/4, Halliwell 0/1.
Sin bin: Clough (53) - interference.
Rugby Leaguer & League Express Men of the Match: *Hornets:* Craig Ashall; *Panthers:* Carl Forber.
Penalty count: 10-8; **Half-time:** 12-14;
Referee: Ronnie Laughton; **Attendance:** 592.

SWINTON LIONS 94 GATESHEAD THUNDER 0

LIONS: 1 Richie Hawkyard; 28 Alex Hurst; 24 Gavin Dodd; 27 Anthony Stewart; 23 Rob Foxen; 34 Craig Harvey; 7 Ian Watson; 31 Anthony Mullally; 9 Phil Joseph; 18 Bruce Johnson; 39 Dale Cunniffe; 36 Darren Hawkyard; 15 Lee Wingfield. Subs (all used): 32 Andy Ainscough; 16 Dana Wilson; 40 Joe Fitzpatrick; 33 Danny Meekin.
Tries: Hurst (4, 18, 66), Cunniffe (11), Johnson (16), Wingfield (21), Harvey (23, 33), Mullally (37), Joseph (39, 53, 68, 78), Dodd (43, 55), Foxen (46), D Hawkyard (63, 73); **Goals:** Dodd 11/18.
THUNDER: 4 Michael Brown; 2 Robin Peers; 31 Matt Garside; 5 Joe Brown; 15 Dan O'Sullivan; 14 Will Bate; 1 Kevin Neighbour; 8 Jason Payne; 9 Ryan Clarke; 13 Matt Barron; 12 Rhys Clarke; 32 Ade Aderiye; 34 Josh Stoker. Subs (all used): 33 Reece Young; 18 Stephen Welton; 17 Chris Parker; 30 Richie Humphries.
Rugby Leaguer & League Express Men of the Match: *Lions:* Phil Joseph; *Thunder:* Will Bate.
Penalty count: 6-8; **Half-time:** 46-0;
Referee: Clint Sharrad; **Attendance:** 331.

HUNSLET HAWKS 32 SOUTH WALES SCORPIONS 24

HAWKS: 29 Stuart Kain; 2 Michael Mark; 4 David Clayton; 21 Wayne McHugh; 26 Waine Pryce; 32 George Rayner; 7 Paul March; 20 Joe Helme; 14 Luke Haigh; 3 James Houston; 12 Steve Dooler; 10 Tom Haughey; 13 David March. Subs (all used): 5 John Oakes; 8 Scott Woodcock; 11 Rob Kelly; 30 Richard Knight.
Tries: Clayton (4), McHugh (21), Dooler (25), Woodcock (32), Houston (69); **Goals:** D March 6/6.
SCORPIONS: 31 Elliot Kear; 14 Jamie Murphy; 11 Christiaan Roets; 3 Lee Williams; 5 Ashley Bateman; 37 Casey Bromilow; 15 Andrew Gay; 24 Liam Roach; 33 Lloyd White; 10 Gil Dudson; 12 Neil Dallimore; 8 Lewis Mills; 13 Aled James. Subs (all used): 7 Steve Parry; 9 Joe McLocklan; 16 Joe Burke; 17 Barrie Phillips.
Tries: Kear (40), Parry (50), Gay (65), Mills (77);
Goals: A James 2/2, Murphy 2/2.
Rugby Leaguer & League Express Men of the Match: *Hawks:* David March; *Scorpions:* Steve Parry.
Penalty count: 9-10; **Half-time:** 24-6;
Referee: Peter Brooke; **Attendance:** 785.

Friday 27th August 2010

LONDON SKOLARS 18 OLDHAM 48

SKOLARS: 31 Neil Thorman; 30 Ade Adebisi; 34 John Paxton; 4 Jason Cook; 25 Smokie Junor; 33 Jy-Mel Coleman; 7 Paul Thorman; 13 Stephen Ball; 32 Sam Gee; 18 James Simon; 3 Matt Thomas; 16 Oliver Bloom; 5 Austen Aggrey. Subs (all used): 11 Oliver Purslow; 38 Michael Sykes; 9 Gareth Honor; 39 Carlern Clement-Pascall.
Tries: Aggrey (23), N Thorman (30), Purslow (46);
Goals: P Thorman 3/3.
Sin bin: Bloom (31) - fighting;
Jy-Mel Coleman (78) - dissent; Honor (80) - dissent.
OLDHAM: 1 Paul O'Connor; 2 Lucas Onyango; 24 Marcus St Hilaire; 4 Mick Fogerty; 5 John Gillam; 7 Matt Ashe; 28 Gregg McNally; 16 Wayne Kerr; 9 Martin Roden; 18 Chris Clarke; 14 John Walker; 13 Joe Chandler; 21 Valu Bentley. Subs (all used): 10 Dave Ellison; 19 Ben Heaton; 17 Danny Whitmore; 20 Mark Brocklehurst.
Tries: Bentley (2), O'Connor (8), Gillam (14, 65), Heaton (34), Clarke (58), McNally (73, 78);
Goals: Ashe 6/6, McNally 2/2.
Sin bin: O'Connor (31) - fighting.
Rugby Leaguer & League Express Men of the Match: *Skolars:* Neil Thorman; *Oldham:* Matt Ashe.
Penalty count: 8-16; **Half-time:** 12-24;
Referee: Tim Roby; **Attendance:** 1,375.

Rochdale celebrate John Cookson's try against South Wales

PLAY-OFFS

ELIMINATION PLAY-OFFS

Sunday 5th September 2010

BLACKPOOL PANTHERS 36 WORKINGTON TOWN 26

PANTHERS: 18 Martin Ainscough; 5 Tom Woodcock; 34 Dean Thompson; 22 Dave Llewellyn; 2 Damian Munro; 6 Carl Forber; 7 Tom Hemingway; 15 Paul Anderson; 9 John Clough; 10 Andy Hobson; 12 Paul Alcock; 27 Danny Halliwell; 32 Mark Roberts. Subs (all used): 14 Martin Keavney; 4 Mark McCully; 28 Neil Holland; 31 Eddie Vaughan.
Tries: Clough (46), Ainscough (49), Keavney (53), McCully (56), Munro (72), Halliwell (75);
Goals: Hemingway 6/6.
Sin bin: Hobson (12) - dissent, (79) - late tackle on Kaighan; Keavney (29) - dissent.
TOWN: 29 Elliot Miller; 17 Neil Frazer; 15 Aaron Low; 31 Jason Mossop; 3 Andrew Beattie; 27 Darren Holt; 7 Scott Kaighan; 28 Ryan McDonald; 9 Jack Pedley; 16 Kris Coward; 11 Mike Whitehead; 12 Jarrad Stack; 21 Paddy Coupar. Subs (all used): 32 Matthew Johnson; 20 James Robinson; 19 Joe McKenna; 22 Ryan Campbell.
Tries: Pedley (13), Stack (20, 77), Miller (67);
Goals: Holt 4/4, Kaighan 1/1.
Sin bin: Miller (35) - punching.
Rugby Leaguer & League Express Men of the Match:
Panthers: Danny Halliwell; *Town:* Scott Kaighan.
Penalty count: 8-17; **Half-time:** 0-14;
Referee: Jamie Leahy; **Attendance:** 308.

ROCHDALE HORNETS 60
SOUTH WALES SCORPIONS 26

HORNETS: 32 Wayne English; 6 Dale Bloomfield; 3 Dean Gorton; 22 Damien Reid; 2 Andy Saywell; 24 Paul Crook; 7 Steve Roper; 4 Adam Bowman; 9 Phil Wood; 36 Peter Fairhurst; 16 Danny Samuel; 12 Danny Smith; 13 Craig Ashall. Subs (all used): 18 John Cookson; 29 Ryan Powell; 10 Gareth Hayes; 25 Dale Blackmore.
Tries: English (4), Bowman (11), Crook (19, 29), Ashall (24, 73), Bloomfield (39, 58), Cookson (45), Hayes (63); **Goals:** Crook 10/11.
SCORPIONS: 31 Elliot Kear; 1 Craig Richards; 5 Ashley Bateman; 3 Lee Williams; 14 Jamie Murphy; 37 Casey Bromilow; 15 Andrew Gay; 8 Lewis Mills; 7 Steve Parry; 24 Liam Roach; 17 Barrie Phillips; 13 Aled James; 11 Christiaan Roets. Subs (all used): 9 Joe McLocklan; 23 Alan Pope; 29 Harri Greville; 22 Curtis Cunningham.
Tries: Parry (32), Murphy (55, 65), Mills (70), A James (79); **Goals:** Kear 0/1, A James 3/4.
Sin bin: McLocklan (22) - interference;
Phillips (52) - interference.
Rugby Leaguer & League Express Men of the Match:
Hornets: Craig Ashall; *Scorpions:* Jamie Murphy.
Penalty count: 17-7; **Half-time:** 38-4;
Referee: Craig Halloran; **Attendance:** 375.

QUALIFYING SEMI-FINAL

Sunday 12th September 2010

OLDHAM 41 YORK CITY KNIGHTS 32

OLDHAM: 1 Paul O'Connor; 2 Lucas Onyango; 24 Marcus St Hilaire; 4 Mick Fogerty; 5 John Gillam; 6 Neil Roden; 28 Gregg McNally; 18 Chris Clarke; 9 Martin Roden; 16 Wayne Kerr; 19 Ben Heaton; 13 Joe Chandler; 21 Valu Bentley. Subs (all used): 7 Matt Ashe; 8 Jason Boults; 10 Dave Ellison; 17 Danny Whitmore.
Tries: Chandler (20, 74), Whitmore (34), Kerr (59), Bentley (71), Clarke (80); **Goals:** McNally 8/8;
Field goal: McNally (67).
CITY KNIGHTS: 1 Danny Ratcliffe; 28 Danny Wilson; 35 Ian Bell; 4 Lee Waterman; 2 Wayne Reittie; 6 Chris Thorman; 32 Paul Stamp; 10 Alex Benson; 33 Jack Lee; 17 Nathan Freer; 29 Ryan Esders; 11 Jordan Ross; 15 Luke Hardbottle. Subs (all used): 26 Steve Lewis; 30 Jack Stearman; 31 James Haynes; 36 Callum Dinsdale.
Tries: Bell (10), Esders (28, 34), Waterman (42, 78), Thorman (76); **Goals:** Waterman 4/6.
Rugby Leaguer & League Express Men of the Match:
Oldham: Gregg McNally; *City Knights:* Ryan Esders.
Penalty count: 10-12; **Half-time:** 16-18;
Referee: Ronnie Laughton; **Attendance:** 1,275.

ELIMINATION SEMI-FINAL

Sunday 12th September 2010

BLACKPOOL PANTHERS 34 ROCHDALE HORNETS 26

PANTHERS: 18 Martin Ainscough; 5 Tom Woodcock; 3 Casey Mayberry; 34 Dean Thompson; 2 Damian Munro; 6 Carl Forber; 7 Tom Hemingway; 15 Paul Anderson; 9 John Clough; 10 Andy Hobson; 22 Dave Llewellyn; 27 Danny Halliwell; 4 Mark McCully. Subs (all used): 14 Martin Keavney; 31 Eddie Vaughan; 28 Neil Holland; 8 David Best.
Tries: McCully (20), Ainscough (26), Mayberry (30, 69), Forber (35), Halliwell (54); **Goals:** Hemingway 5/8.
HORNETS: 32 Wayne English; 2 Andy Saywell; 15 Dayne Donoghue; 3 Dean Gorton; 6 Dale Bloomfield; 24 Paul Crook; 7 Steve Roper; 4 Adam Bowman; 9 Phil Wood; 36 Peter Fairhurst; 16 Danny Samuel; 12 Danny Smith; 13 Craig Ashall. Subs (all used): 29 Ryan Powell; 18 John Cookson; 28 Chris Hough; 10 Gareth Hayes.
Tries: Samuel (15), Crook (39), Wood (44), Gorton (79); **Goals:** Crook 5/5.
Sin bin: Bowman (68) - holding down.
Rugby Leaguer & League Express Men of the Match:
Panthers: Casey Mayberry; *Hornets:* Craig Ashall.
Penalty count: 13-11; **Half-time:** 22-14;
Referee: Jamie Leahy; **Attendance:** 453.

FINAL ELIMINATOR

Sunday 19th September 2010

YORK CITY KNIGHTS 38 BLACKPOOL PANTHERS 18

CITY KNIGHTS: 31 James Haynes; 2 Wayne Reittie; 3 Mike Mitchell; 4 Lee Waterman; 28 Danny Wilson; 1 Danny Ratcliffe; 6 Chris Thorman; 17 Nathan Freer; 33 Jack Lee; 10 Alex Benson; 11 Jordan Ross; 29 Ryan Esders; 15 Luke Hardbottle. Subs (all used): 32 Paul Stamp; 26 Steve Lewis; 36 Callum Dinsdale; 30 Jack Stearman.
Tries: Waterman (3), Benson (13), Ratcliffe (21, 59), Wilson (27), Thorman (63); **Goals:** Waterman 7/9.
PANTHERS: 18 Martin Ainscough; 2 Damian Munro; 3 Casey Mayberry; 34 Dean Thompson; 5 Tom Woodcock; 6 Carl Forber; 7 Tom Hemingway; 15 Paul Anderson; 9 John Clough; 10 Andy Hobson; 27 Danny Halliwell; 12 Paul Alcock; 4 Mark McCully. Subs (all used): 14 Martin Keavney; 22 Dave Llewellyn; 8 David Best; 28 Neil Holland.
Tries: Forber (18), Anderson (51), McCully (79);
Goals: Hemingway 3/3.
Rugby Leaguer & League Express Men of the Match:
City Knights: Chris Thorman; *Panthers:* Tom Hemingway.
Penalty count: 11-4; **Half-time:** 20-6;
Referee: Gareth Hewer; **Attendance:** 673.

GRAND FINAL

Sunday 26th September 2010

OLDHAM 4 YORK CITY KNIGHTS 25

OLDHAM: 1 Paul O'Connor; 2 Lucas Onyango; 24 Marcus St Hilaire; 4 Mick Fogerty; 5 John Gillam; 6 Neil Roden; 28 Gregg McNally; 8 Jason Boults; 9 Martin Roden; 16 Wayne Kerr; 18 Chris Clarke; 13 Joe Chandler; 21 Valu Bentley. Subs (all used): 10 Dave Ellison; 19 Ben Heaton; 17 Danny Whitmore; 7 Matt Ashe.
Try: Fogerty (20); **Goals:** McNally 0/1.
CITY KNIGHTS: 31 James Haynes; 2 Wayne Reittie; 3 Mike Mitchell; 4 Lee Waterman; 28 Danny Wilson; 6 Chris Thorman; 1 Danny Ratcliffe; 17 Nathan Freer; 33 Jack Lee; 10 Alex Benson; 11 Jordan Ross; 29 Ryan Esders; 15 Luke Hardbottle. Subs (all used): 32 Paul Stamp; 36 Callum Dinsdale; 26 Steve Lewis; 30 Jack Stearman.
Tries: Reittie (7), Haynes (26), Thorman (64), Lewis (74); **Goals:** Waterman 2/3, Thorman 2/2;
Field goal: Thorman (69).
Rugby Leaguer & League Express Men of the Match:
Oldham: Neil Roden; *City Knights:* Chris Thorman.
Penalty count: 2-7; **Half-time:** 4-10;
Referee: Gareth Hewer.
(at Halliwell Jones Stadium, Warrington).

York's Chris Thorman on the attack against Oldham during the Championship One Grand Final

NORTHERN RAIL CUP 2010
Round by Round

ROUND 1

Sunday 31st January 2010

POOL 1

BLACKPOOL PANTHERS 22 KEIGHLEY COUGARS 24

PANTHERS: 24 Paul Ballard; 2 Damian Munro; 3 Casey Mayberry; 18 Martin Ainscough; 5 Tom Woodcock; 6 Carl Forber; 7 Tom Hemingway; 15 Paul Anderson; 14 Martin Keavney; 10 Andy Hobson; 17 Kris Ratcliffe; 12 Paul Alcock; 11 Kurt Haggerty. Subs (all used): 8 David Best; 9 John Clough; 16 Simon Svabic; 4 Mark McCully.
Tries: Woodcock (8), Munro (23), Ainscough (44), Ratcliffe (58); **Goals:** Hemingway 3/4.
Sin bin: Best (48) - interference.
COUGARS: 20 Dan Belcher; 2 Craig Moss; 3 Tom Burton; 4 Daley Williams; 5 Gavin Duffy; 6 Jon Presley; 7 Danny Jones; 8 Andy Shickell; 9 James Feather; 10 Scott Law; 11 Will Cartledge; 12 Oliver Pursglove; 15 Greg Nicholson. Subs (all used): 14 Jamaine Wray; 16 Brendan Rawlins; 17 Ryan Benjafield; 18 James Haythornthwaite.
Tries: Rawlins (51), Belcher (55), Haythornthwaite (62), Duffy (68); **Goals:** D Jones 4/5.
Rugby Leaguer & League Express Men of the Match: *Panthers:* Tom Hemingway; *Cougars:* Andy Shickell.
Penalty count: 8-12; **Half-time:** 12-2;
Referee: Dave Merrick; **Attendance:** 468.

POOL 2

DEWSBURY RAMS 50 LONDON SKOLARS 4

RAMS: 2 James Haynes; 15 Bryn Powell; 18 Chris Spurr; 10 Scott Turner; 3 Stewart Sanderson; 13 Pat Walker; 8 Dominic Brambani; 23 Keegan Hirst; 9 Mike Emmett; 24 Anthony England; 20 Rob Spicer; 21 Andrew Bostock; 19 Adam Hayes. Subs (all used): 4 Rob Lunt; 6 Ryan Smith; 11 Adam Robinson; 12 Scott Watson.
Tries: Spicer (2), Lunt (15, 57), Emmett (19), Powell (24), Turner (27), Watson (32), Robinson (39), Haynes (51), Bostock (69);
Goals: P Walker 1/1, Brambani 2/5, Lunt 0/1, Turner 2/3.
Dismissal: England (79) – fighting.
SKOLARS: 1 Josh Welsh; 2 Dave Arnot; 3 Matt Thomas; 22 Curtis Cunningham; 5 Austen Aggrey; 17 Chad Isles; 7 Paul Thorman; 10 Tony Williams; 19 Liam Prescott; 20 Dave Williams; 11 Oliver Purslow; 12 Matt Carter; 13 Stephen Ball. Subs (all used): 24 Lamont Bryan; 4 Jason Cook; 25 Smokie Junor; 8 Liam Roach.
Try: Junor (72); **Goals:** P Thorman 0/1.
Dismissals: Carter (79) - fighting; Prescott (79) – gouging.
Rugby Leaguer & League Express Men of the Match: *Rams:* Dominic Brambani; *Skolars:* Lamont Bryan.
Penalty count: 8-4; **Half time:** 34-0;
Referee: Tim Roby; **Attendance:** 887.

LEIGH CENTURIONS 24 OLDHAM 12

CENTURIONS: 20 Ian Mort; 2 Steve Maden; 18 Adam Higson; 4 Mick Nanyn; 22 Martyn Ridyard; 6 Tim Hartley; 7 Robbie Paul; 8 Chris Hill; 15 Dave McConnell; 13 Dave Armitstead; 11 James Taylor; 14 Tommy Goulden; 12 Macgraff Leuluai. Subs (all used): 9 John Duffy; 23 Dale Cunniffe; 24 Andy Ainscough; 19 Danny Meekin.
Tries: Maden (24, 51), McConnell (35), Goulden (39), Cunniffe (67); **Goals:** Nanyn 2/5.
Sin bin: Armitstead (3) – dissent.
OLDHAM: 1 Paul O'Connor; 2 Lucas Onyango; 3 Craig Littler; 4 Mick Fogerty; 5 John Gillam; 6 Neil Roden; 7 Matt Ashe; 8 Jason Boults; 9 Martin Roden; 10 Dave Ellison; 13 Joe Chandler; 18 Chris Clarke; 21 Valu Bentley. Subs (all used): 16 Wayne Kerr; 23 Ben Mellor; 17 Danny Whitmore; 19 Ben Heaton.
Tries: Littler (57), Gillam (61), Fogerty (79);
Goals: Ashe 0/3.
Sin bin: Fogerty (33) – interference.
On report:
Clarke & Fogerty (74) – alleged high tackle on Higson.
Rugby Leaguer & League Express Men of the Match: *Centurions:* Dave McConnell; *Oldham:* Dave Ellison.
Penalty count: 12-10; **Half-time:** 14-0;
Referee: Ronnie Laughton; **Attendance:** 1,627.

Tuesday 2nd February 2010

POOL 1

WIDNES VIKINGS 50 GATESHEAD THUNDER 6

VIKINGS: 1 James Ford; 18 Scott Yates; 20 Chris Dean; 15 Shane Grady; 19 Matt Gardner; 6 Anthony Thackeray; 7 James Webster; 8 Steve Pickersgill; 9 Mark Smith; 10 Jim Gannon; 11 Lee Doran; 12 Dave Allen; 13 Chris Gerrard. Subs (all used): 14 Thomas Coyle; 17 Ben Kavanagh; 21 Matthew Strong; 23 David Houghton.
Tries: Thackeray (4), Ford (11, 16, 27, 48), Pickersgill (19), Gardner (22), Dean (33, 68), Grady (34), Allen (76); **Goals:** Yates 1/5, Grady 2/6.
THUNDER: 5 Joe Brown; 2 Robin Peers; 3 Tom Wilson; 4 Michael Brown; 15 Richard Lopag; 6 Liam Duffy; 1 Kevin Neighbour; 17 Chris Parker; 9 Ryan Clarke; 18 Stephen Welton; 30 Richie Humphries; 12 Rhys Clarke; 13 Matt Barron. Subs (all used): 14 Will Bate; 24 Mark Walker; 26 David Cash; 11 Jonny Scott.
Try: Peers (72); **Goals:** Neighbour 1/1.
Rugby Leaguer & League Express Men of the Match: *Vikings:* Steve Pickersgill; *Thunder:* Joe Brown.
Penalty count: 8-5; **Half-time:** 34-0;
Referee: Warren Turley; **Attendance:** 2,200.

ROUND 2

Sunday 7th February 2010

POOL 1

BARROW RAIDERS 34 BLACKPOOL PANTHERS 8

RAIDERS: 1 Gary Broadbent; 21 Chris Larkin; 20 Danny Halliwell; 4 Liam Harrison; 5 James Nixon; 7 James Coyle; 18 Liam Campbell; 8 Andy Bracek; 9 Andrew Henderson; 24 Richard Fletcher; 12 Ned Catic; 11 Michael Knowles; 13 Zebastian Luisi. Subs (all used): 10 Chris Young; 17 Paul Noone; 19 Nathan Mossop; 15 Rob Roberts.
Tries: Halliwell (12), Young (32), Campbell (39, 79), Catic (45), Bracek (65); **Goals:** Knowles 3/4, Fletcher 2/2.
PANTHERS: 24 Paul Ballard; 2 Damian Munro; 18 Martin Ainscough; 22 Dave Llewellyn; 5 Tom Woodcock; 16 Simon Svabic; 7 Tom Hemingway; 21 Peter Fairhurst; 9 John Clough; 10 Andy Hobson; 23 John Boland; 12 Paul Alcock; 4 Mark McCully. Subs (all used): 14 Martin Keavney; 15 Paul Anderson; 6 Carl Forber; 17 Kris Ratcliffe.
Tries: Munro (37, 50); **Goals:** Hemingway 0/2.
Rugby Leaguer & League Express Men of the Match: *Raiders:* Zebastian Luisi; *Panthers:* Damian Munro.
Penalty count: 11-9; **Half-time:** 16-4;
Referee: Greg Dolan; **Attendance:** 1,474.

BATLEY BULLDOGS 30 WIDNES VIKINGS 30

BULLDOGS: 5 John Campbell; 1 Ian Preece; 3 Mark Barlow; 4 Danny Maun; 2 Lee Greenwood; 6 Paul Handforth; 7 Gareth Moore; 8 Byron Smith; 9 Kris Lythe; 10 Sean Hesketh; 23 Chris Buttery; 17 Craig Potter; 13 Ashley Lindsay. Subs (all used): 14 John Gallagher; 20 David Tootill; 21 James Martin; 26 Jason Walton.
Tries: Preece (6), Campbell (20, 50), Martin (28), Greenwood (37); **Goals:** Moore 5/6.
VIKINGS: 1 James Ford; 26 Shaun Ainscough; 4 Toa Kohe-Love; 15 Shane Grady; 19 Matt Gardner; 6 Anthony Thackeray; 7 James Webster; 8 Steve Pickersgill; 9 Mark Smith; 10 Jim Gannon; 11 Lee Doran; 12 Dave Allen; 13 Chris Gerrard. Subs (all used): 17 Ben Kavanagh; 23 David Houghton; 27 Liam Farrell; 31 Ben Davies.
Tries: Doran (12), Kavanagh (33, 40), Ainscough (56, 69), Thackeray (77); **Goals:** Grady 3/6.
Sin bin: Thackeray (59) – punching.
Rugby Leaguer & League Express Men of the Match: *Bulldogs:* Paul Handforth; *Vikings:* James Webster.
Penalty count: 10-10; **Half-time:** 24-16;
Referee: Gareth Hewer; **Attendance:** 1,004.

GATESHEAD THUNDER 12 WORKINGTON TOWN 26

THUNDER: 1 Kevin Neighbour; 2 Robin Peers; 3 Tom Wilson; 4 Michael Brown; 5 Joe Brown; 6 Liam Duffy; 14 Will Bate; 17 Chris Parker; 9 Ryan Clarke; 10 Tabua Cakacaka; 18 Stephen Welton; 30 Richie Humphries; 13 Matt Barron. Subs (all used): 11 Jonny Scott; 24 Mark Walker; 26 David Cash; 27 Luke Watson.
Tries: Wilson (13), Ryan Clarke (16), J Brown (41);
Goals: Neighbour 0/3.
Sin bin: Scott (77) – late tackle.
TOWN: 1 John Lebbon; 5 Brett Carter; 15 Aaron Low; 3 Andrew Beattie; 2 Mike Backhouse; 6 Liam Finch; 7 Scott Kaighan; 8 Lee Dutton; 9 Jack Pedley; 10 Kris Coward; 11 Mike Whitehead; 12 Jarrad Stack; 21 Paddy Coupar. Subs (all used): 14 Jamie Marshall; 25 Stewart Rhodes; 4 James Finch; 20 James Robinson.
Tries: Pedley (3), Beattie (19), Backhouse (25, 71), Marshall (37); **Goals:** Kaighan 3/6.
Sin bin: Stack (9) - obstruction.
Rugby Leaguer & League Express Men of the Match: *Thunder:* Ryan Clarke; *Town:* Andrew Beattie.
Penalty count: 11-8; **Half-time:** 8-20;
Referee: Tim Roby; **Attendance:** 404.

KEIGHLEY COUGARS 17 WHITEHAVEN 16

COUGARS: 20 Dan Belcher; 2 Craig Moss; 3 Tom Burton; 4 Daley Williams; 1 George Rayner; 6 Jon Presley; 7 Danny Jones; 8 Andy Shickell; 9 James Feather; 10 Scott Law; 21 Richard Jones; 12 Oliver Pursglove; 22 Ben Sagar. Subs (all used): 14 Jamaine Wray; 18 James Haythornthwaite; 16 Brendan Rawlins; 17 Ryan Benjafield.
Tries: Haythornthwaite (33), Belcher (58);
Goals: D Jones 4/5; **Field goal:** D Jones (78).
WHITEHAVEN: 1 Craig Benson; 5 Derry Eilbeck; 17 Andy Thornley; 3 Rob Jackson; 2 Craig Calvert; 6 Carl Rudd; 14 Dylan Skee; 33 Kyle Amor; 9 Graeme Mattinson; 10 David Ford; 12 Spencer Miller; 11 Howard Hill; 7 Leroy Joe. Subs (all used): 13 Mick Govin; 24 Ryan McDonald; 8 Marc Jackson; 19 Dexter Miller.
Try: Mattinson (6), Calvert (48), S Miller (55);
Goals: Rudd 2/3.
Rugby Leaguer & League Express Men of the Match: *Cougars:* Danny Jones; *Whitehaven:* Mick Govin.
Penalty count: 13-11; **Half-time:** 10-6;
Referee: Peter Brooke; **Attendance:** 750.

SWINTON LIONS 30 DONCASTER 20

LIONS: 24 Gavin Dodd; 23 Rob Foxen; 3 Sam Reay; 5 Dave Hull; 25 Barry Hamilton; 14 Gary Hulse; 7 Ian Watson; 16 Dana Wilson; 9 Phil Joseph; 17 Andrew Isherwood; 12 Paul Smith; 11 Tommy Grundy; 13 Aaron Smith. Subs (all used): 6 Graham Holroyd; 20 Chris Hull; 10 Danny Heaton; 18 Bruce Johnson.
Tries: P Smith (4), Isherwood (7), Foxen (43), Joseph (69), Holroyd (80); **Goals:** Dodd 5/5.
Dismissal: Joseph (71) - high tackle on Stanley.
DONCASTER: 1 Tommy Griffiths; 22 Scott Wilson; 17 Jarryn Osborne; 3 Lee Gomersall; 5 Ben Collins; 13 Grant Edwards; 7 Craig Fawcett; 10 David Bates; 20 Jack Ely; 15 Danny Stanley; 12 Ryan Steen; 11 Liam Brown; 4 Shaun Leaf. Subs (all used): 14 Jake Bassinder; 16 Paul Shaw; 9 Paul Brown; 18 John Winter.
Tries: Wilson (14), Osborne (21), Leaf (30), Gomersall (37); **Goals:** Stanley 0/2, Fawcett 2/2.
Rugby Leaguer & League Express Men of the Match: *Lions:* Rob Foxen; *Doncaster:* Craig Fawcett.
Penalty count: 11-11; **Half-time:** 12-20;
Referee: Robert Hicks; **Attendance:** 380.

POOL 2

LONDON SKOLARS 12 HUNSLET HAWKS 60

SKOLARS: 1 Josh Welsh; 22 Curtis Cunningham; 4 Jason Cook; 3 Matt Thomas; 14 Luke May; 17 Chad Isles; 7 Paul Thorman; 10 Tony Williams; 19 Liam Prescott; 8 Liam Roach; 11 Oliver Purslow; 12 Matt Carter; 13 Stephen Ball. Subs (all used): 18 James Simon; 32 Aran Quinn; 25 Smokie Junor; 33 Jaroslaw Obuchowski.
Tries: M Thomas (33), Quinn (64); **Goals:** P Thorman 2/2.
HAWKS: 29 Stuart Kain; 1 Nathan Larvin; 21 Wayne McHugh; 4 David Clayton; 5 John Oakes; 6 Danny Grimshaw; 7 Paul March; 15 Adam Sullivan; 9 Richard Chapman; 3 James Houston; 11 Rob Kelly; 12 Steve Dooler; 33 Tom Haughey. Subs (all used): 31 Luke Haigh; 16 Neil Lowe; 8 Scott Woodcock; 23 Jake Wilson.
Tries: Houston (10), McHugh (12, 27, 58, 71), P March (21), R Kelly (30), Chapman (47), Clayton (53), Sullivan (69), Larvin (78); **Goals:** McHugh 8/11, Wilson 0/1.
Rugby Leaguer & League Express Men of the Match: *Skolars:* Liam Prescott; *Hawks:* Richard Chapman.
Penalty count: 8-12; **Half-time:** 6-28;
Referee: Warren Turley; **Attendance:** 328.

FEATHERSTONE ROVERS 18 SHEFFIELD EAGLES 18

ROVERS: 1 Ian Hardman; 5 Jon Steel; 4 Liam Welham; 3 Sam Smeaton; 2 Tom Saxton; 6 Kyle Briggs; 7 Andy Kain; 8 Iain Morrison; 9 Liam Finn; 10 Stuart Dickens; 12 Jon Grayshon; 11 Matty Dale; 13 Jamie Field. Subs (all used): 17 Tony Tonks; 18 Tim Spears; 19 Ross Divorty; 22 Jack Lee.
Tries: Welham (6, 43, 46), Steel (11); **Goals:** Briggs 1/4.
EAGLES: 1 Jonny Woodcock; 26 Tim Bergin; 25 Jason Mossop; 23 Tangi Ropati; 5 Ashley Thackeray; 6 Brendon Lindsay; 21 Dane McDonald; 8 Jack Howieson; 9 Craig Cook; 10 Mitchell Stringer; 11 Alex Szostak; 12 Ged Corcoran; 16 Trevor Exton. Subs (all used): 7 Aaron Groom; 15 Sam Barlow; 18 Michael Haley; 17 Alex Rowe.
Tries: Stringer (18), Rowe (30), Cook (78);
Goals: Woodcock 3/4.
Sin bin: Barlow (58) - dissent.
On report: Stringer (50) - alleged high tackle on Steel.
Rugby Leaguer & League Express Men of the Match: *Rovers:* Iain Morrison; *Eagles:* Brendon Lindsay.
Penalty count: 10-13; **Half-time:** 8-12;
Referee: Ronnie Laughton; **Attendance:** 1,175.

HALIFAX 24 DEWSBURY RAMS 0

HALIFAX: 4 Shad Royston; 20 Paul White; 2 Lee Paterson; 5 James Haley; 23 Rob Worrincy; 6 Luke Branighan; 12 Stanley Gene; 10 Neil Cherryholme; 14 Mark Gleeson; 22 David Wrench; 24 Steve Bannister; 3 Jon Goddard; 13 Bob Beswick. Subs (all used): 9 Sean Penkywicz; 16 Said Tamghart; 17 Frank Watene; 18 Dylan Nash.
Tries: Haley (18, 49), Nash (37), Paterson (58), Royston (61); **Goals:** Paterson 2/5.
RAMS: 2 James Haynes; 15 Bryn Powell; 18 Chris Spurr; 10 Scott Turner; 3 Stewart Sanderson; 13 Pat Walker; 8 Dominic Brambani; 23 Keegan Hirst; 9 Mike Emmett; 24 Anthony England; 20 Rob Spicer; 21 Andrew Bostock; 19 Adam Hayes. Subs (all used): 4 Rob Lunt; 11 Adam Robinson; 14 Luke Stenchion; 12 Scott Watson.
Sin bin: Haynes (48) – holding down.
Rugby Leaguer & League Express Men of the Match: *Halifax:* Stanley Gene; *Rams:* Adam Hayes.
Penalty count: 12-10; **Half-time:** 8-0;
Referee: Matthew Thomasson; **Attendance:** 2,141.

YORK CITY KNIGHTS 13 LEIGH CENTURIONS 12

CITY KNIGHTS: 1 Danny Ratcliffe; 2 Wayne Reittie; 3 Mike Mitchell; 4 Lee Waterman; 28 Danny Wilson; 6 Chris Thorman; 27 Casey Bromilow; 17 Nathan Freer; 9 Joe McLocklan; 10 Alex Benson; 11 Jordan Ross; 35 Danny Hill; 13 Richard Blakeway. Subs (all used): 25 Brett Waller; 12 Chris Clough; 16 Carl Barrow; 32 Paul Stamp.
Tries: Mitchell (9, 35); **Goals:** Waterman 2/2;
Field goal: Thorman (78).
CENTURIONS: 1 Stuart Donlan; 2 Steve Maden; 3 David Alstead; 4 Mick Nanyn; 5 Nicky Stanton; 6 Tim Hartley; 7 Robbie Paul; 16 Mike Morrison; 9 John Duffy; 13 Dave Armitstead; 11 James Taylor; 14 Tommy Goulden; 12 Macgraff Leuluai. Subs (all used): 22 Martyn Ridyard; 15 Dave McConnell; 19 Danny Meekin; 18 Adam Higson.
Tries: Alstead (65), McConnell (76); **Goals:** Nanyn 2/3.
Rugby Leaguer & League Express Men of the Match: *City Knights:* Chris Thorman; *Centurions:* Dave Armitstead.
Penalty count: 7-12; **Half-time:** 12-2;
Referee: Dave Merrick; **Attendance:** 911.

Monday 8th February 2010

POOL 2

OLDHAM 22 ROCHDALE HORNETS 14

OLDHAM: 1 Paul O'Connor; 2 Lucas Onyango; 3 Craig Littler; 4 Mick Fogerty; 5 John Gillam; 6 Neil Roden; 7

Matt Ashe; 8 Jason Boults; 9 Martin Roden; 10 Dave Ellison; 13 Joe Chandler; 18 Chris Clarke; 19 Ben Heaton. Subs (all used): 17 Danny Whitmore; 23 Ben Mellor; 16 Wayne Kerr; 11 Saqib Murtza.
Tries: Ellison (10), Chandler (44), Onyango (54); **Goals:** Ashe 4/4, O'Connor 1/1.
Sin bin: Ellison (80) - professional foul.
HORNETS: 32 Wayne English; 1 Craig Johnson; 12 Danny Smith; 19 Ryan McPaul; 5 Bolu Fagborun; 7 Steve Roper; 29 Ryan Powell; 10 Gareth Hayes; 9 Phil Wood; 8 Paul Raftrey; 15 Dayne Donoghue; 16 Danny Samuel; 13 Craig Ashall. Subs (all used): 18 John Cookson; 17 Michael Ostick; 27 Craig Tunstead; 28 Chris Hough.
Tries: Smith (14), Samuel (64), Fagborun (76); **Goals:** Roper 1/2, Hough 0/1.
Dismissal: Donoghue (42) - late tackle on Ashe.
Rugby Leaguer & League Express Men of the Match: *Oldham:* Paul O'Connor; *Hornets:* Danny Samuel.
Penalty count: 15-18; **Half-time:** 8-4; **Referee:** Jamie Leahy; **Attendance:** 540 *(at Park Lane, Sedgley Park).*

ROUND 1

Wednesday 10th February 2010

POOL 1

WHITEHAVEN 26 BATLEY BULLDOGS 34

WHITEHAVEN: 1 Craig Benson; 5 Derry Eilbeck; 3 Rob Jackson; 15 Reece Fox; 2 Craig Calvert; 6 Carl Rudd; 14 Dylan Skee; 8 Marc Jackson; 9 Graeme Mattinson; 11 Howard Hill; 12 Spencer Miller; 19 Dexter Miller; 17 Andy Thornley. Subs (all used): 30 Carl Sice; 22 Richard Farrer; 33 Kyle Amor; 32 Daniel Barker.
Tries: Skee (3), Thornley (20), R Jackson (31, 71), Eilbeck (54); **Goals:** Rudd 3/5.
Sin bin: Mattinson (76) - holding down.
BULLDOGS: 5 John Campbell; 1 Ian Preece; 3 Mark Barlow; 4 Danny Maun; 19 Eddie Kilroy; 6 Paul Handforth; 7 Gareth Moore; 8 Byron Smith; 9 Kris Lythe; 10 Sean Hesketh; 17 Craig Potter; 23 Chris Buttery; 13 Ashley Lindsay. Subs (all used): 12 Mark Toohey; 26 Jason Walton; 20 David Tootill; 21 James Martin.
Tries: Campbell (7, 27), Handforth (10, 75), Moore (24); **Goals:** Moore 7/8.
Rugby Leaguer & League Express Men of the Match: *Whitehaven:* Dylan Skee; *Bulldogs:* Gareth Moore.
Penalty count: 6-12; **Half-time:** 18-24;
Referee: Robert Hicks; **Attendance:** 888.

ROUND 3

Sunday 14th February 2010

POOL 1

BATLEY BULLDOGS 46 SWINTON LIONS 10

BULLDOGS: 5 John Campbell; 2 Lee Greenwood; 3 Mark Barlow; 4 Danny Maun; 1 Ian Preece; 6 Paul Handforth; 7 Gareth Moore; 16 Jon Simpson; 9 Kris Lythe; 10 Sean Hesketh; 23 Chris Buttery; 26 Jason Walton; 14 John Gallagher. Subs (all used): 11 Tommy Gallagher; 13 Ashley Lindsay; 17 Craig Potter; 12 Mark Toohey.
Tries: Preece (4, 48, 52), T Gallagher (23), Campbell (27, 70), Simpson (44), Lindsay (62), Greenwood (79); **Goals:** Moore 5/9.
LIONS: 2 Darren Bamford; 23 Rob Foxen; 5 Dave Hull; 3 Sam Reay; 25 Barry Hamilton; 6 Graham Holroyd; 7 Ian Watson; 10 Danny Heaton; 9 Phil Joseph; 16 Dana Wilson; 12 Paul Smith; 17 Andrew Isherwood; 13 Aaron Smith. Subs (all used): 20 Chris Hull; 18 Bruce Johnson; 19 Neil Rigby; 21 Chris Tyrer.
Tries: P Smith (13), Foxen (72); **Goals:** Holroyd 1/2.
Rugby Leaguer & League Express Men of the Match: *Bulldogs:* Jason Walton; *Lions:* Ian Watson.
Penalty count: 8-8; **Half-time:** 14-4;
Referee: Ronnie Laughton; **Attendance:** 507.

BLACKPOOL PANTHERS 74 GATESHEAD THUNDER 6

PANTHERS: 1 Jonny Leather; 2 Damian Munro; 24 Paul Ballard; 18 Martin Ainscough; 5 Tom Woodcock; 6 Carl Forber; 7 Tom Hemingway; 21 Peter Fairhurst; 14 Martin Keavney; 10 Andy Hobson; 23 John Boland; 17 Kris Ratcliffe; 11 Kurt Haggerty. Subs (all used): 4 Mark McCully; 9 John Clough; 15 Paul Anderson; 12 Paul Alcock.
Tries: Ainscough (2, 6), Keavney (8, 53, 55), Munro (12, 79), Haggerty (15), Clough (22), Ballard (25, 73), Hemingway (61), Leather (64), Forber (76); **Goals:** Hemingway 9/14.
THUNDER: 28 Jason Elliott; 19 Crawford Matthews; 3 Tom Wilson; 1 Kevin Neighbour; 7 Richard Lopag; 4 Michael Brown; 14 Will Bate; 13 Matt Barron; 9 Ryan Clarke; 17 Chris Parker; 30 Richie Humphries; 22 Rob Harvey; 15 Dan O'Sullivan. Subs (all used): 20 Phil Wall; 10 Tabua Cakacaka; 18 Stephen Welton; 29 Jimmy Atkinson.
Try: Cakacaka (46); **Goals:** Ryan Clarke 1/1.
Rugby Leaguer & League Express Men of the Match: *Panthers:* Andy Hobson; *Thunder:* Will Bate.
Penalty count: 7-12; **Half-time:** 34-0;
Referee: Clint Sharrad; **Attendance:** 194.

KEIGHLEY COUGARS 38 WORKINGTON TOWN 10

COUGARS: 20 Dan Belcher; 2 Craig Moss; 3 Tom Burton; 12 Oliver Pursglove; 1 George Rayner; 6 Jon Presley; 7 Danny Jones; 8 Andy Shickell; 9 James Feather; 10 Scott Law; 21 Richard Jones; 22 Ben Sagar; 23 Chris Baines. Subs (all used): 14 Jamaine Wray; 18 James Haythornthwaite; 16 Brendan Rawlins; 17 Ryan Benjafield.
Tries: Belcher (3), Sagar (10, 15), Presley (21, 61, 69), Rawlins (34); **Goals:** D Jones 3/5, Belcher 2/4.
TOWN: 1 John Lebbon; 2 Mike Backhouse; 3 Andrew Beattie; 15 Aaron Low; 5 Brett Carter; 6 Liam Finch; 7 Scott Kaighan; 8 Lee Dutton; 9 Jack Pedley; 10 Kris Coward; 11 Mike Whitehead; 12 Jarrad Stack; 21 Paddy Coupar. Subs (all used): 14 Jamie Marshall; 4 James Finch; 18 Martyn Wilson; 31 Ruairi McGoff.
Tries: J Finch (55), Beattie (74); **Goals:** Kaighan 1/2.
Rugby Leaguer & League Express Men of the Match: *Cougars:* Jon Presley; *Town:* James Finch.
Penalty count: 14-10; **Half-time:** 26-0;
Referee: Greg Dolan; **Attendance:** 654.

WHITEHAVEN 54 DONCASTER 10

WHITEHAVEN: 1 Craig Benson; 5 Derry Eilbeck; 3 Rob Jackson; 15 Reece Fox; 2 Craig Calvert; 6 Carl Rudd; 14 Dylan Skee; 8 Marc Jackson; 9 Graeme Mattinson; 11 Howard Hill; 12 Spencer Miller; 19 Dexter Miller; 32 Daniel Barker. Subs (all used): 22 Richard Farrer; 33 Kyle Amor; 10 David Ford; 21 Chris Smith.
Tries: Eilbeck (1, 15, 79), S Miller (5, 29), R Fox (21), Benson (24), Farrer (35), Calvert (45), Amor (74); **Goals:** Rudd 0/1, Skee 6/7, M Jackson 1/2.
DONCASTER: 1 Tommy Griffiths; 22 Scott Wilson; 3 Lee Gomersall; 17 Jarryn Osborne; 18 John Winter; 13 Grant Edwards; 7 Craig Fawcett; 10 David Bates; 9 Paul Brown; 15 Danny Stanley; 11 Liam Brown; 12 Ryan Steen; 20 Jack Ely. Subs (all used): 5 Ben Collins; 16 Paul Shaw; 14 Jake Bassinder; 21 Scott Howlett.
Tries: Edwards (55), Wilson (59); **Goals:** Fawcett 1/2.
Rugby Leaguer & League Express Men of the Match: *Whitehaven:* Derry Eilbeck; *Doncaster:* Paul Shaw.
Penalty count: 6-0; **Half-time:** 40-0;
Referee: Warren Turley; **Attendance:** 808.

WIDNES VIKINGS 22 BARROW RAIDERS 20

VIKINGS: 1 James Ford; 26 Shaun Ainscough; 4 Toa Kohe-Love; 15 Shane Grady; 19 Matt Gardner; 6 Anthony Thackeray; 7 James Webster; 16 Gareth Haggerty; 9 Mark Smith; 10 Jim Gannon; 27 Liam Farrell; 17 Ben Kavanagh; 13 Chris Gerrard. Subs (all used): 14 Thomas Coyle; 3 Richard Varkulis; 21 Matthew Strong; 23 David Houghton.
Tries: Farrell (21), Houghton (61), Coyle (77), Ainscough (80); **Goals:** Grady 3/4.
Dismissal: Kavanagh (73) - use of the forearm.
RAIDERS: 1 Gary Broadbent; 2 Andy Ballard; 4 Liam Harrison; 20 Danny Halliwell; 5 James Nixon; 6 Jamie Rooney; 13 Zebastian Luisi; 8 Andy Bracek; 9 Andrew Henderson; 15 Rob Roberts; 17 Paul Noone; 12 Ned Catic; 24 Richard Fletcher. Subs (all used): 10 Chris Young; 11 Michael Knowles; 19 Nathan Mossop; 21 Chris Larkin.
Tries: Nixon (12), Harrison (25), Mossop (28); **Goals:** Rooney 4/5.
Sin bin: Roberts (73) - retaliation.
Rugby Leaguer & League Express Men of the Match: *Vikings:* Jim Gannon; *Raiders:* Zebastian Luisi.
Penalty count: 17-10; **Half-time:** 6-18;
Referee: Jamie Leahy; **Attendance:** 3,432.

POOL 2

LEIGH CENTURIONS 36 FEATHERSTONE ROVERS 6

CENTURIONS: 1 Stuart Donlan; 2 Steve Maden; 3 David Alstead; 4 Mick Nanyn; 5 Nicky Stanton; 6 Tim Hartley; 7 Robbie Paul; 8 Chris Hill; 9 John Duffy; 16 Mike Morrison; 12 Macgraff Leuluai; 34 Lee Mitchell; 11 James Taylor. Subs (all used): 14 Tommy Goulden; 15 Dave McConnell; 35 Jacob Emmitt; 13 David Armitstead.
Tries: Hill (4), Leuluai (11), Alstead (30), Nanyn (45, 47), Mitchell (61); **Goals:** Hartley 6/6.
On report:
Armitstead (57) – alleged high tackle on Morrison.
ROVERS: 1 Ian Hardman; 5 Jon Steel; 3 Sam Smeaton; 21 Michael Coady; 2 Tom Saxton; 6 Kyle Briggs; 7 Andy Kain; 8 Iain Morrison; 9 Liam Finn; 10 Stuart Dickens; 16 Dane Manning; 18 Tim Spears; 14 Danny Allan. Subs (all used): 27 Aaron Dobek; 19 Ross Divorty; 20 Tom Lynch; 11 Matty Dale.
Try: Finn (20); **Goals:** Briggs 1/1.
Rugby Leaguer & League Express Men of the Match: *Centurions:* Tim Hartley; *Rovers:* Iain Morrison.
Penalty count: 9-9; **Half-time:** 18-6;
Referee: Gareth Hewer; **Attendance:** 1,729.

LONDON SKOLARS 0 HALIFAX 68

SKOLARS: 4 Jason Cook; 25 Smokie Junor; 3 Matt Thomas; 14 Luke May; 22 Curtis Cunningham; 17 Chad Isles; 7 Paul Thorman; 28 Ben Jones; 1 Josh Welsh; 20 Dave Williams; 11 Oliver Purslow; 24 Lamont Bryan; 13 Stephen Ball. Subs (all used): 18 James Simon; 31 Ben Kaye; 32 Aran Quinn; 10 Tony Williams.
HALIFAX: 20 Paul White; 23 Rob Worrincy; 5 James Haley; 3 Jon Goddard; 2 Lee Paterson; 6 Luke Branighan; 7 Ben Black; 10 Neil Cherryholme; 9 Sean Penkywicz; 22 David Wrench; 24 Steve Bannister; 15 Mark Roberts; 13 Bob Beswick. Subs (all used): 4 Shad Royston; 21 Anthony Bowman; 16 Said Tamghart; 17 Frank Watene.
Tries: Penkywicz (8, 74), Worrincy (13, 46, 58, 70), Tamghart (35), Bowman (36), Beswick (40, 80), Watene (44), Goddard (50), Haley (55); **Goals:** Paterson 8/13.
Rugby Leaguer & League Express Men of the Match: *Skolars:* Jason Cook; *Halifax:* Rob Worrincy.
Penalty count: 4-5; **Half-time:** 0-24;
Referee: Chris Leatherbarrow; **Attendance:** 416.

ROCHDALE HORNETS 12 DEWSBURY RAMS 48

HORNETS: 32 Wayne English; 1 Craig Johnson; 11 Mark Hobson; 6 Dale Bloomfield; 5 Bolu Fagborun; 29 Ryan Powell; 7 Steve Roper; 10 Gareth Hayes; 9 Phil Wood; 17 Michael Ostick; 16 Danny Samuel; 23 Wayne Corcoran; 28 Chris Hough. Subs (all used): 8 Paul Raftrey; 18 John Cookson; 14 Liam Bostock; 21 Jay Duffy.
Tries: Roper (38), Samuel (78); **Goals:** Roper 2/2.
RAMS: 2 James Haynes; 15 Bryn Powell; 26 Ayden Faal; 10 Scott Turner; 18 Chris Spurr; 13 Pat Walker; 8 Dominic Brambani; 23 Keegan Hirst; 9 Mike Emmett; 24 Anthony England; 21 Andrew Bostock; 20 Rob Spicer; 4 Rob Lunt. Subs (all used): 30 Luke Menzies; 25 James Lockwood; 6 Ryan Smith; 36 Paul Hughes.
Tries: P Walker (8), Brambani (15), Turner (24, 65, 69), Bostock (31), Spurr (35), Menzies (62), Faal (72); **Goals:** P Walker 6/9.
Rugby Leaguer & League Express Men of the Match: *Hornets:* Steve Roper; *Rams:* Dominic Brambani.
Penalty count: 8-7; **Half-time:** 6-28;
Referee: Peter Brooke; **Attendance:** 575.

SHEFFIELD EAGLES 40 YORK CITY KNIGHTS 10

EAGLES: 1 Jonny Woodcock; 5 Ashley Thackeray; 25 Jason Mossop; 23 Tangi Ropati; 24 Misi Taulapapa; 6 Brendon Lindsay; 21 Dane McDonald; 8 Jack Howieson; 9 Craig Cook; 10 Mitchell Stringer; 13 Peter Green; 16 Trevor Exton; 19 Joe Hirst. Subs (all used): 7 Aaron Groom; 17 Alex Rowe; 12 Ged Corcoran; 15 Sam Barlow.
Tries: Stringer (8, 54, 68), McDonald (14), Ropati (43), Hirst (51), Cook (61, 72); **Goals:** Woodcock 4/8.
Dismissal: Rowe (48) – use of the elbow.
CITY KNIGHTS: 1 Danny Ratcliffe; 2 Wayne Reittie; 3 Mike Mitchell; 4 Lee Waterman; 28 Danny Wilson; 6 Chris Thorman; 27 Casey Bromilow; 17 Nathan Freer; 9 Joe McLocklan; 10 Alex Benson; 11 Jordan Ross; 35 Danny Hill; 13 Richard Blakeway. Subs (all used): 25 Brett Walker; 12 Chris Clough; 16 Carl Barrow; 32 Paul Stamp.
Tries: Reittie (23), Waterman (75); **Goals:** Waterman 1/2.
Rugby Leaguer & League Express Men of the Match: *Eagles:* Mitchell Stringer; *City Knights:* Chris Thorman.
Penalty count: 10-9; **Half-time:** 8-6; **Referee:** Robert Hicks; **Attendance:** 814 *(at Don Valley Stadium).*

HUNSLET HAWKS 28 OLDHAM 14

HAWKS: 29 Stuart Kain; 2 Michael Mark; 21 Wayne McHugh; 4 David Clayton; 5 John Oakes; 6 Danny Grimshaw; 7 Paul March; 15 Adam Sullivan; 9 Richard Chapman; 3 James Houston; 11 Rob Kelly; 33 Tom Haughey; 13 David March. Subs (all used): 8 Scott Woodcock; 14 Gareth Firm; 16 Neil Lowe; 18 Charlie Wabo.
Tries: McHugh (3), Mark (38), Lowe (53), Chapman (60), Haughey (63, 79); **Goals:** McHugh 2/6.
OLDHAM: 1 Paul O'Connor; 2 Lucas Onyango; 3 Craig Littler; 4 Mick Fogerty; 24 Marcus St Hilaire; 6 Neil Roden; 7 Matt Ashe; 8 Jason Boults; 9 Martin Roden; 10 Dave Ellison; 13 Joe Chandler; 18 Chris Clarke; 19 Ben Heaton. Subs (all used): 11 Saqib Murtza; 16 Wayne Kerr; 17 Danny Whitmore; 23 Ben Mellor.
Tries: Fogerty (13, 44); **Goals:** Ashe 3/3.
On report: Alleged spear tackle (67).
Rugby Leaguer & League Express Men of the Match: *Hawks:* Paul March; *Oldham:* Mick Fogerty.
Penalty count: 7-13; **Half-time:** 8-6;
Referee: Craig Halloran; **Attendance:** 519.

ROUND 1

Wednesday 17th February 2010

POOL 1

WORKINGTON TOWN 18 SWINTON LIONS 19

TOWN: 5 Brett Carter; 2 Mike Backhouse; 3 Andrew Beattie; 15 Aaron Low; 17 Neil Frazer; 6 Liam Finch; 7 Scott Kaighan; 31 Ruairi McGoff; 23 Phil Hewitt; 10 Kris Coward; 11 Mike Whitehead; 12 Jarrad Stack; 22 Ryan Campbell. Subs (all used): 18 Martyn Wilson; 20 James Robinson; 16 Scott Burgess; 21 Paddy Coupar.
Tries: Low (10), Kaighan (76); **Goals:** Kaighan 5/5.
Sin bin: Carter (58) – interference.
LIONS: 24 Gavin Dodd; 23 Rob Foxen; 3 Sam Reay; 4 Carl Sneyd; 2 Darren Bamford; 6 Graham Holroyd; 7 Ian Watson; 26 Dave Newton; 20 Chris Hull; 16 Dana Wilson; 12 Paul Smith; 19 Neil Rigby; 13 Aaron Smith. Subs (all used): 14 Gary Hulse; 15 Lee Wingfield; 18 Bruce Johnson; 17 Andrew Isherwood.
Tries: Hulse (35), Dodd (63), Sneyd (64); **Goals:** Dodd 3/3; **Field goal:** Holroyd (74).
Sin bin: Isherwood (51) – interference.
Rugby Leaguer & League Express Men of the Match: *Town:* Scott Kaighan; *Lions:* Gary Hulse.
Penalty count: 11-9; **Half-time:** 10-6;
Referee: Dave Merrick; **Attendance:** 286.

DONCASTER 0 BARROW RAIDERS 60

DONCASTER: 1 Tommy Griffiths; 17 Jarryn Osborne; 4 Shaun Leaf; 3 Lee Gomersall; 5 Ben Collins; 13 Grant Edwards; 7 Craig Fawcett; 10 David Bates; 20 Jack Ely; 16 Paul Shaw; 11 Liam Brown; 21 Scott Howlett; 12 Ryan Steen. Subs (all used): 24 Jamie Bovill; 32 Gareth Burns; 31 Nathan Anderson; 9 Paul Brown.
RAIDERS: 1 Gary Broadbent; 2 Andy Ballard; 20 Danny Halliwell; 4 Liam Harrison; 5 James Nixon; 13 Zebastian Luisi; 6 Jamie Rooney; 16 Brett McDermott; 9 Andrew Henderson; 10 Chris Young; 11 Michael Knowles; 12 Ned Catic; 24 Richard Fletcher. Subs (all used): 8 Andy Bracek; 15 Rob Roberts; 19 Nathan Mossop; 17 Paul Noone.

Tries: Henderson (13), Nixon (15, 66), Knowles (17), Catic (21, 41, 51), Luisi (30), Rooney (33), Mossop (76); **Goals:** Rooney 8/8, Knowles 2/2.
Rugby Leaguer & League Express Men of the Match: *Doncaster:* Tommy Griffiths; *Raiders:* Jamie Rooney.
Penalty count: 5-3; **Half-time:** 0-36;
Referee: Peter Brooke; **Attendance:** 285.

POOL 2

SHEFFIELD EAGLES 13 HALIFAX 6

EAGLES: 1 Jonny Woodcock; 5 Ashley Thackeray; 25 Jason Mossop; 23 Tangi Ropati; 24 Misi Taulapapa; 6 Brendon Lindsay; 21 Dane McDonald; 8 Jack Howieson; 9 Craig Cook; 10 Mitchell Stringer; 11 Alex Szostak; 12 Ged Corcoran; 19 Joe Hirst. Subs (all used): 20 Matty Brooks; 18 Michael Haley; 16 Trevor Exton; 22 Ryan Hepworth.
Tries: Ropati (25), Howieson (38);
Goals: Woodcock 2/3; **Field goal:** Cook (78).
HALIFAX: 4 Shad Royston; 2 Lee Paterson; 3 Jon Goddard; 5 James Haley; 23 Rob Worrincy; 6 Luke Branighan; 21 Anthony Bowman; 10 Neil Cherryholme; 9 Sean Penkywicz; 22 David Wrench; 11 David Larder; 12 Stanley Gene; 13 Bob Beswick. Subs (all used): 14 Mark Gleeson; 16 Said Tamghart; 17 Frank Watene; 24 Steve Bannister.
Try: Goddard (7); **Goals:** Paterson 1/1.
Rugby Leaguer & League Express Men of the Match: *Eagles:* Alex Szostak; *Halifax:* Stanley Gene.
Penalty count: 11-7; **Half-time:** 12-6; **Referee:** Gareth Hewer; **Attendance:** 851 *(at Don Valley Stadium).*

ROCHDALE HORNETS 12 YORK CITY KNIGHTS 36

HORNETS: 32 Wayne English; 1 Craig Johnson; 3 Dean Gorton; 12 Danny Smith; 26 Andy Taylor; 29 Ryan Powell; 21 Jay Duffy; 16 Danny Samuel; 14 Liam Bostock; 17 Michael Ostick; 13 Craig Ashall; 11 Mark Hobson; 15 Dayne Donoghue. Subs (all used): 25 Andy Hore; 20 Semisi Cocka; 30 Dean Hatton; 7 Steve Roper.
Tries: Bostock (15), Hatton (70);
Goals: Ashall 1/1, Hatton 1/1.
Sin bin: Donoghue (11) – late tackle.
CITY KNIGHTS: 1 Danny Ratcliffe; 2 Wayne Reittie; 3 Mike Mitchell; 4 Lee Waterman; 26 Steve Lewis; 6 Chris Thorman; 7 Jonathan Schofield; 8 Mark Applegarth; 9 Joe McLocklan; 10 Alex Benson; 11 Jordan Ross; 12 Chris Clough; 13 Richard Blakeway. Subs (all used): 35 Danny Hill; 15 Luke Hardbottle; 25 Brett Waller; 32 Paul Stamp.
Tries: Waterman (6, 30, 61), Schofield (40), Waller (43, 48), Clough (75); **Goals:** Waterman 4/7.
Rugby Leaguer & League Express Men of the Match: *Hornets:* Michael Ostick; *City Knights:* Lee Waterman.
Penalty count: 6-6; **Half-time:** 6-12;
Referee: Craig Halloran; **Attendance:** 362.

ROUND 4

Sunday 21st February 2010

POOL 1

SWINTON LIONS 12 WIDNES VIKINGS 36

LIONS: 1 Richie Hawkyard; 24 Gavin Dodd; 3 Sam Reay; 4 Carl Sneyd; 23 Rob Foxen; 20 Chris Hull; 7 Ian Watson; 16 Dana Wilson; 13 Aaron Smith; 26 Dave Newton; 11 Tommy Grundy; 12 Paul Smith; 19 Neil Rigby. Subs (all used): 14 Gary Hulse; 27 Anthony Stewart; 17 Andrew Isherwood; 15 Lee Wingfield.
Tries: R Hawkyard (2), Dodd (18); **Goals:** Dodd 2/3.
VIKINGS: 1 James Ford; 26 Shaun Ainscough; 4 Toa Kohe-Love; 15 Shane Grady; 19 Matt Gardner; 6 Anthony Thackeray; 7 James Webster; 16 Gareth Haggerty; 9 Mark Smith; 17 Ben Kavanagh; 11 Lee Doran; 27 Liam Farrell; 12 Dave Allen. Subs (all used): 13 Chris Gerrard; 14 Thomas Coyle; 23 David Houghton; 31 Ben Davies.
Tries: Kohe-Love (7, 52), Gardner (11), Grady (27), Ainscough (38), M Smith (54), Thackeray (75);
Goals: Grady 4/7.
Rugby Leaguer & League Express Men of the Match: *Lions:* Gavin Dodd; *Vikings:* Gareth Haggerty.
Penalty count: 4-12; **Half-time:** 12-20;
Referee: Warren Turley; **Attendance:** 816.

WORKINGTON TOWN 22 WHITEHAVEN 14

TOWN: 5 Brett Carter; 2 Mike Backhouse; 3 Andrew Beattie; 15 Aaron Low; 17 Neil Frazer; 6 Liam Finch; 7 Scott Kaighan; 31 Ruairi McGoff; 9 Jack Pedley; 10 Kris Coward; 11 Mike Whitehead; 12 Jarrad Stack; 21 Paddy Coupar. Subs (all used): 14 Jamie Marshall; 4 James Finch; 19 Joe McKenna; 24 Dean Bragg.
Tries: Kaighan (45, 76), Frazer (66); **Goals:** Kaighan 5/7.
Sin bin: Marshall (62) – holding down.
WHITEHAVEN: 1 Craig Benson; 5 Derry Eilbeck; 15 Reece Fox; 3 Rob Jackson; 2 Craig Calvert; 6 Carl Rudd; 13 Mick Govin; 8 Marc Jackson; 9 Graeme Mattinson; 33 Kyle Amor; 12 Spencer Miller; 19 Dexter Miller; 28 Daniel Barker. Subs (all used): 30 Carl Sice; 22 Richard Farrer; 24 Ryan McDonald; 17 Andy Thornley.
Tries: Mattinson (39), Calvert (60); **Goals:** Rudd 3/3.
Rugby Leaguer & League Express Men of the Match: *Town:* Scott Kaighan; *Whitehaven:* Graeme Mattinson.
Penalty count: 12-12; **Half-time:** 4-6;
Referee: Matthew Thomasson; **Attendance:** 736.

Monday 22nd February 2010

POOL 2

OLDHAM 22 SHEFFIELD EAGLES 24

OLDHAM: 1 Paul O'Connor; 2 Lucas Onyango; 24 Marcus St Hilaire; 4 Mick Fogerty; 20 Mark Brocklehurst; 6 Neil Roden; 7 Matt Ashe; 8 Jason Boults; 9 Martin Roden; 16 Wayne Kerr; 19 Ben Heaton; 13 Joe Chandler; 18 Chris Clarke. Subs (all used): 17 Danny Whitmore; 15 Craig Robinson; 10 Dave Ellison; 11 Saqib Murtza.
Tries: O'Connor (7), Brocklehurst (10), N Roden (45), Onyango (47); **Goals:** Ashe 3/4.
EAGLES: 5 Ashley Thackeray; 26 Tim Bergin; 4 John Coleman; 3 Menzie Yere; 27 Richie Barnett; 21 Dane McDonald; 20 Matty Brooks; 22 Ryan Hepworth; 9 Craig Cook; 18 Michael Haley; 11 Alex Szostak; 13 Peter Green; 16 Trevor Exton. Subs (all used): 14 Kyle Kesik; 17 Alex Rowe; 25 Jason Mossop; 15 Sam Barlow.
Tries: Barlow (24, 63), Coleman (32), Green (59);
Goals: Coleman 4/5.
Sin bin: Szostak (19) – late tackle.
Rugby Leaguer & League Express Men of the Match: *Oldham:* Ben Heaton; *Eagles:* Sam Barlow.
Penalty count: 6-10; **Half-time:** 10-12; **Referee:** Robert Hicks; **Attendance:** 340 *(at Park Lane, Sedgley Park).*

Tuesday 23rd February 2010

POOL 2

FEATHERSTONE ROVERS 56 ROCHDALE HORNETS 10

ROVERS: 1 Ian Hardman; 5 Jon Steel; 14 Danny Allan; 4 Liam Welham; 24 Larsen Marabe; 6 Kyle Briggs; 9 Liam Finn; 17 Tony Tonks; 27 Aaron Dobek; 10 Stuart Dickens; 12 Jon Grayshon; 16 Dane Manning; 13 Jamie Field. Subs (all used): 19 Ross Divorty; 23 Jode Sheriffe; 22 Jack Lee; 15 Jessie Joe Parker.
Tries: Steel (2, 30), Grayshon (6, 32), Dobek (25), Divorty (39), Marabe (45, 60), Hardman (50), Briggs (65), Parker (68); **Goals:** Briggs 5/9, Dobek 1/2.
HORNETS: 1 Craig Johnson; 19 Ryan McPaul; 3 Dean Gorton; 22 Damien Reid; 27 Adam Wayne; 28 Chris Hough; 30 Dean Hatton; 8 Paul Raftrey; 9 Phil Wood; 10 Gareth Hayes; 11 Mark Hobson; 23 Wayne Corcoran; 12 Danny Smith. Subs (all used): 24 Paul Crook; 18 John Cookson; 25 Andy Hore; 20 Semisi Cocka.
Tries: Gorton (62), Corcoran (78); **Goals:** Hatton 1/2.
Rugby Leaguer & League Express Men of the Match: *Rovers:* Jon Grayshon; *Hornets:* Dean Hatton.
Penalty count: 5-4; **Half-time:** 36-0;
Referee: Craig Halloran; **Attendance:** 777.

Wednesday 3rd March 2010

POOL 2

DEWSBURY RAMS 22 LEIGH CENTURIONS 44

RAMS: 2 James Haynes; 3 Stewart Sanderson; 18 Chris Spurr; 10 Scott Turner; 32 Martin Woodhead; 6 Ryan Smith; 13 Pat Walker; 23 Keegan Hirst; 36 Paul Hughes; 33 James Walker; 41 Andrew Moody; 28 Liam Crawley; 19 Adam Hayes. Subs (all used): 11 Adam Robinson; 37 Luke Blake; 27 Allister McMaster; 7 Tom Wandless.
Tries: Sanderson (13), P Walker (30), Woodhead (53), Smith (73); **Goals:** P Walker 3/5.
CENTURIONS: 1 Stuart Donlan; 3 David Alstead; 36 Matty Blythe; 4 Mick Nanyn; 2 Steve Maden; 37 Tyrone McCarthy; 7 Robbie Paul; 8 Chris Hill; 9 John Duffy; 13 Dave Armitstead; 14 Tommy Goulden; 34 Lee Mitchell; 11 James Taylor. Subs (all used): 15 Dave McConnell; 22 Martyn Ridyard; 12 Macgraff Leuluai; 35 Jacob Emmitt.
Tries: Maden (20), Duffy (24, 34), Blythe (39), Emmitt (46), McCarthy (48), Hill (76), Armitstead (79);
Goals: Nanyn 6/8.
Sin bin: Hill (64) – obstruction.
Rugby Leaguer & League Express Men of the Match: *Rams:* Pat Walker; *Centurions:* John Duffy.
Penalty count: 8-10; **Half-time:** 12-20;
Referee: Jamie Leahy; **Attendance:** 888.

ROUND 1

Thursday 4th March 2010

POOL 2

HUNSLET HAWKS 0 FEATHERSTONE ROVERS 68

HAWKS: 1 Nathan Larvin; 31 Corey Challenger; 25 Danny Cook; 30 Richard Knight; 2 Michael Mark; 17 Stuart Young; 34 Nigel Scott; 10 Nicko Slain; 19 Darren Robinson; 20 Joe Helme; 23 Jake Wilson; 32 Michael Kelly; 18 Charlie Wabo. Subs (all used): 14 Gareth Firm; 16 Neil Lowe; 24 Steve Brook; 35 Russ Dale.
ROVERS: 26 Zak Hardaker; 24 Larsen Marabe; 14 Danny Allan; 2 Tom Saxton; 28 Thomas Carr; 15 Jessie Joe Parker; 27 Aaron Dobek; 8 Iain Morrison; 31 Ben Kaye; 23 Jode Sheriffe; 11 Matty Dale; 16 Dane Manning; 22 Jack Lee. Subs (all used): 21 Michael Coady; 17 Tony Tonks; 19 Ross Divorty; 29 Gareth Williamson.
Tries: Parker (6, 79), Allan (30), Hardaker (32, 60, 72), Dobek (41), Saxton (44), Divorty (50), Williamson (55), Marabe (64), Lee (66); **Goals:** Dobek 10/12.
Sin bin: Williamson (36) - holding down.
Rugby Leaguer & League Express Men of the Match: *Hawks:* Michael Mark; *Rovers:* Aaron Dobek.
Penalty count: 8-6; **Half-time:** 0-18;
Referee: Dave Merrick; **Attendance:** 513.

ROUND 4

Wednesday 10th March 2010

POOL 1

BARROW RAIDERS 62 KEIGHLEY COUGARS 18

RAIDERS: 1 Gary Broadbent; 21 Chris Larkin; 12 Ned Catic; 4 Liam Harrison; 2 Andy Ballard; 13 Zebastian Luisi; 6 Jamie Rooney; 8 Andy Bracek; 9 Andrew Henderson; 15 Rob Roberts; 14 Martin Ostler; 11 Michael Knowles; 24 Richard Fletcher. Subs (all used): 23 Jamie Butler; 17 Paul Noone; 16 Brett McDermott; 19 Nathan Mossop.
Tries: Harrison (4, 25, 53), Knowles (11), Roberts (16), Ballard (22), Larkin (29, 31), Rooney (46), Mossop (50), McDermott (78); **Goals:** Rooney 9/11.
COUGARS: 1 George Rayner; 33 Luke Rayner; 3 Tom Burton; 4 Daley Williams; 5 Gavin Duffy; 6 Jon Presley; 7 Danny Jones; 21 Richard Jones; 24 Tom Hall; 19 Sam Crowther; 15 Greg Nicholson; 25 Jamie Shepherd; 13 Carl Hughes. Subs (all used): 9 James Feather; 17 Ryan Benjafield; 23 Chris Baines; 8 Andy Shickell.
Tries: Presley (38), D Jones (57), G Rayner (67);
Goals: D Jones 3/3.
Rugby Leaguer & League Express Men of the Match: *Raiders:* Liam Harrison; *Cougars:* Danny Jones.
Penalty count: 7-4; **Half-time:** 40-6;
Referee: Craig Halloran; **Attendance:** 1,277.

POOL 2

YORK CITY KNIGHTS 34 LONDON SKOLARS 12

CITY KNIGHTS: 4 Lee Waterman; 22 Tom Stancliffe; 26 Steve Lewis; 18 Matty Duckworth; 5 Tom Lineham; 27 Casey Bromilow; 7 Jonathan Schofield; 10 Alex Benson; 9 Joe McLocklan; 36 Jon Fallon; 11 Jordan Ross; 19 Kris Peacock; 20 Chris Williams. Subs (all used): 8 Mark Applegarth; 15 Luke Hardbottle; 16 Carl Barrow; 33 Mark Falkingham.
Tries: Schofield (11), Bromilow (26, 62), Applegarth (37), Duckworth (43), Waterman (74);
Goals: Waterman 5/6.
Sin bin: Barrow (56) – late tackle.
SKOLARS: 31 Ade Adebisi; 25 Smokie Junor; 14 Luke May; 36 Oliver Bloom; 35 Jaroslaw Obuchowski; 17 Chad Isles; 39 Jamie Boston; 20 Dave Williams; 1 Josh Welsh; 10 Tony Williams; 33 Nathan McLoughlin; 38 Rob Montgomerie; 13 Stephen Ball. Subs (all used): 34 Aaron Small; 32 Aran Quinn; 12 Matt Carter; 3 Matt Thomas.
Tries: Montgomerie (58), Ball (78); **Goals:** Boston 2/2.
Rugby Leaguer & League Express Men of the Match: *City Knights:* Lee Waterman; *Skolars:* Josh Welsh.
Penalty count: 5-10; **Half-time:** 18-0;
Referee: Tim Roby; **Attendance:** 439.

Wednesday 17th March 2010

POOL 1

GATESHEAD THUNDER 4 BATLEY BULLDOGS 100

THUNDER: 28 Jason Elliott; 34 Richard Lopag; 1 Kevin Neighbour; 4 Michael Brown; 5 Joe Brown; 6 Liam Duffy; 9 Ryan Clarke; 17 Chris Parker; 14 Will Bate; 26 David Cash; 16 Dan O'Sullivan; 30 Richie Humphries; 20 Phil Wall. Subs (all used): 33 Reece Young; 13 Matt Barron; 3 Tom Wilson; 25 Gareth Barron.
Try: M Brown (38); **Goals:** Ryan Clarke 0/1.
BULLDOGS: 5 John Campbell; 1 Ian Preece; 3 Mark Barlow; 4 Danny Maun; 2 Lee Greenwood; 25 Kyle Wood; 7 Gareth Moore; 8 Byron Smith; 9 Kris Lythe; 10 Sean Hesketh; 23 Chris Buttery; 26 Jason Walton; 13 Ashley Lindsay. Subs (all used): 14 John Gallagher; 17 Craig Potter; 11 Tommy Gallagher; 20 Dave Tootill.
Tries: Moore (3, 27), Buttery (11), Wood (13, 15), Tootill (30, 46), Walton (32, 78), Barlow (48), Campbell (51, 55, 71), Hesketh (60), Preece (73, 80), Potter (75); **Goals:** Moore 16/17.
Rugby Leaguer & League Express Men of the Match: *Thunder:* Reece Young; *Bulldogs:* John Campbell.
Penalty count: 6-4; **Half-time:** 4-42;
Referee: Chris Leatherbarrow; **Attendance:** 237.

Sunday 21st March 2010

POOL 2

HALIFAX 36 HUNSLET HAWKS 42

HALIFAX: 20 Paul White; 5 James Haley; 3 Jon Goddard; 2 Lee Paterson; 23 Rob Worrincy; 6 Luke Branighan; 7 Ben Black; 8 Makali Aizue; 13 Bob Beswick; 10 Neil Cherryholme; 18 Dylan Nash; 15 Mark Roberts; 24 Steve Bannister. Subs (all used): 19 Dominic Maloney; 14 Mark Gleeson; 17 Frank Watene; 21 Anthony Bowman.
Tries: Nash (26, 50), Bowman (39), Worrincy (45), Watene (75), Branighan (78); **Goals:** Paterson 6/6.
HAWKS: 1 Nathan Larvin; 22 Tom Sheldrake; 5 John Oakes; 4 David Clayton; 2 Michael Mark; 6 Danny Grimshaw; 7 Paul March; 15 Adam Sullivan; 9 Richard Chapman; 3 James Houston; 30 Richard Knight; 11 Rob Kelly; 13 David March. Subs (all used): 19 Darren Robinson; 16 Neil Lowe; 18 Charlie Wabo; 20 Joe Helme.
Tries: Knight (5), Larvin (12), Lowe (20), Wabo (33), Houston (43), Chapman (56), Mark (79);
Goals: Knight 4/5, Robinson 1/1, Sheldrake 2/2.
Dismissal: Chapman (72) - high tackle on Branighan.
Sin bin: Larvin (33) - holding down.
Rugby Leaguer & League Express Men of the Match: *Halifax:* Rob Worrincy; *Hawks:* Paul March.
Penalty count: 11-5; **Half-time:** 12-22;
Referee: Ronnie Laughton; **Attendance:** 1,771.

Northern Rail Cup 2010 - Round by Round

Wednesday 24th March 2010

POOL 1

DONCASTER 20 BLACKPOOL PANTHERS 40

DONCASTER: 2 Aaron Henry; 17 Jarryn Osborne; 3 Lee Gomersall; 18 John Winter; 33 Nick Cooper; 34 Danny Allan; 6 Simon Brown; 10 David Bates; 9 Paul Brown; 19 Garry Ellery; 11 Liam Brown; 21 Scott Howlett; 14 Jake Bassinder. Subs (all used): 15 Danny Stanley; 16 Paul Shaw; 35 Mark Ward; 26 Gary King.
Tries: Osborne (27), P Brown (41), Ellery (58), King (64); **Goals:** S Brown 1/2, Stanley 1/1, Allan 0/1.
PANTHERS: 1 Jonny Leather; 2 Damian Munro; 18 Martin Ainscough; 22 Dave Llewellyn; 5 Tom Woodcock; 6 Carl Forber; 7 Tom Hemingway; 21 Peter Fairhurst; 9 John Clough; 23 John Boland; 27 Danny Halliwell; 12 Paul Alcock; 4 Mark McCully. Subs (all used): 14 Martin Keavney; 11 Kurt Haggerty; 10 Andy Hobson; 24 Paul Ballard.
Tries: Clough (12), Hemingway (20), Woodcock (30, 52), Munro (38, 46), Boland (55), Keavney (74); **Goals:** Hemingway 0/2, Forber 2/4, Leather 2/2.
Sin bin: Keavney (26) - late tackle.
Rugby Leaguer & League Express Men of the Match: *Doncaster:* Danny Stanley; *Panthers:* Martin Ainscough.
Penalty count: 5-6; **Half-time:** 4-20;
Referee: Tim Roby; **Attendance:** 192.

FINAL TABLES

POOL 1

	P	W	D	L	BP	F	A	Diff	Pts
Batley Bulldogs	4	3	1	0	0	210	70	140	11
Widnes Vikings	4	3	1	0	0	138	68	70	11
Barrow Raiders	4	3	0	1	1	176	48	128	10
Keighley Cougars	4	3	0	1	0	97	110	-13	9
Blackpool Panthers	4	2	0	2	1	144	84	60	7
Workington Town	4	2	0	2	1	76	83	-7	7
Whitehaven	4	1	0	3	3	110	83	27	6
Swinton Lions	4	2	0	2	0	71	120	-49	6
Doncaster	4	0	0	4	1	50	184	-134	1
Gateshead Thunder	4	0	0	4	0	28	250	-222	0

POOL 2

	P	W	D	L	BP	F	A	Diff	Pts
Sheffield Eagles	4	3	1	0	0	95	56	39	11
Leigh Centurions	4	3	0	1	1	116	53	63	10
York City Knights	4	3	0	1	0	93	76	17	9
Hunslet Hawks	4	3	0	1	0	130	130	0	9
Featherstone Rovers	4	2	1	1	0	148	64	84	8
Halifax	4	2	0	2	2	134	55	79	8
Dewsbury Rams	4	2	0	2	0	120	84	36	6
Oldham	4	1	0	3	2	70	90	-20	5
Rochdale Hornets	4	0	0	4	1	48	162	-114	1
London Skolars	4	0	0	4	0	28	212	-184	0

Top four teams from each Pool progressed to Quarter Finals.

QUARTER FINALS

Thursday 3rd June 2010

WIDNES VIKINGS 26 BARROW RAIDERS 12

VIKINGS: 1 James Ford; 2 Dean Gaskell; 4 Toa Kohe-Love; 19 Matt Gardner; 5 Paddy Flynn; 33 Chaz I'Anson; 6 Anthony Thackeray; 10 Jim Gannon; 32 Kirk Netherton; 28 Ben Davies; 15 Shane Grady; 12 Dave Allen; 11 Lee Doran. Subs (all used): 13 Chris Gerrard; 17 Ben Kavanagh; 29 Jordan James; 23 David Houghton.
Tries: Grady (4), Netherton (12, 76), Gaskell (26, 40), Kohe-Love (51); **Goals:** Grady 1/3, C Gerrard 0/2, Thackeray 0/1.
RAIDERS: 1 Gary Broadbent; 2 Andy Ballard; 32 Andreas Bauer; 12 Ned Catic; 4 Liam Harrison; 6 Jamie Rooney; 18 Liam Campbell; 16 Brett McDermott; 19 Nathan Mossop; 15 Rob Roberts; 11 Michael Knowles; 24 Richard Fletcher; 13 Zebastian Luisi. Subs (all used): 8 Andy Bracek; 10 Chris Young; 17 Paul Noone; 23 Jamie Butler.
Tries: Catic (18, 41); **Goals:** Rooney 2/2.
Rugby Leaguer & League Express Man of the Match: *Vikings:* Kirk Netherton; *Raiders:* Ned Catic.
Penalty count: 5-6; **Half-time:** 16-6;
Referee: Gareth Hewer; **Attendance:** 1,718.

Sunday 6th June 2010

BATLEY BULLDOGS 26 SHEFFIELD EAGLES 16

BULLDOGS: 5 John Campbell; 24 Alex Brown; 12 Mark Toohey; 4 Danny Maun; 2 Lee Greenwood; 6 Paul Handforth; 7 Gareth Moore; 8 Byron Smith; 9 Kris Lythe; 10 Sean Hesketh; 26 Jason Walton; 31 John Gallagher; 13 Ashley Lindsay. Subs (all used): 33 Mick Govin; 17 Craig Potter; 23 Chris Buttery; 20 David Tootill.
Tries: Hesketh (13), Potter (28), Campbell (33), Lindsay (35); **Goals:** Moore 5/5.
EAGLES: 24 Misi Taulapapa; 2 Danny Mills; 3 Menzie Yere; 23 Tangi Ropati; 27 Richie Barnett; 6 Brendon Lindsay; 7 Aaron Groom; 18 Michael Haley; 9 Craig Cook; 10 Mitchell Stringer; 16 Trevor Exton; 13 Peter Green; 21 Dane McDonald. Subs (all used): 12 Ged Corcoran; 15 Sam Barlow; 22 Ryan Hepworth; 17 Alex Rowe.
Tries: McDonald (7), Cook (57), Mills (62); **Goals:** Lindsay 2/3.

Widnes' Matt Gardner pursues Barrow's Jamie Rooney

Rugby Leaguer & League Express Men of the Match: *Bulldogs:* Sean Hesketh; *Eagles:* Dane McDonald.
Penalty count: 7-8; **Half time:** 24-4;
Referee: Robert Hicks; **Attendance:** 708.

KEIGHLEY COUGARS 32 YORK CITY KNIGHTS 6

COUGARS: 2 Craig Moss; 5 Gavin Duffy; 33 Tom Sheldrake; 4 Daley Williams; 31 James Hutchinson; 6 Jon Presley; 7 Danny Jones; 10 Scott Law; 9 James Feather; 17 Ryan Benjafield; 23 Chris Baines; 11 Will Cartledge; 13 Carl Hughes. Subs (all used): 14 Jamaine Wray; 18 James Haythornthwaite; 16 Brendan Rawlins; 8 Andy Shickell.
Tries: Sheldrake (15), Wray (36), Williams (45, 62), Shickell (68); **Goals:** D Jones 6/6.
CITY KNIGHTS: 28 Danny Wilson; 29 Danny Tuffour; 3 Mike Mitchell; 4 Lee Waterman; 5 Tom Lineham; 6 Chris Thorman; 1 Danny Ratcliffe; 36 Jon Fallon; 33 Jack Lee; 30 Jack Stearman; 18 Matty Duckworth; 15 Luke Hardbottle; 31 Danny Allan. Subs (all used): 20 Chris Williams; 34 Mike Embleton; 10 Alex Benson; 25 Brett Waller.
Try: Duckworth (28); **Goals:** Waterman 1/1.
Rugby Leaguer & League Express Men of the Match: *Cougars:* Jon Presley; *City Knights:* Luke Hardbottle.
Penalty count: 8-7; **Half time:** 14-6;
Referee: Ronnie Laughton; **Attendance:** 712.

HUNSLET HAWKS 6 LEIGH CENTURIONS 42

HAWKS: 29 Stuart Kain; 2 Michael Mark; 21 Wayne McHugh; 4 David Clayton; 5 John Oakes; 6 Danny Grimshaw; 7 Paul March; 15 Adam Sullivan; 14 Luke Haigh; 3 James Houston; 12 Steve Dooler; 10 Tom Haughey; 13 David March. Subs (all used): 8 Scott Woodcock; 16 Neil Lowe; 19 Darren Robinson; 32 Michael Kelly.
Try: McHugh (1); **Goals:** D March 1/1.
Sin bin: D March (80) - interference.
CENTURIONS: 1 Stuart Donlan; 3 David Alstead; 2 Steve Maden; 4 Mick Nanyn; 18 Adam Higson; 22 Martyn Ridyard; 9 John Duffy; 8 Chris Hill; 15 Dave McConnell; 27 Jacob Emmitt; 11 James Taylor; 14 Tommy Goulden; 37 Tyrone McCarthy; 16 Mike Morrison; 36 Anthony Nicholson.
Tries: Taylor (11), Nicholson (37), Nanyn (43, 78), Morrison (50), Alstead (74), Emmitt (80); **Goals:** Nanyn 7/7.
Rugby Leaguer & League Express Men of the Match: *Hawks:* Paul March; *Centurions:* Mick Nanyn.
Penalty count: 9-8; **Half-time:** 6-12;
Referee: Matthew Thomasson; **Attendance:** 770.

SEMI-FINALS

Thursday 17th June 2010

LEIGH CENTURIONS 4 BATLEY BULLDOGS 25

CENTURIONS: 1 Stuart Donlan; 2 Steve Maden; 12 Macgraff Leuluai; 25 Matty Blythe; 3 David Alstead; 22 Martyn Ridyard; 7 Robbie Paul; 10 Ricky Bibey; 15 Dave McConnell; 27 Jacob Emmitt; 11 James Taylor; 14 Tommy Goulden; 26 Lee Mitchell. Subs (all used): 8 Chris Hill; 28 Tyrone McCarthy; 13 Dave Armitstead; 18 Adam Higson.
Try: Maden (12); **Goals:** Ridyard 0/1.

BULLDOGS: 5 John Campbell; 24 Alex Brown; 12 Mark Toohey; 4 Danny Maun; 2 Lee Greenwood; 6 Paul Handforth; 7 Gareth Moore; 8 Byron Smith; 9 Kris Lythe; 10 Sean Hesketh; 26 Jason Walton; 31 John Gallagher; 13 Ashley Lindsay. Subs (all used): 33 Mick Govin; 17 Craig Potter; 23 Chris Buttery; 20 David Tootill.
Tries: Maun (31, 77), Hesketh (52), Lythe (80); **Goals:** Moore 4/5; **Field goal:** Moore (75).
Rugby Leaguer & League Express Men of the Match: *Centurions:* Stuart Donlan; *Bulldogs:* Paul Handforth.
Penalty count: 7-8; **Half-time:** 4-8;
Referee: Robert Hicks; **Attendance:** 2,058.

Sunday 20th June 2010

KEIGHLEY COUGARS 18 WIDNES VIKINGS 48

COUGARS: 2 Craig Moss; 5 Gavin Duffy; 33 Tom Sheldrake; 4 Daley Williams; 31 James Hutchinson; 9 James Feather; 7 Danny Jones; 8 Andy Shickell; 14 Jamaine Wray; 10 Scott Law; 23 Chris Baines; 12 Oliver Pursglove; 11 Will Cartledge. Subs (all used): 15 Greg Nicholson; 16 Brendan Rawlins; 17 Ryan Benjafield; 32 Barry Eaton.
Tries: Wray (75), Eaton (77), Cartledge (79); **Goals:** D Jones 3/3.
VIKINGS: 5 Paddy Flynn; 26 Shaun Ainscough; 4 Toa Kohe-Love; 19 Matt Gardner; 2 Dean Gaskell; 6 Anthony Thackeray; 9 Mark Smith; 10 Jim Gannon; 32 Kirk Netherton; 17 Ben Kavanagh; 15 Shane Grady; 12 Dave Allen; 11 Lee Doran. Subs (all used): 3 Richard Varkulis; 13 Chris Gerrard; 23 David Houghton; 31 Tom Kelly.
Tries: Thackeray (21, 35, 51), Allen (40), Flynn (47), Ainscough (59), M Smith (64), Houghton (68); **Goals:** Grady 8/8.
Rugby Leaguer & League Express Men of the Match: *Cougars:* James Feather; *Vikings:* Anthony Thackeray.
Penalty count: 6-9; **Half-time:** 0-18;
Referee: Ronnie Laughton; **Attendance:** 1,686.

FINAL

Sunday 18th July 2010

BATLEY BULLDOGS 25 WIDNES VIKINGS 24

BULLDOGS: 5 John Campbell; 24 Alex Brown; 12 Mark Toohey; 4 Danny Maun; 2 Lee Greenwood; 6 Paul Handforth; 7 Gareth Moore; 8 Byron Smith; 9 Kris Lythe; 10 Sean Hesketh; 26 Jason Walton; 31 John Gallagher; 13 Ashley Lindsay. Subs (all used): 33 Mick Govin; 11 Tommy Gallagher; 20 David Tootill; 21 James Martin.
Tries: Walton (3), Hesketh (8), Brown (68, 78); **Goals:** Moore 4/5; **Field goal:** Moore (33).
VIKINGS: 5 Paddy Flynn; 26 Shaun Ainscough; 19 Matt Gardner; 15 Shane Grady; 2 Dean Gaskell; 6 Anthony Thackeray; 14 Thomas Coyle; 16 Gareth Haggerty; 32 Kirk Netherton; 10 Jim Gannon; 11 Lee Doran; 13 Chris Gerrard. Subs (all used): 8 Steve Pickersgill; 9 Mark Smith; 17 Ben Kavanagh; 28 Ben Davies.
Tries: Davies (14), Thackeray (17), Flynn (50), C Gerrard (65); **Goals:** Grady 4/4.
Rugby Leaguer & League Express Men of the Match: *Bulldogs:* Paul Handforth; *Vikings:* Ben Davies.
Penalty count: 7-7; **Half-time:** 15-12;
Referee: Robert Hicks; **Attendance:** 8,138.
(at Bloomfield Road, Blackpool).

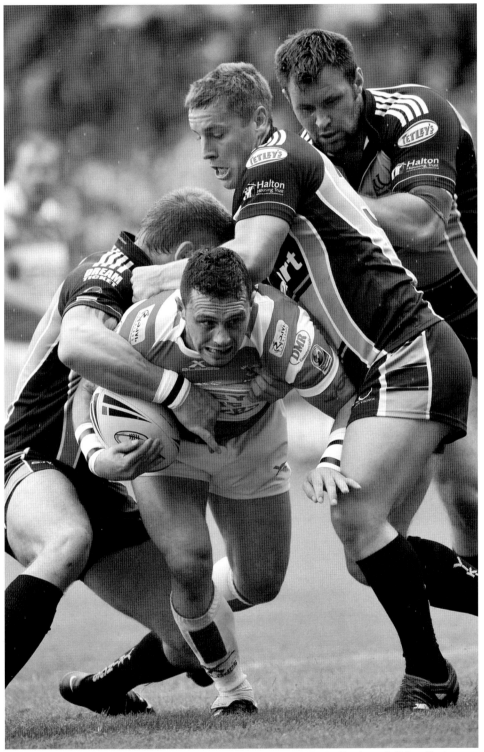

Batley's Ashley Lindsay on the charge against Widnes during the Northern Rail Cup Final

CHALLENGE CUP 2010
Round by Round

ROUND 3

Friday 5th March 2010

LEIGH MINERS RANGERS 20 WHITEHAVEN 40

MINERS RANGERS: 1 Johnny Youds; 2 Daryl Flannery; 3 Leon Brennan; 4 Kieran Dainty; 5 Tom Bradbury; 6 Scott O'Brien; 7 Ryan Smith; 8 Dean Balmer; 9 Danny Jones; 10 Darryl Kay; 11 Luke Murfin; 12 Liam Coleman; 13 Aaron Gorton. Subs (all used): 14 James Muir; 15 Danny Jackson; 16 Tom Dawson; 17 Tom Eckersley.
Tries: O'Brien (8), Smith (17, 47); **Goals:** Bradbury 4/4.
WHITEHAVEN: 30 Carl Sice; 26 Stephen Dawes; 15 Reece Fox; 5 Derry Eilbeck; 2 Craig Calvert; 6 Carl Rudd; 25 Scott George; 24 Ryan McDonald; 9 Graeme Mattinson; 11 Howard Hill; 12 Spencer Miller; 19 Dexter Miller; 32 Daniel Barker. Subs (all used): 8 Marc Jackson; 22 Richard Farrer; 17 Andy Thornley; 10 David Ford.
Tries: Calvert (28), Mattinson (31), M Jackson (36), R Fox (40), Farrer (71), Sice (75), D Miller (80);
Goals: Rudd 6/7.
Rugby Leaguer & League Express Men of the Match:
Miners Rangers: Scott O'Brien; *Whitehaven:* Carl Sice.
Penalty count: 13-13; **Half-time:** 14-22; **Referee:** Warren Turley; **Attendance:** 491 *(at Leigh Sports Village).*

WARRINGTON WIZARDS 22 SWINTON LIONS 34

WIZARDS: 1 Chris Campbell; 2 David Yii; 3 Danny Shaw; 4 Matt Taylor; 5 Stuart Pirrie; 6 Ian Stephenson; 7 Warren Ayres; 8 Tom Wild; 9 Wes Lawton; 10 Matt Clarke; 11 Scott Davidson; 12 Jono Smith; 13 Alan Reddicliffe. Subs (all used): 14 Anthony Braide; 15 Carl Leach; 16 Shaun Gilmour; 17 Nick Braide.
Tries: Smith (21), Shaw (63, 68), Pirrie (66);
Goals: Ayres 3/4.
LIONS: 24 Gavin Dodd; 5 Dave Hull; 3 Sam Reay; 27 Anthony Stewart; 23 Rob Foxen; 20 Chris Hull; 7 Ian Watson; 16 Dana Wilson; 1 Richie Hawkyard; 21 Chris Tyrer; 11 Tommy Grundy; 12 Paul Smith; 19 Neil Rigby. Subs (all used): 13 Aaron Smith; 14 Gary Hulse; 17 Andrew Isherwood; 15 Lee Wingfield.
Tries: D Hull (12, 26), Foxen (29, 55), Wilson (47), Dodd (50); **Goals:** Dodd 5/6.
Dismissal: D Hull (33) - dangerous tackle on Yii.
Sin bin: Rigby (43) - late tackle.
Rugby Leaguer & League Express Men of the Match:
Wizards: Jono Smith; *Lions:* Sam Reay.
Penalty count: 11-10; **Half-time:** 6-16; **Referee:** Brandon Robinson; **Attendance:** 430 *(at Wilderspool).*

Saturday 6th March 2010

DONCASTER 0 SIDDAL 26

DONCASTER: 1 Tommy Griffiths; 22 Scott Wilson; 12 Ryan Steen; 4 Shaun Leaf; 26 Gary King; 6 Simon Brown; 20 Jack Ely; 24 Jamie Bovill; 32 Kyle Kesik; 10 David Bates; 23 Craig Lawton; 11 Liam Brown; 16 Paul Shaw. Subs (all used): 9 Paul Brown; 19 Gary Ellery; 21 Scott Howlett; 18 John Winter.
SIDDAL: 1 Brad Attwood; 2 Gareth Blackburn; 3 Chris Marsh; 4 Andy Bowman; 5 Scott Caley; 6 Shaun Garrod; 7 Lee Gudor; 8 Jamie Wrigley; 9 Simeon Hoyle; 10 Mark Boothroyd; 11 James Simeunovich; 12 Nick Smith; 13 Luke Simeunovich. Subs (all used): 14 Stuart Proctor; 15 Adie Leek; 16 George Ambler; 17 Luke Garrett.
Tries: Caley (1, 77), Attwood (36, 71), Blackburn (46);
Goals: Attwood 3/5.
Rugby Leaguer & League Express Men of the Match:
Doncaster: Craig Lawton; *Siddal:* Lee Gudor.
Penalty count: 13-11; **Half-time:** 0-10;
Referee: Ronnie Laughton; **Attendance:** 561.

LEIGH EAST 14 HUNSLET HAWKS 30

EAST: 1 Ryan Fieldhouse; 2 Andrew Groves; 3 Carl Redford; 4 Gareth Pemberton; 5 Gavin Hunter; 6 Ryan Peters; 7 Mark Ballard; 8 Craig Winfield; 9 Danny Kilshaw; 10 Lee Rowley; 11 John Taylor; 12 Craig Millington; 13 Gary Middlehurst. Subs (all used): 14 Adrian Dootson; 15 Steven Grundy; 16 Carl Mort; 17 Brett Longstaff.
Tries: Groves (30, 42), Fieldhouse (54); **Goals:** Peters 1/3.
Sin bin: Middlehurst (70) - punching.
On report: Rowley (78) - fighting.
HAWKS: 29 Stuart Kain; 2 Michael Mark; 30 Richard Knight; 21 Wayne McHugh; 5 John Oakes; 13 David March; 7 Paul March; 15 Adam Sullivan; 19 Darren Robinson; 3 James Houston; 11 Rob Kelly; 12 Steve Dooler; 33 Tom Haughey. Subs (all used): 16 Neil Lowe; 8 Scott Woodcock; 17 Stuart Young; 18 Charlie Wabo.
Tries: Dooler (15), P March (47), Mark (57, 62), Robinson (72); **Goals:** McHugh 5/6.
On report: Wabo (78) - fighting.
Rugby Leaguer & League Express Men of the Match:
East: Gary Middlehurst; *Hawks:* David March.
Penalty count: 12-20; **Half-time:** 4-8; **Referee:** Matthew Kidd; **Attendance:** 694 *(at Leigh Sports Village).*

KEIGHLEY COUGARS 26 TOULOUSE OLYMPIQUE 35

COUGARS: 1 George Rayner; 2 Craig Moss; 3 Tom Burton; 4 Daley Williams; 5 Gavin Duffy; 6 Jon Presley; 7 Danny Jones; 8 Andy Shickell; 9 James Feather; 10 Scott Law; 23 Chris Baines; 12 Oliver Pursglove; 18 James Haythornthwaite. Subs (all used): 14 Jamaine Wray; 13 Carl Hughes; 16 Brendan Rawlins; 17 Ryan Benjafield.
Tries: Benjafield (27), Burton (30), Presley (34), G Rayner (46), Shickell (59); **Goals:** D Jones 3/5.
OLYMPIQUE: 1 Rory Bromley; 22 Clement Bienes; 3 Sebastien Planas; 4 Vincent Duport; 5 Carlos Mendes Varela; 16 Sylvain Houles; 7 Nathan Wynn; 8 Brendan Worth; 31 Yohann Gigord; 11 Tim Wynn; 18 Yoan Tisseyre; 14 Antoni Maria; 13 Eric Anselme. Subs (all used): 15 Jerome Gout; 19 Romain Mencarini; 33 Kevin Larroyer; 20 Bruno Ormeno.
Tries: Planas (14, 50), Bienes (16), Tisseyre (38), N Wynn (52), Bromley (77); **Goals:** N Wynn 5/7;
Field goal: N Wynn (78).
Rugby Leaguer & League Express Men of the Match:
Cougars: Andy Shickell; *Olympique:* Nathan Wynn.
Penalty count: 6-6; **Half-time:** 14-18;
Referee: Gareth Hewer; **Attendance:** 543.

Sunday 7th March 2010

BATLEY BULLDOGS 70 LEEDS MET UNIVERSITY 6

BULLDOGS: 5 John Campbell; 1 Ian Preece; 3 Mark Barlow; 4 Danny Maun; 19 Eddie Kilroy; 6 Paul Handforth; 7 Gareth Moore; 20 David Tootill; 9 Kris Lythe; 11 Tommy Gallagher; 23 Chris Buttery; 17 Craig Potter; 31 John Gallagher. Subs (all used): 13 Ashley Lindsay; 12 Mark Toohey; 21 James Martin; 2 Lee Greenwood.
Tries: Toohey (2), Barlow (6), Kilroy (8), Buttery (13), Tootill (26), J Gallagher (28), Campbell (43, 63), Moore (46, 77), Greenwood (79, 80); **Goals:** Moore 11/12.
LEEDS MET: 1 Ashley Huck; 2 Jack Sampson; 3 Nick Walker; 4 Rhys Griffiths; 5 John Paxton; 6 Jy-Mel Coleman; 7 Nigel Scott; 8 Matt Carbutt; 9 Scott Ellam; 10 Adam Scott; 11 Jason Hurt; 12 Kris Hodson; 13 Steve Gibbons. Subs (all used): 14 Mark Wool; 15 Chris Clarke; 16 Dom Lespierre; 17 Ben Parker.
Try: Hodson (53); **Goals:** N Scott 1/1.
Rugby Leaguer & League Express Men of the Match:
Bulldogs: Gareth Moore; *Leeds Met:* Adam Scott.
Penalty count: 10-4; **Half-time:** 34-0;
Referee: Jamie Leahy; **Attendance:** 502.

ROYAL NAVY 16 BLACKPOOL PANTHERS 50

ROYAL NAVY: 1 Dane Smallbone; 2 John Humphries; 3 Tom Boyce; 4 Tim Voneravalu; 5 Aaron Hanson; 6 Kevin Botwood; 7 Wayne John; 8 Jamie Goss; 9 Johnny Platt; 10 Lewis Taylor; 11 Gareth Cadmore; 12 Mark Robinson; 13 Danny Johnson. Subs (all used): 14 Richard Sharp; 15 Manasa Tamoi; 16 Ryan Chivernor; 17 Ben Cartwright.
Tries: Humphries (10), Boyce (39), Hanson (76);
Goals: Botwood 2/3.
Sin bin: Goss (36) - fighting.
PANTHERS: 1 Jonny Leather; 2 Damian Munro; 3 Casey Mayberry; 18 Martin Ainscough; 24 Paul Ballard; 6 Carl Forber; 7 Tom Hemingway; 17 Kris Ratcliffe; 14 Martin Keavney; 10 Andy Hobson; 23 John Boland; 4 Mark McCully; 11 Kurt Haggerty. Subs (all used): 12 Paul Alcock; 15 Paul Anderson; 9 John Clough; 16 Simon Svabic.
Tries: Hobson (1, 51), Mayberry (3, 20, 56), McCully (46), Munro (61), Leather (68), Svabic (72);
Goals: Hemingway 7/9.
Sin bin: Boland (36) - fighting.
Rugby Leaguer & League Express Men of the Match:
Royal Navy: Aaron Hanson; *Panthers:* Andy Hobson.
Penalty count: 7-7; **Half-time:** 12-16;
Referee: Bob Everitt; **Attendance:** 250
(at United Services Sports Ground, Portsmouth).

BARROW RAIDERS 62 HUNSLET WARRIORS 10

RAIDERS: 1 Gary Broadbent; 21 Chris Larkin; 12 Ned Catic; 4 Liam Harrison; 2 Andy Ballard; 18 Liam Campbell; 6 Jamie Rooney; 8 Andy Bracek; 9 Andrew Henderson; 15 Rob Roberts; 24 Richard Fletcher; 11 Michael Knowles; 13 Zebastian Luisi. Subs (all used): 23 Jamie Butler; 14 Martin Ostler; 16 Brett McDermott; 19 Nathan Mossop.
Tries: Campbell (7), Ballard (9, 53), Henderson (11), Catic (16, 71), Larkin (32), Ostler (38), McDermott (45), Mossop (47, 64);
Goals: Rooney 6/7, Fletcher 1/1, Knowles 2/3.
Dismissal: Roberts (71) - punching.
WARRIORS: 1 Gary McClelland; 2 Chris Hartley; 3 Mark Cunningham; 4 Tony Swift; 5 Scott Walker; 6 Chris Peach; 7 Aaron Pratt; 8 Paul Sebine; 9 Jim Baker; 10 Johnny Dawson; 11 Joe Howey; 12 Omar Medhi; 13 Caldon Bravo. Subs (all used): 14 Shaun Kehoe; 15 Oliver Graham; 16 Karl Featherstone; 17 Jason Milner.
Tries: McClelland (3), Featherstone (42);
Goals: McClelland 1/2.
Rugby Leaguer & League Express Men of the Match:
Raiders: Nathan Mossop; *Warriors:* Tony Swift.
Penalty count: 9-6; **Half-time:** 34-6;
Referee: George Stokes; **Attendance:** 1,330.

FEATHERSTONE ROVERS 74 WORKINGTON TOWN 0

ROVERS: 1 Ian Hardman; 5 Jon Steel; 15 Jessie Joe Parker; 4 Liam Welham; 2 Tom Saxton; 6 Kyle Briggs; 9 Liam Finn; 19 Ross Divorty; 31 Ben Kaye; 10 Stuart Dickens; 12 Jon Grayshon; 11 Matty Dale; 13 Jamie Field. Subs (all used): 17 Tony Tonks; 8 Iain Morrison; 7 Andy Kain; 22 Jack Lee.
Tries: Welham (1), Parker (14, 19, 42), Grayshon (16, 72), Saxton (29, 52, 75), Hardman (39), Steel (46), Kain (58), Finn (68); **Goals:** Briggs 2/4, Finn 9/9.
TOWN: 17 Neil Frazer; 2 Mike Backhouse; 3 Andrew Beattie; 15 Aaron Low; 18 Martyn Wilson; 6 Liam Finch; 7 Scott Kaighan; 31 Ruairi McGoff; 14 Jamie Marshall; 11 Mike Whitehead; 4 James Finch; 12 Jarrad Stack; 22 Ryan Campbell. Subs (all used): 21 Paddy Coupar; 19 Joe McKenna; 16 Scott Burgess; 20 James Robinson.
Rugby Leaguer & League Express Men of the Match:
Rovers: Liam Finn; *Town:* Mike Whitehead.
Penalty count: 6-7; **Half-time:** 32-0;
Referee: Matthew Thomasson; **Attendance:** 1,215.

GATESHEAD THUNDER 12 YORK CITY KNIGHTS 44

THUNDER: 28 Jason Elliott; 29 Jimmy Atkinson; 1 Kevin Neighbour; 4 Michael Brown; 2 Robin Peers; 6 Liam Duffy; 9 Ryan Clarke; 17 Chris Parker; 14 Will Bate; 10 Tabua Cakacaka; 26 David Cash; 30 Richie Humphries; 32 Ade Aderiye. Subs (all used): 33 Reece Young; 13 Matt Barron; 18 Stephen Welton; 31 Matt Garside.
Tries: Peers (15), Atkinson (28), Neighbour (49);
Goals: Ryan Clarke 0/3.
CITY KNIGHTS: 1 Danny Ratcliffe; 2 Wayne Reittie; 3 Mike Mitchell; 4 Lee Waterman; 26 Steve Lewis; 6 Chris Thorman; 27 Casey Bromilow; 8 Mark Applegarth; 32 Paul Stamp; 36 Jon Fallon; 35 Danny Hill; 11 Jordan Ross; 13 Richard Blakeway. Subs (all used): 9 Joe McLocklan; 25 Brett Waller; 12 Chris Clough; 17 Nathan Freer.
Tries: Bromilow (6, 22), Waterman (12, 59), McLocklan (33), Reittie (36), Hill (70), Blakeway (78);
Goals: Waterman 6/8.
Sin bin: Applegarth (53) - interference.
Rugby Leaguer & League Express Men of the Match:
Thunder: Chris Parker; *City Knights:* Lee Waterman.
Penalty count: 11-8; **Half-time:** 8-30;
Referee: Craig Halloran; **Attendance:** 336.

LEIGH CENTURIONS 52 WATH BROW HORNETS 4

CENTURIONS: 1 Stuart Donlan; 3 David Alstead; 2 Steve Maden; 4 Mick Nanyn; 5 Nicky Stanton; 22 Martyn Ridyard; 7 Robbie Paul; 10 Ricky Bibey; 15 Dave McConnell; 16 Mike Morrison; 14 Tommy Goulden; 12 Macgraff Leuluai; 11 James Taylor. Subs (all used): 8 Chris Hill; 13 David Armitstead; 24 Andy Ainscough; 6 Tim Hartley.
Tries: Goulden (7, 68), Alstead (12, 38, 62, 70), Stanton (34), Nanyn (43, 79), Hill (54); **Goals:** Nanyn 6/10.
HORNETS: 1 Ryan Amor; 2 Peter Caddy; 3 Glen Riley; 4 Dale Bell; 5 Jamie Devine; 6 Craig Johnstone; 7 Ryan Robb; 8 Mark Troughton; 9 James Toman; 10 Scott Teare; 11 Richard Huby; 12 Matty Huby; 13 David Pettit. Subs (all used): 14 Graham Lupton; 15 Jamie Martin; 16 Mickey McCallister; 17 Mally Caton.
Try: Caddy (4); **Goals:** Robb 0/1.
Rugby Leaguer & League Express Men of the Match:
Centurions: Martyn Ridyard; *Hornets:* Dale Bell.
Penalty count: 11-7; **Half-time:** 22-4;
Referee: Tom Crashley; **Attendance:** 1,370.

LONDON SKOLARS 16 LIMOUX 42

SKOLARS: 22 Curtis Cunningham; 23 Olu Iwenofu; 4 Jason Cook; 2 Dave Arnot; 31 Ade Adebisi; 6 Jermaine Coleman; 7 Paul Thorman; 8 Liam Roach; 9 Gareth Honor; 18 James Simon; 3 Matt Thomas; 13 Stephen Ball; 11 Oliver Purslow. Subs (all used): 37 Rob Montgomerie; 1 Josh Welsh; 17 Chad Isles; 12 Matt Carter.
Tries: Honor (20), Cunningham (32), M Thomas (66);
Goals: P Thorman 2/3.
LIMOUX: 1 Adam Innes; 2 Bastien Almarcha; 3 Mathieu Mayans; 4 Sam Key; 5 Stephane Selles; 6 Phil Ramage; 7 Mickael Murcia; 8 Artie Shead; 9 Sylvain Teixido; 10 Aaron Wood; 11 Joris Casal; 12 Mathieu Almarcha; 13 Nicolas Piccolo. Subs (all used): 14 Thibaud Braconnier; 15 Gregoire Dela Rose; 16 Jerome Laffont; 17 Herve Marrot.
Tries: Wood (8), Mayans (15, 54), Key (36, 57), Shead (47), Casal (62), Ramage (75); **Goals:** Ramage 5/8.
Sin bin: Braconnier (28) - punching.
Rugby Leaguer & League Express Men of the Match:
Skolars: Curtis Cunningham; *Limoux:* Aaron Wood.
Penalty count: 16-7; **Half-time:** 12-16;
Referee: Peter Brooke; **Attendance:** 376.

OLDHAM 80 BLACKWOOD BULLDOGS 6

OLDHAM: 1 Paul O'Connor; 2 Lucas Onyango; 24 Marcus St Hilaire; 4 Mick Fogerty; 20 Mark Brocklehurst; 6 Neil Roden; 7 Matt Ashe; 8 Jason Boults; 9 Martin Roden; 16 Wayne Kerr; 19 Ben Heaton; 13 Joe Chandler; 21 Valu Bentley. Subs (all used): 17 Danny Whitmore; 15 Craig Robinson; 10 Dave Ellison; 11 Saqib Murtza.
Tries: Chandler (2, 14, 72), Brocklehurst (7, 23, 39), O'Connor (11, 56), Murtza (33, 45), Onyango (51), Ashe (61, 75), Ellison (77), Fogerty (79); **Goals:** Ashe 10/15.
BULLDOGS: 1 David James; 2 Aaron Humphries; 3 Luke Knight; 4 Gareth Price; 5 Gareth Dare; 6 Kristian Perry; 7 Jeremy Lloyd; 8 Chris Williams; 9 Byron Williams; 10 Adam Coupe; 11 Gareth Rusby-Davies; 12 Stuart Vokes; 13 Andrew Coupe. Subs (all used): 14 Matthew McGovern; 15 Aaron Elliott; 16 Clark Morgan; 17 Craig Clements.
Try: James (41); **Goals:** Price 1/1.
Rugby Leaguer & League Express Men of the Match:
Oldham: Matt Ashe; *Bulldogs:* Jeremy Lloyd.
Penalty count: 11-3; **Half-time:** 36-0; **Referee:** Tim Roby; **Attendance:** 455 *(at Park Lane, Sedgley Park).*

OVENDEN 10 HALIFAX 88

OVENDEN: 1 Mick Holden; 2 Luke Brown; 3 Tom McAdam; 4 Brett Steele; 5 Kurt Sutcliffe; 6 Gareth Jones; 7 Liam Walsh; 8 Gareth English; 9 Luke Sutcliffe; 10 Matty Collins; 11 Matt Turner; 12 Danny Snowden; 13 Chris Geoghegan. Subs (all used): 14 Matthew Short; 15 Shaun Dyson; 16 Chris Sykes; 17 Dean Robertshaw.
Tries: Short (29), K Sutcliffe (47); **Goals:** Holden 1/2.
HALIFAX: 4 Shad Royston; 20 Paul White; 2 Lee Paterson; 5 James Haley; 23 Rob Worrincy; 6 Luke Branighan; 7 Ben Black; 19 Dominic Maloney; 9 Sean Penkywicz; 10 Neil Cherryholme; 24 Steve Bannister; 15

Mark Roberts; 21 Anthony Bowman. Subs (all used): 3 Jon Goddard; 8 Makali Aizue; 13 Bob Beswick; 17 Frank Watene.
Tries: Branighan (2, 37, 50, 65), White (9, 67), Royston (18, 21, 23), Worrincy (25), Watene (31), Bowman (57), Roberts (59, 71), Penkywicz (74), Goddard (77); **Goals:** Paterson 12/16.
Rugby Leaguer & League Express Men of the Match: *Ovenden:* Gareth English; *Halifax:* Shad Royston.
Penalty count: 6-5; **Half-time:** 6-42; **Referee:** Clint Sharrad; **Attendance:** 2,319 *(at The Shay).*

ROCHDALE HORNETS 22 LEZIGNAN 32

HORNETS: 32 Wayne English; 1 Craig Johnson; 19 Ryan McPaul; 12 Danny Smith; 2 Andy Saywell; 29 Ryan Powell; 7 Steve Roper; 17 Michael Ostick; 14 Liam Bostock; 8 Paul Raftrey; 16 Danny Samuel; 13 Craig Ashall; 15 Dayne Donoghue. Subs (all used): 10 Gareth Hayes; 23 Wayne Corcoran; 9 Phil Wood; 4 Adam Bowman.
Tries: Saywell (16, 22, 28), English (36), Ashall (49); **Goals:** Roper 0/1, Ashall 1/4.
LEZIGNAN: 1 Jye Mullane; 2 Nicolas Piquemal; 3 Florian Quintilla; 4 Cedric Bringuier; 5 Olivier Janzac; 6 Mickael Tribillac; 7 James Wynne; 8 Chris Beattie; 9 Cedric Lacans; 10 Franck Rovira; 11 David Romero; 12 Phillipe Laurent; 13 Thibault Ancely. Subs (all used): 14 Jordi Ligneries; 15 Aurelien Bourell; 16 Adel Fellous; 17 Pierre Negre.
Tries: Mullane (1, 54), Janzac (12, 75), Tribillac (46), Negre (64); **Goals:** Wynne 4/6.
Dismissal: Rovira (67) – headbutt.
Rugby Leaguer & League Express Men of the Match: *Hornets:* Wayne English; *Lezignan:* Mickael Tribillac.
Penalty count: 10-6; **Half-time:** 18-12;
Referee: Robert Hicks; **Attendance:** 398.

SHEFFIELD EAGLES 54 THATTO HEATH CRUSADERS 0

EAGLES: 5 Ashley Thackeray; 27 Richie Barnett; 3 Menzie Yere; 23 Tangi Ropati; 24 Misi Taulapapa; 20 Matty Brooks; 6 Brendon Lindsay; 22 Ryan Hepworth; 9 Craig Cook; 10 Mitchell Stringer; 15 Sam Barlow; 13 Peter Green; 21 Dane McDonald. Subs (all used): 1 Jonny Woodcock; 16 Trevor Exton; 12 Ged Corcoran; 19 Joe Hirst.
Tries: Stringer (16), Cook (18, 61), Yere (25), Green (37), Hirst (47), Taulapapa (67, 75), Lindsay (71), Brooks (78); **Goals:** Stringer 5/7, Ropati 2/3.
CRUSADERS: 1 Shaun Quinn; 2 Darren Woods; 3 Jamie Hill; 4 John Hudges; 5 Adam Walsh; 6 Andy Scott; 7 Chris Frodsham; 8 Michael Ledger; 9 Kieron Maddocks; 10 Martin Shea; 11 David Johnson; 12 Mark Beech; 13 Steven Ward. Subs (all used): 14 Kenny Hughes; 15 Carl Lamb; 16 David Bates; 17 Glenn Holland.
Rugby Leaguer & League Express Men of the Match: *Eagles:* Mitchell Stringer; *Crusaders:* Mark Beech.
Penalty count: 11-5; **Half-time:** 24-0; **Referee:** Greg Dolan; **Attendance:** 502 *(at Don Valley Stadium).*

DRIGHLINGTON 10 DEWSBURY RAMS 42

DRIGHLINGTON: 1 Kevin Doyle; 2 Tom Moorby; 3 David Patterson; 4 Andrew Jackson; 5 Sean Coughlan; 6 Michael Sanderson; 7 Ryan Jackson; 8 Andrew Jarrett; 9 Sam Pickles; 10 Andy Kilbride; 11 Luke Pennington; 12 Ryan Burton; 13 Lee Mulhern. Subs (all used): 14 Andrew Brearley; 15 Liam Coughlan; 16 Alex Bedford; 17 John Gallagher.
Tries: Mulhern (24), R Jackson (58);
Goals: Sanderson 0/1, R Jackson 1/1.
RAMS: 2 James Haynes; 15 Bryn Powell; 26 Ayden Faal; 18 Chris Spurr; 10 Scott Turner; 13 Pat Walker; 8 Dominic Brambani; 23 Keegan Hirst; 37 Luke Blake; 24 Anthony England; 25 James Lockwood; 21 Andrew Bostock; 19 Adam Hayes. Subs (all used): 11 Adam Robinson; 14 Luke Stenchion; 6 Ryan Smith; 9 Mike Emmett.
Tries: Lockwood (1), Haynes (17), Spurr (42), Hayes (55), Faal (62), Stenchion (68), Robinson (76);
Goals: P Walker 7/7.
Rugby Leaguer & League Express Men of the Match: *Drighlington:* Lee Mulhern; *Rams:* Pat Walker.
Penalty count: 10-9; **Half time:** 4-12; **Referee:** Dave Merrick; **Attendance:** 1,222 *(at Tetley's Stadium).*

Tuesday 9th March 2010

WIDNES VIKINGS 64 WIGAN ST JUDES 12

VIKINGS: 18 Scott Yates; 5 Paddy Flynn; 22 Dean Thompson; 15 Shane Grady; 19 Matt Gardner; 6 Anthony Thackeray; 14 Thomas Coyle; 16 Gareth Haggerty; 9 Mark Smith; 11 Lee Doran; 3 Richard Varkulis; 21 Matthew Strong; 12 Dave Allen. Subs (all used): 17 Ben Kavanagh; 13 Chris Gerrard; 24 Danny Hulme; 23 David Houghton.
Tries: Allen (12, 72), Thackeray (18), Doran (21), Yates (26), Houghton (31), Grady (41), Hulme (48, 54), Varkulis (59, 68), Coyle (75); **Goals:** Grady 8/12.
ST JUDES: 1 Paul Pendlebury; 2 Ryan Ainscough; 3 Gavin Corfield; 4 Darley King; 5 Nathan Jones; 6 Dave Picton; 7 Dean Lunt; 8 Martin Riley; 9 Glen Hunt; 10 Peter Cain; 11 Lee Maiden; 12 Darren Banks; 13 Mark Whittaker. Subs (all used): 14 Kevin Howells; 15 Danny Clayton; 16 Tye Ford; 17 John McMullen.
Tries: Maiden (5), King (45); **Goals:** Picton 2/2.
Rugby Leaguer & League Express Men of the Match: *Vikings:* Dave Allen; *St Judes:* Gavin Corfield.
Penalty count: 8-5; **Half-time:** 26-6;
Referee: Chris Leatherbarrow; **Attendance:** 1,622.

ROUND 4

Friday 16th April 2010

SWINTON LIONS 4 HALIFAX 56

LIONS: 1 Richie Hawkyard; 25 Barry Hamilton; 27 Anthony Stewart; 3 Sam Reay; 4 Carl Sneyd; 6 Graham Holroyd; 7 Ian Watson; 16 Dana Wilson; 14 Gary Hulse; 8 Paul Southern; 12 Paul Smith; 15 Lee Wingfield; 9 Phil Joseph. Subs (all used): 18 Bruce Johnson; 17 Andrew Isherwood; 26 Dave Newton; 23 Rob Foxen.
Try: Hamilton (32); **Goals:** Holroyd 0/1.
Sin bin: Joseph (57) - dissent.
HALIFAX: 4 Shad Royston; 2 Lee Paterson; 3 Jon Goddard; 5 James Haley; 23 Rob Worrincy; 6 Luke Branighan; 7 Ben Black; 25 Michael Ostick; 13 Bob Beswick; 22 David Wrench; 18 Dylan Nash; 24 Steve Bannister; 21 Anthony Bowman. Subs (all used): 9 Sean Penkywicz; 15 Mark Roberts; 16 Said Tamghart; 17 Frank Watene.
Tries: Branighan (16, 37), Royston (41, 54), Tamghart (49), Roberts (58), Black (60, 65), Penkywicz (75), Bannister (78); **Goals:** Paterson 8/10.
Rugby Leaguer & League Express Men of the Match: *Lions:* Graham Holroyd; *Halifax:* Shad Royston.
Penalty count: 6-11; **Half-time:** 4-12;
Referee: Tim Roby; **Attendance:** 633.

Saturday 17th April 2010

HULL FC 24 LEEDS RHINOS 48

HULL: 1 Jordan Tansey; 24 Craig Hall; 21 Richard Whiting; 4 Kirk Yeaman; 3 Tom Briscoe; 14 Danny Washbrook; 6 Richard Horne; 11 Lee Radford; 20 Danny Houghton; 10 Mark O'Meley; 16 Willie Manu; 12 Danny Tickle; 13 Craig Fitzgibbon (C). Subs (all used): 15 Epalahame Lauaki; 8 Ewan Dowes; 17 Peter Cusack; 19 Jordan Turner.
Tries: Briscoe (8), Tansey (20), Whiting (54, 75), Turner (67); **Goals:** Tickle 1/2, Fitzgibbon 1/3.
On report:
Lauaki (57) - alleged dangerous tackle on Webb.
RHINOS: 1 Brent Webb; 28 Lee Smith; 3 Brett Delaney; 4 Keith Senior; 5 Ryan Hall; 6 Danny McGuire; 7 Rob Burrow; 16 Ryan Bailey; 14 Matt Diskin; 8 Kylie Leuluai; 18 Carl Ablett; 11 Jamie Jones-Buchanan; 13 Kevin Sinfield (C). Subs (all used): 9 Danny Buderus; 17 Ian Kirke; 19 Luke Burgess; 10 Jamie Peacock.
Tries: Ablett (12), Webb (25, 60), Kirke (29), Hall (33, 38, 46, 72); **Goals:** Sinfield 8/9.
Sin bin: Burrow (66) - punching.
Rugby Leaguer & League Express Men of the Match: *Hull:* Jordan Tansey; *Rhinos:* Carl Ablett.
Penalty count: 11-7; **Half-time:** 10-30;
Referee: Richard Silverwood; **Attendance:** 15,109.

HARLEQUINS 23 WAKEFIELD TRINITY WILDCATS 16

HARLEQUINS: 26 Ben Jones-Bishop; 1 Chris Melling; 3 Tony Clubb; 4 David Howell; 5 Will Sharp; 21 Luke Gale; 9 Chad Randall; 10 Louie McCarthy-Scarsbrook; 7 Danny Orr; 17 Danny Ward; 11 Luke Williamson; 13 Rob Purdham (C); 25 Lamont Bryan. Subs (all used): 14 Oliver Wilkes; 8 Karl Temata; 6 Luke Dorn; 18 Ryan Esders.
Tries: Jones-Bishop (10), Clubb (13, 40), Howell (37);
Goals: Orr 3/4; **Field goal:** Gale (79).
Sin bin: Dorn (57) - interference.
WILDCATS: 18 Aaron Murphy; 3 Sean Gleeson; 13 Jason Demetriou (C); 5 Luke George; 2 Damien Blanch; 21 Paul Cooke; 6 Ben Jeffries; 25 Richard Moore; 24 James Davey; 19 Paul King; 16 Paul Johnson; 11 Dale Ferguson; 32 Danny Kirmond. Subs (all used): 4 Darryl Millard; 14 Sam Obst; 10 Michael Korkidas; 31 Ben Gledhill.
Tries: Blanch (17), Kirmond (32), George (45);
Goals: Cooke 2/3.
Rugby Leaguer & League Express Men of the Match: *Harlequins:* Oliver Wilkes; *Wildcats:* Luke George.
Penalty count: 6-12; **Half-time:** 22-10;
Referee: Phil Bentham; **Attendance:** 2,355.

LIMOUX 20 LEIGH CENTURIONS 32

LIMOUX: 1 Russell Bussian; 2 Herve Marrot; 3 Mathieu Mayans; 4 Sam Key; 5 Bastien Almarcha; 6 Phil Ramage; 7 Mickael Murcia; 8 Artie Shead; 9 Sylvain Teixido; 10 Aaron Wood; 11 Joris Casal; 12 Mathieu Almarcha; 13 Nicolas Piccolo. Subs (all used): 14 Maxime Herold; 15 Thibaud Braconnier; 16 Jerome Laffont; 17 Stephane Selles.
Tries: Herold (22), B Almarcha (37), Bussian (42), M Almarcha (68); **Goals:** Ramage 2/4.
CENTURIONS: 1 Stuart Donlan; 2 Steve Maden; 3 David Alstead; 4 Mick Nanyn; 5 Nicky Stanton; 22 Martyn Ridyard; 7 Robbie Paul; 8 Chris Hill; 15 Dave McConnell; 10 Ricky Bibey; 11 James Taylor; 12 Macgraff Leuluai; 14 Tommy Goulden. Subs (all used): 9 John Duffy; 13 Dave Armitstead; 16 Mike Morrison; 18 Adam Higson.
Tries: Alstead (6), Stanton (13), Nanyn (48, 78), Morrison (58), Hill (65); **Goals:** Nanyn 4/6.
Rugby Leaguer & League Express Men of the Match: *Limoux:* Sylvain Teixido; *Centurions:* Ricky Bibey.
Penalty count: 7-7; **Half-time:** 12-10; **Referee:** Warren Turley; **Attendance:** 2,000 *(at Stade de l'Aiguille).*

SHEFFIELD EAGLES 34 WIGAN WARRIORS 50

EAGLES: 24 Misi Taulapapa; 27 Richie Barnett; 3 Menzie Yere; 23 Tangi Ropati; 5 Ashley Thackeray; 6 Brendon Lindsay; 21 Dane McDonald; 8 Jack Howieson; 9 Craig Cook; 10 Mitchell Stringer; 11 Alex Szostak; 13 Peter Green; 19 Joe Hirst. Subs (all used): 25 Jason Mossop; 15 Sam Barlow; 17 Alex Rowe; 18 Michael Haley.
Tries: Yere (6), Barnett (11, 57, 72), Rowe (68), Lindsay (79); **Goals:** Stringer 5/6.
On report: Barlow (75) - alleged dangerous tackle.
WARRIORS: 1 Cameron Phelps; 24 Darrell Goulding; 3 Martin Gleeson; 4 George Carmont; 5 Pat Richards; 13 Sean O'Loughlin (C); 6 Sam Tomkins; 8 Stuart Fielden; 9 Mark Riddell; 14 Paul Prescott; 16 Phil Bailey; 12 Joel Tomkins; 23 Lee Mossop. Subs (all used): 10 Andy Coley; 15 Michael Mcllorum; 17 Iafeta Palea'aesina; 25 Liam Farrell.
Tries: Richards (1), Gleeson (17), Carmont (30), Palea'aesina (34), O'Loughlin (37), S Tomkins (47, 49, 64), Coley (53); **Goals:** Richards 7/9.
Rugby Leaguer & League Express Men of the Match: *Eagles:* Mitchell Stringer; *Warriors:* Sam Tomkins.
Penalty count: 6-9; **Half-time:** 10-26;
Referee: Ian Smith; **Attendance:** 2,950.

ST HELENS 56 TOULOUSE OLYMPIQUE 16

SAINTS: 6 Leon Pryce; 2 Ade Gardner; 19 Chris Dean; 21 Gary Wheeler; 30 Jamie Foster (D); 16 Scott Moore; 7 Kyle Eastmond; 8 Nick Fozzard; 9 Keiron Cunningham (C); 15 Bryn Hargreaves; 17 Paul Clough; 13 Chris Flannery; 11 Tony Puletua. Subs (all used): 14 James Roby; 18 Matty Ashurst; 22 Andrew Dixon; 23 Maurie Fa'asavalu.
Tries: Dean (5), Flannery (10, 39), Wheeler (25, 71), Fa'asavalu (32, 68), Gardner (46), Dixon (54), Puletua (60); **Goals:** Eastmond 0/2, Foster 8/8.
OLYMPIQUE: 22 Clement Bienes; 2 Sebastien Payan; 3 Sebastien Planas; 4 Vincent Duport; 5 Carlos Mendes Varela; 1 Rory Bromley; 7 Nathan Wynn; 8 Brendan Worth; 9 Martin Mitchell; 25 Teli Pelo; 18 Yoan Tisseyre; 12 Simon Worrall; 13 Eric Anselme. Subs (all used): 10 Mathieu Griffi; 14 Antoni Maria; 16 Sylvain Houles; 23 Kevin Larroyer.
Tries: Duport (2), Mendes Varela (29), Mitchell (78);
Goals: N Wynn 2/3.
Rugby Leaguer & League Express Men of the Match: *Saints:* Kyle Eastmond; *Olympique:* Nathan Wynn.
Penalty count: 4-4; **Half-time:** 26-10;
Referee: Gareth Hewer; **Attendance:** 4,043.

Sunday 18th April 2010

HUDDERSFIELD GIANTS 40
HULL KINGSTON ROVERS 12

GIANTS: 1 Brett Hodgson (C); 2 Leroy Cudjoe; 3 Jamahl Lolesi; 4 Paul Whatuira; 5 David Hodgson; 6 Kevin Brown; 34 Danny Brough; 10 Keith Mason; 7 Luke Robinson; 16 Darrell Griffin; 11 Lee Gilmour; 12 David Fa'alogo; 22 Martin Aspinwall. Subs (all used): 8 Eorl Crabtree; 9 Shaun Lunt; 15 Andy Raleigh; 20 David Faiumu.
Tries: Lolesi (16), Fa'alogo (27, 74), Robinson (30), D Hodgson (36), Brough (66), Aspinwall (78);
Goals: B Hodgson 6/7.
ROVERS: 1 Shaun Briscoe; 2 Peter Fox; 3 Kris Welham; 4 Jake Webster; 28 Ben Cockayne; 19 Chaz I'Anson; 7 Michael Dobson; 20 Michael Vella (C); 9 Scott Murrell; 30 Joel Clinton; 11 Clint Newton; 16 Jason Netherton; 13 Ben Galea. Subs (all used): 22 Liam Watts; 8 Rhys Lovegrove; 17 Ben Fisher; 14 Matt Cook.
Tries: Webster (56), Briscoe (69); **Goals:** Dobson 2/2.
Rugby Leaguer & League Express Men of the Match: *Giants:* Kevin Brown; *Rovers:* Shaun Briscoe.
Penalty count: 8-5; **Half-time:** 22-0;
Referee: Richard Silverwood; **Attendance:** 7,241.

BLACKPOOL PANTHERS 24 WHITEHAVEN 18

PANTHERS: 1 Jonny Leather; 2 Damian Munro; 22 Dave Llewellyn; 18 Martin Ainscough; 24 Paul Ballard; 6 Carl Forber; 7 Tom Hemingway; 34 Neil Holland; 9 John Clough; 10 Andy Hobson; 4 Mark McCully; 27 Danny Halliwell; 11 Kurt Haggerty. Subs (all used): 14 Martin Keavney; 15 Paul Anderson; 12 Paul Alcock; 17 Kris Ratcliffe.
Tries: Ainscough (17, 52, 69), Leather (46), Keavney (79); **Goals:** Leather 2/3, Forber 0/1, Hemingway 0/1.
WHITEHAVEN: 1 Craig Benson; 29 Stephen Dawes; 3 Rob Jackson; 28 Tom Philip; 2 Craig Calvert; 6 Carl Rudd; 7 Leroy Joe; 8 Marc Jackson; 9 Graeme Mattinson; 33 Kyle Amor; 19 Dexter Miller; 11 Howard Hill; 26 Daniel Barker. Subs (all used): 30 Carl Sice; 27 Mike Darby; 17 Andy Thornley; 12 Spencer Miller.
Tries: Rudd (21), D Miller (27), Philip (35);
Goals: Rudd 3/4.
Rugby Leaguer & League Express Men of the Match: *Panthers:* Martin Ainscough; *Whitehaven:* Daniel Barker.
Penalty count: 6-10; **Half-time:** 6-18;
Referee: Greg Dolan; **Attendance:** 471.

CATALANS DRAGONS 30 SALFORD CITY REDS 8

DRAGONS: 5 Dimitri Pelo; 2 Steven Bell; 15 Jean-Phillipe Baile; 3 Sebastien Raguin; 28 Frederic Vaccari; 9 Casey McGuire; 7 Thomas Bosc (C); 8 David Ferriol; 20 Kane Bentley; 10 Jerome Guisset; 11 Olivier Elima; 17 Cyrille Gossard; 12 Gregory Mounis. Subs (all used): 24 Remi Casty; 18 Dane Carlaw; 21 Sebastien Martins; 25 Tony Gigot.
Tries: Guisset (10), Vaccari (12, 54), Bell (44), McGuire (57), Casty (77); **Goals:** Bosc 2/5, Gigot 0/1, Mounis 1/1.
CITY REDS: 1 Karl Fitzpatrick; 2 Jodie Broughton; 4 Willie Talau; 3 Mark Henry; 5 Ashley Gibson; 6 Stefan Ratchford; 21 Daniel Holdsworth; 8 Ray Cashmere; 9 Malcolm Alker (C); 19 Ryan Boyle; 17 Adam Sidlow; 12 Luke Adamson; 13 Luke Swain. Subs (all used): 11 Ian Sibbit; 14 Matty Smith; 15 Stuart Littler; 18 Lee Jewitt.
Tries: Broughton (36, 38); **Goals:** Holdsworth 0/2.
Rugby Leaguer & League Express Men of the Match: *Dragons:* Remi Casty; *City Reds:* Jodie Broughton.
Penalty count: 7-7; **Half-time:** 10-8;
Referee: James Child; **Attendance:** 5,238.

SIDDAL 2 BATLEY BULLDOGS 34

SIDDAL: 1 Brad Attwood; 2 Gareth Blackburn; 3 Chris Marsh; 4 Andy Bowman; 5 Scott Caley; 6 Shaun Garrod; 7 Chris Brook; 8 Luke Simeunovich; 9 Simeon Hoyle; 10 Luke Garrett; 11 James Simeunovich; 12 Nick Smith; 13 Lee Gudor. Subs (all used): 14 Stuart Proctor; 15 Mark Boothroyd; 16 Adie Leek; 17 Ben Kendall.
Goals: Blackburn 1/1.
Sin bin: Kendall (35) – interference.
BULLDOGS: 5 John Campbell; 3 Mark Barlow; 23 Chris Buttery; 26 Jason Walton; 24 Alex Brown; 12 Mark Toohey; 6 Paul Handforth; 8 Byron Smith; 9 Kris Lythe; 10 Sean Hesketh; 17 Craig Potter; 11 Tommy Gallagher; 31 John Gallagher. Subs (all used): 13 Ashley Lindsay; 21 James Martin; 20 David Tootill; 7 Gareth Moore.
Tries: T Gallagher (16), Brown (29), Barlow (61), Moore (63), Handforth (65), Walton (76);
Goals: Handforth 2/2, Moore 3/4.
Sin bin: Lythe (26) – dangerous tackle.
Rugby Leaguer & League Express Men of the Match: *Siddal:* Luke Simeunovich; *Bulldogs:* Ashley Lindsay.
Penalty count: 10-15; **Half-time:** 2-12; **Referee:** Dave Merrick; **Attendance:** 1,926 *(at The Shay, Halifax).*

YORK CITY KNIGHTS 8 CRUSADERS 58

CITY KNIGHTS: 1 Danny Ratcliffe; 29 Dennis Tuffour; 3 Mike Mitchell; 4 Lee Waterman; 5 Tom Lineham; 6 Chris Thorman; 7 Jonathan Schofield; 8 Mark Applegarth; 32 Paul Stamp; 17 Nathan Freer; 35 Danny Hill; 13 Richard Blakeway; 9 Joe McLocklan. Subs (all used): 11 Jordan Ross; 19 Kris Peacock; 16 Carl Barrow; 23 Luke Helliwell.
Tries: Schofield (7), Tuffour (76); **Goals:** Waterman 0/2.
CRUSADERS: 26 Clinton Schifcofske (C); 1 Gareth Thomas; 14 Luke Dyer; 27 Rhys Hanbury; 2 Nick Youngquest; 23 Peter Lupton; 6 Michael Witt; 18 Jamie Thackray; 9 Lincoln Withers; 10 Mark Bryant; 12 Jason Chan; 16 Frank Winterstein; 13 Rocky Trimarchi. Subs (all used): 22 Elliot Kear; 28 Gil Dudson; 20 Ben Flower; 21 Lloyd White.
Tries: Hanbury (2, 36), Youngquest (13), Thackray (21), Chan (25, 63), White (46, 52), Flower (48), Thomas (59); **Goals:** Witt 9/10.
Rugby Leaguer & League Express Men of the Match: *City Knights:* Chris Thorman; *Crusaders:* Michael Witt.
Penalty count: 4-7; **Half-time:** 4-30;
Referee: Matthew Thomasson; **Attendance:** 719.

DEWSBURY RAMS 0 BRADFORD BULLS 50

RAMS: 2 James Haynes; 15 Bryn Powell; 10 Scott Turner; 21 Andrew Bostock; 26 Ayden Faal; 13 Pat Walker; 8 Dominic Brambani; 14 Luke Stenchion; 9 Mike Emmett; 23 Keegan Hirst; 25 James Lockwood; 11 Adam Robinson; 19 Adam Hayes. Subs (all used): 33 James Walker; 40 Ed Barber; 37 Luke Blake; 1 Lee Lingard.
Sin bin: Lingard (69) – interference.
BULLS: 1 Dave Halley; 2 Rikki Sheriffe; 15 Michael Platt; 11 Steve Menzies; 19 Jason Crookes; 6 Brett Kearney; 7 Matt Orford; 8 Nick Scruton; 14 Wayne Godwin; 12 Glenn Hall; 16 Michael Worrincy; 20 Elliott Whitehead; 13 Jamie Langley (C). Subs (all used): 24 Tom Olbison; 32 Danny Addy (D); 9 Heath L'Estrange; 18 Craig Kopczak.
Tries: Whitehead (4), Scruton (9), Hall (15, 29), Kearney (23, 35), Godwin (39), L'Estrange (50), Addy (75); **Goals:** Orford 5/7, Addy 2/2.
Rugby Leaguer & League Express Men of the Match: *Rams:* James Lockwood; *Bulls:* Brett Kearney.
Penalty count: 5-11; **Half-time:** 0-38;
Referee: Peter Brooke; **Attendance:** 3,995.

CASTLEFORD TIGERS 28 BARROW RAIDERS 34

TIGERS: 21 Jordan Thompson; 2 Kirk Dixon; 17 Ryan Clayton; 4 James Evans; 5 Michael Wainwright; 23 Ryan McGoldrick; 6 Rangi Chase; 16 Paul Jackson; 19 Kirk Netherton; 10 Craig Huby; 14 Stuart Jones; 12 Steve Snitch; 13 Joe Westerman. Subs (all used): 8 Mitchell Sargent; 9 Ryan Hudson (C); 26 Oliver Holmes; 32 Joe Arundel.
Tries: Thompson (16), Westerman (33, 42), Sargent (39), Dixon (45); **Goals:** Westerman 4/5.
RAIDERS: 1 Gary Broadbent; 2 Andy Ballard; 3 Anthony Blackwood; 4 Liam Harrison; 25 Jermaine McGillvary; 7 James Coyle; 6 Jamie Rooney; 31 Matt James; 9 Andrew Henderson; 8 Andy Bracek; 11 Michael Knowles; 12 Ned Catic; 13 Zebastian Luisi. Subs (all used): 17 Paul Noone; 15 Rob Roberts; 18 Liam Campbell; 14 Martin Ostler.
Tries: Rooney (9, 65), McGillvary (20, 57), Ballard (60), Catic (80); **Goals:** Rooney 5/6.
Rugby Leaguer & League Express Men of the Match: *Tigers:* Joe Westerman; *Raiders:* Jamie Rooney.
Penalty count: 7-11; **Half-time:** 18-12;
Referee: Thierry Alibert; **Attendance:** 5,285.

HUNSLET HAWKS 42 OLDHAM 12

HAWKS: 29 Stuart Kain; 2 Michael Mark; 21 Wayne McHugh; 5 John Oakes; 26 Waine Pryce; 13 David March; 7 Paul March; 15 Adam Sullivan; 9 Richard Chapman; 3 James Houston; 12 Steve Dooler; 30 Richard Knight; 33 Tom Haughey. Subs (all used): 8 Scott Woodcock; 14 Luke Haigh; 16 Neil Lowe; 18 Charlie Wabo.
Tries: D March (14), Mark (22, 73), Lowe (39), Chapman (76), McHugh (78), Knight (80);
Goals: Knight 5/7, McHugh 2/2.
Sin bin: D March (37) - retaliation.
OLDHAM: 1 Paul O'Connor; 2 Lucas Onyango; 24 Marcus St Hilaire; 4 Mick Fogerty; 20 Mark Brocklehurst; 6 Neil Roden; 7 Matt Ashe; 8 Jason Boults; 9 Martin Roden; 10 Dave Ellison; 15 Craig Robinson; 13 Joe Chandler; 18 Chris Clarke. Subs (all used): 16 Wayne Kerr; 17 Danny Whitmore; 19 Ben Heaton; 27 Jamie l'Anson.
Tries: Brocklehurst (47), O'Connor (59); **Goals:** Ashe 2/2.
Dismissal: Fogerty (70) - kicking.
Sin bin: Heaton (37) - holding down, (68) - late tackle.
Rugby Leaguer & League Express Men of the Match: *Hawks:* Steve Dooler; *Oldham:* Neil Roden.
Penalty count: 13-7; **Half-time:** 16-0;
Referee: Craig Halloran; **Attendance:** 509.

WARRINGTON WOLVES 48 FEATHERSTONE ROVERS 24

WOLVES: 1 Richard Mathers; 29 Rhys Williams; 3 Matt King; 23 Ryan Atkins; 2 Chris Riley; 4 Chris Bridge; 7 Richard Myler; 8 Adrian Morley (C); 14 Mick Higham; 16 Paul Wood; 11 Louis Anderson; 12 Ben Westwood; 17 Simon Grix. Subs (all used): 18 Michael Cooper; 27 Vinnie Anderson; 26 David Solomona; 13 Ben Harrison.
Tries: Grix (3), Riley (6, 80), Myler (8, 39, 66), V Anderson (32), Solomona (35, 53);
Goals: Westwood 4/7, Bridge 2/2.
ROVERS: 1 Ian Hardman; 5 Jon Steel; 15 Jessie Joe Parker; 4 Liam Welham; 26 Zak Hardaker; 6 Kyle Briggs; 9 Liam Finn; 8 Iain Morrison; 31 Ben Kaye; 10 Stuart Dickens; 18 Tim Spears; 16 Dane Manning; 11 Matty Dale. Subs (all used): 7 Andy Kain; 23 Jode Sheriffe; 19 Ross Divorty; 12 Jon Grayshon.
Tries: Parker (15, 22), Hardaker (71), Dickens (74);
Goals: Briggs 4/4.
Rugby Leaguer & League Express Men of the Match: *Wolves:* Richard Myler; *Rovers:* Jessie Joe Parker.
Penalty count: 7-4; **Half-time:** 32-12;
Referee: Robert Hicks; **Attendance:** 7,754.

Thursday 22nd April 2010

WIDNES VIKINGS 44 LEZIGNAN 24

VIKINGS: 1 James Ford; 5 Paddy Flynn; 19 Matt Gardner; 15 Shane Grady; 18 Scott Yates; 6 Anthony Thackeray; 7 James Webster; 17 Ben Kavanagh; 14 Thomas Coyle; 10 Jim Gannon; 3 Richard Varkulis; 11 Lee Doran; 13 Chris Gerrard. Subs (all used): 24 Danny Hulme; 23 David Houghton; 31 Jack Smith; 32 Tom Kelly.
Tries: Coyle (3), Thackeray (21), Gardner (24), C Gerrard (26), Yates (32, 37, 77), Kavanagh (72);
Goals: Grady 6/8.
LEZIGNAN: 1 Jye Mullane; 2 Fabien Poggi; 3 Damien Cardace; 4 Cedric Bringuier; 5 Vincent Michau; 6 Nicolas Munoz; 7 James Wynne; 8 Chris Beattie; 9 Nicolas Manessi; 10 Adel Fellous; 11 Phillipe Laurent; 12 Charly Clottes; 13 Mickael Tribillac. Subs (all used): 14 Jordi Ligneries; 15 Julian Bousquet; 16 Thibault Ancely; 17 Aurelien Cologni.
Tries: Fellous (6), Munoz (9), Mullane (40), Laurent (51); **Goals:** Munoz 4/5.
Rugby Leaguer & League Express Men of the Match: *Vikings:* Anthony Thackeray; *Lezignan:* Nicolas Munoz.
Penalty count: 6-4; **Half-time:** 32-18;
Referee: Ronnie Laughton; **Attendance:** 1,349.

ROUND 5

Friday 7th May 2010

BRADFORD BULLS 58 LEIGH CENTURIONS 16

BULLS: 1 Dave Halley; 2 Rikki Sheriffe; 11 Steve Menzies; 4 Chris Nero; 5 Stuart Reardon; 3 Paul Sykes; 6 Brett Kearney; 8 Nick Scruton; 9 Heath L'Estrange; 10 Andy Lynch (C); 20 Elliott Whitehead; 16 Michael Worrincy; 12 Glenn Hall. Subs (all used): 22 James Donaldson; 14 Wayne Godwin; 15 Michael Platt; 18 Craig Kopczak.
Tries: Nero (4, 54, 62), Sykes (11), Menzies (13, 56), Kearney (28), Worrincy (42), Godwin (65), Hall (74);
Goals: Sykes 8/9, Hall 1/1.
CENTURIONS: 1 Stuart Donlan; 2 Steve Maden; 12 Macgraff Leuluai; 4 Mick Nanyn; 5 Nicky Stanton; 22 Martyn Ridyard; 7 Robbie Paul; 8 Chris Hill; 15 Dave McConnell; 10 Ricky Bibey; 14 Tommy Goulden; 11 James Taylor; 13 Dave Armitstead. Subs (all used): 21 Jamie Durbin; 16 Mike Morrison; 20 Ian Mort; 19 Danny Meekin.
Tries: Ridyard (24), Donlan (67), Armitstead (77);
Goals: Nanyn 2/3.
Rugby Leaguer & League Express Men of the Match: *Bulls:* Chris Nero; *Centurions:* Stuart Donlan.
Penalty count: 6-7; **Half-time:** 24-6;
Referee: Thierry Alibert; **Attendance:** 4,250.

LEEDS RHINOS 70 BLACKPOOL PANTHERS 22

RHINOS: 28 Lee Smith; 22 Michael Coady; 3 Brett Delaney; 4 Keith Senior; 5 Ryan Hall; 13 Kevin Sinfield (C); 1 Brent Webb; 19 Luke Burgess; 9 Danny Buderus; 24 Luke Ambler; 20 Jay Pitts; 17 Ian Kirke; 27 Chris Clarkson. Subs (all used): 15 Greg Eastwood; 10 Jamie Peacock; 8 Kylie Leuluai; 12 Ali Lauitiiti.
Tries: Webb (1, 17, 42, 54, 79), Hall (27), Lauitiiti (38), Delaney (44), Coady (48, 51, 58), Eastwood (71);
Goals: Sinfield 11/12.
PANTHERS: 2 Damian Munro; 20 Marlon Miller; 22 Dave Llewellyn; 18 Martin Ainscough; 5 Tom Woodcock; 6 Carl Forber; 7 Tom Hemingway; 34 Neil Holland; 23 John Boland; 21 Peter Fairhurst; 27 Danny Halliwell; 12 Paul Alcock; 11 Kurt Haggerty. Subs (all used): 9 John Clough; 17 Kris Ratcliffe; 19 Adam Thomas; 4 Mark McCully.
Tries: Ainscough (8), Clough (23), Munro (39), Ratcliffe (57); **Goals:** Hemingway 3/4.
Rugby Leaguer & League Express Men of the Match: *Rhinos:* Brent Webb; *Panthers:* Kurt Haggerty.
Penalty count: 4-6; **Half time:** 24-16;
Referee: Robert Hicks; **Attendance:** 5,316.

Saturday 8th May 2010

HUDDERSFIELD GIANTS 4 WARRINGTON WOLVES 60

GIANTS: 1 Brett Hodgson (C); 2 Leroy Cudjoe; 3 Jamahl Lolesi; 4 Paul Whatuira; 5 David Hodgson; 6 Kevin Brown; 34 Danny Brough; 16 Darrell Griffin; 7 Luke Robinson; 10 Keith Mason; 11 Lee Gilmour; 15 Andy Raleigh; 20 David Faiumu. Subs (all used): 8 Eorl Crabtree; 22 Martin Aspinwall; 21 Scott Grix; 33 Graeme Horne.
Try: Aspinwall (45); **Goals:** Brough 0/1.
WOLVES: 1 Richard Mathers; 5 Chris Hicks; 4 Chris Bridge; 23 Ryan Atkins; 3 Matt King; 6 Lee Briers; 7 Richard Myler; 8 Adrian Morley (C); 9 Michael Monaghan; 13 Ben Harrison; 11 Louis Anderson; 12 Ben Westwood; 17 Simon Grix. Subs (all used): 14 Mick Higham; 16 Paul Wood; 26 David Solomona; 2 Chris Riley.
Tries: Atkins (14), Bridge (20, 35, 48, 53, 57), Myler (25), Hicks (29, 66, 72), Riley (61), Higham (69);
Goals: Westwood 4/9, Briers 2/4.
Rugby Leaguer & League Express Men of the Match: *Giants:* Kevin Brown; *Wolves:* Chris Bridge.
Penalty count: 4-9; **Half-time:** 0-26;
Referee: Phil Bentham; **Attendance:** 6,641.

WIDNES VIKINGS 10 WIGAN WARRIORS 64

VIKINGS: 1 James Ford; 5 Paddy Flynn; 4 Toa Kohe-Love; 15 Shane Grady; 19 Matt Gardner; 13 Chris Gerrard; 7 James Webster; 23 David Houghton; 6 Anthony Thackeray; 17 Ben Kavanagh; 21 Matthew Strong; 3 Richard Varkulis; 11 Lee Doran. Subs (all used): 24 Danny Hulme; 32 Tom Kelly; 18 Scott Yates; 31 Alex Gerrard.
Tries: Gardner (48, 68); **Goals:** Grady 1/2.
WARRIORS: 5 Pat Richards; 24 Darrell Goulding; 3 Martin Gleeson; 4 George Carmont; 20 Karl Pryce; 6 Sam Tomkins; 7 Thomas Leuluai; 8 Stuart Fielden; 15 Michael Mcllorum; 10 Andy Coley; 25 Liam Farrell; 12 Joel Tomkins; 13 Sean O'Loughlin (C). Subs (all used): 9 Mark Riddell; 14 Paul Prescott; 21 Eamon O'Carroll; 23 Lee Mossop.
Tries: Pryce (6, 39, 41), Leuluai (9), J Tomkins (13, 24), Gleeson (16, 34), O'Loughlin (45), S Tomkins (62, 66, 79); **Goals:** S Tomkins 2/4, Riddell 6/8.
Rugby Leaguer & League Express Men of the Match: *Vikings:* Lee Doran; *Warriors:* Sam Tomkins.
Penalty count: 12-6; **Half-time:** 0-36;
Referee: James Child; **Attendance:** 5,504.

Sunday 9th May 2010

HARLEQUINS 10 ST HELENS 30

HARLEQUINS: 6 Luke Dorn; 3 Tony Clubb; 13 Rob Purdham (C); 4 David Howell; 5 Will Sharp; 9 Chad Randall; 21 Luke Gale; 10 Louie McCarthy-Scarsbrook; 7 Danny Orr; 17 Danny Ward; 11 Luke Williamson; 8 Karl Temata; 1 Chris Melling. Subs (all used): 14 Oliver Wilkes; 27 Ben Jones; 24 Dave Williams; 18 Ryan Esders.
Tries: Howell (26), Gale (40); **Goals:** Orr 1/2.
SAINTS: 1 Paul Wellens; 2 Ade Gardner; 3 Matt Gidley; 13 Chris Flannery; 5 Francis Meli; 6 Leon Pryce; 7 Kyle Eastmond; 10 James Graham; 9 Keiron Cunningham (C); 15 Bryn Hargreaves; 22 Andrew Dixon; 17 Paul Clough; 11 Tony Puletua. Subs (all used): 8 Nick Fozzard; 14 James Roby; 16 Scott Moore; 18 Matty Ashurst.
Tries: Cunningham (13), Gardner (41), Meli (44, 50), Pryce (78); **Goals:** Eastmond 5/7.
Rugby Leaguer & League Express Men of the Match: *Harlequins:* David Howell; *Saints:* James Graham.
Penalty count: 6-7; **Half-time:** 10-6;
Referee: Ben Thaler; **Attendance:** 3,381.

BARROW RAIDERS 42 HUNSLET HAWKS 24

RAIDERS: 1 Gary Broadbent; 2 Andy Ballard; 12 Ned Catic; 4 Liam Harrison; 25 Jermaine McGillvary; 6 Jamie Rooney; 18 Liam Campbell; 8 Andy Bracek; 19 Nathan Mossop; 15 Rob Roberts; 11 Michael Knowles; 24 Richard Fletcher; 13 Zebastian Luisi. Subs (all used): 16 Brett McDermott; 17 Paul Noone; 10 Chris Young; 21 Chris Larkin.
Tries: Mossop (5), Campbell (9, 32), Catic (27), Ballard (35), Knowles (57), Luisi (75); **Goals:** Rooney 7/7.
HAWKS: 6 Danny Grimshaw; 2 Michael Mark; 4 David Clayton; 5 John Oakes; 26 Waine Pryce; 13 David March; 7 Paul March; 15 Adam Sullivan; 1 Nathan Larvin; 3 James Houston; 12 Steve Dooler; 10 Tom Haughey; 9 Richard Chapman. Subs (all used): 14 Luke Haigh; 18 Charlie Wabo; 16 Neil Lowe; 20 Joe Helme.
Tries: Haughey (17), Helme (37), Pryce (60), Lowe (64), Mark (71); **Goals:** D March 2/5.
Rugby Leaguer & League Express Men of the Match: *Raiders:* Zebastian Luisi; *Hawks:* David March.
Penalty count: 6-7; **Half-time:** 30-10;
Referee: Ronnie Laughton; **Attendance:** 2,241.

CRUSADERS 34 CATALANS DRAGONS 35

CRUSADERS: 26 Clinton Schifcofske; 1 Gareth Thomas; 4 Vince Mellars; 27 Rhys Hanbury; 2 Nick Youngquest; 6 Michael Witt; 7 Jarrod Sammut; 8 Ryan O'Hara (C); 9 Lincoln Withers; 10 Mark Bryant; 11 Weller Hauraki; 12 Jason Chan; 13 Rocky Trimarchi. Subs (all used): 23 Peter Lupton; 18 Jamie Thackray; 16 Frank Winterstein; 20 Ben Flower.
Tries: Schifcofske (7), Mellars (36), Winterstein (49), Lupton (61), Sammut (66), Youngquest (69);
Goals: Witt 2/2, Schifcofske 3/4.
DRAGONS: 5 Dimitri Pelo; 2 Steven Bell; 3 Sebastien Raguin; 4 Setaimata Sa; 28 Frederic Vaccari; 9 Casey McGuire; 7 Thomas Bosc (C); 8 David Ferriol; 15 Jean-Phillipe Baile; 10 Jerome Guisset; 11 Olivier Elima; 12 Gregory Mounis; 13 Dallas Johnson. Subs (all used): 18 Dane Carlaw; 20 Kane Bentley; 22 Jamal Fakir; 24 Remi Casty.

Tries: Sa (11, 28, 59), Bell (16), Bosc (22), Carlaw (32);
Goals: Bosc 5/6. **Field goal:** Bosc (80).
Rugby Leaguer & League Express Men of the Match:
Crusaders: Jarrod Sammut; *Dragons:* Thomas Bosc.
Penalty count: 4-8; **Half-time:** 12-30;
Referee: Ian Smith; **Attendance:** 1,817.

POSTPONED: Halifax v Batley Bulldogs
(due to Rugby Football League investigation of Halifax fielding an ineligible player in Round 4).

Halifax were disqualified from the Challenge Cup on May 11th, 2010, for fielding illegible player Michael Ostick in their Round 4 win against Swinton Lions. Ostick had previously played for Rochdale Hornets, against Lezignan in Round 3. The Lions were reinstated into the competition and played a home tie against Batley Bulldogs.

Wednesday 19th May 2010

SWINTON LIONS 6 BATLEY BULLDOGS 58

LIONS: 1 Richie Hawkyard; 25 Barry Hamilton; 11 Tommy Grundy; 27 Anthony Stewart; 5 Dave Hull; 6 Graham Holroyd; 29 Mick Govin; 26 Dave Newton; 7 Ian Watson; 18 Bruce Johnson; 15 Lee Wingfield; 17 Andrew Isherwood; 9 Phil Joseph. Subs (all used): 23 Rob Foxen; 12 Paul Smith; 20 Chris Hull; 19 Neil Rigby.
Try: Joseph (2); **Goals:** Holroyd 1/1.
BULLDOGS: 5 John Campbell; 3 Mark Barlow; 12 Mark Toohey; 4 Danny Maun; 2 Lee Greenwood; 6 Paul Handforth; 7 Gareth Moore; 8 Byron Smith; 9 Kris Lythe; 10 Sean Hesketh; 26 Jason Walton; 31 John Gallagher; 11 Tommy Gallagher. Subs (all used): 23 Chris Buttery; 17 Craig Potter; 21 James Martin; 20 David Tootill.
Tries: Maun (8), Moore (18), Martin (24), Campbell (30, 80), J Gallagher (33), Greenwood (37, 77), Potter (42), Tootill (67), Hesketh (71); **Goals:** Moore 7/11.
Rugby Leaguer & League Express Men of the Match:
Lions: Richie Hawkyard; *Bulldogs:* Paul Handforth.
Penalty count: 4-12; **Half-time:** 6-30;
Referee: Gareth Hewer; **Attendance:** 636.

QUARTER FINALS

Saturday 29th May 2010

LEEDS RHINOS 12 WIGAN WARRIORS 10

RHINOS: 28 Lee Smith; 2 Scott Donald; 3 Brett Delaney; 4 Keith Senior; 5 Ryan Hall; 13 Kevin Sinfield (C); 6 Danny McGuire; 8 Kylie Leuluai; 9 Danny Buderus; 16 Ryan Bailey; 17 Ian Kirke; 18 Carl Ablett; 11 Jamie Jones-Buchanan. Subs (all used): 10 Jamie Peacock; 15 Greg Eastwood; 14 Matt Diskin; 27 Chris Clarkson.
Try: Smith (78); **Goals:** Sinfield 4/8.
WARRIORS: 5 Pat Richards; 2 Amos Roberts; 3 Martin Gleeson; 4 George Carmont; 20 Karl Pryce; 6 Sam Tomkins; 7 Thomas Leuluai; 8 Stuart Fielden; 9 Mark Riddell; 10 Andy Coley; 12 Joel Tomkins; 16 Phil Bailey; 13 Sean O'Loughlin (C). Subs: 14 Paul Prescott; 15 Michael McIlorum; 25 Liam Farrell; 29 Chris Tuson (not used).
Goals: Richards 5/6.
Sin bin: Farrell (47) - late tackle on McGuire.
On report:
Coley (9) - alleged dangerous tackle on Delaney.
Rugby Leaguer & League Express Men of the Match:
Rhinos: Jamie Jones-Buchanan; *Warriors:* Andy Coley.
Penalty count: 13-10; **Half time:** 4-6;
Referee: Phil Bentham; **Attendance:** 9,242.

ST HELENS 32 BARROW RAIDERS 12

SAINTS: 6 Leon Pryce; 24 Jonny Lomax; 3 Matt Gidley; 13 Chris Flannery; 21 Gary Wheeler; 16 Scott Moore; 7 Kyle Eastmond; 10 James Graham; 9 Keiron Cunningham (C); 15 Bryn Hargreaves; 18 Matty Ashurst; 17 Paul Clough; 14 James Roby. Subs (all used): 8 Nick Fozzard; 11 Tony Puletua; 22 Andrew Dixon; 25 Jacob Emmitt.
Tries: Clough (12, 34), Lomax (39, 59), Roby (50), Gidley (74); **Goals:** Eastmond 1/1, Lomax 3/5.
RAIDERS: 1 Gary Broadbent; 2 Andy Ballard; 32 Andreas Bauer; 4 Liam Harrison; 25 Jermaine McGillvary; 6 Jamie Rooney; 18 Liam Campbell; 16 Brett McDermott; 19 Nathan Mossop; 15 Rob Roberts; 11 Michael Knowles; 12 Ned Catic; 24 Richard Fletcher. Subs (all used): 8 Andy Bracek; 10 Chris Young; 17 Paul Noone; 23 Jamie Butler.
Tries: Catic (21, 47); **Goals:** Rooney 2/2.
Rugby Leaguer & League Express Men of the Match:
Saints: Paul Clough; *Raiders:* Ned Catic.
Penalty count: 6-4; **Half-time:** 16-6;
Referee: James Child; **Attendance:** 4,972.

BATLEY BULLDOGS 12 CATALANS DRAGONS 74

BULLDOGS: 5 John Campbell; 3 Mark Barlow; 22 Josh Griffin; 4 Danny Maun; 2 Lee Greenwood; 6 Paul Handforth; 7 Gareth Moore; 8 Byron Smith; 9 Kris Lythe; 10 Sean Hesketh; 26 Jason Walton; 31 John Gallagher; 13 Ashley Lindsay. Subs (all used): 23 Chris Buttery; 11 Tommy Gallagher; 21 James Martin; 20 David Tootill.
Tries: Walton (40), Lythe (50); **Goals:** Moore 2/2.
Sin bin: Hesketh (1) - late tackle on Bosc.
DRAGONS: 5 Dimitri Pelo; 2 Steven Bell; 3 Sebastien Raguin; 4 Setaimata Sa; 28 Frederic Vaccari; 7 Thomas Bosc (C); 30 Brent Sherwin; 8 David Ferriol; 20 Kane Bentley; 10 Jerome Guisset; 11 Olivier Elima; 18 Dane Carlaw; 13 Dallas Johnson. Subs (all used): 22 Jamal Fakir; 24 Remi Casty; 25 Tony Gigot; 29 Andrew Bentley.
Tries: Guisset (9), Fakir (22, 74), Casty (25), Carlaw (30), Vaccari (36), Elima (57, 70), Raguin (62), Bell (64), Ferriol; A Bentley (77), Gigot (80); **Goals:** Bosc 11/13.

Warrington's Chris Hicks upended against Bradford

Rugby Leaguer & League Express Men of the Match:
Bulldogs: Paul Handforth; *Dragons:* Brent Sherwin.
Penalty count: 5-9; **Half time:** 6-26;
Referee: Ian Smith; **Attendance:** 2,132.

Sunday 30th May 2010

BRADFORD BULLS 22 WARRINGTON WOLVES 26

BULLS: 1 Dave Halley; 2 Rikki Sheriffe; 11 Steve Menzies; 4 Chris Nero; 15 Michael Platt; 3 Paul Sykes; 7 Matt Orford; 8 Nick Scruton; 9 Heath L'Estrange; 10 Andy Lynch (C); 20 Elliott Whitehead; 12 Glenn Hall; 22 James Donaldson. Subs (all used): 29 Joe Wardle (D); 16 Michael Worrincy; 14 Wayne Godwin; 18 Craig Kopczak.
Tries: Sheriffe (23), Halley (29), Nero (35), Menzies (64); **Goals:** Sykes 3/4.
WOLVES: 1 Richard Mathers; 5 Chris Hicks; 3 Matt King; 23 Ryan Atkins; 2 Chris Riley; 6 Lee Briers; 4 Chris Bridge; 8 Adrian Morley (C); 9 Michael Monaghan; 13 Ben Harrison; 26 David Solomona; 12 Ben Westwood; 17 Simon Grix. Subs (all used): 14 Mick Higham; 18 Michael Cooper; 19 Lee Mitchell; 27 Vinnie Anderson.
Tries: Briers (2), Atkins (15), V Anderson (33), Hicks (42, 61); **Goals:** Bridge 3/5.
Rugby Leaguer & League Express Men of the Match:
Bulls: James Donaldson; *Wolves:* Ben Westwood.
Penalty count: 6-5; **Half-time:** 16-18;
Referee: Richard Silverwood; **Attendance:** 7,092.

SEMI-FINALS

Saturday 7th August 2010

LEEDS RHINOS 32 ST HELENS 28

RHINOS: 1 Brent Webb; 28 Lee Smith; 3 Brett Delaney; 4 Keith Senior; 5 Ryan Hall; 6 Danny McGuire; 7 Rob Burrow; 8 Kylie Leuluai; 9 Danny Buderus; 16 Ryan Bailey; 11 Jamie Jones-Buchanan; 27 Chris Clarkson; 13 Kevin Sinfield (C). Subs (all used): 14 Matt Diskin; 19 Luke Burgess; 8 Kylie Leuluai; 15 Greg Eastwood.
Tries: Hall (21, 41), McGuire (59, 74), Webb (63); **Goals:** Sinfield 6/6.
SAINTS: 1 Paul Wellens; 30 Jamie Foster; 3 Matt Gidley; 5 Francis Meli; 2 Ade Gardner; 12 Jon Wilkin; 16 Scott Moore; 10 James Graham; 14 James Roby; 15 Bryn Hargreaves; 13 Chris Flannery; 18 Matty Ashurst; 28 Shaun Magennis. Subs (all used): 9 Keiron Cunningham (C); 11 Tony Puletua; 7 Paul Clough; 25 Jacob Emmitt.
Tries: Wellens (27), Cunningham (34), Meli (39), Gidley (46), Graham (71); **Goals:** Foster 4/5.
Rugby Leaguer & League Express Men of the Match:
Rhinos: Danny McGuire; *Saints:* Keiron Cunningham.
Penalty count: 8-9; **Half-time:** 8-18;
Referee: Phil Bentham; **Attendance:** 15,267
(at Galpharm Stadium, Huddersfield).

Sunday 8th August 2010

CATALANS DRAGONS 12 WARRINGTON WOLVES 54

DRAGONS: 1 Clint Greenshields; 2 Steven Bell; 3 Sebastien Raguin; 18 Dane Carlaw; 23 Chris Walker; 7 Thomas Bosc; 30 Brent Sherwin; 24 Remi Casty; 9 Casey McGuire; 22 Jamal Fakir; 11 Olivier Elima; 12 Gregory Mounis; 4 Setaimata Sa. Subs (all used): 8 David Ferriol; 10 Jerome Guisset; 17 Cyrille Gossard; 27 Michael Simon.
Tries: Greenshields (38, 76); **Goals:** Bosc 2/2.
WOLVES: 1 Richard Mathers; 5 Chris Hicks; 3 Matt King; 23 Ryan Atkins; 2 Chris Riley; 6 Lee Briers; 9 Michael Monaghan; 8 Adrian Morley (C); 15 Jon Clarke; 10 Garreth Carvell; 11 Louis Anderson; 12 Ben Westwood; 13 Ben Harrison. Subs (all used): 16 Paul Wood; 26 David Solomona; 27 Vinnie Anderson; 7 Richard Myler.
Tries: Harrison (6), L Anderson (12, 59, 63), King (28), Riley (31), Briers (45), Myler (61), Clarke (69); **Goals:** Westwood 7/7, Briers 1/1, Myler 1/1.
Rugby Leaguer & League Express Men of the Match:
Dragons: Clint Greenshields; *Wolves:* Louis Anderson.
Penalty count: 8-8; **Half-time:** 6-24;
Referee: Richard Silverwood;
Attendance: 12,265 *(at Stobart Stadium, Widnes).*

FINAL

Saturday 28th August 2010

LEEDS RHINOS 6 WARRINGTON WOLVES 30

RHINOS: 1 Brent Webb; 28 Lee Smith; 3 Brett Delaney; 4 Keith Senior; 5 Ryan Hall; 6 Danny McGuire; 7 Rob Burrow; 8 Kylie Leuluai; 9 Danny Buderus; 16 Ryan Bailey; 11 Jamie Jones-Buchanan; 13 Kevin Sinfield (C). Subs (all used): 14 Matt Diskin; 15 Greg Eastwood; 17 Ian Kirke; 18 Carl Ablett.
Try: Smith (66); **Goals:** Sinfield 1/1.
WOLVES: 1 Richard Mathers; 5 Chris Hicks; 3 Matt King; 23 Ryan Atkins; 2 Chris Riley; 6 Lee Briers; 9 Michael Monaghan; 8 Adrian Morley (C); 15 Jon Clarke; 10 Garreth Carvell; 11 Louis Anderson; 12 Ben Westwood; 13 Ben Harrison. Subs (all used): 16 Paul Wood; 26 David Solomona; 14 Mick Higham; 27 Vinnie Anderson.
Tries: Atkins (4, 35), Hicks (18, 62, 72), L Anderson (76); **Goals:** Westwood 3/6.
Rugby Leaguer & League Express Men of the Match:
Rhinos: Lee Smith; *Wolves:* Lee Briers.
Penalty count: 5-6; **Half-time:** 0-14;
Referee: Richard Silverwood;
Attendance: 85,217 *(at Wembley Stadium).*

Leeds' Brett Delaney soars above Warrington's Chris Riley during the Challenge Cup Final

AMATEUR, RESERVES & ACADEMY 2010

Queens - BARLA National Cup Winners

THE CO-OPERATIVE RUGBY LEAGUE CONFERENCE PREMIER

YORKSHIRE

	P	W	L	D	F	A	D	Pts
East Leeds	12	9	3	0	319	169	150	18
Scarborough Pirates	12	7	5	0	347	232	115	14
Milford Marlins	12	7	5	0	302	238	64	14
Rotherham Giants	12	6	5	1	267	224	43	13
Moorend Thorne	12	6	5	1	314	279	35	13
York Lokomotive	12	5	7	0	272	279	-7	10
Haworth Park	12	1	11	0	110	510	-400	2

MIDLANDS

	P	W	L	D	F	A	D	Pts
Coventry Bears	14	12	2	0	638	228	410	24
Bristol Sonics	14	9	5	0	397	340	57	18
Leicester Storm	14	8	6	0	370	288	82	16
Birmingham Bulldogs	14	8	6	0	357	328	29	16
Gloucestershire W	14	3	11	0	240	522	-282	6
Derby City	14	2	12	0	146	442	-296	4

NORTH WEST

	P	W	L	D	F	A	D	Pts
Widnes West Bank	10	10	0	0	318	106	212	20
Lymm	10	6	4	0	237	206	31	12
Wirral Warriors	10	4	6	0	208	200	8	8
Wigan Riversiders	10	4	6	0	178	251	-73	8
New Broughton R	10	1	9	0	83	261	-178	2

WALES

	P	W	L	D	F	A	D	Pts
Bridgend Blue Bulls	10	9	1	0	550	246	304	18
Valley Cougars	10	9	1	0	556	254	302	18
Cardiff Demons	10	6	4	0	296	320	-24	12
Blackwood Bulldogs	10	3	7	0	291	328	-37	6
CPC Bears	10	2	8	0	188	508	-320	4
Newport Titans	10	1	9	0	232	457	-225	2

SOUTH

	P	W	L	D	F	A	D	Pts
St Albans Centurions	14	13	1	0	692	240	452	26
Hammersmith Hill H	14	10	2	2	430	312	118	22
West London Sharks	14	10	4	0	520	276	244	21
Eastern Rhinos	14	7	6	1	328	364	-36	15
South London Storm	14	4	8	0	386	416	-30	12
Hainault Bulldogs	14	4	10	0	311	492	-181	8
Portsmouth Navy S	14	3	11	0	228	428	-200	6
London Skolars	14	1	13	0	132	499	-367	2

HARRY JEPSON TROPHY - GRAND FINAL

Sunday 12th September 2010

Coventry Bears 4 ....St Albans Centurions **56**
Bears: T - Viggars
Centurions: T - Brown, Fountain 3, O'Rourke, Rampling, Maloney, Kramer 2, van der Merwe, Westhead;
G - Kramer 6

(at Haslams RFC, Derby)

THE CO-OPERATIVE RUGBY LEAGUE CONFERENCE REGIONAL

YORKSHIRE

	P	W	L	D	F	A	D	Pts
Shaw Cross Sharks	14	12	2	0	550	223	327	24
Parkside Hawks	14	11	1	2	516	249	267	24
Leeds Akkies	14	9	5	0	412	335	77	18
Bradford Victoria R	14	8	6	1	382	320	62	15
Barnsley Broncos	14	5	7	2	277	418	-141	12
Lincoln City Knights	14	4	9	1	272	348	-76	9
Scunthorpe Barbarians	14	4	9	1	316	422	-106	9
Wetherby Bulldogs	14	0	13	1	134	544	-410	1

MIDLANDS

	P	W	L	D	F	A	D	Pts
Leamington Royals	12	10	2	0	417	212	205	20
Telford Raiders	12	9	3	0	280	122	158	18
Nottingham O 'A'	13	8	4	1	326	217	109	17
Birmingham B 'A'	11	4	6	1	244	272	-28	9
Coventry Bears 'A'	12	3	9	0	268	388	-120	6
NE Worcestershire R	12	1	11	0	124	448	-324	2

NORTH WEST

	P	W	L	D	F	A	D	Pts
Mancunians	10	7	2	1	327	184	143	15
Chester Gladiators	10	6	4	0	266	220	46	12
Blackpool Sea Eagles	10	6	4	0	236	191	45	12
Wigan Riversiders Eels	10	4	5	1	178	216	-38	9
Crewe & Nantwich S	10	1	9	0	110	306	-196	2

WALES

	P	W	L	D	F	A	D	Pts
Torfaen Tigers	6	4	2	0	190	150	40	8
Neath Port Talbot S	6	3	3	0	156	126	30	6
Dyffryn Devils	6	3	3	0	160	212	-52	6
Tydfil Wildcats	6	2	4	0	180	198	-18	4

SOUTH WEST

	P	W	L	D	F	A	D	Pts
Devon Sharks	10	9	1	0	630	248	382	18
East Devon Eagles	10	8	2	0	568	268	300	16
Exeter Centurions	10	7	3	0	402	255	147	14
South Dorset Giants	10	6	4	0	338	340	-2	12
Somerset Vikings	10	5	5	0	366	324	42	10
South Somerset W	10	2	8	0	236	343	-107	4
North Devon Raiders	10	2	8	0	180	498	-318	4
Plymouth Titans	10	1	9	0	134	578	-444	2

Northampton Demons - Conference Regional Champions

SOUTH EAST

	P	W	L	D	F	A	D	Pts
Elmbridge Eagles	14	13	1	0	788	168	620	26
Guildford Giants	14	9	4	1	416	304	112	19
Southampton Spitfires	14	9	5	0	518	318	200	18
Greenwich Admirals	14	8	6	0	578	250	328	16
Sth London Storm 'A'	14	7	7	0	358	482	-124	14
Sussex Merlins	14	5	9	0	322	508	-186	10
Swindon St George	14	3	10	1	164	780	-616	7
Oxford Cavaliers	14	1	13	0	246	580	-334	2

EAST

	P	W	L	D	F	A	D	Pts
Northampton Demons	10	9	1	0	451	164	287	18
Bedford Tigers	10	8	2	0	338	222	116	16
Bury Titans	10	5	5	0	254	215	39	10
St Ives Roosters	10	5	5	0	256	276	-20	10
Norwich City Saxons	10	3	7	0	234	346	-112	6
St Albans C 'A'	10	0	10	0	140	450	-310	0

NORTH EAST

	P	W	L	D	F	A	D	Pts
Peterlee Pumas	14	14	0	0	798	202	596	28
Jarrow Vikings	14	10	4	0	602	242	360	20
Sunderland	14	9	5	0	515	462	53	18
Newcastle Storm	14	7	6	1	462	357	105	15
Wallsend Eagles	12	7	5	0	390	288	102	14
Cramlington Rockets	14	6	7	1	402	541	-139	13
Winlaton Warriors	14	6	8	0	530	461	69	12
Northallerton Stallions	12	4	8	0	424	500	-76	8
Durham Demons	12	2	10	0	260	576	-316	4
Whitley Bay B	12	0	12	0	128	882	-754	0

SCOTLAND

	P	W	L	D	F	A	D	Pts
Edinburgh Eagles	7	7	0	0	234	112	122	14
Carluke Tigers	7	6	1	0	350	100	250	12
Moray Eels	7	4	2	1	246	206	40	9
Ayrshire Storm	7	4	3	0	250	200	50	8
Fife Lions	7	3	4	0	246	240	6	6
Easterhouse Panthers	7	2	4	1	188	252	-64	5
Falkirk	7	1	6	0	130	408	-278	2
Forth & Clyde Nomads	7	0	7	0	118	244	-126	0

REGIONAL GRAND FINAL

Sunday 12th September 2010

Northampton Demons 16 ....Parkside Hawks **12**
Demons: T - Ward, Goodman, Fewster; G - Fewster 2
Hawks: T - Banks, West; G - West 2

(at Haslams RFC, Derby)

VALVOLINE CUP *(Under 20s)*

FINAL TABLE

	P	W	D	L	F	A	D	Pts
Warrington Wolves	20	16	1	3	832	359	473	33
St Helens	20	15	1	4	744	444	300	31
Wigan Warriors	20	15	0	5	727	340	387	30
Huddersfield Giants	20	11	2	7	510	560	-50	24
Hull FC	20	8	1	11	457	456	1	23
Salford City Reds	20	9	2	9	596	564	32	20
Bradford Bulls	20	10	0	10	552	570	-18	20
Wakefield T Wildcats	20	8	1	11	468	498	-30	17
Hull Kingston Rovers	20	5	2	13	505	671	-166	12
Leeds Rhinos	20	5	2	13	396	720	-324	12
Castleford Tigers	20	5	0	15	488	638	-150	10
Harlequins	20	4	0	16	366	821	-455	8

ELIMINATION PLAY-OFFS

Thursday 2nd September 2010
Huddersfield Giants 33 ....Hull FC 14
Saturday 4th September 2010
Wigan Warriors 62 ....Salford City Reds 0

QUALIFYING SEMI-FINAL

Saturday 11th September 2010
Warrington Wolves 16 ....St Helens 34

ELIMINATION SEMI-FINAL

Friday 10th September 2010
Wigan Warriors 26 ....Huddersfield Giants 10

FINAL ELIMINATOR

Saturday 18th September 2010
Warrington Wolves 0 ....Wigan Warriors 10

GRAND FINAL

Saturday 25th September 2010

St Helens 22...........................Wigan Warriors **30**
Saints: T - Ashurst (40), Fa'asavalu (50), Magennis (54), Armstrong (80); G - Ellis 3/4
Warriors: T - Howarth (11), Dandy (25), Veivers (28), Charnley (38), Russell (46, 72); G - Veivers 3/6
(at GPW Recruitment Stadium)

RESERVES CHAMPIONSHIP

FINAL TABLE

	P	W	D	L	F	A	D	Pts
Whitehaven	16	14	0	2	718	318	400	28
Featherstone Rovers	16	13	0	3	550	338	212	26
Leigh Centurions	16	12	0	4	592	292	300	24
Widnes Vikings	16	12	0	4	575	298	277	24
Oldham	16	10	0	6	539	376	163	20
Keighley Cougars	16	8	0	8	467	474	-7	16
Sheffield Eagles	16	8	0	8	466	496	-30	16
Dewsbury Rams	16	4	1	11	308	627	-319	9
Hunslet Hawks	16	4	0	12	340	504	-164	8
York City Knights	16	2	0	14	300	640	-340	4
Barrow Raiders	16	0	1	15	122	614	-492	1

ELIMINATION PLAY-OFFS

Saturday 21st August 2010
Leigh Centurions 58 ....Keighley Cougars 6
Widnes Vikings 46..Oldham 24

QUALIFYING SEMI-FINAL

Saturday 4th September 2010
Whitehaven 48.........................Featherstone Rovers 26

ELIMINATION SEMI-FINAL

Sunday 5th September 2010
Leigh Centurions 16 ....Widnes Vikings 36

FINAL ELIMINATOR

Saturday 11th September 2010
Featherstone Rovers 32....................Widnes Vikings 16

GRAND FINAL

Sunday 19th September 2010

Whitehaven 46 ....Featherstone Rovers **12**
Whitehaven: T - Hamzat (8, 23), Cook (18), Benson (21), Dalton (31, 38), Jackson (61), Smith (64);
G - Jackson 5/6, Cook 2/2
Rovers: T - Johnson (52), Bassinder (68); G - Carr 2/2
(at The Recreation Ground)

GRAND FINALS
1998-2009

1998

DIVISION ONE GRAND FINAL

Saturday 26th September 1998

FEATHERSTONE ROVERS 22 WAKEFIELD TRINITY 24

ROVERS: 1 Steve Collins; 2 Carl Hall; 3 Shaun Irwin; 4 Danny Baker; 5 Karl Pratt; 6 Jamie Coventry; 7 Ty Fallins; 8 Chico Jackson; 9 Richard Chapman; 10 Stuart Dickens; 11 Gary Price; 12 Neil Lowe; 13 Richard Slater. Subs: 14 Paddy Handley for Coventry (70); 15 Asa Amone for Lowe (50); 16 Micky Clarkson for Jackson (50); 17 Steve Dooler (not used). **Tries:** Baker (15), Jackson (45), Collins (49), Hall (69); **Goals:** Chapman 3.
TRINITY: 1 Martyn Holland; 2 Josh Bostock; 3 Adam Hughes; 4 Martin Law; 5 Kevin Gray; 6 Garen Casey; 7 Roger Kenworthy; 8 Francis Stephenson; 9 Roy Southernwood; 10 Gary Lord; 11 Ian Hughes; 12 Sonny Whakarau; 13 Matt Fuller. Subs: 14 Sean Richardson for I Hughes (32); 15 Andy Fisher for Lord (26); 16 David Mycoe (not used); 17 Wayne McDonald for Whakarau (70); Lord for Stephenson (40); Stephenson for Lord (70).
Tries: Southernwood (2), Bostock (7, 25), Casey (58), Stephenson (76); **Goals:** Casey 2.
League Express Men of the Match:
Rovers: Richard Chapman; *Trinity:* Garen Casey.
Penalty count: 8-3; **Half time:** 6-12; **Referee:** Nick Oddy (Halifax); **Attendance:** 8,224 *(at McAlpine Stadium, Huddersfield).*

SUPER LEAGUE GRAND FINAL

Saturday 24th October 1998

LEEDS RHINOS 4 WIGAN WARRIORS 10

RHINOS: 1 Iestyn Harris (C); 22 Leroy Rivett; 3 Richie Blackmore; 4 Brad Godden; 5 Francis Cummins; 13 Daryl Powell; 7 Ryan Sheridan; 8 Martin Masella; 21 Terry Newton; 25 Darren Fleary; 11 Adrian Morley; 17 Anthony Farrell; 12 Marc Glanville. Subs: 20 Jamie Mathiou for Masella (25); 24 Marcus St Hilaire for Powell (40); 14 Graham Holroyd for Newton (49); 27 Andy Hay for Fleary (54); Powell for Godden (58); Masella for Mathiou (71).
Try: Blackmore (20).
WARRIORS: 1 Kris Radlinski; 2 Jason Robinson; 3 Danny Moore; 4 Gary Connolly; 5 Mark Bell; 6 Henry Paul; 7 Tony Smith; 16 Terry O'Connor; 9 Robbie McCormack; 10 Tony Mestrov; 20 Lee Gilmour; 17 Stephen Holgate; 13 Andy Farrell (C). Subs: 8 Neil Cowie for O'Connor (18BB, rev 48); 14 Mick Cassidy for McCormack (19BB, rev 27); 25 Paul Johnson for Moore (37); 12 Simon Haughton for Gilmour (27BB, rev 33); Haughton for Holgate (33); Cowie for Mestrov (54); Cassidy for Haughton (64); Holgate for Cowie (68); Haughton for Gilmour (71BB, rev 75); Mestrov for O'Connor (75BB).
Try: Robinson (37); **Goals:** Farrell 3.
League Express Men of the Match:
Rhinos: Iestyn Harris; *Warriors:* Jason Robinson.
Penalty count: 7-13; **Half-time:** 4-6; **Referee:** Russell Smith (Castleford); **Attendance:** 43,553 *(at Old Trafford, Manchester).*

1999

NORTHERN FORD PREMIERSHIP GRAND FINAL

Saturday 25th September 1999

DEWSBURY RAMS 11 HUNSLET HAWKS 12

RAMS: 1 Nathan Graham; 2 Alex Godfrey; 3 Paul Evans; 4 Brendan O'Meara; 5 Adrian Flynn; 6 Richard Agar; 7 Barry Eaton; 8 Alan Boothroyd; 9 Paul Delaney; 10 Matthew Long; 11 Andy Spink; 12 Mark Haigh; 13 Damian Ball. Subs: 14 Brendan Williams for Eaton (5BB, rev 15); 15 Sean Richardson for Haigh (50); 16 Simon Hicks for Long (25); 17 Paul Medley for Spink (50); Williams for Evans (61); Long for Boothroyd (71); Spink for Long (78).
Tries: Flynn (27), Ball (54); **Goal:** Eaton; **Field goal:** Agar.
HAWKS: 1 Abraham Fatnowna; 2 Chris Ross; 3 Shaun Irwin; 4 Paul Cook; 5 Iain Higgins; 6 Marcus Vassilakopoulos; 7 Latham Tawhai; 8 Richard Hayes; 9 Richard Pachniuk; 10 Steve Pryce; 11 Rob Wilson; 12 Jamie Leighton; 13 Lee St Hilaire. Subs: 14 Mick Coyle for Wilson (57); 15 Phil Kennedy for Pryce (35); 16 Jamie Thackray for St Hilaire (25); 17 Richard Baker for Higgins (55); Higgins for Fatnowna (62); Pryce for Kennedy (65).
Tries: Cook (31), Higgins (46);
Goal: Ross; **Field goals:** Tawhai, Leighton.
League Express Men of the Match:
Rams: Barry Eaton; *Hawks:* Latham Tawhai.
Penalty count: 8-5; **Half-time:** 7-7; **Referee:** Steve Ganson (St Helens); **Attendance:** 5,783 *(at Headingley Stadium, Leeds).*

SUPER LEAGUE GRAND FINAL

Saturday 9th October 1999

BRADFORD BULLS 6 ST HELENS 8

BULLS: 28 Stuart Spruce; 2 Tevita Vaikona; 20 Scott Naylor; 5 Michael Withers; 17 Leon Pryce; 6 Henry Paul; 1 Robbie Paul (C); 10 Paul Anderson; 9 James Lowes; 29 Stuart Fielden; 15 David Boyle; 23 Bernard Dwyer; 13 Steve McNamara. Subs: 14 Paul Deacon for R Paul (53); 4 Nathan McAvoy (not used); 12 Mike Forshaw for McNamara (18); 22 Brian McDermott for Anderson (18); Anderson for Fielden (61); Fielden for Dwyer (65); R Paul for Deacon (72).
Try: H Paul (18); **Goal:** H Paul.
SAINTS: 1 Paul Atcheson; 14 Chris Smith; 3 Kevin Iro; 4 Paul Newlove; 5 Anthony Sullivan; 13 Paul Sculthorpe; 20 Tommy Martyn; 8 Apollo Perelini; 9 Keiron Cunningham; 10 Julian O'Neill; 2 Fereti Tuilagi; 21 Sonny Nickle; 11 Chris Joynt (C). Subs: 26 Paul Wellens for Martyn (52); 6 Sean Hoppe for Newlove (43); 16 Vila Matautia for O'Neill (20); 7 Sean Long for Perelini (24); Perelini for Matautia (46); O'Neill for Perelini (69).
Tries: Iro (65); **Goals:** Long 2.
League Express Men of the Match:
Bulls: Henry Paul; *Saints:* Kevin Iro.
Penalty count: 4-7; **Half-time:** 6-2; **Referee:** Stuart Cummings (Widnes); **Attendance:** 50,717 *(at Old Trafford, Manchester).*

2000

NORTHERN FORD PREMIERSHIP GRAND FINAL

Saturday 29th July 2000

DEWSBURY RAMS 13 LEIGH CENTURIONS 12

RAMS: 1 Nathan Graham; 2 Richard Baker; 4 Dan Potter; 3 Brendan O'Meara; 5 Adrian Flynn; 6 Richard Agar; 7 Barry Eaton; 8 Shayne Williams; 9 David Mycoe; 10 Mark Haigh; 11 Sean Richardson; 12 Daniel Frame; 13 Damian Ball. Subs: 14 Gavin Wood (not used); 15 Paul Delaney for Mycoe (53); 16 Ryan McDonald for Haigh (30); 17 Matthew Long for Williams (23); Haigh for McDonald (64).
Tries: Eaton (2), Long (23); **Goals:** Eaton 2; **Field goal:** Agar.
Sin bin: Williams (66) - use of the elbow.
On report: Richardson (20) - high tackle on Donlan.
CENTURIONS: 1 Stuart Donlan; 5 David Ingram; 3 Paul Anderson; 4 Andy Fairclough; 2 Alan Cross; 6 Liam Bretherton; 7 Kieron Purtill; 8 Tim Street; 9 Mick Higham; 10 Andy Leathem; 11 Simon Baldwin; 12 Heath Cruckshank; 13 Adam Bristow. Subs: 14 James Arkwright for Cross (68); 15 Paul Norman for Street (36); 16 Radney Bowker (not used); 17 David Whittle for Leathem (24); Street for Norman (62).
Tries: Higham (29, 69); **Goals:** Bretherton 2.
Sin bin: Whittle (66) - retaliation.
League Express Men of the Match:
Rams: Richard Agar; *Centurions:* Mick Higham.
Penalty count: 4-4; **Half-time:** 10-6; **Referee:** Robert Connolly (Wigan); **Attendance:** 8,487 *(at Gigg Lane, Bury).*

SUPER LEAGUE GRAND FINAL

Saturday 14th October 2000

ST HELENS 29 WIGAN WARRIORS 16

SAINTS: 17 Paul Wellens; 24 Steve Hall; 3 Kevin Iro; 15 Sean Hoppe; 5 Anthony Sullivan; 20 Tommy Martyn; 7 Sean Long; 8 Apollo Perelini; 9 Keiron Cunningham; 10 Julian O'Neill; 11 Chris Joynt (C); 22 Tim Jonkers; 13 Paul Sculthorpe. Subs: 14 Fereti Tuilagi for O'Neill (20); 12 Sonny Nickle for Perelini (28); 26 John Stankevitch for Jonkers (50); 23 Scott Barrow (not used); Perelini for Nickle (52); Jonkers for Stankevitch (66); Stankevitch for Perelini (67BB); O'Neill for Hall (74).
Tries: Hoppe (7), Joynt (28, 50), Tuilagi (69), Jonkers (80);
Goals: Long 4; **Field goal:** Sculthorpe.
WARRIORS: 5 Jason Robinson; 2 Brett Dallas; 1 Kris Radlinski; 3 Steve Renouf; 26 David Hodgson; 6 Tony Smith; 7 Willie Peters; 8 Terry O'Connor; 9 Terry Newton; 10 Neil Cowie; 11 Mick Cassidy; 12 Denis Betts; 13 Andy Farrell (C). Subs: 23 Brady Malam for Cowie (30); 17 Tony Mestrov for O'Connor (43); 19 Chris Chester for Cassidy (47BB, rev 69); 14 Lee Gilmour for Betts (51); O'Connor for Mestrov (61); Cowie for Malam (67); Chester for Newton (75).
Tries: Farrell (13), Hodgson (58), Smith (61); **Goals:** Farrell 2.
League Express Men of the Match:
Saints: Chris Joynt; *Warriors:* Andy Farrell.
Penalty count: 10-6; **Half-time:** 11-4; **Referee:** Russell Smith (Castleford); **Attendance:** 58,132 *(at Old Trafford, Manchester).*

2001

NORTHERN FORD PREMIERSHIP GRAND FINAL

Saturday 28th July 2001

OLDHAM 14 WIDNES VIKINGS 24

OLDHAM: 1 Mark Sibson; 2 Joey Hayes; 3 Anthony Gibbons; 4 Pat Rich; 5 Joe McNicholas; 6 David Gibbons; 7 Neil Roden; 8 Leo Casey; 9 Keith Brennan; 10 Paul Norton; 11 Phil Farrell; 12 Bryan Henare; 13 Kevin Mannion. Subs: 14 Mike Ford for Mannion (27); 15 Jason Clegg for Casey (18); 16 John Hough for Brennan (44); 17 Danny Guest for Norton (40BB, rev 54); Mannion for Henare (66); Guest for Clegg (73).
Tries: Brennan (9), Ford (74), Mannion (80); **Goal:** Rich.
VIKINGS: 1 Paul Atcheson; 2 Damian Munro; 3 Craig Weston; 4 Jason Demetriou; 5 Chris Percival; 6 Richard Agar; 7 Martin Crompton; 8 Simon Knox; 9 Phil Cantillon; 10 Stephen Holgate; 11 Steve Gee; 12 Sean Richardson; 13 Tommy Hodgkinson. Subs: 14 Andy Craig for Percival (65); 15 Chris McKinney for Gee (41); 16 Joe Faimalo for Knox (32); 17 Matthew Long for Holgate (23); Knox for Long (49BB, rev 61); Holgate for Long (74).
Tries: Gee (17), Demetriou (38, 60), Cantillon (50), Munro (69); **Goals:** Weston 2.
League Express Men of the Match:
Oldham: Jason Clegg; *Vikings:* Phil Cantillon.
Penalty count: 8-5; **Half-time:** 4-10; **Referee:** Steve Ganson (St Helens); **Attendance:** 8,974 *(at Spotland, Rochdale).*

SUPER LEAGUE GRAND FINAL

Saturday 13th October 2001

BRADFORD BULLS 37 WIGAN WARRIORS 6

BULLS: 5 Michael Withers; 2 Tevita Vaikona; 20 Scott Naylor; 23 Graham Mackay; 3 Leon Pryce; 6 Henry Paul; 1 Robbie Paul (C); 8 Joe Vagana; 9 James Lowes; 22 Brian McDermott; 11 Daniel Gartner; 19 Jamie Peacock; 12 Mike Forshaw. Subs: 29 Stuart Fielden for McDermott (21BB, rev 65); 10 Paul Anderson for Vagana (22); 15 Shane Rigon for Pryce (40); 7 Paul Deacon for R Paul (69); Vagana for Anderson (53); Fielden for Gartner (72); Anderson for Vagana (74).
Tries: Lowes (9), Withers (11, 27, 31), Fielden (65), Mackay (72); **Goals:** H Paul 5, Mackay; **Field goal:** H Paul.
WARRIORS: 1 Kris Radlinski; 2 Brett Dallas; 4 Gary Connolly; 3 Steve Renouf; 5 Brian Carney; 6 Matthew Johns; 7 Adrian Lam; 8 Terry O'Connor; 9 Terry Newton; 20 Harvey Howard; 11 Mick Cassidy; 14 David Furner; 13 Andy Farrell (C). Subs: 15 Paul Johnson for Carney (12BB); 10 Neil Cowie for Howard (17); 12 Denis Betts for O'Connor (32); 19 Chris Chester for Farrell (59); O'Connor for Cowie (55); Howard for Newton (64); Cowie for Cassidy (72).
Try: Lam (63); **Goal:** Furner.
League Express Men of the Match:
Bulls: Michael Withers; *Warriors:* Adrian Lam.
Penalty count: 6-7; **Half-time:** 26-0; **Referee:** Stuart Cummings (Widnes); **Attendance:** 60,164 *(at Old Trafford, Manchester).*

2000...
Paul Wellens takes on Jason Robinson

2001...
Stuart Fielden tackled by Neil Cowie

2002

NORTHERN FORD PREMIERSHIP GRAND FINAL

Saturday 12th October 2002

HUDDERSFIELD GIANTS 38 LEIGH CENTURIONS 16

GIANTS: 1 Ben Cooper; 2 Hefin O'Hare; 3 Eorl Crabtree; 4 Graeme Hallas; 5 Marcus St Hilaire; 6 Stanley Gene; 7 Chris Thorman; 8 Michael Slicker; 9 Paul March; 10 Jeff Wittenberg; 11 David Atkins; 12 Robert Roberts; 13 Steve McNamara. Subs: 14 Heath Cruckshank for Roberts (24BB); 15 Chris Molyneux for Slicker (53); 16 Darren Turner for March (21); 17 Andy Rice for Cruckshank (57); Roberts for Wittenberg (34); Wittenberg for Roberts (74).
Tries: O'Hare (12, 78), St Hilaire (34, 53), Thorman (46), Gene (57); **Goals:** McNamara 7.
Sin bin: Roberts (47) - fighting.
CENTURIONS: 1 Neil Turley; 2 Leon Felton; 4 Jon Roper; 3 Dale Cardoza; 5 Oliver Marns; 6 Willie Swann; 7 Bobbie Goulding; 8 Vila Matautia; 9 Paul Rowley; 10 David Bradbury; 11 Simon Baldwin; 12 Andrew Isherwood; 13 Adam Bristow. Subs: 14 Gareth Price for Bradbury (24BB, rev 35); 15 John Duffy for Swann (32); 16 John Hamilton for Bristow (46BB, rev 57); 17 David Whittle for Matautia (22); Matautia for Bradbury (53BB); Swann for Goulding (58); Hamilton for Whittle (67); Bradbury for Turley (72); Goulding for Swann (75).
Tries: Cardoza (9), Marns (18), Hamilton (70); **Goals:** Turley 2.
Sin bin: Whittle (47) - fighting; Bristow (74) - interference.
On report: Isherwood (66) - high tackle on Roberts.
Rugby Leaguer & League Express Men of the Match:
Giants: Chris Thorman; *Centurions:* Adam Bristow.
Penalty count: 5-4; **Half-time:** 14-10;
Referee: Karl Kirkpatrick (Warrington);
Attendance: 9,051 *(at Halton Stadium, Widnes).*

SUPER LEAGUE GRAND FINAL

Saturday 19th October 2002

BRADFORD BULLS 18 ST HELENS 19

BULLS: 6 Michael Withers; 2 Tevita Vaikona; 20 Scott Naylor; 15 Brandon Costin; 5 Lesley Vainikolo; 1 Robbie Paul (C); 7 Paul Deacon; 8 Joe Vagana; 9 James Lowes; 29 Stuart Fielden; 11 Daniel Gartner; 12 Jamie Peacock; 13 Mike Forshaw. Subs: 14 Lee Gilmour for Gartner (21); 10 Paul Anderson for Vagana (25); 22 Brian McDermott for Fielden (34); 3 Leon Pryce for Vainikolo (53); Fielden for Anderson (55); Vainikolo for Paul (77).
Tries: Naylor (3), Paul (44), Withers (47); **Goals:** Deacon 3.
SAINTS: 1 Paul Wellens; 5 Darren Albert; 3 Martin Gleeson; 4 Paul Newlove; 19 Anthony Stewart; 13 Paul Sculthorpe; 7 Sean Long; 8 Darren Britt; 9 Keiron Cunningham; 10 Barry Ward; 23 Mike Bennett; 15 Tim Jonkers; 11 Chris Joynt (C). Subs: 2 Sean Hoppe for Wellens (3); 12 Peter Shiels for Ward (27); 14 John Stankevitch for Britt (31BB, rev 58); 17 Mick Higham for Joynt (54); Stankevitch for Shiels (58); Joynt for Britt (75); Shiels for Jonkers (77).
Tries: Bennett (24), Long (32), Gleeson (56);
Goals: Long 3; **Field goal:** Long.
Rugby Leaguer & League Express Men of the Match:
Bulls: Paul Deacon; *Saints:* Mike Bennett.
Penalty count: 5-4; **Half-time:** 12-8; **Referee:** Russell Smith (Castleford); **Attendance:** 61,138 *(at Old Trafford, Manchester).*

2002...Sean Long celebrates St Helens' Grand Final win

2003

NATIONAL LEAGUE TWO GRAND FINAL

Sunday 5th October 2003

KEIGHLEY COUGARS 13 SHEFFIELD EAGLES 11

COUGARS: 1 Matt Foster; 2 Max Tomlinson; 3 David Foster; 4 James Rushforth; 5 Andy Robinson; 6 Paul Ashton; 7 Matt Firth; 8 Phil Stephenson; 9 Simeon Hoyle; 10 Danny Ekis; 11 Oliver Wilkes; 12 Ian Sinfield; 13 Lee Patterson. Subs (all used): 14 Chris Wainwright; 15 Richard Mervill; 16 Mick Durham; 17 Jason Ramshaw.
Tries: M Foster (7), Robinson (74); **Goals:** Ashton 2;
Field goal: Firth.
EAGLES: 1 Andy Poynter; 2 Tony Weller; 3 Richard Goddard; 4 Tom O'Reilly; 5 Greg Hurst; 6 Gavin Brown; 7 Mark Aston; 8 Jack Howieson; 9 Gareth Stanley; 10 Dale Laughton; 11 Andy Raleigh; 12 Craig Brown; 13 Wayne Flynn. Subs (all used): 14 Peter Reilly; 15 Simon Tillyer; 16 Nick Turnbull; 17 Mitchell Stringer.
Try: O'Reilly (51); **Goals:** G Brown 3; **Field goal:** Reilly.
Rugby Leaguer & League Express Men of the Match:
Cougars: Simeon Hoyle; *Eagles:* Andy Raleigh.
Penalty count: 6-8; **Half-time:** 9-4; **Referee:** Peter Taberner (Wigan). *(at Halton Stadium, Widnes).*

NATIONAL LEAGUE ONE GRAND FINAL

Sunday 5th October 2003

LEIGH CENTURIONS 14 SALFORD CITY REDS 31

CENTURIONS: 1 Neil Turley; 2 Damian Munro; 3 Alan Hadcroft; 4 Danny Halliwell; 5 Leroy Rivett; 6 John Duffy; 7 Tommy Martyn; 8 Sonny Nickle; 9 Patrick Weisner; 10 Paul Norman; 11 Sean Richardson; 12 Willie Swann; 13 Adam Bristow. Subs (all used): 14 David Bradbury; 15 Lee Sanderson; 16 Bryan Henare; 17 Ricky Bibey.
Tries: Richardson (33), Halliwell (38), Swann (65);
Goal: Turley.
On report: Nickle (60) - late tackle on Clinch.
CITY REDS: 1 Jason Flowers; 2 Danny Arnold; 3 Stuart Littler; 4 Alan Hunte; 5 Andy Kirk; 6 Cliff Beverley; 7 Gavin Clinch; 8 Neil Baynes; 9 Malcolm Alker; 10 Andy Coley; 11 Simon Baldwin; 12 Paul Highton; 13 Chris Charles. Subs (all used): 14 Steve Blakeley; 15 David Highton; 16 Martin Moana; 17 Gareth Haggerty.
Tries: Hunte (3, 52), Beverley (23), Littler (73);
Goals: Charles 6, Blakeley; **Field goal:** Blakeley.
Rugby Leaguer & League Express Men of the Match:
Centurions: Willie Swann; *City Reds:* Gavin Clinch.
Penalty count: 10-10; **Half-time:** 10-16;
Referee: Richard Silverwood (Dewsbury);
Attendance: 9,186 *(at Halton Stadium, Widnes).*

SUPER LEAGUE GRAND FINAL

Saturday 18th October 2003

BRADFORD BULLS 25 WIGAN WARRIORS 12

BULLS: 17 Stuart Reardon; 2 Tevita Vaikona; 6 Michael Withers; 4 Shontayne Hape; 5 Lesley Vainikolo; 15 Karl Pratt; 7 Paul Deacon; 8 Joe Vagana; 9 James Lowes; 29 Stuart Fielden; 11 Daniel Gartner; 12 Jamie Peacock; 13 Mike Forshaw. Subs (all used): 10 Paul Anderson; 18 Lee Radford; 3 Leon Pryce; 1 Robbie Paul (C).
Tries: Reardon (51), Hape (59), Lowes (75);
Goals: Deacon 6/6; **Field goal:** Deacon.
WARRIORS: 1 Kris Radlinski; 5 Brian Carney; 18 Martin Aspinwall; 14 David Hodgson; 2 Brett Dallas; 15 Sean O'Loughlin; 20 Luke Robinson; 30 Quentin Pongia; 9 Terry Newton; 10 Craig Smith; 11 Mick Cassidy; 12 Danny Tickle; 13 Andy Farrell (C). Subs (all used): 4 Paul Johnson; 8 Terry O'Connor; 23 Gareth Hock; 17 Mark Smith.
Tries: Tickle (17), Radlinski (72); **Goals:** Farrell 2/3.
Rugby Leaguer & League Express Men of the Match:
Bulls: Stuart Reardon; *Warriors:* Kris Radlinski.
Penalty count: 7-6; **Half-time:** 4-6; **Referee:** Karl Kirkpatrick (Warrington); **Attendance:** 65,537 *(at Old Trafford, Manchester).*

2004

NATIONAL LEAGUE ONE GRAND FINAL

Sunday 10th October 2004

LEIGH CENTURIONS 32 WHITEHAVEN 16
(After extra time)

CENTURIONS: 1 Neil Turley; 2 Rob Smyth; 3 Danny Halliwell; 4 Ben Cooper; 5 David Alstead; 6 John Duffy; 7 Tommy Martyn; 8 Simon Knox; 9 Paul Rowley; 10 Matt Sturm; 11 David Larder; 12 Oliver Wilkes; 13 Ian Knott. Subs (all used): 14 Dave McConnell; 15 Heath Cruckshank; 16 Richard Marshall; 17 Willie Swann.
Tries: Cooper (27, 83), Martyn (61), Turley (87); **Goals:** Turley 6/8; **Field goals:** Turley 2, Rowley, Martyn.
WHITEHAVEN: 1 Gary Broadbent; 2 Craig Calvert; 3 David Seeds; 4 Mick Nanyn; 5 Wesley Wilson; 6 Leroy Joe; 7 Sam Obst; 8 Marc Jackson; 9 Aaron Lester; 10 David Fatialofa; 11 Paul Davidson; 12 Howard Hill; 13 Craig Walsh. Subs (all used): 14 Spencer Miller; 15 Carl Sice; 16 Chris McKinney; 17 Ryan Tandy.
Tries: Wilson (2, 71), Calvert (45); **Goals:** Nanyn 2/6.
Rugby Leaguer & League Express Men of the Match: *Centurions:* Neil Turley; *Whitehaven:* Aaron Lester.
Penalty count: 5-9; **Half-time:** 7-6;
Referee: Ronnie Laughton (Barnsley);
Attendance: 11,005 *(at Halton Stadium, Widnes).*

SUPER LEAGUE GRAND FINAL

Saturday 16th October 2004

BRADFORD BULLS 8 LEEDS RHINOS 16

BULLS: 6 Michael Withers; 17 Stuart Reardon; 16 Paul Johnson; 4 Shontayne Hape; 5 Lesley Vainikolo; 18 Iestyn Harris; 7 Paul Deacon; 8 Joe Vagana; 1 Robbie Paul (C); 29 Stuart Fielden; 12 Jamie Peacock; 13 Logan Swann; 11 Lee Radford. Subs: 10 Paul Anderson for Vagana (14); 15 Karl Pratt for Paul (23); 27 Rob Parker for Anderson (24); 19 Jamie Langley for Peacock (32); Paul for Withers (ht); Peacock for Radford (48); Radford for Swann (54); Vagana for Parker (56); Parker for Fielden (63); Fielden for Vagana (67); Swann for Langley (68).
Tries: Vainikolo (7), Hape (43); **Goals:** Deacon 0/2.
RHINOS: 21 Richard Mathers; 18 Mark Calderwood; 5 Chev Walker; 4 Keith Senior; 22 Marcus Bai; 13 Kevin Sinfield (C); 6 Danny McGuire; 19 Danny Ward; 9 Matt Diskin; 8 Ryan Bailey; 3 Chris McKenna; 29 Ali Lauitiiti; 11 David Furner. Subs: 16 Willie Poching for Furner (19); 10 Barrie McDermott for Ward (22); Ward for Bailey (29); 7 Rob Burrow for Lauitiiti (30); Bailey for McDermott (41); 20 Jamie Jones-Buchanan for McKenna (48); Lauitiiti for Ward (50); Furner for Sinfield (60); McKenna for Poching (63); Sinfield for Diskin (67); Poching for McKenna (72); Ward for Bailey (73).
Tries: Diskin (15), McGuire (75); **Goals:** Sinfield 4/4.
Rugby Leaguer & League Express Men of the Match: *Bulls:* Lesley Vainikolo; *Rhinos:* Richard Mathers.
Penalty count: 5-5; **Half-time:** 4-10; **Referee:** Steve Ganson (St Helens); **Attendance:** 65,547 *(at Old Trafford, Manchester).*

2005

NATIONAL LEAGUE ONE GRAND FINAL

Sunday 9th October 2005

CASTLEFORD TIGERS 36 WHITEHAVEN 8

TIGERS: 1 Michael Platt; 2 Waine Pryce; 3 Michael Shenton; 4 Jon Hepworth; 5 Damien Blanch; 6 Brad Davis; 7 Andrew Henderson; 8 Adam Watene; 9 Aaron Smith; 10 Richard Fletcher; 11 Tom Haughey; 12 Steve Crouch; 13 Deon Bird. Subs (all used): 14 Paul Handforth; 15 Craig Huby; 16 Adrian Vowles; 17 Frank Watene.
Tries: Huby (22), Crouch (24), Blanch (26), Davis (33, 45), Haughey (52); **Goals:** Fletcher 2/3, Huby 3/4, Hepworth 1/1.
WHITEHAVEN: 1 Gary Broadbent; 2 Craig Calvert; 3 David Seeds; 4 Mick Nanyn; 5 Wesley Wilson; 6 Leroy Joe; 7 Joel Penny; 8 Ryan Tandy; 9 Carl Sice; 10 David Fatialofa; 11 Spencer Miller; 12 Howard Hill; 13 Aaron Lester. Subs (all used): 14 Carl Rudd; 15 Aaron Summers; 16 Craig Chambers; 17 Marc Jackson.
Tries: Seeds (56), Calvert (78); **Goals:** Nanyn 0/2.
Sin bin: Joe (16) - late tackle on Davis.
On report: Joe (16) - late tackle on Davis; Sice (40) - alleged biting.
Rugby Leaguer & League Express Men of the Match: *Tigers:* Brad Davis; *Whitehaven:* Wesley Wilson.
Penalty count: 4-9; **Half-time:** 26-0;
Referee: Steve Ganson (St Helens);
Attendance: 13,300 *(at Halton Stadium, Widnes).*

SUPER LEAGUE GRAND FINAL

Saturday 15th October 2005

BRADFORD BULLS 15 LEEDS RHINOS 6

BULLS: 6 Michael Withers; 3 Leon Pryce; 13 Ben Harris; 4 Shontayne Hape; 5 Lesley Vainikolo; 18 Iestyn Harris; 7 Paul Deacon; 12 Jamie Peacock (C); 9 Ian Henderson; 29 Stuart Fielden; 16 Paul Johnson; 10 Brad Meyers; 11 Lee Radford. Subs (all used): 24 Adrian Morley for Johnson (5); 19 Jamie Langley for Peacock (24); 8 Joe Vagana for Fielden (24); Johnson for Radford (24); 1 Robbie Paul for Henderson (31); Peacock for Vagana (45); Fielden for Morley (49); Henderson for Paul (54); Radford for Meyers (60); Morley for Peacock (62); Meyers for Langley (73); Peacock for Johnson (74).
Tries: L Pryce (29), Vainikolo (53); **Goals:** Deacon 3/5;
Field goal: I Harris.
RHINOS: 1 Richard Mathers; 2 Mark Calderwood; 3 Chev Walker; 12 Chris McKenna; 5 Marcus Bai; 6 Danny McGuire; 7 Rob Burrow; 8 Ryan Bailey; 14 Andrew Dunemann; 15 Danny Ward; 20 Gareth Ellis; 16 Willie Poching; 13 Kevin Sinfield (C). Subs (all used): 10 Barrie McDermott for Ward (17); 11 Ali Lauitiiti for Poching (21); 18 Jamie Jones-Buchanan for Bailey (31); Ward for McDermott (34); 9 Matt Diskin for Ellis (48); Poching for Lauitiiti (48); McDermott for Ward (54); Ellis for Poching (54); Lauitiiti for McDermott (61); Poching for Dunemann (65); Ward for Jones-Buchanan (68); Dunemann for Ellis (71).
Try: McGuire (22); **Goals:** Sinfield 1/2.
Rugby Leaguer & League Express Men of the Match: *Bulls:* Leon Pryce; *Rhinos:* Danny McGuire.
Penalty count: 6-8; **Half-time:** 8-6; **Referee:** Ashley Klein (Keighley); **Attendance:** 65,537 *(at Old Trafford, Manchester).*

2004...Ian Knott and Tommy Martyn lift the NL1 Trophy

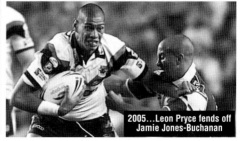

2005...Leon Pryce fends off Jamie Jones-Buchanan

2006

NATIONAL LEAGUE TWO GRAND FINAL

Sunday 8th October 2006

SHEFFIELD EAGLES 35 SWINTON LIONS 10

EAGLES: 1 Johnny Woodcock; 5 Greg Hurst; 4 Jimmy Walker; 3 James Ford; 2 Rob Worrincy; 6 Brendon Lindsay; 7 Gavin Brown; 8 Jack Howieson; 9 Paul Pickering; 10 Mitchell Stringer; 11 Andy Hay; 12 Dale Holdstock; 13 Andy Smith. Subs (all used): 14 Craig Poucher; 15 Martin Ostler; 16 Sean Dickinson; 17 Waisale Sovatabua.
Tries: Worrincy (21, 43), Lindsay (38), Woodcock (39), Walker (51), Hay (60); **Goals:** Woodcock 5/6;
Field goal: G Brown.
LIONS: 1 Wayne English; 2 Andy Saywell; 3 Darren Woods; 4 David Alstead; 5 Marlon Billy; 6 Martin Moana; 7 Chris Hough; 8 Bruce Johnson; 9 Phil Wood; 10 Dave Newton; 11 Kris Smith; 12 Ian Sinfield; 13 Lee Marsh. Subs (all used): 14 Liam McGovern; 15 Chris Morley; 16 Danny Aboushakra; 17 Ian Parry.
Tries: Saywell (35), Alstead (74); **Goals:** McGovern 1/2.
Rugby Leaguer & League Express Men of the Match:
Eagles: Johnny Woodcock; *Lions:* Wayne English.
Penalty count: 3-4; **Half-time:** 16-4;
Referee: Peter Taberner (Wigan).
(at Halliwell Jones Stadium, Warrington).

Dewsbury Rams were National League Two Champions in 2006. This game was to determine who took the second promotion place.

NATIONAL LEAGUE ONE GRAND FINAL

Sunday 8th October 2006

HULL KINGSTON ROVERS 29 WIDNES VIKINGS 16

ROVERS: 1 Ben Cockayne; 2 Leroy Rivett; 3 Gareth Morton; 4 Jon Goddard; 5 Byron Ford; 6 Scott Murrell; 7 James Webster; 8 Makali Aizue; 9 Ben Fisher; 10 David Tangata-Toa; 11 Iain Morrison; 12 Michael Smith; 13 Tommy Gallagher. Subs (all used): 14 Pat Weisner; 15 Dwayne Barker; 16 Jason Netherton; 17 Dave Wilson.
Tries: Ford (6), Goddard (18, 36), Murrell (24), Weisner (43); **Goals:** Morton 4/6; **Field goal:** Murrell.
VIKINGS: 1 Gavin Dodd; 2 Damien Blanch; 3 Sean Gleeson; 4 Daryl Cardiss; 5 John Kirkpatrick; 6 Dennis Moran; 7 Ian Watson; 8 Terry O'Connor; 9 Mark Smith; 10 Barrie McDermott; 11 Mick Cassidy; 12 David Allen; 13 Bob Beswick. Subs (all used): 14 Aaron Summers; 15 Oliver Wilkes; 16 Jordan James; 17 Ryan Tandy.
Tries: Dodd (32), Tandy (57), Blanch (70); **Goals:** Dodd 2/3.
Rugby Leaguer & League Express Men of the Match:
Rovers: James Webster; *Vikings:* Mark Smith.
Penalty count: 8-5; **Half-time:** 22-4;
Referee: Phil Bentham (Warrington);
Attendance: 13,024 *(at Halliwell Jones Stadium, Warrington).*

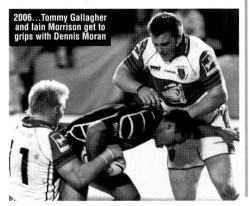
2006...Tommy Gallagher and Iain Morrison get to grips with Dennis Moran

SUPER LEAGUE GRAND FINAL

Saturday 14th October 2006

HULL FC 4 ST HELENS 26

HULL: 1 Shaun Briscoe; 14 Motu Tony; 4 Sid Domic; 3 Kirk Yeaman; 5 Gareth Raynor; 13 Paul Cooke; 7 Richard Horne; 8 Ewan Dowes; 9 Richard Swain (C); 10 Garreth Carvell; 11 Lee Radford; 12 Shayne McMenemy; 24 Danny Washbrook. Subs: 15 Paul King for Carvell (17); 19 Graeme Horne for Radford (23); 26 Scott Wheeldon for Dowes (27); 6 Richard Whiting for McMenemy (29); Dowes for Wheeldon (49); Carvell for King (49); Radford for G Horne (51); McMenemy for Whiting (54); King for Carvell (68); Wheeldon for Dowes (73); Whiting for Tony (76); G Horne for Radford (77).
Try: Domic (24); **Goals:** Cooke 0/1.
SAINTS: 1 Paul Wellens; 2 Ade Gardner; 3 Jamie Lyon; 4 Willie Talau; 5 Francis Meli; 6 Leon Pryce; 7 Sean Long (C); 17 Paul Anderson; 9 Keiron Cunningham; 10 Jason Cayless; 11 Lee Gilmour; 12 Jon Wilkin; 16 Jason Hooper. Subs: 23 Maurie Fa'asavalu for P Anderson (12); 19 James Graham for Cayless (25); 15 Mike Bennett for Fa'asavalu (28); 14 James Roby for Cunningham (31); P Anderson for Wilkin (33); Cunningham for Gilmour (49); Cayless for P Anderson (52); Wilkin for Hooper (56); Fa'asavalu for Cayless (58); Gilmour for Graham (66); Cayless for Fa'asavalu (72); P Anderson for Wilkin (75).
Tries: Meli (17), Pryce (29), Gardner (52), Cunningham (62); **Goals:** Lyon 3/5.
Rugby Leaguer & League Express Men of the Match:
Hull: Shaun Briscoe; *Saints:* Paul Wellens.
Penalty count: 4-2; **Half-time:** 4-10;
Referee: Karl Kirkpatrick (Warrington);
Attendance: 72,582 *(at Old Trafford, Manchester).*

2007

NATIONAL LEAGUE TWO GRAND FINAL

Sunday 7th October 2007

FEATHERSTONE ROVERS 24 OLDHAM 6

ROVERS: 1 Loz Wildbore; 2 Danny Kirmond; 3 Jon Whittle; 4 Wayne McHugh; 5 Ade Adebisi; 6 Andy Kain; 7 Paul Handforth; 8 Gareth Handford; 9 Joe McLocklan; 10 Stuart Dickens; 11 Jamie Field; 12 Richard Blakeway; 13 Tom Haughey. Subs (all used): 14 Jamie Benn; 15 Ian Tonks; 16 James Houston; 17 Gavin Swinson.
Tries: McHugh (39, 49), Handforth (46); **Goals:** Dickens 5/6;
Field goals: Wildbore (66, 70).
Dismissal: Blakeway (64) – head butt on Roberts.
OLDHAM: 1 Gareth Langley; 2 Byron Ford; 3 Craig Littler; 4 Adam Hughes; 5 Lucas Onyango; 6 Neil Roden; 7 James Coyle; 8 Anthony Tonks; 9 Simeon Hoyle; 10 Richard Mervill; 11 Ian Sinfield; 12 Robert Roberts; 13 Geno Costin. Subs (all used): 14 Ian Hodson; 15 Alex Wilkinson; 16 Said Tamghart; 17 Matty Brooks.
Try: Hughes (31); **Goals:** Langley 1/2.
Rugby Leaguer & League Express Men of the Match:
Rovers: Paul Handforth; *Oldham:* Robert Roberts.
Penalty count: 9-5; **Half-time:** 10-6; **Referee:** Gareth Hewer.
(at Headingley Carnegie, Leeds).

Celtic Crusaders were National League Two Champions in 2007. This game was to determine who took the second promotion place.

NATIONAL LEAGUE ONE GRAND FINAL

Sunday 7th October 2007

CASTLEFORD TIGERS 42 WIDNES VIKINGS 10

TIGERS: 1 Stuart Donlan; 2 Danny Williams; 3 Michael Shenton; 4 Ryan McGoldrick; 5 Kirk Dixon; 6 Anthony Thackeray; 7 Danny Brough; 8 Liam Higgins; 9 Andrew Henderson; 10 Awen Guttenbeil; 11 Joe Westerman; 12 Ryan Clayton; 13 Peter Lupton. Subs (all used): 14 Mark Leafa; 15 Chris Charles; 16 Michael Wainwright; 17 Ryan Boyle.
Tries: Wainwright (20), McGoldrick (29), Guttenbeil (44, 76), M Shenton (52), Westerman (62), Clayton (66);
Goals: Brough 6/9; **Field goals:** Brough (25, 55).
VIKINGS: 1 Scott Grix; 2 Damien Blanch; 3 Toa Kohe-Love; 4 Mick Nanyn; 5 Gavin Dodd; 6 Dennis Moran; 7 Joel Penny; 8 Mick Cassidy; 9 Mark Smith; 10 Oliver Wilkes; 11 Joel Tomkins; 12 Paul Noone; 13 Bob Beswick. Subs (all used): 14 Aaron Summers; 15 Jordan James; 16 Ian Webster; 17 Lee Doran.
Tries: Nanyn (35), Wilkes (69); **Goals:** Nanyn 1/2.
Rugby Leaguer & League Express Men of the Match:
Tigers: Danny Brough; *Vikings:* Scott Grix.
Penalty count: 7-2; **Half-time:** 13-4; **Referee:** Phil Bentham;
Attendance: 20,814 *(at Headingley Carnegie, Leeds).*

SUPER LEAGUE GRAND FINAL

Saturday 13th October 2007

LEEDS RHINOS 33 ST HELENS 6

RHINOS: 1 Brent Webb; 5 Lee Smith; 3 Clinton Toopi; 4 Keith Senior; 2 Scott Donald; 6 Danny McGuire; 7 Rob Burrow; 8 Kylie Leuluai; 9 Matt Diskin; 10 Jamie Peacock; 11 Jamie Jones-Buchanan; 12 Gareth Ellis; 13 Kevin Sinfield (C). Subs (all used): 14 Ali Lauitiiti for Diskin (23); 16 Ryan Bailey for Leuluai (18); 18 Ian Kirke for Jones-Buchanan (33); 22 Carl Ablett for Kirke (57); Leuluai for Bailey (55); Jones-Buchanan for Lauitiiti (60); Diskin for Ablett (63); Kirke for Leuluai (65); Bailey for Kirke (76).
Tries: Webb (19), Lauitiiti (50), Donald (52), Smith (69), Jones-Buchanan (80); **Goals:** Sinfield 6/7;
Field goal: Burrow (55).
SAINTS: 1 Paul Wellens; 2 Ade Gardner; 3 Matt Gidley; 4 Willie Talau; 5 Francis Meli; 6 Leon Pryce; 7 Sean Long; 8 Nick Fozzard; 9 Keiron Cunningham (C); 10 Jason Cayless; 11 Lee Gilmour; 30 Chris Flannery; 12 Jon Wilkin. Subs (all used): 17 James Graham for Cayless (15); 14 James Roby for Cunningham (23); 23 Maurie Fa'asavalu for Fozzard (23); 15 Mike Bennett for Wilkin (31); Cayless for Fa'asavalu (34); Cunningham for Flannery (51); Wilkin for Bennett (55); Fa'asavalu for Cayless (55); Fozzard for Graham (57); Cayless for Fozzard (68); Graham for Fa'asavalu (68); Bennett for Gilmour (72).
Try: Roby (27); **Goals:** Long 1/2.
Rugby Leaguer & League Express Men of the Match:
Rhinos: Rob Burrow; *Saints:* Sean Long.
Penalty count: 4-5; **Half-time:** 8-6; **Referee:** Ashley Klein;
Attendance: 71,352 *(at Old Trafford, Manchester).*

2007...Ryan McGoldrick shows his delight at scoring

2008

NATIONAL LEAGUE TWO GRAND FINAL

Sunday 28th September 2008

DONCASTER 18 OLDHAM 10

DONCASTER: 1 Zebastian Luisi; 2 Dean Colton; 3 Andreas Bauer; 4 Shaun Leaf; 5 Wayne Reittie; 6 Kyle Wood; 7 Luke Gale; 8 Nathan Freer; 9 Corey Lawrie; 10 Alex Benson; 11 Peter Green; 12 Craig Lawton; 13 Josh Weeden. Subs (all used): 14 Kyle Briggs; 15 Chris Buttery; 16 Michael Haley; 17 Mark Castle.
Tries: Buttery (44), Gale (49), Briggs (73); **Goals:** Gale 3/4.
OLDHAM: 1 Paul O'Connor; 2 Gareth Langley; 3 Marcus St Hilaire; 4 Mick Nanyn; 5 Daryl Cardiss; 6 Phil Joseph; 7 James Coyle; 8 Adam Robinson; 9 Matty Brooks; 10 Richard Mervill; 11 Tommy Goulden; 12 Danny Halliwell; 13 Robert Roberts. Subs (all used): 14 Ian Hodson; 15 Luke Menzies; 16 Chris Baines; 17 Said Tamghart.
Tries: Hodson (34), Nanyn (62); **Goals:** Nanyn 1/4.
Rugby Leaguer & League Express Men of the Match:
Doncaster: Luke Gale; *Oldham:* Adam Robinson.
Penalty count: 7-8; **Half-time:** 2-6; **Referee:** Ronnie Laughton. *(at Halliwell Jones Stadium, Warrington).*

Gateshead Thunder were National League Two Champions in 2008. This game was to determine who took the second promotion place.

NATIONAL LEAGUE ONE GRAND FINAL

Sunday 28th September 2008

CELTIC CRUSADERS 18 SALFORD CITY REDS 36
(after extra-time)

CRUSADERS: 1 Tony Duggan; 2 Luke Dyer; 3 Josh Hannay; 4 Mark Dalle Cort; 5 Anthony Blackwood; 6 Damien Quinn; 7 Jace Van Dijk; 8 Jordan James; 9 Neil Budworth; 10 David Tangata-Toa; 11 Chris Beasley; 12 Darren Mapp; 13 Terry Martin. Subs (all used): 14 Aaron Summers; 15 Ian Webster; 16 Mark Lennon; 17 Neale Wyatt.
Tries: Blackwood (38), Dyer (50), J James (54), Tangata-Toa (66); **Goals:** Hannay 0/1, Lennon 1/3.
CITY REDS: 1 Karl Fitzpatrick; 2 Matt Gardner; 3 Stuart Littler; 4 John Wilshere; 5 Paul White; 6 Robbie Paul; 7 Richard Myler; 8 Paul Highton; 9 Malcolm Alker; 10 Craig Stapleton; 11 Ian Sibbit; 12 Luke Adamson; 13 Jordan Turner. Subs (all used): 14 Stefan Ratchford; 15 Steve Bannister; 16 Lee Jewitt; 17 Phil Leuluai.
Tries: White (5, 86), Gardner (26), Fitzpatrick (63), Sibbit (83), Myler (99); **Goals:** Wilshere 6/7.
Rugby Leaguer & League Express Men of the Match:
Crusaders: Tony Duggan; *City Reds:* John Wilshere.
Penalty count: 5-5; **Half-time:** 4-10; **Full-time:** 18-18;
Referee: Ben Thaler; **Attendance:** 7,104
(at Halliwell Jones Stadium, Warrington).

SUPER LEAGUE GRAND FINAL

Saturday 4th October 2008

LEEDS RHINOS 24 ST HELENS 16

RHINOS: 5 Lee Smith; 22 Ryan Hall; 19 Carl Ablett; 4 Keith Senior; 2 Scott Donald; 6 Danny McGuire; 7 Rob Burrow; 8 Kylie Leuluai; 9 Matt Diskin; 10 Jamie Peacock; 11 Jamie Jones-Buchanan; 12 Gareth Ellis; 13 Kevin Sinfield (C). Subs (all used): 17 Nick Scruton; 14 Ali Lauitiiti; 18 Ian Kirke; 16 Ryan Bailey.
Tries: Smith (23), Hall (37), McGuire (49, 63);
Goals: Sinfield 4/4.
SAINTS: 1 Paul Wellens; 2 Ade Gardner; 3 Matt Gidley; 4 Willie Talau; 5 Francis Meli; 6 Leon Pryce; 7 Sean Long; 18 Bryn Hargreaves; 9 Keiron Cunningham (C); 17 James Graham; 11 Lee Gilmour; 12 Jon Wilkin; 16 Chris Flannery. Subs (all used): 8 Nick Fozzard; 21 Paul Clough; 14 James Roby; 23 Maurie Fa'asavalu.
Tries: Graham (6), Gidley (43), Gardner (59); **Goals:** Long 2/3.
Rugby Leaguer & League Express Men of the Match:
Rhinos: Jamie Peacock; *Saints:* Sean Long.
Penalty count: 6-8; **Half-time:** 12-6; **Referee:** Ashley Klein;
Attendance: 68,810 *(at Old Trafford, Manchester).*

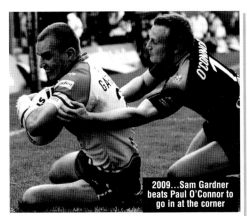

2009...Sam Gardner beats Paul O'Connor to go in at the corner

2009... Andy Bracek brings down Rob Worrincy

2009

CHAMPIONSHIP ONE GRAND FINAL

Sunday 4th October 2009

KEIGHLEY COUGARS 28 OLDHAM 26

COUGARS: 1 George Rayner; 2 Sam Gardner; 3 Dan Potter; 4 Oliver Pursglove; 5 Gavin Duffy; 6 Jon Presley; 7 Danny Jones; 17 Scott Law; 14 Jamaine Wray; 8 Andy Shickell; 11 Will Cartledge; 18 Greg Nicholson; 13 Carl Hughes. Subs (all used): 21 Ryan Smith; 28 Ryan Benjafield; 9 James Feather; 16 Brendan Rawlins.
Tries: Gardner (24), Jones (42, 50), Presley (63), Pursglove (67); **Goals:** Jones 4/5.
OLDHAM: 4 Paul Reilly; 21 Lucas Onyango; 24 Marcus St Hilaire; 22 Phil Joseph; 1 Paul O'Connor; 18 Neil Roden; 7 Thomas Coyle; 15 Jason Boults; 30 Martin Roden; 16 Wayne Kerr; 23 Chris Baines; 12 Tommy Goulden; 28 Craig Lawton. Subs (all used): 10 Jamie I'Anson; 25 Luke Menzies; 27 Matt Ashe; 29 Ben Heaton.
Tries: Menzies (35, 76), N Roden (54), St Hilaire (70), Kerr (78); **Goals:** Baines 3/4, Ashe 0/1.
Rugby Leaguer & League Express Men of the Match: *Cougars:* Danny Jones; *Oldham:* Luke Menzies.
Penalty count: 9-2; **Half-time:** 4-6; **Referee:** Ronnie Laughton. *(at Halliwell Jones Stadium, Warrington).*

Dewsbury Rams were Championship One Champions in 2009. This game was to determine who took the second promotion place.

CHAMPIONSHIP GRAND FINAL

Sunday 4th October 2009

BARROW RAIDERS 26 HALIFAX 18

RAIDERS: 1 Gary Broadbent; 36 Andy Ballard; 32 Andreas Bauer; 4 Liam Harrison; 5 James Nixon; 24 Jamie Rooney; 31 James Coyle; 34 Rob Roberts; 9 Andy Ellis; 8 Brett McDermott; 33 Dave Allen; 22 Ned Catic; 26 Zebastian Luisi. Subs (all used): 15 Chris Young; 13 Andy Bracek; 35 Danny Halliwell; 14 Paul Noone.
Tries: Harrison (33), Ballard (37), Allen (61), Bauer (66, 78); **Goals:** Rooney 3/5.
HALIFAX: 4 Shad Royston; 5 James Haley; 15 Mark Roberts; 2 Lee Paterson; 23 Rob Worrincy; 19 Mick Govin; 7 Ben Black; 21 Neil Cherryholme; 9 Sean Penkywicz; 22 David Wrench; 11 David Larder; 27 Steve Bannister; 12 Paul Smith. Subs (all used): 13 Bob Beswick; 14 Mark Gleeson; 16 Said Tamghart; 26 Dominic Maloney.
Tries: Haley (12), Royston (31), Black (45), Govin (70); **Goals:** Paterson 1/5.
Rugby Leaguer & League Express Men of the Match: *Raiders:* Gary Broadbent; *Halifax:* Mick Govin.
Penalty count: 8-5; **Half-time:** 10-10; **Referee:** Phil Bentham; **Attendance:** 11,398 *(at Halliwell Jones Stadium, Warrington).*

SUPER LEAGUE GRAND FINAL

Saturday 10th October 2009

LEEDS RHINOS 18 ST HELENS 10

RHINOS: 1 Brent Webb; 2 Scott Donald; 3 Lee Smith; 4 Keith Senior; 5 Ryan Hall; 6 Danny McGuire; 7 Rob Burrow; 8 Kylie Leuluai; 14 Matt Diskin; 10 Jamie Peacock; 11 Jamie Jones-Buchanan; 18 Carl Ablett; 13 Kevin Sinfield (C). Subs (all used): 16 Ryan Bailey for Leuluai (19); 19 Luke Burgess for Peacock (29); 17 Ian Kirke for Jones-Buchanan (29); 12 Ali Lauitiiti for Ablett (29); Jones-Buchanan for Lauitiiti (36); Peacock for Burgess (46); Leuluai for Bailey (53); Ablett for Kirke (57); Burgess for Diskin (62); Bailey for Leuluai (67); Diskin for Burgess (69); Kirke for Jones-Buchanan (76).
Tries: Diskin (30), Smith (37, 72); **Goals:** Sinfield 2/4;
Field goals: Sinfield (42), Burrow (78).
SAINTS: 1 Paul Wellens; 2 Ade Gardner; 3 Matt Gidley; 18 Kyle Eastmond; 5 Francis Meli; 6 Leon Pryce; 7 Sean Long; 10 James Graham; 9 Keiron Cunningham (C); 16 Tony Puletua; 12 Jon Wilkin; 11 Lee Gilmour; 13 Chris Flannery. Subs (all used): 14 James Roby for Cunningham (25); 15 Bryn Hargreaves for Puletua (24); 17 Paul Clough for Gilmour (31); 23 Maurie Fa'asavalu for Graham (31); Graham for Fa'asavalu (48); Puletua for Hargreaves (50); Gilmour for Wilkin (55); Cunningham for Clough (61); Wilkin for Roby (65); Roby for Flannery (73).
Try: Eastmond (13); **Goals:** Eastmond 3/3.
Rugby Leaguer & League Express Men of the Match: *Rhinos:* Kevin Sinfield; *Saints:* James Graham.
Penalty count: 8-7; **Half-time:** 8-8; **Referee:** Steve Ganson; **Attendance:** 63,259 *(at Old Trafford, Manchester).*

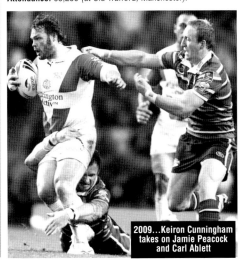

2009...Keiron Cunningham takes on Jamie Peacock and Carl Ablett

SUPER LEAGUE 2011 FIXTURES

ROUND 1 - Millennium Magic

Saturday, 12 February
Huddersfield Giants v Warrington Wolves 13:00
Catalans Dragons v Harlequins 15:00
Castleford Tigers v Wakefield Trinity Wildcats ..17:00
St Helens v Wigan Warriors 19:00
Sunday, 13 February
Crusaders v Salford City Reds 12:00
Bradford Bulls v Leeds Rhinos......................14:00
Hull FC v Hull Kingston Rovers 16:00

ROUND 2

Friday, 18 February
Hull FC v Leeds Rhinos 20:00
Salford City Reds v St Helens 20:00
Saturday, 19 February
Catalans Dragons v Wakefield Trinity Wildcats ..18:30
Harlequins v Crusaders 15:00
Sunday, 20 February
Bradford Bulls v Wigan Warriors 15:00
Castleford Tigers v Huddersfield Giants 15:30
Warrington Wolves v Hull Kingston Rovers 15:00

ROUND 3

Friday, 25 February
Crusaders v Bradford Bulls 20:00
Leeds Rhinos v Harlequins............................20:00
St Helens v Warrington Wolves 20:00
Sunday, 27 February
Huddersfield Giants v Hull FC.......................15:00
Hull Kingston Rovers v Catalans Dragons 15:00
Wakefield Trinity Wildcats v Salford City Reds..15:30
Wigan Warriors v Castleford Tigers
(date & KO TBC)

WORLD CLUB CHALLENGE

Sunday, 27 February
Wigan Warriors v St George Illawarra Dragons ..19:15
(at DW Stadium, Wigan)

ROUND 4

Friday, 4 March
Hull FC v Crusaders 20:00
Salford City Reds v Wigan Warriors...............20:00
Saturday, 5 March
Catalans Dragons v St Helens 18:30
Harlequins v Huddersfield Giants 15:00
Sunday, 6 March
Bradford Bulls v Wakefield Trinity Wildcats 15:00
Castleford Tigers v Hull Kingston Rovers.......15:30
Warrington Wolves v Leeds Rhinos 15:00

ROUND 5

Friday, 11 March
Leeds Rhinos v Salford City Reds 20:00
St Helens v Harlequins 20:00
Wigan Warriors v Hull FC..............................20:00
Sunday, 13 March
Castleford Tigers v Catalans Dragons 15:30
Huddersfield Giants v Bradford Bulls 15:00
Hull Kingston Rovers v Crusaders 15:00
Wakefield Trinity Wildcats v Warrington Wolves..15:30

ROUND 6

Friday, 18 March
Crusaders v Catalans Dragons 20:00
Hull FC v Wakefield Trinity Wildcats 20:00
Leeds Rhinos v St Helens 20:00
Salford City Reds v Hull Kingston Rovers 20:00
Sunday, 20 March
Bradford Bulls v Castleford Tigers 15:00
Huddersfield Giants v Wigan Warriors 15:00
Warrington Wolves v Harlequins 15:00

ROUND 7

Friday, 25 March
St Helens v Bradford Bulls 20:00
Wigan Warriors v Warrington Wolves 20:00
Saturday, 26 March
Catalans Dragons v Salford City Reds 18:30
Harlequins v Hull FC.....................................15:00
Sunday, 27 March
Castleford Tigers v Crusaders 15:30
Hull Kingston Rovers v Huddersfield Giants ..15:00
Wakefield Trinity Wildcats v Leeds Rhinos......15:30

ROUND 8

Friday, 1 April
Hull FC v Castleford Tigers 20:00
Leeds Rhinos v Wigan Warriors.....................20:00
Salford City Reds v Crusaders 20:00
St Helens v Hull Kingston Rovers 20:00
Sunday, 3 April
Bradford Bulls v Harlequins 15:00
Huddersfield Giants v Wakefield Trinity Wildcats ..15:00
Warrington Wolves v Catalans Dragons 15:00

ROUND 9

Friday, 8 April
Crusaders v St Helens 20:00
Hull FC v Bradford Bulls 20:00
Wigan Warriors v Catalans Dragons 20:00
Sunday, 10 April
Castleford Tigers v Salford City Reds.............15:30
Huddersfield Giants v Warrington Wolves 15:00
Hull Kingston Rovers v Leeds Rhinos 15:00
Wakefield Trinity Wildcats v Harlequins 15:30

ROUND 10

Friday, 15 April
Harlequins v Castleford Tigers ....KO TBC
Hull Kingston Rovers v Wigan Warriors ......KO TBC
Leeds Rhinos v Huddersfield Giants 20:00
Salford City Reds v Bradford Bulls.................20:00
St Helens v Wakefield Trinity Wildcats 20:00
Warrington Wolves v Crusaders ....KO TBC
Saturday, 16 April
Catalans Dragons v Hull FC 18:30

ROUND 11

Thursday, 21 April
Bradford Bulls v Leeds Rhinos ....KO TBC
Friday, 22 April
Castleford Tigers v Wakefield Trinity Wildcats..KO TBC
Crusaders v Huddersfield Giants..................KO TBC
Harlequins v Catalans Dragons ....KO TBC
Hull FC v Hull Kingston Rovers ....KO TBC
Salford City Reds v Warrington Wolves ......KO TBC
Wigan Warriors v St Helens ....KO TBC

ROUND 12

Monday, 25 April
Catalans Dragons v Bradford Bulls ....KO TBC
Hull Kingston Rovers v Harlequins...............KO TBC
Leeds Rhinos v Crusaders ....KO TBC
St Helens v Castleford Tigers ....KO TBC
Wakefield Trinity Wildcats v Wigan Warriors ..KO TBC
Warrington Wolves v Hull FC ....KO TBC
Tuesday, 26 April
Huddersfield Giants v Salford City Reds ......KO TBC

ROUND 13

Saturday, 30 April
Catalans Dragons v Huddersfield Giants 18:30
Sunday, 1 May
Bradford Bulls v Warrington Wolves 15:00
Castleford Tigers v Leeds Rhinos..................15:30
Crusaders v Wigan Warriors ....KO TBC
Harlequins v Salford City Reds ....KO TBC
Hull FC v St Helens ....KO TBC
Wakefield Trinity Wildcats v Hull Kingston Rovers ..15:30

CHALLENGE CUP ROUND 4

Weekend of 6/7/8 May

ROUND 14

Friday, 13 May
Crusaders v Wakefield Trinity Wildcats 20:00
Leeds Rhinos v Catalans Dragons 20:00
Salford City Reds v Hull FC 20:00
Wigan Warriors v Harlequins ....KO TBC
Sunday, 15 May
Huddersfield Giants v St Helens....................15:00
Hull Kingston Rovers v Bradford Bulls............15:00
Warrington Wolves v Castleford Tigers 15:00

CHALLENGE CUP ROUND 5

Weekend of 20/21/22 May

ROUND 15

Friday, 27 May
Hull FC v Huddersfield Giants..........................20:00
Leeds Rhinos v Warrington Wolves 20:00
St Helens v Crusaders 20:00
Wigan Warriors v Hull Kingston Rovers.........20:00
Sunday, 29 May
Bradford Bulls v Salford City Reds..................15:00
Castleford Tigers v Harlequins 15:30
Wakefield Trinity Wildcats v Catalans Dragons..15:30

ROUND 16

Friday, 3 June
Crusaders v Warrington Wolves......................20:00
Salford City Reds v Wakefield Trinity Wildcats..20:00
St Helens v Leeds Rhinos 20:00
Saturday, 4 June
Catalans Dragons v Wigan Warriors
(venue & KO TBC)
Harlequins v Bradford Bulls 15:00
Sunday, 5 June
Huddersfield Giants v Castleford Tigers 15:00
Hull Kingston Rovers v Hull FC 15:00

ROUND 17

Sunday, 12 June
Bradford Bulls v St Helens 15:00
Castleford Tigers v Wigan Warriors 15:30
Catalans Dragons v Crusaders
(date & KO TBC)
Hull FC v Harlequins ....KO TBC
Leeds Rhinos v Hull Kingston Rovers..........KO TBC
Wakefield Trinity Wildcats v Huddersfield Giants..15:30
Warrington Wolves v Salford City Reds 15:00

ROUND 18

Friday, 17 June
Crusaders v Leeds Rhinos 20:00
Salford City Reds v Castleford Tigers..............20:00
St Helens v Wigan Warriors 20:00
Saturday, 18 June
Harlequins v Wakefield Trinity Wildcats 15:00
Sunday, 19 June
Bradford Bulls v Hull FC...................................15:00
Huddersfield Giants v Catalans Dragons 15:00
Hull Kingston Rovers v Warrington Wolves 15:00

ROUND 19

Friday, 24 June
Crusaders v Salford City Reds 20:00
Leeds Rhinos v Bradford Bulls........................20:00
Wigan Warriors v Huddersfield Giants 20:00
Saturday, 25 June
Catalans Dragons v Castleford Tigers 20:00
Harlequins v Hull Kingston Rovers..................15:00
Sunday, 26 June
Wakefield Trinity Wildcats v Hull FC................15:30
Warrington Wolves v St Helens 15:00

ROUND 20

Friday, 1 July
Salford City Reds v Harlequins........................20:00
St Helens v Hull FC...20:00
Wigan Warriors v Leeds Rhinos......................20:00
Sunday, 3 July
Bradford Bulls v Catalans Dragons 15:00
Castleford Tigers v Warrington Wolves 15:30
Huddersfield Giants v Crusaders.....................15:00
Hull Kingston Rovers v Wakefield Trinity Wildcats ..15:00

ROUND 21

Friday, 8 July
Crusaders v Hull Kingston Rovers 20:00
Hull FC v Salford City Reds 20:00
Saturday, 9 July
Catalans Dragons v Leeds Rhinos 20:00
Harlequins v Wigan Warriors 15:00
Sunday, 10 July
Castleford Tigers v Bradford Bulls 15:30
Wakefield Trinity Wildcats v St Helens 15:30
Warrington Wolves v Huddersfield Giants 15:00

ROUND 22

Friday, 15 July
Crusaders v Castleford Tigers 20:00
Leeds Rhinos v Hull FC 20:00
St Helens v Catalans Dragons 20:00
Wigan Warriors v Wakefield Trinity Wildcats ..20:00
Saturday, 16 July
Harlequins v Warrington Wolves 15:00
Sunday, 17 July
Bradford Bulls v Huddersfield Giants 15:00
Hull Kingston Rovers v Salford City Reds 15:00

CHALLENGE CUP QUARTER FINALS

Weekend of 22/23/24 July

ROUND 23

Friday, 29 July
Hull FC v Wigan Warriors................................20:00
Salford City Reds v Leeds Rhinos 20:00
Saturday, 30 July
Catalans Dragons v Harlequins 20:00
Sunday, 31 July
Castleford Tigers v St Helens 15:30
Huddersfield Giants v Hull Kingston Rovers ..15:00
Wakefield Trinity Wildcats v Crusaders 15:30
Warrington Wolves v Bradford Bulls 15:00

CHALLENGE CUP SEMI-FINALS

Weekend of 5/6/7 August

ROUND 24

Friday, 12 August
Crusaders v Harlequins 20:00
Hull FC v Catalans Dragons 20:00
Leeds Rhinos v Castleford Tigers....................20:00
St Helens v Huddersfield Giants......................20:00
Wigan Warriors v Salford City Reds................20:00
Sunday, 14 August
Bradford Bulls v Hull Kingston Rovers............15:00
Warrington Wolves v Wakefield Trinity Wildcats..15:00

ROUND 25

Friday, 19 August
Crusaders v Hull FC 20:00
Salford City Reds v Huddersfield Giants 20:00
Wigan Warriors v Bradford Bulls 20:00
Saturday, 20 August
Catalans Dragons v Warrington Wolves 20:00
Harlequins v Leeds Rhinos 15:00
Sunday, 21 August
Hull Kingston Rovers v St Helens 15:00
Wakefield Trinity Wildcats v Castleford Tigers ..15:30

CHALLENGE CUP FINAL

Saturday, 27 August
(at Wembley Stadium)

ROUND 26

Friday, 2 September
Leeds Rhinos v Wakefield Trinity Wildcats......20:00
St Helens v Salford City Reds 20:00
Saturday, 3 September
Catalans Dragons v Hull Kingston Rovers 20:00
Sunday, 4 September
Bradford Bulls v Crusaders 15:00
Castleford Tigers v Hull FC..............................15:30
Huddersfield Giants v Harlequins 15:00
Warrington Wolves v Wigan Warriors 15:00

ROUND 27

Friday, 9 September
Hull FC v Warrington Wolves 20:00
Salford City Reds v Catalans Dragons 20:00
Wigan Warriors v Crusaders 20:00
Saturday 10 September
Harlequins v St Helens 15:00
Sunday, 11 September
Huddersfield Giants v Leeds Rhinos 15:00
Hull Kingston Rovers v Castleford Tigers........15:00
Wakefield Trinity Wildcats v Bradford Bulls 15:30

PLAY-OFFS

Weekend of 16/17/18 September
Qualifying Play-offs
Elimination Play-offs

Weekend of 23/24/25 September
Preliminary Semi-finals

Weekend of 30 September, 1/2 October
Qualifying Semi-finals

GRAND FINAL

Saturday, 8 October
(at Old Trafford, Manchester)

2010 SEASON
Stats round-up

Pat
Richards

Michael
Dobson

TRIES *(play-offs in brackets, included in total)*

1	Pat Richards	Wigan Warriors	31 (2)
2	Darrell Goulding	Wigan Warriors	29 (4)
3	Chris Riley	Warrington Wolves	25 (0)
4	Leroy Cudjoe	Huddersfield Giants	24 (2)
	David Hodgson	Huddersfield Giants	24 (0)
	Ryan Hall	Leeds Rhinos	24 (1)
	Danny McGuire	Leeds Rhinos	24 (1)
	Chris Hicks	Warrington Wolves	24 (2)
9	Francis Meli	St Helens	23 (2)
10	Paul Wellens	St Helens	19 (3)
	Matt King	Warrington Wolves	19 (2)

GOALS *(play-offs in brackets, included in total)*

1	Pat Richards	Wigan Warriors	155 (19)
2	Michael Dobson	Hull Kingston Rovers	112 (7)
3	Kevin Sinfield	Leeds Rhinos	90 (6)
4	Joe Westerman	Castleford Tigers	82 (-)
5	Brett Hodgson	Huddersfield Giants	78 (12)
6	Danny Tickle	Hull FC	77 (0)
7	Kyle Eastmond	St Helens	63 (0)
8	Jamie Foster	St Helens	60 (14)
9	Clinton Schifcofske		
		Crusaders	54 (4)
10	Danny Orr	Harlequins	52 (-)

GOALS PERCENTAGE *(play-offs included)*

			G	Att	%
1	Kirk Dixon	Castleford Tigers	9	10	90
2	Clinton Schifcofske				
		Crusaders	54	62	87.1
3	Michael Dobson	Hull Kingston Rovers	112	129	86.8
4	Danny Tickle	Hull FC	77	92	83.6
5	Kevin Sinfield	Leeds Rhinos	90	108	83.3
6	Thomas Bosc	Catalans Dragons	42	51	82.3
7	Rob Purdham	Harlequins	12	15	80
	Stefan Ratchford	Salford City Reds	8	10	80
	Lee Smith	Leeds Rhinos	12	15	80
10	Ben Westwood	Warrington Wolves	47	60	78.3

(10 minimum attempts to qualify)

POINTS *(play-offs in brackets, included in total)*

			T	G	FG	Pts
1	Pat Richards	Wigan Warriors	31	155	0	434 (46)
2	Michael Dobson	Hull Kingston Rovers	11	112	3	271 (14)
3	Kevin Sinfield	Leeds Rhinos	4	90	4	200 (17)
4	Joe Westerman	Castleford Tigers	8	82	0	196 (-)
5	Kyle Eastmond	St Helens	15	63	2	188 (0)
6	Danny Tickle	Hull FC	4	77	1	171 (0)
7	Brett Hodgson	Huddersfield Giants	2	78	0	164 (24)
8	Jamie Foster	St Helens	7	60	0	148 (28)
9	Leroy Cudjoe	Huddersfield Giants	24	13	0	122 (8)
10	Danny Orr	Harlequins	4	52	0	120 (-)
	Clinton Schifcofske					
		Crusaders	3	54	0	120 (8)

CONSECUTIVE APPEARANCES
(Super League, including play-offs, and Challenge Cup)

1	Michael Dobson	Hull Kingston Rovers	76
2	Clint Newton	Hull Kingston Rovers	62
3	Luke Swain	Salford City Reds	58
	Pat Richards	Wigan Warriors	58
	Joel Tomkins	Wigan Warriors	58
6	Mark Bryant	Crusaders	50
7	Ryan Atkins	Warrington Wolves/	
		Wakefield Trinity Wildcats	45
8	Peter Fox	Hull Kingston Rovers	43
9	Oliver Wilkes	Harlequins/Wakefield Trinity Wildcats	42
	Michael Korkidas	Wakefield Trinity Wildcats	42

FINAL TABLE

	P	W	D	L	F	A	D	Pts
Wigan Warriors	27	22	0	5	922	411	511	44
St Helens	27	20	0	7	946	547	399	40
Warrington Wolves	27	20	0	7	885	488	397	40
Leeds Rhinos	27	17	1	9	725	561	164	35
Huddersfield Giants	27	16	1	10	758	439	319	33
Hull FC	27	16	0	11	569	584	-15	32
Hull Kingston Rovers	27	14	1	12	653	632	21	29
Crusaders	27	12	0	15	547	732	-185	24
Castleford Tigers	27	11	0	16	648	766	-118	22
Bradford Bulls	27	9	1	17	528	728	-200	19
Wakefield Trinity Wildcats	27	9	0	18	539	741	-202	18
Salford City Reds	27	8	0	19	448	857	-409	16
Harlequins	27	7	0	20	494	838	-344	14
Catalans Dragons	27	6	0	21	409	747	-338	12

AVERAGE ATTENDANCES

	2010 Avg	2009 Avg	Diff
Leeds Rhinos	15,237	15,312	-75
Wigan Warriors	15,177	13,695	+1,482
Hull FC	14,014	13,226	+788
St Helens	11,569	11,027	+542
Warrington Wolves	10,738	9,228	+1,510
Bradford Bulls	8,436	9,677	-1,241
Hull Kingston Rovers	8,234	8,501	-267
Huddersfield Giants	7,233	7,641	-408
Catalans Dragons	6,814	9,104	-2,290
Castleford Tigers	6,616	7,490	-874
Wakefield Trinity Wildcats	5,984	5,891	+93
Crusaders	4,621	3,603	+1,018
		(Celtic Crusaders)	
Salford City Reds	4,166	4,390	-224
Harlequins	3,380	3,436	-56
2010 Average	8,730		
2009 Average	8,730		
Difference	0		

BEST ATTENDANCES

		Round	Date
71,526	St Helens v Wigan	GF	2/10/10
	(at Old Trafford, Manchester)		
22,701	Wigan v Warrington	22	16/7/10
20,498	Wigan v St Helens	18	20/6/10
20,079	Hull v Hull KR	22	15/7/10
18,605	Wigan v Harlequins	12	23/4/10
17,883	Wigan v Leeds	8	26/3/10
17,699	Hull v Hull KR	EPO	11/9/10
17,500	St Helens v Warrington	7	19/3/10
17,500	St Helens v Wigan	9	2/4/10
17,244	Leeds v Bradford	9	1/4/10

WORST ATTENDANCES

		Round	Date
1,122	Crusaders v Harlequins	9	6/8/10
	(at The Gnoll, Neath)		
1,495	Crusaders v Castleford	23	25/7/10
	(at The Gnoll, Neath)		
2,330	Harlequins v Catalans	2	14/2/10
2,381	Harlequins v Crusaders	16	6/6/10
2,395	Harlequins v Salford	6	14/3/10
2,412	Crusaders v Salford	24	1/8/10
2,624	Harlequins v Huddersfield	7	20/3/10
2,672	Salford v Harlequins	20	2/7/10
2,819	Harlequins v Hull KR	10	5/4/10
2,837	Crusaders v Wakefield	19	27/6/10

* Super League attendance figures include play-offs.

CHALLENGE CUP

TRIES

1	Brent Webb	Leeds Rhinos	8
	Chris Hicks	Warrington Wolves	8
3	Ryan Hall	Leeds Rhinos	7
4	Ned Catic	Barrow Raiders	6
	Luke Branighan	Halifax	6
	Sam Tomkins	Wigan Warriors	6

GOALS

1	Kevin Sinfield	Leeds Rhinos	30
2	Gareth Moore	Batley Bulldogs	23
3	Thomas Bosc	Catalans Dragons	20
	Lee Paterson	Halifax	20
	Jamie Rooney	Barrow Raiders	20

POINTS

			T	G	FG	Pts
1	Gareth Moore	Batley Bulldogs	4	23	0	62
2	Kevin Sinfield	Leeds Rhinos	0	30	0	60
3	Jamie Rooney	Barrow Raiders	2	20	0	48
4	Thomas Bosc	Catalans Dragons	1	20	1	45
5	Mick Nanyn	Leigh Centurions	4	12	0	40
	Lee Paterson	Halifax	0	20	0	40

BEST ATTENDANCES

		Round	Date
85,217	Leeds v Warrington	F	28/8/10
	(at Wembley Stadium)		
15,267	Leeds v St Helens	SF	7/8/10
	(at Galpharm Stadium, Huddersfield)		
15,109	Hull v Leeds	4	17/4/10
12,265	Catalans v Warrington	SF	8/8/10
	(at Stobart Stadium, Widnes)		
9,242	Leeds v Wigan	QF	29/5/10

WORST ATTENDANCES

		Round	Date
250	Royal Navy v Blackpool	3	7/3/10
	(at United Services Sports Ground, Portsmouth)		
336	Gateshead v York	3	7/3/10
376	London Skolars v Limoux	3	7/3/10
398	Rochdale v Lezignan	3	7/3/10
430	Warrington Wizards v Swinton	3	5/3/10
	(at Wilderspool)		

NORTHERN RAIL CUP

TRIES

1	John Campbell	Batley Bulldogs	10
2	Damian Munro	Blackpool Panthers	7
	Anthony Thackeray	Widnes Vikings	7
4	Ned Catic	Barrow Raiders	6
	Ian Preece	Batley Bulldogs	6
	Wayne McHugh	Hunslet Hawks	6

GOALS

1	Gareth Moore	Batley Bulldogs	46
2	Shane Grady	Widnes Vikings	25
3	Danny Jones	Keighley Cougars	23
	Jamie Rooney	Barrow Raiders	23
5	Mick Nanyn	Leigh Centurions	17
	Lee Paterson	Halifax	17

POINTS

			T	G	FG	Pts
1	Gareth Moore	Batley Bulldogs	3	46	2	106
2	Shane Grady	Widnes Vikings	3	25	0	62
3	Jamie Rooney	Barrow Raiders	2	23	0	54
4	Danny Jones	Keighley Cougars	1	23	1	51
5	Mick Nanyn	Leigh Centurions	4	17	0	50

BEST ATTENDANCES

		Round	Date
8,138	Batley v Widnes	F	18/7/10
	(at Bloomfield Road, Blackpool)		
3,432	Widnes v Barrow	3	14/2/10
2,200	Widnes v Gateshead	1	2/2/10
2,141	Halifax v Dewsbury	2	7/2/10
2,058	Leigh v Batley	SF	17/6/10

WORST ATTENDANCES

		Round	Date
192	Doncaster v Blackpool	4	24/3/10
194	Blackpool v Gateshead	3	14/2/10
237	Gateshead v Batley	4	17/3/10
285	Doncaster v Barrow	1	17/2/10
286	Workington v Swinton	1	17/2/10

CHAMPIONSHIP

Kyle Briggs

TRIES *(play-offs in brackets, included in total)*

1	Shad Royston	Halifax	24 (2)
2	Kyle Briggs	Featherstone Rovers	19 (4)
	Rob Worrincy	Halifax	19 (3)
4	Zak Hardaker	Featherstone Rovers	18 (2)
5	Andy Ballard	Barrow Raiders	17 (1)
6	John Campbell	Batley Bulldogs	16 (-)
7	Anthony Thackeray	Widnes Vikings	15 (0)
8	Liam Finn	Featherstone Rovers	14 (1)
	Craig Cook	Sheffield Eagles	14 (1)
	Menzie Yere	Sheffield Eagles	14 (2)
	Rory Bromley	Toulouse Olympique	14 (-)

GOALS *(play-offs in brackets, included in total)*

1	Lee Paterson	Halifax	106 (12)
2	Kyle Briggs	Featherstone Rovers	104 (10)
3	Jamie Rooney	Barrow Raiders	88 (7)
4	Mick Nanyn	Leigh Centurions	74 (4)
5	Nathan Wynn	Toulouse Olympique	73 (-)
6	Shane Grady	Widnes Vikings	61 (0)
7	Danny Jones	Keighley Cougars	56 (-)
8	Gareth Moore	Batley Bulldogs	52 (-)
9	Pat Walker	Dewsbury Rams	36 (-)
10	Carl Rudd	Whitehaven	31 (-)

POINTS *(play-offs in brackets, included in total)*

			T	G	FG	Pts
1	Kyle Briggs	Featherstone Rovers	19	104	0	284 (36)
2	Lee Paterson	Halifax	12	106	0	260 (28)
3	Jamie Rooney	Barrow Raiders	11	88	1	221 (14)
4	Mick Nanyn	Leigh Centurions	12	74	0	196 (12)
5	Nathan Wynn	Toulouse Olympique	6	73	0	170 (-)
6	Shane Grady	Widnes Vikings	9	61	0	158 (0)
7	Danny Jones	Keighley Cougars	6	56	2	138 (-)
8	Gareth Moore	Batley Bulldogs	5	52	0	124 (-)
9	Pat Walker	Dewsbury Rams	7	36	0	100 (-)
10	Shad Royston	Halifax	24	0	0	96 (8)

FINAL TABLE

	P	W	D	L	BP	F	A	D	Pts
Featherstone Rovers	20	18	0	2	2	735	334	401	56
Halifax	20	16	0	4	2	684	509	175	50
Leigh Centurions	20	12	1	7	5	580	403	177	43
Barrow Raiders	20	12	1	7	1	607	449	158	39
Widnes Vikings	20	11	0	9	5	619	488	131	38
Sheffield Eagles	20	10	1	9	3	503	545	-42	35
Batley Bulldogs	20	7	0	13	8	479	488	-9	29
Toulouse Olympique	20	8	0	12	3	486	649	-163	27
Dewsbury Rams	20	6	0	14	8	444	505	-61	26
Whitehaven	20	4	0	16	4	281	707	-426	16
Keighley Cougars *	20	4	1	15	5	362	703	-341	10

* 9 points deducted for entering administration

AVERAGE ATTENDANCES

	2010 Avg	2009 Avg	Diff
Widnes Vikings	2,858	3,412	-554
Halifax	2,345	2,330	+15
Leigh Centurions	2,026	1,917	+109
Featherstone Rovers	1,822	1,754	+68
Barrow Raiders	1,790	2,206	-416
Toulouse Olympique	1,323	2,372	-1,049
Sheffield Eagles	1,228	1,090	+138
Dewsbury Rams	1,145	1,263	-118 (Ch1)
Keighley Cougars	1,045	916	+129 (Ch1)
Batley Bulldogs	992	856	+136
Whitehaven	984	1,599	-615
2010 Average	1,596		
2009 Average	1,720		
Difference	-124		

BEST ATTENDANCES

		Round	Date
9,443	Featherstone v Halifax	GF	26/9/10
	(at Halliwell Jones Stadium, Warrington)		
4,795	Halifax v Batley	21	15/8/10
3,448	Widnes v Featherstone	9	30/4/10
3,392	Leigh v Widnes	11	13/5/10
3,356	Widnes v Leigh	18	25/7/10
3,286	Widnes v Halifax	3	18/3/10
3,071	Halifax v Leigh	4	28/3/10
3,033	Widnes v Whitehaven	6	5/4/10
2,958	Widnes v Barrow	14	13/6/10
2,871	Sheffield v Featherstone	7	11/4/10

WORST ATTENDANCES

		Round	Date
504	Whitehaven v Dewsbury	20	8/8/10
666	Batley v Whitehaven	11	16/5/10
689	Batley v Toulouse	13	22/6/10
706	Whitehaven v Batley	22	22/8/10
736	Keighley v Toulouse	18	24/7/10
739	Keighley v Whitehaven	21	15/8/10
747	Batley v Sheffield	16	4/7/10
802	Batley v Barrow	17	11/7/10
825	Whitehaven v Featherstone	18	25/7/10
835	Sheffield v Dewsbury	3	19/3/10
	(at Don Valley Stadium)		

* Championship attendance figures include play-offs and Northern Rail Cup. Challenge Cup not included.

CHAMPIONSHIP ONE

TRIES *(play-offs in brackets, included in total)*

1	Wayne McHugh	Hunslet Hawks	21 (-)
	Waine Pryce	Hunslet Hawks	21 (-)
3	Steve Parry	South Wales Scorpions	19 (1)
4	Casey Mayberry	Blackpool Panthers	18 (2)
	Lee Waterman	York City Knights	18 (3)
6	Damian Munro	Blackpool Panthers	16 (1)
	Lucas Onyango	Oldham	16 (0)
8	Mick Fogerty	Oldham	15 (1)
	John Gillam	Oldham	15 (0)
	Paul O'Connor	Oldham	15 (0)

GOALS *(play-offs in brackets, included in total)*

1	Tom Hemingway	Blackpool Panthers	106 (14)
2	Lee Waterman	York City Knights	83 (13)
3	Paul Crook	Rochdale Hornets	67 (15)
4	Gavin Dodd	Swinton Lions	61 (-)
5	Matt Ashe	Oldham	56 (0)
	David March	Hunslet Hawks	56 (-)
7	Paul Thorman	London Skolars	47 (-)
8	Darren Holt	Workington Town	46 (4)
	Gregg McNally	Oldham	46 (8)
10	Lloyd White	South Wales Scorpions	45 (0)

POINTS *(play-offs in brackets, included in total)*

			T	G	FG	Pts
1	Tom Hemingway	Blackpool Panthers	7	106	0	240 (28)
2	Lee Waterman	York City Knights	18	83	0	238 (38)
3	Paul Crook	Rochdale Hornets	7	67	2	164 (42)
4	Gavin Dodd	Swinton Lions	9	61	0	158 (-)
5	David March	Hunslet Hawks	11	56	0	156 (-)
6	Matt Ashe	Oldham	6	56	0	136 (0)
7	Wayne McHugh	Hunslet Hawks	21	22	0	128 (-)
8	Gregg McNally	Oldham	7	46	1	121 (17)
9	Lloyd White	South Wales Scorpions	7	45	0	118 (0)
10	Scott Kaighan	Workington Town	10	34	0	108 (2)

FINAL TABLE

	P	W	D	L	BP	F	A	D	Pts
Hunslet Hawks	20	18	0	2	1	828	305	523	55
Oldham	20	17	0	3	1	694	438	256	52
York City Knights	20	12	0	8	3	617	534	83	39
Blackpool Panthers *	20	15	0	5	3	805	370	435	38
Rochdale Hornets	20	10	0	10	7	630	498	132	37
South Wales Scorpions	20	9	0	11	7	576	468	108	34
Workington Town	20	8	1	11	7	494	498	-4	33
Swinton Lions	20	9	1	10	4	570	581	-11	33
Doncaster	20	8	0	12	4	518	588	-70	28
London Skolars	20	2	0	18	4	444	900	-456	10
Gateshead Thunder **	20	1	0	19	1	236	1232	-996	-2

* 10 points deducted for operational rules breach
** 6 points deducted for entering administration

AVERAGE ATTENDANCES

	2010 Avg	2009 Avg	Diff
Oldham	808	983	-175
York City Knights	730	1,096	-366
South Wales Scorpions	631	N/A	N/A
Rochdale Hornets	567	637	-70
Hunslet Hawks	550	655	-105
Doncaster	509	705	-196
			(Ch)
London Skolars	501	412	+89
Workington Town	470	474	-4
Swinton Lions	419	519	-100
Gateshead Thunder	373	679	-306
			(Ch)
Blackpool Panthers	368	502	-134
2010 Average	**539**		
2009 Average	**746**		
Difference	**-207**		

BEST ATTENDANCES *(figure unavailable for Grand Final)*

		Round	Date
1,412	Rochdale v Oldham	5	2/4/10
1,375	London Skolars v Oldham	22	27/8/10
1,350	London Skolars v York	14	12/6/10
	(at Twickenham Stoop)		
1,275	Oldham v York	QSF	12/9/10
1,127	Doncaster v Workington	22	22/8/10
1,110	Oldham v York	10	9/5/10
1,005	Oldham v Rochdale	21	15/8/10
1,004	Oldham v Hunslet	12	23/5/10
1,002	York v Hunslet	11	16/5/10
987	York v Rochdale	8	25/4/10

WORST ATTENDANCES

		Round	Date
248	Blackpool v Workington	14	13/6/10
253	Blackpool v Doncaster	8	23/4/10
253	Blackpool v Gateshead	11	16/5/10
258	Gateshead v South Wales	10	8/5/10
265	Gateshead v Rochdale	13	30/5/10
266	Blackpool v South Wales	16	3/7/10
276	London Skolars v Swinton	2	14/3/10
277	Swinton v London Skolars	13	30/5/10
286	Gateshead v Workington	12	23/5/10
287	Swinton v Workington	5	20/6/10

* Championship One attendance figures include play-offs and Northern Rail Cup. Challenge Cup not included.

2010 TOP SCORERS - ALL COMPETITIONS

Chris Hicks

TRIES

1	Chris Hicks	Warrington Wolves	32
	Pat Richards	Wigan Warriors	32
3	Ryan Hall	Leeds Rhinos	31
4	John Campbell	Batley Bulldogs	30
	Shad Royston	Halifax	30
6	Chris Riley	Warrington Wolves	29
	Darrell Goulding	Wigan Warriors	29
8	Wayne McHugh	Hunslet Hawks	28
9	Danny McGuire	Leeds Rhinos	27
10	Francis Meli	St Helens	26

GOALS

1	Pat Richards	Wigan Warriors	167
2	Lee Paterson	Halifax	143
3	Jamie Rooney	Barrow Raiders	131
4	Tom Hemingway	Blackpool Panthers	128
5	Gareth Moore	Batley Bulldogs	121
	Kevin Sinfield	Leeds Rhinos	121
7	Kyle Briggs	Featherstone Rovers	117
8	Michael Dobson	Hull Kingston Rovers	114
9	Mick Nanyn	Leigh Centurions	103
10	Lee Waterman	York City Knights	102

POINTS

			T	G	FG	Pts
1	Pat Richards	Wigan Warriors	32	167	0	462
2	Lee Paterson	Halifax	13	143	0	338
3	Jamie Rooney	Barrow Raiders	15	131	1	323
4	Kyle Briggs	Featherstone Rovers	20	117	0	314
5	Lee Waterman	York City Knights	25	102	0	304
6	Tom Hemingway	Blackpool Panthers	9	128	0	292
	Gareth Moore	Batley Bulldogs	12	121	2	292
8	Mick Nanyn	Leigh Centurions	20	103	0	286
9	Michael Dobson	Hull Kingston Rovers	11	114	3	275
10	Kevin Sinfield	Leeds Rhinos	4	121	4	262

FIELD GOALS

1	Lee Briers	Warrington Wolves	4
	Kevin Sinfield	Leeds Rhinos	4
3	Michael Dobson	Hull Kingston Rovers	3
	Danny Jones	Keighley Cougars	3
	Chris Thorman	York City Knights	3